A History of Preaching

A History of Preaching

O. C. Edwards Jr.

ABINGDON PRESS / Nashville

A HISTORY OF PREACHING:
VOLUME 1

This book is printed on acid-free paper.

Volume 1 ISBN 9781501833779
Volume 2 ISBN 9781501833786

16 17 18 19 20 21 22 23 24 25—10 9 8 7 6 5 4 3 2 1

MANUFACTURED IN THE UNITED STATES OF AMERICA

Dedicated
with much love and gratitude

to
Carl and his Jane,
Sam, Patricia, Adrian, and Phoebe,
and
Louise, Russell, Jane, and Charlie

CONTENTS

Part III: From the Renaissance and Reformation to the Enlightenment

PREFACE

The determination to write this history of preaching came to me in the summer of 1983. I had just returned from a sabbatical in Nigeria that ended nine years of administrative duty and was preparing to assume my new duties as professor of preaching that fall. Although I had already written a couple of books on exegesis as a resource for preaching, it seemed appropriate (to say the least) to read more widely in the literature of the field before occupying the chair.

Among the stack of books on my desk was one recommended by a student with an evangelical bent, John Stott's *Between Two Worlds*.[1] Stott is of a generation that considers it improper to write a book about anything without including a chapter on the history of the subject matter. Stott warmly recommended the history of preaching as a discipline helpful to the practitioner, and mentioned his devotion to the two-volume work of Edwin C. Dargan, which by then was already more than seventy years old.[2]

Stott's chapter intrigued me so much that I stopped reading his book to open the only work on my bookshelves devoted to the subject: Yngve Brilioth's *Brief History of Preaching*.[3] Reading what the archbishop of Uppsala had to say about the preaching of the Fathers of the early church activated my instincts as someone trained in patristics, so I began pulling off the shelves the works to which Brilioth referred. And Brilioth and the Fathers together reminded me that all the great preachers of the early church had been trained as professional rhetoricians before their ordination. That drove me to Aristotle, Cicero, and Quintilian.

Apparently launched on an infinite regress of reading books to understand other books, I began to look around for a major work more recent than Dargan's and came rapidly to understand that there was none. The last thorough investigation of the subject had been made when the century that was about to close had just begun. Surely the intervening years had seen research in the area comparable to the progress made in other fields of study over the same period! An update of the history of preaching seemed a book just aching to be written.

Further, while in many ways I liked the work of Dargan very much, in other ways it frustrated me. He had written about preachers, trying to include everyone who had a reputation for excellence in Christian proclamation throughout history. Thus he gave as much biographical information about each as space and the state of knowledge would allow, and then made some observations about that person's preaching. He reflected a Romantic understanding of such oeuvre as a product of the genius of an individual.

But I was more interested in preaching than in preachers; compiling a homiletical prosopography had no appeal to me. My understanding of the historical enterprise is accounting for change over time. I wanted to know about movements, about what the sermons of an era had in common rather than how they differed. I wanted to know what preachers of a period thought they were accomplishing in the pulpit (or chair, or ambo[4]), and the strategy of persuasion they used to achieve that end. I wanted to know when there had been major shifts and why those had occurred.

This desire to understand what preachers were trying to do and how they went about doing it meant that I could not start out with my own theory of what constituted good preaching and use that as a criterion for distinguishing the "good guys" from the "bad guys" throughout history. To do so would be to display the provincialism of the cultural stay-at-home. Whether a sermon can be read with edification today does not really tell us much about how effective it was in the context in which it was originally delivered.

Allegorical biblical interpretation is a case in point. Brilioth refers to it as "one of the hereditary taints of scriptural preaching."[5] Yet, while some Reformers thought sermons should expound the literal grammatical sense[6] of the biblical passage on which they were based, allegorical interpretation remained a common ingredient in sermons well through the nineteenth century. It was not until 1888–89, for instance, that Adolf Jülicher succeeded in convincing most of the scholarly world that Jesus' parables were not to be understood that way.[7] Thus if one is to rule preaching based on allegorical biblical interpretation out of court, one will excommunicate the proclamation of well over three-quarters of the Christian era, including that of most of the Fathers of the early church. And this is but one example of the exclusions that will have to be made if a chronicler of preaching claims to know what distinguishes the good from the bad and goes through history sorting all sermons into these two categories.

However, once I had decided to have a go at bringing the history of preaching up to date, it soon became obvious that in several respects I would have to scale down my original hope. For example, even though the book would cover the Christian era, I could not consider all Christian preaching. I could try to treat preaching in both Latin and Greek through the Golden Age of the Greek Fathers, but would have to overlook sermons in Syriac. Through the Middle Ages, I could study only Western sermons in Latin and vernacular languages. I could discuss all the major traditions of the Reformation, but after that I would confine the history to preaching done in English. And for the twentieth century, I would pay more attention to American than British pulpit work. And so my intention became to produce a homiletical genealogy for those who preach the faith today in English—especially Americans, but British as well.

It was immediately obvious, however, that no one—and certainly not I—could do original research in every period. In fact, the most I could expect to accomplish was to summarize the available monographic literature. That meant the aspects of preaching considered would vary from period to period, because the specialists writing about them had not taken their cues from me about what to concentrate on! It also meant that my distinction between preachers and preaching could not always be scrupulously observed, since the characteristic preaching of a period or the transition to it is often epitomized in one individual or a few, so that talking about preaching in their time is to talk about what they did. In these ways, the book as originally conceived differs from the book that came to be written.

One thing that was clear to me all along, however, was that the historical survey had to be accompanied by a collection of documents—both sermons and theoretical treatments—that illustrated the development being traced. To do anything else would have been as senseless as a history of painting in which there were no pictures. And the selections would have to be complete. A collection of extended quotations would convey little sense of what it was like to be one of those who heard the sermon when it was originally delivered. Even then the experience would fall far short of the reality; a sermon is not black marks on paper but a transaction involving a preacher, a congregation, and, one hopes, the Holy Spirit. This collection of documents appears on the CD-ROM accompanying this volume.

An additional way of clarifying the purpose of this book is to distinguish it from others in the same field. I have already mentioned those of Dargan and Brilioth. When I began, a helpful short work was already available in German: Werner Schütz's *Geschichte der christlichen Predigt*,[8] but it is hardly more than an outline. Among multivolume treatments, the most obvious was *20 Centuries of Great Preaching*, edited by Clyde E. Fant Jr. and William M. Pinson Jr.[9] The great virtue of this set is the many sermons for which it provides an English text. Each of these is prefaced by a short biography of the preacher, but little effort was made to develop an interpretation of the overall development of preaching; only individuals are discussed.

And some of these individuals get more adequate treatment than others. The coverage of Rauschenbusch, for example, is an important contribution to the literature. But the editors admit to using seventeen "men" (who appear to have been seminarians) as aiding in preliminary research;[10] inadequate revision of their efforts could account for the way some of the biographies hardly rise above the level of hagiography.

An even more critical shortcoming in Fant and Pinson's treatment of the entire history of preaching is that the first seventeen and a half of the twenty centuries are dispatched in the first two volumes. Almost ten of the twelve volumes are confined to preaching in the nineteenth and twentieth centuries.[11]

During the eighteen years in which I wrote the present book, many works were published that provided important data and perspective to the history, but they are mostly monographs about a period or a person. There have been, however, two attempts to cover the entire history, and I have tried to distinguish between their purposes and that of this work.

One of the two projects was frustrated by the untimely death of the author, Ronald E. Osborn. A minister and pastor of the Disciples of Christ, Osborn had academic and editorial responsibilities for most of his ministry, teaching church history at the seminary level and serving as dean of Christian Theological Seminary in Indianapolis before his retirement. He was able to finish only one of the four volumes planned for his history, while another is to be completed by Joseph R. Jeter, who teaches preaching at the Brite Divinity School of Texas Christian University.

Thus the only volume to be published so far is Osborn's *Folly of God:*

The Rise of Christian Preaching,[12] which takes the history of preaching through the third century of the Common Era, the time of persecution. The book has many virtues, and it is sad that the author was not able to complete the task on which he had worked so long. The only caveat to be entered against it is that Osborn does not distinguish carefully between what is preaching and what is some other genre of writing. Thus this valuable work could have as easily been titled *Early Christian Literature and Its Greco-Roman and Jewish Antecedents*.

Hughes Oliphant Old, the author of the other survey, has been more fortunate than Osborn: so far four of the seven projected volumes of his *Reading and Preaching of the Scriptures in the Worship of the Christian Church*[13] have appeared. Old conducted his survey on the assumption that there are correct and incorrect ways of worship, and so he goes through history separating the sheep from the goats.

The correct ways are classified as those that treat preaching as an act of worship and see the reading and interpretation of scripture to be the major elements in the offering of the liturgical assembly of the faithful. While Old claims to find this pattern in the earliest traditions of Israel, what he really appears to treat as normative is the standard of American heirs of the Reform tradition. As fellow Presbyterian Thomas G. Long has said:

> Occasionally . . . Old is too eager to find biblical and patristic support for a Reformed understanding of the centrality of the preached Word in worship. The great march of preachers he presents (over 60 in [the first] two volumes) sometimes looks vaguely like a parade of precocious Presbyterians.[14]

In distinguishing my work from others, I have no illusion of its adequacy, much less perfection. Only one who has struggled with the vast expanse of the data can realize how difficult, if not impossible, it is to bring it into terse coherence. I make only three claims. The first is that trying to write this book has been the most enjoyable task I have ever undertaken. The second is that, since publication will occur in my seventy-seventh year, I have the sense of ars longa, vita brevis that must come to anyone who tries to survey two thousand years of the history of anything. And the third is that this is the best I can do.

Having stated how the idea for my history of preaching originally came to me, described what it intends to do and how that is gone about, and distinguished this from other works in the field, it is now necessary to acknowledge my indebtedness to a long list of persons and institutions whose help has made it possible for me to complete this undertaking. This should begin with an expression of gratitude for financial assistance. I was granted two sabbatical leaves from Seabury-Western Theological Seminary, where the Right Reverend Mark Sisk was dean at the time. Generous study grants were provided me by the Conant Fund of the Executive Council of the Episcopal Church in 1987 and 1989; the Pew Charitable Trust through the Association of Theological Schools in 1989–90; and the Lilly Fund of St. Paul's Episcopal Church, Indianapolis, in 1989.

The Newberry Library graciously made me a research associate in 1989–90, the College of Preachers welcomed me as Scholar in Residence and chaplain in 1994, and Seabury-Western accepted me back as Scholar in Residence in the fall of 2000. My thought on the history of preaching was developed through courses taught in that field at Seabury-Western, the University of Notre Dame, the Summer School of Vancouver School of Theology, the Association of Chicago Theological Schools' Doctor of Ministry in Preaching Program, the Divinity School of Duke University, the Doctor of Ministry Program at Emmanuel School of Religion, and the College for Seniors at the University of North Carolina-Asheville. I was also invited to give endowed lectures at Bexley Hall and the School of Theology of the University of the South.

In addition to the libraries of the institutions mentioned above, I am grateful for access to the libraries of the following: Northwestern University, the University of Chicago, Jesuit-Krause-McCormick, Cambridge University, Wesley Theological Seminary, the Virginia Theological Seminary, and Mars Hill College. There are three librarians who must be thanked personally: Newland Smith of the United Library of Seabury-Western and Garrett-Evangelical, Thomas Stokes of Emmanuel School of Religion, and James Dunkly of the University of the South. Without their constant help, this work could not have been completed in retirement in the mountains of North Carolina. Jim Dunkly, especially, was tireless in making bibliographical searches and doing other things to see that I had the books I needed. A different sort of bibliographical help came from Benjamin Cothran, who scanned and turned into editable text most of the documents reproduced on the CD-ROM, saving me many hours of work.

I have never ceased to be amazed at the helpfulness of other scholars, a number of whom—some perfect strangers—have sent me prepublication photocopies of their books. Others have provided me with copies of articles, read over parts of this work and made suggestions, supplied me with bibliographical leads, and otherwise assisted me in my research.

Their assistance is acknowledged in footnotes at the relevant places, an inadequate indication of my gratitude. They, of course, are not to be blamed for any misuse I have made of their erudition.

Colleagues in the Academy of Homiletics and Societas Homiletica have offered suggestions, criticisms, bibliographical leads, encouragement, friendship, and fellowship.

During most of the eighteen years I have worked on this book, I have benefited from the advice, skill, and warmth of my editor at Abingdon Press, Ulrike Guthrie. Only she knows the depth of my debt.

The support of Jane, my wife for forty-five years, has been the sine qua non of this, as well as of all my other undertakings.

Finally, this work is dedicated to our three children: Carl Lee Edwards, Samuel Adams Trufant Edwards, and Louise Reynes Edwards-Simpson. This is a long-delayed acknowledgment of what they mean to me. I had hoped to honor them before with my part in *The Bible for Today's Church,* but the official nature of that volume precluded my doing so. And then I had intended to dedicate a mystery novel I wrote to them, but that remains unpublished. The advantage of this deferred homage, however, is that they can now be joined by their spouses and children—for all of whom, I am profoundly grateful.

Notes

1. John Stott, *Between Two Worlds: The Art of Preaching in the Twentieth Century* (Grand Rapids, Mich.: Eerdmans, 1982).

2. Edwin C. Dargan, *A History of Preaching,* 2 vols. (1905–12; reprint, New York: Burt Franklin, 1968).

3. Yngve Brilioth, *A Brief History of Preaching,* trans. Karl E. Mattson, The Preacher's Paperback Library (Philadelphia: Fortress, 1965).

4. The architectural forerunner of a pulpit or lectern.

5. Ibid., 9.

6. This is a long way from what is meant today by the historical sense.

7. The fact that the Gospels themselves supply such interpretations gave the practice much authority. Nor is allegorical preaching yet dead. I once heard a fundamentalist radio preacher treat the ministrations of the good Samaritan allegorically because he could not believe that Jesus would have spoken approvingly of wine, even as a topically applied medicine.

8. Werner Schütz, *Geschichte der christlichen Predigt,* Sammlung Göschen, Band 7201 (Berlin: Walter de Gruyter, 1972).

9. Clyde E. Fant Jr. and William M. Pinson Jr., eds., *20 Centuries of Great Preaching,* 13 vols. (Waco, Tex.: Word, 1971).

10. Ibid., 1:viii-ix.

11. Volume 13 is devoted to an index.

12. Ronald E. Osborn, *Folly of God: The Rise of Christian Preaching* (St. Louis: Chalice, 1999). See my review in *STR* 44.1 (2000): 103-5.

13. Hughes Oliphant Old, *The Reading and Preaching of the Scriptures in the Worship of the Christian Church* (Grand Rapids, Mich.: Eerdmans, 1998–2002). See my reviews in *STR* 44.1 (2000): 105-8, and *PSB* 20 (1999): 351-52.

14. Thomas Long, review of *The Reading and Preaching of the Scriptures in the Worship of the Christian Church*, by Hughes Oliphant Old, *Christian Century* (December 2, 1998): 1154.

LIST OF ABBREVIATIONS

APR	Abingdon Preacher's Library
ASS	*Acta sanctae sedis*
AARDS	American Academy of Religion Dissertation Series
ARR	American Academy of Religion Studies in Religion
AJP	*American Journal of Philology*
AmUS	American University Studies
ABD	*The Anchor Bible Dictionary*
ACW	Ancient Christian Writers
ANQ	*Andover-Newton Quarterly*
ANF	*Ante-Nicene Fathers*
1 Apol.	*Apologia i (First Apology)*
ARG	*Archiv für Reformationsgeschichte*
AT	Author's Translation
ATR	*Anglican Theological Review*
BCP	Book of Common Prayer
CHR	*Catholic Historical Review*
CFS	Cistercian Fathers Series
CSS	Cistercian Studies Series
CWS	Classics of Western Spirituality
CO	*Calvini Opera*
CEP	*Concise Encyclopedia of Preaching*
Conf.	*Confessionum libri XIII* (Augustine: *Confessions*)
De Sacr.	*De sacramentis* (Ambrose: *The Sacraments*)
EncJud	*Encyclopaedia Judaica*
EEC	*Encyclopedia of Early Christianity*
ER	*The Encyclopedia of Religion*
ERE	*Encyclopedia of Religion and Ethics*
Ep.	*Epistulae* (Augustine: *Letters*)
FC	The Fathers of the Church
FZPhTh	*Freiburger Zeitschrift für Philosophie und Theologie*

GAO	Great American Orators
GOTR	*Greek Orthodox Theological Review*
Hist. eccl.	*Historia ecclesiastica* (Eusebius: *Ecclesiastical History*)
Hom. Act	*Homiliae in Acta apostolorum* (Chrysostom)
Hom. Col.	*Homilae in epistulam ad Colossenses*
Hom. 1 Cor.	*Homiliae in epistulam i ad Corinthios*
Hom. Matt.	*Homiliae in Matthaeum*
IDB	*The Interpreter's Dictionary of the Bible*
JHI	*Journal of the History of Ideas*
LCC	Library of Christian Classics
LPT	Library of Protestant Thought
LCL	Loeb Classical Library
LXX	Septuagint
MQR	*Mennonite Quarterly Review*
MGH	Monumenta Germaniae Historiae
NCB	New Century Bible
NIB	*The New Interpreter's Bible*
NovTSup	Supplements to Novum Testamentum
NPNF[1]	*Nicene and Post-Nicene Fathers*[1]
NPNF[2]	*Nicene and Post-Nicene Fathers*[2]
Or. Bas.	*Oration in laudem Basilii* (Gregory: *Orations*)
OBT	Overtures to Biblical Theology
ODCC	*The Oxford Dictionary of the Christian Church*
OECT	Oxford Early Christian Texts
PG	Patrologia graeca (= Patrologiae cursus completus: Series graeca) (J.-P. Migne)
PL	Patrologia latina (= Patrologiae cursus completus: Series latina) (J.-P. Migne)
PPL	The Preacher's Paperback Library
PSB	*Princeton Seminary Bulletin*
RB	*Revue biblique*
SBLSBS	Society of Biblical Literature Sources for Biblical Study
STRev	*Sewanee Theological Review*
SC	Sources chrétiennes
SWR	Studies in Women and Religion
NovTSup	Supplements to Novum Testamentum
TS	Texts and Studies in Religion
TDNT	*Theological Dictionary of the New Testament*
ThH	Théologie historique
TCP	*20 Centuries of Great Preaching: An Encyclopedia of Preaching*
VC	*Vigiliae christianae*

Part I

Homiletical Origins

CHAPTER 1

THE EARLIEST CHRISTIAN PREACHING

There is no activity more characteristic of the church than preaching. Along with the sacraments, most Christian bodies consider the proclamation of the Word of God to be the constitutive act of the church.[1] No other major religion gives preaching quite the central role that it has in Christianity. Most major religions authorize persons to ritualize and storify their integrating myths; to preserve, interpret, and teach the current relevance of their sacred writings; to connect the past with the present and the future; and, in most cases, to win converts to the faith. But in the Christian religion, "the preacher, by and large, plays a more central role."[2] Judaism[3] and Islam[4] are the two other great monotheistic faiths in which homiletical activity approximating that of Christianity is most common.

The material included within or excluded from this account of the history of preaching was shaped and/or determined by the following basic definition of a "sermon":

> a speech delivered in a Christian assembly for worship by an authorized person that applies some point of doctrine, usually drawn from a

> biblical passage, to the lives of the members of the congregation with the purpose of moving them by the use of narrative analogy and other rhetorical devices to accept that application and to act on the basis of it[5]

The overwhelming majority of Christian sermons have been delivered at regular worship services, especially those conducted on Sundays. Even most of the efforts to convert non-Christians through preaching have occurred at regular meetings of the Christian assembly. While there have been exceptions, such as open-air preaching, even that has often been accompanied by Scripture reading, prayer, and hymn singing, which turn the event into a service of worship. In addition to sermons in the ordered round of worship and those preached in missionary or evangelistic contexts, the other main category has aimed at instruction in the faith. Not all catechesis has been preaching within the definition given above, but at least the instructions in preparation for Christian initiation given by such early church fathers as Ambrose, Cyril of Jerusalem, and John Chrysostom fit within the genre of sermon. The subject of this investigation, then, is Christian preaching at the regular liturgy and in missionary/evangelistic and catechetical situations that falls within the definition of a sermon.[6]

Many will undoubtedly wonder why anyone would wish to bother writing or reading a history of preaching. Certainly the reputation of the activity in some quarters is such as to cause curiosity about it to appear perverse. Thus the third definition of *preach* in the first edition of the *Oxford American Dictionary* is "to give moral advice in an obtrusive way." Nor is it a compliment to call any discourse "preachy." The early-nineteenth-century wit Sydney Smith, himself a priest and even a canon of St. Paul's, said that

> preaching has become a by-word for long and dull conversation of any kind; and whoever wishes to imply, in any piece of writing, the absence of every thing agreeable and inviting, calls it a sermon.[7]

Even the most committed Christian has to acknowledge that there is more justice to such complaints than one wishes were the case. In spite of all that may be said against preaching, however, its history has proved to be of enormous interest to many scholars who have no personal bias in favor of the church. Indeed, most of the monographs in the field, those that make up so much of the bibliography of the present study, are the work of scholars whose field is not church history or homiletics. Many have been historians in other fields, whether political, social, or literary. Folklorists have studied African American preaching, scholars of Middle English have searched manuscripts for sermon illustrations that furnished the plot for early secular writings in the vernacular, and students of the American Revolution have read sermons to see how the decision to take up arms against the Crown was formed. Those interested in the evolution of public speaking have found secular rhetoric influencing homiletical theory, and styles in preaching shaping the work of those who engaged in other forms of public address. Nor has preaching been studied only for the light it could cast on something else; literary critics have found the styles of preachers in various periods to be worthy of attention in their own right. Thus many who have made no personal religious commitment have found *some* Christian preaching, at any rate, worthy of all the attention they could give it.

The attitudes toward preaching of "those who profess and call themselves Christians," however, are of a wholly different order. The most extreme claims have been made for the value of the activity. Paul, for instance, said:

> "Everyone who calls on the name of the Lord shall be saved." But how are they to call on one in whom they have not believed? And how are they to believe in one of whom they have never heard? And how are they to hear without someone to proclaim[8] him? And how are they to proclaim him unless they are sent? As it is written, "How beautiful are the feet of those who bring good news!" (Rom. 10:13-15)

Thus he can say: "God decided, through the foolishness of our proclamation, to save those who believe" (1 Cor. 1:21) and say of himself: "Woe to me if I do not proclaim the gospel!" (1 Cor. 9:16). The interpretation of the early church fathers that was collected into the most authoritative biblical commentary of the Middle Ages, the *Glossa Ordinaria,* found preaching represented allegorically on almost every page of the sacred text. The two greatest of the Reformers, Luther and Calvin, both assumed that the ordinary medium by which election to salvation is effected was preaching. Finally, the *Decree on the Ministry of Priests* of the Second Vatican Council says that "the primary duty of priests is the proclamation of the Gospel of God to all." Thus there are many, believers and nonbelievers alike, for whom investigating the development over time of Christian preaching is a worthy effort.

PREACHING IN THE NEW TESTAMENT

The obvious place to begin a history of Christian preaching would seem to be the New Testament, but when one investigates the matter closely, it becomes clear that there is little in the New Testament that fits the definition given above for Christian preaching. It is true, of course, that there is a larger sense in which everything in the New Testament is preaching. This has been recognized since at least 1918, when Martin Dibelius wrote:

> At the beginning of all early Christian creativity there stands the sermon: missionary and hortatory preaching, narrative and parenesis, prophecy and the interpretation of scripture.[9]

Norman Perrin has summarized the point of view by characterizing the New Testament literature as fundamentally proclamation *(kerygma)* and exhortation *(parenesis),* admitting at the same time that within these two major categories there are many subdivisions.[10] The proclamation involves both the preaching of the kingdom of God by Jesus and the early church's message that Jesus is the one through whom God acted decisively for the salvation of human beings, and the *parenesis* is exhortation that grows out of the proclamation. Hence the indicative declares the history of the Christ event, and the imperative spells out the implications of that event for living.

There is a sense, therefore, in which everything in the New Testament is preaching. And yet, paradoxically, there is another sense in which none of it is. In the strict terms of the definition above, there are probably no sermons as such in the New Testament, no texts that had been delivered orally to an assembly for evangelization, instruction, or worship.

Jesus' preaching could be thought to provide an exception, but it fails to do so on at least two counts. First, since its content was the breaking in of the reign of God and it refers only by implication to its proclaimer's role in that incursion, it is not, strictly speaking, Christian preaching. Second, while the Gospels contain long speeches that are placed on the lips of Jesus, scholars doubt that any of them reflect the content of a discourse he gave on any single public occasion. The Q material presented in Matthew and Luke as continuous speeches of Jesus is, on closer inspection, obviously made up of what seem a series of "one-liners" rather than a developed presentation of thought. Indeed, each verse could be a distillation of an entire sermon. By the same token, the discourses in the Fourth Gospel, which do sound like consecutive speeches, could have grown out of the evangelist's meditation over the years on a single statement of Jesus such as one of the synoptic verses.[11] Thus, while it is certain that preaching was the main form of communication employed by the founder of Christianity, none of his actual sermons are available to be studied for insight into the nature of Christian preaching.

Nor is it likely that any of Paul's sermons *as such* have survived. Paul makes it very clear that he had a strong sense of vocation to preach to the Gentiles the gospel of Christ crucified and risen, and he nowhere gives any indication of a similar sense of vocation to write letters to distant congregations. Yet the letters are what remain and not his missionary, catechetical, and presumably liturgical sermons. Many questions that have plagued New Testament scholars could be answered if we knew how Paul persuaded his Gentile converts to accept Christianity. Certainly there could be a more balanced understanding of his theology if we knew the content of the instruction he gave those converts in preparation for baptism. All that can be reconstructed, however, is what is implied in his letters. While a certain amount of overlap might be expected between the contents of the two kinds of communication, and it can be assumed that what was written later was consistent with what had been said earlier, it cannot be assumed that what he delivered orally was the same as what he wrote. To repeat, none of Paul's sermons have been preserved in a form in which they can be identified as such and analyzed as specimens of his preaching.

An exception to this conclusion is thought to be found in the Acts of the Apostles. A considerable portion of Acts, after all, is taken up with speeches of one sort or another,[12] many of them claiming to be the missionary sermons of Paul—or Peter or some other representative of the primitive church. All of these missionary sermons, however, have the same outline:[13] they begin with what is taken to be a prophecy from the Hebrew Bible, go on to claim that the prophecy was fulfilled in and by Jesus, document that claim by saying that the apostles were witnesses of its fulfillment, and call upon members of their audience to repent and believe the gospel. The unlikelihood that all of these preachers always followed the same outline means that the reports in Acts cannot be taken as transcripts of actual sermons. Indeed, since in a few short verses they present discourses that could have taken hours to deliver, their evidential value is further diminished. Their sounding so much like real speeches is evidence not of their historicity but of Luke's extraordinary literary skill in creating such convincing scenes. Thus, if the sermons in Acts convey any information at all about preaching in the early church, the most that can be assumed is that they tell what Luke thought the missionary preaching of his own day should be like.

Some scholars do believe that at least two New Testament books contain material that originated in oral proclamation: 1 Peter[14] and the Epistle to the Hebrews.[15] Even if those claims are justified, however, there seems to be little reason to think that the shape of Christian preaching in the New Testament period can be reconstructed—which is to say that, while true Christian preaching began much earlier, the *history* of Christian preaching cannot be traced back earlier than the middle of the second century.

While Christian preaching itself cannot be traced earlier, however, there are two pre-Christian movements, Jewish synagogue preaching and Greco-Roman rhetoric, that must be studied before we can understand the way Christian preaching developed.

SYNAGOGUE SERMONS

The New Testament suggests that the first Christian congregations did not understand themselves as part of a new religion, but rather as Jewish synagogues differing from their co-religionists only in claiming that Jesus was the Messiah. Thus it can be expected that their organization and worship would develop along the lines that were already established, making, at first, only the adaptations required by their devotion to Christ, such as initiation by baptism and celebration of the Eucharist. Since other synagogues were accustomed to sermons, it was only natural that churches should have them too. Passages from holy Scripture read at worship assemblies were interpreted and applied to the lives of the people. This knowledge, however, does not contribute as much to clearing away the mist that hovers over the origins of Christian homiletics as might be hoped, because little trace has been left of either the beginnings of the synagogue as an institution or the earliest kinds of preaching done in synagogues.

While most scholars still think the synagogue originated during the Exile in Babylon (sixth century B.C.E.) to provide the people of God with a way to "sing the Lord's song in a strange land" (Ps. 137:4 KJV), no evidence exists to prove that is so. Indeed, the earliest traces of the institution go back only as far as the Hellenistic period. The word *synagogue* itself is Greek *(synagōgē)*, which has a root sense of gathering or assembly. The other early term is *proseuchē*, a Greek word meaning either "prayer" or "a place of prayer." The first appearance in this connection of *proseuchē*, the older of these terms, is in the third century B.C.E.[16] The oldest synagogue building to have been identified was built on the island of Delos during the second century B.C.E. In Israel itself, the oldest synagogue remains are on the Golan Heights at Gamla; they date from just before or after the beginning of the Common Era. The next oldest are in two fortresses erected by Herod the Great, Masada and the Herodium (built on a hilltop near Bethlehem), but the religious use of these buildings may date only to their occupation during the revolt against Rome, 66–70 C.E. Yet by the first century of the Common Era, synagogues were very common both within Israel and throughout the Diaspora, as literary references in the New Testament, from Josephus, and elsewhere attest. It has been estimated, for instance, that there were 365 synagogues within Jerusalem itself by that time.

Our knowledge of the worship conducted in synagogues at the time of Christian beginnings is very slim, yet the little that is known of the patterns developed after the destruction of the Temple suggests that "a Jew of the first century would find himself at home in a synagogue of the twentieth century."[17] The Sabbath morning service was dominated by readings from the Torah and the Prophets (the latter called the *haftarah*), a homily, weekly hymns, and the fixed prayers that "constituted but a small, though significant part of the day's liturgy."[18]

While "nothing is known of [the] beginnings" of the synagogue sermon,[19] it may have begun with the *Targum*, the extempore translation of the reading from the Torah into Aramaic for the benefit of worshipers who did not understand Hebrew. The Targum was nearer a paraphrase than an exact translation, and it was often embellished with haggadic[20] expansion. By the time the Temple was destroyed, however, the Targum had become a much more straightforward translation, and the instruction and edification that had been incorporated into it had been transferred to the sermon. The sprightliness that had characterized the haggadic features of the Targum, however, was not completely lost in the sermon. Haggadic interpretation continued to make more obvious the relevance of Torah to daily life.

> By using at times daring methods of interpretation, the preachers succeeded in making the Bible an unceasing source of ever-new meaning and inspiration in which answers to the problems of every generation could be found.[21]

The preachers also knew that to get their messages across, they had to make them entertaining as well as edifying. They enlivened their sermons with all the techniques of popular speech that Christian preachers of later centuries also would employ.

While elements of thousands of synagogue sermons from the first four or five centuries of the Common Era have been preserved in later collections, seldom do any appear in exactly the form in which they were delivered. And most of those that do survive come from a period that was too late to influence the evolution of Christian preaching. While there was undoubtedly a period in the early days of the church when sermons heard in its assemblies would have closely resembled in form those heard in the synagogues, none from either tradition exist today to be compared.

The oldest synagogue sermons that have been passed down are very different from any Christian sermons. We can see this by taking a quick look at the two main forms of synagogue sermons in the ancient collections. One is called the *proem* type, taking its title from the term used by Greek rhetoricians to refer to the introduction of a speech. What is introduced in this homily form, however, is not the rest of the sermon, but the lection from the Torah. Such a sermon begins with another verse entirely, one from another section of the canon, that makes a point similar to that made in the first verse of that day's reading.[22] "From the 'remote' verse the preacher gives a series of explanations and clarifications that succeed in shedding new light on the Torah reading."[23] Such a sermon would end with the first verse of the Torah lection, and then that passage would be read by those assigned that responsibility.[24]

While the other sermon form to be examined is more like Christian sermons in that it involves exposition of the lection itself rather than serving as an introduction to its reading, it probably represents an even later development. Surviving examples are in collections known as *Tanchuma,* which have been so radically edited that what remains is a "literary" production that was never preached in the form in which it has come down. Nevertheless, it is possible to reconstruct the form of the sermon and even occasionally to extrapolate something close to what must have been delivered. The sermons in the *Tanchuma* seem to have been created as responses to questions about Jewish law, because they begin with the expression "Let our rabbi teach us" *(yelammedenu rabbenu).*

In presenting an example of the genre, Stegner lists the elements that were generally included in sermons of this type:

> 1. The sermon begins with a statement of the first verse of the passage or several words from the first verse....
> 2. A key word or words are explained and emphasized throughout the sermon.

3. Other words and phrases from the whole passage (not just the initial verse) are explained and repeated in the sermon.

4. Other biblical verses are cited for purposes of illustration or for developing side points, etc.

5. Illustrations are drawn from Scripture or contemporary life.

6. If scriptural illustrations are used, the biblical story is frequently retold with imaginative additions to the text.

7. In the conclusion a word or words from the opening verse are repeated to indicate the sermon is ended.

8. Frequently, the main thrust of the sermon is summarized in the conclusion.[25]

Such an abstract description could leave the impression that *yelammedenu* sermons were very similar to patristic Christian homilies, but actually they were quite different in form and, especially, in content. This can be seen clearly in the example of the type examined by Stegner. (**See Vol. 2, pp. 3-6,** for a translation of this sermon.) Its text is Genesis 9:20, "And Noah became a man of the soil."[26] For the preacher, the word *soil* carries a sense of defilement; it is as though the text read "And Noah became dirty," with all the connotations that expression might have. Thus the sermon is an exhortation to ritual purity and the study of Torah rather than to the lesser activities of human life. While the allegorical interpretation of Christian preaching from at least Origen on was as figurative as this, the difference in the way the case is argued and the ideal of the religious life held up have a very different atmosphere and bespeak quite different communities and cultures.

In short, while Christians learned from the synagogue to have sermons at their worship services and to base those sermons on biblical passages that were read at the services, the oldest synagogue sermons that have survived occurred too late to resemble the earliest Christian preaching very closely.

GRECO-ROMAN RHETORIC

The oratorical tradition of classical culture was another influence from the environment of the early church that, through the centuries, proved almost as powerful a force in shaping Christian preaching as the textual commentary of synagogue sermons. What is important for the history of preaching is not so much the *history* of Greco-Roman rhetoric as introducing *concepts* and *vocabulary* that will recur in the history of Christian preaching—especially in the golden age of the Fathers, when all of the great preachers had been trained as rhetoricians, and in the Renaissance, Reformation, and Romantic periods, when the recovery of classical rhetoric had considerable influence on preaching.[27]

Most cultures in the history of the world have produced great oratory. The difference between the ancient Greeks and the others is that Greece also developed a technical vocabulary about oratory that facilitated analysis of it. This conceptualization of public speaking was a result of there being no professional lawyers in Greece. Citizens had to argue their own cases in court, and some were better at it than others. Thus the conceptualization began in the fifth century B.C.E. when little handbooks about effective techniques to use started to appear. The great synthesis of Greek thought on the subject was the work of Aristotle,[28] who defined the aim of rhetoric as the discovery of the available means of persuasion. While many others also wrote on the topic, the Roman appropriation of rhetorical theory is best seen in the compilations of Cicero[29] and Quintilian.[30]

The three sorts of occasions on which Athenians might be called upon to speak in public were in the courts of law, in the legislative assembly, and at ceremonial events. Each required its own appropriate manner of speaking (what the Romans called *genus dicendi*). The law courts, for instance, had to decide what had happened in the past, the *boule* had to agree upon what needed to be done in the future, and ceremonial occasions called for praising or blaming someone or something in the present. These three types of oratory came to be called, respectively, the forensic, the deliberative, and the demonstrative or "epideictic."[31]

Classical thought divided the task of preparing to speak into five stages: invention (figuring out what to say to make one's case), disposition (the outline the speech should follow), elocution (style, especially in the sense of deciding what figures of sound and thought would best contribute to making one's case), memory (preparation for delivery), and delivery itself. Invention recognized the existence of three kinds of "proof": the trustworthiness of the speaker *(ethos)*, reason *(logos)*, and appeal to the emotions *(pathos)*. Each of these seemed generally more appropriate to one part of a speech than another: *ethos* should be established in the introduction, *logos* was necessary for the body,[32] and *pathos* was most effective in the conclusion. Instead of kinds of proof, Cicero spoke of the orator's duties. Since, however, these are to prove *(probare)*, to delight *(delectare)*, and to stir or move *(flectere)*, he obviously meant something very similar. Each of these duties could be connected with one of the levels of style: the plain for proof, the middle for pleasure, and the grand for moving. (The grand is not the most flowery; that is the middle, which is intended for the pleasure of the audience. The grand style aims at moving the audience to believe or do what the speaker is calling upon them to believe or do.)

"Disposition" identified the elements thought to be required for each type of speech. Since the forensic speech was taken as normative from the beginning, the textbooks usually did not discuss in such detail the outline of either of the other types. A forensic speech was expected to have six parts: introduction, narration, partition, confirmation, refutation, and conclusion. In the introduction the speaker had to make the audience well disposed, attentive, and receptive. The narration set the facts of the case before the jury. In the partition the audience was told what would follow in a list of either the points of disagreement or the points the speaker would try to prove. In the confirmation those points were made, and in the refutation the opponent's case was attacked. The conclusion involved a combination of summarizing what had been said and arousing feeling against the opponent and in favor of the speaker. The appropriateness of such a pattern for arguing a case in court at a time when each of the two speakers was given only one opportunity to speak is immediately apparent. What is not so apparent is the helpfulness of this pattern to a preacher trying to write a sermon, since this outline provides no place for the explication of the biblical text on which the sermon is based. However, that would not prevent many homiletical authorities in the future from insisting that preachers should follow it exactly.

The elements of a deliberative speech were essentially the same as those of a forensic speech, although stating the way the speech was divided into its points was not required, nor was a narration, although one could be included. The proof was divided into a series of "headings" *(kephalaia)*. Epideictic speeches had only three main parts—the introduction, body, and conclusion—but there were elaborate lists of topics that should be included in the body, dealing with the life of the person being celebrated or attacked or the quality being praised or blamed.

Good style was thought to have four virtues: (1) grammatical correctness; (2) clarity in expression and arrangement of ideas; (3) propriety in matching style to content; and (4) ornamentation with figures of sound and thought to amplify what was said, give it emphasis and distinction, and maintain contact with the audience. The three levels of style have already been mentioned. Over the centuries in which rhetorical theory was being refined, different writers disagreed over taxonomy, but one way to discuss the tasks of style was to divide the subject into the selection of individual words and of combinations of words. Issues in the choice of separate words included using the *mot juste,* how classical the word had to be, and figurative uses ("tropes") such as synecdoche, metonymy, hyperbole, metaphor, or deliberate misuse of a word.[33]

The combination of words was called *composition* and involved figures of sound, figures of thought, and groupings of phrases. Modern usage tends to combine the first two into "figures of speech," but the ancients recognized that some of these forceful uses of language work through their effect on the ear. Thus anaphora, alliteration, assonance, and *homoiteleuton* were called figures of sound. Other figures of speech, however, depended on the ideas they expressed. Such figures of thought included antithesis, rhetorical question, apostrophe, climax, chiasmus, and lingering on a subject while appearing to say something else *(expolitio)*. Words usually were grouped in periodic sentences, that is, sentences consisting of a "number of elements, often balanced or antithetical, and existing in perfectly clear syntactical relationship to one another."[34] The opposite of such a way of organizing sentences is the "running" or "run-on" iterative style.

The two remaining stages in the preparation of a speech recognized by classical rhetoric were memory and delivery. It was assumed that speeches not given impromptu[35] were to be memorized, and the rhetoricians devised elaborate techniques for such feats of memorization; techniques that are taught today by authors of self-improvement books promising better memory. These, however, had little influence on the history of preaching. And advice on delivery then was not very different from what is familiar today. As such, little needs to be said about these topics to prepare the way for the appropriation of classical rhetoric by Christian homiletics.

THE OLDEST KNOWN CHRISTIAN SERMON

That there was preaching at Christian assemblies for worship from the earliest days is clear from a description of such assemblies written by Justin Martyr in the middle of the second century:

> On the day called Sunday all who live in cities or in the country gather together in one place, and the memoirs of the Apostles or the writings of the prophets are read, as long as time permits. Then when the reader has finished, the Ruler in a discourse instructs and exhorts to the imitation of these good things.[36]

After that the Eucharist continued. We know something of what that preaching was like from two works from the mid- to late-second century that meet the criterion of being texts written for oral delivery to a Christian congregation assembled for worship.

The first has been known since the fourth century as *The Second Epistle of Clement to the Corinthians,* under the belief that it was written by Clement of Rome.[37] Both 1 Clement and 2 Clement were associated with each other in the thought of the time and in the manuscripts.[38] Analysis of style, however, shows that they do not have the same author. And explicit references in the text identify 2 Clement as a sermon rather than a letter, e.g., such indications of the oral nature of the document as "now while we are being exhorted by the presbyters" (17.3).[39]

This sermon fills about ten pages of a modern book and can be read aloud in approximately half an hour. It begins with the strong christological claim that "we ought to think of Jesus Christ just as we do of God."[40] It appears that the sermon was a response to the reading of Isaiah 54:1, which says:

> Sing, O barren one who did not bear;
> burst into song and shout,
> you who have not been in labor!
> For the children of the desolate woman will be more
> than the children of her that is married, says the LORD.

This verse is understood here, as it is in Galatians 4:27, to refer to the relative situations of the church and Israel. With that, however, the parallels of 2 Clement with Paul cease, since the sermon comes close to preaching salvation by works rather than grace.

The argument of the sermon is that since Jesus has shown such mercy on Christians by calling them to salvation, they must demonstrate their gratitude by living in a manner consistent with their calling so they will receive the reward that can be theirs. "If we do the will of the Father and keep the flesh pure and keep the commandments of the Lord, we shall receive eternal life" (8.4).[41] While the sermon rambles a bit, it has a relatively clear thread of thought, which is summarized by Grant and Graham:

1. God's gracious, creative action in Christ on our behalf (1:1–2:7)
2. The response of acknowledging him in deed (3:1–4:5)
3. The Christian warfare in this world (5:1–7:6)
4. Repentance in expectation of the world to come (8:1–12:6)

5. Repentance and faithful obedience in gratitude and in hope (13:1–15:5)

6. While we have time, then, let us repent, using present opportunities to prepare for the judgment to come (16:1–20:5)[42]

The sermon ends with a doxology:

> To the only invisible God, the father of truth, who sent forth to us the Saviour and prince of immortality, through whom he also made manifest to us truth and the life of heaven, to him be the glory for ever and ever. Amen.[43]

The argument is developed by frequent quotations from Scripture. These are remarkable not only for their quantity but also for the range of material regarded as canonical. In the twenty chapters, each of which is hardly more than a paragraph long, there are about sixty explicit quotations from or allusions to the Bible, not to mention other possible echoes. Most references to the Hebrew Bible are to the Prophets or Psalms. More surprisingly at so early a date, most of the books of the New Testament are also cited, the most obvious exception being all of the Johannine literature.[44] There are even a few quotations from apocryphal gospels, especially the Gospel of the Egyptians. Karl Paul Donfried has pointed out that many of the chapters in the midsection of the sermon (chaps. 3–14) follow the pattern of (1) statement of theme, (2) scripture quotation, (3) exhortation, and (4) scripture quotation. As to the way the quotations are used,

> they are illustrations of the point being made, yet, the very fact that these quotations are not simply taken from ancient worthies but carry the authority of the Jewish and early Christian traditions, allows them not only to illustrate but to support authoritatively that which is being said.[45]

Different scholars have assigned the provenance of 2 Clement to every major center of the early church, but, with the exception of Donfried, they agree that it was written in the middle of the second century. This makes it the oldest surviving Christian sermon. Wherever it was written, the author, to be literate, would necessarily have had some exposure to classical rhetoric, on which the educational system of the time was built. The effect on him of that exposure, however, was minimal. In this regard he was just the opposite of the writer of the next oldest sermon that has been preserved.

MELITO'S PASCHAL HOMILY

Known only by title and unidentified fragments before 1940, Melito of Sardis's *Homily on the Passover*[46] (**see Vol. 2, pp. 6-18**, for a translation) has become widely recognized for the light that it sheds on the early history of the Christian calendar and liturgy. Melito, bishop of a church in eastern Asia Minor during the last third of the second century, was the author of about twenty other works that are still lost except for fragments.[47] His contemporaries regarded him as one of the "great luminaries" of Asia, and Tertullian admired his prose style. Beyond his belonging to the Quartodeciman party, little else is known about him except what may be deduced from his homily.

Another source of insight into Melito's sermon, however, is knowledge of the situation in Sardis. Situated about sixty miles inland from Smyrna (modern Izmir) and Ephesus, Sardis was built as the capital city of the Lydian Empire, the last king of which had been the Croesus of legendary wealth. The city retained its importance under the Persians and Seleucids, and under Roman rule it was one of the leading cities of the province of Asia. Sardis was one of the seven churches of the Revelation: the seer was instructed to tell the angel of that church that it had a name for being alive, but was really dead (3:1). The most important thing about Sardis as background to Melito's homily, however, is the size and influence of the Jewish community there. The enormous synagogue that has been excavated there, which had a main hall that could accommodate as many as a thousand worshipers, was not acquired by the Jews until the early third century, but it nevertheless indicates how large the community must have been half a century earlier when Melito was bishop.

Awareness of the size of this community is necessary for understanding Melito, because "almost a third of the text of the Homily on the Passion is preoccupied with the condemnation of 'Israel.'"[48] While persecution of Christians in the Roman Empire was not nearly so intense as it would become in a little more than a century, theirs was not a religio licta, and they could be and were persecuted and martyred. Although such incidents were sporadic, local, and often mob actions rather than the result of judicial process,[49] they seem to have intensified in that area during this period. Another work of Melito, an apology[50] directed to Marcus Aurelius of which a fragment is preserved in Eusebius,[51] calls attention to this intensification in stating that "something that has never happened at all before, the race of the godly is persecuted, being harassed by new decrees throughout Asia."[52]

Near the time of Melito's sermon, eleven Christians from nearby

Philadelphia were martyred at Smyrna, as was also Smyrna's venerable bishop, Polycarp. And the *Martyrdom of Polycarp* links Jews with Greeks as those who agitated for his death (12.2). This was not unusual in Melito's time and area. "In the persecutions which were to wrack Asia in the reign of Marcus Aurelius [A.D. 161–80] the Jew was often in the background."[53] This should be remembered when one reads Melito's statement that "God is murdered. The king of Israel is destroyed by an Israelite hand" (96).[54] This fact does not excuse Melito's statement, but it does point to an extenuating circumstance.

Melito's sermon dates from the period when the paschal mystery was celebrated as a unified event including not only everything from trial to resurrection and ascension, but all Christ's work of redemption, including the incarnation. Thus the exact occasion on which it was preached cannot be tied down neatly according to the Christian calendar of today. The one night on which Melito preached celebrated everything from Christmas to Pentecost.

Melito's Quartodecimanism[55] is also important for understanding his sermon. The name of the group is derived from the Latin word for "fourteen" because of their distinctive belief that Easter—or, more properly, the Christian Passover—should be celebrated on the same day as the Jewish Passover. As long as the Temple existed, Passover lambs were slaughtered on the fourteenth day of the month of Nisan in preparation for the *Pesach,* which began at sundown that day. This is to say that the paschal observance did not ordinarily occur on a Sunday; the fast began on whatever day of the week Nisan 14 fell. It also means that the early part of Melito's liturgical celebration ran simultaneously with that of the synagogue in Sardis.

The paschal observance began with a fast during the day of Nisan 14 followed by a vigil that night.[56] At "cock crow" (the third watch of the night, which lasted from midnight until 3:00 A.M.) the fast was broken by an *agape* meal followed by the Eucharist.[57] During the vigil there was a reading of Exodus 12, and Melito's homily commented on that passage. For a fuller picture of the liturgical context, we should remember that in Melito's time, Christian assemblies were still held in private homes, there were no distinctive garments for clergy, and the bishop probably sat while he preached.

Essentially, the sermon is an interpretation of the account of the Passover in Exodus as a foreshadowing or "type" of the death and resurrection of Christ. It begins with a long account of salvation history, showing the necessity for a redeemer. That is followed by a statement of the principles of typological interpretation, which leads into an identification of the salvation wrought through Christ with all that was prefigured in the exodus, especially the Passover. Next comes an extended apostrophe to Israel, in which Israel is blamed for rejecting Christ and necessitating the crucifixion. The peak of emotional intensity occurs when Melito speaks in the voice of Christ, proclaiming and offering the salvation he brings. There follows an almost creedal summary of the work of Christ that leads into the doxological conclusion.

The homily is notable for the thoroughness with which it introduces classical rhetoric into Christian preaching, the indebtedness it may have had to Jewish Passover celebration, and the way it anticipates later Christian liturgical forms. Campbell Bonner, who published the text of Melito's homily in 1940, considered it to be the first example of Christian art prose, but he attributed its style to biblical and Oriental sources. Since then, patristic scholars have suggested instead that it represents the Asian school of classical rhetoric prominent in the Second Sophistic.[58]

The Asianic style of the Second Sophistic is notable for its use of what are called Gorgian figures. A representative of the First Sophistic and one of the first teachers of rhetoric in Athens, Gorgias went there originally as an ambassador from his native city, Leontius, in Sicily. The impression he made was striking enough to provoke Plato to write a dialogue against him.[59] What made Gorgias's public speaking so striking was his use of what have since been known as his "figures":

> These include phrases or clauses with contrasting thought (antithesis), often of equal length (parison); rhyme at the ends of clauses (homoeoteleuton); and a fondness for sound play of all sorts (paronomasia).[60]

In Melito's sermon we can find these figures and others as well, with anaphora, apostrophe, and personification being among the more conspicuous.

Most of these can be seen in the first three sentences of the homily:

> The scripture from the Hebrew Exodus has been read
>   and the words of the mystery have been plainly stated,
>   how the sheep is sacrificed
>   and how the people is saved
>   and how Pharaoh is scourged through the mystery.
> Understand, therefore, beloved,
>   how it is new and old,
>   eternal and temporary,

perishable and imperishable
    mortal and immortal, this mystery of the Pascha:
old as regards the law,
    but new as regards the word;
temporary as regards the model,
    eternal because of the grace;
perishable because of the slaughter of the sheep,
imperishable because of the life of the Lord;
mortal because of the burial in earth,
immortal because of the rising from the dead.[61]

Antithesis gives the passage its basic structure, the contrasted clauses are of similar length, and the parallel phrases have the same ending in Greek. In the first sentence, for instance, the words for "stated," "sacrificed," "saved," and "scourged" all end in *-etai*.[62] Anaphora occurs in the way the last three phrases in that sentence begin with "how." Apostrophe occurs in Melito's address to Israel, and personification when he speaks in the voice of Christ. This small sample does not exhaust the rhetorical devices used in the homily but only indicates the density with which they occur.

Efforts to evaluate the homily say as much about the taste of the critic as they do the quality of the homily. Some consider the homily eloquent and beautiful while others find it showy. It can be said objectively, however, that the homily reflects both the influence of the Septuagint, especially the poetic books, and also that of the sort of rhetoric with which professional orators were dazzling Asia Minor at the time. From this point on, classical rhetoric will shape Christian preaching.

But, as noted above, this homily has liturgical as well as homiletical significance. It has been argued, for instance, that it reflects the influence of Jewish liturgy. Hall says that it "shows signs of direct debt to the Jewish Passover recitation called the Haggadah."[63] It has also been argued[64] that the homily is a direct ancestor of the *Exultet* sung at the Easter vigil in the Western rite, which begins:

> Rejoice now, all ye heavenly legions of Angels: and celebrate the divine mysteries with exultation: and for the King that cometh with victory, let the trumpet proclaim salvation.[65]

Assuming Talley's date for Melito's homily of "around 165,"[66] one can see that by Melito's time Christian preaching had been going on for more than a century and a quarter. Already it had begun to show two of the main characteristics that would characterize it throughout the patristic period: (1) it would be based on the continuous exposition of a biblical text, and (2) it would utilize the techniques of Greco-Roman rhetoric. The remaining chapters of this section will explore how these characteristics were refined.

FOR FURTHER READING

Grant, Robert M. *First and Second Clement.* Vol. 2 of *The Apostolic Fathers: A New Translation and Commentary.* New York: Thomas Nelson, 1965.

———. *Greek Apologists of the Second Century.* Philadelphia: Westminster, 1988.

Kennedy, George A. *Classical Rhetoric and Its Christian and Secular Tradition from Ancient to Modern Times.* Chapel Hill: University of North Carolina Press, 1980.

Meyers, Erich L. "Synagogue." Pages 252-60 in vol. 1 of *ABD*. Edited by David Noel Freedman et al. New York: Doubleday, 1992.

Stegner, Richard. "The Ancient Jewish Synagogue Homily." In *Greco-Roman Literature and the New Testament.* Edited by David E. Aune. SBLSBS, no. 21. Atlanta: Scholars Press, 1988.

Sur la Pâque et fragments Méliton de Sardes. Introduction, critical text, translation, and notes by Othmar Perler. SC, no. 123. Paris: Cerf, 1966.

Notes

1. Some bodies speak of "ordinances" rather than sacraments, but most of them observe at least baptism and the Lord's Supper, the main exception being the Society of Friends, or Quakers.

2. Charles Rice, "Preaching," in *ER,* ed. Mircea Eliade (New York: Macmillan, 1987), 11:494. It is possible, however, that this position is overstated. Professor Frank Reynolds of the University of Chicago has informed me in a letter dated April 30, 1997, that preaching as defined in this chapter "has always and continues to be a central component in Buddhism." He is also of the opinion that preaching is important in Jainism, but says that little has been published on the subject. Mr. Alok Gupta told me that preaching is a regular part of the worship of his Hindu tradition and his congregation in Mysore, India.

3. I will say more about early Jewish preaching later in this chapter.

4. See D. S. Margoliouth, "Preaching (Muslim)," in *ERE,* ed. James Hastings et al. (Edinburgh: T&T Clark; New York: Scribner's, 1910), 10:221-24.

5. This is an adaptation of a definition I first gave in my *Elements of Homiletic: A*

Method for Preparing to Preach (New York: Pueblo, 1982), 7, and restated in my article "History of Preaching," in *Concise Encyclopedia of Preaching,* ed. William H. Willimon and Richard Lischer (Louisville: Westminster John Knox, 1995), 184. Each part of the definition is analyzed in *Elements of Homiletic,* 7-16. The version of the definition given above seeks to make it general enough to include the preaching that occurs in non-Christian religions, yet the present work will consider very little other than Christian preaching.

6. Standard Roman Catholic publications also list theological argument as a type of preaching and there have indeed been sermons in the history of the church that consisted largely of that. On the Roman Catholic classifications, see Fred A. Baumer, "Toward the Development of Homiletic as Rhetorical Genre: A Critical Study of Roman Catholic Preaching in the United States Since Vatican Council II" (Ph.D. diss., Northwestern University, 1985).

7. Saba Holland, *A Memoir of the Reverend Sydney Smith, by His daughter, Lady Holland* (London: Longman, Brown, Green, and Longmans, 1855), 1:43.

8. "To proclaim" and "to preach" are interchangeable translations of the verb Paul uses here, *kērussein.*

9. Dibelius's words are quoted by Norman Perrin in *The New Testament: An Introduction* (New York: Harcourt Brace Jovanovich, 1974), 19.

10. Ibid., 19-21.

11. See, for example, Barnabas Lindars, *The Gospel of John,* NCB (London: Oliphants, 1972).

12. "The speeches in Acts—Dibelius (*Studies in the Acts of the Apostles*, ed. Heinrich Greeven, trans. Mary Ling [New York: Scribner's, 1956], 150) has counted 24, of which 8 belong to Peter, 9 to Paul—occupy, in round figures, 300 of the book's 1000 verses." Ernst Haenchen, *The Acts of the Apostles: A Commentary,* trans., rev. and brought up to date by R. McL. Wilson (Philadelphia: Westminster, 1971), 104 n. 1.

13. For a summary of research on the speeches in Acts up until the time of writing, see Werner Georg Kümmel, *Introduction to the New Testament,* trans. Howard Clark Kee, rev. ed. (Nashville: Abingdon, 1975), 167-69.

14. Kümmel, however, does not believe any part of 1 Peter was ever a sermon. See ibid., 419-21.

15. Yet Kümmel does believe that Hebrews is a sermon to which there has been added an epistolary conclusion. See ibid., 398. Johann Berger proposed the homiletical origin of Hebrews as early as 1797.

16. This information on the history of the synagogue is based on Erich L. Meyers, "Synagogue," in *ABD,* ed. David Noel Freedman et al. (New York: Doubleday, 1992), 6:252-60. I also consulted Geoffrey Wigoder, *The Story of the Synagogue: A Diaspora Museum Book* (San Francisco: Harper & Row, 1986).

17. Wigoder, *The Story of the Synagogue,* 17.

18. Ben Zion Wacholder, "Prolegomenon" to Jacob Mann, in *The Bible as Read and Preached in the Old Synagogue* (1940; reprint, New York: KTAV, 1971), 1:xi.

19. Joseph Heinemann, "Preaching. In the Talmudic Period," in *Encyclopaedia Judaica* (Jerusalem: Keter, 1971), 13:994.

20. To oversimplify, rabbinic exegesis is usually classified as either *Halakah* or

Haggadah (also transliterated as *Aggadah*). Halakic interpretation is an analytical process aimed at deriving rules and principles, stating clearly what is involved in the observance of Torah. Haggadic interpretation is freer, more creative, analogical, and homiletic, and involves stories and examples. To make the matter more confusing, Haggadah is also the term used to refer to the liturgy for the Passover Seder.

21. Heinemann, "Preaching. In the Talmudic Period," 13:994.

22. The nearest Christian equivalent to the proem form comes in the thematic sermons of the late Middle Ages in which a "sermonette" (horrible word!) on a protheme (a biblical text differing from the text of the sermon proper) is preached while the congregation is assembling. The protheme had to make the same point that the theme of the sermon proper would make. In contemporary worship, children's sermons often seem to serve a similar purpose.

23. William Richard Stegner, "The Ancient Jewish Synagogue Homily" in *Greco-Roman Literature and the New Testament,* ed. David E. Aune, SBLSBS, no. 21 (Atlanta: Scholars Press, 1988), 53. Stegner provides a translation and an analysis of a proem homily, 55-58.

24. In time there would be lectionary cycles established, but it is not clear that those existed when the church was still under the influence of the synagogue. The cycles of Torah and Haftarah developed separately. The one-year cycle still in use began in Babylon, but a four-year (actually longer) cycle was followed in Palestine.

25. Stegner, "The Ancient Jewish Synagogue Homily," 58-62. The sermon translated is found on 60-62.

26. Modern English translations treat "man of the soil" as an appositive of Noah, but the homily depends on a more literal consideration of the Hebrew text.

27. The easiest access to the history of Greco-Roman rhetoric is through the numerous writings of George A. Kennedy, including *Classical Rhetoric and Its Christian and Secular Tradition from Ancient to Modern Times* (Chapel Hill: University of North Carolina Press, 1980); *New Testament Interpretation Through Rhetorical Criticism* (Chapel Hill: University of North Carolina Press, 1984); and *A New History of Classical Rhetoric* (Princeton: Princeton University Press, 1994). Also invaluable is Richard A. Lanham, *A Handlist of Rhetorical Terms,* 2nd ed. (Berkeley and Los Angeles: University of California Press, 1991); Brian Vickers, *In Defence of Rhetoric* (Oxford: Clarendon Press; New York: Oxford University Press, 1988); and James L. Golden, Goodwin F. Berquist, and William E. Coleman, *The Rhetoric of Western Thought,* 3rd ed. (Dubuque, Iowa: Kendall/Hunt, 1983).

28. The most common edition of the Greek text is that which appears in Aristotle, *The "Art" of Rhetoric,* trans. J. H. Freese, Loeb Classical Library (Cambridge: Harvard University Press, 1926; London: William Heinemann, 1926). George A. Kennedy has translated it more recently, with an introduction, notes, and appendices in *Aristotle on Rhetoric: A Theory of Civic Discourse* (New York: Oxford University Press, 1991).

29. In addition to being an orator, Cicero wrote extensively on the subject of rhetoric. His works on the subject, all of which are available in Loeb editions, include *On Invention,* written while he was still in his teens and destined to be the most popular rhetorical textbook of the Middle Ages; *On the Orator,* written as a dialogue; *Brutus,* a history of Greco-Roman rhetoric in the form of a dialogue; and *Orator,* in

which he states his own taste in rhetoric. A convenient English edition of *On the Orator* and *Brutus* is *Cicero on Oratory and Orators,* trans. or ed. by J. S. Watson, Landmarks in Rhetoric and Public Address (Carbondale: Southern Illinois University Press, 1970). Another handbook long thought to have been by Cicero and very influential in the Middle Ages is the anonymous *Rhetorica ad Herennium,* translated for the Loeb Classical Library by Harry Caplan (1954).

30. The Latin text of Quintilian's *Institutio Oratoria* and a translation by H. E. Butler appear in four volumes in the Loeb series (1921–36).

31. There are other English translations of these and indeed most of the technical terms of rhetoric.

32. Needless to say, a good bit of invention consisted of the discovery of arguments to be used in proof. Earlier, this was done by reviewing the appropriate *topoi* (Latin, *loci*), the "places" to look for arguments. Later, however, more attention was concentrated on *stasis* (Latin, *status*), which made the identification of the basic issue of the case the determining factor in the kinds of argument sought.

33. All of these differ from the "figures" proper in that they involve only one word. This is one of the more confusing distinctions to modern readers.

34. Lanham, *A Handlist of Rhetorical Terms,* 112-13. For an idea of how complex such a sentence could be, see the diagram of a sentence of Isocrates made by Kennedy in *Classical Rhetoric,* 36.

35. As declamations of the Second Sophistic were given.

36. *1 Apol.* 67. The translation used is that of *St. Justin Martyr: The First and Second Apologies,* trans. with intro. and notes by Leslie William Barnard, ACW, no. 56 (Mahwah, N.J.: Paulist Press, 1997).

37. Scholars often point out that *The Second Epistle of Clement to the Corinthians* is not by Clement, is not an epistle, and was not written to the Corinthians.

38. They were even considered by some in the early church to be part of the New Testament canon, as may be seen from their inclusion in Codex Alexandrinus, an important Greek manuscript of the entire Bible from the early fifth century.

39. Karl Paul Donfried claims we cannot call 2 Clement a sermon or homily because we cannot give a firm form-critical description for either classification. Then he calls it a deliberative speech, ignoring the classical form of that *Gattung* and at the same time discerning in the work a pattern altogether different from that of a deliberative speech. Finally, he says that the probable sociological setting for the pattern he discovers was "oral exhortation to an assembled Christian congregation" (48), which sounds remarkably close to the definition of preaching proposed above for this history of preaching. *The Setting of Second Clement in Early Christianity,* NovTSup, no. 38 (Leiden: E. J. Brill, 1974).

40. Quotations from 2 Clement are taken from either Kirsopp Lake's translation of *The Apostolic Fathers,* vol. 1, in the LCL (1912–13), or Robert M. Grant and Holt H. Graham's *First and Second Clement,* vol. 2 of *The Apostolic Fathers: A New Translation and Commentary* (New York: Thomas Nelson, 1965), depending on which makes clearest the sense to which attention is being called. The critical perspective taken is very close to that of Grant and Graham.

41. Grant and Graham, *First and Second Clement,* 120.

42. Ibid., 111.

43. Lake, *The Apostolic Fathers,* 1:163.

44. Some deviations of quotations from the text of the canonical Gospels raise the question of whether the author was quoting from oral tradition, written textual variants not otherwise known, or from inaccurate memory of the canonical text.

45. Donfried, *The Setting of Second Clement in Early Christianity,* 96-97.

46. The translation ordinarily quoted will be that in *The Christological Controversy,* trans. and ed. Richard A. Norris Jr., Sources of Early Christian Thought (Philadelphia: Fortress, 1980).

47. The fragments are collected, translated, and commented upon in *Melito of Sardis:* On Pascha *and Fragments,* texts and translations edited by Stuart George Hall, OECT (Oxford: Clarendon Press, 1979).

48. John Griffiths Pedley, "Sardis," in *ABD,* 5:984.

49. The process itself almost encouraged that since Roman law did not provide for governmental agencies to detect the commission of crimes and to prosecute the perpetrators. Rather, charges were brought into court by *delatores,* citizens who made the accusations.

50. The Apologists were the second group of Christian writers after the New Testament period. Whereas the Apostolic Fathers wrote practical treatises addressed to the church, the Apologists wrote defenses (which is what "apologies" means in this context) of Christianity. Many of the treatises were, like that of Melito, addressed to the current emperor and presented arguments against the persecution of Christians. On the Apologists in general see Robert M. Grant, *Greek Apologists of the Second Century* (Philadelphia: Westminster, 1988). His treatment of Melito is on pp. 92-99.

51. *Ecclesiastical History* 4.26.5-11. The Greek text of the fragment and an English translation appear in *Melito of Sardis:* On Pascha *and Fragments,* 62-65.

52. Ibid., 63.

53. W. H. C. Frend, *Martyrdom and Persecution in the Early Church: A Study of a Conflict from the Maccabees to Donatus* (Garden City, N.Y.: Anchor Books, 1967), 194.

54. Norris, *The Christological Controversy,* 46.

55. This term is slightly anachronistic since Quartodecimans were only labeled as such later in the century during the synods over the date of Easter. It is used here, however, because it calls attention to the nature of Melito's paschal celebration. I am grateful to Professor Thomas J. Talley for pointing this out.

56. By Jewish reckoning a day began at sundown rather than midnight, as in the modern usage, or at daybreak, as in the Gospels.

57. *Sur la Pâque et fragments Méliton de Sardes,* intro., critical text, trans., and notes by Othmar Perler, SC, no. 123 (Paris: Cerf, 1966), 25. For a thorough analysis of the observance of the paschal vigil up until the time of Nicaea, see Thomas J. Talley, *The Origins of the Liturgical Year* (New York: Pueblo, 1986), 1-37. What is known of the Quartodeciman vigil comes from a second-century apocryphal work, *Epistula Apostolorum,* which appears in *New Testament Apocrypha,* ed. Wilhelm Schneemelcher; English trans. R. McL. Wilson (Philadelphia: Westminster, 1963), 1:189-227. The relevant section is on pp. 199-200.

58. Hall provides the references to the literature in *Melito of Sardis* On Pascha *and*

Fragments, xxiii-xxiv. On the Second Sophistic see George Kennedy, *A New History of Classical Rhetoric,* 230-41; on Asianism, see pp. 95-96.

59. Brian Vickers concludes a devastating analysis of the dialogue by saying: "In a careful reading, then, Plato's case against rhetoric in the *Gorgias* is based on a calculated perversion of his own principles of dialectic. We can no longer be taken in by Socrates' claim that he is pursuing the truth." *In Defence of Rhetoric,* 84-120, with the quoted words appearing on the last page.

60. Kennedy, *A New History of Classical Rhetoric,* 20. In *Classical Rhetoric and Its Christian and Secular Tradition,* 29-30, Kennedy comes as close as one can in English to giving the effect of one of Gorgias's Greek sentences (taken from his description of Helen of Troy): "Born from such stock, she had godlike beauty, which taking and not mistaking, she kept. In many did she work much desire for her love, and her one body was the cause of bringing together many bodies of men thinking great thoughts for great goals, of whom some had greatness of wealth, some the glory of ancient nobility, some the vigor of personal agility, some command of acquired knowledge. And all came because of a passion which loved to conquer and a love of honor which was unconquered. . . ."

61. Hall, *Melito of Sardis:* On Pascha *and Fragments,* 3. Hall's translation is followed here, because he arranges it typographically to show the rhetorical structure.

62. The first has an *eta* instead of an *epsilon,* but the difference in sound would be small.

63. Hall, *Melito of Sardis:* On Pascha *and Fragments,* xxvi. He goes on to spell out what he means by that and to summarize other theories.

64. Perler, *Sur la Pâque et fragments Méliton de Sardis,* 24-29.

65. The translation used is that of *The People's Anglican Missal in the American Edition* (Mt. Sinai, N.Y.: Frank Gavin Liturgical Foundation, Inc., 1961), A 185.

66. Talley, *Origins of the Liturgical Year,* 32.

CHAPTER 2

THE HOMILY TAKES SHAPE

THE PATTERN OF CLASSICAL EDUCATION

While it is true that training in Greco-Roman rhetoric such as Melito of Sardis received was to have enormous influence on Christian preaching, another element of the classical education system was to play an even more decisive role in its development. Like the modern pattern of formally socializing children into a culture, classical *paidea* also had its elementary, secondary, and advanced stages. "In Rome as in Greece rhetoric belonged to the sphere of higher education and was its chief manifestation."[1] Elementary education in antiquity strikes modern people as very elementary indeed, consisting of little more than learning how to read, write, and count a little through a regimen of mechanical drill and corporal punishment.[2]

For the future of Christian preaching, it was secondary education that was decisive in its importance. For the Greeks and, in a derivative way, for the Romans, this schooling was initiation into the culture through study of its classic literature. Primarily this was a study of poetry, which was thought to be the best expression and summary of what the society was about. And among the poets the epic poets reigned supreme: Homer for the Greeks and Virgil for the Romans. But the lyric poets and the dramatists were read as well. Generally, the only prose writings studied were those of the historians, since the works of the orators were deferred to higher education in rhetoric.

The aspect of this education that was to be so determinative for preaching was the way the literature was taught by the schoolmaster, or grammarian *(γραμματικός)*. First, students were given a plot summary of the passage they were to study, an ancient Greek equivalent of Cliffs Notes. Next, since the copies the students had of the work being studied were handwritten, there was a certain amount of variation between them, and the instructor had to lead the students laboriously through the text to be sure they were all reading the same words. After that, other difficulties imposed by the manuscripts had to be dealt with. Since writing at the time did not separate words and did not make use of punctuation, students were required, after thorough preparation, to read the passage aloud expressively to show that they could make up for these deficits. Then, after the students had gone over the text so closely several times, they took the next step by memorizing it. With such preliminary work out of the way, students undertook the real task—the explanation of the text—which was called exegesis *(ἐξήγησις)*, the word Christians have taken over to mean "biblical interpretation." Explanation involved, first of all, defining words in the text; no small task since Homer's vocabulary was archaic by then. Next, the inflected forms of the words had to be noted and the grammatical structures indicated by those forms. Students studied etymologies as guides to meaning, and pointed out figures of speech. Then the persons (divine as well as human), places, times, and events mentioned in the text had to be identified, a process that was called "historical" study.

All of this analysis, however, was not considered to be an end in itself, nor was its purpose merely aesthetic. The program was designed to initiate the young into their culture and its values. Its end, therefore, was moral education. Teachers completed their presentation of a reading by pointing to the ethical example it held up. Over time, however, readers recognized that Homer, whose writings were valued as scripture to the Greeks, often depicted the immortal gods as engaged in unedifying activities. This meant that pointing out the moral was not always a straightforward task. It was often supposed that the poet was speaking symbolically and calling for an allegorical interpretation. This program of secondary education was, therefore, socialization into the life of a community. And the method by which the grammarian taught had great influence on the way the homily developed.[3] Before that can be considered, however, it will be necessary to say something about what happened to preaching after Melito, especially in Egypt.

INTERPRETING THE WORD IN ALEXANDRIA

Several Latin homilies have come down from the early third century, most of pseudonymous attribution to Cyprian, and a few Greek homilies under the name of Hippolytus. The most influential homiletic development of the early church, however, came from Greek-speaking Egypt. As its name implies, Alexandria was founded by Alexander the Great when he conquered Egypt in 332 B.C.E. Located at the mouth of the Nile, Alexandria had access to all the Mediterranean area. Its strategic importance was recognized by Ptolemy I, one of Alexander's three *diadochoi* who inherited that part of his empire and who built it into one of the world's great cities. Ptolemy's descendants ruled his section of the empire until it passed into Roman hands after the well-known suicide of Cleopatra VII.

From the beginning Alexandria was intended to be a great cultural and intellectual hub. Ptolemy had erected there a large center dedicated to the Muses of all the arts and intellectual endeavors. In Greek the name of the center was the *Mouseion*, which, transliterated into its Latin form of *Museum,* passed on to so many later institutions. Ptolemy invited about a hundred scholars to make their homes in Alexandria, where they were supported by generous salaries. He also built and stocked the famous library there whose collection ran into hundreds of thousands of volumes. Thus from its beginning, Alexandria was the intellectual capital of the Mediterranean world, a title it continued to hold under the Romans most of the way through the third century of the Common Era.

The city had great commercial significance as well: its excellent harbor made it possible for Egypt to become the granary of the Roman Empire. The wheat trade, in addition to a variety of other products and forms of commerce, meant that the city was very prosperous, which, in turn, meant that it drew immigrants from other countries. Thus Alexandria had a Jewish population of nearly one million persons, more than twelve times the population of Jerusalem,[4] and certainly the largest community of the Diaspora. It was for this population that the Greek translation of the Hebrew Bible, the Septuagint, was made. Furthermore, several books written in Alexandria came to be included in copies of this translation. Among these apocryphal books are the Wisdom of Solomon and some of the books of Maccabees.

The most prolific author of the Alexandrian Jewish community was Philo, called "the Jew" *(Judaeus),* who lived in the last two decades before and the first five of the Common Era. During his time there was considerable strife between the Jews and the other inhabitants of Alexandria, and Philo worked hard to overcome that. At the same time he was worried that many young Jews seemed dazzled by Greco-Roman philosophy and literature and were in danger of leaving their ancestral faith. Since he himself was deeply immersed in such studies, Philo wrote a number of books showing that Judaism and the Bible were consistent with the deepest insights of Stoic, Pythagorean, and Platonic thought.

In order to do this, he used the method by which the philosophers interpreted Homer to study the Hebrew Bible. The sort of allegorical interpretation made by the grammarians mentioned above began with Stoic philosophers who assumed that any anthropomorphic descriptions of the gods and their behavior in the Homeric poems were an indication that the passages were to be understood symbolically. For the Stoics, the names of gods were references to elements or forces of nature. While philosophers of other traditions did not adopt these Stoic interpretations, they did take readily to the hermeneutical method by which they were made, and allegorical interpretation became a standard technique for getting around stories whose literal meaning offended their sensitivities.[5]

No one is certain when or how Christianity first arrived in Alexandria. Eusebius cites an anonymous "they" as saying that "Mark was the first to be sent to preach in Egypt the gospel which he had also put in writing, and was the first to establish churches in Alexandria itself" (*Hist. eccl.* 2.6).While that legend is late, a recently discovered letter of Clement of Alexandria shows that it was believed in Egypt itself in the late second century.[6] What this probably means is that by the time of Clement, even the church in Alexandria did not remember how Christianity had been planted. The earliest Christian writers from the city who can be definitely identified were the early second-century gnostic heresiarchs Basilides and Valentinus.

The first orthodox teacher there whose name has come down to us was Pantaenus. Little is known about him other than that he had traveled in India and was involved in preparing catechumens for Christian initiation in Alexandria. An older generation of scholars liked to refer to "the catechetical school of Alexandria," but too little is known to claim the sort of succession in office they described. Clement appears to have arrived in Alexandria around 180 to study under Pantaenus and stayed on to teach, possibly holding school on the model of pagan philosophers and such Christian teachers as Justin Martyr. He appears to have left

Alexandria before 215 and possibly as early as 202. There is no direct evidence that Clement taught Origen, although the influence of his thought is unmistakable. All of this is to say that remarkable Christian teachers, heretical and orthodox, are known to have been in Alexandria in the second century. While a good bit is known about some of their thoughts through their writings, little is known about either the circumstances under which they taught or the church in the city at that time.

The earliest sermon-like document from Alexandria is a delightful piece produced by Clement of Alexandria near the beginning of the third century. Many scholars consider it a homily because it is a verse-by-verse analysis of Mark 10:17-31 that seeks to provide an answer to the question *Who Is the Rich Man Who Shall Be Saved?* It even ends with a wonderful legend about John. But, since it would take a couple of hours to deliver and it is not known whether Clement was ever ordained, the most that can be said is that, while it follows the literary pattern of a homily and does so remarkably well, one cannot know whether it was delivered orally to a congregation.

ORIGEN THE ORIGINAL

Credit for creating the classical form of the homily has to go to the one who is also known as "the first Christian systematic theologian," Origen. With him the study of Christian preaching moves from the vague to the definite. After the handful of sermons that remain from an earlier time—2 Clement and Melito's homily, and the few others attributed to Cyprian and Hippolytus—there is suddenly a preacher from whose ministry more than two hundred sermons have survived. Admittedly, all but about twenty of them are preserved only in Latin translations that are by no means literal. Nevertheless, there is a large enough body of work to analyze. And from such analysis it is clear that he practiced a definite homiletical method. That method gave to Christian preaching the basic shape it was to keep until the High Middle Ages, the pattern of what is called the homily.[7] Since the preacher involved was one of the two or three greatest minds in the history of the church, there is no reason to assume that the pattern was created by anyone else. With Origen, Christian preaching not only emerges into the clear light of history, it can also be said to take shape.

Though I have already used superlatives to describe Origen, a sampling of what scholars have said about him might still be in order. One called Origen and Augustine the two greatest geniuses of the early church.[8] Another judged that "his only peers are Augustine and Thomas Aquinas and he remains the greatest theologian the Eastern Church has produced."[9] Another said:

> When changed conditions call the church's message into question, a theologian must develop an all-encompassing religious vision that enables other Christians to interpret their experience. Two theologians, more than any others, have accomplished this for the entire Christian church. Paul of Tarsus is one of them. . . . The other is Origen.[10]

The scholars quoted are the authors of the three general book-length studies of Origen that appeared in the last half of the twentieth century. A less specialized patristics authority, however, says that "compared with the achievement of Origen, the work of the earlier Fathers of the Church seems a mere prelude."[11] And a professional writer who has produced well-received books in diverse fields says, "No one ever wrestled with the inner meaning of Christianity with such formidable energy, such titanic power."[12]

While more is known about the life of Origen than the lives of most other ante-Nicene fathers, there are still major disagreements about many aspects of his life, most of which relate to how much credence should be given to later charges that he was a heretic. There is no doubt that he held opinions inconsistent with later orthodoxy. First of all, no Christian writer before the councils that established the norms in the doctrines of Christ and the Trinity had views completely consistent with the conciliar definitions. Beyond that, even those who admire Origen most have to admit that his speculations included the preexistence of human souls and the ultimate salvation of everyone. While there is general agreement that the teachings condemned as his by the emperor Justinian I and by the Second Council of Constantinople in 553 are more those of his later admirers than his own, the remaining question has to do with the extent to which his attachment to the teachings of Plato shaped the way he articulated Christian doctrine. These interpretations of Origen have divided along denominational lines. "Roman Catholic and Anglican scholars have tended to rely on the Origen of the Latin homilies and the *De Principiis* while Protestants have often used Greek fragments of the *De Principiis* and restricted themselves to works preserved in Greek."[13] Thus the latter have inclined to the more Platonic interpretation.

Present purposes, however, do not require coming down hard on one side or the other. One requires here only enough knowledge of Origen's life to understand how he developed into the preacher he came to be. It appears that he was born ca. 185 into a Christian family. His father, Leonidas, was probably a Roman citizen while his mother, whose name has not been preserved, may have been an Egyptian. His father may have been a grammarian. Certainly he educated his son thoroughly through the secondary level and also saw to it that he studied the Bible. When the boy was almost seventeen, his father perished in the persecution of Septimius Severus. His ardent adolescent son wrote urging him to be steadfast, and apparently was prevented from being martyred himself only by his mother's hiding all his clothes. In fact, martyrdom seems to have exercised a fascination for Origen all his life.

When Leonidas died, his property was forfeited to the state and the support of his mother and six younger brothers fell to Origen. He was enabled by the patronage of a wealthy woman to complete enough of his education to begin teaching grammar himself. Soon, however, the bishop of Alexandria, Demetrius, placed him in charge of preparing catechumens for baptism. In that role he thought he should put aside all secular study and sold his library of classical literature to provide himself with an annuity. His youthful zeal was such that he led a very ascetic life; indeed, he went so far as to take Christ's saying that "there are eunuchs who have made themselves eunuchs for the sake of the kingdom of heaven" (Matt. 19:12) in what Eusebius delicately describes as "too literal and extreme a sense" (*Hist. eccl.* 6.8.2).

Origen's teaching of the faith in Alexandria met with such an enthusiastic response that eventually he had to turn over basic catechesis to one of his pupils, Heraclas, while he himself concentrated on more advanced pupils and on his own scholarship. Somewhere along the way he also continued his own education by studying under the well-known Platonist philosopher Ammonius Saccas. His doing so calls attention to something important in his eventual homiletical development. It reminds us that the death of his father meant that Origen's education was interrupted at the end of the secondary level. He had mastered that well enough to teach its subjects and, out of necessity, he went to work, postponing his higher education. When his own teaching duties required more knowledge than he possessed, he went back to school. At that point, however, he did not begin rhetorical training, which was the standard form of advanced training, but instead devoted himself to philosophical study.

As H. I. Marrou points out, those who did so broke with the usual culture, which was literary, rhetorical, and aesthetic, and devoted themselves to an ascetic way of life as much as to an intellectual system.[14] This understanding meant that Christianity was considered a philosophy at the time, and the ascetically inclined Origen would have found Platonism with its rigorous intellectual and personal demands a far more promising road to improvement than was rhetoric. Indeed, the influence of Clement had already set him moving in that direction.

Thus he began to attend the lectures of Ammonius, who later taught the founder of Neo-Platonism, Plotinus.

> It is impossible to say just what Origen learned from Ammonius. It may be that, like other great teachers, Ammonius influenced his students more by instilling in them a sympathetic yet critical approach to a great tradition than by passing on his particular doctrines.[15]

What was probably most appealing to Origen about Platonism was the defense that it gave against the gnostic heresies that had been such a threat to Christianity for over half a century. Platonism insisted, as did Christianity, on the goodness of creation and the compatibility of divine providence with human freedom. It also offered something that Christianity lacked: "a rational understanding of God's purpose in which all of these seemingly disparate and contradictory doctrines formed a coherent whole."[16]

The theological equipment that Origen was acquiring was adequate for its purpose, as may be seen in the numbers who flocked to him for instruction in the faith. One of these, Ambrose,[17] a Valentinian gnostic he converted to orthodoxy, was to hold great significance in the rest of Origen's life and work. Ambrose, who was well-to-do, was so grateful for Origen's instruction that he provided him for the rest of his life with a team of stenographers to take down every word he said and copyists and calligraphers to publish what was recorded. This, among other things, accounts for the large number of Origen's surviving sermons.

Origen put all of his erudition to use in the service of the church not in theology proper, as one might expect from his philosophical training, although he did write what has been called the church's first systematic theology, as we shall see below. Rather, his overwhelming interest was biblical interpretation. He accomplished the amazing feat of writing on all the books of the Bible in one or more of three literary genres: commentaries, the sort of marginal notes called *scholia,* and homilies. To be sure, most of these works were never completed, and most of what was written down has perished, but the size of the undertaking and the relatively small numbers of his works in other fields indicate that he saw his basic vocation as that of an exegete—the first major exegete in the history of the church.

Some of his major works in other fields are closely related to his biblical study. What has been called his systematic theology, *On First Principles* (Peri Archōn; *Περὶ Ἀρχῶν, De principiis*), was apparently written to answer criticisms on his method of biblical interpretation that arose after some of his commentary on Genesis was first published. (For the section of *On First Principles* dealing with biblical interpretation, see **Vol. 2, pp. 19-40.**)

> *On First Principles* announces itself as simultaneously a philosophical treatise on the relation of God to the world (*archē* in the first range of meaning) and as a development of a coherent body of doctrine from the logical elaboration of the implications of the rudimentary doctrines of the Christian faith (*archē* in the second range of meaning), the implication being, as Origen intended, that the two procedures are identical.[18]

On First Principles begins with a statement of Origen's view of reality, which starts with the three divine persons of the Trinity and proceeds to consider rational creatures, including animate beings, angels, demons, and human beings. After that he looks at particular issues raised by the system stated in the first part. The last of these issues to be discussed, which is of a different order from the rest since it justifies the procedure by which the system had been arrived at, is how the Bible should be interpreted. Essentially this exegetical method was to dominate in the church until the Reformation. I will defer discussion of it, however, until it is seen in practice in the homilies.

While Origen worked for the church in Alexandria he was not ordained. His emasculation would have been an impediment to that. And, admittedly, over the years of his great productivity and popularity, he did not grow closer to Demetrius, the bishop who had appointed him. While it is commonly asserted that Demetrius was jealous of Origen's fame, there was probably an even more basic conflict, that between an intellectual and an organizer, as Joseph Trigg has pointed out.[19] Nor was the blame one-sided. While Demetrius was apparently unaware of what a treasure he had on his staff, Origen was equally blind to the necessity for other gifts in the church. The grace of baptism he attributed mainly to the discipline of the catechumenate, and he considered the Eucharist to be basically a symbol of the knowledge of God that comes through hearing the teaching of God's word. Nor was the church's penitential discipline the best way for a sinner to receive forgiveness; the pastoral attentions of a spiritual person were far more effective.[20] All this to say that the gifts most appreciated by either Demetrius or Origen were those each had.

By the time the break between the two had actually occurred, Origen had become known throughout the Mediterranean world and had even traveled through a good bit of it. In 215 he had been to Rome. For some reason, around 222 the governor of the Roman province of Arabia (modern Jordan) sent a military escort to accompany Origen on a visit to him.[21] Then in 230 Origen moved to Caesarea, possibly because it was in the Holy Land and also was a place where Origen could consult with Jewish scholars. At any rate, he was met with an official reception there very different from what he had at home. The bishop of Caesarea, Theoctistus, invited him to preach at a Eucharist over which the bishop presided and at which the bishop of Jerusalem was present. Demetrius heard of it and was furious. He fired off an angry letter to Theoctistus about the breach of ecclesiastical discipline involved in letting a layman preach in the presence of bishops. But he also sent two deacons to invite Origen to return home, which he did, if only temporarily.

The next year he left Alexandria again. Julia Mammaea, the mother of Alexander Severus, the emperor, was very interested in all religions and especially Christianity. Having heard of Origen's great brilliance, she arranged for him to visit her at Antioch. Not long after returning to Alexandria, Origen set out again, this time for Greece. While en route he passed again through Caesarea and while he was there, Theoctistus ordained him to the presbyterate. While Origen was spending a couple of years in Athens, Demetrius did everything in his power to have him deposed and declared a heretic. Eventually all of that got straightened out and Demetrius died before he could cause any more trouble, but Origen returned to Caesarea rather than Alexandria.

Once there he settled into an extremely productive period in which he taught, wrote, and functioned as a priest. Apparently he was able to teach on a fuller scale than had ever been possible in Alexandria. A testimonial to Origen survives in the form of a *Speech of Appreciation* given in 245 by one of his students at the end of five years of residential study.[22] It has been customary to attribute the speech to Gregory Thaumaturgus, but the more likely author was named Theodore. The oration outlines an elaborate curriculum designed to prepare the student for interpreting the Bible. The course of study began with all the branches of philosophy: logic, "physics" (the study of the natural world), and ethics, which were considered to be prerequisites for being able to understand theology. The theology Origen taught, which apparently Theodore did not stay for, was undoubtedly close to what he wrote in *On First Principles,* because there is little indication that he ever changed his basic beliefs.

By the time Theodore gave his valedictory address, Origen was probably sixty years old. For the rest of his life he continued in the activities that had occupied him up to that point: he continued to produce long and learned biblical commentaries; he traveled a little, going to Athens again; and he ran afoul of the hierarchy, with the bishop of Alexandria especially trying to prove that he was a heretic. He also wrote the work which, after *On First Principles,* was his most important book that was not a biblical study. His patron Ambrose brought to his attention an attack on Christianity called *The True Doctrine,* which had been written about seventy years earlier by a pagan philosopher named Celsus. Origen set out to refute it in the tradition of the apologies for Christian faith that had been written by such second-century worthies as Justin Martyr. Trigg is probably right in his conclusion that the *Contra Celsum* "did more than any other work of its time to make Christianity intellectually respectable," but not all specialists will agree with him that "it defended it as Platonism for the masses."[23]

Not long afterward, Origen almost got what he had longed for much of his life: martyrdom. Decius, the emperor who ascended the throne in 249, was determined to restore Rome's inner strength by a return to traditional values, especially those of Roman religion. He declared that everyone in the empire had to sacrifice to the gods and produce a certificate that proved they had done so. While many Christians did submit, leaving an enormous problem to the church of deciding what to do about them, Origen was made of different metal. Indeed, he was called *Adamantios*—the man of diamond or steel (*Hist. eccl.* VI.xiv.10). His judge thought the cause would be better served by Origen's recantation than by making a martyr of him, so he ordered the rack and threatened fire. While Origen survived the ordeal and outlived Decius, he was disabled the rest of his life, and his injuries were undoubtedly the cause of his eventual death. There is no definite information about him after he was released from prison. He probably died around 253, perhaps in Tyre.

THE PREACHER

As devoted as he was to biblical study, Origen did not preach until he was in his midfifties, and even then he appears to have preached for only a three-year period beginning in 239 or 240. The reason for the delay, of course, is that he was not ordained earlier. Why he stopped preaching is a matter of speculation. His sermons indicate that they were not always well received. Some objected to his allegorical interpretation, others to his altering the familiar text of the Septuagint. His belief in the preexistence of souls and in the ultimate salvation of everyone may have offended some, while others may have taken issue with his criticisms of the clergy in Caesarea. Some scholars have assumed that Theoctistus, the bishop of Caesarea, may have relieved him of his pulpit duties, and even suggest that his doing so caused ill feelings between them for the rest of Origen's life. This is only inference; there is no explicit evidence that things happened this way. It is, however, consistent with the evidence that exists. If this explanation is accurate, it is replete with irony. It would mean that when the homily form was first introduced, it was not well received, and the preacher who gave to sermons the shape they would keep for almost a thousand years was not able to hold his audience.

All this brings up the question of what Origen's preaching was like. That subject has been treated so well and exhaustively by one scholar, Pierre Nautin, that what follows will simply summarize his findings.[24] He begins with a consideration of the circumstances under which Origen preached. The church in Caesarea in his time apparently celebrated the Eucharist every Sunday and Friday. On the other days of the week there was an assembly at which there was a sermon but no celebration of the sacrament. These weekday services took place before the workday began. The sermon was given by a priest, but not necessarily the same priest every day. There are passages not treated in the collections of Origen's homilies on a particular book, but it is not known whether those were handled by other priests or that there simply was not enough time to cover everything. On Sundays there were readings from the Hebrew Bible and from one of the Gospels, with a homily on each; there may have also been a lection from Acts or an epistle with an explanation of that as well. For the weekday services, however, only an Old Testament lesson was read and preached on. Such services concluded with a prayer.

All services took place in the church with the bishop and priests seated in a semicircle around the altar, the bishop's chair being distinct from the benches on which the priests sat. Deacons were at the door, among the congregation, or at the altar, depending on their duties for the day. The people sat for the sermon. Catechumens also were present for the sermon, this being a major part of their preparation for baptism. The daily services lasted about an hour, but the sermons varied in length. Of the twenty homilies on Jeremiah in Nautin's edition, six are longer than forty pages of the relatively small Sources chrétiennes volumes, in which half of the pages contain the Greek text while the other half carry the translation. One homily, however, is only four pages long, while the rest seem to average about twenty pages. And, as in all churches at all times, not everyone present paid attention to the sermon; some even left early. The deacons kept order much as others were to do during Puritan sermons in colonial New England.

When Origen preached he did so from a position raised above the congregation. His sermons were in effect a rereading of the text with a running commentary on it. This meant that he had a copy of the text open before him from which he read and to which he returned after commenting on each passage. Origen's preaching differed from that of anyone else because of the text that he had before him. As a good grammarian, he needed to begin by establishing the text of the passage on which he commented. Yet he knew that the Septuagint was a translation. For his text to be accurate, it had to match the original Hebrew. To this end, he had some time before prepared a copy of the Old Testament that set in parallel columns with the Septuagint a Greek transliteration of the Hebrew, the word-by-word translation of the Hebrew made by Aquila, a more idiomatic Greek translation by Symmachus, and another by someone named Theodotion.[25] After moving to Palestine he added two more Greek translations, producing what has been called the *Hexapla.* He had also developed a set of symbols that told him at a glance which words from one text were present in another. Thus while he was preaching he could correct the text of the Septuagint to match the Hebrew.[26] While he depended on the *Hexapla* for the text of the passage on which he was preaching, he quoted freely from other parts of the Bible in which the same words or a similar thought appeared, demonstrating a knowledge of Scripture that few have ever been able to match as he explained the Bible by the Bible.

The structure of Origen's homilies owed nothing to rhetorical theories of disposition; he confined himself to the grammarian's task of explicating a text. The nearest he came to providing any formal structure was often to have an introduction and to follow a set pattern for his conclusion. The introduction would begin with something other than the first verse of his passage in order to raise a question to be addressed in his interpretation. Usually these prologues were very short unless he was introducing a point of doctrine. Quite often, however, even such minor preliminaries were skipped. His conclusion, on the other hand, was usually a doxology based on 1 Peter 4:11, "To him [i.e., Jesus Christ] belong the glory and the power forever and ever." To get from biblical explication to these words there would often be a transition of several phrases that was usually an invitation to prayer and perhaps a reminder of death and judgment. Sometimes the shift was more abrupt.

The body of most of the sermons had no logical or rhetorical pattern, but consisted simply of verse-by-verse or phrase-by-phrase explications of the text. In dividing his comments, Origen paid particular attention to grammatical indications of transitions in the text's sentences. He had ways of signaling that he was returning to the text to take up the next bit. Thus he continued through the passage that had been read until either he had commented on its last verse or the time ran out.

In summarizing his description of the sermon form by Origen, Nautin said Origen wished only to explain Scripture as well as he could, and that he was inspired in that task by what he had done previously when he had been a grammarian and was explicating a text his students had in their hands, a passage from Homer or Hesiod rather than from the Bible.[27] Then Nautin goes on to remark how the content as well as the form of Origen's homilies reflect the practice of the grammarian. Origen establishes the correct text, he notes the order of words, he identifies who is speaking and who is spoken to in dialogue and how that relates to the character of each, he is aware when the narrator is not one of the characters, he attends to the significance of the order and choice of words, paying attention to the meaning of a word by noting its etymology or looking at parallel passages in which it appears, he points out figures of speech, and, while doing all of this, he uses the technical vocabulary of the grammarian.[28]

Thus, Nautin deserves credit for observing that the pattern of Origen's homilies is that of a grammarian's lecture. He does not, however, point out two reasons why that is significant. First, Origen's falling into that pattern is a function of the way that his education was interrupted by the death of his father and his teaching at the secondary level as soon as he had completed that level himself. There is a degree of good fortune to the church in his not having gone on to higher education in rhetoric because, as so many homiletical theoreticians failed to note later, none of the *genera dicendi* of classical rhetoric provided for the explication of a text. Origen's training as a grammarian provided him with precisely the genre of speech in the Greco-Roman world that was adaptable to preaching from the Bible. Second, most Christian preaching thereafter until the High Middle Ages and a good bit afterward would continue to follow the pattern of Origen's homily. Much preaching ever since has imitated Origen in giving grammarian's lectures on biblical texts.

Origen's purpose in preaching, however, was no more merely explaining a text than was the grammarian's. Both were concerned that the texts they explicated have the moral and spiritual effect they were intended to, that their intention *(βούλημα)* be realized. For Origen, therefore, two principles governed his interpretation. The first was the recognition that, since all Scripture is inspired by God, its meaning ought to be worthy of God and thus useful for edifying and nourishing the soul. The second principle was that nothing in the Bible—not a word, the choice of a word, even the repetition of a word—was there by accident. Everything had been placed in the text by God for a particular purpose.

Sometimes the edifying purpose of a passage could be achieved by interpreting it in its simple literal sense. That sense, however, was not always obviously and immediately edifying. For instance, at times the Bible reports scandalous events; at others it makes anthropomorphic references to God. In such cases it was assumed that the text should be interpreted allegorically because the allegorical meaning was the true meaning of the text, the meaning the Holy Spirit intended. As noted above, the grammarians did the same with Homer; Origen the Christian continued to practice his trade as a grammarian. He called his methods of application *moral* and *mystical*. The moral sense looked for the meaning of the passage for the soul, and the mystical sense sought what the passage meant in regard to Christ and the church. At other times Origen would refer to the *letter* and the *Spirit,* a distinction he borrowed from Paul (2 Cor. 3:6).

Allegorical interpretation had a long history when Origen began using it in preaching. We have already seen the way that it developed among Greek philosophers, and how Philo applied the method to the Hebrew Bible. He, however, was not the innovator. This method may already be seen in the book of Wisdom, the so-called *Letter of Aristeas,* and in Philo's predecessor Aristobulus. Now its firm place in the history of Christian biblical interpretation prior to Origen has to be acknowledged. Most of the New Testament bases its theology on interpreting passages in the Hebrew Bible as predictions of redemption in Christ. This kind of interpretation, which uses common principles operating between the historical situations in two periods to treat the first as a prediction of the second, was already in use by the community that produced the Dead Sea Scrolls, as seen in their *Habakkuk Commentary*. While this kind of *pesher* or typological interpretation is not identical with the allegorical method, the two at least share the assumption that the real meaning of some biblical texts is other than the literal, grammatical, historical sense; the New Testament has plenty of both. While the Gospel parables that are given allegorical interpretation (such as the parable of the sower in Mark 4 and parallels) were not scripture at the time the interpretation was given, they quickly came to be. Paul often resorted to allegorical interpretation of the Hebrew Bible, for example, in Galatians 4 when he interpreted the sons of Abraham by Sarah and Hagar as referring to the Jewish and Christian covenants. And the Epistle to the Hebrews could be described as an extended allegory. Thus, Origen may have pushed allegorical interpretation farther than any of his predecessors, but he did not invent anything new.

While Origen has been accused of arbitrary biblical interpretation down to the present century, several things need to be said to set such evaluations in perspective. First, "history," as the term is understood today—the verifiable reconstruction of past events—is an invention of the nineteenth century. When the Reformers, for instance, called for literal instead of allegorical biblical interpretation, they still assumed that the Christian creed was the hermeneutical key to the Hebrew Bible. Further, since the historical meaning of biblical passages is always in reference to their first readers, the only way that any preacher has ever been able to transfer those passages to the lives of latter-day parishioners has been to assume that there were analogies between the original situation and the situation in the congregation that made such a transfer of perspective valid. Analogical application is not very far from allegorical application.[29]

Next, to treat all allegorical application as invalid is to excommunicate most of the preaching in the history of the church. While it is true that allegorical interpretation cannot be used to prove Christian doctrine, it was seldom ever used for that purpose. More often it was used to illustrate Christian beliefs that had been arrived at on the basis of other evidence. Mostly it was a tool for extending the meaning of biblical passages to the lives of Christians of later periods. The impetus for allegorical interpretation both in the time of Origen and later was the basic assumption of biblical inspiration, the belief that God gave the Bible to the church as the main hermeneutical instrument for understanding its own life. Thus it was Origen's preaching that furnished the model for biblical interpretation that dominated for many centuries to come.

There are recurrent themes in Origen's preaching: the preacher's important role; defense of Christian faith against such opponents as those who deny Providence, the Jews, and gnostics; and Christian doctrine.[30] But we can gain a more immediate sense of what he was like as a preacher by examining one of his homilies. The question is how to choose among two hundred homilies. At first one might think one of the twenty on Jeremiah that have survived might be best since they are written in the Greek that Origen spoke, which was duly recorded by his stenographers. There are others, however, that better reveal him at his most typical: the two on the Song of Songs that have survived in Latin translation.[31] While we have noted above the shortcomings of Latin translations of Origen's homilies, those by Jerome are generally much closer to the original than those by Rufinus.[32] And in his prologue to these particular sermons, Jerome claims that he translated them "with greater faithfulness than elegance."[33] This is probably near enough to the Greek to justify looking at a homily on a theme so close to Origen's heart.[34] We will therefore examine the first of these two homilies.

In this homily, at any rate, Origen did not check his Septuagint closely against the Hebrew, for there are major differences between them, and the text he interprets is the Greek. To make what he says comprehensible to anyone who may check his commentary against an English Bible, it appears wise to set a modern translation of the passage based on the Hebrew text in parallel with an English translation of the Latin Vulgate, which is very close to the Septuagint.

NRSV	Vulgate
1:1 The Song of Songs, which is Solomon's. 2 Let him kiss me with the kisses of his mouth! For your love is better than wine, 3 your anointing oils are fragrant, your name is perfume poured out; therefore the maidens love you. 4 Draw me after you, let us make haste. The king has brought me into his chambers. We will exult and rejoice in you; we will extol your love more than wine; rightly do they love you. 5 I am black and beautiful, O daughters of Jerusalem, like the tents of Kedar, like the curtains of Solomon. 6 Do not gaze at me because I am dark, because the sun has gazed on me. My mother's sons were angry with me; they made me keeper of the vineyards, but my own vineyard I have not kept! 7 Tell me, you whom my soul loves, where you	1:1 Let him kiss me with the kiss of his mouth, for thy breasts are better than wine, (2) smelling sweet of the best ointments. Thy name is as oil poured out. Therefore, young maidens have loved thee. (3) Draw me; we will run after thee to the odor of thine ointments. The king has brought me into his storerooms. We will be glad and rejoice in thee, remembering thy breasts more than wine. The righteous love thee. (4) I am black but beautiful, O ye daughters of Jerusalem, as the tents of Cedar, as the curtains of Solomon. (5) Do not consider me that I am brown, because the sun hath altered my color. The sons of my mother have fought against me, they have made me the keeper in the vineyards; my vineyard I have not kept. (6) Show me, O thou whom my soul

pasture your flock, where you make it lie down at noon; for why should I be like one who is veiled beside the flocks of your companions? 8 If you do not know, O fairest among women, follow the tracks of the flock, and pasture your kids beside the shepherds' tents. 9 I compare you, my love, to a mare among Pharaoh's chariots. 10 Your cheeks are comely with ornaments, your neck with strings of jewels. 11 We will make you ornaments of gold, studded with silver.	loveth, where thou feedest, where thou liest in the midday, lest I begin to wander after the flocks of thy companions. (7) If thou know not thyself, O fairest among women, go forth and follow after the steps of the flocks, and feed thy kids beside the tents of the shepherds. (8) To my company of horsemen, in Pharao's [*sic*] chariots, have I likened thee, O my love. (9) Thy cheeks are beautiful as the turtledove's, thy neck as jewels. (10) We will make thee chains of gold, inlaid with silver.

Origen begins by pointing out the privilege of considering the song that is beyond all others, the Song of Songs, and then moves to determine the genre of the book, deciding with a critical acumen rare for his time that it is a drama and a marriage song, an epithalamium, in which there are four characters: the husband, the bride, her maidens, and the groom's companions. Immediately he identifies the allegorical significance of each: the groom is Christ, the bride the church, the maidens souls of believers, and the companions angels and "those who have come unto the perfect man" (268). In the commentary Origen wrote on the Song of Songs, he allows for two readings, this corporate reading and an individual reading in which the groom is the Logos and the bride a soul. In this homily, however, he gives only the corporate interpretation. That, however, is consistent with an individual application in that Origen calls upon his listeners to "make haste and understand it and to join with the bride in saying what she says, so that you may hear also what she heard" (ibid.).

He understands the bride's words "Let him kiss me with the kisses of his mouth" to be a prayer to God the Father to send the Son. "Thy breasts are better than wine . . . ," etc., is addressed to the Son himself, however. The odor of his perfumes refers to his being the Anointed, the Messiah, the Christ.[35] Such spiritual understanding of Scripture is needed to become worthy of spiritual mysteries, "of spiritual desire and love" (270). The superiority of Christ's breasts to wine indicates that such thoughts "do inebriate and make the spirit glad" (271).[36] The name of Jesus is "as a perfume poured forth" (272), as may be seen in the way that Jesus was anointed by two women, one a sinner and the other not. "As perfume when it is applied scatters its fragrance far and wide, so is the name of Jesus poured forth" (273).

At this point the bridesmaids show up, but they demonstrate their inferiority to the bride by only following the groom instead of walking beside him. They are "standing without because their love is only just beginning" (274), while the bride is able to say to them, "The king brought me into his chamber" (275). They, however, are happy in their subordination, being glad and rejoicing in her, loving her breasts more than wine. They tell the groom that Equity has loved him, thus indicating the sum of her virtues. But the bride's response to being praised is to say that she is "black but beautiful . . . as the tents of Cedar, as the curtains of Solomon," and she tells them not to look at her because she has been blackened by the sun's looking down on her. Her blackness, of course, means that she is not yet fully cleansed from sin, and members of the congregation should be careful not to be black with sin. *Cedar*[37] is a Hebrew word meaning "darkness," as Origen has been told by his Jewish teachers.

When the bride says that the sons of her mother have fought against her, she is referring to Jewish persecution of the church. This may be seen in the apostle Paul, of whom it could also be said that he was a keeper of the vineyard of others rather than of his own, because "he made himself the servant of all that he might gain all" (279). In one of the touching references to his own spiritual life that he makes from time to time in the homilies, Origen sees a parallel to the bride's experience in his own when the groom leaves her, as he often does in the Song.

> God is my witness that I have often perceived the Bridegroom drawing near me and being most intensely present with me; then suddenly He has withdrawn and I could not find Him, though I sought to do so (280).

Continuing in the first person, she asks the groom where he eats lunch and takes his noonday nap. "I ask about the full day-time, when the light is brightest and Thou dwellest in the splendour of Thy majesty" (280). Noting that Joseph's brothers ate at noon, the same hour Abraham entertained the angels, Origen makes his characteristic claim that "Holy Scripture never uses any word haphazard and without a purpose" (ibid.). We, like the bride, must see Christ at his most glorious so that we will not be tempted to leave him for others. Thus the groom warns the bride of the danger that leaving him would place her in, a danger of being among the goats rather than the sheep.

The groom then tells the bride that she is as superior to all other women as his own cavalry is superior to Pharao's[38] chariots. Her cheeks, the place where a woman's beauty supremely resides, are like those of a turtledove. The cheeks reveal the beauty of the soul while her lips and tongue are references to her intelligence. So great is her beauty that the bride's naked neck is adorned as if she wore a necklace. Having said all that, the groom takes his rest, but then his companions promise to make her "likenesses of gold with studs of silver" (LXX), but when the groom awakens, he will make for her not likenesses but the real thing.

From this homily it is easy to see that the goal of all of Origen's preaching was the spiritual formation of the congregation.[39] In sermons like this, Origen, the Christian grammarian, set the shape of preaching for centuries to come.

FOR FURTHER READING

Crouzel, Henri. *Origen*. Trans. by A. S. Worrall. San Francisco: Harper & Row, 1989.

Grant, Robert M. *The Letter and the Spirit*. New York: Macmillan, 1957.

Marrou, H. I. *A History of Education in Antiquity*. Trans. by George Lamb. New York: New American Library, 1964.

Origen. *The Song of Songs: Commentary and Homilies*. Trans. and annotated by R. P. Lawson. ACW. Westminster, Md.: Newman Press, 1957.

Trigg, Joseph Wilson. *Origen: The Bible and Philosophy in the Third-century Church*. Atlanta: John Knox, 1983.

Notes

1. H. I. Marrou, *A History of Education in Antiquity*, trans. George Lamb ("Mentor Books"; New York: New American Library, 1964; Madison, Wisc.: University of Wisconsin Press, 1982), 380. This study has become classic. A description of this form of advanced education is given on pp. 267-81, 381-90.

2. Ibid., 210-22, 358-68.

3. Ibid.

4. Jerusalem had a population of around eighty thousand in Jesus' time. "Jerusalem," *ABD*, 3:753.

5. On allegorical interpretation in Greek philosophy and education see Robert M. Grant, *The Letter and the Spirit* (New York: Macmillan, 1957), 1-30, and *The Earliest Lives of Jesus* (London: SPCK, 1961), 38-49.

6. The letter was published by Morton Smith in *Clement of Alexandria and a Secret Gospel of Mark* (Cambridge: Harvard University Press, 1973). Most scholars have accepted the document as a genuine letter of Clement, but are very dubious about the inferences Smith drew from it.

7. To the extent that "homily" is a technical term, it refers neither to the length of the sermon nor to the conversational nature implied by the word's etymology as some have claimed, but to verse-by-verse interpretation and application of a biblical passage. Thus, a homily is what would be called expository preaching today.

8. Jean Daniélou, *Origen,* trans. Walter Mitchell (New York: Sheed & Ward, 1955), vii.

9. Henri Crouzel, *Origen,* trans. A. S. Worrall (San Francisco: Harper, 1989), xi.

10. Joseph Wilson Trigg, *Origen: The Bible and Philosophy in the Third-century Church* (Atlanta: John Knox, 1983), 8.

11. Hans Freiherr von Campenhausen, *The Fathers of the Greek Church,* trans. Stanley Godman (New York: Pantheon, 1955), 40.

12. Robert Payne, *The Holy Fire: The Story of the Fathers of the Eastern Church* (New York: Harper, 1957), 43. Anyone without special training who would like to begin a study of the early church fathers could not ask for a more readable and painless introduction than this book.

13. Robert M. Grant in his foreword to Trigg, *Origen,* 1.

14. Marrou, *A History of Education in Antiquity,* 282.

15. Trigg, *Origen,* 67.

16. Ibid., 73.

17. Not, of course, to be confused with the great fourth-century bishop of Milan.

18. Trigg, *Origen,* 93.

19. Ibid., 130.

20. Ibid., 140-46, 191-200.

21. Scholars disagree over the dates of events in the life of Origen. The opinions of Joseph W. Trigg, which are those of Nautin, are accepted here.

22. A translation of the speech may be read in *ANF,* 6:21-39.

23. Trigg, *Origen,* 239.

24. Origen, *Homélies sur Jérémie,* ed. Pierre Nautin, trans. Pierre Husson and Pierre Nautin, Sources chrétienne (Paris: Cerf, 1976), 1:100-191. For other good treatments of the subject, see Trigg, *Origen,* 176-88; Joseph T. Lienhard, S.J., "Origen as a Homilist," in *Preaching in the Patristic Age: Studies in Honor of Walter J. Burghardt, S.J.,* ed. David G. Hunter (New York: Paulist Press, 1989), 36-52; and Origen, *Homilies on Luke, Fragments on Luke,* trans. Joseph T. Lienhard, S.J., FC (Washington: Catholic University of America Press, 1996), xxiv-xxxvi. For Origen's other homilies in English, see Ronald E. Heine's translation of *Homilies on Genesis and Exodus* (2002), and that of Gary Wayne Barkley for *Homilies on Leviticus 1–16* (1990). Both volumes appear in FC from Catholic University of America Press.

25. Apparently Origen got the idea from synagogues in Alexandria, which used the transliteration and the translations of Aquila and Symmachus in parallel columns.

26. Scholars argue over how much Hebrew Origen knew. Most will admit that he knew some, but doubt that he was very fluent in it.

27. Origen, *Homélies sur Jérémie,* 1:131.

28. Later on, Nautin points out that Origen's style is not oratorical, but pedagogical. Ibid., 183-91.

29. I am delighted to discover my position unintentionally supported by Richard B. Hays in his commentary on *Galatians* in *The New Interpreter's Bible:* In writing of the allegory in Gal. 4:21–5:1, he says: "Paul's figurative reading strategy depends from start to finish on delineating correspondences between the scriptural story and the events of his own time.... This sort of imaginative discernment of parallels between past narrative and present situation...is invariably employed whenever preachers see the circumstances of their own day illumined or prefigured by the stories of scripture. Thus all Christian preaching is inescapably allegorical in the Pauline sense. The function of preaching is not to give factual historical reports; rather, it is to make metaphors, linking the ancient text with the present life of the congregation in fresh imaginative ways so that the text reshapes the congregation's vision of its life before God" (Nashville: Abingdon, 2000), 11:309.

30. Origen, *Homélies Sur Jérémie,* 1:151-83.

31. Origen, *The Song of Songs: Commentary and Homilies,* trans. and annotated by R.P. Lawson, ACW (Westminster, Md.: Newman Press, 1957).

32. Lienhard's introduction to the *Homilies on Luke,* xxxii-xxxvi.

33. "*Fideliter magis quam ornate.*" Origen, *The Song of Songs*, 265.

34. Of Origen's commentary on this book, Jerome says: "While Origen surpassed all writers in his other books, in his *Song of Songs* he surpassed himself." (Ibid.)

35. Messiah and Christ are transliterations of the Hebrew and Greek words that mean "anointed."

36. Philo referred to mystical experience as a "sober inebriation."

37. This refers not to the tree but to the Latinized spelling of *Kedar*.

38. "Pharao" is another Vulgate spelling.

39. For an excellent summary of Origen's spirituality, see Crouzel, *Origen,* 87-149.

CHAPTER 3

ELOQUENCE IN CAPPADOCIA

CHRISTIANITY BECOMES RESPECTABLE

The development of the homily form by Origen was the first major step in giving preaching the shape it would have for the first half of the Christian era. The next step was not taken for another century and a half and occurred in a church with a greatly altered position in the Roman world. From being a persecuted minority, Christianity had become the religion of the emperor, with all the favor and privilege that entailed. Under these new circumstances, bishops came to be chosen from the best-educated people of the time, the graduates of schools of rhetoric. Thus it happened that those who preached to the Christian community were thoroughly grounded in the techniques of effective public speaking. Verse-by-verse interpretation of a Scripture passage took on an eloquence it seldom had before. To understand how that came about, it is necessary to trace seismic social upheavals.

The Challenge of Size to the Empire

When Hadrian succeeded Trajan as Roman emperor in 117, he decided to draw back a little from boundaries established by his predecessor in order to keep the empire a manageable size.[1] In the west and north he built a wall near what is England's Scottish border, and in the east he withdrew across the Euphrates from Parthian territory in Mesopotamia. The Rhine and Danube became the empire's northern borders. Roman settlement of Africa had never penetrated deeply beyond its Mediterranean coast and he left it that way. Palestine and Syria were as far east as he needed to go.

Even at that, the territory proved too unwieldy for easy government. This was reflected in changes in the way the empire was ruled. For some time emperors had been drawn from and imposed by the army. Their ethnic stock ceased to be Roman in the urban sense or even the Italian. Their effective capital was no longer the eternal city but wherever their headquarters were located. By 286 it was necessary to have two Caesars, one in the West and one in the East. The empire threatened to come apart under its own weight. The only person who succeeded in unifying it was Constantine, who reigned alone from 324 to 337.

Roman Unity, Christianity, and Arianism

Before Constantine became sole emperor, at the battle of the Milvian Bridge in 312, he converted to Christianity, and from then on, with the exception of the brief reign of Julian the Apostate (360–63), Christianity enjoyed governmental support.[2] Constantine had hoped that he could reunite the empire around his new religion, but found to his chagrin that Christianity itself was badly divided over its understanding of the person and work of Christ. The belief that was eventually to win out and become the orthodox Christian view was that our Lord was at once completely divine and completely human—that he, the Father, and the Holy Spirit were the one God in three hypostases.

The powerful countervailing view was the position of the Arians that Christ was inferior to the Father, occupying a position between full divinity and full humanity. Constantine tried to heal the breach by calling a council of bishops at Nicaea in 325 to settle the matter. The council accepted the orthodox position, but that did not cause Arianism to disappear. It was not ejected from the empire until 381, and even after that it held on to life among some Germanic tribes until the end of the fifth century. Meanwhile several emperors, including Constantine's son, Constantius II, took the Arian side and bestowed governmental favor upon it. Therefore, the empire remained divided religiously, but the contending forces were no longer pagan and Christian but variant Christian expressions instead.[3]

New Patterns of Leadership

During this time, the East became progressively more important in the control of the empire and thus Constantine built its new capital city, Constantinople, on the Golden Horn where Europe almost touches Asia. As a result of all these factors, the next important chapter in the history of preaching was written in the Roman province of Cappadocia, located in what today is east-central Turkey.[4] The province was largely rural and agricultural, and its social organization was feudal. Its population was largely peasant except for the few landowning families.

Sons of these families were the only Cappadocians who could afford rhetorical education, which had recently taken on a new significance. Under Constantine a new career pattern had been created for administrators in Roman governmental service: standard preparation for such a career came to be education in Greek rhetoric.[5] This meant that those who worked in the central bureaucracy, those sent out as provincial governors, and the local notables in the provinces to which the governors were sent shared a common background and common standards of behavior. No matter what part of the empire one came from, people like oneself would be found wherever one went. Most of the members of this new "aristocracy of service" were Christians. Not surprisingly, it was from the same talent pool that bishops came to be selected.[6]

THE CAPPADOCIAN FATHERS

Christian preaching finally became completely integrated with classical rhetoric in Asia Minor in the second half of the fourth century. Three of the greatest preachers of all time not only appeared in the same remote province of the empire, but were very close: two brothers and their best friend. All became bishops, and they are known to history by the names of their sees. The brothers were Basil of Caesarea (330–79) and Gregory of Nyssa (ca. 331–ca. 395), and their friend was Gregory of Nazianzus (ca. 329–390). The three exemplified many of the motifs that have occupied this chapter so far: they were all born into wealthy landowning Christian families, they were thoroughly trained in rhetoric and practiced as Sophists, they all felt a strong call to the contemplative life, they all became bishops, they were deeply involved in the christological controversies of their time, and they all were brought into close contact with emperors (negatively so for Basil, but positively so for the Gregorys).

Basil the Great

Life and Work

As closely related as these Cappadocian Fathers were, it is simpler to look at their lives and their contributions to preaching individually. Basil was the center of the group. His father, also named Basil, was a professional rhetor, originally from Pontus, who married into a Cappadocian family even wealthier than his own. Basil had nine siblings, two of whom also became bishops, and a sister, Macrina, who became a nun.[7] Under his father Basil began the rhetorical training that was the standard form of higher education at the time. The elder Basil died, however, when the younger was a teenager, and so the son went into Caesarea to continue his education. There he met Gregory Nazianzus, who was to become his closest friend. From Caesarea he went to Constantinople where he probably studied under the great Libanius and then finished up with six years of study in Athens where Gregory, also known as Nazianzen, was his classmate.

After returning home and teaching for a year, he toured the monasteries that had recently come into being in Mesopotamia, Syria, Palestine, and Egypt, and developed a strong attraction to the contemplative life. In his day, most believers in Christ feared the danger of postbaptismal sin and so delayed initiation until late in life, but after his tour, Basil was baptized and went to his father's estate in Pontus to found an ascetic community that included Macrina, their mother, and eventually Nazianzen. His love of the ascetic life and his understanding of it caused him to write a monastic rule that gives Greek and Slavonic monasticism its basic shape to this day. He and his friend Gregory also published a collection of passages from Origen, the *Philocalia,* that is still regarded as a spiritual classic.

Though he continued to feel drawn to the ascetic life, Basil was ordained a priest in Caesarea in ca. 362 and an auxiliary bishop in 364. He was devoted to the poor, and he helped avert a disaster in Cappadocia during the famine of 368. With an Arian emperor, Valens, on the throne, he felt a call to do battle with heresy both intellectually and politically. Inheriting the diocese in 370,[8] he soon had to cope with its division by the emperor and the assignment of the other half to an Arian. He and his opposite number each began a mad scramble to strengthen his cause by creating new bishoprics in his territory. Basil assigned his brother Gregory to the town of Nyssa and his friend Gregory to the village of Sasima, an injury his friend never forgot.

On the intellectual front, Basil wrote a treatise on the Holy Spirit and one against Eunomius. He and his two cohorts are credited with developing what was to be the ultimate Eastern statement of the doctrine of the Trinity as Augustine's was to be the ultimate Western statement. Theirs used the principle of coinherence *(perichorēsis)* to do justice to both the unity and the individuality of the three divine persons. Basil's death in 379 meant that he did not see the triumph of the Cappadocian position at the Council of Constantinople in 381. His contributions to theology, monasticism, social service, and the practical life of the church combine to make him truly deserving of the title "the Great" by which he is called.

Preaching

In considering the preaching of the three Cappadocians, Basil's best represents the types of priestly and episcopal preaching that were ordinary at the time—and even these are extraordinary in their quality. The exegetical homily, the most common sermon form from the patristic period, was the form in which the preponderance of Basil's sermons were cast, and slightly more than half of the few that have been preserved are in this form. There are two major collections of sermons on single books of the Bible: those on the *Hexameron,* the six days of creation in the book of Genesis, and those on Psalms.

His homilies, *On the Psalms,*[9] were not a continuous series, but appear to have been preached between 368 and 375, during the last years before and the first years after his consecration as bishop. Fewer than 10 percent of the psalms are interpreted in the collection that has come down, but these few appear to be real sermons that were delivered to a congregation. There are indications of orality in many of them and even of improvisation in some, so they must have been recorded in shorthand. His method of preaching was to explain every word of every sentence of the particular psalm, so he obviously could not have preached on a long psalm in the time available.

Although Christian congregations of the time were very familiar with the psalms, Basil appears to have preached with a text before him, possibly some form of Origen's *Hexapla.* The sermons are addressed to the general Christian public, many of whom would have been unbaptized, and they reflect the social conditions of the time. The theme of some of the homilies is that the righteous person should give thanks to God for the power that enabled that person to triumph over temptation. The overall thesis of the collection is that all other activity should be abandoned for the contemplation of God.[10]

The sermons on the *Hexameron*[11] are longer than those on the psalms: on average, fifty as opposed to fifteen minutes long. They were delivered as a series, probably during Lent, after Basil had become bishop; indeed, Jean Bernardi believes they were preached March 12-16, 378, the year before Basil's death, with two sermons each on Monday, Tuesday, Thursday, and Friday, and only one on Wednesday.[12] The series was not finished because his final illness was already troubling him.[13]

The series was preached to the congregation at Caesarea. In fact, Basil made reference to members of the congregation who were artisans, for whom the sermons had to be short so they could get to work on time. While Basil was still enough under the influence of Origen to use allegorical interpretation when he preached on the psalms, he had abandoned that method by the time he preached on the creation narrative. Charming comments on each work of the Creator reveal Basil as deeply informed of the science of his time and probably also a close observer of nature himself.[14]

Twenty-two of the sermons in the collection called *Diverse Homilies* are regarded as genuine works of Basil, some preached while he was still a priest but most from his episcopate.[15] Those delivered while he was still a presbyter aroused the envy of his bishop, a feeling the bishop eventually transcended when he recognized the value of Basil's gifts to the church. The sermons Basil preached after he became bishop show his awareness of pastoral problems. An Epiphany sermon urged those who were delaying baptism to receive their catechetical instruction that Lent. The fast was apparently observed by many of the unbaptized; there are two sermons on preparation for it, one for the rich and one for slaves. And there is a complimentary homily on avoiding excess in celebrating Easter. All of these sermons take the form of a liturgical homily.

Some of the *Diverse Homilies* take a different shape. Four of them are for feasts of martyrs; they are notable in several respects. They call attention to the development of the cult of the martyrs and also to the exchange of relics taking place between churches at the time and expressing networks being formed by bishops.[16] They also serve as a reminder that the danger of persecution still existed for the orthodox during the reign of the Arian emperor Valens. They also are clear examples of the way that Basil's rhetorical training prepared him for preaching, exemplifying as they do the genus of epideictic (praise or blame) in a scrupulous observance of its rules. Only a few of the *Diverse Homilies* deal with questions related to the doctrines of Christ and the Trinity, since most of Basil's hearers were as yet unbaptized and had not been initiated into the mysteries of these doctrines.

Basil's sermons clearly reflect his pastoral responsibilities. The spirituality they inculcate is deeply biblical. Forty-six of the eighty-nine sermons in the three series are exegetical homilies in form. Many of the others have Scripture as their point of departure, and biblical language permeates all of them. "In almost every line there appears a citation, a reminiscence, or an allusion to a passage of scripture" (AT).[17] The Bible was the reservoir of Basil's ideas and images; he used it the same way his pagan contemporaries used the literature of classical Greece. In his sermons he used the Bible to provide his congregation with a program of reflection and of life. While the eighty-nine sermons that remain are only a small sample of the total amount of preaching Basil did, they are representative of the ways in which he tried to build up his flock morally and spiritually through his preaching.

Gregory of Nazianzus

For several reasons the corpus of Gregory's sermons selected for preservation is very different from that of his friend Basil. First, his basic sense of vocation was to the contemplative life, so he did not have the years of continued pastoral activity in one place that his friend had. Second, the sermons he allowed to be published are intended more for special occasions than for the regular Sunday eucharistic assembly and thus have a more elevated rhetorical style.[18] And, as we shall see, he had different criteria for deciding which of his sermons would be published, a different purpose for the collection that dictated the inclusion of some types and the exclusion of others.

Activities and Contributions

Gregory's criteria for sermon selection, however, can best be understood in the context of his life story. Gregory's father, with whom he shared his name, was not only a Christian but a bishop. The family was affluent; the elder Gregory constructed the church building in Nazianzus largely at his own expense. The father had not been born into the faith, however; he had begun life in a hellenized Jewish sect called the Hypsistarians.[19] Shortly after his baptism, sometime around his son's birth, he was chosen as bishop of Nazianzus.[20]

In being chosen while still a layman, the elder Gregory represented the system that was usual before his distinguished son and his friends changed the rules. In the older generation a leader for a congregation was raised up from its midst with no prior training, his only qualification being the character of Christian leadership recognized by the congregation.[21] It was not even necessary that he serve as a deacon or priest before being chosen as bishop. And many of those chosen were married and had families. Basil and the two Gregorys, however, were to break that tradition. Ordained ministry became a vocation for which one prepared by receiving rhetorical education and ascetic formation in the contemplative life. The contemplative aspect of the life made it also a vocation to celibacy.[22] Thus an important shift in the nature of the episcopate took place between the Gregorys elder and younger.

Gregory's education was very similar to Basil's, though he began school in Nazianzus rather than at his father's knee, and between his stays at the Cappadocian Caesarea and Athens he studied at Caesarea in Palestine and Alexandria rather than at Constantinople. His famous teachers include Thespesius, Himerius, Proaeresius, and possibly Didymus the Blind. In his panegyric on Basil (*Or. 43*) he painted an idyllic picture of their friendship and achievements during their student days.[23] He was in Athens before Basil arrived and stayed after he left; he even taught there for a while before departing.

After Gregory returned home, he was baptized and joined Basil in Pontus in his ascetic retreat. All his life Gregory vacillated between his desire for the contemplative life and the conflicting desire to use his great natural talent for oratory and his excellent education in the service of his faith. He remained in Pontus less than a year and even wrote Basil a satirical letter about the experience, but he continued to go back for extended retreats and took refuge there on several of the flights that were his characteristic response to a crisis in his life.[24]

The first of these flights occurred at Christmastime 361,[25] a couple of years after he returned home from Pontus, when his aging father, in need of assistance in the church, imposed priestly ordination on him. Gregory returned home in time to help his father with Easter services the following spring, and preached his first sermons. He then remained in Nazianzus most of the time until 370, dividing his time between taking as much of the burden off his father as he could and trying to keep up "some of the monastic routine of prayer, vigils, and fasting within the semi-seclusion of his home."[26]

His friendship with Basil was severely tested in 370 when Eusebius died and Basil wanted to succeed him as bishop of Caesarea. Basil considered becoming bishop of Caesarea a necessary defense of the church against Arianism, but Gregory regarded it as "the business of power-mongers."[27] To make matters worse, the following year when Valens divided his jurisdiction, Basil began creating new sees within his remaining territory and consecrated Gregory as bishop of Sasima. Although he accepted the consecration, Gregory despised his assignment, considering it a "stopping-place . . . without water or vegetation, not quite civilized, a thoroughly deplorable and cramped little village."[28] Another flight ensued. After several months, however, he did consent to return to Nazianzus and help his father. Then, when his father died in 374 and there was an effort to make him successor to the see, he fled again, this time to Seleucia, where he lived for four years in the convent of St. Thecla.

From there he was called in 379 to the most productive period of his life as a preacher: half of his surviving forty-four[29] orations were sermons preached during the following two years. After the Arian emperor Valens died and was succeeded by the orthodox Theodosius I, the church in Constantinople was still in the hands of its Arian bishop, Demophilus. Gregory was called to the small orthodox Church of the Anastasis (Resurrection). When Theodosius finally came to Constantinople, however, he placed Gregory on the city's episcopal throne. Gregory's preaching did much to prepare for the triumph of Nicene orthodoxy at the Council of Constantinople in 381. Indeed, his five *Theological Orations* (*Or.* 27–31) have earned him the title in the Eastern Church of "the Theologian," an honor he shares with only the Fourth Evangelist.[30]

When the council actually convened, however, Gregory was caught in the ecclesiastical politics he so disdained. The bishop of Alexandria and his cohorts claimed that it was uncanonical for Gregory to leave Sasima and go to Constantinople. Rather than fight, he resigned as bishop—and president of the council—and went back home to Nazianzus. Finally, he agreed to be bishop there and served until he could train a cousin to succeed him. He then retired to the family estate at Arianzus and the contemplative life for which he had always yearned. During this period he also edited his writings, selecting and revising those to be published. He died in 390.

Orations

The effect of Gregory's editing is obvious in the corpus of his *Orations* as it has been handed down. Some of the speeches, like many others in the history of preaching, have been revised for publication, although not all of them have. But the most impressive aspect of the editing is its high degree of selectivity. While it is true that Gregory was often not involved in regular Sunday preaching, there were whole years when he was, and the number of sermons he preached must have been several times more than the amount that have come down. There is the further issue of the kinds of sermons Gregory edited for publication. While Basil's sermons are representative of pastoral preaching to a congregation, Nazianzen's are not. Indeed, there is only one exegetical homily among them (*Or.* 37). More were written for great public occasions than for ordinary Sunday assemblies.

In his study of the preaching of the Cappadocian Fathers, Bernardi has undertaken to account for Gregory's having chosen to publish just these sermons and no more. First, Bernardi points to the extraordinarily autobiographical character of the sermons in the collection. He says that the preacher seems to have intended to familiarize us with the main periods of his life[31] and the essential aspects of his personality.[32] Beyond that, however, he appears to have selected orations that would be a sampler[33] of rhetorical preaching to show bishops how to go about their work of Christian proclamation. The sermons, then, were chosen to serve as models for other bishops in parallel situations; therefore they include most of the genres of Christian public address.

Gregory's entire oeuvre seems to have a similar purpose: his letters to his great-nephew Nicobolus furnish a guide to letter writing,[34] and his poetry shows how Christian verse should be composed. He had, after all, lived through the reign of Julian the Apostate, who had said that Christians should not teach or study classical literature because it told of pagan gods.[35] More important, the publication of Gregory's sermons and other writings served his desire to see the episcopate transformed in the way I discussed above, in which the vocation to ordained ministry would be prepared for through rhetorical education and contemplative formation.

Ruether identifies the genres of Nazianzen's speeches as "occasional orations, *apologiae* for his own actions, festal orations, and doctrinal sermons" in addition to eight orations of praise and two of invective.[36] These categories are useful. The occasional orations occur at such events as his becoming his father's auxiliary bishop (*Or.* 16), the consecration of Eulalius of Doara (*Or.* 13), or Gregory's enthronement in the Church of the Holy Apostles in Constantinople (*Or.* 36). The defenses of his own actions are generally given after flight from a crisis: *Or.* 1–3 after his ordination to the priesthood, 9–12 after his consecration to the episcopate, and 42 to the bishops assembled for the council just before he left Constantinople.

The festal orations are for feasts of the church year: *Or.* 1 and 45 for Easter; 38–40 for Christmas, Epiphany, and the Sunday after Epiphany (all on baptism); and 41 on Pentecost. Doctrinal sermons include the great *Theological Orations* (27–31) and the synopsis of the first three of these for the bishops of the council (20). The eight orations of praise should be divided into those for saints' days[37] and those for family members and friends.[38] The two invectives are against Julian the Apostate (4, 5), who was a student in Athens at the same time as Gregory.[39]

These categories, however, do not exhaust the genres of the *Orations*. Almost half of Gregory's sermons are models of preaching for the Sunday assembly, although most of these put more emphasis on doctrine than morals or exegesis. Yet both morals and exegesis are included, as, for example, in *Or.* 14, on love of the poor, and the famous *Or.* 37, his surviving exegetical homily, which is on Matthew 19:1-12, Jesus' teaching on divorce.[40] This homily, however, illustrates the difficulty of assigning many of his sermons to a single genre.[41] Although the basic subject is divorce, Gregory uses allegorical interpretation to apply the passage to heretical preaching, asking the Emperor, who was present, to put an end to it (which the Emperor did).[42]

The form of the sermon is a homily, in that it proceeds in verse-by-verse exegesis, but there is literal as well as allegorical interpretation, and that of an extraordinary sensitivity for his time. Gregory called upon Theodosius to make adultery as much a crime for men as for women and to give women authority over their children—revolutionary proposals in Roman society. Yet his ascetic convictions also come to the fore and he still regarded marriage as inferior to virginity.

In other orations he undertook even more tasks. His *Or.* 19, for instance, was intended both for a feast of martyrs when visiting clergy were present as well as for the local faithful. He addressed each of the groups separately and spoke to them of what obedience involved in their state of life. But the provincial tax assessor, an old friend of Gregory's, was also present, and the bishop publicly exhorted him to continue the tax benefits the clergy had enjoyed.

Apologies

While it is impossible in the space available to look at all genres of Nazianzen's preaching, much less each oration, we should pay attention to at least three of his sermon categories: his apologias, his doctrinal preaching, and his encomia. The apologias are defenses of his conduct, normally his fleeing in a time of crisis. Such crises usually occurred when someone was trying to force him to take a more public role than he felt comfortable with, one that would call him from the contemplative life he craved. While modern readers may get the impression that these speeches involved a good bit of rationalization, he was far too talented and too Christian to make them merely that.

A case in point is *Or.* 2,[43] one of his three efforts to account for his departure for Pontus when his father ordained him to the priesthood. Among his other orations, only his panegyric on Basil is as long as this one, but this one was probably not delivered orally. After beginning with several lesser reasons for his flight, he states the main reason: "I did not, nor do I now, think myself qualified to rule a flock or herd, or to have authority over the souls of men" (2.9). While admitting that unworthy persons have undertaken this ministry,[44] he dared not do so himself; one needed to be much farther advanced in the spiritual life than he to undertake so awesome a responsibility. In demonstrating the appropriateness of his attitude, he wrote the first great treatise on the priesthood in the history of the church.

> S. Chrysostom in his well-known treatise, S. Gregory the Great in his Pastoral Care, and Bossuet in his panegyric on S. Paul, have done little more than summarise the material or develop the considerations contained in this eloquent and elaborate dissertation.[45]

Doctrinal Preaching

The most obvious examples of Gregory's doctrinal preaching are his *Theological Orations* (*Or.* 27–31) delivered in Constantinople. As they have come down, these sermons betray the fact that they were turned into a treatise by an editing process that Bernardi refers to as "dissolving" or "melting."[46] The second of the orations does not appear to have been a part of the original series, but to have been fitted in during the editing process. The original oral character of the orations remains obvious enough, however, for their inclusion in a history of preaching.

These sermons reflect the theological ferment of the capital in the years just before the council when an Arian still sat on the episcopal throne in the Church of the Holy Apostles. Nazianzen acknowledged that theological chitchat had almost replaced gossip as the small talk of the social elite of Constantinople when he said:

> Every marketplace must buzz with their talking; and every dinner party must be worried to death with silly talk and boredom; and every festival be made unfestive and full of dejection, and every occasion of mourning be consoled by a greater calamity.[47]

The opponents Gregory attacked in these orations are sometimes identified as Eunomians or Anomoeans and Pneumatomachians.[48] It is more accurate to refer to them generally as Neo-Arians because Gregory seems more concerned to address the "pop" Arianism in Constantinople at the time than to refute the technical treatises of heresiarchs.[49] He makes it clear that he thinks many of his opponents are present for his sermon. Yet not all of those he spoke against were of one opinion or even one heresy.

The five orations differ from one another considerably. The first lays down the ground rules for who should dare to argue a position on such exalted subjects. "Not to everyone, my friends, does it belong to philosophize about God; not to everyone—the subject is not so cheap and low—and, I will add, not before every audience, not at all times, nor on all points" (27.3). The second, which was not originally a part of the series, is on God and begins by discussing the impossibility that an unaided human mind should understand the nature of God and moves on to the strange things that human beings, in their ignorance, have considered gods. Next he gives a list of worthies mentioned in the Bible who have received revelation, but insists that even they did not know God as God is in the divine being. The sermon ends with a demonstration of how God's unknowable richness can be seen in the diversity of creation. This passage (28.22-30) is reminiscent of Basil's sermons on the *Hexameron* in its knowledge of and fascination with nature; Kennedy rightly regards it as the high point of this oration and possibly that of the series as a whole.[50]

The third oration is the first of two on the Son. Gregory begins by stating the orthodox position of consubstantiality and then refutes the doctrines of his opponents. Its high point (29.19-20) is another list, like the *ekphrasis* (vivid description) of nature in the second sermon. This is a collection of antitheses and paradoxes involved in our Lord's two natures, and recalls the Gorgian figures of Melito's *Paschal Homily.*

The fourth oration is also on the Son, but Kennedy is wrong in calling it a homily.[51] While it is true that Gregory shows that ten biblical proof texts cited by his opponents do not have the Arian implications they claim, that is very different from a verse-by-verse exegesis and application of a continuous passage of Scripture, which is the form of a homily. Rather, the oration is a simple refutation of individual points in the first half and a consideration of the titles given Christ in the Bible in the second half. It has little rhetorical form, simply being an effort to cover a lot of ground and to get a number of issues out of the way.

In the fifth oration Gregory faced a major challenge. The Cappadocians were among the first Christian theologians to recognize the consubstantiality of the Holy Spirit, and they were faced with the difficulty that there is not nearly as much about that in the Bible as there is about the status of the Son. Most of the sermon, then, is an effort to show that the scarcity of explicit reference should not lead to negative conclusions. At the end Gregory quickly summarizes the positive evidence from Scripture in support of the position and ends by referring briefly to the lack of adequate symbols of the Trinity in the natural world—rejecting some that continue to be used to this day.

Thus he ends one of the important treatises on the Trinity in the history of the church. The *Theological Orations* are a rare demonstration of the extent to which the church's understanding of its faith can be advanced, not by technical treatises written for experts, but in a pastor's regular proclamation of the Word to his or her congregation. But, of course, clarifying the faith continuously through proclamation demands an extraordinary pastor.

Encomia

Among the many genres in which Gregory spoke, his funeral orations for family members and friends are probably the most cherished. They have a narrative quality that permits readers to feel that they are being given an inside view of the life of the early church. This effect is only increased by the way that Gregory reveals more of his own emotional involvement than almost any other writer from the period. (For an example of an enconium on a family member, the funeral oration for his brother Caesarius, see **Vol. 2, pp. 41-56.**) Of the encomia in praise of saints, family members, and friends, the greatest is undoubtedly the panegyric[52] on Basil. Indeed, George Kennedy, the great historian of classical rhetoric, says that this speech is "probably the greatest piece of Greek rhetoric since the death of Demosthenes."[53]

There are many reasons for its greatness. A uniquely gifted orator who reveals himself in his speeches takes as his subject by far the best friend he ever had, one who himself had made so many and such varied contributions to the life of the church that all succeeding generations have labeled him "the Great." Expressing grief and paying tribute, however, were not his only motives for the speech. One short section is another of Gregory's apologies. Much more important, however, is the purpose of using the fall of the great leader as an occasion to rally others behind the orthodox Trinitarian doctrine that Basil taught.

Beyond even that, Bernardi sees this speech as integral to the purpose for which Gregory edited his orations for publication: to turn them into a call for a new breed of bishops, far better qualified than their predecessors. He notes that the panegyric (*Or.* 43) is Gregory's first speech after the one he gave to the bishops at the Council of Constantinople upon his resignation and departure (*Or.* 42). That was a scathing attack on their lack of qualification. By painting Basil as the ideal bishop, Gregory is able to show what the council fathers should have been like and were not. Thus Basil is treated as exemplifying the ideal shape of the episcopate for the future. By concentrating on Basil's preparation for his vocation through his wide rhetorical education, his mastery of theology, and his ascetic formation as a contemplative, Gregory demonstrated what it would take to enable bishops to measure up to the demands of their office.[54]

It is interesting to go section by section through this great testimony to a friendship to see how the master rhetorician adapted the requirements of the classical rhetorical genre to serve his Christian purpose, as both Kennedy[55] and Ruether[56] have done. It is enough here to refer the reader to their treatments and even more to the panegyric itself. There, more than anywhere else, one can learn what Christian preaching's marriage to classical rhetoric did to enrich Christian preaching.

Gregory of Nyssa

Johannes Quasten, the great compiler of patristic handbooks, has succinctly summarized the distinctive contributions of each of the Cappadocian Fathers:

> Gregory of Nyssa was neither an out-standing administrator and monastic legislator like Basil, nor an attractive preacher and poet like Gregory of Nazianzus. But as a speculative theologian and mystic he is certainly the most gifted of the three great Cappadocians.[57]

He goes on to say that Nyssa is "by far the most versatile and successful author" of the three and that "his writings reveal a depth and breadth of thought," which surpass that of the other two.[58]

Yet the fact remains that Nyssa does not have the importance for the history of preaching that Basil and Nazianzen have. Only twenty-six of his sermons survive, and they date from a relatively short period of his episcopate, 379 to 388. Nothing remains from the first or the last seven years he was a bishop. The reasons why the early and late periods are not represented in the existing corpus are probably clear enough. During the latter years he was working on his great spiritual commentaries such as *The Life of Moses.*[59] For the early years, he was in exile part of the time, his attention may have been on other things, and he probably did not yet have the fame to merit a scribe to take down what he said. The main reason, though, is likely to be that most of his sermons during that time were exegetical homilies that were recycled into the spiritual commentaries.

Nyssa mastered rhetoric through private study rather than schooling, but went on to practice it professionally for about seven years. During this period he married and had a son. Strangely, he had great devotion to the ascetic ideals of his brother and their friend, and, at Basil's request, even wrote a treatise on the glories of virginity. Then, in 372, when Basil was trying to populate his territory with bishoprics, he asked his brother to go to the little town of Nyssa. At first Gregory was not an outstanding success. He was not an effective administrator, and he found that his flock took offense at his efforts to correct them.[60] The Arians were even able to have him deposed over alleged financial irregularities, but he was restored two years later.

His real prominence began after Basil's death when he was assumed to be his brother's successor in the campaign against heresy. He had a visible role in the Council of Constantinople and was often sent by the Emperor on diplomatic missions for the church. After his wife died in 385 he devoted himself to practicing and writing about the ascetic life. The only event known from his last years is his participation in the synod of Constantinople in 394, which was probably the year before his death.

Much of the interest in the small body of his extant sermons lies in their furnishing early evidence of preaching for liturgical occasions: Lent and the great feasts of the church year. His Lenten preaching during the first weeks seems to have been devoted to issues of morality. After that it was probably given over to teaching doctrine on the basis of a systematic exegesis of Scripture. In any case, what remains is but a small sample, since, for a number of years, he preached twice daily during the Lenten season, and only five Lenten sermons remain. Three are against the sins of usury, fornication, and not accepting reprimands, while the other two encourage love of the poor. These last two show Gregory at his best. Bernardi says that in them Gregory reveals himself to be a great master of preaching, which he defines as one who knows how—by the close blending of ideas, images, and feelings—to create an emotion and direct it toward efficacious action because he knows how those who hear him live and feel, and he observes carefully the people he passes in the streets of his town.[61]

The sermons for feasts include three for Easter[62] and one for the ascension that is probably the first record of the observance of that feast.[63] There is also one for Pentecost, but none for any other calendrical date until Christmas, which was also a new feast in the East. Already, however, the days immediately after Christmas were being observed. December 26 was the Feast of Stephen, and the next day commemorated

Peter and James as well as John (to whom alone the feast is assigned today in the Western calendar). And there are two Epiphany sermons, although some scholars think one is for the day after. Other feast days include those of martyrs. Three sermons have come down from Nyssa on the Feast of the Forty Martyrs of Sebaste, a commemoration that he says his mother introduced into Cappadocia. The other is for a soldier named Theodore, who, like the Forty, refused to participate in pagan worship. Only one of the sermons was delivered in a church, the others being given in the appropriate martyria. We can learn much from them about the development of the cult of martyrs.

Also in the epideictic genre are Nyssa's funeral sermons. Three of these are for bishops. That for Gregory Thaumaturgus (miracle worker) was a commemoration in his hometown of Neocaesarea in Pontus more than a hundred years after his death. Gregory Thaumaturgus had personal significance for Gregory because the elder Gregory had instructed his grandmother Macrina in the faith. Needless to say, Gregory's *paramythētikos* for his brother Basil is much closer to home, but, unlike the *epitaphios* by Nazianzus, his speech does not allude to a personal relation. Rather, it presents the case for Basil's canonization and suggests that his day should be December 28, immediately following the Feasts of Stephen and Peter, James, and John.

The funeral sermon was for Meletius of Antioch, which shows the prominence to which Nyssa had risen as his brother's heir, because he delivered it at the Council of Constantinople, at which Meletius had been presiding when he died. This status is further documented in Nyssa's having preached *paramythētikoi* for the emperor Theodosius's wife Flacilla and their seven-year-old daughter, Pulcheria. Two speeches by Nyssa at the council have also survived; from one of them comes one of Gregory's best-known utterances, a description of the atmosphere of Constantinople at the time as one in which one could not buy bread or order a bath without receiving Arian slogans in response.[64]

As Bernardi says, the twenty-six sermons that have been preserved show little of the personality or originality of the bishop of Nyssa.[65] As much as anything else, they show how much he traveled and how responsive he was to the life of the church at large. They may also show how little he was appreciated at home. At any rate, there is little indication in them of continuing pastoral activity. Rather, many of the sermons that have come down were preached somewhere other than Nyssa, generally for some big public occasion. Thus, as Bernardi also says, they show much of the accomplished orator, but little of Gregory himself.[66]

CONCLUSION

The sermons of the Cappadocian Fathers show the sort of marriage between Christian preaching and classical rhetoric that could occur after the church was not only no longer persecuted, but actually favored by the state. Sons of landowning families who had received rhetorical educations that would qualify them for the highest offices of government service could prepare themselves spiritually for ministry by ascetic retreat at a time when monasticism was already being regarded as "the moral equivalent of martyrdom." As a result, there was an extraordinary rush of talent and training into the episcopate. None represented that trend better than the Cappadocians.

Yet, as close as they were to one another, their surviving sermons give very different impressions. Basil's sermons reflect ongoing pastoral activity in a way those of the others do not. And he understood his pastoral task in preaching to be dispensing moral lessons on the basis of Scripture. Conversely, Basil chose few sermons that were used for grand public occasions for preservation; none, for instance, for funerals.

While Nyssa's sermons are also those of a bishop in charge of a flock, the exegetical homilies that were a majority among Basil's sermons are seldom found. Instead there are sermons for great public events. Part of the differences between these sermon collections has to do with the time of their writers' episcopates. Basil died before the triumph of orthodoxy in the accession of Theodosius and the victory at the Council of Constantinople. He always represented a tolerated minority while Nyssa was the voice of the dominant party.

In other respects, however, the two brothers' preaching topics show similar concerns that differ from those of Nazianzus's preaching. Nazianzus chose which of his sermons were to be published on the basis of their being examples for other bishops, used in instructing them how to preach in a variety of genres. In this way he contributed to changing the sort of person chosen to be bishop, a cause to which he was so devoted. In relating to their audiences, Nyssa was probably least successful. Basil shows himself closely in touch with his flock, and Nazianzen's sermons are so deeply personal that they inevitably made contact with his audience.

In summary, Bernardi says that *kerygma* does not exist in a pure state,[67] it is always the preaching of particular persons at certain places at given times, and always reflects that conditioning. The preaching of the Cappadocians—especially the minority of their sermons that were chosen for preservation—is by no means typical of preaching through the ages. Their corpus, for instance, includes few of the exegetical homilies that must have been their standard homiletical form, as it was almost the only sermonic genre in the church before the High Middle Ages. Rather, their sermons have a preoccupation with teaching morals, a concern appropriate for an age in which primary evangelization was no longer necessary, but deep teaching had not yet become possible. Nevertheless, their sermons are invaluable for showing the communicative skill by which rhetorical education can increase the effectiveness of preaching. And the very eccentricity of the selections published reminds later generations that the early church had a richer variety of homiletical genres than is usually apparent. The deepest legacy of the Cappadocians, however, is the way their preaching bears the fruit of the spirituality to which they were committed. Their contemplative asceticism still has power to call readers to a life of deeper holiness.

FOR FURTHER READING

Basil. *Exegetic Homilies.* Translated by Agnes Clare Way. FC. Washington, D.C.: Catholic University of America Press, 1963.

Bernardi, Jean. *La prédication des pères cappadociens: Le prédicateur et son auditoire.* Publications de la Faculté des Lettres et Sciences Humaine de l'Université de Montpellier, no. 30. Paris: Presses Universitaires de France, 1968.

The Easter Sermons of Gregory of Nyssa: Translation and Commentary: Proceedings of the Fourth International Colloquium on Gregory of Nyssa, Cambridge England, 11–15 September, 1978. Edited by Andreas Spira and Christoph Klock, with introduction by G. Christopher Stead. Patristic Monograph Series, no. 9. Cambridge, Mass.: Philadelphia Patristic Foundation, 1981.

Funeral Orations by Saint Gregory Nazianzen and Saint Ambrose. Introduction by Martin R. P. McGuire and translated (Gregory's orations only) by Leo P. McCauley et al. FC. New York: Fathers of the Church, Inc. 1953.

Gregory of Nyssa. *The Life of Moses.* Translated with introduction and notes by Abraham J. Malherbe and Everett Ferguson; preface by John Meyendorff. CWS. New York: Paulist Press, 1978.

Ruether, Rosemary Radford. *Gregory of Nazianzus, Rhetor and Philosopher.* Oxford: Clarendon Press, 1969.

Notes

1. Hugh Elton, *Frontiers of the Roman Empire* (Bloomington: Indiana University Press, 1996).

2. Averil Cameron studies how Christians attained power in the society through their use of traditional forms of oratory during this period, thus identifying themselves with deep roots in the culture. See *Christianity and the Rhetoric of Empire: The Development of Christian Discourse,* Sather Classical Lectures (Berkeley and Los Angeles: University of California Press, 1991), 55:120-54.

3. Paganism also continued as a force until 416 when non-Christians were not allowed to serve in the army. Within a generation, most of the holdouts in aristocratic families had converted.

4. While Christian Cappadocia is best known to travelers for the churches carved out of tall cones eroded from volcanic rock in the area of Göreme, those churches with their marvelous frescoes came along several centuries after the Cappadocian Fathers and are not located in the same region.

5. Much as Englishmen of the eighteenth and nineteenth centuries were prepared for administering their colonial empire by attending public schools where they studied Greek and Latin literature.

6. Peter Brown, *The World of Late Antiquity: From Marcus Aurelius to Muhammed* (London: Thames & Hudson, 1971), 22-33; *Power and Persuasion in Late Antiquity: Towards a Christian Empire* (Madison: University of Wisconsin Press, 1992); and *The Cult of the Saints: Its Rise and Function in Latin Christianity* (Chicago: University of Chicago Press, 1981).

7. Theirs must have been one of the few families in history to produce three siblings with feast days in the church calendar.

8. His predecessor was named Eusebius, but he should be distinguished from the church historian of the same name whose Caesarea was the Palestinian port city and who died when Basil was only ten years old.

9. For an English translation, see Basil, *Exegetic Homilies,* trans. Agnes Clare Way, FC (Washington: Catholic University of America Press, 1963).

10. I owe much of what I say on the sermons of Basil and the two Gregorys to Jean Bernardi, *La prédication des pères cappadociens: Le prédicateur et son auditoire,* Publications de la Faculté des Lettres et Sciences Humaine de l'Université de Montpellier, no. 30 (Paris: Presses Universitaires de France, 1968).

11. Also translated in Basil, *Exegetic Homilies*. An older translation is available in vol. 8 of *NPNF*[2].

12. Bernardi, *La prédication des pères cappadociens,* 47.

13. Some scholars believe that the homilies found in the works of Gregory of Nyssa under the Latin title of *In verba faciamus* are based on notes given by Basil on what he would have said in the final sermons on the days of creation.

14. Way provides some delightful examples of this in her introduction to Basil, *Exegetic Homilies,* x-xiii.

15. PG 31:164-617. See Bernardi, *La prédication des pères cappadociens,* 55.

16. See Brown, The *Cult of the Saints*, especially chapter 5.

17. "*Presque à chaque ligne apparaît une citation, une réminiscence ou une allusion à un passage de l'Ecriture.*" Bernardi, *La prédication des pères cappadociens,* 89.

18. Indeed, they are referred to as "orations" rather than as "sermons" or "homilies," and they are collected with speeches of other sorts.

19. From the Greek *hypsistos,* the "Most High."

20. *Or.* 18.5-16.

21. While the choice of the congregation designated who would become bishop, it was, of course, ordination by other bishops that made the person a bishop.

22. Gregory of Nyssa was the only one of the three who married, but even he wrote treatises about the superiority of virginity over the married state.

23. *Funeral Orations by Saint Gregory Nazianzen and Saint Ambrose,* intro. Martin R. P. McGuire and trans. (of Gregory's orations only) Leo P. McCauley, S.J., FC (New York: Fathers of the Church, Inc., 1953), 27-99; the section dealing with Athens is on pp. 39-49. An earlier translation is in *NPNF*[2] 7:395-422.

24. Rosemary Radford Ruether, *Gregory of Nazianzus, Rhetor and Philosopher* (Oxford: Clarendon Press, 1969), 28-33.

25. Although this particular date is not disputed, the authorities disagree by a year or so over a number of other dates in Gregory's life.

26. Ruether, *Gregory of Nazianzus,* 33.

27. *Epistle* 40, quoted ibid., 34.

28. *Carm. de vita sua,* quoted ibid., 36.

29. There are forty-five orations assigned to Gregory in Jacques Paul Migne, *Patrilogia Graeca,* vol. 35, 36 (Paris: n.p., 1857–66), the standard printed edition of the Greek text, but *Or.* 35 is generally recognized to be spurious.

30. Another translation of *ho theologos* is "the Divine." The translators of the *Orations* in *NPNF*[2] say that the term is used "in the narrower sense of 'Defender of the Godhead of the Word.'" 7:200 n. 1.

31. The *Orations* come from every stage of Gregory's ordained ministry and include his first and last sermons.

32. Bernardi, *La prédication des pères cappadociens,* 256. See also Gerhard H. Ettlinger, S.J., "The Orations of Gregory of Nazianzus: A Study in Rhetoric and Personality," in *Preaching in the Patristic Age: Studies in Honor of Walter J. Burghardt, S.J.,* ed. David G. Hunter (New York: Paulist Press, 1989), 101-18.

33. Bernardi, *La prédication des pères cappadociens,* 256.

34. Gregory appears to have been the first Christian to preserve his letters for posterity. On Gregory's letters see Ruether, *Gregory of Nazianzus,* 123-28. A large number of his letters are translated in vol. 7 of *NPNF*[2].

35. In response to the same challenge, Apollinarius of Laodicea rewrote much of the Bible in the genres of classical literature.

36. Ruether, *Gregory of Nazianzus,* 107. George Kennedy cuts the number of genres down to three—moral, dogmatic, and panegyric—on the basis of what Gregory said about the sermons of Cyprian (*Or.* 24), and goes on to suggest that these correspond to the classical *genera dicendi*: deliberative, forensic, and epideictic (*Greek Rhetoric Under Christian Emperors* [Princeton: Princeton University Press, 1983], 217).

37. The Maccabees (*Or.* 15), Athanasius (21), Cyprian (24), and Hero (25).

38. His brother Caesarius (*Or.* 7), his sister Gorgonia (8), his father (18), and Basil (43).

39. Translations of twenty-four of the forty-four *Orations* can be found in vol. 7 of *NPNF*[2]. A slightly edited form of the *NPNF* translation of the *Theological Orations* appears in *Christology of the Later Fathers,* ed. E. R. Hardy with Cyril C. Richardson, Library of Christian Classics, vol. 3 (Philadelphia: Westminster, 1954), 128-214. Another translation appears in Frederick W. Norris, *Faith Gives Fullness to Reasoning: The Five Theological Orations of Gregory Nazianzen,* trans. Lionel Wickham and Frederick Williams, Supplements to *Vigiliae Christianae,* vol. 13 (Leiden: E. J. Brill, 1990), 217-99. The orations on Caesarius, Gorgonia, Gregory the elder, and Basil appear in McGuire and McCauley, *Funeral Orations of Saint Gregory and Saint Ambrose.*

40. This is not to say that no exegesis occurs in any of the other orations. *Or.* 17, for example, begins as a homily on Jeremiah 4:19, moves into a moral exhortation to the congregation, and ends with an address to the provincial governor who was present. And, of course, there are frequent quotations from or allusions to the Bible, although the incidence of these varies with the subject and genre.

41. Although those that are in a distinct classical form, such as the *epitaphios,* observe its rules as scrupulously as possible when the subject is a Christian.

42. Nazianzen was the first bishop ever to have an opportunity to preach before a baptized emperor, and he took advantage of it to urge legislation supportive of Christian standards.

43. For classical influences on this oration (referred to as the *Apologeticus*), see Kennedy, *Greek Rhetoric Under Christian Emperors,* 218-21.

44. His dissatisfaction with many of the clergy who were contemporaries of his is part of the reason he edited his *Orations* to be both a collection of model addresses for bishops and a dissertation on the model of ministry he shared with Basil and Nyssa.

45. Browne and Swallow, "Introduction to Oration II," *NPNF*[2] 7:204. The practical guidelines and criteria that Gregory used in his preaching are summed up in a section of his autobiographical poem, *Carm. de vita sua* (ll. 1190-1262), a translation of which appears in Ruether, *Gregory of Nazianzus,* 43-44.

46. Jean Bernardi, *"Sermons fondus en un traité," La prédication des pères cappadociens,* 181.

47. *Or.* 27.2. Bernardi interprets references made at the beginning and end of this oration to refer to the women's quarters of high imperial officials as being hotbeds of such theological discussion, agitated by the eunuchs who were attendants there. *La prédication des pères cappadociens,* 186.

48. Eunomius was a late Arian whose position has been caricatured as "anomoean." The Nicene position to which Gregory was loyal insisted that the Son and the Holy Spirit were of the same substance *(homoousion)* as the Father, while earlier Arians had said that the Son, at any rate, was of *like* substance *(homoiousion)* with him. A truly Anomoean position, then, would be that the Son was of *unlike* substance with him.

Pneumatomachians, sometimes mistakenly referred to as Macedonians, were said to have "warred against the Spirit" because they denied the consubstantiality of the Holy Spirit with the Father.

49. Norris, *Faith Gives Fullness to Reasoning,* 53-71.

50. Kennedy, *Greek Rhetoric Under Christian Emperors,* 225.

51. Ibid., 226.

52. Kennedy and Ruether disagree on the genre of this speech. Ruether says that "since it was preached some time after Basil's death and lacks any *threnos* or *paramuthetikos,* we must class it as an encomium rather than an *epitaphios*" (*Gregory of Nazianzus,* 120). Kennedy, on the other hand, follows Menander Rhetor in saying that an *epitaphios* was usually given some time after the death, "in contrast to a *paramythetikos* or monody, which reflects more immediate feelings of grief" (*Greek Rhetoric Under Christian Emperors,* 228). The explanation for this disagreement is probably that the rhetorical handbooks that set forth these definitions and rules were not always consistent with one another in the distinctions they drew.

53. Kennedy, *Greek Rhetoric Under Christian Emperors,* 237.

54. Bernardi, *La prédication des pères cappadociens,* 238-39.

55. Kennedy, *Greek Rhetoric Under Christian Emperors,* 228-37.

56. Ruether, *Gregory of Nazianzus,* 120-23.

57. Johannes Quasten, ed., *The Golden Age of Greek Patristic Literature from the Council of Nicaea to the Council of Chalcedon,* vol. 3 of *Patrology* (Utrecht: Spectrum, 1960; Westminster, Md.: Newman Press, 1960), 254.

58. Ibid., 255.

59. Gregory of Nyssa, *The Life of Moses,* trans. with intro. and notes by Abraham J. Malherbe and Everett Ferguson, and pref. by John Meyendorff, Classics of Western Spirituality (New York: Paulist Press, 1978). Extensive excerpts appear in Jean Daniélou and Herbert Musurillo, *From Glory to Glory: Texts from Gregory of Nyssa's Mystical Writings* (New York: Scribner's, 1961).

60. The problem continued. He preached a sermon "against those who do not bear reprimands" when he had been a bishop almost ten years.

61. Bernardi, *La prédication des pères cappadociens,* 279.

62. Five sermons for Easter are attributed to Nyssa in PG, but only the first, third, and fourth are regarded as authentic. These are among the few of his sermons that have been translated into English. The translation and a collection of essays about them appear in *The Easter Sermons of Gregory of Nyssa: Translation and Commentary: Proceedings of the Fourth International Colloquium on Gregory of Nyssa, Cambridge, England, 11–15 September, 1978,* ed. Andreas Spira and Christoph Klock, with intro. by G. Christopher Stead, Patristic Monograph Series, no. 9 (Cambridge, Mass.: Philadelphia Patristic Foundation, 1981). One of his Epiphany sermons and his funeral sermon for Meletius are translated in *NPNF*[2] 5:513-24.

63. Thomas J. Talley, *The Origins of the Liturgical Year* (New York: Pueblo, 1968), 67-68.

64. Quoted in Hardy, *Christology of the Later Fathers,* 117, and Bernardi, *La prédication des pères cappadociens,* 328, translating PG, vol. 46, col. 557.

65. Bernardi, *La prédication des pères cappadociens,* 331.

66. Ibid., 332.

67. Ibid., 407.

CHAPTER 4

HOMILETICS AND CATECHETICS: CHRYSOSTOM AND OTHERS

This chapter will deal with two different kinds of preaching that were practiced with a rare degree of virtuosity by one man: John of Antioch and Constantinople, known to later generations as Chrysostom *(Chrysostomos)*, the Golden Mouth. His work alone will be considered in the discussion of the homily form in this chapter, but his contribution to catechetical preaching will be examined alongside that of others.

Although the homily was the standard form of preaching before the High Middle Ages, we have not studied it in its characteristic form so far in this volume. While the genre seems virtually to have been created by Origen, he had none of the rhetorical training and flourish that most of the great Fathers showed. The Cappadocians undoubtedly used this genre of preaching more than any other genre, but, as we saw in the last chapter, the homily is not prominently featured in the sermons they chose to have published.[1] The most common sort of homily will not even be seen in the works of John, though most of his surviving sermons are in the genre.[2] Ironically, John's reason for writing his homilies in a form other than the most common of the day—his lack of enthusiasm for the allegorical interpretation employed by most of the other homileticians—makes them more accessible to people today than most other patristic preaching.

The most typical form of homily with allegorical hermeneutics will be the subject of the next chapter, in which we will consider the work of Augustine. These two preachers, Chrysostom and Augustine, have an otherwise unequaled significance for the history of patristic homiletics, which we can see in the way that their writings alone take up the entire fourteen volumes of the first series of the *Nicene and Post-Nicene Fathers*—as much space as is devoted in the second series to the works of all the other writers of their period.[3]

THE GOLDEN MOUTH

Early Life

The one destined to be designated by a future pope as the patron saint of Christian preachers[4] was born in 349, give or take five years,[5] in Antioch on the Orontes River, into an affluent and socially prominent Christian family. His father, a highly placed civil servant in the secretariat of the commander in chief[6] of the Roman army in the Oriens diocese,[7] died while John was an infant, so he was brought up by his mother. His education was the common one of the time, the only exception being that he did not have to leave home to complete it. After elementary and grammar school he was able to remain in Antioch and study under one of the most distinguished rhetoricians of his day, Libanius.[8] He also studied philosophy with Andragatius. He must have been gifted because he learned to speak and write with an eloquence few have attained, causing one modern critic to say that he was "the only prose author of his epoch who could stand comparison with Demosthenes."[9] Indeed, an ancient account quotes the dying Libanius as saying that his successor "ought to have been John had not the Christians stolen him from us."[10]

The career for which John was preparing was probably not the law, as is generally believed, but, as J. N. D. Kelly says, service in the *sacra scrinia,* the Roman civil service responsible for phrasing imperial documents in "clear and dignified prose," a career that could be crowned with the award of senatorial rank.[11] That was not to be, however, for by the time he finished his studies at the age of eighteen, John already felt the attraction of another calling far more deeply, that of ascetic service to his Lord. He was baptized the following Easter (probably 368) and soon began to serve as an aide to Meletius, bishop of the main body of orthodox Christians in Antioch, a capacity in which he served for three years.

During this same period he undertook an ascetic life not unlike that which had been the ideal of Basil and Nazianzus. He was considered a monk *(monachos),* although he was not at that time either a hermit or a member of a community. Rather, he was what was called in Syria a "son of the covenant," one who had taken vows to wear a habit, remain celibate, abstain from meat and wine, and devote his life to prayer. While doing this he lived at home, but he and some friends had agreed to meet together and place themselves under the guidance of Diodore, an ascetic and biblical scholar who was later to become bishop of Tarsus.[12]

Attraction to Asceticism

After three years, when John was about twenty-three, the bishop made him a reader, a member of the order just below the diaconate in the East. The specific duty of the order was to read the lections other than the Gospel at the Eucharist, but it made John a member of the clergy and probably involved other liturgical, pastoral, and administrative duties. About this time, however, John was frightened by an effort of the church authorities to impose the priesthood upon him and his close friend Basil.[13] By a ruse John saw that their efforts were successful with his friend, but he eluded ordination himself, considering himself unworthy of so high an office at that stage of his spiritual development.

The outrage that greeted his refusal was undoubtedly one of the factors in his decision to pursue the ascetic life even more fully by joining the monks on nearby Mount Silpios.[14] There he placed himself under a spiritual director for four years while he struggled for mastery over his youthful sexuality and other desires of the flesh, striving as his fellow monks did to achieve uninterrupted communion with God. After that he felt sufficiently grounded to go off to a cave by himself, where he fasted as much as possible and tried to go entirely without sleep. During this period he learned the Old and New Testaments by heart, a feat that accounts for the extraordinary facility with which he could cite parallel passages in his extempore preaching.

Not surprisingly, his frail body could not take such punishment for more than two years. When his health finally forced him to return to Antioch, he did not feel that he had ceased to be a monk, but only that he was practicing his vows under the different set of circumstances that God had imposed upon him. Indeed, he regarded asceticism as the norm for all Christians. For the rest of his life he lived as abstemiously as possible, even when he became bishop in the capital city of the empire, though his asceticism horrified many he met there.

Ordained Life in Antioch

When John got back to Antioch, he discovered that Meletius had returned from exile under an Arian emperor to be sole bishop of the city. John resumed his old duties as reader for two years, after which he was elevated to the diaconate. This gave him a much more visible liturgical role and very demanding pastoral duties. Essentially, deacons were in charge of all the church's eleemosynary responsibilities, which were quite extensive at the time. The church in Antioch

> had to maintain upward of three thousand widows and virgins, not to mention a host of prisoners in gaol, people who were sick or hospitalized, others who were impoverished or maimed, others still who crouched by the altar in desperate need of food and clothing.[15]

It was while he was busy with those overwhelming responsibilities that John, not yet allowed to preach,[16] began his work as a Christian writer, producing some eight treatises on various subjects.

After serving as a deacon for five years, John was ordained priest in 386, when he was thirty-seven years old. This was the beginning of what must have been the happiest and most fulfilling period of his life. Now he concelebrated the Eucharist with the bishop and sometimes presided for him when he was absent. With the other priests he also continued to assist the bishop in his administrative responsibilities. But chiefly his duties were to preach and to instruct the people. It was the work for which he was born. "So for almost twelve years . . . John stood out as the leading pulpit orator of Antioch, building up an unrivalled reputation."[17] I will defer the discussion of his preaching, however, until I complete this biographical sketch. While Kelly refers to the years of his priesthood as John's "decade of development,"[18] we know little about his activities during that period other than what we can infer from his preaching. Therefore, it is time to move on to the next phase of his life, on which all too much information is available.

Episcopate

Near the end of 397, John was urgently summoned by the local governor, quietly gotten out of town, and then driven to Constantinople where he was told that he was to be the new bishop.[19] He had been chosen by the eunuch Eutropius, superintendent of the sacred bedchamber, who was the power behind the imperial throne. Arcadius, the Eastern emperor at the time, had none of the commanding stature of Theodosius I, and was likely to be dominated by someone, whether his eunuch or his beautiful, capable, and determined wife Aelia Eudoxia. The royal couple were at first very welcoming to their new bishop, a man just under fifty years of age with an unprepossessing appearance,[20] a puritanical outlook, and an almost unparalleled ability to move Christian congregations by his preaching. John quickly won the hearts of the people by the obvious love he felt for them, a love he freely communicated in his preaching. Indeed, his standard way of addressing the congregation was to call them "love."

Yet his austerity and imperiousness evoked a resistance that eventually brought him down. He expected that all the clergy would live as simply as he did and assumed that they had not been doing so and had to be brought into line. He wanted monks to be subordinate to him rather than their founder, to be more like the ascetics in the mountains around Antioch than the monks who had adapted their life to the capital city of the empire. The large number of bishops who were either living in Constantinople or were there temporarily on business, those who came to be called "the resident synod," had trouble relating to a bishop who preferred to dine alone and who provided only abstemious entertainment for guests. He offended Theophilus, the bishop of Alexandria, who had pushed his own candidate for the chair of Constantinople and who was eager to maintain his own as the most influential see in the East.

While he endeared himself to the masses by decrying the luxuries of the wealthy and saying that they should give their resources to the poor rather than lavish them upon themselves, the rich were less enthusiastic about his message. Aracadius and Eudoxia vacillated in their devotion to him, giving him passionate support one moment and turning against him the next. It was hard for the queen, for instance, to be too pleased when he preached against ornate and expensive feminine attire and called attention to hers as an example of what he meant, or, when she expropriated the property of an ordinary citizen and he spoke in a sermon of the sin of Jezebel, who had done the same thing.

Neither tact nor compromise seemed to be a part of his vocabulary or character. While one has to admire both his own self-denial and his fearlessness in opposing what he considered to be evil, it is hard to resist the feeling that he did a great deal to render inevitable his own undoing. It took only about five years for all the powerful persons he had offended to form a coalition against him. In trying to help out other churches in the area, he overstepped canonical authority and gave an entrée to his enemies. He was sent into exile once, brought back, and sent again, this time permanently. After four years of great hardship and deprivation, he finally died in 407 when he was only fifty-eight years old. The entire story of the downfall of this holy but forbidding genius who gave his enemies too much ammunition to use against him is one of the saddest in the annals of the church, but the details are not relevant enough to the history of preaching as such to warrant recounting here.

HIS HOMILIES[21]

Chrysostom's congregations frequently broke out in applause when he preached. His sermons are peppered with remonstrations with them for doing so, saying that if they approved of what he said, they should show it by doing what he told them rather than by anything so easy as clapping. He was there for their salvation rather than their entertainment. Although he turned against Greek culture as a pagan and worldly distraction from the way to heaven, his talent had been honed by Libanius to reflexive virtuosity, and he probably could not state the time of day without some mark of rhetorical grace.

By and large, however, he did eschew the classical *genera dicendi,* speaking only in the rather amorphous homiletic genre that offers less room for oratorical display than most other types of speeches. As Robert C. Hill, the translator of his *Homilies on Genesis* said, there was "little of the original and spectacular in the structure of the homilies."[22]

> Normally, there was the opening reading of the day's verse(s). Chrysostom would then link the day's sermon with the previous day's, often through some such figure as the laying of a table; this [linking] could occasionally develop into a lengthy moral/dogmatic/polemical excursus unrelated to the *Gn* text and supported from other Scriptural loci. Then—sometimes with abruptness and difficulty after such a lengthy digression (disproportionate enough to discourage again an impression of perfect planning beforehand)—he would take up the day's text for exegesis/commentary. Finally, after a substantial time on the text, he would move to a parenetic conclusion, quite perfunctorily done by way of "supplying you with the customary *paraklēsis,*" and not always arising naturally from the exegetical material.[23]

Other things being equal, this description will serve for any of his series of homilies. Sometimes there was no introduction and John began immediately to exegete the text verse by verse. The effect is strange to modern taste, because it often seems like a commentary being read aloud, and often there was no obvious connection between the interpretation of the biblical passage and the concluding exhortation. Even less fathomable to contemporary consciousness was John's habit of building the application not on the passage as a whole, nor on the most profound issues raised in the pericope, but on the last verse to be exegeted, whichever it happened to be.

Biblical Interpretation

As I noted above, however, John's biblical exposition is much more attractive to contemporary taste than the allegorical interpretation so common elsewhere at the time. In part, allegorical interpretation was so popular because anomalies in the text were as obvious to interpreters then as they are now. Yet those who used this method assumed that the discrepancy was inserted by the Holy Spirit to indicate that spiritual interpretation was called for. For someone like John, however, who did not take that way out, the anomaly was apparent and had to be dealt with in ways very similar to those used today.

Therefore, John raises questions about authorship and why only two of the apostles and two of their followers wrote Gospels, and shows familiarity with the tradition that Matthew was originally written in Hebrew and that Mark went to Egypt.[24] Inconsistencies between the Gospel accounts are regarded as an asset rather than a liability: "that discordance which seems to exist in little matters delivers [the Gospels] from all suspicion and speaks clearly in behalf of the character of the writers."[25] John also undertakes to explain why the only three women mentioned before Mary in Matthew's genealogy have something questionable about them.[26] In the second of the *Homilies on St. John,* Chrysostom says, in effect, that a sermon on the author should have the form of an encomium and deal with his family, country, and education, but the lack of anything remarkable about any of these is itself remarkable and indicative of the miracle of inspiration.

In the only extended patristic treatment of Acts, he notes that the Holy Spirit is the special topic of the book, that the greater part of it deals with Paul, and that it was written by Paul's companion Luke, referring to evidence that has been rehashed by most commentators since.[27] He notices that most of Paul's letters begin with thanking God for the congregation to which he writes.[28] And he deduces that Colossians must have been written after Romans and before 2 Timothy.[29] Modern scholars may question the Pauline authorship of some of these epistles, yet they continue to argue over the order in which the genuine ones were written. By being concerned with such matters, John seems more like a colleague to New Testament scholars today than most of his contemporaries.

Chrysostom's literal rather than allegorical interpretation was not just a personal proclivity but was characteristic of the church in Antioch in which he had been formed. Eustathius, the bishop who represented Antioch at the Council of Nicaea in 325, wrote *On the Witch of Endor Against Origen,* a book in which he claimed that Origen's allegorical exegesis deprived the Bible of its historical character. Diodore of Tarsus, under whom John and his friends had placed themselves for spiritual and theological formation in their youth, was the author of a book, now lost, called *What Is the Difference Between Theory and Allegory?* The key term of the debate was "theory," which the two schools understood very differently.

> Where the Alexandrines use the word *theory*[30] as equivalent to allegorical interpretation, the Antiochene exegetes use it for a sense of scripture higher or deeper than the literal or historical meaning, but firmly based on the letter.[31]

Thus, both schools thought that there was more meaning to the Bible than the simple literal sense, but the Antiochenes felt that any such meaning was rooted in and consistent with that sense.

John's friend Theodore, who had studied with him under Diodore and became bishop of Mopsuestia, was the greatest exegete and theologian of this school, but his reputation was clouded later when he was held responsible for the teaching of his pupil Nestorius.[32] It is now generally agreed that Nestorius did not teach the heresy associated with his name and that the school of Antioch was as orthodox as that of Alexandria, but two very different ways of doing theology made it virtually impossible for representatives of one school to understand those of the other.

There are many parallels between the careers of John and Nestorius, including their both serving as bishop of Constantinople and their being ousted from that position by a cabal in which the bishop of Alexandria at the time played a leading part. Church politics as much as anything else made it hard for historical biblical interpretation to receive its due in the fourth century.[33] Even then, however, Jerome, the greatest and most influential exegete among the Western fathers, was persuaded by

Chrysostom's biblical interpretation to abandon the allegorism that he had originally practiced.

Content and Style

One of the reasons John was not as profound a biblical interpreter as his friend Theodore was that he did not have as deep an interest in the meaning of the biblical text in its own right. What he sought in his scriptural study, and certainly what he wished to leave with his congregation, was moral and spiritual guidance to help them live the Christian life. Sometimes, as noted above, that guidance would be based on the day's last exegeted verse. At other times it grew out of something going on in the city and congregation. Or he might have a single virtue he wished to recommend or vice to oppose during the entire liturgical season and homily series. On occasion he would make one moral appeal in the introduction and another in the conclusion. His one overriding interest was in persuading the people of God to live consistently with their calling. As he said in his treatise *On the Priesthood,* "this is the ultimate aim of teaching: to lead their disciples, both by what they do and what they say, into the way of that blessed life which Christ commanded" (4.8).[34]

John's various homilies display a considerable difference in their degree of stylistic polish. Indeed, the lack of such finish is one of the main criteria by which critics have distinguished the series preached in Constantinople from those delivered at Antioch, the assumption being that the busy and often beleaguered bishop had less time to devote to his sermons. This rule of thumb is not completely reliable, however, there being some unpolished works with internal indications that they were produced in Antioch and some more refined works that clearly date from his episcopate. John did not write his sermons out in advance. Instead, his, like those of the Cappadocians, were taken down by a scribe during delivery. Hence, much of the difference in literary elegance depended on whether the author found time to revise a series before publication.

A lack of such editing is not entirely a disadvantage to those who are interested in how John actually preached. As John A. Broadus says:

> You see the sermon in about as imperfect, and sometimes distorted, a condition as it is seen in the actual delivery by many of the congregation. You see the frequent questions, the abrupt turns of phrase, the multiplied repetitions, by which a skilled and sympathetic preacher, keenly watching his audience, strives to retain attention and to insure a more general comprehension. You are drawn near to him, and almost stand by his side.[35]

In all that has been said about the Golden Mouth's preaching, there has been little to account for his great reputation in his own day and since. Partly that is because much of what made him so impressive can no longer be experienced. His sermons were transactions with a live congregation, not words on paper, much less translations of those words into other languages. We can know nothing of his electrifying presence as he sat in his chair in the ambo, much nearer to his audience than if he had preached from the customary position of the bishop's chair behind the altar in the apse. The interaction with the congregation, mentioned by Broadus, cannot be recaptured. What John's delivery was like, the way he used either his body or his voice, is unavailable to history. What the voice that came from the Mouth of Gold sounded like cannot be known. And those who experience his words only in translation cannot guess at the magic of sound or the precision of expression in his choice of words. All that is left is the judgment of his contemporaries that he was the best there was at a time when oratory was one of the most highly developed and critically appreciated art forms there was.

Even from printed translations it is possible, however, to see some of the ways in which John achieved his oral effectiveness. He made great use of metaphor and simile to help his hearers understand the points he was making, drawing especially on athletic, military, maritime, and agricultural images. He also made "abundant, even excessive, use of the stylistic devices of the sophists, especially tropes and figures involving pleonasm, such as anaphora, or sound, such as paronomasia, or vivacity, such as rhetorical question or question and answer."[36]

He created vivid scenes *(ekphrasis)* that brought things to life for his audience. He made comparisons *(synkrisis)* and employed the techniques of the Cynic-Stoic diatribe. Paradox was a common form of expression for him as for all Christian speakers. As much as he claimed to despise Greek culture, he was nevertheless aware that "the art of speaking comes, not by nature, but by instruction, and therefore even if a man reaches the acme of perfection in it, still it may forsake him unless he cultivates its force by constant application and exercise."[37] He constantly honed the skills in which Libanius had trained him.

The Sermons on the Statues

We can see an example of his preaching power in one of his most famous series of sermons, the one called *Concerning the Statues.* Considered by Kennedy to be John's most striking homilies,[38] these were preached when John had been a priest for only a year. (For a sermon in this series, see **Vol. 2, pp. 57-70.**) Just after he began his Lenten sermon series in 387,[39] an event occurred that placed the entire city of Antioch in great danger. When notice of a new and exorbitant tax was read out at the courthouse, a mob led by a claque erupted in widespread vandalism against public buildings, culminating in portraits and statues of the emperor and his family being pulled down and defaced. As Kelly says, "To insult or show disrespect to the images of the reigning emperor was equivalent to insulting him personally, and therefore counted as high treason."[40] The emperor would have been within his rights to obliterate the city and its inhabitants, and he certainly seemed likely to exact some sort of terrible vengeance.[41] The aged bishop Flavian set off to Constantinople at once to beg Theodosius in the name of the God he worshiped to spare the city, leaving his priest to minister to his terrified flock.

In the weeks that followed, John preached twenty[42] sermons, most of which began with an effort to help the anxious congregation see the latest turn of events in a theological perspective. There is an almost breathless quality to these reports, a feel of bulletins from the front lines. John's basic attitude toward the series of events is to consider it a visitation for the city's sins. It does not seem to have occurred to him to suggest that the emperor was being too demanding in levying taxes. Those to blame for the immediate dangers were, in effect, outside agitators. For all his tendency to blame the problems of his congregation on themselves, there is still something very pastoral in John's message, something that must have given many Antiochene Christians the courage to endure a very frightening period.[43]

The modern reader may be astonished, however, to realize that the sermons are not all about the crisis. They are called homilies and correctly so, since most of them are expositions of lections for the Lenten liturgy, largely from Genesis. After the daily update on the crisis, John discussed the reading with very little transition or effort to interconnect these two parts of the sermon. Finally, the concluding exhortation for almost all of the homilies concerned one subject: swearing. It seemed as though, come hell or high water, Chrysostom wanted to stamp out cursing in Antioch that Lent.[44]

One can see John's eloquence in all of the sermons, but perhaps it is in its purest form in the first, the one preached before the riot occurred. It begins, as Kennedy says, with "a splendor worthy of Pindar."[45]

> Ye have heard the Apostolic voice, that trumpet from heaven, that spiritual lyre! For even as a trumpet sounding a fearful and warlike note, it

> both dismays the enemy, and arouses the dejected spirits on its own side, and filling them with great boldness, renders those who attend to it invincible against the devil! And again, as a lyre, that gently soothes with soul-captivating melody, it puts to slumber the disquietudes of perverse thoughts; and thus, with pleasure, instills into us much profit. Ye have heard then today the Apostle discoursing to Timothy of divers necessary matters![46]

He continues to introduce the lection from 1 Timothy 5 that had just been read. After summarizing it he says that, because it would be impossible for him to interpret all of it, he will allow the congregation to pick the text on which he will preach.

The verse they chose was 5:23, "Drink a little wine for thy stomach's sake, and thine often infirmities" (KJV). He then tells them they have chosen a text so simple that it seems to have little promise, but they will be amazed at the riches it contains. He begins by asking how God could permit someone who trusted him as much as Timothy did to fall into chronic illness. That question is further complicated by the way the illness interfered with the work Timothy had to do for the Lord. Why did God allow the work to be interfered with? And, since both Timothy and Paul performed many healing miracles, why did they not heal Timothy?

John begins his response by calling attention to Timothy's great virtue and Paul's loving care. Yet Timothy did not presume on his virtue. Rather, knowing the dangers of youth, he preferred suffering of the body to that of the soul. In that perspective it becomes clear that Paul's admonition to Timothy was a counsel of abstinence rather than indulgence: not "use wine," but "a little wine." For "it is not the use of wine, but the want of moderation which produces drunkenness."[47] With that background John goes on to give eight reasons why God allowed Timothy to suffer. He follows that by citing a long paragraph of scripture supporting each of these reasons. (How could he keep the list in his memory at the time that he was searching it for so many parallel verses of scripture?)

John then begins the shift to his concluding moral exhortation by saying that we should not call God into account for what he does. Even Job did not do that, nor did many others who lost their fortunes while they were using them to help the poor. For a Christian to question God in that way would be blasphemy. With that transition negotiated, John is able to announce what will be his recurring theme throughout the twenty-one sermons: "But since our discourse has now turned to the subject of blasphemy, I desire to ask one favor of you all, in return for this my address, and speaking with you; which is, that you will correct on my behalf the blasphemers of this city."[48] He even gives them permission to use physical force in carrying out that mission. He promises them a spiritual reward for discharging the task and arranges to segue into the doxology with which he closed most of his sermons.

What a tour de force! One of the exercises by which future Sophists were trained in schools of rhetoric was extempore speaking on an assigned subject. Chrysostom took the practice into the pulpit and asked his congregation to tell him from which verse in the passage that had been read he should preach. The complex structure he gave the treatment of the verse by listing the reasons why God allowed Timothy to suffer are *topoi* and the long citing of scriptural parallels showed that he already knew which biblical passages treated each of the topics, that he had furnished his mind to speak on all these subjects—and many more besides. And, in the end, he brought the subject around to the exhortation he wanted to be thematic for that Lent. However much he may have liked to discredit Greek culture, in sermons like this he demonstrated how thoroughly he had mastered everything Libanius had to teach.

PREPARATION FOR INITIATION

While a few of John's sermons in various genres other than homiletic have come down, the catechetical are the only ones that can be mentioned here. Basic instruction in the faith is a task that has been performed in all the Christian centuries, but not all such teaching is preaching. To begin with, preaching requires a more or less formal occasion in which one person is making a continuous presentation, rather than one in which there is discussion back and forth. Beyond that, however, the difference between catechetical sermons and lectures informing or explaining is the purpose of forming the congregation through the medium of the speech, enabling them to experience change, to undergo at least a "mini-conversion." It is not enough for them to know and understand what Christians believe on a particular subject; they must come to accept that as their own belief, and allow that belief to become the motivating factor for their behavior.

Not all catechetical preaching has been immediate preparation for baptism. That done by Aelfric in Anglo-Saxon England, for instance, occurred at a time when infant baptism was the rule.[49] The period of Chrysostom, however, is unique because it was a time when Christians were no longer persecuted and former pagans were flocking to the church for initiation. It was also a time when many if not most Christians were deferring baptism until the storms of youth were over from fear of postbaptismal sin.

Shortly before the late-fourth century there would not have been the numbers desiring baptism that would make catechetical preaching the obvious preparation. Shortly afterward, infant baptism became the norm and candidates could not be catechized. For a while, though, preaching was the favored method of preparation in a number of locations. While it is impossible to know how widespread the method was, it is nevertheless true that four sets of catechetical sermons from that period have been preserved.[50] One was preached by John when he was still at Antioch, one by his friend Theodore of Mopsuestia, one by Cyril and possibly another preacher at Jerusalem, and one by Ambrose in Milan. These series differ enough from one another to make it impossible to treat them synthetically,[51] so we must consider each individually.

John Chrysostom

Most of the catechetical sermons by Chrysostom were unknown until 1955, when they were found in the Stavronikita monastery on Mount Athos in Greece by Antoine Wenger.[52] The discovery called attention to three others that had been published in an obscure Russian series in 1909.[53] Prior to that, only two of John's catechetical homilies were known, one of which is in the Russian publication.[54] It is now believed that the four sermons in the Russian work and in PG are part of the instruction John gave candidates in Antioch in 388, while the newly discovered series was delivered in 390.[55] John was still a priest then, and the task of catechizing seems to have been shared with other priests; his sermons were only part of the total preparation of the Antioch catechumens.

The preacher of the *Baptismal Instructions* is clearly the preacher of the homilies. In demonstrating that the Stavronikita instructions are the work of John, Wenger pointed to characteristics he considered "trademarks" of Chrysostom's preaching:

> the richness and concrete character of his language, the abundance of examples taken from the political and social life of his times, the predominance of moral considerations over speculative theology, the primacy of pastoral preoccupations, and, finally, an unflagging eloquence.[56]

Harkins also points to what he calls John's "almost invariable method of development."[57] It consists of: "(a) an affirmation often linked with an image or supported by a comparison; (b) proof of the affirmation drawn from Scripture, most often from St. Paul; and (c) a conclusion and further developments by which the thought progresses." These two characterizations are consistent with the description of Chrysostom's Sunday preaching in the previous section.

How, then, does his catechetical preaching differ enough from what we've already discussed to warrant separate treatment? To begin with, these sermons do not involve verse-by-verse exegesis of a biblical lection. These are occasional sermons, the occasion for which is preparing catechumens for baptism and the beginning of life as a Christian. But here John's instructions also differ from those of the other three catechetical preachers. Most have as their topics sections of the Lord's Prayer, the local baptismal creed, or the sacraments of baptism and Eucharist. John discusses only some elements of the baptismal rite in a few of his sermons, but even there the emphasis is on exhortation to lead the Christian life rather than on the rite itself.[58]

We can see the special quality of John's catechetical preaching in the topics treated in the longer series of sermons he is thought to have delivered in 390. The first is a welcome to the candidates and almost a pep talk to get them enthusiastic for the challenge that lies ahead—although it does show some of the preacher's characteristic concerns in warnings about women's dress and omens, oaths, and spectacles. The second is more similar to others' mystagogical sermons in that it analyzes the initiatory rites. The third is addressed to neophytes and is much like the first in spirit, although its metaphor is a wrestling match with Satan rather than a spiritual marriage with Christ. Baptism is also compared to the exodus. The fourth is more of the same, saying that the neophyte should shine especially by his conduct, and using an image that will recur often, that of baptism as a brightly clean garment. The title the manuscript gives to the fifth is: "Exhortation to the Neophytes to Abstain from Softness, Extravagance, and Drunkenness, and to Esteem Moderation in All Things."

The sixth is truly occasional, a diatribe against those who skipped church to go to the chariot races and gladiatorial games held that day. The seventh is also occasional, since it was preached on a feast of martyrs in the *Martyrion* where all the instructions were given. And the final instruction serves several purposes: it pays respect to monks who had come down from the mountain to be present, it holds before those about to be baptized the infinite superiority of invisible to visible goods, and makes the practical suggestion that the initiates stop by the church to pray at the beginning and end of their working day. This is all vintage

Chrysostom, but very unlike the mystagogy given by the other three catechetical preachers.

Theodore of Mopsuestia

John's catechetical sermons are as different as possible from those of Theodore, his old friend, fellow student of Diodore, and brother priest. Since the two of them must have been catechizing the neophytes at Antioch at about the same time, it is fascinating to imagine receiving one's instruction from the two in alternation. It would be like riding in a wagon drawn by a spirited racehorse yoked with a powerful ox. Both had great gifts, but not at all the same gifts.

John did not share Theodore's interest in biblical interpretation as a goal in itself. Both, however, were very much in the Antiochene tradition of literal interpretation, as opposed to the allegorism of Alexandria. The two sees also had their characteristic emphases in their understanding of the person and work of Christ. Alexandrine Christology stressed the unity of our Lord's human and divine natures, but in doing so often seemed to do less than justice to his full humanity. That of Antioch, on the other hand, affirmed Jesus' complete humanity so staunchly that at times it was hard to see how that was joined to his divinity.

Theodore's instructions were as doctrinal as John's were moral and ascetic. There were sixteen of them in all: ten on the creed, one on the Lord's Prayer, and five on the sacraments. With almost two-thirds of them being on the creed, a theological emphasis was inevitable. The future controversialist wished none who heard him to be mistaken in their beliefs. His care appears overdone. "His style is exceedingly diffuse and repetitive, and his homilies are more often quarried for information about the rites than read as sermons."[59] So much was this the case that Edward Yarnold removed some of the repetitions from his translation, carefully indicating, however, where he did so.[60] Even at that, his edition of the homilies of Theodore about the sacraments[61] takes eighty-eight pages, while those of the other three on the same subjects total only ninety-seven. Yet, translated into Syriac, Theodore's homilies became a catechetical textbook for the Nestorian church after it broke away.

Cyril of Jerusalem

If any of the series of catechetical homilies was prototypical, it was the one by the least famous preacher. Very little is known about Cyril other than that he wished to have an orthodox Christology without using the word *homoousios*.[62] Cyril was born near 313, the year in which Constantine began to side with Christianity, so Cyril's life and ministry were under the shadow of that emperor. Not only was the theological agenda for his lifetime set by the Council of Nicaea that Constantine called, the material conditions of Cyril's church were also greatly affected by him. One of the marks of Constantine's favor to his new faith was a number of churches he built in the Holy Land, especially in Jerusalem, the scene of Cyril's ministry.

Growing up in the Holy City, Cyril was ordained deacon around 335, served in that order for about ten years, and then for about five more years in the priesthood before he was made bishop. Cyril was exiled a few times, the last and longest being 367 to 378, because of a controversy over whether the church in Jerusalem was subordinate to that in Caesarea or instead had special honor because of its historical importance. Before the Council of Constantinople in 381, Cyril had become reconciled to the unbiblical term designating Christ's shared divinity with the Father and was one of the honored participants in those deliberations. He died five years later as a venerated leader, but left few writings other than his catechetical sermons.

These sermons take on a special interest because of where they were preached. While interest in the holy places stretches back at least to the time of Melito of Sardis,[63] it had been given a new vitality by imperial support for Christianity after 313, especially Constantine's building program in Jerusalem. The centerpiece of the building program was the complex made possible by the proximity to one another of the traditional sites of Jesus' crucifixion and resurrection and the place where Constantine's mother, Helena, discovered what was thought to be the true cross.[64] There was a rotunda called the *Anastasis* (the Greek word for "resurrection") built over the tomb of Joseph of Arimathea from which Jesus rose.[65] Next to it was the walled-in atrium or courtyard of the Holy Cross. In a corner of that stood the rock of Calvary, Golgotha, which was about twelve feet high and enclosed in a grille; this was known as *Ad Crucem* ("at the cross"). A cross was erected nearby to indicate where the crucifixion was thought to have occurred (*Ante Crucem*, "before the cross"). Behind that was a chapel called *Post Crucem*. The courtyard shared its west[66] wall with the *Anastasis,* while its east wall was the wall behind the apse of the main church, the *Martyrion,* built over the cave in which Helena was said to have found the cross. Other churches in Jerusalem erected by Constantine were Sion, on the traditional site of the Last Supper; the *Imbomon,* on the Mount of Olives where the ascension was believed to have occurred; and the nearby *Eleona* (from the Greek word for "olives"), the church built over a cave where Jesus was thought to have taught the apostles.

Less than twenty years after Cyril's death, a Spanish nun named Egeria spent about three years in the Holy Land in an effort to see the places where all the things narrated in the Bible happened.[67] About half of the account of her experiences, which she wrote for her sisters back in Spain, is devoted to describing "the ritual observed day by day in the holy places"[68] of Jerusalem. Included in this is a report on the way candidates for initiation were prepared. While her visit occurred after Cyril's death, it is believed that conditions had not altered. Thus she furnishes a rare eyewitness account of patristic preaching.

During the forty days of Lent,[69] those preparing for baptism would attend the early morning office at the *Anastasis* and be exorcised by the bishop when it was over. Then they would move into the *Martyrion* and cluster around the bishop's throne while he lectured, introducing them to the Bible during Lent. After five weeks[70] they were given the creed, which the bishop then began to explain phrase by phrase. These daily sessions lasted three hours and ended with hymns on the way back to the *Anastasis* for the office for Terce. On the Saturday before Holy Week, the catechumens would show they had learned the creed by reciting it to the bishop. The elaborate liturgies of Holy Week did not leave time for further instruction, but during Easter week the bishop explained to the newly initiated the sacraments of baptism and the Eucharist, which they had now experienced.[71]

Cyril's sermons have an interest of their own beyond that of their setting. They begin with a Procatechesis on the occasion of the solemn enrollment of the catechumens. The first two instructions are hortatory preparations of the candidates for what lies ahead, and the third is a discussion of baptism, although not the sort of detailed explanation of the rite that will follow their initiation on Easter. Then Christian belief is summarized in the fourth lecture as "Ten Doctrines." The fifth speaks of faith both as a system of belief and as an inward disposition; it ends with the impartation of the system of belief as summarized in the local form of the baptismal creed.

Lectures six through eighteen are devoted to phrase-by-phrase explication of the creed. The catechumens recite the creed back to the bishop the day before Palm Sunday, and there is no more instruction until Easter Monday when the five mystagogical lectures (i.e., those on the sacraments) begin. Some scholars think that the mystagogical lectures were not written by Cyril but by his successor in the see, John. For our understanding of how catechetical preaching was done in Jerusalem, the issue is not important, especially since Cyril's catechetical lectures seem to have set the pattern in Jerusalem for at least a century. Nor would it make any difference if, as seems likely, Cyril was still a priest when he first delivered his lectures.

The sermons are true homilies in the sense that each of them is based on a lesson read before it was preached. The texts cited at the beginning of each of the lectures are those assigned to those days in two Armenian lectionaries that reflect the usage of Jerusalem in the fifth century. Yet, while the readings do summarize the theme of the sermons, the true texts on which the sermons are based are the articles of the creed or the elements of the baptismal or eucharistic rites that are being explicated. The preacher shows a good bit of skill in weaving all these together for a unified impact. There is also a certain amount of rhetorical artistry that turns each of the homilies into an appeal for a commitment. And each of the instructions has a hortatory conclusion and ends with a doxology. It is easy to get as excited as Egeria about initiation in Jerusalem and to think about what a nice way that was to be formed as a Christian.

Ambrose of Milan

There are few figures in the early church about whom so much is known and so little understood as Ambrose. Biographers who try to move from the known events to the man behind come up with diametrically opposed interpretations.[72] The basic outline of his life, however, is clear enough. Ambrose's father was praetorian prefect in Trier when his son was born ca. 339, but he seems to have died the next year. His mother took the family to Rome so that Ambrose and his older brother Satyrus could receive the typical education in rhetoric that sons of landowning families received. During their stay in Rome, Ambrose's sister Marcellina, about ten years his senior, was accepted by Pope Liberius as a consecrated virgin. Ambrose was, in fact, the first of the Latin Fathers to have been born into a Christian family, as he was also the first to have come from the aristocracy.[73] After completing their education ca. 365, the two brothers became lawyers at the court of the praetorian prefect of Sirmium, the capital of the province of Illyria and thus the meeting place of East and West. Five years later Ambrose was appointed *consularis* (governor) of Aemilia and Liguaria, with his headquarters at Milan, which was often the seat of imperial government in the West.

The church in Milan had been under the control of Arians until the death of their bishop Auxentius in 374. Yet somehow the orthodox were meeting with them to elect his successor and a riot almost broke out. To prevent it the governor appeared and was suddenly elected by acclamation. He had to not only pass through the other orders but also be baptized before he could be consecrated. As a bishop he took a strong stand against Arians and traditional Roman religion. He had a good deal to do with the removal of the pagan Altar of Victory from the Roman senate house, and he refused to let the emperor's mother have a church in Milan for her Arian congregation. When Theodosius ordered the massacre of seven thousand citizens of Thessalonica for rioting, Ambrose required public penance of him before he was allowed to receive communion. Ambrose has many other claims on the church's memory: he is known, for example, as "The Father of Liturgical Hymnody" because of his innovations in that area, and he is one of the four Doctors of the Western Church.

Most of his many writings are series of homilies that he edited as treatises. While he was not an original thinker, he was an influential one. Part of the explanation is that he was one of the few Western bishops of the time who knew Greek and read the works of the Eastern Fathers. Although his own interests were primarily practical—a characteristic attitude of the Western church at the time—his study of the Greek Fathers made him aware, as few of his Western colleagues were, of the importance of the theological controversies in the East. Thus he became an ardent promoter of orthodox Trinitarian doctrine. Ambrose was greatly influenced by Alexandrine biblical interpretation and became an inveterate allegorizer. He also drew on Greek and Roman philosophy in his writings although, like many preachers, he seldom identified his sources.

Estimates of the quality of his preaching vary. It is common to see such comments as: "His rhetorical style, characterized by long periodic sentences interspersed with direct and pithy statements, was rich in imagery derived from nature, scripture, and classical sources."[74] Yet it is also recognized that the editing done before publication makes it difficult to know exactly what his sermons were like when delivered. Even so sympathetic a critic as Angelo Paredi misses the "lively particulars and spontaneous observations" that must have been eliminated in the editing process. The result, he says, "is like having a glass of champagne which has been standing too long, and which has lost its seething, sparkling bubbles."[75]

The present purpose, however, is not to discuss his preaching in general, but only his catechetical instruction. That is an extensive enough topic by itself, however, since the corpus of his works includes two treatments of the sacraments and a sermon in which the creed was delivered to the catechumens.[76] Although he left no detailed instruction on the creed and Lord's Prayer like those of Cyril or Theodore, Ambrose did direct his Lenten preaching to the preparation of the catechumens. Several of his series of exegetical homilies were also catechetical preaching, a function they must have shared with many exegetical homilies by other Fathers.[77]

His two works on the sacraments give insight into the difference between his homilies as they were delivered and the treatises into which some were edited, since *De Sacramentis* appears to be a stenographic transcript of six homilies as they were delivered and *De Mysteriis* a treatise edited from another series of the same sort. The thought of the two is very similar, and both show Ambrose's great facility in citing Scripture and the remarkable allegorical interpretations that he gives to the verses cited. The shorthand record of *De Sacramentis* is characterized as having such a "lack of cohesion . . . frequent repetitions, and . . . careless style"[78] that many scholars thought it the work of someone else until Otto Faller, Bernard Botte, and Henry Chadwick demonstrated its true nature. Yarnold says that "in these half-extempore sermons A[mbrose] often rambles away from the logical order,"[79] and Yarnold finds the argument so intuitive at times that he feels called upon to explicate it. The extreme example of this is the way that both the fifth and sixth homilies begin discussing aspects of the Eucharist and end explaining the Lord's Prayer rather than finishing one topic before the other is taken up.

We can see something of the effect of this in the second homily. It begins with a discussion of prefigurations of baptism and notes that while both pagans and Jews had ritual washings, they did not have real baptism.[80] This leads to a digression in which the story of the healing at the pool of Bethesda, which had been read the day before but had not been commented on, is recalled. Ambrose makes a christological interpretation of John 5:4, which is not in the best manuscripts of the Fourth Gospel. Next follows an allegorical interpretation of the way that only the first person to go down into the water was healed. He then explains the sick man's lack of someone to carry him to the pool as meaning that he had no mediator with God.

Next the story of the cleansing of Naaman, which had been discussed the day before, is seen as a type of baptism. "There you have one kind of baptism; the flood is another. You have a third kind when our fathers were baptized in the Red Sea. You have a fourth in the pool when the waters moved" (*De Sacramentis* 2.9). This discussion of prefigurations of baptism is followed by other discussions of the presence of the Trinity in the rite, the effects of the rite, and the elements of the rite itself, including the second anointing, to complete this homily. Yet so discriminating a critic of public speaking as Augustine said that when he first went to Milan as imperial professor of rhetoric, he "hung on" Ambrose's words intently, and "was delighted with the pleasantness of his speech, more erudite, yet less cheerful and soothing in manner, than that of Faustus."[81] Something must have been lost in the transcription.

CONCLUSION

These four examples show the variety of catechetical preaching being done in the short period in which it was the means used to socialize adults at last ready to make a full Christian commitment. These series of sermons suggest there must have been many more that were not preserved, including many exegetical homilies designed for the purpose of catechesis. While the time was unique and exactly that sort of catechetical preaching has rarely recurred, these early examples do serve as a reminder that the need to teach Christian faith by sermons that call for conversion and commitment would appear often in the centuries ahead. Along with regular Sunday preaching, which can be called homiletic, and evangelistic preaching, catechetical preaching makes up the third major genre of Christian proclamation.

In considering the four catechetical preachers, a major transition in the history of preaching has passed without comment. Ambrose was the first preacher who preached in Latin to have been considered. Yet from here on until the Reformation, we will study only Western preaching. One reason for that is that with the passing of the great men treated so far, Eastern preaching became derivative.

> The two generations from the middle of the Fourth Century to the beginning of the Fifth constitute the Golden Age of Greek Christian Eloquence. . . . A great deal of subsequent Greek preaching not only imitates Gregory and John, but quarries phrases, sentences, and whole passages from their works. Their achievements were never surpassed and rarely equaled. Already in the Fifth and Sixth Centuries there is a falling off.[82]

Yet, as we shall see, similar things could be said about Western preaching as well. The main reason for the shift is that since the whole history of Christian preaching cannot be studied in so short a work, I made the decision to make this a homiletical genealogy for contemporary preachers in English. Thus, the rest of this work will be confined to Western Christendom, with further tapering in store down the line.

FOR FURTHER READING

Kelly, J. N. D. *Golden Mouth: The Story of John Chrysostom: Ascetic, Preacher, Bishop*. Ithaca, N.Y.: Cornell University Press, 1995.

Paredi, Angelo. *Saint Ambrose: His Life and Times*. Translated by M. Joseph Costelloe. Notre Dame: University of Notre Dame Press, 1964.

St. John Chrysostom: Baptismal Instructions. Translated and annotated by Paul W. Harkins. ACW, no. 31. Westminster, Md.: Newman Press, 1963.

St. John Chrysostom: The Homilies on Genesis 1-17. Translated and edited by Robert C. Hill. FC, vol. 74. Washington, D.C.: Catholic University of America Press, 1986.

Westerhoff, John H., III, and O. C. Edwards Jr., eds. *A Faithful Church: Issues in the History of Catechesis*. Wilton, Conn.: Morehouse-Barlow, 1981.

Wiles, Maurice. "Theodore of Mopsuestia as a Representative of the Antiochene School." In *From the Beginnings to Jerome*. Vol. 1 of *The Cambridge History of the Bible*. Edited by P. R. Ackroyd and C. F. Evans, 489-510. Cambridge: Cambridge University Press, 1970.

Yarnold, Edward. *The Awe-Inspiring Rites of Initiation: Baptismal Homilies of the Fourth Century*. Slough: St. Paul Publications, 1972.

Notes

1. With the exception of Basil's sermons on the *Hexaemeron* and the Psalms.

2. Around seven hundred homilies survive, in contrast to just over one hundred in other genres. These numbers were tabulated from Johannes Quasten, ed., *The Golden Age of Greek Patristic Literature from the Council of Nicaea to the Council of Chalcedon,* vol. 3 of *Patrology* (Utrecht: Spectrum, 1960; Westminster, Md.: Newman Press, 1960), 433-59.

3. Six of the volumes are devoted to John. It takes eighteen volumes of the PG to contain all his writings, more than are required for any other Greek Father.

4. Pope Pius X, *Acta sanctae sedis* (1908), 594-95.

5. J. N. D. Kelly, *Golden Mouth: The Story of John Chrysostom: Ascetic, Preacher, Bishop* (Ithaca, N.Y.: Cornell University Press, 1995), 4. For the rationale for the

dates Kelly accepts for John's early life, see Appendix B, 296-98. The sources for John's life are Palladius's *Dialogue on the Life of St. John Chrysostom*, and the church histories of Socrates (6.21-23, 7.25-45), Sozomen (8.8-28), and Theodoret (5.27-36).

6. Not, as often thought, the commander in chief himself, according to Kelly, *Golden Mouth*, 4-5.

7. The emperor Diocletian divided the empire into twelve administrative districts called dioceses. That of the Oriens stretched from the Red Sea to the southeastern part of modern Turkey.

8. For the significance of Libanius, see George Kennedy, *Greek Rhetoric Under Christian Emperors* (Princeton: Princeton University Press, 1983), 150-63.

9. O. Bardenhewer, *Geschichte der altkirchlichen Literatur,* as cited by Kelly, *Golden Mouth,* 7 n. 4.

10. Sozomen, *Hist. Eccl.*, 8.2. Quoted in Kelly, *Golden Mouth,* 8.

11. Kelly, *Golden Mouth,* 15-16.

12. Ibid., 18-20. It was through the training of Diodore that John became committed to the Antiochene school of biblical interpretation, which did not embrace allegorical explanation.

13. About twenty years later, John wrote of this experience in his dialogue *On the Priesthood*. While most modern scholars have taken this account to be the sort of fictional setting that was common in the dialogue genre, the reasons Kelly sets forth (*Golden Mouth,* 27-28) for considering it historical are persuasive. He is also right in regarding the order to which the two were to be ordained as the priesthood rather than the episcopate.

14. For the location of Mount Silpios, see the map in Kelly, *Golden Mouth,* 303.

15. Ibid., 39.

16. In the introduction to his translation of *The Homilies on Genesis of St. John Chrysostom*, FC, vol. 74 (Washington, D.C.: Catholic University of America Press, 1986), 6, Robert C. Hill raises the possibility that these were preached during John's diaconate, but most scholars doubt a bishop at that time would delegate his authority to preach to a deacon.

17. Kelly, *Golden Mouth*, 57.

18. This is the title of chapter 7 of Kelly, *Golden Mouth*.

19. The titles "archbishop" and "patriarch" were not yet used in Constantinople.

20. The mosaic portrait in Hagia Sophia, though from a later period, is consistent with the unflattering description in the office books for the feasts of saints in the Eastern Orthodox Church. Ibid., 106.

21. Kelly, *Golden Mouth*, 55-71, 83-103, 128-44; Kennedy, *Greek Rhetoric Under Christian Emperors*, 241-54; R. A. Krupp, *Shepherding the Flock of God: The Pastoral Theology of John Chrysostom*, American University Studies, series 7, Theology and Religion, vol. 101 (New York: Peter Lang, 1991), 51-69; Geoffrey Wainwright, "Preaching as Worship" and "The Sermon and the Liturgy," *GOTR* 28 (1983): 325-49.

22. Hill, *St. John Chrysostom*, 10.

23. Ibid. So sympathetic and insightful a critic as John A. Broadus said that it was misleading to compare Chrysostom's sermons with the more tightly integrated

expository sermons favored at the end of the nineteenth century, claiming that prayer-meeting talks furnished a better analogy. "St. Chrysostom as a Homilist," *NPNF*[1] 13:6.

24. *Hom. Matt.* 1.5-7.

25. Ibid., 1.6.

26. Ibid., 3.5.

27. *Hom. Acts* 1.

28. *Hom. 1 Cor.* 2.1.

29. *Hom. Col.* 1.

30. The root meaning of *theôria* is "sight," and the cognate verb has extended meanings of watching, looking on, observing, perceiving, noticing, and experiencing.

31. Robert M. Grant and David Tracy, *A Short History of the Interpretation of the Bible*, 2nd ed., rev. and enl. (Philadelphia: Fortress, 1984), 66.

32. Maurice Wiles, "Theodore of Mopsuestia as a Representative of the Antiochene School," in *From the Beginnings to Jerome*, vol. 1 of *The Cambridge History of the Bible,* ed. P. R. Ackroyd and C. F. Evans (Cambridge: Cambridge University Press, 1970), 489-510.

33. G. L. Prestige, *Fathers and Heretics: Six Studies in Dogmatic Faith with Prologue and Epilogue* (London: SPCK; New York: Macmillan, 1940), 120-49.

34. Graham Neville, trans. *Saint John Chrysostom: Six Books on the Priesthood* (London: SPCK, 1964).

35. Broadus, "St. Chrysostom as a Homilist," *NPNF*[1] 13:v. As Kennedy said, "It must be remembered that he was primarily an orator and not a writer and that he was speaking to a congregation of varied intellectual abilities: he must dwell on his points if they are to be grasped." See *Greek Rhetoric Under Christian Emperors,* 252.

36. Kennedy, *Greek Rhetoric Under Christian Emperors,* 248. Cf. Sister Mary Albania Burns, *Saint John Chrysostom's Homilies on the Statues: A Study of Their Rhetorical Qualities and Form,* The Catholic University of America Patristic Studies, vol. 22 (Washington, D.C.: Catholic University of America Press, 1930).

37. *On the Priesthood, 5.5.*

38. George A. Kennedy, *Classical Rhetoric and Its Christian and Secular Tradition from Ancient to Modern Times* (Chapel Hill: University of North Carolina Press), 145.

39. At that time the Antiochene Lent lasted eight weeks.

40. Kelly, *Golden Mouth*, 74.

41. His initial decision was to strip the city of its status as a metropolis (provincial capital); close its theaters, racetracks, and public baths; and suspend the distribution of bread to the poor.

42. The first of the twenty-one was preached before the riot.

43. Kelly, *Golden Mouth*, 72-82.

44. The *Homilies on the Statues* have been interpreted in a number of different ways by scholars. See, e.g., David Hunter, "Preaching and Propaganda in Fourth-Century Antioch: John Chrysostom's *Homilies on the Statues*" in *Preaching in the Patristic Age: Studies in Honor of Walter J. Burghardt, S.J.,* ed. David G. Hunter (New York: Paulist Press, 1989), 119-38; Peter Brown, *Power and Persuasion in Late Antiquity* (Madison: University of Wisconsin Press, 1992), 106; and Averil Cameron,

Christianity and the Rhetoric of Empire: The Development of Christian Discourse (Berkeley and Los Angeles: University of California Press, 1991), 136-37.

45. Kennedy, *Greek Rhetoric Under Christian Emperors,* 247.

46. *NPNF*[1] 9:331.

47. Ibid., 9:335.

48. Ibid., 9:343.

49. See part 2, chapter 7, below. On trends in the methods by which Christians were formed in their faith see *A Faithful Church: Issues in the History of Catechesis,* ed. John H. Westerhoff III and O. C. Edwards Jr. (Wilton, Conn.: Morehouse-Barlow, 1981).

50. To these may be added four sermons on the Lord's Prayer preached by Augustine to *competentes* (*Sermons on Selected Lessons of the Gospels,* 6-9, *NPNF*[1] 7:274-89).

51. For an introduction to these series and for examples of homilies preached in this genre, see Edward Yarnold, *The Awe-Inspiring Rites of Initiation: Baptismal Homilies of the Fourth Century* (Slough: St. Paul Publications, 1972); see also Leonel L. Mitchell, "The Development of Catechesis in the Third and Fourth Centuries: From Hippolytus to Augustine" in Westerhoff and Edwards, *A Faithful Church,* 49-78. Yarnold's volume is the most convenient way to sample catechetical sermons from each of the four preachers, but he does not provide a full text from any. For that, see *St. John Chrysostom: Baptismal Instructions,* translated and annotated by Paul W. Harkins. ACW, no. 31 (Westminster, Md.: Newman Press, 1963); *The Works of Saint Cyril of Jerusalem,* 2 vols., trans. and intro. Leo P. McCauley and Anthony A. Stephenson. FC (Washington, D.C.: Catholic University of America Press, 1969); or *St. Cyril of Jerusalem's Lectures on the Christian Sacraments: The Procatechesis and the Five Mystagogical Catecheses,* ed. F. L. Cross (1951; reprint, Crestwood, N.Y.: St. Vladimir's Seminary Press, 1986); *St. Ambrose: Theological and Dogmatic Works,* trans. Roy J. Deferrari. FC (Washington, D.C.: Catholic University of America Press, 1963); Theodore of Mopsuestia, *Commentary on the Nicene Creed,* ed. and trans. A. Mingana (Cambridge: Woodbrooke Studies 5, 1932); Theodore of Mopsuestia, *Commentary on the Lord's Prayer and on the Sacraments of Baptism and the Eucharist,* ed. and trans. A. Mingana (Cambridge: Woodbrooke Studies 6, 1933). On the theology of these four series of catechetical homilies, see Enrico Mazza, *Mystagogy: A Theology of Liturgy in the Patristic Age,* trans. Matthew J. O'Connell (New York: Pueblo, 1989).

52. John Chrysostom, *Huit Catéchèses Baptismales.* SC, no. 5 (Paris: Cerf, 1957).

53. A. Papadopoulos-Kerameus, *Varia graeca sacra* (St. Petersburg, 1909). This volume contains a fourth homily that is the same as one of those in the Stavronikita manuscript. Cf. Paul W. Harkins, *St. John Chrysostom: Baptismal Instructions,* 10, 201 n. 14.

54. PG 49:221-40.

55. These appear in reverse order in Harkins's translation, the 390 series includes homilies 1-8, and the 388 series includes homilies 9-12. The dates, of course, are not certain.

56. Cited in Harkins, *St. John Chrysostom: Baptismal Instructions,* 14.

57. Ibid., 205 n. 1. Harkins goes on to say that the vocabulary is also typical of John.

58. Mitchell, "The Development of Catechesis in the Third and Fourth Centuries," 66.

59. Ibid., 70. The form of an individual homily began with a "Synthesis" that was a narrative of what was to be discussed—the succession of actions in a sacramental celebration, for instance. The body of the homily was a series of annotations on the text of the Synthesis with the tone of so many footnotes on the subject.

60. Yarnold, *The Awe-Inspiring Rites of Initiation,* 74.

61. As we shall see below, there is some variation between the series in which topics were lectured on before and which after Easter. John and Theodore instructed their catechumens on baptism before they received it, while Cyril and Ambrose thought it better for them to have the experience first and explanation afterward. All, however, postponed discussing the Eucharist until after their hearers had participated in it.

62. For Cyril's theological position, see Anthony A. Stephenson and Leo P. McCauley, introduction to *The Works of St. Cyril of Jerusalem,* especially 34-60.

63. Ibid., 17-21.

64. All of these are now enclosed in the Church of the Holy Sepulchre built by the Crusaders.

65. The surrounding rock was cut away so that what remained was little more than walls of the tomb formed by what was left of the living rock.

66. I am speaking geographically not ecclesiastically.

67. Most of the assertions in this sentence have been contested, but it represents the majority opinion of contemporary scholarship.

68. *Peregrinatio*, 24, trans. and annotated by George E. Gingras in *Egeria: Diary of a Pilgrimage*, ACW (New York: Newman Press, 1970), 89.

69. Since the Jerusalem church did not fast on Saturdays as well as Sundays, the forty days of Lent were spread over eight weeks. While Egeria says that instruction occurred every day, Cyril's series consists of only twenty sermons. The best explanation seems to be that the catechumens would include Syriac- as well as Greek-speaking persons, so each lecture had to be given twice.

70. There is some inconsistency here between Egeria's report and Cyril's instructions in which the creed was imparted immediately following the fifth lecture rather than after the fifth week.

71. *Peregrinatio,* 45-47. In Jerusalem and Milan, unlike Antioch, baptism was not explained until the *photizomenoi* (those being enlightened) had experienced it, both because of the tradition of withholding information from the uninitiated *(disciplina arcani)* and because of an assumption that it could not really be understood before one had undergone it.

72. Thus Angelo Paredi (*Saint Ambrose: His Life and Times*, trans. M. Joseph Costelloe [Notre Dame: University of Notre Dame Press, 1964]) interprets everything about Ambrose in the best light possible, while Neil B. McLynn (*Ambrose of Milan: Church and Court in a Christian Capital* [Berkeley and Los Angeles: University of California Press, 1994]) sees it all in the worst light. For a good short study by someone who has also written a longer one, see Hans von Campenhausen, *Men Who Shaped the Western Church*, trans. Manfred Hoffman (New York: Harper & Row, 1964), 87-128.

73. Specialists debate how aristocratic they were, but even the most skeptical concede to them a place on the margins of the Roman elite.

74. Lewis J. Swift, "Ambrose," in *EEC*, ed. Everett Ferguson et al. (New York and London: Garland, 1990), 30.

75. Paredi, *Saint Ambrose*, 258. McLynn goes so far as to accuse him of cultivating a biblical sound to his sermons so that in preaching he assumed the mantle of biblical authority and also says he acquired learning in order to parade it in his sermons. See *Ambrose of Milan*, 238-40.

76. The sermon on the creed is called *Explanatio symboli*, "symbol" being a term for a creed. The delivery of the creed was known as *traditio symboli,* and its recitation back to the bishop was called *reditio symboli.*

77. Mitchell, "The Development of Catechesis in the Third and Fourth Centuries," 72.

78. Maria Grazia Mara, "Ambrose of Milan, Ambrosiaster, and Nicetas," in *The Golden Age of Latin Patristic Literature from the Council of Nicea to the Council of Chalcedon*, vol. 4 of *Patrology*, ed. Angelo di Berardino, intro. Johannes Quasten, trans. Placid Solari (Westminster, Md.: Christian Classics, 1986), 172.

79. Yarnold, *The Awe-Inspiring Rites of Initiation,* 103 n. 17.

80. Ambrose thought Christian sacraments were older than the rites of the Jews. See, e.g., *de Sac.* 4.9.

81. Augustine, *Confessions* 5.13.23, *NPNF*[1], 88.

82. Kennedy, *Greek Rhetoric Under Christian Emperors*, 255-56.

CHAPTER 5

AUGUSTINE: THE SIGN READER

THE CHURCH LEARNS LATIN

With the exception of Ambrose's catechetical sermons, all of the preaching studied so far was done in Greek. This would have been true for a long time even if preaching at Rome had been notable enough to be included in this history, because Greek was the language of the Christian community there for some time after the church in Rome was founded. When the eternal city was first evangelized, it had more foreign than native inhabitants. This proportion shifted as time went on, but it was not until the middle of the third century that papal correspondence was in the local language, and it took another century for the liturgy to be translated into what had become the vernacular again.

The first theological treatise in Latin that may have been written in Rome was the *Octavius* of Minucius Felix, from the late-second or early-third century. Yet this work defends monotheism, immortality, and morality on a philosophical rather than a biblical or theological basis, and its author seems to have come from Africa rather than the Italian peninsula, so its claim to be either Roman or theological is somewhat qualified. The first major theologian in Rome to write in Latin[1] was Novatian, who went into schism in the middle of the third century over the easy restoration to communion of persons who had apostatized under persecution.

All of this is to say that a distinctly Latin Christian culture did not originate in Rome itself but in the empire's colonies in North Africa, especially around Carthage. It was there that a Latin version of the Bible first appeared, the liturgy was first celebrated in Latin, practical discussions of church affairs were held in Latin, and a Latin vocabulary for theology was coined.[2] Thus we may see that Latin was the standard language of the church and culture in North Africa, while it was exceptional in Rome. It was in Africa, therefore, that preaching in Latin first became the norm.

Roman Africa (to be distinguished from Egypt and Cyrenaica) was a strip along the Mediterranean coast of the continent that stretched from modern Libya through Tunisia and Algeria to Morocco. The area had been populated by the Berbers for several millennia by the time the Romans arrived. After the Berbers, the seafaring Phoenicians (descended from the ancient Canaanites) invaded and colonized North Africa in the ninth century of the previous era, building Carthage and other port cities. Their descendants were the Punic people with whom the Romans clashed. Carthage was destroyed by the Romans in 146 B.C.E., but was later refounded by Augustus to become the center of Roman administration and the only large city in the territory. Agriculture was the reason for the area's importance to Rome. As hard as it is to believe today, the area was very fertile then, producing grain and olive oil, foodstuffs badly needed by Rome.

To provide the services needed for this agriculture and commerce, there developed a network of country towns.

> For all their pride, these little Romes would have had populations of only a few thousand, living off the land in exactly the same way as the present inhabitants of a Spanish *pueblo* or a South Italian township.[3]

Great estates worked by tenant farmers and slaves occupied part of the area between the towns; as one moved inland, they became the norm. The first several centuries of Roman occupation were a time of great prosperity for the region, but during the fourth century, when Rome was constantly at war, taxes siphoned off much of what discretionary money there was. The Latin culture of North Africa was largely that of the townspeople and the owners of the estates. The language of tenants, slaves, and villagers was the local Berber dialect that the Romans anachronistically called Punic.

It was in this world that Latin Christianity developed as a culture. It was not confined to this world, however; as Latin became the language of the Western Empire, so it became the language of the Western church as a whole. By the end of the fourth century there had been a great deal of preaching in that tongue throughout the West. Yet very few examples of it survive. We have sermons of neither Tertullian, Cyprian, nor Hilary of Poitiers. There are sermon fragments of some sort from Zeno of Verona and two sermons by Pacianus of Barcelona. Nor is the quality of what remains uniformly high, as is shown by, for example, a number of sermons by Gaudentius of Brescia.[4] And, as I noted in the previous chapter, it is hard for modern students to accord Ambrose's preaching the respect that it received from Augustine. It is to Augustine himself, therefore, that one must go to see what preaching in Latin could be like at its best. As I also noted above, it was Augustine who completed the marriage of Christian preaching with Greco-Roman rhetoric by using allegorical biblical interpretation. It was in his proclamation of the Word of God that the homiletic sermon form took its classical shape.

MONICA'S SON

Aurelius Augustinus (354–430), known to history as Augustine of Hippo, was born into a family of the petty gentry in the Numidian town of Thagaste. His father was a pagan at the time, although he later became a Christian under the influence of his ardently devout wife, Monica. While few would quarrel with the judgment of Agostino Trapè that "Augustine is undoubtedly the greatest of the Fathers and one of the great geniuses of humanity, whose influence on posterity has been continuous and profound,"[5] this does not mean that his behavior was impeccable when he was young.[6] It is not too surprising that the young Augustine got into mischief, since most boys do in most places. It is less expected that the possessor of one of the great intellects of all time should have hated school. Nevertheless, his promise was obvious and his father made considerable financial sacrifice to send him to Carthage to acquire the rhetorical education that could open the way to a brilliant career and great financial reward.[7]

He was seventeen when he went to Carthage. His first couple of years there were spent in delayed adolescent rebellion, but then he settled down in relative respectability with a concubine with whom he was to live for fifteen years and by whom he had a son, Adeodatus. With that accommodation, he was able to concentrate on his studies. Among the books he read was the *Hortensius,* in which Cicero argues that happiness is not to be gained by indulging in physical pleasures but by devoting oneself to the pursuit of truth—or, in other words, to philosophy as it was understood at the time. In writing of the experience later Augustine said: "Suddenly every vain hope became empty to me, and I longed for the immortality of wisdom with an incredible ardour in my heart. I began to rise up to return to you."[8]

His return to God was sidetracked, however, when he associated himself with the Manichaeans, a radically dualistic sect resembling the gnostics of the second century. Doing so gave him a perspective through which he could reconcile having a mistress with his devotion to philosophy. A good bit of his later conversion, therefore, had to be disassembling the structure of his Manichaean belief.

After completing his training, Augustine set himself up as a teacher of rhetoric, first in Thagaste and later back in Carthage. In time, though, dissatisfaction with the students in Carthage led him to try his luck in Rome. His greatest success there was to attract the patronage of Symmachus, one of the most influential men in the empire, one who was able to appoint Augustine to the chair of rhetoric in the city of Milan.

> As the Imperial court resided in Milan, this was an important appointment. A professor of rhetoric would deliver the official panegyrics on the Emperor and on the consuls of the year. . . . The successful rhetorician would have found himself, in many ways, a "Minister of Propaganda."[9]

Thus, at the age of thirty, Augustine had arrived at the top of his profession.

He was to stay there for only a couple of years. As he later came to see it, God had other plans for him. And one of the main earthly instruments God used to effect those plans was his mother, Monica. She had determined notions of what her talented son should be and do, notions that combined sacred and secular ambitions for him, notions that were reinforced by dreams she interpreted as revelations from God. When as a boy he had a life-threatening disease, she tried unsuccessfully to get him baptized, and she did not let that intention go until it was eventually accomplished, although she had to wait most of the rest of her life. When he became an adolescent, she urged him to remain chaste; the most she was ever willing to settle for was that he be legally and advantageously married.

When he returned from Carthage to teach at Thagaste, it took a vision to persuade her to let him live in her house while he was a Manichaean.[10] When he went to Rome, he had to lie to her about his departure time to keep her from going with him. She did join him in Milan, however, when he became a professor there. Deciding that he was to become a provincial governor, she knew that he needed a rich wife and set out to find him one, insisting that he send home his Carthaginian concubine to clear the way for the marriage. She was happy to abandon that project when he became a Christian and committed himself to a celibate life. Her mission in life complete, she died in Ostia on their way home to Africa less than a year after his baptism. One of the last things the mother and son were to do together was to share in a mystical experience.[11] She was easily the most influential person in his life.

AUGUSTINE THE CHRISTIAN

Soon after he moved to Milan, Augustine was disillusioned about the Manichaean position and decided that being a Catholic catechumen was as good a thing as any to do while he was seeking the truth. In his quest he received help from a number of directions. He went to hear Ambrose, the bishop of Milan, preach, not so much for religious instruction as to study a capable orator, but he got more than he bargained for. Ambrose introduced him to allegorical interpretation in a way that overcame all his prejudices against the Bible.[12] At the same time, Augustine developed a group of friends who shared the ideal of philosophical retirement. With them he began to read the works of the Neoplatonists, from whom he learned the philosophical framework in which he was to state his theology the rest of his life. He also began to study Paul.

Then he was informed about the life of Anthony and the monks of Egypt who practiced a Christian form of retirement. In his reaction to that discovery, he had the experience regarded as his conversion, the impression of hearing a child's voice chanting, "*Tolle, lege; tolle, lege.*" Pick up and read, pick up and read. He took up the copy of Paul's letters next to him and it fell open to the thirteenth chapter of Romans: "not in reveling and drunkenness, not in debauchery and licentiousness. . . ." Immediately he was released from bondage to his sexual appetite and ready not only to be baptized but also to retire from his profession and devote himself to cultivating the Christian life. Soon his friends and he were on their way back to Africa.

At first they lived in community on some property Augustine owned in Thagaste. There they practiced a Christian form of retirement that was shaped by the African understanding of being a "Servant of God": "a baptized, dedicated layman, determined to live, in the company of bishops, priests and noble patrons, the full life of a Christian."[13] As time went on, their ideal approximated more and more closely that of monks.

This idyll lasted only three years. Then the thing happened of which Augustine had been afraid. Bishops in Africa were chosen then much as Ambrose had been in Milan, by acclamation of the congregation. It was not unusual for the episcopate to be forcibly imposed on a person thus chosen, so Augustine had become careful not to enter a town that had no bishop. But he went to Hippo Regius, a town of thirty or forty thousand inhabitants—second only to Carthage in Roman Africa—to bring spiritual counsel to someone who had asked for it. It ought to have been safe enough, because there was a bishop there, Valerius. But he was an old man and a Greek who did not speak Latin well. As he told the community, they needed someone who could speak their language and speak it eloquently. This was especially so because, like most Catholic churches in Africa, the local congregation was greatly outnumbered by that of the Donatists, the schismatic perfectionist movement that had swept through the region. Augustine, therefore, was made a priest so that he could stand in for Valerius, which made Augustine the first priest allowed to preach in Africa.

After four years, however, Valerius died and Augustine succeeded him as bishop of Hippo Regius, the position in which he was to remain the last thirty-five years of his life. It is hard to imagine someone who had known the glamour of the imperial court in Milan settling down in a small seacoast city in Africa, but most of the talented Africans who went to Rome and Milan in those days did return home to stay. Among these were Augustine's friends who had been his companions in retreat in Thagaste and followed him to Hippo as the monastic community in which he would live.[14]

Augustine settled in and devoted the rest of his life to being pastor to the Catholic community of Hippo. Aurelius, the bishop of Carthage, recognized the talent of his junior colleague and used him in every way possible to advance the Catholic cause in Numidia, often inviting him to preach in the capital city. Augustine became the Catholic champion in theological controversy, acting as chief spokesman against the Manichaean, Donatist, and Pelagian heresies. By his writings, Augustine achieved a worldwide prominence and authority. He was linked in correspondence to church leaders throughout the Mediterranean area. Yet his main and ordinary activity was to serve as head of the Catholic community in Hippo, counseling the anxious, settling disputes between members, and, most of all, thrilling his small-town flock week after week with some of the greatest preaching in the history of the church.

HOW TO TEACH THE FAITH

The way Augustine preached must be studied in detail. For that study a tool exists of a sort that has not been available for the analysis of the homiletical practice of any of his predecessors. Augustine provided a guide to his preaching method in the form of the first homiletics textbook ever written. Its title, *De doctrina christiana,* is often translated as "Concerning Christian Doctrine," which is misleading. It suggests that the book is concerned with the content of Christian teaching, its "doctrines." A brief glance, however, is enough to see that the book is about something else. The real subject is made clear by the author in the *Retractiones,* in which he reviewed and corrected all his writings near the end of his life. There he says of this work:

> I also added the last book, and thus completed this work in four books, of which the first three help in the understanding of the scriptures, while the fourth suggests how what we have understood is to be passed on to others.[15]

Edmund Hill, the most recent translator, says:

> *Teaching Christianity* is how I think the title of the work should be translated. Christianity is, or ought to be, pre-eminently taught by preaching; so the work leads up to the fourth book as to its goal. But Christian preaching is, or ought to be, in terms of scripture; so the would-be preacher must first be taught how to interpret the Bible.[16]

Augustine begins his hermeneutical methodology by saying that all teaching is about either things or signs. Things are not mentioned to signify something else but mean only themselves, while signs mean things other than themselves.[17] Thus, ultimately, all teaching is about things. The most important distinction to be made about things is between those that are to be used and those that are to be enjoyed. The only thing to be enjoyed—the only thing that is an end in itself—is the three-personed God. All other things are a means to the end of enjoying God. Sin keeps people from doing that; so many things have to be used in order to reopen the possibility of enjoying God. The whole Bible, therefore, is about using everything else as a means to enjoy God, to love God. God is to be loved for the sake of God, and neighbors are also to be loved for the sake of God. The Summary of the Law—love God and love your neighbor—is therefore the key to interpreting the whole Bible. Any interpretation that is not consistent with that message is a misinterpretation.

The subject of the first book of *Teaching Christianity* is things and that of the second book is signs.[18] A sign is defined as "a thing, which besides the impression it conveys to the senses, also has the effect of making something else come to mind" (2.1). There are two kinds of signs, natural and conventional. Natural signs are those that signify without intending to, the way that smoke signifies fire. The most common kind of conventional sign is words, with which the interpreter of Scripture is most involved. Difficulties in interpreting Scripture come from signs that are either unknown or ambiguous. This book deals with those unknown; much of the difficulty unknown words cause can be dealt with by learning Greek and Hebrew, the original languages of the Bible.[19] Readers very often have difficulty understanding signs that are metaphorical because they are not familiar with what the biblical thing is compared with. To solve that difficulty they must acquire knowledge of these things,[20] often from books by pagan authors.[21] One must take care in using such books, however, not to be contaminated with pagan errors.

Book 3 deals with signs that are ambiguous, a condition that may result either from the way that words are pronounced or a figurative use of them. The ambiguities of sound are either those dealt with by grammarians as they cope with the lack of punctuation and spacing between words in the manuscripts in use at the time of Augustine, or those that result from the mere fact that the words can be understood in more than one way. The dangers connected with figurative signs are that an expression intended to be understood literally is taken figuratively, or the opposite, that a figurative expression is understood literally. Augustine's rule of thumb for resolving these ambiguities is to say that whenever the literal meaning is inconsistent with Christian faith or morals, the words are to be interpreted figuratively—that is, what others call "allegorically." As noted in Book 1, everything in the Bible means that people should love God and their neighbors.[22]

Since the sermon form presupposed by Augustine is the exegetical homily, the first three books of *Teaching Christianity* are about preaching rather than a separate discipline of biblical interpretation. They deal with the classical rhetorical task of Invention when the task of deciding what to say in a speech is not the discovery of arguments but the explication of a text. Since Book 4 is about discovering "a way to put across to others what has been understood" (1.1), it approximates a little more closely than the first three books, however, what is usually understood as the subject matter of homiletics. (For the text of Book 4, see **Vol. 2,**

pp. 77-102.) Yet even there Augustine makes it clear that he has no intention of merely writing a treatise on rhetoric. Whatever value such treatises have, rhetoric is the sort of thing that is best learned in the schools. Those who did not learn it there can probably do better reading and listening to those who speak well.[23] Among the models of eloquence that one could study, the best are the writers of holy Scripture.

The only aspect of classical rhetoric to which Augustine gives extended attention in Book 4 is the three duties of the orator identified by Cicero: to prove, to delight, and to move. These Augustine relates to the three levels of style, with the plain for proving or teaching, the middle (the most ornate) for pleasing, and the grand for moving. While all have their purpose in preaching, the ultimate goal is conversion, and thus the grand style for moving is the most crucial. Finally, he says that the Christian teacher must practice what he preaches, and also emphasizes the importance of prayer for preaching effectively.

The most obvious thing about *Teaching Christianity* is that Augustine considered the Bible to be basically a book of signs that need to be interpreted. His choice of vocabulary demands attention. He did not use the traditional term "allegory," nor did he refer to the multiple senses of Scripture that were to be so much studied from Gregory the Great on.[24] Rather, he chose to think through in a new and disciplined way the whole matter of how meaning is conveyed in the Bible and how that meaning is to be discovered. In doing so he took as his key term the important biblical term "sign."[25]

While it is common to deplore the nonliteral interpretation of Augustine and most other preachers and exegetes before the rise of the modern historical-critical method, it is important to recognize that they had little choice. To begin with, they really believed the interpretations they came up with were what the passages meant, what God intended for them to learn from the words of the prophet or apostle. The New Testament itself used allegorical interpretation to arrive at the meaning of the Hebrew Bible and, even more consistently, interpreted it typologically and christologically. Further, that was one of the main ways the ancients knew to interpret any book, since grammarians used it to explain the meaning of the classical texts they taught schoolboys. And Augustine had an additional difficulty in the version of Scripture that was available to him. He believed as a matter of faith that every word in the Bible had been put there by God to convey some meaning, but a good bit of the text before him did not make any obvious literal sense. Writing before Jerome made the Latin Vulgate translation, he was dependent on the Old Latin version. Therefore,

> the text of Scripture he used was a rather slavish Latin translation of a rather slavish Greek translation of a Hebrew original that was often corrupt, especially in the Psalms. It was therefore full of both Greek and Hebrew modes of speech which had been quite distorted through translation into more or less meaningless expressions.[26]

No wonder he thought his task was decoding signs!

Peter Brown sees a further explanation of Augustine's interest in signs in the literary culture of the Late Roman period:

> Such a man [as Augustine] lived among fellow-connoisseurs, who had been steeped too long in too few books. He no longer needed to be explicit: only hidden meanings, rare and difficult words and elaborate circumlocutions, could save his readers from boredom, from *fastidium,* from that loss of interest in the obvious, that afflicts the overcultured man.[27]

Such an interpretation finds support in Augustine's statement to the effect that God placed obscurities in the text "in order to break in pride with hard labor, and to save the intelligence from boredom."[28]

Yet Brown saw the main reason for Augustine's regarding the Bible as a book of signs to be the nature of a subject that could not be approached too directly. "The mind must move from hint to hint, each discovery opening up yet further depths."[29] He also took a giant step in making Augustine's biblical interpretation comprehensible to contemporary consciousness by comparing his deciphering of biblical signs to Freud's interpretation of dreams.

We can achieve further insight into Augustine's figurative interpretation by noting when he thinks it is called for. In earlier works it appeared that his criterion for believing figurative interpretation was needed was that the passage otherwise would have a meaning that was absurd. This criterion was common not only to earlier Christian writers, but to pagan ones as well. Yet the criterion invoked in *Teaching Christianity* is much broader: "Anything in the divine writings that cannot be referred either to good, honest morals or to the truth of the faith, you must know is said figuratively" (3.10, 14). There are several reasons for Augustine's adopting this more inclusive criterion. One is that he took very seriously 2 Timothy 3:16, which says: "*All* scripture is inspired by God and is useful for teaching, for reproof, for correction, and for training in righteousness" (emphasis added). Furthermore, the method of examining a text taught in schools was sentence by sentence, word by word, rather than as part of a coherent document. This led to an atomistic exegesis in which a passage did not have to have a consistent meaning all the way through.

Perhaps the most important reason, though, is Augustine's assumption that the whole Bible has a consistent meaning, which is the Christian creed and the ethic of love.

> Given Augustine's view that the essence of Scripture is contained in the Creed and the commandments to love God and neighbor, the vast majority of the Bible would be *superfluum* and *stultum* unless it contained hidden meanings, enigmata, and figures to be understood by those who would seek to understand the word of God at a more profound level.[30]

While contemporary historical consciousness can doubt that the only things the sacred writers ever intended to teach were Christian faith and love, it is important to notice the spiritual maturity of Augustine's hermeneutical key to Scripture.

> The exhortation to look beyond the letter to the deeper spiritual meaning that had been issued by the more moderate representatives of the Alexandrian school reappears therefore in Augustine, but it is made here in the name of charity rather than of wisdom.[31]

While that which Augustine derived from the Bible through his hermeneutical method may not be the meaning historically minded contemporary readers believe the sacred writers intended, it is nevertheless so essentially Christian that they can still agree with the teaching he derived and even be deeply moved by it.

As valuable a document as *Teaching Christianity* is, it is not the best way to learn how Augustine interprets Scripture. "A complete treatise on Augustinian exegesis would have to start from his exegetical practice rather than from his rules for interpretation."[32] Since this principle applies to his preaching as well, it is time to turn from theory to practice.

SERMON TIME IN HIPPO REGIUS

While there is little in the way of eyewitness accounts of Augustine's preaching, a combination of archaeological study of North Africa and the countless topical references that occur in his sermons makes possible the reconstruction of a rather detailed picture of the bishop in action.[33] His basilica was situated in a complex of buildings that included residences for the bishop and his monastic community, for nuns, and for visitors. The church would not have been elaborately decorated. On great occasions as many as two thousand people could be in the congregation, all of whom stood, the men separated from the women. In the apse the presbyters sat on a semicircular dais, in the middle of which the bishop's chair was elevated. In front of the apse in the center aisle was the altar, surrounded by the chancel screens.[34] A fresco in the Lateran Library dating from around 600 depicts Augustine sitting on his *cathedra* in the center of the bench for the presbyters with an open Bible before him, looking little different from a grammarian teaching in a secondary school. There is no reason to doubt the essential accuracy of this portrayal.

The eucharistic liturgy would have begun with the peace and then the psalm. On set days the three lections were prescribed, but on others Augustine could indicate to the lector or, for the Gospel, the deacon the passage to be read. After standing for the Gospel, the bishop would preach from his chair, rising occasionally for emphasis.[35] Often the congregation would break into applause, but, like Chrysostom, Augustine was more interested in changed lives. Depending on the elaborateness of the liturgy to follow and other factors, including the preacher's voice, the sermon could last anywhere from a few minutes to an hour and a half. After the sermon Augustine and his clergy would move down to the chancel for the Great Thanksgiving.

Certain generalizations can be made about Augustine's preaching. Most of his sermons were extempore, growing out of no more immediate preparation than prayer or a short meditation on the biblical passages that had just been read.[36] That was possible because his remote preparation included not only a mastery of rhetoric, but memorization of much of the Bible, theological reflection that is almost unparalleled in the history of the church, and a deep life of prayer as well. Because he used the form of the homily, his outlines were developed by his explication of the biblical text rather than according to a rhetorical *dispositio*. Ideas would come to him as he went along, so digressions were not rare. But neither were they boring, and he usually got back to the subject. His sermons "were not speeches but talks like those which became common in the medieval pulpit, though they were woven according to the stylistic pattern of Antiquity and used Antiquity's vocabulary."[37]

As Augustine spoke he got progressively more into his subject, and his words came alive with an eloquence that grew out of his ardor for his subject rather than from any intentional display of virtuosity. He did not regard his speech as "a harmonious assemblage of prefabricated parts, which the connoisseur might take to pieces, but rather as the inseparable welding of form and content in the heat of the message."[38] One of the many qualities that separated his preaching style from the canons of the rhetoric he had taught and could practice with ease was that his speech was always popular. His vocabulary was that of everyday life, and he used figures of speech such as puns, assonance, rhymes, alliteration, and antithesis to give zest to his thought. He could always find an apt analogy that would make the most abstruse point seem clear and even obvious. His instinct for the right word was infallible, and well-turned phrases were the rule rather than the exception.

> This is the secret of Augustine's enormous power as a preacher. He will make it his first concern to place himself in the midst of his congregation, to appeal to their feelings for him, to react with immense sensitivity to their emotions, and so, as the sermon progressed, to sweep them up into his own way of feeling.[39]

Yet he never used his power of speech to wound his hearers; instead, he was reflexively pastoral. And, surprisingly, although it was an affliction he shared with many of the world's great orators, his voice was not strong.

What can one say of his subject matter? First, that it was always centered on the meaning of the Bible as he understood it, the elucidation of individual words and phrases in the manner of the grammar teacher expounding classical literature. The difference between what he did and what the grammarian did, however, was not just in the text explicated but in the quality of the thought as well.

> There is always wealth in that thought; there are almost always surprises, and the average reader will almost always be overwhelmed by it. Nobody can fail to be astonished at what Augustine can get out of a single text. . . . *His real secret, which he shares with all orators who really succeed in fascinating us, is that he has such an enormous amount to say.*[40]

That "enormous amount" is the system of spirituality he found in the Bible, which he stated in a vocabulary derived from Neoplatonism. "And what Plotinus had struggled to convey to a select classroom in Rome, the Christians of Hippo and Carthage could hear any Sunday in the sermons of Augustine."[41] The remarkable thing about his presentation is that what he communicated was his own best thought on the subject; there is no watering down here. While he did administer his teaching in bite-size units, the whole system was communicated. Ordinary citizens in a small North African town were deemed as capable of holiness as the most rarified spirits.

THE THEORY APPLIED

The method by which Augustine derived his system of spirituality from biblical texts is, of course, interpretation of the passages as figurative signs. We can see an example of how he went about that in the second of his sermons on Psalm 31.[42] (**See Vol. 2, pp. 102-23,** for the text of the second sermon after this one.) To understand the interpretation, however, it will help to set a translation of the relevant verses of Old Latin text on which he commented in parallel with a modern translation (NRSV) from the Hebrew original.

Psalm 31:9-15*a*

Augustine	NRSV
Have mercy upon me, O Lord, for I am being harried,	9 Be gracious to me, O LORD, for I am in distress;
Vexed with wrath is my eye, my soul, and my belly.	my eye wastes away from grief, my soul and body also.
For my life has pined away in pain, And my years in sighs.	10 For my life is spent with sorrow, and my years with sighing;
My strength is weakened in want,	my strength fails because of my misery,
And my bones are vexed.	and my bones waste away.
I have become a disgrace over all my enemies,	11 I am the scorn of all my adversaries,
An excessive one to my neighbors, and a fear to my acquaintances.	a horror to my neighbors, an object of dread to my acquaintances;
Those who used to see me, ran away from me out of doors,	those who see me in the street flee from me.
I am forgotten like one dead, from the mind, I have become like a pot that is scrapped.	12 I have passed out of mind like one who is dead; I have become like a broken vessel.
For I have heard the blame of many who are settled round about,	13 For I hear the whispering of many—terror all around!—
While they gathered together against me, they plotted to catch my soul.	as they scheme together against me, as they plot to take my life.
But I have hoped in you O Lord, I have said: "You are my God,	14 But I trust in you, O LORD; I say, "You are my God."
In your hands are my lots."	15a My times are in your hand.

Augustine begins his exposition by stating that in the psalms the speaker is Christ and reminding his congregation of one of Tyconius's principles, that what is said of Christ applies to his body the church as well.[43] Since the last verse commented on in the previous sermon said that the speaker's feet had been set in an open space, and the first verse here complains of being harried, the meaning is that churches have different experiences: some are in peace and others in trouble. The cause of trouble for those that experience it is that their love has grown cold (Matt. 24:12). The number of holy people in the church has always been small; there are many others who come on Easter but go to the amphitheaters or playhouses on Low Sunday.

The psalmist's reaction to the trouble is anger ("My eye is vexed with wrath") at the sins of others who brought the trouble on them. "Yet from that seemingly worthless pile of chaff a great heap of grain can be winnowed."[44] Nor should we let our anger become a sin of our own. With psychological insight that sounds modern, Augustine says, "When we are angry and can't let fly, but have to keep it in, we fume inwardly, our insides are vexed."[45] Those who have become holy remain on earth only to help others, so when they see others not profiting from their preaching and example, they feel their "life is weakened in want."[46] Bad Christians are worse than pagans, because there is hope for the pagans. "Something can still be made of them, just as something can be made from the logs in a carpenter's yard, in spite of all the knots and the twists and the bark.... But from the twigs and trimmings he cleans off the carpenter can make nothing, they are only fit for firewood."[47] "Bad Christians" are "an excessive disgrace to my neighbours, namely to those who were drawing nearer to me, and were on the verge of believing."[48] But the anger of the righteous is a serious temptation. "It is difficult to say which is worse, this self-satisfied pride, or that wicked life. So never go and say that you are the only one."[49]

Another concern of the righteous is Christians who have deserted to heretical and schismatic bodies. These are the ones referred to in the verse: "Those who used to see me, ran away from me out of doors." They (especially the Donatists) do not realize that the Scriptures foretold that the church would be a worldwide society. They should imitate the obedience of Abraham in the sacrifice of Isaac.

> What does it all mean? It means Christ, but all wrapped up and hidden, tied up in riddles. To get at this meaning the story has to be shaken apart, the riddles untied, the wrapping unwrapped. Then we see that Isaac, his father's beloved only son, stands for the Only Son of God, and

> he carries the wood for his own sacrifice, just as Christ carried the cross.[50]

While what this story teaches about Christ is hidden, what it says about the church is clear—a contrast that is characteristic of Scripture. Because of his obedience, God promised Abraham that "in your seed shall all the nations of the earth be blessed" (Gen. 22:18),[51] an obvious prophecy of the church.

Because of the sins of bad Christians, a good one feels like "a pot that is scrapped," because all Christians are blamed indiscriminately for such inconsistent behavior by outsiders, those who are "settled round about."[52] Those who stay outside the church, by their taunts, hope to lure the Christians out from it.

Some of the bad Christians had been taken as models before their lapse, but we should not depend on human examples. Rather, the psalmist says, "I have hoped in you, O Lord." To depend on human examples "is to be a milk-sop, as they call big boys who are still being breast-fed."[53] But the bad conduct of fallen role models can be like the bad-tasting stuff wet nurses put on their breasts to wean milksops: it can break an unhealthy pattern of dependency. The one thus liberated can say, "In your hands are my lots."[54] Casting lots to decide on a course of action is seeking divine guidance and thus is not sinful in the way that consulting an astrologer would be. This verse reminds us of God's election: "[The psalmist] is calling the grace of God a sort of lottery, because in a lottery things happen not by choice but by the will of God. . . . Not finding in us any merits he could decide on, he saves us by the lottery of his own will."[55] Scripture confirmed this interpretation when Peter told Simon Magus, "You have no lot nor part in this [faith]" (Acts 8:21).[56] He thought he could buy grace with money, but grace is free. A lot means a portion, a share. "What is my share? The inheritance of the Church. And what are its limits? The ends of the earth."[57] And that is as much as there is time for. The rest of the psalm will be interpreted tomorrow.

So goes a fairly typical sermon by Augustine. One could have read over the six and a half verses of the psalm and never thought they contained so much. Nor would they if Augustine had not been an interpreter of signs. What he found was very different from the intention of the psalmist, but it is certainly consistent with the faith of the New Testament. What he came up with is the sort of thing one immersed in Christian faith and spirituality is likely to think when reading a psalm. The psalmist did not know all that was true, but the Christian does. So Augustine brings it all out and makes it available to his congregation. And he does so in a homily that is much more unified than many expository sermons—certainly more so than a homily of Chrysostom, who would go through interpreting verse by verse and only apply the last verse commented upon to the life of the people. It is easier to understand why the Catholic congregation in Hippo Regius considered their bishop to be an extraordinarily good preacher than it is to know why one who had enjoyed international fame as a speaker should seem so contented to remain in his sleepy North African seacoast town for thirty-nine years ministering to his small flock. Unless, of course, he was practicing what he preached.

FOR FURTHER READING

Brown, Peter Robert Lamont. *Augustine of Hippo: A Biography.* Berkeley and Los Angeles: University of California Press, 1967.

Nine Sermons of Saint Augustine on the Psalms. Translated and introduction by Edmund Hill. London: Longmans, Green, and Co., 1958.

St. Augustine: Confessions. Translated with introduction and notes by Henry Chadwick. Oxford World's Classics. Oxford and New York: Oxford University Press, 1991.

The Works of St. Augustine: A New Translation for the 21st Century. Sermons III/11: Newly Discovered Sermons. Translation and notes by Edmund Hill, edited by John E. Rotelle. Brooklyn, N.Y.: New City Press, 1997.

The Works of St. Augustine: A Translation for the 21st Century. Part I, Vol. 11: Teaching Christianity: De doctrina christiana. Introduction, translation, and notes by Edmund Hill, edited by John E. Rotelle. Brooklyn, N.Y.: New City Press, 1996.

Wills, Garry. *St. Augustine.* New York: Viking, 1999.

Notes

1. Hippolytus was earlier, but he wrote in Greek.

2. The two most influential ante-Nicene theologians to write in Latin were the Carthaginians Tertullian (ca. 150–ca. 220) and Cyprian (ca. 205–258). African Christian Latinity may be synchronized with Roman by noting that scholars debate over whether Tertullian influenced Minucius Felix or if it was the other way around and whether or not Novatian corresponded with Cyprian. Tertullian, it should be noted, was a transitional figure who also wrote a few treatises in Greek.

3. Peter Robert Lamont Brown, *Augustine of Hippo: A Biography* (Berkeley and Los Angeles: The University of California Press, 1967), 20. In 2000 Brown issued a

new edition of this standard biography to which he added an epilogue in which he reviewed the advances in scholarship since the first edition. These advances include two discoveries of unknown or partially known works of Augustine, a collection of twenty-nine letters discovered by Johannes Divjak (*St. Augustine: Letters, Vol. 6*, trans. Robert B. Eno. FC, vol. 81 [Washington, D.C.: Catholic University of America Press, 1989]), and a collection of thirty sermons identified by François Dolbeau (*The Works of St. Augustine: A New Translation for the 21st Century. Sermons III/11: Newly Discovered Sermons*, trans. and notes Edmund Hill, ed. John E. Rotelle [Brooklyn, N.Y.: New City Press, 1997]). Both the sermons and the letters permit a more intimate view of Augustine than had been available before. Other advances in scholarship occur in new information about Augustine's contemporaries, the time and place of his ministry, and particular aspects of his works. Another important recent work on Augustine is Garry Wills's short but perceptive *St. Augustine* (New York: Viking, 1999). These works appeared too late to affect more than the footnotes of this chapter.

4. Their "style, thought, and oratory" did not impress Edwin Dargan, *A History of Preaching* (1905–12; reprint, New York: Burt Franklin, 1968), 1:98.

5. Agostino Trapè, "St. Augustine," in *The Golden Age of Latin Patristic Literature from the Council of Nicea to the Council of Chalcedon,* vol. 4 of *Patrology,* ed. Angelo di Berardino, intro. Johannes Quasten, trans. Placid Solari (Westminster, Md.: Christian Classics, 1986), 342.

6. Such a statement can be made with some certainty because more is known of Augustine's life from birth through his first professional activity than of any other person in antiquity, especially from an interior perspective. His autobiographical *Confessions* gives an account of the developing consciousness of an individual that is unparalleled before the modern era. (Wills is correct, however, in saying that *The Testimony* is a more accurate translation of the title than *Confessions* [*St. Augustine,* xiii-xiv].) Although his *Confessions* was written as a prayer praising God for preveniently directing him toward conversion throughout his early life, it is also very informative about what he was like as a boy. For the Latin text, see *Augustine: Confessions*, trans. William Watts. LCL, vols. 26-27 (Cambridge: Harvard University Press, 1912). An excellent translation into contemporary English is *St. Augustine: Confessions*, trans. with intro. and notes Henry Chadwick, Oxford World's Classics (Oxford and New York: Oxford University Press, 1991).

7. Part of the cost of his education was borne by his friend Romanianus, one of the wealthiest citizens of Thagaste.

8. *Conf.* 3.4.7, Chadwick trans.

9. Brown, *Augustine of Hippo,* 69.

10. Her husband had died three years earlier.

11. *Conf.* 9.10.24-26. Most of Book 9 from 8.17 on is about Monica's life and death.

12. Like everyone trained in classical literature, he had regarded the Bible as crudely written.

13. Brown, *Augustine of Hippo,* 132.

14. Most of them, however, were called to be bishops of other towns in the region, and therefore had to be replaced in the monastery.

15. *The Works of St. Augustine: A Translation for the 21st Century. Part I, Vol.*

11: Teaching Christianity: De doctrina christiana, intro., trans., and notes Edmund Hill, ed. John E. Rotelle (Brooklyn, N.Y.: New City Press, 1996), 98. This edition also contains three introductory essays by different scholars, although the rationale for including just these three is not stated. The translator's study of this work and of Augustine's preaching extends over forty years.

16. Ibid., 97. Hill also theorizes why Augustine wrote the book and accounts for the thirty-year lapse between the writing of the first three books and the completion of the fourth. Briefly, Hill says that Augustine was asked to write it by Aurelius, his primate, to train clergy who were to have the responsibility of preaching. After completing the third book, he wrote to Aurelius to get his approval for using the rules of Tyconius (see note 22 below). Either Aurelius never answered or he disapproved, so Augustine set the book aside and forgot about it until he wrote the *Retractiones* thirty years later. That reminded him of the value of the project, and he completed it at that time. Ibid., 96-97.

17. "Thing" is used here in a sense much broader than "an inanimate object." So broad, in fact, that it stands for "whatever is or may be an object of perception or knowledge or thought." First meaning, *Oxford American Dictionary,* 1st ed. In this sense, even God is a thing—without, of course, being reified.

18. A convenient precis of *De doctrina* appears in J. F. Shaw's translation in *NPNF*[1] 2:517.

19. Augustine, although he didn't have an enormous knowledge of Greek, knew enough of the language to translate the Septuagint Psalter into Latin. His knowledge of Hebrew was limited to the explanation of a few words that he had picked up from someone else.

20. What German exegetes refer to as *Sachkritik.*

21. Augustine does not mention it, but he refers to works like Pliny's *Natural History,* which contains most of the information (and misinformation) the ancient world had about nature.

22. Augustine ends the third book of *Teaching Christianity* with a list of seven rules for resolving ambiguities in the Bible that he borrowed from a Donatist theologian named Tyconius. The first of these is "About the Lord and his body," and states that "since Christ and his church form a single person, it is perfectly legitimate to pass from the head to the body." The second is "About the twofold body of the Lord," which takes cognizance of the way that saints and sinners will coexist in the church until the end of time and says that passages that seem to praise or curse Israel or the church are to be understood as referring only to the appropriate group within it and not to all its members. Rule Three, "About the promises and the law," is what Augustine called "about the spirit and the letter" or "about grace and commandments." Augustine considered this "as more a very large question than a rule to be applied to the settling of questions." "About species and genus," Rule Four, Augustine understands as "about the part and the whole." Whatever Scripture says about a part of a whole may be applied to the whole. Although neither he nor Tyconius says so, this is simply the rhetorical figure known as *synecdoche.* The next rule, Five, "About times," seems to be synecdoche used in statements of time. Rule Six, "Recapitulation," means that "when the scriptures do not carefully observe the temporal order of events or confuse the before and after, it is up to the reader to

restore the missing order." The final rule, "About the devil and his body" is the same principle as the first, but applied to the wicked rather than the church.

23. The two methods of learning are roughly equivalent to Kennedy's distinction between "technical rhetoric" (the sort learned from the handbooks) and "sophistic rhetoric" (the sort acquired by apprenticing oneself to a master). George A. Kennedy, *Classical Rhetoric and Its Christian and Secular Tradition from Ancient to Modern Times*, rev. and enl. (Chapel Hill: University of North Carolina Press, 1999), 16-17.

24. Multiple, that is, in the sense of Literal, Allegorical, Tropological, and Anagogical. Augustine believed that a given passage could mean more than one thing and delighted in that realization.

25. For the significance of the term see, for example, the article on *semeion* in *TDNT*, ed. Gerhard Kittel and Gerhard Friedrich, trans. Geoffrey W. Bromiley, abridged in one volume by Geoffrey W. Bromiley (Grand Rapids, Mich.: Eerdmans, 1985), 1015-22.

26. Edmund Hill, trans. and intro., *Nine Sermons of Saint Augustine on the Psalms* (London: Longmans, Green & Co., 1958), 27. Of course, only the Old Testament had a Hebrew original.

27. Brown, *Augustine of Hippo*, 259.

28. Hill, *Teaching Christianity*, 2.6, 7.

29. Brown, *Augustine of Hippo*, 260.

30. Roland J. Teske, "Criteria for Figurative Interpretation in St. Augustine," in De doctrina Christiana: *A Classic of Western Culture*, ed. Duane W. H. Arnold and Pamela Bright (Notre Dame: University of Notre Dame Press, 1995), 118. Teske's article is the basis for this paragraph and the one before.

31. Luigi Alici, "Sign and Language," in *Teaching Christianity*, 45.

32. Prosper Grech, "Hermeneutical Principles," ibid., 92.

33. Brown, *Augustine of Hippo*, 244-58; George Lawless, O.S.A., "Augustine of Hippo as Preacher," *Saint Augustine the Bishop: A Book of Essays*, ed. Fannie LeMoine and Christopher Kleinhenz (New York and London: Garland, 1994), 13-37; and, most important, Frederik van der Meer, *Augustine the Bishop: The Life and Work of a Father of the Church*, trans. Brian Battershaw and G. R. Lamb (London and New York: Sheed & Ward, 1961). While Part 3 of this work (405-67) is devoted to Augustine's preaching practice and his two books on teaching the faith, *De doctrina christiana* and *De catechizandis rudibus* (Instructions for Beginners), almost the entire book is helpful to anyone wishing to imagine what it must have been like to hear Augustine preach. There is a description of the region, its population, and its history; a report of other religious bodies in the area; an account of pastoral activity; an examination of the laity, clergy, and ascetics who made up the community; a description of liturgical practice in Hippo; and a study of popular piety in North Africa.

34. In *Augustine the Bishop*, facing p. 25, there is a drawing of a reconstruction of an African town church that must be very much like that of Hippo.

35. Brown says that from his *cathedra*, Augustine was only about five yards from the first row of the congregation and roughly at their eye level. *Augustine of Hippo*, 251.

36. Since Augustine wrote out few of his sermons, the fact that almost a thousand

of them survive is due to the scribes who took them down. For a breakdown of this figure into the various categories of Augustine's sermons, see Lawless, "Augustine of Hippo as Preacher," 13-15.

37. Van der Meer, *Augustine the Bishop,* 419. This paragraph is largely based on his chapter on the subject.

38. Brown, *Augustine of Hippo,* 256.

39. Ibid., 251.

40. Van der Meer, *Augustine the Bishop,* 432. Emphasis added.

41. Brown, *Augustine of Hippo*, 245. Augustine's basic understanding of what he was doing when he preached was "breaking bread" and "feeding the multitude." Ibid., 252.

42. Psalm 30 in the Vulgate and Septuagint. The translation of the sermon that follows is from Edmund Hill, *Nine Sermons of Saint Augustine on the Psalms,* 122-35. Another translation appears in *St. Augustine on the Psalms*, vol. 2, trans. and notes Dame Scholastica Hebgin and Dame Felicitas Corrigan. ACW, no. 30 (Westminster, Md.: Newman Press; London: Longmans, Green & Co., 1960), 2:28-44, where it is called the third sermon on the psalm, the first being "brief, dry notes of exegesis" probably dictated to a stenographer early in Augustine's ministry. The translation of *Enarrationes in Psalmos* in *NPNF*[1] vol. 8, is painfully abridged. *NPNF* does better by the *Tractates on the Gospel of John* and the *Homilies on the First Epistle of John* (vol. 7) and *Sermons on Selected Lessons of the New Testament* (vol. 6; these are Sermons 51-147 on the Gospel(s) in the Benedictine edition). John Burnaby included ten homilies on 1 John in his *Augustine: Later Works.* LCC, vol. 8 (Philadelphia: Westminster, 1955). Festal sermons are translated in *St. Augustine, Sermons for Christmas and Epiphany,* trans. and notes Thomas Comerford Lawler. ACW, no. 15 (Westminster, Md.: Newman Press; London: Longmans, Green & Co., 1952), and *Selected Easter Sermons of Saint Augustine,* intro., text of thirty sermons, notes, and commentary Philip T. Weller (St. Louis: Herder, 1959). These are the only sermon translations I have consulted, although others exist, some of which are listed in Lawless, "Augustine of Hippo as Preacher," 36. See also *Patrology*, vol. 4, 398-99.

43. As offensive as the notion is to contemporary historical consciousness, that is the way the psalms are always understood liturgically and homiletically. Otherwise, the monastic offices could not have had the Psalter as their core for all these centuries, nor could clergy be so nourished by the recitation of the daily offices or sermons be preached on texts from the psalms. This christological interpretation of the Psalter is already well developed in the New Testament.

44. Hill, *Nine Sermons of Saint Augustine,* 124.

45. Ibid., 125.

46. Ibid.

47. Ibid., 126-27.

48. Ibid., 127.

49. Ibid., 128.

50. Ibid., 130. This quotation from the sermon is an excellent summary of Augustine's understanding of the interpretation of signs. His interpretation of the sacrifice of Isaac is the standard patristic one. New Testament allusions to the passage see Abraham as exemplifying obedience (Jas. 2:21) and faith (Heb. 11:17).

51. Ibid., 130-31.
52. Ibid., 131.
53. Ibid., 132.
54. Ibid., 133. This is an example of the corrupt and at times meaningless Latin text Augustine had to comment on. As we can see in the parallel column above, the Hebrew says, "My *times* are in your hands."
55. Ibid., 132.
56. Ibid., 134.
57. Ibid.

PART II

THE MIDDLE AGES

CHAPTER 6

THE TREK TO THE MIDDLE AGES

In Augustine the Latin homily reached its peak. By the time of his death on August 28 in A.D. 430, the Vandals, who were Arian Christians, had already begun their conquest of North Africa. A year later they captured Hippo and burned part of it. The town was evacuated. Catholic Christians were persecuted by these Arians for a century before Africa was reconquered by Justinian's general, Belisarius. Then, a little over a century and a half later, the Muslims took Carthage, and Latin-speaking Christianity became almost extinct in North Africa, where it had begun.

By that time, the circumstances under which Latin Christianity existed elsewhere were vastly changed. The year 476 saw the abdication of the last Roman emperor in the West. For a while, exarchs in Ravenna provided the church and people in the West with some sort of contact with the imperial government in Constantinople, but even that became less as years passed. The time in which these changes took place was the beginning of what used to be called the Dark Ages, under the illusion that it was a period of intellectual stagnation.[1] Much more is known about the era now and it is recognized as a time of vigorous life.[2]

The titles of two historical surveys, *The End of Ancient Christianity,*[3] which deals with the period from 400 to 600; and *The Rise of Western Christendom,*[4] which traces events to 1000, show this shift. The end of ancient Christianity was the beginning of Western Christendom. These titles serve to divide the time between the era of the empire in the West after Diocletian and the era of the Germanic kingdoms that emerged in what had been the Western provinces of the empire. We will study the transition period, during which the inhabitants of the territory moved from understanding themselves to be part of the Western Roman Empire to thinking of themselves as Europeans.[5]

We may perceive other dynamics as well. Mediterranean civilization had been a civilization of cities, but this new world had few with as many as twenty thousand people; towns of five thousand were much more the rule. By the late-sixth century, Rome itself had fewer than fifty thousand inhabitants. Or, again, it is customary to refer to the movements of peoples that so disrupted the empire as "barbarian" invasions, but the designation is value charged.[6] The important distinction to be made is between *nomads* such as the Huns, who made occasional forays into civilized areas, and the *settled farmers,* who moved nearer to Roman territory for protection when they were disrupted by the nomads. As effective administration from the central government declined, the Romans on the frontier mixed with these Germanic peoples until the two populations became indistinguishable.[7]

The conversion of the population to Christianity adds a further dynamic of crucial importance to this study. Estimates as to the portion of Roman citizens who were Christians at the time of Constantine's conversion are as low as 10 percent.[8] But by A.D. 800,

> a peculiarly determined form of Catholic Christianity became the mandatory faith of all the regions, Mediterranean and non-Mediterranean alike, that had come together to form a post-Roman western Europe. . . . Large regions of northwestern and central Europe came to be joined, slowly but irrevocably, to the former territories of the Roman Empire in a shared Catholicism, that would soon stretch as far as Scandinavia and into parts of eastern Europe.[9]

The time, then, when the patristic period of church history shifted into the medieval, was an era of great vitality. One of the changes that occurred during this era, however, is the basis for the assumption that the age was dark: the decline of classical Roman culture, particularly of the Latin language, literacy, an educational system, and Greco-Roman rhetoric.[10] What remained was being blended with Germanic cultures into the rich mix that would become the medieval synthesis, but for the time being, much that had been regarded by the Romans as the core of their heritage was in abeyance.

This decline of Latin culture was of great significance for the history of preaching. This is not to say that preaching stopped. Far from it! Such mass evangelization could not have occurred without it. But the sermons were in many languages, they were preached by persons who had not been trained in rhetoric—or much else that was academic, and they were not written down. Thus evidence is lacking for reconstructing most of what was occurring in homiletics during this period. What remains is limited to preaching in Latin and is thus highly atypical.

It is possible, on the other hand, to see how the minor amount of preaching that was done in Latin survived. We can gain that knowledge by looking at four preachers who mark its trajectory. Two of them were popes: the only two ever called "the Great" and the only two from the patristic period from whom we have a body of sermons, Leo I and Gregory I. Leo's reign began ten years after Augustine's death. He was the last pope of the patristic era to use the full range of rhetorical effects taught in classical education. While Gregory came from the most exalted circles of Roman society and had a good education, an audience capable of appreciating such art was not available just 150 years after Leo. The third preacher, Caesarius of Arles, was born halfway between the two pontiffs, and he reflects what was happening to preaching in non-Italian territory that had been a part of the empire for centuries. Finally, the Venerable Bede indicates the degree of classical culture that came to be preserved in and by the monasteries of Britain at the edge of what had been the Roman world.

LEO THE GREAT (CA. 390–461)

Virtually nothing is known of Leo's early life and very little of anything he did before his pontificate. While there is a suggestion that he was a Tuscan, it seems more likely that he was born in Rome during the last decade of the fourth century. The only evidence of his having received a first-rate education is the elegant prose that he came to write.[11] He became archdeacon of Rome and was alert, as few Westerners were, to the seriousness of the christological controversies going on in the East. It was he who warned Pope Celestine against Nestorius and also helped Sixtus III deal with the Pelagian Julian of Eclanum. Leo was on a peacemaking mission in Gaul when Sixtus died and he was elected to succeed him.

Even for the period of his pontificate there is little personal information about Leo. Neither his sermons nor his letters, the two genres of his writing, reveal Leo the man. What is known instead are the official acts, which were noteworthy indeed, justifying his designation as "the Great." One of his accomplishments was to cause the papacy to become "self-conscious."[12] Previously the church at Rome had emphasized its foundation by two apostles, Peter and Paul, and bishops elsewhere had assumed that Jesus' naming Peter as the rock on which he would build his church was their corporate charter rather than that of Rome alone. Now Leo insisted that only Rome spoke with the voice of Peter and that doing so gave her authority *(principatus)* over the whole church.[13] While no one ever subordinated himself to his role more than Leo, it is also true that few have ever so maximized their role.

That maximization is clear in his participation in the Council of Chalcedon (451), which gave the definitive formula for Catholic teaching about the person and work of Christ. This council had been called to undo the work of the "Robber Council"[14] of Ephesus in 449, which had been controlled by Monophysites who upheld the heresy of Eutyches.[15] Leo had prepared a statement for Ephesus that set out in Western terms the position that Chalcedon was to affirm, but it was ignored. At neither Ephesus nor Chalcedon did Leo sit down as a peer or even *primus inter pares,*[16] but was represented by legates instead. He expected them to preside over the council as his representatives and that the council would not debate the issue, but merely subscribe to the letter ("Tome") he had prepared for Ephesus on the subject. It was to be a case of *Roma locuta, causa finita* (Rome has spoken, the case is closed). But the Eastern bishops did not see it that way. The patriarch of Constantinople presided and, while Leo's Tome was eventually accepted as an adequate statement of orthodox Christology, that occurred only after long discussion. "The *Tome* of Leo to Flavian was accepted *on merits,* and not because it was issued by the pope."[17]

Leo was a very eloquent man. He persuaded Attila the Hun not to invade Italy and even did something to ameliorate the effects of the Vandal capture of Rome. We can see the same persuasiveness in his sermons. Ninety-six of his sermons have been preserved.[18] The odd assortment is the result of Leo's arranging for two collections to be made to preserve their dogmatic content.[19] This accounts for the fact that a great majority of them were preached in the first five years of his pontificate and most of the rest were preached in the next nine.

It probably accounts also for most of them having been delivered on the fasts and great feasts of the church year. Five were preached for the anniversary of his consecration (September 29), six for the collection for the poor taken in November at the time of a pagan celebration, nine for the December Ember Days,[20] ten for Christmas, eight for Epiphany, twelve for the Lenten Ember Days, one for the transfiguration, twenty-one for Holy Week,[21] two for the ascension, three for the Feast of Pentecost, and four for the Ember Days after it, two for the Feast of Peter and Paul, one in commemoration of Alaric's sack of Rome, one in honor of the Maccabees, one for St. Lawrence, nine for the September Ember Days, one on the Beatitudes, and one against Eutyches.

The first thing that strikes the modern reader about Leo's sermons is how short they are. They average slightly less than four pages each in the Fathers of the Church translation.[22] This brevity could be related to the pope's liturgical duties at that time. The surviving documents do not permit detailed reconstruction of the papal liturgy during this period, but when Leo was pope there were already at least twenty churches in the city of Rome. Although the full system of station days[23] does not appear to have developed before Gregory the Great, it seems likely that the pontiff was already presiding regularly at different churches in the time of Leo. Thus, he and his retinue would proceed to the designated church as a group. Entering it, they would make their way toward the apse, with Leo perhaps greeting those he knew as he passed among them. All this means that the bishop of Rome did not have a regular congregation of his own to preach to each Sunday. He was the distinguished visitor who had come in such pomp. Even more, the voice in which he spoke and the words that he said were more Peter's than his own.

These words take on a kind of objectivity and sound like liturgical prayers. "The rhythm of his phrases is accommodated to the sound of the liturgy, its forms are similar to many preserved by the Roman missal, which, through the sacramentaries, is often inspired by him."[24] As Lietzmann observed, Leo's expression is concise and apposite, and often has a brilliant terseness and a painstakingly formal development that would well repay careful study.[25] He also cited studies that point out Leo's punctiliousness in observing the rules for the cadence of final clauses in periodic sentences—an attention to the rhythms of speech important in classical rhetoric that has not received the attention it deserves in modern public speaking.[26] According to Yngve Brilioth, Leo furnished the model for the "majestic and polished style" of later popes and the *cursus leoninus*: "His balanced prose rhythm became normative for the style of the Roman curia and also set its stamp on the construction of the Roman collects."[27]

A surprising feature of Leo's preserved sermons to those familiar with patristic preaching is that they are not exegetical homilies. They are very biblical in the sense that they are saturated with allusions to the sacred text.[28] Yet there is more to it than that; Jean Leclercq is undoubtedly correct in saying that while Leo does not give a commentary on the text of the Gospel passage read at the liturgy, his teaching in the sermon is nevertheless in respect to it. And while Leo does not follow its text strictly, he explains its content as a whole and pays attention to the details in it that are needed to understand the "mystery" of the day. Therefore, regarding the form of the sermons, it can be said that

> Leo constructed his sermons very carefully—with an introduction, a theme with examples, and a definite conclusion. Content and structure form an admirable, logical whole.[29]

If one wishes to study what Leo's sermons are like, a good place to begin is with his thirtieth, preached on Christmas Day in 454. He begins by saying that although he has often preached to his flock on that occasion, no human eloquence is adequate to the event commemorated. Yet something must be said because so many have gone astray in their understanding of what happened. He will summarize the heresies into which people have fallen concerning the relation between our Lord's divine and human natures. Since Christ's birth proved that "he was the real son of a human being," some have decided that he was "nothing more than a mere man." Others have been so impressed with his teaching and miracles that they feel there could be nothing human in so divine a being, and that his flesh, therefore, must be an illusion. And still others adopted an intermediate position by which "the humanity in Christ would have been false by virtue of the fact that it did not have its own substance, and the divinity would have been untrue by virtue of the fact that it was defective through mutability."

The church, however, has crushed such heresies, and, since the church is his body, "we are his flesh, the flesh that had been taken up from the Virgin's womb." Thus, as Paul said, "In him dwells all the fullness of the divinity according to the flesh, and you have been filled in him" (Col. 2:9-10).[30] "As nothing of his majesty remains that does not dwell in the dwelling filled by it, so nothing of the body remains unfulfilled by his indwelling."[31] This means that the miracle of Christ's birth infinitely exceeds all the miraculous births of the old dispensation, including those of Adam, Eve, Isaac, Jacob, Jeremiah, Samuel, and John the Baptist.

Heretical Christologies should "go far away and recede into their own shadows" and Christians should not be "weakened . . . in the plan of God's mercy." As John 5:25-27 shows, "the Son of God is also the son of a human being." That truth is in no danger of contradiction. And it was to justify human beings that God's Only Begotten became one of them himself. Thus, "although one [of our Lord's natures] remains from eternity and the other began in time, both have nevertheless come together in a unity." Those who believe that are true Christians, as the Gospels show. No one can doubt, therefore, that "there is no other name under heaven given to human beings by which they can be saved" (Acts 4:12).[32]

CAESARIUS OF ARLES (CA. 470–542)

The difference between the world in which Leo lived and that of Caesarius is greater than one would anticipate, even allowing for the time that had elapsed or the distance between them. The territory of classical Gaul was roughly that occupied by modern France. Caesar's *Gallic Wars* is the last chapter of the story begun centuries earlier of the incorporation of this land and its Celtic population into the Roman Empire. By the middle of the second century there were Christian communities in Lyons and Vienne, as Irenaeus, their bishop at the end of the century, indicates. Sixteen Gallic bishops attended the Council of Arles in 314, while a similar number could not be present. The Gallic church even produced a widely known saint, Martin, the soldier who became bishop of Tours late in the fourth century.

Germanic peoples, the Franks, Visigoths, and Burgundians began to move into the territory in the early-fifth century, being accepted as allies of Rome at first, and establishing kingdoms of their own when Roman authority in the West flickered out. The newcomers accommodated themselves to the culture they found in Gaul and in time became hardly distinguishable from the Romanized Celtic natives. Not only did they accept Latin as their language, they even shared the Christian religion, although they were Arians.

Caesarius of Arles, who was born a few years before Romulus Augustus stepped down as emperor in the West in 476, had to contend with these Germanic settlements; his see passed from under Visigothic rule to that of the Ostrogoths and then to that of the Franks. He was not originally from Arles, but came instead from a prosperous family in Châlon (Latin: Cabillonum), a busy port on the Saône river about seventy-five miles north of Lyons. When he was seventeen he took minor orders and transferred from his father's authority to that of his bishop. Two years later, however, he went to test his vocation at the monastery of Lérins,[33] which had become the cradle of the Gallic episcopate.

Caesarius spent only a few years at the monastery before his austerities necessitated his being nursed back to health. He was sent to Arles to recuperate rather than home to Châlon: it was much closer and Aeonius, the bishop there, was a relative. But Lérins had made its mark on him: "a set of habits, ideas, and values that would have a profound impact on his career as a bishop, preacher, pastor, and reformer."[34] These included an ascetic way of life, knowledge not only of the spiritual tradition of his monastery but of all Latin patristic literature, and an Augustinian understanding of the nature of Christian community as an imperfect but nonetheless real manifestation of the true *civitas dei*.

The city where he went to recover his health was very different from his home in Châlon on the edge of the Roman world or the peaceful island monastery to which he had gone. Arles was in Provence, the "province" that had been Roman for six centuries and was as much a part of the Roman world as Italy. Located at the first crossable spot on the Rhône as it left the Mediterranean and moved into the heartland of Gaul, Arles was almost as important a port as nearby Marseilles. And, as to be expected of a city so strategically located, Arles was always a political and administrative center. It had been the capital of Gaul under Rome and had great if lesser importance under the Visigothic rule that began in 476. It is not surprising that the bishop of Arles had metropolitan rights over surrounding dioceses, although these were constantly being contested.

As Caesarius was recovering his health, his kinsman Aeonius had opportunity to observe him and discover his promise. He asked the abbot of Lérins to release him so that he could become one of the diocesan clergy of Arles. Caesarius served for about eight years, first as a deacon and then as a priest, before Aeonius appointed him to succeed the recently deceased abbot of the local monastery in 499. He was about thirty at the time, and Aeonius began to make it clear that he wanted this young relative to become his successor, which did happen in 502.

By the time he was consecrated, Caesarius already had a clear idea of what he or any other bishop ought to be like. One of the people he had come to know in Arles was the distinguished rhetor Julianus Pomerius. Caesarius became his student. Although it is not mentioned in his *Life*,[35] he must have already received a good secondary Latin education or he could never have written so correctly in both simple and sophisticated prose forms.[36] The *Life* also records, however, that Caesarius had a dream not unlike that in which Jerome came to fear that he was not a Christian but a Ciceronian (1.9). In response, he is reported to have discontinued his training under Pomerius.

Rhetoric, however, was not the main thing that he learned from his teacher. Pomerius was a Christian ascetic as well as a teacher of oratory and had written a treatise called *The Contemplative Life,* in which he set forth the Augustinian ideal of a bishop as a monk who lived in community with his clergy. This was in contrast to what had been the practice in Gaul: electing a local aristocrat who would continue to live in much the way he had before. By this time churches were wealthy and had estates that needed to be administered. It was easy for bishops to give more attention to such responsibilities than to teaching the faithful and caring for the poor. Indeed, they could say that the prestige of the church required that they dress richly and entertain at sumptuous banquets. But Pomerius taught Caesarius that all that should change.

At this point the reader could have a sense of having sat through this before, since the Cappadocians, Chrysostom, and Augustine all represented a stage in the development of their churches when the monk was replacing the aristocrat as the favored type of candidate in episcopal elections.[37] But the earlier Fathers represent a time when the empire was still functioning and changes were being made from a more local to a more central form of administration. The Gallic shift in favor of monks, on the other hand, reflects developments that occurred between the late-fourth and the early-sixth centuries. By the later date there was no longer a Roman government in the West, and the rulers of Germanic kingdoms in Gaul needed to rely heavily on bishops for effective local administration. Luckily, a "graduate" of Lérins who had been further schooled under Pomerius was well prepared for such responsibilities.

During his forty-year episcopate, Caesarius upheld the Augustinian and Pomerian ideal both by having its principles turned into law by a number of councils in Gaul and also even more radically by practicing it himself. He was known, for instance, for buying people out of captivity, whether they had been on his side of the conflict in which they had been captured or the other. He also fed the poor and is famous for having founded a monastery (as it was called) for women that was to be free of the control of the local bishop. But, as is appropriate for one espoused to the Augustinian ideal of the episcopate, there is no cause to which Caesarius gave himself so wholeheartedly as that of preaching.

Some 250 of his sermons have been preserved,[38] but only a few were identified as his before the painstaking and groundbreaking work of the Maurists in the seventeenth century—who found about half of them among works attributed to Augustine—and Dom Germain Morin, who identified most of the rest. Much of that obscurity is due to Caesarius's own actions. He not only believed that he himself should preach, but that all bishops and priests should, and that even deacons could read sermons of the Fathers.[39] Therefore, the form of his sermons that has been preserved is not that in which he delivered them, but that into which he edited them to be used by any cleric who could not or would not compose sermons of his own.

This accounts for two peculiarities of the series. One is that he often borrowed wholesale from the Fathers in composing his own sermons, simplifying their words for Gallic audiences. The other is that he often identified one of his own sermons as being the work of an eminent patristic authority, in the hope of making it more likely to be read in church (**See Vol. 2, pp. 127-32,** for an example). The purpose of what Morin called this "pious ruse" was not pride of authorship but a desire for the edification of the people of God.[40]

Not all of the sermons were preached by Caesarius himself; some were only compiled to be distributed for use by others. At his cathedral he had a training center for future clergy, and he used the students there to produce collections of fifteen to fifty sermons to be passed on in this way. The better students would pick out passages from the Fathers they thought would be helpful to Gallic congregations and the bishop would edit them, adding an introduction or conclusion, simplifying the vocabulary and eliminating unnecessary words. These collections proved quite popular and were used over and over again, for instance, by the great missionary bishops in the seventh to ninth centuries.[41]

Caesarius's sermons were sorted by Morin into five groups: 1-80, admonitions on various topics (which do not have the form of homilies); 81-186, exegetical sermons (which do); 187-213, sermons for seasons of the church year; 214-32, those for saints' days and other feasts; and 233-38, addresses to monastic communities.[42] The admonitions cover a wide range of concerns for the behavior of Gallic Christians. The first eight have to do with the value of the written and the proclaimed Word of God. These are followed by a few on creedal or doctrinal subjects, which in turn lead into a group on the Christian life. A series on charity then prefaces a group on almsgiving, which is followed by several on loving one's enemies. Next come warnings against sexual sins and drunkenness and against superstitious pagan practices. Then come admonitions that Christians be prepared for judgment day, followed by some on the value of confessing one's sins and discussions of penitence. The volume ends with instructions on how to behave in church, whether it be how to chant the psalms or the value of such devotional gestures as genuflecting or bowing the head.

While all of these sermons teem with frequent scripture citations, the next 106 are exegetical homilies as such, commenting on the readings at the liturgy and applying them to the lives of the people. In those based on lections from the New Testament as well as the Old, the method of interpretation is uniformly allegorical. Following Origen and Augustine, for instance, the ten plagues of the exodus are related to the Ten Commandments in Sermons 99 and 100. The range of his preaching is well summarized in his *Life:*

> He delivered sermons suited to particular feasts and scriptural passages, and also against the evils of drunkenness and lust, against discord and hatred, against anger and pride, against the sacrilegious and fortune-tellers, against the utterly pagan rite of the Kalends of January, and against augurs, worshipers of trees and springs, and vices of different kinds. (*Life* 1.55)

Unlike other bishops of the time who came from prosperous families and had been educated in rhetoric, Caesarius did not preach in the high style that could be understood only by those with similar backgrounds, but preached instead in the Latin of ordinary people: "What is said to simple souls can, indeed, be understood by the educated, but what is preached to the learned cannot be grasped at all by the simple."[43]

Another way in which Caesarius strove to make his preaching effective was by doing it extemporaneously. The term used in his *Life* (1.54, 2.20), *memoriter,* could suggest that he memorized his sermons, but the more likely meaning is that he remembered an outline and preached from that. This would have been true even of sermons in which he incorporated large sections from the sermons of the Fathers, since he had a "wonderfully retentive memory" (*Life* 1.16) and could recite at will long passages from these works he had studied so attentively.[44]

Other ways in which he tried to make his preaching more effective were to speak loudly enough to be heard, to reinforce his words with gestures and facial expressions, and to keep his sermons short. As Klingshirn said, "Caesarius worked hard to deliver sermons that were clear, convincing, and above all memorable."[45] In doing so he used all the rhetorical techniques advocated by Augustine in *De doctrina christiana*. Even in the way he preached, Caesarius practiced what he preached. It is no wonder that his sermon collections were copied often and used extensively in the centuries to come.

Yet in some ways his preaching forebodes the decline of proclamation at the beginning of the Middle Ages. To a degree, his Latin is already on the way to becoming French[46]—not a bad thing in itself, but evidence that the culture is changing. Caesarius's borrowing from the sermons of his predecessors also prepares the way for the homiliaries at a time when clergy will not trust their own exegesis, but will only repeat what has been said by one of the giants of the past. Additionally there is an emphasis on the miraculous in his sermons as well as in his *Life* that is more akin to the spirit of the age that lies ahead than to that of the age gone before. Caesarius was at once a voice crying in the wilderness of his own generation and a harbinger of the future, a prophet in both the senses of forthtelling and foretelling.

GREGORY THE GREAT (CA. 540–604)

The year in which Caesarius died was close to that in which Gregory was born, but Gregory lived in a world different from that of Caesarius and even more different from that of Leo, his predecessor on the throne of Peter of a century and a half before. Leo had been pope before the Roman Empire in the West had ended. Caesarius flourished in the time when Germanic tribes were in control of the West. Shortly before Gregory was born, however, much of Italy had been reclaimed from the Ostrogoths by the Eastern emperor Justinian. That did not mean, however, that life in Rome had become more secure. The hold of the Eastern emperors on the Italic peninsula never became sure. It was constantly being challenged by the Germanic tribes, and control of Rome itself was not nearly so important to Constantinople as dealing with threats in the East. Even the emperor's exarchs in Ravenna did not give the welfare of Roman citizens in Italy significant priority.[47]

Constant wars and imperial indifference were not the only problems, however. In 542, possibly the year of Gregory's birth, there began a series of outbreaks of the plague that would trouble Europe for the rest of the century, the first killing about a third of the population of the affected areas. During his lifetime there were also famine, disease, floods of the Tiber, inflation, panic, and at times even riots.

After Gregory was consecrated in 590, he had to cope with all these distresses to a degree unprecedented in previous papacies. Before I turn to address the way he did that, however, it is appropriate to consider his life before his elevation to the Holy See. He came from an old and wealthy Roman family, although not one of the highest aristocracy.[48]

They were also deeply involved in the life of the church; indeed, his great-great-grandfather was Felix III, who served as pope a little over a century before Gregory did.

Gregory, however, was the first member of the family to hold an important civil office in Rome. When he was in his midthirties, he became one of the last prefects of the city. While it is hard to know exactly what Gregory's duties as prefect were, it seems likely that a good bit of the responsibility for government rested on his shoulders during the short term of his office.

His reaction to that responsibility is the first statement of a theme that would become dominant in his life, the struggle between his own desire to devote himself to the life of prayer and the many calls he received to look after the needs of others. This time he responded by doing what he must have wanted to do for a long time; he became a monk after his term of office was over.

He sold all of the family property he had inherited and used the proceeds to establish six monasteries in Sicily and a seventh at his family home on the Caelian Hill in the center of Rome, which he himself entered. Founding it, however, did not mean that he wished to govern it. Such duties must have seemed too much like what he was trying to get away from. He wished to begin the contemplative life of a monk; that is what he was fleeing *to*.

The needs of the church in those tumultuous times were too great, however, for so talented a person to be allowed to devote himself uninterruptedly to the life of prayer. He could have been a monk for only five years or so when the pope at the time made him a deacon. This is probably to say that he was put in charge of ecclesiastical administration for one of the seven districts into which Rome was divided. In 579 Pope Pelagius sent him to be his representative *(apocrisiarius)* to the imperial court in Constantinople, a duty with which he was charged for seven years. Gregory took to Constantinople with him a large group of his fellow monks, and his first major book, his *Morals on the Book of Job,* was begun there as conferences he led for his brothers.[49] Yet he was faithful as well in the duties for which he was sent to the capital.[50]

In 590, when he had been back in Rome about four years, one of the victims of that year's outbreak of the plague was Pope Pelagius. Gregory succeeded him as soon as imperial approval was received. The difficulties with which he would have to cope were enormous. Not only had the plague returned, but so had war. The Lombards, who occupied much of the peninsula, were attacking again. Floods of the Tiber devastated the countryside. And, with no effective civil government in the West, all the responsibility for the safety and welfare of the people would fall on Gregory's shoulders.

The Roman church at that time had the most extensive landholdings in Italy, not to mention others in Corsica, Sardinia, Dalmatia, Gaul, and North Africa. These resources made it possible for the church to assume responsibility for most of the services provided at other times by civil government—everything from feeding thousands to bankrolling imperial military operations. This, of course, was in addition to providing for all the expenses of the church, its clergy and religious, buildings, cemeteries, and charities. As one scholar put it, "The capital had become, especially economically, a papal Rome."[51]

It was possible for Gregory to oversee all of that because by talent and, undoubtedly, experience—especially that of being urban prefect, but also the management of the family estates—he was a marvelous administrator. He created an effective bureaucracy for the administration of the papal estates, seeing that everything was under a unified central control. The overall impression is that one of the reasons Gregory found administration so onerous was that he did it so thoroughly and efficiently.

This should not leave the impression, however, that he capitulated completely to his organizational duties and put aside his spiritual life. Rather, he remained a monk and continued to live in community, being the first to take the episcopal ideal of Augustine and Pomerius to the Holy See, the first monastic pope. Thus he still understood the church's main business as the salvation of souls. Indeed, his consciousness of that priority was intensified by his conviction that the world would end very soon.

Granted, then, that he continued to feel acutely the tension between his own desire for the contemplative life and the care for all the churches, which fell upon him daily, it is not surprising that he devoted much thought to how not only he but others as well should resolve that conflict and exercise authority in the church. An outgrowth of his thought on the subject is his conviction of the importance of preaching[52] and his understanding of what makes it important.[53] That understanding and acceptance were not arrived at immediately, however, or without a struggle. It is significant that when he was returned to the active life by being sent as *apocrisiarius* to Constantinople, the biblical figure with whom he most identified was long-suffering Job.[54] And it is also significant that in the first few months of his pontificate, he devoted himself to writing his treatise on pastoral care, his *Regula pastoralis*.

Gregory's eventual resolution of the conflict was more experiential than theoretical. He came to recognize that precisely what is needed by those under one's pastoral care is the fruit of one's contemplation of holy scripture. Thus, instead of seeing the active and contemplative lives as two different stages in spiritual development, he came to regard them as serving one another reciprocally. "The two lives are dynamically related, they foster and nourish each other in the individual person, as well as in the community."[55]

Gregory achieved this ideal on two levels. On the first, he conveyed the fruits of his own contemplation directly to the laity (the *coniugati*, the "married," as he called them)[56] in sermons he preached at the public liturgy. On the second, he preached about his understanding of how they all should carry out their joint responsibility to others with the duty of preaching.[57] Two very different kinds of sermons are involved.

Of his popular preaching there remain only the *Forty Gospel Homilies*.[58] These appear to have been preached early in his pontificate. Some are for Sundays spread through the Christian year, others for the feasts of martyrs and other saints, and still others are for ordinary weekdays. Some were probably preached in stational churches or martyria while others were delivered in the "Golden Basilica" of the Lateran, which served as Rome's cathedral at the time.[59] It would be hard to characterize these homilies better than Jeffrey Richards has: "simple, straightforward and accessible to ordinary people, a pastoral, allegorical, inspirational form of culture which laid great stress on the character, spirituality and endurance of the holy man."[60]

While no one was a more important theological influence on Gregory than Augustine, there are many differences between what they have to say. Most of them are functions of the differences between the worlds in which they lived.[61] In Augustine's North Africa, there were still many non-Christians and also many heterodox Christians. Accordingly, Augustine preached theological sermons not only because of his own disposition but also because of the needs of his hearers.

By the time of Gregory, however, Christian faith could be assumed to be what sociologists of knowledge refer to as "reality taken for granted." Thus the subject matter of Gregory's preaching was very different from that of Augustine's.

> Compared with Augustine, Gregory could take for granted the settled contours of his spiritual landscape. Christianity had come to give definitive shape to a "totalizing discourse." The boundaries of Gregory's intellectual and imaginative worlds were thus the horizons of the scriptures. How to be a Christian, how to live the fullest Christian life: this was Gregory's central preoccupation in all his preaching; and this was the question into which the anxieties of his

> age had shaped themselves. Naturally, it helped to give his exegesis a predominantly moral direction.[62]

Gregory's exegesis, however, was more complex in his "metapreaching" than it was in his popular preaching, and consideration of that needs to be deferred. Before moving on to his preaching to preachers, it is necessary to note one way in which his popular preaching was extraordinarily influential on all later preaching. As Dudden said, "Gregory was the first great preacher who attempted, in anything like a systematic fashion, to introduce non-scriptural illustrations into his instructions, to drive home a religious truth with the help of an apposite story."[63] (**See Vol. 2, pp. 133-40,** for a sermon with two of these illustrations.) These illustrations reflect Gregory's expectation that the world would soon end and thus have much in common with many stories told through the ages by preachers urging sinners to repent while there was still time.

There is a story of a man who did not begin his deathbed repentance in time and another of one who did. A beggar has a holy death, and a sinner who becomes a monk in repentance is forgiven. Angels surround a devout abbot at his death, and the funeral of a saintly nun is celebrated by the angels while she is dying. In a number of the stories, the death of a virtuous person is accompanied by the odor of sanctity. The flavor of these *exempla* may be sampled in the shortest of the lot:

> In the time of the Goths there was a married woman of good family, very religious, who used to come frequently to the church of these martyrs. On a certain day, when she had come to pray as her custom was . . . she saw two monks clothed as pilgrims. She believed them to be pilgrims, and ordered that they be given alms. Before the one who performed this service for her had approached to bestow the alms, they stood close to her and said: "You are helping us now. On the day of judgment we will seek you out, and do whatever we can for you." When they had said this, they were taken out of her sight. Frightened, she returned to her prayers, shedding more copious tears. After this she became more zealous in her prayers, as she was convinced of the promise.[64]

This, then, was the beginning of what has become an important ingredient of sermons.

Gregory became so fond of these anecdotes that he wrote a collection of them, setting it in a genre of philosophical writing that had been popular since Plato. These *Dialogues*[65] contain stories about miracles of the saints of Italy. Most of the stories told in the homilies are repeated in Book 4 of the *Dialogues*. Book 2 is the earliest available account of the life of the great monastic pioneer Benedict of Nursia. The *Dialogues* went on to become, in effect, a "cyclopedia of sermon illustrations" for the great revival of preaching by friars in the thirteenth and fourteenth centuries, offering as they did some of the first *exempla* to be widely incorporated into thematic sermons.[66]

Gregory's metapreaching, his "preaching to preachers about preaching," occurs in such works as his *Morals on the Book of Job* and his *Homilies on Ezekiel,* but is also presented in nonsermonic form in his *Regula pastoralis.*[67] It is well known that the third book of the *Regula,* which is almost twice as long as the other three books put together, consists of suggestions for constructing what later came to be called *ad status* sermons, sermons for persons in various stations in life.[68] In addition, the short fourth book deals with the temptations that come to a preacher after a sermon is delivered.

Preaching is also greatly emphasized in the first two books. The first has to do with "the difficulties of the pastoral office and the requirements it places on him who is called to it."[69] While it refers more generally to the *pastor* and speaks of "the pastoral office" *(magisterium pastoralis)* and "the government of souls" *(regimen animarum),* it nevertheless contrasts those who wish only to withdraw to contemplation with those who are "of service to the neighbor by preaching" (*Regula pastoralis* 1.5).

While the moral qualifications of *rectores* discussed in Book 2 can be seen to fit one with any sort of responsibility in the community, some of them, such as being discreet in silence and speech (chap. 4), exercising sternness toward the vices of those who do evil (chap. 6), not being too eager to please (chap. 8), and meditating on the Scriptures (chap. 11), seem particularly relevant to preachers. Hence it could be said that preaching is the main subject of the *Regula.* This is not surprising, since, as noted above, the importance of preaching is one of the most consistent themes in Gregory's writings.[70] It was one of the most consistent themes in his preaching to preachers.

In his metapreaching as well as his popular preaching, Gregory anticipates trends of medieval homiletics. For his metapreaching, that anticipation is in interpreting Scripture in several senses. While at least three senses had been mentioned as early as Origen, in practice most preachers had confined themselves to two, the historical and the allegorical. Gregory did not yet have the fourfold system that was to be so popular throughout the Middle Ages, but he was moving in that direction. This may be seen in the letter he wrote to Leander as the dedication of the *Moralia:*

> Be it known that there are some parts, which we go through in a historical exposition, some we trace out in allegory upon an investigation of the typical meaning, some we open in the lessons of moral teaching alone, allegorically conveyed, while there are some few which, with more particular care, we search out in all these ways together, exploring them in a threefold method. (Ep. iii)

This program is not carried out in a consistent manner. Indeed, Markus calls the *Moralia* a "scarcely penetrable jungle,"[71] and says that

> Little is to be gained by attempting to disentangle the oddly haphazard vocabulary; the moral sense sometimes appears as part of the historical, sometimes as part of the allegorical; his language is fluid. Gregory cared little for neatness of terminology, and was in any case apt to conflate his three senses of the scriptures with a dichotomy he thought more fundamental.[72]

This is merely to say that in his understanding of the multiple meanings of Scripture, Gregory is a transitional figure. Even so, the understanding of ministry and especially of preaching that he finds in his interpretation of Job is essentially the same as he states in his *Pastoral Care,* an understanding that has a great deal to be said for it.

Scholars enjoy debating whether Gregory is the last of the Fathers or the first great medieval theologian. In his preaching he was very important for what was to come. Few of the Fathers were quoted more often in, for example, the *Glossa ordinaria,* the great patristically annotated volume that was for all practical purposes the Bible of the Middle Ages. For him the work of the pastor in communicating the Bible's hope of salvation through preaching was the one necessary thing. In the allegorical interpretation of the *Morals,* the sons of Job stand for the apostles, the definitive work of whom is preaching (1.14.18), an interpretation that is developed consistently throughout the whole work. The reason preaching is so important is that it is the means by which pagans are converted, the faithful are instructed in the Christian life, heretics are reconciled, and the church reformed.

As Gregory says:

> The church is called "adult" when being wedded to the Word of God, filled with the Holy Spirit, by the office of preaching she is with young in the conception of children, with whom by exhorting she travails, whom by converting she brings forth.[73]

THE VENERABLE BEDE (CA. 673–735)

Britain had been part of the Roman Empire for about four centuries before it was abandoned in 410, and Roman Christians had taken their faith to Britain with them. While the tradition that Joseph of Arimathea brought the Holy Grail to Glastonbury shortly after the death of Christ is unreliable, it does appear that the gospel arrived in the island quite early. The first British martyr, Alban, seems to have died around 208. Writing in the third century, both Hippolytus and Origen refer to Christians in Britain, and British bishops were present at the Council of Arles in 314.

When the Romans withdrew, the British felt a need for protection of the sort the legions had provided and contracted with warriors from Germanic tribes—designated by Bede as the Angles, Saxons, and Jutes—to serve as mercenaries. The newcomers liked what they saw and decided not only to stay themselves but to bring their relatives as well. The process was long and drawn out, but by the end of the seventh century the English, as they could be called by then, had succeeded in confining the British to what is now Wales (where they became the Welsh) and occupied all of what is England today.[74]

While some of the British remained Christian, they apparently made no effort to share their faith with their conquerors. They did, however, share it with a number of other groups, other Celtic peoples in Wales, Brittany, Scotland, and Ireland. The missionary zeal of these Celtic Christians was shown in the fruit of their efforts in the lands they evangelized. This zeal was communicated to their mission territory, and produced there other missionaries who even spread the faith to the Anglo-Saxon (or English) conquerors of Britain.

All of this was taking place near the beginning of the seventh century, the very time that Roman missionaries sent by Gregory the Great were arriving in Kent. Thus while the English conquest of Britain was still going on, the invaders were being converted to Christianity by two groups of missionaries representing different traditions of their religion. The differences between the two groups were settled at the Synod of Whitby in 664, however, and after that there was one English church, embracing most of the country's people, in communion with the Catholic Church in the West under the bishop of Rome.

Evangelization often began with the conversion of a king and his nobles. The church then prospered intellectually and materially, especially in its monasteries. A case in point is the sister monasteries in which Bede spent his life, Wearmouth and Jarrow. They were founded by

Benedict Biscop, who had been a thane before becoming a monk. In his lifetime he made five trips to Rome, each time returning with things and people to enrich his monasteries: paintings, vestments, glaziers, and the archchanter of St. Peter's in Rome, who would teach his monks to conduct their worship in the Roman manner. Most important of all, however, were the books he brought back, the foundation of a library that was at the time one of the best in the world.[75]

And so it came about that in a monastery in the back of beyond, Christian learning was preserved. Indeed, a monk there became one of the last polymaths in history, one of the last people to know almost everything that was known at his time. He is the last of the preachers to be studied in this tracing of the survival of learned Latin rhetorical patristic preaching in the West after its acme in Augustine, and he by no means represents its nadir. The monk Bede has been known as "the Venerable" at least since the Council of Aachen in 836. This honorific did not mean that he was an archdeacon as it would in the English church today. Indeed, he held no office, not even in his monastery. Rather, in reference to him the term "venerable" has a root meaning of one worthy of respect, a sense in which he applied the designation to many others. Yet for him the term seemed so apt that history has treated it as part of his name.[76]

It is extraordinary that one whose name is so well known and for whom so many have a sense of affection should have left so little information about his life. Most of the biographical information that exists, however, comes from a short section at the end of his history:

> I was born on the lands of this monastery, and on reaching seven years of age, I was entrusted by my family first to the most reverend Abbot Benedict and later to Abbot Ceolfrid for my education. I have spent all the remainder of my life in this monastery and devoted myself entirely to the study of the Scriptures. And while I have observed the regular discipline and sung the choir offices daily in church, my chief delight has always been in study, teaching, and writing.
>
> I was ordained deacon at the age of nineteen, and priest at the age of thirty, receiving both of these orders at the hands of the most reverend Bishop John at the direction of abbot Ceolfrid. From the time of my receiving the priesthood until my fifty-ninth year, I have worked, both for my own benefit and that of my brethren, to compile short extracts from the works of the venerable Fathers on Holy Scripture and to comment on their meaning and interpretation.[77]

After that follows a list of his writings. Beyond this very little is known. A story recorded by someone else that must be about Bede is that of a "little lad" who was the only member of the community besides the abbot left at Jarrow after the outbreak of the plague in 686. The two of them, however, continued to sing the offices alone until new monks were recruited.[78] From his writings it is possible to discover that Bede did go to Lindisfarne once and to York and that he visited another monastery, but there the information ends. Otherwise, he appears to have settled into the monastic life to which his parents gave him as an oblate and happily spent all his years within the walls of his monastery.

Despite so little biographical data, it is possible, as Benedicta Ward has said, "to know Bede more intimately than any man of his time, whether in his relationship to Christ and his view of salvation or in his opinions on sex and his admiration for the fashion in beards." The reason this is so, as she pointed out, is that "it is through his writings that Bede is known in this face to face encounter."[79] Through all of them shines the personality of the author and, with his as with other favorite books, the reader would very much like to know the author personally and yet, at the same time, in a deeper sense knows her or him already.

The list of writings that follows the short autobiographical entry in the history is a long one indeed. While it is for his *History of the English Church and People* that he is best known, Bede did not consider it the most important of his writings. He understood his primary role to be that of an interpreter of Scripture. His list of works includes sixteen titles[80] on the Old Testament and eight on the New. These works usually take the form of commentaries and combine a summary of patristic interpretation with his own insights. They seem to be designed, on the one hand, to help monks in their meditation on the lections read at their offices throughout the day and, on the other, to furnish biblical insight to English clergy who were involved in the evangelization of their people.

Moreover, equipping clergy for their work seems the primary motivation of all his writing. "His pupils were monks who had a definite purpose in mind in studying at all and their learning is best understood as part of their work in the conversion of England rather than as essential to their monastic life."[81] His efforts fit into a program of education for ministry inaugurated by the great Greek archbishop of Canterbury, Theodore of Tarsus (668–90), and his African companion, Hadrian, who founded a school at their see city.[82]

Bede seems to have been charged with the responsibility of training novices at Jarrow, where their education extended from the basic three R's to Latin, which opened to them the wider world of Christian knowledge. He taught them about poetry both in Latin and in their own language, how to calculate the dates of feasts in the church year (involving some astronomy as well as mathematics), and about the world they lived in as understood by science at the time. He even encouraged translations into Anglo-Saxon for people who did not have the leisure to learn Latin. And, in order to be able to teach these subjects, he wrote textbooks on many of them.

All of this other study, however, was, as noted above, mere preparation for the study that would be useful in the evangelistic task. Such study, as indicated, was basically study of the Bible, but it included other things as well. Especially it included getting a vision of what the Christian life was to accomplish. This is to say that it involved learning about the holiness of the saints.

Included in the list of Bede's writings on the Bible are two books of *Homilies on the Gospels*. The first question prompted by the appearance of that title is: why would Bede have preached, since most monastic preaching was done by abbots and he was not an abbot?[83] As one of the priests of the community, Bede would have presided at Eucharist on occasion. He could thus have preached his homilies during one of his abbot's frequent absences from the monastery or when he was prevented from celebrating and preaching by some other reason. Since all the homilies are on the Gospel pericopae appointed for the eucharistic lectionary, that would have been a natural occasion for their being preached, but they could also have been preached at chapter or at the night office.[84]

There are fifty homilies, so the collection does not cover the entire church year. Rather, it clusters around the two great seasons of the nativity and resurrection, with a few homilies provided for some saints' days and other holy days. For the Christmas season there are: four for Advent, one for Christmas Eve, three for the different masses of Christmas Day, one each for the Feasts of St. John and the Holy Innocents, one for the octave day[85] of Christmas, one for the Feast of the Epiphany and five for the following Sundays, and one for the Purification (or Presentation, or Candlemass).

The cycle for the paschal mystery includes: seven homilies for Lent, four for Holy Week, one for the Vigil, one for Easter, five for Sundays after Easter, one for the Rogation Days, one for ascension and another for the following Sunday, one for Pentecost and one for its octave. Bede provided three homilies for the feasts of John the Baptist, one for the Roman martyrs James and John, one for Peter alone and another shared with Paul, and one for the founder of Bede's monastery, Benedict Biscop. There were also two homilies for the dedication of a church.

Precisely this selection raises the question of why these and not others. Part of the explanation may lie in the fact that Bede admired Gregory the

Great above all people, and only one of Bede's fifty homilies is on the same pericope as any of Gregory's forty. Thus he may have had a sense of supplementing the legacy of Gregory. It is certainly true that in general development the homilies of Bede are very similar to those of Gregory—although Bede does not imitate his model in the use of narrative illustrations. It is also obvious that Bede had read Augustine's *De doctrina christiana* and followed its precepts both in the interpretation of Scripture and in the use of rhetoric. While there is a simplicity to these homilies, they often achieve real eloquence. But Bede's homilies follow the story line of the pericope more closely than Augustine's and are perhaps even more integrated than Gregory's.

The outline of Bede's homilies is very simple. There is a short introduction, stating why his congregation should ponder the words of the Gospel passage that has just been read to them. Then the passage is examined, but Bede does not feel compelled to comment on every word or even every verse, because it is the pericope as a whole that he wishes to be understood. He explicitly teaches a fourfold interpretation, but seldom deals with more than the literal and perhaps one spiritual meaning. He uses allegorical interpretation regularly but with restraint, and he has the capacity to cite parallel passages from the entire canon without leaving a modern reader feeling that the meaning is forced.

The chief difference between his homilies and his commentaries is that the sermons do not cite nonbiblical authors, while the commentaries scrupulously note from which church father a particular insight comes. This does not mean, however, that the homilies are not indebted to previous interpreters; the lack of citation is rather a function of the difference of genre. In an oral communication for edification, bibliographical references are simply distracting.

Bede has been unfairly accused of having no original thoughts and of merely repeating what was said by his elders and presumably betters. Lawrence Martin, however, has shown how unjust that assessment is. In a detailed analysis of Bede's homily for the Feast of the Purification (2.18),[86] he shows that, while Bede's use of sources differs between the commentaries and homilies, in neither case is it simply a matter of parroting what others thought and said. In the commentaries, he uses the Fathers to strengthen the position he arrived at in his own study, while in the homilies, "Bede often draws on the fathers for motifs to enrich and ornament his own words, quite freely adapting his predecessors' work to suit his own homiletic themes and purposes."[87]

The third part of a homily by Bede is a short application of the teaching of the Gospel lection to the lives of his congregation. It is here that his preaching differs most markedly from that of his predecessors, because he had a different audience. He did not preach to a lay congregation as the bishops did, nor was he doing the sort of metapreaching—preaching to preachers—that Gregory did. Although most of the patristic preachers studied thus far were monks, no great series of monastic conferences has come down from them.[88] Bede thus is a precursor of the Middle Ages when a great deal of such preaching was done, much of which survives.

> Bede's main concern is with the spiritual meaning of the gospel stories, their meaning for the spiritual life of the monk. There is little exhortation about specific moral problems, as we find, for example, in the sermons of Caesarius of Arles. Bede does, however, refer to the specific details of the prayer life of the monastery, and he includes passages of direct address which speak to the concerns of his monastic audience.[89]

Bede's influence on the spiritual life of monks was not of the uninterrupted sort for which he would have hoped. Within a century of his death, England came to be harassed by Viking raids that were especially devastating to the coastal retreats and islands where many monasteries were located. Since *Norman* means "Northman," it could be argued that these disruptions did not end before the victory of William the Conqueror in 1066. By then, however, Bede was well known on the Continent, and most of his works have survived. He was honored in many ways, such as having much of his commentary incorporated into the *Glossa Ordinaria* and in such works of the friars as Thomas Aquinas's *Catena Aurea*. His writings are abundantly quoted in the Roman breviary. The judgment of the ages upon him is summed up in his having been declared a Doctor of the Church by Leo XIII in 1899.

This completes the path followed by the learned Latin rhetorical homily after Augustine. It represents only a fraction of the preaching done during the period that saw the conversion of Europe to Christianity, but its very literary character ensured its preservation, while the more abundant vernacular preaching can only be inferred from its results. While a minority tradition, this is by no means an ignoble one. Its practitioners saved from extinction a Christian cultural inheritance that would reemerge during the Middle Ages and at the Renaissance.

Those who preached at this time share much with their distinguished predecessors regarding Latin rhetorical culture. They also are signs of things to come in medieval preaching. Of the four men studied, the first, Leo the Great, has least in common with the others. He still preached in an elegant Latin that would set the style for the curia in later centuries. Caesarius, Gregory, and Bede were all well trained in rhetoric, but they knew their congregations were not, and they preached to them in words they could understand. The three in their various ways all showed great concern for encouraging others to preach. They also anticipated later preaching in several ways, especially in their elaboration of the multiple senses in which Scripture was to be understood and their emphasis on miracles. And all three were monks on the eve of a era in which Latin Christian culture, both classical and patristic, would remain alive only in the monasteries. The four, then, are key figures in the transition from the end of ancient Christianity to the rise of Western Christendom.

FOR FURTHER READING

Bede the Venerable: Homilies on the Gospels, 2 vols., trans. Lawrence T. Martin and David Hurst, pref. Benedicta Ward, intro. Lawrence T. Martin, Cistercian Studies Series 111. Kalamazoo, Mich.: Cistercian Publications, 1991.

Blair, Peter Hunter. *An Introduction to Anglo-Saxon England*. 2nd ed. Cambridge and New York: Cambridge University Press, 1977.

Brown, Peter Robert Lamont. *The Rise of Western Christendom: Triumph and Diversity A.D. 200–1000* (The Making of Europe). 2nd ed. Oxford and Cambridge, Mass.: Blackwell Publishers, 1996.

Gregory the Great: Forty Gospel Homilies. Translated by David Hurst. Cistercian Studies Series, no. 123. Kalamazoo, Mich.: Cistercian Publications, 1990.

Klingshirn, William E. *Caesarius of Arles: The Making of a Christian Community in Late Antique Gaul*. Cambridge and New York: Cambridge University Press, 1994.

St. Leo the Great: Sermons. Translated by Jane Patricia Freeland and Agnes Josephine Conway. FC. Washington, D.C.: Catholic University of America Press, 1995.

Straw, Carole. *Gregory the Great: Perfection in Imperfection*. Berkeley and Los Angeles: University of California Press, 1988.

Notes

1. See, for example, the definition of "Middle Ages" in *Merriam Webster's Collegiate Dictionary*, 10th edition.

2. Peter Robert Lamont Brown, *The Rise of Western Christendom: Triumph and*

Diversity A.D. 200–1000 (The Making of Europe), 2nd ed. (Oxford and Cambridge, Mass.: Blackwell Publishers, 1996), xi.

3. R. A. Markus, *The End of Ancient Christianity* (Cambridge and New York: Cambridge University Press, 1990).

4. Brown, *The Rise of Western Christendom.*

5. The term "Europe" came to be applied to the territory in the tenth century, although references to "Europeans" go back as early as the eighth century. J. M. Roberts, *History of the World* (New York: Oxford University Press, 1993), 312.

6. The term "barbarian" comes from a Greek word involving the nonsense syllables that foreigners' speech seemed to consist of.

7. Brown, *The Rise of Western Christendom,* 3-17.

8. This figure seems much too low to other scholars.

9. Brown, *The Rise of Western Christendom,* 17.

10. The very things that make up "civilization," as the term is understood in Thomas Cahill's popular book, *How the Irish Saved Civilization: The Untold Story of Ireland's Heroic Role from the Fall of Rome to the Rise of Medieval Europe* (New York: Nan A. Talese [Doubleday], 1995).

11. Even at that, Leo never alludes to pagan classical literature in any of his writings.

12. John Meyendorff, *Imperial Unity and Christian Divisions: The Church 450–680 AD,* The Church in History, vol. 2 (Crestwood, N.Y.: St. Vladimir's Seminary Press, 1989), 148.

13. Ibid., 148-58. As Meyendorff points out, however, it would be anachronistic to see in Leo's position an anticipation of the papal infallibility and universal ordinary jurisdiction promulgated by the First Vatican Council (1870).

14. *Latrocinium,* so designated by Leo.

15. While Eutychianism is a heresy, most of the Monophysites who did not accept the Council of Chalcedon and went into schism were not heretical and could have remained in communion but for some tragic mistakes on both sides of the controversy.

16. "First among equals."

17. Meyendorff, *Imperial Unity and Christian Divisions,* 156.

18. The excellent article by Francis X. Murphy, C.SS.R., "The Sermons of Pope Leo the Great: Content and Style," in *Preaching in the Patristic Age: Studies in Honor of Walter J. Burghardt, S.J.,* ed. David G. Hunter (New York: Paulist Press, 1989), 183-97, has more to say about content than style. Dom Jean Leclercq's introduction to the Sources chrétiennes edition of Leo's sermons is also more concerned with theology than homiletical method. See the introduction to *Léon le Grand: Sermons*, trans. and notes Dom René Dolle, 2nd ed., SC, no. 22 (Paris: Cerf, 1964). The introduction to *St. Leo the Great: Sermons*, trans. Jane Patricia Freeland, and Agnes Josephine Conway, FC (Washington, D.C.: Catholic University of America Press, 1995) is so restricted in its page allotment that it furnishes little guide to what follows.

19. Basil Studer, "Italian Writers Until Pope Leo the Great," in *The Golden Age of Latin Patristic Literature from the Council of Nicea to the Council of Chalcedon*, vol. 4 of *Patrology,* ed. Angelo di Berardino, intro. Johannes Quasten, trans. Placid Solari, 597.

20. The Ember Days were fast days observed in the church four times a year: the

Wednesday, Friday, and Saturday of the first week of Lent; the week following Whitsunday (Pentecost); and the first weeks after the middle of September and the middle of December. Their emphasis has varied over the centuries, and they have been optional observances since Vatican II. "Ember" is the English corruption of *Quattuor Tempora* (four seasons), as is the German *Quatember* and even the Japanese *tempura.*

21. Most of the Holy Week sermons were preached in two parts, one on Sunday and the other on Wednesday, the exception being three for Good Friday and two for Holy Saturday. One of the Good Friday sermons is paired with one of those for Holy Saturday. All the Holy Week sermons have the same theme, the passion, while the other sermon for the vigil on Holy Saturday is on the resurrection; there are no Easter sermons as such.

22. Hans Lietzmann says that Sermons 6 and 7 could not have lasted more than three minutes each. "Leo I, der Grosse," A. F. von Pauly and Georg Wissowa, *Real-Encyclopädie der classischen Altertumswissenschaft* (Stuttgart: J. B. Metzler, 1894–1963), Halband XXIV, cols. 1971-72. In translation these two sermons take less than a page each.

23. Station days were the eighty-seven or so days in the year for which the pope celebrated the liturgy at a designated church.

24. "*Le rhythme de ses phrases est accordé au ton de la liturgie, ses formules sont semblables à beaucoup de celles qu'a conservée le Missel romain qui, à travers les sacramentaires, s'est souvent inspiré de lui.*" Leclercq, intro. to *Léon le Grand,* 1:22-23.

25. *Dafür ist der Ausdruck knapp und treffend, von oft glänzender Prägnanz und sorgfältiger formaler Durchbildung, die eindringendes Studium wohl lohnen würde.* "Leo I, der Grosse," XXIV, 1972.

26. Leo's precise expression led John Henry Newman to conclude that he preached from a manuscript. *The Idea of a University*, ed., intro., and notes Martin J. Svaglic (Notre Dame: University of Notre Dame Press, 1982), 315.

27. Yngve Brilioth, *A Brief History of Preaching*, trans. Karl E. Mattson (Philadelphia: Fortress, 1965), 62. On the issue of Leo's influence on the collects, Josef Jungmann says, "Many Sunday orations [prayers, that is, the Sunday collects] and several prefaces [the seasonal introductions to the *Sanctus*] which we still recite today contain terms and phrases strikingly in accord with Leo the Great's phraseology. Even the rhythm of the language is the same. Thus the assumption that he is the author of many of the prayers in the Leonine Sacramentary is well founded." Josef A. Jungmann, *The Early Liturgy to the Time of Gregory the Great*, trans. Francis A. Brunner, Liturgical Studies, vol. 6 (Notre Dame: University of Notre Dame Press, 1959), 236.

28. A random check of ten pages revealed forty-four quotations or allusions.

29. Freeland and Conway, *St. Leo the Great: Sermons,* 13.

30. Ibid., 127.

31. The original of this sentence is an excellent example of the way Leo used the Latin language: "*Totum igitur corpus implet tota divinitatis; et sicut nihil deest illius majestatis, cujus habitatione repletur habitaculum, sic nihil deest corporis, quod non suo habitatore sit plenum.*"

32. Freeland and Conway, *St. Leo the Great: Sermons,* 131.

33. Located on an island off what today is the coast of Cannes.

34. William E. Klingshirn, *Caesarius of Arles: The Making of a Christian Community in Late Antique Gaul* (Cambridge; New York: Cambridge University Press, 1994), 31.

35. This *Vita* was written by friends and appeared just a few years after his death (*Caesarius of Arles: Life, Testament, Letters*, trans. with notes and intro. William E. Klingshirn, Translated Texts for Historians, vol. 19 [Liverpool: Liverpool University Press, 1994]). See also "Introduction," in *St. Caesarius of Arles: Sermons*, trans. Mary Magdeleine Mueller, , FC, vols. 31, 47, 66 (Vol. 1, New York: Fathers of the Church, Inc.; Vols. 2 and 3, Washington, D.C.: Catholic University of America Press, 1956–73), 1:v-xxvii; and Klingshirn, *Caesarius of Arles*. Another important volume synthesizing over twenty-five years of intensive study of medieval preaching by a number of scholars is *The Sermon,* directed by Beverly Mayne Kienzle, *Typologie des sources du moyen âge occidental,* fasc. 81-83 (Turnhout, Belgium: Brepols, 2000). The chapter covering the period of this and the next chapter is Thomas N. Hall, "The Early Medieval Sermon," 203-69. Hall's point of view is similar to the one I've taken here.

36. Klingshirn, *Caesarius of Arles,* 19.

37. Although admittedly many of the monks came from aristocratic families.

38. The 238 sermons in G. Morin's standard edition, *Sancti Caesarii episcopi arelatensis Opera omnia nunc primum in unum collecta,* 2 vols. (Maretoli, 1937–42), plus an additional sermon published by Anna Maria Giorgetti Vichi in *Academie e biblioteche d'Italia* XXI (1953), 335-42, are included in Mueller's translation of *St. Caesarius of Arles: Sermons*. Klingshirn, however, says that more than 250 of his sermons have survived. Introduction to *Caesarius: Life, Testament, Letters,* xiv. The others may be found in the bibliography to his *Caesarius of Arles,* with their editors listed on p. 288 and the sermons listed in the Secondary Sources section under the names of their editors.

39. Sermon 1.12-15, in *Sermons,* 1:6-16. This sermon, which is four or five times as long as any of Caesarius's others, concerns the duties of bishops and focuses especially on seeing that preaching occurs. It may not have ever been delivered orally; it could have been passed around as a circular letter instead. At the Council of Vaison in 529, his suffragan bishops gave permission for priests to preach and deacons to read patristic sermons. Klingshirn, *Caesarius of Arles,* 230.

40. In his edition, Morin used typography to indicate the degree of Caesarian authorship, using full-size type for sermons that were almost entirely the work of the bishop of Arles, smaller type for those to which he had contributed only an introduction or conclusion, and regular type set off by a dagger (†) for those in which there were extensive borrowings, but not such as to obscure their author/editor's style and thought. Mueller's translation, however, uses an asterisk (*) to indicate both the second and third categories. By the time she got to her third volume she realized that something more was needed, so for each of the sermons in that volume she supplied a footnote indicating Morin's conclusions about it and gave similar notes for the sermons in the first two volumes in an appendix. This makes it possible to know what non-Caesarian material is used in sermons attributed to the bishop, but the only indication that a sermon attributed to someone else is really by Caesarius is that it has a

title like "St. Augustine's Sermon on Charity" while nevertheless appearing among the collected sermons of Caesarius with none of Morin's typographical indications of another provenance.

41. This paragraph is based on a long passage from Morin, "The Homilies of St. Caesarius of Arles," in *Orate Fratres* XIV (1939–40), 481-86, quoted in Mueller, *St. Caesarius of Arles: Sermons,* 1:21-23. On "The Legacy of Caesarius," see Klingshirn, *Caesarius of Arles,* 273-86.

42. The first volume of Mueller's translation comprises the first category, the second volume comprises the second, and the third volume the last three.

43. Mueller, *St. Caesarius of Arles,* Sermon 86.1. Cf. Klingshirn, *Caesarius of Arles,* 81-82.

44. Klingshirn, *Caesarius of Arles,* 12-14.

45. Klingshirn, *Caesarius of Arles: The Making of a Christian Community in Late Antique Gaul,* 150. This sentence begins a paragraph in which Klingshirn gives an excellent summary of the rhetorical techniques Caesarius used to make his preaching effective. This paragraph comes at the end of a very fine discussion of his preaching overall, 146-53.

46. Mueller, *St. Caesarius of Arles: Sermons,* 1:xx, citing a study by Morin.

47. For the general historical background, see John Julius Norwich, *A Short History of Byzantium* (New York: Knopf, 1997), 57-97. For the implications of the political history for the church, see Meyendorff, *Imperial Unity and Christian Divisions,* 207-332, especially 293-332.

48. The most helpful secondary source for this section has been R. A. Markus, *Gregory the Great and His World* (Cambridge; New York: Cambridge University Press, 1997). The classic biography is still F. Homes Dudden, *Gregory the Great: His Place in History and Thought,* 2 vols. (London and New York: Longmans, Green & Co., 1905). Other works will be cited in reference to particular points.

49. Translated as *Morals on the Book of Job by S. Gregory the Great, the First Pope of that Name, Translated with Notes and Indices,* 3 vols. (Oxford: John Henry Parker; London: J. G. F. and J. Rivington, 1844–50).

50. While there he even refuted the heresy of the ecumenical patriarch Eutychius, who had denied the resurrection of the body.

51. Erich Caspar, *Geschichte des Papsttums von den Antängen bis zu Höhe der weltherrschaft* (Tübingen: JCB Mohr, 1930–33), 2 vols. 1:338. Quoted in Markus, *Gregory the Great and His World,* 122 n51.

52. On this issue, see O. C. Edwards Jr., "Preaching in the Thought of Gregory the Great," *Homiletic* XVIII (1993), 5-8.

53. Gregory's spirituality is excellently presented in Carole Straw, *Gregory the Great: Perfection in Imperfection* (Berkeley and Los Angeles: University of California Press, 1988).

54. This should not be pressed too far, because in the letter to Leander of Seville by which he begins the *Morals,* Gregory sees physical suffering to be the main thing he has in common with Job.

55. Markus, *Gregory the Great and His World,* 24. Cf. Gregory's statement in *Morals on the Book of Job,* 2:ii.11.

56. Gregory recognizes three categories of members within the Christian community, the married laity *(coniugati)*, those under religious vows *(continentes)*, and the *ordo praedicatorum*. This order of preachers includes all those who have the *officium praedicationis*. These groups, however, are not mutually exclusive.

57. Jean Batany has distinguished between Gregory's works of *exégèse parénétique (Homilies on the Gospels)* and *<<métaparénétiques>> qui prêchent aux prêcheurs* (*Morals, Regula pastoralis,* and *Homilies on Ezekiel*). *"Le vocabulaire des fonctions sociales et ecclésiastiques chez Grégoire le Grand,"* in *Grégoire le Grand: Chantilly, Centre culturel Les Fontaines, 15-19 septembre 1982:* Actes / publiés par Jacques Fontaine, Robert Gillet, and Stan Pellistrandi, Colloques Internationaux du Centre nationale de la recherche scientifique (Paris: Éditions du Centre national de la recherche scientifique, 1986), 171.

58. *Forty Gospel Homilies,* trans. David Hurst, Cistercian Studies Series, no. 123 (Kalamazoo, Mich.: Cistercian Publications, 1990). The Latin text is in PL, LXXVI.

59. Gregory's is one of the few episcopal thrones or *cathedrae* surviving from the early church. Its present location is a chapel on the south side of the sanctuary of San Gregorio Magno church in Rome (built on the grounds of his family estate). It is the earliest piece of church furniture from which any of the sermons discussed in this book were delivered. A picture of it may be seen in Jeffrey Richards, *Consul of God: The Life and Times of Gregory the Great* (London and Boston: Routledge & Kegan Paul, 1980), plate 4; or F. van der Meer and Christine Mohrmann, *Atlas of the Early Christian World,* trans. and ed. Mary F. Hedlund and H. H. Rowley (London: Nelson, 1958), 136.

60. *Consul of God,* 261. Richards was talking about not only the homilies but Gregory's *Dialogues* as well, which, he said, "epitomize the new folk-preaching that was so influential in the Middle Ages and represent the new form of learning that Gregory and the Gregorians stood for" (ibid.). While there is truth to his statement, it is now being recognized that Gregory's own education was surprisingly good for the time. Compare, for example, Markus, *Gregory the Great and His World,* 34.

61. Markus, *Gregory the Great and His World,* 40-41. Markus was so impressed by those differences when he originally set out to write his study of Gregory, he realized that before doing so he would first have to account for them. This resulted in his writing *The End of Ancient Christianity* (see p. xi of this work).

62. Markus, *Gregory the Great and His World,* 41.

63. Dudden, *Gregory the Great,* 1:255. This statement concludes a discussion of how Gregory's preaching practice differed from that of those who preceded him and of the influence of Gregory's example on later homiletics.

64. Homily 32 in both Migne's edition and Hurst's translation. The order of the first twenty homilies in the manuscripts varies, so Hurst arranged these twenty in the sequence of the liturgical year rather than following the order in which they appear in Migne, but kept Migne's order for the last twenty. *Exempla* may be found in the following homilies (Migne's number first followed by Hurst's in parenthesis where it differs): 12 (10), 15 (12), 19 (11), 32, 34, 35, 36, 37, 38 (in which there are two, one of which is the same as that in 19 [11]), 39, and 40.

65. *Life and Miracles of St. Benedict: Book Two of the Dialogues,* trans. Odo J. Zimmermann, FC, no. 39 (Washington, D.C.: Fathers of the Church, Inc., 1959).

66. See below, 217-32.

67. *Pastoral Care,* trans. and annotated Henry Davis, ACW, no. 11 (Westminster, Md.: Newman Press, 1950).

68. This list of opposed pairs of types of person puts flesh on a skeletal outline in *Morals* XXX:iii, which in turn is developed from a list by Gregory Nazianzen, *Orat.* 2, 16-34. See Batany, "Le vocabulaire des fonctions sociales et ecclésiastiques chez Grégoire le Grand," 173.

69. Davis, *Pastoral Care,* 4.

70. Inflected forms of *praedicare, praedicator,* and *praedicatio,* for instance, appear over thirty-three hundred times, according to the index of *Thesaurus Sancti Gregorii Magni,* curante CETEDOC, Universitatis Catholica Lovaniensis Lovani Novi, Corpus Christianorum Thesaurus Patrum Latinorum (Turnhout, Belgium: Brepols, 1986). Or, to resort to an older guide, the entries related to preaching in the index of subjects and opinions in PL run to almost twelve columns, which is to say, four folio pages of references.

71. Markus, *Gregory the Great,* 16.

72. Ibid., 46-47. This quotation is from an excellent chapter on the importance of the Bible to Gregory and his method of interpreting it, 34-50.

73. *Morals on the Book of Job,* 2:409. Citations in Gregory's works supporting the statements made in this paragraph can be found conveniently in Claude Dagens, *Saint Grégoire le Grand: Culture et expérience chrétiennes* (Paris: Études augustiniennes, 1977), 312-44, by following paragraph titles.

74. For a description of this process see Peter Hunter Blair, *An Introduction to Anglo-Saxon England,* 2nd ed. (Cambridge; New York: Cambridge University Press, 1977), 1-54.

75. Bede wrote of Benedict Biscop not only in his history, but more extensively in his *Lives of the Abbots of Wearmouth and Jarrow,* 1-7 (translated in *The Age of Bede,* ed. with intro. D. H. Farmer, trans. J. F. Webb [Harmondsworth, Middlesex, England; New York: Penguin Books, 1965; reprint, with a new introduction, 1983; reprint, 1988], 185-91), and in a sermon for his feast day (Homily 1:13 in *Homilies on the Gospels,* 2 vols., trans. Lawrence T. Martin and David Hurst, with preface by Benedicta Ward, and introduction by Lawrence T. Martin [Kalamazoo, Mich.: Cistercian Publications, 1991], 1:125-33).

76. John Marsden, *The Illustrated Bede,* rev. ed., with translation by John Gregory, photography by Geoff Green (Edinburgh: Floris Books, 1996), 202. Marsden also reports the more charming if less likely explanation of the term's application to Bede, that it was supplied by the monastic mason carving his epitaph when his bones were moved to Durham cathedral. The stone carver wished to use the rhyme "*Hic sunt in fossa/ Baedae... ossa*" and the blank was miraculously filled during his absence with *venerabalis,* which fit his meter perfectly.

77. Bede, *A History of the English Church and People,* trans. with intro. Leo Sherley-Price (Baltimore: Penguin, 1955), 5:24.

78. The story appears in an anonymous life of Ceolfrid translated by D. S. Boutflower and is quoted in Benedicta Ward, *The Venerable Bede,* Outstanding Christian Thinkers Series (London: Geoffrey Chapman, 1990), 4.

79. Ibid., 2.

80. "Titles" is used to refer to these works because, on the one hand, some cover only a section of one biblical book while others treat a number of canonical writings, and, on the other, the length of these works varies, and Bede's list often gives the number of books into which each title is divided.

81. Ward, *The Venerable Bede,* 2.

82. It is due to their influence that Bede knew Greek better than the other preachers studied in this chapter and, indeed, better than Augustine.

83. Monastic preaching as such is treated in part 2, chapter 8, below.

84. Martin seems to favor the idea that the homilies were not composed for delivery but for being read, for example, as *lectio divina.* While that is possible, the reasons advanced for questioning delivery are a good bit short of persuasive.

85. One week later than the feast.

86. The fifty homilies are divided equally between the two volumes and thus are cited by volume number (1 or 2) followed by homily number (1-25 for each volume, although the break between the volumes is arbitrarily in the middle of sermons for Lent).

87. Martin and Hurst, *Bede the Venerable,* 1:xxii. In his analysis Martin showed the difference between what Bede said and what each of the fathers on whom he had drawn had written. In his translation of the homilies, footnotes indicate all the resonances between Bede's work and that of earlier preachers and commentators so that the reader can look up the citations and perform the sort of comparison Martin made in his analysis of 2°:18.

Ward distinguishes between the format of the homilies and that of the commentaries in regard to their purpose: "The special mark of the homilies is the direct application of biblical passages to a specific audience; whereas the commentaries gave other preachers the material for sermons, here Bede himself made the application" (Ward, *The Venerable Bede,* 65).

88. With the exceptions mentioned above of Gregory's *Moralia* and *Homilies on Ezekiel,* which are treated here as metapreaching rather than monastic conferences.

89. Martin and Hurst, *Bede the Venerable,* 1:xi.

CHAPTER 7

THE EARLY MEDIEVAL PERIOD

MISSIONARY PRELUDE

Periodization in historiography is always somewhat arbitrary. Life is a continuum and it is only in retrospect that points in the flow are labeled as "starts" and "stops," and even these apply only to severely restricted sets of phenomena within the total activity of that moment. Observers correlate beginnings and ends that are relatively synchronistic and seem to them to be interdependent and call these by titles such as "era" and "period," but the patterns discerned are at least as much a function of the organizing intelligence of the observer as they are intrinsic to the events observed. As a result, individual interpreters can and do consider different patterns of synchronicity to be significant. For example, while historians generally concur that there was an "age" that can appropriately be called "middle," they disagree by numbers of centuries about when that age began.

For the purposes of this history of preaching, the shift to the Middle Ages seems to have occurred when the language of preaching in the West shifted from Latin to vernacular tongues. The previous chapter traced the survival of learned Latin preaching through the period in which it had become the exception. This one will recount a time that overlaps that one to some extent, the time when vernacular preaching became the norm.

The easiest point from which to trace this is the evangelization of northern Europe by missionaries from Britain. A contemporary of Bede, Willibrord (658–739) carried the gospel to the Frisians in what is now Holland and Belgium, and Boniface (680–754) became the apostle of Germany. The next stage of missionary expansion would owe more to armies than to monks as Charlemagne began to make conversion one of the terms of peace with the peoples he conquered. The so-called Dark Ages were a time when many new peoples were being led to the Light, were being included in the Christian faith.

Yet, while one cannot doubt that all this missionary activity involved a good deal of preaching, unfortunately no written trace of it survives. Migne contains fifteen sermons attributed to Boniface (PL 89, 843-72). The first fourteen of these seem to be catechetical instruction of the sort called for by Carolingian reforms to be considered below. The last, which seems to have been written earlier, deals catechetically with what is renounced and what is promised in baptism. There is also a pastoral manual written to serve as a model for preachers that has been attributed to St. Pirmin, the founder of the monastery at Reichenau ca. 724, but this attribution seems to derive from the desire of a copyist to have transcribed some work of this worthy rather than from any direct connection with him. Thus missionary sermons prior to the time of Charlemagne do not appear to have survived.[1]

HOMILIARIES

The lack of surviving missionary sermons from the period before Charlemagne means that the study of medieval preaching in the vernacular must begin somewhere else. Before that can be considered, however, it is necessary to look at the way Latin sermons were given an afterglow in collections called homiliaries.[2] These collections come from a time when preachers were experiencing a loss of nerve. With the demise of Latin culture, clergy no longer considered themselves or their contemporaries to be competent to interpret the Scriptures. Instead, they ransacked the sermons of the Fathers for words through which their own generation could be guided safely into the harbor of truth. It is these gleanings that scholars have labeled "homiliaries." More precisely, homiliaries are collections of homilies arranged to follow the liturgical lectionary. The category does not include all collections of patristic sermons made during the Middle Ages; anthologies of sermons by the same author, for instance, or those of homilies on the same topic would not be homiliaries. The collection of sermons by different church fathers must be arranged according to the liturgical calendar.

This is not to say, however, that the only or major purpose of such collections was to provide clergy with sermons to deliver at the liturgy in place of those of their own composition. As we shall see, they were used for a variety of purposes that ranged from being read aloud at the Night Office or during meals in monasteries, to being read privately for personal edification, to being studied by clergy who were composing their own sermons.

One may question the inclusion of such material in a history of preaching on the grounds that activities other than proclamation at the liturgical assembly are being contemplated. Yet these homiliaries constitute the most abundant homiletical remains from the early Middle Ages, when almost no new sermons were being written. Since, then, they are what we have, since their contents originated in proclamation, and since these texts were very influential on later preaching, they must be discussed.

The compilation of homiliaries seems to have begun in Africa with such works as the mid-fifth-century homilies that Victor of Cartenna composed for the edification of his brothers and the eighty sermons from the fifth or sixth century incorrectly ascribed to Fulgentius. From Africa such collections were taken by exiles into Europe where they had their principle diffusion from Naples and Arles. Indeed, as I noted in the previous chapter, the sermons of Caesarius of Arles had much in common with those in a homiliary, often being largely reworkings of sermons by the Fathers. By this time, although the bishop was still regarded as the normative preacher and teacher of the flock, there were places where bishops were not numerous enough to be the head of the congregation in every town and village, and in such places presbyters[3] could preach and deacons could at least read sermons of the Fathers.[4] And Caesarius's own collection of sermons demonstrates the value of having a supply of patristic sermons on hand for anyone responsible for composing sermons.

The usefulness of such collections as homiliaries for monasteries is made apparent in the *Rule of St. Benedict* where it discusses how many psalms and lessons are to be read at the Night Office (chap. ix).[5] There it is stated that

> the books to be read at the Night Office shall be those of divine authorship, of both the Old and New Testament, and also the explanations of

them which have been made by well known and orthodox Catholic Fathers.[6]

Monasteries also drew upon homiliaries for reading during the silence at meals.[7]

From Benedict's reference to the texts to be read as *expositiones* it is clear they were not to function so much homiletically as exegetically; they were to serve in an auxiliary role to *lectio divina,* the meditative study of scripture that was such a basic part of the monastic discipline. Here the use of homiliaries moves in the direction of private devotion, and prefaces to some of the collections make it clear that those responsible for compiling them expected them to be used devotionally as well as exegetically.

Many homiliaries have been preserved. The more important ones are identified briefly by Barré and are discussed at length by Grégoire, being designated either by the name of their collector or by the provenance or locality of the manuscripts in which they have been preserved. These include St. Peter of Rome, Verona, Fleury-sur-Loire, Wolfenbuettel 4096, Vatican lat. 3828, Vienna 1616, Toledo, Agimond, Alan of Farfa, Paul the Deacon, Alcuin, and Ottobeuren. One of the most significant of these, that of Paul the Deacon, will furnish an example of what such collections were like.[8] His was drawn up at the request of Charlemagne because the text of other homiliaries used by monks for the Night Office was so corrupt as to be unintelligible.

Paul's efforts were so successful that his collection continued to be used for a thousand years. It consists of 244 sermons and homilies for every Sunday and feast day in the entire liturgical year, with several provided for occasions when more preaching was expected. He includes fifty-seven sermons or homilies attributed to Bede, fifty to Maximus, thirty-five to Leo the Great, thirty-two to Gregory the Great, nineteen to Chrysostom, eighteen to Augustine, eight to Jerome, six to Origen, five to Ambrose, four to Fulgentius, two to Isidore of Seville, and one each to Severianus and Eusebius of Caesarea. Cyril Smetana considers Paul to have been very discriminating for his time in being able to recognize which sermons are correctly attributed and which are not.[9] One can see that this collection of one or more homilies for each of the Gospel pericopes for the liturgical year, taken from respected Fathers and presented with accurate texts, would have proved very popular not only for readings at the Night Office but for a number of other uses as well. It is no wonder that it was copied as often as it was over so long a period.

Scholars make a distinction between patristic homiliaries, which were basically intended for liturgical use, and Carolingian ones assembled for private reading. These latter were not comprised of complete sermons but consisted instead of quotations from patristic commentaries. This personal usage meant that these homiliaries could be expanded very naturally to include lectionary epistles along with Gospels. Among the more important Carolingian types are the Mondsee homiliary, two composed by Hrabanus Maurus, the homiliary of Chartres, and those of Haymo and Heric of Auxerre.[10] By referring, however, to Paul the Deacon, Carolingian homiliaries, and Hrabanus Maurus, this discussion has already reached a point where it is necessary to take stock of the reforms in the church in general and in preaching in particular that are associated with the reign of Charlemagne.

THE CAROLINGIAN REFORM

There is no more romantic figure in history than Charlemagne, yet surviving documents do not make it possible to learn what he was really like as a person.[11] It is possible to see, however, that during his reign the territory of the Franks was doubled, that he was crowned by the pope as the Roman emperor, and that he built his capital at Aachen and tried to administer his empire from there. He associated his program closely with that of the church and made great use of clergy in his administration, from Alcuin, Theodulf, and Paul the Deacon, who were among his closest advisors, to the bishops he had appointed as ecclesiastical heads of the territories (whereas counts served as civil ones), down to the clerics who were also paired with laymen as his *missi dominici*, "the lord's emissaries." His armies evangelized the lands through which they moved, making conversion one of the conditions of peace. His *Admonitio generalis* tried to set standards for Christian education and behavior for all his territory and many of his captularies deal with programs to implement those standards. (**See Vol. 2, pp. 141-43,** for an example.) At the center of his reforms was a program for educating the clergy, providing them with the skills and tools they needed to do their job of conducting the church's worship and educating their people in Christian faith and morals.

Although it is possible to speak of a Carolingian renaissance, one must be very careful about what the expression means.

> This was no New Athens finer than the Old: it was intellectual reform and textual criticism as the indispensable preliminary to the reform of the clergy and to the performance of the *Opus Dei*.[12]

And, it should be noted, at the same time that Charlemagne was making it possible for the church to be the church, he was also supplying himself with enough literate people to make the administration of his empire possible.

An emphasis on preaching was a necessary part of the Carolingian reform.[13] Preaching was expected to furnish basic catechesis in the Christian faith for Saxons and even Franks who had but recently been converted from paganism and who had only the most rudimentary knowledge of what it means to be a Christian. Preaching could be included with the learning and good letters that J. M. Wallace-Hadrill says were no mere hobbies of the Carolingians and their friends. "They were conditions of survival."[14] Indeed, one of the things that makes learning and good letters necessary is that they are preconditions of the preaching.

"Charlemagne and his clergy legislated for the propagation of the Christian faith, and promoted the sermon to be one of the principal vehicles for the instruction of the people."[15] In his *Admonitio generalis* of 789 Charlemagne instructed his bishops that they should see that the presbyters whom they sent to parishes should preach rightly and virtuously.[16] The content of this preaching is also prescribed. As Rosamond McKitterick summarizes it, it should be:

> the "Triune God, omnipotent and sempiternal," of his Son Jesus Christ, who "was made man and came to judge men according to their respective merits," and of the resurrection of the dead and the eternal rewards to be received.[17]

The *Admonitio* also specified the sins against which the people were to be warned: fornication, uncleanness, lust, witchcraft *(veneficia)*, enmities, controversies, jealousies, animosities, wraths, quarrels, dissensions, heresies, sects, envies, grudges, murder, drunkenness, revelries, and similar things. The opposing virtues to be encouraged were also listed. What it all boils down to is that the people were to be thoroughly instructed in Christian faith and morals.

Sermons were expected at Mass on all Sundays and holy days.[18] The Council of Arles in 813 made it clear that this was not to be done only in cathedrals *(civitatibus)* but in parish churches *(paroechiis)* as well.[19] This expectation is expressed in the communications of such bishops as Gerbald of Liège, his successor Waltcaud, Riculf, Hincmar of Reims, and the author of "All glory, laud, and honor," Theodulph of Orléans. Council attendees also expected their clergy to have such homiletical aids as Gregory the Great's *Forty Homilies on the Gospels* and a homiliary containing sermons for all Sundays and holy days.

The Reform Councils of 813 are also quite insistent that this preaching occur in the language of the people.[20] By the Carolingian period Latin seems to have disappeared as a spoken language in Frankish territory and it was only the renaissance of learning Charlemagne encouraged that made it possible for his clerics to use it; any understanding of it by the laity would have been unlikely.[21] The sort of accommodation made in the sermons' language was also necessary in their content. One of the purposes of the preaching the Carolingian reform urged was to make it possible for laypeople to understand the creeds, but that had to be done a step at a time. McKitterick has compared surviving vernacular sermons with both the complex exposition in Heiric of Auxerre's homily for Trinity Sunday and the use of homiliaries made by Aelfric. She concludes that

> the subject matter of each sermon was simplified and reduced to the most directly relevant essentials, not because the language could not cope, but because the priests felt that they would be more readily comprehensible to an illiterate audience unused to, and possibly not vitally interested in, the deeper profundities of Christian doctrine.[22]

Even though there have been intermittent centuries in which preachers could expect their congregations to follow the most intricate theological arguments, the situation in the time of Charlemagne does not seem greatly different from that of today; in both ages the basics in Christian doctrine could not be assumed to be a part of the common culture of the people.

HRABANUS MAURUS

For insight into what the preaching of the Carolingian reform was actually like it is helpful to turn to one of those most deeply involved in encouraging it, Hrabanus Maurus (ca. 776–856). Hrabanus, a pupil of Alcuin at Tours, was a member of the second generation of reformers. He went on to become abbot of Fulda and then archbishop of Mainz where his activities as an encourager of the reform won for him the title of *praeceptor Germaniae*.[23] A very prolific author for the time, Hrabanus wrote books on most of the theological disciplines; this work is not original, but is instead mostly a retelling of patristic lore. He is an excellent figure in whom to study the reform as it related to preaching because he not only compiled two homiliaries but also provided in his *De clericorum institutione* what is in effect the first in a long line of medieval textbooks on preaching.

De clericorum institutione is virtually a curriculum in pastoral theology by itself. The first book deals with major and minor orders of ministry, their vestments, and the two "dominical" sacraments, with a section on the catechumenate incorporated into the discussion of Christian initiation. The second is largely liturgical, and deals with the full round of daily offices; confession, litanies, fasts, penance, and reconciliation; the feasts and seasons of the church year; and church music and the lectionary. The final book concerns what those in holy orders ought to know, but concentrates on the two closely related topics of biblical interpretation and preaching.[24] This first medieval preaching manual would be more exciting if there were anything new in it, but as Joseph M. Miller has pointed out,

> none of the material is original; he merely takes large chunks of Augustine's *De doctrina christiana,* IV, and reproduces them almost verbatim, sometimes rearranging sections, but never altering the text. . . . One who wishes to read [Hrabanus], then, will do well to return to Augustine.[25]

Hrabanus's two homiliaries were compiled forty years apart, the first begun in 814 when he was master of the monastery school of Fulda and the second in 854 when he was archbishop of Mainz.[26] The collections also are very different: the first was dedicated to Haistulf, a predecessor in Mainz, and was intended to be preached by parish clergy to their congregations[27] while the second was dedicated to the Emperor Lothar and was verse-by-verse catenae of patristic exegesis of the epistles and Gospels for every day of the church year assembled for the devotional reading of the Emperor—although Lothar said that clergy could profitably preach these sermons to their people. This is to say that, according to the distinction made above, the first is a "patristic" and the second a "Carolingian" homiliary.

Hrabanus is very explicit about the purposes of the seventy sermons in the first collection:

> I have composed a book of sermons to be preached to the people, on all subjects which I considered necessary for them. That is, firstly, in what manner they ought to observe the principal festivals which occur in the course of the year. . . . After that, we have written discourses for them concerning the various kinds of virtue. . . . And after this we

> have added another series of discourses on the various seductions of errors and vices. . . .[28]

(**See Vol. 2, pp. 143-44** for a specimen of his preaching.) Hrabanus did not assemble these sermons into a book but sent them to the archbishop as they were written. For that reason, they have not often been copied as a unit and there is only one manuscript that has most of the collection, which is printed in Migne.[29] These sermons borrow heavily from those of Caesarius of Arles, Augustine, Gregory the Great, Bede, Maximus of Turin, and the *Vitae Sanctorum*.

McKitterick has summarized the technique of the sermons for feasts by saying that

> Hrabanus' method . . . was to divide his instruction into two parts. First there was a statement and exposition of the Gospel for the day, followed by an exhortation on whatever subject the pericope or event had suggested.[30]

This description is accurate if one recognizes that the exposition of the Gospel did not look anything like verse-by-verse exegesis; that was much more characteristic of the homilies in the collection made for the Emperor.

Since the first half of the sermons in the first collection ended in exhortations and since the others were about virtues and vices, one may deduce what is indeed true, that these sermons were aimed at encouraging Christian living among masses recently converted from paganism. The main inducement for doing so is eschatological: that they may escape hell and enjoy heaven.[31] Thus the homilies of Hrabanus meet the stipulations set forth by the Synod of Tours in 813:

> It is our unanimous opinion that each bishop should have homilies containing needful admonitions by which his subjects may be taught, that is, concerning the catholic faith, in order that they may be able to embrace it, concerning the perpetual retribution of the good and the eternal damnation of the evil, concerning the coming general resurrection and last judgment and by what works one may merit eternal life and by what works be excluded from it. And that each should be diligent to translate clearly the same homilies into the rustic Romance language or German, in which all may the more easily be able to understand the things that are said.[32]

Hrabanus sent his homiliary for Lothar in three sections: from Christmas through Lent, from the Easter vigil to the fifth Sunday after

Pentecost, and the rest of the year. A single manuscript of the first part survives, the second is printed in PL[33], and the third section may be hidden in the manuscript in which the first section appears.[34] Its technique of verse-by-verse exegesis has already been mentioned. Since, however, it was intended for private devotional reading rather than delivery to congregations, it need not be considered here.

ANGLO-SAXON CATECHETICAL PREACHING

A major goal of promoting preaching in the Carolingian reform was socializing new peoples into the Christian faith. The success of that effort depended on teaching the basic elements of the Christian faith to people in their own languages. One may see from Hrabanus's first homiliary that such efforts were successful to a degree, but surviving texts document an even fuller realization of those accomplishments in England 150 years after Hrabanus's death.

On the eve of the end of the first Christian millennium a political and religious situation had developed in which such preaching could take place. During the last century or so of their occupation of Britain, the Romans had invited in Germanic tribesmen to assist them as mercenaries in maintaining Roman control. These mercenaries and their families stayed and they were followed by great numbers of their kinsmen—Angles, Saxons, Jutes, and Frisians—in the fifth century. Together they drove the Celtic-speaking British people back into what is now Wales, Ireland, and Scotland, and made their own language the language of the land. Scholars call this language "Old English" and they call "Anglo-Saxon" the culture that lasted until the Norman invasion.

So much for political conditions. The religious situation was the English manifestation of the monastic expansion that is associated in Europe with the Cluniac reform. The English version, however, was not closely connected with Cluny, which was fiercely independent of external connections. Instead, it derived from Ghent and was encouraged by and gave great support to the Crown. This monasticism did not seclude itself in cloisters but replaced secular priests in cathedral chapters[35] with monks. It was not long before England's bishops came to be recruited from these communities.[36] This attachment of religious to congregations of laypeople meant that the learning of the monks could be harnessed for the instruction of the laity. The monks had already begun to translate some of their own documents into Old English and there had been effort to furnish Anglo-Saxon people with vernacular religious instruction since the days of Bede and King Alfred. Thus monastic expansion in England created a climate in which learned monks could turn their attention to the religious instruction of the laity in their own language.

Another factor in the religious situation that called for increased teaching of the laity was the replacement of adult baptism with that of infants, a change that involved the separation of catechesis from initiation. With the loss of instruction such as that in the catechetical preaching of Cyril of Jerusalem and Ambrose, it became necessary to devise new ways in which laypeople could be socialized into the Christian faith.[37] The result was replacing the preaching done to catechumens during the Lent and Easter of their baptism with basic instruction on the Christian faith in sermons to the entire congregation who had already been baptized.

Aelfric, "the greatest scholar and literary leader of the English Benedictine Revival" responded to this need for basic Christian catechesis in Old English.[38] While he was still a monk of Cerne Abbas in Dorset and before he became abbot of Eynsham, Aelfric translated into Old English a series of forty sermons that was followed later by a second series. (**See Vol. 2, pp. 144-51** for one of his catechetical sermons.) He stated his reason for doing this in his preface:

> I have seen and heard of much error in many English books, which unlearned men, through their simplicity, have esteemed as great wisdom: and I regretted that they knew not nor had not the evangelical doctrines among their writings, those men only excepted who knew Latin, and those books excepted which king Alfred wisely turned from Latin into English, which are to be had.[39]

Aelfric's preaching has been studied extensively and given a suggestive interpretation by Milton McC. Gatch.[40] He sees it as contributing to the call of the Reform Councils for replacing liturgical preaching with catechetical instruction. This catechetical preaching was to be done at a vernacular office developing at the time that came to be called "Prone." This office, although it could occur separately, usually took place after the Gospel at the Eucharist. It "consisted of a translation and brief explanation of the pericope, announcements of forthcoming liturgical events, catechetical instruction based on the Creed and Lord's Prayer, and biddings of prayers and other devotions."[41]

Gatch sees this tendency to replace the liturgical homily with catechetical preaching in the office of Prone manifested in several features of Aelfric's *Sermones catholici.* A number of these are "sermons" in the strict sense of not being exegetical liturgical homilies. Series 1, for instance, begins with a sermon on the beginning of creation that is reminiscent of the great patristic catechetical expositions of the six days of creation. Moreover, the title matter of this sermon has the rubric that it is to be preached *quando volueris*, "whenever you wish."[42] Therefore it was not an exposition of a lectionary reading. Further, the sermons for the Rogation Days[43] in the first series are the most basic catechesis possible, expositions of the Lord's Prayer, Apostles' Creed, and Nicene Creed.

Gatch argues that Rogationtide "became in the late-Saxon church a conventional collecting-place for general catechetical and parenetic or hortatory sermons."[44] And he finds in the *Sermones* what are in effect the sort of liturgical announcements that are only to be expected at Prone. Finally, he points to the material tacked on to the end of the manuscript on which Thorpe's edition was based, which includes translations into Old English of the creeds, the Lord's Prayer, a collection of prayers, an instruction on Lenten penitence, and other things, all of which are appropriate to a collection of essentially catechetical materials.[45] Thus he is able to argue that the *Sermones,* rather than being liturgical homilies, are catechetical preaching of a purer form than had been developed earlier on the continent. And he can say this in spite of the fact that many of Aelfric's sermons include the verse-by-verse exegesis of a pericope characteristic of a homily.

Aelfric apparently expected such preaching at Prone to occur every other week and he provided two series of sermons to be preached so that the faithful would not become bored by frequent repetition. The second series provided for even greater variety since it gave the preacher some choice about which of the materials provided were to be used in the sermon, while the sermons in the first series were expected to be read to the congregation largely as Aelfric had written them.[46]

Yet what Aelfric does in his catechetical sermons is not a totally new departure in the history of preaching. He used patristic comments on his biblical texts to guide his interpretation, and his source for those comments seems to have been a form of the homiliary of Paul the Deacon.[47] Gatch's argument, which seems cogent, is that while Aelfric used traditional materials from homiliaries, he did not use them to create exegetical liturgical homilies but to write catechetical sermons to be delivered at Prone instead.

The preaching of Aelfric's contemporary Wulfstan shares a similar concern for basic Christian instruction just as there is also a shared eschatological emphasis. There is, however, a great deal of difference between the preaching of the two—in spite of the fact that Wulfstan often used Aelfric's sermons as a source for his own. Much of the difference can be attributed to a difference of responsibility since Aelfric became an abbot but Wulfstan left the cloister to become first bishop of London and then bishop of Worcester and eventually archbishop of York. Wulfstan was always the practical man of affairs, one who became an invaluable counselor of kings, and there was an attendant moral emphasis to all of his preaching.

He did not, as Aelfric did, write sermons to be delivered by others throughout the Christian year, and there are indeed few of his sermons that can be assigned to particular liturgical occasions, nor did he have even the exegetical interest that Aelfric did. Instead, he left us with the sort of general sermons that would do for many occasions that busy prelates often produce to this very day. His editor Dorothy Bethurum has grouped his sermons into categories that she labels as (1) eschatological, (2) the Christian faith (including catechetical), (3) episcopal functions, and (4) evil days (including especially the *Sermo ad Anglos*[48] in response to the Danish invasions of the time).[49] Among the catechetical sermons, 8 a, b, and c deal directly with baptism; 7 and 7 a concern the Lord's Prayer and the Creed; 9 with the gifts of the Holy Spirit; and 10 a, b, and c spell out the implications of the baptismal vows for Christian living. Bethurum concludes that these catechetical sermons must have been some of Wulfstan's first compositions after becoming an archbishop, and notes that, while he probably wrote them for his own use, he would not have been blind to the possibility that his diocesan clergy might take them for models as well.[50]

This survey has not said all that could be said about Old English preaching in Anglo-Saxon England. It has not dealt with all of the sermons of Aelfric and Wulfstan, being limited to their catechetical preaching. And the other sermons that have survived from that period, such as the anonymous ones in the Blickling and Vercelli collections, have not even been mentioned.[51] Since, however, the purpose of this section has not been to give a definitive review of Anglo-Saxon preaching but rather to take a look at a particular movement in the history of preaching, a particular kind of catechetical preaching, such omissions are inevitable.

CONCLUSION

In trying to survey the various kinds of preaching in the vernacular that are the homiletical legacy of the early Middle Ages, one senses a very mixed batch. We have considered a number of different kinds of sermons. Yet there is an underlying theme that gives unity to the period: the incorporation of newly converted pagans into the Christian faith. Missionary preaching (of which we have no surviving samples) attempted to precipitate such acceptances of the gospel. A good bit of the Carolingian reform was precisely about socializing the newly conquered and christianized masses into their new religion, as the preaching of Hrabanus Maurus shows. Anglo-Saxon catechetical preaching, then, was a response to much the same situation as earlier preaching on the Continent. Even the Latin homiliaries were not irrelevant to catechetical preaching in the vernacular, serving as they did as some of the sources most frequently mined by its practitioners for their teaching material. The homiletical goal of the early Middle Ages was, to use Peter Brown's title, "the rise of Western Christendom."

FOR FURTHER READING

Barré, Henri. "Homéliaires," Columns 597-606 in *Dictionnaire de Spiritualité. Ascétique et mystique, doctrine et histoire. Publié sous la direction de Marcel Viller, S.J., assisté de F. Cavallera et J. de Guibert, S.J., avec la concours d'un grand nombre de collaborateurs*. Paris: G. Beauchesne et ses fils, 1932–95, 7.

Gatch, Milton McC. *Preaching and Theology in Anglo-Saxon England: Aelfric and Wulfstan.* Toronto and Buffalo: University of Toronto Press, 1977.

Grégoire, R. *Homéliaires liturgiques médiévaux*: *Analyse de manuscrits,* Biblioteca degli. 'Studi Medievali,' no. 12. Spoleto: Centro italiano di studi sull'alto Medioevo, 1980.

The Homilies of the Anglo-Saxon Church: The First Part, Containing the Sermones Catholici, or Homilies of Aelfric in the Original Anglo-Saxon, with an English Version. 2 vols. Edited and translated by Benjamin Thorpe. London: Aelfric Society, 1844; reprinted New York: Johnson Reprint, 1971.

McCracken, George E. Pages 302-13 in *Early Medieval Theology*. LCC, vol. 9. Philadelphia: Westminster, 1957.

McKitterick, Rosamond. *The Frankish Church and the Carolingian Reforms, 789–895*. London: Royal Historical Society, 1977.

Neale, J. M. *Mediæval Preachers and Mediæval Preaching*. London: J. C. Mozley, 1856.

Notes

1. Jean Longère, *La prédication médiévale* (Paris: Études augustiniennes, 1983), 48-51.

2. The best short introduction to homiliaries is the article on that subject by Henri Barré in *Dictionnaire de Spiritualité* 7, 597-606. See also R. Grégoire, *Homéliaires liturgiques médiévaux: Analyse de manuscrits,* Biblioteca degli 'Studi Medievali,' no. 12 (Spoleto: Centro italiano di studi sull'alto Medioevo, 1980), 3-39.

3. It is less confusing for this period to refer to the three major orders as bishop, presbyter, and deacon since, for example, Caesarius can refer to bishops as priests.

4. Longère, *La prédication médiévale,* 30-31.

5. For a fuller discussion of monastic preaching, see chapter 8.

6. *". . . Expositones earum quae a nominatis et orthodoxis catholicis Patribus factae sunt."* St. Benedict, *Rule for Monasteries,* trans. Leonard J. Doyle (Collegeville, Minn.: The Liturgical Press, 1948), 30.

7. Barré, *"Homéliaires," Dictionnaire de Spiritualité* 7, col. 603.

8. Cyril L. Smetana, "Paul the Deacon's Patristic Anthology" in *The Old English Homily and Its Backgrounds,* ed. with intro. Paul E. Szarmach and Bernard F. Huppé (Albany: State University of New York Press, 1978), 75-97.

9. Paul's collection grew as it was recopied through the centuries and the version of it in PL 95 (1159-1566) is taken from a printed edition of the sixteenth century to which fifty-four sermons have been added and other changes made. Ibid., 87-88.

10. Longère, *La prédication médiévale,* 41-46.

11. J. M. Wallace-Hadrill, *The Barbarian West, 400–1000,* 3rd. ed. (Oxford and New York: Basil Blackwell, 1967), 87-114.

12. Ibid., 102.

13. Rosamond McKitterick, *The Frankish Church and the Carolingian Reforms, 789–895* (London: Royal Historical Society, 1977), 80-114.

14. Wallace-Hadrill, *The Barbarian West,* 99.

15. McKitterick, *The Frankish Church and the Carolingian Reforms,* 81.

16. *Recte et honeste. Admonitio generalis,* c. 82, MGH Cap. I, p. 61.

17. McKitterick, *The Frankish Church and the Carolingian Reforms,* 82.

18. *Ut omnibus festis et diebus dominicis unusquisque sacerdos evangelium Christi populo praedicet. Capitula a sacerdotis poposita,* c. 4. MGH Cap. I, p. 106. Any citations of the capitularies in MGH not explicitly referred to may be found in the notes to the McKitterick chapter noted above.

19. This distinction could also be translated as being between cities and rural areas, but for all practical purposes there is no difference between the two translations. Indeed, it could be argued that one could just as well see this as a distinction between the preaching of bishops and that of presbyters.

20. Tours, "in *rusticam romanam linguam, aut thiotiscam* (Germanic) *quod facilius cuncti possint intellegere*"; Rheims, "*secundum proprietatem linguae*"; the summary of the councils, *"iuxta quod intellegere vulgus possit."*

21. McKitterick, *The Frankish Church and the Carolingian Reforms,* 85. See also Longère, *La prédication médiévale,* 161-64.

22. McKitterick, *The Frankish Church and the Carolingian Reforms,* 86-87.

23. This title was later given to Luther's disciple Melanchthon as well.

24. The chapter on rhetoric is translated and annotated by Joseph M. Miller in *Readings in Medieval Rhetoric,* ed. Joseph M. Miller, Michael H. Prosser, and Thomas W. Benson (Bloomington: Indiana University Press, 1973), 125-27.

25. Ibid., 127.

26. Hrabanus's homiliaries are discussed in Henri Barré, *Les homéliaires carolingiens de l'école d'Auxerre: authenticité, inventaire, tableaux comparatifs, initia,* Studi e testi, 225 (Vatican City: Biblioteca apostolica vaticana, 1962), 13-17; Longère, *La prédication médiévale,* 41-42, and McKitterick, *The Frankish Church and the Carolingian Reforms,* 97-102.

27. Hrabanus's prefatory letter to Haistulf is translated by John Mason Neale in *Mediæval Preachers and Mediæval Preaching* (London: J. C. Mozley, 1856), 30-31.

28. Ibid.

29. PL 110. That manuscript is Clm 14629 from St. Emmeram.

30. McKitterick, *The Frankish Church and the Carolingian Reform,* 98.

31. Several sermons from this collection are translated respectively by Neale, *Mediæval Preachers and Mediæval Preaching,* 32-43, and George E. McCracken in *Early Medieval Theology,* LCC (Philadelphia: Westminster, 1957), 9:302-13.

32. Canon vii, trans. Milton McC. Gatch, "Basic Christian Education from the Decline of Catechesis to the Rise of Catechisms," in *A Faithful Church: Issues in the History of Catechesis,* ed. John H. Westerhoff III and O. C. Edwards Jr. (Wilton, Conn.: Morehouse-Barlow Co., 1981), 92.

33. PL 110, 135-468.

34. The remark of Longère, *La prédication médiévale,* 42, is not clear.

35. A cathedral chapter was its staff of clergy.

36. P. A. Stafford, "Church and Society in the Age of Aelfric," in Szarmach and Huppé, *The Old English Homily and Its Backgrounds,* 11-42.

37. Gatch, "Basic Christian Education from the Decline of Catechesis to the Rise of Catechisms," 79-91.

38. "Aelfric," *ODCC,* 2nd ed. (New York: Oxford University Press, 1974).

39. *The Homilies of the Anglo-Saxon Church: The First Part, Containing the Sermones Catholici, or Homilies of Aelfric in the Original Anglo-Saxon, with an English Version,* ed. and trans. Benjamin Thorpe (London: Aelfric Society, 1844), 1:3.

40. Milton McC. Gatch, *Preaching and Theology in Anglo-Saxon England: Aelfric and Wulfstan* (Toronto; Buffalo: University of Toronto Press, 1977).

41. Ibid., 37.

42. Thorpe, *The Homilies of the Anglo-Saxon Church,* 1:8-9.

43. The Monday, Tuesday, and Wednesday before the feast of the Ascension, days of solemn supplication, at the time of planting, for a good harvest.

44. Gatch, *Preaching and Theology in Anglo-Saxon England,* 53.

45. Thorpe, *The Homilies of the Anglo-Saxon Church,* 2:594-609.

46. Gatch, "Basic Christian Education from the Decline of Catechesis to the Rise of Catechisms," 98.

47. Cyril L. Smetana, "Aelfric and the Early Medieval Homiliary," in *Traditio* 15 (1959): 163-204.

48. For a detailed discussion of this sermon see Rachel Jurovics, "*Sermo lupi* and the Moral Purpose of Rhetoric" in Szarmach and Huppé, *The Old English Homily and Its Backgrounds,* 203-20.

49. Dorothy Bethurum, *The Homilies of Wulfstan* (Oxford: Clarendon Press, 1957).

50. Ibid., 299. Bethurum discusses Wulfstan's preaching on pp. 85-98. Gatch also gives an excellent short introduction to the preaching of Wulfstan in *Preaching and Theology in Anglo-Saxon England,* 18-22.

51. For a perspective on these sermons see Gatch, ibid., 119-28. They are discussed in their own right in two articles in Szarmach and Huppé, *The Old English Homily and Its Backgrounds:* Marcia A. Dalbey, "Themes and Techniques in the Blickling Lenten Homilies," 221-40, and Paul E. Szarmach, "The Vercelli Homilies: Style and Structure," 241-67. The Early English Text Society published R. Morris's edition of *The Blickling Homilies of the Tenth Century* (London: published for Early English Text Society by N. Trübner & Co., 1880) and reprinted it as one volume in 1967. For printed editions of the Vercelli manuscript, see the notes at the end of Szarmach's article.

CHAPTER 8

THE RENAISSANCE OF THE ELEVENTH AND TWELFTH CENTURIES

THE PERIOD

The title of this chapter is borrowed from a great historian of monasticism and medieval thought, David Knowles.[1] As applied to the history of preaching, it refers to a shift in consciousness away from the traditionalism that hardly dared to create sermons that were more than a pastiche of patristic quotations. Loyalty to patristic authority remained, but with a difference. There was coming to be the kind of confidence that is reflected in a well-known statement of Bernard of Chartres to the effect that he and his contemporaries were like dwarfs sitting on the shoulders of giants. Though their stature was obviously much, much less than that of their predecessors, the mere fact that they looked out from the vantage point of the accomplishments of the Fathers enabled them to see farther than the Fathers had. While Bernard's words did not refer to preaching in their original context, they nevertheless exemplify the new willingness to risk originality that distinguishes the preaching of this period from what preceded it.

THE REEMERGENCE OF TEXTBOOKS

Guibert of Nogent

We may see the new spirit characteristic of this period in a thirty-year-old monk of St. Geremar Abbey who began to write a commentary on Genesis shortly before 1084. Guibert, who was later to become abbot of Nogent himself, shocked his abbot by daring at such an early age to begin comment on such an exalted topic as the Hexaemeron, the six days of creation, a task undertaken previously by only the most learned and holy Fathers.[2] He continued with the project in secret and was able to complete it shortly after his abbot's death. To this commentary he added what he called "A Book About the Way a Sermon Ought to Be Given."[3] (For the text of this work, **see Vol. 2, pp. 152-63.**)

With the stipulation that Hrabanus's work[4] was a catena of quotations rather than an original work, one can agree with the judgment of Joseph M. Miller that

> none of the writers from the period between the death of Augustine (430) and the First Crusade (1095) had attempted any organized manual for preachers; rather they had confined themselves to exhortations concerning the need for the preacher to live a virtuous life and to know the Bible.[5]

Thus Guibert's homiletical addition to his commentary on Genesis is the first new homiletics textbook since Augustine's *De doctrina christiana.*

Guibert begins his treatise with the sound statement that "it is extremely dangerous for (one) who has the obligation of preaching ever to stop studying." Then he immediately goes off on a digression about the reasons why people try to avoid preaching, apparently under the impression that the duty of preaching should not be confined to bishops or abbots or even to priests, but should be extended to all who "live virtuously and continently" and who "have acquired any knowledge of the sacred page."[6] He even introduces a numerological argument that would lay the duty of preaching on all who are baptized and confirmed.

Such an assumption raises the question of what Guibert meant. Does it include personal witness and private moral instruction? Since Guibert himself was a Benedictine monk, he would not ordinarily have been expected to preach publicly, but he does dedicate his work to a bishop and it may therefore reflect the bishop's needs more than his own. The point is small and the question unanswerable, but it is also nagging because Guibert devotes so much of his discussion to arguing that some persons who were not doing so should be preaching. Who were they? Whatever the answer may be, Guibert reinforces his position by arguing that even preaching undertaken for such an unworthy motive as a desire for fame can be efficacious.

With his exhortation to reluctant preachers out of the way, Guibert then settles down to a lot of sound practical advice on preaching that would be worth following in any age. Preachers are advised to begin their sermons with prayer so that their own devotion will kindle the hearts of their hearers, "for a tepid sermon, delivered half-heartedly, cannot please even the preacher."[7] Sermons that are not going well should not be allowed to go on too long; indeed, even the best should be brief since repetitions and irrelevancies anger the audience and cause them to forget the good they have heard. Only after spiritual and intellectual preparation should the preacher give thought to issues of style. The preacher, however, should always keep in mind those who will hear the sermon. "Though he preaches simple and uncomplicated matter to the unlettered, at the same time he should try to reach a higher plane with the educated."[8]

For Guibert as for Augustine, a preaching manual needs to say something about biblical interpretation because for both preaching is essentially teaching, *doctrina,* and that teaching consists of helping the congregation to know and understand what the Bible teaches. Yet what the Bible teaches is not immediately apparent to all who read it; this teaching must be ascertained through interpretation. Medieval biblical interpretation was based completely on patristic interpretation, and there is very little difference between the hermeneutics of Guibert and Augustine.

Since, however, the Middle Ages did organize the theory of the Fathers more systematically than they themselves had done, the concise statement of the abbot of Nogent is interesting as one of the first clear enumerations of the four senses of Scripture universally accepted in the medieval period.

> There are four ways of interpreting Scripture; on them, as though on so many scrolls, each sacred page is rolled. The first is *history,* which speaks of actual events as they occurred; the second is *allegory,* in which one thing stands for something else; the third is *tropology,* or moral instruction, which treats of the ordering and arranging of one's life; and the last is *ascetics,* or spiritual enlightenment, through which we who are about to treat of lofty and heavenly topics are led to a higher way of life (italics added).[9]

This accords very well with a little verse in circulation as late as the sixteenth century that has been translated as follows:

The letter shows us what God and our fathers did;
The allegory shows us where our faith is hid;
The moral meaning gives us rules of daily life;
The anagogy shows us where we end our strife.[10]

In actual practice, however, sermons seldom dealt with more than one sense. On the whole, the literal, historical sense held little interest, nor were the doctrines that grew out of allegorical interpretation in the strict sense thought appropriate subject matter for preaching. The real concern was the daily lives of Christians and so the tropological sense was emphasized, although occasional glances were given to the anagogical (eschatological) as a way of reinforcing the moral application. Guibert voiced a strong preference in favor of these. And he thought it well to preach negatively about vices as well as positively about virtues:

> It seems to me that no preaching is more efficacious than that which would help man to know himself, that which brings out into the open all that is deep within him, in his innermost heart, that which will shame him, finally, by forcing him to stand clearly revealed before his own gaze.[11]

Such preaching can grow out of what the preacher learns of the interior life from reading Gregory and Cassian, but this reading has to be measured against the preacher's own experience. Just as stories of battle are told very differently by those who have been in battle and those who have not, so preaching about moral struggle also profits from obvious existential involvement. The purpose of Guibert's commentary is to supply material for such tropological preaching.

Alan of Lille

After Guibert's, the next textbook on preaching we have is from roughly a century later, *The Art of Preaching* by Alan of Lille.[12] Alan's learning was so conspicuous in his time that he was given the title *Doctor universalis*. He taught at Paris and possibly at Montpellier prior to becoming a Cistercian before his death in 1202, and he wrote a vast number of works ranging not only from philosophical to practical theology but even to poetry as well.[13] While he was basically a theologian, he apparently had, as Gillian Evans has said, "an eye for a gap in the literature of any subject which he himself was competent to fill"[14] and thus he produced works in a number of fields of practical theology, including his preaching manual.

Although there are senses in which the works of Guibert and Alan are very similar, and while Alan's is very different from the technical *artes praedicandi* that would begin to appear in such proliferation less than a generation after his death, so much had transpired in the century after Guibert wrote that the two books seem to represent different thought worlds. This was the period in which higher education was passing from monastic and cathedral schools through the era of individual teachers to the beginning of the universities. It was also the time in which dialectic began to dominate theological discussion.[15] This becomes very clear in Alan's discussion of the outline *(dispositio)* of the sermon. While Alan's directions for sermon construction and his own homiletical productions do not yet achieve anything like the formality and complexity recommended for thematic sermons so soon after his death, it is nevertheless true to say that "several features of Alan's method, especially in the *Sermons* themselves, suggest that the manuals of the thirteenth century formalized a method of preaching which had already been well-tried in practice."[16]

One of the distinctions of Alan's *Ars* is that in it he gives what James J. Murphy has described as "the first formal definition (of preaching) in the 1200-year history of the church":[17]

> Preaching is an open and public instruction in faith and behavior, whose purpose is the forming of [persons]; it derives from the path of reason and from the fountainhead of the "authorities."[18]

What Alan meant by this definition, especially the roles of reason and authorities, will emerge as we analyze his method.

The preface to the work is an allegorical interpretation of Jacob's ladder.

> The ladder represents the progress of the catholic man *(viri catholici)* in his ascent from the beginning of faith to the full development of the perfect man. The first rung of this ladder is confession; the second, prayer; the third, thanksgiving; the fourth, careful study of the scriptures; the fifth, to inquire of someone more experienced if one comes upon any point in scripture which is not clear; the sixth, the expounding of scripture; the seventh, preaching.[19]

This high evaluation of preaching is something that had not been heard in the church for quite some time, but shows that it was coming to be in vogue. The saying has a contemporary parallel in Peter the Chanter's enumeration of the three stages of biblical study as reading, disputation, and preaching, "which, like a roof, completes the building of which *lectio* is the foundation and *disputatio* the walls."[20]

Alan begins his manual with a list of what he hopes to accomplish that sounds promising:

> First, then, we must see what preaching is, what form it should take—in the surface aspects of its words, and in the weight of its thoughts—and how many kinds of preaching there are. Secondly, we must consider who the preachers should be; thirdly, to whom the sermon should be delivered; fourthly, for what reasons, and fifthly, in what place.[21]

The question of what preaching is seems to be settled in the definition quoted above, which immediately follows this outline. The form that preaching should take appears also to be dealt with in the treatment of *dispositio* in the first chapter. In the same chapter the three kinds of preaching are said to be that by the spoken word, by the written word, and by deed. At the end of that chapter, though, the treatise seems to get off track with a couple of chapters giving material for sermons about spiritual attitudes. These are followed by seven chapters (4 to 10) supplying homiletical ammunition against vices, after which there are two more on spiritual attitudes, and thirteen on virtues (13-25). Next there are preaching notes on three evil practices followed by nine on devout practices (29-37).

Only in chapter 38, then, does Alan get to his second question of who should preach (prelates, by which he apparently means bishops and abbots, since he refers to the symbolism of their pastoral staffs pointing back toward themselves).[22] In the next chapter he lists the classes to whom preaching should be delivered, following that with chapters on how to preach to eight of the classes mentioned (40-47). All that he says about the reasons for and the site of preaching seems to be in the first chapter: it is for the edification of people and should be done in public.

Why does so much of the treatise seem to be devoted to something other than the topics in the outline? Murphy refers to these chapters as "sample sermonettes" like those provided by Gregory in the *Regula pastoralis* and says elsewhere that Alan's "method in respect to his own definition is the same one he uses elsewhere to amplify ideas in the forty-seven sample sermonettes."[23] Gillian Evans, however, must be correct when she argues that these chapters are not model sermons or sermons in miniature, but are instead rhetorical *topoi,* "stock examples, illustrations, and other commonplaces."[24] Alan's own sermons are always based on only one text, but often in these chapters he suggests a number of possible additional texts. Together with the other material in these chapters, the various texts are,

> as Cicero defines them (in Aristotelian terms), "seats of argument," not arguments fully developed into sequences of argumentation. They are simply collections of source material, and the preacher is intended to draw upon them selectively, taking what he needs for a particular sermon, rather than expanding them as they stand into full-length sermons.[25]

In other words, they are very similar in function to many homiletical aids published today.

Alan begins describing the form of preaching by saying that it should develop from a theological authority, that is, from a quotation from an authoritative document such as the Bible or a work by one of the church fathers. To use the vocabulary of a more modern era, the patristic homily was expository preaching while sermons of the High Middle Ages tended to be textual.

The authority—the biblical verse—that furnished what today would be called the text of the sermon was in those days called the theme. A difference between Alan's preaching textbook and the *artes praedicandi* to come is that sermons constructed according to his method did not develop by dividing the text into three or more parts, and then commenting on several aspects of each. He was more interested in developing the content of the authority/theme/text than in verbal analysis of its component parts. In his opinion, the best texts for preaching come from the Gospels, the psalms, Paul's Epistles, or the books of Solomon. Although Alan does not say so in so many words, the Gospel verses he recommends as texts are Jesus' sayings rather than stories about him, since authorities had to be abstract rather than narrative statements.[26]

Next Alan says that "the preacher must win the good will of his audience through the humility he shows in his own person (what Aristotle called the proof of *ethos*), and through the profitableness of his subject matter."[27] The initial development of the text should not be done in too great a hurry. Other authorities should be used to confirm the first, and even the words of pagan writers can be introduced to good advantage. The preacher "may introduce moving words which soften hearts and encourage tears"[28]—which is to say that the proof of *pathos* may be employed. And the use of examples is encouraged (although by the end of the Middle Ages the church will have had enough of them for a while). Yet, however good the contents of the sermon, it should not be too long. This is the counsel that Alan has to give about developing a sermon.

How well did he follow his own advice? A large number of sermons attributed to him have survived.[29] Unfortunately, relatively few of them have been published. A number of manuscripts contain a *Liber sermonum* of twenty-eight sermons, which accompany *The Art of Preaching* and are intended to exemplify its principles.[30] Evans has translated these, but they have not yet been published. (For one of the sermons from Evans's translation, see **Vol. 2, pp. 163-67.**) Until they are, the best place to sample Alan's preaching is in d'Alverny's book.[31] There she edits:

> three sermons from the *Liber sermonum* (for Epiphany, Palm Sunday, and Michaelmas);
> Six from the *Sermones varii* (for Trinity Sunday, the Birth of St. Augustine, and Ash Wednesday, and occasional sermons for: scholars, a crusade *[de cruce Domini]*, and priests at a synod); and
> A cosmological sermon on a pagan text to the effect that God is an intellective sphere of which the center is everywhere and the circumference nowhere.[32]

With the exception of the last mentioned sermon, Alan shows himself to be a good and at times eloquent practitioner of his own principles. In the sermon on the Epiphany, he interprets the gifts of the magi allegorically as representing three of the four senses of Scripture (historical, tropological, and anagogical), showing how basic to biblical interpretation the four senses had become. The sermon on St. Michael and All Angels is also theological, being a homiletical treatise on angelology.

The "authority" or text for his Palm Sunday sermon is Matthew 21:2, "Go into the citadel over against you."[33] The sermon is based on an analogy Alan sees between the governance of a city and the rule of the universe. In a city, those who have wisdom govern, the knights defend the city, and the people obey. In the universe, the Trinity reigns, the angels execute God's orders, and the people are subject to God. With that background Alan proceeds to recite salvation history as though it were a medieval romance in a manner that must have been quite comprehensible and fascinating to a popular audience. This is an example of the way that Alan's sermons are based on a single verse of scripture rather than on an extended passage as a patristic homily would have been. And yet, unlike the later thematic sermon, his is not developed by a division of the authority, but by an exploration of its content. This is to say that he is a transitional figure in the history of preaching.

He preached his sermon promoting the third crusade on the Feast of the Exaltation of the Cross, which celebrated the recovery of the cross from the Persians by the emperor Heraclius in 629. This, of course, was the cross discovered by Helena, the mother of Constantine, which occasioned the erection of the Church of the Holy Sepulchre in Jerusalem in 335. Alan was urging his auditors to do again what Heraclius had done, but he also took time to attribute the loss of the cross to the characteristic sins of different groups of Christians, the sort of *ad status* preaching suggested by his *Ars*.

Alan's synod sermon, based on the Song of Solomon 3:8, identifies Solomon with Christ and the guards of Solomon's litter with the high church officers attending the synod, and is a fearless attack on the sins of the clergy. For all of his mastery of the contemporary hermeneutical and rhetorical arts, Alan shows himself to be committed to the moral improvement of Christian people of all ranks, and both his sermons and his textbook on preaching are means to that end.

MONASTIC PREACHING[34]

While the manuals of Guibert of Nogent and Alan of Lille are principally concerned with preaching to the laity, much of the preaching done during the eleventh and twelfth centuries was addressed to monks. This, of course, had been the case for some time, as we can deduce from the development of homiliaries used in connection with the Night Office.[35] While it is hard to know exactly how much preaching was done on a regular basis in either parishes or monasteries, clearly there was a great renewal of monastic life in the eleventh and twelfth centuries, and preaching was an important aspect of that renewal.

During this period the revival occurred not so much in the great classical order from the patristic period, the Benedictines, as in new forms the religious life was taking.[36] The Benedictines had begun to devote so much of their energy to the elaboration of their liturgy that the amount of time left for the activities that formed the basis of their Rule was diminished. Further, their endowments came to support progressively smaller numbers of monks.

Two kinds of movements arose to fill the gap left by the departure of the Order of St. Benedict from its original vision, the one more practical and the other more contemplative. The more practical reflected the desire of groups of clergy and laity alike who felt called by God to follow a life devoted to good works in the world while living together under a rule. The rule required them to share their possessions completely, wear identical habits, observe set times of prayer together, and obey a superior. Such groups are called Augustinian[37] canons because their very general rules are based on a letter of advice that Augustine wrote to a group of women who wished to live together in community.[38] A good example of this sort of order is that formed by St. Norbert at Prémontré called Norbertines or Premonstratensians.

The more contemplative tendency of these orders is reflected in their desire to return to what was considered a stricter interpretation of the Rule of St. Benedict than contemporary Benedictines seemed capable of making. The principal manifestation of this tendency was formed in 1098 by Robert of Molesme and his companions at Citeaux, who were thus called Cistercians.[39]

What the monastic movement at its best was about was precisely an attempt to "press on toward the goal for the prize of the heavenly call of God in Christ Jesus" (Phil. 3:14). Or, as it was expressed very simply by a modern writer who has sought to discover what the Rule of St. Benedict has to offer laypersons trying to live out their Christian vocation in the world: "the Rule is simply an aid for us to live by the Scriptures."[40] In the prologue of his Rule, Benedict says: "This message of mine is for you, then, if you are ready to give up your own will, once and for all, and armed with the strong and noble weapons of obedience to do battle for the true King, Christ the Lord" (*RB* 1980, 157).

That he was not advocating works rather than grace is seen a little later when he addresses the question raised in Psalm 15:1, "Who will dwell in your tent, Lord, who will find rest upon your holy mountain?" (*RB* 1980, 161). Part of his answer is as follows:

> These people *fear the Lord,* and do not become elated over their good deeds; they judge it is the Lord's power, not their own, that brings about the good in them. *They praise* (Ps 14[15]:4) the Lord working in them, and say with the Prophet: *Not to us, Lord, not to us give the glory, but to your name alone* (Ps 113[115:1]:9). In just this way Paul the Apostle refused to take the credit for the power of his preaching. He declared: *By God's grace I am what I am* (1 Cor 15:10). And again he said: *He who boasts should make his boast in the Lord* (2 Cor 10:17). [*RB* 1980, 163]

The monastic movement at its best was always a way presented to souls so in love with Christ that they would leave all to follow him. Not surprisingly, then, its preaching was always counsel on how that might be done most efficaciously. Indeed, Benedict calls his monastery "a school for the service of the Lord" and a "workshop."[41]

The Sanctification of Time

In order to understand monastic preaching, it is necessary to know something about the context in which it occurred. The daily schedule of the monastery was built around carrying out in the most literal way possible the words of the psalmist: "Seven times a day have I praised you" (118[119]:164 RSV) and "At midnight I rose to give you praise" (118[119]:62 RSV). Thus there is the Morning Office[42] (called Lauds because the psalms of praise are recited). That is followed by Prime at the first hour of the day, Terce at the third, Sext at the sixth, None at the ninth, Vespers in the evening, and Compline before retiring. The monks rise at the eighth hour of the night (2:00 A.M.) for the Night Office (Vigil or Matins).[43]

The monastic day is built around the schedule of the oratory.[44] During these offices the entire Psalter is recited every week, and almost the entire Bible is read during the course of a year. To these biblical elements are joined hymns, responses, and prayers, but the psalms are the core of the office. It is, therefore, no wonder that all monastic preaching is thoroughly sprinkled not only with allusions, especially to the psalms, but also to the rest of the Bible as well. In contemporary American homiletics, probably only African American preachers in the classical tradition are so immersed in biblical language. This life of constant corporate prayer was called *opus Dei,* the "work of God."

Just as prayer is considered to be work, so physical labor is understood as a form of prayer. *Opere est orare,* "to work is to pray," is one of the monks' sayings. The Rule of St. Benedict calls for a number of hours a day to be spent in manual labor on the grounds that "idleness is the enemy of the soul" (chap. 48).[45] As time went on monasteries began to produce, in addition to agricultural products, such things as manuscripts for their own use and that of others, and nonmanual labor came to replace manual labor for some monks, though some sort of work was always expected from all.

The third sort of activity by which monks were expected to fill all their waking hours except those set aside for eating or rest was called *lectio divina,* "sacred reading" in the sense that what was read was sacred. However, this reading involved much more than is normally encompassed today in the concept of spiritual reading. To begin with, people generally read aloud in those days, and there was a good deal of bodily engagement in the process. The reading was a very reflective kind of reading, an activity close to meditation, an activity that involved thinking about what was being read, fixing it in memory, and learning it. This reading was basically biblical but it also included works of some by the Fathers, especially such spiritual writers as Basil and Cassian.[46]

To complete this total preoccupation with the things of the Spirit, silence was observed most of the time and there was reading aloud during meals. It is hard to imagine a life more calculated to remove everything that distracts one from wholehearted concentration upon the things of God.

An enormous amount of monastic homiletical literature has survived from the eleventh and twelfth centuries. In his treatment of it, Jean Longère has parceled it out among the various orders as a means of allowing himself to list the members of each whose sermons have been preserved, enabling him to make concise observations about the preaching of each.[47] Jean Leclercq, however, has argued in *The Love of Learning and the Desire for God* that there is essentially one monastic theology for this period, a theology that stands in marked contrast with the scholastic theology that developed shortly afterward. Since the purpose of this book is to understand movements in the history of preaching rather than to list the names of all famous preachers, it will be convenient to study all of monastic preaching in the work of its greatest practitioner, Bernard of Clairvaux.[48]

Bernard's Life and Significance

Jean Mabillon, the seventeenth-century patristics scholar responsible for the edition of Bernard's works taken over by Migne, made an estimate of Bernard's significance that still has cogency. He called Bernard "the last of the Fathers, but certainly not unequal to the earlier ones."[49] His meaning is similar to Leclercq's thesis that monastic theology is very different from the scholastic theology that succeeded it because monastic theology is simply a continuation of the spirituality of the patristic *expositores* of the Latin Bible.[50] Any just estimate of Bernard's significance must begin with his stature as a spiritual master since all his other accomplishments that made him one of the most respected persons of his age derive from the authenticity and authority of that spirituality.

His life through his early maturity, however, gave no one reason to believe that he would become one of the most influential people in Europe. Born near Dijon in 1090 into a noble family, he seems not to have been intended for the knightly military career followed by his father and commenced by his brothers. He was sent instead to a nearby school of the Canons Regular where he received the sort of good basic education in Latin that was more characteristic of those going into the church than of those who were to bear arms. When he was twenty-one he not only became a monk himself but also took along thirty others to be professed with him. Four of these were his brothers; another brother and his father would follow them later. Some of the thirty left wives, and Bernard also persuaded his sister to trade her husband's house for a convent. His great powers of persuasion were obvious from an early age.

Reflecting the changes in the monastic life that were taking place at the time, he did not go nearby to the historic and powerful Benedictine abbey of Cluny, but instead went a little farther to Citeaux, where Robert of Molesme had founded the Cistercians only fourteen years before. When Bernard arrived, the infant order seemed likely to succumb to an early death, but his recruits gave it a renewed vigor. In only three years he was sent off with a group of companions to found another monastery at Clairvaux. By the time of Bernard's death the order had grown to 350 houses, slightly fewer than half of which were under his authority; he had founded sixty-eight of these himself.

The Rule of St. Benedict depicts the abbot's primary responsibility as forming the monks under him spiritually by his teaching and example (chap. 2), primarily through preaching. At Cluny, for instance, and in other monasteries, this preaching took place twice a day. In the morning before manual labor was begun, the abbot preached to the monks in the cloister, probably on the book being read at meals in the refectory. Then, in the evening when the day's work was over, he delivered, in the fields or wherever the work had been done, a "conference" or "collation" on a text from Scripture, the Rule, or some patristic writing.[51]

For the first nine years after Clairvaux's founding, this preaching was Bernard's main channel of influence. By 1124, however, his reputation for spiritual wisdom had become so widespread that his own monks wanted him to write down some of the things he said to them, and other religious communities began asking him to undertake writing assignments for them, sharing his deep insight into the religious life. By letters and treatises his influence began to radiate even at a time when his austerities were taking their toll on his frail body.

From teaching on the monastic life he expanded first to talk about the differences between the visions of the Cistercians and those of Cluny. Then he was asked to say what the life and work of bishops should be like. He became involved in the organization of the Knights Templar, trying to show how an order of military men could live a communal life of devotion even when engaged in warfare. Next he rallied the French church and then the Italian church behind Innocent II against the antipope Anacletus, a struggle that took eight years.

During all this time he still taught his monks when he was able to stay in Clairvaux, wrote books that have become spiritual classics, and even persuaded a number of students at the University of Paris to become monks. He became involved in trying to point out errors in faith; his role in the condemnations of Abelard and Gilbert de la Porrée is almost the only aspect of his life that is ever criticized—and even then the importance of the theological issues he raised is recognized. He was sent to the south of France to preach against the heretical teachings of Peter of Bruy and his disciple Henry of Lausanne, who were in some respects predecessors of the Waldensians. When one of his former disciples became pope as Eugenius III, Bernard acceded to his request and preached the second crusade. After his unsuccessful efforts to give the crusade the spiritual dimension that had become obscured, he was blamed for the crusade's failure.

In response to another request from Eugenius, he wrote a treatise on papal spirituality entitled *Consideration*—which, among other things, contained a violent attack on the Curia. Time and time again he was called from the monastery he loved to serve the church in some reconciling faction. He lived a life so devoted to the love of God that, less than a century after his death, Dante would see him replacing even the beloved Beatrice as guide when the poet arrived at the Empyrean. Bernard was the one who introduced Dante to the Blessed Virgin Mary, preparing the way for his beatific vision of God. Few preachers in the history of the church have been so admired as he both by his contemporaries and by Christians of all varieties who came after him.

Bernard the Preacher

As Gillian Evans has said: "Bernard was above all a talker; almost everything he wrote arose out of his sermons or discourses."[52] The standard edition of his works runs to thirty-five hundred pages, of which roughly twenty-one hundred purport to be sermonic literature, and even more grew out of what had originally been sermons.[53] How close any of this is to the words this great talker actually spoke, however, is a question of enormous complexity.[54] The question has less to do with whether Bernard is the author of these works than it does with their literary genre.

While there are at least three major manuscript traditions for most of his works, these usually represent different stages in his writing process rather than efforts of others to create bernardine pseudepigrapha. There is often an earlier, shorter recension; a later, longer one; and then a final version that he edited near the end of his life. So most of the works are genuine enough; the real question is whether they are sermons in the sense of being words that he spoke to a congregation. Certainly they follow the literary genre of sermons and include many conventions of oral presentation, such as an aside to his audience that he had to break off his talk because visitors to the monastery were waiting for him. Nevertheless, the systematic treatment given to topics, often extended over a number of sermons, indicates that in the developed form in which we have them, these writings are to be understood as treatises cast in the literary genre of sermons.[55]

That being the case, one might ask whether such writings should be considered in a history of preaching. There are cogent reasons why they should. First, it seems likely that these works usually had their origin in Bernard's preaching, giving us some indication not only of what he said but also of how he talked about it. Second, they are still the best indication we have of what the sermons of one of the great preachers of all time must have been like. Furthermore, there is one section of the literature that gives good promise of going back to the actual oral delivery of Bernard himself.

The materials categorized as *Sentences* and *Parables* seem to represent either sketches of the arguments of Bernard's sermons or stories that he told in their course taken down by members of his audience either while he was delivering them or shortly afterward. They give us an authentic flavor of Bernard's actual preaching and furnish criteria to distinguish between the elements of his treatises in the genre of sermons that reflect his preaching practice and those that do not.

Finally, treatises written in the genre of sermons were often intended either to be read aloud to monks in the place of live preaching or to be used by them in their *lectio divina;* in either case they served much the same function as actual sermons in the spiritual formation of monks. For instance, Bernard's *Homilies in Praise of the Virgin Mary,* which are among his earliest works, were written when illness caused him to be separated from the monks of his monastery and were used as a substitute for what he would have said to them if he had been with them.[56]

From the remaining materials a picture emerges showing the way that Bernard preached to his monks. As noted above, the purpose of this preaching was to enable them to forsake all bondage in self-will so that they could give themselves completely to God. The content of this preaching was profoundly biblical and patristic, and it dealt much more with practical issues of the spiritual life than it did with speculative thought. Most of his sermons were in the form of commentary—usually on a passage from the Bible, although a text could be taken from the Rule of St. Benedict or the writings of the Fathers.

Although Bernard's sermons at times involved the detailed study of short passages (he wrote a commentary on the Song of Songs consisting of eighty-six sermons without getting past the first verse of the third chapter), his exegesis was spiritual rather than academic. He certainly did not engage in multiple divisions of texts of the sort that thematic preachers would carry to excess a few years after his death. Rather, his preaching shared the fruits of his own *lectio divina,* his own meditation on the Scriptures to which he, like other monks, devoted time not required for corporate prayer and work. The purpose of modeling his own *lectio* was to show the monks how to deepen their own. As Gillian Evans has said,

> No one who had heard Bernard expound the text of the Bible could read it afterwards without perceiving new depths in it. This is what Bernard intended—to form habits of perceptive and reflective reading in his monks which they could use in their own private *lectio divina*.[57]

Bernard's Homiletical Writings

With this background it is now possible to look at Bernard's various preaching materials either grouped together by him as continuous works or collected by others. This survey will illustrate not only the range of Bernard's proclamation but the variety of monastic preaching in general as well. It will show especially what portions of Scripture were most influential in the spiritual formation of religious, both male and female.

Sentences and Parables

The word *sententia* has a number of possible meanings in classical and medieval Latin, but when used to describe Bernard's work it has the sense of résumé or outline. Since many of the sermons summarized are organized around a number of different categories of something (two advents, three degrees of obedience, four animals, etc.), one may assume that the outline is accurate enough. There are many sermon collections in monastic literature, some taken entirely from one preacher and others from a variety. The content of the sermons thus epitomized is typical monastic preaching, summing up the accepted wisdom of what it means to be faithful to one's vocation in a manner reminiscent of *Words of the Elders* in the earliest monastic tradition.

These sermons tend to be quite short, especially in the first two series of Bernard's *sententiae* that were already collected as early as Mabillon and therefore appeared in Migne. Sometimes they are no longer than a "sentence" in its modern English sense of one complete statement; the 231 *sententiae* of the first two series occupy only fifty-one pages of the Leclercq and Rochais edition. Those collected and established as authentic since the time of Mabillon, which make up the third series of Leclercq-Rochais, tend to be much fuller (127 *sententiae* in 196 pages). However detailed the outline, the content still consists of practical advice on how to advance in the spiritual life by fidelity to one's monastic vows.

As the name suggests, the *Parabolae* are not sermon outlines but sermon illustrations taken from Bernard's preaching.[58] While the Leclercq-Rochais edition of Bernard's works has only eight of these grouped together under this rubric, others appear in the *sententiae* and elsewhere in Bernard's sermons. The titles of these eight suggest the kinds of stories they are: the king's son, the conflict of two kings, the king's son sitting on a horse, the church that was captive in Egypt, a king's three sons, the Ethiopian woman married by the king's son, the eight beatitudes, and the king and the beloved servant. To anyone acquainted with New Testament scholarship, these illustrations will seem more like allegories than true parables in that they are decoded term by term. Unlike Anselm, who told his story first and then applied it, Bernard made his identifications as he went along, which gave him greater narrative spontaneity.

Sermones per Annum

Bernard's sermons for use throughout the church year[59] include some for both Sundays and saints' days. The *temporale* covers the time from the first Sunday in Advent to Pentecost, including the fixed feasts between Christmas and Epiphany, but makes little provision for the Sundays after Pentecost. Lent is provided for by the series on "Qui habitat," the Ninety-first Psalm,[60] which also appears as a separate work in the manuscript tradition. The *sanctorale* is largely limited to New Testament saints and events, with provision for only a few postbiblical commemorations: those of Benedict, Malachy (an Irish archbishop who had recently died), Martin, Clement, and the superior general of the Dominicans, Humbert of Romans.

Leclercq has discovered two kinds of evidence that point overwhelmingly to the literary character of the collections of liturgical sermons. First, all the sermons for a particular season, such as, for instance, Epiphany, fit together as a "logical and organized treatise" on the significance of that season.[61] Further, the sequence of thought within individual sermons and the collection as a whole indicates that the entire collection was envisaged by Bernard as a vast commentary on the liturgical year, given its shape by the succession of seasons and feasts.

The other sort of evidence is the degree of literary polish in the sermons. Bernard was one of the greatest preachers of all time, but even he could not have attained such literary perfection speaking from a brief outline. And, even if he could, no one at the time could have taken it all down, since there was no system of shorthand in use then. Besides, we have examples of Bernard's familiar style, and it is not similar to the style of these sermons. Thus the great liturgical sermons are to be viewed as examples of Bernard's written rather than oral art.

Sermones de Diversis

The *Sermons on Various Subjects* are exactly what the name suggests, a collection lacking homogeneity.[62] Sometimes this has also been called "Short Sermons," but that description does not fit everything included in the collection. The variegated nature of the material and its history of having been garnered by a succession of editors from many sources render it inevitable that every stage between oral and literary sermons be represented here.[63] This variety also means that it is much harder in this collection to distinguish what is genuinely bernardine than it is in other series. About all that can be said about these sermons is that most are based on biblical texts, they often receive their outline from a list of categories, and they are applied to the spiritual lives of monks.

Sermones super Cantica Canticorum

Bernard's *Sermons on the Song of Songs*[64] are at once his acknowledged masterpiece and the portion of his work that is most alien to contemporary consciousness. It is hard for people who have been brought up on historical-critical biblical interpretation to take seriously the idea that the Bible's great paean to human sexual love is about the soul's growing attachment to God. Many find it embarrassing to take an expression so graphically carnal as "Let him kiss me with the kiss of his mouth" as an expression of their feelings about God. Yet this tradition goes back far beyond Bernard. The doubt in Origen's mind was whether the bride referred to the individual soul or to the church. In the latter interpretation he had the precedent of Jewish exegesis that understood the bride as Israel. As Brevard Childs has said,

> The theological reasoning behind the allegorical interpretations was not obscure. The Song of Songs formed part of the canon of sacred scripture, indeed, in the Jewish tradition it was read as part of the passover liturgy. Did it not then follow that the book must have a sacred meaning if it had been incorporated into this sacred context?[65]

Add to that the fact that the best analogy human beings have ever been able to find to the love of God has always been their own erotic/romantic love, and the perennial appeal of such spiritual interpretation of the Canticles is not hard to understand.[66]

Certainly the theme was popular enough in Bernard's day. Bernard himself testifies to that in what is probably his best-known work, his treatise *On Loving God (De diligendo Deo)*.[67] Longère is able to list five other commentators on the Canticles from Bernard's Cistercian order alone.[68] Bernard lived, after all, in the age of the troubadours and minstrels, the age of courtly love. It was not only in Christian Europe, however, that a spirituality of love emerged in the twelfth century. During this same period Jewish kabbalistic mystics were also writing commentaries on the Song of Songs; Muslim Sufi masters were celebrating the lovableness of God in the divine beauty; Hindus were composing their own equivalent to the Canticles, their *Gita Govinda;* and Buddhists were experiencing their Tantric and Pure Land movements.[69] How fascinating it would be if historians using the methodology of the sociology of knowledge could come up with an explanation for why this same powerful motif sprang up in so many different and widely separated cultures simultaneously.

Refuting the conclusion of previous research that "St Bernard's *Sermons on the Song of Songs* appeared in book form and were also delivered as talks," Leclercq has argued cogently from a variety of evidence that the sermons as we have them constitute a treatise on the monastic life in the literary genre of a series of homilies.[70] In this series, however, it is possible to see how a treatise of Bernard disguised as sermons related to sermons he had really preached. In his account of the life of Bernard, William of St. Thierry tells of how the two of them lay sick together shortly after Bernard became abbot and Bernard expounded to him the moral sense of the Canticles.[71] Further, various disciples of Bernard have recollected hearing him preach on the Canticles, and there are several sermons in the *Sentences* on texts from this biblical book, some of which employ illustrations that are used in the *Sermons* for the same texts. Finally, Mabillon and Migne after him published William's work entitled *Brevis Commentatio ex Sancti Bernardi Sermonibus Contexta* that appears to be "the frame on which Bernard wove his work on the *Sermons*."[72]

Thus Leclercq concludes:

> We do not have the actual spoken sermons which Bernard delivered on the Song of Songs. But we can well believe that they were more developed than the text of the *Brevis Commentatio,* and on the other hand less polished than the text of the published *Sermons*.[73]

In both his literary *Sermons* and the homilies that he actually delivered in chapter, Bernard wooed monks to progress in their spiritual lives through the love of God, "devotion to the sacred humanity" of Christ.[74]

Sermones in laudibus Virginis Matris

"To this fervent love for Jesus Christ was joined a most sweet and tender devotion toward his glorious mother."[75] This estimate of Pope Pius XII is confirmed by Henri Barré, who called Bernard the "Marian Doctor *par excellence*."[76] This is not to say, however, that Bernard contributed anything to the elaboration of Marian doctrine, especially not in the three developments occurring during his lifetime, the belief that Mary was conceived without inheriting original sin, that her body was assumed into heaven when she died, and that she is the spiritual mother of all Christians. Instead, Bernard drew all of his understanding of the Blessed Mother from the Bible and the Fathers. "But what our author lacks in theological adventuresomeness (a lack which some of us will be inclined to applaud), he more than makes up for in intensity and beauty of expression."[77] This intensity and beauty of expression are probably seen at their best in the second of his homilies when he picks up on Jerome's etymological interpretation of the name Mary as meaning "Star of the Sea."

Bernard's *Four Homilies in Praise of the Virgin Mother* are his earliest writing on the subject and his most complete treatment of it.[78] They were written shortly after he became abbot at a time when he had become ill over his exertions and also over some estrangement from his monks that was already being healed. The bishop of Châlons, William of Champeaux, asked that the young abbot be placed under his spiritual direction for a year, an extremely unusual measure justified by the need to save Bernard's life. This time was spent in retreat and recuperation in a shack similar to those built for lepers.

There, in order to maintain some contact with his monks, he composed these sermons.[79] Because they are on texts from the story of the annunciation, they are also known as the sermons on *Missus est,* the first words of the story in the Vulgate ("The angel Gabriel *was sent*"). Obviously, because he wrote them for his monks when he was away from the monastery, these sermons were not delivered, but they were written to be read to the community in his absence. They nevertheless serve the same essential purpose as all his monastic preaching: "The purpose of all Bernard's preaching on the Virgin and her Son is to make the reader alive to the detailed implications of the Nativity story for his own spiritual and active life."[80]

Ad Clericos de Conversione

Bernard not only preached to those who were already monks but to secular clerics as well to persuade them to become monks. The clergy in question were not all in major orders; most students of the time were at least in minor orders, and it was to students that the original oral form of this "sermon" was addressed. The "conversion" in question was not that of becoming Christians but of becoming monks. As Marie-Bernard Saïd has pointed out, the situation Bernard was addressing was essentially that described in Helen Waddell's *The Wandering Scholars:* "Among the vagrant student population there were genuine scholars, but there were also those of the 'baser type, the unfrocked or runaway monk or clerk.'"[81]

Bernard was debatably the most influential person in Europe when his duties took him through Paris sometime between Lent 1139 and early 1140. The bishop asked him to preach, but at first he refused. The next day, however, he felt moved by God to do so, and a number of clerics gathered to hear him. At least three of them were persuaded to become monks, including Geoffrey of Auxerre, who later became his secretary and then biographer.[82]

On Conversion: A Sermon to Clerics exists in two manuscript editions, one shorter and the other longer. The shorter ends with section 31 at the conclusion of a commentary on the Beatitudes where Bernard says, "But I am tiring you with this rambling sermon."[83] It is assumed that this shorter version is what Bernard actually preached and that the longer version represents his later polishing of the text for publication, together with the addition of some remarks about the morals of clergy at the time and a depiction of the faithful pastor's life. Saïd observes that Bernard makes this treatise do for the priesthood what *De moribus et officio episcoporum* does for bishops and *De consideratione* does for the pope.[84]

This, however, is an afterthought, because the basic thrust of the preached shorter edition, which is approximately four-fifths the length of the longer, is the affirmation that the surest way to heaven is afforded by the opportunity the monastic life gives to rid oneself of every distraction and devote oneself completely to the love of God.

Bernard's Other Sermons

Not all of Bernard's preaching was monastic, but all that has been preserved is. It is especially regrettable that all examples of his preaching in support of the crusades against heresy and for the recovery of the tomb of Christ are lost. There are, however, some indications of the sorts of things he might have said. Sermons 65 and 66 on the Canticles seem to have been written in response to a request from Eberwin (or Evervin) of Steinfeld, prior of a Premonstratensian community near Cologne, for Bernard to speak out against heretics of a Catharist variety in his vicinity.[85] There are also several indications of what Bernard's preaching of the second crusade may have been like. It was Bernard who wrote the Rule for the great crusading order, the Knights Templar, and he also wrote a treatise, *In Praise of the New Knighthood*.[86] There also exists an exciting account of his preaching the crusade at Vézelay on Palm Sunday 1146, when so many came forward to receive the cloth cross that signified their enlistment that Bernard had to tear up his own clothing to make more crosses.[87] At first he opposed the crusade, but when his former pupil Pope Eugenius III asked him to preach it, he complied without question. Yet Bernard's feeling for the Templars was a result of their being a religious order so that even in preaching the crusade there is some sense that Bernard's preaching was monastic preaching.

De Psalmo "Qui habitat"

So far this section has looked at the various collections of Bernard's sermonic material rather than at any particular sermon. It has also emphasized types of monastic preaching rather than the specific content of such sermons. Justice is done to this tradition and its greatest exemplar only by looking at an individual sermon. A good example of the body of work in general, and one that comes closer to oral preaching than many, is the sixth of the Lenten sermons on Psalm 91. (For this sermon, **see Vol. 2, pp. 167-71.**)

Manuscripts of this sermon series fall into three categories: (1) a short form in which commentary is made on only the first six verses of Psalm 91, (2) a longer form that extends the commentary through verse 10, and (3) the final form that makes this series a commentary on the sixteen verses of the psalm, the only commentary from Bernard other than the sermons on the Song of Songs.[88] Since the short manuscripts divide their six sermons into thirty fragments, these may closely resemble notes from which Bernard actually preached to his monks over one Lenten season. The complete form of the work, however, shows too many signs of overall design and finished prose style to be anything but a treatise written in the literary genre of the sermon. Or, more properly, it is written in the literary genre of the homily, since the sermons are verse-by-verse expositions of the passage.

The commentary, of course, is not so much concerned with the literal, historical meaning of the psalm as it is with applying the psalm's meaning to the lives of monks.[89] We may see the way that is done in Sermon 6 on the second part of verse 5 and all of verse 6,[90] which read as follows:

> You will not fear the terror of the night;
> nor the arrow that flies by day,
> nor the bogy that prowls in the darkness,
> nor assault, nor the noonday devil.[91]

The sermon identifies the four dangers listed with temptations faced by monks. The terror of the night is fear of the vexations of the body that appear as temptations during the night. The arrow that flies by day is the vainglory of those who have overcome carnal temptations and thus appear fervent. The bogy that prowls in the darkness is not considered to be an external enemy like the first two, but the treason from within of ambition. These three are equated with the three temptations that came to Jesus (in the Matthean order), but the Tempter did not try on him the fourth: the noonday devil. This is the temptation to regard what is evil as though it were not only good but perfect. After showing how these temptations have beset the church throughout its history, Bernard ends by reminding the brothers that he had dealt with these temptations in one of his sermons on the Song of Songs (Sermon 33), where he connected the noonday devil with the noonday rest of the bridegroom.

Scripture is used here not to inquire into how this psalm reflects the experience of those who journeyed to Jerusalem for one of the pilgrim feasts, the literal, historical meaning of the text. Rather, it borrows familiar language that is recited at least once a week to put into words the monks' experiences in evading temptation. Bernard belonged to a community so saturated with the vocabulary of the Bible that it was the most natural thing in the world to borrow its phrases to describe whatever was going on.[92] In this sermon he makes use of the words not only of Psalm 91 but of much of the rest of the canon as well; Sermon 6 fills only seven pages printed with very wide margins, but there are fifty-seven biblical allusions. This incidence of allusion is by no means exceptional.

Jean Leclercq is able to say that Bernard uses Scripture in both senses of the word:

> First, it is a text that predates his own experience and thinking. . . . He was able to interpret his experience only because it had its continual source in the Church. He could thus similarly understand the solution that the Spirit of God brought to his problems, or more exactly, to the problem that he had with himself.[93]

It is also a pretext in that it becomes an occasion to talk about God's love for souls. "God continues to speak in the words he has left us and through his Spirit, who continues in us the work he began with the biblical writers."[94] Thus

> We are asked to remove the cover and find the hidden contents within; in this way, sacred history, which is universal, objective, impersonal, and external, becomes *our* history.

This is to say that Bernard did what all good preachers have done down through the ages: he applied the Scriptures to the lives of his hearers. This shows the fundamental kinship of monastic preaching with all effective preaching. It also shows that monastic preaching was an important expression of the homiletic aspect of the eleventh- and twelfth-century renaissance.

"YOUR DAUGHTERS SHALL PROPHESY"[95]

Another aspect of this renaissance was the appearance of women who preached with the approval of the Catholic Church in the West. While it seems very likely that women preached in the subapostolic church and perhaps into the second century,[96] records of who they were, what they said, and how they said it have been lost or expunged.[97] Through the ages, schismatic and heretical bodies—from the early Montanists to the Waldensians and Catharists to be studied in the next chapter—have been much more open to women's voices than the Great Church. The twelfth century, however, proves an exception to the rule: a number of women are known to have preached with church approval. Some of these were abbesses addressing their own nuns in the absence of a priest, but the best-documented examples are of women who invoked a different justification for their activity in the face of culturally engrained misogyny, tradition, and explicit biblical statements such as the Pauline prohibition: "Women should be silent in the churches" (1 Cor. 14:34). As Carolyn Muessig has said, "When a teaching or preaching woman is encountered in twelfth- or thirteenth-century medieval sources, her ability to speak about divine matters is generally attributed to a charism of prophecy rather than intelligence."[98]

These women include Rose of Viterbo[99] and Umiltà of Faenza.[100] There is no doubt, however, that their most impressive representative was Hildegard of Bingen. This is true not only because of her preaching, but also because of the range of her activities. No other medieval woman and few men of the time wrote as extensively as she did, or in as many genres. She produced three massive theological tomes in a visionary format. She wrote works of science, including a medical guide. She provided the words and music for liturgical texts and created the first morality play—the only one in which all parts are sung except that of the devil. She was consulted personally and through correspondence by a variety of persons, including bishops and heads of religious houses, members of the nobility, and ordinary people. Her correspondents included a pope, an emperor, and even Bernard of Clairvaux. And, besides preaching to her sisters, she went on several long preaching tours, stopping at monasteries, convents, and cathedral cities as a welcome guest of the hierarchy. She overcame obstacles of opposition by male officials and held on to what she thought she should do. And all of this was accomplished despite her being sick a great deal of the time.

Born in 1098 as the tenth child of wealthy and well-connected parents, Hildegard was precociously religious, having her first visionary experience before she was five. When she was eight, her parents offered her as a tithe of their children to the religious life. She was enclosed—literally, walled up—as an anchoress in a cell attached to the Benedictine monastery of Disibodenberg, where she served as a sort of apprentice hermit under Jutta, the young, beautiful, talented, devout, and determined daughter of a local count. The deep spirituality of the pair quickly attracted disciples, and their cell was transformed into a Benedictine community for women. Hildegard made her profession when she was fifteen.

Almost nothing is known of her next twenty-three years. But in 1136 Jutta died, and Hildegard succeeded her as abbess. Although she had continued to have visions, she had revealed them only to Jutta, who in turn spoke of them to Volmar, one of the monks there who was destined to become one of Hildegard's closest collaborators. In 1141, however, she had a vision that surpassed anything she had experienced before. It left her with the feeling that she "knew the meaning of the exposition of the scriptures, namely the Psalter, the Gospel, and the other catholic volumes of both the Old and the New Testaments."[101] With the understanding came a command from God to write the visions she had received. For a long time she resisted the command, but when she fell into sickness, she interpreted that as a sign of divine disfavor, so she began the ten-year-long process of writing what she had seen and heard and the understanding of it she had received. While she was writing, her project came to the attention of Pope Eugenius, who read what she had done and commanded her to finish the work.

While she was still at work on this book, which she called *Scivias* (a contraction of the Latin for "Know the ways of the Lord"), the project attracted a great deal of attention. Suddenly Hildegard announced that God had commanded her to move the convent thirty kilometers away to Rupertsberg, a hill overlooking the Rhine near the town of Bingen. When the abbot of Disibodenberg refused to let them go for various reasons, she fell ill again, until he was convinced that her illness was a sign and allowed them to make the move. *Scivias* is an enormous book, running to just under five hundred pages in the Hart and Bishop translation. It recounts twenty-six visions and their much longer interpretations, but the subject, as the name implies, is the virtues needed by persons in various walks of life to attain paradise.

Her second great work, *Liber vitae meritorum (The Book of Life's Merits)* on which she worked from 1158 to 1163, is devoted to the vices that oppose the virtues considered in the *Scivias*. Then, from 1163 to 1174 she composed her most ambitious work, *Liber divinorum operum (Book of Divine Works)*. This book

> can be seen as a triumph of synthesis in which Hildegard brings together her theological beliefs, her physiological understanding, her speculations on the working of the human mind and of structure of the universe, into a unified whole.[102]

During the time she was at work on these three volumes of her visionary *summa,* she was also busy as the head of a religious community, occupied with an international correspondence and preaching tours, composing music for the liturgy, and aging—turning seventy-six the year she finished the *Liber divinorum operum*. This makes it all the more astonishing that during the same period, she also summed up and may even have contributed to her age's knowledge of nature in two large scientific works, her *Physica (Natural History)* and a medical treatise, *Causae et curae (Causes and Cures)*. The *Physica* has sections on plants, the elements, trees, jewels and precious stones, fish, birds, animals, reptiles, and metals, and is primarily concerned with their medical use. This work and *Causae et curae* have led to speculation over whether Hildegard filled her spare time by serving as the convent's infirmarian.

While it would be interesting to discuss the haunting beauty of Hildegard's liturgical music, now accessible through a number of recordings, or the vivid illustrations that illuminate her visionary trilogy, it is her preaching that is the proper concern of these pages. Although she took four preaching tours, preaching before both religious houses and the clergy and laity at large, what is best preserved is the preaching she did as the one responsible for the formation and ultimately for the salvation of her own community. While she included copies of some of her sermons in her correspondence, the main source for her sermons is *Expositiones evangeliorum (Expositions of the Gospels)*.[103] These are homilies on the Gospels for twenty-four days in the liturgical calendar.

In addition to her mandate as an abbess, Hildegard based her authority to preach on the prophetic calling responsible for her great visionary trilogy, which also was the justification for her advising a pope, an emperor, bishops and abbots, members of the nobility, and laypersons through correspondence. It is not surprising, therefore, that some of the main themes of the *summa* recur in both the letters and in the homilies.[104] These themes are also reflected in the fact that, while there is only one homily in the *Expositiones* for many of the feasts, for others there are two, three, and even four, each with its distinctive interpretation.

While Hildegard's interpretation is invariably allegorical, it does not correspond to the traditional four levels of meaning in medieval exegesis: literal/historical, allegorical, moral, and anagogical. Rather, she is closer to Origen's distinction between literal and spiritual meaning. But there are four themes or patterns to her interpretation, themes that are tantalizingly and confusingly close to the four traditional meanings, but are never coextensive with them. These themes are: (1) the collective struggle of humankind in salvation history, (2) the journey of the faithful soul, (3) the individual and collective battles against sin that the nun and her community wage in monastic life, and (4) the cosmological theme of the harmony of cosmic elements reestablished with the soul's restoration.[105]

We may see how this plays out in Hildegard's reading of the Gospel for the First Sunday of Advent, Luke 21:25-33, the only Gospel on which four homilies have been preserved. (For the text of these sermons, see **Vol. 2, pp. 172-77.**) There are two elements in this pericope from Luke's version of "the Little Apocalypse," the signs of the end of the age and the *Parousia,* and the parable of the fig tree's leaves as a sign of the times. Hildegard is rare among medieval exegetes in interpreting the parable and connecting it with the signs of the end.

While the first of her homilies for the day is designated in a manuscript as dealing with the literal meaning, it also has a cosmological dimension. The signs of the end are seen as indications of the reaction of the cosmos and angels to human sin. In the fourth homily, the interpretative pattern is that of the drama of the individual soul. A typical theme of the war between virtues and vices can be observed in this psychodrama of both the individual nun and the community as a whole. We can see in these two homilies a familiar Hildegardian theme of playing off microcosm versus macrocosm. The second homily, designated in the manuscript as allegorical, demonstrates Hildegard's concern in resisting the spread of Catharism from France to the Rhineland. And the third homily, which employs the motif of the battle between vices and virtues, seems to have been an expression of Hildegard's concern over the schism in Germany from 1159 to 1177 when her patron, the emperor Frederick Barbarossa, supported anti-popes against the one to whom she was loyal.

As Kienzle says,

> The set of four homilies highlights the spiritual meaning of the text. One is primarily historical-literal, concerned with salvation history, Christ's coming and redemption; another, a psychodrama, is highly allegorical with elements of anagogy. Two moral interpretations relate to contemporary society. . . .[106] Nonetheless, all are primarily spiritual and three of four include a cosmological dimension. These four homilies . . . demonstrate the richness of Hildegard's exegetical range in the entire corpus of *Expositiones*.[107]

There have been many attempts to account for Hildegard's visions psychologically or medically. Sabina Flanagan, for example, offers a plausible case for regarding them as a function of migraines.[108] Since allowing women to preach not only then but down through the twentieth century has been justified by stating they were prophets rather than clergy, such interpretations need assessment. There is no need to reject such analyses: much of what God does in human history is mediated through the ordinary processes of nature (themselves the creations of God). But the analysis alone can be reductionistic, implying that the visions were nothing but migraine, or hallucination, or delusion. The difficulty with this analysis is that from biblical times onward, some of the human beings most honored for their contributions to human spirituality and morality have claimed that their insights were communicated to them in manners that today could result in their being certified as insane. If these people were crazy, we all should be so crazy. Yet there have been those who insisted that they were prophets who were either victims of pathology or charlatans. The question becomes how to distinguish between true and false prophets. The only criterion still seems today to be the pragmatic one offered by Jesus: "You will know them by their fruits" (Matt. 7:16, 20).

The stage in the history of preaching represented by Guibert, Alan, Bernard, and Hildegard was truly a renaissance. As such, it was the homiletical manifestation of the vigorous intellectual awakening of the eleventh and twelfth centuries, and its quality was consistent with all the best of the movement's other aspects. Thus it has significance in its own right and also constitutes necessary preparation for the great outburst of preaching that was about to occur.

FOR FURTHER READING

Alan of Lille: The Art of Preaching. Translated with an introduction by Gillian R. Evans. Cistercian Studies Series, no. 23. Kalamazoo, Mich.: Cistercian Publications, 1981.

Bernard of Clairvaux. *Bernard of Clairvaux, Sermons on Conversion: On Conversion, A Sermon to Clerics, and Lenten Sermons on the Psalm, "He Who Dwells."* Translated with an introduction by Marie-Bernard Saïd. Cistercian Fathers Series, no. 25. Kalamazoo, Mich.: Cistercian Publications, 1981.

Evans, G. R. *Alan of Lille: The Frontiers of Theology in the Later Twelfth Century.* Cambridge and New York: Cambridge University Press, 1983.

Flanagan, Sabina. *Hildegard of Bingen, 1098–1179: A Visionary Life.* London and New York: Routledge, 1989.

Guibert of Nogent. "The Way a Sermon Ought to Be Given." In *Readings in Medieval Rhetoric.* Translated by Joseph M. Miller, edited by Joseph M. Miller, Michael H. Prosser, and Thomas W. Benson, 162-81. Bloomington and London: Indiana University Press, 1973.

Hildegard of Bingen. *Hildegard of Bingen: Expositions of the Gospels.* Translated by Beverly Mayne Kienzle and Fay Martineau. Kalamazoo, Mich.: Cistercian Publications, forthcoming.

Leclercq, Jean. *The Love of Learning and the Desire for God: A Study of Monastic Culture.* Translated by Catharine Misrahi. New York: Fordham University Press, 1961, 1974.

Notes

1. David Knowles, *The Evolution of Medieval Thought* (New York: Vintage Books, 1962), 71-149.

2. Guibert's account of this event is recorded in a portion of his *Memoirs* in *Rhetoric in the Middle Ages: A History of Rhetorical Theory from St. Augustine to the Renaissance,* trans. James J. Murphy (Berkeley and Los Angeles: The University of California Press, 1974), 301. For the complete work, see *A Monk's Confession:*

The Memoirs of Guibert of Nogent, trans. with intro. Paul J. Archambault (University Park, Pa.: Pennsylvania State University Press, 1996).

3. *Liber quo ordine sermo fieri debeat*, PL 156, cols. 21-32. A translation of this by Joseph M. Miller appeared in *Today's Speech* 17 (1969), 46ff.; reprinted in *Readings in Medieval Rhetoric,* ed. Joseph M. Miller, Michael H. Prosser, and Thomas W. Benson (Bloomington: Indiana University Press, 1973), 162-81.

4. Discussed in chapter 7.

5. Miller, Prosser, and Benson, *Readings in Medieval Rhetoric,* 162.

6. Ibid., 164-65. *Sacra pagina* was a technical term for the study of the Bible made by medieval students who had completed their studies of the liberal arts. It was undertaken both for instruction in their private religious duties and as preparation for a pastoral charge. See Beryl Smalley, *The Study of the Bible in the Middle Ages* (Notre Dame: University of Notre Dame Press, 1964), xv.

7. Miller, Prosser, and Benson, *Readings in Medieval Rhetoric,* 168-69.

8. Ibid., 170.

9. Ibid.

10. *Littera gesta docet, quid credas allegoria, Moralis quid agis, quo tendas anagogia.* Quoted in Robert Grant and David Tracy, *A Short History of the Interpretation of the Bible,* 2nd ed., rev. and enl. (Philadelphia: Fortress, 1984), 85.

11. Miller, Prosser, and Benson, *Readings in Medieval Rhetoric,* 173.

12. *Alan of Lille: The Art of Preaching,* trans. with intro. Gillian R. Evans, Cistercian Studies Series, no. 23 (Kalamazoo, Mich.: Cistercian Publications, 1981) from *Ars praedicandi,* PL 210, cols. 109-35. In Latin, Alan's name is Alanus de Insulis and is sometimes translated into English as Alan of the Isles as, for example, in the translation of chaps. 1, 38, 39, and 41 (the theoretical chapters) by Joseph M. Miller, which appears in Miller, Prosser, and Benson, *Readings in Medieval Rhetoric,* 228-39. The term, however, refers to the French city of Lille.

13. While all of PL 210 is devoted to Alan, it does not include all of his works. A list of the known works and editions of them is given in G. R. Evans, *Alan of Lille: The Frontiers of Theology in the Later Twelfth Century* (Cambridge and New York: Cambridge University Press, 1983), 14-19.

14. Evans, *Alan of Lille: The Frontiers of Theology,* 87.

15. Knowles, *The Evolution of Medieval Thought,* 71-149. See also Mark Zier, "Sermons of the Twelfth Century Schoolmasters and Canons," in *The Sermon,* directed by Beverly Mayne Kienzle (Turnhout, Belgium: Brepols, 2000), 325-62.

16. Evans, *Alan of Lille: The Art of Preaching,* 6.

17. Murphy, *Rhetoric in the Middle Ages,* 307.

18. *Praedicatio est, manifesta et publica instructio morum et fidei, informationi hominum deserviens, ex rationum semita, et auctoritatum fonte proveniens.* Alanus de Insulis, *Ars praedicandi,* PL 210 (cols. 109-35).

19. Evans, *Alan of Lille: The Art of Preaching,* 15.

20. Evans, *Alan of Lille: Frontiers of Theology,* 89-90. The work of Peter referred to is his *Verbum abbreviatum,* which, in the opinion of Evans, "has, on the face of it, a strong claim to be set beside Alan's *Art of Preaching* as the first manual of preaching in the university tradition" (89).

21. Evans, *Alan of Lille: The Art of Preaching,* 16.

22. This limitation seems strange since Alan himself, who was neither a bishop nor an abbot, has left a number of sermons.

23. Murphy, *Rhetoric in the Middle Ages,* 304, 307.

24. Evans, *Alan of Lille*, 95.

25. Ibid.

26. Alanus de Insulis, *Ars praedicandi* 210 (PL col. 113). This discussion of form *(dispositio)* begins in col. 113 of PL 210 and on p. 20 of Evans's translation.

27. *Alan of Lille: The Art of Preaching,* 20-21.

28. Ibid., 22.

29. Johannes Baptist Schneyer listed 227 in *Repertorium der lateinischen Sermones des Mittelalters für die Zeit von 1150–1350 (Autoren: A-D)*, Beiträge zur Geschichte der Philosophie und Theologie des Mittelalters, Band 43, Heft 1; Münster Westfalen: Aschendorffsche Verlagsbuchhandlung,1969), 699-83. A shorter list is given in M. T. d'Alverny, *Alain de Lille: Textes inédits avec une introduction sur sa vie et ses oeuvres,* Études de philosophie médiévale, no. 70 (Paris: Librairie philosophique J. Vrin, 1965), 125-40.

30. I am grateful to her for sending me a copy.

31. D'Alverny, *Alain de Lille: Textes inédit,* 241-87, 297-306. Printed editions of Alan's other sermons are listed in Evans, *Alan of Lille: The Art of Preaching,* 19.

32. *Deus est sphaera intelligibilis cuius centrum ubique, circumferentia nusquam.* This is a pseudo-hermetic text that Alan, depending on a florilegium, thought was from Cicero.

33. As rendered in Gillian Evans's unpublished translation.

34. Important works on this topic that appeared too late to influence this chapter are *Medieval Monastic Preaching,* ed. Carolyn Muessig, Brill's Studies in Intellectual History, vol. 90 (Leiden and Boston: Brill, 1998), and Beverly Mayne Kienzle, "The Twelfth-Century Monastic Sermon," in *The Sermon,* directed by Kienzle.

35. See p. 159 above.

36. "Religious" is used here in its technical sense of persons bound by life vows, usually of poverty, chastity, and obedience, to be members of a community. This use of the word is based on the derivation of the Latin noun *religio* from the verb *religo,* "to bind fast." Thus it has the same sense as "regular," which means living under a rule. It is contrasted with "secular" in the sense of living "in the world." That is, a religious or regular priest is one who is a member of an order, while a secular priest is under a diocesan bishop and usually serves in a parish. Many of the religious were (and are) members of the laity, of course.

37. Or, using an earlier English form of the word, "Austin."

38. Augustinus, *Ep.* 211:33 (PL col. 958-68). An English version is *The Rule of Saint Augustine, Masculine and Feminine Versions,* introduction and commentary Tarsicius J. Van Bavel, trans. Raymond Canning (Garden City, N.Y.: Image Books, 1986).

39. A clear introduction to this revival, especially in its social and economic aspects, is given in R. W. Southern, *Western Society and the Church in the Middle Ages*, Penguin History of the Church, vol. 2 (Harmondsworth: Penguin, 1970), 214-

72. In succeeding sections Southern also discusses other developments in the religious life, the rise of the mendicant orders and what he calls "fringe orders and anti-orders," which will be important later in the history of preaching. See also George Zarnecki, *The Monastic Achievement,* Library of Medieval Civilization (New York: McGraw-Hill, 1972).

40. Esther de Waal, *Seeking God: The Way of St. Benedict* (Collegeville, Minn.: Liturgical Press, 1984), 32.

41. *Rule,* prologue, chap. 5. The authoritative edition is *RB 1980: The Rule of St. Benedict,* trans. Timothy Fry, O.S.B. (Collegeville, Minn.: Liturgical Press, 1981).

42. These services are called "offices" because the Latin *officium* has a range of meanings that includes a kindness or favor, a ceremonial occasion, and an obligation or duty, all of which are nuances of the way that these liturgical acts are understood.

43. This scheme varied both seasonally, depending on how close dawn was to six o'clock, and locally, when some services were combined. E. C. Ratcliff, "The Choir Offices," in *Liturgy and Worship: A Companion to the Prayer Books of the Anglican Communion,* ed. W. K. Lowther Clarke and Charles Harris (London: SPCK, 1932), 257-66. Modern readers may be surprised by the lack of obvious reference to the Eucharist in the Rule of St. Benedict, but apparently in the sixth century Benedict himself expected it to be celebrated only on Sundays and feast days, if that often. See *RB 1980,* 410-12.

44. Since the Latin verb *orare* means both to give a speech and to pray, the English transliteration is identical for *oratoria,* the art of public speaking, and *oratorium,* a place of prayer.

45. *RB 1980,* 249-53.

46. Jean Longère, *La prédication médiéval, Séries Moyen Âge et Temps Modernes,* 9 (Paris: Études Augustinienne, 1983), 54-68.

47. Jean Leclercq, *The Love of Learning and the Desire for God: A Study of Monastic Culture,* trans. Catharine Misrahi (New York: Fordham University Press, 1961, 1974), 16-22.

48. The names of the others can be garnered either from the section of Longère cited in the previous note or from Leclercq's notes.

49. Jean Mabillon, *Bernardi Opera, Praef. generalis,* n. 23 (PL 182:26 n23). Pope Pius XII picked up this phrase in *Doctor Mellifluus,* the encyclical he wrote in 1953 to commemorate the eight-hundredth anniversary of Bernard's death. One of the best short studies of Bernard's life and importance is Thomas Merton, *The Last of the Fathers: Saint Bernard of Clairvaux and the Encyclical Letter, Doctor Mellifluus* (1954; reprint, New York: Harcourt Brace Jovanovich, 1981).

50. Leclercq, *The Love of Learning and the Desire for God,* 111.

51. Ibid., 207.

52. Gillian Evans, *The Mind of St. Bernard of Clairvaux* (Oxford: Clarendon Press; New York: Oxford University Press, 1983), 49.

53. *Sancti Bernardi Opera,* ed. J. Leclercq, C. H. Talbot, and H. Rochais, 8 vols. (Rome: Editiones Cistercienses, 1957–78). See also Jean Leclercq, *Recueil d'études sur St. Bernard et ses écrits*, 3 vols. (Rome: Edizioni di Storia e litteratura, 1966–92).

54. This is a major problem with all medieval preaching and, indeed, with written sermons from all ages.

55. The exact situation of Bernard's sermons varies from series to series, but the general process is very similar in all and is well presented in Marie-Bernard Saïd's introduction to the volume she translated, *Bernard of Clairvaux, Sermons on Conversion: On Conversion, A Sermon to Clerics, and Lenten Sermons on the Psalm, "He Who Dwells,"* Cistercian Fathers Series, no. 25 (Kalamazoo, Mich.: Cistercian Publications, 1981), 90-94.

56. *Magnificat: Homilies in Praise of the Blessed Virgin Mary by Bernard of Clairvaux and Amadeus of Lausanne,* trans. Marie-Bernard Saïd and Grace Perigo with intro. Chrysogonus Waddell, Cistercian Fathers Series, no. 18 (Kalamazoo, Mich.: Cistercian Publications, 1979), xiv, 3.

57. Evans, *The Mind of St. Bernard of Clairvaux,* 106. Cf. p. 99.

58. Evans gives a detailed analysis of Bernard's use of *parabolae* in ibid., 52-69.

59. Leclercq, Talbot, and Rochais, *Sancti Bernardi Opera,* vols. 4-6. Some or all of them appear in *St. Bernard's Sermons for the Seasons and Principle Festivals of the Year,* trans. Priest of Mount Melleray (Westminster, Md.: Carroll Press, 1950), vols. 1-3, a work I know only from citation in Clyde E. Fant Jr. and William M. Pinson Jr., eds., *20 Centuries of Great Preaching: An Encyclopedia of Preaching* (Waco, Tex.: Word, 1971), 1:149.

60. Psalm 90 in the Vulgate.

61. *Recueil d'études sur St. Bernard et ses écrits,* III, 139.

62. Leclercq, Talbot, and Rochais, *Sancti Bernardi Opera,* 6:1.

63. Ibid., 6:59.

64. Leclercq, Talbot, and Rochais, *Sancti Bernardi Opera,* vols. 1-2. While there are many English translations of excerpts, the most scholarly translation of the complete work is *Bernard of Clairvaux: On the Song of Songs,* trans. Kilian Walsh and Irene Edmonds, with intro. M. Corneille Halfants, 4 vols., Cistercian Fathers Series, nos. 4, 7, 31, and 40 (Kalamazoo, Mich.: Spencer, Mass., 1971–80).

65. Brevard S. Childs, *Introduction to the Old Testament as Scripture* (Philadelphia: Fortress, 1979), 571.

66. On the novelty that Bernard introduced into Christian spirituality and the possible dangers of excess in this innovation, see the chapter entitled "Eros: Or, Devotion to the Sacred Humanity," in G. L. Prestige, *Fathers and Heretics: Six Studies in Dogmatic Faith with Prologue and Epilogue* (London: SPCK, 1958), 180-207.

67. *Bernard of Clairvaux: Selected Works,* trans. with foreword G. R. Evans, intro. Jean Leclercq, and preface Ewert H. Cousins, Classics of Western Spirituality (New York: Paulist Press, 1987), 173-205.

68. Gilbert of Hoyland, Geoffrey of Auxerre, John of Ford, William of St. Thierry, and Alan of Lille, found in Longère, *La prédication médiévale,* 58-60.

69. Ewert H. Cousins in his preface to *Bernard of Clairvaux: Selected Writings,* 5-7. For his information he draws on an apparently unpublished paper by Richard Payne entitled "A Mystical Body of Love."

70. "Were the Sermons on the Song of Songs Delivered in Chapter?," introduction to vol. 2, *Bernard of Clairvaux: On the Song of Songs*, vii-xxx. The quotation is from p. xxx. In "The Making of a Masterpiece," his introduction to vol. 4, Leclercq makes a fascinating reconstruction of the way that the writing and editing of the *Sermons* can be correlated with what is known of Bernard's life (ix-xxiv).

71. William of St. Thierry, *Vita Sancti Bernardi* (PL 185:258-59).
72. Ibid. (PL 184:407-36). This work is also referred to as *Brevis Commentatio in Cantica*. The quotation from Leclercq is from Bernard of Clairvaux: *On the Song of Songs*, 2:xxx.
73. William of St. Thierry, *Brevis Commentatio ex Sancti Bernardi Sermonibus Contexta,* 2:xxx.
74. This phrase comes from the title of one of G. L. Prestige's 1940 Bampton Lectures, *Fathers and Heretics: Six Studies in Dogmatic Faith with Prologue and Epilogue* (London: SPCK, 1958), 180.
75. From the encyclical *Doctor Mellifluus,* trans. Thomas Merton in *The Last of the Fathers,* 112.
76. Quoted by Chrysogonus Waddell in his introduction to *Magnificat,* xviii.
77. Ibid., xvii.
78. Leclercq, Talbot, and Rochais, *Sancti Bernardi Opera,* 4:1-58; trans. Saïd, *Magnificat,* 1-58.
79. Preface, translated in *Magnificat,* 3.
80. Evans, *The Mind of St. Bernard of Clairvaux,* 136.
81. Bernard of Clairvaux, *Sermons on Conversion*, 18.
82. Geoffrey of Auxerre, *Vita Prima* IV.ii.10 (PL 183, 327).
83. Bernard of Clairvaux, *Sermons on Conversion,* 69.
84. Ibid., 19.
85. Eberwin of Steinfeld, *Epistolae* (PL 182:676-80). See the note in Bernard of Clairvaux, *On the Song of Songs,* 3:189. See also Leclercq's statement in 2:xi-xiii.
86. *De Laude Novae Militiae,* trans. Conrad Greenia in *The Works of Bernard of Clairvaux: Volume 7, Treatises III,* Cistercian Fathers Series, no. 19 (Kalamazoo, Mich.: Cistercian Publications, 1977), 125-67. The Rule of the Templars is found in PL 166:853-76.
87. Author, *Vita prima* 3.iv.9 (PL 185:308-9). On the whole issue of Bernard's involvement with the crusade, see Evans, *The Mind of St. Bernard of Clairvaux,* 24-36.
88. Leclercq, Talbot, and Rochais, *Sancti Bernardi Opera*, 4:119-22; Saïd, *Bernard of Clairvaux, Sermons on Conversion*, 97-99. There are seventeen sermons on the sixteen verses; sermon six continues the discussion of verse five begun in sermon five and also discusses verse six.
89. "This is to be more than an exegetical exercise. It is to change men's hearts. Bernard says that he has chosen the Psalm expressly because it is concerned with the battle with temptation which is fought especially hard in Lent." Evans, *The Mind of St. Bernard of Clairvaux,* 101.
90. *"De ultima parte eiusdem et de sexto versu."* The form of the Psalter Bernard used did not have the same verse divisions as modern editions of the Hebrew and translations made from them. As a result, what Bernard considers to be only the last part of verse 5 of Psalm 91 is the entire verse in modern editions. His edition puts the words "his truth will cover you with a shield" in verse 5, while they are the ending of verse 4 in modern editions. (They are more correctly translated in the RSV as meaning, "his faithfulness is a shield and buckler" [Ps. 91:4*b*].) Sermon 5 was devoted to these words and Sermon 6 comments on what are verses 5 and 6 in

modern editions. Verse divisions were not introduced until Robert Estienne ("Stephanus") placed them in his 1551 edition of the Greek New Testament. Chapter divisions were created by Stephen Langton, the archbishop of Canterbury who brought about the signing of the Magna Carta in 1215.

91. Saïd, *Bernard of Clairvaux, On Conversion,* 143.

92. Rather in the way that those who engage in amateur theatricals find that lines from the current play make appropriate observations on a wide variety of occasions.

93. Leclercq, *Bernard of Clairvaux: Selected Works,* 32.

94. Ibid.

95. "Then afterward I will pour out my spirit on all flesh; your sons and your daughters shall prophesy, your old men shall dream dreams, and your young men shall see visions" (Joel 2:28).

96. Elisabeth Schüssler Fiorenza, *In Memory of Her: A Feminist Theological Reconstruction of Christian Origins* (New York: Crossroad, 1983); Karen Jo Torjesen, *When Women Were Priests: Women's Leadership in the Early Church and the Scandal of Their Subordination in the Rise of Christianity* (San Francisco: HarperSanFrancisco, 1993).

97. There is no complete history of preaching by women. The best treatment of the subject available is a collection of essays by different scholars, *Women Preachers and Prophets Through Two Millennia of Christianity,* ed. Beverly Mayne Kienzle and Pamela J. Walker (Berkeley and Los Angeles: The University of California Press, 1998).

98. Carolyn Muessig, "Prophecy and Song: Teaching and Preaching by Medieval Women," in ibid., 147.

99. Darlene Pryds, "Proclaiming Sanctity Through Prescribed Acts: The Case of Rose of Viterbo," in ibid., 173-95.

100. Catherine M. Mooney, "Authority and Inspiration in the *Vitae* and Sermons of Humility of Faenza," in *Medieval Monastic Preaching,* ed. Carolyn Muessig, Brill's Studies in Intellectual History, vol. 90 (Leiden and Boston: E. J. Brill, 1998).

101. *Hildegard of Bingen: Scivias,* trans. Mother Columba Hart and Jane Bishop, intro. Barbara J. Newman, pref. Caroline Walker Bynum (New York: Paulist Press, 1990), 59.

102. Sabina Flanagan, *Hildegard of Bingen, 1098–1179: A Visionary Life* (London and New York: Routledge, 1989), 142.

103. The standard edition of the Latin text is in *Analecta Sanctae Hildegardis*, ed. Jean-Baptiste Pitra, *Analecta Sacra,* vol. 8 (Monte Cassino, 1882), 245-347. Beverly Mayne Kienzle and Carolyn Muessig are preparing a new edition from the best manuscripts for Corpus Christianorum Continuation Mediaevalis. Kienzle is also translating the *Expositions* for Cistercian Publications with Fay Martineau. I am indebted to Professor Kienzle for copies of her articles on Hildegard's preaching and for her Latin text and translation of the twenty-fourth set of homilies.

104. In what follows I depend on Beverly Mayne Kienzle's article "Hildegard of Bingen's Teaching in her *Expositiones evangeliorum* and *Ordo virtutum*" in *Medieval Monastic Education*, ed. George Ferzoco and Carolyn Muessig (London and New York: Leicester University Press, 2000), 72-86.

105. While Hildegard's visions were communicated in vivid symbolic experience, their result was not mystical experience as in Meister Eckhart or apocalyptic scenar-

ios as in Savonarola (for the two, see chapter 10), but solid intellectual understanding of issues of faith and morals.

106. Such external reference is a very rare thing in monastic preaching.

107. Kienzle, "Hildegard of Bingen's Teaching in her *Expositiones evangeliorum* and *Ordo virtutum*," 81.

108. Flanagan, *Hildegard of Bingen*, 193-213.

CHAPTER 9

THE EXPLOSION OF PREACHING IN THE THIRTEENTH AND FOURTEENTH CENTURIES

THE CONTEXT

Seldom in the history of the church has there been such a rapid and widespread increase in the amount of preaching along with a corresponding proliferation of interest in that preaching as that which began early in the thirteenth century and continued through the fourteenth. One way of documenting this increase is to point to the sheer volume of sermons that have survived from the time. A compiled list of sermons from the years 1150 to 1350 consists of nothing other than the beginnings and endings of sermons along with an identification of the manuscripts in which those sermons are to be found. Nonetheless, the list runs to nine volumes that have a cumulative seventy-three hundred pages. If the average number of sermons per page is consistent with a sample of more than forty pages, more than eighty thousand sermons have been preserved in manuscripts.

In those days when writing materials were so precious and the time needed to inscribe a manuscript was so great, it is doubtful that any of those were written down to be preached just once or even by only one preacher. (Originality was valued less highly then than it is now!) And, of course, it is likely that far more manuscripts have been lost than have been preserved. When all of these factors are taken into consideration, it becomes obvious that the total amount of preaching during this period must have been enormous.[1]

Many of the reasons for such an outburst of preaching are well known. A period of economic expansion had been going on in Europe since before the first crusade (1096–99). An expanding population and more efficient farming methods had produced both prosperity and the need for developing trade. That in turn caused cities to spring up.

Since the parochial system had been tied to the land under feudalism, the church was ill prepared to minister to the new urban masses until a new kind of religious order had developed that could take the gospel to these people where they were. The most notable of these orders, the Franciscans (founded 1209) and the Dominicans (founded 1215), were not, at first, tied to monasteries in remote places as the Cistercians were, but rather lived as wandering beggars who were free to go where the people were.

In order to prepare themselves for this ministry of preaching, these mendicants took advantage of the universities being founded at the time, institutions stimulated by the recovery in the West of the thought of Aristotle. Thus the friars, as members of these orders were called, developed a system that had never existed before for training preachers. In this intellectual and evangelical ferment, a complete support system or infrastructure, one that included the provision of numerous homiletical aids, was established to enable these preachers to do their work. I will address this in more detail later. First, it is necessary to notice that the friars were not the first to respond to the evangelical impulse that seemed to be in the air at the time.

Irregular Preachers

The social ferment described above caused the dislocation of great numbers of people and psychological displacement among others. Old institutions and ways of thinking were brought into question. Not surprisingly, the church and its teaching were among those up for reassessment. The church had grown so large, rich, and powerful that it had been able to challenge even the authority of kings. It began to occur to many, especially among the homeless poor, that such pomp and luxury was a strange development of the religion of the Son of Man who had no place to lay his head (Matt. 8:20; Luke 9:58).

As early as the mid-eleventh century, the Augustinian canons had announced their standard to be the apostolic life *(vita apostolica);* for them, the primary sense of this phrase was the community of goods.[2] In the last quarter of the century, though, the ideal came to be expressed first in the lives of hermits and then in the lives of wandering preachers. Even before their message became heretical, there was great indignation against it among the clergy because these itinerants were often laypersons who were not licensed to preach. The preachers responded by questioning the worthiness of the priests, accusing them of simony, luxury, and unchastity. Inevitably, charges of disobeying spiritual authorities when they refused to give up their preaching drove many of these *Wanderprediger* out of the church so that heresy followed almost inevitably. Originally, though, the charges against them were disciplinary rather than doctrinal.[3]

The period under discussion is that in which the Augustinian canons and the Cistercians were founded and the lay preaching movements reflect some of the same impulses in the piety of the time. Indeed, other religious orders grew out of these beginnings. Robert of Arbissel was a priest who became a hermit before becoming a wandering preacher. The large number of followers who responded to his preaching—"Christ's Poor," as they called themselves—forced him to settle down and form a double monastery[4] at Fontevrault around 1100. Not all wandering preachers, however, were able to stay within the church as Robert did. An Augustinian canon and pupil of Abelard, Arnold of Brescia, taught that the church should give up its wealth and power. He led in the founding of communes in Brescia and Rome to oppose clerical abuses until he was burned at the stake under Hadrian IV. Peter of Bruys and his disciple Henry the Monk preached in France that individuals are responsible for their own salvation and that the entire sacramental and ecclesiastical systems are therefore of no use. Peter was burned by a crowd for what it regarded as sacrilege, and Henry's followers were the targets of a preaching mission by Bernard of Clairvaux (**see chap. 8, pp. 187-97**).

These movements in the first half of the twelfth century were paving the way for much larger ones that dominated the last half of the century, the Waldenses and the Cathars or Albigensians. The Waldenses are the only medieval sect that still exists—although it has changed much through the centuries. In the mid-1170s, its founder, a wealthy merchant of Lyons named Valdès,[5] responded to Christ's "counsel of perfection" to sell all that he had (Matt. 19:21) by making provision for his family and giving the rest of his goods to the poor. Taking Jesus' instructions to the apostles (Matt. 10:5-23) as his standard, he began to travel around preaching repentance, receiving his support entirely from alms.

Soon he attracted followers who assisted in this ministry; they were known as "the Poor in Spirit" or "the Poor of Lyon" and quickly spread through France and over into what are modern Germany and Italy. In Italy they attracted into their company similar local groups, both those known as the *Humiliati* and former followers of Arnold of Brescia.

At first the church's only objection to their work was that they preached without license, and they were excommunicated around 1182 for this disobedience. Even afterward their main doctrinal variations were directed toward a biblical literalism that objected to anything in the church that lacked explicit scriptural warrant. Their leaders were a group called the Seventy who obeyed all the Gospel instructions for the apostolic mission. Since these passages in the New Testament say nothing of gender, women as well as men were permitted to preach and to officiate at the Eucharist.[6]

Very different are the Cathars, who were heretics from the beginning.[7] And that beginning could have been very early; one may trace an unbroken succession between them and the Gnostics of the second century.[8] In the classical way, they were dualists who saw two opposing principles or even two gods fighting against one another in the universe. One was spiritual and therefore good, and the other responsible for the existence of the material universe and therefore evil. Salvation came through receiving the *consolamentum,* a sort of "waterless baptism," and committing themselves to celibacy and to eating no foods regarded as products of sexual intercourse (eggs, meat, milk, and cheese, but not, according to their thought, fish).

Only a few, the "Perfects," received this consolation before death appeared imminent; those who did became, in effect, the clergy of the Cathars and had the duties of preaching, teaching, and administering the *consolamentum*. Ordinary believers *(credentes)* were not expected to practice such asceticism; their hope lay in receiving the *consolamentum* before they died and supporting the Perfects in the meanwhile. Considering human sexuality as a creation of the Evil One, the Cathars regarded distinctions of gender as even less important than the Waldenses did. Women could receive the *consolamentum* as well as men. Having received it, they had the duties of administering it to others and preaching. They were not itinerant, however, and thus did not become deacons or bishops, though the rationale for that restriction seems to have been a practical one of the hardship of the life rather than a theoretical one of their not being qualified.

In Montaillou, at any rate, the main inclination to heresy arose from resentment of the tithes imposed by the church.[9] The combined impact of the Cathars and Waldenses was so great that between them they "threatened to carry the entire region from the Alps to the Pyrenees out of communion with the Roman Catholic Church."[10] To oppose their preaching, the church had to have even more effective preachers of its own.[11] The need for these preachers is one of the immediate causes for the mendicant orders' formation.

The Coming of the Friars

It is hard to imagine two men more different than the founders of the two orders most responsible for the explosion of preaching, the Franciscans and Dominicans,[12] orders that inevitably get lumped together. Francis was still in his late twenties when his personal example began to attract others to imitate his way of life. The son of a wealthy merchant, he had given up earlier ambition to become a knight and, thus, to enter the nobility, in order to practice a simple, direct, and apparently naive spirituality. He had an ardent desire to lead the apostolic life that caused him to embrace poverty, pray constantly, and show love to outcasts to the extent of kissing the sores of lepers. He obeyed Gospel injunctions literally to the extent that he rebuilt decayed churches with his own hands. He had a mystic ardor and charism that make it easy for modern Christians, on the one hand, to regard him as the most obvious saint who ever lived and, on the other, to be uncomfortable with what today seem like symptoms of pathology. He was not an organizer and administrator; he was much more an envisioner, and even before he died it had become obvious that it would be as easy to institutionalize his vision as to domesticate a rainbow.[13]

Dominic, on the other hand, was in his midforties when he established his order. He was a well-trained scholar and a member of the Augustinian canons, from whom he had learned the ideal of the apostolic life. As a canon associated with the cathedral of Osma, he entered a period of close association with the bishop of the diocese, Diego of Acevedo. In 1206 when the two were traveling through France, an incident occurred that was determinative for the rest of Dominic's life.

> In the land of the Albigensians [Bishop Diego] met the legate of Pope Innocent, with a great council of archbishops and bishops and twelve Cistercian abbots; they received him with honor and asked his advice about what ought to be done for the defense of the faith. On his advice, they abandoned all their splendid horses and clothes and accoutrements, and adopted evangelical poverty, so that their deeds would demonstrate the faith of Christ as well as their words.[14]

Diego knew that it would be impossible to compete with the heretics' preaching without matching their example of apostolic living.

He and Dominic joined in this ministry for two years before Diego started for home to raise funds to support it. Along the way, however, Diego died and Dominic was left to carry on without him. He continued with the support of Fulk, the bishop of Toulouse, and Simon de Montfort, the Englishman in charge of the military crusade against the heretics. As time went on he was joined by others who wished to assist. When he was given three houses for his followers in 1215, it appeared to be time to begin regularizing their efforts. In the same year the Fourth Lateran Council forbade the creation of new religious orders, but the next year when Dominic proposed a modification of the Rule of St. Augustine under which he already lived, Pope Honorius III recognized his order.

It was the pope himself who recommended that they be called the order of preaching brothers, a recognition that from the beginning the Dominicans understood themselves as a group committed to a homiletical mission. This was less true of the Franciscans, who saw themselves following Francis in his imitation of Christ. For Francis, "the initial motivation of his preaching is basically the recognition that it is part of the whole program of Luke 10. . . . Diego and Dominic, by contrast, start preaching because preaching is needed."[15]

Dominic lived only a few years after his order was recognized, but he had already discovered before he died that the need for preaching was not confined to the Languedoc with its Albigensian crisis. In 1217 he sent seven of the brothers to Paris and two to Spain while he himself went to Rome, leaving only four to carry on the work in Toulouse. He had also recognized that preaching requires thought and thought requires study. At first he had asked for theological scholars to come from Paris so that his friars could be trained, but he recognized later that it was better for the friars to go to the universities than for the universities to come to them. By the third quarter of the century Dominic's spiritual sons, Albert the Great and Thomas Aquinas, would dominate the intellectual life of Paris.

Preaching by the Friars

This multiplication of preachers raises the question of who was permitted to preach in the church at that time. The answer is simple: bishops were still regarded as the only ones who could preach in their own right. Others were only auxiliary preachers, preachers *per accidens*. Almost a century after the event, Jordan of Pisa could say that when Dominic proposed an order of preachers, the pope wondered to himself,

"Who is this man, who wants to found an Order consisting entirely of bishops?"[16] Yet as Innocent III had said, bishops at the time were like "dumb dogs" (Isa. 56:10 Vg.), not daring to bark because they were ignorant, and leaving the church in a condition of "evil silence" *(pessima taciturnitas)*.[17]

Obviously, many people other than bishops had preached for some time. But that raises the question of what qualifies as preaching. "Public preaching exercised for the enlightenment of a whole assembly of the faithful, generally gathered for liturgy" qualifies.[18] One could see that the mission of parochial priests constituted an extension of the bishops' ministry, and the authority to preach could be assumed to be delegated. But did priests have the authority by virtue of order, or by virtue of having a pastoral responsibility? Could priests without "a cure of souls," such as monks, preach? And what about self-appointed preachers like Valdès, or priests who left their parishes to become wandering preachers? Admittedly, bishops and even popes leaned over backward at times to encourage what seemed beneficial.

The preaching orders emerged in the context of this chaotic lack of universally accepted criteria, though the situation was very different for the two. Dominic was a learned priest and attracted similar sons. Thus in 1221 Honorius III gave members of his order authority to preach everywhere; it was their own constitutions that set limits as to who among them could preach, what education they needed to do so, and where they could preach. The decision as to who could preach was based on evidence of the candidate's having the "grace of preaching" *(gratia praedicationis),* understood as a charism, "the super-natural vocation of one who is certain that the Spirit may speak in him and through him."[19]

Francis had preached since he had heard the Gospel containing Christ's instructions to the apostles for their mission and had responded by saying, "This is what I want; this is what I long for with all my heart."[20] In 1210 Innocent III gave permission for the Franciscans to preach, under the conditions that their preaching be concerned with penitence and not doctrine, and that each friar who was to preach be given personal permission by Francis. The earlier form of the Rule said that only those who had been given permission should preach. "All the brothers, however, should preach by their deeds" (chap. xvii). Yet Francis provided an "exhortation and praise" that could be used as a model sermon by those who were not licensed to preach (chap. xxi); penitence is a major theme in it.[21] By 1219, though, Honorius III wrote to bishops, saying that he wanted the friars to "sow the seed of the divine word after the manner of the apostles,"[22] and from then on there were Franciscan preachers of doctrine as well as exhortation. By then there were also educated friars, and it became harder and harder to distinguish their preaching from that of anyone else.

PREACHING AS AN ART

Franciscans and Dominicans were prominent among those who developed a new way to preach. Previously, most preaching had been done in the form of homilies that expounded one of the biblical readings appointed for the liturgy and applied it to the lives of the people. Now a new style of sermon was developed. Its form can be conveyed from an analogy of the way that a tree branches. For example, there is a drawing of a tree in a fifteenth-century manuscript illumination; its trunk and limbs are labeled to show which parts of the tree correspond to which parts of a sermon. About halfway up, the trunk separates into three large boughs, each of which later divides into three limbs. This tree represents the way that a sermon should be based on a text, which, like the tree, is divided into three points, with each point then broken down into three subpoints.[23]

One can understand more easily when one sees how a particular text could be developed; the illumination shows that in relation to the Summary of the Law (Matt. 22:37, 39, 40). The text (or *thema,* as it was called) is divided into three questions, to each of which three answers are given:

- I. (Why should you love God?) . . .
  - A. Because of His creation of the world.
  - B. Because of His goodness.
  - C. Because of His fatherhood.
- II. (How does one love his neighbor?)
  - A. Favor and good-will.
  - B. Compassion.
  - C. Acts of love.
- III. Why do the whole Law and Prophets hang on these two commandments?
  - A. Because love is the avoidance of all evil.
  - B. Because love is the doing of all good.
  - C. Because love is also the happy and eternal consummation.

The pattern can be completed with three additions. First, there are a couple of sawn-off limbs under the main division; these indicate the possibility of a protheme (a "mini-sermon" on an entirely different text that makes the same point as the theme), which leads into a prayer. Second, there may be a "prelocution," a sort of introduction consisting of an analogy, a moralization, or a proverb. Finally, each of the nine subdivisions may use a different means of "dilating" or developing the point.[24] Although not indicated by the illumination, there is an expectation that each affirmation made in the sermon will be confirmed by at least one "authority" *(auctoritas),* a quotation of a biblical proof text. This, in turn, may be backed up by a quotation from one of the Fathers, and then possibly even a quotation from a pagan writer. (For an example of such a sermon, see **Vol. 2, pp. 202-6.**)

This kind of sermon has been variously designated. The most common term has been "university sermon," but that seems less than appropriate because (1) this is a technical term referring to sermons preached before a university, and (2) it appears uncertain that the style originated in university circles. "Scholastic sermon" connects this style of preaching with the contemporary philosophical and theological method of that name, but, as we shall see below, that connection's validity is unclear. For want of a better term, Richard Rouse and Mary Rouse have called it the "school sermon," but the identity of the schools in question is not obvious.[25] The textbooks that taught the method for preaching such sermons refer to them as "modern," but that relative term is even more confusing here than elsewhere.

The two least misleading terms seem to be those used by James J. Murphy: "artistic sermons" and "thematic sermons."[26] While "artistic" calls to mind the designation of the manuals in which this preaching style is taught as *artes praedicandi* ("arts of preaching"), artistic preaching is suggestive of a wider aestheticism. Since "thematic sermon" indicates that this type of sermon is based on interpretation of a *thema*—a text, a verse from the Bible—it appears to be the term that is least likely to lead to confusion and is thus the one that I will follow here.

The form of thematic sermon depicted in the tree illumination represents its fully evolved state. The sermons of Alan of Lille (**see above chap. 8, pp. 177-82**) represent a starting point. There the outline is a sequence of lists rather than formal divisions and subdivisions. These early sermons also lack both the *auctoritates* and the frequent use of *exempla* characteristic of the fully developed thematic sermon.[27] This development from the end of the twelfth century to the full complexity of the form in the middle of the fourteenth century is gradual but steady.[28]

Before concluding this discussion of the thematic sermon genre, it is necessary to deal with three other questions: (1) Were such sermons addressed exclusively to learned audiences? (2) What language was used for popular preaching? and (3) Was thematic preaching the only genre practiced during the period? The answer given by recent research to the first of these questions is surprising: Far from appealing only to learned audiences, thematic sermons have a number of features that made them especially appealing to popular lay audiences.[29] In order to help the most popular audience to follow, understand, and remember a sermon, speakers would divide the sermon into numbered parts; divide the sermon into a few broad parts; number them; use the protheme to introduce the visiting preacher to his new audience, giving time for latecomers to arrive, and leading the congregation into prayer; and use scriptural authorities to give instruction in the Scriptures, vary the preacher's language, and lend authority to the points made; in addition to using exempla.

The question of popular preaching's language would seem to be a non-issue were it not for one particular sort of evidence. One must agree with David d'Avray: "That the friars achieved their undoubted successes by preaching in a language which their audience could not understand is so wildly implausible that the onus of proof is on those who propose it."[30] Yet the embarrassing fact is that very few surviving thirteenth-century manuscripts contain sermons in vernacular languages. The explanation seems to be that sermon manuscripts were created for the clergy and not for the laity.[31] These manuscripts were used as model sermons from which outlines, authorities, and other matter could be taken for creating new sermons. Having the original in the friars' basic language made it easier for them to draw on it when they put together sermons in a variety of vernacular languages. A possible exception to this rule is "macaronic" sermons, that is, sermons in a mixture of Latin and a vernacular. While it is clear that such sermons were written (manuscripts of them exist), it is not so evident that these sermons were preached in this confusion of tongues.[32]

Knowing whether thematic sermons were the only preaching genre of the period is more important than it sounds. This leads one to question who was preaching. Thematic preaching was overwhelmingly the style of the mendicants, who were itinerants. What sort of preaching, if any, were the secular clergy doing? D'Avray has argued that the lack of elementary instruction in the Christian faith, basic catechesis, in the sermonic literature of the friars implies that such instruction was done by parish priests in catechetical sermons much like the *prônes* of seventeenth-century France. Such catechetical preaching, reminiscent of Aelfric's sermons, had ordinarily replaced homilies (in the technical sense) as the standard pulpit fare from parochial clergy.[33] The very existence of thematic preaching, then, implies that local pastors were laying down a solid foundation in the Christian faith, the foundation upon which the friars built.

Artes praedicandi

Amazingly early in the development of the thematic sermon a profusion of textbooks began to appear telling preachers how to construct this type of sermon.[34]

> By the year 1200 . . . the Christian Church had produced only four writers who could by any stretch of the imagination be called theorists of preaching: Saint Augustine, Pope Gregory, Guibert of Nogent, and Alain de Lille. . . . But within twenty years of 1200 a whole new rhetoric of preaching leaped into prominence, unleashing hundreds of theoretical manuals written all over Europe during the next three centuries. . . . Several hundred such preceptive manuals still survive in various European libraries.[35]

As often as not, the title of one of these textbooks was *Ars praedicandi.* Thus the plural form, *artes praedicandi,* refers to the entire group.

Throughout the history of instruction in public speaking, there have been two main ways in which people learned, the "technical" and the "sophistic."[36] "Technical" is derived from the Greek *technē,* which is close to being a synonym for the Latin *ars*. Technical rhetoric instructs through "how-to-do-it" manuals; by studying such books and applying their principles, almost anyone can become a competent speaker. Yet one cannot acquire virtuosity in this way; that comes only from following the example of acknowledged artists. In ancient Greece these were the Sophists, from whom the sophistic tradition takes its name. The sophistic method consisted of being apprenticed to one of these acknowledged virtuosos. In terms of this distinction, the *artes praedicandi* obviously inculcated a technical rhetoric.

The first *artes* seem to have appeared almost out of thin air. Not only do they predate the earliest manuscripts of sermons constructed according to the method, "there is reason to believe that the basic elements of this new approach were available outside the universities before they were taken up and popularized by academics."[37] Alexander of Ashby, an Englishman, produced such a treatise around the year 1200, stating the whole theory of thematic preaching when he said: "The mode of preaching consists in the parts of a sermon, and in its delivery. There are four parts of a sermon, to wit: prologue, division, proof, and conclusion. The entire material of the sermon is proposition and authority."[38]

An important and easily overlooked aspect of this new form is that it represents the beginning of the assumption that sermons ought to have a pattern instead of taking their shape from the biblical passage expounded. Within a few years of Ashby's work, there appeared an even greater work that both discusses the new nomenclature of preaching (theme, antetheme, division, etc.) and also sets such preaching within the intellectual framework of the period, the *Summa de arte praedicandi* of Thomas (Chabham or Chobham) of Salisbury.[39] The *artes* of Thomas Waleys and Robert of Basevorn, coming a century to a century and a half after those of Alexander and Thomas, represent the full flowering of the form. (For an abstract of the *Ars* of Basevorn, **see Vol. 2, pp. 179-93.**)

With this background, it is possible to look at the preaching method it inculcates.[40] The first step in preparing such a sermon is to choose an appropriate theme (i.e., text). To be a good theme the text has to be from the Bible—using its exact wording—and it must be a passage that has significant meaning and uses words that recur often in Scripture. It should also have three main words so that it may easily be divided into points with the preacher citing the biblical book from which it comes by chapter alone, since verses have not yet been numbered. To give latecomers time to gather, the sermon should begin with a protheme (also called an antetheme), which will culminate smoothly in a prayer for grace, such as the *Veni sancte Spiritus,* the Lord's Prayer, or the Hail Mary.

The prayer said, the preacher will repeat his text, introduce the sermon, divide the text, and then proceed to develop the parts into which the theme has been divided. The introduction should be short, and it should really introduce (*ducere intro,* "lead into") what follows. Introductions may be in either the "narrative" or the "argumentative" mode, although neither of these terms means in this regard exactly what it signifies to modern readers. Narrative introductions make use of an analogy or a quotation that employs one of the words of the theme. The argumentative mode may be built around an induction, an illustration,[41] a syllogism, or an enthymeme.[42] Illustrations may be drawn from nature (e.g., the busyness of bees), history (classical or hagiographic), or art. (It may seem picayune to list these, but apparently these sermons were judged on the basis of the rigidity with which they adhered to the form, and faults and merits were as obvious to cognoscenti of the medium as they are to judges at a dog show.)

After the theme is introduced, it is divided. The three or more "branches" into which the sermon is going to split must be announced in advance, often by some phrase such as "in which words (i.e., the text) three things are touched upon" *(in quibus verbis tria tanguntur)*.[43] The preacher may be assisted in such divisions by making use of distinctions between the various possible meanings of a word in the text (e.g., genuine and feigned penitence) or accepting a plurality (as in noting that there are three requisites for genuine penitence: contrition, confession, and satisfaction).

There are also other conditions that an "artistic" division must satisfy. First, "the words which correspond to the three parts of the division must terminate in syllables which give the same sound."[44] Then the division also should be made in the right cadence, that is, each punctuation mark should be preceded by the right number of the right kind of metric feet (but this works only for someone preaching to clergy in Latin). The key words of the theme or text are the basis of the division, but these words are not used to name the parts into which the text is divided. Even words built on the same roots are not used. Rather, synonyms of the key words that are built on different roots must be used. The parts of the division must be presented in the order in which the words come in the text. Finally, the division will take into proper account the meaning of the theme and of the individual words in it.

The division is followed by the declaration and confirmation of the parts in which the division is paraphrased, justified, and proved by the citation of biblical "authorities" or proof texts. After all of that, each of the points is developed (the *dilatatio*); for this phase, "everything that has gone before is merely a preamble, a skeleton."[45] There are three means by which this dilation is done:

1. The citation of biblical authorities.
2. The advancement of rational arguments.
3. The use of *exempla*.

This seems almost anticlimactic in its simplicity—and, indeed, Basevorn does go on to discuss such "ornaments" of the sermon as digression, correspondence, congruence of correspondence, circulation, convolution, and unification—but the method of constructing a thematic sermon has been communicated.

Presented like this, the method seems artificial in the extreme. Thomas-Marie Charland, a scholar close to the medium, could conclude his analysis of it by saying, in effect, that "one would have to know 'a hell of a lot' to preach so badly."[46] Yet contemporaries did not understand the style that way. One has only to read the introductory chapter to Waleys's *ars praedicandi* to recognize what a deeply spiritual man he was and how seriously he took the vocation of preaching.[47] Interpreting Jesus' preaching on the mountain allegorically, he says that the preacher must live on a higher plane than the congregation, that anyone in a state of mortal sin should not preach. He then says that the preacher should not preach to show off but for the glory of God and the edification of the faithful. Thus the most important preparation for preaching is the spiritual preparation of prayer.

Thereafter, Waleys begins to discuss practical issues of homiletics: The preacher's dress should be neither showy nor contemptible. This is followed by some sound advice on delivery. Gestures should be used in moderation so that the preacher is neither "an immobile statue" nor does his bodily movement suggest that he is "in a duel with someone."[48] The preacher should speak neither too loudly nor too softly, nor should his voice go up and down in a singsong way. And the preacher should avoid speaking so fast that no one understands what he says. Waleys is opposed to memorizing sermons; rather, their substance should be so familiar that the preacher can easily find language in which to express the gospel naturally and forcefully.

> When he is in the fervor of his spirit, his heart is so immediately joined to the hearts of his hearers that he will not perceive his tongue nor his hearers' ears, but it will appear to him almost as if his words flowed and proceeded into the hearts of his hearers without any mediation.[49]

The preacher should not even pay too much attention to *artes praedicandi* out of a desire to preach impressive sermons. Nor should sermons be allowed to go on too long; preachers in danger of going overtime should have a friend signal them when the time is up. Finally, new preachers should practice off in the woods by themselves until they have enough skill for preaching to people.

Thematic Preaching and Scholasticism

For over a century it has been popular to associate thematic preaching with the scholastic movement in theology. The reasons for the association are obvious enough: at about the time scholasticism had its beginning, there appeared a new form of preaching that, instead of being formless as previous preaching had been, had its parts carefully coordinated according to a central plan.[50] Thus what thematic preaching and scholasticism have in common would be systematic division of one form or another.

Yet scholasticism as such did not use just any form for division. Scholasticism was a method of arguing theological questions based on the dialectic of Aristotle and the rhetoric of Cicero. It proceeded by posing *quaestiones* formally, presenting the conflicting points of view held by different authorities and the arguments by which these were supported, and arguing to a solution that did justice to all the issues raised.[51] But thematic preaching did not proceed by formal argument to establish propositions. Rather, it proceeded by dividing a theme into progressively smaller portions and confirming each stage of division or subdivision by quoting authorities. Therefore, scholastic method as such is not used in thematic preaching.

What this preaching and scholasticism do have in common is "a passion for dividing and subdividing."[52] This common element is seen more readily in scholastic commentaries than in the *quaestiones,* since the latter do not lend themselves to numbered sections and subsections. Both the sermons and the commentaries show the working of minds that like to begin with a single point and fan out artistically. D'Avray speaks of such an attitude as exhibiting "the subdividing mentality."[53]

While he argues correctly that any theory about how this subdividing mentality came to penetrate preaching in the thirteenth century would have to be based on a still-unmade study of the sermons themselves, it is not surprising that the same minds could be capable of arguing *quaestiones* and preaching thematic sermons. After all, Aristotle himself insisted that dialectic and rhetoric have their distinctive methods of persuasion. One thing at stake is the difference between written and oral discourse. What one detects in both scholasticism and thematic preaching is an exuberant joy in the God-given powers of the human intellect.[54]

Preaching Aids

One index of the importance assigned to preaching by the mendicant orders is the variety and great abundance of tools provided to assist preachers in their sermon preparation. The *artes praedicandi* already mentioned are a case in point. Although they have received a great deal of scholarly attention, d'Avray argues that in comparing the relatively small number of *artes* manuscripts with the quantity of other preaching aids, these may not have been so important as has been thought.[55]

Reference books are so taken for granted today that the achievement of the human intellect in creating the genre may be overlooked. Many of the techniques helpful in producing searchable reference tools to make it possible for preachers to produce thematic sermons were developed during the thirteenth century and have been in common use ever since. Richard Rouse and Mary Rouse distinguish between the attitudes toward reference works held in the twelfth century and those held in the thirteenth century. They say that the first "represent efforts to assimilate and organize inherited written authority in a systematic form" while "the tools of the thirteenth century represent efforts to search written authority afresh."[56] This new interest in searching written authority was closely connected with the emerging understanding of the preaching task.

To make such searches possible, techniques had to be devised, including alphabetical arrangement, layout, and reference symbols, including Arabic numerals.[57] There even developed among the stationers of the University of Paris, the most important center for the diffusion of these preaching tools, a system by which these reference works could be mass-produced. When a work was in demand, the stationers would provide themselves with exemplars that were written in *peciae,* quires of four or eight folios. Scholars who wished to copy the work would rent the *peciae* a few at a time until they had as much of the work reproduced as they wished.[58]

The first sort of preaching tool to be devised, the *collection of distinctions*, is not surprising in an age with a "subdividing mentality." For example, the number of different senses in which a word is used in the Bible could provide an outline for a sermon. We can see an example of the way lists of such distinctions worked in a compilation of the meanings of the word "horse" in various passages: preacher, temporal dignity, the easy life, and the present age.[59] It was not until this period that verbal concordances to the Scriptures came into existence; they hardly could have existed earlier since the Bible was not divided into chapters until Stephen Langton did so in the early-thirteenth century. Since verses were not numbered until much later, the relative location in a chapter citation was signified by a letter between A and G in the original concordance produced by the Paris Dominicans in 1239. The practice of providing alphabetical subject indexes to books can also be dated to this time. Even such obvious tools as library catalogs owe their origin to the needs of preachers during the thirteenth century.

Another genre of preaching aids was the *florilegium* ("gathering of flowers"), an anthology of earlier writers, a collection of quotations that could serve as *auctoritates* to confirm the points made by preachers. One of the greatest of these was Thomas of Ireland's *Manipulus florum*, a collection of six thousand extracts from the works of the church fathers, a few classical writers, and Maimonides. These are arranged under an alphabetical list of 266 topics, most of which were moral or ethical. The extracts vary from several lines to half a column in length. Within the topic the quotations are arranged alphabetically by author, and cross-references are made to related topics.[60]

Another collection of quotations was made by John of Wales, who did a great deal more besides. A British Franciscan, who studied and taught at Oxford and Paris in the last half of the thirteenth century, John served as Regent Master of Theology at Paris and went on an embassy to Wales for Archbishop Pecham. In his lifetime he was as well known as his contemporaries at Paris: Roger Bacon, John Pecham, Bonaventure, and Thomas Aquinas. What he was principally known for was his production of preaching aids. Scholars now recognize some eighteen works as being his; they include biblical commentaries and sermon collections, themselves useful to preachers, but reference books as well. Among these are a book of advice to princes consisting largely of *exempla* about the virtuous behavior of rulers in classical antiquity, a collection of material useful for creating sermons for different types of people,[61] a summary of the lives and sayings of pagan philosophers, and a similar volume on Christian saints. These handbooks

> aimed to cover all sorts of topics, giving an authoritative view, a number of named authorities in support of this view, a series of *exempla* and appropriate extracts for use in preaching, and suggestions for further reading.[62]

His *Communiloquium*, for instance, contains 2,389 quotations from biblical, classical, and patristic writings, fruits of his own study used to make cogent points. The erudition that went into the production of these reference books for preachers is remarkable.

Treatises on virtues and vices were another common type of homiletical tool. Rouse and Rouse say that eleventh-century preaching not intended for monks had a largely missionary function; it was aimed at converting nonbelievers. A thematic sermon of the style that developed in the thirteenth century, however, "never strays far from the function of teaching."[63] A great deal of that teaching was moral. Siegfried Wenzel has made available to English readers one of these treatises, *Fasciculus morum*, an early-fourteenth-century tool for preaching on the seven deadly sins and their opposing virtues.[64] It takes the form of a series of sermons on each of the sins and its opposing virtue.

The subdividing mentality is seen in the way that each of the sins and virtues is broken down into its components. Lechery, for example, has its nature delineated, its occasions listed (sight, conversation, touching, kissing, and the sex act itself), its branches enumerated (fornication, violating a virgin, adultery, incest, and sodomy), and the reasons it is to be hated (it is offensive to God, hateful to the angels, harmful to the person who commits it, harmful to one's neighbor, and renders service to the devil). Then chastity is discussed, examples of it are given, the method of acquiring it described, and its end effect noted.

The treatment of each of these topics is a sermon, beginning generally with a distinction between the various forms of the phenomenon under consideration,[65] the offering of theses on that subject, and the support of each thesis by biblical, patristic, and classical authorities, and by appropriate *exempla*.

One may see from several features that this collection is intended as a tool for preachers rather than merely a collection of edifying sermons to be read. Frequently a biblical passage or an *exemplum* is introduced without expansion; instead there is interjected the instruction *"expone"* (explain or expound). Then the prologue says that the collection was made "to comfort you and to help the unlettered." Finally, the book ends with the words *"Finis sermonum fit hec collectio morum,"* which Wenzel says can mean, "This collection of moral matters is for the end (purpose) of sermons."[66] Thus the translator has given the person who does not know Latin a rare opportunity to study a medieval preaching tool in its entirety.

What may be regarded as "the most important single genre of preaching aid," however, is *collections of model sermons*.[67] Such collections generally include sermons for the Sundays or the saints' days of the church calendar, that is, ordinary liturgical sermons. Others, however, are collections of *ad status* sermons, sermons addressed to different categories of persons on their state of life. Sermons on the dead appear as well. The pattern of all these sermons, however, is that of the thematic sermon rather than that of the homily. These collections are usually published in a very small format, the sort of "vade-mecum books" that friars could take—along with other preaching material, confessional handbooks, Bibles, and breviaries—as they went from place to place in their preaching travels. Produced in the *peciae* system at the University of Paris, these sermon collections were used by Franciscans especially to enable them to preach on very short notice, whatever the occasion.

Often the model sermons are simply outlines, sometimes in rhyming form, with a scriptural text to confirm each heading.

> The contents of preachers' vade-mecum books brings it home to us that the preaching offensive of the friars, which was

> undoubtedly successful, depended to a significant extent on ready-made sermons and other kinds of stereotyped material.[68]

The sort of preaching aid that has been even more studied than the *artes praedicandi,* however, is *collections of* exempla. Folklorists have combed through these collections looking for popular tales, social historians have sought details of medieval life in them, and literary scholars have studied them to find sources for early creative writing in various vernacular languages. While these efforts called attention to this type of preaching aid and made it accessible to scholars by their producing editions and analyses, they tended at the same time to draw attention away from the primary function of these collections, their usefulness to the writers of sermons.

Before looking at that usefulness, however, it is necessary to specify more precisely the kinds of illustrations and support material that are included in the category of *exempla.* There have been many efforts to enumerate the appropriate categories for such a taxonomy, but more recent study has suggested that the elements that go into the classification of *exempla* are: (1) their source or origin, (2) the nature of the information, (3) the nature of the characters in the story, and (4) the formal or logical structure of the exemplum.[69]

While this bare list may seem dull enough, the variety of data embraced by these categories is consistent with the liveliness of the genre itself. Sources, for instance, can be as diverse as the Bible, the patristic writings most influential in shaping medieval thought (Boethius, Cassiodorus, Gregory the Great, Isidore of Seville, Bede, and *Vitae Patrum*), stories from classical antiquity, *illustrations* from the Carolingian renaissance, and stories collected by the compilers of *exempla* collections from their own contemporaries.

Even this does not adequately suggest the variety. An older listing has presented the variety of sources in the following way, one that does greater justice to the wealth represented here:

> (1) such incidental material as was afforded by
> historical works, secular and ecclesiastical;
> poems and prose fiction, ancient and medieval;
> contemporary events;
> incidents and stories brought personally to the attention of the writer;
>
> (2) collections of tales, fables, anecdotes, and saints' lives, not originally designed to serve as exempla but offering plentiful and convenient matter for such; these are represented respectively by

the numerous early collections of Latin stories,
Aesopic fable collections,
the historical anecdotes of Valerius Maximus, and
the *Legenda Aurea* of Jacobus de Voraigne;

(3) elaborate moral and didactic treatises which make use of a large number of exempla in illustration of the points discussed; to this class belong

the *Dialogues* of Gregory,
the *Disciplina Clericalis* of Petrus Alphonsus,
and *Jacob's Well*;

(4) collections especially designed for the use of preachers and moralists and properly designated as "example-books"; of this class there are four varieties:

(a) collections containing exempla unclassified and without accompanying moralizations, such as the early compilations from the sermons of Jacques de Vitryo;

(b) collections containing exempla classified under topics alphabetically but without moralizations, such as the *Alphabetum Narrationum* formerly ascribed to Étienne de Besançon;

(c) collections containing exempla moralized but not classified, such as the *Gesta Romanorum;*

(d) collections containing exempla both alphabetically classified and moralized, such as the *Scala Celi* of Johannes Junior.[70]

The other issues in classification (nature of the information, sort of characters involved, and formal and logical structure) are directly related to the usefulness of *exempla*. While some illustrative materials had been used in sermons before, they became an important element in the strategy of persuasion of the thematic sermon. To understand this it is necessary to look at the elements that go into defining the *exemplum*. These begin with its narrative character, which makes it more consistent with the proclamation of a faith that looks back historically to its founding and forward eschatologically to its consummation rather than to abstract reasoning from eternally valid principles.

A second element is the brevity necessary for oral presentation. Then there is the element of authenticity given by relating what is either historical or history-like. The example is not the whole argument; it is a component of a total presentation of an argument. Yet it does occupy the culminating position in the argument; it climaxes and completes it. The sort of argument involved is essentially sermonic; thus the use of *exempla* in other forms of medieval literature is derivative from homiletical use.

This homiletical use presupposes a rapport between the preacher and the audience, a community of the faithful. In this situation, the purpose of the *exemplum* is always to teach, its function is pedagogical. Yet this teaching is never for any merely temporal benefit, whether entertainment or moral suasion, but is always directed toward the eternal welfare, the salvation, of the souls of the congregation. From these elements one may construct a definition of the *exemplum*. It is a short narration given as truthful and intended to be inserted into a speech (usually a sermon) to convince an audience by means of a salutary lesson.[71]

With this background, it is possible to see how the other criteria for classifying *exempla* assist in understanding how these stories do their work in thematic sermons. The "nature of the information" refers to the means through which the preacher or collector acquired the *exemplum,* through either reading or conversation. This information is contained in the way the illustration is introduced, whether by the words, "I have heard," or by "it is written."[72] In either case this introduction makes the argument more persuasive by giving it one of the two great forms of cultural authority known in the Middle Ages, that of the written word and that of the word of persons with credibility (clergy, elders, neighbors, and distinguished people). Further, the types of characters who spoke in *exempla,* whether supernatural beings, humans, or animals, were all vested with authority in this kind of story.

The formal or structural logic of these stories could be of one or two sorts. In the first case the argument is analogical and is thus authoritative for whoever falls into a position parallel to that of a character in the story. That is, what is said in a fable about an animal carries a message to all who behave like that animal. In the second category of stories the argument is metonymic: what is said in the tale about one member of the class has implications for all members of the class; for example, what is said about a member of a religious order in a personal narrative is a warning to all religious.[73] All of which is to say that the rhetorical function of *exempla* in thematic sermons contributes greatly to their effectiveness.

While the variety of *exempla* collections is too great to permit cataloging, it is worthwhile to look at one of the most highly developed to get some idea of what the genre was like at its pinnacle. It is the work of John (de) Bromyard, an English Dominican who was chancellor of Cambridge University in the late fourteenth century, vicar of the Dominicans at Oxford, and staunch opponent of Wyclif. A widely traveled man, Bromyard brings to his vast collection a cosmopolitan perspective. This work is entitled "a treatise on preaching that is by far the most useful and indispensable for all shepherds of the Lord's flock, proclaimers of the divine Word, ministers of faithful souls, and planters of the sacred writings,"[74] a title that seems to incorporate a publisher's blurb.

Yet the work itself almost lives up to this billing. In a printed edition it occupies almost one thousand folio pages and has illustrations arranged alphabetically under 189 headings. The seven under the letter "L," for example, are: *labor, laus, lex, liber, loqutio, ludus,* and *luxuria* (work, praise, law, book, speaking, play, and lust). Each of these topics has a series of *exempla* provided under titles that are theses proved by the illustration. Under the heading of *praedicator* there are thirty-eight such theses that could provide a theology of preaching by themselves, all in narrative form. Happy indeed was the preacher who had such an aid in sermon preparation!

Popular Preaching

With such an armory of tools, the itinerant preacher of thematic sermons was well prepared to preach the Word "in season, out of season" (2 Tim. 4:2 KJV) to people in the new cities. Many who did were enormously successful. If this were a work devoted to preachers rather than preaching, it would be a pleasant indulgence to recount the accomplishments of Jacques de Vitry, William of Auvergne, Bernardino of Siena, Juan of Capistrano, Anthony of Padua, and many others. None, however, seems to have been more effective than the one reported by the inveterate chronicler of the friars, Salimbene:

> Take note that Brother Bertold had the special grace of preaching from God. And everybody who has heard him says that from the days of the Apostles till the present day he has not been matched in the German tongue. A great multitude of men and women followed him, sometimes from as much as sixty or a hundred miles around, sometimes from a large number of cities, in order to hear the eloquent and saving words which came forth from the mouth of him who gives "his voice the voice of power" [Ps. 67:34] and who gives "the word to them that preach good tidings with great power" [Ps. 67:12]. He would go up in a *bettefredum* or a wood tower built like a bell tower which he used in the fields as his pulpit. And in the top of this tower had been constructed a wind-indicator, so that the people could tell by the direction of the wind where to sit in order to hear best. Thus, marvelously, he could be heard and understood as well by those sitting at a distance as those near at hand. And nobody got up and left until his sermons were ended. And when he preached on the Last Judgment, they all trembled like a reed in the water. And they begged him for the love of God not to preach on such subjects, because it terrified them so much to hear him.[75]

Salimbene goes on to confirm the power of Berthold's preaching by telling of two miracles accomplished by it. One occurred to a peasant who wished to hear Berthold, but was prevented from doing so by his lord, who insisted that he spend the day plowing. But when Berthold preached, the peasant heard him as clearly from thirty miles away as if he had been right under the tower. Not only that, but he memorized the entire sermon and, when he resumed plowing, got as much done during the day as he would have if he had not been interrupted. The other involved a noble lady who had followed Berthold for six years, not missing a sermon. In doing so she used up her fortune. When, at the end of that time, she had her first audience with him, he instructed her to go to a certain dishonest banker whom she was instrumental in converting. Supporting her then became one of the ways he repaid his ill-gotten gains.

These stories seem to be hyperbolic ways of testifying to the real power of preaching to the masses done by the sons of Francis and Dominic, who utilized the thematic form of the sermon and their abundant array of preaching aids to assist them in their proclamation. This truly was an explosion of preaching. This was the medium through which the church responded to the crisis of the time and the new urban masses of the High Middle Ages had their commitment to the Christian faith reinforced. Although the medium was effective for its age, no single strategy of persuasion is effective at all times and in all places. The time was coming when the friars, with their thematic sermons, their subdividing mentality, the exempla, and their whole infrastructure for preaching, would come under attack.

FOR FURTHER READING

D'Avray, D. L. *The Preaching of the Friars: Sermons Diffused from Paris before 1300.* Oxford: Clarendon Press; New York: Oxford University Press, 1985.

Early Dominicans: Selected Writings. Edited with introduction by Simon Tugwell, and preface by Vincent de Couesnongle. CWS. New York: Paulist Press, 1982.

Murphy, James J. *Rhetoric in the Middle Ages: A History of Rhetorical Theory from Saint Augustine to the Renaissance.* Berkeley and Los Angeles: The University of California Press, 1974.

Rouse, Richard H., and Mary A. Rouse. *Preachers, Florilegia, and Sermons: Studies on the Manipulus florum of Thomas of Ireland.* Studies and Texts, no. 47. Toronto: Pontifical Institute of Mediæval Studies, 1979.

Smyth, Charles. *The Art of Preaching: A Practical Survey of Preaching in the Church of England 747-1939*. London: SPCK; New York: Macmillan 1940.

Wenzel, Siegfried, ed. and trans. *Fasciculus Morum: A Fourteenth-Century Preacher's Handbook*. University Park: Pennsylvania State University Press, 1989.

Notes

1. The list in question is found in J. B. Schneyer, *Repertorium der lateinischen Sermones des Mittelalters für die Zeit von 1150-1350*, Beiträge zur Geschichte der Philosophie und Theologie des Mittelalters, Band 43, Heften 1-9 (Münster Westfalen: Aschendorffsche Verlagsbuchhandlung, 1969-80). Two more volumes of the *Repertorium* have appeared since 1980, but, since they are index volumes for the first nine, they do not change the total number of sermons. See also D. L. d'Avray, *The Preaching of the Friars: Sermons Diffused from Paris Before 1300* (Oxford: Clarendon Press; New York: Oxford University Press, 1985), 1.

2. They appealed to the authority of Isidore of Seville, who says that monks should be "keeping the apostolic life, having all things in common after the apostolic example." *Regula monachorum* 83 (PL col. 870).

3. Stanislaw Trawkowski, "Entre l'orthodoxie et l'hérésie; Vita apostolica et le problèm de la désobéissance," in *The Concept of Heresy in the Middle Ages (11th-13th c.): Proceedings of the International Conference, Louvain, May 13-16, 1973*, ed. W. Lourdaux and D. Verhelst, Mediaevalia Lovaniensia, series 1, studia 4 (Leuven: University Press, 1976), 157-66.

4. That is, one for both men and women.

5. The designation of him as Peter comes more than a century after his death and is the result of an effort to link him with the apostle.

6. No early Waldensian sermons have survived; indeed, by the nature of the case, it is doubtful that any were ever written down. For contemporary records of the movement see Walter L. Wakefield and Austin P. Evans, *Heresies of the High Middle Ages: Selected Sources Translated and Annotated* (New York: Columbia University Press, 1969), 189-241.

7. Also known as Albigensians in southern France from the town of Albi that was one of their important centers. The term *Cathar* is often related etymologically to the Greek word *katharos* ("clean" or "pure"), although some scholars account for it differently.

8. Steven Runciman in *The Medieval Manichee: A Study of the Christian Dualist Heresy* (Cambridge: Cambridge University Press, 1947; reprinted 1960). For a different interpretation of Catharism, see Anne Brenon, "The Voice of the Good Women: An Essay on the Pastoral and Sacerdotal Role of Women in the Cathar Church," in *Women Preachers and Prophets Through Two Millennia of Christianity*, ed. Beverly Mayne Kienzle and Pamela J. Walker (Berkeley and Los Angeles: The University of California Press, 1998). A detailed reconstruction of the life of a Cathar

community is given in Emmanuel LeRoy Ladurie, *Montaillou: The Promised Land of Error,* trans. Barbara Bray (New York: Vintage Books, 1979). See also John Arnold, "The Preaching of the Cathars," in *Medieval Monastic Preaching,* ed. Carolyn Muessig (Leiden; Boston: Brill, 1998), 183-205. Although representing a later period, a remarkable novel by the medievalist and semioticist, Umberto Eco, recreates the religious confusion of tongues of this age: *The Name of the Rose,* trans. William Weaver (San Diego: Harcourt Brace Jovanovich, 1983).

9. Ladurie, *Montaillou,* 327-41 and *passim.*

10. Williston Walker, Richard A Norris, David W. Lotz, and Robert T. Handy, *A History of the Christian Church,* 4th ed. (New York: Scribner's, 1985), 300.

11. Two preachers already studied, Bernard of Clairvaux and Hildegard of Bingen, preached against the Cathars and Waldenses. See Beverly Mayne Kienzle, "Defending the Lord's Vineyard: Hildegard of Bingen's Preaching Against the Cathars" in Muessig, *Medieval Monastic Preaching,* 163-81.

12. The official name of the Dominicans is *Ordo Praedicatorum,* the Order of Preachers, and that of the Franciscans is *Ordo Fratrum Minorum,* literally, the Order of Smaller Brothers, but generally rendered as the Order of Friars Minor. The Dominicans are also known as Black Friars from the color of their cloaks. Franciscans are called Gray Friars from the original color of their habits (which are now brown).

13. The sources for the life of Francis are the two *vitae* written by Thomas of Celano, a document produced by some of Francis's first associates *(Scripta Leonis et Sociorum Eius),* and the *Legenda maior* of St. Bonaventure. This last is translated in *Bonaventure: The Soul's Journey into God, The Tree of Life, The Life of St. Francis,* trans. and intro. Ewert Cousins, pref. Ignatius Brady, CWS (New York: Paulist Press, 1978). Much of the charm associated with Francis comes across in a historically less reliable source from the fourteenth century, *The Little Flowers of St. Francis,* available in numerous translations and editions. See John R. H. Moorman, *The Sources for the Life of S. Francis of Assisi* (Manchester: Manchester University Press, 1940).

14. Jean de Mailly, "Life of St. Dominic," in *Early Dominicans: Selected Writings,* ed. with intro. Simon Tugwell, pref. Vincent de Couesnongle, CWS (New York: Paulist Press, 1982), 54. Biographical materials for the less charismatic Dominic are rarer than they are for Francis; most of the contemporary accounts are included in the Tugwell volume. A sound modern treatment is M.-H. Vicaire, *Saint Dominic and His Times,* trans. Kathleen Pond (New York: McGraw-Hill, 1964).

15. Tugwell, *Early Dominicans*, 18.

16. Quoted in ibid., 14.

17. Quoted in Guy Bedouelle, *Saint Dominic: The Grace of the Word,* trans. Mary Thomas Noble (San Francisco: Ignatius Press, 1987), 121. On the importance of Innocent and the Fourth Lateran Council for preaching, see Richard H. Rouse and Mary A. Rouse, *Preachers, Florilegia, and Sermons: Studies on the Manipulus florum of Thomas of Ireland,* Studies and Texts, no. 47 (Toronto: Pontifical Institute of Mediæval Studies, 1979), 55-59.

18. Much of what follows is based on Bedouelle, *St. Dominic,* 121-29.

19. Ibid., 125.

20. Bonaventure, *Legenda maior,* 3.

21. *Francis and Clare: The Complete Works,* trans. and intro. Regis J. Armstrong and Ignatius C. Brady, pref. John Vaughn, CWS (New York: Paulist Press, 1982). Quote of xvii on 122, quote of xxi on 126.

22. Quoted in John R. H. Moorman, *A History of the Franciscan Order from Its Origins to the Year 1517* (Oxford: Clarendon Press, 1968), 273.

23. Otto A. Dieter, "*Arbor picta*: The Medieval Tree of Preaching," in *The Quarterly Journal of Speech* 51 (1965), 123-44.

24. Those indicated on the tree branches in the illumination are: concordance of authorities, discussion of the words, properties of things, exposition of more than one sense of interpretation, parables and facts of nature, alleging the opposite (making a correction), comparing adjectives, interpreting a name, and multiplying synonyms. There is nothing sacrosanct about this order nor are these the only "ornaments" recognized.

25. Rouse and Rouse, *Preachers, Florilegia, and Sermons,* 66 n. 1.

26. James J. Murphy, *Rhetoric in the Middle Ages: A History of Rhetorical Theory from Saint Augustine to the Renaissance* (Berkeley and Los Angeles: The University of California Press, 1974), 311-44.

27. I will explain *exempla* in greater detail below, but for the moment they may be thought of simply as sermon "illustrations."

28. Rouse and Rouse trace this development stage by stage in *Preachers, Florilegia, and Sermons,* 68-90.

29. Ibid., 76-77, 84-87. Cf. D'Avray, *The Preaching of the Friars,* 193-95. Since this chapter was written, thematic sermons have been treated in N. Bériou, "Les sermons latins après 1200" in *The Sermon,* directed by Beverly Mayne Kienzle (Turnhout, Belgium: Brepols, 2000), 363-447, and in most of the chapters on vernacular sermons in that volume.

30. David d'Avray, *The Preaching of the Friars,* 94. On the language in which popular preaching was done, see 91-95. Giles Constable notes that the question is very complicated in "The Language of Preaching in the Twelfth Century," in *Viator,* Medieval and Renaissance Studies, 25 (1994), 131-52. I am grateful to A. Gary Shilling for bringing this article to my attention. Kienzle discusses the matter in the conclusion of *The Sermon,* 971-74, summarizing the views of the other contributors to the volume expressed *passim.*

31. An exception is German sermons copied in the vernacular as spiritual reading for nuns. D'Avray, *The Preaching of the Friars,* 91-93. For reason to believe that exceptions were more extensive, see Kienzle, *The Sermon,* 968-70.

32. This conclusion is brought into doubt by Siegfried Wenzel, *Macaronic Sermons: Bilingualism and Preaching in Late-Medieval England,* Recentiores: Later Latin Texts and Contexts (Ann Arbor: The University of Michigan Press, 1994).

33. D'Avray, *The Preaching of the Friars,* 82-90. The catechetical sermons of Thomas Aquinas referred to below would have served as an excellent model for this kind of preaching.

34. The earliest surviving collection of such sermons was published in Marie Magdeleine Davy, *Les sermons universitaires parisiens de 1230–1231: Contribution à l'histoire de la prédication médiévale.* Études de Philosophie Médiévale, no. 15 (Paris: Librairies philosophique J. Vrin, 1931). But, as we shall see, the oldest surviving *artes* go back before that.

35. Murphy, *Rhetoric in the Middle Ages,* 309-10. The study of these textbooks has gone through a number of different stages. The first major work on thematic preaching in England was G. R. Owst, *Preaching in Medieval England: An Introduction to Sermon Manuscripts of the Period c. 1350–1450,* Cambridge Studies in Medieval Life and Thought (Cambridge: The University Press, 1926); the *artes* are dealt with on 309-54. A list of the manuscripts containing these textbooks is found in Harry Caplan, *Mediæval Artes Praedicandi: A Supplementary Handlist,* Cornell Studies in Classical Philology (Ithaca, N.Y.: Cornell University Press; London: H. Milford, Oxford University Press, 1934) and its *Supplement,* which appeared in 1936. Thomas-Marie Charland edited the Latin texts of two of the most important of the *artes*, those of Thomas Waleys and Robert of Basevorn, in *Artes Praedicandi: Contribution à l'histoire de la rhétorique au moyen âge,* Publications de l'Institute d'Études Médiévales d'Ottawa, no. 7 (Paris: Librairie Philosophique J. Vrin; Ottawa: Institute d'Études Médiévales, 1936). The Murphy volume is the major study of developments within this literature. Murphy has provided translations of *artes* in *Three Medieval Rhetorical Arts* (Berkeley and Los Angeles: The University of California Press, 1971).

36. George A. Kennedy, *Classical Rhetoric and Its Christian and Secular Tradition from Ancient to Modern Times,* rev. and enl. (Chapel Hill: The University of North Carolina Press, 1999), 16-17. What Kennedy calls "technical" rhetoric is designated as "preceptive" in Murphy, *Rhetoric in the Middle Ages,* 296.

37. Murphy, *Rhetoric in the Middle Ages,* 311.

38. Quoted in ibid., 313.

39. Ibid., 317-26.

40. This summary is based on Charles Smyth, *The Art of Preaching: A Practical Survey of Preaching in the Church of England* 747–1939 (London: SPCK; New York: The Macmillan Company, 1940), 20-35.

41. An *exemplum.* See below.

42. According to Aristotle, dialectic uses syllogisms while rhetoric uses enthymemes, which are incomplete or implied syllogisms; that is, only one of the premises is explicit in an enthymeme, the other being presupposed as something the audience believes. For him, rhetoric is oratory, and audiences cannot be expected to follow rigorous argument when it is presented orally. Thus the enthymeme is the syllogism accommodated to oral presentation.

43. There is still a proverbial homiletical wisdom to the effect that you should "tell them what you are going to tell them, tell them, and tell them what you've told them." Many homileticians today (including the author) question the desirability of doing this, but some highly regarded preachers still practice it, for example, the distinguished Jesuit patristics scholar, Walter Burghardt. One of his *divisiones* is as follows: "Three stages to my journey into Jonahland: (1) the man, (2) the meaning, (3) the message. Who was he? What was his importance for Israel? What might he say to you and me now?" See Burghardt, *Grace on Crutches: Homilies for Fellow Travelers* (New York: Paulist Press, 1986), 100.

44. Smyth, *The Art of Preaching,* 27. He illustrates this principle by dividing a sermon to be preached to bishops on Psalm 141:5 (Vulgate 140:5): "Let the righteous strike me in mercy" *(Corripiet me justus in misericordia),* which I translate as follows:

A prelate is described
with respect to state *(statUM)*:
"righteous" *(justus)*,
with respect to deed *(actUM)*:
"let him strike" *(corripiet)*,
with respect to manner *(modUM)*:
"in mercy" *(in misericordia)*.

45. Ibid., 34.

46. *"Il fallait savoir prodigieusement pour prêcher si mal."* See *Artes Praedicandi*, 224.

47. O. C. Edwards Jr., "Thomas Waleys: A Fourteenth-Century Colleague," in *Homiletic* 14 (1989), 1-4.

48. Ibid., 2.

49. Ibid., 3.

50. This section is based on d'Avray, *The Preaching of the Friars*, 163-80. Although d'Avray denies that thematic preaching is scholastic, Daniel R. Lesnick unsuccessfully refutes that claim in *Preaching in Medieval Florence: The Social World of Franciscan and Dominican Spirituality* (Athens: University of Georgia Press, 1989), 96-97.

51. One has only to open one of Thomas Aquinas's *Summae* to any page to see the method in full form.

52. D'Avray, *The Preaching of the Friars*, 176.

53. Ibid., 177.

54. For a long time it was believed that there was an *ars praedicandi* written by Thomas Aquinas, but that appears to be the work of a later Thomist, according to Harry Caplan, *Of Eloquence: Studies in Ancient and Mediæval Rhetoric*, ed. with intro. Anne King and Helen North (Ithaca, N.Y.: Cornell University Press, 1970), 48-76. There are, however, sermons preached by Thomas that have survived: Lenten sermon conferences on the Apostles' Creed, the Ten Commandments, the Lord's Prayer, and the Hail Mary. See *The Sermon-Conferences of St. Thomas Aquinas on the Apostles' Creed* trans., ed., and intro. Nicholas Ayo (Notre Dame, Ind.: University of Notre Dame Press, 1988).

55. D'Avray, *The Preaching of the Friars*, 78.

56. Rouse and Rouse, *Preachers, Florilegia, and Sermons*, 4.

57. Ibid., 26-36.

58. Ibid., 169-80.

59. Ibid., 8. Allegorical interpretation is needed to account for some of these. For example, the understanding of the horse as a preacher comes from Gregory the Great's exegesis of Job 39:19: "Wilt thou give strength to the horse, or clothe his neck with neighing?" (Rheims-Douay).

60. The work of Rouse and Rouse is an important pioneering study of such a preaching tool. It could be said to have focused attention of medieval sermon studies on tools other than *artes praedicandi* and collections of *exempla*.

61. *Ad status* sermons.

62. Jenny Swanson, *John of Wales: A Study of the Works and Ideas of a Thirteenth-Century Friar,* Cambridge Studies in Medieval Life and Thought, 4th series (Cambridge; New York: Cambridge University Press, 1989), 16.

63. Rouse and Rouse, *Preachers, Florilegia, and Sermons,* 43, 67.

64. *Fasciculus Morum: A Fourteenth-Century Preacher's Handbook,* ed. and trans. Siegfried Wenzel (University Park: Pennsylvania State University Press, 1989). The popularity of the genre is reflected in a quotation from a manuscript of the time: "There be so many books and treatises of vices and virtues and diverse doctrines, that this short life shall rather have an end of any man, than he may either study them or read them" (spelling modernized). See Owst, *Preaching in Medieval England,* 278.

65. For example, incest includes intercourse not only between those who are related by blood but also between those related by spiritual kinship. Thus it is the sin of religious who break their vow of chastity. See Wenzel, *Fasciculus Morum,* 682-83.

66. Ibid., 731.

67. D'Avray, *The Preaching of the Friars,* 78.

68. Ibid., 61.

69. Jean-Claude Schmitt, *L'"Exemplum,"* Typologies des sources du moyen âge occidental, fasc. 40 (Turnhout, Belgium: Brepols, 1982), 27-38. For a summary of their general perspective see *Prêcher d'exemples: Récits de prédicateurs du Moyen Age,* intro. Jean-Claude Schmitt (Paris: Stock, 1985), 9-24.

70. Joseph Albert Mosher, *The Exemplum in the Early Religious and Didactic Literature of England,* Columbia University Studies in English (New York: Columbia University Press, 1911), 6-7. Tabular presentation added.

71. Schmitt, *L'"Exemplum,"* 37-38.

72. A cartoon in *The New Yorker* some years ago showed several clergy sitting together on a train like a group of traveling salesmen. One of them was saying, "Let me tell you a parable I heard in Scranton." This conveys the mood of the personal *exempla,* which, as Smyth says, "are mostly at second or third hand, the godly gossip of the cloister or of the preaching tour." See *The Art of Preaching,* 60.

73. Schmitt, *L'"Exemplum,"* 41-42.

74. *Summa Praedicantium omnibus dominici gregis pastoribus, divini verbi praeconibus, animarum fidelium ministris, et sacrum literarum cultoribus longe utilissima ac pernecessaria.* From the title page of the printed edition of 1614 published by Hieronymus Verdussi in Antwerp.

75. *The Chronicle of Salimbene de Adam,* trans. Joseph L. Baird, Giuseppe Baglivi, and John Robert Kane (Binghamton, N.Y.: Medieval & Renaissance Texts & Studies, 1986), 566. So great was Berthold's reputation that most mendicant sermons from Germany, whether in Latin or German, are attributed to him, although only a few can be assigned to him with certainty. Hans-Jochen Schiewer, "German Sermons in the Middle Ages," in *The Sermon,* directed by Kienzle, 868-69.

CHAPTER 10

A HOMILETIC MISCELLANY

While the designation of periods is always arbitrary, there is often an ebb and flow of events that makes it easy to feel as though history does occur in eras. After the preaching explosion of the thirteenth and fourteenth centuries, there seems to have been a settling down, the calm before the next storm, that of the Protestant Reformation. This chapter, therefore, will deal with odds and ends, the wisps of mist that appeared on the horizon, wisps that could either be burned out by the sun on a clearing day or instead burgeon into massive thunderheads that would darken and then drench the landscape. This meteorological mixed bag is filled with spirituality, on the one hand, and negative responses to either thematic preaching or the institutional life of the church or both, on the other.

A SPIRITUALITY OF PREACHING

The first of the phenomena to be surveyed is wispy indeed, a single volume, and one that was so little valued at its appearing that only four manuscripts of it remain, none of which contain the entire work.[1] Yet it had every reason to be received enthusiastically, having been written by the fifth master of the Order of Preachers after his resignation from that post. The skill with which he had discharged that responsibility is perhaps suggested by his having been offered the patriarchate of Jerusalem when he stepped down; he had also received a few votes in a papal election. His duties even involved him with royalty. When he was elected master, one of his first duties was to receive a daughter of the king of Hungary as a Dominican nun. He became godfather to a son of the king of France and advised the king on how to settle disputes between some of the most powerful families of his realm. There is no doubt about the respect in which his contemporaries and successors held the author, Humbert, from the town of Romans-sur-Isère[2] (ca. 1200–1277).

Why, then, was his book not more popular? The opinion of the editor and translator of the work, Simon Tugwell, is that "its failure as a book is one symptom of the originality (eccentricity, some would say) and difficulty of the whole notion of a religious order defined as an Order of Preachers."[3] Dominican spirituality never had the emotional fervor of Bernard's exhortations to Cistercians who had gone into the wilderness to give their souls completely to God. The Dominicans' "spiritual exercises were designed to make them better preachers, and their own spiritual progress was not sought as a goal in its own right, but rather as a kind of spin-off from their service of others."[4] They sought not the desert, but the marketplace where the people were. The concept, however, was so novel that even the Dominicans themselves were not ready for a book spelling out the principle: "For those called to be preachers, it is precisely the *gratia praedicationis*, the 'grace to be a preacher,' that must be the nucleus of their whole spiritual life."[5]

Such a book, however, is *The Formation of Preachers*.[6] Appearing two-thirds of the way through the thirteenth century, it was written very much in the manner of the sermons of the time. A point is stated but hardly developed. It may be paraphrased or a reason for it may be stated and then an authority for it quoted, but there is no "dilation" beyond that. What d'Avray calls "the subdividing mentality"[7] is the obvious principle of organization. Each topic is broken down into a number of subheadings—which often sound like a list of all the permutations the author could think of.

Modern logic is offended by a considerable overlap of categories; it seems as though everything that could be said is said, even if its substance has been included in what was said before. This is especially true when biblical metaphors for a thing are being cataloged (e.g., the scriptural symbols of the preacher in 2.6). Biblical interpretation may reflect any of the four senses and quite often depends on the exegesis of the passage in question given in the *Glossa Ordinaria*, that great collection of patristic commentary that was, for all practical purposes, what the Bible meant to the Middle Ages.

This, too, can be disconcerting for modern readers, as when the point that without preaching the church would never have been established is being made on the basis of Job 38:4: "Where were you when I laid the foundation of the earth?" Gregory says: "When scripture refers to foundations, we understand the preachers, who were the first to be established in the church by the Lord, so that the whole structure which follows rests upon them."[8] When, however, one becomes accustomed to the form of reasoning employed, one can see that it is not so superficial as it first appears. Indeed, the spiritual principles involved are very deep and still valid.

Humbert was not reflecting on the vocation to preach in general, but on what it meant to be a member of the Dominican order that had been founded precisely as a preaching order. The treatise is about the implications of that identification. Thus he begins with the nobility of the preacher's job and goes on to the necessity of preaching, its acceptability in the sight of God, and the benefits that accrue to the preacher both in this life and the life to come. Then he speaks of the usefulness of preaching, which is coextensive with that of the Word of God. This means that it is needed by many categories of people. Then the difficulties of the job are discussed, with a recognition at the end that they can be relieved by study, learning from others, and prayer. The requirements to be a preacher (**see Vol. 2, pp. 207-19,** for this section) are compiled under the headings of quality of life, knowledge, speaking ability, and merit, which can be lost in a number of ways. The preacher's person is exhausted in a short list of physical requirements (including maleness). Next, the scriptural symbols of the preacher are set down, and then right and wrong ways of becoming a preacher are detailed.

The section devoted to the actual performance of preaching is not concerned with the how-to-do-it issues covered in such profusion by the *artes praedicandi*, but looks instead at cases in which one should preach, inadequate reasons for failing to do so, undiscriminating ways of preaching and the conditions under which it is done well, ending with the reasons that those with the vocation should preach gladly. An analysis is made of the ways in which people come to be deprived of preaching and the harm occasioned by that lack. Then all the possible results of preaching, good and bad, are examined together with the conditions that make for each.

Since Dominicans were an itinerate preaching order, all the dangers and opportunities of travel must be noted. Further, the conduct of the traveling preachers while out of the pulpit comes in for a lot of discussion, focusing especially on their conversation. Finally, a bit of advice is given over such purely practical issues as the hearing of confessions, whether prothemes are used, and the kinds of homiletical aids to be taken in the friar's knapsack.

When spirituality is understood not just as a set of devotional exercises, but as the total way of life by which a Christian's vocation is lived out, it becomes clear that a spirituality can be built that derives entirely from the obligation to preach. By clearly delineating the purposes of preaching and then discussing the way life must be organized and lived out by persons who are called to accomplish those purposes, Humbert did indeed set forth a spirituality growing out of what it means to be a member of an order of preachers.

SPIRITUALITY THROUGH PREACHING

Meister Eckhart

In addition to the possibility of a spirituality growing out of the obligation to preach, there can also be a spirituality communicated largely through preaching. A spirituality of this sort also developed within the Dominican order, but it was preached as much to nuns as to friars. The setting for this development was the Rhineland in the early fourteenth century. The form of preaching that was the medium for this spirituality is an exception to the rule that says thematic preaching replaced classical patristic homilies as the genre of preaching during this period. Indeed, a technical description of the sermons of these mystics would be reminiscent in many ways of the monastic preaching of Bernard and his contemporaries. Most of the distinctions to be drawn between these two periods of preaching to religious have first to be made on the basis of content before they can be spelled out in terms of form. That, however, will come out as the homiletical careers of two of the leading Rhineland mystics, Meister Eckhart (ca. 1260–1327) and John Tauler (ca. 1300–1361), are presented.

Eckhart's first name may have been Johannes, but he has been called so exclusively by the title of Master given him by the University of Paris that certainty about what his parents called him is impossible. He was born around 1260 in the Thuringian town of Hochheim and entered the Dominican order in nearby Erfurt. After preliminary formation and education, he was sent to Cologne, where he may have studied under Albert the Great. From there he went to Paris and began his career as a writer and teacher.

Under the Dominican practice of rotating its university lecturers, Eckhart was next returned to Erfurt for the first in a series of administrative positions. He began as prior of Erfurt and then became the Thuringian representative of the Dominicans' provincial prior of Germany. Next he directed the newly created subdivision of Saxony, becoming after that the general vicar of the province in Bohemia. In 1310 he was elected prior provincial of Teutonia, but the general chapter of the order decided that he should return to Paris instead. After a three-year stint he was sent back to Germany, first to Strasbourg and then Cologne. In both places he attracted great attention for the essential Dominican work of preaching, being especially popular in convents of Dominican nuns.

He also caught the unfavorable attention of the archbishop of Cologne, a Franciscan, who began raising questions about his orthodoxy, questions that resulted in a papal condemnation for heresy not published until after his death in 1327.[9] The extent of any lapses from orthodoxy was a matter of debate at the time and has remained so. The questions arose out of the perennial difficulty mystics have of putting their experiences into words. One of Eckhart's favorite expressions referred to the birth of the Son in the soul of the Christian. Some of his paradoxical ways of talking about that sounded like a unitive mysticism in which the worshiper becomes so at one with the worshiped that the union is ontological and the two are no longer distinguishable. A pantheistic interpretation of the same doctrine was given by some.

Whatever the case, Eckhart expressed regret before his death for any heretical interpretations to which his statements could have given rise; his own intention was always devoutly orthodox. His condemnation did not terminate his influence; Tauler and Henry Suso (Heinrich Seuse) carried on with more judicious expressions of his thought. In this century his ideas have again become an occasion of controversy; "at different times Eckhart has been viewed as a pantheist, a forerunner of the Reformation, a prophet of German national religion, a Zen master in disguise, and a proto-Marxist."[10]

The present relevance of Eckhart, however, is not in his possible heresy, but in his homiletics. Perhaps the best approach to that is to look at the way he develops a particular sermon.[11] The second in the collection of his German sermons is preached from the text of Luke 10:38 (**See Vol. 2, pp. 219-24,** for this sermon). The text was read to its audience of religious in the Latin of the Vulgate: "He entered into a certain village *(castellum)*; and a woman named Martha welcomed him to her house." Despite the use of a word for the village that has as its primary meaning "a fort, camp, or castle," there is little surprising in that. The surprise begins, however, when Eckhart translates the text into German: "Our Lord Jesus Christ went up into a little castle and was received by a virgin who was a wife." That begins to sound like a text from which a mystic might wish to preach!

The sermon is a commentary on this verse and gives no evidence of the subdividing mentality of thematic sermons. Instead, it is a straightforward treatment of the words of the text. These words are understood allegorically,[12] of course, but so were the texts from which Bernard preached. The difference almost seems to be in the spiritualities of the two preachers, the classical patristic and monastic approach of Bernard and the more mystical and philosophical approach of Eckhart.

From this it should not be assumed, however, that Eckhart is to be thought of as a mystic or philosopher who followed his personal interests while wearing the habit of the Order of Preachers. His understanding of his vocation, and indeed that of biblical interpretation, was homiletical and Dominican to the core.

> True philosophy—what we would call theology—is based on the study of the scriptures and has as its goal the work of the preacher, however much it may strive to make use of natural reasons and examples. This is the perspective from which Eckhart wrote and preached. . . . The majority of his surviving Latin works are exegetical in character, and his numerous Latin and German sermons are also based on biblical texts.[13]

"Martha" is understood to mean "wife" through a traditional method of interpreting biblical names. Since she received Jesus into *her* house, she was the mistress of the house, so she is assumed to be a wife. The means by which the "woman" is identified as a virgin depends on Eckhart's principle of finding the hidden meaning under the letter. Neither "wife" nor "virgin," however, is to be applied in its literal sense. *Virgin* here is to mean "a human being who is devoid of all foreign images and who is as void as he was when he was not yet."[14]

Behind this lies Eckhart's belief, derived from Albert the Great, in the preexistence of human beings in their ideal state before birth. In that state they did not know by images, but knew things in their own nature as God knows them. A return to that virginal state of pure knowing is the goal of human beings, and that is to be achieved by detaching oneself completely from these images and thus from any sense of things as one's own property.

Jesus, by his knowing as God knows, was virginal in this sense. To be united with him, a soul must be pure, as he is pure. In order to be united, though, the virgin must become a wife, must become creative and conceive, so that the Son of God is born in the soul. This is the fruit of complete detachment: "to reintegrate the primitive freedom before the self disperses itself among images."[15] Freedom from images is much more fruitful than attachment to them; it can give birth "a hundred, a thousand times a day"[16] rather than just once a year. The difference is between the fruit the *attached* person conceives and the fruit the *detached* person conceives in union with God.

Eckhart goes on to show that the power in which this conception occurs is neither in the intellect nor the will. It occurs in the one and simple ground of the mind that he calls the "little castle" *(castellum)*. This is to say that it consists of regaining "the original identity with the self, in the ground of the mind to which God gives himself in his being."[17] While this doctrine is appropriately called mystical, it is not otherworldly; it is not flight from this world but a call to find God by being in the world but not of it. The Meister's interpretation is not the first thing that pops into one's mind today when reading Luke 10:38, but it was the "hidden meaning under the letter"[18] that he saw in this passage.

John Tauler

Although greatly influenced by Eckhart, John Tauler did mystical preaching in a very different way. A fellow Dominican, he nevertheless was always much more the spiritual director than the professor and philosopher, more the *Lebmeister* than the *Lesmeister* (director of studies). Born around 1300, twenty-seven years before the death of Eckhart, Tauler grew up in a prosperous family in Strasbourg and spent most of the rest of his life as a friar in his native city and in Basle. His work was largely with the seven convents of Dominican sisters in Strasbourg and with the communities there of Beguines (women living together in a religious community without taking life vows). These religious houses had a combined population of almost a thousand women, about 5 percent of the total population of Strasbourg.[19] His sermons to them were also open to the laity. Tauler and Henry Suso, his friend and fellow disciple of Eckhart, were leaders of the Friends of God, a movement in the

Rhineland and Switzerland of mystics who stressed transformation through the union of their souls with God.

Little is known about the life of Tauler, but several pieces of evidence come together to suggest a spiritual crisis around the time of his move to Basle in 1339.[20] The first is that a visit to Cologne that year seems to have been the occasion of a revived interest in the work of Eckhart. Also, he says in one of his sermons that "until a man has reached his fortieth year, he will never attain lasting peace, nor be truly formed into God, try as he may."[21]

These two reports are consistent with a beautiful legend about Tauler. It tells of a devout layman who had been instructed in a dream to go hear him preach. Following this instruction, making his confession to Tauler and receiving his Communion from him, the man then asked him to preach on "how a man may attain to the highest and utmost point it is given to us to reach in this present time." When Tauler had done so, the layman returned to him and told him that the sermon was excellent, but that the preacher himself did not live by its precepts. Shocked, Tauler asked for instruction. After a discipline of two years' silence in the pulpit, he began to preach again with the power that he is known to have had.[22]

Not much in addition to that is known about his life, although he lived in the exciting years of the Avignon papacy and the Black Plague, dying during its second outbreak in 1361. During his lifetime his orthodoxy, unlike that of Eckhart, was never in doubt. When, after the Reformation, his works were translated into Latin along with a number of others attributed to him (only about sixty of his genuine sermons remain), he was interpreted in a quietistic way and Pope Sixtus V temporarily placed his works on the Index.[23]

While Tauler drew much of his understanding of the spiritual life from Eckhart, his sermons are very different from those of the Meister. In form, they are fairly straightforward biblical homilies much in the pattern of the monastic preaching of Bernard, the difference being in the spirituality inculcated rather than in the rhetorical form. Taking a text from one of the liturgical lections for the occasion, Tauler would draw out the lessons he found in it for the development of the spiritual lives of the nuns and laypersons in his congregation. These are far more accessible than the teaching of Eckhart.

Indeed, Tauler's are some of the few sermons that have come down from previous centuries that can still be read today with a sense of immediate applicability, so great is their simplicity, directness, and complete commitment to doing "the one thing necessary." They are less abstract, philosophical, and theoretical than those of Eckhart. Then, too, they seem to depend less on Neoplatonism and more on the example of Jesus.

Gabriele von Siegroth-Nellessen has conducted a study of the styles of Eckhart, Tauler, and Suso that involved a statistical analysis of syntactic patterns and idiosyncrasies. She came to the conclusion that Tauler is "the most spontaneous and audience-oriented preacher of the three." She says that while Eckhart uses the written style of the treatise even when he is preaching, Tauler "relates to the everyday context of the audience."[24]

There is no doubt, however, that the basic mystical thought of Tauler comes from Eckhart. That thought is expressed in Eckhart's own words:

> Whenever I preach, I usually exhort detachment and that man should free himself of himself and of everything. Secondly, that one should become embedded . . . into the one-fold good that is God. And thirdly, that one should contemplate the great nobility that God has implanted into the soul so that man comes in mysterious ways into God. And fourthly, of the purity of divine nature—of the light that is in divine nature, which is truly ineffable.[25]

There are important differences between the mystical thought of Tauler and that of his teacher, and these undoubtedly had implications for the differences in their preaching styles, but they need not concern us here. For the moment it is enough to recognize that the two of them in their mystical fervor created a distinctive genre of preaching in fourteenth-century Germany. Through his influence on the *Theologia Germanica*, Tauler was an inspiration even to Martin Luther as he was an influence on spiritual renewals and mystical-theological controversies as late as the eighteenth century.[26] Any history of preaching would be incomplete without some reference to the homiletical activity of the Rhineland mystics.[27]

A PULPIT OF PROTEST

Wyclif

A late contemporary of Tauler was engaged in a very different sort of production of sermons in England. Not a Dominican like the other major figures studied in this chapter, John Wyclif[28] (ca. 1330–84) was a secular priest. Having grown up in a comfortable Yorkshire family, he arrived at Oxford in the mid-1350s, where he was first a fellow of Merton and then master of Balliol. Being master of Balliol at the time amounted to little more than heading a lodging house for students, and the position provided him with scant support; he gave it up as soon as he could. In 1365, however, he was given a more prestigious appointment; he was made head of Canterbury Hall, an experimental college in which both monastic and secular clergy would live together (there being few members of the laity in the university then). When, however, he tried to eject all of the religious from the college, he was relieved of his position.

During Wyclif's era (and for centuries after the Reformation), it was possible for a cleric to receive the income from a church appointment without living in the place or performing the ministry. Someone else could be hired to do the actual work while the incumbent did something else, such as studying in a university. Indeed, one might be appointed to several such benefices and live in none of them. Such absentee pluralism was the major source of Wyclif's income while he was at Oxford.

Since the Oxford degree nomenclature at the time was the same as it is in modern universities, Wyclif's career can sound a bit confusing. Advancement from the bachelor to the master of arts involved several years of lecturing, and the master's, given after a total of six or eight years of study, was the standard teaching degree. Wyclif did not receive his doctorate until he had been at Oxford almost eighteen years.

His first lectures were in logic; he quickly identified himself as a realist, in opposition to the nominalists who had ruled the turf at Oxford since William of Ockham had taught there in the previous generation. While his argument is too subtle to be explored here, it is enough to note that he claimed an ethical motivation for it:

> All envy or actual sin is caused by the lack of an ordered love of universals . . . because every such sin consists in a will preferring a lesser good to a greater good, whereas in general the more universal goods are better.[29]

Stated in terms of simple ethical choices, the acknowledgment of categories of persons could lead one to promote the welfare of the entire class of human persons rather than of just those closely related to oneself. However foreign such a philosophical vocabulary sounds today, it was very much that of the time—and it is hard to argue with the conclusion. This and other ventures in the field of logic led in time to Wyclif's becoming one of the most influential minds in the university. For most of his career, any fame he had rested on his skill as a logician. With the completion of his first work in theology as such, a study of the incarnation, he received his doctor of divinity degree in 1372.[30] After that he began work on a theological *summa*, an undertaking that occupied eight years. Before it was completed, however, his life underwent a number of changes.

Like many scholars of today, Wyclif's reputation for learning caused him to be called into government service. Popes had long claimed the right to tax clergy anywhere in the Western world. When, however, the papacy moved to France and came under the protection of the French Crown, the English began to feel that such taxes were taking their money to arm their enemies against them. In 1371, Parliament had just levied a large tax on the English clergy to help pay for the war against France when the pope levied another to finance a war to recover papal territories in Italy. Wyclif was invited to be a member of the second of two unsuccessful English delegations to Bruges to negotiate the matter with papal officials.

This involvement led Wyclif to begin to think about government. In the treatise on civil dominion in his *Summa*, he argued the thesis that no one in a state of sin has a right to exercise authority. God may allow someone to occupy such a position in a state of sin, but that person does so without any divine claim to the position. He drew a number of inferences from this, including the principle that Christians ought to have all things in common. Yet he applied his thesis very differently to civil and church governments. Even a bad king should be obeyed, as Christ obeyed Pilate, but

> whenever an ecclesiastical community or person habitually abuses its wealth, kings, princes and temporal lords can take it away, however much it may be established by human tradition.[31]

By the time of publication in 1376, when Wyclif was in his mid-forties, he took the first step toward his later recognition as a heretic, that of siding with the Crown against church government at any level when the latter could be accused of using its wealth for itself rather than to help the poor. Why he chose to work out the implications of his thesis for church government alone and not for civil as well, no one knows.[32]

Needless to say, his opinions were more welcome to political than to religious leaders. As a result, Wyclif enjoyed the protection of John of Gaunt, son of the king and one of the most influential men at court. John invited him to London to preach a series of sermons against the worldliness of the bishops of London and Winchester. When the bishop of London summoned him to trial for these sermons, Wyclif was accompanied not only by four advocates but also by John and the marshal of England, and the trial ended in a riot.

By this time the pope had condemned eighteen propositions from Wyclif's *On Civil Dominion* and had asked the king, the senior bishops, and Oxford to condemn him. The king died, but the royal council hired Wyclif as a consultant; the bishops forbade only his teaching those doctrines in a way that might scandalize the laity; and Oxford found the condemned theses to be true. Then the pope died and was succeeded by one from whom reform was expected. When that pope inspired the election of an anti-pope, Wyclif was safe from prosecution by Rome until after his death.

After this London episode Wyclif turned his attention to the doctrine of holy Scripture. His lectures on the Bible had already allowed him to complete a commentary on every book in it that was rich in knowledge of patristic interpretation, the only such commentary that survives from the second half of the fourteenth century. His treatise *On the Truth of Sacred Scripture* (1377–78) argues that the Bible is free from error and thus authoritative, that all truth is in it, and that it is thus the yardstick by which all other claims to truth are to be evaluated. Because it is the inerrant statement of truth, it should be available to all Christians.

Yet Wyclif was no fundamentalist; all his life he used allegorical interpretation, and he considered patristic interpretation to be the guide to true biblical understanding. He certainly did not believe in what was later to be called "plenary verbal inspiration."

> What is on the paper is not scripture without its relation to the mental understanding; and what is in the mind is not holy unless it is a grasping of the objective scripture. Hence the need to compare manuscripts together, and check them against the common faith of the whole Church.[33]

His belief that Scripture should be open to all Christians does not mean, as was long thought to be the case, that he himself translated any of it or even supervised the translating activity of others. There is no doubt, however, that the two English translations from his time were made by his followers. After he left Oxford in 1381, the leader of his party at the university, Nicholas of Hereford, did a pedestrian rendering that employed Latin cognates and constructions; and his companion at Lutterworth, John Purvey, was probably the one who revised that into a more idiomatic version.[34]

In 1378–79 Wyclif continued to develop his thoughts about civil and religious government. In doing so he worked out his doctrine of the church, which he defined as consisting of the predestined, those elected to salvation. He distinguished between being in a state of grace and being predestined. At a given moment someone not predestined may be in a state of grace, while someone who is predestined may be in a state of sin. No matter; only those who will persevere are considered actually to be part of the church. Thus he approaches the distinction between the visible and the invisible church.

Yet, in connecting these thoughts with what he has to say about civil dominion, he makes it clear that it is being in a state of grace rather than being predestined that entitles a leader to obedience. Thus if the pope is in grace, even if he is not predestined, he should be obeyed by as much of the Western church as is in communion with him (although this is a "poor particular church cramped in a corner" rather than the holy catholic church).[35] Not being head of the universal church, the pope has no claim to the obedience of all secular lords.

Grace can be communicated to Christians without its having to go through the pope. Nonpredestinate clergy can administer valid sacraments so long as they are in a state of grace (a variation on the Donatist view). Thus, while it is necessary that there be a pope, an actual pope not in a state of grace may even be an Antichrist and thus forfeit any right to be obeyed. A true pope would leave secular matters entirely alone and be a model of charity and holiness. Because of this it had been hard for a bishop of Rome to be a true pope ever since the Donation of Constantine endowed the Roman church and made it wealthy.

Up through this attack on the papacy, Wyclif had the support of many leaders in the church as well as the government, especially the friars who agreed with his standard of apostolic poverty. When, however, he turned his critical eye to eucharistic doctrine, he lost this following. His quarrel was not with the real presence of Christ in the Eucharist; indeed, he died hearing Mass. But he could not make logical sense of the claim that while all the accidents of bread and wine remained, the substance had been totally transformed into the body and blood of Christ. He did not believe that accidents can subsist without a substance, nor did he believe that any substance can be annihilated. Further, as he pointed out, the early fathers had not believed or known the unscriptural doctrine of transubstantiation. All of these arguments depend, of course, on an analysis of reality that grows out of Aristotle's distinction between substance and accident.

Friars at Oxford caused a university commission of twelve doctors to be set up in 1380 to examine this doctrine, which they found to be heretical and dangerous to Catholic faith and the reputation of the university.

Anyone teaching it should be imprisoned, suspended from university functions, and excommunicated. This doctrine also cost Wyclif the support of John of Gaunt. Meanwhile, one of the leaders of the Peasants' Revolt, John Ball, claimed to have learned from Wyclif the doctrines that justified the rebellion. While Wyclif would not have condoned this application of his theory, the association of his name with the revolt did him no good.

Soon afterward he withdrew from Oxford and settled in the nearby parish of Lutterworth, a benefice he had held for a number of years. From there he continued to pour out polemical writings for the three years that remained of his life, although many of his closest followers were either recanting or fleeing. Meanwhile, in 1382 his old enemy the bishop of London, who had become archbishop of Canterbury, called a conference of bishops and theologians to meet at Blackfriars' and examine twenty-four of Wyclif's teachings. Ten were declared heretical and the other fourteen erroneous.

One of Wyclif's activities during the waning days of his life was to edit his Latin sermons for publication. It is ironic that the reason for his consideration in this volume is hardly mentioned before he was near to death. As an absentee pluralist, however, he would have done little preaching in the parishes to which he had been presented. Some of his Latin sermons were preached to the university and numbers of them have no distinctive Wycliffite doctrines, yet most represent his short stay at Lutterworth and the majority of these were never preached by him. They "were a literary production, composed in the sequence in which they now stand, and were probably intended for the use of other preachers."[36] "Of sermons actually preached by Wyclif only a relatively small number survive as the *Sermones Quadriginta*,"[37] which appear in the last volume of the Loserth edition.

There also exists in English a cycle of 294 sermons that are homilies in form and constitute a series (for an example of these sermons, see **Vol. 2, pp. 224-27**). The series comprises sermons on both the Epistles and Gospels for every Sunday in the Sarum calendar,[38] including Gospels shared by the feast days of a number of saints ("commons"), those for a particular saint's day ("propers"),[39] and Gospels for certain weekdays in the church year ("ferias").

Until recently, it was assumed that Wyclif wrote these sermons or that they were translations made by others of the similar series of Latin sermons he had composed but not preached at Lutterworth. Now, however, "it seems clear that, whatever their debt to Wyclif's Latin works, and whatever the link with his *Sermones* in their extant or previous forms, the English sermons as they stand are very unlikely to have been written by Wyclif himself."[40] Indeed, they seem to have been written after his death, with 1389–90 the most likely date.[41] The series appears to have had either an unknown single author or at least an overseer of the entire project. That person was someone closely related to a university who was familiar (a) with most of the corpus of Wyclif's writings, (b) with many works of patristic and earlier medieval biblical scholarship, and (c) with issues before the church at the time of writing. Yet that person was also capable of lapses in Latin usage and showed other gaps in learning.[42]

The manuscripts of these series are very fine and appear to have been produced under tight control. This fact has a number of implications. First, it appears that there were wealthy Wycliffites (or Lollards, as they were called) who could bear the expense and provide the facilities where such manuscripts could be produced in safety.[43] Next, the preaching to be done was neither the extempore nor the written efforts of the preachers, nor even their variations on appointed themes; the sermons were to be read as official teaching.[44] They were bound into handsome volumes appropriate for use at liturgical assemblies and so were not prepared for street preaching, but for the regular worship of congregations who followed the official calendar. From this fact it would appear that there was an organized circuit of Lollard congregations, congregations, moreover, that were prepared to listen to four or more sermons a week.[45]

While it used to be thought that Wyclif himself organized groups of "poor priests" to wander over England giving extempore sermons based on his English translation of the Bible, little of that belief is now credible. The translation was made by others, only a few of Wyclif's supporters have left records of preaching tours in his lifetime, and no evidence exists to prove that he organized them. Yet, obviously, congregations did come into existence, and they were founded by people influenced by the teaching of Wyclif. It does not push the evidence too far to suggest that he was in favor of such developments, but there is no ground for saying that he was responsible for their initiation.

Little is known about how the movement spread. One scholar has suggested that it did so through the efforts of sympathetic Oxford colleges to appoint Wycliffites to parishes to which they had the power of appointment.[46] At any rate, the doctrines did spread until the failure of Sir John Oldcastle's[47] Lollard rebellion against Henry V in 1413–14.[48]

The English cycle, however derivatively, reflects Wyclif's thought about preaching. He never tired of saying how important he thought it was.[49] That, of course, does not make him very different from the friars. Indeed, on the whole, his thoughts about preaching remind one of nothing so much as the early days of the friars. Their emphasis on having learned priests go about preaching from the Bible is very similar, as is also their emphasis on poverty and their objections to avarice and worldliness among the clergy. Even the picture that has survived of the "poor priests" Wyclif was supposed to have sent out (which could be an accurate representation of Lollards who went out later) sounds very Franciscan:

> Bare-foot, clad in a long coarse cloak of dark-red colour which was the symbol of hard labour and poverty, a long staff in hand signifying their pastoral office, they wandered in the dioceses of Leicester (and of London) from town to town, from village to village. In churches, chapels and alms-houses, wherever they could get a few hearers together, they preached of the glory of God's law. Although mocked at by some for their coarse garb and for their manner of teaching, they were beloved by the people.[50]

This raises the question of why Wyclif opposed the friars so much. It can be pointed out that he did not do so until his eucharistic doctrine met their disfavor. After that he began to teach against begging; he also criticized thematic preaching and, especially, the use of *exempla*. While it does appear likely that, as time went on, some *exempla* were a bit coarse and others appear to have been told more for their entertainment than their illustrative value, it is hard to know what Wyclif had against *exempla* in general, unless it was merely that his philosopher's mind preferred the abstract to the concrete.

The form of Wycliffite sermons, both those of the master in Latin and those of his followers in English, was essentially that of old-style homilies that fell into two divisions, exegesis and application. The former was the shorter of the two and was by no means confined to the literal, historical meaning of the passage. Yet, as Kinney says: "All too often Wyclif uses an episode in Christ's life, or a scriptural text, merely as a peg on which to hang an attack on his *bêtes noire*."[51]

Since Wyclif's preaching has often been claimed to be "sermons of the Reformation age rather than of medieval times,"[52] it is interesting to read the evaluation of a distinguished mid-twentieth-century Lutheran historian of preaching:

> We expect great things of Wycliffe and his school; the study of his extant sermons has, however, disappointed those who wish to see in him a "precursor" of the Reformation. Though his Latin sermons are wholly Scholastic in character, the English sermons are a practical, popular proclamation based upon the Bible. The allegorical method does,

> however, hold him in its sway and when he interprets scripture literally it becomes primarily a law of God which demands application to the contemporary situation in church and state. Because of this Wycliffe did not find the true living water of the gospel. It was in rapture over the law of God that the Lollards left on their travels.[53]

The significance of Wyclif and his preaching is seen not only in his inspiration of the Lollards, but also in his having been the primary theological and homiletical influence on John Hus and his Bohemian followers. Whole passages of the sermons of Hus can be set down in parallel with those of Wyclif and be seen to have extensive verbal dependence.[54] Thus Anne Hudson has summarized Wyclif's importance in the history of preaching by saying:

> Directly, Lollardy prepared the ground for the reformation in England, by establishing groups of men who were accustomed to radical ideas on the church and authority within it, and who regarded the text of the Bible in the vernacular with special reverence. Indirectly, Wyclif's theories, through the medium of Hus's writings and of Hussite copying, reinforced those of the later reformers.[55]

Pulpit Apocalypse

It could be thought that any history of preaching, even one devoted to movements rather than practitioners, would be incomplete without reference to so famous a preacher as Girolamo Savonarola (1452–98). One of the most authoritative interpreters of the Florentine friar, however, has insisted that the attention he deserves generally and not just homiletically does not spring so much from his uniqueness as from his being at home in his environment. As Donald Weinstein says:

> The central methodological problem has been the tendency to treat Savonarola monolithically, either as a man without a history or as one whose history serves to illustrate a solid, unchanging core of personality, rather than, as with ordinary men, to provide the experience that shaped his personality.[56]

That experience, as Weinstein noted a few pages earlier in *Savonarola and Florence,* is very much a part of the Florentine world of his time. "He is just such a combination of popular zealot, conservative theologian, and radical millenarian as could have existed only in the milieu of Italy before the Reformation and the conquest of Hapsburg Spain."[57] He could have also said that Savonarola exemplifies the apocalyptic preaching so common in the Middle Ages.

Few persons in the history of preaching, including Meister Eckhart and Wyclif, have been the subject of more varied interpretations offered by more fervent partisans. In an excellent summary of scholarship over the last century, Weinstein refers to those who love Savonarola as "the New *Piagnoni*," the term by which his contemporary followers were designated.[58] They are those who think that the church should regard him as a saint rather than as the heretic he was burned for being. These devotees could be divided into those who consider him a precursor of the Reformation and those who think he should be canonized by the Roman Catholic Church. Others consider him proud and deluded, not to mention doctrinally devious and dangerous. More secular modern interpreters are apt to regard anyone who claimed to be the recipient of divine revelation as emotionally disturbed. Others are content to think of Fra Girolamo as a political thinker: the restorer of the Florentine republic, a herald of Italian unification in the nineteenth century, or a dictator. Variations have been played on all these themes.

Whatever the interpretation, there is general agreement on the data. Born in 1452 into a middle-class professional family in Ferrara, Savonarola was always a serious and severe person, even when he was studying philosophy as part of his premedical education. His love of Thomas Aquinas undoubtedly had something to do with his running away from home to join the Dominicans when he was twenty-two. In 1482 he was sent to Florence for the first time.

He did not show great promise as a preacher, however, until he was preaching in the church at San Gimignano near Siena two years later. There, for the first time, he began to incorporate into his preaching what he considered to be the revelations he was receiving, revelations to the effect that the church was to be scourged,[59] then it would be renewed, and all of that was going to happen very soon. After several years on a preaching tour in northern Italy, he was ready to return to the Dominican community of San Marco as prior in 1491 and see the beginning of his remarkable success in the city of Florence.

From the beginning, his prophecies seem to have been closely related to the political scene. His predictions of the death of Lorenzo de Medici and the conquest of Florence by the king of France, Charles VIII, were seen by the people as signs that his message came from God. He was a member of the embassy that Florence sent to arrange terms with Charles, and, when those terms were lenient, he was regarded as the savior of the city. So high was his stock that he not only played an important role in the establishment of a sort of theocratic democracy, but also began a period of ascetical moral reform there.

His attacks on the church continued, however, and brought him to the unfavorable attention of Pope Alexander VI.[60] By this time, too, political, economic, and financial difficulties in Florence, as well as restiveness under his puritanical standards, had begun to foster disaffection among powerful elements within the citizenry. In 1495 the pope suspended the friar from preaching, a ban he observed for about six months. On the whole, Alexander was very patient and did not excommunicate Savonarola until 1497. The friar's response was to start requesting the secular powers to call an ecumenical council to depose an unworthy pope. After that there seemed no alternative but to arrest him, wring a confession out of him by torture, and turn him over to the secular authorities for execution.

In order to understand the sermons of Savonarola, it is necessary to know something about the apocalyptic framework in which they were set. Learning that is not as simple as it could have been because, as Weinstein pointed out, the framework changed in midcourse. His original revelation had been little more than that the church was to be purged by God from its wickedness and then restored to purity in the near future. But

> at a certain moment his Christian universalism narrowed to a partisan civic focus, with Florence taking shape in his mind as the New Jerusalem and the future of her government and worldly fortunes becoming part of the divine plan.[61]

As Weinstein has shown, the new elements in Savonarola's vision were derived from "the myth of Florence" widely believed at the time. "Strongly optimistic millenarian hopes centered on Florence as the harbinger of the renovated church" had been a motif in Florentine self-understanding for some time,[62] and the seer came to this more positive view of his adopted city as the very success of his earlier prophecies generated a wider acceptance of him and his message within the city.

Savonarola's confidence in his own revelation, however, demanded that he see his point of view as having been consistent all along. The way he explained it to himself and others was as follows:

> As Almighty God saw the sins of Italy multiply, especially in her ecclesiastical and secular princes, he was unable to bear it any longer and decided to cleanse his Church with a great scourge. . . . Since Florence is located in the middle of Italy, like the heart in a man, God himself

> deigned to choose her to receive this proclamation so that from her it might be widely spread through the other parts of Italy, as we have seen fulfilled in the present. Among his other servants he chose me, unworthy and unprofitable as I am, for this task, and saw to it that I came to Florence in 1489 at the command of my superiors. That year, on Sunday, August first, I began to interpret the book of the Apocalypse in public in our Church of San Marco. Through the whole of the same year I preached to the people of Florence and continually stressed three things: first, the renovation of the Church would come in these times; second, God would send a great scourge over all Italy before that renovation; and third, these two things would happen soon. I worked at proving and establishing these three conclusions by firm arguments, by figures from the Holy Scriptures, and by other likenesses or parables formed from the things that are now happening in the Church.
>
> I urged the case at that time only with these arguments and kept secret the fact that I had also received knowledge of them from God in another way, because it seemed that the state of souls was not then ready to receive that mystery. In the following years, finding minds more ready to believe, I sometimes introduced a vision, not disclosing that it was a prophetic vision but setting it forth to the people only in the manner of a parable.[63]

Savonarola says that he received his revelations in all of the ways that such things come. He always received a supernatural light that was a form of participation in God's eternity; from this he learned that the revelation was true and came from God. The medium of the revelation varied, however: sometimes it came directly into the intellect without any images, sometimes the imagination was imprinted with different figures and images, and sometimes God set forth things to the exterior senses.

Beginning with a sermon at Santa Reparata's in Florence during 1490, however, he came to realize that God sent him the visions so that he could make them known. From that time on he did so, and the response was overwhelming. "My faithful listeners know how fittingly my expositions of the scriptures always agreed with the present times."[64] A climax in this process came when everyone knew that Charles VIII was about to invade Italy. In his continuing exposition of Genesis he came to the text "Behold, I will bring waters upon the face of the earth." When he announced that text, "many were immediately astonished and acknowledged that this passage of Genesis had been gradually prepared by God's hidden inspiration to fit the times."[65]

With most of Savonarola's recorded sermons, there is some difficulty in knowing exactly how closely they approximate what he actually said in delivery, because his faithful amanuensis, Lorenzo Violi, did not always seek to write down what he said word for word.[66] In part Violi's interest grew and in part his skill improved, especially after the friar began to assist him by looking over what he had taken down in a shorthand that appears illegible to others.[67] For some of Savonarola's sermons before Violi began to record them there remain the author's Latin notes, but these are very sketchy and incomplete. Later scholars have published some of these earlier series of sermons in a form that seems imaginative expansions from such notes into full sermons. It can be assumed, however, that for the last sermons on which Violi had the cooperation of the preacher, the text is close to what was actually delivered.

When one looks at the sermons of Savonarola,[68] it is obvious that the friar returned to a patristic practice of *lectio continua*, doing series of sermons on individual books of the Bible rather than preaching on one of the lections for the liturgical occasion. Yet the sermons are preached from a short text rather than from an extended passage, and the preacher shows virtually no interest in the historical meaning of the text. Rather, he is concerned with its applicability to the situation in Florence as that is understood within the framework of his basic revelation.

Thus, after pointing out that Savonarola adhered to the traditional medieval fourfold interpretation, Weinstein goes on to say:

> But not even skill in the fourfold exegetical method was enough to reveal all the mysteries contained in Scripture. Only the prophet illuminated by God could uncover the history of the future recorded therein; Savonarola's Biblicism was inseparably linked with his prophetism and inevitably subordinated to it: "And this I have not by Scripture nor by the revelations of any man who is under heaven."[69]

The only way in which the flavor of that can be communicated is through extended quotation. This sample comes from his sermon for All Saints' in 1494 when Charles VIII was threatening to attack:

> *Vox dicentis clama*. A voice cries out saying: O Italy, *propter peccata tua venient tibi adversa*. All you cities of Italy, now is the time for all your sins to be punished. O Italy, for your lust, your avarice, your pride, your ambition, your thieving and extortion, there will come upon you many adversities and many scourges. *Vox dicentis clama*. A voice cries out saying: *O Florentia, propter peccata tua venient tibi adversa*. O Florence, O Florence, O Florence, for your sins, for your brutality, your avarice, your lust, your ambition, there will befall you many trials and many tribulations. *Vox dicentis clama*. On whom do you call? O Clergy, Clergy, Clergy, *propter te orta est haec tempestas*—O clergy,

> who are the principal cause of so many evils, through your evildoing comes this story; by your sins have been prepared so many tribulations; woe, woe, I say unto those that bear the tonsure! *Vox dicentis clama,* a voice still calls. On whom further should I call? *Clama, ne cesses, annuntia populo huic scelera eorum*, cry out without ceasing, declare unto the people their wickedness. It calls and says, keep on: *Annuntia populo huic scelera eorum*. . . . I have said it so many times, I have cried out so often, I have wept for you so many times, Florence, that it should suffice. *Orate*, pray for me to the Lord, *ut Deus consoletur me*. O Florence, I have wished to speak this morning to you and each and every one openly and sincerely, for I could do no other. And still the voice cries out: *vox dicentis clama,* the voice of One speaks forth and calls. And whom else should I call? I have called each one to repentance. *Clama ad Dominum Deum tuum*, call and cry out to the Lord, thy God. I turn to thee, O Lord, Who died for love of us, and for our sins. *Parce, Domine, populo tuo*. Forgive, forgive, Lord, this Thy people; forgive, Lord, the people of Florence, who desire to be Thy people![70]

All preaching is predicated on the assumption that a common principle is operating between the situation in the text and the situation in the congregation. That is what justifies the transference of the perspective in the text to the congregational situation. But even if one assumes that the Holy Spirit inspires the preacher into awareness of these parallels, only an apocalyptic preacher, one who assumed that he or she had a direct message from God, would ever suggest that the only reason the Holy Spirit had inspired the biblical writer to say something was because of its future applicability to the situation of the apocalyptist. That is what Savonarola did when he said that the Genesis text "Behold, I will bring waters upon the face of the earth" had been "gradually prepared by God's hidden inspiration to fit the times."[71] In doing this he points to what makes apocalyptic preaching a distinct homiletical genre. While his own apocalyptic preaching received extraordinary attention both while it was occurring and ever since, it is representative of the genre not only in the Middle Ages but whenever it has appeared, from New Testament times on.

Revolutionary Conservatism

With the exception of the homiletical spirituality of Humbert of Romans, this chapter has dealt with movements in preaching that have not followed the supremely medieval pattern of the thematic sermon. The Rhineland mystics used a form of preaching little different from that of Bernard of Clairvaux; the difference that did exist was in the content. The reform preaching of the Wycliffites and the apocalyptic sermons of

Savonarola also employed variations on the traditional pattern of the homily. At least the latter two represented movements critical of the mainstream life of the church at the time, and thus the change of homiletical pattern was probably not entirely an accident.

There were other oscillations of the weathercock on the steeple of the medieval church, suggesting that winds of change were in the air. The "subdividing mentality" seen alike in scholasticism and thematic preaching was probably an effect of the confidence in the powers of the human mind given to the medieval world by the recovery of Aristotle, especially his logic. The distinctions it allowed theologians to make opened to them the possibility of breaking down issues into their component parts. By the middle of the fifteenth century, however, the minds of Europe were being excited by the recovery of other writings from classical antiquity, especially the rhetorical works associated with the names of Cicero and Quintilian. This recovery was, of course, a part of a passionate interest in every aspect of classical antiquity, that movement of the human spirit known as the Renaissance. The coincidence of that with the movement known as the Reformation marks the next turning point in the history of preaching.

FOR FURTHER READING

Early Dominicans: Selected Writings. Edited, translated, and introduction by Simon Tugwell, and preface by Vincent de Couesnongle. CWS. New York: Paulist Press, 1982.

Johannes Tauler: Sermons. Translated by Maria Shrady, with introduction by Josef Schmidt and preface by Alois Haas. CWS. New York: Paulist Press, 1985.

Kenny, Anthony. *Wyclif*. Past Masters. Oxford: Oxford University Press, 1985.

Meister Eckhart: The Essential Sermons, Commentaries, Treatises, and Defense. Translated and introduction by Edmund Colledge and Bernard McGinn, with preface by Huston Smith. CWS. New York: Paulist Press, 1981.

Selections from English Wycliffite Writings. Edited and introduction, notes, and glossary by Anne Hudson. Medieval Academy Reprints for Teaching, no. 38. Cambridge: Cambridge University Press, 1978; repr., Toronto: University of Toronto Press for the Medieval Academy of America, 1997.

Weinstein, Donald. *Savonarola and Florence: Prophecy and Patriotism in the Renaissance*. Princeton, N.J.: Princeton University Press, 1970.

Notes

1. *Early Dominicans: Selected Writings,* ed. with intro. Simon Tugwell, and pref. Vincent de Couesnongle, CWS (New York: Paulist Press, 1982), 181.

2. Near Valence.

3. Tugwell, *Early Dominicans,* 2.

4. Ibid., 2.

5. Ibid., 6.

6. The Latin title is *De eruditione praedicatorum* and the standard edition is Humbertus de Romanus, *Opera de vita regulari,* ed. J. J. Berthier, 2 vols. (1889; reprint, Turin: Marietti, 1956). Another element in the mystery of the lack of notice that *The Formation of Preachers* received is the fact that Humbert joined to it a collection of model sermons, mostly of the *ad status* variety. Since it represented a more familiar genre, the model sermon collection was copied more often than the work on spirituality.

7. D. L. d'Avray, *The Preaching of the Friars: Sermons Diffused from Paris Before 1300* (Oxford: Clarendon, 1985), 177.

8. *The Formation of Preachers* 1.3.12. in Tugwell, *Early Dominicans,* 188. Gregory's exegesis here obviously reflects Ephesians 2:20 and a hermeneutical principle acknowledged since at least the time of Hillel that a word means the same thing whenever it appears in the canon, the word in this case being *foundation.* Also involved is Gregory's identification of the essential task of the apostles as being preaching.

9. The year 1327 is not known with certainty.

10. *Meister Eckhart: The Essential Sermons, Commentaries, Treatises, and Defense,* trans. and intro. Edmund Colledge, and Bernard McGinn, pref. Huston Smith, CWS (New York: Paulist Press, 1981), xvii. The entry in *ODCC* adds that he has also been regarded as a forerunner of Kantian critical idealism.

11. Cf. *Meister Eckhart: Mystic and Philosopher,* trans. and commentary Reiner Schürmann, Studies in Phenomenology and Existential Philosophy (Bloomington: Indiana University Press, 1978), 3-47.

12. "Allegorical" here is used in the general sense of any figurative meaning. Eckhart did not refer to the four senses of Scripture (literal, allegorical, topological, and anagogical) in the commonly accepted way, but instead spoke of two senses, the "more evident" and that hidden "under the shell of the letter" (McGinn in Colledge and McGinn, *Meister Eckhart,* 28). A convenient presentation of this perspective in Eckhart's own words occurs in the prologue to *The Book of the Parables in Genesis,* ibid., 92-95.

13. Ibid., 28.

14. Schürmann, *Meister Eckhart,* 3.

15. Ibid., 47.

16. Ibid., 5.

17. Ibid., 47.

18. Ibid., 10.

19. In the collection of *ad status* sermons included as the second half of *The Formation of Preachers,* Humbert of Romans provided a number for women in various states of life.

20. Strasbourg had sided with Louis of Bavaria against Pope John XXII, and so was one of the cities placed under Interdict. Thus Dominicans there had to be transferred to cities not under the ban.

21. "Sermon for Ascension II," trans. Maria Shrady, in *Johannes Tauler: Sermons*, intro. Josef Schmidt and pref. Alois Haas, CWS (New York: Paulist Press, 1985), 72.

22. *The History and Life of the Reverend Doctor John Tauler of Strasbourg; with Twenty-five of His Sermons,* trans. Susanna Winkworth (London: Smith, Elder & Co., 1857), 1-71.

23. Haas, *Johannes Tauler: Sermons,* xiv.

24. *Versuch einer exacten Stiluntersuchung für Meister Eckhart, Johannes Tauler, und Heinrich Seuse,* Medium Aevum Philosophische Studien (Munich: Wilhelm Fink Verlag, 1979). Schmidt reviews her analysis in *Johannes Tauler: Sermons,* 18-19.

25. Translated by Schmidt from Eckhart's Middle High German in a passage cited by Alois Haas, "Meister Eckharts geistliches Predigtprogramm," *FZPhTh* 29 (1982), 192-93. (*Johannes Tauler: Sermons,* 13). The final line of the quotation has been altered in the interest of intelligibility in English.

26. Haas, *Johannes Tauler: Sermons,* xiii.

27. To set this in the context of German homiletics, see Hans-Jochen Schiewer, "German Sermons in the Middle Ages" in *The Sermon,* dir. Kienzle, 861-961.

28. There are variations on the spelling of the name, but Wyclif is that preferred by specialists.

29. *De Universalibus,* ed. I. Mueller, P. Spade, and A. Kenny (Oxford: University Press, 1978), 77. Quoted in Anthony Kenny, *Wyclif,* Past Masters (Oxford: University Press, 1985), 10.

30. To this day, the D.D. is not an honorary degree in England as it is in the United States, but is rather a very high earned degree.

31. *De civili dominio,* ed. R. L. Poole (London: Wyclif Society, 1885), 286. Quoted in Kenny, *Wyclif,* 49-50.

32. Scholars disagree drastically about the reasons, depending on their overall attitude toward Wyclif. Herbert B. Workman sees Wyclif as more interested in metaphysical groundwork than in working out in life the doctrine of lordship. *John Wyclif: A Study of the Medieval Church* (Oxford: Clarendon Press, 1926), 1:259. K. B. McFarlane considers his motivation to have been pique at being passed over for a canonry in *John Wycliffe and the Beginnings of English Nonconformity,* Teach Yourself History (London: English Universities Press Ltd., 1952), 30, 66-69, 84-85. Gordon Leff insists that it is important to remember that "Wyclif was also a theorist who gave to his hostility to the church a far-reaching theoretical framework." *Heresy in the Later Middle Ages: The Relation of Heterodoxy to Dissent c. 1250–c. 1450* (Manchester: University Press; and New York: Barnes and Noble, 1967), 2:497.

33. Kenny, *Wyclif,* 61.

34. Margaret Deansley, *The Lollard Bible and Other Medieval Biblical Versions,* Cambridge Studies in Medieval Life and Thought (Cambridge: At the University Press, 1920), 252-67; *Selections from English Wycliffite Writings,* ed., with intro., notes, and glossary Anne Hudson, Medieval Academy Reprints for Teaching, no. 38 (Cambridge: Cambridge University Press, 1978; reprint, Toronto: University of Toronto Press for the Medieval Academy of America, 1997), 163.

35. Kenny, *Wyclif,* 71.

36. Hudson, *Selections from English Wycliffite Writings,* 3. For the Latin sermons, see *Iohannis Wyclif Sermones Now First Edited from the Manuscripts with Critical and Historical Notes,* ed. Johann Loserth, 4 vols. (London: Trübner & Co. for the Wyclif Society, 1887–90).

37. Ibid.

38. The calendar used in the Diocese of Salisbury, which, with most other liturgical usage there, became standard for Britain in the late Middle Ages.

39. In the Wycliffite tradition, only New Testament saints are provided for (with rare exceptions).

40. *English Wycliffite Sermons*, ed. Pamela Gradon and Anne Hudson, vol. 4 (Oxford: Clarendon Press, 1996), 28.

41. Ibid., 21.

42. Ibid., 28-37.

43. Sir Thomas Latimer is a case in point.

44. Although, as with other model sermons, there are times when a particular point is left to be developed by the preacher.

45. Anne Hudson, "A Lollard Sermon-Cycle and Its Implications," *Medium Aevum* 40 (1971): 142-56.

46. A. K. McHardy, "The Dissemination of Wyclif's Ideas," *From Ockham to Wyclif,* ed. Anne Hudson and Michael Wilks (Oxford: Basil Blackwell for the Ecclesiastical History Society, 1987), 361-68.

47. It is ironic that this Lollard leader should have been in his youth the companion of the future Henry V, on whom the character of Falstaff is based.

48. McFarlane, *John Wycliffe and the Beginnings of English Nonconformity,* 146; Anne Hudson, *Selections from English Wycliffite Writings,* 1:7.

49. Loserth, *Iohannis Wyclif Sermones,* 1:iii-vi.

50. Quoted by Loserth, *Iohannis Wyclif Sermones,* 1:xviii, from R. Buddensieg, *Johann Wiclif und seine Zeit* (Gotha: n.p., 1885), 169-70. Workman says that Wyclif "copied the methods of St. Francis" (*John Wyclif,* 1:201).

51. *Wyclif,* 97.

52. Workman, *John Wyclif,* 2:213-14.

53. Brilioth, *Brief History of Preaching,* 91-92. Brilioth obviously thought that Wyclif wrote the English as well as the Latin sermons. Much of this evaluation is conceded by Workman, who says: 'The student who turns from these glowing precepts (i.e., Wyclif's theory of preaching) to Wyclif's actual sermons will be disappointed, even if he bears in mind that there is nothing which so changes from age to age as the standard of effective pulpit oratory." *John Wyclif,* 2:212. Workman's understanding of Wyclif's preaching and his responsibility for the work of the "poor preachers" is presented in ibid., 2:201-20.

54. Loserth, *Iohannis Wyclif Sermones,* 1:xxii-xxvii.

55. Hudson, *Selections from English Wycliffite Writings,* 4. In a survey of preaching in English between ca. 1370 and ca. 1500, H. Leith Spencer says compilers of English sermon collections generally appear to have been persons of Wycliffite sympathies before the clamp-down on Lollardy by Archbishop Arundel in his *Constitutions* of 1407, but after that the more traditional influence of John Mirk's *Festial* was more prevalent. *English Preaching in the Late Middle Ages* (Oxford: Clarendon Press, 1993). Spencer expresses this view more concisely in "Middle English Sermons" in *The Sermon,* dir. Kienzle, 597-660.

56. Donald Weinstein, *Savonarola and Florence: Prophecy and Patriotism in the Renaissance* (Princeton: Princeton University Press, 1970), 18.

57. Ibid., 15.

58. Ibid., 3. The term means "the tearful ones" or "the mourners" and was originally used pejoratively, but it soon lost negative connotations. The summary of recent scholarship is found on pp. 3-26.

59. It is often thought that Wyclif and Savonarola were lone voices condemning the sins of the clergy of their day, but G. R. Owst has made it clear that the corrupt morals of some of them was one of the standard topoi of late medieval preaching. *Literature and Pulpit in Medieval England: A Neglected Chapter in the History of English Letters and of the English People* (Cambridge: University Press, 1933), 236-86.

60. An entertaining journalistic (but generally reliable) account of the clashes of Savonarola with the pontiff whose name has become a symbol for everything wrong with the Renaissance papacy is Michael de la Bedoyere, *The Meddlesome Friar: The Story of the Conflict between Savonarola and Alexander VI* (London: Collins, 1958). Alexander's reputation is not entirely deserved.

61. Weinstein, *Savonarola and Florence,* 77. This is the essential thesis of Weinstein's study.

62. Ibid., 27-66. The phrase quoted is from Bernard McGinn's preface to his translation of Savonarola's Compendium of Revelation in his book *Apocalyptic Spirituality: Treatises and Letters of Lactantius, Adso of Notier-en-Der, Joachim of Fiore, Franciscan Spirituals, Savonarola,* pref. Marjorie Reeves, CWS (New York: Paulist Press, 1979), 188.

63. McGinn, *Apocalyptic Spirituality,* 195-96.

64. Ibid., 196-97.

65. Ibid., 197.

66. *Savonarola: Prediche Italiani ai Fiorentini,* ed. Francesco Cognasso, Documenti di Storia Italiana (Perugia, Venice: Nuova Italia, 1930), 1:xiii. See also Roberto Ridolfi, *The Life of Girolamo Savonarola,* trans. Cecil Grayson (London: Routledge and Kegan Paul, 1959), 111-12.

67. E.g., Pierre Van Paassen, *A Crown of Fire: The Life and Times of Girolamo Savonarola* (New York: Scribner's, 1960), 174.

68. By no means an easy thing for the English reader to do. I know of only three translated sermons that are generally available. Petry has sections of the "Sermon for All Saints," 1494, in *No Uncertain Sound,* 296-99. An Ascension Day sermon appears in *20 Centuries of Great Preaching: An Encyclopedia of Preaching,* ed. Clyde E. Fant Jr. and William M. Pinson Jr. (Waco, Tex.: Word, 1971), 1:273-81. Then a "Sermon for the Octave of the Annunciation" is incorporated into Savonarola's *Compendium of Revelation,* in McGinn, *Apocalyptic Spirituality*, 208-70. Whole paragraphs of sermons are translated, however, in the English version of Ridolfi's *Life,* which also discusses the various series of sermons. The best critical edition of the sermons in Italian is that of "Edizione nazionale delle opere di Girolamo Savonarola" published in Rome by A. Berladetti (1955–74); the individual volumes in this series have different editors. Since Petry gives only an excerpt from a sermon, the sermon in McGinn occupies sixty-two printed pages, and the sermon in Fant and

Pinson has been reprinted often since it first appeared in 1908, no sermon from Savonarola is included in Volume 2. The flavor of Savonarola's preaching, however, is communicated in the excerpt from his sermon for All Saints' Day in 1494 that is included in this chapter.

69. Weinstein, *Savonarola and Florence,* 184. The internal quotation is from the *Sermons on the Psalms*, 1:45, in the edition that Weinstein was using.

70. Ridolfi, *Life,* 80-81.

71. McGinn, *Apocalyptic Spirituality,* 197.

Part III

From the Renaissance and Reformation to the Enlightenment

CHAPTER 11

ERASMUS AND THE HUMANISTS

CHANGING TIMES

At the height of the Middle Ages there was a universal culture in Europe that found its unity expressed in the papacy. By their end, however, that culture was in disarray. Factors that contributed to the dissolution of the medieval synthesis include the growth of national sentiment among the European nations, skepticism about the hierarchy of the church, a resort to mysticism as an alternative to the sacramental spirituality of the church, the success of nominalism in undercutting scholastic theology, and the rise of humanism.[1] Most of these factors' impact on preaching were discussed in the previous chapter; the impact of humanism will begin this one.

The significance of the dissolution, however, is not so much that something old had ended as that something new was about to begin. A spiritual vacuum had been created that many exciting new movements would rush in to fill. Since this process resulted in divisions in Western Christianity that still exist, some effort is necessary at this point to evade the partisanship that has characterized many discussions of these monumental changes in the past. One way of going about that is to note that systems do not have to be treated as wholes; they may be separated into aspects that can be studied individually. For example, no one denies that there was much wrong with the church in the West at the beginning of the sixteenth century, but we do not have to see efforts to improve that situation as so confined to one group that a horrible past can be contrasted to an ideal present or that faith communities are seen as either heroes or villains.

Major aspects of changes in church life in the sixteenth century include at least morality, theology, and scholarly method. To begin with the first, the inconsistency that can exist between the ethical ideals of the church and its own behavior was most conspicuous at the highest level. From a time when popes could appear to make good their claim to have power over kings and emperors, they had moved to one in which they could be pawns of rulers and there could be two or even three popes at the same time, each chosen by and for different political interests. In this milieu they often functioned like other monarchs, even to the extent of leading troops into battles over territory. Thus secularized, their interests and means assimilated to those of their opponents. The church's lands and treasures were treated as personal possessions, and efforts were made to create dynasties by the appointment of relatives and even offspring to key posts in civil and religious governments. Vast funds were needed to support both these efforts to acquire or maintain power and extensive building operations that expressed the glory and the taste of the papacy. The power to forgive sins came to be treated as a marketable skill, and the hawking of indulgences was the distribution system devised to maximize its profitability.

No one at any time, however, considered such conditions to be ideal. This can be seen in Alexander VI, Savonarola's nemesis, who appeared to incarnate all that was wrong with the Renaissance papacy but yet was capable of designing an excellent program for purifying the church when he was devastated by the murder of his son Juan. Both before and after the separation of others, there were always persons of the highest standards who remained loyal to the papacy at the very moment that they called for its reform. In the Counter or Catholic Reformation their standards of ecclesial rectitude were put into practice and have remained in force to an extraordinary degree to this day. Furthermore, church bodies that originated in the sixteenth century and continued in existence have discovered that all religious institutions have their ups and downs, times when they exemplify their ideals more and less adequately. Therefore, while moral reform of the church was very much an issue at this time, it cannot be identified as the agenda of any one group to the exclusion of all others.

In addition to the impetus for moral improvement, there was in the air a call for theological change. This is the area in which the greatest differences can be discerned between the various faith communities that existed at the end of the period. And, while these theological positions had serious implications for the way that preaching was understood and practiced and will have to be considered at the appropriate juncture, this is not the forum in which to adjudicate among them and to opt for the superiority of one over the others. Rather, it will be assumed that faithful representatives of all traditions held their convictions in integrity and with intelligence.

The third noteworthy aspect of the changes of the sixteenth century is in scholarly method. This is closely connected with the effort to recover classical antiquity that was so prominent a characteristic of the Renaissance.[2] The scholars involved in this quest are known as "humanists," not because of any implied contrast with interest in the Divine, but because of their preoccupation with the "humanities": the liberal arts of grammar, rhetoric, poetry, history, and moral philosophy.[3] For present purposes the most relevant aspect of their recovery of antiquity is Greco-Roman rhetoric. Manuscripts of the major works by or attributed to Cicero and Quintilian were discovered and published, and Aristotle's treatise came once again to be regarded as a textbook on eloquence instead of being read primarily as a work on politics and morals.[4] This interest in rhetoric was central to the humanists. As Hanna Gray says:

> It is essential to understand the humanists' reiterated claim, that theirs was the pursuit of eloquence. That claim, indeed, reveals the identifying characteristic of Renaissance humanism. The bond which united humanists, no matter how far separated in outlook or in time, was a conception of eloquence and its uses.[5]

EPIDEICTIC AT THE VATICAN

The implications of Renaissance humanism for other aspects of scholarly method will be considered as they come up. For the moment, however, the implications for preaching can easily be imagined. By changing notions of what was to be admired in public speaking in general, this newly recovered classical theory of rhetoric was bound to have its impact on the way people thought preaching ought to be done. Although the medieval *artes praedicandi* would continue to influence preaching in some quarters for centuries to come, a major shift in homiletical theory was already under way.

The question was not whether thematic preaching would be replaced by sermons shaped according to the standards of classical rhetoric, but which classical standards should apply. Renewed study of classical rhetorical theory caused homileticians to reflect on the three genres into which public speaking had been divided by the ancients: the forensic oratory of the law courts, the deliberative oratory of legislative bodies, and the epideictic oratory used for praise and blame. In Christian adaptations of this theory, many practitioners accepted the view that since preaching did not call upon its listeners to decide what happened in the past, its genre was not forensic. Nor were they to come to decisions about future policy, so it was not deliberative. Instead, sermons urged upon them sets of positive and negative value judgments about persons (divine as well as human) and patterns of behavior, and thus their genus was epideictic.

John W. O'Malley has demonstrated that this shift can be traced at the very heart of the medieval church, the papal court.[6] The shift from thematic to epideictic preaching can be seen in the manuscripts and printed copies of sermons preached at solemn masses in the papal chapel during the period under investigation.

In order to argue his case, O'Malley established six categories for analyzing the differences between thematic and epideictic preaching: Latin style, sources, structure, unity, *res* or materials preached about, and purpose. Differences in Latin style could easily be seen in the use of a scholastic or a classicizing vocabulary. Further, the epideictic genre (known in Latin as the *genus demonstrativum*) has a lyrical quality.

Epideictic did not quote statements from the Bible or ancient writers as proof texts or "authorities" as thematic sermons did. Instead, it incorporated allusions and paraphrases into a more literary use of these sources. Like thematic preaching, epideictic preaching cited the Bible and the church fathers, but, unlike it, the new style did not draw directly on medieval theologians. Classical writers were cited less frequently, though classical history was occasionally invoked. In neither case, though, was the pagan writing thought to be the source of the Christian point of view; rather, the argument was *quanto magis,* "how much the more!"

In epideictic, the thematic sermon's shape of the spreading tree has been replaced by the *dispositio* of the pagan orator's speech. Such sermons began with an *exordium* emphasizing the impossibility of the orator's task and ended with a peroration that summarized the speech and roused the congregation to an emotional climax. When the sermon was for a saint's day, it often followed all the *topoi* of a classical speech of praise.[7] Going through these *topoi* gave a unity to the speech that the thematic sermon had lacked with its "fanning out." Indeed, it was assumed in all the genera of classical oratory that every element of the speech would contribute to a single unified impact and conclusion—that a person had been guilty or not guilty, a proposed policy should be accepted or rejected, or that a person or thing was to be praised or blamed. The Christian *genus demonstrativum,* like its classical exemplar, was a unified call upon its audience to join the speaker in being grateful for or alarmed about the sermon's subject.

The subject matter of thematic preaching was points of doctrine or ethics. The form of argument was thus abstract. That of epideictic preaching, on the other hand, was very concrete. It was more historical in its orientation, dealing with the deeds, acts, mighty works, or benefits of God. The verbs used in reference to such things are "look," "view," "gaze upon," or "contemplate." In other words, argument has been replaced by narrative and word pictures. This is to say that while the principal source of both types of preaching was the Bible, the way that it was used had changed considerably. It was no longer treated as a data bank for doctrine; it had come instead to be regarded as a book of sacred history.[8] With the Bible viewed in this way, the purpose of preaching based upon it was to evoke a response from the congregation of "veneration," "admiration," and "praise." The audience was called upon to imitate. Since the liturgy of the papal solemn masses was supposed to approximate as nearly as possible the worship of the heavenly sanctuary, it is no wonder that the sermons preached at them also sought to draw the listeners into a sense of awe and wonder at beholding and praising the very glory of the divine presence.

While such preaching has value, there are ways in which it can be a disservice. The admiration that it elicits can make people complacent even if solemn warnings are intercalated into it, as they were in the papal court. Such complacency can cause people not to take seriously enough the signs in the outside world that conditions are changing rapidly and that others elsewhere do not find the status quo such an occasion for rejoicing. Yet, ironically, the change in the style of preaching itself should have shown that the world was no longer satisfied with the way things had been. Sermons at the solemn masses in the court of Renaissance popes could have alerted the court to the truth that the Middle Ages were over.[9]

THE ERASMIAN WATERSHED

With the recovery of Greco-Roman rhetoric, it became inevitable that *artes praedicandi* would be replaced with textbooks that advocated the construction of sermons in accordance with the standards of classical oratory. The earliest efforts to produce such works did not meet with much response. The *Margarita eloquentiae castigatae* of Lorenzo Guglielmo Traversagni seems to have been "singularly ignored by his contemporaries," the effort of the great Hebraist Johann Reuchlin "did not have much impact on contemporaries," and the works on preaching as such by Philipp Melanchthon and Veit Dietrich were "sketchy, partisan, and extremely brief works of pamphlet size that did not have immediate or broad influence."[10]

Therefore, since the text published by Erasmus in 1535, *Ecclesiasticus,* was a long and thorough work (a modern edition would run to about a thousand pages without notes)[11] and a successful one (going through ten editions in as many years and thus "one of the best sellers of the decade"),[12] O'Malley is able to call the text "the great watershed in the history of sacred rhetoric."[13] (For a résumé of this work, **see Vol. 2, pp. 231-47.**)

Such a judgment might be surprising to anyone who has not kept up with recent scholarship about Erasmus, since an earlier generation of scholars tended to regard him either as a Reformer who did not have the courage to go all the way with Luther or as a precursor of the Enlightenment. That his character had many sides cannot be denied. Roland Bainton has suggested that each of the three artists who depicted his features caught a different aspect of the man: Dürer showed the scholarly editor of the church fathers, Holbein the ironical author of satires, and Metsys the author of *Contempt of the World* and *Preparation for Death.*[14]

> No matter how one chooses to label Erasmus, however, one can no longer deny that he was deeply concerned about ministry, doctrine, theology, and theological method and that he saw all those as closely related to *pietas*, to *pie beatque vivendi ars.*[15]

Thus it is that his last and longest work was a treatise on preaching.

The title of the work is *Ecclesiastes, sive Concionator evangelicus.*[16] These alternative designations are important clues to Erasmus's understanding of how preaching should be done. The first is the same as the Greek title of the biblical book that he took as the equivalent of the Hebrew *Koheleth* and the Latin *Concionator,* all of which can be rendered in English as "Preacher." He had a particular sort of preaching in mind, however, the sort of sermon he calls *concio*. "The *concio* was a specific type of deliberative oratory in which a leader addressed, not sophisticated statesmen gathered in the Senate, but a popular and perhaps unruly audience of ordinary people."[17] Before his time, this term had seldom been used to designate Christian preaching, but afterward it became quite common. More will be said later of the significance of this choice of term when Erasmus's understanding of the relation of preaching to the genera of classical oratory is discussed.

The first of the four books of *Ecclesiastes* is devoted to the importance of preaching and the consequent virtues and training needed by the one who preaches.[18] Indeed, it would not be too much to call it a spirituality of preaching. Erasmus says preaching is the most important duty of clergy and more important than any task of rulers.

> The most important function of the priest is teaching by which he may instruct, admonish, chide, and console. A layman can baptize. All the people can pray. The priest does not always baptize, he does not always absolve, but he should always teach. What good is it to be baptized if one has not been catechized, what good to go to the Lord's Table if one does not know what it means?[19]

The skills of preaching can be taught: "If elephants can be trained to dance, lions to play, and leopards to hunt, surely preachers can be taught to preach."[20] Even more important than the skills, however, are the virtues the preacher ought to have.

> The preacher should exhibit purity of heart, chastity of body, sanctity of deportment, erudition, wisdom, and above all eloquence worthy of the divine mysteries. Let him remember that the cross will never be lacking to those who sincerely preach the gospel. There are always Herods, Ananiases, Caiaphases, Scribes and Pharisees. There are men of Ephesus who incite the mob and there are those like the Jews before Pilate who cried, "Crucify him! Crucify him!"[21]

Hence the life of the preacher must be a lived sermon.[22]

In Book 2, Erasmus follows Augustine in deeming the three duties of the preacher to be to teach, to please, and to move. For him the first is the most important, although after the turgidity of thematic sermons, a humanist like Erasmus has to find a place, however humble, for pleasing. These duties are to be met by following the techniques of classical rhetoric. Thus the parts of a speech, the genera of speeches, and the topics to be discussed are presented. Book 3, like Book 2, shows great debt to Cicero and Quintilian, dealing as it does with disposition and style. "In Book IV, Erasmus presented a *topicon* for the Christian orator, 'an index of materials in which the Christian orator must be versed.'"[23] These include most of the tracts of theology.

Weiss has analyzed *Ecclesiastes* brilliantly, showing that in it Erasmus not only advocates rhetorical training for the preacher but also models its benefits in a virtuoso manner and thus reveals that for him, rhetoric is an entire epistemology, greatly superior to dialectic, a way of knowing especially congenial to a man as irenic as he.

In the construction of his last and longest book, Erasmus was able to bring together the themes of most of the other works that he had given a lifetime to writing.

> *Ecclesiastes'* style and method reveal not only the richness of the rhetorical approach in itself but also the very texture of Erasmus' mind. We find this thread of method running through the fabric of all his thought. Or rather, this thread discloses the seamless quality of the fabric. In talking ostensibly about one thing, the rhetorician can talk about many things. And in a comprehensive handbook of Christian rhetoric, Erasmus talked about everything.[24]

And, although Erasmus never preached a sermon himself that we know about,[25] James Weiss is able to say that "the mirror of the Christian orator reflects the full-length image of Erasmus himself."[26]

Saying this, however, is not the same as saying that *Ecclesiastes* is a satisfactory homiletics textbook. Even O'Malley, who considers the book to represent a watershed in the history of sacred rhetoric, recognizes faults in it. He points out that however little entitled Alfonso Zorilla was to say so, some truth lies in his charge that *Ecclesiastes* was "diffuse, prolix, and confused."[27]

The other main contemporary question about the work had to do with the propriety of Christians drawing on pagan sources. While having no quarrel with that propriety as such, O'Malley raises four questions that grow from the difficulty of constructing an adequate Christian preaching method out of pagan rhetoric. The first is, granting Christian belief in "the divine, or supra-human, nature of the word of God," one must recognize that this belief "requires that any treatise on preaching must have a component lacking in the classical treatises on rhetoric: a theology of the divine word and the minister of that word."[28] This issue was recognized by Erasmus and addressed by him to a degree in Book 1, but such considerations do not appear to greatly influence the rest of the book.

The next difficulty has to do with the way that most Christian preaching has been a "text-related enterprise," involving as it does a desire to bring words of scripture to bear on the lives of the people of God.[29] Classical oratory has no genre related to *explication de texte*. Rather, as noted often above, the preacher needs to turn from the rhetorician to the *grammaticus* for classroom techniques of exegesis.

In the Renaissance, however, there was an additional resource to be drawn upon. In the ancient world, rhetoric had been the theory of oratory, speaking effectively in public, but by the sixteenth century the term came also to be applied to the analysis of works of literature. The earlier, more exclusive use of the term is "primary rhetoric" while the later, literary use is "secondary rhetoric." This secondary rhetoric of Erasmus's time also offered preachers help in their exegetical task. Before that time, however, from the age of Origen to the development of the thematic sermon, Christians had not used any of the classical genera for preaching, but had instead employed the homily form. This was done also by Erasmus's much admired friend, the Franciscan Jean Vitrier.[30]

The extent to which Erasmus dealt with this problem, however, was in his treatment of the three genera of classical rhetoric. He understood the basic task of preaching to be teaching, and he believed that teaching could be accomplished in all three genera: judicial, deliberative, and epideictic. He felt, however, that the adversarial relations demanded by judicial rhetoric were inappropriate to Christian preaching. To meet the needs of Christian proclamation, he developed the deliberative genus into four others: the persuasive, the exhortative, the admonitory, and the consolatory. Retaining epideictic as the laudatory genus, he thus had a system of five genera of preaching.[31] These subdivisions, however, concentrate on the purpose of the various types of sermon rather than on how text commentary is to be incorporated into them. Perhaps Erasmus's own lack of experience in preaching left him insufficiently aware of the practical problems posed by squeezing biblical interpretation into classical rhetorical forms.

Further, Erasmus also seems insensitive to the liturgical setting of the sermon in the Eucharist. He appears unaware that it should, in the words of William Skudlarek, tell the congregation why they should lift up their hearts.[32] Thus the sermon is reduced to mere instruction and exhortation, "just an address on a sacred subject to a popular audience, which would be a fair rendering of Erasmus' understanding of it."[33]

The last problem that John O'Malley found with Erasmus's preaching theory also has to do with genera, but is different from that of making allowance for the sermon's need to explain a biblical text. The Lutheran Melanchthon, as will be seen below, created a distinctive genus, the *genus didascalicum* or *didactium,* in order to treat doctrinal instruction as the characteristic purpose of preaching. Erasmus, however, "was more concerned with inculcating and persuading to good morals and ethically correct behavior,"[34] thus helping to promote a moralistic strain in Catholic preaching that was already strong.

Although he located preaching within the charism of prophecy, "not confrontation, but the teaching of prescriptive and ethics-related wisdom was the task of the Erasmian prophet." This understanding of the preaching task undoubtedly has something to do with his hitting upon the classical category of *concio* as that to which preaching should be assigned. The purpose of such speeches was "to explain to the promiscuous multitude the edicts, promises, and will of the supreme prince and to persuade that multitude to accept them."[35] With such a definition, it is not surprising that a moralistic model of preaching occurs. But Erasmus must have felt something of the inadequacy of such an understanding, for he seems to have shown some nostalgia for the homily even though it did not fit comfortably among the classical genera.[36]

If *Ecclesiastes* fell short of being a perfect homiletics textbook, what can be made of O'Malley's claim that it represents "the great watershed in the history of sacred rhetoric"?[37] A surprising amount, actually. First of all, it appears to have represented the death knell of thematic preaching. Although the form continued in use for a while, no new *artes praedicandi* seem to have been published after Erasmus's work appeared.[38]

Then, too, Erasmus's *Ecclesiastes* was innovative in the extent to which it drew explicitly on classical rhetoric. While Augustine presupposed the discipline, he used only elements of it in *De doctrina Christiana* because, on the one hand, the genre in which he preached, the patristic homily, did not fit any of the classical *genera dicendi,* and, on the other, he thought that rhetoric could be studied profitably only as a schoolboy. In his huge textbook, Erasmus was the first to attempt to teach the entire discipline of classical rhetoric as an element in preparing readers to preach.

But what of its influence on later homiletical literature? Since, as has been seen, all of Erasmus's works were placed on the index in 1549, and *Ecclesiastes* is not quoted in Catholic manuals after that, there would seem to be little chance of its shaping the future of that tradition. And, since Luther disagreed so strongly with Erasmus on theology, one would not expect his followers to quote Erasmus with approval. Frederick J. McGinness, however, has studied the reforms in preaching made by the Council of Trent, reforms that have shaped Catholic preaching down almost until the present, and he concludes that although the name of Erasmus is not invoked, the ideas are largely his:

> No one other than Erasmus had anticipated so clearly every single component in the Tridentine decree on preaching, and had spelled out thoroughly what each component entailed: that bishops and their preachers be feeders of their flocks—teachers—concerning themselves with the gospel of Jesus Christ, preaching the things one needs to know for salvation, [word omitted] upon them with briefness and plainness of speech the vices that they must avoid and the virtues they must cultivate, in order that they may escape eternal punishment and obtain the glory of heaven.[39]

The influence on Lutheran homiletics is also very probable. As will be seen in the next chapter, Luther's own preaching was not much imitated by his followers. Rather, the rhetorical manuals of his disciple Melanchthon, a humanist who was indebted to Erasmus, set the standard. Certainly Erasmus was very influential on the English Reformation, and he helped to create an atmosphere in which the public school curriculum was to be shaped by classical literature and rhetoric. The main Reformation tradition not directly shaped by Erasmus was the Calvinist. Although Calvin was certainly formed by humanism, and even wrote a commentary on a work of Seneca before he turned to theology, his approach to preaching was much more in the tradition of the *lectio continua* of the patristic homily (i.e., the tradition of the grammarian) rather than that of the rhetorician.

With such innovation in content, such replacement of the previous norms, and such influence on most succeeding homiletics, it is by no means too much to claim that *Ecclesiastes* represents a watershed in textbooks on preaching. That will become more evident in the chapters ahead.

FOR FURTHER READING

Bainton, Roland H. *Erasmus of Christendom.* New York: Crossroad, 1982.

Erasmus, Desiderius. *Ecclesiastes, or the Evangelical Preacher.* Translated by James Butrica, edited by Frederick J. McGinness. Collected Works of Erasmus. Toronto: University of Toronto Press, forthcoming.

O'Malley, John W. *Praise and Blame in Renaissance Rome: Rhetoric,*

Doctrine, and Reform in the Sacred Orators of the Papal Court, c. 1450–1521. Duke Monographs in Medieval and Renaissance Studies, no. 3. Durham, N.C.: Duke University Press, 1979.

———. "Erasmus and the History of Sacred Rhetoric: The *Ecclesiastes* of 1535." In vol. 5 of *Erasmus of Rotterdam Society Yearbook,* 1-29. 1985.

Renaissance Eloquence: Studies in the Theory and Practice of Renaissance Rhetoric. Edited by James J. Murphy. Berkeley: University of California Press, 1983.

Notes

1. Justo L. González, *A History of Christian Thought* (Nashville: Abingdon, 1975), 3:11-24.

2. For a dated and misleading but still exciting treatment of this see Jacob Burckhardt, *The Civilization of the Renaissance in Italy*, trans. S. G. C. Middlemore, int. Benjamin Nelson and Charles Trinkaus, Harper Torchbooks (New York: Harper & Brothers, 1958 [German original, 1860; Eng. trans. of 15th ed., 1890]), 1:175-278. The introduction to the volume indicates what aspects of the treatment are upheld by modern scholarship. Much of the mood of the period is captured in *Romula,* George Eliot's novel set in the Florence of Savonarola. For a contemporary view, see Ronald Witt, "The Origins of Italian Humanism," *Centennial Review* vol. xxxiv (1990): 91-109.

3. Hanna H. Gray, "Renaissance Humanism: The Pursuit of Eloquence," *JHI* 24 (1963): 499.

4. George A. Kennedy, *Classical Rhetoric and Its Christian and Secular Tradition from Ancient to Modern Times* (Chapel Hill: University of North Carolina Press, 1980), 190. For the recovery of classical rhetoric in the Renaissance, see ibid., 195-219. See also Brian Vickers, *In Defence of Rhetoric* (Oxford: Clarendon Press; New York: Oxford University Press, 1988), 254-93. On the difficulties in writing a complete history of rhetoric in the Renaissance, see the essays in *Renaissance Eloquence: Studies in the Theory and Practice of Renaissance Rhetoric,* ed. James J. Murphy (Berkeley: University of California Press, 1983), especially Paul Oskar Kristeller, "Rhetoric in Medieval and Renaissance Culture," 1-19; James J. Murphy, "One Thousand Neglected Authors: The Scope and Importance of Renaissance Rhetoric," 20-36; and Dominic A. LaRusso, "Rhetoric in the Italian Renaissance," 37-55.

5. Gray, "Renaissance Humanism," 498. By "eloquence," of course, she means rhetoric and goes on to say: "By 'rhetoric' the humanists did not intend an empty pomposity, a willful mendacity, a love of display for its own sake, an extravagant artificiality, a singular lack of originality, or a necessary subordination of substance to form and ornament.... True eloquence, according to the humanists, could only arise out of a harmonious union between wisdom and style; its aim was to guide men toward virtue and worthwhile goals, not to mislead them for vicious or trivial purposes."

6. John W. O'Malley, *Praise and Blame in Renaissance Rome: Rhetoric, Doctrine, and Reform in the Sacred Orators of the Papal Court, c. 1450–1521,* Duke Monographs in Medieval and Renaissance Studies, no. 3 (Durham, N.C.: Duke University Press, 1979).

7. For a list of these, see the description of *epideictic* in the orations of Gregory of Nazianzus in Kennedy, *Classical Rhetoric and Its Christian and Secular Tradition from Ancient to Modern Times,* 228-37, or Rosemary Radford Ruether, *Gregory of Nazianzus, Rhetor and Philosopher* (Oxford: Clarendon Press, 1969), 120-23.

8. For this insight, I am indebted to a letter from Father O'Malley written December 7, 1990.

9. John A. McManamon has detected in funeral sermons a similar shift from thematic to epideictic preaching in "Innovation in Early Humanist Rhetoric: The Oratory of Pier Paolo Vergerio the Elder," *Rinascimento* 22 (1982): 1-32, arguing that the transition was pioneered by Vergerio (who also figures in O'Malley's treatment). For a fuller treatment of Renaissance funeral sermons, see McManamon's *Funeral Oratory and the Cultural Ideals of Italian Humanism* (Chapel Hill: University of North Carolina Press, 1989).

10. John W. O'Malley, "Erasmus and the History of Sacred Rhetoric: The *Ecclesiastes* of 1535," *Erasmus of Rotterdam Society Yearbook,* vol. 5 (1985), 6-8. On textbooks for this period, see also his "Content and Rhetorical Forms in Sixteenth-Century Treatises on Preaching" in *Renaissance Eloquence,* 238-52.

11. Ibid., 18.

12. Ibid., 2.

13. Ibid., 13. Compare his statement on p. 29: "The *Ecclesiastes* is not simply a major work by Erasmus. It is a major monument in the long history and continuing influence of classical tradition in western culture. Above all, it is a major monument—perhaps *the* major monument—in the history of sacred rhetoric." He sees its only rival to be Augustine's *De doctrina christiana.*

14. Roland H. Bainton, *Erasmus of Christendom* (New York: Crossroad, 1982), 237-38.

15. John W. O'Malley, "Introduction," *Spiritualia: (vol. I) Enchiridion, De Contemptu Mundi, De Vidua Christiana,* Collected Works of Erasmus, vol. 66 (Toronto: University of Toronto Press, 1988), xiv.

16. Originally published by Froben at Basel in 1535 and, as noted above, reprinted often in the next ten years in both authorized and pirated editions, *Ecclesiastes* fell on hard times afterward. Luther's opposition to Erasmus and the placing of all Erasmus's books on the first Index of Prohibited Books by a fanatical pope in 1559 caused the work to fall into obscurity. Thus the standard Latin edition was still *Opera omnia,* ed. J. Clericus, vol. 5 (Leiden: 1703–6), until a new one appeared, *Opera Omnia Desiderii Erasmani Roterodami recognita et adnotatione critica instructa notisque illustrata,* ordo 5, tome 4 (Amsterdam: North-Holland, 1991–). Thomas Bray, founder of both the SPCK and the Society for the Propagation of the Gospel, published a Latin edition of the first part of the work in London in 1730 (Robert Kleinhans, "Erasmus' Ecclesiastes and the Church of England," *Historical Magazine of the Protestant Episcopal Church* 39 [1970]: 307-14). No English translation of the entire work has been published before now, but that oversight will soon

be remedied with a translation by James Butrica and edited by Frederick J. McGinness that is forthcoming in the Collected Works of Erasmus being published by the University of Toronto Press. I am grateful to Professor McGinness for a copy of the page proofs. The Latin edition consulted for the first draft of this chapter was the Froben of 1554.

17. O'Malley, "Erasmus and the History of Sacred Rhetoric," 14-15.

18. The following summary is based on James Michael Weiss, "*Ecclesiastes* and Erasmus: The Mirror and the Image," *ARG* 65 (1965): 83-108; Marc Fumaroli, *L'Age de l'éloquence: Rhétorique et <<res literaria>> de la Renaissance au seuil de l'époque classique,* Hautes études médiévales et modernes 43 (Genève: Librairie Droz, 1980): 106-9; and Charles Béné, *Érasme et Saint Augustin ou influence de Saint Augustin sur l'humanisme d'Érasme,* Travaux d'humanisme et renaissance," no. 103 (Genève: Librairie Droz, 1969), 372-425.

19. Translated in Bainton, *Erasmus,* 268-69. He takes the statements *passim* from volume five of the Leiden edition, giving page numbers on p. 275.

20. Ibid., 268.

21. Ibid.

22. Weiss, "*Ecclesiastes* and Erasmus," 87, citing the Leiden edition, 783-90.

23. Ibid., 88. The interior quotation is from the Leiden edition, 5:1071C.

24. Ibid., 107.

25. O'Malley, "Erasmus and the History of Sacred Rhetoric," 21.

26. Weiss, "*Ecclesiastes* and Erasmus," 107.

27. O'Malley, "Erasmus and the History of Sacred Rhetoric," 18. Zorilla's *De sacris concionibus recte formandis,* published in 1542, plagiarized Erasmus's work—not to mention that of Melanchthon, Dietrich, and Johannes Hepinus (Hoeck)—on a wholesale basis.

28. Ibid., 19.

29. Ibid.

30. Ibid., 20. See also Bainton, *Erasmus of Christendom,* 64ff.

31. Weiss, "*Ecclesiastes* and Erasmus," 98-101. The relevant sections of *Ecclesiastes* are found in the Leiden edition, 858-92.

32. *The Word in Worship: Preaching in a Liturgical Context,* Abingdon Preacher's Library (Nashville: Abingdon, 1981), 70.

33. O'Malley, "Erasmus and the History of Sacred Rhetoric," 22.

34. Ibid., 24.

35. Ibid., 26, quoting from the Leiden edition, 770.

36. Ibid.

37. Ibid., 13.

38. Ibid. See also a paper delivered by Frederick McGinness at the Sixteenth Century Studies Conference, Cleveland, Ohio, on November 3, 2000, "Erasmus and the Reform of Preaching Between Luther and the Council of Trent," 10. I am indebted to Professor McGinness for a copy of this paper, which is a draft of part of the Introduction he was preparing for the University of Toronto translation of *Ecclesiastes.*

39. McGinness, "Erasmus and the Reform of Preaching Between Luther and the Council of Trent," 16. Professor McGinness said in his cover letter that he would probably make last-minute changes in the text of the paper before he delivered it.

CHAPTER 12

THE REFORMATION PREACHING OF LUTHER AND MELANCHTHON

GENESIS

Few people in history have been more influential or effective in shaping the future development of preaching than Martin Luther. So it comes as a surprise both that his followers did not imitate his style more and that his own preaching has not been much studied.[1] Yet every student of preaching, of whatever ecclesial allegiance, must admit that there is much in his style worthy of study and imitation. Part of the explanation for this neglect must be that his talent was so individual that the challenge of measuring up to his example was daunting.

Luther's preaching and theology were shaped to a large extent by his personal experience. The basic story is well known. Being frightened by a thunderstorm in 1505 when he was twenty-one years old, the moody young man made and kept a vow to Saint Anne that he would become a monk in order to prepare for a holy death. Even though he became a very ascetic member of the Augustinian Hermits, he was never able to quiet his conscience, and so he lived with the conviction that he merited damnation. To assist him in dealing with his scrupulosity, his superior assigned him the task of earning his doctorate and becoming a professor of Scripture. At some point between receiving his degree and beginning his teaching career in 1511, and his being made vicar over eleven monasteries in 1515, he had what is called his "tower experience" *(Turmerlebnis)*, which resolved all his doubts and at the same time gave him the theological basis for his eventual break with Rome.

His own words best describe that event and its significance for him:

> I greatly longed to understand Paul's Epistle to the Romans and nothing stood in the way but that one expression, "the justice of God," because I took it to mean that justice whereby God is just and deals justly in punishing the unjust. My situation was that, although an impeccable monk, I stood before God as a sinner troubled in conscience, and I had no confidence that my merit would assuage him. Therefore I did not love a just and angry God, but rather hated and murmured against him. Yet I clung to the dear Paul and had a great yearning to know what he meant.
>
> Night and day I pondered until I saw the connection between the justice of God and the statement that "the just shall live by his faith." Then I grasped that the justice of God is that righteousness by which through grace and sheer mercy God justifies us through faith. Thereupon I felt myself to be reborn and to have gone through open doors into paradise. The whole of Scripture took on a new meaning, and whereas before the "justice of God" had filled me with hate, now it became to me inexpressibly sweet in greater love. This passage of Paul became to me a gate to heaven.[2]

Luther felt that the basic hermeneutical key to understanding Christian theology had been communicated to him through this experience. Christians do not have to earn their salvation through ascetic and charitable works, but rather it is freely given by God. It took some time, however, for him to work out the implications of that view to the point where a breach with the pope seemed necessary. Salvation through works had involved a calculus in which the exact value of all acts, evil or virtuous, could be ascertained and expressed in terms of the number of days a soul would have to spend in purgatory as temporal punishment for sins. Such punishment had to be endured even if the sins had been forgiven. On the other hand, days of plenary remission of such punishment were given as reward for merit.

Much of this calculus was based on an understanding of Matthew 16:18-19 that saw the pope, by virtue of his succession from Peter, as having the "keys of the kingdom" that would allow him to bind or loose the sins of Christians and thus to increase or decrease the time they would have to spend in purgatory. This view was connected with another in which the saints were regarded as persons who had accumulated more merit than was required to expiate for their own sins. Their surplus, therefore, was translated to the "treasury of merit," which the pope could apply to sinners. His remissions of this temporal punishment for sins were called indulgences.

Indulgences at first were given for such major acts of penance as participation in a crusade, but during the Renaissance when papal need for money became acute, they came to be sold outright on a wholesale scale. As early as his trip to Rome in 1511, Luther had come to doubt the efficacy of various pious activities connected with pilgrimages to holy places as a means of reducing time to be spent in purgatory. When Johann Tetzel preached at nearby Jüterbog in 1517 and offered an indulgence granted by Leo X to raise money to renovate St. Peter's basilica at Rome, parishioners in Wittenberg were disturbed. Luther was driven to post his Ninety-five Theses on the church door, inviting the debate that ended in his break with Rome and the beginning of the Reformation.[3]

LUTHER'S UNDERSTANDING OF SALVATION

Martin Luther's theological thought developed in such an integrated way that it is impossible to understand his theory of preaching without knowing the overall dynamic of his thought. A convenient way of entering the dynamic that immediately reveals the enormous importance of preaching in Luther's thought is to begin with his doctrine of the Word of God.[4] God's Word is seen in three manifestations: the second person of the Trinity (the incarnate Word), the Holy Scriptures (the written Word), and the preaching of the church (the proclaimed Word). Thus he was completely traditional in his understanding of the Trinity and the person and work of Christ. The Word who became flesh and dwelled among us is also the Word by which the Father created the universe. The intimate connection between God the Son and the Bible is that the whole purpose of Scripture, Hebrew and Christian, is to reveal Christ. The authority of Scripture for Luther is therefore not that of the canon, the authoritative list of writings, but that of the writings that proclaim the gospel. While any biblical book is to be interpreted in light of the intention of its author, that intention was always basically to proclaim the gospel. Finding that proclamation, then, is the hermeneutical key to the book. Such discovery is not basically an exercise of the human intellect, however, because the guidance of the Holy Spirit is necessary for finding and receiving that gospel.

The written Word has two aspects, law and gospel. Law is God's will, God's moral requirement of human beings. It cannot be identified exclusively with the Hebrew Bible, nor is the gospel to be associated exclusively with the New Testament. Each may be found in either testament and indeed in the same passage, but law is found outside the Bible as well, while gospel is discerned only with the aid of the Spirit. Law, for instance, can be known by the unaided human intelligence as natural law. It is enacted as positive law, civil law, to restrain the wicked and provide the order necessary both for people to live together in society and for the gospel to be proclaimed.

At the same time, since no one can live up to its standards, law also serves the function of convincing all human beings that they deserve damnation and are in need of redemption. When they hear the gospel, though, they know that God has shown his love for them in the redemption made available through Christ and thus they are liberated from the law by God's attribution to them of the righteousness of Christ. This attribution is their justification—which does not mean that they cease to be sinners, but does mean that they are redeemed sinners, justified (accounted righteous) by the grace and faith given to them.

Such extreme measures are necessary because fallen humanity has entirely lost its capacity to respond to God or to do good. Human sin is so all-encompassing that persons cannot even learn of their sinful state without its being revealed to them. And, knowing about it, they have no power of their own to resist it. The only capacity left to them is to be turned in a new direction by God.[5] That capacity, however, has no inherent virtue. It is only the place where the power of God can be exerted. That power is God's absolution, God's reclassifying of human beings as saved rather than damned.

While this justification is appropriated by faith, faith is not to be understood as an intellectual or volitional good work, but rather as the work of the Holy Spirit in the soul. This justification is absolution, but it is not a restoration of the pre-fall capacity to live without sin. Yet by it God does lead the justified into righteousness, allowing them to have some experience of the status attributed to them. Luther described the state of such a person as *simul justus et peccator*—a righteous person and a sinner at the same time. Good works then become not a way to earn salvation, but a demonstration that it has been freely given. To the person who has been justified, the law ceases to be the hateful reminder of damnation and becomes the sweet will of the loving Father.

Luther's doctrine of justification is not individualistic. Rather, he believes that there is no salvation outside the church. The church, however, is not constituted by apostolic succession, but by the Word of God. Both preaching and sacraments are functions of the Word, through which the Spirit speaks to human beings and they are justified. Since this church is not invisible but an institution on earth, many of the Word's means of grace had been preserved in the papal church and there was even true Christianity and sanctity in that body.

LUTHER'S THEORY OF PREACHING

Luther considers preaching to be the most important office in the world, more important than even that of officiating at sacraments.[6] It is more important than prayer (21:228). It is a matter of life and death (3:347) because it is the medium through which salvation is bestowed. Unlike the Muslim religion, which is spread by the sword, Christian faith is spread by preaching (44:179). People who are deprived of preaching often lose their faith (44:175). Thus David, in saying, "I shall not want" (Ps. 23:1), means that he will have all the bodily and spiritual blessings bestowed through preaching (12:157). Preaching constitutes the church (32:73). For that reason, "the Word of God does not assail trifles, baubles, or bubbles, but kingdoms, great kings, and nations on earth, as Psalm 2:2 declares" (23:387). Preaching is the means by which Christ will slay the antichrist (35:387). So, clergy who do not preach do not deserve the name of clergy (36:91).

Because preaching is the one necessary thing, Luther took his own proclamation with the utmost seriousness. He said, "I, Dr. Luther, am convinced that the birds, the stones, and the sand of the sea will have to attest to my preaching" (23:239). And he made a number of references to the frequency with which he did preach. He walked to church to preach so often that it would not be surprising if, in addition to wearing out his shoes, he had worn out his feet as well (54:206). Often he preached four times a day; one whole Lent he preached at two services and gave a lecture every day (54:282). (The lecture involved was the sort of course preaching he did, giving expositions of entire books of the Bible [48:320].) This commitment to preaching did not begin with the Reformation, but already existed when he was a vicar of the Augustinians (48:27-28, 113).

For Luther, preaching is as fully the Word of God as the incarnate Lord and the written Scripture. Therefore, any preacher who has finished a sermon should not pray for the forgiveness of its deficiencies, but should rather say, "In this sermon I have been an apostle and a prophet of Jesus Christ." Anyone who cannot boast like that should give up preaching, "for it is God's Word and not (the preacher's) and God ought not and cannot forgive it, but only confirm, praise, and crown it" (41:216). The distinction between the incarnate and the proclaimed Word is that "the former Word is in substance God; the latter word is in its effect the power of God, but isn't God in substance, whether it's spoken by Christ or by a minister" (54:395). Thus it can be said that "the preaching of the gospel is nothing else than Christ coming to us, or we being brought to him" (35:121).

Luther placed great emphasis on the orality of preaching. In an allegorical interpretation, he identified the star of Bethlehem as "the new light, preaching, and the gospel, oral and public preaching." (For Luther, allegory always relates to the Word; he never entirely ceased doing allegorical interpretation.) Oral preaching took precedence over even the written Word. "In the New Testament, preaching must be done orally and publicly, with the living voice, to produce in speech and hearing what prior to this lay hidden in the letter and in secret vision" (52:205). Such oral preaching is "the way the Lord, our Ruler, establishes his kingdom" (12:114; cf. 170). The superiority of the oral to the written Word is developed at length in Luther's exegesis of Malachi 5:7: "For the lips of a priest guard knowledge" (18:401).[7]

With this perspective, then, he can say:

> For just as in legal disputes whatever judgment is passed on the basis of the reports of witnesses is arrived at by hearing alone and believed because of faith, since it cannot be known in any other way, neither by perception nor by reason, so the Gospel is received in no other way than by hearing. (29:145)

When one moves from Luther's view of the importance of preaching to his understanding of how it should be done, it becomes apparent how accurate Carl Braaten's statement is that "the law/gospel distinction is the classical Lutheran homiletical principle."[8] This distinction is phrased in other ways as well by Luther; it is the same as the letter/Spirit and the *Schrift/Predigt* dichotomies, and the basic difference between the Old and New Testaments.

This does not mean, however, that Christian preaching should include no element of law. Quite the contrary, such preaching is necessary before the gospel can be heard, and every valid sermon will contain both law and gospel. Such preaching of the law leads people to an awareness of their need for the gospel and opens them to hearing its word of forgiveness and grace.

> Even though we are already in the New Testament and should have only the preaching of the Spirit, since we are still living in flesh and blood, it is necessary to preach the letter as well, so that people are first killed by the law and all their arrogance is destroyed. Thus they may know themselves and become hungry for the Spirit and thirsty for grace. So [the letter] prepares the people for the preaching of the Spirit. (39:188)[9]

Hence the proof for the seventeenth theological thesis in the *Heidelberg Disputation* reads: "It is apparent that not despair, but hope, is preached when we are told that we are sinners. Such preaching concerning sin is a preparation for grace" (31:51).

Since law is preached to enable people to recognize that they are sinners, the basic content of the gospel and, therefore, Christian preaching is the forgiveness of sins. "This is the gist of your preaching: *Behold your God!* Promote God alone, his mercy and grace. Preach Me alone" (17:14). Those New Testament books that reflect this emphasis are to be preferred: in Romans and 1 Peter "you do not find many works and miracles of Christ described, but you do find depicted in masterly fashion how faith in Christ overcomes sin, death, and hell, and gives life, righteousness, and salvation" (35:362). For the same reason, John is "the one, fine, true and chief gospel."

More is required for such preaching to be effective than merely hearing it physically, however eloquently it is proclaimed. Faith is also necessary. "For whoever does not accept the Word on its own account, is never inclined to accept it on account of any preacher, even if all the angels were preaching to him" (52:32). Yet it is through preaching that faith is communicated. Christendom, the people of the King, is constituted by "the Word of the gospel (that) brings them to the point where they willingly cling to him by faith" (13:291). This faith, however, is no achievement of their own, but is a gift of God administered through preaching: "God has so ordered it that the Holy Spirit ordinarily comes through the Word."[10]

Election occurs through preaching: "When the Word is revealed from heaven, we see that some are converted and freed from condemnation" (2:16-17). Their own unwillingness is the reason some are not converted, but faith is given only to those God chooses.

> The Holy Spirit, ordinarily, gives such faith or his gift to no one without preaching or the oral word or the gospel of Christ preceding, but ... through and by means of such oral word he effects and creates faith where and in whom it pleases him (Romans 10[:14ff.]). (38:87)
>
> Thus to the end of the world we preach to those who await the coming of Christ, but we preach not at all to the others, the ungodly. (17:344)

Election, however, does not mean that one ceases to sin (23:234). The Christian is *simul justus et peccator.* As a result, "every preacher and minister of the Word is a man of strife and judgment and because of his office he is compelled to reprove whatever is wrong" (2:20). This is the preaching of the law that must take place before the gospel can be heard.

Since preaching is the very vehicle of salvation, it is the most important duty of clergy and the main purpose for which people are ordained. "Whoever does not preach the Word, though he was called by the church to do this very thing, is no priest at all, and that sacrament of ordination can be nothing else than a certain rite by which the church chooses its preachers" (36:113; cf. 23:342; 38:186).

That clergy are ordained to preach, however, does not mean that only the ordained preach. Luther understood the priesthood of all believers to mean that all the faithful are capable of preaching. Thus if Adam had not fallen, he would have preached publicly to his family (1:82, 105). The sacrifices of Cain and Abel were not offered without preaching because "God is not worshiped by a speechless work" (1:248). Noah and Abraham are also seen as preachers (2:22, 26, 84, 93, 333). "The only true, genuine office of preaching, like priesthood and sacrifice, is common to all Christians.... Not many of you are to preach at the same time, although all have the power to do it" (36:149).

In order to show that laity could preach, Luther wished to persuade Melanchthon to do so (48:308). Yet his understanding of preaching was much broader than such formal proclamation in assemblies for worship; he recognized that in the apostolic church, preaching was not confined either to worship services or to the ordained clergy (48:311). The preaching office extended not only to pastors and preachers, but also to teachers, lectors, chaplains, sacristans, schoolmasters, and others (46:220). Heads of households had a responsibility for seeing that members, whether children or servants, attended the preaching service (51:145). "Father, mother, master, or mistress" can also preach at home (41:264).

Although the Roman Catholics quote 1 Corinthians 14:34 as authority for denying that believers who are women can preach, Luther replies that while all have the right to preach, only those who are most skilled should exercise that right:

> Because it is much more fitting for a man to speak, a man is also more skilled at it. . . . Therefore order, discipline, and respect demand that women keep silent when men speak; but if no man were to preach, then it would be necessary for the women to preach. (36:152)

He even lists a number of women in the Bible who may be said to have preached and elsewhere sums up his position by saying, "If the Lord were to raise up a woman for us to listen to, we would allow her to rule like Huldah" (28:280).

While all the faithful may preach, there is a procedure for deciding which ones will.

> We are the Christian Church, or a segment of it. This church has the power to engage pastors. The church selects such as are able and competent, not for their own sakes but for the welfare of the church. And in an emergency everyone must take care of his own needs. Yet not all are authorized to preach, but only one is to preach to the entire congregation. (22:480)

If any Christian is the only one in a certain place, "here it is his duty to preach and to teach the gospel to erring heathen or non-Christians." If there are others, however, the preacher should wait until he is called and chosen (39:310).

The call is based upon skill, and some talents are required: "The person who wishes to preach needs to have a good voice, good eloquence, a good memory, and other natural gifts" (36:152). But education is needed as well: "A preacher must be instructed in the Word of God in order that he may be able to defend the church" (51:182). Luther thought that his doctorate conferred authority to preach (54:100), and he was greatly annoyed by "these fellows who know nothing and yet dispute our preaching" (51:223). To see that there was always an ample supply of clergy was one of the reasons children needed to have more than the minimum education required by business (46:251). One of the uses to which old monasteries could be put was as school buildings in which young people could prepare to be "bishops, pastors, and other servants of the church" or other Christian vocations (37:364).

Education, however, is not the only essential qualification for preaching: "No matter how learned a man may be, if he has no sure call and does not rightly teach the scriptures, he may talk as he will but there is nothing behind it" (51:224).

The preacher should not be intimidated by the presence in the congregation of people better educated than he; rather, "think of yourself as the most learned man when you are speaking from the pulpit" (54:158). Besides, when preaching, one should not aim the sermon at scholars.

> I spoke to Bucer in Gotha and suggested that he and Osiander should refrain from erudite preaching. Philip (Melanchthon) doesn't need to be instructed, and I don't teach or lecture for his sake, but we preach publicly for the sake of plain people.... Good God, there are sixteen-year-old girls, women, old men, and farmers in the church, and they don't understand lofty matters!... Someday I'll have to write a book against artful preachers. (54:383-84; cf. 235-36)

Furthermore, "practice must agree with preaching" (52:243).

> The preacher's first message is to teach penitence, remove offenses, proclaim the Law, humiliate and terrify the sinners. No one can do this but a godly preacher. Hypocrites cannot preach this way because they do not truly feel sins (17:277).

Even when preaching is completely sincere and skillful, however, the response to it is not always positive. Luther can say of his own experience,

> I would rather be stretched upon a wheel or carry stones than preach one sermon. For anyone who is in this office will always be plagued.... If I were to follow my own impulse I would say, "Let the damned devil be your preacher!" (51:222)

Indeed, he hardly preached at all for the first nine months of 1530.

In the last sermon of his life, he said that people get tired of preaching when it occurs often (51:390). At another time he observed that certain "bigwigs and towns" despise the office of ministry and "trample the ministers and preachers underfoot and treat them more cruelly than the peasants treat their hogs" (21:226). "The nearer the punishment, the worse the people become; and ... the more one preaches to them, the more they despise his preaching" (35:281). The devil wants preachers to become despondent over their work so that they will give it up (24:289; cf. 29:9).

On top of everything else, clergy are not even paid well: "We have let the peasants and noblemen starve us" (51:222; cf. 17:343; 23:7). That should not be too surprising since "God's Word must suffer persecution in the world"; "where God's Word, the dear gospel is preached and proclaimed, the devil does not rest or take a holiday" (12:183). Hence the lack of persecution is a sign that one is not preaching the gospel (51:112).

Much of the resistance to what Luther considered good preaching came from the two fronts on which he was constantly fighting, from Roman Catholics on the one hand and those he called *Schwärmer* on the other. Roman priests were objected to either because they said private Masses and did not preach at all or because of the sort of preaching they did. On the one hand it might be said: "A priest was a man who could say mass, even though he could not preach a word and was an unlearned ass" (46:221). Or, on the other,

> the reason why the world is so utterly perverted and in error is that for a long time there have been no genuine preachers. There are perhaps three thousand priests, among whom one cannot find four good ones—God have mercy on us in this crying shame! And when you do get a good preacher, he runs through the gospel superficially and then follows it up with a fable about the old ass or a story about Dietrich of Berne, or he mixes in something of the pagan teachers, Aristotle, Plato, Socrates, and others, who are all quite contrary to the gospel and also contrary to God. (51:63-64)[11]

The radical reformers whom Luther called *Schwärmer* were originally limited to Münzer, Karlstadt, and the others who pushed changes in Wittenberg after the Diet of Worms when he was seeking asylum in Wartburg, but later he came to include Zwingli in this category. Usually translated "enthusiasts" or "fanatics," the word is derived from the verb used to refer to the swarming activity of bees, which had taken on a secondary sense of "raving" (37:18 n). Luther was willing to include Oecolampadius in this category for saying that since the Word is available through preaching, the Eucharist is rendered redundant (140). These people "take the greatest offense if unworthy men baptize, celebrate Mass, preach, etc. They do not see that they themselves may be more offensive before God" (188). "Sectarians," "fanatics," and "visionaries" of a spiritualist tendency "despise the oral word" because they do not realize that "it takes toil and trouble to engender faith in people by the God-ordained means of the preaching ministry, absolution, and the sacrament" (22:48). Yet such divisions were inevitable: "If the preaching is God's Word, sects arise, and the same thing happens" as that reported in John 7:43 (23:290).

In short, Luther considers preaching the most important activity in the world because it is the instrument by which election occurs, and he gives a great deal of attention to how it should be done. In doing so, he raises the question of who can preach and what qualifications they should have. Preaching is not always effective, however, when all due precautions are taken. There will always be people who resist the Word of God, whether they be papists or enthusiasts, or merely ordinary sinners.

LUTHER'S HOMILETICAL PRACTICE

About twenty-three hundred of the more than four thousand sermons Luther preached are included in the twenty-two volumes devoted to them in the Weimar edition of his works. By this count, a very high percentage of his sermons have survived, although, as will be seen below, we have almost nothing in the exact form in which it was delivered from the pulpit. Such prodigious homiletical production, even stretched out over half a century, represents frequent preaching. Although Luther was neither the pastor nor the only preacher at the church in Wittenberg, its preaching schedule accounts for the quantity. The first service on Sunday began at 5:00 A.M. and included a sermon on the Epistle appointed for that day in the lectionary. The text for the ten o'clock morning sermon was the Gospel, while the afternoon sermon was either on a passage from the Hebrew Bible or on the catechism.[12] There were also catechetical sermons on Mondays and Tuesdays, with Matthew furnishing the text for Wednesdays, the Apostolic Letters for Thursday and Friday, and the Gospel of John for Saturday afternoon. It is known that Luther also did courses of homiletical lectures on books from both Testaments and that he preached to his household, including whoever might be staying with him, on Sunday afternoons.[13]

Involved in this preaching were a number of different genres of sermons. Sunday sermons were generally on lectionary passages; their form will be discussed below. In the traditional way, catechetical sermons expounded texts from the Creed, the Lord's Prayer, or the Ten Commandments. Course lectures on individual books of the Bible took the homiletical form of verse-by-verse exposition.[14] Occasional sermons varied with the demands of the occasion.

Since Luther preached from an outline (from which he departed frequently), there are no manuscripts containing the full text of what he said. What have survived are notes taken by members of his inner circle; sometimes several produced reports of the same sermon and the printed edition is a synthesis of these. Such notes were usually macaronic, combining the German words that Luther uttered with Latin terms that the scribes could fill in more quickly. About the only sermons published by Luther himself were literary revisions of what he had preached, which he issued when he did not like the notes published by someone else. On the whole, though, it is thought that the printed versions of sermons come very close to what Luther actually said in church, especially when the transcriber was Georg Rörer.

There is, however, a significant body of sermonic material, material that has exercised influence on Lutheran preaching through most of the succeeding centuries and can be traced in its existing form to the pen of Luther. Unfortunately, for the purpose of re-creating his homiletical practice, this material is entirely literary and was never delivered in precisely that form by Luther at divine service. Rather, it was written as an aid to clergy in their sermon production. The work in question is Luther's *Church-* or *Wartburg Postil.* The word *postil* comes from the Latin *postilla*, which has the sense of "exposition," being itself a corruption of *post illa verba sacrae scripturae* ("after these words of sacred scripture"), the words with which expository sermons usually began.

Luther completed only the portion of the postil that covers Advent through Lent. Stephan Roth provided for the remaining Sundays of the year and for feast days in a form that was only partially acceptable to Luther; eventually he commissioned Kaspar Cruciger Sr. to redo the summer postil. Confusingly, the term "postil" is also used to refer to an additional body of Lutheran homiletical material. Between 1531 and 1535, when Luther's health prevented public preaching, his household sermons for the church year were published as the "house postil."[15]

Like most other great preachers, Luther did not emerge with his style full-blown, but had to evolve one. Naturally, he began in the medieval tradition of the thematic sermon. One of the oldest two surviving sermons is outlined on the medieval scheme[16] of: Who, What He Gave, To Whom, With What Motive, What He Accomplished, For What. Another characteristic of thematic preaching that appears in the early sermons of Luther is numbering points. Then, too, he also reflected the medieval sense of the multiple meanings of scripture.[17] Indeed, he only gradually and incompletely restrained himself from allegorical interpretation.

In time, however, Luther developed a method of preaching that was virtually unique. It has often been compared to the patristic homily, but ordinarily he did not engage in verse-by-verse exegesis. Rather, it was the method of *schriftauslegende Predigt,* "expository preaching." Instead of looking at every word in the text sequentially in the sermon, he would discover in his own exegetical preparation what could be called the *Sinnmitte* (center of meaning), *Herzpunkt* (heart point), or *Kern* (kernel) of the passage.[18]

Then, rather than having a formal introduction, he would begin by stating that point, the message he felt the text had for his congregation that day. To illustrate, he begins a Lenten sermon based on the story of the raising of Lazarus with these words:

> Dear Friends of Christ. I have told you the story of this Gospel in order that you may picture in your hearts and remember well that Christ our

> God, in all the Gospels, from beginning to end, and also all writings of the prophets and apostles, desires of us nothing else but that we should have a sure and confident heart and trust in him. (51:44)

The sermon consists of his efforts to extract that meaning from the story.[19]

Other than that, there is no set pattern by which his sermons are developed. Indeed, Johann Gerhard characterized their structure as "heroic disorder."[20] Luther would take an outline *(Konzept)* into the pulpit, but he was notorious for departing from it. Yet that is not to say he did not prepare thoroughly for his preaching. That preparation, however, consisted of immersing himself in the text until he had penetrated to its *Sinnmitte* and developed a *Konzept* that would allow him to get that point across. His favorite structural device was to set up an antithesis,[21] to set things in opposition to one another. As noted above, the law/gospel contrast is the most characteristic form of this, but he also used sin/grace, Satan/God, and bound will/free will.

There is more to this than rhetoric, however. Preaching was a life-and-death matter for Luther because he believed that it was the medium through which election occurred, and in every sermon judgment and gospel were experienced anew. As John Doberstein says:

> Luther's sermons are therefore real battles in the eschatological struggle between Christ and the adversary; their aim is to make Christians of the hearers through the Word of God and thus hurl the power and victory of Christ against the power of evil.[22]

This accounts for the popular, conversational style, his "characteristic use of direct address, dialogue, and the dramatic form."[23] This accounts, too, for his addressing his sermons not to the forty or so doctors and masters in the congregation, but to the hundreds and thousands of young people and children in attendance (54:235). It is for their souls that the eschatological struggle is being waged and its outcome is eternal. (For an example of a sermon by Luther, see **Vol. 2, pp. 248-54.**)

One could deduce from this description that the study of rhetoric had nothing to do with Luther's preaching, that he was unaffected by the humanist movement. Recent investigation, however, has cast important new light on this issue, light that also helps clarify both the relation of Luther to his disciple Melanchthon and part of the reason that Luther's followers did not more closely imitate his homiletical style. John O'Malley has summarized and added to this literature in an important article[24] in which he points to the humanistic studies of grammar and rhetoric going on in Luther's time and notes that each of the two categories can be subdivided. The distinction between primary and secondary rhetoric has long been taken to be that between rhetoric as the study of oratory and rhetoric as other uses of oratorical strategies, such as, for example, in letter writing and historical narration.

This sort of secondary rhetoric moves in the direction of grammar, which traditionally taught more than the elementary skills of reading and writing. "The 'grammarian' taught literature, especially poetry, for it was from poetry that the rules of grammar were originally derived."[25] This study of literature involved the interpretation of texts at two levels: a word-by-word or line-by-line philological reading and a search for philosophical or theological meaning that was determined allegorically or "poetically."

With O'Malley's distinctions, we can say immediately that Luther "fits, first and foremost, into the tradition of 'the Christian grammarian,' and that it is in this category that he was most palpably influenced by the patristic and Renaissance adaptation of the classical tradition."[26] From there it becomes clear that Luther understood the Bible primarily as a book of doctrine. As a scholastic he had been trained in dialectic, and he had defined preaching as *doctrina et exhortatio*. This is to say that preaching is a pedagogical art involving dialectics for persuasion.

Adding to that insight Luther's emphasis on popular preaching, one is reminded of the definition of *contio*[27] as deliberative speech addressed to popular assemblies, as Birgit Stolt has pointed out.[28] This association connects Luther to primary rhetorical theory, theory that, as will be shown, was easily available to him through Melanchthon. It also associates his preaching with the kind recommended by Erasmus 274-79. Thus Luther combined the grammarian's concern for explicating a text with the rhetorical techniques of the *contio* for persuading popular audiences to take a course of action.

On the basis of this analysis, O'Malley is able to point out three features of Luther's sermons that make them rhetorically effective, features that are not only good rhetorical practice, but also very appropriate to the Reformer's personality, theology, and existential situation:

1. "Clear and untiringly repeated doctrine" ("his message, in other words, had a clear center" and Lutheran preaching ever since has aimed at "precise doctrinal content").
2. Clear isolation of enemies (papists and *Schwärmer*), giving a sense of "present danger," and, therefore, urgency.

3. "An agenda for the hearers that was specific and immediate, yet fraught with implications for a better order to come."[29]

In the preaching of Luther, then, there was a perfect marriage of content and method. His grammarian's analysis of the text allowed him to discover its meaning for the congregation, and the form of the *contio* enabled him to direct that insight powerfully to their attention. And the doctrine of justification itself was not just something to be explained; it was a call for a response, a demand for a decision.

> Abstract though the doctrine of justification might be in its slogan-like formulation, it had, as expounded by Luther, an immediate impact on the way those who heard it viewed themselves and acted. It clashed dramatically with received opinions and with what other preachers had been saying. As such, it had to make an impression.[30]

MELANCHTHON'S INFLUENCE ON LUTHERAN PREACHING

In his effort to account for the relative neglect of Luther's preaching art—even within Lutheran circles—John O'Malley points out that "unlike so many of his contemporaries and near-contemporaries, he left no specific treatise on how to preach."[31] He could well have gone on to say that Luther's right-hand man, Philipp Melanchthon, did leave such a treatise; indeed, he left a number of them.

Insight into Melanchthon can be garnered by noting that the etymology of his family name is Greek rather than German. He had been baptized as Philipp Schwarzerd, but, while he was receiving attention as a prodigy during his university training, he indulged in the scholarly fad of adopting a Greek equivalent of his family name. Since *Schwarzerd* means "black earth," he combined the genitive forms *melanos* (of the black) and *chthonos* (soil). In those days of humanist excitement over all things Greco-Roman, it was natural that this grandnephew of Johann Reuchlin should follow the graecicizing fashion by which, for example, Neumanns were becoming Neanders.

Envy of his brilliance as a young classical scholar caused his superiors at first Heidelberg and then Tübingen to deny him the advancements he so obviously deserved. Recognition finally came, however, when he was called in 1518, at the age of twenty-three, to become professor of Greek at a center of humanism, Frederick the Wise's new university in Wittenberg.[32] That was ten years after Luther had begun to lecture there, seven after he had become a doctor and professor, and a year after he had begun to preach against Tetzel and indulgences. So quickly did Melanchthon become a friend of Luther and a party to his cause of reform that the following year he supported him in the Leipzig Disputation. His *Loci communes* of 1521 was "the first ordered presentation of Reformation doctrine."[33] In later years he was one of the chief Lutheran representatives in various important negotiations (e.g., he was the leading presence at the Diet of Augsburg in 1530 and the main author of the Confession produced by it).

The humanism of Melanchthon was not abandoned in his enthusiasm for the Reformation cause, nor was it unimportant for the history of Lutheran preaching. Indeed, the epithet by which Melanchthon is known is "the preceptor of Germany." The educational system he devised was essentially rhetorical, and it not only furnished the basic pattern of German education for centuries to come, but that of English and American education as well.[34]

Much of his continuing influence was through the textbooks he wrote on rhetoric. He did write a book solely on preaching, *De officiis concionatoris,* the third edition of which, appearing in 1535, was the first one dated. Up until that time, it could be said of this work and a similar textbook by Viet Dietrich that they were "sketchy, partisan, and extremely brief works of pamphlet size that did not have an immediate or broad influence."[35] The real influence of Melanchthon on preaching was thus exercised through his treatment of it in his work in rhetoric.

> In 1519, Melanchthon published his first book on rhetoric, *De rhetorica libri tres.* Two years later his lectures on rhetoric at Wittenberg were published as the *Institutiones Rhetoricae.* In 1531, he produced his own textbook, the *Elementa rhetorices* and revised it slightly in 1542.[36]

Thus Luther himself accepted Melanchthon's secondary rhetoric as the major tool of biblical exegesis, but made use of his primary rhetoric only to the extent of adopting the *contio* form for his sermons. Yet it was Melanchthon's primary rhetoric, his theory of preaching, that was more determinative for the future shape of Lutheran homiletics than was the preaching of Luther himself. As a humanist, Melanchthon was committed to the revival of classical rhetoric. Instead of accepting the *contio* form favored by Luther and Erasmus for Christian preaching, he dealt with the essential difficulty of fitting *explication de texte* into the three classical genera by creating a fourth genus especially for preaching and classroom lecture, which he called *genus didascalicum.* (For

Melanchthon's treatment of this, see **Vol. 2, pp. 254-61.**) But this designation reflects Luther's understanding that preaching is essentially the teaching of sound doctrine and that the method for doing so is dialectic, a combination of *doctrina et exhortatio.*

In classical dialectic there are both simple and complex questions. The *loci* for a simple question are: What is the thing, what are its parts or species, what are its causes, what are its effects, what things are related to it, and what things are opposed to it?[37] Using these *loci,* the preacher can "invent" (i.e., discover) what is to be said about any simple question. The *loci* for complex questions are essentially the same. By asking themselves such questions, clergy can find what needs to be said about every biblical topic.

The three classical genera are the judicial or forensic *(genus iudicialis),* the legislative or deliberative *(genus deliberativum),* and the epideictic *(genus demonstrativum).* Melanchthon did not think that the judicial had any part in Christian preaching and felt that epideictic did so only to the extent that it was an "ornamented" version of the *didascalicum.* The deliberative, however, was homiletically useful if it was broken up into two sub-genera: the *epitrepticum,* which exhorts to faith; and the *paraneticum,* which exhorts to good morals.[38]

In his textbooks, Melanchthon taught pastors to write sermons in the didascalic, the epitreptic, and the paranetic genera. These homiletical forms, rather than the *contio* of Luther, became the standard patterns of Lutheran preaching for centuries to come. The man who influenced Luther by his knowledge of secondary rhetoric influenced the followers of Luther with his primary rhetoric.[39] In doing so, he became the preceptor not only of Germany but of the majority of Lutheran preachers for centuries to come.

FOR FURTHER READING

Bainton, Roland H. *Here I Stand: A Life of Martin Luther.* New York: Abingdon-Cokesbury, 1950.

La Fontaine, Mary Joan. "A Critical Translation of Philipp Melanchthon's *Elementorum Rhetorices Libri Duo,*" Latin text with English translation and notes. Louisville: Westminster John Knox, 1995.

Luther, Martin. *Luther's Works.* American ed. Edited by Jaroslav Pelikan and Helmut T. Lehmann. Vols. 51-52, *Sermons I-II,* edited by John A. Doberstein. St. Louis: Concordia Publishing House; Philadelphia: Fortress, 1959.

Meuser, Fred W. *Luther the Preacher.* Minneapolis: Augsburg, 1983.

O'Malley, John. "Luther the Preacher," *The Martin Luther Quincentennial,* ed. Gerhard Dünnhaupt. Detroit: Wayne State University Press for *Michigan Germanic Studies,* 1985.

Wengert, Timothy J. *Philipp Melanchthon's Annotationes in Johannem in Relation to Its Predecessors and Contemporaries.* Travaux d'Humanisme et Renaissance, no. 220. Geneva: Librairie Droz S.A., 1987.

Notes

1. The reason that Luther's style was not copied is that his disciples followed instead the pattern set forth in the textbooks of his assistant Melanchthon, as will be seen below (pp. 298-300). That his preaching has not been studied is a commonplace (see, e.g., Elmer Carl Kiessling's University of Chicago dissertation, *The Early Sermons of Luther and Their Relation to the Pre-Reformation Sermon* [Grand Rapids, Mich.: Zondervan, 1935], 5; and Fred W. Meuser, *Luther the Preacher* [Minneapolis: Augsburg, 1983], 9).

2. Roland H. Bainton, *Here I Stand: A Life of Martin Luther* (New York and Nashville: Abingdon-Cokesbury, 1950), 65, from the Weimar edition of Luther's works, 54:185. In his book, written in English, Bainton provided the English translation of the passage on 455 cited in this note, which was originally in German.

3. Historians are no longer sure the breach occurred in precisely this way, but there is no doubt that it did occur at that time over these issues.

4. The presentation of Luther's thought that follows is based on Justo L. González, *A History of Christian Thought: From the Reformation to the Twentieth Century,* vol. 3 (Nashville: Abingdon, 1975), 25-62.

5. Luther does not speak of "the capacity to be turned in a new direction," but the phrase seems to express his thought.

6. Documentation for this section will be drawn from *Luther's Works,* American ed., Jaroslav Pelikan and Helmut T. Lehmann, eds. (St. Louis: Concordia Publishing House; Philadelphia: Fortress, 1958–86). Citations appear parenthetically in the text with the volume number followed by a colon and the page number (e.g., the documentation for the statement for which this note is given is 39:314).

7. Luther even sees a powerful homiletical dimension to sacraments. See 35:105; 13:377.

8. Carl E. Braaten, *Justification: The Article by Which the Church Stands or Falls* (Minneapolis: Fortress, 1990), 148.

9. See also 12:17, 71; 13:316-17; 17:7-8, 210, 260, 277; 23:278; 31:241, 364; 35:166.

10. 23:174. The Word here is not just the proclaimed Word, but is the incarnate and written Word as well.

11. Passages of the sort quoted in this paragraph are too common to list.

12. The view stated is that of Meuser, cited below, 37-38. But Prof. Timothy

Wengert told me during conversations held over March 13-16, 1991, that catechetical sermons were preached only during the Ember seasons—a traditional time for such sermons from at least the time of Aelfric. Wengert said that when Luther preached such sermons, he was filling in for the pastor of the church. He referred to the 5:00 A.M. service as Matins, the 10:00 A.M. as Mass, and the afternoon as Vespers. His reference was Bruno Jordahn, "Katechismus-Gottesdienst im Reformationsjahrhundert," *Luther: Mitteilungen der Luthergesellschaft* 30 (1959): 64-77.

13. Meuser, *Luther the Preacher,* 37-38.

14. For example, it took Luther twenty-eight lectures to get through the first four chapters of Galatians (26:ix).

15. Hans J. Hillerbrand, "Introduction," in *Luther's Works,* 52:ix-xiii. This volume contains a translation of slightly more than half of the *Christmas Postil.* See also Yngve Brilioth, *A Brief History of Preaching,* trans. Karl E. Mattson, The Preacher's Paperback Library (Philadelphia: Fortress), 108-9; and Meuser, *Luther the Preacher,* 37. Other short treatments of Luther's preaching occur in Bainton, *Here I Stand,* 348-58; Werner Schütz, *Geschichte der christlichen Predigt* (Berlin: Walter de Gruyter, 1972), 90-96; Harold J. Grimm, "The Human Element in Luther's Sermons," in *ARG* 49 (1958): 50-60; James Mackinnon, *Luther and the Reformation* (London, New York, and Toronto: Longmans, Green & Co., 1930), 4:304-18; and John W. Doberstein, "Introduction," in *Luther's Works,* 51:xi-xxi. Volume 51 is a good collection of characteristic sermons preached at various periods of Luther's career.

16. Based on the dialectics of Aristotle, from which Melanchthon was to derive the *loci* of his Didactic genus of speaking.

17. Kiessling, *The Early Sermons of Luther and Their Relation to the Pre-Reformation Sermon,* 60-67.

18. Although scholars at times refer to this as "literal, historical, grammatical" interpretation, these terms can be misleading, since Luther was not involved in the task of modern historical-critical exegesis, that of discovering what the sacred writer intended his/her first readers to understand. Rather, the Scriptures were taken as addressed to the contemporary church. The "literal" meaning of a passage from Galatians, for instance, would not be what it had meant to Christians in the community founded by Paul in the region of Ancyra, but what it meant to Wittenbergers.

19. Meuser, *Luther the Preacher,* 46-48.

20. Quoted by Kiessling, *The Early Sermons of Luther and Their Relation to the Pre-Reformation Sermon,* 60.

21. Meuser, *Luther the Preacher,* 48.

22. Doberstein, "Introduction," in Luther's Works, 51:xix-xx.

23. Ibid., 51:xi-xxi.

24. "Luther the Preacher," *The Martin Luther Quincentennial,* ed. Gerhard Dünnhaupt (Detroit: Wayne State University Press for *Michigan Germanic Studies,* 1985), 3-16.

25. Ibid., 6. O'Malley's interpretation is consistent with what was said above about Origen, 31-46. Indeed, his "secondary rhetoric" is essentially the concerns of the classical *grammatikos.*

26. Ibid., 8.

27. A variant spelling of *concio.*

28. O'Malley, "Luther the Preacher," 9. The reference is to Stolt's *"Docere, delectare, und movere bei Luther," Deutsche Viertejahresschrift für Literaturwissenschaft und Geistesgeschichte* 44 (1970): 433-74.

29. O'Malley, "Luther the Preacher," 12.

30. Ibid., 12.

31. Ibid., 3.

32. For the atmosphere of the university at the time, see Maria Grossmann, *Humanism in Wittenberg 1485–1517* (Nieuwkoop: B. DeGraaf, 1975). It must be admitted, however, that Grossmann stresses more than most recent scholars an anti-Christian spirit in humanism and an opposition to humanism on the part of Luther. For German humanism, see also Mary Joan La Fontaine, "A Critical Translation of Philipp Melanchthon's *Elementorum Rhetorices Libri Duo,*" Latin text with English translation and notes (unpublished Ph.D. dissertation, University of Michigan, 1968), 6-18; and Helmut Schanze, "Problems and Trends in the History of German Rhetoric" in *Renaissance Eloquence: Studies in the Theory and Practice of Renaissance Rhetoric,* ed. James J. Murphy (Berkeley: University of California Press), 105-25.

33. *ODCC,* 898.

34. La Fontaine, "A Critical Translation of Philipp Melanchthon's *Elementorum Rhetorices Libri Duo,*" 30-38.

35. John W. O'Malley, "Erasmus and the History of Sacred Rhetoric: The *Ecclesiastes* of 1535," in *Erasmus of Rotterdam Society Yearbook,* vol. 5 (1985), 8.

36. Timothy Wengert, "Melanchthon, Philipp," in *Concise Encyclopedia of Preaching,* ed. William Willimon and Richard Lischer, 328-29.

37. La Fontaine, "A Critical Translation of Philipp Melanchthon's *Elementorum Rhetorices Libri Duo*" (Louisville: Westminster John Knox, 1995), 99.

38. O'Malley, "Sixteenth-Century Treatises," in *Renaissance Eloquence: Studies in the Theory and Practice of Renaissance Rhetoric,* ed. James J. Murphy (Berkeley: The University of California Press, 1983), 242-43.

39. This is not to say that his secondary rhetoric was not also very influential on subsequent Lutheran exegesis. The *Loci communes* was even more of an exegetical tool of secondary rhetoric than it was a theological treatise as such. For the use of rhetorical categories in Melanchthon's exegesis, see Timothy J. Wengert, *Philipp Melanchthon's Annotationes in Johannem in Relation to Its Predecessors and Contemporaries,* Travaux d'Humanisme et Renaissance, no. 220 (Geneva: Librairie Droz S.A., 1987), 167-212. For a translation of *Loci communes,* see *Melanchthon and Bucer,* ed. Wilhelm Pauck, LCC, vol. 19 (Philadelphia: Westminster, 1969), 18-152.

CHAPTER 13

CALVIN AND THE REFORM TRADITION

THE SWISS REFORMATION

Luther's particular type of reforming activity, although the inspiration or occasion of the efforts that followed, succeeded only in spreading to other Germanic-language areas. The tradition that was to influence the rest of the world arose in Switzerland. The movement there began very soon after that in Germany, but apparently without Lutheran influence in the beginning. Indeed, Ulrich Zwingli, its first founder, was eager to escape association with Luther even after he became acquainted with his writings; he considered the Wittenberg Reformer to have been too conservative, too supportive of aspects of the old religion. Besides, they were operating out of different presuppositions and preoccupations. Zwingli had never been a monk involved in an effort to achieve a sense of acceptance by God, and he never acquired the deep immersion in scholasticism that Luther's doctorate betokened. Rather, his training had alerted him to the revival of classical and patristic learning among the humanists. Instead of Luther's emphasis on justification, he was more involved in the humanist's desire to return to the sources *(ad fontes),* and thus he wanted to emphasize the Bible as the exclusive source of Christian doctrine. His battle cry was not *sola fide,* but *sola scriptura.*[1]

Although Zwingli's reform teaching was the earliest in Switzerland, it was not to be the form that predominated. Nor was his own example of preaching to be the most influential. In fact, very few of his sermons have survived. Only two aspects of what was to become the standard pattern of Swiss preaching can be traced to him. The first is that he did not preach from the lectionary for the church year but instead did course preaching through books of the Bible. The second is that he designed a liturgy for which the sermon, rather than the Eucharist, provided the shape.[2]

> The Sunday service was again given a new form with the sermon as the central point. The sermon itself, loosed from its liturgical context, became the basic motif in the creation of new liturgy.[3]

As important as these changes were, the initiative for innovation was to lie elsewhere. Zwingli's early death as a casualty of the second war between Switzerland's Catholic and Protestant cantons in 1531 meant that he was no longer on the scene when John Calvin, the Frenchman who was to give the Swiss Reformation and its preaching their distinctive patterns, made his appearance.

Radical Reform

Calvin's, however, was not the first attempt to alter the pattern Zwingli had begun to construct in Zurich. That impulse came from Zwingli's own city and from his circle of friends. The ostensible issue of the first disagreements was the legitimacy of infant baptism, although more was at stake than the nature of one sacrament; the whole nature of the church and its relation to the state was involved.[4] The first disagreement was in debates about the Mass, especially Zwingli's decision to let the town council decide the timing for discontinuing the Mass. Anabaptists felt the council had no right to legislate on an issue governed by the Word of Scripture—it was thus a disagreement about the relationship of church and state.

Yet the event has traditionally been discussed in terms of stands on infant baptism. Those who quarreled with Zwingli claimed that it had no legitimacy (a point on which he agreed with them at first), and thus argued that adults should be baptized even if they had been christened as babies. From this position they came to be known as "Anabaptists," advocates of rebaptism. They rejected the term, however, saying that no one could be rebaptized if the ceremony through which they had previously gone was not true baptism.

The argument still goes on about the proper way to refer to the groups that grew out of or otherwise resemble Zwingli's opponents at Zurich. For a while it was popular to refer to the movement as "the left wing of the Reformation," a tendency growing out of Ernst Troeltsch's analysis, which envisioned

> a spectrum of religious practice ranging from medieval and reactionary, on the far right, to liberal and modern, on the far left.... By this measure Catholics were the most medieval and reactionary; Lutherans, conservative to moderate; Calvinists and Zwinglians, moderate to liberal; and the radical reformers—Anabaptists, Spiritualists, and Evangelical Rationalists—liberal and modern.[5]

Part and parcel of this interpretation has been assigning to these groups the credit for three principles that are taken for granted in contemporary North American Christianity: "the voluntary church, the separation of church and state, and religious liberty."[6] For Troeltsch, this makes them forerunners of modern humanism and liberal Protestantism, but it disregards their differences from modern groups and ignores how much they had in common with medieval Christianity.[7]

The appropriateness of retrojecting contemporary political categories into the sixteenth century has been further questioned by George H. Williams, who has suggested instead that the groups be referred to collectively as "the radical Reformation."[8] As a way of avoiding the confusion of some of these groups with others that have very different views and dynamics, Williams also proposed a taxonomy that distinguishes between a number of different types of radical reform movements. It lists three kinds of Anabaptists (revolutionary, contemplative, and evangelical), three kinds of Spiritualists (revolutionary, evangelical, and rational), and Evangelical Rationalists.[9]

Before the recent scholarship reflected in the previous paragraphs, there was a tendency to lump all of these groups together and to study them in terms not of their own writings, but of what their enemies, especially Lutherans, Calvinists, and Zwinglians, had to say about them.[10] Luther tended to confuse later movements with the group who had disturbed the Wittenberg church while he was in Wartburg after the Diet of Worms and with radicals in the north German town of Münster. In 1534 these latter instituted a theocracy that put into practice many positive Old Testament social ideals, providing work for everyone, which at the same time revived charismatic prophecy and polygamy. Luther thus dismissed all radical reform movements as "enthusiasts" *(Schwärmer)*, and assumed that all were revolutionary and antinomian. Yet there seems to have been little if any influence of either group on the Zurich, southwest German, and Dutch radicals from whom later Anabaptists appear to have originated.

The basic doctrines of at least evangelical Anabaptistry begin with a primitivist assumption that the apostolic age was the golden age of the church, a normative period in which the church enjoyed a perfection from which it later fell. That fall was often associated with the time of Constantine, when indiscriminate baptism occurred and unbelievers were allowed into the church. This was seen as the beginning of the use of coercion by the state for religious conformity.

The Radical Reformers, however, saw themselves as called by God to inaugurate a new period in history, the time of the restitution of Christianity to its New Testament pattern. They were energized by an eschatological belief that the end was at hand.[11] In their system, religious behavior was to be voluntary and therefore sincere. This meant not only that there would be no use of police power to enforce conformity, but also that only adults who freely chose to make the commitment would be baptized. The Anabaptists thus called for an end to religious establishment enforced by the state and a beginning of tolerance for dissent. They themselves foreswore any use of force and committed themselves to a pattern of pacifism and passive resistance, even when they knew that it could very well lead to martyrdom.[12]

As in the time of Tertullian, the blood of martyrs proved to be seed from which the church sprang up in vigorous new growth. The "Fourth Reformation"[13] became an aggressive missionary movement. The Anabaptists' missionary activity, like the rest of their ministerial activity, involved a great deal of lay participation. Those who had taken on responsibility for their own religious commitment also took on responsibility to share it with others.

Since the historical recovery of the Radical Reformation is still under way, it is not surprising that there have not been many studies of its preaching so far.[14] Furthermore, the nature of the case is such that few written sermons have survived from the early days of the movement. While the founders had been ordained as Catholic priests and were often learned, almost all were included among the martyrs of the first generation. After that, those chosen for ministerial office (by lot at first, though later by election) came from the congregation and had no academic training in theology. Further, sermons that were not extempore were distrusted at first. There is little surprise, then, that few were taken down by stenographers and published.

> The early Anabaptist sermons were without doubt conceived as simple forthright declarations of a hortatory and devotional character, except when used for evangelistic purposes. They were certainly not expected to be rhetorical orations prepared and finished according to the practice of learned men. It was assumed that any member of the church could admonish the congregation out of his general knowledge of the Scriptures, his experience in life, and the help of the Holy Spirit.[15]

The life pattern of such congregations probably means that what Roy Umble said about the American preachers of 1864–1944, whom he studied, could apply equally well to any generation after the first (except for the extent to which it suggests a central place for the sermon):

> With the Bible as the background and focus of the preaching, these men illustrate a certain uniformity in method of organization and proof. Sermons usually followed a lengthy devotional period consisting of congregational singing, Scripture reading and prayer. The minister began with a Scripture text, announced a theme or related the Bible verse to the occasion, and proceeded to explain or expand and then apply the teaching.[16]

In time and in various places, this pattern changed. While the extempore pattern continued in Switzerland and south Germany, there developed in Prussia and Russia a practice of writing out sermons and reading them. This was followed by a time when it was thought prideful to preach a sermon of one's own composition, so only the written sermons of the past could be read. At least as late as the 1950s, in Hutterite congregations of Canada and the northwest United States, newly elected preachers copied by hand notebooks full of sermons from mid-seventeenth-century Slovakia to read at worship services.[17]

In the Anabaptist tradition, on the other hand, only one sermon in German survives from the sixteenth century and one in Dutch from the seventeenth. By the eighteenth century, though, sermons were printed frequently. These were not read from the pulpit, although they probably were thought of as models. Their main purpose was to be read in family devotions; by the beginning of the twentieth century, such collections were published with the explicit statement that they were *zum Gebrauch für Hausgottesdienst.*[18] This custom reflected the influence of Pietism.

Regrettably, this is about all that can be learned about a preaching tradition that was rich, and very meaningful to those who experienced it.

THE CAREER OF A REFORMER

When Luther did or did not post his Ninety-five Theses on the door of the Wittenberg church on All Hallows' Eve, 1517, John Calvin was an eight-year-old boy, the fourth son of a notary in service of the clergy in the cathedral town of Noyon in Picardy. Recognizing the opportunities for advancement that the church offered to a young man of talent, Gérard Cauvin[19] began early to plan on a priestly career for his precocious son. The father's connections made it possible for young John to receive the tonsure and to be appointed to several benefices when he was only twelve.

Two years later, the lad was enrolled in the Collège de la Marche at "the Sorbonne," the University of Paris. This meant that he found himself "in the greatest of universities and at the heart of the greatest of nations."[20] Five years after that, when he had completed his M.A., his father, now involved in quarrels with the cathedral clergy that would eventually result in his excommunication, caused John to take up the study of law. He was enrolled first at Orléans and then at Bourges, although he returned to Paris for regular intervals of study during the five years that he was a law student. After John became *licencié* in the law in 1533, he was free to pursue his own interests, his father having died the year before.

While Calvin was well exposed to scholasticism during his years of study, he was most impressed by the humanists among his teachers.[21] His ideals during those days were Erasmus and Jacques Lefèvre d'Étaples (latinized as Jacobus Faber Stapulensis), librarian of the monastery of St. Germain-des-Prés and humanistic biblical scholar.[22] The greatest monument of Calvin's own humanistic activity and his first book as well was a commentary on Seneca's treatise, *De clementia,*[23] which he published the year before he finished his legal studies.

The teachers who influenced him most during this period were humanists who were critical of abuses within the Roman Catholic Church while remaining loyal to it. That seems to have been the situation of his close friend Nicholas Cop, who took advantage of his position as rector of the University of Paris to preach a sermon on All Saints' Day, 1533, criticizing the scholasticism of the Sorbonne faculty from an Erasmian perspective that Bouwsma calls "evangelical humanism."[24] In the fallout from this sermon, not only Cop but also Calvin had to flee Paris. Authorities disagree over whether Calvin's danger was the result of his having shared in the composition of the sermon or was merely guilt by association. In any case, most scholars now believe that Cop's sermon, critical as it was of the religious establishment, stopped short of recommending a breach with Rome.

In point of fact—and remarkably so—one of the most disputed issues in the study of Calvin's life is that of exactly when his own criticism of the Catholic Church's conduct and thought led him to decide that conscience required him to leave it. It has long been recognized that virtually the only autobiographical evidence on the question is contained in the dedication at the beginning of his commentary on the Psalms:[25]

> I was called back from the study of philosophy to learn law. I followed my father's wish and attempted to do faithful work in this field; but God, by the secret leading of his providence, turned my course another way.
>
> First, when I was too firmly addicted to the papal superstitions to be drawn easily out of such a deep mire, by a sudden conversion He brought my mind (already more rigid than suited my age) to submission [to him]. I was so inspired by a taste of true religion and I burned with such a desire to carry my study further, that although I did not drop other subjects, I had no zeal for them. In less than a year, all who were looking for a purer doctrine began to come to learn from me, although I was a novice and a beginner.

But what exactly does that mean? It obviously involved the reorientation of his life, but if it also involved a cataclysmic emotional experience, he does not describe it. Clearly it was not his passing over from a dissolute life of irreligion or atheism to a life of Christian belief and commitment. Indeed, Bouswma seems to deny that he had a conversion at all, at least in the manner of Paul or Augustine. Pointing out that Calvin always seemed to minimize Paul's experience and to emphasize "the gradualness rather than the suddenness of conversion," he makes the startling claim that "Calvinism was the creation of a devout sixteenth-century French Catholic."[26] More measured and probably nearer the truth is his statement on the following page that Calvin's conversion "did not obliterate but built upon his evangelical humanism."[27] I would prefer to say that his conversion occurred when it became obvious to him that his loyalty to evangelical humanism forced him to leave the Roman church and become one of its critics and opponents.

The date for this reorientation of Calvin's life is also a matter of dispute. At present, however, most scholars consider the first act that decisively indicates a change of heart to have been Calvin's visit in May 1534 to his hometown of Noyon to surrender his benefices; apparently he felt that he could not receive income from a system in which he did not believe. This dating is supported negatively by the lack of any distinctively Protestant sentiments in his Seneca commentary of 1532. It is easy to speculate that Calvin's visit to Lefèvre d'Étaples near the time he went to Noyon must have been for the purpose of consulting his aging humanistic ideal about his decision to abandon the Roman communion.

Calvin spent the next two years traveling in France and Italy and putting his newfound convictions into expression. During this time he produced the first edition of *Institutes,* his "instruction" in the reformed faith that he used also as an apologia to the French king Francis I, urging him to grant amnesty to returning religious exiles. The book did not succeed in its apologetic purpose, and so its patriotic author had to spend the rest of his life as an exile. As a textbook in Protestant thought, however, it has no near rival. Continuing to revise and expand it (to five times its original length) until five years before his death in 1564, Calvin had already decided by the second edition that it was not to be merely a handbook for the faithful; it was also to be the authoritative guide for theological students in their interpretation of the Bible.[28]

Calvin had tried to remain anonymous out of a desire for scholarly retreat, but his name on the title page of the *Institutes* made that impossible. A temporary amnesty for religious exiles permitted him to return briefly to settle his affairs in France. From there he set out for Strasbourg in hopes of finding the peace and quiet that study requires. He was, however, forced to take a detour through Geneva, and word of his overnight presence there brought to his inn the local Reformer, Guilliaume Farel. The religious situation in the city was tense. Its traditional ruler had been its prince-bishop, who had exercised his oversight through a town council. Huguenot exiles, however, had negotiated an alliance with Fribourg and Bern that toppled the prelate and handed his power over to a concentric series of councils. Bern then sent Reform missionaries to the city under the leadership of Farel. After a series of disputations, the town council accepted the Reformation on May 25, 1536. Two months later, Calvin arrived in town. Farel, who is described by McNeill as "Lefèvre's most aggressive pupil, a second-rate scholar, and a hot gospeler,"[29] recognized both the tenuousness of the religious situation in Geneva and his own limitations. He tried to persuade Calvin, who was twenty years his junior, to stay and help.

How Farel overcame Calvin's reluctance is best stated in Calvin's own words in the preface to his Psalms commentary that also contains the story of his "conversion":

> Since the wars had closed the direct road to Strasbourg, I had meant to pass through Geneva quickly and had determined not to be delayed there more than one night.

> A short time before, by the work of the same good man [Farel], and of Peter Viret, the papacy had been banished from the city; but things were still unsettled and the place was divided into evil and harmful factions. One man, who has since shamefully gone back to the papists, took immediate action to make me known. Then Farel, who was working with incredible zeal to promote the gospel, bent all his efforts to keep me in the city. And when he realized that I was determined to study in privacy in some obscure place, and saw that he gained nothing by entreaty, he descended to cursing, and said that God would surely curse my peace if I held back from giving help at a time of such great need. Terrified by his words, and conscious of my own timidity and cowardice, I gave up my journey and attempted to apply whatever gift I had in defense of my faith.[30]

After that, it would be appropriate to say, "And the rest is history," except for one thing, namely, that in less than two years the town council expelled Farel and Calvin from Geneva, unwilling to grant them the power of excommunication they felt their reform program called for. Thus Calvin finally got to Strasbourg, where he assisted Martin Bucer by serving as pastor to a congregation of French exiles. There he accomplished many things, including writing his first biblical commentary (on Romans),[31] revising and expanding the *Institutes,* and learning much from Bucer about how to be a Reform leader in a Swiss city.

After a little more than three years, however, he reluctantly accepted the recall of the Genevan town council and went back to the position of leadership that he was to keep until his death in 1564. During that time he met with opposition, but gradually those who opposed him emigrated. Meanwhile, Geneva became the city of refuge for many whose zeal for reform had necessitated their flight from other countries; in time these refugees totaled 30 percent of the population. For them Geneva was the epitome of all their hopes and dreams because Calvin had succeeded in getting accepted there his full program of religious reform.

Le Prédicateur Méconnu de Genève

After Calvin returned to Geneva in 1541, he asked the council to appoint a committee to draft *Les Ordonnances ecclésiastiques de l'Église de Genève* to govern the religious practices of the city and its citizens. These ordinances, as approved by the council, called for a rich diet of preaching. On Sundays at daybreak there was a sermon in the larger two of the three churches. There were sermons in all three churches at nine o'clock and again at mid-afternoon. Then there were sermons during the week on Mondays, Wednesdays, and Fridays.[32] In 1549 the sermons during the week became daily. Calvin's associate and successor, Theodore Beza, estimated that Calvin preached an average of 290 sermons a year.[33]

Preaching was very important to Calvin's understanding of what the church exists to do. In listing his criteria by which a genuine church was to be recognized, he said:

> Wherever we see the Word of God purely preached and heard, and the sacraments administered according to Christ's institution, there, it is not to be doubted, a church of God exists.[34]

He never did achieve his sacramental ideal of having the Eucharist every Sunday. It was not until 1557, when the power of excommunication was granted to the Consistory, that he realized his disciplinary ideal for the administration of the sacraments.[35] He could hardly complain, however, that the Word of God was not purely preached.

This singular success in the area of preaching makes it all the more amazing that Richard Stauffer could claim that Calvin the preacher is unappreciated and ignored. This inattention goes back to Calvin's lifetime. While it is true that arrangements were made for Denis Raguenier to take down Calvin's extemporaneously delivered sermons in shorthand, that was not done until 1549. Only eight hundred of the transcribed sermons were published before Calvin died. These amounted to only a fraction of the contents of the forty-four folio volumes of these transcripts made by Raguenier; his catalog of Calvin's sermons lists 2,042.

These manuscripts remained in the Public and University Library of Geneva until 1806 when the librarian sold them by the pound as wastepaper. In 1823 eight of the volumes were discovered in a used clothing shop by some theological students, who recognized them for what they were and began the effort to reassemble the collection. Although other volumes have been recovered, it is estimated that around a thousand sermons were lost. The Corpus Reformatorum edition of *Calvini Opera* contains 872 sermons. More than two hundred others began to see the light of day, however, in 1961 when the series of *Supplementa Calviniana* started to appear.[36] Such tardiness in the publication of these sermons supports Stauffer's claim that Calvin the preacher has been unappreciated and ignored.[37]

Calvin's Doctrine of Preaching

Calvin did not go as far as Luther did in identifying preaching as the Word of God.[38] The minister cannot assume that God is speaking through his[39] preaching:

> A man whose holy life is given up to the service of God may preach irreproachably scriptural doctrine, applied with a profound psychological insight to the needs of the congregation, and yet nevertheless it cannot be taken for granted that God is speaking to His Church. Rather, Calvin would say, preaching *becomes* Revelation by God adding to it His Holy Spirit.[40]

Nevertheless, preaching is the ordinary channel through which the Holy Spirit speaks:

> Outward preaching is vain and useless unless the Spirit himself acts as the teacher. God therefore teaches in two ways. He makes us hear his voice through the words of men, and inwardly he constrains us by his Spirit. These two occur together or separately, as God sees fit.[41]

When the Spirit speaks internally to someone, however, no insight is granted that is not already expressed in Scripture. "The Spirit will not be a maker of new revelations."[42] Yet through this preaching it may be expected that the older revelation will be extended to the congregation:

> The task of the preacher of the Word is to expound the scripture in the midst of the worshipping Church, preaching in the expectancy that God will do, through his frail human word, what He did through the Word of His prophets of old, that God by His grace will cause the word that goes out of the mouth of man to become also a Word that proceeds from God Himself, with all the power and efficacy of the Word of the Creator and Redeemer.[43]

In this perspective it may be said that preaching is the Word of God in at least two senses. The first is that "it is an exposition and interpretation of the Bible, which is as much the Word of God as if men 'heard the very words pronounced by God himself.'"[44] The Bible and nothing but the Bible is the matter of preaching; Calvin was determined to speak where the Scriptures speak and to be silent where they are silent. Thus "the teaching of a minister should be approved on the sole ground of his being able to show that what he says comes from God."[45] When such preaching occurs, it can be taken as a sign of the presence of God and the instrument through which Christ's rule is established, a Word that is effective to accomplish its commands and promises. This is to say that it is "efficacious for the salvation of believers (and) abundantly efficacious for the condemning of the wicked."[46]

The second sense in which it may be said that preaching is the Word of God is that the minister is called precisely for the proclamation of the Word of God. His vocation comes through the Holy Spirit and is ratified by his call to serve in a congregation. In the confidence of this double calling, he speaks as an ambassador of God and as though God personally were speaking.

> Now we must not find this strange, for when the servants of God speak thus, they attribute nothing to themselves, but show to what they are commissioned and what charge is given them; and thus they do not separate themselves from God.[47]

Calvin's conviction that it takes the Holy Spirit's ratifying of the sermon to make it the Word of God, his belief in double predestination, and his generally low estimate of the value of human activity did not mean that he considered the qualifications of pastors to be a matter of indifference.

> Clearly not everyone is fitted to be a pastor; knowledge of the Scriptures and soundness of doctrine must be joined to faithfulness, zeal, and holiness. As important as any of these, however, and without which no man can be a good preacher, is the gift of teaching.[48]

Such qualities are external evidences of an inward call and are thus prerequisites for ordination. And the most important duty of the minister is preaching the Word of God; that was believed to be "the constituting essential of the ministry."[49]

Purely Proclaiming the Word of God

Anyone moving from Calvin's theory of preaching to his practice of it will not be surprised at the consistency between them. His own knowledge of the Scriptures, theological erudition, high standards of personal behavior, and pedagogical skill are well known. Further, his humanistic training developed all of his natural rhetorical ability. He knew the misuses to which rhetoric could be put, but knew as well its value when rightly used:

> That eloquence, then, is neither to be condemned nor despised, which has no tendency to lead Christians to be taken up with an outward glitter of words, or intoxicate them with empty delight, or tickle their ears with its tinkling sound, or cover over the Cross of Christ with its empty show as with a veil; but, on the contrary, tends to call us back to the

> native simplicity of the Gospel, tends to exalt the simple preaching of the Cross by voluntarily abasing itself, and, in fine, acts the part of a herald.[50]

His rhetorical skill may not be immediately apparent to modern readers of his sermons, however, for two reasons: (1) his preaching, though carefully prepared for, was always extempore, and (2) he used the homily form of verse-by-verse analysis, which undercuts the overall unity of a sermon. He used the homily form as he engaged in course preaching through entire books of the Bible, having theological qualms about chopping the Scriptures into liturgical lections. Doing that, he felt, suggested that parts of Scripture were unnecessary, less inspired, and not of a unity with the rest of the canon in their teaching.

Parker has drafted the outline of a typical Calvin sermon on a text of two phrases or clauses:

1. Prayer.
2. Recapitulation of previous sermon.
3. (a) Exegesis and exposition of first member.
   (b) Application of this, and exhortation to obedience or duty.
4. (a) Exegesis and exposition of second member.
   (b) Application of this, and exhortation to obedience or duty.
5. Bidding to prayer, which contains a summary of the sermon.[51]

This diagram, however, suggests a sharper division between exegesis and application than one often feels in reading one of Calvin's sermons. Rather, Parker captures that experience much more adequately when he analyzes the construction of a particular sermon, that on Job 21:13-15. (For another sermon in the same series, see **Vol. 2, pp. 263-76.**) His outline is as follows:

> The text is chapter 21. 13-15: "They pass their days in good, and in a moment they descend to the sepulchre. Yet they say to God, 'Depart from us, for we do not wish to know thy ways. What is the Almighty that we should serve him? or what profit will there be to pray to him?'"

1. He reminds the congregation of what he said yesterday.
2. Verse 13. "God will permit the despisers of his majesty *to go to the sepulchre in a minute of time,* after they have had a good time all their life." Psalm 73:4ff. (of which a brief exposition) may be compared with this passage.

   There is a "contrast between frequently easy deaths of the ungodly and pains of believers."

But God defers his judgments to the next world; and therefore we must raise our minds above this fleeting world, when God will judge the ungodly.

Therefore, let us not be like those who despise God and have all their happiness in this world. But rather let us prefer to be wretched here and look to God to give us his bounty hereafter.

"See what believers are admonished of here."

3. Verse 14. "Now Job consequently declares how the wicked reject God entirely. *They say to him, 'Depart from us, for we do not wish to know thy ways.'*"

The wicked wish to be free from God. We see them trying to get away from him by claiming they can do as they like.

"*We do not wish for thy ways.*" To be near God or far from him does not refer to his essence and majesty. It is to be obedient or disobedient to his Word.

"Now *voici* a passage from which we can gather good and useful teaching."

(1) The root and foundation of a good life is to have God always before us.

- (a) How can a man leave the evil to which he is prone?
- (b) He must be reformed by God, since he cannot reform himself.
- (c) We are so blind that we do not know the right way. We think evil is good "until God enlightens us."

"So then, do we wish to walk as we should? Let us make a start at this point—that is, of drawing near to our God. How do we draw near? First of all, let us know that nothing is hidden from him; everyone must come to a reckoning before him, and he must be the Judge, even of our thoughts" (CO 34:232[7-13]).

"*Voilà,* so much for the first."

(2) "God will judge us by His Word," the two-edged sword.

- (a) Therefore we must draw near to Him.
- (b) And this means, to him in his Word, in which he comes to us.
- (c) Therefore "our greatest misery" is to be without God's Word; "our greatest blessing" is when he gives it to us.
- (d) "Those who will not submit to the Word" show that they are God's enemies.
- (e) Let us always be willing and obedient.

"*Voilà* what we have to note from this passage—that we may not only have God before our eyes, but also love him to care for us and lead us" (CO 34.234[8-11]).

4. Verse 15. "Now, after Job has shown here such blasphemy on the part of the wicked and the despisers of God, he adds that they say, '*What is*

the Almighty, that we should serve Him? and what profit" will it bring *us to "pray unto him?'"*

(1) "The pride of the wicked."
  (a) "Pride is the chief vice" of the wicked, as humility is the sovereign virtue in believers—"the mother of all virtues."
  (b) "Their pride is ... trust in their own wisdom."
  (c) Swollen with presumption, they do just what they like.

(2) "*What is the Almighty, that we should serve Him?*"
  (a) They do not use these words, but this is in their mind; and sometimes God makes them betray themselves.
  (b) They "acknowledge God's existence, but not His authority."
  (c) "But believers must submit themselves to God" as those that are his children, "created in His image," "redeemed by the death" and passion of his only Son, and called to be his household, as "children and heirs."

"When, then, we have made all these comparisons—I pray you, if we have hearts of iron or steel, ought they not to be softened? If we are swollen with arrogance and bursting with it, must not all that poison be purged, that so we may come with true humility to obey God?" (*CO* 34.236[33-40]).

  (d) He refers to the preface to the Ten Commandments: "I am the Eternal, thy God."
    (i) "The Eternal—that is, the Creator."
    (ii) "Thy God"—the Father of his people.
    (iii) "that brought thee out of the land of Egypt, out of the house of bondage"—that is, redeemed us from the depths of hell by our Lord Jesus Christ.
    (iv) Therefore we must dedicate ourselves entirely to the service of God.
    (v) God adds promises to his service, that he will be our Father, the protector of our life, that he will pardon our sins, and will accept our feeble service without examining it rigorously and hypercritically.

(3) "*What is the profit of serving God?*"
  (a) If we flee from God, we become servants to our own desires or to the devil.
  (b) "Freedom from God's service is bondage."
  (c) The service of God is more honorable than possessing a kingdom.

(4) "Moreover, let us extend this even further, as Job has done."
  (a) The wicked think they can live well or ill as they like, because God's punishments are not apparent.
  (b) But we must hold to the truth of what Isaiah said: "There is good fruit for the righteous" (5:10). When we see con-

fusion in the world and it seems a mockery to serve God, we must trust in him that he will not disappoint our hope.

(c) God himself is our reward, as it says in Ps. 16:5 and Gen. 15:1.

5. "Now, there is still one word to note. It is that after Job had spoken of the service of God, in the second place he put prayer."

(1) Although service to our fellows is service to God, more is required—"prayers and orisons."

(2) A life unstained by gross vices and yet without religion or faith is not acceptable to God.

(3) The principal service of God is to call upon him.

(4) The conclusion: A life approved and accepted by God is one that trusts in him and has recourse to him and is loving towards our neighbors. "When, then, our life is thus ruled, it is the true service of God."

Bidding to prayer, relevant to the substance of the sermon.

The style in which Calvin constructed such sermons is exceedingly plain, but also exceedingly clear:

> Thought follows thought in careful, orderly arrangement without muddle, and each idea is expressed clearly, and often in two or three different ways, so that every member of the congregation might be able to understand.[52]

He is, indeed, one of the pioneers of French prose and the original model of that *clarté* on which the language has always prided itself.

Yet, as Parker has said, "He walks, and rarely soars."[53] His style of preaching is conversational and, in the service of being clearly understood, he sacrifices most of the ornaments that decorate writing. For instance, he seldom quotes anyone, although he was arguably the most learned man of Europe in his time. Yet neither does his preaching descend to the coarseness of Luther's—although he does employ the invective conventional in the polemical writing of the period. Nor does he often illustrate his points with stories or even employ imagery.

> His sermons are characterized by a gravity and earnestness springing from a profound realization of the urgency of the situation. Those to whom he preached were, he believed, either in a fearful plight under the wrath of God for their sin, or they were believers who needed to be encouraged and urged to strain every effort to arrive at the salvation which was theirs in heaven.[54]

So great was Calvin's earnestness that people asked: "Can they not preach without being angry?"[55] All of which is to say that his style was matched perfectly to his understanding of what he was hoping would be accomplished through the pulpit.

Preaching as Exegesis

Since Calvin understood preaching to be the exposition of the Word of God to the people assembled for worship, it is important to know how he went about the task of exegesis. Otherwise there is a danger of evaluating his accomplishment anachronistically. His humanistic training had developed in him a deep sense of need to return *ad fontes,* to the original languages of the texts he was interpreting, in order to recover the original meaning of the sacred writers. And his mastery of biblical languages was impressive.

Yet his understanding of "original meaning" was not the same as that of historical-critical biblical scholars of today. He lived before the Enlightenment, and he certainly did not have a modern fear of historical relativism. Furthermore, he acted out of two hermeneutical assumptions that are contrary to contemporary biblical interpretation: he postulated without question the unity and perfection of the Scriptures.[56] For instance, he presupposed without question the christological interpretation of the Hebrew Scriptures made by New Testament writers. This was not only their interpretation but the true interpretation—inspired by the Holy Spirit, who can be accurately spoken of as having dictated the sacred writings.

Thus what Calvin understood as the original meaning of a passage could be very different from what a modern exegete might understand. Nor would he assume that his interpretation of any key passage was just one theory proposed among many. The Spirit guided the faithful interpreter (and thus Calvin *a fortiori*) to discover in a passage the meaning the Spirit intended that passage to have. And this passage would be completely consistent with any other in the Holy Book because all had been dictated by the same Spirit to communicate the same gospel, and it was impossible for such divine efforts to meet with ambiguous or inconsistent results. Therefore, any apparently natural interpretation of a passage at odds with this overall teaching of the Bible was illusory and had to be explained away.

The overall teaching of the Bible is related to what Calvin meant by one of his key concepts, that of knowledge. He began the *Institutes* with the statement: "Nearly all the wisdom we possess, that is to say, true and sound wisdom, consists of two parts: knowledge of God and of ourselves" (1.1.1). Since this knowledge is acquired from Scripture, it amounts to the faith system Calvin found in the Bible. For him this most important knowledge, which he called the knowledge of faith, had to do with the doctrine of salvation of the elect through grace.

> In understanding faith it is not merely a question of knowing that God exists, but also—and this especially—of knowing what is his will toward us. For it is not so much our concern to know who he is in himself, as what he wills to be toward us. Now, therefore, we hold faith to be a knowledge of God's will toward us, perceived from his Word.[57]

This understanding of the meaning of the Bible is not only communicated through true preaching but is also given to the elect believer by the Holy Spirit. Indeed, it could almost be said that justification and the communication of this knowledge are the same act. For the elect believer, this knowledge, then, is knowledge of the gratuitous mercy of God.

> This knowledge of faith contains within itself the broad outlines of a more or less complete system of theology. It suggests a doctrine of man as incapable of saving himself. It points to Jesus Christ as the revelation of the divine will. Moreover, it proclaims that man's ineptness is overcome and Christ's work made effective through the work of the Holy Spirit. In short, one may say that Calvin's doctrine of faith summarizes in a general way the major themes discussed in Book II and Book III of the *Institutes.*[58]

In addition to this knowledge of faith, however, there is, as suggested above, a wider knowledge that includes knowledge of the Creator (the subject of Book 1) as well. Calvin also recognized a very propositional kind of knowledge, a kind of *fides quae creditur* in addition to the *fides qua creditur,* which was the knowledge of faith.[59] This knowledge is also important because the perfection of the Bible means there is nothing in it that it is not necessary for believers to know—otherwise the Spirit would not have dictated it.

Thus there is a full range of knowledge that is a matter of cognition, knowledge that may be arrived at deductively from reading the Bible. But the knowledge of faith, on the other hand, is a "firm and effectual confidence," a knowledge that has its seat in the heart rather than the head.[60] The knowledge of faith is saving knowledge, through which the believer is secure in being the object of the grace of Christ, and thus is enabled to participate in Christ.

This knowledge is communicated to the elect in two ways. One is directly into the heart by the Spirit. But the other is through preaching. These two reinforce one another. No wonder that Calvin, believing this, preached with such earnestness and solemnity.[61]

FOR FURTHER READING

Bouwsma, William J. *John Calvin: A Sixteenth-Century Portrait.* New York and Oxford: Oxford University Press, 1988.

Calvin, John. *Sermons from Job.* Translated by Leroy Nixon. Grand Rapids, Mich.: Eerdmans, 1952.

Calvin: Institutes of the Christian Religion. Edited by John T. McNeill, translated and indexed by Ford Lewis Battles. LCC. Philadelphia: Westminster, 1960.

Parker, T. H. L. *Calvin's Preaching.* Edinburgh: T&T Clark, 1992.

Spiritual and Anabaptist Writers. Edited by George H. Williams and Anjel M. Mergal. LCC. Philadelphia: Westminster, 1957.

Notes

1. Steven E. Ozment, *The Age of Reform (1250–1550): An Intellectual and Religious History of Late Medieval and Reformation Europe* (New Haven, Conn.: Yale University Press, 1980), 318-24.

2. Calvin, who gave the definitive form to Swiss Reform preaching, did not want this sort of liturgy, preferring instead for the Eucharist to be celebrated every Sunday. He could never persuade the town council of Geneva to support him in this ideal, however.

3. Yngve Brilioth, *A Brief History of Preaching,* trans. Karl E. Mattson, The Preacher's Paperback Library (Philadelphia: Fortress, 1965), 152.

4. This chapter has been revised in the light of a conversation with Prof. Thomas Finger of Eastern Mennonite Seminary, held over March 13-16, 1991, in Irving, Texas. Assertions growing out of that discussion will be documented as "Finger conversation."

5. Ozment, *The Age of Reform,* 340.

6. Ibid., 341, quoting from Roland H. Bainton, *Studies in the Reformation,* collected papers in church history, series 2 (Boston: Beacon Press, 1963), II, 199.

7. Bainton, *Studies in the Reformation.* See the Finger conversation.

8. *Spiritual and Anabaptist Writers,* ed. George H. Williams and Anjel M. Mergal, LCC (Philadelphia: Westminster, 1957), 21. Williams's interpretation of these movements is developed on an impressive scale in *The Radical Reformation* (Philadelphia: Westminster, 1959).

9. *Spiritual and Anabaptist Writers,* 19-38.

10. For an account of this recent process of rehabilitation see Franklin H. Littell, *The Origins of Sectarian Protestantism: A Study of the Anabaptist View of the Church* (New York: Macmillan, 1964, 1958, 1952). This work was originally published as *The Anabaptist View of the Church.*

11. Finger conversation.

12. This reconstruction is based on Littell, *The Origins of Sectarian Protestantism,* and is in accord with what is said by Williams and others. It should be noted, however, that not all accept this understanding. See Ozment, *The Age of Reform,* 340-51.

13. So called to distinguish it from the Lutheran, Calvinist, and Anglican movements.

14. In "An Annotated Bibliography on Published Mennonite Sermons," *Mennonite Quarterly Review* 27 (1953): 144, Harold S. Bender and N. P. Springer say, "The only known published discussion of the history of Mennonite preaching outside of Holland is that by H. G. Mannhardt in *Mennonitische Blätter,* 38:18f., 22f., 37f. (1891)." Reference is then made to Roy Umble's Northwestern University dissertation, "Mennonite Preaching," which is summarized in the same issue of *MQR,* pp. 137-42. Bender, however, was to expand his bibliographical annotations into the article on "Sermons" in *The Mennonite Encyclopedia* (1959), occasionally using the same phraseology. This article, in turn, is followed by one on "Sermons, Hutterite" by Robert Friedmann, thus extending the coverage to the other main body existing today that grew out of Anabaptistry per se. Evangelical Rationalism did influence modern English and American Unitarianism through Socinius's impact on England. Hans J. Hillerbrand includes a reference to C. J. Dyck, "The Role of Preaching in Anabaptist Tradition," *Mennonite Life* 27 (1962): 21-26, in *A Bibliography of Anabaptism, 1520–1630. A Sequel—1962–1974,* Sixteenth Century Bibliography 1 (St. Louis: Center for Reformation Research, 1975), 51, but I have not been able to see the Dyck article.

15. Bender, "Sermons," 4:503. Finger says that evangelism was probably the chief use of sermons. Anabaptist gatherings probably consisted of informal teaching, prayer, and mutual exhortation in which many participated. Holy Communion was also held frequently. The centrality of preaching in Reformation worship grows out of an assumption that many church members were unconverted, an assumption the Anabaptists did not make. Further, it presupposes one main leader in worship, which the Anabaptists did not have. Finger conversation.

16. Umble, "Mennonite Preaching," 141.

17. Friedmann, "Sermons, Hutterite," 4:505. Actually, two types of sermons were copied and read, *Lehren* and *Vorreden.* The *Lehren* were verse-by-verse exegeses of entire chapters of the Bible, while the *Vorreden* were expositions of single verses. Seldom are *Lehren* read in their entirety anymore, although sections from them make up the second half of the service, with a *Vorrede* serving as a part of the devotional first half. The sermons are read in High German, although the community speaks a Tyrolean-Bavarian dialect in ordinary conversation. Yet they are very fond of this preaching that they call "sharp" because of "the outspokenness of the instruction concerning the meaning of the scriptural texts and its application to everyday life, realizing that it is this biblical radicalism which distinguishes their piety and life from all their surroundings" (ibid.).

18. "For use in home worship."

19. John (Jean, Joannes) latinized the family name to Calvinus when he went to the University of Paris.

20. John T. McNeill, *The History and Character of Calvinism* (New York: Oxford University Press, 1954), 94. This biographical sketch is derived from McNeill, 93-234, and William J. Bouwsma, *John Calvin: A Sixteenth-Century Portrait* (New York and Oxford: Oxford University Press, 1988). Not long after arriving at Paris, Calvin transferred to the Collège de Montaigu, a college noted for its orthodoxy and discipline that numbered both Erasmus and Rabelais among its disgruntled alumni.

21. For a list of the teachers and their individual contributions, see McNeill, *The History and Character of Calvinism,* 95-106. For another good but slightly different analysis of the intellectual influences on Calvin during his student days, see Thomas F. Torrance, *The Hermeneutics of John Calvin* (Edinburgh: Scottish Academic Press, 1988). See also the chapter on "John Calvin and the Rhetorical Tradition" in Quirinius Breen, *Christianity and Humanism: Studies in the History of Ideas,* ed. Nelson Peter Ross (Grand Rapids, Mich.: Eerdmans, 1968), 107-29.

22. Calvin consulted him on the eve of his break with Rome, but nothing is known of Lefèvre's advice.

23. *Calvin's Commentary on Seneca's De Clementia,* ed. with intro., trans., and notes Ford Lewis Battles and André Malan Hugo (Leiden: E. J. Brill for the Renaissance Society of America, 1969). For a concise statement of the nature of the commentary and Calvin's purposes in writing it, see pp. 72-74.

24. Bouwsma, *John Calvin: A Sixteenth Century Portrait,* 9 and *passim.*

25. The Dedication to the commentary on the Psalms is quoted in the translation of Joseph Haroutunian in *Calvin: Commentaries,* LCC (Philadelphia: Westminster, 1958), 51-57, especially p. 52. The standard edition of the works of Calvin in the original Latin and/or French is *Joannis Calvini Opera quae supersunt omnia,* ed. G. Baum, E. Cunitz, and E. Reuss, Corpus Reformatorum (Brunswick and Berlin: C. A. Schwetschke et filium, 1863–1900; reprint, New York and London: Johnson Reprint Corp., 1964). Not included in this are a number of sermons to be discussed later. The standard English version of Calvin's Old Testament commentaries is the nineteenth-century Calvin Translation Society edition published in Edinburgh. There is a translation of the New Testament commentaries edited by David W. and Thomas F. Torrance, published in Grand Rapids between 1963 and 1974.

26. Bouwsma, *John Calvin: A Sixteenth Century Portrait,* 11.

27. Ibid., 12.

28. John T. McNeill, "Introduction," *Calvin: Institutes of the Christian Religion,* ed. John T. McNeill, trans. and indexed Ford Lewis Battles, LCC (Philadelphia: Westminster, 1960), 1:xxxv.

29. McNeill, *The History and Character of Calvinism,* 131.

30. Haroutunian, *Calvin: Commentaries,* 53.

31. I regret that I was not able to consult Benoit Girardin, *Rhétorique et Théologique: Calvin, Le Commentaire de l'Épitre aux Romans,* ThH, no. 54 (Paris: Éditions Beauchesne, 1979), before writing this chapter. It would have contributed a great deal to my understanding of Calvin's humanistic perspective and the way that theology and rhetoric were intertwined in his biblical interpretation and, therefore, preaching.

32. T. H. L. Parker, *The Oracles of God: An Introduction to the Preaching of John Calvin* (London and Redhill: Lutterworth, 1947), 33. Since this chapter was written, Parker has published a much longer study, *Calvin's Preaching* (Edinburgh: T&T Clark, 1992). It was impossible to recast the entire chapter in the light of this later work, but insights from it are incorporated where they seemed most to demand inclusion.

33. Richard Stauffer, *Un Calvin méconnu: le prédicateur de Genève, Bulletin de Société de l'histoire du Protestantisme français* 23 (1977): 188.

34. *Institutes,* 4.1.9.

35. McNeill, *The History and Character of Calvinism,* 188.

36. The series, under the general editorship of Erwin Mülhaupt, is published by Neukirchener Verlag des Erziehungsvereins in Neukirchen-Vluyn. Accounts of the misadventures of the manuscripts can be found in Stauffer, *Un Calvin méconnu;* Erwin Mülhaupt, "Calvin's 'Sermons inedits': *Vorgeschichte, Überlieferung und gegenwärtiger Stand der Edition,*" in *Der Prediger Johannes Calvin: Beiträge und Nachrichten zur Ausgabe der Supplementa Calviniana,* ed. Karl Halaski (Neukirchen-Vluyn: Neukirchener Verlag des Erziehungsvereins, 1966), 25-33; and T. H. L. Parker, *Supplementa Calviniana: An Account of the Manuscripts of Calvin's Sermons Now in the Course of Preparation* (London: Tyndale, 1962). See also John H. Leith, "Calvin's Doctrine of the Proclamation of the Word and Its Significance for Today," in *John Calvin and the Church: A Prism of Reform,* ed. Timothy George (Louisville: Westminster John Knox, 1990), 207.

37. When one turns to English translations of Calvin's sermons, the neglect is even more obvious. An advertisement of *A Selection of the Most Celebrated Sermons of John Calvin, Minister of the Gospel, and One of the Principal Leaders of the Protestant Reformation,* ed. John Forbes (New York: S. & D.A. Forbes, Printers, 1830), says that "Calvin's Sermons were translated and published in England, about the year 1580; since which date we have no account of an edition having been published." When William B. Eerdmans of Grand Rapids reprinted the Forbes edition in 1950, their advertisement said that it was "the only sizeable collection of John Calvin's sermons translated into the English language since the sixteenth century and the only volume ever published in America." The Forbes volume was copied in 1831 by T. Desilver Jr. of Philadelphia. In 1950 Eerdmans began to issue a series of volumes of sermon translations by Leroy Nixon. These include *The Deity of Christ, and Other Sermons* (1950), *Sermons from Job* (1952), and *The Gospel According to Isaiah* (1953). To this all too short list may be added *Sermons on Micah by Jean Calvin,* trans. Blair Reynolds, Texts and Studies in Religion, vol. 47 (Lewiston: Edwin Mellen, 1990), a translation of vol. 5 of *Supplementa Calviniana* and thus a volume that allows English readers to get a sense of what Calvin's course preaching must have been like.

38. This section is based on Parker, *The Oracles of God,* 45-64, and Haroutunian, *Calvin's Commentaries,* 392-406.

39. Calvin did not believe that women should speak in church. *Inst.* 4.15.20-22.

40. Parker, *The Oracles of God,* 55.

41. Commentary on John 14:26, *Calvini Opera* (hereafter referred to as CO) 47:334-35. Quoted in Haroutunian, *Calvin: Commentaries,* 397. This volume is

arranged to present topically the doctrine Calvin teaches in the commentaries, with the squibs quoted following citation of the biblical verse on which the comment is made. Thus the only indication of the particular commentary from which the quotation is extracted is the naming of the book from which the verse is taken.

42. Ibid.

43. Ronald S. Wallace, *Calvin's Doctrine of the Word and Sacrament* (Edinburgh and London: Oliver & Boyd, 1953), 83.

44. Parker, *The Oracles of God,* 50. His reference is to CO. 25:646.

45. Haroutunian, *Calvin's Commentaries,* 396.

46. Calvin's comment on Isaiah 55:11 as quoted in Wallace, *Calvin's Doctrine of the Word and Sacrament,* 93.

47. CO 26:66.

48. Parker, *The Oracles of God,* 57.

49. J. L. Ainslie, *The Doctrine of Ministerial Order in the Reformed Churches of the Sixteenth and Seventeenth Centuries,* 43, quoted by Parker, *The Oracles of God,* 61.

50. Quoted from the translation of the commentary on 1 Corinthians in the Calvin Society edition of the *Works,* 77 (CO 49:322) by Parker, *The Oracles of God,* 65. This section will draw heavily upon ibid., 65-80. Virtually useless for an understanding of the manner (as opposed to the content) of Calvin's preaching is Leroy Nixon, *John Calvin, Expository Preacher* (Grand Rapids, Mich.: Eerdmans, 1950), 27-45, which consists almost exclusively of extended quotations from hagiographic turn-of-the-century histories of preaching.

51. Parker, *The Oracles of God,* 71-72. The following outline is taken from Parker, *Calvin's Preaching,* 133-36.

52. Parker, *The Oracles of God,* 77.

53. Ibid., 75.

54. Ibid., 75-76.

55. Ibid., citing CO 35:12.

56. What follows is closely based on H. Jackson Forstman, *Word and Spirit: Calvin's Doctrine of Biblical Authority* (Stanford: Stanford University Press, 1962), 106-23. His treatment of Calvin's understanding of the unity and perfection of the Scriptures occupies pp. 109-12.

57. John T. McNeill, translation of *Inst.* 3.2.6 in *The History and Character of Calvinism.*

58. Forstman, *Word and Spirit,* 92.

59. Ibid., 89-105.

60. Ibid., 101. Quoted from Calvin's commentary on Romans 10:10.

61. For a very similar interpretation but one that grows out of an analysis of Calvin's thought in terms of influences upon it, see Torrance, *The Hermeneutics of John Calvin,* Part II: "The Shaping of Calvin's Mind," 61-165. See also Parker, *Calvin's Preaching,* 93-107.

CHAPTER 14

THE PREACHING OF CATHOLIC REFORM

In this more ecumenical age of church historiography, the sixteenth-century reforming activities of those who remained within the communion of Rome are no longer seen as merely a reaction to the threat to the church posed by Protestant separation.[1] Rather, they are seen to have antedated that and to have a validity of their own, representing the same impulses as those reflected in the work of the Reformers. Thus Steven Ozment can say:

> Modern historians interpret the Counter Reformation of the sixteenth century as less a reaction to the success of Protestantism than the continuation of late medieval efforts to reform the medieval church.[2]

He goes on to cite the conclusion of H. O. Evennett:

> The Reformation on its religious side and the Counter Reformation on its religious side can reasonably be regarded as two different outcomes of the [same] general aspiration toward religious regeneration which pervaded late fifteenth and early sixteenth century Europe.[3]

So much is this the case that the traditional term, "Counter Reformation," is now questioned as the definitive categorization to use when discussing this movement. Originated by polemical German Protestant scholars to suggest that any reforming activity within Rome was a purely defensive reaction to what Luther and Calvin had done, the term was picked up by other scholars to refer to what was considered to be the repressiveness of the movement's institutions. Then Italian intellectuals like Benedetto Croce adopted it to designate Italian baroque, a cultural decline they blamed on the church after the Council of Trent.[4]

So pervasive has this negative understanding of Counter Reformation been that it has affected the judgment of even Catholic scholars on the worth of its products. An example of this trend in the area of homiletics is the way that J. B. Schneyer "dismisses the whole phenomenon of Renaissance preaching in Italy and Spain with four pages in his *Geschichte der katholischen Predigt* (Freiburg, 1969)."[5]

It would, however, be possible to overcorrect, to act as though none of the motivation for reform within the Roman communion were occasioned by the successes of Protestants. Hubert Jedin has proposed using the term "Catholic Reform" to designate the movement in its aspect of continuity, and "Counter Reformation" when referring to it as a response to the Protestant Reformation.[6] This distinction makes it easier to be precise and to avoid value-laden vocabulary.

THE ROLE OF PREACHING

A very important place is assigned to preaching in both of these aspects of Catholic renewal. This may be seen in four of the most important channels of reform: religious orders in general, the Jesuits in particular, the Council of Trent, and missionary activity.

The Religious Orders

Besides humanism, the three reforming movements that A. G. Dickens traces back to the fifteenth century are all related to communities of monks and friars.[7] These include the *devotio moderna,* developed among the Augustinian canons of Windesheim and spread to the Brothers of the Common Life; the Observant movement, arising among the Franciscans; and the renewal of the Carthusians. In addition to these, the fire of Savonarola and the passion of Luther testify to spiritual vitality among the Dominicans and Augustinian friars. While it was among these groups that the real vitality remaining in the religious life at the end of the fifteenth century was to be found, all of these were more concerned with developing the spiritual lives of their members than with reforming the church at large. The mendicant orders still supplied most of the trained and skillful Catholic preachers, but it was time for new orders to be created to minister to the overwhelming needs of a new generation.

The first indication of the changes to come was not an order as such, but only a confraternity for laity and clergy interested in working to increase their personal holiness and practical charity, the Oratory of Divine Love.[8] The first Oratory was founded at Vicenza in 1494 and the second at Genoa. The movement spread to Rome and between 1517 and 1527 came to involve a group of outstanding persons who were to have significant roles in the reforming activity that changed the religious face of the Roman church. Among these were a number of bishops: Jacopo Sadoleto of Carpentras, Giovanni Matteo Giberti of Verona, and Giovanni Pietro Caraffa of Chieti.[9] Luigi Lippomano was one of Giberti's successors in Verona while Gaetano da Tiene, along with Caraffa, was founder of the Theatine order and was later to be canonized as Saint Caejetan. When driven from the city by the sack of Rome in 1527, this group fled to Venice, where they added a number of other distinguished colleagues to their ranks.

Pope Paul III recognized their abilities and made six of them cardinals. Later he largely committed to them the task of drawing up a plan for reform of the church. Presented to the pope in 1537, the plan bore the title of *Consilium delectorum cardinalium ... de emendanda ecclesia*. After stating that the main cause of everything wrong with the church was the belief that the pontiff could sell benefices as though they were personal property, they listed particular abuses, most of which had to do with practices that interfered with the effectiveness of clergy. The spiritual welfare of the people in their care should be the only consideration in their appointment. Other abuses such as absenteeism and pluralism were also attacked, and stricter discipline was advocated for religious orders. The ability to teach the faith and to deal with sin was crucial to the effectiveness they sought. Thus the *Consilium* said: "Care must be taken that their preachers and confessors are fit men, and not admitted to their office except after examination by their bishop."[10] The report was so devastating and so embarrassing to the papacy that it was not published officially, but it undoubtedly did a great deal to prepare the way for Trent.[11]

As important as the Oratory of Divine Love was, there existed a widespread recognition that the cause of reform needed stronger ties than the loose association of a sodality; the life vows of religious communities seemed called for. Gaetano da Tiene considered the poor quality of secular clergy to be the main thing wrong with the church. His idea for reform was not unlike that of the Augustinian canons of the early Middle Ages: an order of clerks regular who would live together in community under vows of poverty, chastity, and obedience while carrying on parochial ministry.[12] In founding the order, the practical skills of Caraffa were united with the vision of Gaetano. Though the Theatines, as they were called, lived the life of the poor, they came from the aristocracy and many became bishops.

Three other orders of regular clerics were formed. The Paulines, who came to be called Barnabites after they took charge of the St. Barnabas church in Milan, were more at home among the masses. They were concerned with the religious instruction of the young and general pastoral care. Open-air preaching missions were one of their most effective tools. The bishop of Milan, Charles Borromeo,[13] made great use of them. The Somaschi were founded to take care of children who were orphaned or rendered homeless in the wars that had ravished the Italian peninsula. Intellectually, one of the most vigorous of the new orders was the Oratorians,[14] founded by Philip Neri through what had started out as informal gatherings of students and young clergy for conferences and music.[15] This order also spread rapidly, although in France it took a form slightly different from its form in Italy.[16]

A different type of new order was the Capuchins, a reform movement within the Franciscans devoted to Saint Francis's ideals of care for the poor and suffering, and preaching to the people. Unfortunately for them, their leader and most popular preacher, Bernardino Ochino, was so attracted to the cause of Reformation that he went over to the Protestants, serving in several countries and churches before ending up as a Polish Unitarian. Yet the Capuchins survived the adverse publicity and were by far the largest and most important of the new orders.

What Owen Chadwick said of the entire movement describes especially well the spirit of these religious communities:

> If we seek a single theme running through the reforming endeavors of the Catholic Reformation, it would be the quest for a more adequate clergy—better-trained and better-instructed priests, priests resident in their parishes, bishops resident in their sees, pastors fervent and self-sacrificing and missionary-minded, trained as confessors, celibate, mortified, able to teach in school, wearing canonical dress; a priesthood uncorrupted and incorruptible, educated and other-worldly.[17]

While he does not explicitly list preaching among these desiderata, others did. The place it occupies in such a program is obvious.

The Society of Jesus

If all the new orders exemplified the ideals of the Catholic Reformation as listed by Chadwick, none did so more than the Jesuits. Indeed, the papal bull confirming the order[18] contains a similar summary, describing the Jesuits as

> a Society founded to concern itself above all for the advancement of souls in Christian life and doctrine, for the propagation of the faith by public preaching, spiritual exercises and works of charity, and in particular for the Christian education of the young and the unlearned, as well as for the hearing of confessions.[19]

When Don Inigo de Onez y Loyola entered adult life, he had no thought of founding a religious order. Fond of the sort of courtly romances that inspired Don Quixote, Inigo lived at a time when there were still wars to be fought. When he was thirty and fighting in Charles V's defense of Pamplona against Francis I, he was wounded in both legs by a cannonball and spent a long time recovering. During his recuperation, a shortage of his favorite literature forced him to read devotional books for lack of anything else.

Being converted in the process, he left his sword on an altar of the Blessed Virgin Mary at Montserrat, took the dress of a beggar, and began a year's retreat in a cave near Manresa. During this time his own meditations gave him the insight to make an initial draft of his *Spiritual Exercises*. After making a pilgrimage to the Holy Land, he returned to Spain where he began to educate himself for the work that he felt lay ahead. In order to make sure that his foundation was firm, he sat in Latin class with schoolchildren in Barcelona before going on to university training in Alcalá and Salamanca. He preached in the streets until he was imprisoned twice by the Inquisition. Transferring to the University of Paris, he began to gather the nucleus of his order.

They left Paris intending to go on a missionary crusade to the Holy Land if possible, but resolving to stay in Rome and put themselves under the pope if the Middle East was closed to them. War between Venice and the Turks rendered eastern travel impossible. Thus they sojourned in Rome, where their distinctive vocation began to emerge in practice and to be spelled out in their preliminary draft of a rule. They felt that most devotions should be performed more often than had become customary.

They advocated more frequent confessions and Communions and even more frequent preaching, it being the custom in Rome at the time to have sermons only in the penitential seasons of Advent and Lent. Once again their enthusiasm caused them to be suspected of heresy, but investigation brought exoneration. Ignatius (he had begun to use this Latin form of his name) was ordained at Venice and thus was able to say his first Mass on Christmas Day in 1538. In less than two years, their preliminary rule was accepted and summarized by the pope in the bull in which he confirmed it.[20]

The apostolic, missionary, catechetical, and homiletical character of the Jesuits' ministry was obvious from the very beginning. Salmeron's sermons at Brescia and Belluno, for instance, began to attract huge crowds. Lainez's congregations at Florence must have rivaled those of Savonarola half a century earlier. Peter Cannisius was able to reclaim southern Germany from the Reformation. Francis Xavier took the gospel to India and Japan.

The tasks of preaching and teaching were combined in one particular homiletical genre, that of the sacred lecture.[21] In addition to preaching both at the liturgy and in the open air, Jesuits who were in a city for a protracted time gave series of lectures on Sunday afternoons or at other convenient times. Most often these would be on consecutive sections of biblical books, although they could be on such other topics as catechetical issues or "cases of conscience."

There were pre-Reformation precedents for such preaching, especially among the mendicant orders; some of the preaching of Savonarola is a case in point. It also resembles the sort of course preaching that Luther and others did at Wittenberg. Not surprisingly, some of the Jesuit lectures were Counter Reformation preaching in the strict sense of being used to refute such Protestant positions as the Lutheran interpretation of the Epistle to the Romans.

These sacred lectures differed from university courses on biblical books in both the popular audience for which they were prepared and the application of the teaching to people's lives. They represent the sort of aggressive effort put forth by the Jesuits to instruct the faithful that characterized the early life of their society.

The Council of Trent

From as early as the thirteenth century, there had been a strain of thought that became quite pronounced in the fifteenth, in which the supreme authority in the church was a general council. During the time of the Avignon papacy, councils were thought of as the way to resolve the claims of rival popes, and the Councils of Pisa (1409) and Constance (1414–18) had been resorted to as the means of healing the Great Schism. After there ceased to be multiple claimants to the papal throne, there then arose the problems associated with the Renaissance holders of the chair of Peter, not the least of which were the political activities that saw the Holy See competing militarily and diplomatically with the world powers of the time. Some conciliar theorists appealed to the example of Constantine assembling the bishops at Nicaea as justification for saying that the initiative for assembling a council lay with the civil authority. Popes had resisted appeals over their head to councils; Pius II went so far in 1460 as to promulgate *Exercrabilis,* a bull forbidding such actions.

After the Reformation had begun to divide his territory into warring factions, the emperor Charles V began to urge a council as a way of reuniting his realm. The empire and the papacy, however, were not the only vested interests within the Catholic world. Francis I was so eager to pursue French interests against the Holy Roman Empire that he would even resort to alliance with Muslim Turks. And, devoted as he was to the defense of the Catholic faith, Philip II also had his own course to pursue in the interests of Spain.

Charles appeared to be on the way to an initial success in 1541 when, concurrently with an imperial diet there, a colloquy was held in Regensberg or Ratisbon, the hometown of the popular medieval preacher Berthold. The Protestants had such distinguished representatives as Melanchthon, Martin Bucer, and a very young John Calvin, while the Catholic delegation included a range of opinion from irenic Erasmians to the aggressive Johannes Eck.

The most influential Catholic, though, and the pope's representative, was Cardinal Contarini, one of the old members of the Oratory of Divine Love. He had enough sympathy with an Augustinian theology to approve a statement on justification, which seemed to open the possibility of compromise and negotiation. When the discussion moved on to sacraments, however, he was so firm in his commitment to transubstantiation that agreement would have been impossible, even if all parties on both sides had been willing to accept the statement on justification—which they were not. And so the most promising effort to reunite European Christendom foundered.

After a great deal of maneuvering back and forth, Paul III called a council that finally convened in 1545 at a town in the Italian Alps called Trent.[22] Contrary to everyone's expectations, it dealt with the issues at hand, spreading its deliberations over three periods and eighteen years.

By the time the council actually met, the emperor was the only one still interested in reunion. The results could be roughly summarized by saying that *theological* decisions in general had the effect of reaffirming medieval positions against Protestant efforts at revision, while *practical* decisions were usually in the direction of reforming abuses.[23] The council's efforts were remarkably successful. Its decisions stood the test of time and in retrospect appear far more nuanced than anyone would have guessed when they were being made. It is quite appropriate, therefore, that the character of church life achieved by the Counter Reformation is called post-Tridentine.

The practical reforms achieved by Trent bear out Chadwick's contention that the most consistent theme of the Catholic Reformation was the search for a more adequate clergy. In this program nothing was more important than preaching. At the Fifth Session (June 17, 1546) there was passed a Decree on Reformation, which began by providing lectureships on Scripture for schools at every level and quickly went on to discuss preachers of the Word of God:

> But seeing that the preaching of the Gospel is no less necessary to the Christian commonwealth than the reading thereof; and whereas this is the principal duty of bishops; the same holy Synod hath resolved and decreed, that all bishops, primates, and all other prelates of the churches be bound personally—if they be not lawfully hindered—to preach the holy Gospel of Jesus Christ.[24]

Those who are "lawfully hindered" must appoint competent substitutes. Anyone with a cure of souls

> shall, at least on the Lord's days, and solemn feasts . . . feed the people committed to them with wholesome words, according to their own capacity, and that of their people; by teaching them the things which it is necessary for all to know unto salvation, and by announcing to them with briefness and plainness of discourse, the vices which they must avoid, and the virtues which they must follow after, that they may escape everlasting punishment, and obtain the glory of heaven.[25]

There follows a provision of disciplinary measures to be taken against those who neglect this duty. Next are regulations concerning the licenses needed by members of religious orders who preach, the steps to be taken when someone preaches heresy, what to do about religious who live outside their houses and try to preach, and prohibition of preaching by anyone in quest of alms.

Many of these provisions are repeated in chapter 4 of the Decree on Reformation promulgated at the twenty-fourth session, with the additional stipulations that daily or at least triweekly sermons be preached during Advent and Lent, that the people be admonished to attend sermons, and that

> the said bishops shall also take care, that, at least on the Lord's Days and other festivals, the children in every parish be carefully taught the rudiments of the faith, and obedience towards God, and their parents, by those whose duty it is.[26]

Closely connected with this concern for preaching is the desire of the council that clergy be trained so that they can exercise responsibly their duty of preaching, which is reflected in the directive that seminaries be established:

> The holy Synod ordains, that all cathedral, metropolitan, and other churches greater than these, shall be bound, each according to its means and the extent of the diocese, to maintain, to educate religiously, and to train in ecclesiastical discipline, a certain number of youths . . . in a college to be chosen by the bishop for that purpose.[27]

The relevance of the curriculum for homiletics is obvious:

> They shall learn grammar, singing, ecclesiastical computation, and the other liberal arts; they shall be instructed in sacred scripture; ecclesiastical works; the homilies of the saints; the manner of administering the sacraments, especially those things which shall seem adapted to enable them to hear confessions; and the forms and rites of the ceremonies.[28]

Provision is then made for the adequate financing of the seminaries and for the appointment of competent faculty.

One can see the extent of change these standards imply by looking at the system in France, where the decree on seminaries was late in being implemented. "The idea that an advanced secular education and a decent family were sufficient qualification for the cleric held good until the second half of the (seventeenth) century."[29] Trent was destined to make a great deal of difference in the emphasis placed on preaching and the training for it in the Roman Catholic Church.

Missionary Activity

For a number of reasons, missionary activity—whether directed at reviving the faithful at home, wooing back adherents who had been proselytized, or evangelizing non-Christian foreigners—was much more characteristic of Catholic Reform than it was of the Protestant Reformation. "It is perhaps in this sphere that true originality and enterprise found their most congenial spheres within the Counter Reformation church."[30] Sufficiently preoccupied with preserving their competitive edge against one another or resisting Counter Reformation efforts to recover lost flocks, the Reformed churches often found themselves left with little attention to devote to new fields. Then, too, efforts to convert the unsaved seemed blasphemous to thoroughgoing double-predestinarians. And most of the voyages of discovery were conducted by representatives of countries that remained in communion with Rome.[31] To give some degree of consistency to this worldwide missionary enterprise, the *Congregatio de Propaganda Fide* was formed in 1622. As always in the history of Christian missionary activity, preaching was an important medium for spreading the faith.

THE BEGINNINGS OF THE REVIVAL

In an essay published in 1988, Peter Bayley discussed the current state of the investigation of preaching from the early modern period in the history of Catholicism. After showing how disadvantaged the historian of preaching in this period is compared with patristic or medieval colleagues, he outlines the work that needs to be done: the search of libraries for sermons and preaching aids from the period, the coordination of knowledge of composition principles followed in sermon writing, and the pooling of information for a more comparative perspective. The completion of these scholarly tasks, he says, will permit the evaluation of the best hypothesis that the current state of knowledge will permit. He phrases his hypothesis in this way:

> that the ideals of Trent, coinciding as they did with the revival of antique rhetoric, evolved into theories in strong Counter Reformation centers like Borromeo's circle in Milan and, fertilized by contact with cultivated Renaissance minds like Luis de Granada in Spain and disseminated by innumerable handbooks, became by those very methods of dissemination the stuff and texture of the European Catholic sermon for two hundred years.[32]

Although Bayley warns that attempts at general surveys in the history of preaching "end up as compilations of out-dated second-hand material and opinions,"[33] the writers of such surveys have little choice but to accept the conventional wisdom in each discrete area of research and synthesize it with findings from other periods. A single scholar could never hope to do for all periods what the combined efforts of specialists in those periods have not been able to accomplish for them individually.

Thus, having observed the factors in Catholic Reform that dictated a renewed emphasis on preaching, it is now time to begin to state what is known about how that preaching developed. After a look at the work of Borromeo, there will be a summary of studies of sermons and the theories on which they were constructed in the two countries on which such investigations have been made, Spain and France.[34] In the look at French preaching, Bayley can at least have the consolation that the "out-dated second-hand materials and opinions" are his own.

Charles Borromeo

Although many of the abuses of the Renaissance papacy resulted from the tendency of its occupants to treat the Holy See as a family business, there is one occasion upon which all authorities will agree that nepotism was a good thing: the time in 1560 when Pius IV made his nephew Charles Borromeo cardinal and archbishop of Milan. This appointment made it possible for Borromeo to become the preeminent example of how a bishop went about translating Trent's decrees into policy and action. (For a sermon about Borromeo, **see Vol. 2, pp. 277-95.**) In no area was his leadership more important than in the implementation of the Tridentine decrees on preaching. Taking seriously the statement that preaching is the principal duty *(praecipuum munus)* of bishops, he was an indefatigable preacher himself, he issued an instruction to his clergy about their obligation, and he encouraged others to write treatises on preaching.[35]

In order to assess the role of Borromeo in the history of Catholic Reform preaching, John O'Malley began by looking at the homiletics textbooks produced under the influence of the archbishop of Milan. He points out that at the beginning of the sixteenth century, the only treatise on the subject in print other than the *Artes praedicandi* of medieval thematic preaching was Augustine's *De doctrina christiana.* The great turning point came in 1535 when Erasmus published his *Ecclesiastes,* which introduced classical rhetoric and patristic homiletics as furnishing alternatives to thematic preaching. While, for a variety of reasons given in chapter 11, Erasmus's work was more important as a milestone than as a ready tool, Catholics were ready for a new method of preaching by the time the Tridentine decrees were published—a method that would move beyond not only the thematic sermon but also the patristic homily, one that would reflect on how the principles of classical rhetoric could be combined with the Christian necessity of explicating biblical texts.

It was at this point Borromeo entered the scene. His contribution reflects his background. Having been only twenty-one when his uncle ascended to the Holy See and, in the Renaissance tradition, immediately appointed him as his secretary of state, Borromeo had a humanistic university education but no formal schooling in theology. In Rome he had helped organize the *Noctes Vaticanae*, a group that studied classical and patristic writers, including rhetoricians and Stoic philosophers.[36] When he took up residence in Milan, then, and began to put the Tridentine legislation into practice, much of his understanding of what preaching, the "principal duty of bishops," should be like was shaped by his study of rhetoric and pagan ethics. This, connected with the Franciscan language of the conciliar decree on preaching, meant that when he was in the pulpit, he continued the moralistic emphasis of the Middle Ages.

Although regard for preaching was characteristic of the provincial synods Borromeo held in Milan, it was not until 1576 that he issued his own developed statement on the subject, *Instructiones praedicationis verbi Dei*.[37] His understanding there of the subject matter of sermons is "sins, occasions of sin, virtues, and, finally, the sacraments and other holy usages of the church"[38]—in other words, the moralistic emphasis expected. Missing is "any developed 'theology of the Word' or 'theology of the minister of the Word.'"[39] He does deal with the *ethos* of the preacher, which turns out to be a very clerical style of life. His lack of theological training made it inevitable that the instruction would be somewhat lacking as a theoretical statement, but, coupled with his indefatigable example[40] in exercising the *praecipuum munus*, it meant that he was extraordinarily influential in recommending the implementation of the Tridentine legislation about preaching.

Like many other preachers, his practice was better than his theory, moving beyond Stoic morality to a deep grounding in the Christian understanding of creation and redemption. The sermons take cognizance of the liturgical occasion and are based on the appointed lections. Francis de Sales pointed out that while Borromeo's theological knowledge was meager, it was sufficient for effective preaching.[41]

More important than his own theoretical work in preaching is that which he inspired and commissioned in others. Since Erasmus's work had been placed on the Vatican's Index of Prohibited Books, several Catholic manuals were published that stressed classical rhetoric and showed various degrees of dependency upon such Protestant writers as Melanchthon and Hyperius. Borromeo, however, asked his friend Agostino Valier (Valerio), Bishop of Verona, to produce a volume of "ecclesiastical rhetoric." Valier's *De rhetorica ecclesiastica* was first published in 1574 and reprinted often. Soon it was followed by similar works by the Spanish authors Luis de Granada and Diego de Estella.

> These three books were characterized by their comprehensiveness, their easy intelligibility, their organizational clarity, and their grasp of both the classical and patristic traditions.... They mark a great watershed not only for the sixteenth century but for the entire history of preaching in the Roman Catholic Church.[42]

All of these works and others as well owe at least some of their inspiration to the archbishop of Milan, but they do not exhaust his contributions to preaching. He also imported effective preachers into his archdiocese to teach his clergy by precept and example. Quoting Fumaroli to the effect that Borromeo created an "atelier for preaching established at Milan," O'Malley corrects him by saying, "It would be more adequate to the reality to speak of a huge 'industry.'"[43] He goes on to conclude that Borromeo "is a major figure and a chief promoter of the extraordinary enthusiasm for the ministry of the Word in the sixteenth century, which . . . was just as characteristic of Catholicism as it was of Protestantism."

Catholic Reform Preaching in Spain

Anticipating O'Malley's comment, Hilary Dansey Smith says:

> Catholics and Protestants seem to have been possessed of an equally voracious appetite for sermons, to judge by the numbers of them to appear in print as the (seventeenth) century progresses, and by the persistent homiletic strain which runs through contemporary prose fiction, particularly in Spain.[44]

These sermons were preached not only in churches but in hospitals and out of doors as well. Even "processions of flagellants and *autos-de-fe* were accompanied by sermons."[45] The sermons were preached by some bishops, by priests with a cure of souls, and by religious who were licensed to do so. During Lent and Advent, there were extra sermons in the afternoon in addition to those preached at Mass. As time went on, the recognition made by Trent that education was required to do such preaching became more general, the increase in the quantity of sermons having created a demand for a similar increase in quality.

Many Spanish sermons from the period were published. Some appeared individually as occasional sermons *(sueltos)* for such events as funerals or saints' days; these were occasionally collected into books. Others were published in *sermonarios* that "represent a preacher's personal selection of his sermons, often spanning the whole of his preaching career."[46] The choice was made on the basis of the sermons' ability to serve as models for young clergy just learning the homiletical craft. While some of the *sermonario* sermons were *ad status,* most had been composed for either the temporal or the sanctoral lectionary cycle.

Since most of the sermons were originally delivered from notes, the published form does not represent a verbatim account of what was actually said. Instead, it could depend either on what the preacher wrote up for publication or on—sometimes quite accurate—notes taken by members of the congregation. Such collections were also used as devotional reading by the laity. From their published form it can be seen that the sermons were delivered in the vernacular; this genre was one of those through which written Spanish was being developed. The average published sermon must have taken about an hour to deliver. In terms of style,

> what distinguishes this genre is a particular form, or *dispositio*, which . . . lends itself to parody by virtue of being quite easy to recognize. There is always a single main text *(thema)*, and always a division of the text, traditionally a tripartite one in honour of the Trinity.[47]

Various types of outlines were followed in these sermons: the *sermón de un (solo) tema*, *homilia*, *paradoxon*,[48] or *panegyrico*.

Whichever sort of sermon was preached, all tried to fulfill Cicero's three duties of an orator: to prove, to please, and to move. These are usually met in the parts of the speech in which they were classically expected, so that pleasure was communicated in the exordium, reason in the proposition and confirmation, and emotional appeal in the peroration. The three most common figures of thought were exempla, comparisons (similes in which "the more concrete, visible term of comparison illuminates the abstract, invisible one"),[49] and conceits.

The textbooks of the time used various poetic ways of talking about all this. They also offered advice about gestures. Some preachers extended these latter to include "audiovisuals" and other dramatic effects, the least of which was holding a crucifix while they preached. Others, however, were willing to rely upon words alone to create what has been called "virtual experience," a sense of having participated in a described event.[50]

While the revival of classical rhetoric was very much an element of the golden age of Spanish speaking, there were inevitable questions about what constitutes the difference between Christian preaching and other forms of public speaking. At times this was phrased in terms of two kinds of "spirits," natural and supernatural. Any good speech depends upon a certain amount of *brío*, but the sanctification of souls is the work of God. Yet that divine work requires a degree of cooperation from the one who preaches, the human instrument through whom the purposes of God are accomplished. Thus holiness of life is more important to effective preaching than any amount of rhetorical talent and training. In the context of such a discussion, there were, of course, differences on what Christian eloquence sounded like:

> On the one hand, the apostolic ideal leads to the conclusion that sincerity and plain-speaking are the only acceptable forms of Christian preaching, and that all the rest is dangerous sophistry.... On the other hand, if one looks back to the Fathers one finds quite another kind of eloquence, and even elegance.[51]

Such considerations of style lead to questions of content: Should Christian preaching draw on pagan thought, especially philosophy? Could one "spoil the Egyptians" without being contaminated? Or, for that matter, could poets—pagan or modern—be quoted from the pulpit? As on most questions, the Spanish preachers were divided, some taking one side, some the other, and most in between. Similar discussions occurred over the use in sermons of that popular seventeenth-century form of imagery, the emblem.[52]

Spanish preaching participates in the pervasive moralism of Catholic Reform, and its homiletical literature deals not only with confronting congregations with their sins, but also with the preacher's need for a blameless life and with issues of professional ethics in the choice of methods by which others' sins are opposed. Yet the preachers also felt obliged to teach the faith, and the popularizations of doctrines they published in their sermons make them useful documents for the historian of doctrine.

In these, as all other aspects of preaching in Spain's golden age, it is possible to see how important preaching was in Catholic Reform and to see also how well it could be done.

The French Experience

Catholic Reform preaching in France has been studied by Peter Bayley.[53] He points out that the sermons that were published and thus have survived were not the relatively short homilies delivered at Sunday Mass:

> The full dress sermon was normally delivered at a separate time, often in the afternoon, on certain major feast days, on Sundays in fashionable town churches, and above all during Lent and Advent.[54]

Other published genres include sermons for preaching missions, for the professions of members of religious orders, and for the funerals of distinguished persons.

These occasions suggest what is indeed the case, that the preaching in question involved more self-conscious virtuoso performances than the regular weekly doses of the proclaimed Word of God. And from this it follows that there had to be a culture to support such an activity, which also proves to be true. One of that culture's bases was the dominance of school curricula by rhetoric in the late-sixteenth and early-seventeenth centuries. The principal difference between one school and another was likely to be whether the rhetoric taught was purely classical or, instead, had been influenced by the theories of Peter Ramus; there was a slight probability that more Roman Catholics were trained in the purely classical tradition and more Protestants in the Ramist tradition.[55]

When one moves beyond general education in the schools and universities to discover the sort of rhetorical training future clergy received, there is less to be learned than might be expected. "The Council of Trent's decree on the subject of the seminarian movement was one of the last to be accepted by the French Church, and the seminarian movement of the 1630s and 1640s aimed at only a very brief training in essentials prior to ordination."[56] All clergy except Jesuits were expected to learn to preach from published treastises on the subject after they had entered the practice of their priesthood. At first these treatises were translations of the Italian and Spanish works mentioned earlier, including those of Granada and Estella, propagated by Borromeo and by their own intrinsic merit. Jesuits, however, did receive preordination training in preaching, and those who demonstrated aptitude were given additional preparation, for which special textbooks were developed within the order.[57]

When post-Tridentine homiletical literature began to originate in

France itself, the works produced fell into two categories, elaborate theoretical works and practical manuals of instruction. While some of the former seem to represent an antirhetorical bias, closer inspection shows that they are really concerned with the spiritual life of the preacher. It is in the "how-to-do-it" manuals that there can be discerned the characteristic element of baroque preaching. Whether these are translations of works by Italian or Spanish writers such as Panigarola or Estella, or the original compositions of a Frenchman like Francis de Sales, what they have in common is an insistence upon the use of preaching aids that is reminiscent of the heyday of thematic preaching.

Perhaps the most important of these is the commonplace book compiled by the preacher himself. One gets the impression that the main reason for a preacher's reading is the discovery of quotations or illustrations that can be copied out against the day when they will be what is needed to "prove" the theme of a sermon. But, in order to assure an adequate *copia* of such material, the preacher will also need encyclopedias, concordances, and digests compiled by others.

With this emphasis on the accumulation of such material, it is not surprising that the major differences between the styles of sermons constructed during this period are in the ways the contents of such collections are employed in the construction of sermons. Most published sermons from the end of the sixteenth and beginning of the seventeenth centuries represent "a kind of preaching which sees the sermon in much the same terms as the long poem or the expository tract"—that is to say, preaching in either the "poetic" or the "plain" style. In the latter part of that period, however, there began to develop "a type of pulpit oratory in which the preacher's main function is the presentation and connection of a wide range of anecdotes, illustrations, and analogies." This is the sort of preaching for which commonplace books and digests are prerequisites. Bayley calls such sermons "thesaurus preaching."[58]

Since it is difficult to communicate the flavor of such preaching without quoting extended passages, Bayley calls upon the most similar works of literature with which the average reader may be familiar, the essays of Montaigne:

> Just as Montaigne's essays developed from a commentary on a selection of favourite anecdotes and passages from the classical writers, so the chief sources of this type of preaching are the thesauri, encyclopedias, and collections of *exempla* which . . . were constantly recommended by the manuals.[59]

Since such preaching had the tendencies of becoming flabby and monotonous on the one hand, and of creating in its published volumes of sermons what are essentially new thesauri to be plundered by other preachers on the other, reactions against it were inevitable. One of these produced what Bayley considers to be "the most highly individual technique of sermon construction in our period," the "catenary preaching" of Jean-Pierre Camus.[60] The catenary style consists of

> the "*enchaînement des images*" . . . the nonchalant linking together of strings of analogies, allusions, anecdotes, Scriptural figures and quotations which combine, [Jean Descrains] says, to form a sort of "*prose poétique.*"[61]

Camus accepts calmly the knowledge that a large part of the public buying volumes of sermons will consist of clergy quarrying inspiration for their own preaching. "He has deliberately shaped his work so that it can serve not only as a model for direct imitation, but as a conceptual framework for the sermons of others."[62]

Etienne Molinier objected to the catenary sermon. He considered writing sermons mainly to serve as resources for others who were writing sermons to be a perversion of the preacher's calling. The purpose of preaching was to inspire souls to flee from sin to the love of God, and the accomplishment of that purpose required an affective development of the sort seen so well in the New Testament preaching of Paul. In catenary preaching Molinier could find no intention to instruct or persuade, duties of a Christian orator recognized since Augustine wrote *De doctrina christiana.* This is not to say that Molinier and his allies objected to the use of material garnered from commonplace books and encyclopedias; instead, they insisted that it be embedded in passages of consecutive writing stating the argument the quotations were to ornament.

It was by such a combination of argument and ornament that the desired emotional appeal could be created. Indeed, the existence of a strong line of argument set the commonplace material free to do its work fully. "Since the *conception* no longer has to play the double role of both proof and ornament, the element of the decorative wittiness can be exaggerated; word-play and ingenious analogies unite to form conceits of extreme brevity."[63] Which is to say that extreme cleverness does not have to be superficial; it can be a strategy of great seriousness. The style advocated by Molinier has much in common with the "wittiness" of English "Metaphysicals" like Donne and Andrewes.[64]

CONCLUSION

From this survey of schools of thought about preaching in France during the first half of the seventeenth century, it is clear that French Catholics shared with co-religionists in other countries and with Protestants the enthusiasm for preaching that was characteristic of the age. Preaching was as important in Catholic Reform as it was in the Protestant Reformation. The need for it had already been stressed in the emphasis of new religious orders on the improvement of parochial ministry. The Jesuits even went so far as to have special training programs in preaching. Leaders in all these orders, however, were among the more active advocates of reform in ministry at the Council of Trent. They also had a missionary vision and zeal that sent their brothers all over the world preaching the gospel at a time when other Christian bodies were content to minister to their members at home.

No one embodied the Tridentine ideal and program for the renewal of ministry, including its emphasis on preaching, so much as Charles Borromeo. He wrote on preaching himself and encouraged others to create both theoretical and practical literature about it. His example was copied in both Spain and France, with the result that in both countries clergy worked energetically to discover more effective ways of preaching, and laypeople flocked to hear the products of their labor. In this preaching of Catholic Reform, there was not the single hermeneutical principle that directed the whole preaching enterprise in the way that justification dominated all Lutheran preaching. Nor was there the emphasis on exegesis that characterized the preaching of Calvinists. Instead, the subject matter—and therefore the form—of early-seventeenth-century Catholic preaching was more diverse than that of the Protestants. It cannot be doubted, however, that a new outpouring of preaching characterized all European Christianity during the period of the Reformation.

FOR FURTHER READING

Bayley, Peter. *French Pulpit Oratory 1598–1650: A Study in Themes and Styles with a Descriptive Catalogue of Printed Texts.* Cambridge: Cambridge University Press, 1980.

———. *Selected Sermons of the French Baroque (1600–1650).* New York and London: Garland, 1983.

Catholicism in Early Modern History. Edited by John O'Malley. St. Louis: Center for Reformation Research, 1988.

Dickens, A.G. *The Counter Reformation.* New York: W. W. Norton & Co., 1968.

O'Malley, John. *The First Jesuits.* Cambridge: Harvard University Press, 1993.

Smith, Hilary Dansey. *Preaching in the Spanish Golden Age: A Study of Some Preachers in the Reign of Philip III.* Oxford: Oxford University Press, 1978.

Notes

1. The first draft of this chapter was revised in light of suggestions made by John O'Malley in a letter dated July 9, 1991.

2. Steven Ozment, *The Age of Reform 1250–1550: An Intellectual and Religious History of Late Medieval and Reformation Europe* (New Haven, Conn.: Yale University Press, 1986), 397.

3. Quoted ibid., citing Henry Outram Evennett, *Spirit of the Counter Reformation,* 1951, Birkbeck Lectures in Ecclesiastical History (Cambridge: Cambridge University Press, 1968), 9.

4. John O'Malley, "Catholic Reform" in *Reformation Europe: A Guide to Research,* ed. Steven Ozment (St. Louis: Center for Reformation Research, 1982), 304.

5. In John O'Malley, "Content and Rhetorical Forms in Sixteenth-Century Treatises on Preaching," in *Renaissance Eloquence: Studies in the Theory and Practice of Renaissance Rhetoric,* ed. James J. Murphy (Berkeley: University of California Press, 1983), 238 n. 2.

6. Originally posed in his 1946 work, *Katholische Reformation oder Gegenreformation?*, his thesis is concisely stated in Erwin Iserloh, Joseph Glazik, and Hubert Jedin, *Reformation and Counter Reformation,* vol. 5 of *History of the Church,* ed. Hubert Jedin and John Dolan, trans. Anselm Biggs and Peter W. Becker (New York: Seabury, 1980), 431-32. An example of an effort to observe this distinction can be seen in a work of the English Lutheran scholar A. G. Dickens, *The Counter Reformation* (New York: W. W. Norton & Co., 1968), 7: "I shall try to use each in its appropriate place: Catholic Reformation for the more spontaneous manifestations, Counter Reformation for the developed movement with resistance and reconquest high on its agenda." Recently, however, John O'Malley has proposed the more inclusive term "Early Modern Catholicism" on the grounds that not all the activity in the Catholic Church during that period was motivated by a desire to reform; the Jesuits, for example, seem to have thought of their work much more in terms of the care of souls. See his 1990 presidential address to the American Catholic Historical Association, "Was Ignatius Loyola a Church Reformer? How to Look at Early Modern Catholicism," *CHR* 77 (1991): 177-93.

7. Dickens, *The Counter Reformation,* 63-65.

8. The Italian name for the group is *Fraternita del divino amore sotte la protezione di San Girolamo.*

9. All three became cardinals, and Caraffa became Pope Paul IV.

10. B. J. Kidd, *The Counter-Reformation 1550–1600* (London: SPCK, 1933), 13-14. For the Latin text, see B. J. Kidd, *Documents Illustrative of the Continental Reformation* (Oxford: Clarendon, 1911), 314.

11. There were, however, a number of pirated editions published. One of these ended up in Germany and was republished by Luther with his sarcastic comments.

12. The Jesuits received this model from them.

13. About whom we shall hear more later.

14. A true religious order, not to be confused with the Oratory of Divine Love, which was only a confraternity or sodality.

15. One of the members of this group was Palestrina, the papal choirmaster. The musical genre of "oratorio" grew out of his compositions for these gatherings.

16. John Henry Newman brought it to England in the nineteenth century. Like Gaetano, Philip Neri was eventually canonized.

17. Owen Chadwick, *The Reformation,* Pelican History of the Church, vol. 3 (Grand Rapids, Mich.: Eerdmans, 1964), 255. Cf. John O'Malley's statement: "For Jedin, the heart of the Tridentine reform was an episcopacy animated by a renewed (or even a new) sense of ministry, as the bishop was transformed from feudatory to pastor" (O'Malley, "Catholic Reform," 297).

18. *Regimini militantis ecclesiae,* promulgated on September 27, 1540, and based upon the society's provisional rule, *Prima summa institute.* See André Ravier, *Ignatius of Loyola and the Founding of the Society of Jesus,* trans. Maura, Joan, and Carson Daly (San Francisco: Ignatius, 1987), 102.

19. Translation in Kidd, *The Counter-Reformation 1550–1600,* 28; Latin in Kidd, *Documents Illustrative of the Continental Reformation,* 337.

20. The quotation at the beginning of this section is taken from that summary.

21. John O'Malley, *The First Jesuits* (Cambridge: Harvard University Press, 1993), 104-10. I am grateful to Father O'Malley for a prepublication copy of his draft for the chapter containing this section.

22. *Trento,* in Italian.

23. For a much more nuanced understanding of the complexities of the council, see Giuseppe Alberigo, "The Council of Trent," in *Catholicism in Early Modern History: A Guide to Research,* ed. John O'Malley (St. Louis: Center for Reformation Research, 1988), 211-26. See also the chapter by Jared Wicks, "Doctrine and Theology," in ibid., 227-51.

24. J. Waterworth, trans., *The Canons and Decrees of the Sacred and Oecumenical Council of Trent, Celebrated Under the Sovereign Pontiffs, Paul III, Julius III, and Pius IV* (New York and London: E. Dunigan & Brother and C. Dolman, 1848), 2:27.

25. Ibid. John O'Malley points out that in this decree "is found a paraphrase of the 'Second Rule' of St. Francis of Assisi, viz., that preaching concerns 'virtues and vices, punishment and reward.'" "St. Charles Borromeo and the *Praecipuum Episcoporum Munus*: His Place in the History of Preaching," in *San Carlo Borromeo: Catholic Reform and Ecclesiastical Politics in the Second Half of the Sixteenth Century,* ed. John M. Headley and John B. Tomaro, Folger Books

(Washington: Folger Shakespeare Library, 1988; London and Toronto: Associated University Presses, 1988), 141, 152 n. 19.

26. Waterworth, *The Canons and Decrees of the Oecumenical Council of Trent,* 2:211-12.

27. Ibid., 2:187.

28. Ibid.

29. Peter Bayley, *French Pulpit Oratory 1598–1650: A Study of Themes and Styles, with a Descriptive Catalogue of Printed Texts* (Cambridge: Cambridge University Press, 1980), 38.

30. Evennett, *Spirit of the Counter Reformation,* 121.

31. "Missions," *ODCC*. For a report on research, see John W. Witek, "From India to Japan: European Missionary Expansion, 1500–1650," in O'Malley, *Catholicism in Early Modern History,* 193-210.

32. Peter Bayley, "Preaching After the Counter Reformation," in ibid., 308-9.

33. Ibid., 299.

34. The limitation of attention to two countries does not imply that there was not abundant homiletical activity in other countries as well, but only that I do not know of studies of that activity. In a letter dated March 25, 1991, John O'Malley listed the places where Catholic Reform preaching has been actively pursued as "Spain, Latin America, Portugal, Italy, Catholic France, Catholic Germany, Poland, etc." The list was intended to be suggestive rather than definitive.

35. O'Malley, "St. Charles Borromeo and the *Praecipuum Episcoporum Munus*" 139. On the importance of Borromeo's example, see Alberigo, "The Council of Trent," 219-21. Not everyone was enthusiastic about what Borromeo was doing, as Alberigo points out. Some of his enemies went so far as to try to have him assassinated, and even saintly Robert Bellarmine saw to it that Borromeo's canonization was for his private virtues rather than his pastoral concerns and activity.

36. Marc Fumaroli, *L'Age de l'éloquence: Rhétorique et res literaria de la Renaissance au seuil de l'époque classique*, Hautes Études Médiévales et Modernes, no. 43 (Geneva: Librairie Droz, 1980), 122-22, 135-36.

37. This is found in *Acta Ecclesiae Mediolanensis* 2:1205-48 and has been reprinted many times, but I have not been able to consult it.

38. O'Malley, "St. Charles Borromeo and the *Praecipuum Episcoporum Munus,*" 142.

39. Ibid.

40. Ibid., 143. He sometimes preached three or four times a day, preparing different sermons for each occasion.

41. In ibid., 144, 154 n. 41, with a reference to de Sales's letter to André Frémyot of October 5, 1604, and a quotation of the French text.

42. O'Malley, "St. Charles Borromeo and the *Praecipuum Episcoporum Munus,*" 147. For more detailed descriptions of these works, see Bayley, *French Pulpit Oratory 1598–1650,* 145-56.

43. O'Malley, "St. Charles Borromeo and the *Praecipuum Episcoporum Munus,*" 149.

44. Hilary Dansey Smith, *Preaching in the Spanish Golden Age: A Study of Some Preachers in the Reign of Philip III* (Oxford: Oxford University Press, 1978), 5. The

years of Philip's reign were 1598–1621. An example of the prose fiction is Padre Isla, *Historia del famoso predicador Fray Gerundio de Campazas,* which Bayley describes as "the satirical novel that did for post-Tridentine preaching what *Don Quixote* did for chivalric romances" (Bayley, "Preaching After the Counter Reformation," 307 n. 44). The only English translations I have been able to learn about were made in the eighteenth century.

45. Ibid., 17.

46. Ibid., 30.

47. Ibid., 44. The medieval practice of division by words or letter-by-letter in cabalistic fashion continued in common but not standard use.

48. Ibid., 54. "This is a term used ... to denote a sermon which weaves together, or contrasts one with the other, a Gospel text and an *Autoridad* (which may be from the Epistle for the day, or from the Breviary)."

49. Ibid., 75.

50. The rhetorical term for this is *ecphrasis.*

51. Ibid., 94-95.

52. Ibid., 109. A picture, usually printed in a collection of such things, accompanied by a statement about its significance, which is essentially enigmatic because true emblems are "composed of a set of secret relationships which at first puzzle the beholder."

53. Bayley, *French Pulpit Oratory,* and its companion volume, *Selected Sermons of the French Baroque (1600–1650)* (New York and London: Garland, 1983), which provides examples of the different kinds of sermons discussed in the first book.

54. Bayley, *French Pulpit Oratory,* 14.

55. Ibid., 19, 22. For more on Ramism, see below, chapters 15 and 18.

56. Ibid., 38.

57. Ibid., 56-60.

58. Ibid., 77.

59. Ibid., 78.

60. Ibid., 85.

61. Ibid. The internal reference is to Jean Descrains, "La Rhétorique dans les homélies de Jean-Pierre Camus aux Etats Généraux de 1616," *XVIIe Siècle,* 80-81 (1968): 61-78.

62. Ibid., 86.

63. Ibid., 94.

64. Bayley goes on, pp. 97-100, to discuss what he calls "orhestrated prose," but since that sort of preaching was found more among Protestants than Roman Catholics, it does not need to be discussed here.

CHAPTER 15

UPHEAVAL IN BRITAIN

CUIUS REGIO

The beginning of this chapter marks a decisive shift in the orientation of my account of the history of preaching because from here on the preoccupation of the narrative will be with preaching in English; the homiletical tradition in other languages will be referred to only to the extent that it casts light on developments in preaching in English. While that shift could be thought to portend some simplification of the story, such optimism is destined for disappointment. From its beginning, the Reformation and post-Reformation history of English-speaking Christianity has been variegated and occasionally many-splendored.

A partial explanation for this complexity is given in a now-classic statement from F. M. Powicke: "The one definite thing which can be said about the Reformation in England is that it was an act of state."[1] In making the statement, however, Powicke was not explicitly contrasting what took place in England with what occurred on the Continent, but rather with medieval traditions of papal authority that had culminated in the pontificate of Boniface VIII (1294–1303). The role of the German princes in the Lutheran Reformation, that of the Swiss city councils in the Calvinist, and the establishment of the principle of *cuius regio eius religio*[2] as the means for settling which territories were to remain Catholic and which were to become Protestant show that all religious developments of the sixteenth century were very much acts of state, whatever superiority over princes previous theory may have given to popes.

At the time it was inconceivable to anyone that there could be a unified state that was religiously divided; indeed, the knowledge that religious pluralism did not entail civil anarchy is one of the eventual contributions of the English experience to Christendom. Furthermore, ever since Constantine had called the Council of Nicaea there had been theorists who were convinced that the state should have supremacy in spiritual as well as temporal matters; conciliarists such as Marsilius of Padua had so argued, and their thought had been persuasive to Catholic monarchs up until the Council of Trent.

Thus, in respect to its involvement with secular government, the essential difference between the Reformation in England and what happened on the Continent resulted from the fact that one English monarch's religious commitments differed so dramatically from another's; and so the pattern that religious reform took varied considerably from reign to reign. Indeed, there had not been such religious instability even in late antiquity when Roman emperors were either orthodox or Arian.

On the whole, Henry VIII had not wished for any religious change in England beyond the replacement of papal authority in the church with royal, even though he was willing to sound more Lutheran when diplomatic dickering with Germany called for his doing so. After Henry was succeeded by his ten-year-old son, Edward VI, in 1547, the two successive protectors, Somerset and Northumberland, moved the English church in a more Calvinist direction for a variety of political and theological reasons. When Edward died in 1553, his half sister Mary, daughter of Catherine of Aragon and wife of Philip II of Spain, acquired the sobriquet "Bloody" from the ardor with which she returned the Church of England to papal obedience.

Five years later when Queen Mary died, Elizabeth inherited a land deeply divided over issues of faith, with some subjects loyal to Rome, others who had lived during Mary's reign as exiles in Geneva where they acquired a vision of a "truly" Reformed church, and many others in between. For forty-five years Elizabeth refused to submit to pressure from either extreme, fostering instead a settlement in which the English church acquired the balance of Catholic and Reformed elements that has characterized it ever since, the balance that came in the nineteenth century to be called Anglicanism.

The Elizabethan Settlement, however, did not mean that matters were settled permanently. When James VI of Scotland became James I of Great Britain in 1603, his experience of the Presbyterianism that had been the religion of Scotland since John Knox had reformed the national church in 1560 led him to resist the pressure of Puritans to make the English church more Calvinistic. Then, under his son Charles I and Charles's archbishop, William Laud, considerable effort was made to emphasize the Catholic aspect of Anglican tradition.

The *religious* resistance to the efforts of this king and his primate by the group called "Puritans" since the reign of Elizabeth,[3] together with the *political* resistance of Parliament to the way Charles acted on his understanding of the divine right of kings, resulted in revolution, with Laud's execution in 1645 and that of the king in 1649. Under the Commonwealth, which lasted from the death of Charles I to the Restoration of Charles II in 1660, the English church (or, at least, the part of it under control of Parliament) was given at first a Presbyterian and then an Independent (Congregationalist) complexion.

At the Restoration it became obvious that the ideal of a realm united religiously as well as politically was no longer achievable. The established church could never again claim to embrace all citizens. Dissent was allowed, but those remaining within the establishment—freed from the necessity of accommodating disagreement—could now emphasize their differences from Presbyterians, Independents, and Baptists. The equilibrium thus established was threatened later when James II used his position to ease the situation of his fellow Roman Catholics, but the "Glorious Revolution" replaced him as monarch with his daughter Mary and her husband, William of Orange.

They, in turn, were followed by Queen Anne, Tory and High Church, but already weariness over religious controversies had made welcome a latitudinarianism to which any "enthusiasm" or fanaticism was foreign. This characterized the mood of the Church of England until it was finally vanquished by the Evangelical revival of the eighteenth century and the Catholic renewal (the "Oxford movement") of the nineteenth. Since then the major influence on the religious life of England has been the secularization of Western thought, which has left churches there as sparsely filled with worshipers as those of Roman Catholics and Protestants on the Continent.

It can be seen that English Christianity has been in a continual state of upheaval since the Reformation and that many of the disturbances upsetting it were induced by the Crown until the reign of William and Mary, when the monarchy became too constitutional to have any real power over the religious life of the realm.[4]

ON AGAIN, OFF AGAIN: THE TUDOR PERIOD

Periods and Characteristics

This ecclesiological flux and vacillation at the behest of sovereigns, especially clear during the reigns of Henry VIII and his three children, had homiletical implications. These have been traced by J. W. Blench in *Preaching in England in the Late Fifteenth and Sixteenth Centuries: A Study of English Sermons 1450–c.1600*.[5] So impressed was Blench with the influence of reign changes on preaching that each of his chapters is divided into four sections:

1. The Pre-Reformation Catholic Preachers, including the Conservative Henricians (1450–1547),
2. The Early Reformers (1547–1553),
3. The Preachers of Mary's Reign (1553–1558), and
4. The Elizabethan Preachers (1558–1603).

Indeed, he gives the impression at times that the preaching of a particular reign was monochrome when in fact, most of the ways of preaching were found in every period.

Tudor Hermeneutics

Blench begins his study by showing what forms of biblical interpretation were in use by preachers of different parties during the various reigns. Before the Reformation, the four medieval senses of Scripture dominated exegesis until Catholic-thinking clergy came under the influence of Erasmus and other humanists, and Reform-minded preachers came to accept Luther's demand for literal interpretation.[6]

As noted in the discussion of Luther (above, chap. 12) the literal sense recognized in the sixteenth century is very different from that of twentieth-century biblical scholars; it is a timeless theological interpretation rather than an effort to discover what the sacred authors intended their first readers to understand—and its hermeneutical key was the theological system of the preacher. Blench is able to say of a construal of scripture in a sermon by Bishop John Hooper that while "it does start with a theological position which it proceeds to find in the words of the sacred writer, it is very far removed from anything resembling the later 'higher criticism.'"[7] He goes on to say: "It is interesting also to notice that Latimer, while he will not admit pro-Catholic allegories, nevertheless introduces anti-

Catholic accommodations."[8] So a great deal of the preaching of the period was polemical, and the needs of controversy often dominated not only sermon strategy but also biblical interpretation as well.

Homiletical Genres

For his discussion of sermon form *(dispositio)*, Blench uses the medieval terms of "ancient" and "modern" to refer to the homily and thematic sermon forms,[9] although, by the time he wrote about, this vocabulary had already become anachronistic: the thematic sermon was no longer modern and the homily was in the process of revival. Thematic sermons were still the norm on the eve of the Reformation, but some preachers inspired by the humanists, such as Colet, had reverted to the patristic homily form. The preferred type for those influenced by continental Reformers was the exegetical homily that proceeded *secundum ordinem textus*.

While there was some resurgence of thematic preaching during the reign of Queen Mary I, the influence of humanism had tamed somewhat the ardor for "the subdividing mentality," with its infinite capacity for elaborate divisions. Preachers of the period, therefore,

> content[ed] themselves with an Exordium, Prayer, Division into (most frequently) three topics (which usually do not depend on the words of the text) and Confirmation of the Division with little if any subdivision. [10]

Blench notes correctly that this simplification of the thematic sermon, which had already begun to appear in the time of Edward, "approximates to the essentials of the classical oration."[11] This is to say that it represents the influence of the sort of ecclesiastical rhetoric that was a primary influence of the Renaissance on both Catholic and Protestant preaching. I will say more about this below.

Blench calls attention to the appearance during Elizabeth's reign of "the new Reformed method" found in the lectures of the extreme Puritans, but he devotes less than a page to this sermon form.[12] While the number of preachers who used it in the Tudor period may have been relatively small, the method later became so influential in both England and New England that I discuss it below.

Plain or Fancy

While Blench's analysis of the exegesis and form of Tudor preaching is generally accepted as accurate, what he has to say about style has recently been brought into question by implication. Classical rhetorical theory spoke of three styles: plain, moderate, and grand. For his period, however, Blench spoke of the "plain, but uncolloquial," the "colloquial," and the "ornate" styles.[13] The difficulty with this taxonomy is that it overlaps without duplicating the classical distinctions and thus misleads the reader into thinking that the traditional categories are being invoked. This danger of confusion is increased by the way Blench uses a good bit of classical vocabulary to talk about style.

What he does is coherent enough in itself. The plain but uncolloquial style is characterized by a spare use of *exempla* and schemata (figures of speech [or sound] as opposed to figures of thought) and these employed "not for display, but as an aid to cogent expression." The colloquial style "used a racy and pungent speech idiom, and avoids the schemata, but is enriched by frequent homely *exempla*." The ornate style, as might be expected, "is highly embellished by the schemata, employs many *exempla* (often from literary sources) and aims distinctly at oratorical display."[14]

The difficulties with this categorization of styles are: (1) the danger of confusion with classical nomenclature, and (2) an importation of value judgments into descriptions in a way that obscures classifications. This latter difficulty is exaggerated by the resemblance of Blench's scheme to a modern critical misunderstanding of the way the three classical styles were distinguished in the ancient world, deriving from the 1905 analysis of G. L. Hendrickson.[15] He claimed there were originally only two ancient styles, one of which he called "oratorical" and the other "plain." The first was an emotional appeal while the second was a rational one.[16]

The whole discussion of style in Tudor sermons has been set on a more sure footing by Debora K. Shuger in *Sacred Rhetoric: The Christian Grand Style in the English Renaissance*.[17] She argues that this interpretation represents a distortion of both classical and Renaissance rhetorical theory. The ancient denotation of grand style was not the use of showy speech forms to convince an audience through psychological manipulation.[18]

> Beginning with the Greeks, the grand style was not described as primarily periodic, schematic, or playful but as passionate. The grand style moves the emotions . . . [It] expresses a passionate seriousness about the most important issues of human life; it is thus the style of Plato and the Bible as well as Cicero and Demosthenes.[19]

In the ancient world, a common way of contrasting the grand style to its alternative was to use the analogy of soldiers and athletes. The contests of athletes may be more aesthetic, but soldiers engage in life-and-death struggles. An audience of Isocrates might have responded by saying, "O how eloquent!" but an audience of Demosthenes would have responded by saying, "Let's go to war against the Macedonians!" Thus it was Demosthenes rather than Isocrates who would have been said to use the grand style.

The preachers of the English Renaissance, however, did not have a grand style that was identical with that of the classical rhetoricians, whose speech making was for courts of law, legislative assemblies, and ceremonial occasions. Nothing in their oratorical theory, therefore, had so exalted a subject as Christian preaching about the triune God. It remained for Augustine to point out that speaking of such a God required an elevated speech aimed at expressing and inculcating love of this God. His theories led medieval homileticians to develop what is called a "passionate plain style." Puritan preaching theory is a development of that medieval approach to proclamation.

Other English preachers, however, under the influence of continental Neo-Latin textbooks of both rhetoric and homiletics, developed a Christian grand style (even if they did not refer to it by that term). It drew on late Hellenistic rhetorical traditions connected with Longinus and Hermogenes, who wrote of "the sublime" and saw the need for a sense of grandeur in religion. They also began to address issues of affective psychology, a type of consideration absent from ancient rhetoric, because Greek and Roman culture had deep distrust of "the passions" as the antithesis of reason. This homiletical emphasis reflected the development of "faculty" psychology.

Shuger's reconstruction is convincing. The one caveat to be entered is that although she gives incidental expression to her familiarity with English Renaissance preaching that did not represent the grand style, on the whole she confines her book to its subject. A careless reader could be left with the impression that grand style was the only sort of homiletical theory or preaching there was. In an excellent chapter on textbooks, however, she indicates that preachers in the grand style were instructed using Latin textbooks from the Continent, whether liberal Protestant and Tridentine works on homiletics or general rhetorics. Hence they are squarely in the tradition of Erasmus and the humanists. Yet she recognizes that there were also textbooks in the vernacular, often very short—like that of William Perkins, to be studied below. These had an entirely different readership, one that was the heir of the medieval passionate plain style, even though it resisted almost every other aspect of medieval theology.

That is to say, the advocates of the plain style were Puritans. Proponents of the grand style were much more central Anglicans. The latter would reach their apogee, not only in eloquence but also in learning and sanctity, in the early seventeenth century with practitioners like Lancelot Andrewes and John Donne.

A DISPLAY OF PREACHERS

The Tudor preaching scene was so kaleidoscopic that it is difficult to hold any picture from it in view long enough to acquire distinct impressions of what it was like. A few thumbnail sketches at this point may be helpful in getting some sense of the phenomena. While these sketches cannot claim to be representative of all elements of the scene, at least they can give a sense of concretion to some of them.

The Book of Homilies

The first is not of a person but a book and the reality that necessitated it. When the power of the Crown was placed behind the Reformation by the regents of Edward VI, two truths were recognized: (1) that the new doctrines needed to be taught in a wholesale way, and (2) that many of the clergy were not well enough trained to teach them. To meet the need, a collection of sermons was published to inculcate the new doctrines. Known popularly as *The Book of Homilies,* it bore the full title of *Certain Sermons, or Homilies, appoynted by the Kynges Maiestie, to be declared and redde, by all Persones,*[20] *Uicars, or Curates euery Sonday in their Churches, where they haue Cure,* a designation stating the program as well as the contents of the work.[21]

The sermons are topical in their construction and constitute a catechetical enterprise, as may be seen from a listing of their titles. These, together with the authors to whom some have been attributed, are: (1) "A Fruitful Exhortation to the Reading of Holy Scripture," Archbishop Thomas Cranmer; (2) "Of the Misery of All Mankind," Archdeacon John Harpesfield; (3) "Of the Salvation of All Mankind," Cranmer; (4) "Of the True and Lively Faith," Cranmer; (5) "Of Good Works," Cranmer; (6) "Of Christian Love and Charity," Bishop Edmund Bonner; (7) "Against Swearing and Perjury"; (8) "Of the Declining from God"; (9) "An Exhortation to Obedience"; (11) "Against Whoredom and Adultery," possibly Cranmer's chaplain, Thomas Becon; and (12) "Against Strife and Contention," possibly by Becon.[22]

It has been cogently argued by John N. Wall Jr. that these homilies reflect a program of religious renewal for England that owes its inspiration not so much to any continental Reformer as it does to the northern tradition of Christian humanism represented by Erasmus.[23] His basic thesis is that these English humanists shared with Erasmus three convictions: that obedience to God is aimed not so much toward holy dying as toward obedience to God in the world as a way that improves social living, that such obedience is to the will of God as revealed in the Bible, and that this reform is communicated through human speech. In this view Wall is following the insight of Marjorie O'Rourke Boyle that "for Erasmus, the Christ is God's eternally thought speech; men imitate the Father when they imitate the divine discourse made flesh in Jesus."[24] On the basis of this theology,

> Cranmer and his followers set out to reform England with a collection of written documents intended to be read aloud, a collection of documents including among them the Bible itself, Erasmus' own commentary[25] on the New Testament heart of it for Christina speakers, and a collection of rhetorically constructed sermons expounding its meaning.[26]

All of these documents were begun during the reign of Henry VIII before the fall of his vicar general, Thomas Cromwell, but Henry's conservatism held back their distribution until the reign of Edward VI. Yet those who sponsored them included not only Cromwell, but Henry's archbishop of Canterbury, Thomas Cranmer, and even Catherine Parr, Henry's last wife, as well. So important was this ministry of the Word to Cranmer that all the books necessary for it were completed before the appearance in 1549 of the first Book of Common Prayer, which provided the English church with its liturgy in the language of the people. Central to this project was a vision of the Christian commonwealth that Erasmus had communicated through his *Enchiridion*. "The *Book of Homilies* is at once the fullest Tudor expression of the vision of a Christian commonwealth attainable through universal humanist education and the basic work in a program of universal education aimed at realizing this vision."[27]

One of the clearest indications of Cranmer and his associates' success in getting the Homilies used was the Puritan opposition to them. Millar Maclure summed it up when he said that "the drone of the Homilies replaced the mutter of the Mass."[28] The grounds for opposing them were that they were not tailor made for the sins of the priest's congregation and that they did not penetrate hearts as did sermons prepared with the particular congregation and occasion in mind. While insisting that the Puritans exaggerated the differences between the effects of reading a sermon from *The Book of Homilies* and preaching one freshly created, even Hooker had to agree that people may not pay too much attention to something they can read themselves at any time and that sermons "come always new."[29] Yet such complaints are a tribute to the extent to which the policy of the English humanists succeeded in providing for sound Anglican doctrine to be delivered orally to the people on a regular basis.

Hugh Latimer

The next representative of Tudor preaching to be considered, the Right Reverend Hugh Latimer (ca. 1485–1555), can be understood as a perfect exemplar of the English Erasmian tradition. He certainly was committed to an understanding of Christian living as devoted to the establishment of the Commonweal, preaching out against what he considered to be the social evils of his day.[30] His preaching shows consistently that he believed the Bible to be the only source of Christian doctrine and shows as well that few were as gifted as he in the oral communication of the biblical faith and its behavioral implications.

The son of a yeoman farmer who could afford to send him to school, Latimer was a fellow of Clare Hall at Cambridge when Erasmus was there. He was already recognized enough for his ability in the pulpit to be selected as one of the university's twelve scholars licensed to preach anywhere in England. Yet at first he did not support the New Learning. It was one of his fellow dons, Thomas Bilney—"Little Bilney," as Latimer called him—who won him to its cause.[31] Not long afterward, his preaching began to get him in trouble with the bishop of Ely, in whose diocese Cambridge is located, but at the time he had an unlikely rescuer in Cardinal Wolsey. Along with Cranmer, Latimer was active in obtaining Cambridge's approval for the annulment of Henry VIII's marriage to Catherine of Aragon, following which he received the first of many invitations to preach at court, and was appointed rector of a parish in Wiltshire.

Even though he continued in his outspoken preaching of the Reformation cause,[32] he was made bishop of Worchester in 1535. When, however, Henry's conservatism effected the enactment of the Six Articles that retained most elements of traditional practice, he resigned his see. Under house arrest for a while, he was then given a pension to live in retirement.

The death of Henry and accession of Edward VI came when he was in the Tower of London for having been supportive of another Reformer, Dr. Edward Crome. Even under the auspicious new reign, however, he did not resume his diocese, although he was continually invited to preach, delivering eight sermons at Paul's Cross and seven Lenten sermons before the king. When he preached another sermon at court the following Lent (1550), he spoke of himself as an old man and suggested that it would be his last at that place. He lived in semiretirement on the estate of his friend the duchess of Suffolk, preaching in the neighborhood twice every Sunday.

When, however, the sickly young king died and was succeeded by his older sister Mary, the fortunes of Latimer changed with those of the Reformation cause. Confined to the Tower with Cranmer and Ridley in September of 1553 and then transferred to prison in Oxford, he and Ridley anticipated Cranmer slightly in their trial for heresy and their deaths at the stake on October 16, 1555. Throughout his ordeal, Latimer maintained a sober gaiety. Foxe tells us that when the flame was set to the pyre he said, "Be of good comfort, master Ridley, and play the man. We shall this day light such a candle, by God's grace, in England, as I trust shall never be put out."[33]

As a preacher, Latimer is more reminiscent of Luther than anyone else because of his colloquial style, his sermons approaching what someone has called "matey chats."[34] Yet, unlike Luther, he had no theory of a single task that all sermons must accomplish. Indeed, some of the conventions of the thematic sermon still linger in his work,[35] such as an occasional protheme followed by a bidding prayer. Some of his longer efforts were delivered in two parts, with the prayer coming at the end of the first. He also used *exempla.* Yet there is nothing of the subdividing mentality in him. Rather, his sermons have been said to "suffer from looseness of structure and (to be) encumbered with digressions."[36] While most are constructed *secundum ordinem textus,*[37] and such expository homilies are not notorious for their coherence, Latimer is also like Luther in his tendency to ramble.

All this may be seen in an analysis of his "Sixth Sermon Preached Before King Edward the Sixth."[38] (For the text of this sermon, **see Vol. 2, pp. 296-312.**) The whole Lenten series shares the common text of Romans 15:4, but little is said about it here. Rather, Latimer begins with a summary of his previous sermon and then, through six long paragraphs, defends himself against a misunderstanding of something he said in it. He next announces that his text for the day will be the story of the miraculous draft of fishes in Luke 5, saying that he will refute a papal interpretation given the passage by Cardinal Reginald Pole, and bids prayer.

In response to the statement that the people pressed upon Jesus to hear him, Latimer wonders at the prevalence of "unpreaching prelates." In the process of doing so he tells an *exemplum* about a woman who went to hear the sermons at a certain church because she needed the sleep. But that reminds him of how Augustine was converted by Ambrose's preaching even though he had gone to church with unworthy motives. The importance of preaching is demonstrated by reference to the devil's efforts to stop it, including hardships in educating sons for the ministry and the impoverishment of clergy through the fee farming of benefices.

The people listened reverently to Jesus, unlike Latimer's restless audience at Westminster Palace. Jesus' getting into Peter's boat did not indicate that he was the future pope; Jesus just chose the most convenient boat in the manner that Latimer had picked his wherry over from Lambeth Palace that day. A good bit of antipapal interpretation is given, interlarded with a tale of a bishop who was angry when he was not rung into town for his visitation because the local bell lacked a clapper, and another story about his own visitation of a town where the people were too busy celebrating Robin Hood's day to gather for his sermon.

The way the fish came to be caught at Jesus' command, but still the disciples had to lower their nets to catch them, shows a synergism between the activity of God and human evangelistic endeavor. Jesus worked at being a carpenter until he began to preach, and then he worked at that. Everyone else should work as well, including the king, who has his own distinctive duties. As disjointed as the sermon may sound from this summary, it was tied together by the motif of the importance of preaching the Word of God.

Even from so sketchy an outline, it is possible to feel both the passion of Latimer's polemic and the pleasure of his style. Blench calls him "the greatest exponent of the colloquial style in the century"[39] and points out some of the stylistic devices by which he achieves this effect. These include the use of humorous compounds such as "claw-backs," "flibbergibs," "by-walkers," "merit-mongers," "bell-hallowers," and "card-gospellers." He frequently places words close together that sound alike but have different meanings (paronomasias), such as homily/homely, or supper/dupper. "Alliteration's artful aid" is employed, as in "boils, botches, blains, and scabs."[40] He loves to quote proverbs and folk wisdom and invents homely comparisons. He has an extremely sharp ear for the sound of conversation. He tells many *exempla* and, a much rarer thing, tells personal anecdotes, especially related to farm life—although he can tell about the perils of the episcopate as well.

From this depiction alone, it would be possible to confuse Latimer with mere entertainers who have taken the pulpit for their stage, a real temptation in times when preaching is popular. But as Horton Davies said:

> Latimer's preaching was too courageous, too direct, and too compassionate ever to be mistaken for demagoguery. It was, whether in denunciation, retelling a Biblical narrative, or in exposition, ... popular preaching at its best.[41]

His passion for the gospel was paramount, his concern for the suffering unending, and his willingness to speak the Word of God in season and out of season, at whatever cost to himself or others, makes the likes of him rare in any age.

Puritan Sermon Form

While Blench calls attention to the appearance of Puritan preaching in the reign of Elizabeth, he says little about it, because it was not yet very popular. Though the number of preachers who used it in the Tudor period may have been relatively small, the method became so influential later both in England and in New England that it deserves identification at its first appearance. From the time of Elizabeth through the beginning of the Commonwealth, most English clergy operated out of an essentially Calvinist theological framework. As a result, Calvin's highly exegetical understanding of the work of the preacher inevitably had its influence, especially among the more thoroughgoing Calvinists, those called Puritans.

The normative statement of Puritan homiletical method in England is generally recognized to have been made in William Perkins's *The Arte of Prophesying*.[42] In Perkins's formula the method was reduced to tabular form:

> 1. To read the Text distinctly out of the canonicall scripture.
> 2. To give the sense and understanding of it being read by the scripture itself.
> 3. To collect a few and profitable points of doctrine out of the naturall sense.
> 4. To applie (if he have the gift) the doctrine rightly collected to the manners of men in a simple and plain speech.[43]

This formula, commonly summarized as "Understanding, Doctrines, and Uses," has been explicated by Perry Miller:

> The Puritan sermon quotes the text and "opens" it as briefly as possible, expounding circumstances and context, explaining its grammatical meanings, reducing its tropes and schemata to prose, and setting forth its logical implications; the sermon then proclaims in a flat, indicative sentence the "doctrine" contained in the text or logically deduced from it, and proceeds to the first reason or proof. Reason follows reason, with no other transition than a period and a number; after the last proof is stated there follow the uses or applications, also in numbered sequence, and the sermon ends when there is nothing more to be said.[44]

The only thing that needs to be added theologically is that while Perkins insisted the "onlie" sense of Scripture is the "literall," he also believed the Holy Spirit inspired the sacred writers in such a way that the meaning of all parts of the Bible is consistent. That means passages not necessarily showing that consistency were still to be interpreted "by the analogie of faith," in other words, in accordance with the Apostles' Creed—and even more with Paul's Epistle to the Romans as interpreted by Calvin. Perkins also divided texts into those of gospel and those of law in a manner reminiscent of Luther.[45]

Philosophically, an extremely important additional insight is that Perkins's homiletical theory reflects the perspective of the French logician Pierre Ramus and his rhetorical aide-de-camp, Omer Talon. Ramus represents a stage of development in logical thought between late scholasticism, on the one hand, and Bacon and Descartes, on the other, that was extremely influential on continental Reform thought and English and American Puritanism.[46] The essence of Ramus's system was to say that the material of any discipline could be classified by going through what today is called a "decision tree," opting between mutually exclusive alternatives.[47]

He also eliminated invention, disposition, and memory from the classical tasks of rhetoric, leaving only style *(elocutio)* and delivery *(actio)*, on the grounds that invention and disposition were parts of logic or dialectic rather than rhetoric. This does not mean that composers of sermons and other speeches no longer engaged in invention and arrangement in their work, but only that they were wearing their dialectical rather than their rhetorical hats when they engaged in such activities. Besides the implied diminution of rhetoric (always a popular pastime), the adoption of Ramist theory (as worked out in reference to rhetoric by Talon) gave sermons the form of logical demonstrations rather than oral persuasions.

Ramist principles were congenial to Puritans for a number of reasons, particularly that since sermons were the usual vehicle of conversion or election, they had to combine logical and emotional appeals. Because logic is a gift of God, the sermons had to be consistent with human reason, but the suggestion that preaching could persuade by force of intellect alone implied that conversion could be a human rather than a divine activity—a blasphemous idea.

This psychology of the Puritans called for election to be accompanied by a physical stimulus, in the belief that this reservation would allow for election to be an exclusively divine act, but one that was at the same time accepted in human freedom. Furthermore, they wanted to avoid any implication that the saving work of God was dependent upon human emotional manipulation or even that preaching was merely an aesthetic experience and thereby a sensual indulgence. Thus they felt that Ramus's humbling of rhetoric was consistent with the needs of the saints: it allowed for preaching that was both reasonable and passionate, but that nevertheless left results entirely in the hands of God.[48]

So much for Ramist theory, but what evidence is there that it is reflected in the "new Reformed method" of Puritan preaching inculcated by Perkins's *Arte of Prophesying*? The case has been well argued by Miller:

> The laws of invention applied to extracting arguments from a Biblical text would teach [a Ramist] how to "open" it and how to formulate the doctrine; Ramus' rules for memory would instruct him to "porte" his text into a few doctrines; the whole of the *Dialecticae* would teach him how to prove them and how to dispose doctrines and proofs in order. Ramus' constant insistence upon "use" would show him the necessity for applying each doctrine to the auditors "as euery heade shall geue the occasion." For the embellishment with figures and tropes and for the methods of oral delivery, Talon's rhetoric would teach him that these are secondary to the analysis of arguments and the genesis of a method, that they are to be added only after the theme and the demonstration are worked out.[49]

It can be seen that, along with the preaching patterns of the patristic homily and the medieval thematic sermon, pulpits of the English Reformation exhibited a third, Puritan pattern based on Ramist logic that received its classical statement in William Perkins's *The Arte of Prophesying*.[50]

"Silver-Tongued" Smith

Very little is known about the life of the third example of Tudor preaching. The "silver-tongued preacher,"[51] as Henry Smith was called, came from a wealthy and well-connected Leicestershire family; William Cecil (Lord Burghley), Elizabeth's treasurer, was the brother of his stepmother, and one of Smith's cousins married Francis Bacon. Although he was an eldest son, he did not inherit the family estate because he lived only a little over thirty years. He studied at Oxford, but his name was far too common for university records to furnish any certainty about whether he received a degree.[52]

An early-nineteenth-century life of John Aylmer, Bishop of London in Smith's time, furnishes what little additional information there is about his training for the ministry:

> Soon after his coming to Oxford, he lived and followed his studies with Richard Greenham, a pious minister in the country, but not thoroughly affected to the orders of the church established; and his principles he seems to have infused into Smith.[53]

Saying that he was not "thoroughly affected" was a quaint Georgian way of saying that Henry Smith was a Puritan. The extent to which he was "Puritan," though, was very different from conventional associations with the term. His only certain ministerial appointment was, to be sure, in that most Puritan of all arrangements, a readership.

> If an incumbent minister could not or would not preach the number and kind of sermons demanded, the laity could hire another minister, the lecturer, to preach at times when the church was not being used for regular services.[54]

Smith became reader at St. Clement Danes church near the Temple Inns of Court in 1587. The next year the bishop of London suspended him under the impression that he was not licensed, and that he had spoken disrespectfully of the Book of Common Prayer and not subscribed to the Articles of Religion. His reply, however, showed that he had no wish to do any of those things, and he was restored.[55] Indeed, in *God's Arrow Against Atheism and Irreligion,* he says that church people should not argue about such perennial Puritan concerns as set prayers, saints' days, fasting, and vestments:

> Inasmuch therefore as we have the preaching of God's holy word, and the right administration of the sacraments, which be the essential marks of the true church, none ought to forsake our church for any other defect, corruption, or imperfection.[56]

He opposed any sort of Separatism, although he believed in working within the Church of England to reform it in some ceremonial matters. Horton Davies has said that the difference between Smith's view of the importance of preaching and Hooker's view was that Smith believed it was "the one thing necessary," while Hooker taught that the gospel was equally conveyed in the reading of the lectionary in church and in the dramatic enactments of the gospel in baptism and the Eucharist.[57]

Certainly Smith's preaching is not preoccupied with controversial theological issues. Rather, his concern is greater for issues of morality, making him sound more like the popular image of a Puritan in the following catalog than many who had better claims to the title:

> What! Do you think that God doth not remember our sins, which we do not regard; for while we sin, the score runs on, and the judge setteth down all in the table of remembrance, and his scroll reacheth up to heaven.
>
> Item, for lending to usury; item, for racking of rents; item, for deceiving thy brethren; item, for starching thy ruffs; item, for curling thy hair; item, for painting thy face; item, for selling of benefices; item, for starving of souls; item, for playing at cards; item, for sleeping in church; item, for profaning the Sabbath day; with a number more hath God to call account, for every one must answer for himself: the fornicator for taking filthy pleasure; O son, remember thou hast taken thy pleasure, take thy punishments; the careless prelate for murdering so many thousand souls; the landlord, for getting money from his poor tenants by racking of his rents.[58]

This list, however, which seems to place on a par breaches of traditional Christian morality, social evils, ecclesiastical conditions that horrified Puritans, and petty vanities, can give an impression of small-mindedness that was by no means typical of Smith. He was concerned with the temptations of his flock. Their station in life can be inferred from the occupations of those who petitioned that Smith be made the incumbent of the parish where he was the reader: the wardens were a grocer and a locksmith, and their cosigners included "ordinary tradesmen, as smiths, tailors, saddlers, hosiers, haberdashers, glaziers, cutlers, and such like." For them, what he said was as practical as it was sweetly reasonable. But he could also keep them alert to the larger issues of society.[59] In its social witness, his sermon on poverty called "The Poor Man's Tears" compares favorably not only with the sermons of Latimer but with the best sermons of today's social prophets.

The style of Smith's preaching eludes easy categorization. Davies, drawing on the categories of Blench, says that Smith used the fully ornate style,[60] but Blench himself invents a category between the plain and the ornate for him:

> The truth surely lies between these extremes, for although his diction is simple, and often his use of the schemata[61] is, as Herr says, "stolid," nevertheless his sermons are given rich and varied colour by very frequent masterly similes, which are often combined in a series, each member of which throws some illumination on the subject.[62]

In speaking of the clarity of Smith's preaching, his nineteenth-century editor says:

> So free are (his sermons) from the affectations that disfigure most of the pulpit productions of the time, that there is scarcely an expression that would require alteration in order to adapt them to the tastes of the present day. They probably do not contain a dozen words that would not be understood by an ordinary modern audience.[63]

In much the same tone, John Lievsay speaks of Smith as a "bright rift in the fog of dullness" of Elizabethan sermons in general.[64] No wonder, then, that Fuller tells us:

> His church was so crowded with auditors, that persons of good quality brought their own pews with them, I mean their legs, to stand thereupon in the alleys.[65]

A look at the popularity Smith acquired, not only with his contemporaries but with succeeding generations as well, brings amazement that this is a response to the ministry of a man who died in his early thirties, a ministry that appears to have lasted only about four years and from which there remain less than sixty sermons.

The Judicious Hooker

The final example of Tudor preaching is very different from the others. Richard Hooker, who was born about the time Latimer died and who himself died three years before Elizabeth, comes nearer to being its definitive theologian than anyone else the Church of England has produced, with his *Treatise on the Laws of Ecclesiastical Polity* being the nearest approximation to an Anglican summa. Nor is he well known or attested as a preacher. Only ten of his sermons survive, and three of those were regarded as the work of Archbishop Ussher until the latest publication of his *Tractates and Sermons*.[66]

These homiletical works owe their survival to being relevant to the controversies of the period. The big issue of the time was the Church of Rome because in 1570 Pope Pius V had excommunicated Queen Elizabeth, declared that she was no longer queen, and forbade Roman Catholic English to obey her "orders, mandates, and laws" upon pain of excommunication themselves. The Spanish Armada and the various plots that centered around Mary Queen of Scots show that the dangers of revolt and regicide were not paranoid fancies. The "Two Sermons Upon S. Jude's Epistle" represent some of Hooker's polemic against Rome; it is, of course, far more measured and theological than most of what was going around at the time. Indeed, the long "Learned Discourse on Justification" (a tractate in the sense defined above) is largely an argument that not only pre-Reformation English forebears but even cardinals and popes were not necessarily excluded from salvation.

A reaction to this liberalism prompted the controversy that eventuated in the writing of the *Ecclesiastical Polity.* Hooker's most prestigious appointment was to be as master of the Temple, the minister in charge of the old Norman round church of the Knights Templar in London that became a parish church when the Templar property was taken over by the Inns of Court of the Inner and Middle Temple. That position, however, had its built-in difficulties, since there was another cleric at the Temple in the position of reader who was employed to preach in the afternoon. The reader in question was Walter Travers, a Presbyterian minister of strict Calvinist persuasion who had been disappointed in not being made master himself. To some extent Travers enjoyed the support of the lawyers who were the parishioners of the Temple, because many of their profession were Puritans.[67] At any rate, Travers began to use the time of his sermons in the afternoon to refute what Hooker had preached in the morning, especially his point that "the Church of Rome might be considered a part of Christ's church whose members might be saved in spite of erroneous official teaching."[68] Thus the situation became what was classically defined by Thomas Fuller as Canterbury speaking in the morning and pure Geneva in the afternoon.

Travers's behavior is not irrelevant to Hooker's "Learned Sermon on the Nature of Pride." "A Remedie Against Sorrow and Fear" is a sermon Hooker preached at the funeral of an otherwise unidentified "virtuous gentlewoman." The "Sermon Found in the Study of Bishop [Lancelot] Andrewes" is, appropriately enough, about prayer. The three sermon fragments previously attributed to Ussher do not specify the occasion of their delivery, but one may have been for Holy Week and another for Easter.

Thomas Fuller, who heard both Hooker and Travers, gives an unencouraging report of the former's delivery:

> His voice was low, stature little, gesture none at all, standing stone-still in the Pulpit. . . . Where his eye was left fixed at the beginning, it was found fixed at the end of his Sermon.[69]

Yet the sermons were masterfully crafted. Hooker had full knowledge of rhetorical theory, and his sermons followed the pattern of a classical oration. His sentences had the periodic structure of Latin prose, so his style has been called "Ciceronian," but his vocabulary was colloquial, candid, and intimate.[70] His range of biblical citation and allusion was enormous. He was concerned with the "on-going struggle within the individual believer's soul,"[71] and his theme was God's infinite love and mercy. As a final assessment, P. E. Forte's judgment has much to recommend it:

> If he rarely matches the eloquence of Donne or Andrewes or Taylor, he lacks their mannerisms as well, so that his sermons are among the least self-conscious and declamatory of the period. . . . Quiet, observant, concerned, he is the most reflective of the great English preachers.[72]

The Metaphysicals

Queen Elizabeth died and was succeeded by James I in 1603, thus ending the Tudor period and inaugurating the Stuart barely into the new century. "The seventeenth century in England was *par excellence* an age of sermons,"[73] but they were not all of a single type. Rather, preaching during this period suffered extraordinary shifts in taste. At the beginning of the century, the vogue was for pyrotechnic displays of amazing virtuosity; it was a time when some of England's best poets were also preachers. The middle of the century reflected the triumph of the Puritans in first the Presbyterian and then the Independent phases of the Commonwealth. Then the century ended with a reaction against theological partisanship in which lucid moral essays became more fashionable in pulpits that were themselves very fashionable. By that time, the period of Renaissance and Reformation had ended and the early modern era had begun.

The style of preaching popular at the beginning of the century when Elizabeth's long reign was ending and that of James I beginning is referred to variously as being "witty" or "metaphysical." The understanding of "wit" in this context is characteristic of that period rather than the current. Instead of designating either intelligence or humor *as such,* it had the ninth meaning assigned to the word in *Webster's*: "felicitous perception or expression of associations between ideas or words not usually connected, such as produce an amusing surprise."[74] Mitchell expresses the idea of wit in preaching as "the facility in discovering resemblances between the most disparate things, especially where one of these happened to be of a religious character."[75] That is to say, wit is the ability to coin *conceits* in the literary sense of the word.[76]

Such preaching could sound supercilious unless one remembers the paradoxical nature of the Christian religion in which the most divine things are communicated through the most mundane media and human values are turned upside down. In the perspective of that memory, however, a peculiar appropriateness and even holiness can be imagined for such preaching.

The description of this style of preaching as "metaphysical" is derived from its association with the poetry that had been given this designation by Samuel Johnson, partially out of recognition that one of the metaphysical poets, John Donne, became one of the most respected witty preachers. The near equivalence of the two terms can be seen in Johnson's complaint that by the metaphysical poets "the most heterogeneous ideas are yoked by violence together."[77]

There is more to the definition than that, though. There is an element of the source of the ideas. Mitchell says:

> When . . . we speak of preaching as "metaphysical" we mean that it is quaint and fantastic, not because it employs unusual or whimsical expressions or images, but that when it does employ such it derives them from a background of remote learning, and adapts them to use by a curious transmutation effected by means of the peculiar temperament or deliberate endeavor of the preacher.[78]

The association of witty preaching with metaphysical poetry suggests what is indeed true, that the homiletical phenomenon does not represent a rarified taste confined to the pulpit, but is instead indicative of a characteristic of English and indeed European culture at the time, a fashion in taste that came and went.

That, in turn, suggests another truth, that the metaphysical style was not confined to one ecclesiastical party. It is the case, however, that it was more characteristic of Anglo-Catholics than of any other group.[79] These

English theologians had reached a stage in their understanding of church reform and renewal in which they no longer regarded Luther and Calvin as new founding fathers. Rather, they believed the Church of England to be in continuity with the church through the ages, the Body of Christ, the Holy Catholic Church. They saw that continuity in the succession of their bishops from the apostles and in the continuation of the sacramental life of the church.

Their objection to Rome, beyond the (as they viewed them) unjust pretensions of the pope, was not that it was catholic, but rather that it was insufficiently catholic. It had made additions to the original and apostolic deposit of faith and practice. The English Reformation, therefore, had been a removal of such accretions without any jettisoning of essentials in the manner of continental Protestants. The English had been careful, as their descendants loved to say, not to throw the baby out with the bathwater. They considered their church to represent a reformed Catholicism "such as Chrysostom or Alfred would feel at home in, and David, Boniface, Chad or Anselm would not repudiate as alien."[80]

This conviction of their continuity with the church through the ages led the Anglo-Catholics to find their theological inspiration not in the continental Reformers but in the Fathers of the early church. Indeed, they did not eschew the medieval theologians either. But in returning to what they regarded as the fonts of their faith, they learned things from their reading in addition to dogmatics. They learned, for instance, a way of writing and speaking.

As noted in part 1, the patristic giants had all been trained as rhetors before they were ordained, and they did not forget the style they had learned when they became Christian authors. The Fathers who most influenced Anglo-Catholic style, such as Tertullian, represented not the balanced periods of Cicero, but the more aphoristic style of the Stoics, especially Seneca. "Senecan brevity, abruptness, and point characterize the sentences of Andrewes, and affect those of Donne."[81] And this at a time when Seneca's appeal was felt by English authors in fields other than theology.

The Anglo-Catholic metaphysical preachers acquired a number of stylistic traits from the Fathers. Basil's *isocola* and *antitheses* were effective vehicles for communicating the paradoxical gospel of the God who became a human being, the immortal God who died in behalf of mortals. Chrysostom, the "Golden-tongued," had "an oriental richness and profusion of epithets and images."[82] Ambrose's rich imagination found full play in allegorical interpretation of the Scriptures. He also introduced his seventeenth-century readers to the Cabalists and, with the aid of his contemporaries, to the natural history of Pliny and the *Physiologus*, from which so many morals could be derived. The Hermetic literature became known in a similar way. A sense of drama was acquired from the "last of the Fathers," Bernard of Clairvaux. The Anglo-Catholics shared the fashion for the use of "conceits" like those employed by the Fathers with Spanish, Italian, and French preachers. With them as well they shared a rhetorical education that taught them to keep commonplace books in which they could note for future use all such wonderful treasures from the Fathers. Thus imitation and quotation of the Fathers were common in the sermons of both Catholic Reform and Anglo-Catholic preachers.

Stella Praedicantium

The first and certainly one of the greatest of the Metaphysicals was Lancelot Andrewes (1555–1626),[83] who was known to his contemporaries as *stella praedicantium,* the "star of preaching," and an "Angell in the Pulpit." Born the year after his friend Hooker, he outlived him by twenty-six years. A London native and the son of a successful mariner who became a master of Trinity House, he was sent to Cooper's Free School and the Merchant Taylors' School. He achieved such a proficiency in Latin, Greek, and Hebrew by the age of sixteen that he became one of the first to receive a Greek scholarship to Pembroke College, Cambridge. There he continued to make rapid progress, receiving his B.A. in 1575. Elected a fellow of his college, he stayed on to receive his B.D. in 1585, and his D.D. around 1588.[84]

A naturally studious youth who allowed himself no recreation beyond walks on which he studied nature,[85] he became one of the most learned men in England. When he was appointed catechist of his college about the time he received his M.A., he quickly attracted a wide following both within and beyond the university. He then became Pembroke's treasurer and showed himself to be an effective administrator.

His fame had already begun to spread beyond Cambridge, and in 1586 he was appointed as one of the chaplains of both the queen and the archbishop of Canterbury, John Whitgift. Three years later he became vicar of St. Giles in the new Cripplegate section of London and also a prebendary (canon) of St. Paul's Cathedral. He was also made master of his Cambridge college at about this time.

Honors and duties were heaped upon him, and he was humble about the one and conscientious about the other. For instance, after his death a manual was published on ministering to the sick that he had drawn up for his pastoral work at St. Giles. Further, his stall at St. Paul's had been traditionally connected with hearing confessions, a responsibility he reinstituted. In 1601 he became dean of Westminster Abbey; in addition to his other activities in connection with the position, he became a beloved teacher of the boys at Westminster School.

King James I was, whatever his other shortcomings, well trained in theology. He took an immediate liking to Andrewes, appointing him to such duties as meeting with the Puritans at the Hampton Court Conference, heading the London group of translators of the Authorized Version of the Bible,[86] and engaging in controversy with Cardinal Bellarmine. Under this royal patronage, Andrewes became successively bishop of Chichester (1605), Ely (1609), and Winchester (1618). His presence at court was highly valued; he was made a privy councilor of England in 1616 and of Scotland the next year. He was appointed dean of the Chapel Royal, and, among other assignments in connection with the royal family, carried the paten in the coronation procession of Charles I in 1626. He died the same year.

He never sought the honors that came to him in such abundance; his first sense of duty was always to God. He was reputed to have spent five hours a day in prayer, a statement that is rendered credible by the manual of prayers he compiled for his own use, his *Preces Privatae,* first published in 1675 and in print to this day.[87]

It was, however, for his preaching that Andrewes was best known. Shortly after his death, King Charles I ordered that his sermon manuscripts be collected and published. Those given the task found ninety-six sermons in the form in which the bishop had delivered them. Most of them had been preached in court: seventeen for Christmas, eight on prayer and fasting for Ash Wednesday, six for other days in Lent, three for Good Friday, eighteen for Easter, fifteen for Whitsunday (Pentecost), and eighteen in thanksgiving for deliverance from conspiracies (eight for the Gowries and ten for the Gunpowder Plot).[88] There is one that was preached at St. Mary's hospital and two at St. Giles, six delivered at court on less solemn days in the Christian year, and three more on state occasions. In addition to his XCVI Sermons there remain his Cambridge catechetical sermons, in which there are nineteen on prayer (especially the Lord's Prayer) and seven on Christ's temptation in the wilderness. Of the court sermons it can be said that those before Elizabeth were for penitential seasons, while, for most of the years of his reign, James I heard Andrewes preach on Christmas, Easter, and Whitsunday, the great feasts of the year.

While some general characteristics of metaphysical preaching have been indicated above, a sample of the sort of thing Andrewes did could be a helpful preface to listing the attributes of his preaching. The passage chosen is from "Sermon IX of the Nativity," on the text: "Behold a virgin shall conceive and bear a Son and she shall call his name Immanuel":

> And now, to look into the name. It is compounded, and to be taken in pieces. First, into *Immanu* and *El*; of which, *El* the latter is the more principal by far; for *El* is God. Now, for any thing yet said in *concipiet* and *pariet,* all is but man with us; not "God with us" till now. By the name we take our first notice that this Child is God. And this is a great addition, and here, lo, is the wonder. For, as for any child of a woman to "eat butter with honey," (Isa. vii.15), the words that next follow, where is the *Ecce*? but for *El,* for God to do it—that is worth an *Ecce* indeed.
>
> *El* is God; and not God every way, but as the force of the word is, God in His full strength and virtue; God *cum plentudine potestatis* as we say, "with all that ever He can do"; and that is enough I am sure.
>
> For the other, *Immanu*; though *El* be the more principal, yet I cannot tell whether it or *Immanu* do more concern us. For as in *El* is might, so in *Immanu* is our right to his might, and to all He hath or is worth. By that word we hold, therefore we to lay hold of it. The very standing of it thus before, thus in the first place, toucheth us somewhat. The first thing ever that we look for is *nos, nobis,* and *noster*, the possessives; for they do *mittere in possessionem,* "put us in possession." We look for it first, and lo, it stands here first; *nobiscum* first, and then *Deus* after.
>
> I shall not need to tell you that in *nobiscum* there is *mecum*; in *nobiscum* for us all a *mecum* for every one of us. Out of this generality of "with us," in gross, may every one deduce his own particular—with me, and me, and me. For all put together make but *nobiscum.*
>
> The Wise Men out of Immanuel, that is *nobiscum Deus,* doth deduce Ithiel (Prov. xxx.1), that is *mecum Deus,* "God with me"—his own private interest. And St. Paul when he had said to the Ephesians of Christ, "Who loved us, and gave Himself for us," (Eph. v. 2). might with good right say to the Galatians, "Who loved me and gave Himself for me." (Gal. ii. 20).
>
> This *Immanu* is a compound again; we may take it in sunder into *nobis* and *cum*; and so then have we three pieces. 1. *El,* the mighty God; 2. and *anu,* we, poor we,—poor indeed if we have all the world beside if we do not have Him to be with us; 3. and *Im,* which is *cum,* and that *cum* in the midst between *nobis* and *Deus,* God and us—to couple God and us; thereby to convey the things of the one to the other. Ours to God; alas, they be not worth the speaking of. Chiefly, then, to convey to us the things of God. For that is worth the while; they are indeed worth the conveying.
>
> This *cum* we shall never conceive to purpose, but *carendo*;[89] the value of "with" no way so well as by without, by stripping of *cum* from

> *nobis.* And so let *nobis,* "us," stand by ourselves without Him, to see what our case is but for this Immanuel; what, if this virgin's Child had not this day been born us: *nobiscum* after will be the better esteemed. For if this Child be "Immanuel, God with us," then without this Child, this Immanuel, we be without God. "Without Him in this world," (Eph. ii. 12), saith the Apostle; and if without Him in this, without Him in the next; and if without Him there—if it be not *Immanu-el,* it will be *Immanu-hell*; and that and no other place will fall, I fear me, to our share. Without Him, this we are. What with Him? Why, if we have Him, and God by Him, we need no more; *Immanu-el* and *Immanu-all.* All that we can desire is for us to be with Him, with God, and He to be with us; and we from Him, or He from us, never to be parted. We were with Him once before, and we were well; and when we left Him, and He no longer "with us," then began all our misery. Whensoever we go from Him, so shall we be in evil case, and never be well till we be back with Him again.
>
> Then, if this be our case that we cannot be without Him, no remedy then but to get a *cum* by whose means *nobis* and *Deus* may come together again. And Christ is that *Cum* to bring it to pass. The parties are God and we; and now this day He is both. God before eternally, and now to-day Man; and so both, and takes hold of both, and brings both together again. For two natures here are in Him. If conceived and born of a woman, then a man; if God with us, then God. So Esay offered his "sign from the height above, or from the depth beneath," (Isa. vii. 11); here it is. "From above," *El*; "from beneath," *anu*; one of us now. And so, His sign from both. And both these natures in the unity of one Person, called by one name, even this name Immanuel.[90]

The first and most obvious comment to make is that the text from which Andrewes preaches is the Latin Vulgate, although he always translates the Latin (or other foreign language) after he quotes it. Anyone at the court of James I could have been expected to know the Latin, but he takes no chance of being misunderstood. The second point to be made, almost as obvious as the first, was stated by the one who did more than anyone else to call Andrewes to modern attention, T. S. Eliot:

> Andrewes takes a word and derives the world from it; squeezing and squeezing the word until it yields a full juice of meaning which we should never have supposed any word to possess.[91]

Other characteristics of Andrewes's preaching come out in the following passage from Mitchell, which characterizes this preaching so concisely that it deserves extended quotation:

> It was not . . . so much the material as the use to which the material was put that distinguished the "metaphysical" preacher; the greater ingenuity with which he adapted his examples, the more unexpected parallels which he produced, and the more subtle, psychological, and learned images which he employed—these were the characteristic traits. Not mere quotation, but quotation leading up to an unexpected "point,"[92] and a "point," which, while it was verbal, conveyed something of much greater import; not punning and quibbling merely for their own sakes, but because amid the jingle of human phrases might be caught the accents of a divine message—these were the things that counted.[93]

In spite of his appreciation for Andrewes, Mitchell does fault him for what he calls the jerkiness or abruptness of his style, "the inability to achieve the *lexis eironmene* on which literary grace so largely depends."[94] This criticism, however, needs to be understood in the perspective of Mitchell's concern with sermons as literature, as representing a written rather than an oral medium. From this perspective, he finds the sermons of John Donne more satisfactory. Yet T. S. Eliot, a literary critic at least as perceptive as Mitchell, has found the advantage the other way in comparing the sermons of the two.[95]

In addition to Andrewes and Donne, many other early seventeenth-century preachers belonged to the metaphysical school. Among them Mitchell discusses the pulpit work of Ralph Brownrig, John Hacket, Richard Corbet, Henry King, Thomas Playfere, John Cosin, and Mark Frank.[96] Before leaving this school, however, it is necessary to pay attention to the rapid loss of respect that it suffered. It is represented in the attitudes of George Bull, who became bishop of St. David's in 1705. Although his theological position was very close to that of the earlier Anglo-Catholics, his former curate wrote of him:

> He abhorred Affectations of Wit, Trains of fulsom Metaphors, and nice Words wrought up with tuneful, pointed Sentences, without any substantial Meaning at the Bottom of them. He looked upon Sermons consisting of these Ingredients . . . as inconsistent with the Dignity of serious and sacred Things, and as an Indication of a weak Judgment.[97]

A similar point of view was expressed by a Scottish lord who heard Andrewes preach at Holyrood during the royal visit of 1617: "He rather plays with his text than preaches on it."[98] The frequent imputation was that the metaphysical preachers were merely showing off.

To anyone who does not recognize the fundamental seriousness of the sermons of Andrewes, about the only thing that can be said is to call attention to the sermon that Archbishop William Laud preached from the scaffold on Tower Hill before he was beheaded by the Roundheads on January 10, 1645. It begins this way:

> *Good People,*
> You'l pardon my old Memory, and upon so sad occasions as I am come to this place, to make use of my Papers, I dare not trust my self otherwise. This is a very uncomfortable place to Preach in, and yet I shall begin with a Text of Scripture, in the twelfth of the Hebrews,
>
> *Let us run with patience that race that is set before us, looking unto Jesus the author and finisher of our faith, who for the joy that was set before him, endured the Crosse, despising the shame, and is set downe at the right hand of the Throne of God.*
>
> I have been long in my race, and how I have looked unto Jesus the Author and finisher of my Faith, is best known to him: I am now come to the end of my race, and here I finde the Crosse, a death of shame, but the shame must be despised, or there is no coming to the right hand of God; Jesus despis'd the shame for me, and God forbid but I should despise the shame for him; I am going apace, as you see, towards the Red-sea, and my feet are upon the very brinks of it, an Argument, I hope, that God is bringing me to the Land of Promise, for that was the way by which of old he led his people; But before they came to the Sea, he instituted a Passeover for them, a Lamb it was, but it was to bee eaten with very soure Herbs, as in the Twelfth of *Exodus.*
>
> I shall obey, and labour to digest the sowre Herbs, as well as the Lamb, and I shall remember that it is the Lords Passeover; I shall not think of the Herbs, nor be angry with the hands which gathered them, but look up only to him who instituted the one, and governeth the other: For men can have no more powre over me, then that which is given them from above; I am not in love with this passage through the red Sea, for I have the weaknesse and infirmity of flesh and blood in me, and I have prayed as my Saviour taught me, and exampled me, *Vt transiret calix ista,*
>
> That this Cup of red Wine might passe away from me, but since it is not that my will may, his will be done; and I shall most willingly drink of this Cup as deep as he pleases, and enter into this Sea, ay and passe through it, in the way that he shall be pleased to leade me.[99]

To imagine that such a witness of faith and demonstration of grace is less than serious requires an uncommon lack of imagination.[100] Although the metaphysical style of preaching, like all other homiletical styles, had its imitators who aped the conventions without aspiring to its substance, later generations' criticism of its true practitioners betrays an extraordinary capacity to miss the point.[101] But perhaps such a lack of imagination was epidemic at the time. T. S. Eliot suggests that "in the seventeenth century a dissociation of sensibility set in, from which we have never recovered."[102] This dissociation is a separation of thought from experience. Perhaps it was necessary for the development of scientific thought and modernism in general, but a price was paid: the loss of the ability of human beings to respond to their world as total persons whose thoughts are felt.

These examples of Tudor and Stuart preaching show that after a beginning in the reign of Edward VI, when the lack of trained preachers required sermons that could be read to congregations, the cause of preaching received considerable impetus. It was certainly supported by Latimer, the colloquial preacher of Reform. By the time of Elizabeth, Puritans were demanding extra preaching through the ministry of readers, and preaching of the clarity and grace of Henry Smith's could acquire an enormous following. Even a philosophical theologian like Hooker, with no skill in delivery, could attract an audience by the profundity of his thought. At the end of the Tudor period and the beginning of the Stuart, some of the greatest theologians, spiritual writers, and poets in the history of England were preaching witty sermons in the metaphysical style. No wonder that

> preaching played a more important role in the life of the times than ever before or since. Not only did the pulpit outdraw bearbaiting and morris dancing, but even in sophisticated London the popular preachers attracted larger audiences week after week than Shakespeare and Jonson in their prime.[103]

By any standard, it must be admitted that the goals of the English Erasmians were met beyond anything they could have imagined.

FOR FURTHER READING

Blench, J. W. *Preaching in England in the Late Fifteenth and Sixteenth Centuries: A Study of English Sermons 1450–c.1600*. Oxford: Basil Blackwell; New York: Barnes & Noble, 1964.

Certain Sermons, or Homilies, appoynted by the Kynges Maiestie, to be declared and redde, by all Persones, Uicars, or Curates euery Sonday in their Churches, where they haue Cure. London: R. Grafton, 1547.

Hooker, Richard. *Tractates and Sermons*. Edited by W. Speed Hill, general; Laetitia Yeandle, text; and Egil Grislis, commentary. Vol. 5 of *Folger Library Edition of the Works of Richard Hooker.* Cambridge: Belknap Press of Harvard University Press, 1990.

Lancelot Andrewes: Sermons. Selected and edited with introduction by G. M. Story. Oxford: Clarendon, 1967.

Selected Sermons of Hugh Latimer. Edited by Allan G. Chester. Folger Documents of Tudor and Stuart Civilization. Charlottesville, Va.: University of Virginia Press for the Folger Shakespeare Library, 1968.

Shuger, Debora K. *Sacred Rhetoric: The Christian Grand Style in the English Renaissance.* Princeton: Princeton University Press, 1988.

The Works of Henry Smith, Including Sermons, Treatises, Prayers, and Poems. Edited by Thomas Smith. Nichol's Series of Standard Divines: Puritan Period, vols. 39, 40. Edinburgh: James Nichol; London: James Nisbet and Co.; Dublin: G. Herbert, 1866.

The Works of William Perkins. Edited and introduction by Ian Breward. The Courtenay Library of Reformation Classics, vol. 3. Appleford, Abingdon, and Berkshire: Sutton Courtenay, 1970.

Notes

1. F. M. Powicke, *The Reformation in England* (London: Oxford University Press, 1941), 1.

2. The principle that the religion of the sovereign determines that of the realm.

3. The Puritans were not uniformly a group of Presbyterian separatists but included as well many who were loyal to the Church of England and who could live comfortably with episcopacy. See Patrick Collinson, *The Religion of Protestants: The Church in English Society 1559–1625* (Oxford: Clarendon, 1982), 1-38.

4. For a concise history of the Church of England, see William P. Haugaard, "From the Reformation to the Eighteenth Century," and Perry Butler, "From the Eighteenth Century to the Present Day" in *The Study of Anglicanism,* ed. John Booty and Stephen Sykes (London: SPCK; Philadelphia: Fortress, 1988), 3-47.

5. J. W. Blench, *Preaching in England in the Late Fifteenth and Sixteenth Centuries: A Study of English Sermons 1450–c.1600* (Oxford: Basil Blackwell; New York: Barnes & Noble, 1964).

6. Although it was not as clear when Blench was writing as it has become recently, both the Catholic and Protestant approaches were indebted to the humanists for their biblical literalism, as the grammatical basis of Luther's exegesis indicates. See above, chapter 12.

7. Blench, *Preaching in England in the Late Fifteenth and Sixteenth Centuries,* 47.

8. "Accommodations" were analogical extensions of biblical texts that theoretically were not claimed to be explicit biblical teaching but only inferences from such teaching or illustrations employing biblical metaphors or narratives. Blench (ibid.,

39) gives an excellent quotation from Tyndale explaining this procedure, although the word *accommodation* does not appear in the passage quoted.

9. Ibid., 71-72.

10. Ibid., 97.

11. Ibid., 88. The *partes* of the classical oration adapted to the sermon form were spelled out in an English translation of a homiletics textbook by Hyperius of Marburg as: (A) "Reding of the sacred scripture," (B) "Inuocation," (C) "Exordium," (D) "Proposition or division," (E) "Confirmation," (F) "Confutation," and (G) "Conclusion" (cited, ibid., 102). As Blench points out, "The last five are the stock parts of the classical oration."

12. Ibid., 101-2. Perhaps one reason for the short shrift given this method of sermon construction is that Blench found the form "unbearably tedious to the modern reader after a few pages."

13. Ibid., 113.

14. Ibid.

15. Ibid., 3. The G. L. Hendrickson article, "The Origin and Meaning of the Ancient Characters of Style," appeared in a journal identified by Shuger as *AJP* XXVI (1905), 249-90.

16. This misunderstanding of style is similar to the way the word *rhetoric* is often used pejoratively today to refer to only flowery or manipulative speech, as though legitimate persuasion were somehow unrhetorical.

17. Debora K. Shuger, *Sacred Rhetoric: The Christian Grand Style in the English Renaissance* (Princeton: Princeton University Press, 1988).

18. What the comic-strip character Pogo once described as "the twenty-four karat bamboozle."

19. Shuger, *Sacred Rhetoric,* 6.

20. That is, "parsons," from the Latin *persona,* the person who represents a parish church in its corporate and ecclesiastical capacities, which is to say, the priest who has been appointed to the benefice.

21. *Certain Sermons, or Homilies, appoynted by the Kynges Maiestie, to be declared and redde, by all Persones, Uicars, or Curates euery Sonday in their Churches, where they haue Cure* (London: R. Grafton, 1547).

22. Horton Davies, *From Cranmer to Hooker, 1534–1603,* vol. 1 of *Worship and Theology in England* (Princeton: Princeton University Press, 1970), 229, citing J. T. Tomlinson, *The Prayer Book, Articles, and Homilies,* an 1897 publication that I have not seen. Most of the same attributions are given in the articles on "Homilies, the Books of" in *ODCC.* Perhaps some of these attributions will have to be revised in the light of John N. Wall Jr.'s unpublished 1973 Harvard Ph.D. dissertation, "The Vision of a Christian Commonwealth in the Book of Homilies of 1547." A "Second Book" of twenty-one more homilies, most written by John Jewel, was issued under Elizabeth I around 1571.

23. "Godly and Fruitful Lessons: The English Bible, Erasmus' *Paraphrases,* and the *Book of Homilies,*" in *The Godly Kingdom of Tudor England: Great Books of the English Reformation,* ed. John E. Booty (Wilton, Conn.: Morehouse-Barlow, 1981), 47-135.

24. Ibid., 56, referring to Marjorie O'Rourke Boyle, *Erasmus on Language and Method in Theology* (Toronto: University of Toronto Press, 1977), 53.

25. The *Paraphrases*.

26. Ibid., 57.

27. Ibid., 93.

28. Millar Maclure, *The Paul's Cross Sermons, 1534–1642,* University of Toronto Department of English Studies and Texts, no. 6 (Toronto: University of Toronto Press, 1958), 54. This study gives an account of a remarkable series of sermons preached outside St. Paul's Cathedral in London.

29. Davies, *From Cranmer to Hooker, 1534–1603,* 296-97. The Hooker reference is to *Ecclesiastical Polity* 5.22.

30. On the social conditions reflected in Latimer's sermons and his recommendations on what to do about them, see A. G. Dickens, *The English Reformation* (New York: Schocken Books, 1964), 151-54, and Charles Montgomery Gray, *Hugh Latimer and the Sixteenth Century: An Essay in Interpretation,* Harvard Phi Beta Kappa Prize Essays (Cambridge: Harvard University Press, 1950).

31. For Latimer's account of his conversion, see the first of his sermons on the Lord's Prayer, *The Works of Hugh Latimer, Sometime Bishop of Worchester, Martyr, 1555,* ed. for the Parker Society by George Elwes Corrie (Cambridge: The University Press, 1844), 2:334-35. For more about Bilney, see "The Seventh Sermon Before Edward VI," 2:222. Both of these sermons are included in *Selected Sermons of Hugh Latimer,* ed. Allan G. Chester, Folger Documents of Tudor and Stuart Civilization (Charlottesville: University of Virginia Press for Folger Shakespeare Library, 1968). Biographies of Latimer tend to be hagiographic, but one that is less so while still admiring is that of Allan G. Chester, *Hugh Latimer, Apostle to the English* (Philadelphia: University of Pennsylvania Press, 1954). Some critical distance is also maintained in Harold S. Darby, *Hugh Latimer* (London: Epworth, 1953). All must draw on John Foxe's *Acts and Monuments of Matters Happening in the Church* ("Foxe's Book of Martyrs"), whose account is reprinted in Latimer's *The Works of Hugh Latimer,* 1:ix-xxxi. I regret that Michael Pasquarello's University of North Carolina dissertation on the preaching of Latimer was not completed in time to influence this chapter.

32. Always, apparently, in the English humanist tradition. At any rate, he said: "I will not take upon me to defend (Luther) in all points. I will not stand to it that all that he wrote was true; I think he would not so himself: for there is no man but he may err. He came to further and further knowledge: but surely he was a goodly instrument." "Sixth Sermon Preached Before King Edward the Sixth" (Latimer, *The Works of Hugh Latimer,* 2:212).

33. John Foxe, *Acts and Monuments,* ed. R. R. Mandham and Josiah Pratt, 4th ed. rev. (London, 1875), 8:289.

34. Quoted without attribution in *The English Sermon, An Anthology,* vol. 1, ed. Martin Seymour-Smith (Cheadle and Cheshire: Carcanet, 1976), 54.

35. Charles Smyth says that Latimer was "a typically medieval preacher," in *The Art of Preaching: A Practical Survey of Preaching in the Church of England, 747–1939* (London: Society for Promoting Christian Knowledge, 1940), 107-8.

36. Blench, *Preaching in England in the Late Fifteenth and Sixteenth Centuries,* 92.

37. "Following the order of the text."

38. On at least one occasion he apologized for not preaching on either the Epistle or the Gospel appointed for the day. Latimer, "Last Sermon Preached Before King Edward the Sixth," in Chester, ed., *Selected Sermons of Hugh Latimer,* 90-113.

39. Blench, *Preaching in England in the Late Fifteenth and Sixteenth Centuries,* 142. He also gives a concise analysis of the construction of all seven sermons preached before Edward VI on pp. 92-94.

40. For the amount of his alliteration and also for the rhythm of his speech see Longinus, *On the Sublime,* trans. with commentary, James A. Arieti and John M. Crossett, Texts and Studies in Religion, vol. 21 (New York: Edwin Mellen, 1985), 207 n.

41. Horton Davies, *From Cranmer to Hooker, 1534–1603,* in *Worship and Theology,* 1:248.

42. Written originally in Latin by Perkins in 1592, *The Arte of Prophesying* was translated into English by Thomas Tuke in 1607. The edition followed here is the slightly condensed version contained in *The Works of William Perkins,* ed. and intr. Ian Breward, Courtenay Library of Reformation Classics (Appleford, Abingdon (Berkshire): Sutton Courtenay, 1970), 3:331-49, supplemented by references to the 1626–31 I. Legatt edition of *The VVorkes of... Mr. William Perkins.* The edition used by Breward, however, is that of John Legate and Cantrell Legge published between 1616 and 1618. Both of these seventeenth-century editions were published in London.

43. Breward, ed., *The Arte of Prophesying, Works of Perkins,* 3:349. The form of seventeenth-century spelling followed is that of Teresa Toulouse, *The Art of Prophesying: New England Sermons and the Shaping of Belief* (Athens: The University of Georgia Press, 1987), 20. A brief form of this method was imposed as a standard for clergy by *A Directory for the Public VVorship of God Throughout the Three Kingdoms of England, Scotland, and Ireland. Together with an Ordinance of Parliament for the taking away of the Book of Common-Prayer and For establishing and observing of this present Directory throughout the Kingdom of England, and Dominion of Wales* (London: Evan Tyler, Alexander Fifield, Ralph Smith, and John Field, 1644), 27-36.

44. Perry Miller, *The New England Mind: The Seventeenth Century* (Cambridge: Belknap Press of Harvard University Press, 1939), 332-33.

45. For a convenient summary of Perkins's theory of interpretation see Toulouse, *The Arte of Prophesying,* 14-23.

46. For an evaluation of the Ramist movement see Walter J. Ong, *Ramus: Method, and the Decay of Dialogue from the Art of Discourse to the Art of Reason* (Cambridge: Harvard University Press, 1958), ix. For a critique of Ong, see Brian Vickers, *In Defence of Rhetoric* (Oxford: Clarendon; New York: Oxford University Press, 1988), 475-77.

47. Bacon's objection to this procedure is that "men of this sort torture things with their laws of method, and whatever does not conveniently fall in these dichotomies, they either omit or pervert beyond nature, so that, so to speak, when the seeds and kernels of science are springing forth, they gather so many dry and empty husks." Quoted from the Spedding, Ellis, and Heath edition of Bacon's *Works,* 1:663, by Perry Miller, *The New England Mind,* 127.

48. For the psychology behind the Puritan understanding of conversion, see the chapter on "The Means of Conversion" in Perry Miller, *The New England Mind,*

280-99. For Ramist influence on Puritan homiletics, see the two following chapters on "Rhetoric" and "The Plain Style," 300-362.

49. Ibid., 338-39.

50. For the popularity of Talon among continental Reformed preachers, see Peter Bayley, *French Pulpit Oratory 1598–1650: A Study in Themes and Styles with a Descriptive Catalogue of Printed Texts* (Cambridge: Cambridge University Press, 1980), 29-31, 97.

51. From Thomas Fuller, "The Life of Mr. Henry Smith," which prefaced his 1675 edition of Smith's works and was reprinted in *The Works of Henry Smith, Including Sermons, Treatises, Prayers, and Poems,* ed. Thomas Smith, Nichol's Series of Standard Divines: Puritan Period, vols. 39, 40 (Edinburgh: James Nichol; London: James Nisbet and Co.; Dublin: G. Herbert, 1866), 1:ix. Unfortunately, the only modern book-length treatment of Smith is R. B. Jenkins, *Henry Smith: England's Silver-Tongued Preacher* (Macon, Ga.: Mercer University Press, 1983), which shows very little knowledge of Smith's period or understanding of the religious scene. For instance, the author thinks Thomas Fuller was a bishop and calls Lancelot Andrewes, Richard Hooker, and even Richard Bancroft "Puritans." He further considers Puritan "prophesyings" to have been only sermons rather than a homiletical training program (see Collinson, *The Religion of Protestants,* 129-30) and thinks the *Book of Homilies* was a set of lay-readers' sermons that were "devoid of theological controversy, political overtones, and sectarianism" (p. 26). Much shorter but far more reliable is John L. Lievsay, "'Silver-Tongued Smith,' Paragon of Elizabethan Preachers," *Huntington Library Quarterly* 11 (1947–48): 13-36. The implication of the epithet "silver-tongued" is that Smith was second in preaching ability only to John of Antioch and Constantinople, who was called *Chrysostomos,* the "Golden-tongued."

52. Thomas Smith argued that the title of "Mr. Henry Smith" under which he published his sermons would have been the equivalent at the time of "Henry Smith, M.A." *The Works of Henry Smith,* 1:xii. Jenkins, *Henry Smith,* 11, credits this opinion to Fuller rather than Thomas Smith, not having noticed, apparently, that the Fuller account ended two pages earlier.

53. Quoted in Thomas Smith, *The Works of Henry Smith,* 1:xiii.

54. Paul Seaver, *The Puritan Lectureships: The Politics of Religious Dissent, 1560–1662* (Stanford: Stanford University Press, 1970), 6. For a slightly different perspective see Collinson, *The Religion of Protestants,* 170-77.

55. No doubt the intercession of his powerful stepuncle also assisted in this restoration.

56. Thomas Smith, *The Works of Henry Smith,* 2:447.

57. *Worship and Theology,* I, 294. *Sed contra,* Smith's statement quoted above that the administration of the sacraments is one of the "essential marks of the true church."

58. Thomas Smith, *The Works of Henry Smith,* 2:328.

59. Ibid., 1:xvi.

60. Davies, *From Cranmer to Hooker, 1534–1603,* in *Worship and Theology,* 1:309. In *Like Angels from a Cloud: The English Metaphysical Preachers, 1588–1645* (San Marino, Calif.: Huntington Library, 1986), 12 *et passim,* Davies treats Smith as one of the Metaphysical preachers.

61. Blench defines schemata as "artificial word patterns" (*Preaching in England in the Late Fifteenth and Sixteenth Centuries,* 113), but the more ordinary term is "figures of speech."

62. Ibid., 184.

63. Thomas Smith, *The Works of Henry Smith,* 1:xx.

64. Lievsay, "Silver-tongued Smith," 13.

65. Thomas Smith, *The Works of Henry Smith,* 1:ix.

66. Hooker, *Tractates and Sermons,* vol. 5 in *Folger Library Edition of the Works of Richard Hooker,* gen. ed. W. Speed Hill, text, Laetitia Yeandle, comm., Egil Grislis (Cambridge: Belknap Press of Harvard University Press, 1990). See my review article in *ATR* 74 (1992), 112-16. In the usage of the time, "sermons" were delivered from notes rather than a full manuscript, "lectures" were read verbatim from the pulpit, and "tractates" were preached in church but published to be read as treatises. Yet the terms were not used with such consistency that one can infer from the title the extent to which a particular Hooker text represents what was actually said from the pulpit.

67. This affiliation reflects in part the objection of the common lawyers of the Inns of Court to their not being allowed to practice in church courts of canon law. Possibly relevant to this partisanship is the fact that Hooker argued from the principles of natural law, which is related to the Roman tradition of civil law (taught in the universities but not at the Inns of Court, where most British barristers received their legal education) while the lawyers were trained in the English tradition of common law.

68. William P. Haugaard, "The Controversy and its Dissemination," in Hooker, *Tractates and Sermons,* 268.

69. Thomas Fuller, *Church History of Britain* (London: 1655; reprint, London: Thomas Tegg, 1842), 9.7.53 (2:216).

70. Fuller says of his style: "The doctrine he delivered had nothing but itself to garnish it. His style was long and pithy, driving-on a whole flock of several clauses before he came to the close of a sentence. So that when the copiousness of his style met not with proportionable capacity in his auditors, it was unjustly censured for perplexed, tedious, and obscure" (ibid.). This Ciceronian complexity of sentence structure has caused, for example, Blench to speak of Hooker as a representative of the "fully ornate style" (Blench, *Preaching in England in the Late Fifteenth and Sixteenth Centuries,* 188), but Shuger is right in seeing that it is rather the passion of his preaching, a passion that results from the union of *magnitudo* and *praesentia* that makes his style "grand" in the sense in which the term was used in the Renaissance (Shuger, *Sacred Rhetoric,* 223). This union is further defined as that of "the greatest object (of love) with the most vivid representation" (199)—which, of course, is what the rhetorical terms *magnitudo* and *praesentia* mean.

71. P. E. Forte, "Hooker as Preacher," in Hooker, *Tractates and Sermons,* 650.

72. Ibid., 682. Cf. W. Fraser Mitchell, *English Pulpit Oratory from Andrewes to Tillotson: A Study of Its Literary Aspects* (1932; New York: Russell & Russell, 1962), 65.

73. Mitchell, *English Pulpit Oratory from Andrewes to Tillotson,* 3. This is the standard work on the period although (a) much new light has been shed in the two generations since it originally appeared, and (b) its primary concern with the literary aspects of seventeenth-century preaching means that the criteria of judgment often reflect written more than oral standards, and aesthetic more than theological.

74. *Webster's New International Dictionary (Unabridged),* 2nd ed., s.v. "wit."

75. Mitchell, *English Pulpit Oratory,* 6.

76. "An elaborate metaphor comparing two apparently dissimilar objects or emotions, often with an effect of shock or surprise." *The Oxford Companion to English Literature,* ed. Margaret Drabble, 5th ed. (Oxford: Oxford University Press, 1985), 222.

77. Quoted without documentation in T. S. Eliot, "The Metaphysical Poets" in *Selected Prose of T. S. Eliot,* ed. with intro. Frank Kermode (New York: Harcourt Brace Jovanovich, 1975), 60. Eliot's essay was originally published in 1921.

78. Mitchell, *English Pulpit Oratory,* 7.

79. While the term "Anglo-Catholic" was coined in 1838, the essential elements of the point of view so labeled go back to the seventeenth century.

80. Douglas Macleane, *Lancelot Andrewes and the Reaction* (London: Allen, 1910), 2. Quoted in Mitchell, *English Pulpit Oratory,* 139.

81. George Williamson, *The Senecan Amble: A Study in Prose Form from Bacon to Collier* (Chicago: University of Chicago Press, 1951), 231-74. The quotation is from p. 239.

82. Mitchell, *English Pulpit Oratory,* 142. The influence of the Fathers on the Anglo-Catholics is discussed on pp. 141-48. Davies, *Like Angels from a Cloud,* 2-3, 45-98, lists eleven characteristics of metaphysical sermons: patristic learning; classical lore; citations from Greek, Latin, and occasionally Hebrew originals; illustrations from "unnatural" natural history; allegorical exegesis; plans with complex divisions and subdivisions; a Senecan and staccato style; the use of paradoxes, riddles, and emblems; fondness for speculation; and the relation of doctrinal and devotional preaching to the Christian calendar. While the way of stating them is different, this list parallels closely the traits listed in the text.

83. The main contemporary biographical sources are the sermon preached at his funeral by the bishop of London, John Buckeridge, and a life written by his secretary and friend Henry Isaacson, both of which are reprinted in the edition of his *Works,* ed. J. P. Wilson and James Bliss, 11 vols., in The Library of Anglo-Catholic Theology (Oxford: John Henry Parker, 1841–54). The locations of these are, respectively, *Works* 5:257-98, and 11:i-xxxiv. The standard modern biography is Paul A. Welsby, *Lancelot Andrewes, 1555–1626* (London: SPCK, 1958), even though his negative view of some of Andrewes's actions is not shared by all scholars. A handy introduction to the man and his preaching is Trevor A. Owen, *Lancelot Andrewes,* Twayne's English Authors Series, no. 325 (Boston: Twayne, 1981). In addition to the complete edition of the sermons in the *Works,* sermons are found in *Seventeen Sermons on the Nativity by the Right Honourable and Reverend Father in God Lancelot Andrewes,* Ancient and Modern Library of Theological Literature (London: Griffith, Farran, Okeden, and Welsh; New York: E. P. Dutton, n.d.), and *Lancelot Andrewes: Sermons,* selected and ed. with intro. by G. M. Story (Oxford: Clarendon, 1967). The latter contains twelve sermons. Marianne Dorman has edited the sermons for devotional reading in *The Liturgical Sermons of Lancelot Andrewes,* 2 vols. (Edinburgh, Cambridge, and Durham: Pentland, 1992–93), but in making the sermons more accessible to modern readers, she has rendered them useless for scholarly study.

84. In the Oxford and Cambridge of Andrewes's time, these English degrees did not have the same meaning as do current American degrees with the same names.

The M.A. represented continuing residence and study, but not a thesis, and principally signified a change of status in the university whereby one became a "senior member" and thus a member of the university's governing body. The B.D. was (and is) not pre-ordination training but represents the completion of a definitive thesis in one of the theological disciplines, being therefore closely akin to our modern Ph.D. The D.D., far from being honorary, represents further publications or a further thesis regarded as embodying original research. The number of years of residence after which one became eligible for such degrees was closely regulated. I am indebted to Prof. Peter Bayley of Cambridge for this information.

85. He is said to have spent his school holidays learning new languages with the help of a tutor.

86. Andrewes and his committee were responsible for Genesis through 2 Kings in the King James version.

87. Although Andrewes compiled his manual from a variety of biblical and liturgical sources in their original languages, the edition most often referred to is the translation with notes and introduction by F. E. Brightman (London: Methuen, 1909; reprint, Gloucester, Mass.: Peter Smith, 1983).

88. Parliament had decreed liturgically observed days of annual national thanksgiving to commemorate the escape of James from the conspiracy of the Gowrie brothers in Perth on August 5, 1600, and the frustration of the plan of Guy Fawkes to blow up the Houses of Parliament on November 5, 1605, when the king and all the lords and commons were there.

89. "By being deprived" of it.

90. *Seventeen Sermons on the Nativity by the Right Honourable and Reverend Father in God Lancelot Andrewes, Sometime Lord Bishop of Winchester. A New Edition.* The Ancient and Modern Library of Theological Literature (London: Griffith, Farrar, Okeden, and Welsh, n.d.), 140-42.

91. Eliot, "Lancelot Andrewes," in *Selected Prose of T. S. Eliot,* 184. This essay was originally published in 1926. The theology, as opposed to the rhetorical form, of Andrewes's sermons is well treated in Nicholas Lossky, *Lancelot Andrewes the Preacher (1555–1626): The Origins of the Mystical Theology of the Church of England,* trans. Andrew Louth (Oxford: Clarendon, 1991). Not as sympathetic to the man or his thought is Maurice F. Reidy, *Bishop Lancelot Andrewes, Jacobean Court Preacher: A Study of Early Seventeenth-Century Religious Thought* (Chicago: Loyola University Press, 1955).

92. "Point" is a key term in the vocabulary about witty preaching, so much so that the style is also called "pointed." It means that the "wit" is used to enhance meaning rather than as a mere ornament.

93. Mitchell, *English Pulpit Oratory,* 149. A more nuanced analysis of the way Andrewes achieved his effects that employs the techniques of modern linguistics appears in Joseph C. Beaver, "A Study of the Sermon Styles of Lancelot Andrewes and John Donne" (unpublished M.T.S. thesis, Seabury-Western Theological Seminary, 1986), 8-15.

94. Mitchell, *English Pulpit Oratory,* 163. Mitchell seems to have misunderstood rhetorical terminology here. This "run-on" or "strung-out" continuous style, far from being the basis of good writing, is contrasted unfavorably with the periodic

style by Aristotle in *Rhetoric* 3.9.1 (1409a). And what Mitchell calls jerkiness or abruptness is simply the Senecan style taken into English.

95. Eliot, "Lancelot Andrewes," 181-88.

96. Mitchell, *English Pulpit Oratory,* 163-94. In *Like Angels from a Cloud,* Davies discusses many more—more than forty.

97. Quoted, Mitchell, *English Pulpit Oratory,* 120-21, from William Lupton as cited in Robert Nelson, *The Life of Dr. George Bull* (London: 1713).

98. Ibid., 161.

99. Reprinted, *In God's Name: Examples of Preaching in England from the Act of Supremacy to the Act of Uniformity, 1534–1662,* chosen and ed. with intro. and annotations by John Chandos (Indianapolis and New York: Bobbs-Merrill, 1971), 415-16.

100. The judgment required in the case of Laud's sermons is not unlike that expected in a cartoon that appeared in the *New Yorker* a number of years ago. Two men were depicted walking on a beach. From the sea they could hear someone shouting, *"Au secours! Sauvez moi!"* In the caption one man observed to the other: "Either he's French or the worst snob I ever saw."

101. See also Davies, *Worship and Theology in England,* 2:142-54.

102. Eliot, "The Metaphysical Poets" in *Selected Prose of T. S. Eliot,* 64.

103. Seaver, *The Puritan Lectureships,* 5. See also the chapter on "The Vogue of the Sermon" in Alan Fager Herr's dissertation, *The Elizabethan Sermon: A Survey and Bibliography* (Philadelphia: University of Pennsylvania, 1940), 11-29.

PART IV

THE MODERN ERA: FROM THE RESTORATION TO WORLD WAR I

CHAPTER 16

THE DAWN OF MODERNITY (A)

THE RESTORATION AND THE AGE OF REASON

There are a few moments in history in which it is possible to discern a shift in consciousness, a point in time when it seems that the whole world has suddenly awakened seeing things in a different way. One such moment occurred in Europe in the late-seventeenth century. That moment can be characterized in a number of ways. One is in terms of the aftermath of the religious wars that followed the Reformation, wars to determine not only whether a particular area would remain under the spiritual jurisdiction of the pope or be given over to the teachings of one of the Reformers, but also to see which of competing versions of Protestantism would prevail. At the end of these wars, the world was sick of bloodshed and devastation and would have been willing to live under any religious system or none, rather than continue what appeared in retrospect to have been a war over iotas.

Then, too, this was the age of Francis Bacon and Isaac Newton, a time when the scientific method was being used for the first time to investigate nature and was producing extraordinary results. It was also the time when philosophy ceased to presuppose revelation and began to depend on human reason alone, the time of Spinoza, Descartes, and Locke. And, finally, this was a time when the interests of the mercantile classes began to take priority over those of the nobility and royalty. The christocentric culture that had begun with the conversion of Constantine had begun visibly to disintegrate.

In Great Britain, when Richard Cromwell proved in 1660 to be lacking in his father's great ability, Presbyterians joined with Royalists to recall Charles II to the throne. Although Charles himself had little interest in religion, under him the Royalists succeeded in excluding Puritans and Independents from the established church. Thus, for the first time, one can speak of the Church of England as Anglican (although the term is of later coinage) and note that there were dissenting churches in the realm, the Presbyterians and Congregationalists. Charles's brother, James II, who succeeded him, was unlike him in that he had a great deal of religious commitment—and it was all Roman Catholic. When the "Glorious Revolution" against him in 1688 brought his daughter Mary to the throne with her husband, William of Orange, a leader of the Dutch Protestants, it became inevitable that dissent should be tolerated. For the first time it was recognized in England that the country could be politically united and yet religiously divided.

HOMILETICAL THEORY

A New Taste in Preaching

Inevitably, this shift in consciousness that was the dawn of modernity came to be reflected in preaching. It expressed itself as a growing distaste for the styles of either Anglo-Catholics like Andrewes or Puritans following the rules of Perkins. Originally, the basis for this change of taste was expressed exclusively in terms of homiletical and rhetorical values without reference to the cultural changes that occasioned the shift.

One of the first to articulate this dissatisfaction with former styles was Robert South (1634–1716), a staunch Anglican who nevertheless seemed to say to both parties from earlier in the century, "A plague on both your houses." The Anglo-Catholics he designated as "such as disparage, and detract from the Grandeur of the Gospel, by a puerile and indecent Levity" and the Puritans as "such as depreciate and (as much as in them lies) debase the same, by a coarse, careless, rude and insipid Way of handling the great and invaluable Truths in it."[1]

Since the canons of taste enunciated by South are, on the one hand, such a reversal of the standards that prevailed earlier in the century, and yet are, on the other hand, so typical of the period that was beginning, there is no better way to state the objections to former tastes more economically than to quote South at length. Of the Anglo-Catholics with whom he shared so many theological positions, he says:

> All vain, luxuriant Allegories, rhiming *Cadences* of similary Words, are such pitiful Embellishments of Speech, as serve for nothing, but to embase Divinity; and the Use of them, but like the Plaistering of Marble, or the Painting of Gold, the Glory of which is to be seen, and to shine by no other Lustre but their own. What *Qunitilian* most discreetly says of *Seneca's* handling Philosophy, that he did *rerum pondera minutissimis sententiis frangere,* break, and (as it were) emasculate the Weight of his Subject by little affected Sentences, the same may with much more Reason be applyed to the Practice of those, who detract from the Excellency of Things Sacred by a comical Lightness of Expression: As when their Prayers shall be set out in such a Dress, as if they did not supplicate, but compliment Almighty God, and their Sermons so garnished with Quibbles and Trifles, as if they played with Truth and Immortality; and neither believed these Things themselves, nor were willing that others should. . . . And as this can by no means be accounted Divinity, so neither indeed can it pass for Wit; which yet such chiefly seem to affect in such Performances. . . . Such are wholly mistaken in the Nature of *Wit:* For *true Wit* is a severe and manly Thing. Wit in Divinity is nothing else, but Sacred Truths suitably expressed. 'Tis not Shreds of *Latin* or *Greek,* nor a *Deus dixit,* and a *Deus benedixit,* nor those little Quirks, or Divisions into the [ ], the [ ], and the [ ], or the *Egress, Regress,* and *Progress,* and other such Stuff (much like the Style of a Lease) that can properly be called *Wit.* For that is not *Wit,* which consists not with *Wisdom.*[2]

As sharp as South was with his fellow High Churchmen, he was much more acerbic in treating the Puritans and Independents, whom he despised, devoting almost five times as much space to his list of their shortcomings as he had to that of their opponents.

> First of all they seize upon some Text, from whence they draw something (which they call a *Doctrine*) and well may it be said to be *drawn* from the Words; forasmuch as it seldom naturally flows, or *results* from them. In the next place, being thus provided, they branch it into several Heads; perhaps twenty, or thirty, or upwards. Whereupon, for the Prosecution of these, they repair to some *trusty Concordance,* which never fails them, and by the Help of that, they range six or seven

> Scriptures under each Head; which Scriptures they prosecute one by one; first amplifying and enlarging upon one, for some considerable Time, till they have spoiled it; and then that being done, they pass to another, which, in its Turn, suffers accordingly. And these impertinent, and unpremeditated Enlargements they look upon as *the Motions and Breathings of the Spirit,* and therefore much beyond those *carnal Ordinances of Sense and Reason,* supported by Industry and Study; and this they call a *saving Way* of Preaching, as it must be confessed to be a Way to save much Labour, and nothing else that I know of. . . . But to pass from these indecencies to others, as little to be allowed in this Sort of Men, can any tolerable Reason be given for those strange new Postures used by some in the Delivery of the Word? Such as *shutting the Eyes, distorting the Face, and speaking through the Nose,* which I think cannot so properly be called *Preaching,* as *Toning of a Sermon.* Nor do I see, why *the Word* may not be altogether as effectual for *the Conversion of Souls,* delivered by one, who has the Manners to look his Auditory in the Face, using his own Countenance, and his own native Voice without straining it to a lamentable and doleful *Whine,* (never serving to any Purpose, but where some religious Cheat is to be carried on). . . . And here, I humbly conceive, that it may not be amiss to take Occasion to utter a great Truth, as both worthy to be considered, and never to be forgot: Namely, That if we reflect upon the late Times of Confusion, which passed upon the Ministry, we shall find, that the grand Design of the Fanatick Crew was to persuade the World, That a standing, settled Ministry was wholly useless. This, I say, was the main Point which they then drove at. And the great Engine to effect this, was by engaging Men of several Callings (and those the meaner still the better) to hold forth, and harangue the Multitude, sometimes in Streets, sometimes in Churches, sometimes in Barns, and sometimes from Pulpits, and sometimes from Tubs. . . . But on the contrary, had Preaching been made, and reckoned a Matter of solid and true Learning, of Theological Knowledge, and long, and severe Study, (as the Nature of it required it to be) assuredly, no *preaching Cobbler* amongst them all, would ever have ventured *so far beyond his Last,* as to undertake it.[3]

Eight years later, in a sermon delivered at the cathedral rather than the university church at Oxford, South stated his ideal of preaching in positive terms. The sermon, on "Christ's Promises to the Apostles," treated the preaching of the apostles as the norm for that of latter-day clergy. He considered them to have miraculously been given an ability to speak that those to come later would have to acquire by study. The speaking enabled by that gift had three properties:

> i. Great clearness and Perspicuity.
> ii. An unaffected Plainness and Simplicity. And
> iii. A suitable and becoming Zeal or Fervour.[4]
>
> In a word, the Apostles Preaching was therefore mighty, and successful, because plain, natural, and familiar, and by no means above the Capacity of their Hearers: nothing being more preposterous than for those, who where professedly aiming at Men's *Hearts,* to miss the Mark, by shooting *over their Heads.*[5]

Foreshadowing

These criteria characterize a homiletical norm and style that was to remain in effect until well into the nineteenth century. It is, therefore, worthwhile to trace its origins.

One of the first groups to call for greater simplicity in preaching was the Cambridge Platonists. During the interregnum, this group of scholars had begun to feel disquiet over the Calvinism that pervaded the university. This theological position, together with the Laudianism of the opposition, was objected to, not so much because of its beliefs, as because of the spirit that promotion of the position seemed to engender, a pride and querulousness foreign to the spirit of Christ. Members of the group combined an irenicism of spirit with a trust in the God-given powers of human reason, a reason that had discovered truth even when employed by practitioners of other religions or by pagan philosophers.

Their philosophical stance, however, was not the Aristotelianism that had been regnant since its reintroduction into Europe in the Middle Ages. Nor was it the contemporary thought of Descartes and Hobbes, both of whom seemed to describe a materialistic and mechanistic universe in which there was little opening to the immanence of God. Instead, they liked Plato and Plotinus and shared with them a mystical orientation.

While the Platonists were not a homiletical movement as such, their contribution to English preaching has been summarized by Mitchell: "From the elevation of their thoughts they supplied it with a new sublimity, and from the necessity of conveying their ideas to the many they materially aided in the fight for simplicity."[6] Their greatest contribution, however, was through the later preachers whom they influenced. Of whom, I will say more later.

It has been claimed in the past that one of the major forces leading to the plain style of preaching was the standard of prose composition the newly founded Royal Society expected of its members in the communication of the results of their scientific investigations:

> They have exacted from all their members a close, naked, natural way of speaking, positive expressions, clear sense, a native easiness, bringing all things as near the Mathematical plainness as they can, and preferring the language of Artizans, Countrymen, and Merchants, before that, of Wits or Scholars.[7]

Their goal, in short, was to deliver "so many *things* almost in an equal number of *words.*" Yet while some of the people calling for the change in preaching style were involved in the formation of the Royal Society, it seems that both movements were responses to the same social forces rather than that one was an outgrowth of the other.

A third influence that might be thought to account for the new demand for plain preaching is that of the contemporary French pulpit. This was, after all, the golden age of French preaching, with such giants as Bossuet, Bourdaloue, Claude, Fénelon, Massillon, and Rapin. And many of the Royalist clergy had been in exile with Charles II in France during the Commonwealth. Yet Charles Smyth is convinced that the first real impact of French homiletics on English preaching did not occur before 1778–79, when Charles Simeon annotated Robert Robinson's translation of Jean Claude's *Traité du la composition d'un sermon.*[8] The main explanation usually given for this lack of influence is what Mitchell has called the French sermon's "declamatory style foreign to the majority of English preachers."[9] This difference in national temperament and taste is well summarized by Hugh Blair's biographer, John Hill:

> The French preacher generally addresses the imagination and passions; rouses his audience by an animated harangue; and is at more pains to embellish a few thoughts thinly spread out, than to exhibit any rich variety of sentiment. The English preacher, on the other hand, who is often of a temper more cold and phlegmatic, tries to accomplish his purpose by very different means. He regards his hearer as an intellectual, rather than as a sensitive, being.[10]

In addition to these matters of temperament, there is a deeper difference in the purpose of preachers, noted by Irène Simon in comparing funeral sermons of Bossuet and Gilbert Burnet:

> Though both preachers agree on what corrupts sacred eloquence, their standards are altogether different: plain, solid, edifying sermons for the one; for the other "la parole de l'Evangile . . . vive, pénétrante, animée, toute pleine d'esprit et de feu."[11]

Thus the influence of French neoclassicism also fails to account for the emergence of the plain style. The most it seems possible to say is that the world woke up one morning with differences of taste that affected different countries as well as different aspects of intellectual life. Perhaps a sociologist of knowledge could account for this broad shift, but so far no historian appears to have done so.

Genesis in Ecclesiastes

The person in whom the demand for a plain style in preaching first makes its definitive appearance is **John Wilkins** (1614–72). The grandson of the great moderate Puritan John Dod and son of an Oxford goldsmith, Wilkins, upon the completion of his education and ordination, became in turn the chaplain of several distinguished political and scientific figures, including the Elector Palatine. In London and later, after he returned to Oxford as warden of Wadham College, he became a leading popularizer of the new science and the key figure in the organization of the Royal Society. After the Restoration he was made bishop of Chester. For his vigorous participation in the intellectual life of the period, ranging from the liberalization of English religious life through the acceptance of the scientific revolution to the advocacy of simpler modes of intellectual communication, he appears to have deserved being called "the most dynamic force in seventeenth-century England."[12]

Wilkins's contribution to preaching theory occurred early in his career with the 1646 publication of *Ecclesiastes: or, A Discourse Concerning the Gift of Preaching, As it falls under the Rules of Art.*[13] The book is divided into five sections, the first of which (after the short introduction) is on homiletical method and the last of which concerns "Expression"—style and delivery, in the vocabulary of classical rhetoric. By far the largest portion of the volume (pp. 32-251 in the edition consulted) is devoted to providing bibliographical assistance to the preacher in finding appropriate content for the sermon: section 3 on "Matter and Authors," and section 4, which provides "*A regular* Scheme *of the chief Heads in* Divinity."

The section on method deals with the parts of a sermon and what may be said in each part to render it most effective. This latter is, of course, what classical rhetoricians called "invention"—discovering in every case the available means of persuasion. It lists the topics that could be discussed in each part of the sermon, stating the alternatives first in an outline form that is typographically reminiscent of Ramist charts. That is not surprising, since Wilkins was influenced by Ramist logic as part of the entire system of Puritan homiletics taught by Perkins.[14] In modern typography and eliminating the distracting brackets Wilkins's printer used, such an outline looks like this:

3. **Application** is either,
    - **Doctrinal,** for our information; whether more
        - **General,** in some truths to be acknowledged;
            - **Dialectical,** for Instruction, by inferring such corollaries as do naturally flow from the truth we have proved.
            - **Elenctical,** by confuting such errors as are inconsistent with what we have asserted.
        - **Particular,** as to the discovery of our own estates and conditions, whether we do really believe such a truth or practice such a duty, to be examined by signs or marks, which are derived either from the
            - **Cause** or Original from which a thing must proceed.
            - **Effects** or Consequences of it.
            - **Properties** belonging to it
    - **Practical,** either for
        - **Reproof,** which may consist of two parts
            - **Dissuasive,** from the aggravation of any sin, as to the
                - **Nature** of it, its unreasonableness, deformity, etc.
                - **Threats** denounced.
                - **Judgments** executed upon it.
            - **Directive,** to be amplified by
                - **Cautioning** against impediments that hinder.
                - **Setting down** the most proper means to promote such an end, whether more remote, immediate.
                - **Consolation,** either in a state of
                    - **Suffering,** by losses, etc.
                    - **Doubt** or desertion. Against which men are to be supported by
                        - The **consideration** of the nature of God, ourselves, afflictions.
                        - **Promises.**

Experience.
Removal of scruples.
Exhortation, to be further enlarged by
Motives, to excite the affections from those general heads of
Benefit or profit,
Hurt or danger.
Means, to direct the actions, whether
General.
Special[15]

Although Wilkins develops all of this in essay form later, most of the possible ways of relating the message of a text to a congregation are already apparent in this outline.

In the Wilkins method, the parts of a sermon are similar to the old Puritan "doctrines and uses." The principal parts are *explication* of the biblical text and its teaching, the *confirmation* of that doctrine by appeal to authority or reason, and the *application* of that teaching to a congregation. These parts may be preceded by a *preface,* although Wilkins did not consider one to be necessary on most occasions. A *transition* should be made from the explication to the confirmation, to render the method more "perspicuous." "The *Conclusion* should consist of some such matter as may engage the hearers to a serious *remembrance* and *consideration* of the truths delivered."[16]

The topics for an explication or confirmation are developed as fully as those of the application in the outline above, and the expository treatment of each part contains further subpoints. Indeed, the section on explication offers an excellent concise handbook on the best exegetical method of the time and on the means for drawing correct theological inferences from the text. Stated in such detail, the method sounds very complex, but what remains after all the options are explored is a simple, straightforward sermon pattern. The minute subdivisions of Puritan homiletics have been eliminated from sermons using the Wilkins method.

Wilkins's insistence upon simplicity of style is as important for the development of the plain sermon as this simplification of sermon outline. Dividing expression into *phrase* and *elocution,* he says the phrase must be:

> plain and natural, not being darkened with the affectation of *Scholastical* harshness, or *Rhetorical* flourishes. Obscurity in the discourse, is an Argument of Ignorance in the mind. The greatest learning

> is to be seen in the greatest plainness. The more clearly we understand anything ourselves, the more easily we may expound it to others. When the notion it self is good, the best way to set it off, is in the most obvious plain expression.[17]

Wilkins seems to have anticipated the way that homiletical taste was ready to turn and set forth a clear method for constructing sermons that would satisfy that taste. The number of editions in which his textbook appeared in such a short time shows that the homiletical world was ready for such an approach. With his emphasis on simplicity of construction and plainness of diction, he was able to articulate norms for sermons that remained unconscious until he stated them. As soon as he put them into print, the world seemed to recognize that this was what they had been waiting for.

The Theory and Message of Eighteenth-Century Preaching

The closest study of neoclassical or latitudinarian British preaching as a whole is that of Rolf Lessenich in his handbook of eighteenth-century homiletics and theology.[18] No simpler way of surveying the subject exists than merely summarizing his treatment. He also writes as something of an advocate, trying to prove that the pulpit literature of the period is not as dull and dry as reputation would have it.

He begins by showing that the objective prose style of the Royal Society was not the ideal of the preachers. Accepting the recent faculty psychology, they knew that it was as necessary to move hearts as it was to convince minds.[19] The call for a plain style was in part motivated by this desire to make an emotional impact, since it was assumed that the two extremes to be avoided—ostentation and rusticity—made a negative impression on a congregation.

Another way of asserting the emotional appeal of eighteenth-century preaching is to note not only its status as literature at the time but also its influence on the prose style of other literature as well. Samuel Johnson was able to say: "Why, Sir, you are to consider, that sermons make a considerable branch of English literature; so that a library must be very imperfect if it has not a numerous collection of sermons."[20] Further, preachers were urged to deepen the appeal of their preaching by studying the best ancient and modern rhetorical handbooks and examples of oratory.

Yet the solemn purpose of preaching was never forgotten, so that the pleasure of listening or reading was always regarded as subordinate to instruction. To have this combined appeal to the mind and to the emotions, sermons had to be comprehensible to persons of a wide range of social status and education.[21]

The strategy by which the mind was persuaded and the passions moved was tandem, with appeal first to the mind and then to the emotions. This task, however, was set within the framework of a forensic speech of classical rhetoric. Thus the pattern was: exordium, explication, proposition, partition, argumentative part, application, and conclusion. Although the pattern was concealed in the outline recommended by Wilkins, the structure was there. His preface was an exordium or introduction, his explication included the statement of a proposition, his transition was a partition, his confirmation the argumentative part, and he used the same terms for application and conclusion.

Eighteenth-century exordia, prefaces, proems, or introductions served the classical purposes of rendering the audience benevolent, attentive, and teachable and of preparing them for what was to come, thus leading smoothly into the explication.

The way the neoclassical preachers solved the historic problem of fitting the explication of a text into the pattern of a forensic oration was by having it serve the function of the narration, the summary of a case made by a lawyer that led up to an identification of the issues to be contested in the trial. This exegetical section, however, was much simpler than it had been in previous Puritan practice. It aimed neither at some abstruse point of doctrine nor at controversy, but at practical moral instruction. This choice of purpose had already determined the choice of the text to be explicated, since lectionary preaching was not an ideal of the day. Indeed, some neoclassical sermons were topical rather than textual.

If, as was most common, there was a text, its explication was not to be technical and complex, but as "artistic" as the rest of the sermon. The explication enabled the preacher to show that the proposition to be proved by the sermon did derive from the scriptural passage on which it was based. Being thus prepared for, the proposition was stated concisely. Then the partition outlined what was to come by giving "a short and precise enumeration of the separate points of view under which the subject was consecutively treated."[22] The purpose of the partition was to help the congregation remember what was said.[23]

In the argumentative part, which was considered the most important, a preacher would either try to teach the congregation the message of the text or would use the text almost as a pretext, as a jumping-off place for the consideration of a wider topic. The first of these two sermon types was called "analytic" and the other was called "synthetic," but by the vocabulary of later generations, they are not very different from textual and topical developments.

Each of these two types could be divided into two more, giving four genera to neoclassical preaching. The subcategories of analytic sermons were "explicatory" and "observatory," while those of the synthetic sermon were "applicative" and "propositional." The *explicatory* seeks to illustrate the doctrine of the text by exploring the meaning of its most important theological terms, solving difficulties raised, and removing obscurities. Such sermons, of course, are on texts of which the meaning is not clear. For those that have an obvious meaning, the argument needed to consist only of observations about that meaning—hence the designation *observatory.* This method was often used for historical texts.

The *applicative* sermon did not develop the explication of the text so much as it did its practical application to the hearers' lives. Such sermons were essentially hortatory, calling upon the members of the congregation to repent or to lead holier lives. Such sermons, however, were not without the support of rational argument, although they did call for more warmth than the other genera. The *propositional* sermon, on the other hand, was in some ways like the explicatory, but differed in deriving a number of propositions from the text rather than just one. But the development of these propositions was not limited to the implications of the one text; it could be expanded to draw in other material. This genus was a favorite medium for systematic theological instruction from the pulpit.

The preaching theorists of the period disagreed about the way arguments should be introduced in a sermon, some holding that there should be a formal statement of each "head" or topic that would be discussed, while others insisted that transitions from point to point should be unobtrusive. The arguments for the first method are pedagogical and mnemonic, while those for the second are essentially aesthetic, an assumption that the best art is that which covers up art *(ars est celare artem).* In either case, however, it was assumed that the arguments should be presented in a logical order, and that arguments of the same kind should be grouped together. By the same token, it was expected that the arguments should be presented in an order that built to a climax. And it was recognized that the multiplication of arguments generated more confusion than persuasion.[24]

The epilogue (peroration, conclusion) of the sermon could either recapitulate what had already been said or it could be an emotional appeal to the congregation to act on what had been said. Many theorists thought the latter method far more effective than the former. A variety of emotional appeals was recognized, as for instance in this catalog of Jean Claude:

> There are three sorts of dispositions, or emotions, the violent—the tender, and the elevated. The *violent* are, for example, indignation, fear, zeal, courage, firmness against temptations, repentance, self-loathing, &c. The *tender* emotions are joy, consolation, gratitude; tender subjects are pardon, pity, prayer, &c. The *elevated* are admiration of the majesty of God, the ways of providence, the glory of Paradise, the expectation of benefits, &c.[25]

A number of these emotional appeals in the conclusion involved references to judgment and eternal life or damnation.[26]

Like all good manuals of rhetoric, the homiletical writings of the eighteenth century were not only concerned with composition but with delivery as well. Their writers accepted the wisdom of Demosthenes, who told an inquirer that the most important aspect of oratory is "delivery." When asked what the second and third most important parts are, he repeated, "delivery," and "delivery." Yet Thomas Sheridan, founder of the elocution movement and father of the playwright Richard, was convinced that this was the most neglected aspect of preaching in England.[27] Delivery (also called "pronunciation" or "elocution") was recognized to consist of two parts, voice and gesture.

In delivery, as in everything else, however, the eighteenth century sought the golden mean between extremes. Dryness was to be avoided on the one hand, ecstasy on the other.[28] The soporific qualities of sermons were proverbial. Yet the enthusiasm of such as the Methodists was equally to be avoided. A liveliness of voice and gesture that did not spill over into hysteria was the ideal. Another Scylla and Charibdes to be steered between were meanness and affectation. One was neither coarse nor pretentious in the pulpit. In delivery as in style, the latitudinarian ideal was naturalness.[29]

To summarize all of this preaching theory, the ideal preacher was seen to be one who combined learning with forceful delivery. "Next to convincing his hearers with solid learning the preacher had to persuade them, to raise their emotions and stir their passions in favor of his cause."[30] Finally, for a preacher to be truly effective, it was necessary that he support these gifts with the moral qualities of sincerity and behavior consistent with what was enjoined. This combination was the ideal of the neoclassical homileticians.[31]

In addition to their thoughts about preaching, it helps to understand the theology of the latitudinarians, since in some ways their homiletic was a function of their beliefs about God—which is probably true of all preaching. The theology of the latitudinarians was probably neither so bad as it is regarded by some (hardly better than deism), nor so good as it is regarded by others (straightforward Christian orthodoxy expressed in the vocabulary of the time). To begin with, those who held it were not Calvinists; they did not believe in predestination or a God of wrath. The order and regularity of the universe as discovered by the new science had convinced these thinkers of God's benevolence toward humanity.

Everything that existed was a provision of an all-wise and all-loving Creator, the God of "the spacious firmament on high." It was assumed that nature revealed the glory of God and that there was, therefore, universal human consent to the existence of such a Being. The Calvinist doctrine of election was seen to be inconsistent with divine benevolence: How could an all-loving God consent even passively to the damnation of most of the human race? Human beings, therefore, must be free to choose good or evil. Inevitably, some would choose evil, and God would reluctantly allow them the fate upon which they had insisted.

Indeed, human reason and will had been incapacitated by the fall, but God's will for the salvation of all expressed in the redemption of the world by God's Son, Jesus Christ, meant that anyone who wished grace to overcome original sin would find it available in abundance. Since human reason had not been so distorted by the fall as to be unable to recognize the advantages of good over evil both here and hereafter, and since in any case the Scriptures revealed these advantages for those who had any difficulty in seeing them, there was nothing really to inhibit the salvation of anyone who wished it.

Accepting this salvation was largely a matter of living in the way of God's will, the practical goodness apparent to natural reason but made abundantly clear in biblical revelation. Holiness could hardly be distinguished from what Jeremy Bentham was later to call "enlightened self-interest." The advantages of righteousness were so patent that it was hard to understand how even a reason and will corrupted by the fall could fail to choose the way of life. But to ensure that this benighted option was even less likely to be elected, sermons were preached urging all people to reform their ways and live the moral life that was the commandment and gift of God. The faith that appropriated this way of life was simply a fervent conviction that this view of the universe was correct.[32]

Popular as such preaching was for a long time, consciousness has shifted again so completely that many modern readers find neoclassical preaching as hard to appreciate as the Restoration congregations found the sermons of the Metaphysicals and Puritans. To contemporary ears it has a sound of smugness, of self-satisfaction, of comfort in the universe and ease in Zion that is almost impossible to empathize with. Its serene good taste and its abhorrence of enthusiasm as nature abhors a vacuum make it guilty of breaking the eleventh commandment for all public speakers: "Thou shalt not bore!" To say that, however, is only to admit that contemporary consciousness is as provincial as any that preceded it, because there can be no doubt that neoclassical latitudinarian preaching fitted the consciousness of its time like a custom-tailored garment. Further, it was the style of preaching that was developed during the Enlightenment, a time when Christianity was very much on the defensive. In an atmosphere in which deists and atheists were attacking the roots of faith, neoclassical preaching may have been as much of the gospel as could be heard.

PRACTICE IN PREACHING

In order to understand the careers and homiletical practice of the Restoration and the eighteenth-century preachers who set the style that was to last so long and be so pervasive,[33] it is necessary to know something about the close involvement of church and state during this period. Since the Reformation, it had been assumed in England that many of the administrative responsibilities of the pope during the Middle Ages had been transferred (or, according to the theory, restored) to the monarch, God's vicegerent in the realm. As constitutional theory came to be debated in the early-seventeenth century, when Puritans began to say that divine authority rested in the law (enacted by Parliament), the issue was not over the legitimate role of the state in the government of the church, but over who should exercise that role.

Thus the two sides in the English Civil War each had characteristic positions on civil and church government. Royalists tended to be Episcopalians, and Puritans were Parliamentarians. (The Independents who were so much at the center of things during the Protectorate were opposed to both doctrines of ministry and to the establishment of any church.) After the Restoration, these coalitions became High Church Tories and latitudinarian Whigs. The High Churchmen were devoted equally to bishops and the monarchy, while the latitudinarians were tolerant toward Dissenters and considered the king to be subordinate to the law.

Throughout the seventeenth century and during the early part of the eighteenth, there were constant changes in which coalition was in power. James I and Charles II had combined a belief that they ruled by divine right with an Anglo-Catholic theology. The Civil War was an effort of a Puritan Parliament to overthrow both the monarchy and the episcopal establishment. As the Commonwealth moved into the Protectorate of Oliver Cromwell, Independency came to the fore. At the Restoration, High Church heirs of Laudian Anglo-Catholicism took control of the church as the reward of their loyalty to the monarchy. The refusal of James II to support the established church and his efforts to restore Roman Catholicism created an intolerable bind for High Church Tories, because it forced them to choose between their doctrine of the church and their theology of government.[34] Under William and Mary, the Whigs were in power. Queen Anne was High Church and Tory and tried to reward those who agreed with her, but the Whig hegemony was restored with the Hanoverian succession and lasted longer than the Georges.

What makes all of this so important for the history of preaching during that period is that most church offices beyond the parochial level were royal (that is to say, governmental) appointments. University positions, cathedral canonries and deanships, and bishoprics were bestowed by the political party in power. Not surprisingly, plums went to their supporters among the clergy. This was especially true with regard to the episcopate because bishops were members of the House of Lords, and a loyal episcopal bench could often swing a close vote to the side that had appointed them. In spite of laws to the contrary, this was still a time when clergy could enjoy appointment to a number of positions simultaneously, even when these were geographically distant from one another. This pluralism rendered absenteeism inevitable. And bishops were absent from their dioceses most of the year because of their need to be in London when Parliament was sitting. Although the ethical standards of a later generation make it hard to credit, many of even the most exemplary clergy of this period (among them most of those to be considered below) were caught up in an endless quest for preferment to influential and lucrative positions in the church.[35]

The Pioneers

It is generally recognized that the style of plain preaching was set in the last third of the seventeenth century by three masters: Robert South, Isaac Barrow, and John Tillotson. A brief look at the contribution of each of them is necessary for an understanding of how the taste was formed.

Robert South (1634–1716)

Although South was slightly the youngest of the three, Mitchell credits him with being the first to achieve the plain style:

> All the competing and, from different points of view, extravagant styles which had fascinated men and absorbed their attention during the first sixty years of the century were successfully fused together [by South], and the result was a plain, perspicuous and harmonious whole.[36]

Certainly he was the most explicit theorist of the style, as may be seen above in his critique of sermons constructed according the methods of the Metaphysicals or Perkins. Yet he was an odd person for this achievement, being far from a latitudinarian. He came from a background of affluence and loyalty to the Royalist cause.[37] Indeed, the most traumatic and significant moment of his life, the execution of Charles I, occurred when he was a youth at nearby Westminster School, where Latin prayers were being said for the king on the morning of his death. Growing up with such passionate convictions when the detested enemy was in power must have been galling for South, but at Westminster he was taught how to survive in such a period. The sincerity of his conviction was shown when he moved on to Christ Church, Oxford, where he was a member of a small group that met for clandestine worship according to the outlawed Prayer Book.

With the Restoration, things began to look up for South. It was during the year in which it occurred that he preached "The Scribe Instructed," the first of his two sermons in favor of the plain style. His brilliance was noted and he became the Orator of the University, the person who made the official Latin addresses upon auspicious public occasions. Preferment came his way: he was made a canon of Westminster in 1663 when he was only twenty-nine, vicar of a Welsh parish in 1667, canon of Christ Church[38] in 1670, and rector of Islip in 1678.

Seven years later, James II came to the throne. Even though he had earlier been one of James's chaplains while he was still Duke of York, South shared with all his fellow English a hysteria about Roman Catholicism; the so-called Popish Plot was quite a recent memory. Yet the accession of William and Mary was no relief to South, since their openness to Dissenters was at least as abhorrent to him as James's attitude toward Roman Catholics. Thus, in his final decades, South's lifelong and passionate devotion to the Royalist cause had to contend with the reality that the kings whom his theology idealized were quite capable of encouraging religious systems deeply at odds with his own. South's brilliant climb had stalled.

In addition to his advocacy of the plain style and his proclamation of his High Church Tory convictions, South's preaching is known for two main characteristics: his use of humor and his elaboration of metaphor. South was "witty" in the modern sense of brilliant joking rather than in the early-seventeenth-century sense of employing conceits.[39] This trait, which can be seen clearly in his criticism of other preaching styles, has drawn disapproval both in his own time and since. Some believed that levity could never be used to press home serious messages and that it was, in any case, inconsistent with the dignity of preaching's divine subject matter. Others have found his biting sarcasm at times to accord ill with Christian charity. Yet others delight simply in his being funny and charming, and recognize the rhetorical effectiveness of the way he used wit to surprise his audience into considering seriously points they might have passed over in a more sober presentation.

South also used metaphors at a time when their legitimate employment in sermons was debated, and he used them more extensively than any of his contemporaries.[40] Some of the metaphors are quite extended; they are often incorporated into broader patterns of imagery. He used metaphor to develop the argument of his sermons, at times employing a complex metaphor in which there was more than one point of comparison. Sometimes a complex pattern of imagery was mixed in with other elements, such as biblical and historical allusions and quotations. His preaching relied as heavily upon metaphor as Jesus' preaching relied upon parable.

As disturbing as elements of his style have been to various people then and now, many others undoubtedly agree with Simon that he was "probably the best preacher of his age, and he had a mind of the highest order"[41] and regret with her that his influence was not more widespread in the century to follow. While one cannot convey the religious depth of much of his preaching by quoting a short passage, something of his charm may be seen in a letter he wrote to respond to an offer of the deanship of Westminster Abbey shortly before his eightieth birthday:

> My Most Honoured Lord,
>
> Could my present circumstances and condition, in any Degree come up to the Gracious, and surpriseing offer lately brought me from her Majesty, I should with the utmost Gratitude, and Deepest Humility Cast my self at Her Royall Feet, and with Both Armes Embrace it.
>
> But alas, my Lord, That Answer which Alexander the Great once gave a Souldier petitioning Him for an Office in his Army may no lesse properly become her majesty to my Poor Self, (though not *Petitioning for,* but *prevented by*[42] her Princely Favour,) *Freind* [*sic*], said He, *I own that I can give thee this Place, but I cannot make thee Fitt for it.* And this, my Lord, is my unhappy case.

For haveing, for now above these *Fourty years,* the Best, the Ablest, and most usefull part of my Age, not bin thought fitt by my Superiors, to serve the Crown or Church in any other way, or Station, than what I have held hitherto, I cannot, but in modesty (and, even, in *Respect to them*) judge myself unworthy and unfitt to serve them in any higher, or greater Post now; being grown Equally superannuated to the *Active,* as well as the *Enjoying* Part of Life.

For Age, my Lord, is not to be *Defyed*, nor forced by All, that Art, or Nature can doe, to retreat one step backward: And even the Richest Spread Table, with the Kindest Invitations to it, Come but too late to one, who has lost both his Stomack, and his Appetite too.

In fine, my good Lord, after the Utmost Acknowledgement, Duty and Devotion paid to the Sacred *Fountain-Head* from which all this Goodnesse flowes, the same Gratitude, in the *very next place,* commands me, with the Profoundest Deference to Own, and Blesse that Noble Channell, by which it has so liberally passed upon,

(Great Sir)

Your Honours most obliged, Humble, and obedient Servant

Robert South.

Westminster Abbey,

8 June, 1713,

Nothing, my Lord, afflicts me more than that I am disabled from bringing your Honour, these my Acknowledgements (and many more with them) in Person my Self.[43]

Isaac Barrow (1630–77)

A Royalist like South, Barrow seems to have been less troubled by his allegiance. Somehow he managed to go through Cambridge during the Puritan reign without having to sign either the Covenant or the Engagement, and he died before either James II or William and Mary could test his conscience. On the whole, he seems to have led a carefree existence in an academic setting most of his life. It is only when one looks at the diversity of his accomplishments that it becomes clear what an extraordinarily gifted person he was.

Apparently his original intention had been to become a physician; he studied science in preparation for such a career. His election as a fellow of Trinity College, however, obligated him to study theology. An interest in biblical chronology led him into astronomy and geometry. Taking up mathematics, he was eventually made a professor of Gresham College, the London center of scientific study so closely related to the founding of the Royal Society (of which Barrow became a member). Elected from there to the first chair of mathematics at Cambridge, he became one of the predecessors of Isaac Newton and Gottfried Leibniz in the discovery of differential calculus. Yet he recognized the superior genius of his pupil and in time resigned the chair in favor of Newton.

At points along the way, his great classical learning caused him to be considered for various chairs before he became regius professor of Greek at the Restoration. He had, after all, gone to Constantinople to study the works of Chrysostom. On the voyage home, pirates attacked his ship and he, who had been notorious for fighting as a schoolboy, joined the struggle against them.

He was ordained shortly before the Restoration, but his other duties kept him from writing the theological treatises that were prerequisite to appointment as a preacher at Trinity College. After resigning in favor of Newton, however, he quickly satisfied that requirement and immediately became much in demand as a preacher at court as well as the university. When he was appointed Master of Trinity in 1672, he devoted himself to refuting Roman Catholic claims and to building up a library for his college, the university not having one at the time. So charmed was his life that it seems inevitable that it should have been he who commissioned Christopher Wren to build Trinity's magnificent library. It would be hard to quarrel with the judgment of Charles II when he appointed Barrow as Master of Trinity: the king called him the best scholar in England.[44]

Since Barrow was appointed a preacher to his college only six years before his death, it is extraordinary that his sermons should have the respect they do. Mitchell calls him "the most continuously and uniformly eloquent of English preachers."[45] What accounts for this reputation? Two things, apparently: the profundity of his mind, which permitted him to treat his subjects comprehensively, not to say exhaustively, and his having learned style from transcribing the works of Demosthenes and Chrysostom until he fell into the English equivalent of the patterns of their speech. Both of these qualities can be seen in a short passage from his sermon on "The Profitableness of Godliness":

> The gain of money, or of somewhat equivalent thereto, is therefore specially termed Profit, because it readily supplieth necessity, furnisheth convenience, feedeth pleasure, satisfieth fancy and curiosity, promoteth ease and liberty, supporteth honour and dignity, procureth power, dependencies, and friendships, rendreth a man somebody, considerable in the world; in fine, enableth to doe good, or to perform works of beneficence and charity.[46]

One is left with the contradictory feelings that, on the one hand, everything has been said that could be, and, on the other, that Barrow could have gone on indefinitely. Apparently he sometimes did; it is reported that one of his sermons lasted three hours and forty-five minutes. His use of appositives, parallel construction, and anaphora allow him to roll along forever, never repeating himself, always saying something worthwhile. To acquire such a reputation for preaching, however, it is usually necessary that spiritual depth be accompanied by literary grace. Although Barrow appears in some ways to have given as little thought to the way his sermons sounded as he did to his own personal appearance, there can be no doubt that the charm was there. Anyone who questions that has but to read his defense of legitimate humor in his sermon "Against Foolish Talking and Jesting."[47]

John Tillotson (1630–94)

The preacher who is universally admitted to have set the style for plain, latitudinarian, neoclassical preaching is one who was in touch with all of the trends and influences that anticipated the taste. Born into the strict Puritan family of a Yorkshire clothier, John Tillotson went to Cambridge where, in addition to some of the leading Puritans of the day, he came under the influence of the Cambridge Platonists and others.

Being of a naturally irenic disposition and willing to consider a number of points of view, he remained for a while within the Puritan camp without presupposing, as so many did, that his was the only position worthy of respect. Although he was in London at the time of Cromwell's death, eventually married Cromwell's niece, and sat with the Presbyterians at the Savoy Conference in its abortive effort to work out a Restoration settlement that would include them, Tillotson was ordained by a bishop and served various appointments in Church of England parishes. His fame began to build in his early thirties, when he was appointed to preach on Sundays to the lawyers at Lincoln's Inn and on Tuesdays at the parish of many who were influential in the city government of London, St. Lawrence Jewry.

During this London ministry he became close to John Wilkins, the author of *Ecclesiastes,* who was his vicar at St. Lawrence. Indeed, the Cromwell niece whom Tillotson married in 1664, a year after arriving at St. Lawrence, was Wilkins's stepdaughter. Tillotson must have been an eager disciple of his father-in-law's homiletical principles; he certainly became deeply involved in another of his causes in communication, that which resulted in the 1668 publication of Wilkins's *Essay Towards a*

Real Character and Philosophical Language. This project was devoted to an effort to help the scientists of the Royal Society achieve their goal of "so many *things* almost in an equal number of *words*."[48] Indeed, Tillotson himself became a member of the society. And when Wilkins was consecrated to be bishop of Chester, his son-in-law preached. He also edited Wilkins's sermons after his death.

Tillotson's broad-mindedness and irenic spirit continued to manifest themselves, especially in his efforts to ease the legal situation of Dissenters and even include them in the establishment. The only area of his thought in which his charity was not apparent was his attitude toward Roman Catholics; like both South and Barrow, he wrote polemical works against them. Barrow was a great friend, and Tillotson also became his posthumous editor.[49] In fact, it is difficult to discover anyone who was not his friend, so universal was his capacity to appreciate fellow human beings!

Inevitably, preferment came his way. In 1668 he became one of the chaplains of Charles II, in 1670 a prebendary, and in 1672 the dean of Canterbury, becoming as well a canon of St. Paul's. When James II came to the throne, he continued to preach passive obedience to the civil magistrate, but he also urged Dissenters not to go along with the king's efforts to grant indulgence to Dissenters as a means of acquiring it for his co-religionists as well. Tillotson was among those called together by Archbishop Sancroft when James ordered the proclamation of the Declaration of Indulgence in churches, but, not being a bishop, he was not one of the seven sent to the tower for refusing to have it read.

Neither was he directly involved in the invitation to William and Mary to take over the throne, but, an old friend of William's, he was invited to preach at court three days after their coronation. He then was made dean of St. Paul's, having refused a bishopric, pleading little taste for "either the ceremony or the trouble of a great place."[50] It was only with great reluctance that he acceded to William's request that he succeed the nonjuring Sancroft as archbishop of Canterbury, becoming, in the words of Charles Smyth, "the only Primate of All England to enjoy the reputation of being the greatest preacher of his day."[51] He found, as he expected, the role to be very onerous, especially as there were many who questioned his orthodoxy, and he survived in the position only three years.

In some ways, his preaching style could be described as meeting an ideal of today: it was conversational. (For a sermon by Tillotson, **see Vol. 2, pp. 329-48.**) That trait, however, is not recognizable to many modern readers because ordinary speech has changed so much since his time. Even then, it was the ordinary speech of a particular social group, that of "gentlemen." It was not the sophisticated parlance that had been popular at the court of James I, where the diction of Lancelot Andrewes could have been considered conversational, nor yet was it the language of "lower classes" in either the city or the country.

Tillotson carried plainness to the extreme of actively seeking to avoid any expression that was either dramatic or poetic. He wished to avoid persuading anyone by any tricks of language, depending instead entirely upon the reasonableness of the thought he presented so calmly. Nor was his thought particularly demanding or profound; he wished to be sure that his audience could understand and accept what was said. Pellucidity, even obviousness, was his great aim.

As for structure:

> He usually begins a discourse with a short proem which seeks to introduce his subject, impress its high seriousness upon his hearers, and prejudice them in his favour. As though outlining a problem in logic, he makes every sentence count; there are no embellishments and no redundant phrases. In turn he considers the several divisions into which his subject logically falls. There is no peroration; no impassioned pleading with sinners; no final "call." When the argument is concluded, the counsel for the Prosecution rests his case.[52]

When his preaching is thus described, it is hard for ordinary people of today to understand how it could have been so popular at the time. It is even hard for specialists who have studied it to understand its appeal. Simon, for instance, says:

> It is doubtful . . . whether such a style could have riveted the attention of less eager listeners. While Barrow's verbal imagination or South's manly wit arouse our interest in the themes they treat, the reader who does not come to Tillotson's sermons for edification is likely to appreciate the clear and easy style only when the matter treated is of particular interest, that is, defines the preacher's position and belief as a Church-of-England man of the time, for the prosaic quality of his thought and mind is made all the more obvious by the plainness and simplicity of his style.[53]

Smyth speaks of "the dull sobriety, the unadventurous reasonableness of Tillotsonian homiletics."[54] He also indicates the theological shortcoming of the content of these sermons: "Beyond a general impression that it was more prudent on the whole to believe the Gospel, in a modified sort of way, than not, what impression does Tillotson convey?"[55] Yet Smyth also recognizes what made such a style so welcome in its generation, "the real horror of fanaticism that lay at the heart of the Anglican piety for more than a hundred years" after the Civil War, Commonwealth, and Protectorate.[56]

The popularity of Tillotson's preaching, however, does not entirely account for the influence of his style on preachers for a century afterward. James Downey says:

> Above all, and herein lies the reason for his influence, Tillotson was imitable. In both structure and language his sermons are easy to emulate. Barrow, South, Burnet, and Stillingfleet were all perhaps better preachers; but none of them was really imitable. Lesser men attempting to emulate their styles were in danger of falling victims to bombast, or bathos, or both.[57]

There must have been more to it than that. Tillotson set a style that was to remain popular for some time, not only for preachers, but for all writers of English prose. There must have been something in the spirit of the age to which such prose spoke.

PREACHING AND THE LIFE OF THE MIND IN THE EIGHTEENTH CENTURY

Several connections have already been suggested between homiletics and the rest of the intellectual life of England at the Restoration and afterward: the number of outstanding preachers closely connected with the new science and the founding of the Royal Society, the influence of the homiletical plain style on essayists such as Addison, Steele, Dryden, and others. There is probably no other time in British history when ties were so numerous between preachers and secular high culture. Thus this chapter would be incomplete without at least a simple listing of preachers who are also well known today for their contributions to literature and philosophy: Swift, Sterne, Johnson, Butler, and Berkeley.

The list begins a little before this exact period with someone who anticipated the plain style. While **George Herbert** is classified as one of the metaphysical poets, his homiletical taste was much simpler than that of the preachers who share that adjective. Born into a noble family active in both government and letters, Herbert was educated at Westminster and Cambridge, was made a Major Fellow of Trinity, gave university lectures in rhetoric, and became Orator of the university. Although devout all his life, he seemed attracted at first to serving God in government; he spent a year as a member of Parliament. That seemed to disillusion him thoroughly with the idea of a unified realm of church and state. At the end of it, late in 1624 when he was thirty-one years old, he was ordained deacon. While he was appointed to livings then,[58] his health seems to have delayed his ordination to the priesthood for six years. By that time he had already been installed for a few months at Bemerton, his only parish. He did not live to serve there a full three years.

His ministry is best known for its ideals, stated in a work that was near completion when he moved to Bemerton, his *A Priest to the Temple, or, The Country Parson, His Character and Rule of Life.* In this spiritual classic, he set forth his standards for preaching and for all other aspects of his ministry. He seemed to consider no work more important than preaching, saying: "The Country Parson preacheth constantly, the pulpit is his joy and his throne."[59] The way in which he anticipated the plain style can be seen in what he had to say about explication.

> The Parson's Method in handling of a text consists of two parts; first, a plain and evident declaration of the meaning of the text; and, secondly, some choice Observations drawn out of the whole text, as it lies entire, and unbroken in the Scripture itself. This he thinks natural, and sweet, and grave. Whereas the other way of crumbling a text into small parts, as, the Person speaking, or spoken to, the subject, and object, and the like, hath neither in it sweetness, nor gravity, nor variety, since the words apart are not Scripture, but a dictionary, and may be considered alike in all the Scripture.[60]

But for the kindness and humility, this could sound like South, although it anticipates "The Scribe Instructed" by twenty-eight years.

A less obviously saintly soul was the satirist and political pamphleteer **Jonathan Swift** (1667–1745). Most literary critics who have studied his work have been able to neglect or dismiss his priesthood.[61] Yet there is plenty of evidence to suggest that the dean of St. Patrick's, Dublin, was not only conscientious in the performance of his official duties by the standards of his time and a High Churchman in his beliefs, but that he was also a man of prayer, a good pastor, and a generous almsgiver.[62] His satire shows him to have been a person of such lofty ideals and such outrage over their contradiction in the way people lived that he could not contain his indignation, having it build up inside him like steam in a pressure cooker until it came hissing out of the safety valve. The epitaph that he wrote for himself says what needed to be said:

> Here lies the body of Jonathan Swift, Doctor of Divinity and Dean of this Cathedral Church, where savage indignation can no more lacerate

> his heart. Go, traveller, and imitate if you can one who strove with all his might to champion liberty.[63]

The homiletical theory and practice of such a person can hardly be expected to be ordinary, nor was it. His "Letter to a Young Clergyman Lately Entered into Holy Orders" states his theory of preaching, but does so with such irony that it would be easy to forget the sound advice in appreciation of the sardonic manner in which it is given.[64] He begins by observing that most clergy do not stay at the university long enough to acquire the learning preaching requires—a minimum of ten years. Then he says that clergy should learn how to deliver sermons in rural congregations before they preach to those in the city.

The study of English is a necessity, including as a minimum the ability to use words that people understand rather than technical jargon (although it is possible to use language that is too common or coarse). Clichés are to be avoided like the plague. Sermons that persuade by reason are more effective in the long run (at least in northern climates) than those that move the emotions:

> A plain convincing reason may possibly operate upon the mind, both of the learned and the ignorant hearer, as long as they live, and will edify a thousand times more than the art of wetting the handkerchiefs of a whole congregation, if you were sure to attain it.[65]

"The two principal branches of preaching," according to Swift, "are, first to tell the people what is their duty, and then to convince them that it is so." The heads of divisions should be expressed in a few clear words so that the outline can be remembered. Clergy should prepare their manuscripts in such a way and practice their delivery so that they may appear to preach without looking at their notes. Few preachers are capable of wit in the pulpit, and the rest should avoid trying.

While Swift is clear that saving truth is a matter of revelation, he nevertheless wishes that clergy would be grateful for the help they can receive from pagan philosophers in teaching practical morality and not bite the hand that feeds them. Yet quotations, except from the Bible, should be kept to a minimum; clergy should never have been encouraged to collect them in commonplace books. The reasoning of the preacher is more convincing than "a manifest incoherent piece of patchwork." The mysteries of the Christian religion should be accepted rather than explained, and controversial preaching against the heresies of the day is pointless since those who hold them are not in church. But at least clergy had given up preaching on the doctrinal issues of the Puritans.

One cannot be entirely sure of the extent to which Swift practiced what he preached, because only about a dozen of his sermons have survived. He was as ironic about his preaching as everything else, telling Thomas Sheridan when he gave him a bundle of them: "They may be of use to you, they never were of any to me."[66] His sermon on the Trinity certainly followed his advice on recognizing that mysteries are mysteries:

> There is some kind of unity and distinction in the divine nature, which mankind can not possibly comprehend; thus the whole doctrine is short and plain, and in itself incapable of any controversy, since God himself both pronounced the fact, but wholly concealed the manner.[67]

The majority of his surviving sermons do deal with Christian behavior. Occasionally his political convictions entered his preaching, but did so because of his deep moral commitments. His sermon on "Brotherly Love," for instance, would seem to the ecumenically minded modern Christian to be commending its opposite in his opposition to political rights for Roman Catholics and Dissenters, but he saw the Whig policy of comprehension to be a cynical indifference to religion for political advantage.[68] His sermon on "Doing Good" (public service) was occasioned by the issue that prompted his *Drapier's Letters,* William Wood's patent to circulate his halfpence in a way that would exploit the Irish for the profit of the English.

The true value of Swift's preaching, however, can best be seen in his sermon on "Mutual Subjection." In a world rife with class consciousness, smugness, and condescension, he undercuts it all:

> It plainly appears from what hath been said, that no human creature is more worthy than another in the sight of God, farther than according to the goodness or holiness of their lives; and that power, wealth, and the like outward advantages, are so far from being the marks of God's approving or preferring those on whom they are bestowed, that, on the contrary, he is pleased to suffer them to be almost engrossed by those who have least title to his favour. Now, according to this equality wherein God hath placed all mankind with relation to himself, you will observe, that in all the relations between man and man, there is a mutual dependence, whereby the one cannot subsist without the other.[69]

A writing cleric whose religious seriousness has been at least as suspect among the critics as Swift's is **Laurence Sterne** (1713–68), the author of *Tristram Shandy* and *A Sentimental Journey.*[70] The morality of both his life and his works was severely attacked by Thackery and other

Victorians. And some question of seriousness could be raised by the way the sermons were published, not as Sterne's own, but as those of the fictitious Mr. Yorick in *Tristram Shandy.* It was only posthumously that any sermons were published under his own name, and those were inferior to Yorick's, consisting largely of borrowings from imminent divines of the day. Apparently the Yorick sermons were his own, preached during the thirty years he had been a parish priest in Yorkshire, the last twenty of which he was a prebendary of York Minster.[71] The sermons published as Yorick's were his best, but after his death, his heirs issued his earlier and less skillful sermons under his own name. He seems to have developed the literary talent manifest in the novels by writing sermons in which he dramatized biblical stories through his ability to imaginatively construct scenes, characters, and dialogue. He appears to have achieved in his preaching the ideal that he set forth in a letter: "Preaching (you must know) is a theological flap upon the heart, as the dunning for a promise is a political flap upon the memory."[72]

Sermons were written by at least one eighteenth-century author who was not ordained, **Samuel Johnson** (1709–84). While the famous doctor was a very devout High Church Tory with an almost encyclopedic knowledge of English homiletical literature, the sermons appear to have been part of the literary work he did to support himself. He claimed to have written around forty, although only twenty-eight have survived. Of these, one was for his friend the Reverend Henry Hervey Aston to deliver to the Sons of the Clergy, another was for a priest convicted of forgery to deliver to fellow prisoners at Newgate.

The rest were for his oldest and closest friend, the Reverend John Taylor, including one for the funeral of Johnson's wife. Taylor, under whose name most of the sermons were originally published, was a sort of Dr. Syntax, though more of a stockbreeding than a hunting parson. Yet it was to him that Johnson himself turned when he was in need of pastoral care. Sometimes the sermons seem to have emerged from a dialectical process in which Johnson would draft something according to the specifications of his client, and the client would then tailor that to make the work his own. In any case, the sermons were consistent with Johnson's own theological principles while being fair to those of the preacher when there was a difference—as there was between Johnson and Taylor.[73]

Finally, to show the extent of homiletical involvement in the intellectual and artistic life of England in the eighteenth century, two bishops need to be mentioned, one of whom was a theologian and the other of whom was a philosopher. **Joseph Butler** (1692–1752), who became bishop first of Bristol and then of Durham, is chiefly remembered for his great refutation of deism: *The Analogy of Religion Natural and Revealed to the Constitution and Course of Nature* (1736). Since, however, all good apologetic builds on principles mutually acknowledged by the opponent and the defender, the *Analogy* lost some of its force as a defense of Christianity when those who attacked it became atheists instead of deists.

Thus Butler's other great work, his *Fifteen Sermons Preached at the Rolls Chapel,* written to oppose Hobbes's position that human behavior is motivated exclusively by self-interest, has continued to have relevance. The abiding interest of these sermons, which argue from the human experience of having a conscience, is even more impressive when one notes that they were preached in Butler's first assignment after ordination during the years between his twenty-sixth and thirty-fifth birthdays.[74]

The philosopher bishop was **George Berkeley** (1685–1753) of the Irish diocese of Cloyne. Known as a philosophical idealist, Berkeley pointed out that there is no necessary connection between our stream of sensation in consciousness and any external universe, thus becoming an important epistemological link between Locke and Hume. He also looked on the Americas as a place where Christianity could begin afresh, served for a while in Newport, Rhode Island, and had a scheme for building a college in Bermuda to train colonists and natives for the ministry and other useful service.[75] Yet in the rationalistic age in which he lived, the sermons of Berkeley the philosopher represent for Downey not so much the latitudinarian beginning of his century as something proleptic of the evangelical preaching of the century's end.[76] This is in part because, for Berkeley, the church was not so much "the temporal custodian of virtue and a bulwark for morality" as it was the mystical Body of Christ, in which souls could be saved from sin and damnation by an appeal to the heart. Unfortunately, only ten of Berkeley's sermons and fourteen sets of pulpit notes have been preserved. Still, they represent yet another way in which preaching has been connected to the very center of eighteenth-century intellectual and artistic life.

FOR FURTHER READING

Downey, James. *The Eighteenth Century Pulpit: A Study of the Sermons of Butler, Berkeley, Secker, Sterne, Whitefield, and Wesley.* Oxford: Clarendon, 1969.

In God's Name: Examples of Preaching in England from the Act of Supremacy to the Act of Uniformity, 1534–1662. Edited with introduction and notes by John Chandos. Indianapolis: Bobbs-Merrill, 1971.

Lessenich, Rolf P. *Elements of Pulpit Oratory in Eighteenth-Century England (1660–1800)*. Cologne and Vienna: Böhlau Verlag, 1972.

Simon, Irène. *Three Restoration Divines: Barrow, South, Tillotson: Selected Sermons.* Bibliotèque de la Faculté de Philosophie et Lettres de l'Université de Liège, Fascicules 171 and 213. Paris: Société d'Editions Les Belles Lettres, 1967–76.

Swift, Jonathan. "Letter to a Young Clergyman Lately Entered into Holy Orders." In *Works,* vol. 5. London: John Nichols, 1801.

The Works of Dr. John Tillotson, Late Archbishop Of Canterbury. With the Life of the Author, By Thomas Birch, M. A. Also, A Copious Index, And The Texts Of Scripture Carefully Compared. In Ten Volumes. London: J. F. Dove for Richard Priestley, 1820.

Notes

1. "The Scribe Instructed, Preached at St. Mary's, Oxford, on 29 July, 1660, Being the Time of the KING'S Commissioners meeting there, soon after the *Restoration,* for the Visitation of that *University,*" in Irène Simon, *Three Restoration Divines: Barrow, South, Tillotson: Selected Sermons,* Bibliotèque de la Faculté de Philosophie et Lettres de l'Université de Liège, Fascicules 171 and 213 (Paris: Société d'Editions Les Belles Lettres, 1967–76), 2.1.245.

2. Ibid. The complaints of South against metaphysical preaching may be compared with the list Mitchell has culled from a considerable body of contemporary criticism: "its partiality for strange and unexpected figures, its 'wit,' its passion for quotations, particularly in Latin and Greek, the exaggerated importance it attached to particular words or expressions, and its illogical and unnecessary divisions and subdivisions" (W. Fraser Mitchell, *English Pulpit Oratory from Andrewes to Tillotson: A Study of Its Literary Aspects* (1932; New York: Russell & Russell, 1962), 352-53). A characteristic interpretation of the time was that the quotations from the Fathers and classical writers were an effort to show off one's scholarship.

3. Ibid., Simon, 2:246-50. South's prejudice can be seen here in the way that he lumps together the preaching of often very learned Puritans with that of many uneducated Independents. For a parody of the preaching of Independents, see *In God's Name: Examples of Preaching in England from the Act of Supremacy to the Act of Uniformity, 1534-1662,* ed., with intro. and notes, John Chandos (Indianapolis: Bobbs-Merrill, 1971), 388-93.

4. "[Christ's Promises to the Apostles] Preached at Christ Church, Oxford, on 30 April, 1668, Being Ascension-Day," ibid., Simon, 2.2.323.

5. Ibid., 2.2.326.

6. Mitchell, *English Pulpit Oratory from Andrewes to Tillotson,* 307.

7. Thomas Sprat, *The History of the Royal Society of London, For the Improving of Natural Knowledge* (London: 1667), 2:20.

8. Charles Smyth, *The Art of Preaching: A Practical Survey of Preaching in the*

Church of England 747–1939 (London: SPCK; New York: Macmillan 1940), 183. Robert Robinson's translation of Claude's work was published in 1688 under the title of *An Essay on the Composition of a Sermon.*

9. Mitchell, *English Pulpit Oratory from Andrewes to Tillotson,* 124.

10. *An Account of the Life and Writings of Hugh Blair* (Edinburgh, 1807), 131-33, as cited in Rolf P. Lessenich, *Elements of Pulpit Oratory in Eighteenth-Century England (1660–1800)* (Cologne and Vienna: Böhlau Verlag, 1972), 62.

11. Simon, *Three Restoration Divines,* 1:11.

12. Barbara J. Shapiro, *John Wilkins 1614–1672: An Intellectual Biography* (Berkeley and Los Angeles: University of California Press, 1969), 2. The quotation is from Grant McColley, "The Ross-Wilkins Controversy," *Annals of Science* 3 (1938): 155.

13. Immediately influential, the book was reprinted in 1646, 1647, 1651, 1653, 1659, 1669, 1675, 1679, 1693, 1704, and 1718, with many revisions and expansions. Shapiro, *John Wilkins 1614–1672,* 272. The edition I have consulted is the eighth of 1704, which incorporates the 1693 additions of John Williams.

14. "Wilkins's *Ecclesiastes* was a part of the Puritan preaching tradition. In time, however, the Puritan's emphasis on plain language was obscured by the tremendous complexity of their 'method,' with its countless subdivisions and their minute discussions of the text. Wilkins and later Restoration writers retained the natural, direct language, but reduced the method to a simple outline form and eliminated textual division." Shapiro, *John Wilkins 1614–1672, 75.*

15. John Wilkins, *Ecclesiastes: or, A Discourse Concerning the Gift of Preaching, As it falls under the Rules of Art* (London: J. Lawrence; A. and J. Churchill, 1704), 10, 11.

16. Wilkins, *Ecclesiastes: or, A Discourse Concerning the Gift of Preaching,* 32.

17. Ibid., 251.

18. Lessenich, *Elements of Pulpit Oratory in Eighteenth-Century England (1660–1800).*

19. One of the ways that Lessenich was able to argue this was to insist that "the theory of preaching and latitudinarian theology remained virtually unchanged from the beginning to the end of the neoclassic era" (p. xi), a point that will be challenged below in the consideration of Hugh Blair and the Belles Lettres movement.

20. Quoted by Lessenich, *Elements of Pulpit Oratory in Eighteenth-Century England (1660–1800),* 13, from James Boswell, *The Life of Samuel Johnson* (1791). He cites the edition of Birbeck Hill (Oxford: Oxford University Press, 1887), 4:105-6.

21. Ibid., 1-36.

22. Ibid., 76.

23. Ibid., 37-81.

24. Ibid., 82-119.

25. Robinson, *An Essay on the Composition of a Sermon,* 2:489-94, quoted in Lessenich, *Elements of Pulpit Oratory in Eighteenth-Century England (1600–1800),* 123.

26. Lessenich, *Elements of Pulpit Oratory in Eighteenth-Century England (1660–1800),* 120-27.

27. Lessenich does not pay enough attention to the elocutionary movement. While its standard for gestures was naturalness, its writers came to think that these could

be reduced to a science. Thus in 1768 James Burgh described seventy-two different emotions and the facial and bodily movements to be used to suggest them. This tendency reached its *reductio ad absurdum* in the 1806 publication of Gilbert Austin's *Chironomia,* which came complete with charts including foot positions for the expression of the entire range of emotions. See *The Rhetoric of Western Thought,* eds. James L. Golden, Goodwin F. Berquist, and William E. Coleman, 3rd ed. (Dubuque: Kendall/Hunt, 1976–83), 174-87.

28. William Hogarth did two satirical engravings of preachers, one showing an Anglican parson putting his flock to sleep with his sermon and the other showing a Methodist preacher whose effects on his congregation were measured by an emotional thermometer registering everything between the high of madness and the low of suicide.

29. Lessenich, *Elements of Pulpit Oratory in Eighteenth-Century England* (1600–1800), 128-50.

30. Ibid., 154.

31. Ibid., 151-61.

32. Ibid., 162-232.

33. While the few individual trendsetters to be discussed below were all clergy of the established church, their style of preaching was adopted by clergy of all denominations. See, for example, Lessenich, *Elements of Pulpit Oratory in Eighteenth-Century England (1600–1800),* x: "The large majority of post-Restoration Protestant preachers quickly forgot their petty differences of belief, as between Anglicans and Dissenters, Congregationalists, Baptists, Presbyterians, and Unitarians, and united their strength in a joint oratorical crusade against vice." As he makes clear in the passage that follows this, Lessenich believed that this agreement included homiletical form as well as content.

34. Many of their best and most capable leaders, including Archbishop Sancroft, went into schism from the Church of England rather than swear allegiance to William and Mary, feeling that their ordination oaths of loyalty to James II were still in effect even though he was deposed. For this refusal to swear, they were called nonjurors.

35. This combination of circumstances made it possible for Professor Norman Sykes to deliver a course of lectures at Cambridge in 1951–52 on church, state, and society in England from the Restoration through the reign of Queen Anne that was structured around a satirical song, "The Vicar of Bray" (*The British Musical Miscellany,* 1734, reproduced in *The Oxford Book of Light Verse,* ed. W. H. Auden [Oxford: Clarendon, 1939]), 260-62:

In good King Charles's golden days,
  When loyalty no harm meant;
A furious high-church man I was,
  And so I gain'd preferment.
Unto my flock I daily preach'd,
  Kings are by God appointed,
And damn'd are those who dare resist,
  Or touch the Lord's anointed.
    And this is law, I will maintain
      Unto my dying day, Sir,

When glorious Ann became our Queen,
  The Church of England's glory,
Another face of things was seen,
  And I became a Tory:
Occasional conformists base,
  I damn'd, and moderation,
And thought the church in danger was,
  From such prevarication.
    And this is law, &c.

That whatsoever King shall reign,
I will be Vicar of Bray, Sir!

When Royal James possessed the crown,
And popery grew in fashion;
The penal law I houted down,
And read the declaration:
The Church of Rome, I found would fit,
Full well my constitution,
And I had been a Jesuit,
But for the Revolution.
And this is law, &c.

When William our deliverer came,
To heal the nation's grievance,
I turned the cat in pan again,
And swore to him allegiance:
Old principles I did revoke,
Set conscience at a distance,
Passive obedience is a joke,
A jest is non-resistance.
And this is law, &c.

When George in pudding time came o'er,
And moderate men looked big, Sir,
My principles I chang'd once more,
And so became a Whig, Sir:
And thus preferment I procur'd,
From our Faith's Great Defender,
And almost every day abjur'd
The Pope, and the Pretender.
And this is law, &c.

The illustrious House of Hanover,
And Protestant succession,
To these I lustily will swear,
Whilst they can keep possession:
For in my faith, and loyalty,
I never once will falter,
But George, my lawful King shall be,
Except the times should alter.
And this is law, &c.

36. Mitchell, *English Pulpit Oratory from Andrewes to Tillotson,* 320-21.

37. The best studies of South and his work are Simon, *Three Restoration Divines,* 1:228-7 (a selection of his sermons makes up 2.1.1-331), and Gerard Ready, *Robert South (1634–1716): An Introduction to His Life and Sermons,* Cambridge Studies in Eighteenth-Century English Literature and Thought, no. 12 (Cambridge: Cambridge University Press, 1992).

38. The chapel of Christ Church, South's college, serves also as the cathedral of the diocese of Oxford.

39. For the best discussion of South's wit, see Simon, *Three Restoration Divines,* 1:253-74.

40. See Ready, *Robert South (1634–1716),* 48-52, 109-10 passim.

41. Simon, *Three Restoration Divines,* 1:231.

42. In the usage of the time, "prevented" meant "preceded."

43. Quoted, Simon, *Three Restoration Divines,* 1:232, from British Museum MS Loan (Portland Papers) 29/200.

44. This section is drawn from Simon, *Three Restoration Divines,* 1:213-28. Barrow's sermons appear ibid., 1:301-510. The other easily accessible source for Barrow is Mitchell, *English Pulpit Oratory from Andrewes to Tillotson,* 321-33 and passim.

45. Mitchell, *English Pulpit Oratory from Andrewes to Tillotson,* 324.

46. Quoted in Simon, *Three Restoration Divines,* 1:219-20, from the 1683 edition of his *Works,* 1:14.

47. Simon, *Three Restoration Divines,* 1:315-26.

48. This ideal seems not unlike the Chinese use of pictograms for writing instead of an alphabet that transcribed the sounds of words.

49. The bad press Tillotson has received for this editing, in which he has been accused in effect of transmitting his own blandness to Barrow's prose, is undeserved. See Simon, *Three Restoration Divines,* 1:303-14.

50. Smyth, *The Art of Preaching,* 104.

51. Ibid., 103.

52. James Downey, *The Eighteenth Century Pulpit: A Study of the Sermons of Butler, Berkeley, Secker, Sterne, Whitefield, and Wesley* (Oxford: Clarendon, 1969), 25.

53. Simon, *Three Restoration Divines,* 1:291.

54. Smyth, *The Art of Preaching,* 146.

55. Ibid., 162. Cf. Horton Davies, *Worship and Theology in England: From Andrewes to Baxter and Fox, 1603–1690* (Princeton: Princeton University Press, 1975), 2:183-84: "Here is an unequalled combination of eudaemonism, utilitarianism, and pelagianism, masquerading as Christianity. It was left to the men of latitude to conceive of a contradiction, Christian discipleship without the taking up of a cross."

56. Smyth, *The Art of Preaching,* 146.

57. Downey, *The Eighteenth Century Pulpit,* 27.

58. That is, given preferment; appointed to receive the income of church positions while hiring someone else to do the actual ministerial work.

59. The edition consulted is that of Western Spiritual Classics, with a preface by A. M. Allchin, ed. and intro. John N. Wall Jr. (New York, Ramsey, and Toronto: Paulist, 1981). The quotation is from p. 62.

60. Ibid., 64.

61. This is true even of so perceptive a critic as David Nokes, who entitled his critical biography *Jonathan Swift, A Hypocrite Reversed* (Oxford: Oxford University Press, 1985). On the title page he quotes the relevant passage from Thomas Sheridan's 1784 *Life of Jonathan Swift:*

> He had, early in life, imbibed such a strong hatred to hypocrisy, that he fell into the opposite extreme; and no mortal ever took more pains to display his good qualities, and appear in the best light to the world, than he did to conceal his, or even to put on the semblance of their contraries. . . . Lord Bolingbroke, who knew him well, in two words summed up his character in that respect, by saying that Swift was a hypocrite reversed.

Yet even Nokes seems incapable of understanding any of the religious activities of Swift in anything but the worst light. In doing so he reminds me of Roland Barthes's description of all biography as inevitably a "counterfeit integration of the subject." (Quoted by Carolyn G. Heilbrun in "Dorothy L. Sayers: Biography Between the Lines" in *Dorothy L. Sayers: The Centenary Celebration,* ed. Alzina Stone Dale (New York: Walker & Co., 1993), 2. The data of a person's life is filtered through the biographer's capacity to perceive.

62. While there may be a rose-colored tint to the lens through which Robert W. Jackson views Swift, there can be no doubt that he has amassed some real and objective

data in *Jonathan Swift, Dean and Pastor* (London: SPCK, 1939) that shows the sincerity of Swift in his exercise of his ministry.

63. *Hic depositum est corpus Jonathan Swift, S.T.D. huius cathedralis decani, ubi saeva indignationio ulterius cor lacerare nequit, abi viator, et imitare, si poteris, strenuum pro virili libertatis vindicatorem.* The translation is that of Nokes, *A Hypocrite Reversed,* 412.

64. The edition consulted is that of 1801 by John Nichols in London, 5:85-110. The date of the original is January 9, 1719–20 (the two years reflect the shift from treating March 25, the Feast of the Annunciation, as the beginning of the New Year to starting it on January 1).

65. Ibid., 5:95.

66. Quoted in Jackson, *Jonathan Swift, Dean and Pastor,* 123.

67. Quoted ibid., 121.

68. This and the other two sermons to be discussed are contained in *The English Sermon: Volume II: 1650–1750,* ed. C. H. Sisson (Cheadle, Cheshire: Carcanet, 1976), 286-313.

69. Ibid., 309.

70. What follows is based on Downey, *The Eighteenth Century Pulpit,* 115-54.

71. In this case, being a prebendary meant being a non-residentiary canon who, among other duties, preached twice a year at the cathedral.

72. Quoted from a letter to George Whateley in Downey, *The Eighteenth Century Pulpit,* 137.

73. James Gray, *Johnson's Sermons: A Study* (Oxford: Clarendon, 1972). With Jean Hagstrom, Gray edited the sermons for *The Yale Edition of the Works of Samuel Johnson* (New Haven: Yale University Press, 1958–85).

74. See Downey, *The Eighteenth Century Pulpit,* 30-57, and *The Works of Bishop Butler: Vol. I: Sermons, Charges, Fragments, and Correspondence,* ed. with intro. and notes J. H. Bernard (London: Macmillan, 1900).

75. For his reaction to his American experience, see his "Sermon Preached before the Incorporated Society for the Propagation of the Gospel in Foreign Parts" in Sisson, *The English Sermon,* 315-30.

76. Downey, *The Eighteenth Century Pulpit,* 58-88. The quoted words appear on p. 62.

CHAPTER 17

THE DAWN OF MODERNITY (B)

THE RECOVERY OF FEELING

"RELIGIONS OF THE HEART"

The beginning of the demand for plainness in preaching was seen in the previous chapter as a response to a number of simultaneous historical conditions: the weariness with theological disputes at the end of the wars of religion, the beginnings of modern science, the emergence of philosophical systems that did not presuppose revelation, and the growing ascendancy of the mercantile class over the aristocracy. The rationalism of the group that became the latitudinarians was only one of the possible responses to the same set of circumstances.[1] Another would strike many people as being as near to diametrically opposed as one could get: an emphasis on emotion instead of reason.

The one response was as widespread as the other.[2] Throughout Europe in the sixteenth and seventeenth centuries, there suddenly emerged in all religious traditions an insistence that in order to be real, religion had to be experienced affectively. It is impossible to account for this diversity of movements in terms of the historical influence of some on others. Rather, there appears to have been a spontaneous emergence of the same demand for an engagement of feelings in a wide variety of religious systems, systems that had little in common with one another beyond this new emphasis that they shared.

All the major religious groups of Europe were involved. Roman Catholic manifestations included Jansenism, quietism, and devotion to the Sacred Heart. In seventeenth-century British Christianity, the hunger for religious involvement that stirred the emotions was observable in strands of Puritanism, the Scots-Irish revivals, and the birth of the Quakers. The form of religion of the heart most related to this history of preaching in the English-speaking world, the Evangelical Awakening, appeared in Great Britain and America in the eighteenth century.

Among continental Protestants the expression was Pietism, first in its Dutch Reformed emergence and then in the German Lutheran. In Russia, some stirrings could be seen that remained within the Orthodox Church, while others separated into sects of varying degrees of radicality. Of all these aspects, some could be attributed to the influence of European Protestantism and Pietism, while others appeared to be entirely indigenous. The emergence of Hasidic Judaism in the eighteenth century has to be reckoned as another example of the tendency to value the affective dimensions of religion.

The preaching of those in groups that found their discriminating characteristic in experience would be very different from the preaching of those who based everything on an appeal to reason. Thus religions of the heart have an important place in the history of preaching. While only the movements from this group that had a direct influence on the development of preaching in the English-speaking world will be considered in what follows, those that do concern this story cannot be understood adequately unless they are seen in the context of this wider spirit of the times.[3]

EARLY STIRRINGS OF BRITISH HEARTS

The first manifestations in Great Britain of the tendency to estimate the value of religion on the basis of its affective dimensions occurred among the Puritans. The treatment of the Puritans in part 3 concentrated on their agenda to bring the Church of England to what they considered the scriptural perfection of the model of Geneva and the way their understanding of how sermons should be shaped had been influenced by Ramist logic. As early as the reign of Charles I, however, a change can be detected in the Puritan program. Preoccupation with purification of the polity and liturgy of the national church gave way to consideration of the life of the individual Christian. As good Calvinists, Puritans agreed that one's salvation is entirely in the hands of God, a matter of the eternal decree of God by which one was elected to salvation or reprobation. But the question arose as to whether those who were elected to grace knew they were.

It came to be Puritan orthodoxy that those who were elected to grace had assurance of their salvation. The pioneers in this line of thought were William Perkins[4] and his disciple, William Ames. Their work in this area grew out of a recognition that the way election occurred was not simply in God's having decided the issue at the dawn of creation or even in the Holy Spirit's causing a person to respond to the proclamation of the gospel in a sermon (which, according to Calvin, was the medium through which justification occurred). Rather, salvation was communicated in an inevitable sequence of stages (*ordo salutis,* the "order of salvation").

Calvinist biblical interpreters had found that pattern in Romans 8:30: "And those whom he predestined he also called; and those whom he called he also justified; and those whom he justified he also glorified." Perkins saw the "degrees" of salvation to be:

1. Effectual calling—or conversion, the event by which someone is brought to repentance and faith by the proclamation of the law and the gospel.
2. Justification—the imputation of Christ's righteousness to the sinner so that the sinner is accounted righteous by God on the basis of faith.
3. Sanctification—the Christian's continuing death to sin (mortification) and coming to life in Christ (vivification).
4. Glorification—the completion of the Christian's conformity to the likeness of Christ that occurs between death and judgment.

While Perkins had already insisted that the highest degree of faith is assurance of one's own salvation, Ames identified the appearance of this assurance as "adoption" and added it to the order of salvation as a stage between justification and sanctification.[5] The lack of assurance that one was saved came to be treated as evidence that one was not, a position that in time would offer a powerful appeal for conversion in evangelistic preaching not only by Calvinists but also by "Arminians" (those like Wesley who believe that human freedom of the will is consistent with the sovereignty of God).

While the doctrine of assurance would give important theological content to the later preaching of revivals, some of the external forms of such preaching also can be traced back to British Calvinists in the early-seventeenth century—although in this case they were not English Puritans, but Scottish and Irish Presbyterians. Among them a tradition had developed of preparing for their infrequent celebrations of the Eucharist by having sacramental meetings at which people were encouraged to ready themselves to receive Holy Communion by repenting of their sins in the assurance that justification should produce a sanctified life. The preaching was often quite emotional, and people came under conviction of their sins and experienced conversion.

Such meetings began as activities of the local congregation, but they came to be such moving experiences that visitors from some distance were attracted. At times the crowds were so large that the meeting had to be moved out-of-doors. These meetings were suppressed by Charles I, but, by the time of the Restoration when they were outlawed again, they had become the principal institutional form of the religious life of the Scottish and Irish Calvinists, who continued to hold such meetings under clandestine conditions. Access to the churches being forbidden them, open-air meetings became the norm. Since their clergy had been ejected from their "livings," they wandered around preaching revivals at these sacramental meetings. These conditions continued until the Glorious Revolution of 1688, when William and Mary came to the throne.

> By 1688 there was a long-established tradition of periodic sacramental meetings, involving enthusiastic preaching and the expectation of experiences of conviction and conversion, hosted by a semi-independent fellowship of traveling (or itinerant) preachers. The precedents for the Evangelical Revival (and American Awakenings) were well in place.[6]

THE EVANGELICAL REVIVAL

Wales

Although the Evangelical revival is explained by some historians against the background of the industrial revolution, deism, Lockean psychology and epistemology, and the emergence of moralism and voluntary societies in the sphere of religion, its first manifestation was in one area of the British Isles least affected by all of these forces, Wales. Unlike the movement a century before among Scottish and Irish Calvinists, this one began (although it did not remain) within the established church. Nor was the Welsh revival unhoped for. **The Reverend Griffith Jones** of the parish of Llandowrer, who served as a sort of godfather for the movement, had been praying for it as far back as 1714. His own way of preparing the way of the Lord was to establish schools in which children could become literate enough to read the Bible in Welsh. He was able to found 3,225 such schools, in which 150,000 had learned to read before he died in 1761; he also distributed 30,000 Welsh Bibles.

Two young men in particular are credited with the first preaching of the revival. One of them, **Howell Harris,** was not ordained. After a dramatic conversion experience in 1735 when he was twenty-one, he went to Oxford with the ministry in mind, but he was so distressed by the low moral level of the university that he stayed only a few weeks. Returning home, he began a ministry of teaching and preaching. He became an overseer of some of Griffith Jones's schools and began evangelizing from house to house, establishing societies of his converts.

Soon his witnessing attracted crowds, and he began preaching out-of-doors and itinerating between his congregations. Harris's preaching drew power from his strongly emotional nature, a nature that also made him hard to get along with. In fact, at one time he dropped out of the Methodist conference for twelve years, establishing instead a community not unlike Zinzendorf's Herrnhut at his home at Trevecka. Later, though, he became reconciled. Through him the Welsh revival was to influence the British revival, especially through his contacts with George Whitefield, John Wesley, and Lady Huntingdon.

The other young man, **Daniel Rowland,** was ordained in the established church and presented to the parish of Llangeitho, which served both as a base for his itinerate preaching and as a center for the revival. Although no direct influence has been traced, Rowland's work bore many resemblances to the Scottish and Irish revivals of the previous century. Harris has left an account of the preaching in preparation for a celebration of the Eucharist in Rowland's parish:

> I was last Sunday at the Ordinance with Brother Rowlands where I saw, felt, and heard such things as I cant send on Paper any Idea of. . . . Such Crying out and Heart Breaking Groans, Silent Weeping and Holy Joy, and shouts of Rejoicing I never saw. Their Amens and Cryings Glory in the Highest &c would inflame your soul was you there. Tis very common when he preaches for Scores to fall down by the Power of the Word, pierced and wounded or overcom'd by the love of God and Sights of the Beauty and Excellency of Jesus, and lie on the ground.[7]

It was upon the foundation of these two men that the Methodist movement, which became the most notable aspect of Welsh culture for generations to come, was built.

A study of the preaching of the Welsh pioneers was made by one of their successors, Gwyn Walters, who taught preaching for many years at Gordon-Conwell Theological Seminary.[8] He described the preaching style of the Welsh folk preachers covering a period of 250 years, demonstrating what remarkable eloquence in the gospel some of them attained. Several characteristics of their style remind one of classical African American preaching, especially a form of dialogue with the elders in the "amen corner" that resembles the black tradition of "call and response," and the way preachers would break out in an extemporaneous singing of their words, what the Welsh call the *hwyl*, which resembles the chanted portions of American folk preaching.

The Homeless Pilgrim with Dubious Name[9]

The link between the Welsh and British expressions of the Evangelical Awakening was in the person of Howell Harris, who came to have close association with both Whitefield, for whom he furnished the model of field preaching and later served as a marriage broker, and Wesley, in an association to be discussed below.[10]

Born to innkeeping parents[11] in Gloucester in 1714, **George Whitefield** showed great interest in both religion and drama as a child. Changing financial circumstances of the family meant that the only way he could go to the university to prepare for ordination was as a "servitor," who had to perform chores for his college and for "gentleman" scholars. There he met the Wesley brothers (who occupied the middle status of "commoners") and became involved in their pious circle, known in the university by such opprobrious terms as the "Holy Club" or "Methodists."

Although the name Methodists was later to be picked up and proudly worn as a badge, what it came to stand for was very different from that to which it was originally applied. The circle at Oxford was typical of a sort of voluntary association being formed at the time, one that owed something to the influence of both the Puritan "conventicles" of the previous century and the *collegia* of Spener and the German Pietists. These "societies," founded on models established by Anthony Horneck and Josiah Woodword, were "a means by which Christians could hold each other accountable for their personal moral behavior and for their pursuit of benevolent enterprises."[12]

Although all forms of the Methodist revival would use societies as one of their basic methods of organization, they would envision them as associations of the converted. The Holy Club at Oxford, however, had its heyday before any of its members had undergone a conversion experience. Its members, therefore, would look back on its activities as fruitless works before grace. Whitefield was the only member of the group who underwent that experience while he was still at the university, which he did under the influence of a book to which Charles Wesley introduced him.

Ordained a deacon on June 20, 1736, about a month before he received his B.A., Whitefield began preaching around London, not having been appointed to a cure. In what Stout calls the "filiopietistic" accounts of the beginning of the Methodist revival, a good bit of shock is expressed over the way that the founders were denied pulpits in the Church of England. Such a reaction is hardly justified. The account of the latitudinarian church in the previous chapter does not reveal it to be seething with zeal, but the synagogue at Nazareth when our Lord preached there may have been the last pulpit open to anyone who wanted to occupy it. The clergy appointed to the parishes were the only persons with an automatic right to preach in them. Those who complain today about the exclusion of Whitefield and the Wesleys probably keep close watch over who preaches in their own churches, and it is only the conviction that the Methodist leaders were voices crying in the wilderness that makes the closed pulpits seem at all exceptional.

The truly extraordinary fact is that they received so many invitations to preach so early in their ministries. That does not happen today to many twenty-two-year-old, newly ordained deacons. Yet young Whitefield seems to have been the sensation of the season. The Wesleys had already gone to Georgia as missionaries of the Society for the Propagation of the Gospel, and Whitefield soon came to see it as his vocation to follow them there. Meanwhile, he took advantage of every opportunity to preach the necessity of the rebirth he had just experienced.

The effects were astonishing: someone complained to the bishop of London that in his first sermon, Whitefield had driven fifteen people mad. The bishop's response was to wish that "the madness might not be forgotten before the next Sunday." Other clergy must have felt the same way because invitations poured in and, wherever he went, the churches were overflowing. In the year and a half before he could sail to America, Whitefield created such a taste for his sermons that it had to be met by printed transcripts for those unable to hear them. Indeed, most of the sermons that he ever edited for publication himself (forty-six out of sixty-three) were written by the time he was twenty-five.[13]

This early adulation was accorded before Whitefield's preaching had acquired two of the characteristics that were to make it most appealing and accessible to mass audiences: it was done without notes and in the open air. Extempore preaching had been an ideal of the Holy Club at Oxford, but Whitefield began it only on the eve of his departure for America. Field preaching was inaugurated after he returned from his short sojourn abroad[14] for ordination to the priesthood and appointment to the orphanage he had founded in Georgia as his cure. Since canon law of the Church of England did not provide for itinerate preaching, Whitefield found his excuse in the need to raise money for the orphans, as John Wesley was to find his in the claim that a fellow of an Oxford college was licensed to preach anywhere.

By this time, however, the publication of Whitefield's *Journal* of his travels had already turned many of the clergy against him so that the popularity he had enjoyed the year before was now withheld. Pulpits were closed to him, especially after an incident in which he appears to have intruded into that of St. Margaret's, Westminster, by force. But he had heard of Howell Harris's field preaching as early as 1737, and now he experimented with it himself.

Less than two weeks after the St. Margaret's affair, Whitefield and his friend William Seward were visiting Bristol and went out to the collieries of nearby Kingswood. There he decided to preach to the miners, about two hundred of whom assembled. A week later he was preaching to five thousand, and that number doubled two days later. In March, the number had doubled again to twenty thousand. After that he was ready to try out this technique developed in the countryside on urban London. He had found his medium. Before moving into London, however, he made two visits to Harris in Wales and preached with him there, establishing in person the friendship already begun by mail.

Thus all the pieces were in place for what must be one of the most extraordinary preaching careers of all time. Soon Whitefield was to preach to a crowd in Hyde Park that he estimated to number eighty thousand. "Even discounting that number substantially leaves a staggering total, a crowd the size of which had not been seen in all England since the great battles of the Civil War."[15] The following October he preached to twenty thousand in Boston, and "there had never been a larger crowd in America to that date."[16]

He was to keep up the pace for thirty years, preaching an average of nine times per week to congregations that regularly ran to the tens of thousands. He toured America seven times, meeting his death on the last round there, and became what Stout has called "an American icon—the first intercolonial hero."[17] He made twice as many trips to Scotland and also visited Wales and Ireland; he even went to Holland and Spain. Inside England he traversed distances that were geographically short but socially cosmic, having been heard on many occasions by the leading members of the nobility and intelligentsia.

Even though there were popular preachers in the Middle Ages who attracted vast crowds, it is doubtful that any human being was heard by as many fellow mortals as Whitefield before the advent of modern mass communication. And it is even more doubtful that as many of any other preacher's listeners experienced what they understood to be conversion as a result of their preaching, until at least the nineteenth century and possibly the twentieth.

As interesting as it would be to follow Whitefield the rest of his journey—to observe his breach with John Wesley, his association with Lady Huntingdon, his friendship with Benjamin Franklin—it is more to the purpose of this book to try to ascertain what made his preaching unique, to determine as far as possible both what made him attract such vast audiences and also why there was at the time and has remained ever since such disagreement about him—what makes his name "dubious," as Whittier called it. (For an example of Whitefield's preaching, **see Vol. 2, pp. 349-62.**)

The first observation to be made is that while Whitefield created the basic pattern that evangelistic preaching has retained ever since, it does not differ greatly in terms of outline from the neoclassical pattern followed by Tillotson and his successors. This is to say that the pattern was essentially topical. The sermon was based on a short text, and, after an introduction and some background, there was an announcement of the points that would be made. Each of the heads would have several subheadings, and all led to a conclusion.

Here, though, the resemblance ended, for the greatest dread of the neoclassicists was what they called "enthusiasm." They did recognize the need for emotional appeals, but these were never to exceed the bounds of good taste. What Whitefield was aiming at, however, was conversion, and he believed that could occur only when people were brought under conviction of their sins, when they were brought to believe in the depths of their being that they were sinners whose only chance of escaping hell was a divine intervention. Hammer away at this as he did, however, his emphasis was not on God's wrath so much as on the divine love and pity that sought the lost sheep and the rejoicing in heaven whenever one was reclaimed. However much the grounds for fear are gone over in the sermon, the conclusion is always joyful doxology. It is no wonder that Whitefield himself was frequently in tears and that most of his hearers were; often the emotional manifestations were more extreme.

In addition to creating a formula, Whitefield also had extraordinary personal gifts. One was a voice that not only carried to audiences larger than any addressed before amplification, but also was the envy of actors because of the feeling it could put into a word. The actor David Garrick is reported to have said that Whitefield could "make his audiences weep or tremble merely by varying his pronunciation of the word Mesopotamia."[18] He also said, "I would give a hundred guineas if I could only say 'O!' like Mr. Whitefield."[19] Another talent he possessed was the ability to register in his face and gestures all of the feelings he invoked; in this he was at one with the elocutionary movement in rhetoric of that time, which sought to bring liveliness to delivery.[20] Beyond that, he had a genius as a raconteur to make a scene from biblical history and other illustrative material palpably present to his hearers.

To these qualities he added the other techniques of popular speakers. One student has enumerated them in this way:

> the element of surprise; travellers' tales; anecdotes to lighten the strain or to point a moral; the selection of the dramatic parts of scripture for his most successful expositions; such rhetorical devices as the formal introduction to an imaginative flight, antithesis, the intermingling of long and short sentences, and the enforcing of a point by a pithy saying; counter-attacks upon his critics by way of declamations; the comic interlude in which wit, satire, and whimsy, humour, and even puns are used; the direct form of address to individuals or to groups in the auditory and particular applications in the exhortations of his sermons; the great range of his appeal to sentiment, arousing pity (he was a master of pathos), indignation, or terror; the use of homely and telling illustrations; and the employment of topical references and impromptu illustrations.[21]

To this must be added the mastery that came through the privilege of an itinerant, that of repeating a sermon many times. Benjamin Franklin said:

> By hearing him often I came to distinguish easily between sermons newly composed and those which he had often preached in the course of his travels. His delivery of the latter was so improved by frequent repetition, that every accent, every emphasis, every modulation of

> voice, was so perfectly well turned, and well placed, that without being interested in the subject, one could not help being pleased with the discourse: a pleasure of much the same kind with that received from an excellent piece of music.[22]

All of this effort to list traits is not intended to explain Whitefield's power, but rather to show that the only possible explanation for it is that in him came together that rare combination of ability called genius. There must be few speakers in human history who have matched his ability to move audiences by eloquence.

Since these and similar gifts in preachers are often described as dramatic, it may be worthwhile to make important distinctions between effective public speaking and acting. The actor says words written by someone else and says them in the role of another person, a character in a play, while preachers speak their own words as their own. The speech of actors is ostensibly spoken to other actors on the stage and is meant to be heard by the audience as interaction between the characters portrayed, while preachers address congregations, usually parishioners, communicating directly with them.

Effective acting, then, is the ability to be convincing in the portrayal of emotions that are not the actor's own, while effective preaching is the ability to convey one's own deepest convictions with power. The two skills are different, and not everyone good at the one activity is good at the other. This, of course, is not to say that preachers cannot improve their delivery by study and application, and even less is it to claim that all preachers, or even all widely heard preachers, have been sincere. But even if they are frauds, it is their own thoughts and feelings that they are feigning, and they intend for their words to be received as direct address. Their performances, then, are not theater, but a confidence game.

The question raised in the Whittier quotation, therefore, is essentially one of Whitefield's sincerity. Yet the issue is more complex. Since the preserved documentation does not furnish explicit evidence of duplicity, the issue is simply one of trust. But trust in such a matter depends largely upon whether one favors or opposes the kind of activity in which the figure in question was engaged. In this case, that means whether one considers dramatic conversion experiences in response to emotional preaching to be the ordinary channel of the grace of God or regards them instead as hysterical responses to manipulative behavior. A mediating position would be that such preaching and conversion experiences are one of the many channels through which God reaches out to reclaim estranged children, the channels differing according to the needs of the individuals.

As for Whitefield, any evaluation must do justice to these data: on the one hand, even many of those who admire him most, the "filiopietists," admit that he was not always judicious. On the other hand, he was convincing to a skeptic like Benjamin Franklin, who knew him well, and many of his converts were permanently changed for the better.[23]

Institutionalizing the Revival

In American folklore there is the story of how the legendary hero of the Southwest, Pecos Bill, lassoed a tornado. **John Wesley** accomplished something on the same order by the way he harnessed the religion of the heart movement in Britain (as his followers were to do in America) and organized it into a denomination. His having done so is not without irony, since he insisted to the end of his life that he was utterly opposed to his movement's separating from the Church of England. There are other ironies as well, including the fact that most of the techniques he used to domesticate the revival had been used by others before him, but without his fixity of purpose, so that they were never as productive for those from whom Wesley copied them as they were for Wesley himself. For instance, Wesley learned field preaching from Whitefield, who, in turn, had learned it from Howell Harris.

In many ways, it appears that Whitefield began most things before Wesley did but that Wesley was the one who hung around and garnered the results. While it can be argued that in his devotion to preaching the revival himself rather than organizing its results, Whitefield was maximizing the gifts he had as Wesley maximized his own, it is nevertheless true that Whitefield was the first of the two to be converted, the first to itinerate, the first to preach in the open, and the first to organize a network of societies. Of course, all these things had been done by Harris and the Welsh revivalists before Whitefield, by the seventeenth-century Scotch and Irish Calvinists before Harris, and many by continental Pietists as well.

Yet Wesley was the one able to launch an international religious movement by these actions. The Welsh Calvinistic Methodists, as they came to be called, were to dominate Welsh culture well into the twentieth century. Whitefield's clergy seem to have become Independents or Congregationalists, and Lady Huntingdon's Connexion became dissenting chapels. As closely connected and intertwined as these movements were at various times—especially before the breach between the "Arminian" Wesleyans and the "Calvinist" others—it is for their association with Wesley's Methodists that the others are chiefly remembered.

For over a third of his long life, however, no one looked less likely to lead a mass religious movement than John Wesley. It would have seemed much more likely that he would develop into the fussy sort of scholarly priest his father was. Educated at Charterhouse and at Christ Church College, Oxford, he was ordained and elected as a fellow of Lincoln College. After taking a couple of years off to serve as his father's curate, he resumed the life of a fellow of an Oxford college. As long as he remained a bachelor he would receive an adequate fellow's stipend while engaging in the educational tasks of the college and pursuing his own studies. While doing so, he also showed himself to be an earnest and pious, not to say scrupulous, Christian. With the kindred souls of the Holy Club or "Bible Moths," he took on a strict regimen of prayer, fasting, self-examination, and corporal works of mercy. It was because he and his friends went about these duties so systematically that they came to be derisively called "Methodists."

Several of the Methodists, including John and his brother Charles, decided to become SPG[24] missionaries to Georgia and set out for that purpose late in 1735 when John was thirty-two. After a voyage of almost four months, they arrived at their destination to begin a ministry that lasted less than two years and was characterized by misguided zeal and pastoral ineptitude. Arriving back in England at the end of January 1737, Wesley's evaluation of his time abroad was expressed in his *Journal*:

> It is now two years and almost four months since I left my native country in order to teach the Georgian Indians the nature of Christianity. But what have I learned myself in the meantime? Why, what I the least of all suspected, that I, who went to America to convert others, was never myself converted to God.[25]

That lesson did not come directly from his time in Georgia but from the voyages over and back. Storms at sea revealed to Wesley his fear of death, a fear obviously not shared by Moravian fellow travelers. Their peace and calm convinced him that he stood in need of conversion, an experience that came to him on the evening of May 24, 1738, when he was attending a meeting of a Moravian society in Aldersgate Street. The following month he began a trip to the Continent for the principal purpose of visiting Zinzendorf's Moravian community at Herrnhut. There he was refused Communion on the grounds that he was *homo perturbatus,* but he was greatly impressed with what he saw. Even though he was eventually to break with the Moravians over their quietism, they provided the occasion on which his previously divided self could be united through a great emotional upheaval. It is probably more accurate to speak of a process rather than a single experience of conversion for Wesley, but the Aldersgate experience was the turning point. Soon after his thirty-fifth birthday, he was ready to begin his life's work.

The direction his work was to take was shown him by Whitefield, who returned from Georgia at the end of 1738. Whitefield had already begun his own experiments in field preaching, and now he called on Wesley to join him. Always a stickler for propriety in many ways, Wesley was at first reluctant to go. Yet he had already begun preaching out of his experience of conversion with two results: (1) people responded in profoundly emotional ways, and (2) the pulpits of staid Anglican parishes came to be closed to him. Thus he joined Whitefield at Bristol, and his *Journal* entry for April 2, 1739, tells the tale:

> At four in the afternoon I submitted to be more vile, and proclaimed in the highways the glad tidings of salvation, speaking from a little eminence in a ground adjoining to the city, to about three thousand people.

The text of his sermon was, "The Spirit of Lord is upon me, because he hath anointed me to preach the gospel to the poor."[26]

And preach it he did. In the remaining fifty-two years of his life, he preached more than forty thousand sermons. Although he did not draw the crowds that Whitefield did, his were large enough, sometimes over twenty thousand. While he left it to his representatives to cross the Atlantic, his travels—on horseback until he was almost seventy—have been estimated at 225,000 miles. And what of the results? When he died three-quarters of the way through his eighty-eighth year, he left behind seventy thousand Methodists in Great Britain. This number represents rolls that he was continually trying to strip of deadwood. There were also sixty thousand of his followers in America—even though he had opposed their Revolution. Nor do these figures represent isolated adherents. The secret of the movement's strength was the complex infrastructure he devised to keep the fires of faith burning ardently among his followers. Ronald Knox has provided an economical list of the components of this infrastructure:

> When he died he left behind him a powerful religious body, Anglican in its inspiration, and for the most part in its membership, but ripe for schism. . . . It had its cadre, not only of itinerate preachers and local preachers, but of class leaders, band leaders, helpers, stewards, and schoolmasters; it had band-meetings, class-meetings, quarterly meetings, love-feasts over and above its ordinary services. Nominally it was

> only an aggregation of "religious societies" organized in various centres. . . . But in fact a church had formed in embryo within the womb of the Establishment, with John Wesley as its visible head.[27]

This unparalleled ministry is not only impressive in its own right but also significant for the history of preaching in at least three ways. First, those forty thousand sermons call for attention, not so much for their number as for the light they cast on the modes of evangelistic preaching. While the outward form of Wesley's sermons was similar to that of Whitefield's, the strategy of persuasion was very different. Looking at Wesley's sermons after examining Whitefield's can offer a sense of the range of expression possible in this genre. Then Wesley also has importance in the history of preaching as a writer of homiletical instruction for his itinerate and local preachers. Manuals on how to preach for those who have not undergone formal theological education are relatively rare, and it is indicative of Wesley's thoroughness that he thought to produce them. Finally, Wesley chose published sermons (many of which had never been delivered orally) as his own most distinctive catechetical form in the library he created to provide all his followers needed to know in addition to the Bible. This use of the sermon form divorced from oral delivery as the most effective pattern for forming his movement intellectually casts some light on the effectiveness of the form itself as a vehicle for the communication of Christian faith and knowledge.

Wesley's Live Preaching[28]

The term "live," taken from modern telecommunications media where it distinguishes performances being broadcast as they occur from a recorded form to be aired later, is chosen to call attention to an issue even more problematic for John Wesley than for others in the history of preaching: the relation of published sermons to what was delivered orally to a congregation. The reason it was more problematic is that his spoken and written sermons are not necessarily different forms of the same composition: "Many of Wesley's favorite texts for oral preaching do not appear at all in the corpus of his written sermons and vice versa."[29] And the reason for that is: "He saw an important difference between the principal aims of an oral and a written sermon: the former is chiefly for *proclamation* and invitation; the latter is chiefly for *nurture* and reflection."[30]

Even though this difference in purpose would suggest a difference in method, which in turn would ordinarily mean a published document would offer an unreliable guide to the oral event, there is at least one printed sermon that probably comes close to what was spoken to congregations. Sermon 43, "The Scripture Way of Salvation," is on Ephesians 2:8, "ye are saved through faith," a text from which Wesley's record tells us he preached over ninety times.[31] Since its form is the neoclassical structure followed by both the latitudinarians and Whitefield, a detailed look at this sermon may give a sense of how variation in content and in the faculties to which appeal is made can produce enormous difference in the dynamics of sermons constructed to satisfy ostensibly the same criteria.

Sermon 43 begins with a short proem that distinguishes between the complexity of religion as it is often described and the simplicity of the "genuine religion of Jesus Christ," which has salvation as its end and faith as the means to that end. In order to see what those important terms mean, he proposes the partition:

I. What is salvation?
II. What is that faith whereby we are saved? and
III. How we are saved by it.

I. What is salvation?

1. First of all, negatively, it "is not what is frequently understood by that word, the going to heaven, eternal happiness." Rather, it is something his hearers already possess.

2. This includes "all that is wrought in the soul by what is frequently termed 'natural conscience,' but more properly, 'preventing grace.'"

3. But the salvation spoken of by the apostle in the text "consists of two general parts, justification and sanctification," with the understanding that "justification is another word for pardon."

4. Sanctification begins at the moment of justification.

5. The experience of pardon at justification leaves those who undergo it with a sense that "all sin is gone."

6. "But it is seldom long before they are undeceived, finding sin was only suspended, not destroyed."

7. Macarius expressed that point well fourteen hundred years previously.

8. The work of sanctification takes place gradually "while we take up our cross and deny ourselves every pleasure that does not lead us to God."

9. The process of sanctification is "go[ing] on to perfection," the perfection of perfect love. "It is love excluding sin; love filling the heart, taking up the whole capacity of the soul."

II. "But what is that 'faith through which we are saved'?"

1. It is what the apostle calls "the evidence of things not seen," which is both a supernatural evidence and a supernatural perception of God, a "twofold operation of the Holy Spirit" by which we see "the spiritual world" and "the eternal world."

2. Most particularly, "faith is a divine evidence and conviction, not only that 'God was in Christ,' . . . but also that Christ 'loved *me*, and gave himself for *me*.'"

3. Such a faith is both the "faith of assurance" and that of "adherence," "for a man cannot have a childlike confidence in God till he knows he is a child of God."

4. "It is by this faith we . . . [are both] justified and sanctified."

III. How are we justified and sanctified by faith?

1. We are justified by faith in the sense that "faith is the condition, and the only condition, of our justification."

2. While both repentance and the fruits of repentance are necessary for justification, they are not necessary in the same sense nor to the same degree as faith.

3. And just as we are justified, so also are we sanctified by faith because "no man is sanctified till he believes; every man when he believes is sanctified."

4. But since Wesley teaches the need for repentance after as well as before justification, is that repentance not then a condition for salvation in addition to faith?

5. This second repentance (as well as good works), rightly understood, is necessary to salvation.

6. This repentance after justification differs from that before in that it is "a conviction wrought by the Holy Ghost of the 'sin' which still 'remains' in our heart," "a conviction of our proneness to evil, of an heart 'bent to backsliding,' of the still continuing tendency of the 'flesh' to 'lust against the Spirit.'"

7. "With this conviction of the sin *remaining* in our hearts there is joined a clear conviction of the sin remaining in our lives."

8. "One thing more is implied in this repentance, namely, a conviction of our helplessness, of our utter inability to think one good thought."

9. Of the good works that must be practiced for sanctification, the first kind is "works of piety."

10. The second kind is "works of mercy."

11. "Hence may appear the extreme mischievousness of that seemingly innocent opinion that 'there is no sin in a believer' . . . By totally preventing that repentance it quite blocks up the way to sanctification."

12. Yet "there is no possible danger in *thus* expecting full salvation."

13. "Though it be allowed that both this repentance and its fruits are necessary to full salvation, yet they are not necessary either in the *same sense* with faith or in the *same degree*."

14. The "faith whereby we are sanctified, saved from sin and perfected in love" is "a divine evidence and conviction, first, that God hath promised it in the Holy Scripture."

15. "It is a divine evidence and conviction, secondly, that what God hath promised he is *able* to perform."

16. It is, thirdly, a divine evidence and conviction that he is able and willing to do it *now*."

17. To this there needs to be added a fourth thing, "a divine evidence and conviction that *he doth it*."

18. This "great work in the soul"... "may be gradually wrought in some," but "it is infinitely desirable, were it the will of God, that it should be done instantaneously."[32]

(At this point, without any change in the division, there is a shift to application/ exhortation.)

> *Thou* therefore look for it every moment. . . . But you shall not be disappointed of your hope: it will come, and will not tarry. Look for it then every day, every hour, every moment.[33]

(This exhortation ends in a call, complete with the verse of a hymn.)

> Do *you* believe we are sanctified by faith? Be true then to your principle, and look for this blessing just as you are, neither better, nor worse; as a poor sinner that has still nothing to pay, nothing to plead but "Christ died." And if you look for it as you are, then expect it *now*. Stay for nothing. Why should you? Christ is ready. And he is all you want. He is waiting for you. He is at the door! Let your inmost soul cry out,
>
> Come in, come in, thou heavenly Guest!
> Nor hence again remove:
> But sup with me, and let the feast
> Be everlasting love.[34]

The contrast with Whitefield is diametrical. Indeed, were it not for the subject matter and the final exhortation, this sermon of Wesley's would have more in common with the rational addresses of the latitudinarians. There is nothing in the way of ornament, nothing that will impede the clear flow of thought. At the end of a detailed analysis of the preaching styles of the two evangelists, Horton Davies says in summary:

> The conclusion of our consideration of the techniques of the discourses of Whitefield and Wesley can only be that Whitefield was the spell-binding orator and preacher par excellence, while Wesley was the best of pulpit teachers.[35]

While this is true as far as it goes, it probably makes the mistake of assuming that the matter and style of the oral and written sermons were the same. Since, however, it is known that Wesley expected them to accomplish different purposes, that assumption cannot be safely made. The oral sermons were for proclamation and invitation. How else can one account for the tens of thousands of persons converted through them? Could this religion of the head appeal successfully to a generation yearning for a religion of the heart? The answer would appear to be no, especially in light of the emotional appeal of the exhortation in the sermon just summarized. Nor does "head work"—to contrast this intellectual appeal to the term "heart work," which Wesley loved to speak of—appear to be all there was to his preaching.

This much is suggested by one of the sophisticates of the time who heard him out of curiosity. The earl of Orford, Horace Walpole, a litterateur and a pioneer in the Gothic revival, wrote an unsympathetic account:

> I have been at one opera, Mr. Wesley's. . . . Wesley is a lean elderly man, fresh-coloured, his hair smoothly combed, but with a *soupçon* of curl at the ends. Wondrous clean, but as evidently an actor as Garrick. He spoke his sermon, but so fast and with so little accent, that I am sure he has often uttered it, for it was like a lesson. There were parts and eloquence in it; but towards the end he exalted his voice, and acted very vulgar enthusiasm; decried learning, and told stories, like Latimer, of the fool of his college, who said, "I *thanks* God for everything."[36]

One does not have to depend, however, on such unsympathetic accounts. In his *Journal,* Wesley often notes that he was powerfully moved while preaching and that his congregation shared that experience. Further, he also notes that some of his hearers shouted, fainted, or were seized with convulsions.[37] The only conclusion is that in his oral preaching Wesley made strong emotional appeals, the nature of which his published sermons do little to suggest. It is hard to believe that he employed any of the rhetorical means that came so naturally to Whitefield; nothing in his writings suggests that he had such weapons in his arsenal. Perhaps it was something about his presence, the sort of overwhelming compassionate concern conveyed in the Hone portrait, or his urgent conviction. It is utterly unlikely that so many would have been converted through his preaching unless it had a large element of enthusiasm. Though whether one would agree with Walpole that the enthusiasm was ugly is another matter.

His Instructions to His Preachers

What has been said about the difference between the preaching style of Wesley and that of Whitefield refers to a difference in personality. It certainly should not suggest that Wesley was unconscious of his manner of speaking or that he had not given considerable thought and study to the principles of effective speech. It would have been entirely out of character for him to overlook anything so important to his mission.[38] He not only applied such insight to his own practice, but also distilled it for the instruction of his lay preachers. While some of his thoughts on the subject are inserted in letters to various persons, most of them are collected in two documents: the "Large Minutes," which served as the nearest approach of his Connexion to being a codex of canon law,[39] and *Directions Concerning Pronunciation and Gesture,* an abridgement he made of an anonymous rhetorical manual of his time.[40]

Before going into his instructions about preaching, it would perhaps be helpful to say something about his cadre of preachers. He does not regard them as clergy. Rather, they are intended to be Helpers of the Ministers of the Church of England. They are "extraordinary messengers," who "provoke regular Ministers to jealousy"[41] and "supply their lack of service toward those who are perishing from lack of knowledge" (Q. 24). Their duties include preaching morning and evening, meeting regularly with societies and bands and their leaders, catechizing families in the method recommended by Richard Baxter in *The Reformed Pastor,* and studying at least five hours a day. They also have records to keep. What they did not do was administer any sacraments, since doing so would imply that they were a dissenting Christian body and not what today would be called a renewal movement within Anglicanism.[42]

There were both local and itinerating preachers, although Wesley thought it bad for anyone to settle down in one place. There were also assistants, who were supervisors somewhat in the manner of modern American district superintendents. All of them owed complete allegiance to Wesley, and any that did not wish to follow the minute rules he laid down were free to leave (Q. 27.5).

The same condition applied to laypeople, so there were frequent departures and the rolls were continually purged—although the founder was never satisfied with the state of purity achieved. Wesley is often spoken of as a good organizer, but that does not mean he delegated authority well. It means rather that he wanted to have oversight of the souls of all his seventy thousand followers and those who preached to them. It was this discipline that lassoed the tornado.[43]

The advice he gives to his preachers on the best general method of preaching is: (1) to invite, (2) to convince, (3) to offer Christ, and (4) to build up, "and to do this in some measure in every sermon" (Q. 36). He follows this with "smaller advices relative to preaching," which include beginning and ending at precisely the time appointed; letting one's whole deportment before the congregation be serious, weighty, and solemn; suiting one's subject to the congregation; choosing the plainest texts possible; not rambling; limiting one's use of allegorical or spiritual interpretation; and avoiding anything either awkward or affected in gesture, phrase, or pronunciation. The list continues after that, but with admonitions that have less and less to do directly with preaching, touching such matters as singing no hymns of one's own composition, not spelling words like "honour" and "vigour" without the *u,* not wearing a slouched hat, and taking care of one's horse (Q. 37).

While such preaching was obviously intended to be evangelistic, Wesley was contemptuous of what were often spoken of as "gospel sermons."[44] The implication is that preaching such can relieve the necessity of requiring behavioral standards consistent with what God had required of converted sinners. He says:

> The most effectual way of preaching Christ, is to preach him in all his offices,[45] and to declare his law as well as his gospel, both to the believers and unbelievers. Let us strongly and closely insist upon inward and outward holiness, in all its branches. (Q. 38)

One of the objections to Calvinism, "the direct antidote to Methodism," and its doctrine of "heart-holiness," is that "it seems to magnify Christ; although in reality it supposes him to have died in vain" (Q. 74). But Methodists had leaned too much in the direction of Calvinism by soft-pedaling the need for redemption to express itself in good works. There was thus a need for them to attend to the strong practical and ethical thrust of Wesley's own preaching and that which he expected of his preachers. For example, to Question 21, "Do not Sabbath-breaking, dram-drinking, evil-speaking, unprofitable conversation, lightness, expensiveness or gaiety of apparel, and contracting debts without due care to discharge them, still prevail in some places?" he responds by saying, "Let us preach expressly on each of these heads."

The content of Methodist preaching, then, was a combination of evangelizing those not yet converted and exhortation on holiness of life to the justified, who were supposed to be "going on to perfection."

To see that these messages get across, the founder also had some sage advice on delivery.[46] Preachers should imitate only good examples. They should develop their voices so that they could be heard, and they should practice their enunciation. Faults to be avoided were speaking either too loudly or too low; speaking in a "thick, cluttering manner," mumbling and swallowing words or syllables; speaking too fast or slow or with an irregular, desultory, and uneven voice; or, the worst fault of all, speaking with a "tone" (and Wesley has an interesting list of the varieties of such affected pronunciation that are available). Instead, one should speak in public as one does in conversation. This involves working to achieve a voice that is soft and sweet. Preachers should not cough or spit while they are speaking.

They should, however, learn to vary their voice so that it is appropriate to their subject matter. There are three qualities of voice in which such variation is possible: volume, vehemence, and speed; and Wesley gives the ways for achieving the proper combination of these qualities for the different moods in sermons (e.g., "In congratulating the happy events of life, we speak with a lively and cheerful accent").[47]

Preachers who wish to improve the way they communicate their thoughts and feelings through the expressions on their faces and their gestures should work with a mirror or a friend who will give them reliable reactions. The preacher should neither be constantly in motion nor stand stock-still. The head is to be "kept modestly and decently upright, in its natural state and position," looking occasionally to the right or left but otherwise straight forward. Facial expressions should be practiced. Preachers should move from looking one hearer in the eye to so looking at another, with "an air of affection and regard."[48]

> The mouth must never be turned awry; neither must you bite or lick your lips, or shrug your shoulders, or lean upon your elbow; all which give just offense to the spectators.[49]

The hands can be used in "a thousand different ways." The preacher should not clap or thump the pulpit. The right hand is used most in gestures; the left is never used alone. When speaking of one's own "faculties, heart, or conscience," one may gently apply the right hand to the breast[50]—and other such advice. But when speaking, one should use the gestures that arise naturally. Wesley trained his preachers with these and other such instructions, apparently giving them little leeway about either what they should say or how they should say it.

Wesley's Printed Sermons

The familiarity of published sermons could blind one to the significance of Wesley's in his total plan for the religious community he founded. Publication for him was not simply an effort to make available to people a transcript of what they had heard and wished to go back over, or what they had not heard and were sorry they missed. Indeed, as has been noted, not all of his oral sermons were published, nor were all his published sermons delivered.

The purpose of this published corpus has to be understood in terms of Wesley's role in relation to his movement. Outler has described this by saying: "His chief intellectual interest, and achievement, was in what one could call a folk theology: the Christian message in its fullness and integrity, in 'plain words for plain people.'"[51] Expanding this, he goes on to say:

> Wesley was a prolific author, editor and publisher. But in his literary work, as in all else, it was the requirements of the Revival that dictated what he wrote and what he published. He regarded himself—and was so regarded—as the chief theological tutor of the Methodist people. In this role he undertook to supply them with an abundance of edifying literature which was cheap enough to buy, concise enough to read.[52]

This means that he personally set out to provide the Methodists, preachers and laity alike, with everything they needed to know—which amounted to a great deal: witness the five hours a day he expected his preachers to read. He did this by writing prolifically himself, but even more by editing others' works for his people's use, sometimes producing a tract of only thirty pages from a volume that ran into the hundreds.

Most of the reading and editing he did on horseback, which prompted Ronald Knox to quip that "he is not a good advertisement for reading on horseback,"[53] suggesting that he had misunderstood what he read. The truth is more likely that his interest was not in passing along the thought of others so much as it was in providing edifying reading for his people. If what he wrote was not what his sources had said, it was what they should have said. In his fifty-volume "Christian Library" of devotional and theological literature drawn from every age, as well as in his *Arminian Magazine,* he set out to supply all his people would need to read—every bit of it predigested for them by the leader himself.[54]

It is in the total context of Wesley's efforts to supply his movement with all the reading material it needed that the purpose of his published sermons is to be understood: they were the keystone of the arch. I noted above that he saw a difference in purpose between oral and published sermons: the first were for proclamation and invitation, and the latter were for nurture and reflection. This didactic purpose lay behind his publication of his sermons. They were to be the distinctive theological literature of his people as creeds, confessions, or theological treatises had been that of other Christian bodies. They were to be his main medium for communicating what he thought Methodists were about.

Wesley began publishing his sermons in collected form less than ten years after his Aldersgate experience. He originally intended a three-volume set of his *Sermons on Several Occasions.* Volume 1, containing those that dealt with his soteriology, appeared in 1746; volume 2, devoted to the *ordo salutis,* appeared in 1748; and volume 3, "a sort of ellipse with its twin foci (:) Wesley's understanding of the graciousness of grace . . . and the fullness of grace,"[55] in 1750. A fourth volume, bringing the total of published sermons to forty-three, appeared in 1760. When he brought out his *Works* in 1770, the four volumes of sermons, now containing an additional nine, appeared first in the set.

Eight years later he felt that his controversy with Calvinists demanded a medium through which he could communicate his views to his people. The medium he chose was the eventually ten-volume *Arminian Magazine,* for which he began to write sermons that had never been delivered orally. Finally, in 1787 he collected these new sermons, along with the older ones, into an eight-volume edition of *Sermons on Several Occasions,* the last four volumes being devoted to what can be lumped together as pastoral theology.

All the various editions of the sermons that appeared over a forty-year period were introduced with the same preface (**see Vol. 2, pp. 362-66**), a document that thus has great importance in indicating the author's intentions in publishing them. Outler has summarized these:

> (1) to describe the enterprise and to explain Wesley's choice of the sermon form as the medium of his theology; (2) to defend his style and role as a folk theologian, renouncing his academic identification; (3) to stress soteriology as the focus of his entire theology; (4) to leave the way open for dialogue and reconciliation. . . .[56]

The sentence in which Wesley explains his choice of sermons as his theological medium is: "Every serious man who peruses these will therefore see in the clearest manner what those doctrines are which I embrace and teach as the essentials of true religion."[57] This seems to be saying that, since preaching has been the normal mode of his teaching, it should also be the normal mode for publishing that teaching.

Whether there are deeper reasons for the choice of the medium is open to question. Outler has suggested at least two reasons. The first is that the standard collection of the Church of England's theological teachings was the two *Books of Homilies*,[58] published under Edward VI and Elizabeth, formularies to which Wesley was ever eager to confess his allegiance. Always anxious to be understood as an Anglican, perhaps he thought sermons were the genre for the expression of Anglican theology. The second reason is that "sermons, as a genre, do not lend themselves to legalistic interpretation."[59] This is related to the fourth purpose stated in the preface, leaving the way open for dialogue and reconciliation. To this could be added the popularity of sermons as a form of literature at the time.[60]

While much more could be said about all of this, enough has already been said to show that the Wesleyan revival was at heart a preaching movement, as may be seen from the indefatigable oral preaching of the founder, the oral preaching also of the cadre of preachers he appointed and trained through his manuals, and the choice of published sermons as the definitive medium for the communication of his thought.

Reviving the Establishment

The early-twentieth-century revivalist Billy Sunday is supposed to have called the Episcopal Church in the USA a "sleeping giant." If that term appropriately described the American expression of Anglicanism of his time, how much more does it apply to the mother church in the wake of latitudinarianism! All that Whitefield and the Wesleys were trying to do could be understood as an effort to arouse Gulliver.

That should not leave the impression, however, that no one else in the Church of England shared their concerns. The same impulse to a religion of the heart was stirring in other clergy who would remain within the established church and try to revive it. They had some contact with the Methodists, but, since most of them had Calvinist leanings, they felt more in common with Whitefield than Wesley. By and large, they did not itinerate or do field preaching; instead, they remained within their parishes, preached the cross of Christ as the only hope of salvation, and hoped to instill in their parishioners an acceptance and assurance of that salvation, and to encourage them to lead lives totally given to living out the implications of their redemption.

Later, through the influence of members of the so-called "Clapham Sect,"[61] especially William Wilberforce, Evangelicals were to be involved in a variety of good works ranging from the abolition of slavery and the slave trade, and reform of child labor, to foreign missions and the organization of the British and Foreign Bible Society.

Some of the pioneers of the movement include John Fletcher, Henry Venn, William Romaine, and John Newton. The most famous name associated with the movement, though, and that which is most important for the history of preaching, belongs to a member of the second generation, **Charles Simeon** (1759–1836), who spent fifty-four years as vicar of Holy Trinity, Cambridge. When Simeon went up to Cambridge from Eton, he discovered that one of the ways in which the universities were still fiefdoms of the established church was that all students were required to receive Holy Communion, and that he would have to do so in three weeks. Although he had not been devout before, he was afraid that unworthy reception would cause him to eat and drink damnation to his soul. He therefore involved himself in a frenzy of preparation.

When he went through that experience without achieving the peace he sought, he continued his search until Easter, not knowing how to relate his sense of guilt to the sacrifice of Christ. The key came to him from Bishop Thomas Wilson's *Instruction for the Lord's Supper,* in which he read that there was wisdom in the Jewish practice of transferring the people's guilt to the scapegoat on the Day of Atonement. He immediately knew that he did not have to bear the weight of his own sins, that he could transfer them to Christ. As he told it,

> Accordingly I sought to lay my sins upon the sacred head of Jesus; and on the Wednesday began to have a hope of mercy; on the Thursday that hope increased; on the Friday and Saturday it became more strong; and on the Sunday morning, Easter Day, April 4th, I awoke early with those words upon my heart and lips, "Jesus Christ is risen today! Hallelujah! Hallelujah!"[62]

After his conversion, Simeon appears to have gone from strength to strength. When he graduated from Cambridge he was ordained deacon and during the summer filled in at St. Andrew's church, where he occupied Latimer's old pulpit and, much to everyone's surprise, drew large congregations. He was also made a fellow of King's, his old college. When he became a priest, the bishop of Ely appointed him vicar of Holy Trinity in the center of both the town and the university. He was to occupy these positions for the rest of his life, living in rooms at King's and ministering to his parish flock. He had not been his parishioners' choice, and for a number of years he was quite unpopular with them; they went so far as to lock their pews so no one could sit in them and tried to lock him out of the church. Evangelicals were so unpopular in the university that students tried to break up his services and threw unpleasant things at him in the street.

In the end, the effects of his conversion and (what may amount to the same thing) his rare sweetness of character won out. He filled his church with his preaching, attracting not only parishioners but undergraduates as well in a way that few clergy in Cambridge have ever been able to. And he sent many "sons in the gospel" out into the ministry. In time, his influence was so great that the historian Thomas Macaulay said:

> If you knew what his authority and influence were, and how they extended from Cambridge to the most remote corners of England, you would allow that his real sway in the church was far greater than that of any primate.[63]

One of the more prominent ways in which he influenced the church of his day was by sharing his conviction of the importance of preaching. He did this through four media: his own preaching, sermon classes and "conversation parties" he held for serious students preparing for ordination, a neoclassical French homiletics text he annotated, and a series of sermon outlines he produced on what he considered to be virtually all the preachable texts in the Bible. While records remain of the impression made by the first two,[64] the others exist today in their full form.

The preaching textbook in question was the *Traité de la composition d'un sermon,* written by Jean Claude in 1688 and translated into English by Robert Robinson, a Baptist minister in Cambridge shortly before the incumbency of Simeon at Holy Trinity.[65] Simeon, however, did not come across the book until he had already been preaching for some years, during the first seven of which he was apparently without any sense of how sermons work. By the time he read Claude, though, he had learned enough to recognize in the work of the Frenchman a systematic presentation of an understanding very similar to his own. He made it the basis of his sermon classes and finally included it as an appendix to his twenty-one volumes of sermon outlines.[66] He called his version of Claude "an improved edition of a translation," which is to say that he found Robinson's violently antiestablishment introduction and notes offensive. Nor was he entirely satisfied with the work of Claude himself, believing that not all the examples of his principles taken from sermons of the

Frenchman were entirely accurate and offering some of his own in their place.

Scholars who are more interested in Simeon than they are in the history of preaching are inclined to give both Claude and Simeon more credit for originality than they are strictly entitled to. First, they fail to recognize that Claude came toward the end of the neoclassical movement in France and that he tended to epitomize the particular development of Protestant homiletics in that movement, a development that had more in common with Roman Catholic preaching at the time than might be expected. Second, as the term "neoclassical" implies, the movement was an effort to apply the insights of Greco-Roman rhetoricians to homiletics. For instance, in the introduction to a selection of sermon outlines from *Horae Homileticae,* James M. Houston says, "Simeon had . . . not two but three aims in his preaching: to instruct, to please, and to affect his audience,"[67] failing to recognize in this list Cicero's enumeration of the *officia* of the orator *(reddere auditores benevolos, attentos, dociles)* as that had been adapted to preaching by Augustine in *De doctrina christiana.* Even more amazing is Hugh Evan Hopkins's conclusion that Claude's conviction that a sermon should be composed of three parts, an introduction, discussion, and conclusion, "was in fact largely original" with Simeon.[68]

The basic sermon pattern advocated by Claude and Simeon has been spelled out by Peter Bayley:

> After the reading of the text, he begins with a general exordium which sometimes discusses the sacred author, sometimes the circumstances in which the sermon is being preached, and sometimes more abstract topics. This is followed by a close examination of the text, its historical background, its context in the book from which it is taken, and the difficulties raised by its language. This is often the place for a display of etymological scholarship. Then comes the *propositio* or division, almost always into three points. The body of the sermon is followed by a sort of extended peroration often entitled "Applications" or "Enseignements et consolations." . . . It is to this model that the majority of the Protestant preachers in the second half of our period approximate. . . . It was, as the sermons of Jean Claude show, to remain the model for many decades.[69]

The basic differences between this type of preaching and the sermon form of the latitudinarians are differences between French and English preaching, summarized in such statements as: "The 'inflamed orations' of the French preachers were no doubt less suited to the English genius than 'the sober reasonings' of British divines."[70] But Evangelistic preaching necessarily calls for more feeling than that of rationalists like Tillotson. What distinguishes the Claude-Simeon method from that of Wesley, however, is that the former is more exegetical and less topical, allowing the sermon's structure to be determined by the text. Yet the form is not simply exegesis.

> Some say, preaching is designed only to make Scripture understood . . . but this is a mistake; for preaching is not only intended to give the sense of Scripture, but also of theology in general; and, in short, to explain the whole of religion.[71]

These transchannel collaborators do insist, however, that the sermon should clearly and purely explain a text and that the sermon should give the entire sense of the whole text.[72] What is most distinctive about their method is the four methods they have of developing the sermon so that it succeeds in giving the entire sense of the text. The first method, *discussion,* as the body of the sermon is called, is by way of explication, in which everything in the text that needs to be explained is explained. The second is by way of *observation,* involving many of the *topoi* of classical rhetoric: from species to genus or vice versa; the diverse characters of something; the relation of one subject to another; the person speaking or acting; time, place, person addressed; and so on, through twenty-seven areas of observation. Explication and observation are called textuary ways of preaching because they keep to the text. That is not true of discussion by *continual or perpetual application* or by *propositions.* The first moves directly from the teaching of the text to the lives of the congregation, while the second reduces the text to between two and four propositions that have mutual dependence and connection.[73]

Simeon recognized that beginning preachers would have difficulty in applying all these principles to the composition of their own sermons. He wished to preserve them from the habit of the time of repreaching the sermons of others, so he tried to provide them with an intermediate alternative, that of preparing sermons following outlines (or "skeletons," as he called them) written by him until they developed sufficient skill to write their own. His collection of these, which began with the publication of 100 in 1796, continually grew until the full edition of *Horae Homileticae* contained 2,536 outlines on what were regarded as all the preachable texts of the Bible. "If one were to read a single sermon a day, it would take seven years to get through them all."[74]

Since the total work went through eight editions within sixteen years, it must have been a success. Indeed, Hopkins notes that Simeon's profits from the sale of the work (all of which he gave to evangelical causes) would amount in time to twice what James Boswell ever received for his famous account of the life of Samuel Johnson.[75] As everyone knows, however, buying a book is not the same as reading it and following its instructions.

> In consequence, Victorian dust collected upon the one and twenty volumes of the *Horae Homileticae*: and Anglican preachers of a later generation forsook the formal intricacies of the Claudian system in favour of a simpler method which had developed naturally under the influence of Tillotson, and which had never been abandoned. This method consisted in the division, not of the text, but of the sermon, into two or three, or at most into four or five, main heads.[76]

Thus, if one is to look for the influence of Charles Simeon on Anglican Evangelical preaching, it will not be so much in the particular method he taught. Nor will it be subsumed into the general preaching of the Evangelical Awakening in England, since the Evangelicals of the established church did not preach in fields, itinerate, or conduct revivals. Most of their preaching was to people who were already baptized and who had come to church on Sunday for an ordinary Prayer Book service. More than anywhere else, Simeon's influence on Anglican Evangelical preaching will be found in the sincerity of the converted man who knew the joy of being a saved sinner and who devoted his life to seeing that as many others as possible would have the same experience. Simeon himself preached in a church crowded with townspeople and undergraduates, whom he inspired to seek the same awareness he had of divine grace poured out efficaciously in one's own behalf. From there the influence went out over all England and the world.

BRINGING THE AWAKENING INDOORS: THE PREACHING OF CHARLES HADDON SPURGEON

The next stage of the religion of the heart movement in British preaching can be seen as a combination of the sort of mass evangelism characteristic of the Methodist revival (Wesleyan and Calvinist) with a parochial base as favored by the Anglican Evangelicals. A church became the site of a revival, and the masses flocked to it instead of having the preacher come to them. Since the preacher himself was one of the extraordinary geniuses who appear from time to time in the history of preaching, it could be thought that discussion of his work does not belong to a narrative more concerned with movements than individuals. Yet it is true that movements are often begun by and summed up in particular preachers and that these preachers are thus determinative for much that is to follow. Such is the case of Charles Haddon Spurgeon.

The basic facts of Spurgeon's life can be told quickly. Born in Essex in 1834 into a working-class family that produced a number of Dissenting clergy, he grew up as a physically awkward child who did well at his books and acquired a precocious taste for John Bunyan and other Puritan writers. As a youth, he was oppressed with such a sense of sin that he began a systematic search for a church and preacher to relieve him of his burden and give him assurance of pardon. His goal was achieved on a Sunday morning in January of his fifteenth year in a Primitive Methodist chapel in Colchester, where he heard a lay preacher expound on Isaiah 45:22: "Look unto me, and be ye saved, all the ends of the earth" (KJV).

Being convinced, however, that only believers should be baptized, he joined a Baptist church. He then secured employment as an usher (assistant teacher) in a Cambridge academy and began to engage in a vigorous program of Sunday school teaching, visitation, and tract distribution.[77] Next he involved himself in the work of the Lay Preachers Association, and served as the pastor of the little chapel at Waterbeach for two years. He remained a lay preacher all his life, refusing ordination and eschewing the title of "Reverend." The little congregation grew under his leadership to four hundred members, and there were other improvements in the community.

The reputation of the "boy preacher" grew so much that he was called to be pastor of New Park Street Baptist Church, which had been a major congregation in London but had diminished because of a changing neighborhood. Even at that, it was an extraordinary invitation for someone who was only nineteen. He remained with the same congregation the rest of his life, forcing it constantly to expand its seating capacity, moving temporarily to music halls or other locations while remodeling was going on, until finally it was necessary to build the Metropolitan Tabernacle which could hold, standees included, almost six thousand people—and Spurgeon filled it twice on Sundays for thirty years. It has been estimated that no other English preacher has been heard in a church building by so many people.

Spurgeon in Action

While he had many other remarkable accomplishments, Spurgeon's importance for the history of preaching lies in three areas: his live preaching to congregations, his published sermons, and his lectures on homiletics. To imagine Spurgeon preaching in his prime is to think of him at the Metropolitan Tabernacle.[78] Although the exterior of the building was Greek Revival, the interior had the form of a long oval given to it by a lower and an upper balcony, both supported by columns rising from the floor and extending just behind their front railings to an architrave above that supported the vaulted ceiling. The pews faced the baptistery, which was set off by rails in front that curved at the sides and ascended to the first balcony level as guards for a flight of stairs on each side. The staircases led up to a platform that projected with a semicircular floor surmounted by a smaller semicircle at its center. The inside stair rails continued and joined in front of the platform. To the left of the smaller semicircle was a table on which a Bible rested.

Imagine all five thousand–plus seats filled and all faces looking toward the semicircular platform at the level of the first balcony, because it was from there that Spurgeon preached in a voice that could be clearly heard by all. The tabernacle had no pulpit because Spurgeon hated pulpits, considering them too confining to permit graceful gesture. The second series of *Lectures to My Students* includes woodcuts contrasting "Paul Preaching at Athens" in the open air with free movement to "The Very Reverend Dr. Paul Preaching in London," which depicts the apostle hedged in by a pulpit that came up over his elbows, with a cushion in front and gas lamps level with the lower part of his face on either side.[79]

This is not to say that Spurgeon strutted and strode like some televangelists today; he had no desire to be compared to "the polar bear, at the Zoological Gardens, which for ever goes backwards and forwards in its den."[80] He just wanted to be unfettered when he proclaimed the Word. He sought a golden mean between excess and woodenness in gesture, following the principles of the elocutionary movement. Photographs and caricatures often showed him with an upper arm extended straight out to the side and parallel to the floor, while the forearm reached up at a right angle, the forefinger pointing to heaven.

Spurgeon had almost certainly prayed the pastoral prayer, involving the congregation in the petitions that he had already been earnestly offering in private. On the table he would have at most an outline of his points and subpoints. He had written that only the night before, although he had been thinking all week about his topic, studying it, setting secretaries to look up information for him. On Saturday afternoon he'd had friends in to tea and then excused himself early to go to his final preparation. That began with choosing the best text to preach from in order to convey the message he had in mind. That done, he would work up an outline. Or, rather, he would usually work up a number of outlines, until he finally found the way of most tellingly and effectively saying what was on his heart. He then would have his wife read to him from various commentaries on the passage from which his text was taken.

Apparently that was all it took to enable him to be fluent in speech the next morning. His words, as they have been transcribed, seem to have come cascading from his mouth; semicolons dot the page, suggesting a cumulative force of urgency in the words that tumble forth, yet each of the words (sturdy Anglo-Saxon words; no Latinisms here) seems as carefully chosen as though a manuscript had been labored over for months. And never does the rush obscure the meaning. The skeleton of the sermon is always visible. Each point or subpoint is illustrated by an anecdote, a quotation, an analogy or metaphor that renders the principle in utter clarity. Even though the message has an eschatological seriousness, there is also time for joy and humor. One could even speak of a breeziness about the enterprise. Finally, at the end comes the invitation, communicated with all the pathos and power of one who believes completely in the reality of the salvation he is offering and in the effectiveness of the means he is extending to his hearers to enable them to experience that reality. There is almost always at least one conversion, and usually there are more.

Then, as now, people had diametrically opposed opinions about the quality of his preaching. Many of the objections were simply to popular preaching as such, to someone more interested in getting the message across than in the decorum with which that is done. Clergy of all denominations, including his own, had vitriolic things to say about him, some undoubtedly in envy of his widespread appeal. For a while, most newspapers pilloried him.[81] Echoing their spirit over a century later are the words of a British poet and literary critic who recently lectured at Cambridge on nonconformist literature:

> Spurgeon's vulgarities led him to misinterpret both the Scriptural text and Scriptural doctrine, and to let his exhortatory didacticism swamp out the sacramental aspects of worship. . . . In any case, it is plain that from a standpoint concerned with the cultural implications of English Dissent, Spurgeon's ministry, and the influence he exerted, were disastrous.[82]

In marked contrast is the advice given by the famous post–World War II pastor and theologian of Heidelberg, Helmut Thielicke:

> I am almost tempted to shout out to those who are serving the eternal Word as preachers, and to those who are preparing to do so, in what I hope will be a productive hyperbole: Sell all that you have (not least of all some of your stock of current sermonic literature) and buy Spurgeon (even if you have to grub through the second-hand bookstores).[83]

These words have been quoted often enough to become a cliché. What is not said nearly so often is where they appear: at the end of the introduction to a volume published by Thielicke and composed of selections from *Lectures to My Students* plus a couple of Spurgeon's sermons. Which is to say that Thielicke thought enough of his advice to make it possible for people to follow it.[84]

About the only response to these differences of opinion that can advance beyond remarks of the *de gustibus* ilk is to notice Lewis Drummond's efforts to account for the popularity of Spurgeon's preaching in terms of its being in service of a revival sent by the Holy Spirit.[85] People will respond to Spurgeon's preaching in the way that they respond to the idea of such revivals. Everything from his Calvinism and absolute conviction that souls will be eternally damned or saved on the basis of whether they have undergone a conversion experience or not, to his use of language that working-class and poor people can understand and respond to, is to be assessed upon the basis of whether one believes that a basic dynamic of God's relation with human beings is the sending of periodic revivals. This is to say that the judgment is theological rather than aesthetic or merely homiletic. In any case, there is no doubt that he was popular and effective. The membership of his congregation in London grew from 313 when he arrived in 1854, to a peak of 5,427 in 1882.

Publish Glad Tidings

Beyond the growth of his own congregation and even the effects upon countless visitors of hearing him preach is the impact of Spurgeon's printed sermons. There must be few preachers in history who have published so many different sermons in so many copies. During his second year in London, a publisher began to print one of Spurgeon's sermons each week and continued that practice until long after Spurgeon's death, up until World War I. These weekly "Penny Pulpit" sermons were annually collected into a book, resulting in six volumes of *The New Park Street Pulpit* and fifty-seven of *The Metropolitan Tabernacle Pulpit*, each of which contains between fifty-two and sixty sermons. That brings the total number of sermons published to around thirty-five hundred. For many years, the average press run of the weekly sermon was twenty-five thousand. Over the years, the number of copies of individual Penny Pulpit sermons published totaled more than one hundred million.[86] This, of course, does not count the bound volumes, the other collections, the American newspaper publication of weekly sermons, or the translations into as many as twenty-three languages.

There are enough stories of people being converted through reading one of Spurgeon's sermons to constitute a *Gattung* for form critics to analyze. Yet the influence of the sermons is wider yet, for one must consider the number of clergy who have imitated the sermons' style in their own preaching or quoted from them—or preached them as their own. Drummond even has a story of Spurgeon himself being helped by one when he was suffering from one of his bouts of depression and wandered into a small church, where he heard the preacher delivering a Spurgeon sermon.[87] It seems safe to say that no other preacher's sermons in history have been read by so many people. And they are still in print. Even as these words are being written, catalogs offer a ten-volume set of 250.

A Teacher of Preachers

Finally, Spurgeon's influence on preaching was exercised through his lectures on homiletics. These had an impact not only on the hundreds of students who heard Spurgeon deliver them in his Friday afternoon visits to the Pastors' College of the Metropolitan Tabernacle, but on the half million people who have purchased copies of *Lectures to My Students* as well. The lectures were published in three series. The first begins with several talks on the spiritual condition of the preacher: He should practice what he preaches. He should have the call to preach, which includes physical as well as spiritual qualifications (e.g., having a chest wide enough to have lung power).[88] Next follows a treatment of the necessity of the preacher's life of private prayer and advice on leading public prayer.

Then Spurgeon shifts to preaching itself, beginning with the content of the sermon. Since he outlined so meticulously himself, it is surprising that the only advice he gives on the subject is that "our matter should be well arranged according to the true rules of mental architecture" (1:80). After that comes a section on how to choose a text to preach upon, which is virtually the same as choosing the subject of a sermon. While it is not surprising that he does not favor following the lectionary (on which he says Church of England sermons were based at the time [1:87]), it is more so that he does not favor course preaching either (1:99-101).

The treatment of the chosen text is dealt with to the extent of saying that occasionally it is permissible to spiritualize it—an admission that horrified many of his contemporaries. Then comes an excellent little section of what may be called the stewardship of the preacher's voice, which is followed by words from a master of the subject on how to get and hold attention and by techniques for acquiring the ability to speak impromptu on the rare occasions when it is necessary and therefore to be allowed.

"The Minister's Fainting Fits" is a touching presentation of the incidence of depression among clergy by one who himself suffered grievously from it. The first series then concludes with notice of how one's preaching ministry carries over into conversations with parishioners and seekers, and a lecture on how preachers who cannot afford one can get by without a large library—a sensitive empathy from a man who had a personal collection of twelve thousand volumes.

The second series of lectures also begins with spirituality, including the necessity of commitment to the truth of the gospel, before going on to deal with the history and value of open-air preaching and then with body language in preaching. In the two lectures on the latter subject, Spurgeon is at the top of his form, caricaturing formalists on the one hand and ranters on the other. To be certain that the point gets across, he even commissioned woodcut illustrations, showing such monstrosities as the preacher who looks like he is boxing or hammering, or whose arms perform the motions of a whirligig. Then, to offer a positive example, he includes several pages of illustrations from that classic of the elocutionary movement, Austin's *Chironomia* (2:137-43). There follows another lecture on spirituality and one on pastoral discretion, followed by a reminder that the conversion of sinners is the aim of preaching, which purpose is to be achieved by preaching the basic doctrines of Calvinism in the manner that the president of Pastors' College details. (For the text of the lecture on conversion, **see Vol. 2, pp. 366-79.**)

The third series of lectures, devoted to illustration, will probably disappoint most modern readers, being occupied as most of it is with Spurgeon's assessment of Puritan and contemporary encyclopedias of support material as quarries for preachers. Of more use to most will be the study of the other lectures to see how Spurgeon himself went about making certain that his meaning would be inescapable. A brilliant case in point is the lecture "Illustrations in Preaching," which is organized by a sustained metaphor: illustrations as the windows of sermons (3:1-14).

When one asks what religion of the heart preaching looked like in the last half of the nineteenth century, no better answer can be given than to point to the "boy preacher" who captivated London and the world by the power of his own preaching, both orally and in printed transcripts, and who tried to show other pulpit fledglings how he went about doing what he did. None of those who followed commanded so large a hearing, but it is doubtful that any in his tradition ever went into the pulpit without carrying with him echoes of Spurgeon. He had shown his generation and several to follow what it meant to preach a revival in one's own congregation.

This account of preaching movements emphasizing affective involvement, which grew up along with and in response to many of the same conditions as rationalist preaching, has traced its development for two hundred years. Any stopping point is arbitrary. The Moody-Sankey revival, which Spurgeon favored, is worth noting but will be considered in the treatment of American evangelical preaching. The Salvation Army developed their own methods for bringing the gospel to the attention of the poorest of the urban poor, but their homiletical tradition was too oral to leave much in the way of written records.

Yet there is a sense that the movement has tamed. While Spurgeon drew many thousands, he drew them to a building. As much as he advocated open-air preaching and even practiced it on occasion, his chief concern seems to have been with his congregation. Nor do we hear of the converts at the Metropolitan Tabernacle being torn by paroxysms of emotion. We are told of no one who yelled, leaped, rolled on the ground, or fainted. Everything appears to have been in good taste; a bourgeois decorum was observed. One almost gets the impression that religion of the heart had evolved from emotion to sentimentality.

Much has changed in the two centuries from the Restoration to the time of Victoria. The next chapter deals with religion of the heart preaching in America, and the two following chapters look at side effects of that preaching. Then it will be time to see that religion of the heart had other manifestations, manifestations not so much of sentimentality as of sentiment. That will call for a survey of the effect of the Romantic movement on preaching.

FOR FURTHER READING

Campbell, Ted A. *The Religion of the Heart: A Study of European Religious Life in the Seventeenth and Eighteenth Centuries.* Columbia: University of South Carolina Press, 1991.

Hopkins, Hugh Evan. *Charles Simeon of Cambridge.* Grand Rapids, Mich.: Eerdmans, 1977.

Select Sermons of George Whitefield, With an Account of His Life by J. C. Ryle. Edinburgh: Banner of Truth Trust, 1958.

Spurgeon, C. H. *Lectures to My Students: Addresses Delivered to the Students of the Pastors' College, Metropolitan Tabernacle.* One-volume edition of the first, second, and third series published in London, 1875–94. Grand Rapids, Mich.: Baker, 1977.

Stout, Harry S. *The Divine Dramatist: George Whitefield and the Rise of Modern Evangelicalism.* Grand Rapids, Mich.: Eerdmans, 1991.

The Works of John Wesley: Volume 1: Sermons I. Edited with introduction by Albert C. Outler. The Bicentennial Edition of the Works of John Wesley. Nashville: Abingdon, 1984.

Thielicke, Helmut J. *Encounter with Spurgeon.* Translated by John W. Doberstein. Philadelphia: Fortress, 1963.

Notes

1. Speaking of these movements as responses to historical situations is in no way intended to preclude other levels of description, including the theological. There is some sense in which Christians have to regard at least some of them as providential, the work of the Holy Spirit. Divine causation, however, is not susceptible to empirical observation and thus not a factor in historical explanation as such.

2. What follows is based upon Ted A. Campbell, *The Religion of the Heart: A Study of European Religious Life in the Seventeenth and Eighteenth Centuries* (Columbia: University of South Carolina Press, 1991).

3. In his tracing of the synchronicity of these movements, Ted Campbell has noted that in addition to their emphasis on the feeling element in religion, they had four concomitant traits, traits that do not define the movements but do show their similarity. These include: "the phenomena of religious excitation, the threats posed to them by sectarianism and mysticism, the leadership roles exercised by women, and their offering of a cultural parallel to the Enlightenment" (ibid., 173-76, with this summary passage on the last of these pages). His explanation of why so many groups should turn to the cultivation of affective piety at the same time is that in each church there were those who were "disgusted with what corporate Christian states had done to one another since the Reformation (and) disillusioned with 'objective' appeals to scripture and tradition." In reaction, these "turned inwardly to a more individualistic and (in a certain sense) 'subjective' appropriation of the Christian faith" (ibid., 177).

4. He has already been encountered as the author of the most influential Puritan homiletics textbook, *The Arte of Prophesying.* See above, p. 365.

5. Campbell, *The Religion of the Heart,* 44-53. The *ordo salutis* was to become one of the most important topics in evangelical theology, and strategies of evangelistic preaching were framed on the basis of theories about that order.

6. Ibid., 53-57.

7. Quoted by Derec Llwyd Morgan, *The Great Awakening in Wales,* trans.

Dyfnallt Morgan (London: Epworth, 1988), 23, from Harris's *Selected Trevecka Letters,* ed. G. M. Roberts (Caernarfon, 1956–62), 1:81. Morgan's book is the fullest treatment of the Welsh revival in English.

8. In the year that he was president of the Academy of Homiletics, he shared his findings in his address (Toronto, 1983). Seven years later, at the twenty-fifth anniversary meeting of the academy at Princeton Theological Seminary on December 8, 1990, he repeated the lecture. The report above is based on the tape recorded by the Audio-Visuals Department of Princeton Theological Seminary. For the conventions of African American preaching, see below, pp. 529-31.

9. Lo, by the Merrimack WHITEFIELD stands
In the temple that never was made by hands,
Curtains of azure, and crystal wall,
And dome of sunshine over all!
A homeless pilgrim, with dubious name
Blown about on the winds of fame;
Now as an angel of blessing classed,
And now as a mad enthusiast.

John Greenleaf Whittier, "The Preacher" (*The Complete Works of John Greenleaf Whittier,* Cambridge ed. [Boston: Houghton Mifflin, 1894], 69-74. See specifically p. 71.

10. Whitefield was eventually to break with Harris after the latter fell so under the influence of Sidney Griffith as to occasion scandal. Harry S. Stout, *The Divine Dramatist: George Whitefield and the Rise of Modern Evangelicalism* (Grand Rapids, Mich.: Eerdmans, 1991), 221.

11. There is disagreement about the social status of the Whitefields. Stout sees his going to Oxford to study for the ministry to have been an effort on his part and that of his mother to reverse the declining social status of the family (ibid., 2-3, and passim). Arnold A. Dallimore, on the other hand, sees the family as one of Gloucester's more prominent families, in *George Whitefield: God's Anointed Servant in the Great Revival of the Eighteenth Century* (Westchester, Ill.: Crossway, 1990), 11. Opinion seems to vary on the basis of whether one approves or disapproves of Whitefield. The work of Dallimore cited is a condensation of a work of 1,200 pages from the same publisher, *George Whitefield: The Life and Times of the Great Evangelist of the Eighteenth-Century Revival* (1970–79), a work described by Stout as "filiopietistic" (i.e., hagiographic).

12. Campbell, *The Religion of the Heart,* 101.

13. The relatively few of his other sermons to be published were taken down and published by others. While some of these are poorly transcribed, probably the best indication of what Whitefield was like in his prime comes from *Eighteen Sermons . . . Taken Verbatim in Shorthand and Faithfully Transcribed by Joseph Gurney,* rev. Andrew Gifford (Newburyport: Edmund Blunt, 1797). This superiority is due in part to being a transcript of what was actually said rather than what was edited for publication, and in part to coming from near the end rather than the beginning of the preacher's career.

14. February 2 to December 8, 1738.

15. Stout, *The Divine Dramatist,* 84.

16. Ibid., 125.

17. Ibid., 252.

18. Joseph Beaumont Wakeley, *The Prince of Pulpit Orators* (New York: Carlton & Lanahan, 1871), 225-26. While Wakeley claims in his preface to use many sources that had not been available before, he does not cite them for particular anecdotes in this very anecdotal account.

19. Ibid.

20. As stated in note 27 of chapter 16.

21. Horton Davies, *From Watts and Wesley to Maurice, 1690–1850,* vol. 3 of *Worship and Theology in England* (Princeton: Princeton University Press, 1961), 162-63.

22. Quoted by Stout, *The Divine Dramatist,* 104, without citation.

23. For other efforts to account for the effectiveness of Whitefield's preaching, see not only those of Stout and Davies already referred to, but also that of Edwin Dargan, *A History of Preaching* (New York: Burt Franklin, 1968), 2:313-15; Edward S. Ninde, *George Whitefield: Prophet-Preacher* (New York: Abingdon, 1924), 161-79; and Clyde E. Fant Jr. and William M. Pinson Jr., eds., *20 Centuries of Great Preaching: An Encyclopedia of Preaching* (Waco, Tex.: Word, 1971), 3:111-16. The most complete edition of the sermons of Whitefield was published in 1771 in the last two of a six-volume set of his works. Oddly enough, they have not been much reprinted. The most available collection is *Select Sermons of George Whitefield, With an Account of His Life by J. C. Ryle* (Edinburgh: Banner of Truth Trust, 1958). For samples of the *Eighteen Sermons* transcribed in shorthand by Joseph Gurney and edited by Andrew Gifford, see Volume 2, chapter 17, and the Fant and Pinson volume.

24. The Society for the Propagation of the Gospel in Foreign Parts, an Anglican voluntary association for missions that sent out a high percentage of the priests who went to America.

25. *John Wesley,* ed. Albert C. Outler, Library of Protestant Thought (New York: Oxford University Press, 1964), 48.

26. Ibid., 17.

27. Ronald A. Knox, *Enthusiasm: A Chapter in the History of Religion* (Oxford: University Press, 1950), 427.

28. W. L. Doughty has published a volume called *John Wesley: Preacher* (London: Epworth, 1955), but since it is more anecdotal and hagiographic than analytical, it is not referred to in the discussion that follows.

29. Albert C. Outler, "Introduction" to *The Works of John Wesley: Vol. 1: Sermons I,* The Bicentennial Edition of the Works of John Wesley (Nashville: Abingdon, 1984), 14. While the sermons of Wesley have been published in many editions both during his lifetime and ever since, the Bicentennial Edition is the first critical edition ever published. Outler's edition, which draws on the textual work of Frank Baker, the first general editor of the series, runs to four volumes. A handy edition of the most important of these sermons is *John Wesley's Sermons: An Anthology,* ed. Albert C. Outler and Richard P. Heitzenrater (Nashville: Abingdon, 1991). Heitzenrater began as assistant editor in chief to Frank Baker for the Bicentennial Edition and now serves as general editor. Outler, a beloved teacher of the present

writer, entered the church expectant before the publication of this latter volume. *Requiescat in pace.*

30. Outler, "Introduction" to *The Works of John Wesley, Vol. 1: Sermons I,* 14.

31. Outler and Heitzenrater, *John Wesley's Sermons,* 371-80.

32. Ibid., 379-80.

33. Ibid., 380.

34. Ibid.

35. Davies, *From Watts and Wesley to Maurice,* 172. This is the closing sentence of a section that begins on p. 160 and that will repay in insight the energy spent reading.

36. In a letter written to John Chute on October 10, 1766. *Horace Walpole's Correspondence with John Chute et al.,* ed. W. S. Lewis et al., The Yale Edition of Horace Walpole's Correspondence, vol. 35 (New Haven: Yale University Press, 1973), 118-19.

37. These entries have been collected and reflected on by Knox in a chapter entitled "Wesley and the Religion of Experience," in *Enthusiasm,* 513-48.

38. It is important to recognize how much Wesley was a man of his time in his interest in all things scientific. His *Journals* have frequent reference to his curiosity about new inventions and, in general, how things work. He shares some of the optimism of his time that almost any skill can be reduced to written law on the basis of observation. "Experimental" has for him the double significance of efforts to gain such knowledge and reference to experience, especially religious experience. Without thinking that evangelism could be done with mechanistic determinism, he nevertheless thought that one could learn how things ought to be done.

39. *Minutes of Several Conversations between the Rev. Mr. Wesley and Others from the Year 1744, to the Year 1789.* The edition consulted was the Zondervan reprint of the Wesleyan Conference Office edition published in London in 1872, 8:299-338. Reference, however, will be made within the text by question rather than page number (e.g., Q. 2). The "Conversations" in question were Wesley's "Conferences" with his preachers, the beginning of that conspicuous feature of Methodist polity. The Methodist term for canon law is "discipline."

40. *The Art of Speaking in Publick: Or an Essay on the Action of an Orator as to His Pronunciation and Gesture* (1727); see Outler, "Introduction," 24. The edition of *Directions* consulted is the Zondervan, 13:518-27.

41. Here "jealousy" probably means "zealousness."

42. Keeping Methodism within the Church of England was one of the areas in which Wesley had the greatest difficulty imposing his will on the Methodists—although it must be admitted that he initiated many of the aspects of Methodist life that made the breach inevitable.

43. Deborah M. Valenze, *Prophetic Sons and Daughters: Female Preaching and Popular Religion in Industrial England* (Princeton: Princeton University Press, 1985). Valenze gives a fascinating account of a few women whom Wesley allowed to preach while he was alive and many more who became preachers in Methodist sects that withdrew from the Wesleyans after his death. Since, however, her interest is in the way their preaching was a form of resistance to social and economic change, she

understandably neglects providing the information about their preaching per se that would be such an enrichment to this history.

44. See Sermon 123, "On Knowing Christ After the Flesh," or Wesley's letter to Mary Bishop of October 18, 1778: "Let but a pert, self-sufficient animal, that has neither sense nor grace, bawl out something about Christ, or his blood, or justification by faith, and his hearers cry out, 'What a fine gospel sermon!' Surely the Methodists have not so learnt Christ. We know no gospel without salvation from sin." See Outler, "Introduction," 25.

45. That is, as prophet, priest, and king.

46. What follows is drawn from *Directions Concerning Pronunciation and Gesture* (Grand Rapids, Mich.: Zondervan), 13:518-27.

47. Ibid., 523.

48. Ibid., 526.

49. Ibid.

50. The influence of the elocutionary movement is to be seen in all of this.

51. *John Wesley*, ed. Albert C. Outler, vii.

52. Ibid., xi.

53. Knox, *Enthusiasm*, 447.

54. For the sources and formative influences of his thought see Outler, "Introduction," 66-96.

55. Ibid., 45.

56. Introductory comment on the Preface, *Sermons*, 1:103.

57. Ibid.

58. See above, p. 358.

59. Outler, "Introduction," 40. Cf. p. 55.

60. See above, pp. 392-414.

61. A group of wealthy evangelical families who lived in the London suburb of Clapham and attended the parish church where John Venn was rector. The best account is the memoir of James Stephen, who grew up in the group, in his *Essays in Ecclesiastical Biography*, Silver Library ed. (London: Longmans, Green & Co., 1907), 2:187-248. For the beginnings of the movement, see L. E. Elliott-Binns, *The Early Evangelicals: A Religious and Social Study* (London: Lutterworth, 1953). For the generation after the Clapham Sect, see Michael Hennell, *Sons of the Prophets: Evangelical Leaders of the Victorian Church* (London: SPCK, 1979). For the theological position of the Evangelicals in contrast to that of the Oxford movement, see Peter Toon, *Evangelical Theology 1833–1856: A Response to Tractarianism*, New Foundations Theological Library (Atlanta: John Knox, 1979).

62. Quoted in Hugh Evan Hopkins, *Charles Simeon of Cambridge* (Grand Rapids, Mich.: Eerdmans, 1977), 28, from a personal memoir quoted in William Carus, *Memoirs of the Life of the Rev. Charles Simeon* (London: Hatchard, 1847), 9.

63. Quoted in Hopkins, *Charles Simeon of Cambridge*, 118, from G. O. Trevelyan, *The Life and Letters of Lord Macaulay* (1876), 1:68 n. "Primate" in this context refers to the archbishop of either Canterbury or York.

64. Abner William Brown has left *Recollections of the Conversation Parties of the Rev. Charles Simeon, Senior Fellow of King's College, and Perpetual Curate of Trinity Church, Cambridge* (1863), which I have not seen. An impression of Simeon's

delivery can be formed from silhouettes cut out at the time that depict him expounding, imparting, acquiring, entreating, imploring, and concluding. These silhouettes, which are the property of King's College, are reproduced in the inside front cover of Hopkins, *Charles Simeon of Cambridge.*

65. John Claude, *An Essay on the Composition of a Sermon,* trans. with notes Robert Robinson, 2 vols. (London and Cambridge, 1778, 1779).

66. Charles Simeon, "Claude's Essay on the Composition of a Sermon," *Horae Homileticae, or Discourses Digested into One Continuous Series, and Forming a Commentary, Upon Every Book of The Old and New Testament,* 8th ed. (London: Henry G. Bohn, 1847), 21:287-435.

67. *Evangelical Preaching: An Anthology of Sermons by Charles Simeon,* ed. John M. Houston with intro. John R. W. Stott (Portland, Ore.: Multnomah, 1986), xvii.

68. Hopkins, *Charles Simeon of Cambridge,* 58.

69. Peter Bayley, *French Pulpit Oratory 1598–1650: A Study in Themes and Styles with a Descriptive Catalogue of Printed Texts* (Cambridge: Cambridge University Press, 1980), 110. More is said of Bayley's contribution in the section above on the preaching of the Catholic Reform, pp. 343-45.

70. Attributed to George Colman and Bonnell Thornton in Rolf P. Lessenich, *Elements of Pulpit Oratory in Eighteenth-Century England (1660–1800)* (Cologne and Vienna: Böhlau Verlag, 1972), 61. His treatment of the differences between the styles of French and English exordia, 60-64, has humor that may be unconscious. This same section indicates more knowledge of French rhetorical thought in England during this period than the observations of Charles Smyth, *The Art of Preaching: A Practical Survey of Preaching in the Church of England 747–1939* (London: SPCK; New York: Macmillan 1940), 181, seem to suggest. Yet Smyth speaks guardedly of "direct and significant influence upon the English pulpit." Hugh Blair showed detailed knowledge of the French literature in his textbook of rhetoric, *Lectures on Rhetoric and Belles Lettres,* that was published a little before Simeon's edition of Claude, but Blair was a Scot. For Blair, see the treatment of belletristic preaching in the discussion of the Romantic movement in preaching in chapter 22.

71. Simeon, "Claude's Essay on the Composition of a Sermon," 292.

72. Ibid., 294.

73. Ibid., 325-97. Simeon gives outlines of four sermons on the same text using each of these methods, pp. 411-27. An excellent summary of the Essay is given by Smyth, *The Art of Preaching,* 179-201.

74. John Stott, in "Introduction" to Houston, *Evangelical Preaching,* xxvii.

75. Hopkins, *Charles Simeon of Cambridge,* 60. Simeon's work, however, was much more than twice as long as Boswell's.

76. Smyth, *The Art of Preaching,* 201.

77. There he became a member of St. Andrew's Baptist Church, where Robert Robinson, the translator of Claude, had been pastor.

78. The following description of the Metropolitan Tabernacle is based on the remarkable collection of photographs in Craig Skinner's biography of Spurgeon's son Thomas, *Lamplighter and Son* (Nashville: Broadman, 1984), 120-57. Some of these are reproduced with better quality in Lewis A. Drummond, *Spurgeon: Prince of Preachers* (Grand Rapids, Mich.: Kregel, 1992). Skinner's Spurgeon scholarship is

also reflected in his article "The Preaching of Charles Haddon Spurgeon," *Baptist History and Heritage* 19 (1984): 16-26.

79. C. H. Spurgeon, *Lectures to My Students: Addresses Delivered to the Students of the Pastors' College, Metropolitan Tabernacle,* one-volume edition of the first, second, and third series published in London, 1875–94 (Grand Rapids, Mich.: Baker, 1977), 2:102-3.

80. Ibid., 2:109.

81. For many quotations from both clergy and the press, see Drummond, *Spurgeon,* 175-274. While this 895-page volume is the most complete source of information on Spurgeon, it has little critical distance on its subject, falling into the genre of hagiography. For the person who would like to search further, there is also the disadvantage that many interesting pieces of information and even quotations are undocumented.

82. Donald Davie, *A Gathered Church: The Literature of the English Dissenting Interest, 1700–1930* (New York: Oxford University Press, 1978), 89.

83. Helmut Thielicke, *Encounter with Spurgeon,* trans. John W. Doberstein (Philadelphia: Fortress, 1963), 45.

84. For praise of Spurgeon from an unexpected source, see the quotation from the leader of the Oxford movement, E. B. Pusey, in Drummond, *Spurgeon,* 320-21. Unfortunately, the admiration was not mutual. For Spurgeon's remarks about the followers of Pusey, see ibid., 492.

85. Drummond, *Spurgeon,* 258-74.

86. These figures are drawn from idid., 320-25.

87. Ibid., 328.

88. Spurgeon, *Lectures to My Students,* 1:34-35. Further references will be inserted parenthetically into the text with the volume number, a colon, and the page number(s).

CHAPTER 18

AMERICAN REVEILLE

THE PURITANS

The first distinctive American homiletical tradition was that of the Puritans—although, to be sure, this tradition had its origins in England.[1] Within it were both of the characteristic English responses to the challenge of early modernism, religion of the head and religion of the heart. Before it can be seen how these two impulses, which seemed so contrary to one another in England, were entwined in the colonies, however, something must be said about the distinctiveness of American Puritanism.

Puritanism as such lasted much longer in America than it did in England. In some sense, Puritanism as a movement ended in England with the Restoration in 1660. Before that time, it had largely been an effort within the established church to change its polity from episcopacy to a presbyterian structure and to pursue other goals of the Calvinist agenda, such as doing nothing in the church not explicitly called for in the Bible. When Puritanism was excluded from the established church in the Restoration settlement, it gained recognition as a tolerated form of dissent. Puritans and Independents became Nonconformists, forming Presbyterian, Congregationalist, and Baptist denominations. For the

Presbyterians and Congregationalists, at any rate, this soon led to a loss of much that had been distinctive about Puritan ethos. In New England, however, the basic pattern of thought and preaching lasted through the Revolution and into the beginning of the nineteenth century.

The Pilgrims landed at Plymouth Rock in 1620 and were soon followed by the Puritans at Massachusetts Bay, whose colony eventually absorbed that of their Pilgrim neighbors. Twenty thousand Puritans eventually migrated to what are now the states of Massachusetts and Connecticut. From the beginning they had their own theological emphases, which distinguished them from Puritans who remained in England.[2] First, while most of the English Puritans believed in a presbyterial polity, those who went to New England appear to have been Congregationalists all along.

That distinction means more than a difference in church government. The English Presbyterian Puritans were like other Anglicans in believing that all citizens should belong to the national church. Those who went to New England, however, thought of the church as a congregation of the elect. They wished to erase the distinction between the visible and invisible church by not extending the possibility of church membership to any but visible saints. To be eligible, a person had to be able to recite his or her story of conversion as a demonstration of election. Churches were formed by the saints in a local area covenanting with one another. The primary ecclesial reality was, therefore, not the holy church universal but a local congregation of those elected to salvation. The even more basic Christian reality was the individual soul predestined to salvation.

This does not mean, however, that those who could not demonstrate their election never darkened the meetinghouse door. Rather, it was assumed that all who immigrated to New England shared in the Puritan construction of reality and wished to be in the covenant. They were required to attend church and thus be exposed to the preaching through which election usually occurred. While they were not guaranteed election, they would nevertheless wish to be in position for it to occur if it were decreed.

So taken for granted was this desire of the not-yet-visibly-chosen that civil law required church attendance. Indeed, since right religious behavior and right behavior as citizens were considered to be obeying two aspects of the law of God, it was further agreed that only the saints, those capable of recognizing God's law, should be allowed to vote in civil elections. As unjust as this may appear to later generations that have different theories of the bases of civil law, it made sense to the New Englanders of the time, both the enfranchised and the disenfranchised.

Perry Miller says:

> The effort of the Massachusetts Bay Company to set up a due form of government both civil and ecclesiastical came ultimately to the one purpose of gathering men and women together in orderly congregations that they might sit under a "powerful" and a literate ministry, that they might hear the Word of God . . . as it was expounded by that ministry.[3]

This shows how important preaching was in their whole scheme of things: the Puritans left England and endured the dangers of sea travel and the hardships of the frontier so that they could guarantee, as far as humanly possible, that the people in their community would be exposed to sermons preached as they ought to be. The reason they felt so strongly about this is an extension of the general Calvinist assumption that preaching was the most common medium through which election was effected.

Their expression of this belief, however, had a few refinements of the Puritans' own. These were functions of Puritan presuppositions about psychology on the one hand, and logic and rhetoric on the other. The psychology was of a faculty variety that could be traced ultimately back to Aristotle. The way the faculties operated has been succinctly and amusingly illustrated by Miller in this example of a man who sees a bear:

> So the bear, encountered in the wilderness, causes in the *eye* a phantasm of the bear, which is identified as belonging to the species bear in *common sense,* recognized as dangerous in *imagination,* associated with remembered dangers in *memory,* declared an object to be fled in *reason,* made the signal of command to the *will,* which then excites the *affection* of fear, which finally prompts the muscles of the legs to run.[4]

The importance of this psychology for the understanding of preaching grows out of the Puritan desire at one and the same time to preserve God's absolute sovereignty in election while making human beings, who are predestined to reprobation, responsible for their own damnation. While more is involved in that effort, the relevant aspects were in the assumption that all of the faculties had been distorted in the fall and that an effect of conversion was the restoration of the faculties to their Edenic accuracy. It is this restored capacity of the faculties that enables a person to accept the salvation extended in preaching. While God has to renew the faculties for them to be able to work aright, nevertheless, the one who rejects or accepts the gospel does so by the employment of all that person's faculties. The one who refuses to accept, therefore, does so naturally, and the results are that person's own fault and not something for which God is to be blamed.

The underlying assumptions are what caused the Puritans to decide preaching that can be an effective medium for election must appeal mainly to the faculties of reason and will. This insistence upon the conversions of both understanding and the will shows how intertwined religion of reason and religion of the heart were in Puritan thought.

Puritan understanding of what is meant by reason and will comes from the theories of Pierre Ramus. While the impact of Ramus's thought on the structure of English Puritan sermons was discussed above, more needs to be said of his system here. Briefly, his dialectic was an effort to simplify the logic of Aristotle. Ramus reduced logic to two, or, more accurately, three operations. The first, which he called *invention,* consisted of identifying the objects of thought and their relations. Confusingly to modern readers, he calls both the "things" and their relations "arguments." The second part of dialectic is *judgment,* which involves taking the arguments (things and their relations) discovered by invention and stating them propositionally as "axioms." Ideally and most often, these axioms will be self-evident propositions. When they are not so evident, however, difficulties are to be resolved by means of syllogisms. Finally, *method* (sometimes treated as a subdivision of judgment) disposes axioms in their best possible order.

Ramist logic was thought to be not the contrivance of a clever man, but the way the universe was constructed by God, which Ramus merely discerned. By this logic, all of the arts arrive at the true depiction of their subject matter and at the laws by which their operations are performed. While *truth* is one, a result of the fall is that humans can only discern it piecemeal as separate arts, but all the arts are consistent with one another, and not the smallest element of that consistency is the way their science is arrived at through the use of Ramist dialectic.

This is as true of rhetoric as it is of other arts. In fact, rhetoric was one of the disciplines most radically redefined by the Ramist system. Ramus saw no need for a special art for oral persuasion, assuming that all persuasion should be by the use of reason (i.e., Ramist logic). Thus the invention of Aristotelian rhetoric (discovering the available means of persuasion) and its disposition (finding the most effective sequence for a speech) should be coextensive with Ramist dialectical invention, judgment, and method. Ramus also saw no need for treating *memory* as a separate part of rhetoric. All that was left as a subject matter proper to rhetoric was *style* (*elocutio*: figures of thought and speech) and *delivery.* Ramus's friend Omer Talon wrote the handbook of rhetoric, which perfectly incorporated Ramus's theories and came to have almost the status of revelation among the Puritans. The specifically homiletical implications of Ramism were worked out by William Perkins in *The Arte of Prophesying.*[5]

Preaching theory built on the foundations of Ramus, Talon, and Perkins was quite consistent with Puritan understanding of the way preaching was the ordinary means through which election occurred. Both reason and the will needed to be converted. Reason that has been restored by election recognizes the truth of axioms derived by Ramist judgment from the arguments it invented. The will is moved by the tropes and schemata recognized by Ramist rhetoric. These are not ornament for the sake of ornament; there is here no "carnall eloquence" from a "blubber-lipt Ministry."[6] Rather, the purpose of figures (mostly metaphors) is to humble sinners by helping them feel the extent to which they deserve damnation.[7]

The exclusion of useless ornamentation is extended to exordia and perorations, introductions and conclusions. All that is necessary or even appropriate is a succession of axioms disposed in their natural order. This is not to say, of course, that the sermon does not have parts. It begins with the "opening" of the text, which generally consists of taking the figurative statements of Holy Scripture and translating them into the literal language of Ramist self-evident axioms. These are *doctrines,* for which there must be *proofs,* which are either (1) parallel biblical passages or principles of systematic theology, (2) principles in nature, universal rules, or (3) common experience and sense. With this establishment of doctrines as sound, it remains only to show their relevance to the life of the congregation, their *uses.*

It is in uses that the will is moved through the appropriate figures. While the basic use was to be the means through which those predestined to salvation were elected, a variety of application types were made. William Ames, who played Elisha to Perkins's Elijah, listed as the main types:

> information in proving a truth; refutation in confuting error; instruction in demonstrating a life to be followed; correction in condemning a life to be shunned; consolation to remove or mitigate grief or fear; exhortation to start or strengthen an inward virtue; and admonition to correct a vice.[8]

Such was the homiletical diet of the Puritans. And it is doubtful that many other groups in history have been so systematically stuffed.

> Twice on Sunday and often once during the week, every minister in New England delivered sermons lasting between one and two hours in length. . . . The average weekly churchgoer in New England (and there were far more churchgoers than church members) listened to something like seven thousand sermons in a lifetime, totaling somewhere around fifteen thousand hours of concentrated listening.[9]

Because of the quantity of preaching to which the average New Englander listened in a lifetime, and because no other opinion-shaping medium came even close to rivaling this saturation, Harry S. Stout has argued that sermons were the most important influence on the way reality was constructed socially among the Puritans:

> Unlike modern mass media, the sermon stood alone in local New England contexts as the only regular (at least weekly) medium of public communication. As a channel of communication, it combined religious, educational, and journalistic functions, and supplied all the key terms necessary to understand existence in this world and the next. As the only event in public assembly that regularly brought the entire community together, it also represented the central ritual of social order and control.[10]

Because he sees preaching to have been so influential in the lives of the settlers in Massachusetts and Connecticut, Stout is eager to correct what he considers to be a misunderstanding on the part of many scholars about the persistence of Puritan theology's great themes in that preaching. A similar misunderstanding exists of the results of the Reforming Synod convoked in 1679.

> Historians from Perry Miller onward have emphasized the reformers' concern with external civil reform and "outward" ritual to the virtual exclusion of their pietistic concern with covenant renewal and revival. From this one-sided examination, they have concluded that the synod's "preoccupation" with external morality signaled a dilution of Puritan thought and piety; having lost their parents' piety, the children settled for outward shows of morality that preserved the husk of religiosity without the nourishing kernel of inner spirituality.[11]

Most such studies are concerned with trying to find the roots of the radical resistance and violence that prompted New Englanders, along with other American colonists, to revolt against the English Crown. The offered explanations include secular "republicanism," "civil millennialism," and class-conscious "popular ideology."[12]

The studies all suffer, however, from the way they have used evidence from sermons to support their arguments. In doing so, they have assumed that the published sermons were the more influential. Stout points out, however, that 85 percent of the sermons published were weekday "occasional" sermons. Yet the regular Sunday sermons were the steady homiletical diet of the people and much more influential than the considerably less frequent weekday sermons that appeared in print.[13] In order to see whether there was any such falling away as has been suggested, it would be necessary to study the manuscripts of ordinary Sunday sermons rather than the published occasional sermons.

Stout himself spent nine years reading more than two thousand Sunday sermons in manuscript form. In doing so, he discovered that the sermons offered little support for previous interpretations of New England culture made on the basis of sermons. For example, he discovered no shift from piety to moralism, no "decline" or subsequent "secularization" of Puritanism. From the landing of the *Mayflower* through the Revolution, the regular Sunday sermons continued to be about the great classical themes of Calvinist Christianity: sin, salvation, and service.

Stout's thesis is that other historians have misunderstood the occasional sermons. They assumed that the published sermons were the most "successful," the most representative of the way public attitudes were developing. He argues that these sermons should instead be understood as variations on the themes of the much more frequent and normative regular Sunday sermons. The basic categories for understanding human existence in general, and covenant experience in New England in particular, were set forth on Sunday. The details were worked out in the occasional sermons when principles were applied to particular circumstances.

A natural disaster, for instance, would indicate that God was angry because the people had been unfaithful. A fast would then be called so the unfaithfulness that accounted for the disaster could be specified and the people could repent, following which the hand of God would be turned.[14] Thus such sermons were preoccupied with external events and issues of morality. When these are the only sermons read by historians, it is not surprising that they assume faith was being replaced by morality and religious explanation was giving way to secular interpretation. If, however, occasional sermons are seen in the perspective of the more massive regular preaching that never departed from the basic themes of Calvinism, they are revealed to document the continuing appeal of Puritanism rather than to bring it into question.

Stout divides preachers into five "generations" based on when they graduated from college, and names the generations after the five divisions of classical rhetoric:

> *Inventio*—"Invention," discovering what to say, 1620–65
> *Dispositio*—Arrangement, 1666–1700
> *Elocutio*—Style, 1701–30
> *Pronuntiatio*—Delivery, 1731–63
> *Memoria*—Memory, 1764–76[15]

As artificial as this sounds, it works astonishingly well as a device for characterizing the issues of the various periods.

It was in the first generation, for instance, that the "founders" developed the basic covenantal theology of this "special people." The second generation worked out the details of what this would look like in practice by instituting such things as the "Halfway Covenant" and the various forms of occasional preaching, as well as founding Harvard College to prepare new preachers. They showed their adaptability in relating the founders' covenantal theology to new situations ranging from King Philip's War to the decline of clerical social status. The third generation was a time of Anglicization when influence of the neoclassical preaching style was felt—and even a dab of latitudinarian thought, which, however, never compromised Calvinist orthodoxy. The period of the Great Awakening was a time of controversies over delivery, whether one preached in the polished neoclassical manner or followed the impromptu method of George Whitefield. Finally, it was precisely the memory of the founders' theology that enabled preachers on the eve of the Revolution to justify opposition to the English Crown through appeals to the parallels between threats to the covenant people of the Old Testament and to those in New England.[16]

A study of New England preaching that overlaps the periods surveyed by Stout and goes beyond, *The Art of Prophesying: New England Sermons and the Shaping of Belief* by Teresa Toulouse,[17] is valuable for showing how much variety there can be in sermons constructed according to the same theory and structure. The theory and structure she studies is the classic for English and American Puritans, that enunciated by William Perkins in *The Arte of Prophesying*. She shows that Perkins himself used it as a way of preparing those who had not yet become aware of their election to receive assurance of it. John Cotton, however, who was of the generation of the founders in New England, used it to reassure those who had already become aware of their election. And Benjamin Colman, of the generation of style that brought the influence of Tillotson back to New England from London, was able to preserve the Perkins form and Calvin's theology in a way that nevertheless undercut the whole Puritan system.

Toulouse's analysis of the preaching of Channing and Emerson will be drawn on below. For now, it is enough to note the perspective her analysis gives on Stout's thesis. One could almost reverse the old French proverb and say that the more Puritan preaching remained the same, the more it changed. Before the Revolution, this can be seen in the Old Light/New Light controversy, and afterward, the extent of the change can be discerned in the Unitarian reaction.

JONATHAN EDWARDS AND THE GREAT AWAKENING

The preacher under whom the Great Awakening was inaugurated, Jonathan Edwards, was a loyal follower of the Perkins sermon form. While, as seen above, the preacher with whom the Awakening is most associated is George Whitefield,[18] the one under whose preaching it began was very different in both preaching style and approach. Enough was said about Whitefield in the discussion of the Evangelical Awakening in Britain. Even though Edwards shared Whitefield's Calvinism, the two of them were even more different in their preaching styles than were Whitefield and Wesley. Whitefield preached in an evangelical adaptation of the neoclassical style, while Edwards was loyal to Perkins's form. Whitefield was one of the most dramatic preachers of all time and Edwards one of the most staid.[19]

This makes it even more ironic that at least in the Anglo-American revival tradition, it was Edwards who seems to have popularized "hell-fire and damnation" preaching and justified it theologically.[20] The primary association with Edwards in the minds of most products of American schools is his sermon "Sinners in the Hands of an Angry God." A reaction to that sermon that is atypical only in the charm of its expression is Phyllis McGinley's poem "The Theology of Jonathan Edwards":

> Whenever Mr. Edwards spake
>   In church about Damnation,
> The very benches used to quake,
>   For awful agitation.
>
> Good men would pale and roll their eyes
>   While sinners rent their garments

To hear him so anatomize
  Hell's orgiastic torments,

The blood, the flames, the agonies
  In store for frail or flighty
New Englanders who did not please
  A whimsical Almighty.

Times were considered out of tune
  When half a dozen nervous
Female parishioners did not swoon
  At every Sunday service;

And, if they had been taught aright,
  Small children, carried bedwards,
Would shudder lest they meet that night
  The God of Mr. Edwards.

Abraham's God, the Wrathful One,
  Intolerant of error—
Not God the Father or the Son
  But God the Holy Terror.[21]

Such an attitude represents a cultural lag in what Henry F. May calls "the nineteenth century revulsion against Edwards as a cruel monster, dangerous because of his great talents." Or maybe it is what May calls the twentieth-century tendency to patronize Edwards.[22]

All things considered, though, Jonathan Edwards seems an odd person to have introduced this innovation in homiletical theory and practice. He was, after all, "the most astute American philosopher up to the time of Charles Pierce," in the opinion of the Dominican scholar Brian Davies,[23] which may differ from a more common view only in stating a *terminus ad quem*. But there is more to it than that: in trying to voice the consensus of contemporary scholarship, May says: "We can agree that Edwards was somehow a great man, whether we admire him most as artist, psychologist, preacher, theologian, or philosopher."[24] How could such a universal genius be responsible for establishing a trend that many find shameful?

This, after all, was the man who expressed his mystical appreciation of the blessings of election and his awareness of the specialness of the woman he would eventually marry when she was only thirteen:

> They say there is a young lady in [New Haven] who is beloved of that Great Being, who made and rules the world, and that there are certain seasons in which this Great Being, in some way or other invisible, comes to her and fills her mind with exceeding sweet delight, and that she hardly cares for any thing, except to meditate on him—that she expects after a while to be received up where he is, to be raised up out of the world and caught up into heaven.[25]

To understand how this could happen, it is necessary to have some knowledge of Jonathan Edwards's life. Born in East Windsor, Connecticut, in 1703, he was the son of one and grandson of another New England cleric of good reputation whose congregation had experienced revival. The only son in a family of eleven children, he grew up as a precociously religious and scholarly boy who was socially awkward. He entered Yale at the age of thirteen and, when he graduated four years later, stayed on for another two years of study. Sometime along the way, he experienced conversion (without, however, experiencing the classical stage of "legal fear") and decided to enter the ministry.

His first call was to the new Presbyterian congregation in New York City, where he stayed less than a year because of the church's financial stress. Returning to Yale as a tutor, he received an M.A., wrote his famous essay on spiders, and, more important, began work on "his central philosophical concept"[26] of excellence. Then he was called to assist his famous grandfather, Solomon Stoddard, in the role of heir apparent at the church in Northampton, Massachusetts. The following year he married Sarah Pierrepont.

Although Northampton at the time was little more than a frontier town, it was known throughout New England for its minister, one of the most articulate theologians and influential clergy of the period, the one known as "the Congregational Pope of the Connecticut Valley." Solomon Stoddard's main claim to fame was that he had taken even further the logic of the "Halfway Covenant," by which the children of visible saints could be baptized before they were capable of narrating the tales of their own conversions, by admitting them to Communion as well if they exhibited godliness. When Edwards arrived, his grandfather had been at the Northampton church for fifty-three years and was a recognized authority on preaching. It must have been intimidating for the twenty-three-year-old to alternate Sundays in the pulpit with his famous grandfather. In two years, though, Stoddard was dead, and young Edwards was the spiritual leader of the congregation.

He had almost twenty good years before the events occurred that would eventually lead to his dismissal. Indeed, he was very popular at first, especially with the young adults in the congregation. He was even given the honor of being invited to preach before the clergy of Boston only two years after he had succeeded Stoddard, a sign that he was already recognized as a brilliant young theologian. A revival that occurred in his parish, and the account of it that he then published, was what brought Edwards to the attention of a wider world. This revival was the immediate occasion of the Great Awakening.

It began in late 1733 when he was disturbed by the way the young people of the congregation spent their Sunday evenings socializing—after, of course, they had attended his afternoon lecture, not to mention the morning worship service and sermon. While to later tastes this activity may seem harmless and even desirable, to their minister it was an unbecoming worldliness, so he suggested their parents see that they stay home instead.

Later he suggested they come together in small groups for religious conversation. Parental intervention proved unnecessary because the young people complied at once on their own. A couple of deaths in the community and a threat of Arminianism that arose helped heighten the atmosphere of religious seriousness. Soon there came to be numerous conversions, at first among the youth but in time among the middle-aged parishioners and children as well, and as much among males as females.[27] Before long, the influence of the revival spread to thirty-two churches in the Connecticut River valley of Massachusetts and Connecticut.[28]

Although the number of communicants at the Northampton church was around 620, which included most of the town's adults, Edwards, using the tests applied by clergy of the time, was convinced that around 300 valid conversions had occurred by the end of 1735, when the revival seemed to have run its course. Several attempts at suicide suggested to some that the atmosphere had become too intense, and much of the movement's momentum was dissipated.

Edwards's part in the inspiration of the Great Awakening was largely in the reception accorded his account of this revival in Northampton, which he called *A Faithful Narrative of the Surprising Work of God in the Conversion of Many Hundred Souls in Northampton, and the Neighboring Towns and Villages of New-Hampshire in New-England.*[29] He was such a meticulous observer that his descriptive morphology of conversion in that work was taken by many at the time and by large numbers of evangelicals ever since as being a normative morphology, an effect that he lived to regret, since it seemed to place more emphasis on the "bodily manifestations" of conversion than on the effect of election on the will. A good bit of the rest of his literary output had to be devoted to redressing the balance, to insisting upon the reality of revivals and their importance while treating the emotional manifestations that often accompanied them as epiphenomena of conversion rather than its essence.

Understanding Edwards's convictions on this subject can take us a long way toward understanding his approach to preaching, including his countenancing and practicing the stirring up of the terror of damnation and hell. The place to begin is with the realization that Edwards was an utter Calvinist in his assumption that there is absolutely nothing any human being can do to contribute toward that person's own conversion and salvation or that of anyone else. While such Calvinism was still the official theology of New England, its erosion was evident in the Halfway Covenant and the admission of persons baptized under that covenant to Holy Communion, which were advocated and practiced by Edwards's grandfather and predecessor, Solomon Stoddard. Such relaxations of the Puritan determination to have churches of the visible elect would lead to further theological derelictions as time went on, first Arminianism and, after the Revolution, even Unitarianism. But the initial vision had not faded one whit for Jonathan Edwards.

This raises the question that has recurred constantly in the history of reactions to predestination: Why preach to those who have already been elected to salvation or reprobation? To the classical Calvinist response that preaching is the normal medium through which election is effected, Edwards added additional understanding of what preaching could contribute. Since people were not converted through persuasion, the preacher's purpose was not to persuade.

> Rather than attempt to persuade the unconverted, Edwards tried by means of his preaching, in addition to offering the Word, (1) to provide the optimal conditions and circumstances within which conversion might take place, (2) to offer the logical connections between guilt and repentance so that those who have been or are being converted might better understand what is happening to them, and (3) to prevent the misinterpretation of pseudo-religious experience, especially by those who believe they have experienced grace but have not.[30]

This theory about what preaching can accomplish grows out of Edwards's understanding of the will. He had abandoned the Puritan faculty psychology that assumed reason inevitably preceded volition. Rather, a person has two wills, the rational and another that is an "inclination arising from the liveliness of the idea of, or sensibleness of the good of, the object presented to the mind."[31] At other times, he refers to what he calls "inclination" here as "appetite," "heart," or "will." The emphasis is on the affective rather than the logical dimension of will.

What is attractive to the will is the perfection of God, the superiority of infinite being to finite being. While this could sound like Aristotle's understanding of the Unmoved Mover as moving the universe by the *eros* of all things for its perfection and beauty, that is precisely what Edwards's understanding is not. For the attractiveness of the Unmoved Mover could be expected to move all things equally, but conversion for Edwards is the divine alteration of the human will of one elected to salvation, which enables it to consent to the infinite will and purpose of God and to find it overwhelmingly attractive.

What is so transcendently beautiful for Edwards is the idea of God's sovereignty, which elects some to salvation and others to reprobation. Election is manifested in the ability to recognize the excellency of that sovereignty and consent to it joyfully.

The excellency of that sovereignty is the central concept in Edwards's thought to which I have already alluded.[32] Edwards's understanding of that concept is stated in a sermon he preached on the eve of the revival in Northampton, "A Divine and Supernatural Light." (For the text, **see Vol. 2, pp. 380-97.**) A look at that sermon will show not only his thought on the subject but also his use of the Perkins sermon form of "doctrines and uses." The text for the sermon is Matthew 16:17 (KJV): "And Jesus answered and said unto him, Blessed art thou, Simon Bar-jona: for flesh and blood have not revealed it unto thee, but my Father which is in heaven."

The sermon begins with the explication of the text. It may be observed in the text that:

> Peter is blessed because of what has been revealed to him.
> What makes him blessed or happy is that God and God alone made the revelation to Peter, since this shows that:
>> God favored him more than others.
>> The knowledge was greater than any of which flesh and blood are capable, any merely natural knowledge.

From this text he draws the doctrine that "there is such a thing as a spiritual and divine light, immediately imparted to the soul by God, of a different nature from any that is obtained by natural means." He expounds this doctrine by showing three things (the "reasons" for the doctrine):

What that spiritual and divine light is. This is first shown negatively by stating what the light is not. It is not

Convictions of their sin and misery that persons have in a state of nature, as from conscience. Such convictions come rather from the Spirit of God who operates very differently in the souls of the redeemed from the way that Spirit operates in the unregenerate (111).

"Any impression made upon the imagination" (although such impressions may accompany such spiritual discoveries) (112).

"New truths or propositions not contained in the word of God" (which would be inspiration of the sort the sacred writers and no one else had) (113).

An "affecting view" of religious things, since those can be received from other human beings and not exclusively from God.[33]

Next, he shows positively what the divine and spiritual light is. It is "a true sense of the divine excellency of the things revealed in the word of God, and a conviction of the truth and reality of them thence arising. . . . There is therefore in this spiritual light . . . ":

1. *"A true sense of the divine and superlative excellency of the things of religion; a real sense of the excellency of God and Jesus Christ, and of the work of redemption, and the ways and works of God revealed in the gospel"* (113). This is not merely notional knowledge, but a sense of the heart. The difference between the two is that between "having a rational judgment that honey is sweet, and having a sense of its sweetness" (114).

2. "A conviction of the truth and reality" of the excellency of the things revealed in scripture that is both indirect and direct. It is indirect in two ways:

When prejudices against the divine truth are removed, the mind is opened to rational arguments for the truth.

Reason is helped positively because the light makes speculative notions more lively.

It is also direct because "the excellency of these things is so superlative" (115).

The truth "is immediately given by God, and not obtained by natural means." This does not mean, however, that

"... the natural faculties are not used in it."

"Outward means have no concern in this affair."

It does mean, though, that

"It is given by God without making use of any means that operate by their own power or natural force" (116).

> The doctrine is true, "there is such a thing as that spiritual light that has been described, thus immediately let into the mind by God" (116). This may be demonstrated
>
> By scripture (with a number of texts cited and inferences drawn from them).
>
> Rationally.
>
>> The superlative excellency of divine things is built into the definition of God.
>>
>> Yet, again by definition, it cannot be expected that wicked persons should be able to see that excellency.
>>
>> Thus the knowledge of this excellency must be communicated by God directly and not obtained through natural means.

With his doctrine thus clearly delineated, Edwards moves on to apply it with a "brief improvement."

> The members of his congregation are led "to reflect on the goodness of God" in so ordering revelation that a knowledge of truth is not limited to the brilliant and well educated, but can be given as well to persons of little ability or training.
>
> The doctrine should lead them to reflect on whether they have received such a revelation or not.
>
> They all should seek that light earnestly, since:
>
>> "This is the most excellent and divine wisdom that any creature is capable of."
>>
>> "This knowledge is that which is above all others sweet and joyful."
>>
>> "This light is such as effectually influences the inclination, and changes the nature of the soul" (122).
>>
>> "This light, and this only, has its fruit in an universal holiness of life" (123).

The second point in the application calls for members of the congregation to reflect on whether or not they have received the divine and spiritual light. This means that Edwards, in this and all sermons, assumes he has two audiences, those who have and those who have not received the light, those who have experienced election and conversion and those who have not, the redeemed and the reprobate.

> The unredeemed are shown to fall short. Their fears, their confusions, their inadequacies, are explained by their departures from biblical

> expectations. In contrast, the redeemed are reminded of their present difference from their past life and from their fellows who remain unsaved.[34]

This twofold audience is as much a presupposition for sermons in which he held up the horrors of damnation as it is for those that speak of the joys of salvation. As time goes on, however, a shift is discernible in his preaching, from emphasizing the latter to making more of the former. Part of that is undoubtedly a matter of young preachers having to preach largely from their own experience because they do not have much knowledge of the experience of others—and the spiritual life of the young Edwards was full of affective satisfaction. As he came to better know parishioners, however, he discovered that they were not so much a company of visible saints as he had expected. And the longer he knew them, the worse they appeared to get. After the revival there were various signs of worldliness: a diminished respect for ministerial authority, the introduction of pews into the meetinghouse with the structuralization of social distinctions that involved, and the erection of a secular building for town meetings that seemed to deny the peculiar vocation of New England.

Yet even these negative sermons presupposed two audiences. And it is the failure to recognize this that causes contemporary readers to assume that all of his hearers must have responded to such preaching with terror.

> Saints may hear his sermons as psalmlike celebrations of God's glory—the rolling thunder and leaping fire may, in Edwards' words, "rejoice" one. . . . Grounded in assurance, saints are able to discern the awesome beauty of God's justice.[35]

As calloused as such a reaction may appear to modern readers, it reached to the heart of Edwards's conviction that election was manifested in a love for the excellency of God, especially in the excellency of God's justice in calling some to election and others to reprobation. Sinners' reactions to such sermons, however, would not likely be of terror. The worst proof of their condition could be a smug assumption that they were of the elect and that the terrible words applied to others and not to themselves; or they might be merely apathetic about the whole business. Stark terror on the part of a listener, then, could be a sign of hope, since it takes the grace of God to realize the extent of the loss that threatens and to realize God's justice in condemning sinners such as oneself.

Not only that, the sermon may aid those who have been awakened to the point of fear, since preaching is the ordinary medium through which election occurs. Stephen Yarborough and John Adams interpret this homiletical strategy of Edwards as a use of what Aristotle considered to be the main characteristic of oral persuasion, the *enthymeme.* An enthymeme is an incomplete syllogism, one with a suppressed minor premise that must be supplied by the audience. The major premise in Edwards's sermons is his description of the way that God works with souls. The minor premise to be supplied is the confirmation or ratification of what has been said from one's own experience. The converting potential of sermons like "Sinners in the Hands of an Angry God" is enthymematic, "the 'missing premise' is in the unwilled inclination of a saint to experience the Word in a saving way—with an uncommon affection."[36]

Such sermons, therefore, do not have a character of their own that causes conversion; that cause lies only in the excellent and inscrutable will of God. Yet such sermons can achieve the first of Edwards's three purposes in preaching: "to provide the optimal conditions and circumstances within which the conversion might take place." Hence in defending such preaching, Edwards says:

> Another thing that some ministers have been greatly blamed for, and I think unjustly, is speaking terror to them that are already under great terrors, instead of comforting them. Indeed, if ministers in such a case go about to terrify persons with that which is not true, or to affright 'em by representing their case worse than it is, or in any respect otherwise than it is, they are to be condemned; but if they terrify 'em only by still holding forth more light to them, and giving them to understand more of the truth of their case, they are altogether to be justified. When sinners' consciences are greatly awakened by the Spirit of God, it is by light imparted to the conscience, enabling them to see their case to be, in some measure, as it is; and if more light be let in, it will terrify 'em still more. . . . Why should we be afraid to let persons that are in an infinitely miserable condition, know the truth, or bring 'em into the light, for fear it should terrify them? 'Tis light that must convert them, if ever they are converted.[37]

In all this may be seen the way it came about that Jonathan Edwards was the great advocate and theorist of hellfire and damnation preaching. Yet not all that was to follow in this genre would have met with his approval. In his high Calvinist way of denying that conversion could be effected by anything human beings do, he would have been aghast at suggestions soon to be made that fear could be used to induce conversion. He may have paved the way for such preaching, but he would never have been willing to walk down the paths by which others extended his route.[38]

FOR FURTHER READING

American Sermons: The Pilgrims to Martin Luther King, Jr. Edited by Michael Warner. The Library of America. New York: Library Classics of the United States, 1999.

The Great Awakening. Vol. 4 of *The Works of Jonathan Edwards.* Edited by C. C. Goen. New Haven and London: Yale University Press, 1972.

Miller, Perry. *The New England Mind: The Seventeenth Century.* Cambridge: Belknap Press of Harvard University Press, 1939.

Sermons and Discourses 1720–23. Vol. 10 of *The Works of Jonathan Edwards.* Edited by Wilson H. Kimnach. New Haven and London: Yale University Press, 1992.

Stout, Harry S. *The New England Soul: Preaching and Religious Culture in Colonial New England.* New York and Oxford: Oxford University Press, 1986.

Yarborough, Stephen R., and John C. Adams. *Delightful Conviction: Jonathan Edwards and the Rhetoric of Conversion.* Great American Orators, no. 20. Westport, Conn., and London: Greenwood, 1993.

Notes

1. See above, chapter 15.
2. What follows is based on Perry Miller, *The New England Mind: The Seventeenth Century* (Cambridge: Belknap Press of Harvard University Press, 1939).
3. Ibid., 298.
4. Ibid., 241. Emphasis added to identify faculties.
5. William Perkins, *The Arte of Prophesying*, trans. Thomas Tuke, in *The Works of William Perkins,* ed. and intro. Ian Breward, Courtenay Library of Reformation Classics (Appleford and Abingdon, Berkshire County): Sutton Courtenay, 1970), 3:331-49.
6. Quoted in ibid., 301.
7. For something of the range of "similitudes" in Puritan sermons, see Babette M. Levy, *Preaching in the First Half Century of New England History* (New York: Russell & Russell, 1967; reprinted from American Society of Church History edition of 1945), 98-130.
8. Quoted by Horton Davies from Ames's *The Marrow of Sacred Divinity,* a 1638

translation of *Medulla Theologica,* in *The Worship of the American Puritans, 1629–1730* (New York, Bern, Frankfort am Main, and Paris: Peter Lang, 1990), 84. Chapter 5 of Davies's work, pp. 77-113, is a useful analysis of Puritan preaching. Others have written about Puritan preaching from a number of different perspectives. Ralph G. Turnbull's effort to write a third volume for E. C. Dargan's *A History of Preaching* that would deal with American preaching as well as European preaching in the first half of the twentieth century (Grand Rapids, Mich.: Baker, 1974) is not really a scholarly work and should be used with caution. Dargan himself produced a manuscript for a third volume that is in the library of Southern Baptist Theological Seminary, Louisville, Kentucky, where he taught. Microfilm copies of the manuscript are in a few other libraries, such as that of the Princeton Theological Seminary. The article of Eugene E. White titled "Puritan Preaching and the Authority of God" in *Preaching in American History: Selected Issues in the American Pulpit, 1630–1967,* ed. DeWitte Holland, assoc. eds. Jess Yoder and Hubert Vance Taylor (Nashville and New York: Abingdon, 1969), deals more with the theology preached by the Puritans, especially their understanding of the various covenants, than with any specifically homiletical issues, but it does have a useful bibliography. In the companion volume, *Sermons in American History,* edited by the same people and published by the same press two years later, White introduces two sermons dealing with those issues: John Cotton's "A Sermon" and Peter Bulkeley's "Three Differences More Betwixt the Two Covenants." Emory Elliott, *Power and the Pulpit in Puritan New England* (Princeton: Princeton University Press, 1975), a learned, interesting, and informative work, is concerned about the way sermons and other Puritan religious literature furnished the symbols and myths that enabled the people to deal with the psychological stress inherent to their situation. Again, the concern of the book is not really germane to the history of preaching as such. For examples of Puritan preaching see *American Sermons: The Pilgrims to Martin Luther King, Jr.,* ed. Michael Warner, Library of America (New York: Library Classics of the United States, 1999), which devotes about half of its 900-plus pages to examples.

9. Harry S. Stout, *The New England Soul: Preaching and Religious Culture in Colonial New England* (New York and Oxford: Oxford University Press, 1986), 3-4. In an endnote to this passage, Stout notes that this lifetime load of sermon listening is about ten times the time spent listening to lectures in a college undergraduate degree program. What is said here about Stout's book and that of Toulouse follows very closely my review article, "Preaching in New England," *ATR* 71 (1989): 191-200.

10. Stout, *The New England Soul,* 3.

11. Ibid., 97.

12. Ibid., 7.

13. The times at which occasional sermons were preached include fast days, days of thanksgiving, and election days. Ibid., 27-31. On occasional services, see Davies, *The Worship of the American Puritans,* 51-73.

14. For a full discussion of such fast-day sermons and their subsequent influence on American literature, see Sacvan Bercovitch's classic study, *The American Jeremiad* (Madison: University of Wisconsin Press, 1978).

15. Stout, *The New England Soul,* 5.

16. An ambitious effort to interpret the last of Stout's periods is made by Donald Weber in *Rhetoric and History in Revolutionary New England* (New York: Oxford University Press, 1988), where he attempts to use an interdisciplinary method to enter the thought world of "New Divinity" preachers like Jonathan Edwards Jr. He does not succeed, however, in making either his thesis or the case for it clear enough for evaluation. See my review "Preaching in New England," 194-96.

17. Teresa Toulouse, *The Art of Prophesying: New England Sermons and the Shaping of Belief* (Athens and London: University of Georgia Press, 1987).

18. The respective influences of Whitefield and Edwards on American revivalism have been distinguished by C. C. Goen: "While Whitefield, by virtue of his flamboyant itinerancy and its consequent influence on evangelistic method, may be called the 'founder' of American revivalism, it was Jonathan Edwards who began the historical documentation and theological defense which have sustained as an ongoing tradition." "Editor's Introduction" in *The Great Awakening,* vol. 4 of *The Works of Jonathan Edwards* (New Haven and London: Yale University Press, 1972), 1.

19. For a comparison of the two homiletical styles, see Stephen R. Yarborough and John C. Adams, *Delightful Conviction: Jonathan Edwards and the Rhetoric of Conversion,* Great American Orators, no. 20 (Westport, Conn., and London: Greenwood, 1993), 43. We owe to Ola Elizabeth Winslow the oft-quoted observation that Whitefield gave New England "its first taste of theater under the flag of salvation" in her foreword to the volume she edited, *Jonathan Edwards: Basic Writings* (New York: Meridian, 1966), xviii.

20. For a demonstration of the rarity of such preaching by the earlier Puritans, see Levy, *Preaching in the First Half Century of New England History,* 25-39. It was not, however, unheard of. For example, Edwards's grandfather, Solomon Stoddard, said: "When men don't Preach much about the danger of Damnation, there is want of good Preaching. Men need to be terrified and have the arrows of the Almighty in them that they may be converted," in *The Defects of the Preacher Reproved* (Boston, 1724), 13, 14, quoted by Wilson H. Kimnach, ed., *Sermons and Discourses 1720–23,* vol. 10 of *The Works of Jonathan Edwards* (New Haven and London: Yale University Press, 1992), 14. Yet it was Edwards's fame as the theologian and harbinger of the Great Awakening that gave widespread currency to the practice.

21. Phyllis McGinley, *Times Three: Selected Verse from Three Decades* (Garden City, N.Y.: Image Books, 1975), 35-36.

22. Henry F. May, "Jonathan Edwards and America," in *Jonathan Edwards and the American Experience,* ed. Nathan O. Hatch and Harry S. Stout (New York and Oxford: Oxford University Press, 1988), 23, 25. This collection of papers read at a conference at Wheaton College in 1984 represents an effort "to pull together some of [the disparate strands of the contemporary proliferation of Edwards studies] and to make accessible the best of the current thinking about this remarkable individual," p. 5.

23. Editorial foreword to John E. Smith, *Jonathan Edwards: Puritan, Preacher, Philosopher* (Notre Dame: University of Notre Dame Press, 1992), vii.

24. May, "Jonathan Edwards and America," 30.

25. Winslow, *Jonathan Edwards: Basic Writings,* 66. For a delightful picture of the home life of the Edwards family and its positive influence on the Edwards children,

see Elisabeth D. Dodds, *Marriage to a Difficult Man: The "Uncommon Union" of Jonathan and Sarah Edwards* (Philadelphia: Westminster, 1971).

26. Yarborough and Adams, *Delightful Conviction,* 4.

27. For a socioeconomic theory of why the young people in Northampton were so responsive to Edwards, see ibid., 24-27.

28. For a list of the churches and their ministers and a map of their dispersion, see Goen, *The Great Awakening,* 22-25.

29. A critical edition of this work is given by Goen in *The Great Awakening,* 97-211.

30. Yarborough and Adams, *Delightful Conviction,* 10.

31. Quoted ibid., 11, from the Edwards notebooks.

32. Ibid., 11-21. This paragraph represents an effort to give a simple and concise summary of a position to which Yarborough and Adams give a nuanced presentation.

33. Yarborough and Adams, *Delightful Conviction,* 113. Page numbers used parenthetically throughout this sermon are also from this work.

34. Ibid., 30.

35. Ibid., 54.

36. Ibid., 56.

37. "Some Thoughts Concerning the Revival" in *The Great Awakening,* ed. C. C. Goen, 389-90.

38. In his introduction to *Sermons and Discourses 1720–23,* which extends over 250 pages, Wilson H. Kimnach contributes greatly to our knowledge of many aspects of Jonathan Edwards's preaching: the influences on his preaching, the way he constructed his manuscripts, his recycling of material in later sermons and books, his thoughts about writing, and his homiletical and literary techniques (the subject of Kimnach's 1971 University of Pennsylvania dissertation). Since, however, the present purpose is not to concentrate on the genius of individual preachers but rather to study movements, this section has been confined to the area in which Edwards was most influential on preaching to come, hellfire and damnation preaching. The stir caused by itinerants such as Gilbert Tennent and James Davenport, while interesting in their own right, had little direct influence on later preaching. For a good short treatment of Edwards's preaching, see chapter 3, "Word and Spirit," in Conrad Cherry, *The Theology of Jonathan Edwards: A Reappraisal* (Garden City, N.Y.: Anchor Books, 1966), 44-55.

CHAPTER 19

THE SECOND CALL

THE SECOND GREAT AWAKENING

The discontinuities between the First and Second Great Awakenings are at least as great as the continuities. Some have to do with the cultural setting. Jonathan Edwards's Northampton and the other sites of the First Awakening were places where there had been almost a century of Puritan culture, while much of the Second Awakening took place beyond the borders of the original thirteen colonies in areas newly opened to white settlement. The first occurred in a British colony not yet grown dissatisfied, while the second was set in a self-consciously independent America that was moving beyond its original boundaries. The first came at a time when Calvinism was still the taken-for-granted construction of reality, and the second was at a time when the whole belief system was up for grabs.

A religious movement can be described in many ways, none of which call into question its religious reality. The fact that sociological, psychological, anthropological, or economic interpretations can be given for the sequence of events is not to say that it is any less a revival sent by God. And many scholars have sought to offer such interpretations of the Second Great Awakening. William G. McLoughlin, for instance, has undertaken to use the tools of social anthropology to gain insight into the dynamics of all "revitalizations," as he calls them.[1] Using analytical tools developed by Anthony F. C. Wallace, he argues that there is a standard pattern in which these occur:

> A great awakening occurs, Wallace says, when a society finds that its day-to-day behavior has deviated so far from the accepted (traditional) norms that neither individuals nor large groups can honestly (consistently) sustain the common set of religious understandings by which they believe (have been taught) they should act.[2]

This statement can be paraphrased in the vocabulary of the sociology of knowledge by saying that when a society can no longer assimilate its experience to its social construction of reality, that construction must be revised to accommodate experience. That revision is normally accomplished by individuals who undergo the accommodation in their own religious experience and then proclaim the transformation to others.

> If they are lucky, [the members of the society] will find leaders able to articulate a new accommodation with "reality," a new sense of reality, of identity, and of self-confidence, and, above all, a revision of their institutional structure that will return daily life to regularity and order.[3]

The Second Great Awakening enabled the new American nation to negotiate the changes listed above by giving the country a new way to articulate the basic myths of its culture so they were consistent with the way life was being experienced at that time, thus making it possible for the culture to continue until the next crisis of discontinuity occurred.[4]

While McLoughlin has a chapter on the Second Great Awakening, the basic thing to be learned from him is the pattern of awakenings in general. Insight into this particular awakening can be gained from Nathan O. Hatch's study, *The Democratization of American Christianity*.[5] Hatch argues against those scholars who have seen the Second Great Awakening as having an essentially conservative social force by looking at the populism unleashed by the Revolution, which he calls "the most crucial event in American history."[6]

> The generation overshadowed by it and its counterpart in France stands at the fault line that separates an older world, premised on standards of deference, patronage, and ordered succession, from a newer one that continues to shape our values. . . . Above all, the Revolution dramatically expanded the circle of people who considered themselves

> capable of thinking for themselves about issues of freedom, equality, sovereignty, and representation. Respect for authority, tradition, station, and education eroded.[7]

This populism was as obvious in religion as in any other aspect of culture. That meant the Puritanism that had predominated in religious life up to that point and had even furnished the rationale for the Revolution was suddenly out of fashion. It represented an elite establishment that was anti-egalitarian. Its clergy expected deference to their authority because of their station and the education they had acquired to prepare for it. Theirs was the way of tradition, but the time had come when that no longer drew any water. One person was thought to be as good an interpreter of the Bible as another, whether ordained or lay, educated or not. And along with this populism went an optimism that was aghast at the assumption that a revival occurred only following the inscrutable decision of Providence to send it. God wanted revivals, and it took only faithful souls devoted to the cause and actively promoting it to bring one about. By the same token, salvation was not open just to those elected to it; it was available to any who would trust and accept God's promises. Thus while the Second Great Awakening shared many presuppositions with the First, there were other presuppositions in which it could not have differed more. These differences gave both a very different dynamic to the later movement and a very different style of preaching to mediate it.

But, as noted above, the explanation of the events given by those who participated in them was theological. To those who were in favor of them, they appeared God-sent. To those who opposed them, they were of infernal inspiration. The issue at stake was whether souls would be saved or damned for all eternity.

SOUTHERN BEGINNINGS

The Cane Ridge Sacrament

There were two major streams of the Second Great Awakening, one coming out of New England and going to the upper Midwest, and one that was southern and moved into the whole area, reaching from the lower Midwest to the Gulf of Mexico. Since the latter was the earlier and also reflected a greater break with tradition, it seems the place to begin.

The southern revival began among Presbyterians, although they were quickly to lose this leadership and were actually to suffer schism because of the revival. While the Presbyterian Church in this country began among Puritan colonists from England, it had its largest growth and fastest spread among Scotch-Irish who settled in Pennsylvania and farther south. These made up more than half of the first white Americans who crossed the Appalachians as pioneer settlers.[8] Since their pattern of settlement met the standard of Daniel Boone, who considered himself crowded if he could see the smoke from a neighbor's chimney, it was hard to find enough people who lived close together to form a church. The learned ministers expected by their tradition were also in short supply. Since a majority of these settlers had come from the ardent tradition of Ulster, being deprived of their church was very hard on them and probably caused them to feel guilty as well.

In some ways it is misleading to separate the two Great Awakenings, because there was no intervening period in which a revival[9] was not going on somewhere. This was especially true of Scotch-Irish Presbyterians, who had brought with them the tradition of sacramental meetings, which had been the occasion of great revivals among them in the seventeenth and eighteenth centuries and which also had been the inspiration of the Welsh revival and had developed most of what were to become the conventions of the Methodist Awakening in Great Britain.[10]

> Nothing was as conducive to cyclical revivals as the traditional communion service, with its day of fasting and prayer, its intensive all-day preparatory services, the careful screening of candidates and allocation of tokens (which very conspicuously identified those outside the church), the intense experience of the sacrament itself, and the follow-up thanksgiving service, all in an intercongregational context with huge throngs of people, outdoor preaching tents, and frequent all-night prayer services.[11]

As Presbyterianism moved down through Virginia into the Carolinas and then over into Kentucky and Tennessee, there was a succession of communion meetings led by clergy who had been converted in such meetings themselves and then acquired the education that allowed them to be ordained. By the summer of 1800, there was a small group of such clergy in Logan County, Kentucky, under the leadership of James McGready, who preached with extraordinary power in spite of using a manuscript. The area clergy planned to have their summer sacramental meetings so synchronized that none would conflict, permitting members of one congregation to attend the meeting of another and create the critical mass of people necessary for such an event.

Much to everyone's surprise, what some consider to be the first camp meeting occurred at the communion of one of McGready's churches, that of Gasper River.[12] People came from more than one hundred miles, which means that they could have come from Tennessee, Illinois, or Indiana, as well as Kentucky. By the time of the opening session on Friday, twenty to thirty wagons were encamped. Four clergy shared the preaching and ministration of the sacrament. The anticipation shown by the flocking of people from such a wide area was not disappointed. Many were caught up in the excitement of the occasion, experiencing a variety of physical manifestations of the grace they felt, and a large number were converted. This spark ignited a flame of revival that spread to Carolina and east Tennessee.

Religious stirrings had been felt not only by the Presbyterian congregations in central Kentucky, but by Methodists and Baptists as well, although the Presbyterian sacraments were always the most explosive. By the time the next summer came, anticipation was intense. The excitement was canalized by the Presbyterians through what they called societies or socials, groups very similar to Methodist classes. Clergy became involved by hearing of the things that were happening in other churches and going to witness them for themselves.

An example of this was Barton Stone, the pastor of Cane Ridge and Concord churches in Bourbon County east of Lexington. He had been in his cure and indeed had been ordained only three years when he visited his old classmates at Gasper River to see what their communion was like in May of 1801. He returned to his flocks and saw signs of a great stirring at the Concord sacrament. The Cane River communion in August, however, was to prove, to the amazement of all concerned, to be the unleashing of the Second Great Awakening in the South.

Since he did not take a leading part in the preaching, it is unclear what Barton Stone's exact role was in what happened at his Cane Ridge sacrament that year. Indeed, it is hard to know the contribution of any or all of the clergy there, since what happened appears to have been, humanly speaking, a function of the expectations of the people who arrived. They came like lemmings eager to drown in a sea of grace.

Although there are a number of eyewitness accounts, some written down at the time and others not until years later,[13] reliable numbers are hard to come by. While estimates range as high as twenty thousand, half that number of attendants seems more likely. Methodists and Baptists came as well as Presbyterians, although the Baptists' practice of close Communion would have excluded them from the sacrament. Blacks participated as well as whites, but in a segregated manner on the grounds. Not all who came were devout; there were many who were curious, cynical, or thrill seekers. Seventeen ministers preached during the course of the event, while hundreds of laity exhorted—including one seven-year-old girl. At this communion meeting it is likely that no more than 200 received, but Stone estimated that somewhere between 500 and 1,000 persons were converted. Many more than that number were said to be "slain" (i.e., to have fainted from religious agitation).

What most impressed contemporary observers as well as historians and their readers ever since was the bodily manifestations[14] of religious emotions displayed at Cane Ridge and in the camp meetings to follow. The descriptions are impressive, as this example from one of the clergy present:

> Sinners dropping down on every hand, shrieking, groaning, crying for mercy, convoluted; professors [of religion] praying, agonizing, fainting, falling down in distress, for sinners, or in raptures of joy! Some singing, some shouting, clapping their hands, hugging and even kissing, laughing; others talking to the distressed, to one another, or to opposers of the work, and all this at once.[15]

The writer's reaction to the events he reported was to say, "No spectacle can excite a stronger sensation," a verdict few would question.

In addition to weeping, shouting, and fainting, the physical manifestations of religious emotion were so varied that a taxonomy had to be created to classify them. One written by Stone is worth quoting at length:

> The jerks cannot be so easily described . . . When the whole system was affected, I have seen a person stand in one place and jerk backward and forward in quick succession, their head nearly touching the floor behind and before. All classes . . . were thus affected. They could not account for it; but some have told me that they were among the happiest seasons of their lives.
>
> The dancing exercise . . . The subject, after jerking awhile, began to dance, and the jerks would cease . . . While thus exercised, I have heard their solemn praises and prayers ascending to God.
>
> The barking exercise (as opposers contemptuously called it) was nothing but the jerks. A person affected with the jerks, especially in his head, would often make a grunt or a bark, if you please, from the suddenness of the jerk.
>
> The singing exercise . . . The subject in a very happy state of mind would sing most melodiously not from the mouth or nose, but entirely in the breast, the sounds issuing thence. Such music silenced everything, and attracted the attention of all.[16]

Then as now, such descriptions have repulsed many people. Some have tried to distance themselves from this type of behavior by attributing it to the effect of the frontier on ignorant people, but, as Paul Conkin has pointed out, "no revivals took place, or could take place, among the first scattered white settlers in any area of the West,"[17] and one of the diary records of the event shows that "the people most stricken were often sturdy landowners or prominent women, leaders in the local congregations, people in the upper ranks of early Kentucky society."[18]

Conkin also has a good perspective on these exercises that sound as alien to many contemporary Christians as they do to religion's "cultured despisers":

> What the exercises revealed were religiously serious people who, in a powerfully suggestive environment, chose, or were forced, to reenact the drama of Jesus' passion and the ever-recurring drama of their own tortured quest for salvation. . . . Tears, either of remorse or of joy, are at the heart of any affectional religion. Beyond tears are the more extreme but equally involuntary effects—verbal or muscular or neurological. These, too, are within the range of almost everyone's experience, as in rare and often unwanted moments of overwhelming feeling, such as at the death of a loved one. Who can then resist tears? Or cries of despair? Or even the writhing and convulsive movements that may provide an outlet for complete personal desolation? Surely no one expects a quiet demeanor or reasonable rationalization at such moments. Nor for those often unsought, often inexplicable moments of sheer exaltation which, for some people, may be approached in a sexual orgasm. In other words, some form of physical expression fitted these occasions, whether in an avowedly religious or a secular setting. Physical effects are not in themselves different whatever the stimulant. After all, some people largely identify swooning with rock concerts or find in Woodstock the clearest parallel to Cane Ridge.[19]

The kind of preaching done at Cane Ridge encouraged responses of ecstatic frenzy. Since the preaching was impromptu, we have no manuscript texts of sermons preached there, but do know of some devices employed:

> Certain repeated and familiar verbal images, those with great resonance for an audience, worked better than others. In many of the greatest revivals the spark was a type of confession—the telling of what had happened to oneself there or at an earlier revival. Some ministers learned the most evocative ways of telling their stories. Several sermonic

> devices—timing, phrasing, pauses, and above all the display of intense feeling—worked.[20]

Undoubtedly the mood of the crowd contributed to an emotional state open to intense religious experience. There is bound to be something contagious about being in the middle of a group caught up in despair or ecstasy. The fact that there were always several clergy preaching at the same time from different platforms on the grounds must have heightened the excitement. Add to that hundreds of people, clergy and lay, "exhorting" groups and individuals, and you have conditions highly conducive to emotional release. This, too, affected the preaching:

> In the tumult the distinction between prepared sermons (with a theme or text taken from the Bible and carefully developed points or arguments) and more spontaneous exhortations (extemporaneous or even impromptu practical advice, or tearful appeals or warnings) dissolved, particularly when outlying members of the audience could not even hear the sermons.[21]

In the Kentucky revivals around the turn of the nineteenth century, a style of preaching was perfected that was very effective for creating revivals in which large numbers of people received the spiritual release for which they were hoping and praying. It was to become characteristic of the camp meetings and most revivals that have taken place since.

Before moving on to the camp meetings, however, a word needs to be said about the immediate effects of Cane Ridge. One is that the camp meeting as such, rather than the Presbyterian sacrament meeting, came to be the characteristic occasion of revivals. This meant, first of all, that the centrality of the Eucharist was lost for Presbyterians.[22] It also meant that the initiative for the Awakening in the South passed from the Presbyterians to the Methodists and, to a lesser extent, the Baptists.

The Presbyterians, indeed, were to suffer two schisms as a result of disagreements over the Kentucky revivals.[23] Most of the clergy involved in the Cane Ridge revival, including Barton Stone, would separate over a nexus of issues that included how worship should be conducted, whether clergy should be given privileged status, the doctrine of Christ, and freedom of the will. In time, the majority of these ministers became involved in the Restoration movement that created the Christian Church,[24] the Disciples of Christ, and the Church of Christ—although some became Shakers.

The heirs of the McGready revivals in Logan County found themselves at loggerheads with less evangelical clergy in the Cumberland Presbytery.

All the issues of decorum versus emotion in worship were involved, but the original issue around which controversy centered was educational qualifications for ordination: Was English education enough or did one need classical and biblical languages as well? In time, however, the issue shifted to Arminianism. The result was that the orthodox pronounced anathemas, and the evangelicals formed the Cumberland Presbyterian Church.

Circuit Riders and Camp Meetings

The growth of Methodists in the years following Cane Ridge was phenomenal. Shortly before the Revolution, they had small groups in New York and Philadelphia and a few in the South, but by 1820 they had a quarter of a million members, and ten years later they doubled that number.[25] The Baptists did almost as well, increasing their membership tenfold by 1813. These two groups would come to claim the allegiance of two-thirds of America's Protestants. By contrast, the Congregationalists, who had two times as many clergy as any other American church at the beginning of the Revolution, had less than one-tenth the number of the Methodists by 1845.

The reason for this rapid increase of the Methodists is that they had the infrastructures that enabled them to grow with the westward expansion of the country. Primary among these were an itinerant ministry recruited from the settlers and the camp meeting. This is to say that the system of Wesley flourished in America at the very time that it was disappearing in England. In its native land, Methodism had gone respectable: "The circuit horse was almost extinct in England by 1815,"[26] and camp meetings were considered egregious breaches of decorum. What makes this especially ironic is that American Methodists actually revoked their former commitment to obey Wesley at their General Conference of 1787 and removed his name from their minutes.[27] Yet they were much truer to his spirit than the parent church.

Bishop Asbury

The main reason the American Methodists were so loyal to the evangelistic method of their founder was a man who resembled him closely in almost every respect other than being a fellow of an Oxford college. Francis Asbury was as tireless in his labors, as thorough an organizer, and as authoritarian in his leadership as John Wesley, the man who had chosen him for his work.[28] He was born in 1745 into the family of a skilled gardener and farmer, and his formal education took place between the ages of seven and twelve. He was apprenticed to a trade, but after his conversion at the age of fourteen and his discovery of the Methodists, preaching came to be his only interest. He was appointed to his first circuit as an itinerant when he was twenty-one.

His lack of formal education does not mean that he was ignorant. Wesley's reading program for his preachers was never more assiduously followed. A commitment of Asbury's rule of life was to read a hundred pages a day, an extraordinary achievement under the most adverse circumstances.[29] He regretted that travel by horseback was not as conducive to reading in America as it was in England, but he used the time to review Hebrew grammar.[30]

In 1771, five years after his first itinerant appointment, Wesley sent him to America in response to a request from Methodists here for help. Since soul winning was the ruling passion of Francis Asbury's life, he became constantly on the alert for ways in which the infant Methodist movement in this country could become more effective. He came to be the best-informed person in the church about its state in every place. His efforts to improve things had its ups and downs until after the Revolution, when Wesley saw the need for clergy in America who could administer the sacraments. In 1784 he said that Asbury and Thomas Coke should be appointed superintendents—by which he meant bishops, although he never admitted it. Since Coke spent more time in England than America, Asbury was virtually dictator of the American branch of the church.

This did not mean that he ceased to be an itinerant preacher. Quite the contrary; it meant only that his circuit was enlarged. In his entire ministry in America, Asbury would travel 270,000 miles, mostly on horseback, but in a carriage after he became infirm. He would preach 16,500 sermons and ordain 4,000 preachers.[31] He never married, he accepted no salary larger than that of his circuit riders, beginning at the rate of sixty-four dollars a year, and most of the time he was sick and in pain. Yet until his death in 1816, American Methodism bore his imprint as clearly as the original movement bore that of John Wesley.

Asbury's journals (for a sample, see **Vol. 2, pp. 398-403**) permit us to know a good bit about his preaching—which was not atypical of Methodist preaching in general at the time. He was always on the go and preached wherever he went. Like Wesley, he often preached at 5:00 A.M. and also preached almost every evening. Frequent notes in his journal not only mention the occasions of his sermons, but also often give the texts and even say how successful the sermon was. Occasionally the outline is given as well. He did not write out his sermons; to preach from a manuscript on the frontier would have been counterproductive. He did believe in preparation, however, which probably consisted of prayer and thinking through the outline he would follow. Yet his constant study also lay behind each sermon.

While he almost always preached from a text, neither the outline nor the content necessarily grew out of the text. Rather,

> Asbury's most common practice was to take the wording of a biblical text and reconstruct from that wording a topical outline of his own for preaching. Where he knew the historical background of the text he might use it. If the text was obviously and directly applicable he might apply it literally. . . . But there was no guarantee that the topical outline drawn from a text would have any direct connection with the primary meaning of the text itself. . . . If the text mentioned salvation, the topic headings would almost certainly cover the full range of crucial Methodist doctrines. . . . The topics of the sermon tended to come out the same no matter what the text. There was (1) conviction—under awful weight of our sin; (2) repentance and justification—to be taken on now; (3) perseverance in good works—no backsliding; and (4) sanctification—going on to perfect love.[32]

When described this way, his sermons do not sound very biblical, but there is a more profound sense in which they were very much so: he was saturated with the Bible and from it drew his most basic thought forms. His illustrations also were taken from Holy Scripture, unless they were taken from current events.

He generally preached for about an hour, although if the response justified it, he could go on for several hours. He was not emotional in his delivery, but if he sensed that his congregation was being stirred, he sometimes allowed himself free rein and continued as long as the response did. He was not a great preacher, but those who heard him most often best appreciated him.

Peter Cartwright and Circuit Riding

No system could have been better devised than Methodist itinerancy for bringing religion to the settlers moving westward. Even the Baptist system of having unpaid preachers who were fellow settlers and farmers did not work as well; their settled condition limited their ability to follow every movement of population. But wherever pioneer families moved, circuit riders found their way to them and established classes with their leaders and local preachers. They would appoint a regular time to preach in a home in an area and make that a point on their circuit, although they may not visit more often than once a month. They would appear at the appointed time, pray, preach, and learn from class leaders the spiritual state of every class member.

The circuit riders, in turn, were visited by their presiding elders, who would meet with them and the lay preachers of the area in quarterly conferences. Then all the clergy of an annual conference would meet annually with Asbury. Every four years there was a General Conference, attended by preachers elected by their annual conference and presided over by Asbury. Further, the Methodist Book Concern, organized by Asbury, turned all the circuit riders into colporteurs of Methodist literature, by which they reinforced their doctrinal preaching and, incidentally, added to their scanty income. It is hard to imagine a system better devised for evangelizing the westward movement of American settlers.

What the life of a circuit rider was like can be learned from a remarkable document written by a remarkable man, *The Autobiography of Peter Cartwright, the Backwoods Preacher.* Cartwright was born in Logan County and converted at one of McGready's sacramental meetings at the age of fifteen. Two years later, when his family moved three counties west and he asked for his letter of transfer of church membership, he discovered that it commissioned him to establish a preaching circuit there. At first he demurred on the basis of his lack of education, but went on to become an autodidact in the great tradition of Wesleyan preachers.

> From then on Peter Cartwright rode circuits in Kentucky, Tennessee, Indiana, Ohio, and Illinois when the distances between preaching appointments were often measured by hundreds of miles and when at times the indefatigable riders were guided only by the evening star or dead reckoning.[33]

Within ten years he was made what modern Methodists call a district superintendent, which eventually enabled him to publish a second autobiographical volume called *Fifty Years as a Presiding Elder.* He became a sort of folk hero and acquired national fame, at least in part because he was willing to use his fists when other means of persuasion failed. He also was a vigorous polemicist, advocating a sectarian exclusiveness shocking to the ecumenical ears of later generations.[34] Although he considered slavery one of the greatest evils in the history of the world, he seemed to think abolitionists ran a close second. He even served in the Illinois legislature, the only opponent ever to win an election over Abraham Lincoln for a seat in that body—although Lincoln was to have his revenge in a congressional election.

Yet Cartwright's passion, his monomania, was soul winning. His *Autobiography* has fascinating accounts of the exposure to weather and other hardships to which circuit riders subjected themselves in their loyalty to their vocation, the sort of experience that gave rise to the proverbial remark about stormy days: "There is nothing out today but crows and Methodist preachers."[35] As absorbing as these are, more to the present purpose are his remarks about the kind of preaching it took (and did not take!) to exercise the vocation of a frontier evangelist. One of the most hilarious of his negative examples is the account of the New School preacher whose response upon being sent to minister to those in anguish on the anxious bench was, "Be composed; be composed, brother."[36] Writing in his early seventies, Cartwright had lived to see Methodism overtaken by the sort of refinement that made Presbyterians so ill-adapted to following the settlers west. More store was set by the education and good taste of clergy than their passion for souls. This was not the spirit that had won a million souls in sixty years.[37]

Although he had devoted much effort to the promotion of education, Cartwright's reaction to this development was an indignant snort. The following passage is typical:

> About this time there were a great many young missionaries sent out to this country to civilize and Christianize the poor heathen of the West. They would come with a tolerable education, and a smattering knowledge of the old Calvinistic system of theology. They were generally tolerably well furnished with old manuscript sermons, that had been preached, or written, perhaps a hundred years before. Some of these sermons they had memorized, but in general they read them to the people. This way of reading sermons was out of fashion altogether in this Western world, and of course they produced no good effect among the people. The great mass of our Western people wanted a preacher that could mount a stump, a block, or old log, or stand in the bed of a wagon, and without note or manuscript, quote, expound, and apply the word of God to the hearts and consciences of the people.[38]

Camp Meetings

So much for the preaching of circuit riders in general. Now for the particular sort of proclamation that was done in that other infrastructure of Methodist expansion during the Second Great Awakening, the camp meeting. While other denominations made some use of camp meetings, it was the Methodists who really capitalized on the opportunities they afforded. With the regular life of the class with its leaders and local preachers, and the regular but less frequent presence of the circuit rider, the Methodist system had need for the occasional sessions of rally and reinforcement that came from having camp meetings around the last quarterly conference of the year and around the annual conference each year.

Such regularity involved a certain "routinization of charisma," as did other aspects of the way the meetings evolved. The two main differentiae between Cane Ridge and true camp meetings were that Cane Ridge was unplanned and had no set rules governing the conduct of those who attended. Rules and planning as characteristics of the events already involve a degree of routinization. A paradox of the camp meeting movement was that, while the emotional extravagance of Cane Ridge and Logan County were the evidences that the Holy Spirit was sending a revival, the emotion itself was regarded as dangerous, and those who wanted to imitate the earlier successes wished at the same time to tame them.[39] Small wonder that camp meetings were progressively refined until they evolved into such programs as Chataqua and summer camping; or that later historians would look on the achievements of the movement more in terms of "civilizing" the West than evangelizing it.[40]

The fire did not leave the backwoods revivals all at once, though. As Charles Johnson says:

> While a public display of one's inner feelings is unthinkable by today's standards [1955], it was regarded as merely the expression of convictions "very pungent and deep" in the harvest time of the camp meeting. This mode of behavior was common even in the populous East. The point at which tension, confusion, and strife between the old sinful ways and the new were overcome by the awesome sermons, prolonged prayers, and crowd pressures was often accompanied by strange bodily manifestations. Automatisms (bodily excitement, crying out, and hallucinations), while not considered positive evidence of conversion, were viewed as probable tokens of God's presence and attested to the power of preaching.[41]

What were the events like that elicited such strong responses? They were held at the end of the summer, when there was a natural lull in farmwork and the weather was still warm enough to permit meeting out-of-doors. An area of two to four acres would be prepared for the camp (**See Vol. 2, pp. 403-4,** for a firsthand report). It had to be near a good source of water. The ground would be laid out in one of several patterns: round, horseshoe, or rectangular. The outer border would contain the horses and mules, and inside their ring were drawn up the wagons and carriages in which participants traveled to the meeting. In front of those, tents were raised, and in front of the tents, campfires were built. At each end of the open area in the middle was erected an elevated speaker's stand, in front of which was usually an area for "mourners" (those under conviction of sin who had not yet been converted). The area in between was filled with benches made of split logs or boards between tree stumps.

The meetings would occupy a four-day weekend or sometimes a longer period. The days would begin early with family prayers and breakfast, followed by a marathon of preaching that lasted into the night. Preaching rotated among the clergy present, with the better known and more accomplished taking the prime times. The intervals between sermons were filled with exhorters and the singing of emotional revival music. Exhorters were also active during the sermons. Those who were "affected" were constantly being ushered into the mourners' area. There they would be surrounded by clergy and others who would try to help pray them through. There were probably as many curiosity seekers as devout in attendance and not a few tradespeople were hawking their wares—including whiskey. Sometimes agitators would try to interrupt the proceedings and would have to be coped with by those in charge. Anything else that brought as much excitement into the backwoods as a camp meeting had the disadvantage of being life-threatening.

The preaching that occurred on these occasions had much in common with other preaching of the circuit riders, but a few generalizations about it are worth making. Naturally, the delivery was extempore. Not only was an inability to preach without manuscript regarded as an indication of practical incompetence, it was also taken as prima facie evidence that the preacher was unconverted: the Spirit would tell the truly called what they should say. The vocabulary and diction of the preachers were in the idiom of those who heard them. Picturesque expression and vigorous delivery were highly prized. A loud voice was necessary to be heard over the hubbub. The vocal endurance of the preachers was remarkable; they could sustain the volume for as many as two or three hours. At the same time, the preachers were capable of great pathos. Poetic imagery and sentimental stories were part of their stock in trade. Much of the spirit of these events was captured by Abraham Lincoln's statement that "when I see a man preach I like to see him act as if he were fighting bees."[42] These backwoods preachers felt they were engaged in an eschatological struggle with evil for the eternal souls of men and women, and they were prepared for strenuous combat. As the evangelist in the film *The Return of Frank James* said: "It's gonna be me and the devil and no holds barred."

Most, but not all, of the sermons were evangelistic in the sense of calling upon those who heard them to escape hell and accept salvation. Altar calls were their climax. Yet many other sermons were preached to the converted, telling them how to live the new lives they had received. In the Methodist tradition, this involved the assumption that they were going on to perfection, and the demands made were stern and uncompromising. A radical difference between the new and old lives was expected.

Whiskey drinking, vanity in dress, and slavery were a triad of evils frequently attacked.

> In pungent language the evils of the day were fearlessly denounced: immorality, intemperance, tobacco, blasphemy, dueling, card playing, horse racing, and gambling.[43]

Hatch's claim that this period in church history was characterized by "the democratization of American religion" is documented by the frequency with which liberty was a sermon topic at camp meetings. There were also doctrinal sermons, especially polemical ones against the perceived shortcomings of other denominations. Thus there was considerable variety in the homiletical diet of a camp meeting. All in all, the camp meeting was one of the most effective means the Methodists used to accomplish their phenomenal growth in the first half of the nineteenth century.

THE URBANIZATION AND UPWARD SOCIAL MOVEMENT OF THE AWAKENING

Stirrings

One of the curious aspects of the northern manifestation of the Second Great Awakening is its ambivalent attitude toward the man whose activity was the occasion of the First, Jonathan Edwards. Indications of this attitude were shown in disagreements about the theological system to which Edwards was in some ways so loyal, Calvinism. As time went on, the great center of Calvinist orthodoxy migrated from Congregationalist New England to Presbyterian Princeton. Those who were closest to Edwards in terms of common history, denomination, and even family ties were no longer so captured as he had been by an overwhelming view of God's absolute sovereignty. They did, however, cling to his devotion to the cause of revival. Indeed, it was their concern for conversions—along with influences from the spirit of the times—that caused them to modify their views on election.

The herald of the Second Awakening in the North was Edwards's grandson, **Timothy Dwight.** A Congregationalist minister who had been a chaplain in the Revolution, Dwight felt that the Puritan world of his ancestors was threatened by many conditions that prevailed in the postwar world. Deism and Unitarianism showed how far gone New England was from original righteousness. Part and parcel with these was the Jeffersonian Republicanism that was disestablishing the church, depriving learned clergy of their elevated position in the community, and banishing respect for all constituted authority. With such an apocalyptic view of the situation, it is no wonder that Dwight thought a revival of religion was needed to get the country back on course. Thus when he became president of Yale in 1795, Dwight immediately began preaching revival in the chapel. Notable outpourings were felt in 1802, 1807, 1812, 1815, and 1820.

The significance of this for the Second Great Awakening was in the graduates who went forth from Yale to spread the revival. There were three who were especially important. The revivalist was **Asahel Nettleton,** who appears to have been launched in that role almost by accident and to have succeeded in it as much by accident as any intention or skill. About the time he became accepted as the very model of a modern gospel preacher, however, illness interrupted his ministry, and his activity was greatly abated from the early 1820s on. He lived to become an embittered man who would find the reason for his existence in resisting the new methods of evangelism that were to sweep the country.

The churchman who would organize the party and rally the troops to the flag was **Lyman Beecher.** He became the most influential leader in the Congregational Church and could succeed in getting accepted almost any program he sponsored. The theologian was **Nathaniel Taylor,** who was the first to occupy Yale's chair in theology, established in 1822. He would furnish a theoretical basis for revivals more congenial than Edwards's assumption that they were sent by an inscrutable Providence for reasons unaffected by human thought or efforts. "For many years in his ministerial study he was absorbed in working on a new system of divinity which left man free to repent and virtually promised that he would be saved if he did."[44]

While these heirs of Edwards were important in the history of the northern expression of the Second Great Awakening, they were not influential on the future of preaching. Of his own preaching, Beecher said:

> I always preached right to the conscience. Every sermon with my eye on the gun to hit somebody. Went through the doctrines; showed what they didn't mean; what they did; then the argument; knocked away objections, and drove home on the conscience.[45]

This is obviously the old Perkins form of "doctrines and uses" and represents no change in preaching style. Nor did the delivery of such sermons violate earlier norms of decorum. While Beecher had a great reputation as a preacher during his lifetime, Nettleton did not attempt to stir the congregation in one of his revivals; "if the meeting began to show signs of violent feeling, Nettleton was apt to break it up."[46]

Charles Grandison Finney, Prosecuting Attorney

Timothy Dwight's disciples were greatly upset when someone came along who changed the rules of the game considerably. As will be seen, they were to put forth energetic effort to set roadblocks in the way of Charles Grandison Finney, who was to adapt the techniques of the southern awakening to the North. The irony is that Finney was to do so in a way that would recommend itself to areas much more stably settled than the southern backwoods and to an audience higher on the social scale than farmer-settlers. Before he finished, Finney numbered among his supporters some of the wealthiest people in the country, and he was invited by them to conduct revivals in the largest cities of the East.

Although Charles G. Finney was actually born in New England, his parents joined the westward migration when he was only two and moved to Oneida County, New York. There the young Finney eventually gained enough education to become a schoolteacher, but he afterward turned to an apprenticeship in law as the path to his chosen career.

Finney's parents had not been religious, and he lived in the region for which he supplied the name that has stuck, "the burned-over district."

> There had been, a few years previously, a wild excitement [passing through that region], which they called a revival, but which turned out to be spurious. It was reported as having been a very extravagant excitement; and resulted in a reaction so extensive and profound as to leave the impression on many minds that religion was a mere delusion.[47]

Finney spent only three years in the study and practice of law. He already attended church, but his motives for doing so were not basically religious. Discovering, however, that the Bible was cited in his legal texts as the authority for many of the principles of common law, he bought his first Bible and began to study it. Yet when he started reading the Bible, he was led to consider the condition of his own soul. He came under deep conviction of sin and remained that way for about a week. At the end of that ordeal, he had an overwhelming conversion experience that filled him with great joy and a sense of being called to preach. On the morning of his conversion, he had been scheduled to appear in court, but he told his client, "Deacon B______, I have a retainer from the Lord Jesus Christ to plead his cause, and I cannot plead yours."[48]

He began studying for the Presbyterian ministry under the guidance of his pastor, having refused to go to seminary because he found seminary graduates so poorly prepared for their work—although his *Autobiography* probably exaggerates the extent to which he differed from his instructor on Calvinism at the time.[49] After two years of study, he was taken under care by the presbytery. Six months later he was licensed, and seven months after that he was ordained as a teaching elder for a ministry of evangelism rather than that of a settled pastor. He began to work in the small villages of the surrounding area, and his preaching met with an enthusiastic response.[50]

He immediately began to acquire a local reputation, and success in one area would lead to an invitation to a larger one. In the rural villages where he began, his method was the sort of sensational hellfire and damnation preaching that was common at first in southern camp meetings, but as he moved to larger towns, he recognized that more restraint was needed if he was going to reach a more refined set of sinners.[51]

Even toned down, however, his methods met the objections of Nettleton, who to that time had been the reigning revivalist in New York and New England. Finney was accused of using "new measures" in evangelism.

> Although opponents such as Asahel Nettleton would later list as many as twenty-nine practices they considered objectionable, only five or six caused widespread controversy: public praying by women in mixed audiences; protracted series of meetings (i.e., daily services); colloquial language used by the preacher; the anxious seat or bench; the practice of praying for people by name; and immediate church membership for converts.[52]

While Methodists and others had used such means for some time, they were, nevertheless, offensive to the sense of decorum of some Presbyterians and Congregationalists. Unitarians and Universalists were also very opposed to Finney, but he could take their disapproval almost as a commendation.

By 1827 Nettleton and Lyman Beecher were involved with others in a conspiracy to halt Finney's influence and had begun publishing attacks on his methods in the church press. A conference was proposed in New

Lebanon, New York, where Finney had been preaching, to see if the two sides could iron out their differences. Each side had nine representatives. When they convened on July 18, it was the hope of the New Englanders that Finney would be so discredited that his effectiveness would vanish. They treated the occasion almost as a trial of him and his methods.

In the end, however, they overextended themselves; they had very inadequate information about what he was actually doing and were abashed to discover that the measures they could get condemned by the group had apparently never been practiced by Finney. The upshot was that he left the conference without a mark against him and thus with the appearance of the blessing of the New England establishment. Beecher was eventually to be somewhat reconciled to Finney and even to join Boston clergy in inviting him to conduct a revival.[53] Nettleton, however, would not accept the inevitable and found himself progressively isolated and embittered. When Finney's measures were next subjected to a major attack, it was not from New School Calvinists but from the Old School tradition of Princeton, after the publication of his *Lectures on Revivals.*

From New Lebanon on he began to have citywide, ecumenically supported revivals in the major metropolitan centers of the East Coast. His successes there, however, were never so overwhelming and unqualified as they were in western New York. His greatest triumph was in Rochester, where he preached from September 10, 1830, to March 6, 1831. Although conditions had been very unpromising when he arrived, the response was total. The establishment backed the revival completely. Church membership increased by almost ten thousand. And, in one of the first major associations of evangelism with social action, a city that was a center of distilleries was converted to the cause of temperance.

The most important results of the revival, however, were not confined to Rochester:

> It was almost singularly responsible for bringing about the national revival of 1831, in which what had been building up for years throughout the country seemed almost to explode in that one year. . . . Between 1800 and 1835 the portion of Protestant church members to the national population almost doubled, from 7 to 12 1/2 percent, but most of that growth came after 1830. . . . Everywhere, ordinary citizens desired to have duplicated in their town what had happened so sanely and so respectably in Rochester.[54]

The Second Great Awakening, which had begun among the widely scattered farmer-settlers of the Trans-Appalachian South, was now completely at home among the business leaders as well as the rank-and-file population of the urban North.

Even though Finney was to continue preaching revivals for many years and was even to make two evangelistic tours of England, the exacting demand of the revival schedule had begun to wear down his health so that in 1832, at the age of forty, he accepted his first appointment as pastor of a congregation, the Second Free Church (also called Chatham Street Chapel) in New York City. Two years later he transferred to Broadway Tabernacle, where a church was built to his specifications.

The following year, he accepted the professorship of theology at the infant Oberlin College and for a while divided his year between his parish and the campus. Although not the founder of Oberlin, Finney was the person around whom it was built. His main understanding of his work there was that he was to raise up a generation of young evangelists who would carry on his work. Finney was deeply involved in the development of "Oberlin perfectionism," a belief similar to Wesley's understanding of sanctification. He became president of Oberlin in 1852, and the college remained his home until his death twenty-three years later.

The key to Finney's success as an evangelist was the power of his preaching. He was a tall, slim, commanding figure, his appearance not unlike that of the film actor Charlton Heston. His most impressive feature was his eyes, which even in printed reproductions of photographs have an amazingly piercing, hypnotic quality.[55] One gets the impression that he must have been a riveting speaker. We can gain an idea of what—beyond the sheer physical impact of his appearance—made his preaching so effective by reading, even more than his sermons, two of his other writings, his *Lectures on Revivals of Religion*[56] and his *Autobiography.*

The *Lectures on Revivals* were not only an end in themselves but also a means to raise money. They were given at his Chatham Street Chapel in New York in 1834, after Finney returned from an unsuccessful voyage to restore his health only to discover that the *New York Evangelist* was almost bankrupt because, contrary to his instructions, the editor had used the newspaper to crusade for abolition.[57] Publication of the lectures in the *Evangelist* did succeed in regaining its lost subscribers. Modern readers who turn to the work expecting to find "how-to" gimmicks will be disappointed. While the work is prescriptive, the perspective is much more spiritual than practical. More than the first third of the book is devoted to the work of prayer that must be done in advance and during the meeting for a revival to occur.

Only the twelfth lecture is devoted to preaching. Its outline shows not only his thoughts on the subject but also the form Finney's sermons usually took:

How to Preach the Gospel

I. Several passages of scripture ascribe conversion to human agency.

II. These are not inconsistent with those that ascribe it to God.

III. Several particulars about preaching the gospel will be listed which show that practical wisdom is needed to win souls for Christ.

First, with regard to the matter of preaching.

1. "All preaching should be *practical.*" Doctrine that does not have practical implications is irrelevant.
2. "Preaching should be *direct,*" preached to people instead of about them.
3. The minister should hunt for sinners and for Christians entrenched in inaction.
4. The preacher should dwell on the points most needed.
5. The minister should not introduce distracting controversy.
6. The whole gospel should be brought to the mind of the people.
7. Sinners should be made to feel their guilt and not left with the impression that they are merely unfortunate.
8. "A prime objective with the preacher must be to make the *present obligation* felt."
9. Sinners should be made to feel that they should repent and repentance is something no one else can do for them.
10. "Ministers should never rest satisfied, until they have ANNIHILATED every excuse of sinners."[58]
11. "Sinners should be made to feel that if they *now* grieve away the Spirit of God, it is very probable that they will be *lost forever.*"

Secondly, a few remarks about the manner of preaching.

1. It should be *conversational.*
2. It must be in the *language of common life.*
3. Preaching should be *parabolical.*
4. The illustrations should be drawn *from common* life.
5. Preaching should be *repetitious.*
6. "A minister should always feel deeply his subject, and then he will suit the action to the word and the word to the action, so as to make the full impression which the truth is calculated to make."
7. "A minister should aim to *convert his congregation.*"

8. The preacher should anticipate and answer the objections of sinners.

9. The preacher must not be monotonous.

10. "A minister should address the feelings enough to secure attention, and then deal with the conscience, and probe to the quick."

Remarks[59]

1. To convert the leading minds of the community, ministers must reason with them so that they see the truth of the gospel.

2. The success of the gospel requires extempore preachers.

a. there is not time to write all the sermons that will be needed.

b. written sermons do not produce the necessary effect.

c. "it is impossible for a man who writes his sermons to arrange his matter, and turn and choose his thoughts, so as to produce the same effect as when he addresses the people directly, and makes them feel that he means them."

3. Education for ministers should all be theological in the sense that secular disciplines should only be studied from a theological perspective.

4. "All ministers should be revival ministers, and all preaching should be revival preaching" in the sense that it promotes holiness, it inculcates doctrines to be practiced.

5. Two mistaken objections have been made to such preaching:

a. it lets down the dignity of the pulpit.

b. it is theatrical.

6. Ministers should be chosen not on the basis of whether they are popular or learned but on that of whether they are wise to win souls.

"Finally It is the duty of the church to pray for us, ministers."[60]

Nearly everything that needs to be said about Finney's understanding of how preaching should be done is included in that outline, but the significance of some of his remarks needs to be underlined by reference to parallel statements in his *Autobiography.* At the outset, the difference between him and his predecessors in the Congregationalist-Presbyterian tradition needs to be noted.[61] He summarized their objections to him in a paragraph:

> They used to complain that I let down the dignity of the pulpit, that I was a disgrace to the ministerial profession, that I talked like a lawyer at the bar, that I talked to the people in a colloquial manner, that I said "you," instead of preaching about sin and sinners, and saying "they," that I said "hell," and with such an emphasis as often to shock people;

> furthermore, that I urged people with such vehemence as if they might not have a moment to live; and sometimes they complained that I blamed people too much.[62]

His opponents considered talking like a lawyer at the bar a shortcoming, but he regarded it as a virtue. He said that he had interpreted the Bible from the beginning "as I would have understood the same or like passages in a law book" (42, cf. 89). The qualities of legal speech that appealed to him were its simplicity, its logic, and the way that it was directed to getting a verdict on the spot. Thus preachers should define their terms and not assume what needs to be proved (8, 7). His hyper-Calvinist opponents did not preach that way; the biblical passages with which they supported their doctrines would not have been considered at all conclusive in a court of law (60).

He quoted against them the remarks of a supreme court judge: "Our object in addressing a jury, is to get their minds settled before they leave the jury box. . . . We are set on getting a verdict. Hence we are set upon being understood." Most ministers, the judge said, do not share that purpose; "They rather seem to aim at making fine literary productions, and displaying great eloquence and an ornate use of language" (85-86). Finney says in another place, "If advocates at the bar should pursue the same course in pleading the cause of their clients, that ministers do in pleading the cause of Christ with sinners, they would not gain a single case" (155).

On the whole, Finney seems to have approved of the members of his former profession more than he did those of his latter. He said, "As a general thing, they take a more intelligent view of the whole plan of salvation, than any other class of men to whom I have preached" (368). In one of his Rochester revivals, he had a special course of sermons for them. He certainly thought more highly of legal than ministerial training (85-97). And he always taught doctrine more like someone with legal than with theological training. There is also in his teaching a certain legalism, as in such remarks as "For me the Law and Gospel have but one rule of life; and every violation of the spirit of the Law, is also a violation of the spirit of the Gospel" (339). (For a sermon that shows how much he was shaped by a legal approach, **see Vol. 2, pp. 405-19.**)

Ways in which his preaching resembled an attorney's efforts to win a verdict are his use of colloquial speech and his illustrations.

> I used to meet from ministers a great many rebuffs and reproofs, particularly in respect to my manner of preaching. . . . They would

> reprove me for illustrating my ideas by reference to the common affairs of men, as I was in the habit of doing. Among farmers and mechanics, and other classes, I borrowed illustrations from their various occupations. I tried also to use such language as they would understand. I addressed them in the language of the common people. (I sought to express all my ideas in few words, and in words that were in common use.) (81)

The result was that "people have often said to me: 'Why, you do not preach. You talk to the people....He don't preach; he only explains what other people preach.' Or, again, 'You talk as if you were as much at home as if you sat in the parlor'" (91). To be effective, sermons must also repeat the main points over and over until they have entered the consciousness of the congregation (83 passim).

His own practice and the response to it gave him distinct opinions about how seminarians should be trained:

> Men cannot learn to preach by study without practice. The students should be encouraged to exercise, and prove, and improve their gifts and calling of God, by going out into any places open to them, and holding Christ up to the people in earnest talks. They must thus learn to preach. Instead of this, the students are required to write what they call sermons, and present them for criticism; to preach—that is, read—them to a class and a professor. Thus they play at preaching. . . . This reading of elegant literary essays, is not to [the people] preaching. . . . The students are taught to cultivate a fine, elevated style of writing. As for real eloquence, that gushing, impressive and persuasive oratory, that naturally flows from an educated man whose soul is on fire with his subject, and who is free to pour out his heart to a waiting and earnest people, they have none of it. (90)

In addition to being in conversational language and clearly illustrated from the experience of the congregation, preaching must be extemporaneous. Finney not only often castigates written sermons, but also describes his own method of sermon preparation.

> My habit has always been to study the Gospel, and the best application of it, all the time. . . . Then, in the light of the Holy Spirit, I take a subject that I think will meet their present necessities. I think intensely on it, and pray much over the subject on Sabbath morning, for example, and get my mind full of it, and then go and pour it out to the people. . . . I think I have studied all the more for not having written my

> sermons. . . . I simply note the heads upon which I wish to dwell in the briefest possible manner, and in language not a word of which I use, perhaps, in preaching. (94)[63]

The frequency of his sermons and the demand of other duties meant that he often did not have opportunity to think of what he was going to say until the last minute.[64]

> Some of the most telling sermons I have ever preached in Oberlin, I have thus received after the bell had rung for church; and I was obliged to go and pour them off from my full heart, without jotting down more than the briefest possible skeleton, and that sometimes not covering half the ground that I covered in my sermon. (96)

For him, this dearth of immediate preparation was not irresponsible, but was instead a dependence upon divine inspiration.

> I held that the Holy Spirit operates in the preacher, clearly revealing these truths in their proper order, and enabling him to set them before the people in such proportion and in such order as is calculated to convert them. (155, cf. 55)

The reason such plain and persuasive language and, even more, such inspiration is necessary is that the eternal destiny of precious souls is at stake:

> A reflecting mind will feel as if it were infinitely out of place to present in the pulpit to immortal souls, hanging upon the verge of everlasting death, such specimens of learning and rhetoric. They know that men do not do so on any subject where they are really in earnest. The captain of a fire company, when a city is on fire, does not read to his company an essay, or exhibit a fine specimen of rhetoric, when he shouts to them and directs their movements. . . . This is the reason why, formerly, the ignorant Methodist preachers and the earnest Baptist preachers produced so much more effect than our most learned theologians and divines. . . . Great sermons lead the people to praise the preacher. Good preaching leads the people to praise the Savior. (90-91)

That, however, was not the way of his opponents:

> You would scarcely get the idea from the sermons that are heard, either in this country or in England, that ministers expect or intend, to be instrumental in converting, at any time, anybody in the house. (410, cf. 43, 155)

> They often preach about the Gospel instead of preaching the Gospel. They often preach about sinners instead of preaching to them. . . . I have often said, "Do not think I am talking about anybody else; but I mean you, and you, and you." (92)

Evangelistic preaching aimed at conversions then and there was the only sort of preaching for which Finney had any use. That preoccupation determined both the way he went about preaching and all of the other "means" that he used in his revivals. His method of preaching was to hammer away at his congregation for two hours at a time or more, to break down the unconverted until they had to admit they were sinners who deserved eternal damnation if they did not repent and accept salvation at that very moment.

It often appeared brutal to others, but he felt that anything else would make him a party to the loss of their souls. "It seemed to myself as if I could rain hail and love upon them at the same time; or in other words, that I could rain upon them hail, in love" (101). "It was a fire and a hammer breaking the rock and as a sword that was piercing to the dividing asunder of soul and spirit" is the way he described his preaching on another occasion (65).

He tried to show his listeners that all delay was only an evasion of present duty (80).

> We insisted then, as I have ever done since, on immediate submission, as the only thing that God could accept at their hands; and that all delay, under any pretext whatever, was rebellion against God. (190)

His message was consistent with his medium:

> Sinners were not encouraged to expect the Holy Ghost to convert them, while they were passive; and never told to wait God's time, but were taught, unequivocally, that their first and immediate duty was, to submit themselves to God, to renounce their own will, their own way, and themselves, and instantly to deliver up all that they were, and all that they had, to their rightful owner, the Lord Jesus Christ. They were taught here, as everywhere in those revivals, that the only obstacle in the way was their own stubborn will; that God was trying to gain their unqualified consent to give up their sins, and accept the Lord Jesus Christ as their righteousness and salvation. . . . [In meetings of inquiry he made a course of remarks] calculated to strip them of every excuse, and bring them face to face with the great question of present, unqualified, universal acceptance of the will of God in Christ Jesus. . . . The doctrine of the justice of endless punishment was fully insisted upon; and not only its justice, but

> the certainty that sinners will be endlessly punished, if they die in their sins, was strongly held forth. (363-64, cf. 77, 134-35, 189)

Finney not only pressed for an immediate decision, but also provided means by which those under conviction could respond then and there. He did not introduce the Methodist mourners' bench or "anxious seat" until his first great revival at Rochester, but he began very early in his ministry to see that people had an opportunity to respond to the pressure for conversion by some simple act such as standing or kneeling (116, 164 passim). The other means he used also reinforced the emotional pressure to submit to his call for conversion:

> The means that I had all along used, thus far, in promoting revivals, were much prayer, secret and social, public preaching, personal conversation, and visitation from house to house; and when inquirers became multiplied, I appointed meetings for them, and invited those that were inquiring to meet for instruction, suited to their necessities. These were the means and the only means, that I had thus far used, in attempting to secure the conversion of souls.[65] (160, cf. 77, 80)

For all that his revivals were designed to be emotional pressure cookers, however, Finney remained enough of a Presbyterian (or was concerned enough about his reputation and influence in the areas to which he wished to take the revival) to see that things were done decently and in order. In his autobiography he often takes pains to show that "converts were sound, and the work permanent and genuine" (105). He also stresses that revivals were not emotionally excessive, as, for example, the meeting at Rome, New York: "It is difficult to conceive so deep and universal a state of religious feeling, with no instance of disorder, or tumult, or fanaticism, or anything that was objectionable" (170). In much the same spirit are countless remarks about the upper-class status of those who were converted or who supported and called for the revivals.

In many ways, the culmination of Finney's work as an evangelist was the Awakening of 1858, which began in Hamilton, Ontario, and quickly spread through the northern United States. Triggered by the financial panic of the previous year, it began in many cities with businessmen gathering spontaneously for noonday prayers; as many as ten thousand met in various places in New York City. James Gordon Bennett and Horace Greeley made coverage of the Awakening a regular feature in their newspapers. College campuses were as affected as business districts.

> Estimates of the total number of converts in the Awakening of 1858 have varied somewhat. Finney declared, "It was estimated that during

> this revival not less than five hundred thousand souls were converted in this country," and this may be one of the lower approximations. At times the reports from various places seemed to indicate that, for the climactic five months from February to June 1858, some fifty thousand persons were making commitments each week, which would raise the estimate considerably above Finney's. The total will never be known, but the fact that the Awakening of 1858 was utterly lacking in fanaticism, solemn, devoted to prayer, and led by laymen, makes it unique in American history.[66]

Largely through the efforts of Charles Grandison Finney, the shape of revivals in America had changed. The Calvinism of the First Great Awakening was dead and buried. The excesses of the southern Second Awakening had been tamed. The decorous demurrals of conservative northern revivalists were silenced. The soul of the North, and especially its urban aristocracies, was reflexively evangelical. And Finney's "new measures" were everywhere accepted as the way to have a revival. Indeed, his *Lectures on Revivals* is still the accepted textbook for almost anyone who wishes to have a protractive meeting.[67]

FOR FURTHER READING

The Autobiography of Peter Cartwright, the Backwoods Preacher. Edited with introduction by Charles L. Wallis. Pierce & Washabaugh, 1956: reprint, Nashville: Abingdon, 1984.

Conkin, Paul K. *Cane Ridge: America's Pentecost.* The Curti Lectures. Madison and London: University of Wisconsin Press, 1990.

Finney, Charles G. *An Autobiography.* Old Tappan, N.J.: Fleming H. Revell, 1876, renewed 1908.

________. *Lectures on Revivals of Religion.* New revised edition. Oberlin, Ohio: E. J. Goodrich, 1868.

Hardman, Keith J. *Charles Grandison Finney, 1792–1875: Revivalist and Reformer.* Syracuse: Syracuse University Press, 1987; republished by Baker Book House in 1990.

Johnson, Charles A. *The Frontier Camp Meeting: Religion's Harvest Time.* Dallas: Southern Methodist University Press, 1955; reprinted in 1985 with new introduction by Ferenc M. Szasz.

Rudolph, L. C. *Francis Asbury.* Nashville: Abingdon, 1966.

Weisberger, Bernard A. *They Gathered at the River: The Story of the Great Revivalists and Their Impact upon Religion in America.* Boston and Toronto: Little, Brown, 1958.

Notes

1. William G. McLoughlin, *Revivals, Awakenings, and Reform: An Essay on Religion and Social Change in America, 1607–1977,* Chicago History of American Religion (Chicago and London: University of Chicago Press, 1978).

2. Ibid., 12.

3. Ibid.

4. The basic American myths that have perdured and been accommodated in each revitalization of our history are: "the chosen nation, the covenant with God, the millennial manifest destiny; the higher (biblical or natural) law, against which private and social behavior is to be judged; the moral law (the Ten Commandments, the Sermon on the Mount); the laws of science, presumed to be from the Creator, and evolutionary or progressive in their purpose; the free and moral responsible individual, whose political liberty and liberty of conscience are inalienable; the work ethic (or 'Protestant ethic'), which holds that equal opportunity and hard work will bring economic success and public respect to all who assert and discipline themselves; and the benevolence of nature under the exploitative or controlling hand of man (i.e., nature was made for man)" (ibid., 103).

5. Nathan O. Hatch, *The Democratization of American Christianity* (New Haven and London: Yale University Press, 1989).

6. Ibid., 5.

7. Ibid.

8. Paul K. Conkin, *Cane Ridge: America's Pentecost,* The Curti Lectures (Madison and London: University of Wisconsin Press, 1990), 27. This admirable monograph is drawn on heavily for this treatment of the Cane Ridge Revival.

9. In the sense that a congregation or an area was experiencing intensified religious emotions. Revival in the sense of a protracted meeting held to bring in such a period is anachronistic for the time.

10. See above, chapter 17. Marilyn J. Westerkamp has seen the Scotch-Irish sacraments as the inspiration of the First as well as the Second Great Awakening in America. She also has identified a lay rather than a clerical impetus for the Awakening. *The Triumph of the Laity: Scots-Irish Piety and the Great Awakening, 1625–1760* (New York and Oxford: Oxford University Press, 1988).

11. Conkin, *Cane Ridge,* 31. Although tents in the modern sense of fabric-covered shelters came to be a standard feature of camp meetings, and even though Charles Finney and others were to hold tent revivals, in the passage quoted "tent" is used in the technical sense of Presbyterians of the time that referred to the permanent outdoor canopied platform from which preaching was done at a communion meeting. Ibid., 19.

12. There is much disagreement over what was the original camp meeting, depending on how one defines that event and other factors, including the denominational allegiance of the particular scholar. Conkin, however, says judiciously that "by most later images of camps, [the Gasper River meeting] scarcely qualified; there had been no planning, no tents or cabins, no regulations." Ibid., 61.

13. Ibid., 97-98 n. 22.

14. "Exercises" was the term used at the time.

15. Quoted, ibid., 93-94, in a letter from a Kentucky minister included in a letter from Moses Hoge to Dr. Ashbel Green, September 10, 1801, in William Wallis Woodward, *Increase of Piety, or Revival of Religion in the United States of America* (Newburyport, Conn.: Angier March, 1802), 53.

16. *The Biography of Eld. Barton Warren Stone, Written by Himself: With Additions and Reflections by Elder John Rogers* (Cincinnati: J. A. and U. P. James, 1847), 39-42. Quoted in Max Ward Randall, *The Great Awakenings and the Restoration Movement* (Joplin, Mo.: College Press, 1983), 51-52. See also Bernard A. Weisberger, *They Gathered at the River: The Story of the Great Revivalists and Their Impact upon Religion in America* (Boston and Toronto: Little, Brown, 1958), 34-35.

17. Conkin, *Cane Ridge,* 65.

18. Ibid., 103.

19. Ibid., 104-5. Nor are such religious exercises confined to the remote past. Near the time this section was being written, a story appeared in a national newsmagazine concerning the spread of the phenomenon known as the "Toronto Blessing," which causes people caught up in ecstatic worship to fall to the floor in uncontrollable laughter, some jerking spasmodically. Apparently more than one hundred thousand persons have already undergone this experience. Furthermore, "Anglicans—known for their reserve at worship—seem especially prone to catching the new spirit" (*Newsweek,* February 20, 1995, 54). Another point Conkin made later about the emotionalism of the Cane Ridge revival was that "such a warm religion enabled humble people, whose lives were so much more insecure and cruel than our own, to have fun. That was not a mean achievement" (*Cane Ridge,* 178).

20. Ibid., 106.

21. Ibid., 91.

22. For a much more extensive discussion of the loss of that centrality, see Doug Adams, *Meeting House to Camp Meeting: Toward a History of American Free Church Worship from 1620 to 1835* (Saratoga, Fla.: Modern Liturgy-Resource Publications; Austin, Tex.: Sharing Company, 1981, 1984).

23. Those who left the Presbyterian Church at that time, of course, were to view their actions not as schisms, but as founding churches in which a more scriptural form of Christianity was taught and practiced.

24. Now part of the United Church of Christ, having merged with Congregationalists in 1931.

25. Hatch, *The Democratization of American Christianity,* 3.

26. Ibid., 91. On this general subject, see also pp. 7, 8, 50-52, and 92.

27. L. C. Rudolph, *Francis Asbury* (Nashville: Abingdon, 1966), 70. Wesley's name was restored in 1789 as a courtesy, but he died without accepting the independence of the American branch of the movement he founded.

28. It is amazing that a critical biography of Asbury has yet to appear. The most often cited work is that of a descendant who was a journalist and not a follower in the faith; Herbert Asbury, *A Methodist Saint: The Life of Bishop Asbury* (New York: Knopf, 1927). Asbury's journal was republished in three volumes by Abingdon Press in 1958 (*The Journal and Letters of Francis Asbury,* ed. Elmer T. Clark, J. Manning Potts, and Jacob S. Payton), but, as informative as that is, it can hardly be considered objective. Perhaps the best treatment available is the short work of Rudolph cited above.

29. Ibid., *The Journal and Letters of Francis Asbury,* for July 29, 1776 (1:195).

30. Ibid. for March 6, 1793 (1:750).

31. Merrill R. Abbey, *The Epic of United Methodist Preaching: A Profile in American Social History* (Lanham, N.Y.: University Press of America, 1984), 20.

32. Rudolph, *Francis Asbury,* 84-85. This description of Asbury's preaching is based on ibid., 80-94.

33. Charles L. Wallis, "Introduction," in *The Autobiography of Peter Cartwright* (Pierce & Washabaugh, 1956; Nashville: Abingdon, 1984), 6.

34. In this he was not unlike Asbury, who thought the Reformation small potatoes beside the Wesleyan awakening and believed that true episcopacy had not existed between the apostle's times and its itinerant restoration by American Methodists. Rudolph, *Francis Asbury,* 171-73, 186-206.

35. Quoted in Charles A. Johnson, *The Frontier Camp Meeting: Religion's Harvest Time* (Dallas: Southern Methodist University Press, 1955, as reprinted in 1985 with new intro. by Ferenc M. Szasz), 151.

36. Wallis, *The Autobiography of Peter Cartwright,* 245.

37. Ibid., 266.

38. Ibid., 236. For similar passages, see pp. 63-66, 114, 204, 212, 236-37, 244-46, 265, 316, and especially 267-68.

39. This is not unlike the fate of the legacy of Jonathan Edwards. It came to be overtaken by the Genteel Tradition, as in Edwards Amasa Park, who wrote: "We bow before this father of our New England theology with the profoundest veneration. . . . Yet we can not help wishing that he had been something more of a brother and somewhat less of a champion." He goes on to say that they needed a theology to take with them into the flower garden. Quoted by Herbert May, "Jonathan Edwards and America," in *Jonathan Edwards and the American Experience,* ed. Nathan O. Hatch and Harry S. Stout (New York: Oxford University Press, 1988), 22.

40. The author of the standard monograph on camp meetings, Charles A. Johnson, begins his preface by saying: "Among all of the weapons forged by the West in its struggle against lawlessness and immorality, few were more successful than the frontier camp meeting" (*The Frontier Camp Meeting,* xix). In this he followed the interpretation of his mentor, William Warren Sweet.

41. Ibid., 173.

42. Quoted ibid., 188. This paragraph and the next are based on pp. 170-91.

43. Ibid., 177.

44. Weisberger, *They Gathered at the River,* 84.

45. Quoted from his *Autobiography,* 1:100-101, in ibid., 72-73.

46. Ibid., 66.

47. Charles G. Finney, *An Autobiography* (Old Tappan, N.J.: Fleming H. Revell, 1876, renewed 1908), 63. Finney's actual term was "burnt district," but the other form has been standard at least since Whitney R. Cross published his book with that title in 1950.

48. Ibid., 24.

49. Keith J. Hardman, *Charles Grandison Finney, 1792–1875: Revivalist and*

Reformer (Syracuse: Syracuse University Press, 1987; republished by Baker in 1990), 52. This is the only modern scholarly biography.

50. For a map of Finney's evangelistic activity, see ibid., 1.

51. Ibid., 82.

52. Ibid., 84.

53. The differences between Beecher and Finney were more political than theological, Beecher being a Federalist defender of the established order of New England and Finney showing a Jacksonian democratic spirit.

54. Ibid., 220.

55. A hint of their effect can be given by saying that they remind one of the eyes of master villains in superhero comic books. They seem to emit X-rays that can see right through you and laser beams that can saw you in half.

56. Charles G. Finney, *Lectures on Revivals of Religion,* new rev. ed. (Oberlin, Ohio: E. J. Goodrich, 1868). Finney regarded these lectures as sermons and they follow his typical sermon outline. Yet the lectures do not represent his *ipsissima verba:* they were taken down while he delivered them by the editor of the *Evangelist,* who did not know shorthand. Finney said that the lectures averaged an hour and three-quarters in length while one in published form can be read aloud in half an hour (Finney, *An Autobiography,* 330).

57. Finney was an ardent opponent of slavery, but he considered promoting abolition to be a distraction from the even more important cause of winning souls. His strategy for eliminating slavery was to have churches universally condemn it as sin, with the expected result that "in three years, a public sentiment would be formed that would carry all before it, and there would not be a shackled slave, nor a bristling, cruel slaveowner, in this land" (ibid., 302).

58. Emphasis in all quotations from this chapter is Finney's.

59. "Remarks" is Finney's usual designation for the application section of his sermons.

60. Finney, *Lectures on Revivals of Religion,* 185-212.

61. By this time, the two traditions were so alike that it was even possible to have united "Presbygational" congregations, although there were groups in both churches that stoutly insisted on differences.

62. Finney, *An Autobiography,* 83. Hereafter in this section, page numbers of quoted material from this work will be cited parenthetically in the text.

63. Finney says that he wrote down nothing for his first twelve years of preaching. His first sermon "skeletons" were written after he preached the sermon rather than before. Yet he found he could never reuse one of those sermon outlines. A specimen skeleton in his handwriting is reproduced in his *Autobiography,* on facing pp. 96-97.

64. At the beginning of his ministry, his presbytery, having heard of his impromptu preaching, arranged an occasion on which he would have to do it before them (ibid., 82).

65. To this list should be added the apparatus and infrastructure created for city-wide revivals, at least from Rochester on.

66. Hardman, *Charles Grandison Finney,* 433.

67. Finney even shaped the architecture of evangelism. In his directions for the construction of Broadway Tabernacle, he anticipated most of the provisions

Spurgeon would make at his Metropolitan Tabernacle to have every eye in the church focused on the preacher, and did so in the year Spurgeon was born (Finney, *An Autobiography,* 326). He even commissioned an enormous tent that was largely used to make up for the lack of an auditorium of adequate size at Oberlin, but it "was used, to some extent also, for holding protracted meetings in the region round about" (ibid., 336), possibly making Finney the first tent evangelist.

CHAPTER 20

"THE FRUITS OF FERVOR" (A)

AMONG AFRICAN AMERICANS

THE SOCIAL IMPLICATIONS OF GOSPEL PREACHING[1]

Revivalism was the dominant influence on all major denominations in the United States between 1840 and 1865, especially in the larger cities. During this period, American Protestantism took on four qualities that have characterized it ever since: (1) lay leadership, (2) interdenominational cooperation, (3) an emphasis on ethics over theology, and (4) the replacement of the Calvinist doctrine of election with belief in the human acceptance of salvation as determinative. Furthermore, this regnant revivalism both reflected and helped shape an interconnected series of elements in the American *zeitgeist* during that era, which included optimism, perfectionism,[2] and millennialism.

These elements of mid-nineteenth-century urban revivalism had inevitable social implications. It used to be assumed that revivalism as a force had pretty well run its course before the Civil War and that it would not reemerge until the end of the century and then only among socially marginal groups. It was further assumed that the emphasis on social ethics in American Christianity owed its origins entirely to the liberal tradition. It is now recognized, however, that "Evangelical Protestantism reached the summit of its influence in America during the last half of the nineteenth century."[3] Furthermore, during the quarter century ending with the end of war,

> a widespread aspiration for Christian perfection complemented in many ways the social idealism which endeavored to reform the drunkard, free the slaves, elevate womankind, and banish poverty and vice from the country.[4]

This is not to say that exclusive credit for these social movements should go to revivalism. Rather, as Timothy Smith has said:

> Whatever may have been the role of other factors, the quest for perfection joined with compassion for poor and needy sinners and a rebirth of millennial expectation to make popular Protestantism a mighty social force long before the slavery conflict erupted into war.[5]

Many of these points can be documented in the persons and movements surveyed in the previous chapter. John Wesley told William Wilberforce in a letter dated February 24, 1791, that he considered American slavery to be "the vilest that ever saw the sun."[6] Almost twenty years earlier he had published his negative *Thoughts upon Slavery.* Thomas Coke and Francis Asbury shared the founder's opinion and did all in their power to make it impossible for anyone who owned slaves to be a Methodist in good standing. Southerners in the General Conference, however, refused to permit rules against slavery to stay on the books. Asbury ultimately had to settle for evangelizing the slaves instead of working to free them.[7]

Peter Cartwright shared the opinion of Brother Axley that "a preacher that was good and true, had a trinity of devils to fight, namely: superfluous dress, whiskey, and slavery."[8] Cartwright moved from Kentucky to Illinois so that his children would not have to grow up in a state where slavery was practiced, and then ran for the legislature in order to oppose efforts to open his new state to slavery.[9]

Charles G. Finney was equally opposed. He wrote:

> Deprive a human being of liberty who has been guilty of no crime; rob him of himself—his body—his soul—his time, and his earnings, to promote the interests of his master, and attempt to justify this on the principles of moral law! It is the greatest absurdity, and the most revolting wickedness.[10]

Finney would not permit slaveowners to receive Communion at Chatham Street Chapel, and he made the admission of African American students one of the conditions of his joining the faculty at Oberlin.

None of these men, however, could be considered an abolitionist in the strict sense. Each saw eternal salvation as a higher good than earthly freedom. Besides, William Garrison and other abolitionists often expressed anti-Christian sentiments, making it hard for clergy to align themselves with the cause. Further, Cartwright was even more committed to preventing the schism of southern Methodists than he was to opposing slavery. And Finney was not an integrationist; he insisted on segregated seating in the Chatham Street Chapel, even over the opposition of his largest donors, Arthur and Lewis Tappan.

Another moral crusade in which all these evangelists were engaged is that of total abstinence, which was just coming into vogue as an easier goal to reach than true temperance. Peter Cartwright admired the wisdom of John Wesley in interdicting dram drinking in the Rules of his United Societies, and, although in the United States the rule was (to misinterpret Hamlet) more honored in the breach than the observance, this prototypical circuit rider was not at all inclined to go along with the laxity of the prevailing fashion—especially when, as was often the case, the offender was ordained.[11]

As noted in the previous chapter, Finney included the cause of temperance in his first great campaign in Rochester. He invited his young convert Theodore Weld to come and lead that aspect of the work. Finney even consented to suspending evangelistic work for a while so that the cause of temperance could be given exclusive attention. Weld later would become one of the leading abolitionists of the Oberlin group. This eventually was to come between Weld and Finney, since the young disciple began to consider ending slavery to be the most urgent demand upon Christian conscience and activity. For Finney, the most pressing insight (and also the most elusive) was to comprehend that all evils afflicting human society—wrongs done to women, slavery, drunkenness, war, and all the rest—were but natural consequences of *sin,* and that if faithful pastors attacked this central evil by the cure of conversion, in time all subordinate evils would begin to diminish.[12]

Nevertheless, Finney did speak out against the other evils, considering it the evangelist's duty not only to convert the unsaved but also to help reborn souls know how to live out the life into which they had been initiated. Thus revival preaching always included a strong dose of attacks upon the ills of the day. What Charles Johnson said of the preachers at camp meetings could apply to all revivalists of the Second Great Awakening and their heirs:

> The itinerants were not socially myopic, as their sermon themes indicate. They considered it their spiritual obligation to strike out against all forms of sin. In pungent language the evils of the day were fearlessly denounced: immorality, intemperance, tobacco, blasphemy, dueling, card playing, horse racing, and gambling.[13]

To contemporary consciousness, that list of evils must appear a curious blend of the personal and the corporate. Yet the lines were not so clearly drawn then as they are today; for example, much of the passion behind the abstinence movement was a conviction that drunkenness was a major cause of poverty. In any case, having these social evils and bad habits blended together so indiscriminately does not weaken Smith's assertion that a major by-product of the Second Great Awakening was the preaching of social reform.

ETHIOPIA STRETCHES OUT HER HANDS UNTO GOD:[14] THE BEGINNING OF AFRICAN AMERICAN PREACHING

The extension of preaching topics to include social reform was not the only fruit of the Second Awakening fervor. One of the most obvious and beneficial was a broadening of understanding about the social groups whose members were eligible to preach. Until this time in America, it had been generally assumed that preaching was beyond the capacity of any but a white male. A result of the Awakening was that there came to be significant numbers of women and African American preachers. Of the two groups, the latter was the larger, and we will consider it first.

The majority of African American slaves did not become Christians until after the second decade of the nineteenth century.[15] There is a variety of reasons for that, including a desire of their owners that they not do so, a shortage of clergy to evangelize them, and an effort to get them to accept Christianity through the uncongenial method of catechesis rather than conversion. The more emotional means of evangelization introduced in the Second Great Awakening—means that had something in common with African traditional religion—however, made Christianity, especially in its Methodist and Baptist manifestations, more attractive to some slaves and free persons of color. And some of their number began to preach; "Black Harry" Hosier, for instance, who accompanied Asbury and other Methodist leaders, was often regarded as a better preacher than the white clergy with whom he traveled.

Black Christians were either included in white congregations or founded their own, and preachers of their race were heard in both configurations.

The founding of African American denominations occurred largely in the North and was the work of free blacks, yet there were congregations in the South composed largely of slaves. The ability of persons in bondage to participate in any public religious activities varied considerably from time to time and place to place. For instance, owners for a long time refused to allow their slaves to be baptized, under the impression that doing so would imply manumission. Most owners also would not allow the people belonging to them to be educated, for fear they would become less subservient. And, after some slave rebellions grew out of Methodist groups, especially those connected with Nat Turner and Denmark Vessey, many southern states passed laws against preaching by slaves. Instead, white missionary activity directed to this human chattel was promoted on the theory that it would make them more obedient servants. At other times, black preaching was permitted, but only when whites were present to make certain nothing subversive was said.

The condition of slavery was so oppressive, however, that such participation in public institutions was not to be the rule of slave religion. The norm was to be the "invisible institution" mentioned by Albert J. Raboteau in the subtitle of *Slave Religion*: secret and illegal gatherings of African Americans for worship on plantations. These often occurred in the middle of the night in fields, gullies, or thickets—places away from the observation of the whites. Even more than their other gatherings, these clandestine praise meetings, or "shouts," were times of fervent emotional outbursts in which tormented people sought the strength to endure their difficult lives. Shouting, hand-clapping, ring dancing, and transports of ecstasy, often choreographed by one of their own who had been called to preach, marked these precious moments of release.

Their own Christian congregations, whether churches or the clandestine gatherings on plantations, were the only institution over which African Americans had complete control.[16] It is not surprising, therefore, that these congregations became a natural sphere for the development of leadership within their number. One of the first to point out the significance of that leadership was W. E. B. DuBois, who wrote in 1903:

> The Preacher is the most unique personality developed by the Negro on American soil. A leader, a politician, an orator, a "boss," an intriguer, an idealist,—all these he is, and ever, too, the centre of a group of men, now twenty, now a thousand in number.[17]

Some of these clergy proved to be among the most eloquent preachers of their day. They seem to have developed two distinct homiletical styles, styles that can be seen in the African American church to this day. One labored (successfully) to show that members of their race were as intellectually capable as whites, and that they could produce sermons that were as eloquent and closely argued as the best white preaching of the time. The other style discovered kinship between the ecstatic preaching of the Second Great Awakening and African religious traditions that enabled them to meet their congregations at the deepest emotional level. Thus the different types of preaching served different social functions within the African American community.

William E. Montgomery has criticized the tendency to speak of "the black church" as though it were monolithic, and has pointed to the social stratification within its different expressions of Christian faith.[18] He designates the two types of congregation—and preaching—as "elite" and "folk." These are not mutually exclusive or polar opposite categories, but instead represent the extreme positions on a spectrum. They are, however, a convenient distinction for looking at African American preaching.

Both preaching methods are worthy of study. Unfortunately, they cannot both be studied in the same way. Inevitably, the literary tradition has left much more extensive documentation. The ecstatic tradition, however, has been so impressive that it has been the object of a great deal of analytical attention. Consequently, the two preaching styles will have to be studied separately. The literary tradition can be examined in the ministries and pulpit work of two of its greatest exemplars: C. T. Walker and Charles Albert Tindley.[19] The ecstatic tradition is accessible mainly through secondhand reports and the efforts of scholars to interpret what they have heard or heard about, although it can be seen in part in the preaching of John Jasper.

Learned Preaching

The elite tradition can be seen as early as the late-eighteenth century in the life of **Lemuel Haynes.** The son of a black father, Haynes was abandoned by his white mother in infancy, but he was taken into the home of a white church deacon and raised as a member of the family. Well educated, he prepared for the ministry after serving in the American army during the Revolution. Apparently his racial mixture did not limit him in any way; he served in several pastorates with great success, had sermons published, and was consulted by the presidents of Yale and Amherst on matters of doctrine. In a famous sermon against the doctrine of universal salvation, he attributed the doctrine to Satan in the Garden of Eden, when he said: "Ye shall not surely die!" This proclamation of doctrine, Haynes said, made Satan a preacher, of whom it could be said that he was old, cunning, laborious, heterogeneous, presumptuous, and successful.[20]

While the preaching of Haynes can be called elite, and it is the work of a man of some African ancestry, it hardly represents the preaching of the black church as such. To see that in its fullest development, it helps to look at the proclamation of a minister who was born into slavery and, to show that talent was not the result of an admixture of white blood, one who was "a Negro in every drop of his blood."[21] Such a person was the preacher who came to be called "the Black Spurgeon," **Charles T. Walker.** The son of a black deacon who was his master's coachman and who died the day before he was born, Walker lived his first seven years as a slave.[22] Two of his uncles were preachers, however, one of whose freedom was purchased by his congregation, Franklin Covenant Baptist Church, founded in 1848 near Hepzibah, Georgia. His mother died during her first year of freedom, and her eight-year-old son was passed from relative to relative until he could care for himself. He worked as a field hand on his pastor uncle's large farm, and was converted at the age of fifteen after a struggle of three days.

His call to preach came not long afterward, and he felt the need to become educated. His mother had taught him his ABC's and how to read John 14. He had also spent two five-month terms in a school operated by the Freedman's Bureau. In the fall of his sixteenth year, he began to study at the Augusta Institute, a school formed to train black preachers by a former slaveowner, which later became Atlanta Baptist Seminary and then Atlanta Baptist College. After two years there he graduated and was ordained. Already popular as a "boy preacher," he soon had four churches to serve. Two years later he married. Moving to LaGrange, Georgia, he preached two revivals in the church he served for three years, during which four hundred were converted, three hundred of whom became church members.

Walker was then called to and eventually became pastor of what later became known as Tabernacle Baptist Church in Augusta. Under his leadership it soon had a new brick building that seated eight hundred and had a pipe organ. It was paid for within two years. During the fourteen years he was pastor at Tabernacle Baptist, there were two thousand conversions and fourteen hundred baptisms. He was also active in civic affairs, helping to found a weekly newspaper as well as a high school and a normal school for his people, and leading an exposition to demonstrate the progress of the Negro. He also saved many from jail; paid fines and rent; furnished food, clothing, and fuel; reconciled marriages; sent children to school; got jobs for adults; and brought many to Christ.[23] During the same period, he conducted revivals throughout the state, served in many church offices, was a trustee of colleges, acted as a member of the State Executive Committee for the Republican Party, and became "the best known Negro minister in the state."[24] He became the first cleric of his race to be sent to Europe and the Holy Land by his congregation, and his lectures about the trip were eventually published as a book.

During all this time, Walker was becoming known nationally. He was a leader of the National Baptist Convention and had been awarded a D.D. by the State University of Kentucky. He served as a chaplain in Cuba during the Spanish-American War, and became a vice president of the International Sunday School Convention in 1899. He also began preaching revivals in many of the major cities of the country. When he preached in the Exposition Park in Atlanta to audiences of eight thousand whites and blacks, the *Constitution* said that he had drawn as many if not more people than the legendary white evangelists Sam Jones and Dwight L. Moody.[25]

These successes resulted in his being called in 1899 to Mt. Olivet Baptist Church in New York City, a church to whose building fund John D. Rockefeller and other prominent Baptists had contributed. Its membership increased from 430 to 1,800 in two years, with the result that Walker preached to "the largest regular congregation of any man in New York City, white or black."[26] Thus, in accordance with the custom of the times, his sermons were regularly and favorably reviewed by the New York press.

His sermon preparation consisted of prayer, Bible reading, and meditation. He said: "I know what I'm going to say before I come into the pulpit. I know the hymns I am going to sing, the chapter I'm going to read, and I know where the text is to be found."[27] The daily newspaper was his favorite source of information outside the Bible. According to his biographer:

> When he enters the pulpit, free from the narrowness that muts [sic] come to the man who uses only his Bible commentary, he seems to feel himself under divine compulsion to deliver a message of transcendent importance to dying men; there is an air about him of a soldier who has a divine commission to fight a great battle for humanity. He speaks directly to the heart, in language all hearts can understand. Humor and pathos, pleading and scorn, impassioned exhortation and cutting sarcasm, are all used in his discourses with tremendous effect.[28]

An example of his preaching that is also informative about the history of the black church can be seen in an excerpt from the sermon he was invited to deliver at the Missionary Baptist State Convention in Georgia to commemorate the one-hundredth anniversary of the Negro Baptist Church in Georgia. His text was Numbers 23:23 (KJV): "According to this time it shall be said of Jacob and of Israel, What hath God wrought!"

> We stand today upon an eminence from which we may take a retrospective view of a one hundred years' journey. This is a glorious day. We have come to celebrate the progress and triumphs of a century. We are here to speak of the vicissitudes through which we have passed, the conflicts we have encountered . . . and the victories yet to be achieved. We are here to pass up and down the line of march from 1788 to 1888. Old fathers, worn and weary with burdens and cares of long and useful lives, their heads whitened by the frosts of many winters, infirm and superannuated, have come up to shake hands with the century, to bid Godspeed to their brethren, and, like Simeon of old, to exclaim, "Lord, now lettest thou thy servant depart in peace, for mine eyes have seen thy salvation." Young men have come to get inspiration from a review of the works of the fathers and to return to their various fields stimulated, electrified and encouraged.
>
> We shall discuss, first, what God has wrought in the permanent establishment of His church. The founder of the true church is Jesus Christ. He is the Son of Abraham, according to the flesh, and He is also the Son of God. Two natures and three offices mysteriously meet his person. He is the foundation of the true church, the chief corner stone, the lawgiver in Zion. He has given us a kingdom which cannot be moved. He began in Asia to ride in the gospel chariot. He sent out twelve small boats at first. On the day of Pentecost, 3,000 were added to the number. In 1630, He sent Roger Williams to America. In the spirit of his Master, he planted churches in New England, and the stone continued to roll until it reached the sunny South. In 1788, the oppressed, rejected and enslaved brother in black, for the first time in Georgia, lifted the Baptist flag under the leadership of Andrew Bryan. The handful of corn was sown not on the high, wild and rocky mountains, but on the seaboard; but the wind carried the seed to every part of Georgia and the barren rocks and sandy deserts became gardens of the Lord. From that handful of corn have sprung more than 1,500 churches, 500 ordained preachers, and 166,429 communicants. The little one has become a thousand. In the entire United States there are today more than 1,250,000 colored Baptists. I make bold to say here and now that the progress of the Baptists in this country has been due to the earnest, faithful and simple preaching of Christ crucified. The

fathers in their preaching did not preach philosophy, nor did they strive to reach the people with rhetorical strains of eloquence, but they strove to reach the people by preaching the plain, old-fashioned, simple truths of the gospel. The gospel declared in its truth and simplicity will make Baptists.

Third, we shall discuss what God has wrought for our race during this century. For our race, this century was one of hardship, oppression, persecution and sore trial. We were slaves; we had no moral training; no intellectual advantages during the greater part of this century and the two preceding; we were run by bloodhounds; sometimes whipped to death; we were sold from the auction block, husbands and fathers being separated from wives and children at the behest of some white man; we had to get a ticket to go to church; we had to get permission from some white man before we could join the church; we were outcasts. But all that has changed. God was against slavery, and in his own time and way He removed the foul blot from the national escutcheon. Emancipated without a dollar, without education, without friends and without competent leaders, like Hagar and Ishmael, we were turned out to die. But despite all obstacles, the Negro in Georgia has today $10,000,000 worth of property and has proven himself worthy of citizenship. We have thousands of children in our public schools. Our men will be found in the law, in the practice of medicine, in legislative halls, among teachers and professors, on the list of authors, skilled musicians, journalists, theologians, and business men. God has wrought wonderfully among us. God is still opening the way for greater progress. The cry is loud and long all the line for consecrated workers. The harvest truly is white, but the laborers are few.[29]

In recording the progress of his people, he incarnates and epitomizes it. Remarkable accomplishments, all of them.

The second example of a preacher in the literary tradition who was born in slavery is **Charles Albert Tindley.** The exact date of Tindley's birth is unknown, and details of his early life are hard to come by. Some records say he was born in 1856, but others say 1851.[30] His parents were among the few slaves owned by a farmer near Berlin on the Eastern Shore of Maryland. His mother died when he was two and his father was unable to keep him, so he was placed in the homes of others to work for his keep.[31] Some of the people who kept him were cruel, and none allowed him to own a book or go to church. He nevertheless developed a great desire for education. He says:

I used to find bits of newspaper on the roadside and put them in my bosom (for I had no pockets), in order to study the A,B,C's from them.

> During the day I would gather pine knots, and when the people were asleep at night I would light these pine knots, and, lying flat on my stomach to prevent being seen by any one who might still be about, would, with fire-coals, mark all the words I could make out on these bits of newspaper. I continued in this way, and without any teacher, until I could read the Bible almost without stopping to spell the words.[32]

Emancipation occurred at some time during his youth, and he grew up to support himself as a hod carrier[33] and to marry. Hearing of better opportunities in Philadelphia (directly north through the state of Delaware), he took his wife there and found lodgings and a job. His landlord invited the young couple to worship with him at John Wesley Methodist Episcopal Church, affiliated with the Delaware Annual Conference, an administrative provision for black congregations in the Middle Atlantic region within a basically white denomination. Tindley threw himself into the life of the congregation, participating in every activity, and even becoming its volunteer sexton when the congregation moved to a location on Bainbridge Street (from which it would take its name in 1890).

His passion for learning continued. Not being able to attend the Institute for Colored Youths because he had to work days when it was in session, he studied at night and was examined by local schoolteachers subject by subject. Somewhere along the way, he discovered his vocation to the ministry and began reading for preordination examinations under the guidance of his pastor and with the approval of his presiding elder and the encouragement of his bishop. To the surprise of the contemptuous seminary graduates with whom he was examined, he scored highly on the tests and was admitted to the conference on probation. He never lost his desire for learning. He completed the theological course at Brandywine Institute and learned both Greek and Hebrew in order to be as well prepared as possible for his ministerial work. In time, he received the doctor of divinity degree from Bennett College and Morgan College. Nevertheless, he was plagued the rest of his life by the detractions of clergy with more formal credentials; indeed, these were to subvert his election to the episcopate.

When he was admitted to the conference on probation in 1885, Tindley was sent to his first charge in Cape May, New Jersey, where he served for two years. At the end of that time, he was ordained deacon and reassigned to South Wilmington, Delaware. After ordination as an elder in 1889, he served in a variety of charges until he became pastor of the prestigious Ezion Church in Wilmington, Delaware, in 1897; he was promoted to presiding elder of that district in 1900.

From the district, Tindley went to the church he would serve the rest of his life, Bainbridge Street Methodist Episcopal—which, during his tenure, would change its name two more times: once to East Calvary and then, in his honor, to Tindley Temple. When he first arrived, however, some parishioners were embarrassed to discover that their former sexton was now their pastor. When he became pastor of the congregation it had only 130 members, but under his leadership it grew to seven thousand.[34] A church building seating thirty-two hundred that he called a cathedral was constructed while he was there, and he filled it twice on Sundays. His congregation came to have a wide variety of programs, from literary societies to the provision of meals for large numbers of the poor. Tindley had an extraordinary street ministry in which he greeted, counseled, and prayed with everyone from derelicts to the sporting crowd.

As pastor of an influential church, he became a power within the city of Philadelphia and had friendships with such figures as Russell Conwell,[35] the founder of Temple University, and John Wanamaker, the department store magnate. He also became very influential in the General Conference of the Methodist Episcopal Church, to which he was a regular delegate and at which he was a frequent preacher. And, on top of everything else, he was a talented musician and composer with more than forty-five gospel songs to his credit, five of which are in *The United Methodist Hymnal.* Two have become popular favorites: "I'll Overcome Someday"[36] and "Stand By Me."

It was for his preaching, however, that Tindley was most famous. He must have been an impressive figure in the pulpit. He was six feet three inches tall, had a booming baritone speaking voice, and a walk that "exuded self-confidence without injecting the least semblance of swagger."[37] He seems to have preached topical sermons[38] that were developed with a list of qualities. His sermon "The World's Conqueror," based upon John 16:33 (KJV) ("I have overcome the world"), has as its points "the forces which heaven employed to conquer the powers of the devil and to bring man, with all his possession, back to God."[39] These are: truth, peace, and love.

We can gain a taste of his eloquence from his definition of *love* in this sermon:

> It is the soul of one person going out, with all of its possession and powers, to make another happy. It is this going out to make others happy that is healing the scars and wiping up the blood caused by Cain's

> murderous club, and Samaritan-like, healing the wounded, providing for their comfort and paying the bill. This is the mightiest possession that any soul can have. It is the sunlight of heaven caught and stored up in the human life to shine among men. Like chunks of coal a heartful of the Love of God has banked the fires that are destined to burn up and melt the coldness of this world into the springtime of heaven. It is a flower garden in every life through which perennial streams flow. It is the songbird whose notes of melody drown the croaking of the frogs, the hiss of serpents and the growl of beast.[40]

This is little more than half of what he says on the subject, but it is enough to show the eloquence of which he was capable. (For another of Tindley's sermons, see **Vol. 2, pp. 420-30.**)

The Folk Tradition of the Chanted Sermon

The elite literary tradition represented above was always eager to distance itself from the tradition to be considered now, which was regarded as undignified, emotional, illiterate, and embarrassing. There is no standard term for referring to a sermon of this second sort. It has been called anything from "the black folk sermon" to "old-time country preaching," but Albert J. Raboteau prefers to call it "the chanted sermon" because, as he says, its defining characteristic is "the metrical, tonal, rhythmic chant with which the preacher climaxes the sermon."[41]

More on the chant later. The place to begin a description of this genre is with the recognition that, as Raboteau points out, verbal skill has always been highly valued in the black community.[42] This is as true of the elite as of the folk portion of the community,[43] but the impressive phenomenon to be noted here is the ability of persons with no access to written language to construct oral music of extraordinary beauty. Because the folk preachers could expect audiences composed of connoisseurs of linguistic sound, those who were most appreciated were virtuosos.

Thus the power of their preaching was felt by many who, in consciousness of their sophistication, were embarrassed by their own reaction of being deeply moved. But others recognized the richness of the resources displayed and went on in time to combine the technique of the folk preachers with a more rigorous theological content.[44]

The classical folk or chanted sermon always began with a text from the Bible, shaped as it was by the example of the preaching of the Great Awakening—and, indeed, most of the Christian tradition. Dependence upon a printed book posed a considerable challenge to slaves whose masters were afraid to allow them to learn to read, but many showed incredible ability to remember not only narratives but also long passages of text they had only heard. The tradition of preaching as an explication of text was so strong that

> some illiterate slave preachers of the antebellum South had their texts read for them or, lacking a Bible, pretended to read scriptural words from their hand or from a handkerchief.[45]

Henry Mitchell has a good bit to say about the use of the Bible in African American preaching. He begins by noting that while the Bible is the ultimate authority for what is preached, the black church has not tended to be Fundamentalist.

> The Black preacher is more likely to think of the Bible as an inexhaustible source of good preaching material than as an inert doctrinal and ethical authority.... His intuitively flexible approach to the Bible leads him to ask, "What is the Lord trying to tell me today in this passage of scripture?"[46]

The basic use of the Scripture is narrative, and details to enliven the story are drawn from the text itself, from biblical scholarship, and from analogy to the lives of the people. Apposite parallels from contemporary life are also used, both to bring the story to life and to show its relevance. Black illustrations tend to stick very close to the gut-level issues of life and death, of struggle and frustration. And black preachers tend to illustrate passages already chosen from the Bible on the basis of the same criteria.[47]

This means that an effective preacher in the tradition must be a first-rate storyteller, which involves dramatizing the story, playing every part in it, and making the congregation feel present at the described events. As entertaining as such storytelling is, it is never done purely for entertainment. Rather, it is through this engagement that the preacher enlists the congregation's commitment to the truth being communicated. For that involvement to occur, the suspense of the story must be maintained, no matter how familiar it is. The preacher must be a master of timing.[48]

Classical folk sermons on particular texts were repreached by others and in this manner were "passed with only slight modifications from preacher to preacher and from locality to locality."[49] These, however, were not "vain repetitions," since in the slave church there was an unspoken recognition that preaching is, among other things, a performance art, and thus the expectation of the community was not so much for originality as it was for "skill, fluency, spontaneity, and intensity."[50] The slave preachers recognized instinctively something understood by the seventeenth-century English metaphysical school of preaching: the content of a sermon cannot be separated from the way in which it is communicated.[51]

To say that the folk sermon began with a text is not to say that it was necessarily confined to its exposition. An old joke has it that clergy preach from a text—often very far from it, and this applies to most traditions. But the Bible was the main source of the language, images, and stories of the slave preachers' sermons. In this appropriation, nothing was more important than the story of Moses and the exodus: "Slaves prayed for the future day of deliverance to come, and they kept hope alive by incorporating as part of *their* mythic past the Old Testament exodus of Israel out of slavery."[52]

The basic outline of these sermons covered the announcement of the text, an elaboration of the context of the passage, and then an application of it to the lives of those who heard it. Mitchell observes that many sermons consist of retelling a Bible story with continuous application as the story unfolds. Certainly the structure is seldom deductive and tightly argued; the preacher "guides his seekers rather than arguing with his opponents."[53]

In addition to this pattern of content, there was also a pattern of sound, the structure of performance style. This justifies the designation of "chanted" sermons.[54]

> The preacher begins calmly, speaking in conversational, if oratorical and occasionally grandiloquent, prose; he then gradually begins to speak more rapidly, excitedly, and to chant his words in time to a regular beat; finally, he reaches an emotional peak in which his chanted speech becomes tonal and merges with the singing, clapping, and shouting of the congregation. Frequently, the preacher ends the sermon by returning briefly to conversational prose.[55]

The only thing that needs to be added to this description is to say that many of the sermons do not have just one peak of intensity, but will reach several minor climaxes before the major one is achieved.

The art of preaching such sermons is improvisational, because it is expected that they will be delivered extempore. This does not mean they are unprepared; indeed, the fact that many of them are repeated shows that all could not be created in the process of delivery. But the preacher must have a capacity to adjust rapidly to the immediate situation. The adjustments call for a high artistry because of the rhythmic pattern that has been established. Words must be composed on the spot to fit that pattern, and any adjustment to an earlier form of the same sermon that adapts it to the new situation has to be made in the full flow of delivery.

Bruce Rosenberg conducted research to see if connections could be made between the improvisational skill involved in the chanted sermons and that of the bards who performed the Homeric poems or *Beowulf,* and with Yugoslav *guslars* of more recent times, all of whom were able to create verse on the spur of the moment that satisfied many formal requirements.[56] While doing so, he became aware of significant differences between the material he was working with and that of the oral poets, and he became more and more interested in American folk preaching in its own right. Rosenberg did, however, see a connecting link between the preachers' art and that of the poem performers in his experience of hearing an African American preacher repeat the same phrases again and again in the course of delivering a chanted sermon.

Albert Lord had argued that what enabled the poets to compose epics spontaneously while performing them was the use of "formulas," which he defined as: "a group of words regularly employed under the same metrical conditions to express a given essential idea."[57] The repeated phrases in the sermons seemed to serve a similar purpose. Rosenberg calls the repeated phrases of the preachers "stall" formulas, meaning that they are interjected in order to give the preacher time to think of what to say next. Closely related to these are what he calls "themes,"[58] "a formulary portion of a sermon," that is, a set piece that can be inserted anywhere—a tape to be played, in current slang. These also put a preacher on automatic pilot as a way of gaining time to think.

Related to this need to establish a rhythmic pattern is the preacher's tendency to gasp for air at the end of each line. This practice and its purpose were noticed as early as James Weldon Johnson. He referred to the gasps as the oral punctuation of sermons by "a certain sort of pause that is marked by a quick intaking and an audible expulsion of breath." He saw it as a part of a "syncopation of speech—the crowding in of many syllables or the lengthening out of a few to fill one metrical foot."[59]

The folklorist Gerald L. Davis has pointed out that the rhythm established by the preachers is not nearly so exact as the meter of the poets. While the sermon is being preached it may seem that all the lines are of the same length, but actually their length may vary widely. He describes the process more precisely by saying that "the principle morphologic unit of the African-American sermon is a *group of hemistich phrases shaped into an irrhythmic metrical unit when performed.*"[60]

In any case, the rhythm is important. The preacher may even rap it out on the pulpit with his hand to emphasize the beat. The preacher may also clap his hands and even dance around the podium. It is in response to the established rhythm and other aspects of the sermon that the congregation becomes involved. They join in the clapping or tap their feet.[61] Their bodies may sway. And they find their own voices. They may moan or shout, but they also become involved in a dialogue with the preacher. This is to say that a black folk sermon is not a solo performance by a preacher, but a verbal activity involving the whole congregation. This flow between the preacher and the congregation is the pattern of "call-and-response" that is distinctive of preaching in this tradition.

Although he does not use the vocabulary of form criticism, Davis treats the performed sermon as a *Gattung* with certain necessary elements. Several of these have to do with the introduction:

- The preacher must indicate that the sermon text was provided by divine inspiration.
- The theme or subject of the sermon must be stated.
- The biblical passage on which the sermon is based must be interpreted, first literally and then more broadly.

The requirements for the body are more complex, but Davis states them as a single element:

> The body of the African-American sermon is constructed of independent theme-related formulas. Each unit of the formula develops or retards a secular and sacred tension and moves between abstract and concrete example. Each generated formula is an aspect of the "argument" of the announced theme and advances the discovery and examination of the sermon theme.

The final element is not so much a conclusion as an end.

> Closure is rarely found at the end of an African-American sermon. The sermon is open-ended.[62]

The successful sermon satisfies these criteria and others as well. It is in the recognition of these formal criteria that the significance of call-and-response is to be seen: the different responses (including relative lack of response) indicate the congregation's judgment of whether the criteria of the genre are being satisfied. They thus constitute either the congregation's permission for the preacher to go ahead or indicate a need to go back and complete the foundation.[63]

There is considerable debate among those who have studied these folk sermons about what they are supposed to accomplish. Most of the early interpreters sided with the elite tradition in seeing the purpose to be emotional release. Johnson, for instance, noted that he had seen congregations "moved to ecstasy by the rhythmic intoning of sheer incoherences."[64] According to William Pipes, the sermons "reflected the need for an escape mechanism by a people held in bondage." In addition to instructing people in biblical teaching and persuading them to live accordingly, the purpose of the preaching is "to impress the audience, so that there will be an outburst (escape) of emotion in shouting and frenzy."[65] And, beginning as he did with his concern for rhythm as the counterpart in folk preaching to the meter of the oral poets, Rosenberg understandably considered the tempo established in the sermon to be more important than semantic content. He thus saw the essential dynamic of such preaching to be an emotional catharsis achieved through crescendo and climax of the rhythm.[66]

For Gerald Davis, on the other hand, the semantic content is primary: "In sermon performance, the African American preacher is primarily concerned with the organization and language of his sermon."[67] The feel of rhythm is a vehicle of content and is generated simultaneously with the sermon's linguistic structure.

The element of overall argument is often lost on the outside observer of African American preaching because of the coded quality of language, a quality necessary in slave times and at least prudent ever since.[68] Over time, the habit of communicating in code became ingrained and reflexive. Therefore,

> both preacher and congregation share in the encoding and deciphering of sermon element. When this complex, concurrent activity is most intense, the only suitable responses are sound or word-absent phrases—those "moans," "cries," and "shouts" so underestimated by [Lawrence] Davis, [Daniel] Crowley, and [William] Pipes and appreciated by [Henry] Mitchell.[69]

What is encoded here is the preacher's exercise of a pastor's role as guide to the congregation in both religious and secular life. In Davis's interpretation, every sermon has to deal with both. But more attention is given to the secular than the sacred. The secular factor in the sermon is "weighted." According to Davis, the preacher "may use the perfection of the Christian life as example, as framework, but his focus is riveted on his congregation's need to live a fully experiencing daily, secular existence."[70] Even this is still somewhat encoded, because it does not say that the daily existence must be lived in a world dominated by whites. Living in such a world is like "living with a hatchet over your head every day," to use a description given a therapist of my acquaintance.

This understanding has been further refined by Cleophus J. LaRue.[71] His thesis is that the power of black preaching comes from a combination of three elements: (1) a particular method of interpreting the Bible, (2) a deep awareness of the black experience, and (3) particular aspects of the life of the black church. The key employed in the interpretation of Scripture is to discern in all its pages the work of "a sovereign God who acts in concrete and practical ways on behalf of the marginalized and powerless."[72] This belief that God is powerful to act and uses that power for those who suffer gives meaning to what black people have experienced, first in slavery and later in prejudice and discrimination. The hope and expectation of power that enable God's people to overcome all obstacles are applied to one of four "domains of experience": (1) personal piety, (2) care of the soul ("encouragement, exhortation, consolation, renewal, instruction, or admonishment"[73] to the wounded and broken), (3) social action, corporate concerns that "particularly and peculiarly affect black life,"[74] and (4) maintenance of the institutional church.

Sermons in the tradition of the black church create a powerful conviction that the people of God will be given the strength to endure and to overcome in all areas of their lives in Christ. Decoded, that means black Christians will be able to survive all the oppression heaped upon them by a white world. As LaRue shows, this purpose is discernible in the whole tradition, whether in slave times or contemporarily, and in the sermons of the learned as well as those of folk preachers. To what LaRue said may be added the point that whites have felt the power of such preaching but because racism is so systemic, they have not identified themselves with the oppressors in the biblical stories and the sermons based upon them, but with the oppressed because of their own life struggles.

It would be a false dichotomy, however, to contrast this emphasis on content with another on the catharsis or ecstasy experienced by worshipers when the traditional folk method of preaching is employed. In defending celebrative climaxes against the charges that they are emotional and manipulative, Henry Mitchell says:

> People live by emotion. Emotions move people, while ideas which do not generate some emotion are powerless to change anybody's life. In the black climax at its best, the idea—the point which has been made—

> is embraced and celebrated. It is, as it were, burned into the consciousness of the hearer. Embrace and celebration are emotional. And a good Black climax will appeal to the highest and noblest emotions of a man, whether Black or white.[75]

The conviction with which those who have participated leave the church is not simply a rational belief in an intellectual proposition about God's power and activity. It is an existential certainty that has been reinforced while doubts have been resolved in the whole process of the experience of the sermon. People are enabled to go back into a hostile world and live another week because of their persuasion of a truth that has been accomplished at every level of their being. "In the chanted sermon, African-American Christians did not merely talk about God, they experienced his power, and found that in the experience their own spirits were renewed."[76]

The remaining question to be discussed about black chanted sermons is whether the predominant influence on their development was white or African. Rosenberg takes the position that it began in the efforts of Africa American preachers to imitate the preaching style of the white preachers of the Second Great Awakening under whom they were converted. As documentation for this thesis, he points out that some white preachers in eastern Kentucky, where the awakening began, continue to preach that way to this very day.[77] In stating his own position, he does not discuss the extensive and prolonged argument over whether traditional African American Christian worship, including preaching, owes more of its inspiration to African traditional religion than to white American Christianity.

The classical debate over the question was between Melville J. Herskovits, who used his anthropological fieldwork in Africa to argue for that origin, and the African American anthropologist E. Franklin Frazier, who insisted that slavery had successfully expunged any memories of African culture.[78] Rosenberg referred to the work of Frazier but not to that of Herskovits.[79] There is, nevertheless, a good bit to be said for the Herskovits position in its basic claim, if not in its detailed argument.

Raboteau has summarized the current status of the debate very judiciously. He notes that there were many survivals of African traditional religion in Caribbean and Latin American countries, but that there were considerable cultural differences between the slave populations there and those in the United States, differences that prevented many detailed influences in this country. The African past, then, is not so determinative of the exact shape of the worship and preaching of African Americans as it is of those in the Caribbean and Latin America.

> Nevertheless, even as the gods of Africa gave way to the God of Christianity, the African heritage of singing, dancing, spirit possession, and magic continued to influence Afro-American spirituals, ring shouts, and folk beliefs.[80]

The ring shout, the dance in which Christian slaves shuffled, clapped, and sang spirituals, closely resembles call-and-response, including the sort of congregational involvement that Rosenberg considers to be the cathartic release toward which the rhythm of folk preaching is aimed.[81] African religious traditions thus predisposed the slaves to respond more readily to the emotional presentation of Christianity made in the Second Great Awakening than to catechetical presentations that were largely rational in their appeal.[82] Anyone who has heard classical African American chanted sermons has reason to be grateful for this fruit of the fervor of the Awakening.[83]

John Jasper: A Case Study in Folk Preaching

Just as Walker and Tindley enable one to have a vision of the elite tradition of African American preaching in action, a similar perspective on the folk tradition can be gained by looking at the life and ministry of John Jasper. Like Walker and Tindley, Jasper was born into slavery. What accounts for the difference in the path he took is probably that he was born so much earlier than they. Instead of being a child or at most an early teenager when he was given his freedom, he was a half century old and had already preached for half that time.

Anyone who writes about Jasper labors under the difficulty that the only source of information about him is a collection of articles[84] written by a Baptist minister who occupied the pulpit of one of the most prominent white churches in Richmond, the city where Jasper's ministry occurred. That cleric, William Eldridge Hatcher, was a Virginian of colonial ancestry and a person of great sophistication.[85] Thus he maintained an ambivalent attitude toward his subject throughout the book. There can be no doubt that he admired and even loved him. Indeed, he almost appears obsessed with him. For twenty-five years he sat under his preaching, even when influential members of his congregation criticized him for doing so. When Jasper died, he preached a eulogy for him to a packed house in his large white church. It is said that Hatcher's dying words were, "John Jasper, we're brothers now, and we'll live forever round the throne of God."[86] Yet he was able to refer to social equality between the races as a "hideous dogma."[87] He shared many of the prejudices of the elite against folk preaching, and much that he says sounds patronizing to modern ears. An example is the way he recorded Jasper's words in conversation and preaching in dialectical spelling, even though at times one cannot distinguish between the sounds of his transcription and standard spelling (e.g., "great palace" sounds exactly like "grate pallis") (178).[88] In depending upon the Hatcher account, therefore, it is a challenge not to sound condescending at times.

John Jasper was born into slavery on the plantation of the Peachy family in Fluvanna County, Virginia, in 1812, the last of the twenty-four children of Philip and Nina Jasper. His father, who was also a preacher, died two months before John was born, but his mother lived until she was almost one hundred and held many responsible positions, from being head of the working women on the Peachy plantation, to serving as chief of the servant force in a wealthy home, to being nurse to the sick in the negro quarters.

John originally served as a field hand, but he was moved around from place to place because of his owners' fluctuating fortunes. After he became an adult, he was sent to live in Williamsburg, and while there he became engaged, but was forced to move on the day he married. Since he could not live with her, his wife eventually asked to be released from the union.

After the Peachy family broke up, he was sold to various masters and used for different kinds of work. When he came to live in Richmond, he worked for a time in foundries and also as a house servant, but his last owner, Samuel Hargrove, put him to work removing stems from tobacco leaves in his plant. Jasper had gone to school for only six weeks, but around the beginning of 1839, he found a man who taught him to read from a *New York Speller.*

On July 4 of that year, he came under conviction of sin and was converted at work one day after six weeks of searching for God. His elation was so great that he wanted to share it, and tried to do so quietly, but his emotion overcame his restraint. The overseer quieted him and sent him back to work, but his owner asked what the commotion was about. On hearing, he sent for Jasper, took his hand, and told him they shared the same faith and were brothers in the Lord (27). Then he told him to witness throughout the factory and to take the rest of the day off to tell his folks and his neighbors about what had happened to him. Afterward, Jasper always regarded this as his call to preach, which came from God but was mediated through his master.

Since slaves were permitted to go only where their owners allowed, it was difficult for one called to preach to get around very much or to make any regular commitments. One concession allowed slaves to take off for a loved one's funeral, and the master would arrange for someone to preach it. Often a white minister was summoned, but a few slave preachers like Jasper achieved a considerable reputation as funeral preachers and received invitations their owners allowed them to accept. Stories remain of how, when he competed with a white preacher on such an occasion, Jasper outshone him by far. In time, his master allowed him to go to Petersburg two Sundays a month, and he acquired a large following there. The war brought that to an end, however. During the war, though, he visited the Confederate hospitals in Richmond to preach to the wounded. Although he preached for twenty-five years before liberation, the oppressive conditions of slavery meant that "his ministry had been migratory, restricted, and chiefly of ungathered fruit" (58).

When freedom came at last, Jasper was like most other released slaves in having no financial resources, and he had to make his way in the world as best he could. His first job was cleaning bricks from ruined buildings so they could be reused. But his great ambition was to build a church. He began preaching on an island in the James River where many of the newly freed lived. Sometimes they met in a house and sometimes in a deserted stable. When the congregation outgrew those meeting places, they found a larger building that was unoccupied. All along, his flock multiplied as sinners were converted and Jasper baptized them in the river. They bought a deserted Presbyterian mission church for $2,025 but soon had to enlarge it at a cost of $6,000. By then the congregation numbered two thousand, and Jasper was more than sixty years old. Yet they went on to build another church that "would be respectable in almost any part of Richmond" (60-61). The name of the church was Sixth Mount Zion Baptist.

While Jasper was a devoted and tireless pastor, the church was built on his preaching. That was in the folk tradition, but he practiced it with rare genius. Hargrove describes the first sermon he ever heard Jasper preach:

> Did ever mortal lips gush with such torrents of horrible English! Hardly a word came out clothed and in its right mind. And gestures! He circled around the pulpit with his ankle in his hand; and laughed and sang and shouted and acted about a dozen characters within the space of three minutes. Meanwhile, in spite of these things, he was pouring out a gospel sermon, red hot, full of love, full of invective,

> full of tenderness, full of bitterness, full of tears, full of every passion that ever flamed in the human breast. He was a theatre within himself, with the stage crowded with actors. He was a battle-field;—himself the general, the staff, the officers, the common soldiery, the thundering artillery and the rattling musketry. He was the preacher; likewise the church and the choir and the deacons and the congregation. (9)

That experience drew the white minister back as long as Jasper lived and led him to write essays during that time as "a tribute to the brother in black—the one unmatched, unapproachable, and wonderful brother" (10).

Of his preaching style, it can be said that he documented every point he made with a quotation from the Bible, citing chapter and verse, and often saying, "If you don't find it just exactly as I tells you, you can meet me on the street the next day and say to me, 'John Jasper, you are a liar,' and I won't say a word" (63). Many of his sermons were retellings of Bible stories that turned each successive scene into a vivid verbal picture. Yet at other times he would give an exposition on a point of Christian doctrine, and his logic was "his tower of strength" (96). "His ministrations fairly covered the theological field, were strongly doctrinal, and he grappled with honest vigour the deepest principles of the Gospel" (66). There were even times when his sermons were "sober and deliberate, sometimes even dull" (67). He studied his Bible with the asceticism of a hermit and came to have an encyclopedic knowledge of its text that he drew upon freely as he preached.

> There was a kinship between the Bible and himself, and, untaught of the schools, he studied himself in the light of the Bible and studied the Bible in the darkness of himself. This kept him in contact with people and whenever he preached he invaded their experience and made conscious their wants to themselves. (48)

His delivery was in the classical style of the chanted sermon, and "he intoned his sermons,—at least, in their more tender passages" (95). And the congregation participated in call-and-response (128). After the preacher died, Hatcher interviewed one of his former parishioners, who said, "It look like Brother Jasper couldn't stop preaching. It was his food and drink" (81). She went on to say what it was like to hear him:

> Brother Jasper was mighty fond of walking in the pulpit. It was a great, large place, and he frisked around most like he was a boy.

> When he was filled up with the arousement of the gospel on him, it was just glorious to see him as he whirled around the stand; the faces of his folks shone with the brightness of the sun, and they often made the house ring with laughter and with their shouts.
>
> One thing that always made his congregations rock with joy, and that was [for him] to sing while he was preaching. He was almost ninety years old, but he never lost his power to sing, and when he struck a tune the note of it shot in the people like arrows from angels' quivers. You couldn't hold still when Jasper sung. Soon as he started, the people would begin to swing and join in till the music filled the house. (82)

He soon attracted a following among Richmond's white population. Members of the legislature, judges, governors, and other distinguished people, including some of the most prominent ministers in the country, thronged to hear him. "He was justly ranked as one of the attractions of Richmond" (107). For many who came for the first time, the expectation was that they would be amused by the ridiculous posturings of an ignorant semi-savage, but those who came to scoff, stayed to pray.

He achieved a national reputation that was based largely on one sermon he preached arguing that when Joshua fought the battle of Gibeon, the sun actually stood still (Josh. 10:13). He did not preach it to seek notoriety, but simply to settle a theological debate between his sexton and another church member. He later repreached it 250 times to raise money to pay off the church debt, and even made an abortive venture on the lecture circuit. While he was ridiculed by many for the position he took, he simply took his stand on the plenary verbal inspiration of the Bible, a doctrine still held by many Christians. Like John Wesley, he was a man of one book. But he knew that book thoroughly, and he arrayed his argument with great logic and rhetorical power. "He had ferreted out of the Bible every passage that bore upon the motions of the sun, and he had them all printed in a sort of tract" (159), which he distributed beforehand so that everyone could follow his argument and its proof. His biographer responded by saying: "I believed in his sincerity, and to me he was a philosopher, sound in his logic, mighty in his convictions, though he might be wrong in his premises" (171).[89]

A final point needs to be made before turning to an example of Jasper's preaching. In the account given above of the first sermon by Jasper that he heard, Hatcher speaks of the preacher's atrocious grammar and pronunciation. In the essays that he collected into a book, Hatcher makes many such slighting remarks. One passage, however, suggests that with Jasper's lifetime of study, his diction grew progressively closer to the norms of standard English:

> During his long ministerial life his reading and contact with educated people rooted out many of his linguistic excrescences. There were times when he spoke with approximate accuracy, and even with elegance; and yet he delighted, if indeed he was conscious of it, in returning to his dialect and in pouring it forth unblushingly in its worst shape, and yet always with telling effect. (96)

In the interview mentioned above, his former church member said much the same thing, noting that many of the white people who came to hear him commented on his elegant language. "I know," she said, "he could handle great words when he wanted to, but he could talk in the old way, and he often loved to do that" (88).

A sample of his preaching can be seen in his sermon on "The Stone Cut Out of the Mountain" (108-20; **see Vol. 2, pp. 430-37**). This is a narrative sermon based upon Daniel 2:45. It begins with an introduction in which Jasper affirms his call to preach and says he knows that it angers the devil to see him ascend the pulpit. Then he moves without transition into the story, saying that God sets up the rulers of the people, even though he does not always pick out good people for the job. Temple-robbing Nebuchadnezzar was a case in point, and he was a very powerful ruler.

But Nebuchadnezzar had a frightening dream that none of the experts in his court could tell or explain to him. When he threatened to have all of them killed, Daniel heard of it and prayed. Receiving the insight for which he prayed (for "one thing the Lord can't do: he can't refuse to answer the cries of his people"), he went to the king and explained the dream. The stone from the rock that struck the idol's feet of clay was the kingdom of God, and it would destroy and replace the Babylonian Empire.

Then Jasper said that Nebuchadnezzar did not learn from this experience but built an image ninety feet high and nine feet wide, which he commanded people to worship on the signal of a musical group. He did so despite the fact that Daniel had already explained that Nebuchadnezzar's kingdom would be destroyed by the kingdom of Jesus Christ. God will destroy all the foundations of sin, and Jasper could hear the Savior saying to his Father that it was time for Gabriel to blow his horn. "I am going out to call my people from the field; they have been abused and laughed at, and made a scoffing long enough for my name's sake." God is going to bring his people home, and Jasper and his people will be among them. Then the proud from whom they have suffered will be told by King Jesus, "I don't know you, and I don't want to know you, and I don't want to see you." The stone out of the mountain will roll through the kingdom of darkness and crush the enemies of God.

Shadrach, Meshach, and Abednego refused to worship Nebuchadnezzar's golden image, and the Chaldeans reported them. When the king offered them another chance, they refused it, so he ordered that the furnace be heated seven times hotter than usual and commanded giants to throw in the Hebrew children. The giants were burned up, but the king looked into the furnace and saw that the three men were totally undamaged and that a fourth man was with them who looked like the Son of God. "The righteous always comes out conquerors and more than conquerors. Kings may hate you, friends despise you, and cowards backbite you, but God is your deliverer."

But Jasper had forgotten that some people believed what he was saying was "old fogy religion." He, however, wanted his church filled with old fogies, who would participate in the unceasing worship in heaven that John of Patmos had foreseen. The "saints of God that was all bruised and mangled by the fiery darts of the wicked" would be there to enjoy it. While Jasper did not have as much religion as he wanted, he had enough to give free salvation to all who wanted it. "If in this big crowd there is one lost sinner that have not felt the cleansing touch of my Savior's blood, I ask him to come today and he shall never die."

In form, this is a fairly standard narrative sermon, but one that could be decoded and seen to have all the power of the tradition, because it used the hermeneutical key to the Bible mentioned by LaRue, combined it with the black experience, and focused it on a particular aspect of life in the church. Anyone reading the entire text can understand why people, black and white, hastened to hear this man who had lived the first half of his life as the possession of another human being.

Thus in the generation before the Civil War, the fruits of the fervor of the Second Awakening came to be visible in a number of efforts at social reform. White evangelicals preached against slavery (without identifying themselves with the strict abolitionists), initiated the campaign against alcoholic beverages that would eventually result in prohibition by constitutional amendment, and pushed other ethical and social implications of their theology. One of the most bountiful fruits of the Awakening, however, was the attraction of significant numbers of African Americans, first to Christianity and then to a preaching ministry. Two manifestations of black Christianity ultimately developed: the elite, which wanted to demonstrate that African Americans are capable of the same achievements as whites, and the folk, which built upon links between the emotionalism of the Awakening and elements of traditional African religion. Both manifestations were to produce preachers of great power. An additional fruit of fervor was the acceptance of women as preachers, which will be the subject of the next chapter.

FOR FURTHER READING

Hatcher, William E. *John Jasper: The Unmatched Negro Philosopher and Preacher.* New York: Fleming H. Revell, 1908.

Johnson, James Weldon. *God's Trombones: Seven Negro Sermons in Verse.* New York: Viking, 1927.

Jones, Ralph H. *Charles Albert Tindley, Prince of Preachers.* Nashville: Abingdon Press, 1982.

McArthur, Robert Stuart. Introduction to *Life of Charles T. Walker, D.D. ("The Black Spurgeon") Pastor of Mt. Olivet Baptist Church, New York City,* by Silas Xavier Floyd. 1902. Reprint, New York: Negro Universities Press, 1960.

Mitchell, Henry H. *Black Preaching: The Recovery of a Powerful Art.* 1970, 1979. Rev. ed. Nashville: Abingdon Press, 1990.

Raboteau, Albert J. *Slave Religion: The "Invisible Institution" in the Antebellum South.* New York: Oxford University Press, 1978.

Smith, Timothy L. *Revivalism and Social Reform: American Protestantism on the Eve of the Civil War.* 1957. Reprint, New York: Harper & Row, 1965.

Notes

1. The title of this chapter is borrowed from a chapter in Timothy L. Smith, *Revivalism and Social Reform: American Protestantism on the Eve of the Civil War* (Nashville: Abingdon, 1957; reprint, New York: Harper & Row, 1965).

2. The theological roots in this belief lie in the theology of John Wesley, who regarded perfection as a second work of grace, an experience parallel to and following conversion. Finney developed a different form of the doctrine as part of his revision of Calvinism. More of this will be considered in the next chapter in the discussion of the Holiness movement.

3. Smith, *Revivalism and Social Reform,* 15.

4. Ibid.

5. Ibid., 149.

6. *John Wesley,* ed. Albert C. Outler (New York: Oxford University Press, 1964), 86.

7. L. C. Rudolph, *Francis Asbury* (Nashville: Abingdon, 1966), 193.

8. Charles L. Wallis, ed., *The Autobiography of Peter Cartwright* (Pierce & Washabaugh, 1956; Nashville: Abingdon, 1984), 72.

9. Ibid., 176.

10. Charles G. Finney, *Lectures on Systematic Theology,* 2:446, quoted in Keith J. Hardman, *Charles Grandison Finney, 1792–1875: Revivalist and Reformer* (Syracuse: Syracuse University Press, 1987), 370.

11. Wallis, *The Autobiography of Peter Cartwright,* 145-46 passim.

12. Hardman, *Charles Grandison Finney, 1792–1875,* 316.

13. Charles A. Johnson, *The Frontier Camp Meeting: Religion's Harvest Time* (Dallas: Southern Methodist University Press, 1955, as reprinted in 1985 with new intro. by Ferenc M. Szasz), 177.

14. "Princes shall come out of Egypt; Ethiopia shall soon stretch out her hands unto God" (Ps. 68:31 KJV). For the interpretation of this verse in the black church, see Albert J. Raboteau, *A Fire in the Bones: Reflections on African American Religious History* (Boston: Beacon, 1995), 37-56.

15. Albert J. Raboteau, *Slave Religion: The "Invisible Institution" in the Antebellum South* (Oxford: Oxford University Press, 1978), 149.

16. On the importance of this institution, see C. Eric Lincoln and Lawrence H. Mamiya, *The Black Church in the African American Experience* (Durham: Duke University Press, 1990).

17. W. E. B. DuBois, *The Souls of Black Folk* (Chicago: A. C. McClurg, 1903; reprint, New York: Blue Heron, 1953; reprint, with intro. Herbert Apteker, Millwood, N.Y.: Kraus-Thomson, 1973), 190-91.

18. William E. Montgomery, *Under Their Own Vine and Fig Tree: The African American Church in the South, 1865–1900* (Baton Rouge: Louisiana State University Press, 1994), 256-66.

19. I am grateful to Prof. Henry Mitchell for the suggestion of these two names.

20. Lemuel Haynes, "Universal Salvation—A Very Ancient Doctrine," in *Black Writers of America: A Comprehensive Anthology,* ed. Richard Barksdale and Keneth Kinnamon (New York: Macmillan, 1972), 226-29. Haynes follows the Perkins sermon form of doctrines and uses, and the characteristics of Satan he lists are aspects of his first point of doctrine, the character of the preacher.

21. Born February 5, 1858. Silas Xavier Floyd, *Life of Charles T. Walker, D.D. ("The Black Spurgeon") Pastor of Mt. Olivet Baptist Church, New York City,* intro. Robert Stuart McArthur (National Baptist Publishing Board, 1902; reprint, New York: Negro Universities Press, 1960).

22. Robert Stuart MacArthur, introduction to ibid.

23. Ibid., 52.

24. Ibid., 57.

25. Ibid., 93.

26. Ibid., 103.

27. Ibid., 182.

28. Ibid.

29. Ibid., 125-28.

30. Ralph H. Jones, *Charles Albert Tindley, Prince of Preachers* (Nashville: Abingdon, 1982). 13. Tindley was less fortunate in his biographer than Walker. Jones wrote largely on the basis of archival information and the memory of former parishioners, and what he wrote is more like a chronicle than a coherent effort to interpret

Tindley's life and ministry. There is, however, an advantage to this approach because information about such things as Tindley's disappointment in not being elected a bishop, the politics behind that, the misbehavior of his children, and factions within his congregation is not filtered out.

31. His memory of this, recorded in a sermon (ibid., 19-20), implies that his father had disposition of him, which sounds inconsistent with his being a slave.

32. Ibid., 20.

33. A workman who carried bricks and mortar to masons.

34. There may have been as many as ten thousand, but his biographer is not consistent in the statistics he provides.

35. A Baptist minister famous for an inspirational speech he gave six thousand times called "Acres of Diamonds."

36. "We Shall Overcome" of civil rights fame.

37. Jones, *Charles Albert Tindley,* 15.

38. I have been able to see only two.

39. Jones, *Charles Albert Tindley,* 157.

40. Ibid., 162.

41. In an essay entitled "The Chanted Sermon" in Raboteau, *Fire in the Bones,* 141-51; the quoted words are from p. 151. There is a wide literature on this subject that begins with James Weldon Johnson's introductory essay to his *God's Trombones* (New York: Viking , 1927) and includes: William H. Pipes, *Say Amen, Brother! Old-Time Negro Preaching: A Study in American Frustration* (New York: William-Frederick, 1951); Bruce Rosenberg, *The Art of the American Folk Preacher* (New York: Oxford University Press, 1970), revised as *Can These Bones Live?* (Urbana and Chicago: University of Illinois Press, 1988); Gerald L. Davis, *I Got the Word in Me and I Can Sing It, You Know: A Study of the Performed African American Sermon* (Philadelphia: University of Pennsylvania Press, 1985); Evans E. Crawford with Thomas H. Troeger, *The Hum: Call and Response in African American Preaching* (Nashville: Abingdon, 1995); and Henry H. Mitchell, *Black Preaching* (San Francisco: Harper & Row, 1970, 1979; rev. ed. Nashville: Abingdon, 1990).

42. Raboteau, *Fire in the Bones,* 142.

43. T. G. Steward, "The Influence of Euphony upon the Employment of Language," *A.M.E. Zion Church Review (Quarterly)* 2 (1885): 41-43.

44. Among those can be numbered such contemporary preachers as James Forbes, senior pastor of Riverside Church and former homiletics professor at Union Seminary, and Michael Curry, bishop of the Episcopal Diocese of North Carolina.

45. Raboteau, "The Chanted Sermon," 143.

46. Mitchell, *Black Preaching,* 113.

47. Ibid., 129.

48. Ibid., 112-47.

49. Johnson, *God's Trombones,* 1.

50. Raboteau, "The Chanted Sermon," 142.

51. See above, chapter 15.

52. Raboteau, *Slave Religion,* 311. On the influence of the Bible in slave religious thought, see ibid., 239-66.

53. Mitchell, *Black Preaching,* 179.

54. Johnson refers to this use of voice as "intoning." "This intoning is always a matter of crescendo and dimuendo in the intensity—a rising and falling between plain speaking and wild chanting" (*God's Trombones,* 10).

55. Raboteau, "The Chanted Sermon," 143-44.

56. Bruce Rosenberg, *The Art of the American Folk Preacher* and *Can These Bones Live?*

57. Albert Lord, *The Singer of Tales* (New York: Athenaeum, 1965), 30, quoted in *Can These Bones Live?,* 84.

58. The term used by folklorists, apparently, although what it means closely approximates what classical rhetoricians called *topi.*

59. Johnson, *God's Trombones,* 11.

60. Davis, *I Got the Word in Me and I Can Sing It, You Know,* 49.

61. A number of studies have been made about the musical aspect of this preaching, including Jon Michael Spenser, *Sacred Symphony: The Chanted Sermon of the Black Preacher* (Westbury, Conn.: Greenwood, 1987); and Marion Joseph Franklin, *The Relationship of Black Preaching to Black Gospel Music* (Unpublished Drew D.Min. thesis, 1982). See also the treatment of spirituals in Raboteau, *Slave Religion,* passim. There have also been linguistic studies such as the unpublished 1976 University of Texas Ph.D. dissertation of Richard Louis Wright, *Linguistic Standards and Communicative Style in the Black Church.*

62. Davis, *I Got the Word in Me and I Can Sing It, You Know,* 64-80. The criteria are stated in Davis's language.

63. Ibid., 26-38. This point is documented in an amusing way by Evans Crawford's use of typical sermon responses to furnish criteria by which a homiletics class can evaluate a student's sermon:

Help 'em, Lord (the search is on for the connections and we start out in need of prayer),

Well? (You're hinting to the witness with a chantable refrain or "riff"),

That's all right! (There are Good News and gospel possibilities; the sermon is becoming persuasive),

Amen! (The truth is affirmed and the pitch is right for the people and Scripture passage),

Glory Hallelujah! (the point of the loudest praise, highest joy, and praise to God). (Crawford, *The Hum,* 13).

64. Johnson, *God's Trombones,* 5.

65. Pipes, *Say Amen, Brother!,* 71-72.

66. Rosenberg, *Can These Bones Live?,* 131; cf. 71-72, 139-40.

67. Davis, *I Got the Word in Me and I Can Sing It, You Know,* 51.

68. On the ambiguity of language in spirituals, see Raboteau, *Slave Religion,* 248-50.

69. Davis, *I Got the Word in Me and I Can Sing It, You Know,* 66.

70. Ibid., 64.

71. Cleophus J. LaRue, *The Heart of Black Preaching* (Louisville, Ky.: Westminster John Knox, 2000).

72. Ibid., 18.

73. Ibid., 22.

74. Ibid., 23.

75. Mitchell, *Black Preaching,* 195.

76. Raboteau, "The Chanted Sermon," 151.

77. Ibid., 21. Cf. Howard Dorgan, *Giving Glory to God in Appalachia: Worship Practices of Six Baptist Subdenominations* (Knoxville: University of Tennessee Press, 1987), 56-85, for an excellent description of such preaching. See also what was said above about Welsh preaching, above, chapter 17.

78. Raboteau, *Slave Religion,* 48-55. See E. Franklin Frazier, *The Negro Church in America* (New York: Schocken, 1964), 1-19, and other books as well.

79. In contrast, see the treatment of Pipes, *Say Amen, Brother!,* 55 n. 13, pp. 169-70.

80. Raboteau, *Slave Religion,* 92.

81. Ibid., 66-73.

82. There is something problematic about the time references of the studies of African American preaching that have been reviewed here. This chapter is concerned with fruits of the Second Great Awakening, and thus is mainly interested in African American preaching during slave times and Reconstruction, the period studied by Raboteau and referred to by DuBois. Johnson was writing just before the Great Depression. Pike wrote during the Korean War, but in an effort to see if preaching in rural Georgia was still like slave preaching. Rosenberg and Davis, however, did their fieldwork mostly in California, the first in the late 1960s and the latter in the early 1980s. To what extent can it be assumed that essentially the same phenomenon is being described? The only answer that can be given is that the qualities to which Rosenberg and Davis call attention are present in the descriptions of the earliest black preaching. Undoubtedly there are differences between times and places, but they do not seem to affect the overall picture that has been presented.

83. I will say more of African American preaching in the section that deals with preaching after World War II, including the civil rights movement, the way that Negro preaching came to the attention of white culture, how black preachers came to occupy positions of national leadership, African Americans giving the Beecher Lectures on Preaching at Yale, and the development of homiletical textbooks and other pedagogical tools in this tradition. See below, chapter 28.

84. William E. Hatcher, *John Jasper: The Unmatched Negro Philosopher and Preacher* (New York: Fleming H. Revell, 1908).

85. *Dictionary of American Biography,* ed. Dumas Malone (New York: Scribner's, 1932), 8:395.

86. Richard Ellsworth Day, *Rhapsody in Black: The Life Story of John Jasper,* A Broad Brim Book (Philadelphia: Judson, 1953), 12.

87. Hatcher, *John Jasper,* 131. Hereafter, references to this work will be given parenthetically in the text by page number alone.

88. On the advice of Prof. Larry Murphy of Garrett-Evangelical Theological Seminary, quotations from Jasper will be given here in standard spelling, but grammatical irregularities will be allowed to stand.

89. It is ironic that Hatcher, a Southern Baptist minister, accepted the scientific explanation one hundred years ago, while today many members of his denomination would agree with Jasper in a creationist understanding.

CHAPTER 21

"THE FRUITS OF FERVOR" (B)

"YOUR DAUGHTERS SHALL PROPHESY"

Women preachers have appeared occasionally throughout the history of the church, but the first significant trend toward making their activity the norm, rather than an exception, in what became the mainline churches in America was another fruit of the Second Great Awakening. Yet, to vary the metaphor, the ground was prepared and a seed was planted that did not achieve its full fruitfulness until the last half of the twentieth century. In the intervening time, sprigs grew into trees that dropped their own seed until, finally, there was an orchard.

There is, however, one major exception to this otherwise accurate generalization.

THE SOCIETY OF FRIENDS

The first tradition in America to have women ministers on a regular basis was the Religious Society of Friends, commonly known as the

Quakers.[1] During the first three-quarters of the eighteenth century, this body became the third largest religious group among Americans of European descent,[2] and their women who "traveled in ministry" were a common sight. Among Quakers, women preachers had been recognized equally with men from the beginning. The principle on which that recognition was based had been stated succinctly by William Penn: "Sexes make no Difference; since in Souls there is none."[3]

This revolutionary attitude originated in the cauldron of social and religious change that was seventeenth-century England. Quakers have been classified as one of the more radical spiritual reform groups that arose during the age of the Puritans and Independents.[4] George Fox, the founder of the Friends, proclaimed that men and women had been restored to their pre-fall purity. Upon the basis of the quotation in Acts 2 of Joel 2:28-32, the existence of women who prophesied was taken as evidence that the last days had arrived.[5] Accordingly, it was necessary and even inevitable that women should preach, but their doing so meant the end of the world was very near. The spirit of Christ had come as Light to dwell in human beings and to fill them with concerns that they should relay to others. By the end of the century, however, these imminent apocalyptic expectations had faded from the movement and the motivating dynamic had become the experience of Light itself, which "had come to be viewed more as a divine spiritual principle working in all people and ages."[6]

The apocalyptic interpretation of Acts 2:17 did not relieve the early Friends from the necessity of justifying the preaching of women in the face of the widely perceived Pauline ban on women speaking in church. Fox himself wrote two tracts on the subject. The first, published in 1656, had the misleading title of *The Woman Learning in Silence: or, the Mysterie of the Woman's Subjection to Her Husband, as Also, the Daughter Prophesying, Wherein the Lord Hath, and Is Fulfilling That He Spake by the Prophet Joel, I Will Pour Out My Spirit unto All Flesh.* The second was titled *Concerning Sons and Daughters, and Prophetesses Speaking and Prophesying in the Law and the Gospel.* Both showed that women in the Bible had prophesied and been the vehicles of messages from God. Another tract, *Womens Speaking Justified, Proved, and Allowed of by the Scriptures,* was published in 1666 by the "Nursing Mother of Quakerism," Margaret Fell.

To say that Quakers had women preachers can be confusing, since the Religious Society of Friends did not have pastors.[7] Furthermore, their meetings for worship were silent gatherings unless someone present—anyone present—felt moved by the Spirit to share some light received. To clarify the matter, it is necessary to distinguish among ministry as order (i.e., conferred by ordination), ministry as office (i.e., a professional appointment), and ministry as function. Only in the functional sense can we speak of early Quakers, male or female, as ministers. From the beginning, they had decried a professional ministerial class as a "hireling" clergy. Those among them who performed ministerial functions had other employment and ministered only occasionally and as they were led by the Spirit.

But, as Carol Stoneburner said, "Over time Quakers created a leadership class."[8] While it was still believed that the Spirit dwelled in all human beings and could lay a concern to speak on any member attending a meeting, experience showed that the Spirit spoke through some persons more often, more effectively, and at greater length than through others. Those whose gifts had been noticed were recorded as ministers. Meetinghouses came to be constructed with a slightly raised bench at the front that faced the other benches. Elders and recorded ministers sat on these. There could be several ministers in one congregation, and there was no expectation that each would speak at every meeting. Only a person who felt that she or he had been given an insight by the Spirit, as well as a command to share it with the meeting, would speak. And when speaking, only the message received was to be communicated and then as concisely as possible, without any rhetorical embellishment or addition of thoughts by the speaker.

In a study of twenty-five women from the first five generations of English Quakers, Elise Boulding writes of stages of call to ministry:

> All the women struggle mightily against being called to the ministry. There are usually three crises. The first is in accepting an inward call to serious holiness. The second is accepting a call to speak in Meeting. Some women struggled so hard against the inner call to speak that they became seriously ill, and the struggle could go on for several years.[9]

The effective preachers among those who responded to this call were "recorded" as ministers. The third crisis mentioned by Boulding was the call to travel in ministry outside one's local meeting.

Again, this call could come to either a woman or a man, and at times came to a wife and husband together. They would report to their local meeting for business that a concern had been laid upon their hearts for a particular task in a particular place. In the seventeenth century, this could be to carry the Quaker message in evangelism or proselytism, but in the eighteenth, it was more often a matter of building up or reforming other

Quaker meetings.[10] The meeting, after a process of discernment as to whether the concern was really a prompting of the Spirit, would decide whether to record in a minute the sense of the meeting that the person should travel in this ministry. Such decisions were often accompanied by a commitment of the meeting to underwrite the travel expenses and to look after the traveling minister's local responsibilities while away. The journey might be short or long. It could be the only one on which a particular person ever went or it could be one of a number, but the commission in the enabling minute was for only the particular trip.

The records of some of these journeys are heroic in the extreme. Seventeenth-century preaching could involve disrupting services of the established church to claim the superiority of Quaker worship, street preaching in the marketplace, or even addressing the king at court. Those who went on such journeys often had to pay severely for their witness, being either beaten or imprisoned. When Mary Fisher and Elizabeth Williams rebuked the undergraduates of Oliver Cromwell's old college at Cambridge, calling them "Antichrists" and "a Cage of Unclean Birds and the Synagogue of Satan," the magistrate ordered them to be whipped until the blood ran down their bodies. This same Mary Fisher was eventually to preach before the sultan of Turkey, by whom she was received with far greater courtesy than was accorded her in either old or New England.

The following year, two others who tried to preach in Cambridge received the same punishment. One, Elizabeth Fletcher, never recovered from the beating, but she did go back the following year and walked naked through the streets "as a sign for the hypocritical profession they made there."[11] Mary Dyer, one of a number of English women Friends who attempted to preach in New England, was eventually hanged in Boston under a law of the Massachusetts General Court banishing Quakers on pain of death.[12]

Not only did British women Quakers receive minutes authorizing them to travel to America, American women also became Public Friends, as those who received such minutes were called, to travel in ministry to England. Women accounted for 42 of the 103 American Public Friends who visited Britain in the eighteenth century.[13] While travel remained hazardous, the danger of outright persecution had lessened, and perhaps the ministries had become more sedate. As noted above, imminent apocalyptic expectations had faded from the movement by the end of the seventeenth century, and its motivating dynamic had become the experience of Light itself. This shift within the movement coincided with a shift in the culture at large toward toleration and other Enlightenment virtues.

As a result, Quaker women who traveled in ministry to America were no longer regarded as witches; instead, some were even welcomed as "celebrated preachers."[14]

As the eighteenth century turned into the nineteenth, the Society of Friends became an established part of American life, but continued to lead in every activity for the amelioration of society, from prison reform to abolition. Two sisters from a slaveowning family in South Carolina, Angelina and Sarah Grimké, moved north to Philadelphia to join the Quakers and speak out against slavery and the oppression of women, although they did not find their own meeting there as supportive as they had hoped.

This speaking on social issues from a religious perspective by the Grimké sisters does not appear to have been mandated by a minute to travel, but some of their coworkers in these causes were definitely women ministers. The most prominent was certainly Lucretia Mott. Many know her primarily for her advocacy of a wide range of reforms, including feminism, abolition, peace, Native American rights, and immigrant welfare, among others. A close study of her correspondence, sermons, and speeches, however, convinced one scholar that "her secret source of strength was her implicit faith in the promptings of the Divine Spirit."[15]

Born Lucretia Coffin in Nantucket in 1793, she was educated at a Quaker school in New York State, where she met and eventually married a young instructor named James Mott. By the time of their marriage they had moved to Philadelphia, which remained their home the rest of their lives. The mother of six children, Lucretia also devoted herself to many activities outside the house. The death of one of her children in 1817 caused her to turn to her faith more deeply than before. It was out of this experience that she became a recorded minister in the Society of Friends. From then on, she traveled in ministry, preached widely, and lectured and otherwise labored for the many causes listed above. Her husband, also a recorded minister, was not nearly as articulate as she, but was content to enable her ministry in any way possible.[16]

Influences on Mott's thought, in addition to the Quaker tradition and the abolitionism of William Lloyd Garrison, were Unitarianism and New England transcendentalism.[17] Her belief system was thus an amalgam that fitted in with the optimistic progressivist liberalism of her time. It is not surprising, then, that Mott's sermons were neither expository nor textual, but topical. She did, however, quote extensively from the Bible and from other sources, especially poetry. She was invited to preach in churches of other denominations and, of course, she gave platform addresses in support of her many causes.

But, in accord with the Quaker tradition, her sermons at regular meetings for worship were delivered extempore, and their preservation is due to stenographic recording. (For an example, **see Vol. 2, pp. 438-44.**) In her sermons, she holds up the superiority of the Quaker tradition to that of other denominations (decrying rites, dogmas, and "hireling" clergy). She exhorts her hearers to act upon the testimony of the Spirit within them, root out their own sin, and extirpate social evil in a manner consistent with their nonviolent tradition. And she looks forward to a time when all of that will be accomplished.

Quaker women proclaimed the message that characterized each century of the existence of their movement: in the seventeenth they were apocalyptic, in the eighteenth they focused on Inner Light and reform in a deeply Christian way, and in the nineteenth they advocated progressive social causes, many also identifying themselves with liberal religion.

THE WESLEYAN/HOLINESS TRADITION

By the nineteenth century, the number of women preaching afforded their being classified according to tradition and typical experience. While an extensive literature upon the subject exists, until recently it has concentrated more upon the effort to have women's eligibility to preach recognized than what made their pulpit activity distinctive from that of their male counterparts.[18] A great service has been done the history of preaching by Catherine A. Brekus, who has rescued from oblivion more than a hundred women preachers in this country before the Civil War. In *Strangers & Pilgrims: Female Preaching in America, 1740–1845*,[19] she has been able to reconstruct a detailed picture of preaching by women in a period when it was believed that little occurred. Very few of these women were ordained clergy, but most had recognized positions within their denominations that allowed them to engage in proclamation, even to "promiscuous" audiences (as those containing both men and women were called at the time).

One of the most useful of Brekus's services is her recognition of periods in which different groups of women preachers were enlisted. Most of the women active in the time of the First Great Awakening were exhorters, who encouraged those under conviction to accept conversion. During the period of the Revolution, two charismatic women started their own sects: Mother Ann Lee, founder of the Shakers; and the woman known as Jemima Wilkinson before the experience in which she was reborn as the Public Universal Friend and began to gather other Universal Friends around her.

The majority of the women preachers chronicled by Brekus, however, were itinerant lay evangelists of the Second Great Awakening who were recognized by denominations that came into existence in America during that time: the Methodists, the African Methodists, the Free Will Baptists, and the Christian Connection.[20] Brekus's essential thesis is that these bodies used women evangelists to help them grow from small sects into flourishing denominations, and then were embarrassed by them as their churches became respectable in the age of the cult of domesticity. In that culture, where women were expected to refine and purify the private sphere and be invisible in the public sphere, the raucous evangelists of the frontier no longer had a place. Indeed, there was an effort to purge denominational histories of any hint they had ever existed.

The preaching of women evangelists did get a new lease on life in the Millerite movement, out of which the Adventists were eventually to be formed, but most of Brekus's study is devoted to the earlier and larger group. In addition to a chapter on their message (typical of evangelistic preaching at the time), other chapters are devoted to their autobiographical writings and their use of marketing techniques being developed at the time while deploring the marketing revolution.

One shortcoming of Brekus's work, however, is a failure to recognize the impetus given to such preaching by the Holiness movement. It could be argued that Mott's understanding of guidance by the Inner Light was an example of the yearning for perfection, which, according to Timothy Smith, characterized so many American religious movements in the quarter century before the Civil War. In the Wesleyan movement, however, the understanding of Christian perfection, sanctification as a second work of grace was on its native soil. And it is not accidental that the number of women who felt called to preach in this tradition and its branches were usually persons who claimed to have undergone that experience.

African American Pioneers

Among the earliest women to preach in the Wesleyan tradition were a number of African American evangelists, several of whom have left accounts of their lives. The best known of these, the woman who received the name Sojourner Truth (1797–1883), was the least typical. In spite of early membership in a Methodist congregation, she was not affiliated with any denomination for most of her life—although she worked with a number—nor was she ever authorized by any to preach. Although Truth was a person of commanding presence and penetrating insight, the relatively short time during which preaching was her main activity suggests that the most appropriate category in which to understand her is that put forward by Marta Tomhave Blauvelt, "wandering seer."[21]

After Sojourner Truth, the best known is probably Amanda Smith, a member of the African Methodist Episcopal Church who was an independent evangelist and served as a missionary in the United States, Great Britain, India, and Africa between 1878 and 1890.[22] As impressive as she was, there are autobiographical accounts of the ministries of several women who labored much earlier than she. Jarena Lee first felt the call to preach in 1811 and was licensed as an A.M.E. exhorter by Bishop Richard Allen in 1819. In the year that Lee was licensed, Zilpha Elaw felt the call to preach at a camp meeting. She did not enter full-time ministry until 1825, however, and, while she was never officially licensed, Elaw did receive endorsement from various Methodist clergy and others. Born later than the other two, Julia Foote did not begin preaching until the early 1840s. She was "read out" of her A.M.E. congregation for preaching, but was nevertheless welcomed into the pulpits of other A.M.E. churches, as well as those of other denominations, including the Methodists. After many years, she became an official missionary for her church and was even ordained elder before her death in 1900.[23]

A number of common threads run through the stories of Lee, Elaw, and Foote. All members of the A.M.E. Church, their common sense of vocation to preach grew out of their experiences of sanctification. All had visionary experiences. Each had difficulty in accepting her call because the assumption of the time was that women should not preach.[24] The husbands of all three opposed their ministries, and it was not until after the spouses' deaths that they were able to give themselves unremittingly to their work. Relations with official church structures were tenuous at best, yet each found willing audiences and was welcomed into the pulpits of many clergy. Their preaching was heard with appreciation by members of different denominations,[25] by white as well as black, the educated and socially prominent as well as the poor and illiterate.

Each suffered from racial bigotry, from prejudice against women in preaching, and from resentment of evangelism.[26] Each traveled many difficult miles, enduring great hardships and dangers. Elaw, for instance, carried her ministry into slave states where she was in danger of being sold into slavery herself and also spent several years preaching in England. Their sense of being led by God to do things opposed in the society of their time means that their autobiographies are accounts of extraordinary heroism in the service of the gospel.

What can be said of the way they preached? For one thing, their styles must have had much in common with the evangelistic preaching of men during the Second Great Awakening. Lee and, even more, Elaw sometimes record the texts from which they preached, and most are the sort that suggest the challenge given by the coming judgment to repent and accept the gospel. The responses to their preaching also sound very much like the responses recorded by men from the *Journals* of John Wesley on.[27] They also proclaimed the blessings of sanctification in such a manner that, at times, mere conversion sounded like only a half-safe step.

The most informative of the three autobiographies from a homiletical point of view is that of Foote. Its title is taken from Zechariah 3:2 (KJV), "a brand plucked out of the fire," and these words recur as a refrain throughout the book to proclaim that the author had been providentially rescued many times.[28] A common homiletical device is thus used in giving structure to a book. Further, many chapters end in an exhortation to the reader that sounds for the world like the end of a sermon, such as:

> Dear reader, have you innocent children, given you from the hand of God? Children, whose purity rouses all that is holy and good in your nature? Do not, I pray, give to these little ones of God the accursed cup which will send them down to misery and death. Listen to the voice of conscience, the woes of the drunkard, the wailing of poverty-stricken women and children, and touch not the accursed cup. From Sinai come the awful words of Jehovah, "No drunkard shall inherit the kingdom of heaven" [1 Cor. 6:10].[29]

Foote also gives evidence in several places of having consulted commentaries or other tools of biblical study in the preparation of her sermons. When, for example, she tries to answer the supposed Pauline ban on women preaching, she refers to the meaning of the Greek term by which Paul refers to Priscilla, notes how the same word is translated in other places, and concludes by saying: "When Paul said, 'Help those women who labor with me in the Gospel,' he certainly meant that they did more than to pour out tea."[30]

Biblical scholarship is used again in a sermon she was asked to preach on Micah 4:13 (KJV), "Arise and thresh, O daughter of Zion," when she contrasts the method of threshing used in biblical times with that utilized in her own day.[31] She seems to give an outline of the sermon (it surely must have been longer), the first of several that occur near the end of her book. She interprets the passage as referring to preachers and says that the metaphor works as well with modern as with ancient means of threshing. Either way, the devil is threshed out of sinners, an unpleasant but necessary experience for all to undergo.

To repeat, the sermons of these African American women evangelists seem to be calls for conversion and sanctification, common themes of Awakening preaching.

Mainstreaming Holiness

Lee, Foote, and Elaw had experienced sanctification some years before it came to be sought by white Methodists, especially those with any social prominence. There were, however, calls for greater holiness from the highest circles of the Methodist Episcopal Church, including a pastoral address on the subject from the bishops at General Conference in 1835. The critical turn occurred that same year when Sarah Lankford combined the prayer meetings of two Methodist churches in New York City to form the "Tuesday Meeting for the Promotion of Holiness." Her sister, **Phoebe Palmer,** soon experienced sanctification and became the leader of the movement. Within five years a number of prominent clergy had been enlisted in the cause, women in other places started similar groups, and expectation of the experience became common rather than rare.

This was about the time that Charles G. Finney and the Oberlin faculty were beginning to teach their doctrine of perfection, which had Wesleyan roots although it also grew out of Finney's teaching on free will. Holiness was an idea whose time had come.

Palmer's understanding of holiness grew out of Wesley's teaching about sanctification as a second work of grace after conversion, but she adapted the doctrine somewhat:

> Wesley's emphasis on the disciplined life that led to an eventual attainment of this "perfect love" was, in her mind, an unnecessary prolongation of a "blessing" that was available the moment a Christian consecrated everything to God and claimed this promise of "perfect love." All an individual needed to do was to become a "living sacrifice on the altar of Jesus Christ."[32]

Part of the explanation for her change was that her approach was more analytical than emotional. She had never felt the affective satisfaction that converted Methodists were expected to enjoy. When she experienced sanctification herself, it came as a matter of faith, of deciding to believe that God could be relied upon to keep the divine promises. "Signs and wonders" were not to be relied upon:

> She would instead rely on nothing except the Bible, which she held to be the word of God to man, and "faith," which she defined as . . . taking "God at his word, whatever [one's] emotions might be."[33]

Phoebe Palmer was quick to express the grace she had received in her life, handing out tracts in the slums, visiting prisons, and doing pioneer settlementhouse work, especially in the Five Points Mission she founded. She also wrote several books to communicate her understanding. And she and her physician husband, Walter, began in the late 1850s to travel around, conducting revivals. They were so successful that by the time she died in 1874, Phoebe Palmer was credited with having brought twenty-five thousand people to Christ.[34]

There is an evolution in the form Palmer's leadership took at religious gatherings. The Tuesday Meetings were largely occasions at which those gathered testified to their experience of grace or the need for it, and at these she presided unobtrusively. As she began to receive invitations to speak, she developed an ability to address a group in a more complex way, so that by the time she began preaching revivals, she was an accomplished speaker:

> In the church or hall meeting . . . Palmer was the preacher of the hour, doing all the things a Finney would do; occupying the pulpit, taking a text, presenting an exhortation calculated to persuade hearers to repent and turn to God or seek to more fully enter the "way of holiness" (always replete with stories and illustrations), issuing an "invitation" to the anxious to pray and be prayed for, and praying with an[d] instructing those who responded to the invitation. According to the evidence, this was perhaps Palmer's *most* effective medium of all, as well as being the one in which the participation of a woman was the most exceptional.[35]

Palmer, then, was one of the great women preachers of the nineteenth century. Yet at first she would have rejected the description, since she did not believe it right for women to preach. In time, however, she came to distinguish between what she did and "technical preaching," the sort of thing done by ordained clergy. (For her discussion of "the gift of prophecy," **see Vol. 2, pp. 446-57.**) Her definition of "nontechnical preaching" was elastic enough to cover anything from the personal witness of one individual to another to addresses from the pulpit to large crowds. She did not so much oppose the ordination of women and technical preaching by them as prescind the questions of their appropriateness. She seemed to think the sort of thing she was doing was much more crucial. As she said,

> The word *preach* taken in connection with its attendant paraphernalia, oratorical display, onerous titles, and pulpits of pedestal eminence,

> means so much more than we infer was signified by the word *preach,* when used in connection with the ministrations of Christ and his apostles, that we were disposed to withhold our unreserved assent to women's preaching in the technical sense.[36]

So modest was she and so traditional in her view of the role of women that at first she did not even allow her name to appear on the title pages of her books. *Promise of the Father,* for instance, says only that it is by the author of her other works. She changed her mind, however, when she was walking past the Bowery Theater one day and saw a lurid placard that listed female as well as male members of the cast. Her reaction was: "Here are the servants of Satan who are not afraid or ashamed to let their names appear. And shall the servants of the Heavenly King be less bold?" From then on, she published under her name.[37]

Palmer was born only sixteen years after the death of John Wesley, the daughter of a man who was proud that he had received his ticket of membership in the Methodist society from the founder himself.[38] She came along at a time when American Methodism

> was seeking its way from an association of "societies" founded for spiritual discovery and fellowship within the Church of England to an autonomous denomination operating according to the American pattern of free-for-all competition among pluralistic religious bodies.[39]

Under Wesley's regime, all Methodist preachers were assumed to be laypersons, but in America they came to be ordained. It was inevitable that the time would come when ordination would be extended to women.

The first Methodist Episcopal woman to be licensed to preach was **Maggie Newton Van Cott.**[40] Born in 1830 into a prosperous middle-class Episcopal family, Margaret Newton married Peter Van Cott a couple of months before her seventeenth birthday. Her husband later contracted tuberculosis and was an invalid on and off for the rest of his life. His illness forced Mrs. Van Cott to help in the support of the family, and she became something of an entrepreneur, manufacturing medicines and selling them to stores.

Converted while riding the Fulton Street ferry, she became a class member at Duane Street Methodist Episcopal Church and began to speak a little at class meetings. After her husband died, she joined The Methodist Church. Before long she began conducting a meeting in an ecumenical mission in Five Points that lasted twenty-one months and included the organization of a Sunday school.[41] Then, early in 1868, she was asked to preach in the Catskills. She accepted the invitation but refused to call what she was doing "preaching," saying that she was only "talking about Jesus." Yet host clergy insisted that she speak from the pulpit.

It seems that wherever Van Cott went to speak, a revival broke out and she had to remain several weeks. Then further invitations would come from the surrounding area. By the middle of 1868, the urgent invitations for her to preach had become so numerous that she had to give up her business. In September of that year, she was licensed as an exhorter by the Methodist Episcopal Church and six months later was licensed to preach by that church—although she herself had little interest in such credentials.

In her first year as an itinerant evangelist, she preached 335 hour-long sermons, traveled 3,000 miles, and saw 500 probationers added to The Methodist Church (222). She expanded the circle of her travels first into New England and then to the Midwest. When she preached in Evanston, Illinois, Frances Willard said that all but two of her "girls" at the Evanston College for Ladies became members of the church. In 1870 she preached 339 times and had a total of 2,949 converts, 1,735 of whom became Methodist probationers (276). She "was on the sawdust trail for thirty years" and was compared to Dwight L. Moody in effectiveness.[42]

It is possible to get an impression of Van Cott's preaching because her biographer included in an appendix a number of press clippings that contain reports of her sermons, and he also reprinted newspaper transcriptions of two of her sermons. A sense of what it was like to hear her can be gained from one of the reviews, that in *Harper's Bazaar.* At the time it was still a Methodist publication in spirit if not officially, and it contained many favorable remarks about her preaching. This report, which describes the qualities indicative of the time's successful revival preaching, justifies extended quotation:

> Like most revivalists, she is more declamatory than argumentative, appealing more to the passions than the reason. Her articulation is distinct and easily heard in any part of the church (we had almost said of the village), and her style being varied does not fatigue the hearer. At times she amuses the fancy with familiar talk, filled with flowery imagery, fixing the attention and winning the confidence of her hearers, till rising with her theme, she rushes on with the excitement of inspiration, breaking down the fortifications of the ungodly and carrying their works by storm. She is not an educated woman, in the strict sense, and her influence, as a consequence, is chiefly felt among her own class. She is gifted with a remarkable flow of language, her gestures are graceful,

and her general style would give rise to the remark that she must have derived her ideas of public speaking from dramatic performers. Her powers of endurance are very remarkable, speaking nearly three hours every evening through the week, and twice on Sundays. (327)

A Return to the Soil

Much humbler were the circumstances of **Lydia Sexton,** a woman who ministered in the church that has been called the "German phase of Methodism in America," the United Brethren in Christ.[43] Born the daughter of a Baptist minister in Rockport, New Jersey, she came to experience extreme deprivation. When her father died, her mother remarried and had to farm out her own children in order to take care of her husband's children by a former marriage and other dependents. Consequently, while growing up, Sexton was exploited as free labor while living in the homes of various relatives. She married out of such dependency twice, only to have her husbands die. When her *Autobiography* was published, however, she had been living with her third husband for more than fifty years. Her story is a fascinating account of life on the frontier as she moved from New Jersey to Ohio to Indiana and finally to Kansas.

Converted in a United Brethren revival, Sexton was eventually urged to begin preaching. She was licensed by her quarterly conference in 1851, a license that had to be renewed every quarter. Eventually, though, she was given not a license but a "recommendation" by her annual conference. She was not appointed to a circuit but gave out appointments to preach (i.e., she accepted invitations). Her preaching was revivalistic, and she held many protracted meetings—the sort of ministry Maggie Van Cott had. Finally, in 1870 she was appointed chaplain to the Kansas State Prison for men, a post in which she was very effective.

One sample of Sexton's preaching is included in her book. There is a gusto and humor about her writing that are seen in her description of the situation in which the sermon was preached:

> I greatly doubted the propriety and actual benefit of my preaching at St. Marys [Indiana]; but the appointment had gone out and I must submit. They had procured the largest room in the place, which was in part used for the storage of groceries and liquors. When I entered the room the fumes of whiskey were very rank—indeed almost intolerable. I had my misgivings as to duty; but I thought of what Brother Griffith said when asked whether he would preach in a Universalist Church. His

> answer was, "I will preach anywhere on this side of hell, if it is a decent place." As the audience was very large I thought it best not to disappoint them. (309)

Her sermon was suited to the setting. She preached mainly on Leviticus 14:33, but actually on all that Leviticus has to say about leprosy. She spent some time talking about how it was diagnosed, how it could attack a house as well as a person, the precautions a priest had to take in visiting the contagion, and what must be done about it—with the destruction of the house as the remedy of last resort. Then she said that various moral failings were like leprosy: swearing, dancing, gambling, and, worst of all, selling liquor.

The sermon is illustrated with anecdotes of people she had known whose lives one or another of these vices had ruined. The language is vigorous, and there is the occasional bit of comic relief, as when she tells a long tale proving that men who are stingy will seldom become drunkards (316-17). She is convinced that woman suffrage would close the saloons (318). Rum sellers should be held accountable for the damage they do in the same way as the owner of an ox that gores someone. The only remedy for sin is the death of Jesus, a point that is made by a catena of verses from all over the Bible.

She heard the next day that the owner of the building "liked [her] sermon first-rate, only he wished [she] had not spoken so strongly against dancing and drinking and grocery-keepers" (321).

Early Pentecostalism

As the century moved on, the Holiness movement became separated from mainline churches and formed into independent denominations and even congregations. While many of these have continued their existence to the present day, they also furnished the environment in which the Pentecostal movement began at the turn of the century.[44] A woman in whose ministry this trajectory of the Wesleyan Holiness tradition can be observed is the proto-Pentecostal preacher, **Maria Beulah Woodworth-Etter.**[45] Almost forgotten for a time, Woodworth-Etter had great success as an evangelist in Indiana and Illinois in the closing decades of the nineteenth century, attracting crowds of as many as twenty-five thousand people. Originally from Ohio, she had been born in Lisbon in 1844. Her family did not become religious until her father almost died when she was twelve. Thereafter they became Disciples of Christ, and although Maria had a conversion of sorts when she was thirteen, it was not until 1879 that she experienced what led her to begin preaching.

By then she had married a Civil War veteran and farmer, Philo Harrison Etter, and had six children by him, five of whom succumbed to illness. Her sense of call came in her bereavement. Or, rather, in that condition she felt a renewal of a call that had stirred her when she was a teenager. She began reviving churches in the area. The Disciples did not ordain women, but several denominations offered her jobs. She began with the United Brethren but soon switched to the Church of God (Winebrenner), which asked her to return her ministerial credentials after she had preached in their connection for twenty years.

She held successful meetings in places like Muncie and Kokomo. She was best known for a sort of trance into which she and some of her converts fell. She also engaged in healing and other displays of charismatic power, but the gift of tongues is not mentioned in connection with her until after the Azusa Street revival in Los Angeles in 1906, the most commonly given date for the beginning of the Pentecostal movement.[46]

She lost credibility in 1909 when she prophesied a tidal wave and earthquake in Oakland, California, that did not happen,[47] but somehow she kept at it until 1914 when she began to identify with Pentecostalism, the movement for which she seems to have been born. Many communities where she held revivals were embarrassed by what they considered to be excesses, and as a result she was often harassed by the law and arrested on trumped-up charges. She finally settled down and built a tabernacle in Indianapolis, where she remained as pastor until she was eighty. And her congregation survived her death.

A skeptical but impressed reporter for the Muncie *Daily News* provided a vivid account of one of Woodworth's revivals for their edition of September 21, 1885.[48] The service described was attended by an estimated twenty thousand people. The preacher's platform, surrounded by mourner's benches, was in a large tent. In order to be seen and heard by the throng, she had to stand on two chairs held together by some men.

The writer gives an account of the sort of trance into which Woodworth[49] went:

> Mrs. Woodworth had risen to a dread and awful majestic grandeur. Her lips moved, but she said nothing. Throwing her head back she gazed upward with a reverential and earnest, though frightful and terrible, yet fascinating,[50] and with an alluring charm her hands supplicantly and helplessly extended in the direction of her gaze and her whole frame was quivering as though laboring under intense excitement.[51]

Woodworth-Etter's biographer includes excerpts from three of her sermons as appendixes to his book. The first, a defense of women in ministry, is based upon most of the same texts that had been used since George Fox and Margaret Fell saw prophesying women as a sign of the end. In this sermon, she says that "Paul worked with women in the gospel more than any of the apostles."[52] Instead of seeing Phoebe as likely to be the owner of a house where the church met, she says that Paul and Phoebe had been holding revivals together and that she had been successful in winning souls to Christ. The Pauline ban on women speaking in church is dealt with by saying that the statement is law, but we are under grace. This direction of Paul is no more binding than that which says it is better not to marry. The response of the Samarian people after the woman at the well told them about Jesus is described as "a great revival there at the well." The sermon ends with an exhortation:

> My dear sister in Christ, as you hear these words may the Spirit of God come upon you, and make you willing to do the work the Lord has assigned to you. . . . The world is dying, the grave is filling, hell is boasting; it will all be over soon.[53]

The next female star to rise in the Pentecostal firmament could easily be the most famous woman preacher of all times, one who did not suffer in comparison with male revivalists such as Dwight L. Moody and Billy Sunday. **Aimee Semple McPherson** attracted an extraordinary amount of attention during her lifetime, having, for instance, her returns to Los Angeles greeted by tickertape parades that rivaled those of the most popular moviestars.[54] Such success inevitably inspired envy on the part of many, making it hard to get a straightforward view of her life. By the same token, Sister's homiletical use of her own life story does not make it any easier to strive after the Rankean will-o'-the-wisp, history "as it actually happened."

Aimee Kennedy grew up on a prosperous farm in southern Ontario, the daughter of an older man and his young second wife, a Salvation Army lassie. A child of ability and attractive appearance, Aimee early on acquired a local reputation for her dramatic and writing abilities as well as her interest in religious questions. It was not, however, until a Pentecostal mission opened in town during 1907, her final year of school, that she found her destiny. It seemed personified in the young Irish evangelist under whose preaching she was converted, Robert Semple. They were married the following summer and, after a short ministry in Canada, went to Chicago, where they both received ordination.

Their deepest sense of call, however, was to missionary work in China, and by the beginning of 1910 they were on their way. They arrived on June 1, and by August 19, Robert had died from dysentery. On September 17, Aimee gave birth to their daughter, Roberta. At the age of nineteen, she found herself in a foreign country, a widow, and a single parent.

Her mother wired her money to come home, but she returned to New York City rather than to the farm in Ontario. Mother Minnie was there, having reached an agreement with her seventy-four-year-old husband that allowed her to go to New York to do administrative work for the Salvation Army. Minnie tried to involve her daughter in this work, but, depressed and lonely, she responded to the attentions of a cashier in a fashionable restaurant, Harold McPherson. They were married in February of 1913.

Harold wanted nothing but domesticity, but his wife had strong guilt feelings about having forsaken the ministry to which she had been called—not to mention energy and creativity her husband could never understand. Her sense of vocation drove her to leave him in June of 1915, going home to her mother, who was temporarily back in Canada. There she became involved in a Pentecostal revival and found that people easily received the gift of tongues through her. She received invitations to conduct revivals and began her first in a town called Mount Forest. This was so successful that she bought a tent, and the future seemed set.

Her husband became reconciled with her and even tried to be her partner in evangelism. In the winter of 1916–17 they made an evangelistic tour of Florida, going north to Long Island and Boston for the summer. Then it was back to Florida again. By this time, Harold had discovered that he was not suited to the life of a revivalist, and the McPhersons separated. Aimee carried on with her ministry, embarking on a transcontinental tour in the fall of 1918. Her mother became, in effect, her business manager or executive officer and took care of all the arrangements necessary for the sorts of campaigns Sister Aimee was now conducting in major cities all over the country.

Such an itinerant life, however, can go on only so long. By February of 1921, McPherson had already purchased land in Los Angeles and broken ground for her permanent mission center, the Angelus Temple. In less than two years, the enormous church complex had been built, paid for, and dedicated. Having a flexible seating capacity of between five thousand and seventy-five hundred, it was filled for three services on Sundays and heavily used every other day of the week as well. Programs proliferated. Sister became one of the first religious broadcasters, opening station KFSG early in 1924. At the end of 1925, she opened a school for ministry, L.I.F.E. Bible College. During the depression, the Temple carried on a huge feeding program for the hungry.

As time went on, the toll of such total dedication began to show. In the spring of 1926, Aimee Semple McPherson disappeared after a swim at Ocean Park and did not appear again until more than a month later. Although scandalmongers then and since have argued that she was with a lover, Edith Blumhofer is right in saying that "the historical evidence is simply too ambiguous to be resolved conclusively in a responsible way."[55] Her final years show the enormous psychic energy demanded by a ministry as vast as hers and the difficulty of sustaining the pace indefinitely. In trying to sum up Sister's impact, Blumhofer gets as close to the reality as one could hope:

> Her singularity resulted more from her extraordinary application of her ordinariness than from unusual traits as such. She found the stamina to persist when others lagged; she had the practical creativity to make or acquire what she wanted while others simply craved it; she had the knack of enlisting cooperation and putting everyone to work. She loved people, and she lived out—at considerable personal cost—dreams many shared but for which few were willing to pay the price.
>
> Perhaps this apparent determination not to consider the personal toll at first set her apart from the crowd.[56]

It was undoubtedly McPherson's power as a preacher that most moved the immense crowds she attracted. The content of her preaching is hardly surprising. Her Foursquare Gospel included the four points of Pentecostalism: (1) justification, (2) Holy Ghost baptism, (3) healing, and (4) the imminent return of Christ, although as time went on she soft-pedaled distinctive Pentecostal emphases for a more general "Bible Christianity" that had a wider appeal.

Her method of presentation was what made her different from hundreds of other preachers. She had a flair for the dramatic and could pick up on the latest slogan and use that as a medium for conveying her traditional message. For instance, during World War I, she took the patriotic expression "Buy a Liberty Bond" and worked it into a catena of biblical expressions that were a call for conversion.[57] The use of a maid's or nurse's uniform as a vestment was originally an expedient of indigence, but she immediately recognized its effectiveness. There was also an erotic element to her appeal that somehow shone through utter decorum. And she used props and devices of all kinds, from musical presentations to flowers to live animals, to make her sermons more vivid.

This use of audiovisual aids in preaching came about in two stages. First was the use of charts to enable congregations to keep track of her outline, a device hit upon when she was developing a core of about sixty sermons that were her basic repertoire.[58] Other revivalists before and since have used similar charts, but she did it with a special flair.

A case in point is the chart used for the sermon "A Certain Man Went Down," based upon the parable of the good Samaritan.[59] At the top of the chart is the legend "A Certain Man Went Down from Jerusalem to Jericho" (**see Vol. 2, pp. 457-71**). Under this appears a picture of a shining walled city with two gates and the name Jerusalem written on the wall. Roads from the two gates merge quickly into a winding road, which leads down to a similar but unshining city labeled Jericho.

Along the road are small numbered signs in two sets, one a group of seven and the other a group of nine. The numbers stand for the letters in the names of the two cities, and on each side there is a list of qualities, the initials of which spell the name of one of the cities. The list used to spell *Jerusalem* is: Jesus, Enjoyment, Rest, Usefulness, Salvation, Adoration, Love, Enrichment, Mercy; and to spell *Jericho*: Jollification, Evil, Restlessness, Indifference, Calousness [*sic*], Hatred, and Obstinacy.

The chart makes the allegorical treatment of the text obvious. Sister begins by saying that the sermon is especially directed to backsliders and admits that she had an experience of their sin herself, not going into detail, but suggesting that it could have been in her marriage to Harold McPherson. What she derives from her text is not the example of the Samaritan as a person of compassion; indeed, the Samaritan signifies Christ. Rather, the two cities represent the two possible eternal destinations of life.

> Let *Jerusalem* on the chart stand for all that is holy and pure and Christlike, for all that is embodied in the New Jerusalem that is soon coming down from God out of Heaven, and *Jericho* for all that is sinful and profane and ungodly.[60]

Within that typology, each word in the story is interpreted anagogically. For instance, after the words "and fell" (among thieves), she says: "Oh you cannot walk a single step without Jesus, no matter how strong you are, or how many years you have been a Christian; the moment you let go of his dear hand, that moment you will cease to stand, and you will fall." The qualities for which the names of the cities are acronyms represent the clothing worn by the citizens of each, with the apparel of

Jerusalem representing what the backslider is stripped of. The beast on which the victim is set is salvation. The inn is the church, and the host is the preacher.

In many ways, the treatment is very patristic, although it is hard to imagine one of the fathers having such an unctuous style as to say in response, "I will repay thee."

> Why! Just one glimpse of his beautiful face—fairer than the lilies, brighter than the sun—just one smile from his tender eyes—just one "well done," and we would be a million times repaid for any little labor of love that is naught but our reasonable service when all is said and done.[61]

Other examples could be given, but the point is clear. A barrel of sixty such sermons would be adequate for a protracted meeting a month long.

After Sister Aimee settled in Los Angeles, built the Angelus Temple, and had a regular congregation, however, it was necessary to employ a wider repertoire and to introduce more variety. While her preaching of weekday sermons remained in her old basic style, the Sunday sermons in time came to be more dramatic—perhaps in keeping with the expectations of Tinseltown. She began to produce what are called "illustrated sermons," complete with costumes, props, and scenery.[62] The message or even the approach does not appear to have changed much; the difference seems to be that she could enlist much more elaborate audiovisual aids than the simple charts of the revival tent. But what she wanted to get across remained the same. As time went on, the productions became extravaganzas, and the streetcar company had to run extra trolleys on the route that led to the Temple when a new illustrated sermon began its run.[63] It was said that with George Whitefield, America got its first taste of theater under the banner of religion. That was not to be its last. But, contrary to the implication of Harry S. Stout's characterization of Whitefield as "the divine dramatist," dramatic presentation is not incompatible with utter sincerity. Few things are so impressive, in fact, as the ring of complete conviction.

This trajectory of women preaching in the Wesleyan Holiness/ Pentecostal tradition can be completed by reference to a study made of the sermons of **contemporary Pentecostal women preachers** in central Missouri by Elaine J. Lawless, a folklorist who teaches English at the University of Missouri.[64] While the current division of this history of preaching is supposed to survey a period that ends with World War II, homiletical conventions within this faith community can be expected to have remained nearly enough the same for an analysis of current practice to be informative about the way earlier preaching was done. Studies by folklorists in the field of contemporary African American preaching certainly contributed to the interpretation of classical preaching in that tradition advanced in the previous chapter.

The women studied by Lawless ministered in small Pentecostal churches in impoverished agricultural communities either as evangelists or, less commonly, as pastors. The most significant result of her study for the concerns of this book is the difference she discovered between the preaching of those who were invited into congregations in which someone else was pastor, and the preaching of those who were the regular minister of a congregation. Lawless says of one woman revivalist's pulpit behavior:

> Sister Linda's style of preaching is close to what we have come to expect from inspired, spontaneous evangelistic preachers in general. . . . She speaks quickly and, for the most part, in a loud dramatic performance style. Her rhythmic, punctuated style yields "line" formations that are balanced symmetrically, metered, and phonetically pleasing. In the most clearly "chanted" portions of her sermons, she terminates each line with the standard sermon performative "ah." She utilizes simple assonance and alliteration and persistently employs "formulas" for emphasis and for transition during certain portions of her sermons. She characteristically repeats formulaic sequences for effect.[65]

As Lawless says, the style is familiar; it sounds like the African American preaching described by Bruce Rosenberg and Gerald Davis and that of white male clergy of Baptist subdenominations in the Appalachians reported upon by Howard Dorgan. What Lawless calls the "cheerleading" approach of Sister Linda is the familiar pattern of "call-and-response."

The main differences Lawless finds between the preaching of the evangelist and that of the pastor result from the intimate acquaintance the latter has with members of the congregation and the different purpose of helping them lead the life of faith rather than converting them to it.[66] Hence there is less need to work up the congregation or to establish a relation with them; instead, everything can be more "businesslike":

> She mentions child abuse, drugs, divorce, adultery, Alcoholics Anonymous, and compromise in an evil and sinful world. These are real-life, everyday issues for the people she knows so well. Poverty and unemployment are common in the lives of her congregation. Unwed

mothers attend her church; young men whose wives have left them with three babies come to Sister Anna for help. She cannot be a stranger talking to an anonymous audience. She knows them too well.[67]

THE PREACHING OF LIBERAL WOMEN

The history of women in preaching is very different from that of women serving as ordained ministers and pastors of congregations, acceptance being far easier to come by in the former role than in the latter. Most of the women studied so far preached as itinerant evangelists rather than as parish clergy.

Even as late as 1888, when Willard published her classic *Woman in the Pulpit,* there were only an estimated twenty women in the United States serving as pastors. That figure did not include the some five hundred women evangelists or the Quaker women "preachers," whose numbers were estimated to be around 350. Nor did it include Salvation Army officers.[68]

Even when women were ordained, they did not necessarily stay in the pastorate very long. Much is made of the fact that Antoinette Brown was "the first fully ordained woman in a recognized American denomination," but less is said about the way her initial parish ministry lasted less than a year.[69] As Edwina Hunter has said:

> Congregationalists (United Church of Christ), Disciples (Christian Church), and American Baptists have ordained women for almost one hundred years; however, real progress in full acceptance of women in parish ministry has come only recently.[70]

There is, however, one group of women clergy in a liberal denomination who functioned over a number of decades, preached regularly in their own congregations, and whose ministry is well enough documented to permit a reconstruction of what they did and how they did it. In *Prophetic Sisterhood: Liberal Women Ministers of the Frontier, 1880–1930,*[71] Cynthia Grant Tucker has traced the growth of a network of Unitarian women clergy that arose in Iowa at the end of the nineteenth century and continued to influence their church for several decades. The pivotal figure was **Mary A. Safford,** who had been born just across the Mississippi near Hamilton, Illinois, the daughter of a religious liberal. Near her home was that of another family with Unitarian connections. Their daughter **Eleanor Gordon** was Safford's best friend. In their early twenties, the two "made a pledge that they would spend their lives together serving the world as a team."[72] Gordon was already a schoolteacher, but Safford soon decided to become a Unitarian minister. Unable to earn degrees, the two began to educate themselves as best they could. The Unitarians' Western secretary, Jenkin Lloyd Jones, helped them to begin a congregation in Hamilton. By the end of the year, the little congregation was flourishing. The Sunday school organized by Gordon had a weekly attendance of more than 150, and Safford had organized another small church eight miles away.

Jones asked Safford to become the minister of a parish in Humboldt, Iowa, where Gordon became school principal. Even with their different professions, the two lived together and worked as a team. As the work grew rapidly, Gordon became more and more involved in the life of the congregation, so that the sensible thing seemed for her to become ordained herself and work full-time for the church. They took into their home four young women who assisted in the parish while attending Humboldt's Normal College, and some of whom entered the ministry. They also began forming a network of women in ministry throughout an area encompassing several states. In time, the women who entered the ministry under the tutelage of Safford and Gordon began to influence others to seek that goal. After five years in Humboldt, the two ministers moved to a parish in Sioux City, leaving a vacancy that was filled by other women.

The "sisterhood" that grew up around Safford and Gordon expanded in time to include twenty-one women engaged in promoting the cause of liberal religion.[73] Not all accepted ordination, and some of those who did were eventually to leave parochial ministry. But for a while, Iowa seemed a Camelot for liberal women ministers. There they engaged in an imaginative and energetic form of ministry that evoked an enthusiastic response. Operating out of an egalitarian perspective, they conceived of the church as a family. This domestic model shaped the way they built churches, conducted worship, and involved parishioners in study projects.

The women had received much of their own vision from eastern male Unitarians, Universalists, and transcendalists including William Ellery Channing, Theodore Parker, and Ralph Waldo Emerson. Yet the heirs of these men in the East, the Unitarian national leadership, disapproved of and eventually discouraged the frontier ministries simply because they were performed by women, even though they were proving more effective than those of male clergy. Many of the women ultimately left for work with other causes where they expected their efforts to meet with a better response. Others remained, but became too hedged in by bureaucracy to be able to exercise much influence. For a while, though, it must have been a heady experience.

These women took their preaching responsibilities very seriously. In this regard, they resembled their male counterparts in the Unitarian ministry. Since their church had accepted the new biblical criticism coming out of Germany, they felt no necessity to engage in traditional exegesis in order to demonstrate a system of orthodox doctrine. Instead, they felt free to range the whole expanse of human experience. And, while they generally took a biblical text to preach from,

> their themes and "proof passages," topical illustrations, and language were just as likely to come from current events and history as from the Bible or to draw on ancient and modern philosophy, world religions, science, and art.[74]

They were excited about ideas, especially those of the new science and contemporary philosophy, yet they resisted some of the fashions of the age such as phrenology, mind cure, and social Darwinism. Their sermons were thoughtful presentations of ideas rather than efforts to stir up emotions. And, although the majority of listeners in their day were no more eager than the majority today to hear sermons advocating social change, these women used their pulpits as platforms from which they could prophetically call for reform.[75]

This overview of their preaching can be made more concrete by a look at a few of their sermons.[76] One preached by Safford on Matthew 19:17 was published in the July 1856 issue of *Old and New,* the journal of the Iowa conference. It begins with a contrast between a former age, in which teachings of the church were considered authoritative in their own right, and the present age, in which demonstration by scientific experiment was required. That did not mean, however, that the day of religion had passed:

> Because religion rests on a sure foundation, because it is as real as the law of gravitation or as the solar system, it will bear the test of reason and experiment, it can be tried in the crucible of life and not be found wanting.

To show the empirical basis of religion, however, one had to go much deeper than what the revivalists meant by experiencing religion. Instant conversion was not deep enough to accommodate all that is involved in religion, "for the religious life is above all things else, the honest, loving, reverent life." Just as flowers need to incarnate sunshine in the very tissues of their being, so human beings must use everything that comes their way to build noble characters. This point is documented first by a quotation from Emerson and then by the text "If thou wouldest enter into life, keep the Commandments."

> Religion has been too divorced from life. Too long have men tried to embody it in creeds and forms and rituals instead of striving to express its divine strength and beauty, its sweetness and light in loyal, loving lives.

Conversion, then, is not the end of religious development, but only its beginning. In the past, conversion has often been the occasion for someone to claim superiority over others, rather than to acquire the sort of humility exemplified by Dickens's "poor little Joe." In contrast to such arrogance, true religious experience is "our delight in finding truth, our satisfaction in honest, faithful work, our joy in noble love." A life devoted to the activities that produce those satisfactions will permit someone eventually to attain to an experimental knowledge of religion.

A sermon by Eleanor Gordon making a similar point but taking a very different form appeared in the February 1906 issue of *Old and New.* (The text of this sermon is in **Vol. 2, pp. 471-75.**) The form has become common since then, but it must have been rare in sermons at the time. Gordon says that her text was an entire novel by Edith Wharton, *The House of Mirth,* which had appeared the previous year. This text could be reduced to several biblical verses, however.

The novel is a "picture of a society where the one aim is pleasure," and thus one in which the one essential is money. Members of the group who did not have money had to devote all their efforts to marrying someone who did. The two characters in the story who did not share this preoccupation remained, nevertheless, unattractive. One of the two was a woman philanthropist, but she did not truly represent the modern settlement worker, because such a person would not fit the environment of the story. The main character in the novel is Lily Bart, who had grace, charm, and beauty, but in order to have money she had to marry it. Hers is a divided self, too good to accept the proposal when it came, but too weak to leave the group to support herself; too good to expose the false friend who smeared her reputation, but too weak to go on living on her own.

Gordon suggests that her congregation must wonder how a depiction of such a social world can offer any insight into their own lives. In reply, she points out that if a line could be drawn separating good from evil, "this line would not pass between any two of us. It would divide each and every one into two parts. . . ." Thus the evils of the more elegant social group found their counterparts in the humbler one. The need for excitement that had turned weekends in the House of Mirth into gambling parties caused the local school to have football and other rough sports so that boys would not be too bored to attend. Unless the young women of Des Moines were trained to support themselves with honest and useful labor, they would not be any better off than Lily Bart. Even those who would inherit means had a debt to the universe that they owed for their subsistence, a debt that should be repaid by usefulness. The suggestion of the novel that "licentiousness and flagrant violation of the moral law" can grow out of seemingly so small a thing as "love of luxury and a desire to take things easy" is absolutely true to life. People must learn that "the one really essential thing in this world is personal honor." The novel is nothing but an extended paraphrase of Jesus' question: "What shall it profit a man if he gain the whole world and lose his own soul?"

Thus the emergence of women preachers can be seen as one of the fruits of the Second Great Awakening. While Quaker women had been accustomed to engaging in ministry on a par with men from their origins in the seventeenth century, it was only with the Awakening that such openness was met in other traditions. The emphasis placed by the Awakening upon religious experience in contrast to theological sophistication meant that the qualifications for preaching became less of a barrier—although there remained much resistance. Since the tradition of which the Awakening was characteristic was a Wesleyan trajectory that went through the African American churches, white Methodist Episcopalians, the United Brethren, and Holiness and Pentecostal denominations, it is not surprising to find a succession of women preachers there. Although some of the liberal denominations pioneered in opening ordination and parish ministry to women, there was so much opposition that these permissions generally fell into desuetude. Yet there are notable exceptions, such as the group of Unitarian women in Iowa who were so active for a time. While the total number of women who preached remained small, the quality of their work was an earnest of good things to come.

CONCLUSION

The three main homiletical fruits of the fervor of the Second Great Awakening were (1) preaching on the social implications of the gospel, (2) the beginnings of African American preaching, and (3) the first admission of a significant number of women to the ranks of those who preached. It would be possible to go on to consider another fruit of the Second Awakening to be the Third.[77] That temptation will be resisted, though, because while D. L. Moody, Sam Jones, and Billy Sunday did have their own distinctive styles of preaching, in many ways what they did can be understood as a decline rather than a development of the "Religion of the Heart" movement.

Certainly the emotionalism that was characteristic of the First and Second Awakenings had so declined that these evangelists would have removed from the congregation anyone who became too excited. Then, too, what was understood as conversion had tamed considerably. Instead of turmoil that included being slain in the Spirit and struggles that could go on for days or even weeks, it came to be nothing more than a willingness to hold up one's hand, sign a card, or walk down the sawdust trail to shake the evangelist's hand. Most of the people who attended these revivals were already active in churches, and their conversion meant little more than committing themselves to living in a way more consistent with the profession of faith they had already made. Revivals had come a long way from Northampton and Cane Ridge. Revival no longer meant any great upheaval in either the culture at large or the lives of individual Christians.

FOR FURTHER READING

Blumhofer, Edith L. *Aimee Semple McPherson: Everybody's Sister.* Library of Religious Biography. Grand Rapids, Mich.: Eerdmans, 1993.

Brekus, Catherine A. *Strangers & Pilgrims: Female Preaching in America, 1740–1845: Gender and American Culture.* Chapel Hill: University of North Carolina Press, 1998.

Larson, Rebecca. *Daughters of Light: Quaker Women Preaching and Prophesying in the Colonies and Abroad, 1700–1775.* Chapel Hill: University of North Carolina Press, 1999.

Lucretia Mott: Her Complete Speeches and Sermons. Edited by Dana Greene. Studies in Women and Religion, vol. 4. Lewiston, N.Y.: Edwin Mellen, 1980.

McPherson, Aimee Semple. *This Is That: Personal Experiences, Sermons, and Writings.* Los Angeles: Echo Park Evangelistic Association, 1923.

Palmer, Phoebe. *Promise of the Father; or, A Neglected Speciality* [*sic*] *of the Last Days, Addressed to the Clergy and Laity of All Christian Communities*. Boston: Henry V. Degen, 1859.

Raser, Harold E. *Phoebe Palmer: Her Life and Thought*. Studies in Women and Religion, vol. 22. Lewiston, N.Y.: Edwin Mellen, 1987).

Sisters of the Spirit: Three Black Women's Autobiographies of the Nineteenth Century. Edited with introduction by William L. Andrews. Religion in North America. Bloomington: Indiana University Press, 1986.

Tucker, Cynthia Grant. *Prophetic Sisterhood: Liberal Women Ministers of the Frontier, 1880–1930*. Boston: Beacon, 1990.

Notes

1. There were, of course, individuals such as Anne Hutchinson who engaged in activity that could be called preaching, but no religious bodies other than the Quakers accepted preaching by women.

2. Rebecca Larson, *Daughters of Light: Quaker Women Preaching and Prophesying in the Colonies and Abroad, 1700–1775* (Chapel Hill: University of North Carolina Press, 1999), 339.

3. William Penn, *Fruits of Solitude* (London: Northcott, 1693), 33, quoted by Margaret Bacon in *Mothers of Feminism: The Story of Quaker Women in America* (San Francisco: Harper & Row, 1986), 2.

4. Horton Davies has graphically set out the various degrees of radicalism in movements of the period by describing the progression of interiorization from Roman Catholics to Quakers in *Worship and Theology in England: 1603–1690* (Princeton: University Press, 1975), 495-96. It should be noted that the Quakers were not the only body at the time to have women preachers: more radical Independents such as the Brownists had them as well. See Antonia Fraser, *The Weaker Vessel* (George Weidenfeld & Nicholson, and Knopf, 1984; New York: Vintage, 1985), 244-64.

5. The passage begins: "In the last days it will be, God declares, that I will pour out my Spirit upon all flesh, and your sons and your daughters shall prophesy."

6. Catherine M. Wilcox, *Theology and Women's Ministry in Seventeenth-Century English Quakerism: Handmaids of the Lord,* Studies in Women and Religion, vol. 35 (Lewiston, N.Y.: Edwin Mellen , 1995), 235. The understanding given above of how the Quakers originally understood the preaching of women is an attempt to summarize the thesis of Wilcox's book.

7. An exception is the heirs of the Gurneyite faction of Quakers, who had pastors after the Second Great Awakening; their meetings for worship were very much like general Protestant services.

8. Carol Stoneburner, "Drawing a Profile of American Female Public Friends as

Shapers of Human Space" in *The Influence of Quaker Women on American History: Biographical Studies,* ed. Carol and John Stoneburner, Studies in Women and Religion, vol. 21 (Lewiston, N.Y.: Edwin Mellen, 1986), 6.

9. Elise Boulding, "Mapping the Inner Journey of Quaker Women," in ibid., 89.

10. A sense of the way this worked can be gained from *The Journal of John Woolman.* The edition consulted was the John Greenleaf Whittier text with intro. Frederick B. Tolles (New York: Citadel, 1961). I am grateful to Dr. Ann Riggs for this insight.

11. Fraser, *The Weaker Vessel,* 365-66; Bacon, *Mothers of Feminism,* 18-19.

12. Ibid., 26. It has been estimated that twenty-nine of the first eighty-seven Friends who traveled in ministry to New England between 1656 and 1700 were women. This does not include those who accompanied their husbands. Ibid., 29.

13. Bacon, *Mothers of Feminism,* 34.

14. Larson, *Daughters of Light,* 232-95, traces this evolution in status.

15. Margaret H. Bacon, "Lucretia Mott: Holy Obedience and Human Liberation," in Stoneburner and Stoneburner, eds., *The Influence of Quaker Women on American History,* 203-4.

16. Mott was in the wool business, having abandoned cotton because it was a product of slave labor.

17. The introductory essay in *Lucretia Mott: Her Complete Speeches and Sermons,* ed. Dana Greene, Studies in Women and Religion, vol. 4 (Lewiston, N.Y.: Edwin Mellen, 1980), 12.

18. This may be seen, for instance, in the section devoted to the topic in the standard history edited by Rosemary Radford Ruether and Rosemary Skinner Keller, *Women and Religion in America* (San Francisco: Harper & Row, 1981). Written by Barbara Brown Zikmund, the chapter is entitled, "The Struggle for the Right to Preach," 1:193-205. A guide to literature in the field is Robert R. Howard, "Women and Preaching: A Bibliography," *Homiletic* 17 (1992): 7-10; 18 (1993): 34-36; 19 (1994): 28-30; 20 (1995): 7-10. Susie C. Stanley has compiled *Wesleyan/Holiness Women Clergy: A Preliminary Bibliography* (Portland, Ore.: Western Evangelical Seminary, 1994). I am grateful to President Zikmund, Dr. Howard, and Professor Stanley for assistance in several ways.

19. Catherine A. Brekus, *Strangers & Pilgrims: Female Preaching in America, 1740–1845: Gender and American Culture* (Chapel Hill: University of North Carolina Press, 1998).

20. Followers of Barton Stone who did not go with him into the merger with Alexander Campbell's denomination that created the Disciples of Christ.

21. Marta Tomhave Blauvelt, "Women and Revivalism," in *Women and Religion in America,* ed. Ruether and Keller, 1:5. Carleton Mabee corrects the tendency to turn Sojourner Truth into a legend by using critical scholarship to establish her real contribution, in *Sojourner Truth: Slave, Prophet, Legend* (New York and London: New York University Press, 1993).

22. Amanda Smith, *An Autobiography: The Story of the Lord's Dealing with Mrs. Amanda Smith the Colored Evangelist,* intro. Jualynne E. Dodson (Chicago: Meyer, 1893; reprint, Schaumburg Library of Nineteenth-Century Women Writers, New York: Oxford University Press, 1988).

23. *Sisters of the Spirit: Three Black Women's Autobiographies of the Nineteenth Century,* ed. with intro. William L. Andrews, Religion in North America (Bloomington: Indiana University Press, 1986). Andrews gives short synopses of the women's lives on pp. 4-10.

24. This and other patterns recur with such consistency in the life stories of these and other women of the period that one wonders how much such statements are the conventions of a literary genre. This, of course, is not to question the historicity of the experience. Such conventions, among other things, tell people what to expect in their own experiences.

25. Lee and Elaw had significant contacts with Quakers and observed some of their conventions.

26. In the introduction to Foote's book, the editor of *Christian Harvester,* Thomas K. Doty, says ironically that Foote was "guilty of three great crimes": color, womanhood, and evangelism. Andrews, *Sisters of the Spirit,* 164.

27. Though seldom in such elegant language as Elaw uses to justify emotional response to preaching. Andrews, *Sisters of the Spirit,* 107.

28. Julia Foote, *A Brand Plucked from the Fire: An Autobiographical Sketch* (Cleveland: privately printed, 1879).

29. Andrews, *Sisters of the Spirit,* 168.

30. Ibid., 209.

31. Ibid., 222.

32. Ruth A. Tucker and Walter L. Liefeld, *Daughters of the Church: Women and Ministry from New Testament Times to the Present* (Grand Rapids, Mich.: Zondervan, 1987), 262.

33. Harold E. Raser, *Phoebe Palmer: Her Life and Thought,* Studies in Women and Religion, vol. 22 (Lewiston, N.Y.: Edwin Mellen, 1987), 47. The internal quotation is from Palmer's *The Way of Holiness, With Notes by the Way* (New York: W. C. Palmer, 1843, ed. of 1867), 37-38.

34. For an enthusiastic estimation of Palmer's place in American church history, see the editorial introduction of Thomas C. Oden to *Phoebe Palmer: Selected Writings,* Sources of American Spirituality (New York: Paulist, 1988), 1-22. Perhaps more measured is the assessment of Raser, *Phoebe Palmer,* 289-98.

35. Raser, *Phoebe Palmer,* 115-16.

36. Phoebe Palmer, *Promise of the Father; or, A Neglected Speciality* [*sic*] *of the Last Days, Addressed to the Clergy and Laity of All Christian Communities* (Boston: Henry V. Degen, 1859), 36.

37. George Hughes, *Fragrant Memories of the Tuesday Meeting and the Guide to Holiness and Their Fifty Years' Work for Jesus* (New York: Palmer & Hughes, 1886), 182.

38. Raser, *Phoebe Palmer,* 23.

39. Ibid., 290.

40. John O. Foster, *Life and Labors of Mrs. Maggie Newton Van Cott, The First Lady Licensed to Preach in the Methodist Episcopal Church in the U.S.A.,* intro. Gilbert Haven and David Sherman, Women in American Protestant Religion 1800–1930 (Cincinnati: Hitchcock & Walden, 1872; reprint. New York: Garland, 1987). Hereafter, references to this work will be given parenthetically in the text by page number alone.

41. I do not know if this was the settlementhouse started by Phoebe Palmer.

42. Van Cott's biography ends in 1872, near the beginning of her ministry. The words in quotation marks appeared as an undocumented quotation in Tucker and Liefeld, *Daughters of the Church*, 269.

43. *Autobiography of Lydia Sexton: The Story of Her Life Through a Period of Over Seventy-two Years, From 1799 to 1872. Her Early Privates, Adventures, and Reminiscences, Clouds and Sunshine, As Child, Wife, Mother, and Widow; As a Minister of the Gospel; As Prison Chaplain,* Women in American Protestant Religion 1800–1930 (Dayton, Ohio: United Brethren Publishing House, 1882; reprint, New York: Garland, 1987). References to page numbers in this source will be indicated parenthetically in the text.

44. Donald W. Dayton, *Theological Roots of Pentecostalism* (Grand Rapids, Mich.: Francis Asbury Press of Zondervan, 1987). See also Robert M. Anderson, *Vision of the Disinherited: The Making of American Pentecostalism* (New York: Oxford University Press, 1979; reprint, Peabody, Mass.: Hendrickson, 1992).

45. Wayne E. Warner, *The Woman Evangelist: The Life and Times of Charismatic Evangelist Maria B. Woodworth-Etter,* Studies in Evangelicalism, no. 8 (Meteuchen, N.J.: Scarecrow, 1986).

46. The other birthday commonly assigned is when Agnes N. Ozman spoke in tongues at Charles F. Parham's Bethel College in Topeka, in late 1900 or early 1901. See Anderson, *Vision of the Disinherited,* 51-58.

47. Warner, *The Woman Evangelist,* 309-11.

48. Ibid., 52-57.

49. Her name at the time.

50. This is one of several places where the reporter omitted words or Warner failed to transcribe them. I incline to the former explanation.

51. Members of the congregation who went into a trance, however, would become stiff and could remain that way for hours. Warner, *The Woman Evangelist*, 54.

52. Ibid., 297-98.

53. Ibid., 300.

54. Two recent biographies are past the muckraking that characterized some earlier ones: Daniel Mark Epstein, *Sister Aimee: The Life of Aimee Semple McPherson* (San Diego: A Harvest Book of Harcourt, Brace & Co., 1993), and Edith L. Blumhofer, *Aimee Semple McPherson: Everybody's Sister,* Library of Religious Biography (Grand Rapids, Mich.: Eerdmans, 1993).

55. Blumhofer, *Aimee Semple McPherson: Everybody's Sister,* 300.

56. Ibid., 21.

57. Described by Epstein, *Sister Aimee,* 130.

58. Blumhofer, *Aimee Semple McPherson: Everybody's Sister,* 155.

59. Aimee Semple McPherson, *This Is That: Personal Experiences, Sermons, and Writings* (Los Angeles: Echo Park Evangelistic Assoc., 1923), 599-614.

60. Ibid., 601.

61. Ibid., 338.

62. The illustrated sermons are discussed in Blumhofer, *Aimee Semple McPherson: Everybody's Sister,* 258-62, and in Epstein, *Sister Aimee,* 253-59.

63. The reality was vivid enough, but journalists could not help improving on something that lent itself so naturally to caricature. Thus they said that one night, dressed

in a traffic cop's uniform, she came down the aisle of the Temple on a motorcycle and roared up a ramp to stop in mid-stage. She merely stood by a motorcycle parked onstage and, while sirens sounded in the background, raised a white-gloved hand and said: "Stop! You've been arrested for speeding." She quickly sketched in a number of vignettes in which persons seemed destined for every success, and then began to list the sort of incident that could arrest any such progress, thus reminding her congregation of the contingency of human life and the necessity of depending upon God at every moment.

64. Elaine J. Lawless, *Handmaidens of the Lord: Pentecostal Women Preachers and Traditional Religion* (Philadelphia: University of Pennsylvania Press, 1988).

65. Ibid., 90.

66. Even the sermons of the pastors end in an altar call, however, as they do when the pastors are male clergy in any strongly evangelistic tradition.

67. Ibid., 105.

68. Zikmund, "The Struggle for the Right to Preach," 208.

69. Tucker and Liefeld, *Daughters of the Church,* 281. It was almost fifty years before she returned to the pastorate, then as a Unitarian, in a church she founded and remained in for twenty years, All Souls' in Elizabeth, New Jersey. She died in 1921.

70. Edwina Hunter, in intro. to "Contemporary Women Preachers," in *And Blessed Is She: Sermons by Women,* ed. David Albert Farmer and Edwina Hunter (San Francisco: Harper & Row, 1990), 88.

71. Cynthia Grant Tucker, *Prophetic Sisterhood: Liberal Women Ministers of the Frontier, 1880–1930* (Boston: Beacon, 1990).

72. Ibid., 18.

73. Biographical sketches of these twenty-one women are given in Tucker, *Prophetic Sisterhood,* 235-40.

74. Ibid., 161.

75. This paragraph is an effort to summarize Tucker's chapter on "Preaching Reform," in ibid., 159-70.

76. I am grateful to Professor Tucker for making the texts of these sermons available to me.

77. The identification of four Great Awakenings is the work of William G. McLoughlin. His designation of the exact period of the Third Awakening changed between his initial presentation of the concept in *Modern Revivalism: Charles Grandison Finney to Billy Graham* (New York: Ronald Press, 1959) and his presentation of it in *Revivals, Awakenings, and Reform: An Essay on Religion and Social Change in America, 1607–1977,* Chicago History of American Religion (Chicago and London: University of Chicago Press, 1978).

CHAPTER 22

THE PREACHING OF ROMANTICISM IN BRITAIN

DEFINITION

The rationalistic preaching inaugurated by the latitudinarians and the emotional preaching of the "Religion of the Heart" were both born in the aftermath of the religious wars at the end of the seventeenth century. Rationalistic preaching lasted into the nineteenth century, while heart preaching is still practiced today in some circles. By the end of the eighteenth century, a third mode of preaching began to appear that had elements in common with both of the others while having a spirit different from that of either. For instance, it stressed emotion, but did not try to furnish the occasion for religious experiences such as conversion. Rather, it saw feeling as a path that ultimately gave greater access to knowledge than reason. This epistemological understanding of feeling, however, did not mean that those who held it were anti-intellectual or opposed to critical thought. To the contrary, it was in their circles that, for instance, historical-critical biblical interpretation developed.

The intellectual movement of which this sort of preaching was a manifestation is called Romanticism. While in many ways it was essentially a literary movement, from its earliest days in Germany and Great Britain it caught the imagination of the day's greatest philosophical minds, and theologians were numbered among its most seminal thinkers. Unfortunately, it seems virtually impossible to get scholars, especially literary critics, to agree on what constitutes the essence of Romanticism. There is, however, no need to supply the correct definition here. It is enough to list qualities that have been associated with Romanticism by reputable scholars and see how these qualities became standard in the preaching that will occupy this chapter and the next two.

The task may be performed by looking at what historians of doctrine have pointed to as characteristics of the thought of theologians admitted to have been Romantic in their outlook. The list compiled by Bernard M. G. Reardon is a good example. He has said that Romanticism can be defined negatively by opposing it to classicism.[1] Its essence, however, is not to be found in this antithesis nor in the horror of reality attributed to it by Emile Faguet, but rather in a deep sense that behind and within the finite there is always "an infinite beyond" that shines through. Thus there is always a coincidence of the finite and infinite. Taken to extremes, this Romantic conviction easily boils over into pantheism; it certainly finds idealistic philosophy congenial. But the basic conviction is that behind the finite and transfiguring it there is always the infinite.

The sense of the ultimate unity of things involved in this stance caused Romanticists to yearn for final reconciliation and peace, although they did not expect to achieve it without endless struggle. And their recognition of the need to strive fitted into the Romantic understanding of perfection as being dynamic rather than static. Thus meaning was found in process, and reality was seen as always being brought into being and never finally achieved.

The struggle to achieve reconciliation and peace was—as all else—considered to be highly individual, and the reality perceived through it was therefore subjective. The ego became the measure of reality. This premium on uniqueness can be illustrated in the way the standard Romantic hero was an exile. An outcome of this egotism was an intense emotionalism. And in this emphasis on emotion, there was an understanding that feeling had an epistemological function: It was through the strength and depth of feeling that knowledge was attained. Religious truth, for instance, was considered to be subjective, but that subjectivity made it more rather than less reliable.

In a similar way, an aestheticism was also related to this emotionalism; indeed, as Reardon says, "aesthetics itself becomes a religion, with art as its dogma and liturgy."[2] Aesthetics itself was highly subjective, and that subjectivity gave it much of its importance. The uniquely individual had never before been so prized.

Since Romanticists believed every moment of the past was, on the one hand, unique and, on the other, a finite moment in which the infinite was present, they also shared a new appreciation for history. Beginning with a taste for the culturally most alien period, the Gothic, this love of the past led in time to the development of critical historiography. Yet it also gave birth to a new respect for tradition and continuity—an ironic turn of events, since nothing was more Romantic than a contempt for convention and a "bohemian" delight in shocking respectability. Still, modern historical consciousness began with Romanticism.[3]

EARLY INFLUENCES

To this list of traits have to be added only a couple of the period's characteristics commonly noted by literary critics—love of nature and interest in common people—in order to have criteria for recognizing that a tradition of preaching deserves to be considered Romanticist. Not surprisingly, most of these traits are apparent in the thought and work of "the father of modern theology," Friedrich Daniel Ernst Schleiermacher (1768–1834), whom Reardon calls the Protestant theologian *par excellence* of the Romantic movement.[4]

As in Germany, the beginnings of the Romantic movement in England had an important connection with preaching. The first major literary monument of the movement in Britain was *Lyrical Ballads,* published in 1798 by William Wordsworth and Samuel Taylor Coleridge. While Coleridge was a poet of genius in his younger days, that muse seems to have deserted him as he aged. In his maturity, however, he became an unusually perceptive critic as well as a theological writer of distinction.

He was one of the few British thinkers of his time to read German, and he kept abreast of what was being written in that language. As a result he became, with Connop Thirlwall, one of the first to introduce German historical-critical biblical scholarship to the British Isles. Yet the efforts of these two were not much heeded, for it was only with the publication of Benjamin Jowett's contribution to *Essays and Reviews* (1860) that the English church became aware enough of that scholarship to be disturbed by it.[5] Nevertheless, since the introduction of historical-critical exegetical perspective was one of the most revolutionary elements of Romanticist preaching, it is worth noting that one of the fathers of Romanticism in Britain was a pioneer in this perspective.

While Coleridge had alluded to the topic in earlier works, the fullest statement of his position (itself quite short) was published posthumously in 1840. *Confessions of an Inquiring Spirit*[6] appears in the form of seven letters written to a friend about biblical inspiration. In this work Coleridge says he cannot accept the doctrine that biblical books were dictated word for word by the Holy Spirit and provides some critical analysis of biblical books to show the reasons why.

The principles that Coleridge had learned from Herder, Eichhorn, Lessing, and Schleiermacher seem self-evident to mainstream Christianity today, Catholic as well as Protestant, but they were shocking then. It was hard for his contemporaries to recognize that he occupied a mediating position between those who idolized the Bible and those who rejected it. He accepted the Bible as the medium through which Christian faith and morals were mediated and valued it above all other books put together. He was grateful for the way it spoke to his deepest needs. Yet he also had to admit that its excellence was not uniform, that there were traces of chaff still in the well-winnowed wheat. And he was convinced that what was valuable in it had a far greater chance of being recognized and lived by if those who found it were not required to treat the rest as having the same level of merit.[7] As his sources indicate, his position was thoroughly Romantic and was to be the view that informed Romanticist preaching.

PRE-ROMANTIC RHETORIC

While it is fairly easy to date the beginning of the Romantic movement, that does not mean it emerged instantly and full-grown. All through the eighteenth century in Great Britain, there were anticipations of attitudes that would be considered to be characteristically Romantic in the following century, and in France these began to appear even earlier.

Longinus

For rhetoric, the most noteworthy harbinger was the publication in 1674 of Boileau's translation of an obscure[8] Greek rhetorical treatise called *On the Sublime* by an otherwise unknown writer whose name was thought to be "Longinus." The impact of this work on the thought of the time, however, has been compared with that of Freud's ideas on contemporary thought.[9] "*On the Sublime* added to Neoclassical rhetorical criticism an element it badly needed, a theory of genius and inspiration to rise above pedantic rules of composition without contradicting them."[10] Nothing could have been better calculated to appeal to the Romantic consciousness that was to emerge than ideas of inspiration, genius, and rising above pedantic rules.

What makes the seventeenth-century publication of this work so important in the history of rhetoric in general and homiletics in particular is that it contained the first statement of the view that persuasion was not the only purpose of oratory. It also had the aim of enabling an audience to experience sublimity. The sublime *(hypsos)* is defined as "a kind of height and conspicuous excellence in speeches and writings."

> What is beyond nature drives the audience not to persuasion, but to ecstasy. What is wonderful, with its stunning power, prevails everywhere over that which aims merely at persuasion and at gracefulness.[11]

Longinus's view that the aim of public speaking was not so much to persuade an audience of the truth of a proposition as it was to enable them to experience ecstasy was to have enormous influence on Romantic thought. In the critical thought of Coleridge, for instance, "we can see the Romantic attempt to adopt Longinus' principle of intense emotion as the central and organic element of art."[12]

British Rhetorical Thought

The influence of Longinus on British preaching, however, was to be mediated by three rhetorical writers, all clergy deeply concerned about preaching whose books were to be the subject's most influential treatments in both England and America through the nineteenth century.[13] The late-eighteenth century was a time when rhetoric occupied some of the best minds of the age—such thinkers as Edmund Burke, Adam Smith, David Hume, Lord Kames, and others—so that writers speak of this as the period of New Rhetoric.

It was also a time when the intellectual life of the Scottish universities was more exciting than that of the ancient English ones. This was the world of the first two authors of textbooks in rhetoric to be noted, Hugh Blair and George Campbell. The third, Richard Whately, was to write half a century later in Oxford. These three, by writing textbooks that would shape the understanding of public speaking of English and American university students and schoolboys through the nineteenth century, furnished the basic understanding of preaching held by those who practiced the skill during the Romantic period.[14] Each influenced this understanding in a way different from that of the other two.

The fullest heir of Longinus was **Hugh Blair** (1718–1800), who for the last half of his life was minister of Edinburgh's prestigious High Church of St. Giles and regius professor of rhetoric and belles lettres at the university. The conjunction in the title of his chair suggests the distinctiveness of his influence. "Belles lettres" was the term used in Blair's day to refer to literature and thus shows that, like Longinus, he combined the discussion of oratory with that of creative writing, and that he thought to engage in either activity one must become a critic in the field. The term also indicates that Blair's Longinian perspective was mediated and filtered through French neoclassical rhetorical thought. In France the belles lettres movement was associated with that of the beaux arts, and thus displayed a self-conscious aestheticism that was to be characteristic of the Romantic period. To all of this Blair was an heir.[15]

It is possible to make too much of the pre-Romanticism of Blair's work on rhetoric. Most of what he has to say about oratory as such is a translation of Quintilian's principles into the vocabulary of eighteenth-century Edinburgh. He was, after all, giving practical instruction to college students, mostly in their mid-teens, on how to write, speak in public, and assess others' attempts to do the same things. The whole effort was considered to be as elementary as college textbooks on rhetoric are today.

Yet the pre-Romanticism of the twenty or so lectures he devoted to oratory is seen in his decision to concentrate on only one of the five tasks the classical rhetoricians saw as necessary in preparing a speech: *elocutio*. His main emphasis, more than half his effort, goes to the details of style. He is almost contemptuous of invention and disposition as set forth in Aristotle's *Rhetoric*. Memory is barely touched on. Delivery is compressed into one lecture.[16]

This focus meant he was preoccupied with an aesthetic interest that was to become characteristically Romantic. The preacher was now to be considered a creative writer, sermons were to be thought of as works of art, their style was to be evaluated critically in terms of taste, and the results of that critique reflected the genius of the preacher or lack of it.[17]

Blair, however, was no mere aesthete. Indeed, he said that the preacher should shun above all things the "air of foppishness" (116).[18] He had a high view of the ministerial calling, and his definition of *preaching* was very serious, even if it was short on theological and christological content for an heir of Calvin.[19] He says, "The end of all preaching is to make men good" (105).[20] Or, again, the proper idea of a sermon is that of "a serious persuasive Oration, delivered to a multitude, in order to make them better men" (114). Or, finally, the "great end for which a Preacher mounts the pulpit" is "to infuse good dispositions into his hearers, to persuade them to serve God, and to become better men" (125).

This understanding of the purpose of preaching dictates that a sermon should be a popular speech in the best sense of the word, one "calculated to make impression on the people; to strike and to seize their hearts" (106). Thus the qualities that distinguish preaching from other forms of public speaking are gravity and warmth. These qualities are hard to combine, but when they are properly joined they create the quality the French call *onction*: "the affecting, penetrating, interesting manner, flowing from a strong sensibility of heart in the Preacher to the importance of those truths which he delivers, and an earnest desire that they may make full impression on the hearts of his Hearers" (107).

Further, to be most effective a sermon should be about a single subject and as concrete as possible. Some of the best sermons are those that follow a biblical character in a way that "can trace and lay open, some of the most secret windings of man's heart" (113), sermons such as Bishop Butler's on the character of Balaam, and, though he would have been too modest to say so, his own on Joseph and on Hazael.[21] The Romantics would share his conviction that truth is experienced more deeply in narratives of individual human lives than in abstract reasoning. Frederick Robertson, for instance, would also preach biographical sermons about biblical characters.

Blair's advice about preaching is very practical. He is aware that a preacher has advantages over other public speakers, such as being free from interruption, but the preacher also has to contend with the fact that "his[22] subjects of discourse are, in themselves, noble and important, but they are subjects trite and familiar" (102). The first rule of homiletical style is that sermons should be perspicuous. No quality of a sermon is so important as its being clear and understandable. Rightly employed, scriptural quotations and allusions are a great ornament to sermons, but "in a Sermon, no points or conceits should appear, no affected smartness or quaintness of expression" (116). Preachers must decide for themselves whether to memorize their sermons, preach them extemporaneously, or speak from notes, but "the practice of reading Sermons, is one of the greatest obstacles to the Eloquence of the Pulpit in Great Britain, where alone this practice prevails" (118).

Blair's knowledge of neoclassical rhetoric allows him to distinguish between French and English preaching:

> The French Preachers address themselves chiefly to the imagination and the passions; the English, almost solely to the understanding. It is the union of these two kinds of composition, of the French earnestness and warmth, with the English accuracy and reason, that would form, according to my idea, the model of the perfect Sermon. (119)

In a brief review of British preaching, Blair notes the traditionally alleged faults of the metaphysical preachers, but insists that they did have "warm pathetic addresses to the consciences of their hearers" (122). And he considers that a much more appealing quality than the "argumentative manner, bordering on the dry and unpersuasive" that was characteristic of the latitudinarians. In Blair's opinion, no finer compliment could be paid to a sermon than that of Louis XIV to Massillon after a sermon at Versailles: "Whenever I hear you, I go away displeased with myself, for I see more of my own character" (126). Such a criterion would probably have seemed "enthusiastic" to the latitudinarians, but it would prove very congenial to the Romantic emphasis on feeling.

The approach of the next New Rhetorician to be considered was very different from the aesthetic emphasis of Blair. Blair had produced what George Kennedy called a technical rhetoric, a "how-to-do-it" manual, but **George Campbell** (1719–96) was, among other things, a philosopher. His *Philosophy of Rhetoric* (1776),[23] as its title indicates, was intended to be what Kennedy calls philosophical rhetoric. To say that Blair wrote a technical and Campbell a philosophical rhetoric is not to say their understandings of rhetoric were fundamentally different. They share many of the same presuppositions and, indeed, often state them in almost the same words. The difference is rather in the aspect of rhetoric to which they devote their attention.

Most of Campbell's life and ministry were spent in Aberdeen. There he attended Marischal College in his youth and became its principal and professor of divinity in his maturity. His writings grew out of his teaching duties; they include volumes on miracles, church history, systematic theology, and pulpit eloquence,[24] as well as his translation of the New Testament.

His *Philosophy of Rhetoric,* however, was not written as a general textbook, nor was its content originally addressed to students. Most of its chapters began as papers he read to a small group he helped found, the Philosophical Society of Aberdeen, which met twice a month to discuss a presentation of one of the members. He had little interest in practical rhetoric; what occupied his thought was the relationship between rhetoric and what was called "human nature" at the time, most of which today would be considered aspects of psychology.[25] Campbell's understanding of human nature was based on the work of the British empiricist philosophers, especially David Hume, whom Bitzer describes as "the absent member of the Philosophical Society of Aberdeen."[26]

The way Campbell understands rhetoric in the light of human nature may be seen in his conviction that what causes attention to be paid to an idea and credence given to it is the idea's vivacity, its liveliness, energy, force, or brilliancy. Rhetoric, which includes all forms of communication for Campbell, may have as its purpose to inform, convince, please, arouse passion, or persuade. In order to fulfill any of these purposes, though, the rhetor must "communicate ideas which feel lively and vivid to his hearers or readers."[27]

For Campbell, there are three kinds of perceptions immediately present to the mind. The first is *sensations,* feelings, which include both sense data and emotions.[28] The next kind of perception is *ideas of memory,* recollections of earlier sensations. The third sort, *ideas of the imagination,* are constructs the mind makes from its ideas of memory. Thus ideas of imagination include everything from hypotheticals[29] to judgments about the real existence of things not being sensed or remembered at the present moment.

It works out that sensations are the perceptions with the greatest vivacity, ideas of memory come next, and ideas of imagination have the least. The challenge to the rhetor is that most of what he wishes to communicate are ideas of imagination. Therefore, the rhetor must find ways of lending vivacity to those perceptions that have the least of it.

Those ways are furnished by the patterns of the association of ideas in the mind, the most important of which, to Campbell's way of thinking, are resemblance, contiguity, and causation. Such associations can transfer vividness from a more to a less lively idea. Most of the work of the rhetor is in finding such associations by which vivacity can be given to the rhetor's ideas of imagination.

The other means by which the rhetor is persuasive involve the use of grammar and language. The phrasing of one's ideas must be "pure" in the sense of expressing them exactly and in not misleading the hearers in any way. It must also be perspicuous. Stylistic devices are another quality of language that gives it vivacity. Rhetorical strategy, then, involves using the association of ideas, purity and perspicuity of language, and stylistic devices to give to one's ideas of imagination the vivacity of sensations, thus providing the passion by which persuasion occurs.

This is the way Campbell draws on contemporary studies of human nature, especially that of Hume, to construct a theory of how rhetoric works. This empiricism makes his understanding of persuasion very different from the rationalism of the latitudinarians. Although his approach to emotion differs from that of Blair, his emphasis on it made it easy for the Romantics who came afterward to use his book.

The third of the New Rhetoricians was even more unlike the other two than they were unlike one another. **Richard Whately** (1787–1863) was born almost seventy years after Blair and Campbell, he was English rather than Scottish, an Anglican rather than a Presbyterian, and affiliated with Oxford rather than a Scottish university. He resembled Campbell in that he was more interested in persuasion than in style, but like Blair in that he wrote a beginner's textbook rather than a philosophical treatise on rhetoric.

He became a fellow of Oriel College on taking his degree and was identified with the "Noetics," the group involved in restoring the intellectual life of Oxford. After marrying he took a parish for several years, but returned to Oxford as principal of St. Alban's Hall. There he remained until he became the Anglican archbishop of Dublin in 1831.

Not a Romantic himself, Whately did have connections with those who were in the previous and following generations. Both his *Elements of Logic* and his *Elements of Rhetoric* were originally created in manuscript form for use with students preparing for ordination.[30] The first published form of both works, however, was as articles in the *Encyclopedia Metropolitana,* a publication for which Coleridge had the idea and was originally to have been the editor.[31] The Romantic link in the following generation was John Henry Newman, a new fellow at Oriel whom Whately had taken in hand. Newman credited Whately with being the one who "opened (his) mind, taught (him) to think and to use (his) reason."[32] Part of that opening was to enlist Newman's help in rewriting Whately's manuscripts on logic and rhetoric for the encyclopedia articles.[33]

The editor of the modern edition of the *Elements* claims that it is essentially an ecclesiastical rhetoric to prepare future clergy for their work.[34] He sees traces of that purpose in such features as the inclusion of a section on oral reading and the selection of a number of illustrations from theological literature. Ehninger identifies the "chief business" of the book to be:

> to arm the pulpit orator for his task of conveying to an unlettered congregation the indisputable doctrines of the Christian faith, and (2) to arm the Christian controversialist who is called upon to defend the evidences of religion against the onslaughts of the skeptic.[35]

Whately considered the preacher's task to be basic catechesis of a particular apologetic sort in which the articles of faith are to be defended against challenges. Outside the pulpit and in other fora, the preacher was to take on the gainsayers themselves.

Whately makes this polemical understanding of rhetoric clear in his introduction. He states that he is going to follow a middle course in his book, neither treating rhetoric exclusively as persuasive speaking nor broadly as any sort of prose composition, but presenting it instead as argumentative composition generally and exclusively (4).[36] The argumentative character of the rhetoric taught by Whately is further brought out by his statement that he considers rhetoric to be "an off-shoot of logic." This prepares the reader for the way roughly the first half of the book is devoted to argumentation, leaving the impression of a textbook on debate more than one on homiletics.

Whately, then, expected polemics and controversy to be the order of the day in preaching. Ehninger describes him as a person who was "by dedication a life-long defender of religion against the attacks of the rationalists and the skepticism of science."[37] He devoted himself to preparing other clergy to continue in the fight that had gone on since the rise of deism, a fight in which the latitudinarians had been engaged with less sense of a sharp line dividing the two sides. Since, however, Whately was an early friend of the leaders of the Oxford movement and he would become their opponent, perhaps he had an awareness that a period was beginning in which a good deal of preaching would be more concerned with controversy than the simple proclamation of the gospel. And, living at a time when geology and evolution as well as biblical criticism would present severe challenges to the faithful, perhaps a rhetoric of argumentative composition was what would be most needed.

THE ROMANTICISM OF VICTORIAN PREACHERS

While it is customary for critics of English literature to distinguish between the Romantic and Victorian periods, from a religious perspective, "the whole of the nineteenth century exudes an aura of Romanticism to a greater or lesser degree."[38] The truth of that claim becomes apparent when one looks at the characteristics of Victorian British preachers. These, as noted by Horton Davies, are: They preached topical sermons in response to the challenges to traditional faith that arose in that era. They made frequent appeals to the emotions, especially pity and fear. They delighted in scenic grandeur. And, perhaps their least Romantic trait, they included wit and humor among the weapons in their rhetorical armory.[39]

John Henry Newman

From the number of eminent Victorian preachers, two can be selected as representative, Frederick Robertson and John Henry Newman. The latter was certainly the better known of the two during their lifetimes, but both continue to be read as homiletical models to this day. Born into a middle-class family of comfortable means, Newman had a conversion experience as a schoolboy, and he arrived at Oxford an earnest Evangelical when he was seventeen.[40] He did well enough academically to be made a fellow of Oriel College after taking his B.A. The senior common room of Oriel at the time was the center of the noetic movement; there the shy and serious Newman was taken in hand by Whately and whipped into shape both intellectually and socially. After ordination in the established church,[41] Newman became Whately's vice-principal at St. Alban's Hall in 1825. Three years later he was made vicar of St. Mary's, the university church.

He toured southern Europe in 1832–33 and returned to Oxford to learn that John Keble had preached an assize sermon at the university, declaring that the effort of the government to suppress ten Irish bishoprics was tantamount to "National Apostasy." For Keble, the issue was not whether so many Anglican bishops were needed in Ireland but whether the state had the right to decide how many bishops the church should have. This and other examples of what was regarded as Erastianism were the precipitating causes of the Oxford movement, the Catholic revival of the Church of England.

Newman quickly became involved in the cause, and he and others began writing a series of "Tracts for the Times,"[42] in which were set forth a renewal of the Anglo-Catholic theology of Caroline divines such as William Laud and Lancelot Andrewes. They claimed that the apostolic succession of the established church's bishops, and the continuity and validity of its sacramental practice, made it the ancient and legitimate branch of the church Catholic in England. The original inspiration for this theology was patristic, and the Tractarians contributed greatly to the study and publication of the Fathers, using their scholarship to assert that the Church of England was the *via media* between Rome and Protestantism. As time went on, a widespread stir arose over the tracts, associating them with Roman Catholicism. A certain number of the younger and more enthusiastic members of the group did begin to find Roman claims persuasive, and even Newman himself was received into the Roman church in 1845.

As a Roman Catholic, Newman joined the Oratorians, an order founded during the Catholic Reformation by Philip Neri, and opened a house in Birmingham. Except for five years when he was in Dublin organizing a short-lived Roman Catholic university, he spent the rest of his life quietly in the Oratory as a priest, preaching to the working-class people who came to church there. For most of this second half of his life he was viewed with suspicion by his co-religionists, although he was made a cardinal by Leo XIII eleven years before his death. His most important theological treatises were written during this period, however, including his *Essay on the Development of Doctrine, A Grammar of Assent,* and *The Idea of a University.* These works have caused some to see anticipations in his thought of some of the most important insights of contemporary Roman Catholic theology. Perhaps his best-known book was the autobiography he wrote to defend himself against Charles Kingsley's charge of dishonesty, *Apologia pro vita sua.* He also wrote novels and poetry.

While he was vicar of St. Mary's, Newman's preaching made him the pied piper of undergraduates. (For a sample of his preaching there, see **Vol. 2, pp. 476-85.**) Accounts of the effect of his preaching have been left by J. A. Froude, Matthew Arnold, and W. E. Gladstone. Perhaps the best description, however, is that of Principal Shairp:

> The service was very simple,—no pomp, no ritualism[43] . . . the most remarkable thing was the beauty, the silver intonation, of Mr. Newman's voice, as he read the Lessons. It seemed to bring new meaning out of the familiar words.... When he began to preach, a stranger was not likely to be much struck, especially if he had been accustomed to pulpit oratory of the Boanerges sort. Here was no vehemence, no declamation, no show of elaborated argument, so that one who came prepared to hear "a great intellectual effort" was almost sure to go away disappointed. . . . The delivery had a peculiarity which it took a new hearer some time to get over. Each separate sentence, or at least each short paragraph, was spoken rapidly, but with great clearness of intonation; and then at its close there was a pause lasting for nearly half a minute; and then another rapidly but clearly spoken sentence, followed by another pause. It took some time to get over this, but, that once done, the wonderful charm began to dawn on you. . . . He laid his finger—how gently, yet how powerfully!—on some inner place in the hearer's heart, and told him things about himself he had never known till then. Subtlest truths, which it would have taken philosophers pages of circumlocution and big words to state, were dropt out by the way in a sentence or two of the most transparent Saxon. . . . And the tone of the voice in which they were spoken, once you grew accustomed to it, sounded like a fine strain of unearthly music. Through the silence of that high Gothic building the words fell on the ear like the measured drippings of water in some vast dim cave.[44]

The appeal to idealistic undergraduates was so magnetic that the dons of other colleges, suspicious of this influence on their students and perhaps jealous of it as well, changed the hour of Sunday dinner in hall to coincide with that of Newman's sermon at St. Mary's. Even then many of the young men chose to satisfy the hunger of their souls rather than that of their bodies.

What did he preach that had such an effect? What was his homiletical theory? It will be easier to first answer the latter question. Newman published two treatises on preaching, one negative on what to avoid and the other positive on what to strive for. The last of his *Lectures on the Doctrine of Justification* (1838) was "On Preaching the Gospel."[45] It grew out of a sense Newman shared with the other Oxford leaders that Anglican Evangelicals had unduly exalted preaching in their understanding of the Christian life. Thus the chapter is a rousing critique of the evangelical theory and practice of preaching.

> It summarizes the Tractarian attitudes toward the Evangelicals: it attacks their emphasis upon feeling, their insistence upon "internal" versus "external" religion, their unnatural and strained idiom, their elevation of preaching to primacy over baptism and other sacraments, their innate tendency to dissent, their substituting faith in faith for faith in Christ—in short, their allegiance to what Newman would see as a human system replacing the system ordained by God for the proclamation of the gospel.[46]

What worries Newman about all this is its subjectivism, its emphasis on the evangelicals' interior state of feeling rather than on Christ, the object of their faith. It is also a reliance on the rhetorical skill of preachers who are able to engender these emotional states in others, a tendency "to rely upon words, vehemence, eloquence, and the like."[47] All of this is a substitute for the means of grace provided by God in the historic church with its catholic faith, apostolic ministry, sacramental system, and disciplinary practices. Thus it substitutes a human program for the divinely ordained program of salvation.

The positive treatise on what a preacher should strive for is called "University Preaching" and appeared first in *Lectures and Essays on University Subjects* (1859), but, like much of that volume's content, it is much more accessible in *The Idea of a University* (definitive edition, 1873).[48] Written when he was rector of the Catholic University of Ireland in Dublin, the article was a response to those invited to preach university sermons who had asked for guidelines.

His advice is given in two stages, the first having to do with preaching in general and the second with specifically university preaching. He begins by noting that "the preacher's object is the spiritual good of his hearers." That immediately leads him to the strategic consideration that "as a marksman aims at the target and its bull's-eye, and at nothing else, so the preacher must have a definite point before him, which he has to hit" (304-5).

This means that any consideration of eloquence, intellect, or learning has to be subordinated to the single purpose of getting across to the congregation the one point identified as the best way at that moment to effect their spiritual good.

Nothing contributes so much to getting that point across as the earnestness of the preacher in trying to. This does not mean that the preacher should strive to be earnest or, even worse, to appear earnest: "He must aim at his *object,* which is to do some spiritual good to his hearers . . . which will at once *make* him earnest" (306). The object of doing some spiritual good involves having before the preacher's mental eye the Four Last Things.[49] "It is this earnestness, in the supernatural order, which is the eloquence of saints; and not of saints only, but of all Christian preachers, according to the measure of their faith and love" (307).

To be effective, the good the preacher tries to do for the congregation must be specific rather than general. "No one will carry off much from a discourse which is on the general subject of virtue, or vaguely and feebly entertains the question of the desirableness of attaining Heaven, or the rashness of incurring eternal ruin." Or, again, "so necessary is it to have something to say, if we desire any one to listen" (308). This involves deciding, before composing a sermon, exactly what one wishes it to communicate.

Every temptation to include anything—however valuable it might be in itself—that does not contribute to the one unified impact must be sternly resisted. Included in this ban on extraneous material is "the habit of preaching on three or four subjects at once," which amounts to "the delivery of three sermons in succession without break between them." The best way of achieving such definiteness is to "select some distinct fact or scene, some passage in history, some truth, simple or profound, some doctrine, some principle, or some sentiment, and . . . study it well and thoroughly, and first make it (one's) own" (ibid.). Making it one's own begins with bringing that point home to oneself.

So much for preaching in general. Why and how should university preaching be different? The why is that a sermon should always be prepared to meet the needs of a specific audience: "We cannot determine how in detail we ought to preach, till we know whom we are to address"

(311). In most important respects, all hearers are the same: redeemed sinners and members of the church. The first thing to be noticed about a university congregation, however, is that it is composed largely of undergraduates: "an assemblage of the young, the inexperienced, the lay and the secular" (312), which means that no Christian doctrine is too basic or simple. Beyond that, however, in Newman's time the university congregation would consist of "men, not women; of the young rather than the old; and of persons either highly educated or under education" (312).

A series of university sermons should not be considered the draft of a book on the subject. Rather, Newman thought, such lectures belonged to the Divinity School instead of the pulpit. "Nevertheless, it is not asking too much to demand for academical discourses a more careful study beforehand, a more accurate conception of the idea which they are to enforce, a more cautious use of words, a more anxious consultation of writers of authority, and somewhat more of philosophical and theological knowledge" (314-15).

Even more important, however, is the principle that university sermons should be addressed to the temptations faced by the congregation.

> The temptations which ordinarily assail the young and the intellectual are two kinds: those which are directed against their virtue, and those which are directed against their faith. . . . As youth becomes the occasion of excess and sensuality, so does the intellect give accidental opportunity to religious error, rash speculation, doubt, and infidelity. (313)

In trying to help students resist such temptations, however, preachers should first be very certain they understand their congregation, or they could do more harm than good. The other caution Newman gives to a university preacher is that "even when he addresses himself to some special danger or probable deficiency or need of his hearers, he should do so covertly, not showing on the surface of his discourse what he is aiming at" (314). This is to say that "infidelity, orthodoxy, or virtue, or the pride of reason, or riot, or sensual indulgence" should not be approached head-on—explicitly, and as a block. Instead, one should preach about such subjects as, for instance, the improvement of time, avoiding the occasions of sin, frequenting the sacraments, divine warnings, the inspirations of grace, the mysteries of the rosary, natural virtue, beauty of the rites of the church, consistency of the Catholic faith, relation of Scripture to the church, the philosophy of tradition, and any others, which may touch the heart and conscience, or may suggest trains of thought to the intellect, without proclaiming the main reason why they had been chosen (314).

The last advice Newman gives to university preachers is that they not use a manuscript in the pulpit if they can possibly avoid doing so. While his approach to the question is strategic, nuanced, and perhaps extended unnecessarily, his conclusion is that it is "no extravagance to say that a very inferior sermon, delivered without book, answers the purposes for which all sermons are delivered more perfectly than one of great merit, if it be written and read" (320-21).

Newman's own observance of this last principle was an accomplishment of his Roman Catholic days. His sermons to the undergraduates of Oxford were delivered from manuscripts, and he began to preach extempore only as a Roman Catholic, apparently because doing so was expected at that time. This is only one of the differences between the eight[50] volumes of *Parochial and Plain Sermons* preached at St. Mary's and the *Discourses Addressed to Mixed Congregations* and *Sermons Preached on Various Occasions* from his Roman Catholic period. Each series is faithful to the principle of being aimed at a particular audience: the *Parochial and Plain* for Oxford, those to *Mixed Congregations* for the working-class neighborhood of Birmingham where the Oratory was, and those *on Various Occasions* for university audiences, his brothers of the Oratory, and distinguished public occasions.[51]

A very different sort of sermon from those in these three series appears in his *Oxford University Sermons,*[52] which deal with the theological issue of the relation of faith to reason, rather than the issues of personal spirituality that are the standard topics of the others. Indeed, the *University Sermons* are considered to be the preliminary working out of the argument developed and completed in *The Grammar of Assent.*

This serves as a reminder that Newman was a complex thinker who wrote in a number of literary genres. Perhaps he was most famous as a controversialist, one of whom Whately could have been proud if their paths had not diverged so greatly. But he also had an acute philosophical mind. And he found different means of persuasion appropriate for different tasks. It has been shown by Jouett L. Powell that Newman's "discourse concerned with 'coming to faith' features implicit persuasive reasoning, that with 'exercising faith' reliance on mental imagery, and that with 'explicating faith' dependence on abstract argument."[53] Thus Newman advocates different strategies of persuasion for different stages of faith.

The majority of the sermons have to do with what Powell calls "exercising faith" and so rely heavily on mental imagery and imagination.[54]

That is responsible for their effect described so vividly by Principal Shairp: "He laid his finger—how gently, yet how powerfully!—on some inner place in the hearer's heart, and told him things about himself he had never known till then."[55]

And in all this we have "the typical Romantic appeal to the past, to tradition, to the continuing organic life of the community, as against the atomistic individualism brought about by the irresponsible use of critical reason."[56] Newman was without doubt one of the great English Romantic preachers.

Frederick Robertson

Even more obviously a Romanticist, however, was Frederick W. Robertson. Robertson, who has been posthumously awarded such superlative homiletical accolades as being called the greatest English-speaking preacher of the nineteenth century, would appear at first blush an unlikely candidate for such laurels. None of the conditions that have usually accompanied such status can be discovered in his life. To begin with, it was too short; he died when he was only thirty-seven after an ordained ministry that lasted a mere thirteen years. He served a curacy among the poor in Winchester, then he filled an assistantship in fashionable Cheltenham for five years, and his last six years were spent in the fashionable watering place of Brighton, not as vicar of the parish church, but as rector of Trinity, a proprietary chapel.[57]

He did none of the things that would have called attention to himself or his ministry. He was stationed neither in London nor at a cathedral or a university. He did not preach at court. He was granted no titles and he did not seek preferment. Only one of his sermons was published while he lived, and he appeared in a London pulpit but once. During his ministry at Brighton he became something of a local celebrity, yet his fame scarcely extended beyond the city limits.

His anonymity, however, faded quickly after his death. His family published four volumes of his sermons, and these did not go out of print for at least a century after his death.[58] Further fame came with the issuance of *The Life and Letters of Frederick W. Robertson, M.A.* by Stopford A. Brooke in 1865.[59] Which is to say that the enormous reputation of Robertson as a preacher is based entirely on the impression made by his printed sermons on people who never heard him. This is the more remarkable because the published form of the sermons is not a transcript of what was spoken from the pulpit. Rather, they are simply "Recollections":

> sometimes dictated by the Preacher himself to the younger members of the family in which he was interested, at their entreaty; sometimes written out by himself for them when they were at a distance and unable to attend his ministry.[60]

To account for the homiletical phenomenon that was Frederick Robertson, it is necessary to understand two things: the effect he had on his Brighton congregation, and his appeal to later generations of preachers. One of a number of possible ways of approaching the first of these issues is to note that Robertson was a perfect Romantic figure. That is apparent in his Byronic good looks. He was a little above average in height, and he had a well-made but not heavy body—the sort of figure one associates with an officer of the guards. His posture was of a military erectness and his gait was sprightly. His thick, wavy brown hair crowned a high forehead, and bushy sideburns set off the features of his face. He had a long, straight nose that began with so little indentation under the brow that it was almost Greek, leaving his dark blue eyes deep set. His lips were gracefully curved and capable of registering a wide range of emotion. The overall impression was of "a man of great moral elevation of character, and of large intellectual power."[61]

The ideal and language of chivalry came naturally to his lips. As a boy, "he loved to fancy himself a knight—seeking adventures, redressing wrongs, laying down his life for maidens in distress" (1:4).[62] He came from a military family and he wanted passionately to be a soldier. When his father suggested the ministry, he replied that he was not good enough for it, but did hope that as an officer he could have a Christian influence on his men like that of Cornelius the centurion. His commission as an officer of the dragoons came through just days after his acceptance at Oxford to study for holy orders, so he could have had a military career. By then, however, he had almost reluctantly admitted that duty lay elsewhere. Much of the military man clung to him the rest of his life.[63]

At the same time that he appeared so vigorous and dashing, his ministry, as noted above, was beset by health problems. Each of his three appointments[64] was terminated by illness: Winchester by problems with his lungs, thought to be, and treated as, the tuberculosis to which other members of his family had succumbed, Cheltenham by what sounds like a bout of deep depression, and Brighton by a fatal illness described as "abscess in the cerebellum" (2:221) or as something that affected "the *ganglia* or bunches of nerves which are at the roots of the brain" (2:223).[65] As early as his year in Winchester he had premonitions of an early death (1:64), and was much impressed with the lives of David

Brainerd and Henry Martyn (1:60), both of whom died young in the service of the gospel.

All this poor health must have had an enormous Romantic appeal at the time. Susan Sontag notes that in the nineteenth century, melancholy and tuberculosis came to be socially regarded as a sign of a special nature: "The melancholy character—or the tubercular one—was a superior one: sensitive, creative, a being set apart."[66] These were the ailments of artists; they made people interesting. Keats, Shelley, and, it seems, half the poets of the time were "consumptive." Robertson's first illness was thought to be tuberculosis; his second seems to have been melancholy. The third was most Romantic of all, a mysterious illness that sapped away life and led to an early death.

None of this is to suggest that Robertson was a poseur or in any way insincere. As James R. Blackwood says, "Intensity was the secret of his power." And he backs up the statement by quoting Lady Byron's statement that "his very calm is a hurricane."[67] There is nothing more obvious than his earnestness. And he agonized over everything. Nor is it to suggest that he was weak. Few clergy have shown greater courage in the pulpit. He did not allow suffering to keep him from his work; he labored on silently in great pain, trying not to let it show to those to whom he was ministering. It is only to say that he would have been recognizable to his contemporaries as a much admired type of the time, the candle that burned so brightly, it had quickly to burn itself out.

Consistent with this intensity was a high degree of sensitivity. He loved friends, had a great need for their support, felt loneliness intensely, and yet had a code or pride that made it nearly impossible for him to confide what was troubling him or the degree of his pain. Thus, not surprisingly, he spent a good bit of his time depressed—and yet tried not to let it show and to work as hard as ever. Preaching was an agony to him, and he seemed useless for a day or so after a Sunday. There was no group for which he had such contempt as popular preachers, those who used their power over crowds to advance their own cause rather than that of the Kingdom.

He was also impatient with party strife in the Church of England at the time, which seemed to be polarized between evangelicals and Tractarians like Newman, and, because he would not repeat the slogans of either side, he was pilloried by both. He felt some sympathy with the liberalism of Thomas Arnold and the Christian socialism of F. D. Maurice and Charles Kingsley, but disagreed with both positions in some matters and resented having their opinions attributed to him. He was an isolated individual who suffered to preserve integrity through much struggle.

He loved poetry and read all the Romantics deeply, offering his critical insight into their work frequently in his letters and occasionally giving public lectures about them. He was also immersed in earlier poetry and especially loved and studied Shakespeare and Dante. Nor was that the end of his reading.[68] In his correspondence he frequently discussed the latest novels, reading not only English books but a surprising number of American works of all kinds as well. In addition to the biblical languages and Latin, he read in French, Italian, and German. The Germans were important to him for their philosophers, notably Kant, Fichte, and Lessing, and for their biblical scholars. He was also conversant with the science of his age, especially enjoying chemistry and ornithology.

Thoroughly Romantic also was his appreciation for the beauty of nature, whether awesome Alpine landscapes[69] or the less dramatic scenery of the hills around Cheltenham or the Brighton seashore. Equally Romantic was his appreciation of common people, but discussion of that will be postponed for inclusion in the treatment of what has made his preaching so influential in recent generations. Enough has been said, however, to indicate that Frederick Robertson summed up most of the cultural themes of his age, he was aware of and evaluated calmly and soundly all that was going on in his society, and he did so utilizing the categories that reflected the spirit of the age. He epitomized a Christian appropriation of Romantic consciousness, and thus what he said spoke directly to most of his hearers.

As to what made him a natural role model to preachers of later generations, that, too, can be approached from a number of directions, but none sums it up so well as saying that he was one of the first to face the issues that have been characteristic for mainline Christianity ever since, and that he dealt with them in ways that were effective. He did so without rejecting the issues, but by presupposing them and going on matter-of-factly to consider their ramifications. In this way he remained relevant to preachers who lived in later times, when it was no longer thought that if the difficulties were ignored, they would go away. While in many ways his age seems as alien to the present as many that are more remote, the situation of the church in the world was so much the same that his example can still be followed with profit.

This is to say that he assumed the people who filled Trinity Chapel Sunday after Sunday found Christian faith hard rather than easy. Their Christian construction of reality had been eroded by their experiences of the week, and they needed to have it reinforced. Thus most of Robertson's preaching can be considered problem solving, but he addressed a range of kinds of problems.

Some of his sermons were essays in apologetics, defending the faith in an age in which new knowledge—scientific, historical, or biblical—seemed to call it into question. Others had to do with the difficulties individuals had in living out their faith, so that he became one of the first great psychological preachers who practiced pastoral care from the pulpit. And others had to do with a society in which the wealth of empire and industrial revolution was distributed very inequitably and in which the gulf between social classes seemed an abyss over which even Victorian engineers could not erect a bridge. Social problems, personal problems, impediments to belief—they all sound very familiar, and Robertson of Brighton showed how all of them could be dealt with helpfully through sermons. It is not surprising that preachers who have come after him have wanted to look back and see how he did it.

While the way he dealt homiletically with each of these three kinds of problems will need to be examined, those examinations must be informed by an awareness of what Robertson considered to be the basic principles of his approach to Christian theology.

> First. The establishment of positive truth, instead of the destruction of error.
>
> Secondly. That truth is made up of two opposite propositions, and not found in a *via media* between the two.
>
> Thirdly. That spiritual truth is discerned by the spirit, instead of intellectually in propositions, and, therefore, Truth should be taught suggestively, not dogmatically.
>
> Fourthly. That belief in the Human character of Christ's Humanity must be antecedent to belief in His Divine Origin.
>
> Fifthly. That Christianity, as its teachers should, works from the inward to the outward, and not *vice versa.*
>
> Sixthly. The soul of goodness in things evil. (2:153)

Such an approach is hard to imagine in any period prior to the Romantic era.

With these principles understood, the approach he made to dealing with the problems of belief, practice, and society that he faced in common with his colleagues in the twentieth century becomes clear. This approach may be seen first in his work as an apologist.

His was the first generation of Christians to deal with the challenges to faith that have become so familiar, the challenges to the historicity of Genesis posed by the study of geology and biological evolution. In the 1830s Sir Charles Lyell and William Buckland[70] had used the evidence of rocks and fossils to show that the world was much older than the six thousand years the standard reconstruction of biblical chronology claimed.[71] And, although Darwin's *Origin of the Species* would not be published until six years after Robertson's death, an anonymous book called *The Vestiges of the Natural History of Creation* had appeared in 1844 with a theory of the development of animal life, with which Darwin's would agree in principle. For the first time, evidence existed that would bring into question the literal historical truth of the Bible.

At the same time, German scholars had begun to study the Bible like any other book and to raise questions about its historical accuracy on literary grounds. Although Coleridge and Thirwall had already introduced the German scholarship to English readers, it remained unnoticed by most clergy and theologians until the publication of *Essays and Reviews* in 1860—seven years after Robertson's death. Ten years earlier, Robertson lectured on Genesis in his parish and, "while declaring that the Mosaic cosmogony could not be reconciled with geological facts, still succeeded in showing its inner harmony, in principle, with the principles of scientific geology" (1:233; cf. 2:139). He also distinguished between the J and E documents and questioned the universality of the flood, but approached all these questions in a positive rather than a negative way, in accordance with his principles. That is what made it possible for people to leave the chapel "deeply opposed, it is true, to the popular theory of Inspiration, but deeply convinced of *an* Inspiration" (ibid.).

Robertson also preached a sermon on inspiration in that same year of 1850.[72] (For the text of this sermon, **see Vol. 2, pp. 486-92.**) In the introduction he listed the kinds of questions to be raised. A sampling includes: "What the Bible is, and what the Bible is not? What is meant by inspiration? Whether inspiration is the same thing as infallibility? When God inspired the minds, did he dictate the words? Did the inspiration of men mean the infallibility of their words? Is inspiration the same as dictation?" In regard to these questions he says:

> Upon these things there are many views, some of them false, some superstitious; but it is not our business now to deal with these; our way is rather to teach positively than negatively; we will try to set up the truth, and error may fall before it.[73]

Instead of exposing erroneous principles of interpretation, he invokes the principles by which the apostles read the Bible, two of them constituting the divisions of the body of the sermon. The first is that Scripture is of universal application. By that he means, while passages in the Bible tell of individual persons, they apply to not just those individuals but to all who are in that "particular state of character." The second point is that all the lines of Scripture converge toward Christ.

> Every unfulfilled aspiration of humanity in the past; all partial representation of perfect character; all sacrifices, nay even those of idolatry, point to the fulfillment of what we want, the answer to every longing—the type of perfect humanity, the Lord Jesus Christ.[74]

In a time when few English Christians knew that science and biblical scholarship had brought the historicity of parts of the Bible into question, when even Maurice still spoke of the universe as only six thousand years old,[75] it is astonishing to see the rector of a proprietary chapel in a fashionable watering place finding no threat to full Christian faith in the issues. He assured his congregation that if the popular theory of inspiration is wrong, the Scriptures are nevertheless the inspired Word of God, from which all true insight into the human condition is derived. He was dealing calmly with the problem before most clergy knew there was a problem.

The first point in his sermon on "Inspiration" is the principle on which Robertson dealt with personal problems from the pulpit. Assuming that "scripture is of universal application," he would identify a personal or spiritual problem on which he thought he ought to preach and then compose the sermon as a study of a biblical character who suffered from it. He brought the issue so to life that his hearers would recognize themselves and their own situations and be given insight accordingly. In this way, he became one of the first "psychological" preachers.[76] Horton Davies lists examples of such sermons when he says that Robertson discoursed on the skepticism of Pilate, on Thomas as the type of the doubter, on Elijah as the victim of despondency, on Christ as the supreme image of heroic loneliness, on religious depression, on the faith of the centurion, on the victory of faith, and on how to attain rest.[77]

What gave Robertson such acute psychological insight was his own experience of many of the problems discussed, experience that caused him acute suffering. Such an understanding of what made the sermons work could not be stated better than it was by their anonymous editor:

> Suppose a preacher goes down into the depths of his own being, and has the courage and fidelity to carry all he finds there, first to God in confession and prayer, and then to his flock as some part of the general experience of Humanity, do you not feel that he must be touching close upon some brother-man's sorrows and wants? . . . Does not the man feel that here is a revelation of God's truth as real and fresh as if

> he had stood in the streets of Jerusalem and heard the Savior's very voice?[78]

The third area in which Robertson's sermons have been an inspiration and model for later preachers is the way they addressed social problems. The radicality of what he did cannot be understood without knowledge of the condition of English Christianity in general, from Roman Catholics to Unitarians, at the time. England had been frightened into reaction by the French and American revolutions, and thus its class system had become yet more rigid. Even Coleridge can be cited as an example of this tendency. He argued in 1829 for a National Church (a temporal body separate from the spiritual Church of Christ), which would have a clerisy whose responsibility would be "to form and train up the people of the country to be obedient, free, useful, organizable subjects, citizens, and patriots, living to the benefit of the state and prepared to die for its defense."[79]

The main difference between Coleridge and many of his clerical contemporaries is that they would see no need for the National Church to be separate from the Church of Christ, or for its clerisy to be a body other than the clergy. To them the most important teachings of the Catechism in the Book of Common Prayer were:

> To honour and obey the King, and all that are put in authority under him: To submit myself to all my governors, teachers, spiritual pastors, and masters, . . . to learn and labor truly to get mine own living, and to do my duty in that state of life, unto which it shall please God to call me.

This was a time of much social unrest, when Chartists and Socialists were threatening the status quo. At the same time, it was a period in which to be a "gentleman" and a member of polite society meant having private income and not having to work or engage in trade, the age of *Vanity Fair.*

Robertson was not a revolutionary. He felt the ambiguity of his position, saying, "My tastes are with the aristocrat, my principles with the mob" (2:118). Nor was he even a Christian Socialist like Maurice or Kingsley, much less a Socialist in the ordinary sense of the word. He felt that Socialism would only create a new ruling class with all the faults of the present one.

> Dragged aside by two extremes, he fell back on Christianity, not as a *via media,* but as declaring truths that embraced in their ample round

> the wisdom of conservatism and the progressive spirit of liberalism, which solved the questions of the day—neither by laying down laws, nor by coercive measures for oppression or for liberty, but by spreading in all classes a spirit of love, of duty, and of mutual respect (1:161).

However unsatisfactory this may seem to contemporary analysts who consider social evil systemic, he was at least as demanding that the upper classes do their Christian duty as he was that the poor do so. In a sermon on Sabbath observance, for instance, he pointed out that clergy have been inconsistent in demanding that the poor not break the day in ways the wealthy were permitted to.[80] In reply to Evangelical threats that God would punish England by a foreign war for its breach of the holy day, he said that God's judgment would not fall because the working class had a few hours recreation, but because "we are selfish men; and we prefer pleasure to duty, and traffic to honor; and because we love party more than our Church, and our Church more than our Christianity; and our Christianity more than truth, and ourselves more than all."[81]

Certainly the poor were a main concern all through his ministry. His work at Winchester was among them, he chafed among the prosperous in Cheltenham, he accepted a poor parish in Oxford before the bishop urged him to go to Brighton instead. There his congregation was largely of the merchant class, but he preached sermons that were appreciated by the working class and servants as well. He was interested in the young men who came to Brighton to work in stores and offices. He helped in the organization of a Working-Man's Institute, which would make a library and reading room available to its members. He visited the poor assiduously and helped as he could in all their troubles. And he preached on social and economic issues.

The one sermon he preached in London was in a series for working people at St. John's, Fitzroy Street, in which Maurice and Kingsley were also to preach. For a text he took the story of David's response following Nabal's refusal to make a contribution to the band that had protected his property. Robertson said that "whenever two classes are held apart by rivalry and selfishness, instead of drawn together by the law of love, . . . there exist the forces of inevitable collision."[82] The sermon division he proposed, then, was: "I. The causes of this false social state. II. The message of the Church to the man of wealth." The cause of the false social state was a social falsehood to the effect that "wealth constitutes superiority, and has a right to the subordination of inferiors." Thus he branded as false what was generally assumed to be the basis of English society at the time. The church's message to the wealthy was that "a

Scientific Political Economy" would coincide with the Christian revelation, which is that "the law, which alone can interpret the mystery of life, is the self-sacrifice of Christ."[83] To be Christian, the wealthy must live by that example. That they have not been aware of that duty was the fault of the clergy: "For three long centuries we have taught submission to the powers that be. . . . Rarely have we dared to demand of those powers that be, justice; of the wealthy man and the titled, duties."

Robertson did not preach that way only when he was out of his parish. The two that follow this example in the *Sermons* were equally forthright and were preached at Trinity Chapel. His biography lists other sermons on social questions at the time (2:2). It also includes letters that demonstrate his willingness to justify such preaching to members of the nobility and the wealthy (e.g., 2:6-8, 54-55).

He did not set himself up as an expert on social conditions, although he was deeply aware of them from his ministry among the poor; nor did he believe that one social group was less tainted by original sin than another. His profound conviction was that the church should participate in the improvement of society by being the channel through which God changed the hearts of its members. As an ordained minister, he thought his field of competence was sin and grace, and that the repentance of one and the acceptance of the other were what was needed to improve society. As a cobbler, he stuck to his last. While later generations may recognize that social structures as well as individuals need to be made more just, no one can deny the prophetic courage with which Robertson took stands rare among the clergy of his age. Thus his sermons on social issues, personal problems, and impediments to faith have made him one of the few preachers of the past with whom today's clergy can feel immediate empathy and from whom they can derive new inspiration and dedication.

FOR FURTHER READING

Brooke, Stopford A. *The Life and Letters of Frederick W. Robertson, M.A.* New ed. of 1868. London: Kegan, Paul, Trench, Trübner, & Co., 1891.

Golden, James L., Goodwin F. Berquist, and William E. Coleman. *The Rhetoric of Western Thought.* 3rd. ed. Dubuque, Iowa: Kendall/Hunt, 1976–83.

Ker, Ian. *John Henry Newman: A Biography.* Oxford: Oxford University Press, 1988.

Longinus. *On the Sublime.* Translated with commentary by James A. Arieti and John M. Crossett. Texts and Studies in Religion, vol. 21. Lewiston, N.Y.: Edward Mellen, 1985.

The Preaching of John Henry Newman. Edited with introduction by W. D. White. The Preacher's Paperback Library. Philadelphia: Fortress, 1969.

Reardon, Bernard M. G. *Religion in the Age of Romanticism: Studies in Early Nineteenth Century Thought.* Cambridge: Cambridge University Press, 1985.

Robertson, Frederick W. *Sermons Preached at Brighton.* New York: Harper & Brothers, 1905.

Notes

1. Bernard M. G. Reardon, *Religion in the Age of Romanticism: Studies in Early Nineteenth Century Thought* (Cambridge: Cambridge University Press, 1985), 1. If it may be said that Romanticism is, in part, a reaction against classicism, then classicism becomes its *terminus a quo*. In that sense, its *terminus ad quem* would be realism.

2. Ibid., 10.

3. The foregoing represents an effort to summarize ibid., 1-15. For a comparable but much terser effort to characterize Romanticism, see the summary of Claude Welch, *Protestant Thought in the Nineteenth Century, Vol. I, 1799–1870* (New Haven: Yale University Press, 1972), 52-55:

> 1. A protest, in the name of freedom and dynamism, against the formalism and structure of neoclassicism, rationalism, and moral asceticism and discipline.
> 2. A stress on individuality that at times amounted almost to worship of originality and genius.
> 3. An exaltation of the immediacy of feeling "in the self, for humanity, and for the world," which involved vitalism and an aesthetic approach to nature.
> 4. A concern and feeling for history.
> 5. The dominance of the twin principles of plenitude (as opposed to the restriction of content by formal rules) and diversity (as opposed to uniformity and simplicity).

4. Reardon, *Religion in the Age of Romanticism,* 29. For a look at his preaching, see *Servant of the Word: Selected Sermons of Friedrich Schleiermacher,* trans. with intro. Dawn De Vries, Fortress Texts in Modern Theology (Philadelphia: Fortress, 1987).

5. Stephen Neill and Tom Wright, *The Interpretation of the New Testament 1861–1986,* 2nd. ed. (Oxford: Oxford University Press, 1988), 3 (Coleridge), 8-10 (Thirlwall), 31-34 *(Essays and Reviews).*

6. *Confessions of an Inquiring Spirit,* intro. David Jasper, 3rd ed. of 1853, Fortress Texts in Modern Theology (Philadelphia: Fortress, 1988).

7. For the influence of Coleridge on later English theology, see Charles Richard Sanders, *Coleridge and the Broad Church Movement: Studies in S. T. Coleridge, Dr. Arnold of Rugby, J. C. Hare, Thomas Carlyle, and F. D. Maurice* (Durham, N.C.: Duke University Press, 1942). Sanders gives a concise statement of Coleridge's understanding of inspiration, pp. 82-83.

8. The work is not mentioned in any classical writing.

9. Longinus, *On the Sublime,* trans. with comm. by James A. Arieti and John M. Crossett, Texts and Studies in Religion, vol. 21 (Lewiston, N.Y.: Edward Mellen, 1985), x.

10. George A. Kennedy, *Classical Rhetoric and Its Christian and Secular Tradition from Ancient to Modern Times* (Chapel Hill: University of North Carolina Press, 1980), 226.

11. Arieti and Crossett, *Longinus,* 9.

12. Ibid., 39.

13. James L. Golden, Goodwin F. Berquist, and William E. Coleman, *The Rhetoric of Western Thought,* 3rd. ed. (Dubuque, Iowa: Kendall/Hunt, 1976–83), 103-87.

14. Nan Johnson, *Nineteenth-Century Rhetoric in North America* (Carbondale: Southern Illinois University Press, 1991).

15. One of the tasks to which Schleiermacher devoted himself in his first parish was translating Blair's sermons into German (*Servant of the Word,* ed. De Vries, 2).

16. Hugh Blair, *Lectures on Rhetoric and Belles Lettres,* ed. with intro. Harold F. Harding with a foreword by David Potter (Carbondale: Southern Illinois University Press, 1965), xviii.

17. *The Rhetoric of Blair, Campbell, and Whately, with Updated Bibliography,* ed. James L. Golden and Edward P. J. Corbett, Landmarks in Rhetoric and Public Address (Carbondale: Southern Illinois University Press, 1990), 37-73.

18. Parenthetical numbers refer to pages in the second volume of the Harding edition of Blair's *Lectures.*

19. He represents the "Common Sense" school of Scottish philosophy and theology regnant at the time. The edition of Blair's *Sermons* consulted is the single volume published in London by T. and J. Allman in 1825 with "A Short Account of the Life and Character of the Author" by James Finlayson.

20. Obviously, Blair lived at a time when "men" was thought to be gender inclusive.

21. Blair, *Sermons,* 269-88.

22. Blair assumes that all preachers will be male.

23. *The Philosophy of Rhetoric,* ed. Lloyd F. Bitzer with foreword by David Potter, Landmarks in Rhetoric and Public Address (Carbondale: Southern Illinois University Press, 1963). Although Campbell's book on rhetoric was published six years before that of Blair, Blair's thought on the subject is earlier, since he had lectured on the subject since 1759 and he made very little change in the text of his lectures prior to their publication.

24. Since, however, it was not these lectures but his book on rhetoric that was to be so influential on future preaching, attention here will be focused on the latter work.

25. This interpretation follows very closely that of Lloyd Bitzer in his introduction to the Southern Illinois edition of Campbell. For alternative approaches, see Golden, Berquist, and Coleman, *The Rhetoric of Western Thought,* 148-63, and Johnson, *Nineteenth-Century Rhetoric,* 20-31.

26. Bitzer, "Introduction," xiii.

27. Ibid., xxv.

28. Campbell recognizes, however, that there is no necessary connection between what the mind perceives as sensation and any external reality.

29. Ranging from a purple cow to the heavenly city.

30. Undergraduates in their teens rather than postgraduates in a professional degree program. It was not even required that they "read" ("major in") divinity; general education was the goal with the assumption that professional readiness could be acquired on one's own.

31. The first publication of the *Logic* as a separate book was in 1826 and that of the *Rhetoric* was in 1828. Whately continued to revise the latter work all his life, seeing it through seven editions, four of which involved at least some revision. Richard Whately, *Elements of Rhetoric, Comprising an Analysis of the Laws of Moral Evidence and of Persuasion, with the Rules for Argumentative Composition and Elocution,* intro. Douglas Ehninger, Landmarks in Rhetoric and Public Address (Carbondale: Southern Illinois University Press, 1963), xvi-xix.

32. The words are from *Apologia pro Vita Sua,* quoted without page citation in Ian Ker, *John Henry Newman: A Biography* (Oxford: Oxford University Press, 1988), 19. For the relation of Whately and Newman, see Geoffrey Faber, *Oxford Apostles: A Character Study of the Oxford Movement* (London: Faber & Faber, 1935; reprint, Harmondsworth: Penguin, 1954) 108-11.

33. Whately also arranged for the twenty-three-year-old Newman to contribute the article on Cicero to the *Encyclopedia,* an article that is held in high regard. Walter Jost, *Rhetorical Thought in John Henry Newman* (Columbia: University of South Carolina Press, 1989), 9. And, when Whately became principal of St. Alban's Hall, he invited Newman to become his vice-principal.

34. Ehninger, "Editor's Introduction," ix.

35. Ibid., xi.

36. Ibid., 4.

37. Ibid., ix.

38. Reardon, *Religion in the Age of Romanticism,* 2.

39. Horton Davies, *Worship and Theology in England, From Newman to Martineau, 1850–1900,* vol. 4, Worship and Theology in England (Princeton: Princeton University Press, 1962), 4:287-301.

40. The standard treatment of his life has become, Ker, *John Henry Newman.* On it and several other recent books about Newman, see my review article, "A Centennial Perspective on Newman as Rhetor," *ATR* 73 (1991), 477-83.

41. The only church possible for a member of either university, since religious tests excluding Dissenters were not abolished until 1871.

42. From which came the designation of the Oxford movement as the Tractarians.

43. The first generation of Tractarians was not liturgically demonstrative. It was the second generation, the "millinerians," who began to imitate the vestments and ceremonial of contemporary Roman Catholics.

44. I have taken the quotation from Faber, *Oxford Apostles,* 187. It is from the *Studies in Poetry and Philosophy* (1868) of John Campbell Shairp, a Scottish scholar who became professor of poetry at Oxford long after Newman left.

45. John Henry Newman, "On Preaching the Gospel" in *Lectures on the Doctrine of Justification* (London: Longmans, Green & Co, 1892). The best analysis of

Newman's preaching I have seen is W. D. White's introduction to *The Preaching of John Henry Newman,* The Preacher's Paperback Library (Philadelphia: Fortress, 1969).

46. Ibid., 14-15.

47. John Henry Newman, "On Preaching the Gospel," 371.

48. *The Idea of a University Defined and Illustrated in Nine Discourses Delivered to the Catholics of Dublin in Occasional Lectures and Essays Addressed to the Members of the Catholic University,* ed. with intro. and notes by Martin J. Svaglic (Notre Dame: University of Notre Dame Press, 1982), 303-21. Further page references to this work will be made parenthetically in the text.

49. Death, judgment, heaven, and hell.

50. Originally seven.

51. For a succinct description of the differences between the three series, see Davies, *Worship and Theology in England,* 4:302-5.

52. John Henry Newman, *Fifteen Sermons Preached Before the University of Oxford Between A.D. 1826 and 1843.* The edition consulted was that of 1898 published by Longmans, Green, & Co.

53. Jouett L. Powell, *Three Uses of Christian Discourse in John Henry Newman: An Example of Nonreductive Reflection on the Christian Faith,* AARDS, no. 10 (Missoula, Mont.: Scholars Press, 1975). The quotation is from Jost, *Rhetorical Thought in John Henry Newman.*

54. Powell, *Three Uses of Christian Discourse,* 90-91.

55. John Campbell Shairp, *Studies in Poetry and Philosophy,* quoted in Faber, *Oxford Apostles,* 187.

56. Reardon, *Religion in the Age of Romanticism,* 14. The extent to which Newman was a man of his time and a Romantic is discussed by David Nicholls and Fergus Kerr in the introduction to the collection of essays they edited titled *John Henry Newman: Reason, Rhetoric, and Romanticism* (Carbondale: Southern Illinois University Press, 1991), 3-4, and by Valerie Pitt in her contribution to that volume, "Demythologizing Newman," 13-27. Most of the essayists of that volume doubt the ongoing significance of Newman's thought (p. 4). A much more thorough effort to understand the life and work of Newman in terms of the great motifs of Romanticism is David Goslee, *Romanticism and the Anglican Newman* (Athens: Ohio University Press, 1996).

57. That is, a church that was not a part of the diocesan structure, but one that was privately organized and supported.

58. *Sermons Preached at Trinity Chapel, Brighton, by the Late Rev. Frederick W. Robertson, M.A., the Incumbent.* The copy consulted was the frequently reprinted Harper & Brothers one-volume edition, which appeared originally in 1870, but I am very grateful to Prof. Sam Hill for the gift of a set of the edition published by Bernhard Tauchnitz of Leipzig, 1861–66.

59. Stopford A Brooke, *The Life and Letters of Frederick W. Robertson, M.A.* The copy consulted is the New Edition of 1868, published in London by Kegan, Paul, Trench, Trübner, & Co., Ltd. in 1891.

60. Frederick W. Robertson, *Sermons Preached at Brighton* (New York: Harper & Brothers, 1905), 5.

61. Brooke, *Life and Letters,* 2:265. The description above is based on the letter from which the quotation was made, a passage from his biography (2:229), an engraving of his bust that is the frontispiece for that volume, and the portrait sketch that is the frontispiece for the Harper & Brothers edition of the *Sermons.*

62. Parenthetical numbers refer to pages of Brooke, *The Life and Letters of Frederick W. Robertson.*

63. It is hard for post–Vietnam Christians to consider anything warlike to be consistent with their religion, but that is simply one of the cultural differences between them and nineteenth-century Europeans, who believed that war kept nations morally healthy. Cf. Owen Chadwick, *The Secularization of the European Mind in the Nineteenth Century,* Canto (Cambridge: Cambridge University Press, 1990), 132-34, although in this passage Chadwick is discussing a period slightly later than that of Robertson.

64. There was a fourth, St. Ebbe's at Oxford, but he was there only two months.

65. Davies says that he died of a brain tumor, but does not cite his authority for that diagnosis. *Worship and Theology,* 4:312. In response to my summary of symptoms, Dr. Samuel A. Trufant, who taught neurology at the medical schools of Cincinnati and Tulane Universities for many years, said that an aneurysm or a cerebellar or other form of cyst seems more likely.

66. Susan Sontag, *Illness as a Metaphor* (New York: Farrar, Straus & Giroux, 1978), 32.

67. James R. Blackwood, *The Soul of Frederick W. Robertson, the Brighton Preacher* (New York: Harper & Brothers, 1947), 117.

68. At the same time, he was an advocate of studying a few books thoroughly rather than reading many superficially.

69. Some of his best descriptions of natural beauty occur in letters he wrote to his wife while walking through the Alps after the collapse of his work in Cheltenham. Brooke, *The Life and Letters of Frederick W. Robertson,* 1:115-33.

70. The Dean of Westminster Abbey!

71. Archbishop Ussher set the date of creation as 4004 B.C.

72. Frederick W. Robertson, *Sermons Preached at Brighton.*

73. Ibid., 826.

74. Ibid., 831.

75. Alec R. Vidler, *The Church in an Age of Revolution: 1789 to the Present Day,* The Pelican History of the Church, vol. 5 (Harmondsworth: Penguin, 1961), 114.

76. Charles Smyth, *The Art of Preaching: A Practical Survey of Preaching in the Church of England 747-1939* (London: SPCK; New York: Macmillan, 1940), 229-30.

77. Davies, *Worship and Theology,* 4:290. For an analytical summary of one such sermon see Smyth, *The Art of Preaching,* 226-29. The sermon treated is "The Skepticism of Pilate," *Sermons,* 226-34.

78. Brooke, *The Life and Letters of Frederick W. Robertson,* ix.

79. "On the Constitution of the Church and State," *Works,* 10:54, quoted in Robert Hole, *Pulpit, Politics, and Public Order in England 1762–1832* (Cambridge: Cambridge University Press, 1989), 253.

80. "The Sydenham Palace, and the Religious Non-Observance of the Sabbath," *Sermons*, 343-52.

81. Ibid., 352.

82. Robertson, *Sermons Preached at Brighton*, 186.

83. Ibid., 195.

CHAPTER 23

TRANSATLANTIC ROMANTICISM

UNITARIAN ROMANTICISM

Although most previous trends in preaching moved from east to west, Romantic preaching was heard in America before it began in Britain. Theological liberalism in the U.S. was receptive to Romantic influence at an earlier date. British radical thought began in the late-seventeenth century with Enlightenment rationalism rather than with Romanticism, which developed later. The eroding tendencies of the Enlightenment, however, were pretty well kept in check in New England through the American Revolution, at least in regard to the doctrine of the Trinity.[1] By the time this traditional orthodoxy came to be questioned, therefore, the mood of the culture had shifted from the Augustan exaltation of reason to one more congenial to the Romantic spirit.

For some time before that, double predestination had ceased to be presupposed by many New England Congregationalists; the sort of Arminianism that developed in the Second Great Awakening could be found even among the more staid clergy of Boston. This left them open to other liberalizing tendencies. Then, near the beginning of the nineteenth century, liberal clergy moving away from Trinitarian orthodoxy took key positions at Harvard. In this way an atmosphere developed, but there was not yet any movement toward institutionalizing it.

Pre-Romantic Liberalism

The catalyst that turned the theological trend into a denomination was a sermon preached by William Ellery Channing (1780–1842) at the 1819 ordination of Jared Sparks in Baltimore. The young minister of the Federal Street Church in Boston had already appeared as the champion of modernist theology in 1815, when he led the defense against a call from the orthodox for the exposure of heretics. In an open letter to Samuel Thatcher, his colleague at the Brattle Street Church, he had warded off that attack and turned a beleaguered position into a positive platform. But the ordination sermon, "Unitarian Christianity,"[2] initiated a movement that culminated in the formation of the American Unitarian Association in 1825.

Channing, however, represented a position that was still pre-Romantic, one that was in transition from neoclassic rationalism. He still showed some of the attitudes of the Enlightenment, but he worked out their implications differently from the way of his British predecessors. His Christology, for instance, was Arian rather than Socinian; that is, he regarded Jesus as a preexistent divine being rather than as a human being with a special divine mission.

He also showed other tendencies that would have a fuller place among the Romantics, nor were these exclusively theological. When he needed to travel for his health, he went to England and looked up William Wordsworth, who introduced him to Samuel Coleridge, who, in turn, induced him to read Friedrich Schelling and Johann Fichte. His interest in Wordsworth and his poetry was a result of his love of nature and a "mystical sense of the universe as the outer garment of God."[3] All this was thoroughly Romantic.

The heart of Channing's theology was not the doctrine of God, nor was it Christology. Rather, his characteristic interest was anthropology, and he entertained a very high understanding of the spiritual capacity of human beings. His reaction against Calvinism is most apparent in his estimate of human capacity. He came "to define the religious life as a continual pursuit of self-culture."[4] The possibilities of self-improvement were infinite; its goal was perfection. This is not to say that he was unaware of the human capacity for evil, but only that he felt it did not have to be indulged.

While the later transcendentalists shared Channing's "intractable faith in the potential divinity of the individual," they carried it farther than he, fitting it in with the pantheism to which Romanticism was always inclined, while he "clung much more firmly to a Christ-centered religion."[5] In other ways as well he remained pre-Romantic in his theology, his rationalism being seen, for instance, in an epistemology derived from John Locke and the Scottish Common Sense philosophers. In early American Unitarianism, the closer one got to Romanticism, the farther one became removed from traditional Christianity. Coming at the very beginning of the process, Channing was thus nearer to historic Christianity and less Romantic than many to follow.

Channing's preaching was shaped by Hugh Blair, in both form and content.[6] With his commitment to self-cultivation, it was only natural that he should find congenial Blair's belief that the purpose of preaching was to make people better. Indeed, one of his major objections to Trinitarianism was that the preaching of its doctrines did not have this effect.[7] Channing used the same criterion to evaluate both doctrines and the rhetorical method by which they were communicated: the value of either was seen in its capacity to improve people morally. Beliefs also needed the unity, consistency, and harmony that Blair required of speeches if they were to contribute to the improvement of human morals.[8]

Emerson's Pastorate

True Romantic preaching in America was first practiced by one whose very Romantic impulses would eventually lead him from the pulpit and even from such a place in the Christian tradition as his Unitarian mentors retained. Ralph Waldo Emerson (1803–82) was the son of a Unitarian minister who died when Waldo was eight, leaving his widow and their children in straitened circumstances. The one of these five who would grow up to be called "the Sage of Concord" showed no particular literary, philosophical, or religious precocity in his youth. One of his earliest vague senses of vocational direction, however, was a desire to "put on eloquence as a robe," and it was from his preacher father that he claimed to derive "a passionate love for the strains of eloquence."[9] Yet when he graduated from Harvard he was not able to pursue that goal, since he had to start working immediately as a schoolteacher to supplement the family income.

The influences on his life pointed him toward the Unitarian pulpit. Among these were the Channing brothers, with William Ellery supplying the theological framework and Edward Tyrrel having taught him how to write and speak. After he decided to enter the ministry and prepare for it at Harvard Divinity School, he contracted tuberculosis, which not only threatened his vision but also left him weak for his studies. When eventually he was licensed to preach, he delayed finding a church of his own and becoming ordained both to protect his health and because it was still expected that a New England minister would be wedded to his parish for life. He wanted to make sure that the place he accepted was one in which he could devote more energy to scholarly preaching than to wider pastoral duties.

His eventual settlement came after he began in July 1828 to fill in at Second Church, Boston,[10] because of the illness of its pastor, Henry Ware Jr., one of the most distinguished Unitarian ministers of the period. The following January he was called to be junior pastor of Second Church.[11] It was recognized that because of Ware's illness, most of the work would fall upon Emerson; he would, however, succeed Ware as senior minister. The succession occurred on July 1, 1829, when Ware joined the Harvard faculty.

Far from being lifelong, his tenure as pastor lasted less than two and a half years. The secular literary scholars who have been the main students of Emerson have assumed that he was miscast as a minister all along, and that his resignation of his pastorate was an escape from the shackles of an institution and its dogmas that he found confining.[12] While it is true that his transcendentalist manifesto, "Nature," was published in 1836, he nevertheless continued to fill pulpits on occasion until 1839.

The transition was far more gradual than has been understood, and the discontinuity less than has been assumed. Wesley Mott, for instance, argues that the roots of Emerson's most transcendental teachings lie not in Platonism or Eastern religions, as has been thought, but in biblical and Puritan theology, and David Robinson takes a very similar position.

The occasion of his resignation was his unwillingness to administer Holy Communion, but this was not because he had lost his religion. The issue, rather, was his concern with the relation of what he called "forms" to religious experience. He was probably not so much a philosophical idealist as someone who was convinced that spirit is much more important than matter. Sacraments or ordinances, the Bible, morality, and church were all in conflict to a certain degree with the experience of the true religion in the soul. The sacramental assumption that forms can be means of grace was foreign to him; such things seemed to Emerson more likely to block than to convey the Spirit. Hence his quarrel with Unitarianism was not that it was too religious but rather that it was not religious enough; in his Romantic antiformalism he saw popular religion, including Unitarianism, as a constable religion.[13]

The important human trait for Emerson was what he called "Mind," which is the same as what Coleridge called "Reason"; this is to be distinguished from the analytical faculty that most people call reason (and Coleridge designated as mere "Understanding").[14] This Mind in the individual participates in the spiritual reality of the universe that Emerson can describe interchangeably as Reason, Universal Mind, or the Oversoul. Therefore, religion can be self-evident to all minds open to perceiving it, and Emerson can say that spiritual religion "has no other evidence than its own intrinsic probability."[15] Such a religion, of course, would have slight need of forms.

Slight, but some—just as Reason would always have need of Understanding. The sort of preaching Emerson believed in and wanted to do while he was still a minister was one of the right sort of forms, because he conceived preaching to be the middle term between Spirit and letter. The preacher enunciates the inner testimony of Spirit that he perceives and thus calls it to the attention of the congregation, who can recognize it because the same Spirit is testifying to the same truth within them.

The Spirit "speaks," makes itself heard, through the medium of the external word, but the hearing is of two kinds. The external word simply helps to activate (not to cause) the inner hearing of the inner Word. Listeners respond initially to external words only by an external hearing, but all who truly desire to do so are capable of hearing the Spirit's voice "through" external words.[16]

Such an understanding of the purpose of preaching would obviously have implications for the form of preaching. To begin with, it meant that a sermon was not complete when the preacher spoke; it had to be completed within and by the hearers. Its meaning had to be recognized and carried further by them. And the medium for enabling that process was not discursive reasoning, but a "suggestiveness" that did not override the audience's freedom. Thus Emerson came to reject Hugh Blair's rhetorical theory, which he had learned from Edward Tyrrel Channing, having a different sense of the hearers' needs and believing that "the individual self must express itself outward in forms that are not imposed from without."[17]

He began to deride what he called the "gingerbread distinctions" of sermons and to recognize that truths to be communicated have their own organic form; in this way, sermons are "composed" as a system of interrelations. "For Emerson, it is the idea, the unity infusing the parts of a lecture, just as it is the law immanent in the parts of nature (such as a shell) that a speaker should suggest."[18]

Emerson went on to experiment with the sermon form in an effort to see how self-evident truth could be relayed to an audience.[19] Before he could perfect that form, however, another, Holy Communion, came to appear too inconsistent with his understanding of ministry for him to continue in that calling. He became a lecturer and a writer as his thought evolved in a more transcendental direction. Even then, however, the degree of his alienation from Christianity can be overestimated. (For an example of a sermon by Emerson, see **Vol. 2, pp. 493-502.**)

Theodore Parker, a Transcendental Preacher

The Unitarian transcendentalist who would remain in the ministry and anticipate many trends of later Romantic preaching in liberal Christianity was Theodore Parker (1810–60), a grandson of the John Parker who led the American minutemen in the first battle of the Revolutionary War. Theodore exhibited throughout his life the spirit of the words his forebear is supposed to have said just before the fighting began: "Don't fire unless fired upon; but if they mean to have a war, let it begin here!"[20]

From his father he inherited an omnivorous appetite for reading but little in a material way, since his father was a not very successful farmer. Theodore had to take his Harvard degree by examination because he could not afford tuition, but both his diligence and his capacity for learning meant that by graduation he was already on his way to becoming a polymath.[21] At first he taught school but had some of the same difficulty with teaching that he was later to have with preaching: he expected from those who heard him commitment, application, and ability equal to his own. Gifted in languages, he read deeply in German Romantic philosophers and biblical criticism, not to mention the sacred writings of other religions in their original tongues.

By the time he took his first pastorate in West Roxbury, he had identified himself with the transcendentalists. Like Channing, he signaled the next stage of Unitarian thought in an ordination sermon; his was later to be published as "The Transient and Permanent in Christianity." His distinction between the permanent and transient was essentially the one others were to make later between "the religion of Jesus" and "the religion about Jesus." The transient elements were forms and doctrines, which had changed in every age and place. Examples of such evanescent dogmas were doctrines of scriptural revelation and Christologies. What was abiding could be reduced to Jesus' summary of the law: love God completely and your neighbor as yourself.

Implicit to all this is a transcendental epistemology. The religion of

Jesus is not reliable because it was taught with either his authority or that of the Bible. "It is hard to see why the great truths of Christianity rest on the personal authority of Jesus, more than the axioms of geometry rest on the personal authority of Euclid or Archimedes."[22] Great religious truth is recognized intuitively because God has constructed the human soul to have that capacity.

> Such ideas, capable of this legitimation, transcend experience, require and admit no further proof; as true before experience as after; true before time, after time, eternally; absolutely true.[23]

People do not differ on these truths; because they were implanted in the human consciousness by God, they are the same for all. That self-evidence, however, was less than self-evident. What Parker said at the ordination of Charles Shackleford was as threatening to the cozy establishment of his fellow Unitarian clergy as what Channing had said was to the orthodox Congregationalists of his day. They wished to exclude him from their fellowship, but they could never muster enough votes, and he refused to resign.

He continued to work on a number of fronts. One of his most important contributions was a heavily revised translation of Wilhelm De Wette's *Critical and Historical Introduction to the Canonical Scriptures of the Old Testament.* Although German thought was influential in Boston at the time,[24] this was one of the first if not the very first translation into English of contemporary German biblical scholarship. In this Parker contributed to the beginning of what was to become a norm in Christian preaching, its relying upon historical-critical biblical scholarship.

As little welcome to the Unitarian clergy as Parker and his message were, they were very welcome to a large number of laity. In 1845 he was called from his West Roxbury pulpit to a new congregation in Boston that would become the Twenty-Eighth Congregational Society there. They had no building in the beginning, nor did they wish to erect one large enough for the crowds they could expect. Instead, they held their services first at the Melodeon theater and then, when it was completed, at the new Music Hall, which held three thousand persons. Parker had one thing in common with successful evangelists of the period like Charles Grandison Finney and Charles Haddon Spurgeon: needing a theater to hold the huge audiences that turned out to hear them.

What Parker considered to be the permanent elements of Christianity, love of God and love of neighbor, determined the content of his preaching. He was, in his opinion, a reformer of faith and a reformer of morals.

His way of reforming faith has already been indicated. Soon after he moved to Boston, however, his way of reforming morals became clear. He saw eight "prominent evils" that needed to be opposed: intemperance, covetousness, ignorance, the condition of women, improper politics, war, slavery, and false theology.[25]

He was deeply concerned about all these issues. For instance, his concern for women is reflected in a practice modern feminists may have thought they invented, praying to "Our Father and Our Mother God."[26] He also anticipated the preaching of the "Social Gospel" to be discussed below. Soon, however, his passionate commitment to the abolitionist cause forced him to neglect other areas of social evil to concentrate on that massive one. His tireless work in the cause of abolition may have contributed to the tuberculosis that forced his early retirement, which was to be shortly followed by his death.

Although he published a great deal, the main medium for the dissemination of Parker's thought was his sermons.[27] These usually lasted about an hour and tended to be deductive, beginning with the widest possible generalization and working down progressively to the point under consideration. Words were chosen to be effective when heard rather than read. A standard technique was classification, which allowed him to break the material discussed into several categories that could be analyzed. Into this rhetorical framework he would fit vast amounts of statistics, history, and arcane lore.

In no case, however, was the appeal to authority, since the only source of religious truth he recognized was innate intuitions and perceptions of the divine. Thus "The Transient and Permanent in Christianity" was an exception among his sermons because it took a biblical text as a point of departure. In this way, Parker's transcendental epistemology led him away from what had always been a main characteristic of Christian preaching, the explication of a biblical text. The next wave of Unitarian theological change would regard theism as optional. And so it happened that the tradition to first produce Romantic preaching in English came in time to abandon anything that with precision could be labeled Christian proclamation.

THE THREE Bs OF AMERICAN PREACHING[28]

Horace Bushnell

By a quirk of fate, the three preachers most highly regarded in America during the middle to the end of the nineteenth century had family names that begin with the letter *B*: Bushnell, Beecher, and Brooks. All three were Romantics who were loyal to the traditional Christian faith, but wished to state it in a vocabulary that would have meaning to the men and women of their day.

Chronologically the first of these, and theologically the most innovative and influential, was Horace Bushnell (1802–76). The son of a farmer in Litchfield County, Connecticut, Bushnell grew up to attend Yale. Upon graduation he worked for a while as a newspaperman before returning to Yale to tutor undergraduates and study law. During the time he was in that capacity in 1831, a religious revival occurred of the sort that had been a regular event at Yale earlier in the century during the presidency of Timothy Dwight.[29] Bushnell, who had been something of a skeptic before, was converted, although as much out of a desire to set a good example, apparently, as from any other internal crisis.[30] Nevertheless, the experience was enough to cause him to transfer to the Divinity School to prepare for ordination. Upon graduation he became the minister of North Congregational Church in Hartford, Connecticut, where he remained until ill health forced him to retire in 1859. Afterward, he was able to write and even to travel; he remained a force until his death in 1876, and his influence lasted on after that.

Even though he never held an academic post and was always contemptuous of academic theology, he came to be regarded as "the American Schleiermacher" and "the father of American religious liberalism,"[31] and has been described as "the greatest theologian of his generation and one of the most important thinkers in the history of American Protestantism."[32] As H. Shelton Smith has pointed out, the main issues on which Bushnell was to reflect theologically had become the agenda for New England theology after being raised by William Ellery Channing in his Baltimore ordination sermon.[33] The issues were the Trinity, Christology, human depravity, and the nature of the redemption brought by Christ. Bushnell's position on these issues was very different from that of Channing, however. He was also careful to distinguish his position from the other two influential systems of the time, Scholastic Calvinist Orthodoxy (as then taught) and revivalism.

Bushnell wished to affirm the Trinity, the divinity of Christ, human sinfulness, and the need for redemption.[34] What made him different from his orthodox contemporaries was a conviction learned from one of the books that influenced his thought most deeply, Coleridge's *Aids to Reflection,* the conviction that "Christianity is not a theory, or a speculation; but a life;—not a philosophy of life, but a life and a living process."[35] This organic perspective on life is typically Romantic. It was shocking to Bushnell's orthodox contemporaries, however, who thought that Christian preaching consisted of accurately arguing the doctrines of Calvin as they had received them. And it was equally unsatisfactory to the Unitarians, whether of Channing's Christian variety or Parker's transcendentalist persuasion.

Bushnell's position was also offensive to the revivalists because his understanding of Christian growth had led him to publish his views on Christian nurture—in many ways merely an extension of the old Puritan concept of the "Halfway Covenant."[36] He assumed that children born into Christian families and baptized could "grow up in love with all goodness, and remember no definite time when they became subjects of Christian principle."[37] This meant that it was not necessary to undergo a dramatic conversion experience in order to be saved. He thought the revivalist understanding "denied the manner in which one could grow into the faith and thereby ignored the need for the structures of family, church, and society, which nurture the person into the religious life."[38] Yet Bushnell—particularly after a near mystical experience in 1848—was convinced that growth had to involve significant change. Otherwise, the "religious nature," a longing for God shared by all human beings, never developed into the "religious life," which for him was the state of salvation.[39] Thus he believed in conversion, but thought that it could be a process spread over a lifetime as well an event of which one could remember the day and the hour.

Bushnell's characteristic medium for developing and communicating his theological positions was his sermons. Even though he published treatises in addition to his volumes of sermons, the longer works generally grew out of his preaching. His theological perspective caused him to object to the major preaching styles of his day, whether the arid rationalism of Orthodoxy, the Romanticism of transcendentalism, or the emotional manipulation of the revivalists.

One of the reasons he opposed Scholastic Orthodoxy was his understanding of the way language works. From his professor of biblical languages at Yale, Josiah Willard Gibbs, he learned that all language began as physical descriptions, which came to be used in abstract thought only as analogies; no abstract language is literal.[40] Yet it took Bushnell to see the implication that theological language therefore cannot be univocal, cannot be literal, objective, or scientific. The Scholastics' insistence that it could be would "only serve to produce a theology even more ambiguous than its metaphorical language already makes it."[41]

Bushnell recognized that the language of theology is artistic and even poetic. While such language does not encapsulate truth in exact formulas, it can do something better: it can get closer to the religious life as it is actually lived. And what is true of the language of theology is true a fortiori of the language of preaching. "Preaching should be an art form which stirs the symbolic consciousness and invites one to undertake the pilgrimage of faith."[42] Thus preaching involves all the instruments of eloquence, but its aim is vastly more serious than that of mere eloquence: it is a call to faith.

These principles can be seen at work in Bushnell's sermons, in which he takes a subject that has become stale in the arid formulas of the orthodox and brings it alive by graphic language, lively analogies, and the sheer power of imagination. For instance, in "The Power of an Endless Life," he admits at the outset that the subject of immortality as usually presented is "one of the dullest subjects," largely because of a concentration on its merely mathematical duration.[43] He wishes it to be understood as growth and sees an analogy in the way gigantic California redwoods develop from tiny seed. The emphasis is on achieving one's full potential. He goes on to show how many areas there are in which human beings develop in addition to the spiritual: "intelligence, reason, conscience, observation, choice, memory, enthusiasm." A catalog of the areas of human achievement made possible by those developments is given. Then he goes on to say, "And yet we have, in the power thus developed, nothing more than a mere hint or initial sign of what is to be the real stature of his personality in the process of his everlasting development."[44]

Having said that, though, he goes on to show how sin has inhibited the realization of this potential. He must speak, therefore, of the redemption wrought in Christ. The greatest impediment to appreciating this is the assumption by human beings that they are too far beneath such attention from God: "The expense of the sacrifice wears a look of extravagance."[45] In the conclusion he says people also fear a diminished humanity in salvation, but, to the contrary, it is far expanded beyond anything they can imagine. He quickly sketches in a virtual presence of humanity in the achievement of its full potential among the principalities and powers of the heavenly kingdom. The overall effect is to take what has been regarded as dullness itself and show it in such vividness that hearers begin to aspire to it with an exalted yearning that is itself a proleptic presence of the glory to be revealed. The hallmark of Bushnell's preaching is his ability to reconceive traditional Christian teaching in a way that brings it startlingly to life and makes it a real option to be sought.

Henry Ward Beecher

The revivalism against which Bushnell reacted was not just that of Finney's heirs, but also that urged by Finney's early opponents: Asahel Nettleton, Nathaniel Taylor, and Lyman Beecher.[46] While they had come to revise Jonathan Edwards's Calvinist belief in predestination, they were as insistent upon divine judgment as the hard-shell Presbyterians of Princeton, the orthodox Scholastics opposed by Bushnell. But when Lyman Beecher's son Henry Ward Beecher (1813–87)[47] entered the ministry, he discovered, after an initial commitment to the revivalist camp, that Bushnell's God of love appealed to him more than his father's God of wrath. Thus, although the younger Beecher was more of a communicator than a thinker, his theology, insofar as it was systematic, developed very much in the spirit of Bushnell's.[48]

The eleven children of Lyman Beecher are a strong argument for the importance of either heredity or environment in the development of talent. Two of Henry Ward's sisters were among the most influential women of the nineteenth century, Catherine being one of the major theoreticians of the cult of true womanhood and Harriet the author of *Uncle Tom's Cabin,* the novel that did more than anything else to galvanize Northern opinion against slavery.[49] Henry was the eighth child born to the Beechers and was not regarded by his parents as one of their more promising. He was not, for instance, considered up to following in the family tradition of Yale. Instead, he was sent to Mount Pleasant School in Amherst, Massachusetts, for his secondary education, and he stayed on in the same town for college. He was a rather weak student in such basic courses as Greek and Latin, but he became thoroughly grounded in rhetoric and developed a power of delivery that was to stay with him and grow for the rest of his life.[50]

When his father accepted the presidency of Lane Seminary in Cincinnati out of a deep sense of mission to evangelize the West with the religion and culture of New England, much of the family followed, including Henry, who enrolled in the seminary. After graduation he stayed in the area to assist in that winning of the West, serving first as minister of the Presbyterian church of Lawrenceville, Indiana (1837–39), and then going on to become pastor of Second Presbyterian in Indianapolis (1839–47). In this work on what was still essentially the frontier, his ministry began to develop emphases for which he would later become famous. In Indianapolis, for instance, he preached his first sermons against slavery, and gave his *Lectures to Young Men,* warning them against the moral dangers of life in the city. He also became involved in editorial work and even wrote for a periodical on agriculture.[51]

In 1847 he was called to be the first pastor of Plymouth Congregational Church in Brooklyn. There his pulpit became what William McLoughlin has called "the spiritual center of the republic for almost half a century."[52] His principal work at Plymouth Church was preaching; he did little pastoral work in the usual sense. The rest of his energy was spent in what could be considered extensions of his preaching: lecturing, writing, and editorial work. So effective was his communication that his preaching came to be regarded as one of the tourist attractions of the metropolitan area that every visitor from this country or abroad had to experience.[53]

The impact of his proclamation was phenomenal, especially as he began to address social issues in general and slavery in particular.[54] He had been concerned about slavery during college, had tried to protect an abolitionist printer against mob action while in seminary, and had begun preaching against slavery in Indianapolis. But now Henry went so far as to raise money to provide rifles (the notorious "Beecher's Bibles") for antislavery settlers in Kansas. Abraham Lincoln is supposed to have greeted Henry's sister Harriet with the words: "So you're the little woman who wrote the book that started this great war!"[55] She and her brother were certainly among the most effective antislavery publicists.

Many at the time thought that Beecher's speaking tour in Britain was the main factor in dissuading the British from recognizing the Confederacy. President Lincoln invited him to be the speaker when the Union flag was raised again at Fort Sumter at the end of the war. After the war, his became an important voice on many issues disrupting the society, issues ranging from woman's rights to the acceptance of evolution. Although he remained a conservative on such questions as the accumulation of wealth and labor unions, he was nevertheless a forerunner of the Social Gospel preaching of Washington Gladden and Walter Rauschenbusch.

The most significant aspect of the preaching of Henry Ward Beecher is that pointed out by Clifford E. Clark Jr. Beecher was the public thinker who provided Americans with the words and ideas to negotiate their transition from a rural agricultural society to an urban industrial one. He was the one who articulated the ideals of American Victorian culture, and he did so by calling upon a core of Romantic Christian themes.

> As espoused by Beecher, romantic Christianity was a religion of the heart, an appeal to the feelings and emotions that replaced the cold, formalistic evangelical theology of the previous generation and accepted the

> new theories of evolution and biblical criticism. Using the natural world as a source of inspiration, Beecher preached a new experiential Christianity that emphasized God's love for man and the availability of salvation for all. It was a cheerful and optimistic faith that gave people the confidence to attack vice and crime and encouraged them to work for a general reformation of society.[56]

This is to say that the significance of Beecher's preaching was that it furnished the thoughts and words from which a generation was able to construct their reality socially and thus to articulate for themselves the meaning of the new world in which they were living.[57] In many ways Beecher was like Lincoln: the attitudes of both men enabled them to win more support for their side than others who were closer to what was later to be called political correctness. Beecher had such a sensitive finger on the public's pulse that he seemed to know the exact moment when they were ready to arrive at a new understanding, and he stood ready to provide for them the words and concepts in which to phrase that understanding. If effective preaching is more a matter of getting people to see something in a new way than it is of stating what they ought to believe before they are willing to accept it, Henry Ward Beecher has to be regarded as one of the most effective preachers in American history.

Phillips Brooks

The influence of the third of the three *B*'s, Phillips Brooks (1835–93), was due entirely to his preaching and the impact of his personality through it. As one scholar noted, he "was not an ecclesiastical statesman, an energetic executive, or an adventurous missionary. He led no movement; he wrought no reforms; and except for his sermons and lectures he wrote no books."[58] Yet it would be hard to think of anyone else who has had as much influence on American preaching. Edgar De Witt Jones has said that Beecher and Brooks are "the two most written about preachers in America" and that their Beecher Lectures on Preaching at Yale are the series most often referred to by other lecturers.[59] One has the impression, however, that the long-term influence of Brooks has been greater than that of Beecher and that his lectures have been reprinted more regularly.[60] Certainly no homiletical mot is more quoted than Brooks's definition of *preaching* as "truth through personality."[61]

His life is quickly summarized because it appears as almost without incident. Born on December 13, 1835, he was the second of the six sons of his parents, both of whom came from old New England families. When he was four, the family changed its membership from a Congregational church that was too Unitarian for their orthodox taste to an evangelical Episcopal parish. Young Brooks went to Boston Latin School and received a thorough grounding in classical languages and then to Harvard, where he was known for writing effective prose.

Almost the only ripple ever to disturb his life's placid surface was connected with his first employment, teaching at the Latin School. He was an utter failure. Unable to maintain discipline, he resigned after only four months and spent the rest of the academic year in depression. By the end of the summer, however, he began to emerge from his gloom and started reading again, especially the English and German Romanticists. "In the midst of his discouragement, the English poet Percy Bysshe Shelley provided him with the kind of heroic defiance of adverse circumstances that he desperately needed."[62] Reading the Romantics was both therapy and a conversion of sorts. Even though he had not yet been confirmed, he enrolled that fall in the Virginia Theological Seminary.

Although Brooks's background was in the Evangelical wing of the Episcopal Church, which had founded the seminary in Alexandria, he was put off by much he found there. He thought his classmates used piety as an excuse to avoid intellectual effort, most of the faculty fell far below the standards of Harvard, and he found slavery abhorrent. Yet he settled in, studied hard on his own, began a lifelong habit of notebook keeping, completed the course, and was ordained to the diaconate in June 1859.

From the beginning, his preaching attracted large crowds. His first call was to the Church of the Advent in Philadelphia, but his success there led to his being called three years later to Holy Trinity in the same city, one of the largest Episcopal churches in the country—an extraordinary appointment for a young man of twenty-six. Even then his preaching was so impressive that it was reported in New York papers. Unlike Beecher, however, he was a devoted pastor. He loved his people—and indeed all people—and gave himself unstintingly to them. During the Civil War years, he ministered to the soldiers in their camps and hospitals as much as he could.

Then, after ten years in Philadelphia, he accepted a call back to Boston to Trinity, the old downtown church. There he remained as rector, preaching three times a week to a full church, for twenty-two years. Having resisted many prestigious calls to other parishes, to the episcopate, and to academic appointments, he agreed to become the bishop of his own diocese. His health held out in that office for only fifteen months. He died on January 23, 1893, deeply mourned by the whole city of Boston and by thousands all over the world who had been blessed by his ministry.

When Brooks was in seminary, his devout Evangelical mother wrote to him, warning against the theology of Horace Bushnell, saying that she would prefer that he never preach the gospel to his perverting it as Bushnell did.[63] She was to be disappointed, for both his theology and his homiletical method were to be closer to Bushnell's than to those of the clergy she admired.

While Brooks has been described as a liberal or a Broad Churchman, the Incarnation was nevertheless the center of his faith, and he had a passionate devotion to the Trinity. But he did accept evolution, finding that it strengthened rather than weakened his faith, and, while he did not put much emphasis on exegesis, he welcomed biblical criticism.

When he was elected to the episcopate, there were accusations of heresy leveled against him by Anglo-Catholics, and efforts were made to prevent his consecration, but today most of what he was charged with would be regarded merely as ecumenism. Although he valued it, he did not consider the threefold ministry of bishops, priests, and deacons to be of the *esse* of the church as the Anglo-Catholics claimed. Even in those days of more conservative theology, however, the necessary number of dioceses and bishops approved his candidacy and he was consecrated. These questions about his orthodoxy were the closest he ever came to being criticized publicly; otherwise, his reputation was without blemish.

Brooks's Beecher lectures on preaching are in some ways more of a spirituality of preaching than a how-to manual. The key is the principle enunciated in the first lecture that "preaching is the bringing of truth through personality."[64] "Personality" here does not so much have its modern sense of charm (as in the expression "He has a good personality") as it does of personhood. In other words, Brooks was as incarnational in his understanding of preaching as he was in his theology. Preaching is interpersonal communication, but it is even more the communication of the deepest truth embodied in the communicator. The preacher, therefore, must be a person who is totally alert in two directions—listening attentively to God and observing people as closely as possible—so that what God has to say to the people can be relayed to them in the most effective manner. For such preaching to occur, the "primary necessity" is "that the Christian preacher should be a Christian first" (16).

Since it is the personality of the preacher that mediates truth, the preacher's own person has to be considered. The work of the preacher is then attended under the heads of its nature, method, and spirit. The nature of the work is that one is at once a preacher and a pastor; one is also a leader. As disastrous as having no method in the work is having the wrong method, too small or narrow, a hobbyhorse that is ridden. "The first necessity for the preacher and the hod-carrier[65] is the same. Be faithful, and do your best always" (101). The preacher's work should be done in the spirit of a servant to one's parishioners, of one who never feels equal to the task, who is profoundly honest, and who is vitally alive.

This concern with the spirituality of the preacher carries over into the lecture on the idea of the sermon. The idea grows out of the purpose. "A sermon exists in and for its purpose. That purpose is the persuading and moving of men's souls" (110).[66] The lecture that sounds as though it will come nearest to nuts and bolts is that on the making of the sermon, but its concern, too, is loftier than that. When speaking of deciding upon a subject, Brooks says:

> Care not for your sermon, but for your truth, and for your people; and subjects will spring up on every side of you, and the chances to preach upon them will be all too few. (152)

Within that framework, factors in the choice of a subject should be the peculiar needs of the people, the symmetry and "scale" of all the preacher's preaching, and the bent of the preacher's inclination. Even in the discussion of style, the issues seem more moral than rhetorical.

In considering the congregation to which one preaches, Brooks calls attention to the categories of people who make it up, but says that sermons should be directed to those who are "earnest seekers after truth" (200). Next he notes special qualities of his age that affected the way one preached: what he calls a fatalism brought on by a scientific worldview, tolerance and relativism, not to mention commercialism, preoccupation with fashion, and sentimentalism. Another condition of preaching in that age was the changed status of the Bible. Evaluating the situation, he says: "While there have been many centuries in which it was easier, there has been none in which it was more interesting or inspiring for a man to preach" (254).

He was able to maintain this enthusiasm and even joy in his vocation because of his deep belief in the value of the human soul, which is the topic of the final lecture (**see Vol. 2, pp. 502-16**). Few passages ever written have this lecture's capacity to rekindle the ardor of a preacher's vocation. Rereading it annually on the anniversary of one's ordination would be a good addition to any cleric's rule of life.

How did the practice of Brooks's preaching match his theory? His power in the pulpit has been well described by one of his friends, an English scholar named James Bryce:

> There was no sign of art about his preaching, no touch of self-consciousness. He spoke to his audience as a man might speak to his friend,

> pouring forth with swift, yet quiet and seldom impassioned earnestness the thoughts and feelings of his singularly pure and lofty spirit. The listeners never thought of style or manner, but only of the substance of the thoughts. They were entranced and carried out of themselves by the strength and sweetness and beauty of the aspects of religious truth and its helpfulness to weak human nature which he presented. There was a wealth of keen observation, fine reflection, and insight both subtle and imaginative, all touched with warmth and tenderness which seemed to transfuse and irradiate the thought itself.[67]

Small wonder that the day of Brooks's death, January 23, has been chosen by the Episcopal Church for inclusion as a day of optional commemoration in its calendar of saints' days and holy days.[68] Truth was brought through his personality.

CONCLUSION

A short summary of the characteristics of Romanticism noted at the beginning of the previous chapter follows:

1. A protest, in the name of freedom and dynamism, against the formalism and structure of neoclassicism, rationalism, and moral asceticism and discipline.
2. A stress on individuality that at times amounted almost to worship of originality and genius.
3. An exaltation of the immediacy of feeling "in the self, for humanity, and for the world," which involved vitalism and an aesthetic approach to nature.
4. A concern and feeling for history.
5. The dominance of the twin principles of plenitude (as opposed to the restriction of content by formal rules) and diversity (as opposed to uniformity and simplicity).

It would be tedious to parcel out this list of traits among the preachers of Britain and America who have exemplified some or all of them. Yet a simple review of the persons encountered should be enough to establish that a major tradition of proclamation of the Word was begun in Britain and America that can be understood only in the context of the Romantic movement. This is especially clear when we remember that the alternatives available at the time were either the rationalistic preaching of the latitudinarians or the "religion of the heart" preaching characteristic of the Evangelical Awakenings. Romantic preaching represents a new consciousness and a new style.

Its great German pioneer, Friedrich Schleiermacher, was both a foundational theoretician of the Romantic movement and a parish pastor and preacher. Samuel Coleridge, who, with William Wordsworth, began the English manifestation of Romanticism, was deeply interested in theology and, among other things, introduced historical-critical study of the Bible to the British Isles.

A necessary precondition for the development of a Romantic rhetoric was Nicolas Boileau's translation of Longinus's treatise *On the Sublime,* which claimed aesthetic experience to be as much a purpose of oratory as persuasion. The pre-Romantic rhetoricians, Hugh Blair, George Campbell, and Richard Whately, enunciated a homiletic that would be an appropriate medium for the new preaching when it appeared. In very different ways, John Henry Newman and Frederick Robertson, among the British, took full advantage of the opportunities this afforded for the expression of Christian faith in the vocabulary of the spirit of the new age.

In America, true Romantic preaching began earlier because of the Unitarians' openness to its spirit. William Channing anticipated this efflorescence, but it was seen in full blossom in the short pulpit ministry of Ralph Waldo Emerson and the longer ministry of Theodore Parker. The great orthodox theologian of Romanticism was Horace Bushnell, and his insights were given voice in the proclamation of his disciples, Henry Ward Beecher and Phillips Brooks.

Partly because of such products of Romanticism as biblical criticism, Protestant Christianity was about to separate into three main branches: (1) the liberal, which would become progressively more radical until it ceased to feel the need to be theistic (by far the smallest of the streams), (2) the critical orthodox, which would become "mainline," and (3) the conservative evangelical, which would be as large, if not as socially prominent, as the mainline. In the mainline, Romantic preaching would become the norm rather than the exception.

FOR FURTHER READING

Abbott, Lyman. *Henry Ward Beecher.* Boston: Houghton Mifflin, 1903. Reprint, with introduction by William G. McLoughlin, New York: Chelsea House, 1980.

Brooks, Phillips. *Lectures on Preaching: The Yale Lectures on Preaching,*

1877. Edited by Ralph G. Turnbull. New York: E. P. Dutton, 1907. Reprint, Grand Rapids, Mich.: Baker, 1969, 1981.
Commager, Henry Steele. *Theodore Parker.* Boston: Little, Brown, 1936.
Horace Bushnell: Sermons. Edited with introduction by Conrad Cherry. Sources of American Spirituality. NewYork: Paulist, 1985.
Mott, Wesley T. *"The Strains of Eloquence": Emerson and His Sermons.* University Park: Pennsylvania State University Press, 1989.
William Ellery Channing: Selected Writings. Edited by David Robinson. Sources of American Spirituality. New York: Paulist, 1985.

Notes

1. William R. Hutchinson, *The Modernist Impulse in American Protestantism* (Cambridge: Harvard University Press, 1976), 14.

2. The sermon has been reprinted often; the edition consulted was in *William Ellery Channing: Selected Writings,* ed. David Robinson, Sources of American Spirituality (New York: Paulist, 1985), 70-102.

3. Van Wyck Brooks, *The Flowering of New England 1815–1865* (New York: E. P. Dutton, 1937), 104.

4. Robinson, ed., *William Ellery Channing*, 6.

5. Ibid., 31.

6. William Ellery's brother, Edward T. Channing, was professor of rhetoric at Harvard and is one of the American teachers whose textbooks were based on the New Rhetoric of Blair, Campbell, and Whately (Nan Johnson, *Nineteenth-Century Rhetoric in North America* [Carbondale: Southern Illinois University Press, 1991], 70 passim). His pupils included the great writers of the period, many of whom gave him credit for teaching them their craft. Brooks, *The Flowering of New England,* 43.

7. This moral criticism of the results of preaching Calvinism may be seen all through "Unitarian Christianity." The following example, however, is sufficient to make the position clear: "(This religious system) tends to discourage the timid, to give excuses to the bad, to feed the vanity of the fanatical, and to offer shelter to the bad feelings of the malignant. By shocking, as it does, the fundamental principles of morality, and by exhibiting a severe and partial Deity, it tends strongly to pervert the moral faculty, to form a gloomy, forbidding, and servile religion, and to lead men to substitute censoriousness, bitterness, and persecution, for a tender and impartial charity" (Robinson, *William Ellery Channing*, 89-90).

8. Channing's homiletical strategy changed over the years as he strove to make his own preaching more effective in enabling the moral development of members of his congregation. Teresa Toulouse, *The Art of Prophesying: New England Sermons and the Shaping of Belief* (Athens: University of Georgia Press, 1987), 75-117.

9. Ralph Waldo Emerson, *Journals and Miscellaneous Notebooks,* 2:242, 238, as quoted by Wesley T. Mott, *"The Strains of Eloquence": Emerson and His Sermons* (University Park: Pennsylvania State University Press, 1989), 4-5. Mott's interpretation of Emerson's preaching is generally consistent with that of Toulouse, *The Art of*

Prophesying, 118-84. The following account also draws on David M. Robinson, "The Sermons of Ralph Waldo Emerson: An Introductory Historical Essay," in *The Complete Sermons of Ralph Waldo Emerson* (Columbia: University of Missouri Press, 1989), 1:1-32. Albert J. von Frank edited vol. 1; Toulouse and Mott edited other volumes.

10. Both Increase and Cotton Mather were numbered among its earlier ministers.

11. He was then ordained the following March 11.

12. "Emerson's resignation of his only full-time pastorate in October 1832 has been seen as a sloughing off of religious orthodoxy and stifling convention." Mott, *"The Strains of Eloquence,"* 2.

13. Emerson, *Journals and Miscellaneous Notebooks,* 4:363-64, quoted in Toulouse, *The Art of Prophesying,* 119. Most of what follows is an attempt to summarize her understanding of Emerson's preaching.

14. "That part of the mind which takes in, classifies, divides, and arranges sensuous information" (ibid., 123).

15. Ibid.

16. Ibid., 125.

17. Ibid., 144.

18. Ibid., 145.

19. Ibid., 148-75. Toulouse analyzes four of Emerson's sermons—his first, two from the middle of his ministry, and his last at Second Church—to show his developing understanding of the preacher's task.

20. R. C. Albrect, *Theodore Parker,* Twayne's United States Authors Series, no. 179 (New York: Twayne, 1971), 17.

21. His personal library would number twenty-five thousand volumes.

22. "The Transient and the Permanent," in *Theodore Parker: American Transcendentalist: A Critical Essay and a Collection of his Writings,* ed. Robert E. Collins (Meteuchen, N.J.: Scarecrow, 1973), 88.

23. "Transcendentalism" (ibid., 70).

24. Brooks, *The Flowering of New England,* 73-88 passim.

25. The list comes from a report he wrote to his congregation after ill health forced his retirement, *Theodore Parker's Experience as a Minister,* which has been preserved in several collections of his works. For citations, see Albrecht, *Theodore Parker,* 132, 148 n. 7.

26. See, for instance, Henry Steele Commager, *Theodore Parker* (Boston: Little, Brown, 1936), 120.

27. For an extended description of his preaching, see Commager, *Theodore Parker,* 115-20.

28. A form of this section appeared as "The Preaching of Romanticism in America," *ATQ: 19th C. American Literature and Culture* n.s. 14 (2000): 297-312.

29. See above, 526-29.

30. His sermon on "The Gentleness of God" tells how souls are led to conversion in a lifelong process of which they are hardly conscious at the time (*Horace Bushnell: Sermons,* ed. with intro. Conrad Cherry, Sources of American Spirituality [New York: Paulist, 1985], 148-62; reprinted from *Christ and His Salvation, In Sermons Variously Related Thereto* [New York: Scribner's, 1864], 28-50). The sermon could be autobiographical in detailing how Bushnell himself came to faith.

31. The two titles are set in quotation marks but not identified as to source by Sidney Ahlstrom, *A Religious History of the American People* (New Haven: Yale University Press, 1972), 610, 613.

32. Gardiner H. Shattuck Jr., "Bushnell, Horace," in *The Encyclopedia of American Religious History,* ed. Edward L. Queen II, Stephen R. Prothero, and Gardiner H. Shattuck Jr. (New York: Facts on File, 1996), 1:93.

33. H. Shelton Smith, *Horace Bushnell*, A Library of Protestant Thought (New York: Oxford University Press, 1965), 4-22. For the Channing sermon, see above, 625-26.

34. Apparently he was not completely successful in the beginning of his efforts to proclaim the traditional form of these doctrines. Ahlstrom, *A Religious History of the American People,* 611-12.

35. Quoted by Cherry in his introduction to *Horace Bushnell: Sermons,* 1. The reference is to *Aids to Reflection* (4th ed. of 1840; reprint, New York: Kennikat, 1971), 201.

36. On the publication history of Bushnell's writings on the subject, see Smith, *Horace Bushnell,* 376-78.

37. Quoted in ibid., 375, from "The Kingdom of God as a Grain of Mustard Seed," *New Englander* 2 (1844): 610. In nothing is Bushnell more Romantic than in his view of education. Jean-Jacques Rousseau, who has been called "the first major Romantic," revolutionized educational theory in his work of 1762, *Émile, ou de l'Éducation.* His protest, however, was against the corrupting effect of society and was a plea for bringing up children naturally. Bushnell was reacting against revivalism more than Enlightenment rationalism, but in his organic view of life and his emphasis on feeling he had much in common with Rousseau.

38. Cherry, *Horace Bushnell,* 4.

39. See the sermon "Religious Nature, and Religious Character," published in his *Sermons on Living Subjects* (New York: Scribner, Armstrong & Co., 1872), 129-47, and reprint, Cherry, *Horace Bushnell,* 26-37.

40. Gibbs, in turn, learned this from Schleiermacher's friend, Karl Ferdinand Becker.

41. Cherry, *Horace Bushnell,* 10.

42. Ibid., 12.

43. In ibid., 119-33 (the quotation is from p. 119); reprint from *Sermons for the New Life* (New York: Scribner, Armstrong & Co., 1873), 304-25.

44. Ibid., 123.

45. Ibid., 129.

46. See above, 507-9.

47. Eleven years after the birth and the death of Bushnell.

48. See Clifford E. Clark Jr., *Henry Ward Beecher: Spokesman for Middle-Class America* (Urbana: University of Illinois Press, 1978), 81-86, for a comparison of the theologies of the two.

49. For information about this remarkable family, see Joan D. Hedrick, *Harriet Beecher Stowe: A Life* (New York: Oxford University Press, 1994). Harriet was Henry's next oldest and his closest sibling.

50. The training he received in preparatory school was in the tradition of the

elocutionary movement, which stressed vocal exercises and gesture. The vocal exercises meant both that he had great nuance of expression and that he knew how to use his voice without straining it. He drilled himself so in gesture that as an adult he never had to think about it, doing automatically what would best communicate his point. See the hagiographic but informative biography by his successor at Plymouth Church, Lyman Abbott, *Henry Ward Beecher* (Boston: Houghton Mifflin, 1903; reprint, with intro. William G. McLoughlin, New York: Chelsea House, 1980), 104-5.

51. His editorial activity had begun in Cincinnati, but in Indianapolis he edited the agricultural section of the *Indiana Journal,* "The Western Farmer and Gardener," displaying a Romantic interest in nature that stayed with him all his life (ibid., 328).

52. Ibid., xvi.

53. An indication of how well known he became and remained is a limerick that puns on his name:

A great Congregational preacher
Said, "The hen is an elegant creature."
The hen, liking that,
Laid an egg in his hat
And thus did the hen reward Beecher.

54. So great was his popularity that his reputation survived both civil and ecclesiastical trials over the charge that he committed adultery with the wife of Theodore Tilton, one of his supporters. Beecher was acquitted in the church trial, but the civil jury was unable to agree, although a majority of them considered him innocent. Nevertheless, many since have believed that he was guilty. Some writers have enjoyed capitalizing on the sensational aspects of the trial of so famous a preacher for actions inconsistent with his profession; a case in point is Robert Shaplen, *Free Love and Heavenly Sinners: The Story of the Great Henry Ward Beecher Scandal* (London: Andre Deutsch, 1956).

55. Hedrick, *Harriet Beecher Stowe,* vii.

56. Clark, *Henry Ward Beecher,* 4. The book that follows is essentially Clark's development of this thesis.

57. That being the case, there is little need to detail the specifics of his homiletical technique. That task has been performed often enough, however, first by Beecher himself. One of Henry's church members endowed what has become the most prestigious series of lectures on homiletics in the country, the Beecher Lectures at Yale, in honor of Beecher's father. Henry himself gave the first three sets, although only the first dealt with preaching. He published these as *Yale Lectures on Preaching* (Boston: Pilgrim, 1874). A good summary of them is given by Abbott, *Henry Ward Beecher,* 353-73. Lionel G. Crocker has published two books on Beecher's homiletics: *Henry Ward Beecher's Art of Preaching* (Chicago: University of Chicago Press, 1934), and *Henry Ward Beecher's Speaking Art* (New York: Fleming H. Revell, 1937). Finally, Halford R. Ryan has written *Henry Ward Beecher: Peripatetic Preacher,* Great American Orators, no. 5 (New York: Greenwood, 1990). Ryan's knowledge of the history of oratory is greater than his familiarity with church history and theology, and thus he often misses the point.

58. James Thayer Addison, *The Episcopal Church in the United States, 1789–1931* (New York: Scribner's, 1951), 262.

59. Edgar De Witt Jones, *The Royalty of the Pulpit: A Survey and Appreciation of the Lyman Beecher Lectures on Preaching Founded at Yale Divinity School 1871 and Given Annually (with Four Exceptions) Since 1872* (New York: Harper & Brothers, 1951), 19.

60. The edition consulted was Phillips Brooks, *Lectures on Preaching: The Yale Lectures on Preaching, 1877,* ed. Ralph G. Turnbull (New York: E. P. Dutton, 1907; reprint, Grand Rapids, Mich.: Baker, 1969, 1981).

61. Ibid., 5.

62. John F. Woolverton, *The Education of Phillips Brooks* (Urbana: University of Illinois Press, 1995), 53. The classical biography is Alexander V. G. Allen, *Life and Letters of Phillips Brooks,* 2 vols. (New York: E. P. Dutton, 1900). The standard modern biography is Raymond W. Albright, *Focus on Infinity: A Life of Phillips Brooks* (New York: Macmillan, 1961).

63. Her letter of November 27, 1864, quoted in Albright, *Focus on Infinity,* 106.

64. Brooks, *Lectures on Preaching,* 5. Hereafter, references to this work will be given parenthetically in the text by page number alone.

65. A menial laborer on construction sites at the time whose duty was to carry bricks and mortar to those who would use them.

66. Brooks obviously lived in an age when it was thought that masculine terms could be generic and therefore inclusive.

67. James Bryce, quoted in Addison, *The Episcopal Church in the United States, 1789–1931,* 267.

68. *The Book of Common Prayer and the Administration of the Sacraments and Other Rites and Ceremonies of the Church Together with the Psalter or Psalms of David According to the Use of the Episcopal Church* (New York: Church Hymnal Corp. and Seabury Press, 1979), 19. Cf. *The Proper for the Lesser Feasts and Fasts, Together with the Fixed Holy Days,* 4th ed. (New York: Church Hymnal Corporation, 1988), 130-31.

CHAPTER 24

THE TRIUMPH OF ROMANTICISM

THE SOCIAL GOSPEL

The Romantic preaching of liberal orthodoxy helped American Protestants to adjust to the great social change of the years after the Civil War, that of moving from an agricultural to an industrial society. Horace Bushnell, Henry Ward Beecher, and Phillips Brooks all were concerned with the social problems they saw, such as slavery and the status of women, but they were too involved in the rise of middle-class Victorian culture and an urban, industrial economy to identify the characteristic evils they entailed.[1] It remained for the next two generations of preachers to help their congregations understand that these new social and economic arrangements had spawned human suffering that Christian conscience could not tolerate. This preaching was to manifest a number of continuing Romantic emphases and outgrowths, including concern for the common people, the influence of German philosophy and theology, historical-critical biblical interpretation, and evolutionary thought.

A group of clergy and social scientists, who came to be known collectively as the "Social Gospel" movement, called attention to the moral crises brought on by the industrial revolution. Charles Howard Hopkins has chronicled the movement from 1865 to 1915, dividing the time into four periods that are characterized as stages in a person's life: birth, youth, coming of age, and maturity.[2] Birth (1865–80) was a time of vague awakenings; youth (1880–90) a period of discussion rather than action, for lack of a well-developed sociology; the coming of age (1890–1900) saw action being taken in the formation of organizations and founding of periodicals; and maturation (1900–15) involved both a theoretical grounding of the movement and its incorporation into the mainstream of American Protestant life, accomplished through denominational agencies committed to its cause and the organization, largely around social concerns, of the Federal Council of Churches.

Washington Gladden

For the purposes of the history of preaching, the first three stages can be seen in the life of one man, Washington Gladden, and the last stage in the life of another, Walter Rauschenbusch.[3]

Gladden[4] (1836–1918) is deservedly known as the "father of the Social Gospel." Orphaned at an early age, he grew up on an uncle's farm near Oswego, New York, where he helped with the chores and acquired a good but irregular basic education. He was apprenticed to a local newspaper publisher when he was sixteen, but became attracted to the ministry and prepared for it through study at Oswego Academy and Williams College. Immediately after college he taught school and privately studied theology. He was called to a small Congregational church in Brooklyn and was ordained on November 15, 1860.

Like most of the Romantic preachers studied above, he had a nervous breakdown. He resigned his church but was soon called to another in suburban Morrisania, New York, where he was able to recuperate, attend lectures at Union, and read Frederick Robertson and Horace Bushnell, thus acquiring the theological perspective from which his life's work would be done.

That work began, in a sense, when he was called to a church in North Adams, Massachusetts, where he witnessed the tension between capital and labor. After serving in North Adams for five years, he became religious editor of the *Independent*, a leading newspaper of the time, and participated in the paper's crusade against the Tweed Ring in New York.[5]

Returning to the pastorate in 1875, he went to North Church in Springfield, Massachusetts. When an economic depression led to widescale unemployment, Gladden tried to speak to the problem in addresses, first to workers in Springfield and then to the employers. The series of lectures so begun was published as *Working People and Their Employers*, the first of his thirty-eight books.[6]

In 1882 he accepted a call to First Congregational Church in Columbus, Ohio, a position in which he remained until his retirement in 1914. There he became one of the best-known clerics in the country and was widely invited to speak at important events. He was, for instance, twice the Beecher lecturer at Yale.

Most of his fame came through his many books, but these, in turn, were by-products of his preaching. He said in his *Recollections*,[7] "Of the thirty-one volumes [as of then] of which the encyclopedias accuse me, all but six have gone through my pulpit, and are printed as they were preached, with almost no revision."[8]

Gladden's pulpit practice is responsible for an unusual twist to his pioneering Social Gospel preaching.[9] His Sunday morning sermons were fairly ordinary, preached on biblical texts and devoted to issues of personal religion. On Sunday and Wednesday evenings, however, he would lecture on a wider range of topics, usually not starting from Holy Scripture, but "keeping the discussion close to the issues of life and character."[10]

Although the Sunday morning sermons were by no means devoid of reference to the social issues of the day, it was in the evening lectures that he dealt most explicitly and fully with the problems of an industrial society. It could be argued that these discourses were not sermons in a strict sense, lacking a scriptural base, but they were proclaimed from the pulpit, and it is obvious that Gladden considered them all part of the same work.

"Thy Kingdom Come," in a series on the Lord's Prayer, is an example of a Sunday morning sermon that includes Christian social teaching (**see Vol. 2, pp. 517-25**).[11] In this sermon, he is able to take the standard Social Gospel position that the kingdom of God is to come on earth as a perfect social order. "When we intelligently offer this petition, then, we are asking for nothing less than this—that the light and love and power of God may increase and abound everywhere in the world."[12]

The petition is seen as not being confined to Christian countries, and it is answered wherever attention is paid to the needs of women, prisoners, the insane, and slaves. He ends this exposition of the meaning of the Lord's Prayer, as he understands it, with a personal challenge to his hearers:

> You pray that the Kingdom of God may come? Do you want it to come to Massachusetts? Do you desire that it should come to Springfield? Do you wish to have it come to your store, your office, your shop, your

> study, your table, your toilet, your closet, your heart? How near to you do you desire that the Kingdom of God should come?[13]

The lectures are very different, in that they do not explain a biblical passage nor apply it to the lives of the congregation, and they are what the name implies: expository speeches that inform their audience about an issue. A case in point is the lecture on "Labor and Capital," given to the working men of Springfield and included in *Working People and Their Employers,* which talks of the three different systems by which capital and labor have been brought together—slavery, wages, or cooperation—with a recommendation of cooperation as the Christian ideal.[14] But even this lecture is from the perspective of Christian theology and ends with an appeal to its audience:

> The power that has stricken the shackles from the laborer, that has lightened his burdens, that has lifted him up to a happier and nobler life, and that has put into his hands the key of a great future, is the power that came into the world when Christ was born.[15]

This shows that even the lectures have a right to be considered as sermons proclaiming the Social Gospel. Thus Gladden appears to have devised a new genre of Christian preaching.

Walter Rauschenbusch

While most of Gladden's ministry was as a parish pastor and much of his self-identity was tied up in preaching,[16] the other great spirit of the movement spent only eleven years in parochial ministry as a regular preacher to a congregation. For most of his professional life, Walter Rauschenbusch (1861–1918) was a member of a seminary faculty, doing the work that entitles him to be known as "the theologian of the Social Gospel." His father was a German pastor who came to this country as a Lutheran missionary, but later changed to Baptist views and ministry and went on to teach at Rochester Theological Seminary. His father also had a drinking problem, which in 1864 caused his mother to take young Walter and two sisters back to Germany for four years.[17]

Indeed, the German connection was to be very important for him. After high school he completed the classics course in the Gymnasium in Gütersloh. Then in 1891 he took a leave from his church to study social movements in England and the New Testament in Germany. His seminary training after the Gymnasium and before ordination was in the German department of Rochester.

His parochial ministry was served in a German Baptist church in the "Hell's Kitchen" area of New York City, a neighborhood where he became an eyewitness of "the terrible human effects of insecurity, unemployment, poverty, wretched housing, malnutrition, disease, ignorance, and crime."[18] In 1897 he returned to Rochester as a member of the faculty, first in the German department and then in the English, a position he held until his death.

In response to the conditions around him when he was a pastor, Rauschenbusch became involved in studying the social situation to see how it could be ameliorated. He became active in the campaign to elect Henry George, the single-tax theorist, as mayor of New York. In 1889 he tried to start a newspaper for working people.

Most of all, though, he tried to find a basis for Christian ministry that was not just interested in saving people's souls, but was concerned for their bodies as well. This he eventually found, with the help of Horace Bushnell, Friedrich Ritschl, Julius Wellhausen, and Adolf Harnack, in the ethical teaching of Jesus:

> When the kingdom of God dominated our landscape, the perspective of life shifted into a new alignment. I felt a new security in my social impulses. . . . I found that this new conception of the purpose of Christianity was strangely satisfying. It responded to all the old and all the new elements of my religious life. The saving of the lost, the teaching of the young, the pastoral care of the poor and frail, the quickening of starved intellects, the study of the Bible, church union, political reform, the reorganization of the industrial system, international peace—it was all covered by the one aim of the reign of God on earth.[19]

While it would be interesting to trace the development of Rauschenbusch's theology,[20] the present purpose is to look at his preaching, most of which occurred before his thought became so theoretical. Until recently it has been hard to study that preaching, because Rauschenbusch published no volumes of sermons and did not even leave complete or easily legible manuscripts. Instead, he left sermon notes that were partly in German and partly in shorthand. Fortunately, eight sets of these notes for sermons on social topics were deciphered and translated by Robert Payne and Clyde Fant Jr. for the section on Rauschenbusch in *20 Centuries of Great Preaching*.[21]

Even these notes, however, are not entirely for sermons preached to his congregation, and some sound more like Gladden's "lectures" than sermons based upon Scripture. For instance, the set on "The Kingdom of God in the Parables of Jesus" (146-54), while an excellent exegetical study from the perspective of the time, was written as a study for the Brotherhood of the Kingdom, a fellowship of socially involved Baptist clergy that was an important support group for Rauschenbusch. Although "The Social Problem, Our Problem" (154-57) gives the first chapter of Isaiah as a text, the passage is referred to only obliquely in the course of this address concerning poverty. Instead, Rauschenbusch calls upon his audience to overthrow poverty by the abolition of privilege and by association (Christian and Socialist). The methods recommended are thought and agitation. "Peace" (158-62) also lists a text, but it is an address given to the International Peace Conference.[22]

There are, however, several sermons for his congregation that show both traditional sermonic structure and concern for social issues. An example is "The Kingship of Christ" (162-64), which is organized by a series of questions about the title of "King" offered to Jesus. Words from the text (Matt. 28:18-20) are given as answers to the questions:

1. Did Jesus claim the title? Yes, *"to me is given all power in heaven and earth."*
2. "Has he an army and ministers to present and enforce his claims? Yes, *'Go ye.'* "
3. "What are the weapons of warfare? *Teach.*"
4. "The extent of the Kingdom. *All nations.*"
5. "Is there a badge of citizenship? *Baptizing them.*"
6. "Is there a law in this kingdom? *All things whatsoever I commanded you.*"
7. "Has it glory and splendor like other kingdoms? Yes, *Lo, I am with you.*"
8. "How long shall it endure?" . . . *"Always, unto the end of the world."*

Rauschenbusch's empathy with his congregation comes out clearly in the introduction to his sermon on "The New Jerusalem":

> We have met together as a band of brothers after a week of toil, weariness, and failing, as an army rallies after one assault to prepare for the next. We have felt weak and starved; we have come to take the bread of life, to have peace and love, and faith, and a brighter hope. It is hope that beckons us on. (164)

Such preaching in a hellish environment must have sounded like good news indeed.

The preachers of the Social Gospel have been criticized by later generations for a number of shortcomings,[23] one of which is that they concentrated only on labor issues and did not deal with the whole range of problems besetting the society, especially issues of race. The only reply that can be made is that the preachers were aware of most of these problems and spoke out about them, but they concentrated upon what seemed the most pressing issue of their time.

More subtly, Janet Forsythe Fishburn has pointed to a number of paradoxes involved in the movement. The major one, she says, is that the Social Gospel

> differs so little from the evangelical piety that Rauschenbusch so disdained in the "conservative" evangelical. Although the social gospel was theoretically the application of humanitarian concern to the social order, in practice the salvation of the social order depended on the influence of individual Christians as the primary mode of evangelism. This was not significantly different from the practice and methods of the conservative evangelical tradition.[24]

This is probably only what was to be expected, since so much of Christian concern with social issues was an outgrowth of the Second Great Awakening, as Timothy Smith pointed out.[25] It also reflects the difficulties Hopkins pointed to in his periodization of the Social Gospel movement.[26] Seeing a need and devising a strategy for meeting it are two very different activities. But both preaching and writing are aimed at the individual member of the audience; they can persuade only one at a time. The hope is that enough will be enlisted in a cause to constitute a group that can effect change. While the civil rights movement of the 1960s and 1970s became much more sophisticated about how change is effected in society, it, too, found social evil to be far less tractable than it had anticipated. "This kind goeth not out but by prayer and fasting" (Matt. 17:21 KJV)—if even then. But the cause of the kingdom—understood either eschatologically or socially—has always depended upon "the foolishness of preaching" (1 Cor. 1:21 KJV). As Rauschenbusch said, teaching is the only weapon in our warfare.

THE ROMANTIC BECOMES ORDINARY: JOHN A. BROADUS

The Social Gospel movement lasted until World War I, but long before that Romantic preaching had become the rule rather than the exception.

This may be seen in a textbook published in 1870 that was to be revised and remain the standard work in the field for more than a century: *A Treatise on the Preparation and Delivery of Sermons* by John A. Broadus.[27]

Almost as informative on the triumph of Romanticism in preaching as a look at this book would be a glance at the life of its remarkable author. Broadus was born in 1827 on a farm in Virginia, where he grew up and helped his father. A major in the county militia and for many years a member of the state legislature,[28] his father had made some bad investments that reduced the family's resources. Yet so great was his commitment to his talented son that he took a position as the steward for boarding state students at the University of Virginia to enable his son to continue his education there.

The university was one of the best in the country at the time, and John stayed on to receive an M.A. in 1850, becoming an excellent classicist and all-around scholar. He also married the daughter of the chair of the faculty. Although he had already begun to receive the invitations to teach at institutions of higher education that would continue throughout his life, he had answered the call to preach. Since seminary training was unavailable, he spent a year as tutor in a private household so that he could study theology on his own.

He was called back to Charlottesville to become pastor of the Baptist church there. The university asked him to teach, as well, and he stayed for eight years, proving effective in various combinations of parochial and university positions. In him, the scholar and the minister were always to be deeply connected. He was finally prevailed upon in 1859 to become one of four learned young clergy to found the Southern Baptist Theological Seminary at Greenville, South Carolina. His teaching responsibilities were in the areas of New Testament and homiletics. The recognition he had already received as a rising scholar was indicated in the two honorary doctorates bestowed upon him at the time, one from William and Mary.

The seminary was just getting started when the Civil War broke out. Although Broadus opposed secession, he did support the Southern cause when hostilities came and even served as a missionary to Confederate troops, winning the admiration of Stonewall Jackson and Robert E. Lee. Meanwhile, it was a struggle to keep the seminary going and his family fed. After the seminary closed in 1862, Broadus supported his family by preaching every Sunday at several small Baptist churches.

Reconstruction was hard on the seminary, but it did get going again. During the first term, which began November 1, 1865, Broadus had only one student in homiletics and that one blind, but the professor gave him his conscientious best, which seemed his only standard for performing any duty. The result of this course was the lectures that became his textbook.

The heroic efforts he had been required to make for so long weakened his health, and in 1870 he was forced, like many other preachers in this period, to travel for the benefit to his health. He spent a year in Britain, Europe, and the Middle East, seeing the sights and making firsthand acquaintance with scholars he had previously known only through correspondence and exchange of writings. In 1877 the seminary moved to Louisville, where it has remained and flourished. When his dear friend James P. Boyce died in 1889, Broadus succeeded him in the seminary's presidency, remaining in that office until his own death in 1895.

Broadus and his friends gave their lives for the seminary, turning down flattering offers elsewhere in order to see that Southern Baptist theological education got off to a good start. Broadus himself was offered the presidencies of Chicago University,[29] Brown University, and Crozer Seminary, as well as teaching positions on many faculties, some of them very prestigious.

During his lifetime, Broadus was more famous as a New Testament scholar than as a homiletician. His best-known work in that field is a commentary on Matthew, but he wrote many articles and was also involved in biblical translation revision and the International Sunday School lessons. Philip Schaff invited him to contribute to the first series of *Nicene and Post-Nicene Fathers* by revising and supplying additional notes for the Oxford translation of Chrysostom's homilies on Philippians, Colossians, and Thessalonians.[30]

Yet he was much in demand as a preacher, supplying in prominent eastern and northern pulpits in the summer, and being invited to preach on significant occasions at churches, universities, and seminaries. His Beecher lectures at Yale were given in 1889, almost twenty years after *A Treatise on the Preparation and Delivery of Sermons* was published. They were given from notes—Broadus's characteristic method of preaching and lecturing—and never published, although E. C. Dargan did integrate much from them into the second edition of the textbook. The five lectures on the history of preaching that Broadus gave at Newton Theological Seminary in 1876 were published, however—after his children copied them with his corrections.[31]

For one who came from a rural area, received all his formal education near to home, served but one church full time, and taught only in a new and struggling seminary of a denomination that was not yet known for its scholarship,[32] his international fame and respect are remarkable.

The claim that *A Treatise on the Preparation and Delivery of Sermons* inculcates a Romantic homiletic can be first established negatively by saying that it does not commend either the rationalistic preaching of the latitudinarians or the emotional preaching of the revivalists. The positive case, however, is to be made on the basis of the book's treatment of imagination.

When Broadus comes to discuss "Application," he says that it is not enough to convince people or to let them see that the message applies to them; they must also be persuaded. And persuasion is largely a matter of supplying them with motives for acting as the preacher recommends (232).[33] Yet

> so mighty is the opposition which the gospel encounters in human nature, so averse is the natural heart to the obedience of faith, so powerful are the temptations of life, that we must arouse men to intense earnestness and often to impassioned emotion, if we would bring them to surmount all obstacles, and to conquer the world, the flesh, and the devil. (235)

How are people so aroused? "In order to excite any passions by speech, we have to operate chiefly through the *imagination*" (238). Thus Broadus includes a section on imagination in its relation to eloquence, which deals not only with the many high uses of imagination but also with how it is to be acquired (395-405) (**see Vol. 2, pp. 526-32**). This section ends his treatment of the preparation of sermons as such. The rest of the book is devoted to delivery and conducting public worship. But to end with imagination is to end in Romantic territory. Romantic preaching has become the norm rather than the eccentricity of a few.

FOR FURTHER READING

Broadus, John A. *A Treatise on the Preparation and Delivery of Sermons*. Philadelphia: Smith, English & Co.; New York: Sheldon & Co., 1870.

Gladden, Washington. *Recollections: An Autobiography.* Boston: Houghton, Mifflin & Co., 1909.

________. *The Lord's Prayer: Seven Homilies.* Boston: Houghton, Mifflin & Co., 1881.

Robertson, A. T. *Life and Letters of John Albert Broadus*. Philadelphia: American Baptist Publication Society, 1910.

The Social Gospel in America 1870–1920: Gladden, Ely, Rauschenbusch. Edited by Robert T. Handy. A Library of Protestant Thought. New York: Oxford University Press, 1966.

"Walter Rauschenbusch, 1861–1918." In *20 Centuries of Great Preaching*. Edited by Clyde E. Fant Jr. and Walter M. Pinson Jr., 7:125-72. Waco, Tex.: Word, 1971.

Notes

1. For a picture of the challenges to faith arising in the last third of the nineteenth century, see Paul A. Carter, *The Spiritual Crisis of the Gilded Age* (DeKalb: Northern Illinois University Press, 1971).

2. Charles Howard Hopkins, *The Rise of the Social Gospel in American Protestantism 1865–1915,* Yale Studies in Religious Education, no. 14 (New Haven: Yale University Press, 1940). For an interesting attempt to set the movement in a wider cultural context, see Janet Forsythe Fishburn, *The Fatherhood of God and the Victorian Family: The Social Gospel in America* (Philadelphia: Fortress, 1981).

3. Gaius Glenn Atkins said these two "did more between them to direct the mind of the churches toward the social problem than any of their contemporaries" (*Religion in Our Times* [New York, 1931], quoted in *The Social Gospel in America 1870–1920: Gladden, Ely, Rauschenbusch,* ed. Robert T. Handy, A Library of Protestant Thought [New York: Oxford University Press, 1966], 15).

4. His first name, Solomon, is seldom used in references to him.

5. A notoriously corrupt group of political leaders in New York City in the third quarter of the nineteenth century headed by William M. "Boss" Tweed.

6. Washington Gladden, *Working People and Their Employers* (Boston: Houghton, Mifflin & Co., 1876); in Handy, *The Social Gospel in America 1870–1920,* 38-48.

7. Washington Gladden, *Recollections: An Autobiography* (Boston: Houghton, Mifflin & Co., 1909).

8. Quoted in Handy, *The Social Gospel in America 1870–1920,* 24.

9. While Gladden epitomizes the movement during this period, he was by no means its sole representative. For a much fuller list, see the names cited by Hopkins in the various stages of *The Rise of the Social Gospel in American Protestantism 1865–1915.*

10. Gladden, *Recollections,* 411.

11. Washington Gladden, *The Lord's Prayer: Seven Homilies* (Boston: Houghton, Mifflin & Co., 1881), 59-81.

12. Ibid., 64. This was before Johannes Weiss and Albert Schweitzer demonstrated the eschatological nature of the term in the teaching of Jesus.

13. Ibid., 80-81.

14. Washington Gladden, *Working People and Their Employers* (Boston: Houghton, Mifflin & Co., 1876), 30-51; in Handy, *The Social Gospel in America 1870–1920,* 38-48.

15. Ibid., 48.

16. Fant and Pinson, *20 Centuries of Great Preaching,* 6:181, quotes him as saying: "I have never tried to do anything else but preach. I have no other ambition."

17. Fishburn, *The Fatherhood of God and the Victorian Family,* 8.

18. Handy, *The Social Gospel in America 1870–1920,* 254.

19. Walter Rauschenbusch, *Christianizing the Social Order* (New York: Macmillan, 1912), 93, quoted in Handy, *The Social Gospel in America 1870–1920,* 255-56.

20. For the development of his theology, see Hopkins, *The Rise of the Social Gospel in American Protestantism 1865–1915,* 215-44.

21. Robert Payne and Clyde Fant Jr., "Walter Rauschenbusch, 1861–1918," in *20 Centuries of Great Preaching,* ed. Clyde E. Fant Jr. and William J. Pinson Jr. (Waco, Tex.: Word, 1971), 7:125-72.

22. This, the only sermon preached at the conference, is printed in full from a newspaper account instead of being mere notes.

23. For an evaluation of the accomplishments of the moment that is extremely nuanced for the time in which it was written (1940), see Hopkins, *The Rise of the Social Gospel in Protestantism 1865–1915,* 318-27.

24. Fishburn, *The Fatherhood of God and the Victorian Family,* 166.

25. See above, 526-29.

26. See above, 648-49.

27. John A. Broadus, *A Treatise on the Preparation and Delivery of Sermons* (Philadelphia: Smith, English & Co.; New York: Sheldon & Co., 1870). The first revision was made in 1897 according to the intentions of the author by his colleague, the noted historian of preaching, E. C. Dargan. The next revision was not made until 1943, this one by J. B. Witherspoon, who still was able to consult a daughter of Dr. Broadus. Vernon L. Stanfield revised the fourth edition in 1979. Dargan could say of the first edition that it had gone through twenty-two printings in this country and two in England, was used in English as a textbook in Japan, and was translated to be used in China and again to be used in Brazil (Dargan's preface to the 2nd ed. as reprinted in Stanfield's 4th ed., xvii).

28. A critical biography of Broadus is badly needed. The standard work is still the original: A. T. Robertson, *Life and Letters of John Albert Broadus* (Philadelphia: American Baptist Publication Society, 1910). While the genre of "life and letters" was popular at the time and could produce good results, as in the case of Stopford A. Brooke's treatment of Frederick Robertson (above, 608-17), this Robertson did not provide enough context for letters to enable the reader to understand what they were about. A good condensation of the *Life and Letters* is given in Fant and Pinson, *20 Centuries of Great Preaching,* 5:43-59.

29. An earlier institution than the University of Chicago, which did not incorporate until 1892. Broadus, however, was known and admired by both William Rainey Harper, the first president of the University of Chicago, and John D. Rockefeller, who endowed it.

30. *NPNF*[1] 13:v-vii. Broadus also provided a short essay on "St. Chrysostom as a Homilist" as a preface to the volume.

31. Robertson, *Life and Letters of John Albert Broadus,* 300.

32. It could be argued now, however, that no other seminary has made quite the contribution to homiletics that Southern Baptist at Louisville has.

33. Broadus, *A Treatise on the Preparation and Delivery of Sermons.* Page numbers cited parenthetically are to the first edition of 1870.

PART V

THE CENTURY OF CHANGE

CHAPTER 25

PASTORAL COUNSELING THROUGH PREACHING

THE LULL BEFORE THE STORM

The twentieth century seems to have seen more changes than most previous centuries put together. In the same way, there has been greater variety in the kinds of preaching developed during these recent decades than appeared in all previous periods. The homily, after all, was nearly the only form available for well over half the Christian era, and the thematic sermon was the only other major development before the Reformation. During the era of Renaissance and Reformation there was a great deal of homiletical creativity, but since then most efforts could be subsumed under the categories of rationalistic, revivalistic, and Romantic preaching. The trends treated in this section, therefore, should lead readers to conclude that preachers during the late-twentieth century tried to accomplish a greater variety of things through their sermons than any of their predecessors attempted.

Yet this creativity was not evenly distributed throughout the century and was by no means evident in the beginning. One way of showing this is to look at the textbooks used to teach clergy to preach, on the assumption that different understandings of the undertaking require different methods of execution. "During the first half of this century, John A. Broadus's *On the Preparation and Delivery of Sermons* dominated the teaching of homiletics. . . . Not until 1958 was its dominance seriously challenged."[1] H. Grady Davis's 1958 *Design for Preaching*[2] was still being used by more than half the homiletics professors polled in 1974. Ten years later, however, the situation had changed completely again. Davis's share of the market was less than one-fourth of what it had been, with eight other books doing as well or better, yet none of them were used by as many as one-seventh of the respondents to a questionnaire on the subject.[3]

All of this suggests that the majority of the new movements in homiletics reported on began after World War II and, indeed, from the Vietnam era on. A corollary to this is that the new kinds of preaching surveyed are closely tied to the changes going on within the larger society. To reflect these changes, the chapters ahead will deal with eight areas of homiletical development: (1) pastoral counseling through preaching, (2) the impact of biblical theology, (3) the influence of the liturgical movement, (4) the emergence of African American preaching in the majority culture, (5) new forms of social protest preaching, (6) the homiletical results of the widespread opening of ordination to women, (7) changes in evangelistic preaching, and (8) the trends referred to collectively as "the New Homiletic."

Since most of these trends are still developing, since they are so numerous, and since they are much more likely than what has preceded to be familiar to anyone with interest in homiletics, no effort will be made to provide as detailed a history for these movements as that given for those that came before them. Instead, what will follow will be more in the nature of progress reports or bulletins and often will pay more attention to the theory enunciated in books than to sermons actually delivered. To attempt more would be to create something intolerably long and something that is bound to be outdated before it could be printed.

THE FIRST CATALYST

Not only were changes in homiletical thought slow to emerge, they were not even always recognized at the time as interruptions of the status quo. The general situation of Protestant churches in general and their preaching in particular seemed better than ever through the first half of the century. Indeed, William B. Lawrence has referred to the years

1930–55 as "the crest of the Protestant mainstream."[4] Exploring the metaphor of "mainstream" as it is commonly applied to these denominations, he says:

> At the beginning of the twentieth century, their level of cultural influence and ecclesiastical domination was rising. At the end of the twentieth century, they are receding. Somewhere during these hundred years, the mainstream denominations crested.[5]

And, as he says, "one only knows that the crest has occurred after it has passed."[6]

Lawrence dates the beginning of the mainstream's crest as October 5, 1930, with the dedication of Riverside Church, constructed at the cost of $4 million by John D. Rockefeller to afford a suitable platform for his pastor, Harry Emerson Fosdick. By then Fosdick was already one of the most influential clerics in the country, and he had developed the theory of preaching that is the subject of this chapter: pastoral counseling through preaching.

The historical significance of this development, however, is not basically that it was the accomplishment of Fosdick. Rather, its relevance is as an early indicator of what Philip Rieff has called "the triumph of the therapeutic."[7]

The present concern, however, is with only the homiletical aspects of that historical movement. There is no need to trace here, for instance, the evolution of pastoral counseling in its own right.[8] The effort to sketch the progress of the pulpit's use for pastoral counseling must begin with Fosdick, however, because "it was Fosdick who persuaded a large section of the liberal Protestant clergy to refashion the sermon in the image of the counseling session."[9]

Harry Emerson Fosdick

Harry Emerson Fosdick[10] (1878–1969) was born into the home of one of the most beloved secondary educators in Buffalo, New York. His parents were devout but not narrow Baptists, and religion was an important element in his upbringing. After going though the local school system, Fosdick attended Colgate University, where he experienced a crisis of faith that ended in a sense of call to the ministry. He started his theological education at Hamilton Theological Seminary, but transferred to Union Theological Seminary, near Columbia University in New York City. Despite a nervous breakdown after his first year at Union, he graduated with an impressive record. He immediately got married, and began his ministry.

His beginning pastorate was First Baptist Church in Montclair, New Jersey, where he remained for eleven years. Most of the things that were to distinguish his ministry were evident in its beginning. Before his Montclair tenure was over, he had seen his church grow, had made an impact on the local community, and was in demand as a speaker all over the country. He also had published six devotional books, two of which were to be printed in millions of copies and translated into many languages.[11] It was also in Montclair that he developed his personal approach to homiletics, which will be considered below.

While still at Montclair he began teaching at Union Seminary, first in Baptist principles and polity and then in homiletics. In 1915 he was invited to become a full-time faculty member. Nine years later he gave the prestigious Lyman Beecher Lectures on Preaching at Yale, although the topic he chose was not preaching as such but biblical interpretation.[12] Yet his academic involvement did not mean that he had quit preaching. In 1918 he went on a six-month mission to minister to American soldiers in France. He later reflected on what he saw of war and became a staunch pacifist, a commitment he maintained throughout World War II.

After his return from France, he was engaged as an interim preacher at First Presbyterian Church in Manhattan, which had just been formed by the consolidation of three historic congregations. When asked to become the pastor, he refused to become a Presbyterian. The search committee then recommended that someone else be designated as pastor, but that Fosdick do most of the preaching. This arrangement was agreed to.

While at First Presbyterian, Fosdick preached a sermon titled "Will the Fundamentalists Win?" This sermon not only established him as one of the most visible leaders in the fundamentalist-modernist controversy,[13] but also occasioned a fierce battle within the Presbyterian Church, U.S.A. The upshot was that Fosdick was given the choice of becoming a Presbyterian or leaving that pulpit. Thus two preaching engagements Fosdick undertook in 1918 eventually resulted in two of the stands for which he was best known, modernism and pacifism.

Fosdick's reluctance to allow First Presbyterian to suffer because of his theological principles left him open to the invitation of Park Avenue Baptist Church to become its pastor. The invitation was all the more welcome because, through the generosity of Rockefeller, one of its lay leaders, the congregation promised to build a new church to be established according to Fosdick's principles. That, of course, became Riverside Church. By then his fame was enormous, but it soon grew even greater when he became a pioneer radio preacher on the National Vespers Radio Hour and had a weekly audience of millions. By this means, he came to be heard by more people than any preacher who had ever lived up until that time.

While Fosdick made many contributions to homiletics, the one to be considered here is his understanding of the way sermons should work and the way he organized his sermons to accomplish that purpose. In his autobiography he tells how he arrived at that insight during his pastorate in Montclair:

> Little by little . . . the vision grew clearer. People come to church on Sunday with every kind of personal difficulty and problem flesh is heir to. A sermon was meant to meet such needs; it should be pastoral counseling on a group scale. . . . Every sermon should have for its main business the head-on constructive meeting of some problem which was puzzling minds, burdening consciences, distracting lives, and no sermon which so met a real human difficulty, with light to throw on it and help to win a victory over it, could possibly be futile.[14]

It is easy for contemporary readers to misunderstand what Fosdick meant by "personal counseling on a group scale," because of the radical change in meaning the expression "pastoral counseling" underwent in the 1950s and 1960s. Then, largely under the influence of Carl Rogers, pastoral counseling was understood as psychotherapy done in the context of the church.[15] Fosdick's list of problems that puzzle minds, burden consciences, and distract lives shows that by pastoral counseling he meant all the kinds of issues parishioners might like to discuss privately with their pastor, whether personal, family, ethical, theological, or what-have-you.

He was interested in the new psychology, aware of William James, the mental health movement, and Freud,[16] but he would not have considered himself competent to do what psychoanalysts, psychiatrists, or psychotherapists did, nor would he have felt theirs was a higher calling.[17]

Fosdick's own experience of having a nervous breakdown gave him an empathy he called "clairvoyant," and there are many records to show that his counseling was penetrating and helpful. Since, however, most of his sessions lasted only fifteen minutes, it is likely that there was as much preaching in his counseling as there was counseling in his preaching.

The most obvious breakthrough in his use of the pulpit to do pastoral counseling on a group scale was in the way he constructed his sermons. While he saw much good in the classical expository sermon that grew out of Puritan homiletics, he worried about the way sermons began with issues of exegesis, saying, "Only the preacher proceeds still upon the idea that folk come to church desperately anxious to discover what happened to the Jebusites."[18] (For the magazine article from which this quotation is taken, **see Vol. 2, pp. 535-47.**) He had less respect for topical preaching, which he associated with a loss of faith that eventually caused clergy to leave the ministry.

He was led to what he called "the project method," which he used as a technical term in educational psychology. He said, "Modern pedagogy starts not with the subject, but with the child."[19] Information is taught by showing the relevance of the information. Hence he began his sermon with a problem he thought some of his hearers might be facing.

It has been thought that Fosdick's sermon arrangement, in which he began with the problem,[20] reflected the thought of John Dewey,[21] but that is only partially true. Dewey believed that the best teaching was done in five steps:

1. A felt difficulty
2. Location and definition of the difficulty
3. Suggestion of possible solutions
4. Development by reasoning of bearings of suggestions
5. Further observation and exploration leading to acceptance or rejection of the solution.[22]

The difficulty with this interpretation is that, while Fosdick's sermons begin with a felt difficulty, they do not follow the rest of the outline.[23]

This can be seen in a fairly typical sermon, "When Life Reaches Its Depths," which was preached after America's entry into World War II.[24] This sermon is based on a clause from Psalm 42:7 (ASV), "Deep calleth unto deep at the noise of thy waterfalls," which is understood analogically to mean: "Every serious life has had that experience, where the profundities within ask for an answering profundity."[25] That experience accounts for "the deathless hold that religious faith has upon the human experience," because irreligion offers no answering profundity to the deep situations in which people find themselves. This is what Fosdick called "the major idea"[26] of the sermon.

The rest of the sermon is a testing of that thesis in five areas of human experience. Was it true when one had to deal with trouble, love, moral need, ethical devotion, and spiritual insight? Fosdick may have learned from Dewey's pedagogical theory to begin with difficulties members of the congregation were feeling, but he did not follow the other four of Dewey's five steps in learning as the rest of his outline.

The opening section of a Fosdick sermon first served to show that the problem being discussed was a problem for his hearers, was important, and was consistent with life as it is depicted in the Bible. Then he went on to state the main idea around which the rest of the sermon was organized.

The way in which the other points related to the main idea were seen by Fosdick as analogous to either a *box,* a *tree,* or a *river.* The points in the first sort of sermon are enumerated one after another, as boards are nailed together in the construction of a box. Those of the second sort fork off from the main idea, as do limbs from the trunk of a tree. "The message with 'riverlike' structure flows along without giving the hearers points sharply marked off from one another. It surges forward, opening up one new vista after another."[27] To repeat, none of these patterns follows Dewey's five steps.

The opening section in which Fosdick stated his main idea is the *introduction* to his sermon, and the points he makes in relation to that idea are thus its *body.* These two sections were there to lead to the *conclusion.* As Fosdick said:

> Starting a sermon with a problem, however vital and urgent, suggests a discussion, a dissertation, a treatise. A sermon, however, is more than that. The preacher's business is not merely to discuss repentance but to persuade people to repent; not merely to debate the meaning and possibility of Christian faith, but to produce Christian faith in the lives of his listeners; not merely to talk about the available power of God to bring victory over trouble and temptation, but to send people out from their worship on Sunday with victory in their possession. A preacher's task is to create in his congregation the thing he is talking about.[28]

Of course, the entire sermon was designed to lead to this result, but it was in the conclusion that Fosdick challenged his listeners to live by what he had said.

PREACHING IN THE HEYDAY OF PASTORAL COUNSELING

This pattern of stating in the introduction a main idea about a problem facing members of the congregation, making points about it in the body of the sermon, and appealing to them to live by that message in the conclusion is Fosdick's main contribution to the effort to do pastoral counseling from the pulpit. It was some time before thought about how such preaching should be done advanced beyond what he had said.[29] Tracing that advance when it came is a matter of surveying the literature in which it appeared.

A pioneering work was Edgar N. Jackson's *A Psychology for Preaching,* which appeared in 1961 with a preface by Fosdick.[30] It is a disappointment, however, to anyone who expects to find in it either a personality theory or much insight into how one can achieve Fosdick's goal of preaching as counseling on a group scale. Instead, it is the sort of book that flooded the market in the years after World War II, one that promised professional practitioners psychological insight to help them understand their customers or clients and thus be more successful.

The next book on the subject, *Preaching and Pastoral Care* by Arthur L. Teikmanis, appeared in a distinguished series of books edited by pastoral counseling pioneer Russell L. Dicks.[31] It did not advance the theory of how counseling was done through preaching, however, consisting as it did of introductory chapters on the importance of preaching, the value of pastoral calling, and aspects of preparing to preach, followed by chapters consisting of nothing but outlines of sermons the author had preached on five categories of problems faced by parishioners. Perhaps the greatest contribution of this book was its defense of the value of preaching, something rare in the counseling field at the time, when the two activities were often viewed as antithetical alternatives.

The first book I have known to relate preaching to the pastoral care movement, which emerged after World War II under the influence of Carl Rogers, did not appear until 1979. David K. Switzer's *Pastor, Preacher, Person: Developing a Pastoral Ministry*[32] is not devoted exclusively to the relation of pastoral counseling and preaching. Rather, it seeks to bring insights from the field of psychotherapy to bear on "ministers' ways of thinking about themselves, their operational context within the church, and two central ministerial functions—preaching and pastoral care."[33] Only two of the five chapters are about preaching, the first having to do with the pastor's sense of his or her role, and the other examining the metaphor of the church as the family of God by applying to it the traits of a healthy family.

Switzer, who taught at Southern Methodist University, thinks that such descriptions of preaching as calling it "counseling on a group scale" are essentially reductionistic (especially after the Rogerian understanding of counseling took over). He does recognize, however, that the two activities share a desire to meet human needs and that both are "interpersonal, primarily verbal processes engaged in by the minister with others, and as such there are *some* common goals and necessary relational ingredients."[34] In reference to meeting human needs, he argues that preaching can change lives, although some authorities in pastoral counseling doubt that. His reasons for thinking so, however, are theoretical and theological rather than empirical.

The necessary relational ingredients held in common by counseling and preaching are also shared with all the helping professions: empathy, respect, concreteness, genuineness, self-disclosure, confrontation, and immediacy. The desirability of such ingredients is self-evident, but may be like other self-evident things: they are only so after being pointed out.

In this way Switzer undertook to illuminate the preaching task with psychotherapeutic insight. In doing so he did not reduce the church's ministry to therapy but recognized the transcendent claims of Christians. It would have been interesting to see what he would have said, however, had he gone on to analyze what is unique to the work of the pastor and thus discontinuous with other helping relationships.

The next major effort to relate pastoral counseling and preaching was *Pastoral Counseling and Preaching: A Quest for an Integrated Ministry,* by Donald Capps of Princeton Theological Seminary.[35] Capps claims that efforts to relate counseling and preaching from Fosdick on had failed to show that they are "two foci of an integrated ministry."[36] His thesis is that counseling and preaching share a formal structure: (1) identification of the problem, (2) reconstruction of the problem, (3) diagnostic interpretation, and (4) pastoral intervention.

His understanding of diagnosis is Rogerian, trying to understand a problem from the counselee's internal frame of reference. Yet he recognizes that there are different types of diagnosis done in preaching, each of which is akin to a type of counseling. The correlations he makes are:

1. "Identify[ing] underlying personal motivations" (psychoanalysis and others, including transactional analysis).
2. "Identify[ing] the range of potential causes" (various social therapies, such as social psychology and family counseling).
3. "Expos[ing] inadequate formulations of the problem" (depth psychology).
4. "Drawing attention to untapped personal and spiritual resources" (humanistic psychology).
5. "Bring[ing] clarity to the problem" (various therapies clarify various things).
6. "Assess[ing] problems in terms of the deepest intentions of shared human experience" (the client-centered approach).[37]

Capps sees value in each of these approaches, but thinks a pastor should be consistent in using only one of them in both preaching and counseling. Though his formal structure is not necessarily significant, his recognition of the theological nature of diagnosis, and of the need for proclamation in counseling, points toward an overarching theological vision of the church and its ministry, one in which pastoral counseling and preaching belong together as parts of the same work.

All the writers since Fosdick surveyed here represent the era of pastoral counseling's hegemony in practical theology. The swing of the pendulum back to the center can be seen in the last book to be studied on the relation of counseling to preaching. In *Pastoral Preaching: Timeless Truth for Changing Needs,*[38] Gary D. Stratman, a Presbyterian pastor in Nashville, Tennessee, looks for a wider definition of "pastoral" that can arise from a study of the biblical image of the shepherd (for which, of course, the Latin word is *pastor*). He draws on a study by David Steere, which sees the essential elements of the biblical concept of shepherding to be:

1. A positive pattern of action meeting need
2. A negative pattern of action constituting a withdrawal of the first
3. A sacrificial expenditure of life
4. Love as spontaneous, creative, and initiating.[39]

Stratman thinks the pastoral counseling approach to preaching has been strong on the first and last of these elements, but weak on the second and third. Weakness on the second element has been seen in an unwillingness to judge. Moral judgments, however, are a necessary part of pastoral leadership. Though counseling sermons have dealt with true and important matters, they have not treated everything of concern to Christians. Thus, Stratman says, "pastoral preaching will be marked by a shepherd's compassion and concern which desires nothing less for Christ's flock than the whole counsel of God."[40]

Stratman is concerned that preaching deal not just with some truth but with the *whole* truth. This, for him, is a theological concern. The source of truth is the Bible, and preaching that presents the whole truth cannot be limited by drawing upon only restricted portions of the Scriptures; for the whole truth, one needs the whole Bible.

Most of the rest of Stratman's book is dedicated to the way he prepares to preach, which does not need to be considered here. It is to be regretted that he did not pursue the biblical metaphor of shepherding further to specify in more detail what he means by "pastoral," and that he did not say more about what is the "whole" truth of the Bible. The development of Stratman's thought is more homiletical than analytical. Since his insights, in an area in which analysis is badly needed, seem so sound, it is to be regretted that he did not go on to make a wider contribution.

THE CURRENT SITUATION

As Stratman's work indicates, the period in which pastoral counseling enjoyed a hegemony in practical theology has passed, and the esteem in which the two pastoral activities of counseling and preaching are held is now more even. Having begun with reference to homiletics textbooks to see what was important in the preaching of a period, this chapter can end the same way by heeding what a popular manual has to say on this subject:

> The distance between preaching and pastoring has been manufactured out of exaggerated descriptions and caricatured portraits of both. On the one hand, the preacher was sketched as a drone, full of authoritarian harangues, moralistic scoldings, sectarian loyalties, and promotional trivia. On the other hand, the pastor was cartooned as a passive pseudo-psychologist, relishing the intimate details of parishioners' private lives.
>
> The past tense was used in the sentences above because preaching and pastoring now enjoy a healthier relationship of mutual enrichment.[41]

In summary, it can be said that it is axiomatic for most preachers today that one of the purposes of their preaching is to do pastoral counseling on a group scale. Furthermore, it seems obvious to many that sermons should begin with issues that are relevant to members of the congregation—whether those of personal psychology or of theology or ethics or whatever else is appropriate to preach about—in order to engage their interest and prepare them to see the relevance of what will be said. And so the influence of Fosdick continues, although it is not as dominant as it was during his ministry.

FOR FURTHER READING

Fosdick, Harry Emerson. *The Living of These Days: An Autobiography.* New York: Harper & Brothers, 1956.

———. *A Great Time to Be Alive: Sermons on Christianity in Wartime.* New York: Harper & Brothers, 1944.

Harry Emerson Fosdick's Art of Preaching: An Anthology. Edited by Lionel Crocker. Springfield, Ill.: Charles C. Thomas, 1971.

Holifield, E. Brooks. *A History of Pastoral Care in America: From Salvation to Self-Realization.* Nashville: Abingdon, 1983.

Stratman, Gary D. *Pastoral Preaching: Timeless Truth for Changing Needs.* Nashville: Abingdon, 1983.

Notes

1. Lucy Atkinson Rose, *Sharing the Word: Preaching in the Roundtable Church* (Louisville, Ky.: Westminster John Knox, 1997), 7.

2. H. Grady Davis, *Design for Preaching* (Philadelphia: Fortress, 1958).

3. Donald F. Chatfield, "Textbooks Used by Teachers of Preaching," *Homiletic* 9 (1984): 2:1-5.

4. William B. Lawrence, *Sundays in New York: Pulpit Theology at the Crest of the Protestant Mainstream 1930–1955,* ATLA Monograph Series, no. 41 (Lanham, Md.: American Theological Library Association and Scarecrow Press, 1996). While this book is a treasure trove of fascinating information, it seems to argue that a good bit of the loss of mainstream Protestantism's influence on American society was due to the "tangentially" Protestant theology of Harry Emerson Fosdick and Ralph W. Sockman; this sounds like a "great man" theory of historical change with a vengeance. See especially pp. 224-26.

5. Ibid., vii.

6. Ibid.

7. Philip Rieff, *The Triumph of the Therapeutic: Uses of Faith after Freud* (New York: Harper & Row, 1966).

8. An excellent account of that has been provided by E. Brooks Holifield in *A History of Pastoral Care in America: From Salvation to Self-Realization* (Nashville: Abingdon, 1983), 210-356.

9. Ibid., 220. What is meant by "pastoral counseling" in this context will be defined below. For the present, it is enough to note that the practice is in part a function of the growing popularity of psychology in America immediately after World War I.

10. The bibliography on Fosdick is enormous. His own account of his life and ministry is *The Living of These Days: An Autobiography* (New York: Harper & Brothers, 1956). The standard biography is Robert Moats Miller, *Harry Emerson Fosdick: Preacher, Pastor, and Prophet* (New York and Oxford: Oxford University Press, 1985). Miller also wrote the article on Fosdick in the *Concise Encyclopedia of Preaching,* ed. William H. Willimon and Richard Lischer (Louisville: Westminster John Knox, 1995), 154-57. The major collection of Fosdick's writings and those of others about his preaching is *Harry Emerson Fosdick's Art of Preaching: An Anthology,* comp. and ed. Lionel Crocker (Springfield, Ill.: Charles C. Thomas, 1971). Two of the most useful essays in that collection are Robert D. Clark, "Harry

Emerson Fosdick: The Growth of a Great Preacher" (pp. 128-85, reprinted from *A History and Criticism of American Public Address,* ed. Marie Kathryn Hochmuth [New York: Russell & Russell, 1955]), and Edmund H. Linn, "Harry Emerson Fosdick and the Techniques of Organization" (pp. 186-209, reprinted from *ANQ* 1 [1961]: 19-40). Linn later went on to construct the sort of homiletics textbook Fosdick might have written had he been inclined to do so, *Preaching as Counseling: The Unique Method of Harry Emerson Fosdick* (Valley Forge, Pa.: Judson, 1966), which incorporates much of the earlier essay. Another study of Fosdick's rhetoric is Halford R. Ryan, *Harry Emerson Fosdick: Persuasive Preacher,* Great American Orators, no. 2 (New York: Greenwood, 1989). Clyde Fant's introduction to the sermons of Fosdick included in Clyde E. Fant Jr. and William M. Pinson Jr., eds., *20 Centuries of Great Preaching: An Encyclopedia of Preaching* (Waco, Tex.: Word, 1971), 9:3-27, is another good summary.

11. Harry Emerson Fosdick, *The Meaning of Faith;* and *The Meaning of Prayer.*

12. Harry Emerson Fosdick, *The Modern Use of the Bible* (New York: Macmillan, 1924).

13. About whether the Bible was to be understood as literally true or to be interpreted by the historical-critical method. While Beecher and Brooks had been strong advocates of critical method a half century before, the clash over biblical interpretation did not really begin to tear Protestant churches apart until the 1920s.

14. Fosdick, *The Living of These Days,* 94.

15. Holifield, *A History of Pastoral Care in America,* 259-306.

16. His knowledge of Freud was superficial and his attitude toward him antagonistic. Miller, *Harry Emerson Fosdick,* 260-64.

17. See ibid., 251-84, and Holifield, *A History of Pastoral Care,* 219-21.

18. Fosdick, "What Is the Matter With Preaching?" in *Harper's Magazine* (July 1928), reprinted in Crocker, *Harry Emerson Fosdick's Art of Preaching,* 30.

19. Ibid., 32.

20. Charles Kemp called this kind of sermon "Life Situation" preaching in "Harry Emerson Fosdick: The Methods of a Master," *Life Situation Preaching* (St. Louis: Bethany Press, 1956), 88, in Crocker, *Harry Emerson Fosdick's Art of Preaching,* 225. I was introduced to this term in the early 1950s in a course on public speaking at Duke Divinity School taught by John J. Rudin III. The concept was summarized as: "You have to start with people where they are in order to get them where you want them to go," but I do not know with whom this statement originated.

21. See, for example, Halford E. Luccock, *In the Minister's Workshop,* Notable Books on Preaching (Whitmore & Stone, 1944; reprint, Grand Rapids, Mich.: Baker, 1977), 52-58. I accepted this theory in my book *The Living and Active Word: One Way to Preach from the Bible Today* (New York: Seabury, 1975), 47-48.

22. Luccock, *In the Minister's Workshop,* 56.

23. A speech outline based on Dewey is Alan Monroe's "Motivated Sequence," for which the five steps are: (1) *Attention.* The creation of interest and desire, (2) *Need.* The development of the problem, through an analysis of things wrong in the world and through a relating of those wrongs to individuals' interests, wants, or desires, (3) *Satisfaction.* The proposal of a plan of action which will alleviate the problem and satisfy the individuals' interests, wants, or desires, (4) *Visualization.* The verbal depiction of the world as it will look if the plan is put into operation, (5) *Action.* The final call for personal commitments and deeds" (David Ehninger, Bruce E. Gronbeck, and

Alan H. Monroe, *Principles of Speech Communication,* 9th Brief Ed. (Glenview, Ill.: Scott, Foresman & Co., 1984), 249. Monroe first published this pattern in 1935.

24. In Harry Emerson Fosdick, *A Great Time to Be Alive: Sermons on Christianity in Wartime* (New York: Harper & Brothers, 1944), 192-200.

25. Ibid., 192.

26. This term was used in a letter to Edmund H. Linn, dated April 15, 1951, and quoted in "Techniques of Organization," in Crocker, *Harry Emerson Fosdick's Art of Preaching,* 189.

27. Ibid., 200. While Fosdick was more concerned with psychological than logical order in his sermons, Gilbert Stillman MacVaugh's idea that his longest point was always his main idea in the introduction and that his subordinate points grew progressively shorter appears not to be true. ("Structural Analysis of the Sermons of Dr. Harry Emerson Fosdick," in Crocker, *Harry Emerson Fosdick's Art of Preaching,* 210-224; reprinted from *The Quarterly Journal of Speech,* 19:531-46). See Linn letter, ibid., 204-5. Linn's analysis of the organization of Fosdick's sermons is the most astute study of *dispositio* as practiced by a particular preacher that I have seen.

28. Fosdick, *The Living of These Days,* 99.

29. The rest of this chapter builds on my essay "Preaching and Pastoral Care," in *Anglican Theology and Pastoral Care,* ed. James E. Griffiss, Anglican Study Series (Wilton, Conn.: Morehouse-Barlow, 1985), 133-58.

30. Edgar N. Jackson, *A Psychology for Preaching* (1961; reprint, San Francisco: Harper & Row, 1981).

31. Arthur L. Teikmanis, *Preaching and Pastoral Care,* Successful Pastoral Counseling, ed. Russell L. Dicks (Englewood Cliffs, N.J.: Prentice-Hall, 1964).

32. David K. Switzer, *Pastor, Preacher, Person: Developing a Pastoral Ministry* (Nashville: Abingdon, 1979).

33. Ibid., 9.

34. Ibid., 53.

35. Donald Capps, *Pastoral Counseling and Preaching: A Quest for an Integrated Ministry* (Philadelphia: Westminster, 1980). He taught at Phillips University at the time of this writing.

36. Ibid., 91-103.

37. This list brings to mind Walker Percy's question: "Can you explain why it is that there are, at last count, sixteen schools of psychotherapy with sixteen theories of the personality and its disorders and that patients treated in one school seem to do as well or as badly as patients treated in any other—while there is only one generally accepted theory of the cause and cure of pneumococcal pneumonia and only one generally accepted theory of the orbits of the planets and the gravitational attraction of our galaxy and the galaxy M31 in Andromeda?" (*Lost in the Cosmos: The Last Self-Help Book* (New York: Washington Square Press Division of Pocket Books, 1983), 11.

38. Gary D. Stratman, *Pastoral Preaching: Timeless Truth for Changing Needs* (Nashville: Abingdon, 1983).

39. Ibid., p. 20.

40. Ibid., p. 37.

41. Fred B. Craddock, *Preaching* (Nashville: Abingdon, 1985), 38.

CHAPTER 26

THE RESURGENCE OF ORTHODOXY

THE RISE OF BIBLICAL THEOLOGY

From the late-nineteenth century through the middle of the twentieth, a prevailing climate had developed in mainstream American—and, to a lesser extent, British—preaching, in which the primary concerns of the pulpit seemed to be pastoral counseling or problem solving à la Fosdick,[1] social reform, and moral exhortation. The last of these reflected, among other things, the concentration during that period of New Testament scholarship upon efforts to reconstruct the life of Jesus historically.[2] Such a preoccupation with the ministry of Jesus led by default to a lessened emphasis on the incarnation, crucifixion, resurrection, and ascension. Thus it came about that clergy, many of whom still held a traditional Christology, found themselves treating Jesus homiletically as the great teacher and example of ethical life.

In the years following World War II,[3] this picture was to undergo considerable change brought about by a number of factors. One was a revolution in the way New Testament scholars looked at Jesus. It was the historian of Life of Jesus research,[4] **Albert Schweitzer** (1875–1965),[5] among others, who showed that Jesus' life and teaching must be understood in light of the belief Jesus shared with most of his contemporaries, that the present age of history was coming to a sudden and cataclysmic end, after which would be ushered in the reign of God. Therefore, sound biblical interpretation did not support the view that Jesus taught a timeless ethic or that the kingdom of God was something human beings were to bring in through their personal and corporate efforts at social reform. While Schweitzer's own evaluation of Jesus' eschatological teaching was to assume that it was brilliantly and gloriously mistaken, scholars were beginning to assume by the mid-1930s that there had to be some way in which Jesus' views were both true and normative for Christianity.

A change in the dominant method of studying the Gospels occurred simultaneously with some of these developments. Life of Jesus research had been predicated upon the assumption that differences in the Gospels were to be explained by differences in the sources available to the Evangelists, and much of synoptic study was directed toward separating and identifying these sources, the assumption being that the earliest was the most reliable historically. During World War I, however, a new method of synoptic study was devised by a trio of German scholars: **K. L. Schmidt** (1891–1956), **Rudolf Bultmann** (1884–1976), and **Martin Dibelius** (1883–1947). This method, called "Form Criticism" in English,[6] investigated the time between Jesus' ministry and when the first account of it was written down in Mark's Gospel, an interval of slightly less than forty years. During that interval, the stories and sayings of Jesus were handed down by word of mouth. When such transmission occurs, as studies in the oral tradition of folkloric material indicate, various kinds of material tend to settle into characteristic patterns. Thus by analyzing the way that such patterns were preserved or altered, it should be possible to establish the relative age of different versions of the same unit of tradition.

When the form-critical method was first applied to the Gospels, the question was raised of why the church preserved some stories and sayings and not others. It was immediately recognized that the only material handed down was that useful to the early church in its effort to evangelize the Greco-Roman world. This means that nothing was passed down just because it satisfied curiosity about Jesus; the purpose was not reminiscence but conversion. Each story or saying was kept because it led to the conclusion that "Jesus is the Messiah, the Son of God, and that through believing you may have life in his name" (John 20:31).

It became an axiom of form criticism that each individual unit of tradition, each story or saying, had such christological implications that it was the entire gospel in a nutshell. And this meant that the whole nineteenth-century quest of the historical Jesus had been based upon a misunderstanding. It had hoped to get behind the supernatural picture of Jesus to show him as a historical person, when the very reason all the sources drawn upon had been preserved was to serve as evidence for the supernatural interpretation. One could not get behind them to a purely historical account; every pericope of the Gospels proclaims the ultimacy of Christ.

New Testament scholars learned the method of form criticism from Old Testament scholars, who had also used it to move behind source criticism. Late in the nineteenth century, **Julius Wellhausen** (1844–1918), professor at Marburg and Göttingen, published a theory of how the Pentateuch was put together, identifying the J (Yahwistic), E (Elohistic), P (Priestly), and D (Deuteronomic) accounts as the sources from which the finished document was assembled. Combined with this literary analysis was a Hegelian and evolutionary interpretation of the history of the religion of Israel that traced its progress from primitive superstition to the enlightened ethical monotheism of the prophets. Form criticism shifted the emphasis to the individual units of tradition that lay behind the sources of not only the Pentateuch but other parts of the Hebrew Bible as well. Sagas from Genesis were analyzed, psalms were sorted into their various types, and the structure of prophetic oracles was studied.

Creedal statements that took the form of recitals of the history of God's dealings with Israel were identified, and these dealings were seen in relation to the succession of covenants God formed with Israel. In this manner, the emphasis shifted from an evolutionary view of Israel's search for God to the proclamation of the God who acted in the history of Israel. In the process, philosophical interpretation of biblical religion was branded as illegitimate, and there was much insistence upon the difference between Hebrew and Greek thought, with an implied claim of the superiority of the former over the latter. Connected with this was an interest in the theological vocabulary of the Bible, such as was manifested in the *Theologisches Wörterbuch zum Neuen Testament,* edited by **Gerhard Kittel** (1888–1948) and Gerhard Friedrich. Although the vocabulary of the New Testament was Greek, it was thought to represent the Semitic thought world from which Jesus and his first followers came.

Another development in biblical scholarship that was to have a profound impact on homiletics was **C. H. Dodd**'s (1884–1973) study of *The Apostolic Preaching and Its Developments.*[7] In the book Dodd argued that the New Testament word for preaching, *kerygma,* and its cognates, did not refer to moral instruction, which instead was designated as *didache* (teaching), *paraklesis* (exhortation), or *homilia* (informal discussion of the Christian life). To preach was to proclaim the good news of

God's saving activity in Jesus Christ. "While the church was concerned to hand on the teaching of the Lord, it was not by this that it made converts. It was by *kerygma,* says Paul, not by *didache,* that it pleased God to save men."[8]

These changes in biblical studies paralleled shifting emphases in theology. A voice crying in the wilderness for such changes had been **Søren Kierkegaard** (1813–55), a Danish philosopher and theologian who challenged the regnant theology of German idealism that derived from Hegel. His concern with the position of a human being existing before God made him the father of existentialism (a term he coined). Furthermore, his criticism of the Danish church of his time for seeking to accommodate the Christian revelation to human desires makes him the ancestor of the "crisis" or "dialectical" theology of the twentieth century, a movement largely identified with the Swiss theologian Karl Barth.

Also influential in English-speaking countries was **P(eter) T(aylor) Forsyth** (1848–1921), a Scottish Congregationalist theologian who in his early life and ministry had espoused the liberal theology of Hegel and Albrecht Ritschl. When he came to be convinced of the inadequacy of that approach, however, he also knew that he could not espouse instead the rigorous biblicism that was the other option in Scottish theology at the time. Although he continued to appreciate much about modernism, he nevertheless insisted upon the radical pervasiveness of human sin and, therefore, the utter dependence of human beings upon the atoning death of Christ, through which God reconciled a lost humanity to God's self.[9] Forsyth has been called "a Barth before Barth," and he did indeed anticipate many of what were to be the characteristic emphases the Swiss theologian would later display.

Generally recognized as the most influential theologian of the twentieth century, **Karl Barth** (1886–1968) demonstrated to the Christian world that the optimistic liberal assumption of inevitable progress was inconsistent with the realities of human nature. Two world wars, separated by a worldwide depression, were to reveal to many the shallowness of liberal Christian theology's optimistic understanding of human nature. For Barth, however, that insight came before even World War I. Trained by the leading liberal theologians of Germany, he found the worldview he had been taught inadequate in his efforts to be a pastor in the Swiss town of Safenwil. To gain a deeper understanding of his parishioners' lives, he turned to a study of Paul's Letter to the Romans.

This study was incorporated into a commentary, and through its revised second edition he both established what was to be his characteristic position and was established as one of the leading theologians in

Europe. Biblical truth could not be understood as progressive human discovery but only as the self-revelation of a holy God who is totally different from sinful human beings. The upshot was that all human activity—whether philosophical, ethical, or religious—was thoroughly compromised by human pride and self-centeredness and thus not to be relied upon for any insight. The only serious truth available to humanity is what God discloses of God's self in biblical revelation.

The response of the theological world to Barth's commentary on Romans was overwhelming; university appointments in Germany came his way, and he began his *Kirkliche Dogmatik,* which was to run to thirteen thick volumes in its English translation.[10]

While the theological world responded to Barth's call to recognize the infinite qualitative distance between God and human beings, most thinkers were not prepared to state the disjunction between divine and human thought so starkly as he. They were more likely to side with **Emil Brunner** (1889–1966) in recognizing the possibility of some natural knowledge of God. The theological school of Barth, Brunner, and others was called "dialectical" and "crisis" theology, but the wider movement that reaffirmed the transcendence of God and the human need for salvation was called "neoorthodoxy." In the United States, the most influential spokespersons for this wider theological movement were the brothers **Reinhold** (1892–1971) and **H. Richard Niebuhr** (1894–1962). By the end of World War II, there was a pervasive rejection of old-school liberalism in American and British theology and a call for a more biblical understanding of God's relations with human beings.

As a result of these and other trends, a characteristic approach to biblical study developed that referred to itself as the **"biblical theology" movement.** While the movement was always very fluid and comprised a great variety of positions, it nevertheless had a number of emphases that were shared by most of those who made it up. These emphases included a reaction against abstract and philosophical thought in general, and a rejection of efforts to systematize the theology of the Bible on the grounds that it was too organic to be susceptible to that sort of presentation without distortion. Instead, it showed a preference for what was considered the more dynamic quality of biblical ("Hebrew") thought over what was believed to be the static quality of Greek thought. It was believed that the New Testament had to be interpreted in light of the Old, since it belonged to the Hebrew thought world. There was, therefore, a deep sense of the unity of the Bible. A favored method for getting at the Hebrew structure of thought was the study of individual words, as in the Kittel *Wörterbuch.*

And, just as New Testament thought was distinguished from that of the Greeks, so Old Testament thought was sharply separated from that of Israel's Near Eastern neighbors. One of the qualities of Hebrew thought admired by the movement was its understanding that revelation occurs in history rather than in the delivery of abstract propositions. Thus the reason for scholars to study the Bible was to discover the theology that had been revealed in history. By the same token, other theological disciplines should have biblical theology as their point of departure. But this theology was not to be remote and academic. It should be concerned with the life of the church in the world and have its most important expression in preaching.[11]

THE INFLUENCE OF EXEGESIS UPON PROCLAMATION

The impact of biblical theology upon preaching was mainly through seminary courses in Bible and theology. There was not, at any rate, a single textbook devoted to the method that dominated the teaching of homiletics from the midforties to the midsixties, the heyday of the movement. There were, however, a number of significant books on preaching that reflected the movement's assumptions. Oddly enough, Barth's own lectures on homiletics were not among the most influential. That was undoubtedly because he did not publish them himself; rather, they survived in the form of student notes. The earlier form of these was not published in English until 1963, and the more complete form did not appear until the movement was over.[12]

A book that was a review of the changed situation in theology and designed to persuade preachers to change their way of preaching was among the more significant. Theodore O. Wedel, who was warden of the College of Preachers at the National Cathedral in Washington, began *The Pulpit Rediscovers Theology*[13] by describing the liberal theology that had been the homiletical staple up until that time, and the doubts that must have arisen in regard to it, especially noting that ethical exhortation that does not grow out of the gospel of grace, is an invitation to despair in the way that it sets perfectionist standards to be met by human effort alone. Jesus must be our Savior before he can be our Master.

Saying that recognizes the need for dogma, however repugnant the word was to liberals. The pulpit needed the biblical theology that was making such an impact at the time, with its recognition of the reality of sin and the need for grace. After summarizing the main tenets of biblical theology and its critique of liberalism, Wedel ended his book by noting the implications of the liturgical movement[14] for preaching and giving a review of the doctrine of the church.

While Wedel tried to persuade preachers of their need for biblical theology, he did not tell them how to preach from its insights. There were, however, a number of textbooks that did attempt to do so—some of which were written by biblical scholars rather than homileticians—although, as noted above, none of these were accepted as the standard work.[15]

One of the clearest examples of such an effort may be seen in two books by Donald G. Miller, *Fire in the Mouth*[16] and *The Way to Biblical Preaching*.[17] Miller was a Presbyterian pastor who also taught in several seminaries and served as president of one, as well as the editor of *Interpretation*, one of the leading journals to grow out of the biblical theology movement. The first of the two books deals with presuppositions behind biblical preaching, and the second tells how to construct sermons that reflect the understanding of the first. *The Way to Biblical Preaching* begins with a summary of the perspective of *Fire in the Mouth*. After criticizing several definitions of biblical preaching and rejecting the older understanding of expository preaching, the author states his ideal:

> Expository preaching is an act wherein the living truth of some portion of Holy Scripture, understood in the light of solid exegetical and historical study and made a living reality to the preacher by the Holy Spirit, comes alive to the hearer as he is confronted by God in Christ through the Holy Spirit in judgment and redemption.[18]

Two aspects of that definition call for attention. The first is that the approach to exegesis is historical-critical, but depends upon the perspective of biblical theology. The second is the implicit understanding of the nature of the preaching event. "The *end* of preaching is that the sermon situation should be transformed from a human encounter between the preacher and his congregation into a divine encounter between God and both preacher and people."[19]

Having set forth such a high doctrine of preaching, Miller goes on to outline a process of sermon preparation. He begins with the exegesis of the biblical text, recognizing the necessity of understanding the passage in its context within the Bible, but focusing more on lexicographical study than any other sort. He has little to say about the historical situation reflected in the passage, for instance. The next task is to discover the theme of the sermon: "Every sermon should have a theme, and that theme should be the theme of the portion of scripture on which it is based."[20]

Miller writes in a homiletical style, finding examples of good and bad usage in published sermons of unidentified preachers, and offering abundant analogies to the principles he states. In successive chapters he argues that preaching should be balanced, reflecting all sides of the truth, and that every sermon's message should be reducible to one sentence and should have a clear structure that is an outgrowth of the biblical passage upon which it is based. And it should have a particular purpose. Finally, the sermon must be delivered in the proper emotional tone. "Fire is kindled by fire. Let us capture the Bible's fire and lay it on the dry faggots of our own lives and those of our people. The world needs to know again that 'our God is a consuming fire.' "[21] While it might be difficult to construct a sermon with no more guidance than this, any that were constructed in this way would certainly represent the perspectives of the biblical theology movement.

The overall success of the movement in influencing preaching can be seen in the way that many of its teachings were presupposed by the next textbook to dominate the field, *Design for Preaching* by H. Grady Davis, which was used by over half the homiletics professors polled in 1974.[22] Yet for Davis, the emphases were presuppositions rather than his main concern. And, in looking at sermons produced in the heyday of the movement, it is hard to find many that seem to have been constructed according to a hard and fast formula. As Brevard Childs says of the impact of the movement upon preaching, "At least for a time, one gains the impression that many pastors tried to put the suggestions into practice while holding on to a typical American homiletical style."[23]

This is to say that the change had more to do with content than pattern. There were fewer sermons of the sort Wedel designated as the "we must" type, sermons that urged ethical imitation of Jesus. And there were more that proclaimed the reality of sin and the need for the grace of God, who acts and who has acted most visibly in Jesus Christ for the redemption of a lost world. There also was a visible shift in pulpit demeanor from that of exhorters, who were earnestly urging more effort in moral practice, to that of proclaimers, who believed that through human words the omnipotent God was communicating urgent messages to the people of God. (**See Vol. 2, pp. 548-52** for an example of British tradition of this sort of preaching.)

Even though many influences of the biblical theology movement continue to be felt in preaching today, there is no question that it has long since ceased to be the dominant consciousness in homiletics. It has not had that prominence since the mid-1960s, when the civil rights movement and other forms of social action came to the forefront of churches' attention. In that period there was a sense, as Childs has said, that "God has abandoned the sanctuary and gone out into the streets."[24] He went on to say:

Many pastors who continued to hold the major tenets of the movement struggled unsuccessfully to apply the theology to concrete issues. Neither the concept of the biblical mentality nor the redemptive history of the people of God provided the needed insights or carried the required authority for the issues of the day. Suddenly the familiar approach to the Bible began to seem as outdated as had Harry Emerson Fosdick's theology to the biblical theologians of the forties. The growing uncertainty regarding the place of the Bible reflected itself again in the form of the sermon. Whatever criticisms one could aim at the older liberals in respect to its content, one had to admit that the preaching of Fosdick, Luccock, and Sockman had at least been interesting, lucid, and relevant. These qualities appeared to many modern preachers to claim top priority.[25]

FOR FURTHER READING

Barth, Karl. *Homiletics.* Translated by Geoffrey W. Bromiley and Donald E. Daniels, with foreword by David Buttrick. Louisville: Westminster John Knox, 1991.

Bonhoeffer, Dietrich. *Worldly Preaching: Lectures on Homiletics.* Edited and translated with critical commentary by Clyde E. Fant. New York: Crossroad, 1991.

Childs, Brevard S. *Biblical Theology in Crisis.* Philadelphia: Westminster, 1970.

Davis, H. Grady. *Design for Preaching.* Philadelphia: Fortress, 1958.

Miller, Donald G. *The Way to Biblical Preaching.* New York and Nashville: Abingdon, 1957.

Wedel, Theodore O. *The Pulpit Rediscovers Theology.* Greenwich, Conn.: Seabury, 1956.

Notes

1. See the previous chapter for the way that Fosdick and those who followed him understood preaching as pastoral counseling on a group scale.

2. The history of nineteenth-century German efforts in this enterprise is recounted in Albert Schweitzer, *The Quest of the Historical Jesus,* trans. W. Montgomery, pref. F. C. Burkitt, 2nd ed. (1911; New York: Macmillan, 1948); the title in German was *Von Reimarus zu Wrede* (1906). For American and English activity in this field, see Stephen Neill and Tom Wright, *The Interpretation of the New Testament 1861–1986,* passim.

3. There was a time lag between what was going on in German biblical scholarship, where most of the new movements were launched, and their acceptance by

American and English scholars. While the main changes discussed here happened in the first quarter of the twentieth century in German scholarship, they were not widely accepted by English and American scholars until the third quarter.

4. *Lebenjesuforschung.*

5. A man of many talents, Schweitzer was considered one of the greatest interpreters of the organ works of J. S. Bach. By midcentury he was widely regarded as a saint for devoting his life to service as a medical missionary in French Equatorial Africa, receiving a Nobel Peace Prize in 1953. Since then his reputation has been diminished by a belief that he had racist attitudes toward his African patients. Yet few people have ever made such distinguished contributions in such diverse fields as biblical scholarship and theology, philosophy and ethics, music (both as a scholar and a performer), and medicine—in which he could have had a brilliant career in research.

6. German: *Formgeschichte.*

7. C. H. Dodd, *The Apostolic Preaching and Its Developments* (Chicago and New York: Willett, Clark & Co., 1937).

8. Ibid., 8.

9. A highly respected preacher himself, Forsyth was invited to give the prestigious Beecher Lectures in Preaching. These were published as *Positive Preaching and the Modern Mind* (London: Independent Press Ltd., 1907).

10. The size of the set together, with the color of the cloth in which the original German edition was bound, led him to refer to it deprecatingly as his Moby Dick, his "great white whale."

11. The most extensive discussion of this movement's rise is in Brevard S. Childs, *Biblical Theology in Crisis* (Philadelphia: Westminster, 1970), 9-87. An excellent short treatment is James Barr, "Biblical Theology," *IDB,* Supplementary Vol., 104-11. Krister Stendahl gave a concise statement of the movement's European background in his article "Biblical Theology," *IDB,* 1:418-32. Childs considered the movement to be more American than British or continental, and attributed its attractiveness to the depth of memories of the still recent fundamentalist-modernist controversy. Barr, on the other hand, saw it as an international and essentially uniform movement. In the discussion of the impact of biblical theology upon preaching that is to follow, I am grateful for bibliographical suggestions from David Buttrick, Don Wardlaw, Bruce Shields, and Richard Lischer.

12. The earlier form was *The Preaching of the Gospel* (Philadelphia: Westminster, 1963), trans. B. E. Hooke from *Le proclamation de l'Évangile,* ed. A. Roulin (Neuchâtel: Delachaux et Niestlé, 1961), while the later was *Homiletics,* trans. Geoffrey W. Bromiley and Donald E. Daniels, with foreword by David Buttrick (Louisville.: Westminster John Knox, 1991). Barth's approach to preaching was to eschew introductions, conclusions, and efforts at relevance or to relate the biblical message to the contemporary thought world. Instead, he called for a reiteration of the text's message. Like many other writers of homiletical textbooks, however, he was not completely consistent in carrying out his own principles. See Clyde Fant in Clyde E. Fant Jr. and William M. Pinson Jr., eds., *20 Centuries of Great Preaching: An Encyclopedia of Preaching* (Waco, Tex.: Word, 1971), 10:104-7. Some of Barth's sermons may be read in the Fant work. Much of his preaching was done at the prison

in Basel. A sampler of these sermons is Karl Barth, *Deliverance to the Captives,* trans. Marguerite Wieser (New York: Harper & Bros., 1961). For thoughts about preaching that are close to those of Barth in many ways while having significant differences, cf. Dietrich Bonhoeffer, *Worldly Preaching: Lectures on Homiletics,* ed. and trans. with critical commentary by Clyde E. Fant (New York: Crossroad, 1991).

13. Theodore O. Wedel, *The Pulpit Rediscovers Theology* (Greenwich, Conn.: Seabury, 1956).

14. The influence of the liturgical movement upon preaching is the subject of the next chapter of this history.

15. Examples include Jean-Jacques von Allmen, *Preaching and Congregation,* trans. B. L. Nicholas, Ecumenical Studies in Worship, no. 10 (Richmond, Va.: John Knox, 1962); Ernest Best, *From Text to Sermon: Responsible Use of the New Testament in Preaching* (Atlanta: John Knox, 1978); Leander E. Keck, *The Bible in the Pulpit: The Renewal of Biblical Preaching* (Nashville: Abingdon, 1978); and Paul Scherer, *The Word God Sent* (New York: Harper & Row, 1965). For a conservative evangelical approach to the subject, see Edmund P. Clowney, *Preaching and Biblical Theology* (Grand Rapids, Mich.: Eerdmans, 1961).

16. Donald G. Miller, *Fire in the Mouth,* Notable Books on Preaching (Pierce & Washabaugh, 1954; reprint, Grand Rapids, Mich.: Baker, 1976).

17. Donald G. Miller, *The Way to Biblical Preaching* (New York and Nashville: Abingdon, 1957).

18. Ibid., 26.

19. Ibid.

20. Ibid., 55.

21. Ibid., 153.

22. See chapter 25, p. 664.

23. Childs, *Biblical Theology in Crisis,* 28.

24. Ibid., 85.

25. Ibid.

CHAPTER 27

PREACHING AS AN ELEMENT OF WORSHIP

THE IMPACT OF THE LITURGICAL MOVEMENT ON ROMAN CATHOLIC PREACHING

Biblical theology was by no means the only influence on the mainline American churches during the 1950s and 1960s. Equally exciting were the ecumenical movement, which had little influence on their homiletics,[1] and the liturgical movement, which had a good bit. This latter movement, however, did not begin among these churches; instead, it began in continental Roman Catholicism.[2]

To understand how drastically Roman Catholic worship has changed in response to the liturgical movement, contemporary readers have to be reminded of what it was like before. The Mass was in Latin. Much of the emphasis was on its daily celebration as part of the priests' rule of life; those who did not preside for a congregation said private Masses. Because of this concentration on the priest, the norm became the "Low" or said celebration. Thus when the service was sung ("Solemn"[3] or "High" Mass), the celebrant would, in effect, say a Low Mass while the choir sang.

For instance, when the priest finished saying the creed, he moved to the sedilia and sat until the choir finished singing it, and often he would be well into the eucharistic prayer before the choir had finished the sanctus. While the choir sang the people's parts in the liturgy, the altar boy said those parts to the priest, whose back was to the congregation. At Low Mass, only the altar boy made the responses while the faithful, who did not understand the Latin, occupied themselves with some other devotion, such as private recitation of the rosary or adoration of the sacrament exposed in a monstrance.

For the laity, the value of assisting at Mass was understood to be receiving remission of days in purgatory. Missing Sunday Mass was considered a mortal sin. Communion by the faithful was infrequent, mainly because one had to be in a state of grace with no mortal sins committed since the last confession in order to receive. Even then, it was often the case at Solemn Masses that only the sanctuary party were communicated. When there was a sermon, which was not always the case, it would likely be a topical treatment of a doctrinal or moral issue, rather than an effort to apply the biblical passages read (in Latin) to the lives of the people.

Thus there was a highly individualistic understanding of the whole affair. The liturgical movement in Roman Catholicism can be understood as the effort to change most of these aspects of eucharistic celebration to those that are the norm today.

The beginning of the movement[4] is generally dated to the restoration of Benedictine monasticism (which had been greatly disrupted during the French Revolution) at the abbey of Solesmes by **Dom Prosper Guéranger** (1805–75). After the fabric of the monastery had been put in order, the full Benedictine life was instituted, with its corporate recitation of the offices and celebrations of the feasts of the church year. For that to be done properly, Guéranger thought it was necessary to revive plainsong, or Gregorian chant as it is called. Prior to this, French liturgical life had been chaotic, with a number of "neo-Gallican" rites being used in addition to that of Rome. After Solesmes became a showcase of the transcendent beauty with which the liturgy could be offered, parishes and cathedrals, as well as monasteries, adopted its model.[5]

Solesmes was also influential at a theoretical level, producing a widely read study of the liturgical year that ran to five thousand pages, the purpose of which was to deepen the congregation's participation through greater understanding of the liturgical texts and the scriptural lectionary. While this emphasis on participation did not entail any desire to revise the Roman liturgy or to translate it into the vernacular, it set in motion a progression of thought that would end there. Another result was that the use of plainsong rather than "concert" Mass settings shortened musical responses drastically, and so provided a far greater synchronicity of the celebrant's actions with those of the choir, making it more obvious that all were involved in a joint undertaking.

The next stage of the movement was to see the Eucharist understood as an action of the entire church. As early as 1883, Dom Gerhard Van Caloen began to advocate lay participation in the rite and published a small bilingual missal that would make it possible for the laity to follow the action of the Mass. Another Belgian Benedictine, **Dom Lambert Beauduin,** believed that the way to restore Christian spirituality was to work for the sung Mass's restoration as the norm for Sundays, with the faithful participating by singing and by an informed following of the rites and texts.

Beauduin's openness to Eastern Christians and Anglicans led in 1926 to his being expelled from the monastery of Mont César and indeed all of Belgium, but his exile's effect was to spread the influence of his thought. Among those who felt the force of his convictions were Virgil Michel, an American Benedictine who returned home to spread the movement here, and the papal nuncio in Paris when Beauduin taught there, the future pope John XXIII.

By the end of World War I, there was considerable lay interest in the liturgy. One of those who did most to satisfy that curiosity was **Pius Parsch** (1884–1954), an Augustinian canon of Klosterneuberg in Austria. While a chaplain in the war, "he discovered the two ideas that were to dominate his later years, the Bible as the people's book and the liturgy as the people's work."[6] He came to advocate many reforms, such as having the Sunday Mass at the center of the life of the people. To be such, it would have to be what was called a dialogue Mass, one in which the faithful made the responses. Congregational hymn singing was another important ingredient of Sunday worship as it ought to be. Parsch even came to encourage use of the vernacular. And, not surprisingly in the light of his devotion to Scripture, he published sermons for both the Sunday cycle and the great feasts, as well as a five-volume commentary on the Sunday Masses and their biblical texts.[7] Michael Mathis said that this latter work may have "won more adherents to the liturgical movement than any other book ever written."[8]

Romano Guardini (1885–1968) was another great popularizer of the movement. He was also one of the earliest priests to set a good example of liturgical preaching.

> He realized that for each homily he needed a "fuse," a burning question that interested him personally. He followed the church year, but chose his subjects based only on his own questions embedded in themes of the feasts and seasons.[9]

He also discovered that the homilist "had to use the same language from the pulpit that he used in the words and deeds of his personal life,"[10] rather than an artificial rhetorical language.

The primary theological insight upon which all the reforms advocated by the liturgical movement were based was that of the church as the mystical body of Christ. This insight, recognizing Christian worship's corporate nature, called for greater participation of all the faithful to make practice consistent with this understanding. The most influential theologian of the liturgical movement was **Odo Casel** (1886–1948), a Benedictine of Maria Laach. Casel's "mystery theology," as it was called, was seen as offering an adequate conceptualization of what the mystical body does in liturgy. His understanding of liturgical theology grew out of his study of pagan mystery religions.[11] He wrote at a time when scholars of the *Religionsgeschichtliche Schule* ("History of Religions School"), such as Richard Reitzenstein and Wilhelm Bousset, were suggesting that sacraments and much else in early Christianity were derived from these mystery religions. As Louis Bouyer said, Casel's "great and courageous feat was . . . to accept all the materials brought forward by the 'comparative' school and to propound new interpretations of these materials, much deeper and richer than that of his opponents."[12]

Casel's theology has been well summarized by Ernest B. Koenker:

> In the liturgical rites of sacrifice and sacrament we meet the mystical making-present-again of the *totum opus redemptionis*;[13] not only the Passion of Christ but his whole life, from the Incarnation to his Second Coming, is rendered sacramentally present in the cultic mysteries. It is not an empty commemoration or pious meditation; neither is this action something psychological or ethical. It is rather ontological action, a *signum efficax,*[14] a reality which efficaciously heightens man's natural existence through an activity in a higher sphere; as such, of course, it works *ex opere operato.*[15]

Through the combined force of its pioneers' insights, the way was paved for total triumph of the liturgical movement's point of view at the Second Vatican Council, as may be seen in its *Constitution on the Sacred Liturgy,* which was ratified on December 4, 1963. Now when the faithful gather for the liturgy, they have a text in their own language and all participate in dialogue with the priest, who presides facing them over the holy table. It is, after all, the action of the whole people of God, the mystical body of Christ, and thus a corporate activity.

On Sundays and during great feasts, at any rate, there is likely to be a great deal of singing—which may be anything from traditional chants of the church, to hymns from the rich tradition of the Protestant Reformation, to songs from the contemporary renewal movement accompanied by a guitar. Laypeople often read biblical lections other than the gospel and may also help in administration of Holy Communion.

A sermon is called for at all major celebrations, and the guidelines for such sermons say that they will help the congregation understand their lives in the light of these scriptures and the liturgy. The importance of such preaching in the liturgy is stated in the council's *Decree on the Ministry and Life of Priests*: "The primary duty of priests is the proclamation of the gospel of God to all."[16]

The revival of biblical scholarship in the Roman Catholic Church was contemporaneous with the liturgical movement's latter phase, and there was much cross-fertilization between the two activities. As far back as the time of Guéranger, the importance of the scripture readings at Mass was recognized. This gave new impetus to biblical interpretation. Some suspicion became attached to use of the historical-critical method developed by Protestant scholars because it had been taken too far by the modernist movement within Roman Catholicism, a movement condemned by Pope Pius X in his 1893 encyclical *Providentissimus Deus*.

By 1943, however, the appreciation of the Bible's importance to the church had sufficiently increased, and the recognition of the value of critical interpretation had sufficiently advanced, that Pius XII could issue *Divino afflante spiritu,* which was a reinterpretation as well as a reiteration of the earlier encyclical. In retrospect, it is recognized that a new era of Catholic biblical scholarship had been opened.[17] That opening was widened by the publication of the Vatican II document on revelation, *Verbum Dei*. A natural culmination of these trends was the publication of a new three-year lectionary cycle to begin with Advent 1971.

This changing climate had made it possible for the liturgical movement to be informed by the biblical theology movement, using many of the latter's insights in its own liturgy interpretations. New Catholic translations of the Bible into English became available at about the time the liturgy itself appeared in the vernacular. These included *The Jerusalem Bible* in 1973, greatly influenced by a French translation prepared by the École Biblique in Jerusalem, and *The New American Bible* in 1970–86. Both have excellent critical notes.

All of these trends come together in comments about preaching in Vatican II's *Constitution on the Sacred Liturgy,* which speaks of "the two parts which, in a certain sense, go to make up the mass, namely, the liturgy of the word and the eucharistic liturgy" and says these two parts are "so closely connected with each other that they form but a single act of worship" (56).

Indeed, the homily "is to be highly esteemed as a part of the liturgy itself; in fact, at those masses which are celebrated with the assistance of the people on Sundays and feasts of obligation, it should not be omitted except for a serious reason" (52). The content of the sermon is also specified:

> The sermon, moreover, should draw its content mainly from the scriptural and liturgical sources, and its character should be that of a proclamation of God's wonderful works in the history of salvation, the mystery of Christ, ever made present and active within us, especially in the celebration of the liturgy. (35)

Similarly, #24 states that "it is from scripture that lessons are read and explained in the homily."

It was, of course, much easier to arrange for a wholesale change in the way the liturgy was celebrated than to see that there was a similarly drastic alteration in the way preaching was done. For the liturgy, a priest had only to receive the revised rites and celebrate them according to the rubrics, but for preaching he almost needed to be "sent back to the factory and reprogrammed."

Some excellent resources were developed to assist in the change, however. Within five years of the *Constitution on the Sacred Liturgy,* a volume on preaching, edited by no less an authority than Karl Rahner, appeared in the Concilium series. Titled *The Renewal of Preaching: Theory and Practice,*[18] it includes articles on such subjects as the New Testament theology of the Word, "translation from the language of scripture and tradition into a language that can be understood today,"[19] an application of communications theory to preaching, an analysis of preaching's relation to sacramental worship, a study of preaching's contribution to reconciliation, a consideration of whether the laity may preach, and an essay on radio preaching. This is followed by reports on preaching in various European and American countries, with another look at preaching in relation to mass media. This volume, therefore, is not so much a statement of how the council's decrees concerning preaching were to be carried out as a look at the issues that have to be considered in making such a statement.

A number of individuals have written "how-to" manuals consistent with the criteria of the *Constitution on the Sacred Liturgy,*[20] but perhaps the best place to gain a post–Vatican II American Roman Catholic perspective on the nature of the homiletical task is a document published by the Bishop's Committee on Priestly Life and Ministry of the United States Conference of Catholic Bishops, *Fulfilled in Your Hearing: The Homily in the Sunday Assembly.*[21] After an introduction in which it is noted that the Sunday homily is "the normal and frequently the formal way in which [the majority of Catholics] hear the Word of God proclaimed" (2), the document looks at the three major elements of liturgical preaching: the assembly, the preacher, and the homily, in that order. This analysis of elements is followed by a consideration of homiletic method; after that the work concludes with an epilogue on "The Power of the Word."

The analysis begins with the assembly not only because communications theory points to the importance of the audience, but even more basically because "the primary reality is Christ in the assembly, the People of God" (4).

> The community that gathers Sunday after Sunday comes together to offer God praise and thanksgiving, or at least to await a word that will give meaning to their lives and enable them to celebrate Eucharist. (8)

The priest helps the people to make connections between their lives and the Word of God by listening prayerfully both to the biblical readings appointed for the Sunday and to his people. For interpretation of the Scriptures, the priest must do the best exegesis he is capable of, and he must study his people with the same attentiveness. Study of either the Word or the people will not be infallible, but "what the Word of God offers us is a way to interpret our human lives, a way to face the ambiguities and challenges of the human condition, not a pat answer to every problem and question that comes along" (15).

The purpose of the liturgical homily is that "a community of believers who have gathered to celebrate the liturgy may do so more deeply and more fully—more faithfully—and thus be formed for Christian witness in the world."[22] Thus one of the major differences between liturgical preaching and other varieties is that this form derives a lot of its meaning from the way it relates to the other liturgical elements. As William Skudlarek said, "To celebrate and offer thanks for the good news we have heard: that ultimately is the reason preaching and liturgy go together. We need to know why we should lift up our hearts."[23] Therefore, it is "preaching that proclaims the good news of the great and wonderful things God has done and is doing for his people, rather than preaching that lists the dos and don'ts that people must follow if they are to gain the favor of God."[24] Such preaching would meet with the approval of the biblical theology movement, rehearsing as it does the mighty acts of God, but it is also preaching that gives meaning and purpose to the eucharistic celebration of which it is an integral part. Implicit in this liturgical grounding is celebration of the *magnalia*[25] that reflect a particular day's theme in the church year and their rehearsal in the lectionary-appointed scriptural lessons.

The method of homily preparation taught in *Fulfilled in Your Hearing* could have been a godsend to the priest who had no idea of how to go about the kind of preaching the council expected him to do, but it is not otherwise innovative enough to require summary here. An appropriate closing to this account of the difference the liturgical movement has made in Roman Catholic preaching, however, is the sense of the joy and privilege of preaching with which the booklet ends:

> We too stand in sacred space, aware of our personal inadequacy, yet willing to share how the scriptural story has become integrated into our thoughts and actions while we walked among those who turn their faces toward us. The words we speak are human words describing how God's action has become apparent to us this week. Is it any wonder then that excitement and tension fill us in the moments before we preach? With a final deep breath may we also breathe in the Spirit of God who will animate our human words with divine power (42).[26]

THE ANGLICAN/EPISCOPAL EXPERIENCE

Among Western churches not in obedience to the pope, the Anglican Communion is unique in that it has "never ceased to be a *liturgical* church." This is to say that "it finds its nexus of unity, its spiritual regimen, its tradition and way of life in the Book of Common Prayer."[27] Moreover, Anglicanism's sense of continuity with the undivided early church had been strengthened for many by the nineteenth-century Catholic revival known as the Oxford or Tractarian movement.[28] That movement, however, had the effect of polarizing the communion into those who identified primarily with either its Catholic or its Protestant heritage. While all Anglican worship was liturgical, and the majority of parishes had an early celebration of the Eucharist without music or sermon, the main service on most Sundays tended in "Low Church" parishes to be choral Morning Prayer with sermon,[29] and in "High Churches" to be the Eucharist, celebrated as nearly as possible to the Roman Catholic manner described at the beginning of this chapter, with the exception that it was usually in English rather than Latin.

There had always been liturgical scholars in Anglicanism, and some of their efforts culminated in a 1928 attempt to revise the Church of England's Prayer Book and bring an end to the chaos into which Anglicanism's liturgical life had degenerated. While the necessary legislation passed the church's governing body, it failed to get through Parliament, which had to approve such major changes in the established church.[30] In the aftermath of that failure, two changes began slowly to occur. One was a reduction of tension between the High and Low Church, and the other was a growing appreciation for the Eucharist as the central act of Christian worship.

The attitude developing toward the Eucharist was given a rallying point in the concept of the "parish communion" publicized in a 1937 book edited by A. G. Hebert.[31] Gabriel Hebert, a monk of the Society of the Sacred Mission at Kelham, had already translated the great study by the Swedish Lutheran archbishop Yngve Brilioth, *Eucharistic Faith and Practice: Evangelical and Catholic.*[32] He had also established himself as a liturgical theologian in *The Liturgy and Society: The Function of the Church in the Modern World,*[33] an effort to consider the continental liturgical movement's implications for the Church of England and, indeed, for modern Europe.

The parish communion, which had originated in the parish of Temple Balsall in rural Warwickshire in 1913, was a manner of celebrating the Eucharist so that its status as the central act of Christian worship would be obvious and honored. It was held around nine o'clock on Sunday morning and was designed to be as participatory as possible. Often it was followed by a parish breakfast, a sort of modern agape meal in which members of the parish could become better acquainted and could interact as fellow members of the body of Christ. Often there was an offertory procession in which the elements were brought to the altar from the back of the church, where each person intending to receive had placed a communion bread in the ciborium when entering.

In other words, the parish communion in the Church of England exemplified most of the liturgical movement's ideals. And, as Horton Davies says, "The parish communion has, in subsequent years, become almost the normative celebration of the eucharist in the Church of England."[34] The practice quickly spread from England to other parts of the Anglican Communion, including the Episcopal Church in the United States.

Father Hebert came to devote more of his energy to biblical theology and less to liturgics, another of many instances when the two movements cross-fertilized each other. Meanwhile, Anglican preaching got a new lease on life from the parish communion, at which priests felt it necessary to teach about the liturgy, especially the seasons of the church year, and about the biblical lections that were read to proclaim the mighty acts of God on which the calendar was based. Thus it is not surprising that one of the most important representatives of the biblical theology movement in England, Reginald H. Fuller, should write a book called *What Is Liturgical Preaching?*[35] (For a later version of Fuller's thought, **see Vol. 2, pp. 553-67.**)

Although scriptural passages read at their services had always been those appointed in the lectionary, Anglican clergy had never been as likely to preach on one of these "propers" as Lutheran pastors were to preach from the "pericopes." Further, as Brilioth has pointed out, after Tillotson, "the Anglican sermon to a disheartening extent became an oral essay on a religious or ethical subject."[36] The result was that, in spite of the occasional great preachers who were exceptions to the rule, Anglican preaching stood in real need of being rescued by the liturgical movement.

Fuller explained that the purpose of the sermon was not merely to explain obscure passages in the Bible, nor to relate them to the lives of modern congregations, nor to be analogous to "the type of public speaking which takes place at the annual festal gathering of a society or club."[37] Neither is it the sort of preaching to non-Christians that the New Testament *kerygma* was, nor the kind of instruction in doctrine and ethics that *didache* was. Rather, it should be *paraklesis*: "a renewal and deepening of the apprehension of the *kerygma* in the already converted."[38] Close to Skudlarek's saying that it should tell us why we should lift up our hearts is Fuller's understanding of the purpose of the sermon:

> to extract from the scripture readings the essential core and content of the gospel, to penetrate behind the day's pericope to the proclamation of the central act of God in Christ which it contains, in order that the central act of God can be made the material for recital in the prayer of thanksgiving.[39]

As the parish communion became the norm in Anglicanism, this sort of preaching accompanied it and has been the basic form of preaching in the communion ever since.

THE LITURGICAL MOVEMENT AND NONLITURGICAL CHURCHES

In the subtitle for the fifth volume of his history of *Worship and Theology in England,* Horton Davies refers to the twentieth as the "ecumenical century." Nowhere is that more obvious than in attitudes toward Christian worship. As Davies said:

> What is fascinating about (the liturgical) movement is that it has enabled Protestant churches to recover in part the Catholic liturgical heritage, while the Catholics seem to have appropriated the Protestant valuation of preaching, of shared worship in the vernacular tongue, and the importance of the laity as the people of God.[40]

These trends in England are traced only to 1965, the year the Davies volume was published.[41] James F. White, however, sees Catholic and Protestant worship traditions growing even closer in the years after Vatican II (1962–65). He says:

> If the postwar period was a time of Protestant ideas coming to the forefront in Roman Catholic thinking, the post–Vatican II era has been a time of Roman Catholic ideas shaping Protestant worship. Protestants have now returned the compliment by borrowing much that is new in Roman Catholic worship. Indeed, new service books from Roman Catholic, Methodist, Lutheran, Reformed, and Anglican traditions seem to be similar recensions of a single text.[42]

The degree of accord that has been achieved may be seen in the *Baptism, Eucharist, and Ministry* document of the Faith and Order Commission of the World Council of Churches, which was completed in January 1982 at Lima, Peru. While the response to this document has not been without dissension, it has, nevertheless, been adequately positive to indicate the high degree of agreement achieved in the three areas of theology indicated by its title, areas in which sharp polemics had raged since the Reformation.[43]

The changes that have occurred in the worship of the Free Churches of Great Britain parallel those in American Protestant churches. As listed by Davies, changes for England have included the following:

1. A loss of prejudice against set forms of worship and, in some places a welcoming of liturgical forms.
2. The increasing use of the seasons and feasts of the Christian year.
3. A diminishing antipathy to the recitation of creeds in worship.[44]
4. A greatly enhanced appreciation of the gospel sacraments of Baptism and the Eucharist.
5. The improvement of the solemnity of ordination services.
6. A better balance between Word and sacrament.[45]

Of these, those that affect preaching the most deeply are concerned with greater acceptance of the Christian year and better balance between Word and sacrament. Wider use of the lectionary is implicit to the acceptance of the liturgical calendar. How widespread that has become may be seen in a popular series of homiletical preparation aids that list in parallel columns the passages to be read on a given Sunday or holy day according to the usage of a number of churches. These include the Lutheran, Roman Catholic, Episcopal, Presbyterian/United Church of Christ/Christian, and United Methodist/COCU lectionaries. To these can be added *The Common Lectionary,* which was drawn up by the North American Committee on a Common Lectionary. All of these are three-year reading cycles that have a high incidence of agreement on the second lessons and Gospels appointed for particular days, but show greater variation in the readings from the Hebrew Scriptures.

A result of the mainline Protestant churches' greater openness to preaching from the lectionary, observing the Christian year, and achieving a better balance between Word and sacrament, has been that the homilies preached by clergy from the different faith communities show the same sort of convergence displayed by the liturgies in their new service books. Therefore, the liturgical movement, combined as it has been with the biblical theology and ecumenical movements, has been a major change agent in twentieth-century preaching.

FOR FURTHER READING

Fulfilled in Your Hearing: The Homily in the Sunday Assembly. Bishop's Committee on Priestly Life and Ministry of the United States Conference of Catholic Bishops. Washington: United States Conference of Catholic Bishops, 1982.

Fuller, Reginald H. *What Is Liturgical Preaching?* Studies in Worship and Ministry. London: SCM, 1957.

How Firm a Foundation: Leaders of the Liturgical Movement. Compiled and introduction by Robert L. Tuzik. Chicago: Liturgy Training Publications, Archdiocese of Chicago, 1990.

The Parish Communion. Edited by A. G. Hebert. London: SPCK, 1937.

Skudlarek, William. *The Word in Worship: Preaching in a Liturgical Context.* Abingdon Preacher's Library. Nashville: Abingdon, 1981.

White, James F. *Protestant Worship: Traditions in Transition.* Louisville: Westminster John Knox, 1989.

Notes

1. Preaching theory had been agreed upon among these churches for some time.

2. The involvement of the Roman Catholic Church in the ecumenical movement did open it to both the biblical theology movement and, as will be seen below, the influence of Protestant homiletics.

3. At a Solemn Mass, a deacon and a subdeacon assisted the officiating priest.

4. A concise history of the continental Roman Catholic phase of the liturgical movement appears in Horton Davies, *The Ecumenical Century, 1900–1965,* vol. 5 of *Worship and Theology in England* (Princeton: Princeton University Press, 1970), 5:13-49. The contribution of individuals is detailed in *How Firm a Foundation: Leaders of the Liturgical Movement,* comp. and intro. Robert L. Tuzik (Chicago: Liturgy Training Publications, Archdiocese of Chicago, 1990). This latter volume is ecumenical, includes Americans as well as Europeans, and traces the movement down to recent times, treating "the dead and the elderly, though a few in their 60s" at the time of writing. See also Louis Bouyer, *Liturgical Piety,* Liturgical Studies (Notre Dame: University of Notre Dame Press, 1955), and the article on "The History of the Liturgical Renewal," by Massey H. Shepherd Jr., in the volume he edited for the Associated Parishes, *The Liturgical Renewal of the Church* (New York: Oxford University Press, 1960), 21-52.

5. The revival of Gregorian chant was greatly aided by a *motu proprio,* published by Pope Pius X in 1903 on music and liturgy.

6. Michael Kwatera, "Pius Parsch, Evangelist of the Liturgy," in Tuzik, *How Firm a Foundation,* 30.

7. *Sermons on the Liturgy for Sundays and Feasts,* trans. Philip T. Weller (Milwaukee: Bruce, 1953), and *The Church's Year of Grace,* trans. William G. Heidt (Collegeville, Minn.: Liturgical Press, 1953–59).

8. Quoted in Kwatera, "Pius Parsch, Evangelist of the Liturgy," 34.

9. Regina Kuehn, "Romano Guardini," in Tuzik, *How Firm a Foundation,* 40.

10. Ibid.

11. Casel wrote two doctoral dissertations, one on the eucharistic theology of Justin Martyr, and the other on mysticism and Greek philosophy.

12. Bouyer, *Liturgical Piety,* 87. Bouyer, however, goes on to say that Casel could have questioned the findings of the History of Religions School far more radically than he did.

13. "The whole work of redemption."

14. "Effective sign."

15. "On the basis of the action performed." Ernest B. Koenker, *The Liturgical Renaissance in the Roman Catholic Church* (Chicago: University of Chicago Press, 1954), 107, quoted in Shepherd, *The Liturgical Renewal of the Church,* 31-34.

16. *Decree on the Ministry and Life of Priests,* Presbyterorum Ordinis, *Promulgated by His Holiness, Pope Paul VI on December 7, 1965,* chapter 2, section 1, paragraph 4, http://www.microbookstudio.com/secondv.htm.

17. Robert Grant and David Tracy, *A Short History of the Interpretation of the Bible,* 2nd ed., rev. and enl. (Philadelphia: Fortress, 1984), 119-25.

18. *The Renewal of Preaching: Theory and Practice,* ed. Karl Rahner, Concilium:

Theology in the Age of Renewal, vol. 33 (New York and Glen Rock, N.J., 1968).

19. Ibid., 23. This article is by Rahner himself and is titled "Demythologization and the Sermon," but the words quoted above are what he means by the title.

20. An excellent example is *The Word in Worship: Preaching in a Liturgical Context,* Abingdon Preacher's Library (Nashville: Abingdon, 1981) written by a Benedictine, William Skudlarek, for an ecumenical series of volumes on preaching. My own *Elements of Homiletic: A Method for Preparing to Preach* (New York: Pueblo, 1982), was commissioned by a Roman Catholic publisher to serve that purpose.

21. *Fulfilled in Your Hearing: The Homily in the Sunday Assembly,* Bishop's Committee on Priestly Life and Ministry of the United States Conference of Catholic Bishops (Washington: United States Conference of Catholic Bishops, 1982). The principal writer was the author of the book listed in the previous note, William Skudlarek, O.S.B. The team included such capable homileticians as David Buttrick and Fred Baumer, C.P.P.S., in addition to members of the hierarchy. The priestly sociologist and novelist Andrew Greeley was a consultant to the project. (Hereafter, parenthetical references in text are to page numbers in this document.)

22. Ibid., 18. In the text there is an extensive footnote commenting on this passage.

23. Skudlarek, *The Word in Worship,* 70.

24. Ibid., 71.

25. The "mighty acts" of God.

26. That the kingdom has no more fully come in the Roman church than any other, however, is suggested by Keith F. Pecklers in *The Unread Vision: The Liturgical Movement in the United States of America: 1926–55* (Collegeville, Minn.: Liturgical Press, 1998). He says: "We are in the midst of a liturgical malaise. Liturgical presiding, preaching, and music are in need of help" (p. 285).

27. Davies, *Worship and Theology in England,* 5:38. Davies gives a convenient summary of the history of the liturgical movement within Anglicanism on pp. 38-44, although he wrote before the Prayer Book revisions made by virtually every province of the communion had appeared. See also Shepherd, "The History of the Liturgical Renewal," 45-50. For the American branch of the Anglican Communion, the Episcopal Church, see Urban T. Holmes, "Education for Liturgy: An Unfinished Symphony in Four Movements," in *Worship Points the Way: Celebration of the Life and Work of Massey H. Shepherd, Jr.,* ed. Malcolm C. Burson (New York: Seabury, 1981), 116-41. For the importance of the Book of Common Prayer for all Anglican understandings of ministry, see my essay "Anglican Pastoral Tradition," in *The Study of Anglicanism,* ed. Stephen Sykes, John Booty, and Jonathan Knight, rev. ed. (London: SPCK; Minneapolis: Fortress, 1998), 378-91.

28. See above, chapter 22, 601-8.

29. Prayer Book rubrics call for a sermon with the Eucharist but do not do so for Morning Prayer.

30. For an account of this process, see Davies, *Worship and Theology in England,* 5:284-306.

31. *The Parish Communion,* ed. A. G. Hebert (London: SPCK, 1937).

32. Yngve Brilioth, *Eucharistic Faith and Practice: Evangelical and Catholic,* trans. A. G. Hebert (London: SPCK, 1930).

33. A. G. Hebert, *The Liturgy and Society: The Function of the Church in the Modern World* (London: Faber & Faber, 1936).

34. Davies, *Worship and Theology in England,* 5:321.

35. Reginald H. Fuller, *What Is Liturgical Preaching?,* Studies in Worship and Ministry (London: SCM, 1957). By the time the book was published, Fuller had already joined the faculty of Seabury-Western Theological Seminary in Evanston, Illinois. As another incidence of the overlap of the biblical theology and liturgical movements, see Theodore O. Wedel, *The Pulpit Rediscovers Theology* (Greenwich, Conn.: Seabury, 1956), 128-58.

36. Yngve Brilioth, *A Brief History of Preaching,* trans. Karl E. Mattson (Philadelphia: Fortress, 1965), 179.

37. Fuller, *What Is Liturgical Preaching?,* 17.

38. Ibid., 22.

39. Ibid.

40. Davies, *Worship and Theology in England,* 5:7.

41. Davies has since written a sixth volume to *Worship and Theology,* entitled *Crisis and Creativity, 1965-Present* (Grand Rapids, Mich.: Eerdmans, 1996), but that is primarily concerned with developments in baptism and the Eucharist and says very little about changes in preaching in the generation covered.

42. James F. White, *Protestant Worship: Traditions in Transition* (Louisville: Westminster John Knox, 1989), 34. White himself is not in favor of too much assimilation of Protestant worship to Catholic forms, however, saying: "If the convergence becomes too prominent, we must ask whether some of the richness of the variety of Protestant worship will suffer. *The richness of Protestant worship consists in its diversity and in its consequent ability to serve a wide variety of people*" (ibid., 212).

43. See *Baptism, Eucharist, and Ministry, 1982–1990: Report on the Process and Responses,* Faith and Order Paper, no. 149 (Geneva: WCC Publications, 1990).

44. Davies did not number this as a separate trend, but he did devote a page to discussing the matter. *Worship and Theology in England,* 5:391-92.

45. These are discussed in ibid., 5:387-97. On the last point of the relation of Word and sacrament, it is interesting to note that the intimate connection between them was maintained by Karl Barth (*Homiletics,* transl. Geoffrey W. Bromiley and Donald E. Daniels, foreword David Buttrick [Louisville: Westminster John Knox, 1991], 56-63).

CHAPTER 28

A HOMILETICAL EPIPHANY

THE EMERGENCE OF AFRICAN AMERICAN PREACHING IN MAJORITY CONSCIOUSNESS

"THE PREACHER KING"

Among the many streams of tradition that converged to form late-twentieth-century understanding of the nature of preaching, none showed the proclaimed word's potentialities to move people and change society as did the classical homiletic of the African American church. As much as its pulpit had done to sustain its people through slavery, reconstruction, and segregation, it was hardly known to the rest of American society until the civil rights movement got under way in the late-1950s. Then, however, it burst on the national scene with dazzling brightness.

The brilliance of that impression is the product of two factors: the homiletical ability of the Reverend Dr. Martin Luther King Jr., and the coverage the news media, especially television, gave to the campaigns in which he was involved. The events were startling enough to be given full coverage, to be served up to white Americans in their living rooms on a daily basis. And always at the center was a man who could articulate the issues in such a way that they had to be taken seriously. Whether the viewers were inspired, reluctantly persuaded, or stirred to rage by him, he and his message could not be ignored.

This is not to say that Martin Luther King was the only civil rights leader, that he was the only Christian minister among the leaders, or even that he was the best preacher of the lot. Working with him were such gifted proclaimers of the word as Ralph Abernathy, Andrew Young, Wyatt Tee Walker, C. T. Vivian, Jesse Jackson, Bernard Lee, Walter Fauntroy, James Lawson, Charles Sherrod, Bernard Lafayette, John Lewis, and James Bevel. Local clergy were involved in every campaign, and other civil rights organizations, some with their own clergy, were engaged in additional campaigns. But the TV cameras focused on King, and, therefore, it was he who showed the rest of the country a homiletical tradition of startling power.

Ironically, King's own preaching at the beginning of his ministry was not in the tradition of the black church, but more akin to that of liberal white clergy at the time. He grew up in the classic tradition and saw it modeled by his father at Ebenezer Baptist Church in Atlanta's "Sweet Auburn" district, and by William Holmes Borders at the nearby Wheat Street Church. Although he and his friends studied the techniques of preachers in the neighborhood, when he went to Morehouse College he undertook the formal study of rhetoric and began to be influenced by the liberal preaching of the college president, Benjamin Mays.[1]

That liberal influence was intensified when King enrolled in the predominantly white Crozer Seminary in Chester, Pennsylvania. And it achieved its ultimate impact when he focused his Ph.D. on the personalist theology of Edgar S. Brightman at Boston University.[2] Thus he absorbed the pulpit tradition of such nineteenth-century figures as Henry Ward Beecher and Phillips Brooks, and that of contemporary luminaries like Harry Emerson Fosdick, George A. Buttrick, and Halford E. Luccock. At the same time, however, he studied the examples of great African American preachers like Gardner Taylor, who could "generate passion while retaining his composure," and J. Pius Barbour, who could combine "theological erudition with old-time religion."[3]

When King arrived in Montgomery, Alabama, to begin his first pastorate in September of 1954, his new congregation included the most distinguished people of his race in the city, and they expected a dignity in their worship that was commensurate with their achievement.[4] Thus the previous January when he preached his trial sermon auditioning for a call to the church, he used a sermon called "The Three Dimensions of a Complete Life," which he had preached in the Boston area several times.[5] It was an allegorical interpretation of Revelation 21:16, which gives the dimensions of the New Jerusalem. He treats a healthy self-respect as the length, love of neighbor as the breadth, and love of God as the height.[6] According to the historians of the church at its centennial, King at some time during his tenure there said: "I revolt against the emotionalism of Negro[7] religion, the shouting and the stamping. I don't understand it and it embarrasses me."[8] At the beginning of his ministry, he and his parishioners apparently saw eye to eye.

This is not to say, however, that he had forgotten his roots. A sermon he preached in Detroit the month after his Dexter trial sermon was much more the combination of traditional homiletic with learned content that was to be the hallmark of his later preaching. More important, his reflexes were ready for the supreme challenge when it came. The occasion of its coming was Rosa Parks's now legendary refusal to give up her bus seat to a white man. Clergy and other leaders in the African American community quickly called a boycott of buses and organized the Montgomery Improvement Association, naming King as their president. He was to speak, virtually without preparation, on the evening after her trial at a mass meeting called at Holt Street Baptist Church.

At that meeting on December 5, 1955, Martin Luther King Jr. discovered his calling, his principle, and his method. The calling was to lead the civil rights movement, his principle was to combine militancy with nonviolence, and his method was to use oratory that combined intellectual content with the power of classical African American preaching. As Stephen Oates said:

> It was as though he had been preparing for that speech all his life . . . He sat down, trembling from his effort. Across the church, people were yelling and waving their arms, clapping and singing as he had never seen them do before. Imagine Martin Luther King, a twenty-six-year-old scholar, making people rock with such emotion.[9]

The bus boycott ended triumphantly a year later when the Supreme Court struck down the laws that segregated public transportation in Alabama. Although Dr. King continued as pastor at Dexter, his presence was continually being sought elsewhere to help in the struggle. Thus King organized the Southern Christian Leadership Conference in August of 1957. Eventually, however, the conflict between being pastor of a local church and heading a movement that covered the Deep South and had international involvement became too great. At the end of January 1960, he resigned from Dexter and moved to Atlanta, where he would receive most of his income from being his father's assistant pastor at Ebenezer and devote most of his time and energy to being president of SCLC.

The story of what was accomplished has been told too often to need recounting here. Besides, at first glance, much of it would appear to have little to do with the history of preaching. Yet overprecise distinctions would be hard to maintain. Lischer has shown that from 1960 on, King practiced three basic forms of public address:[10] he preached often at Ebenezer and other African American churches, he addressed mass meetings held nightly during campaigns, and he occupied distinguished public rostra in the white world.[11]

Yet there was not as much difference among these genres of speech as might be expected. The mass meetings were held in churches, hymns were sung and prayers offered, and ordained men who often based what they said on a biblical text gave most of the speeches.[12] And, while the public addresses argued from civic rather than biblical texts and were intended to appeal to a wider audience, even in them appear many of the preacher's mannerisms and techniques. A small example of this is his "adroitly juxtaposing quotations from the scriptures with the lyrics of patriotic anthems" in the most famous of such occasions, his "I Have a Dream" speech at the March on Washington of August 28, 1963.[13] Hence the key to all of King's rhetorical activity is an understanding of his preaching.

To understand the preaching of the mature King, it is necessary to look at the sermons he preached during the eight and a quarter years he served as his father's assistant at Ebenezer Baptist Church in Atlanta. While he did not preach there every Sunday during that period, he did so often enough to reveal a clear pattern to his sermons:[14]

> The bent of King's gospel follows the contours of the Christian story of redemption. It begins with the human condition, which is nothing other than the experience of one of life's many perplexities. The perplexity suggests a larger problem, the problem yields a sin, the sin opens onto a social concern (always related to race or war), the concern invites a generalization about "man" or "life," and the stage is set for the next phase of the message.[15]

By "sin," King means a human effort to accomplish what only God can do. What starts out as the presentation of a problem always ends up as a cry for redemption. Along the way, however, the universal problem is particularized in ways that it is experienced by the African American community, both in terms of what has been done to them (the "triple ghetto" of poverty, race, and misery) and also in the sinful responses these crimes evoke in their victims.

The only answer to any of these problems is the God of the Bible: the Creator of the world, the liberator of Israel, and the Father of Jesus Christ. "It goes without arguing that God wills to liberate Negroes from captivity in America because that is the kind of God we have."[16] This God of love grants deliverance through Jesus Christ, the caring one who can heal all personal wounds and overcome all social problems, the one who can not only forgive sins but also change sinners. King's hearers could be transformed into people who love their enemies, and their love would be the means God used to transform those who persecuted them.

Thus the vision of a glorious future kingdom of God that he held up to his congregation was not of a heavenly home but of a transformed society. And the agent of that deliverance was not the Christian church in general—he had seen too many failures of white Christians—but the African American church, with its willingness to suffer in order to bring about reconciliation.

King's Ebenezer sermons always ended with a celebration of the glory and goodness of God, the ecstatic climax of African American preaching, but this element was consistently eliminated when he preached to a white congregation and from printed editions of his sermons. Also at Ebenezer, he always ended with that staple of Southern evangelical churches, an altar call. The "doors of the church" were opened, but, more important, the possibility of a personal relation with Jesus was extended. The way to achieve that was through repentance and conversion. And then, "the services at Ebenezer often ended on a chaotic note when the invitation would degenerate into general announcements."[17] This, too, was standard in thousands of churches, black and white.

Dr. King seldom had time to prepare his Ebenezer sermons in detail, and his ability to virtually extemporize homiletical masterpieces depended on his having available in his memory a variety of sermon titles and outlines, and a collection of set pieces that he could interject wherever they were needed. This is not to say that his sermons were simply rehashes of his own and other preachers' previous efforts, but rather that having available such a useful collection of frameworks left him free to devote his creativity to the immediate situation and its needs.

The titles and outlines generally went together, and he had been using most of them since at least his first year at Dexter; many had been borrowed or adapted from other preachers. In this use of borrowed materials, King was like all preachers of his time:

> A survey of the sermon volumes of the 1950s reveals a pronounced lack of originality among the twentieth-century princes of the pulpit not only in the canned illustrations that circulated among them but also with regard to their themes.[18]

What is impressive, however, is not his sources but his use of them. They were merely hooks on which he was able to hang his analysis of the racial situation in the country. The real content of his sermons was uniquely his. This can be seen especially by comparing the recordings made over a period of years of sermons involving the same title and outline, such as the "Three Dimensions" sermon he used for his audition at Dexter. These are versions of the same thing only in the most limited sense. In terms of real content and effect, each version is unique, and thus entitled to respect from even the perspective of the Romantic preoccupation with originality. (For a version of this sermon, **see Vol. 2, pp. 568-79.**)

More important for his oratory's effectiveness than King's reused titles and outlines was what Lischer calls his "set pieces"—the "enormous disassembled inventory of rhetorical parts ready for immediate installation."[19] The more usual rhetorical term is "commonplaces," a literal translation of both the Latin *loci communes* and the Greek *koinoi topoi.* This term is defined as "a general argument, observation, or description a speaker could memorize for use on a number of possible occasions."[20] King's quiver of commonplaces embraced a range of complexity, the simplest form of which was the epithet, a brief metaphoric expression such as "the iron feet of oppression."

> In addition to the Homeric epithet, King developed a repertoire of borrowed formulas that included assemblages of poems, paragraphs drawn from popular white preachers, gospel climax formulas absorbed in the black church, and much longer poetic-like pieces of his own composition.[21]

"Commonplace" is a basket term, embracing the two meanings "of the things that people generally consider persuasive, and of methods that have persuasive effects."[22] King's collection of set pieces were sermonic elements that he knew from experience would elicit a response, would stir up the sort of emotion that would cause people to identify with the cause and enlist in its program. And his whole purpose in preaching was to achieve that result.

It would be possible to think of the stylistic elements in King's sermons as a collection of techniques he had amassed in general that could be applied to the specific goal of participation in the movement. In doing so, however, one would miss the strategic dimension of all King did in his preaching. It was all motivated behavior, intended to accomplish the particular task and to do so in the most efficient way possible. He recognized with Cicero that the purposes of the orator are to teach, to please, and to move—and that teaching and pleasing are done in order to move, to enlist one's hearers in the cause.

A basic goal was to enable all to realize that their particular campaigns were not small struggles on local issues, but were instead key episodes in the eternal struggle between right and wrong. These were not things "done in a corner," but events of cosmic significance. A key element of King's rhetorical strategy was to indicate by the elevated tone of his discourse the importance of what was at stake in the struggle.

A case in point is the use of epithets noted above. Many of these involve metaphors: gradualism is a drug, despair a "dark and desolate valley," pessimism a chamber, etc. In these epithets, "King often combines an archetypal image, for example, a *valley* or a *sunlit path,* with an equally universal value, such as *despair* or *peace.*"[23] In so doing he indicates the universal scope of the issues at stake in the local struggle. "King framed what was an exceedingly mean-spirited conflict between protesters and state troopers in the abstract language of light and darkness, justice and injustice."[24] At the same time, by his elevated diction, King showed that he—and, by implication, all members of his race—were not servile, but persons of intelligence and ability, deserving of a place in society as good as their oppressors'. His diction was so elevated that many passages of his sermons could be set down in stanza form and read as poetry.

The elevation of his style involves use of all the standard figures of sound. One encounters alliteration and assonance. Anaphora, which begins successive clauses with the same group of words, is balanced by its opposite, epistrophe, where the repetition occurs at the end. Key to these figures is repetition, which is also seen in such forms of amplification as copiousness (saying the same thing in a number of different ways) and intensification (statements in an ascending order of gravity). His strategy of elevation also involves sacred or heroic association, at times in explicit and logical ways, but at others through unexpected parataxis.

These are devices of sound, but they represent only a fraction of King's ability to pattern sound to achieve his effect. In addition to these, for instance, he was able to establish rhythm in his sermons by the way he spoke them. This effect was heightened by his use of anaphora and other repetitive figures. He would often rap out the cadence on the side of the pulpit or its Bible. He would reinforce the effect by variations in the stress and pitch he gave to syllables. Then he would emphasize the pattern by altering it in places with a syncopated stammer or a run-on effect, as when the third time around he said "I have a dream" at the close of one sentence rather than the beginning of the next.

Much of the way he was able to pattern sound was a function of the total control he had of his magnificent voice:

> The gradual ascendancy of his pitch from a low growl at the beginning of the sermon to a piercing shout at the upper range of his high baritone, the predictable rhythm of the rise and fall of his voice, and the relentless increase in the *rate* of his speech—all contribute to the melodiousness, the songlike quality, of his voice.[25]

Among the musical techniques that he, in common with other African American preachers, employed vocally were blue notes, glissando, grace notes, falloffs, and tremolo. The range of his power of expression was extraordinary.

Blend all of this with the antiphony of the call-and-response interaction between a black preacher and his congregation, and the effect was hypnotic and ecstatic, especially when the sermon rose to the final climax in which the goodness and glory of God were celebrated. There is no doubt that King was a rhetorical and vocal artist who could carry out a strategy for enlistment. In the end, however, all the technique was just a vehicle for his message. More than his rhetorical ability but reinforced by it, what really allowed him to demonstrate to the wider public the power of classical African American preaching was a combination of two factors: the axiomatic nature of his appeal's moral principles and his unhesitating, undeviating, fearless commitment to carrying them out.

TEACHERS TO THE NATION: AFRICAN AMERICAN BEECHER LECTURERS

While the television coverage of Martin Luther King Jr.'s leadership of the civil rights movement revealed to the nation at large the richness of the African American church's classical homiletical tradition, it was through different channels that those who practiced other preaching methods were instructed in how to acquire for themselves something of the black pulpit's power. One of these channels—and, even more, an indication of the extent to which such instruction was sought—were the invitations extended to African American clergy to deliver the Lyman Beecher Lectures at Yale, the most distinguished forum in the country for the imparting of homiletical wisdom. Eight sets of lectures have been delivered by African Americans, all given in the second half of the twentieth century.[26]

James H. Robinson

The first series stands apart from the others in a number of ways. Given in 1955, it preceded the next set by almost twenty years. And it was delivered a few months before the bus boycott in Montgomery, and so was prior to when the civil rights movement seized the general public's attention. Further, the lecturer, the Reverend Dr. James H. Robinson, was a minister of the Presbyterian Church, rather than one of the historic African American denominations, and had trained at Union seminary. Although possibly the youngest person ever to give the lectures, he was already a world-famous speaker who often had been invited to address prestigious white groups.

His parish, the Church of the Master on the western edge of Harlem, was large enough to justify having assistant pastors and a number of other professional staff who administered a number of social and pastoral programs. The church was located in a changing neighborhood in which the black population had increased from 25 to 65 percent in a decade. But the congregation still drew faculty and students from not only Union but Columbia and City College of New York as well. Reinhold Niebuhr wrote the preface to his published lectures.

Shortly after giving the lectures, Dr. Robinson went on to found and become executive director of Operation Crossroads Africa, a program that arranged for a number of students to spend the summer in Africa after their graduation from prep school.[27]

Thus for all his concern about race relations, Robinson was not really a representative of the classical African American homiletical tradition. Further, his lectures deal more with what to preach about than how to do it.[28] The first is devoted to the loss of status in the culture that clergy had experienced for some time, even though at the time of writing, during the Eisenhower administration, there was at least a superficial "revival of religion." The next has to do with the preacher's need for a deep spiritual life; for a relation with God, laypeople, and fellow clergy, with whom could occur a "fellowship of confession." The third is a passionate call for urban churches to remain in changing neighborhoods and minister to the people around them. Then follows an analysis of the deteriorating condition of Western civilization and the church in the post–World War II world, with challenges to Christianity from Communism and from other religions, especially in Asia and Africa, where the integrity of the gospel had been compromised by its association with Western exploitation. After that there is a prophetic insistence on the inseparability of religion and politics. The book ends with lectures on the gospel's inclusiveness and the grounds for hope given by faith in situations that encourage despair. An excellent set of lectures by a very impressive man, but not one that extends to others the resources of the classical African-American homiletic.

Henry H. Mitchell

The next African American Beecher lecturer attended both the same university and the same seminary as Robinson, but remained closer to the black church. Indeed, he was one of the first to pay serious homiletical attention to classical African American preaching, and it was the publication of his *Black Preaching* in 1970 that led to his invitation to give the lectures in 1974.[29] Published as *The Recovery of Preaching*,[30] his lectures had the purpose of assisting the white pulpit to preach with the power of the black. Sermons in the classical African American tradition "have had great impact and given great support and guidance in both communal and individual life."

> By way of contrast it may at least be argued that this has not been true of White middle-class Protestant preaching, which has been carried on in an academically oriented counterculture to the folk idiom of America's majority.[31]

The reason Mitchell sees for white preaching's failure, as implied in the quotation, is that it has been directed too exclusively to the intellect instead of to the whole person. In this vein, he begins his lectures with a sermon from Ezekiel 3:15 on the way the prophet sat where the people sat before he began preaching to them. Drawing on depth psychology and the history of religions, he says that the whole person includes what Jung inaccurately calls the "unconscious," and Eliade more accurately describes as "transconsciousness."

In order to reach the depth dimension of human persons, an artistic homiletic is necessary, one that makes use of stories and images: "vivid and realistic pictures or dramas of truth and symbol and of experience" (32). The goal is not achieved by art alone, however, since no one can communicate an experience that he or she has not had. The stories to be told are mainly from the Bible, and the preacher must combine information and imagination, first internalizing a story in order to make it meaningful to others. The meaning of these biblical stories is not separable from the stories themselves; rather, "Moses and David and Jeremiah and Jesus are their own content" (40).

At the same time, however, the sermons must relate to the congregation's deepest needs, corporately and individually. "The desperate need is for patterns of life-sustaining meaning, targeted to reach 'what's happening' and hurting *now*" (40). For this storytelling to be effective at the meaning level, the congregation has to be given time to experience each important point, and no point should be made that cannot be expressed in a story or word picture filled with graphic details.[32] The ability to supply those details is the fruit of a life devoted to searching them out.

Such preaching is not only proclamation, but celebration as well—both literal celebration and a symbolic and ritual expression of praise and joy. This type of celebration enhances the retention of the gospel and contributes to the way the congregation understands it and acts on it. This ecstasy also contributes to the hearer's personhood and identity by giving it free expression. The celebration also transforms a congregation into a community. Further, it can be recalled and drawn on as a spiritual resource. And, finally, it is an appropriate climax to a well-balanced sermon. Such celebration, then, is not just one of the conventions of African American preaching, it is an effective ingredient for all good preaching.

Celebration like this occurs only when a sermon is on a great theme. It must also minister effectively to deep-seated human needs, offering fulfillment to persons. In addition to having such seriousness of purpose and content, a sermon must be rhetorically effective to engender celebration. Specifically, it must have good timing and provide a medium for summing up and celebrating the theme. An ingredient of good timing, an appropriate emotional pace, is introducing new insights early rather than dragging them in at the last minute. And the celebration at the end should be of what the sermon is about: "the climactic utterance should be especially characterized by celebrative feelings matching the ideas" (64).[33]

Recognizing that something so emotionally powerful can be used manipulatively, Mitchell gives a list of safeguards to prevent that misuse, ending with the caution that "the preacher who would ask God to confer on his or her feeble utterance the charismatic gift of climactic celebration must diminish or hide self, and be possessed by the message and its Giver" (67). He then goes on to give the criteria for material to be used in the climax, noting the necessity for imagination and the preacher's deep involvement.

This ends the summary of the first four chapters of *The Recovery of Preaching,* the only ones given as Beecher lectures. The other chapters, however, presented as lectures elsewhere, also serve the intention to help white preachers achieve the homiletical power of their black colleagues. As Dr. Mitchell says, "The rest of this work is devoted to a kind of unpacking of the three preceding chapters."[34] The remaining chapters give practical instruction on effective biblical storytelling, preaching in the folk vocabulary of the congregation, and achieving dialogue through a cultural equivalent to call-and-response.

Like many good sermons, the book ends with a summary of all that has been said. Ministers from other racial or ethnic groups who wish to learn from African American colleagues how to make their sermons come alive could hardly find a better place to begin than with this book, written for the specific purpose of offering them such help.[35]

Gardner Taylor

The next African American Beecher lecturer was Dr. Gardner C. Taylor. Originally asked to be a colecturer with Mitchell,[36] Taylor was reinvited to deliver the series in 1976. In doing so he became the first lecturer who was pastor of a large congregation in a traditional black denomination. Concord Baptist Church in Brooklyn has a congregation of twelve thousand members. During the forty years of his pastorate, ten thousand have been added to the church rolls. Destroyed by fire in 1952, the church was rebuilt at a cost of $2 million before runaway inflation. Deeply involved in the life of its community, Concord has a fully accredited elementary school, a 121-bed hospital, a clothing exchange, and a credit union.

Although he has taught homiletics at Colgate Rochester, Harvard, and Union, Taylor's reputation is based mainly on his preaching to his own congregation. The effectiveness of that proclamation has been recognized in countless other ways as well, including his election as president of his denomination, the Progressive National Baptist Convention; presidency of the New York City Council of Churches; appearance on the National Radio Pulpit; and being selected by *Time* magazine as one of the top seven preachers in the country.[37]

Educated at Leland College and Oberlin Graduate School of Theology, Taylor is a master of the grand style of preaching in the African American tradition. Thus he was a homiletical model for many other preachers, including Martin Luther King Jr. Comparing them, Lischer deems Taylor to have been better than King both in the use of his voice and in his rhetoric. In comparing their capacity for vocal expression, Lischer cites many qualities they have in common, but goes on to say: "Taylor's high is purer, his low more richly resonant, and the mastery of his vocal instrument more complete than King's."[38]

In comparing the two rhetorically, he says:

> Taylor's allusions . . . are more organic to his sermons, his metaphors more original and intellectually satisfying, and his powers of biblical reportrayal far more vivid than young King's.[39]

High praise indeed!

In his lectures, Dr. Taylor is like Phillips Brooks in that he does not so much seek to instruct in the mechanics of homiletics as he does to provide a spiritual perspective on the preaching task. Accordingly, his first lecture deals with the presumptuousness of preaching and his second treats its foolishness. The third seems more likely to give practical advice, bearing as it does the title of "Building a Sermon."

It begins by recognizing that "the heart of the preacher's dilemma is how to trust God wholly and at the same time to prepare diligently."[40] Ideas for sermons come in many ways, with Bible study being the first. But ideas can come from anywhere, with the observation of nature being a good source. And,

> any preacher greatly deprives himself or herself who does not study the recognized masters of pulpit discourse, not to copy them but rather to see what has been the way in which they approached the scriptures, their craftsmanship, their feel for men's hearts.[41]

To preach well, human hearts must be studied, beginning with one's own. Such study will note not only "the sense of melancholy which possesses most of the ablest preachers"[42] but the sense of being visited by God as well. In this lecture there is much that every preacher needs to hear, but little that relates to what the rhetoricians call invention, disposition, and style.

The final lecture is called "Preaching the Whole Counsel of God" and deals with the duty of preaching to cover the full range of biblical teaching and all the needs of "people who are solitary-social animals."[43] Even here, however, one suspects that what must have been most valuable in this series, certainly to those present but to readers as well, is the sense of being in contact with a great soul who personifies a great tradition. Even in the lecture format, the conventions of the African American preaching genre shine through.[44] There is wonderfully imaginative retelling of the biblical narratives, there is involvement of the audience—at least in the range of human experience addressed, and there are even celebratory climaxes.

The only one of Mitchell's criteria for the classic tradition of African American preaching that Taylor's writing does not meet is that of "folk language." Or, if it does, it is a very special category, because, as Lischer said, Taylor belongs to the "grand" tradition. He uses an elevated diction that he attributes to home influence:

> I am thankful that I was born to parents who, though not highly educated by today's standards, had a natural feel for the essential music of the English language wedded to an intimate and emotional affection for the great transactions of the scriptures. Somehow, in the way they thought and spoke, what is African found a cordial meeting with what is Anglo-Saxon.[45]

His way of putting things can be imagined from this and other quotations from his writings, although the sustained beauty of his expression can only be seen in extended passages, especially from the sermons.[46] It is no wonder that so many sought to imitate him.

Kelly Miller Smith

The next African American Beecher lecturer not only set out to help the white pulpit achieve something of the black pulpit's power, but did so specifically in the area of social justice preaching. Kelly Miller Smith, the lecturer for 1982–83, had studied at Morehouse College and Howard University Divinity School. After an early pastorate in Vicksburg, he went to First Baptist Church, Capitol Hill, in Nashville. While in Nashville, he also served as assistant dean of the Divinity School of Vanderbilt University, where he lectured in church, ministry, and community. Having been a close associate of Martin Luther King Jr., Smith's lectures, published under the title of *Social Crisis Preaching,*[47] draw liberally upon King's preaching for illustration.

His four lectures, titled with homiletical alliteration, deal with the Purview, Perception, Perspective, and Proclamation and beyond of social crisis preaching.

> Under the caption of "Purview," the terrain was observed in order to see its composition. Questions were asked as to what and where the danger points are and what can be learned of the topography. (79)

Noting that a number of previous Beecher lecturers had been characterized as "prophets of social change," Smith states that there has been such preaching all through church history and that, indeed, all religion is concerned with the social problems people face. "The social relevance of Christianity is axiomatic" (8), growing as it does from the tradition of the Hebrew prophets and Jesus of Nazareth. The black church owes its existence to social crisis.

That is not to say, however, that preaching on social issues is always expected or welcome. Nor, on the other hand, does everyone think preaching is capable of effecting social change. To do so, its quality must be high, it must be courageous, and it must be "proclamation of *what God continues to say* to the present condition" (18). Through the impact of the ancient Word of God in preaching, "the oppressed become aware that they are not hapless orphans deserted on the doorsteps of destiny, but are sons and daughters of a caring God" (23).

In his lecture on Perception, which deals with how social crisis preaching is perceived both by the preacher and by the congregation, Smith defines such preaching as "the proclamation of that which is crucially relevant within the context of the Christian gospel in times of social upheaval and stress." As part of the definition, he goes on to say that such preaching "aims at setting corrective measures into motion" (33). To get his own perception straight, the preacher needs to ask: What social crisis? Recognizing that there is one, the preacher must recognize his or her own limitations of experience and theological orientation and deal honestly with the pressure of practical considerations. To overcome those limitations, the preacher should call on those who better understand the situation, study what is written on the issue, and become directly involved in working toward a solution.

Acquiring a more accurate perception of the congregation involves recognizing that "they are people who are not excited about the social issue that the preacher is going to present in sermon context. They are people with their own priorities" (41). The preacher must know what those priorities are, and what the people's needs are as well—which may not be the same thing. To avoid answering questions that no one is asking, the preacher has the task of showing the congregation how the crisis reflects their own needs as well as those of the people more directly involved. With that correct perception of the preacher and the congregation, the preacher can then see that one of the most effective things that can be done is to preach about the crisis. "The power inherent in that word conjoined with the perceptiveness, commitment, and faithfulness of the preacher who proclaims that word and the people who hear it, will bring results" (45).

For social crisis preaching to be done effectively, it must be seen in Perspective, it must take cognizance of the dimensions of history, the Bible, and the black experience. History shows that such preaching characterized the prophets of the Old Testament, the writers of the New Testament, the great Fathers of the early church, the Social Gospel movement, and, especially those who are victims of the crisis. The biblical perspective on social crisis preaching demands that it demonstrate the relationship between experience and exegesis, that between extrabiblical tradition and the Word of God in Scripture, and that between exegesis and proclamation. The perspective of the black experience recognizes that

> the Black church in America not only provides the care necessary for those wounded in the fray; it also provides the experience of liberation itself for an oppressed people. (73)

Coming as it does out of that experience, "the preaching of Dr. Martin Luther King, Jr. represents social crisis preaching at its best" (74).[48]

Smith's final lecture, on Proclamation, gives practical advice on social crisis sermons. He begins by saying that for the individual sermon on a social issue to be effective, it must not be an isolated event, but instead must be part of an ongoing effort to involve the congregation in social ministry. The sermon itself should be based on an idea "rooted in an expression of God's concern for some human condition" (82). In crafting the sermon, the preacher needs to pay careful attention to language to make sure that what is said is clear, that the emotional freight of words is not overlooked, that what is offered as the Word of God is no mere venting of the preacher's spleen, and that the power of language to move people is drawn upon positively. Even then, however, the words will "still fail to convey the total message which is in the heart of one committed minister" (85).

Like all good preaching, social crisis sermons will have focus and structure. Homiletical strategy will determine the kind of structure chosen. A "miniature inductive"[49] form will move a reluctant congregation "gently but positively onto the basic thesis of the sermon," but at times "the abruptly direct order may be chosen for its shock value." And an inductive structure may work best with a conservative congregation. There are outlines that are also especially appropriate for social crisis sermons, including the interrogative, the problem solving, and the Hegelian pattern of thesis, antithesis, and synthesis.[50]

Delivery may be from or without a manuscript, if proper safeguards are taken against the dangers of each method. The preacher's emotion should be controlled but obvious. Different preachers have different gifts, but variety in pitch and force is always appropriate, and diaphragmatic breathing, clarity of enunciation, and projection of the voice always help. Finally, the sermon must be consistent with the life of the preacher: "effective social crisis preaching requires life commitment to the cause of justice and liberation" (99). One hears in Smith the voice of experience in effective preaching on social issues.

James Forbes

If it is true that Gardner Taylor's Beecher lectures were a spiritual perspective on the preaching task, then the same description may be applied a fortiori to those of James Forbes in 1986.[51] Indeed, they constitute a homiletical pneumatology, since Forbes's thesis is that in order to preach effectively, one must have been anointed by the Holy Spirit. The son of a bishop in the United Holy Church of America, a Pentecostal denomination, Forbes was educated at Howard and Union Seminary. He found at Union, in the teaching of H. Pitney Van Dusen, Paul Tillich, and others, an openness to the work of the Spirit that allowed him to state his Pentecostal convictions in the language of academic theology at that time. After graduation, he served as assistant pastor at a large Southern Baptist church in Chapel Hill, North Carolina, and then went on to pastor churches of his own denomination in Wilmington and Roxboro, North Carolina, and in Richmond, Virginia. From Richmond he was called back to Union to teach preaching, which he continued to do until he succeeded William Sloane Coffin Jr. as senior minister at Riverside Church. He has been an extremely popular visiting preacher, lecturer, and workshop conductor all over the country.

Forbes sees much of the weakness of contemporary preaching to be attributable to a Holy Spirit shyness among many Christians. Since it is the Spirit who inspired the Bible at every stage of its origin and transmission, and it is the Spirit who guides both preachers and congregations today in their understanding of how its message applies to them, not to be aware of the Spirit's action is to miss a great deal of what is going on. And, as a result, "many of the biblical provisions for Holy Spirit empowerment often are left unrealized like unclaimed packages and unopened letters" (22).

For that power to be reclaimed, there must be preachers who have been anointed by the Holy Spirit in much the way that Jesus was. While the relation of Jesus to God was unique, there is also a sense in which the relation of anyone to God is unique. In calling for this anointing, Forbes is not suggesting that there is only one pattern for its bestowal; he is open ecumenically to all the ways the gift of the Spirit has been understood in church history. Nor does he wish to say that it has to come in an unvarying series of steps. He finds that Tillich's reference to dimensions of spiritual growth gives a more accurate sense of the way things happen.

The marks of the Spirit's anointing include, first, its wholeness in the sense that it covers every aspect of the anointed. Thus "the anointed person is *willing to witness* in word and deed to the lordship of Jesus and the kingdom of God" (48). Then, faithfulness makes one attentive to the Spirit's guidance. With the guidance comes power from on high. Therefore, "those who testify to the anointing of the Spirit will go forth in ministry fully convinced that their efforts will make a difference" (51).

With these marks of the anointed, a preacher should be able to raise the dead in the way that Ezekiel saw the Spirit giving life to dry bones.[52] Taking a physician's definition of *death* as the point at which "there is no longer any prospect of meaningful, powerful, human existence" (59), Forbes points to conditions in the lives of individuals and society that can only be called death. It is in such situations that the anointed preacher must prophesy, not knowing what to say but depending upon guidance. In such moments, the preacher is gripped by a fear of losing control, but love casts out fear. The preacher says what God says, but before giving that word, "God gives the prophet the sense of the despair of the people"—the death from which they are yearning to be raised (64).

Speaking from such an orientation, it is not surprising that when Forbes comes to writing a chapter titled "Sermon Preparation and Preaching," he does not give "how-to" instructions, but rather talks about waiting on the Spirit for the message one is to proclaim. That does not mean, however, that he thinks the anointed preacher can avoid the hard work of exegesis and the other preparation tasks. Rather, he tells what may be expected in that process: the guiding presence of the Spirit. And the same Spirit will be preparing the congregation to receive the message the Spirit gave the preacher.

Forbes's final chapter, "The Spiritual Formation of Anointed Preachers," is a homiletical tour de force. It is an interpretation of the sixteenth chapter of Mark, a traditional problem for exegetes. Most believe that Mark ended his Gospel with verse 8 of chapter 16, which has the women fleeing the empty tomb, saying nothing to anyone because of their fear. It is usually thought that a later redactor added verses 9-20 as a summary of the resurrection appearance stories in the other Gospels. These verses also state that believers will be able to speak in tongues, handle snakes, not be overcome by poison, and cure the sick. Forbes treats the blank space between verses 8 and 9 in modern translations as the hiatus in which the anointing of the disciples occurred and their fear of speaking was taken away. Then he interprets these abilities of believers as the effects of anointed preaching, the sort of results that one should be able to expect. It is a glorious vision of the difference preaching can make.

Samuel D. Proctor

The 1990 Beecher lectures, given by Samuel D. Proctor,[53] are like those of James H. Robinson in that they have more to do with the content than the method of preaching[54] and that little distinguishes them as representative of African American preaching. Born in Norfolk in 1921, Proctor graduated from Virginia Union University and preceded Martin Luther King Jr. at both Crozer and Boston, studying at Penn and Yale as well along the way.

After an early pastorate in Providence, Proctor spent most of his career in education, government, and institutional service. Returning to his alma mater, he taught religion and ethics at Virginia Union, and became first dean of the School of Religion and then president of the university. After that he was president of North Carolina A & T State University. Then came work with the Peace Corps and O.E.O., and offices in the National Council of Churches and the Institute for Services to Education. A deanship at the University of Wisconsin and a professorship at Rutgers followed. While remaining on the Rutgers faculty, he succeeded Congressman Adam Clayton Powell Jr. as pastor of Abyssinian Baptist Church in Harlem. In retirement he taught preaching at Vanderbilt, Duke, and United Seminary in Dayton.[55]

The content Proctor recommends for sermons comprises four propositions that he developed as his lecture topics:

> First, basic to the Christian belief system is the understanding of God as absolute, wholly "other," yet present, participating, and aware of the details of all creation, history, and human endeavor, and who can and does intervene on our behalf in the affairs of the world.
>
> Second, it is also basic to our faith that human nature can be renewed; we can be born again and become new creatures.
>
> Third, is the conviction that, dismal and remote as it may seem at the moment, the human family can become a genuine community.
>
> Fourth, also basic is the belief that our earthbound condition, our mundaneness, is given meaning and purpose by the dimension of eternity that is the ever-present potential in our midst. Immortality begins now; eternity flows in the midst of time.[56]

Proctor's lectures include reminiscences of classical African American preaching through his frequent completion of a point in a quotation from Scripture, poetry, or a hymn, and in his use of language reminiscent of Taylor's. And there is certainly notice taken of racial justice issues and the contributions of African Americans. Yet, on the whole, while Proctor's recommendations about sermon content are worthy contributions to homiletics,[57] there is little reminder that this help is coming from the black church.

Thomas Hoyt

The Beecher lecturer in 1993 was Thomas Hoyt, a New Testament scholar and ecumenist. Born in Fayette, Alabama, Hoyt received his Ph.D. from Duke University. He was a pastor in Chapel Hill, North Carolina, and then taught at the Interdenominational Theological Center, an African American seminary consortium in Atlanta, before becoming professor of Biblical Studies at Hartford Seminary, the position he held at the time of the lectures. Since then he has become bishop of the Christian Methodist Episcopal Church[58] in Shreveport, Louisiana, and president of the National Council of Churches of Christ in the U.S.A. An ardent ecumenist, he has served on the Faith and Order Commissions of both the National and the World Councils of Churches.

Titled "The Church's Preaching in a Pluralistic and Ecumenical Context,"[59] Hoyt's three lectures[60] have three foci that represent his commitments. The first, on tradition, reflects his work as a New Testament scholar. His thesis is that Christian proclamation has focused too exclusively on Paul's understanding of the crucifixion and resurrection and has not done justice to Jesus' teaching about the kingdom of God, a theme important for the hope it gives to all oppressed peoples.[61]

His second lecture, titled "Particularity: Let the Church Say Amen," begins with the recognition that biblical interpreters look for a hermeneutical key that will unlock the meaning of Scripture. Such a key, however, is often "a canon within the canon" for the interpreter. All such approaches are partial and need to be supplemented with others to do justice to the full gospel. Each particular expression must be heard as a part of the whole and he will present the African American tradition. The African American approach to biblical interpretation has emphasized such biblical motifs as the exodus, creation in the image of God, Jesus' suffering and overcoming, and hope for those struggling ("after awhile" and "by-and-by"). The emphasis on these motifs in preaching has been the way in which the biblical tradition has been made contemporary to the black church.

While the preaching of the African American pulpit has been too rich, diverse, and creative to be characterized in a simple formula, it can be said that it is an oral tradition that cannot be fully understood from sermon manuscripts or transcripts.[62] That orality is only one aspect of the way black preaching grew out of a history of slavery and oppression. Black people have gone to church to hear the good news that they are somebodies in a land where they are called nobodies. As diverse as the congregations and their preachers are, however, certain generalizations can be made. Hoyt agrees with Eugene Stratton that black sermons are marked by congregational participation, prophetic boldness, creativity on the part of the preacher, storytelling, spontaneity and movement of the Spirit, and accompaniment by a liturgy of singing, praying, and general celebration.[63] The congregation becomes involved in the end of the sermon as well.

Hoyt's third lecture is on "Universality: What, in View of the World's Disorder, Shall We Preach?" The black church does not agree with white politicians who have seen "a new world order." Their experience has been of disorder instead. There has been a need, as Walter Wink has said, to confront the powers, those who spread the delusions that those who hold power in society deserve to and are entitled to its rewards by their virtue. But for this disorder to be overcome, differing Christian and religious traditions will have to cooperate rather than compete. White people of Europe and America have dominated and exploited the rest of the world for their comfort and convenience, and this cannot continue. Even an assumption of the religious superiority of white Christians can no longer be made.

In the face of this world disorder, however, is the amazing truth pointed out by Kelly Miller Smith[64] that these issues can be addressed by the preaching of the gospel. Such preaching, though, cannot be from the perspective of an ideology. It must have as its content what God has done and will do in Jesus Christ, it must challenge the powers that be, and it must expect a cross. And, as Smith said, it must get over Cartesian compartmentalization and preach to the whole person and to a pluralistic society.

The church is called upon to go into all the world where there is a need for repentance, and to proclaim the inauguration of the reign of God. In doing so, it must resist the temptation of power and assume the role of a servant in a world where violence and force have been determinative of all outcomes.

Along with this proclamation must also go teaching, calling people to obedience as well as belief, and recognizing that an evangelism that does not address the social order is not evangelism. Such preaching will share with the fifth chapter of Revelation a vision of community that is multiethnic, multinational, multiracial, and multilinguistic. God is creating such a community in the secularity of life, and if we do not get it now, we will by-and-by.

Peter Gomes

The most recent Beecher lectures delivered by an African American resemble the first in that they are "an excellent set of lectures by a very impressive man, but not one that extends to others the resources of the classical African American homiletic." Although he has worked for causes important to the black community,[65] the homiletical tradition that lay behind the lectures of Peter Gomes was that of Harvard's Memorial Chapel, where he had preached for twenty-eight years, rather than the African American pulpit. Building on his popular volume *The Good Book: Reading the Bible with Mind and Heart,*[66] Gomes's 1999 lectures[67] deal with preaching from the Psalms, Epistles, and parables.[68]

This brings up to date the efforts of African American preachers through Beecher lectures to tutor their colleagues of other traditions in how to appropriate some of the power that has traditionally been attached to black preaching. The lecturers are a variegated group. Several of them (Robinson, Gomes, and, to an extent, Proctor) have shown in their lectures little that was distinctively African American. Only Mitchell has concentrated exclusively on preaching method. Robinson, Smith, Proctor, and Gomes have dealt instead with the content of preaching, while Taylor and Forbes were concerned with homiletical spirituality.

The lecturers represent a variety of denominations: three come from black Baptist churches, two are American Baptists,[69] one is from a historical black Methodist body, one began in a black Pentecostal church but is now a Baptist, and one is a Presbyterian. Most of them represent the hybrid sort of black congregation in that they have combined the emotion of the folk tradition with the rationality of bourgeois parishes.

All of them, however, further document what was first revealed to the majority culture through television coverage of Dr. Martin Luther King Jr.: the existence of a homiletical tradition with sufficient power to effect change.

FOR FURTHER READING

A Knock at Midnight: Inspiration From the Great Sermons of Reverend Martin Luther King, Jr. Edited by Clayborne Carson and Peter Holloran. New York: Warner, 1998.

Lischer, Richard. *The Preacher King: Martin Luther King, Jr. and the Word That Moved America*. New York: Oxford University Press, 1995.

Mitchell, Henry H. *The Recovery of Preaching*. Harper's Ministerial Paperback Library. San Francisco: Harper & Row, 1977.

Smith, Kelly Miller. *Social Crisis Preaching*. Macon, Ga.: Mercer University Press, 1984.

Taylor, Gardner C. *How Shall They Preach?* (Elgin, Ill.: Progressive Baptist Publishing House, 1977).

Notes

1. Richard Lischer, *The Preacher King: Martin Luther King, Jr. and the Word That Moved America* (New York: Oxford University Press, 1995), 42-44. I am grateful to Professor Lischer for a prepublication copy of the book manuscript. Most of the interpretation of King's preaching that follows is based on Lischer's insights. He also wrote the article on King in the *Concise Encyclopedia of Preaching,* which he edited with William Willimon (Louisville: Westminster John Knox, 1995), 288-90. For other biographical information, I have relied on Stephen B. Oates, *Let the Trumpet Sound: The Life of Martin Luther King, Jr.,* A Plume Book (New York: New American Library, 1982).

2. Like any public figure, especially one who has effectively challenged entrenched social patterns, King has his detractors. One of the more frequent charges made against him is that of plagiarism. The most thorough statement of the case for that charge is in Keith D. Miller, *The Voice of Deliverance: The Language of Martin Luther King, Jr. and Its Sources* (New York: Free Press, 1992). While it would be hard to question the facts Miller presents, his interpretation of them is another matter. He says, for example, that "his professors' ivory-tower formalism failed to engage his mind" (ibid., 62).

What Lischer says in response to a charge made by David Garrow that King was out of his element in an academic environment applies to Miller's view as well: "The problem with this portrait is that it does not square with King's academic record at Crozer, including his top examination scores." Nor does it accord with the memory of his fellow students at Boston that he "had the intellectual capacity to carry on prolonged theological debates with his professor while the rest of the class respectfully watched" (Lischer, *The Preacher King,* 63). As Lischer says, "The dilemma [of his plagiarism] cannot be resolved, but for the purposes of understanding King's preaching two points must be made. The first is that despite carelessness and lapses in academic honesty, King's immersion in academic theology was real and significant for his development as a preacher.... The second point is closely related to this observation. He approached all intellectual learning as raw material for the rhetoric of his sermons" (ibid., 63-64).

It is also true, as Miller shows, that King appropriated other preachers' sermon outlines and much of their language. Partly, that is a tradition of both black and white homiletics. As William Sloane Coffin said: "While most preachers are incurable magpies, I am a shameless one" (*Living the Truth in a World of Illusion* [San Francisco: Harper & Row, 1985], Preface). The other point to be made relates to the use King made of his sources. Shakespeare, after all, used as a source for *Hamlet* a play that is now lost and forgotten. None of the sermons on which King drew had the impact that his own did.

3. Lischer, *The Preacher King,* 51, 68.

4. Something it had not always had from King's erudite, brilliant, and unpredictable predecessor, Vernon Johns—the first African American to have his work published in one of the annual volumes of *Best Sermons.*

5. Many clergy have had popular sermons they preached frequently, and King was no exception. Caught up as he became in his duties as a leader of the civil rights movement, King found less and less time to prepare for sermons or any other kind of public speaking. Though he went through most of his life repreaching the sermons he composed during his first year at Dexter, a given sermon was never simply repeated; it was always altered to fit the circumstances of its delivery and in the light of King's evolving understanding of the world. When word-for-word documentation is not available, and all we have is the sermon title, it is hard to know what he said on a particular occasion. Besides, his sermons were edited for publication. Many of the Dexter sermons were published in *Strength to Love* (New York: Harper & Row, 1963), but, as Lischer says, "King and his editors removed all local and personal references from these sermons and polished them up as timeless masterpieces of the pulpit. In their printed form, they are scarcely distinguishable from the liberal commonplaces of the white, mainline pulpit during the Eisenhower era. Anything resembling the African-Baptist gospel in which King was nurtured or the prophetic rage that often seized him was removed in order to lend his utterances universality and to recommend his Movement to as wide a reading audience as possible" (Lischer, *Preacher King,* 4-5).

The transcriptions in *A Knock at Midnight: Inspiration from the Great Sermons of Reverend Martin Luther King, Jr.,* ed. Clayborne Carson and Peter Holloran (New York: Warner, 1998) follow, with a few exceptions, the editorial principles developed by the Martin Luther King Jr. Papers Project, and thus are much more accurate representations of what was actually said. But, precisely because of that, the form of each sermon is only the one preached on the occasion of the recording; there is no way the countless variations could be included. The best anthology of King's other writings is *A Testament of Hope: The Essential Writings of Martin Luther King, Jr.,* ed. James M. Washington (San Francisco: Harper & Row, 1986).

6. According to Miller, he took the outline from Phillips Brooks's sermon "The Harmony of Life" (Miller, *The Voice of Deliverance,* 75).

7. This was still the preferred way of referring to his race during most of King's ministry.

8. Quoted in Lischer, *The Preacher King,* 82, from *The Dexter Avenue Baptist Church, 1877–1977,* ed. Zelia S. Evans with J. T. Alexander (1978), 69.

9. Oates, *Let the Trumpet Sound,* 72.

10. Of course, he had practiced all of them before, but during his time at Dexter the roles were not so clearly separated. In addition to recognizing the different gen-

res in which King spoke, it is necessary to be aware of the periodization of his public utterances. During the first period, he spoke from a strategy of identification with the values of mainstream Western virtues to develop a consensus between all whites and blacks except what he originally believed was only a minority of racists. Next was a period in which he recognized that the movement had to provoke racists to engage in acts of violence that would elicit white sympathy when they were shown on television, and thus become a force for change. The last period was when the Vietnam War revealed to King that American society was and always had been racist to the core. Then he began to attack the system rather the shortcomings of individuals (Lischer, *The Preacher King,* 142-62).

11. Ibid., 221-66.

12. King's associates said that his speeches in these meetings were all the same (ibid., 253). Lischer gives a nine-point outline of the typical mass-meeting speech (ibid., 257).

13. The quoted words are from ibid., 178. The text of the speech can be found in Washington, *A Testament of Hope,* 217-20.

14. What follows is based on Lischer, *The Preacher King,* 221-42.

15. Ibid., 221-22.

16. Ibid., 225.

17. Ibid., 241.

18. Ibid., 106. Such mutual dependence is characteristic not only of all preachers in all times, but of others whose profession requires frequent public expression, including politicians and stand-up comics. In his analysis of King's usage of "What He Received: Units of Tradition," Lischer gives a masterful analysis of what is involved in sermon composition for all preachers (ibid., 93-118).

19. Ibid., 102.

20. Richard A. Lanham, *A Handlist of Rhetorical Terms,* 2nd ed. (Berkeley and Los Angeles: University of California Press, 1991), 169. Lanham's entire article on commonplaces is informative.

21. Lischer, *The Preacher King,* 104.

22. Kenneth Burke, quoted in Lanham, *A Handlist of Rhetorical Terms,* 169.

23. Lischer, *The Preacher King,* 123. In this passage, Lischer speaks of metonymy as a "predictable metaphor" (ibid.), apparently in dependence on Bernard Brandon Scott (ibid., 292). More commonly, *metonymy* denotes the substitution of one "name" for another, for example, *cause* for *effect* or vice versa. This confusing use of terms, however, does not make his analysis of King's strategy of elevation any less perceptive.

24. Ibid., 124.

25. Ibid., 133.

26. I am grateful for the assistance of Prof. Harry Adams of Yale Divinity School, Prof. Richard Lischer of Duke, and Prof. Henry Mitchell of the Interdenominational Theological Center in Atlanta for assistance in the identification of these lecturers. The last two of these advisers are themselves Beecher lecturers.

27. See James H. Robinson's *Africa at the Crossroads,* Christian Perspectives on Social Problems (Philadelphia: Westminster, 1962), and *Education for Decision,* eds. Frank E. Gaebelein, Earl G. Harrison Jr., and William L. Swing, for which he and

D. Elton Trueblood, Ernest Gordon, and John Crocker are listed as authors (New York: Seabury, 1963).

28. James H. Robinson, *Adventurous Preaching,* The Lyman Beecher Lectures at Yale (Great Neck, N.Y.: Channel, 1956).

29. Henry H. Mitchell, *Black Preaching* (San Francisco: Harper & Row, 1970, 1979; rev. ed. Nashville: Abingdon, 1990). This book is discussed above, chapter 20. For Mitchell's biography, see his *Festschrift, Preaching on the Brink: The Future of Homiletics,* ed. Martha J. Simmons (Nashville: Abingdon, 1996), 16-25.

30. Henry H. Mitchell, *The Recovery of Preaching,* Harper's Ministerial Paperback Library (San Francisco: Harper & Row, 1977).

31. Ibid., 11. This point is stated even more strongly on p. 98 where Mitchell says, "Everyone in the ghetto fancies that white preachers 'can't preach a lick,'" reminding one of a 1992 humorous film about pickup basketball games, *White Men Can't Jump.* (Parenthetical references that follow in this text section are to page numbers in *The Recovery of Preaching.*)

32. In an arresting simile of his own, Mitchell compares stories as they appear in the Bible with dried milk: they do not become palatable until they are mixed with an ordinary substance like water (ibid., 47).

33. A similar point will be made by Thomas Hoyt (see below), who said that he prefers his gravy to be made with the juice of the meat.

34. Ibid., 73. It will be recalled that the first chapter was a sermon.

35. In many ways, Mitchell's Beecher lectures were brought up to date in his *Celebration and Experience in Preaching* (Nashville: Abingdon, 1990). In 1993, Martha J. Simmons collaborated with him in writing a privately published *Studyguide to Accompany Celebration and Experience in Preaching.* Dr. Mitchell's colleague in all his homiletical enterprises is his wife, Dr. Ella Pearson Mitchell. In her own right, she has called attention to the homiletical achievements of African American women, as in the two volumes she edited titled *Those Preaching Women: (More) Sermons by Black Women Preachers* (Valley Forge, Pa.: Judson, 1985). In 2000, the Mitchells were copresidents of the Academy of Homiletics.

36. Dr. Mitchell told this to me in a telephone conversation.

37. This information was garnered from the dust jackets of Dr. Taylor's Beecher lectures, *How Shall They Preach* (Elgin, Ill.: Progressive Baptist Publishing House, 1977); his collection of sermons, *Chariots Aflame* (Nashville: Broadman, 1988); and the homiletical aid volume on which he and I collaborated, *Proclamation 2: Aids for Interpreting the Lessons of the Church Year: Pentecost 3* (Philadelphia: Fortress, 1980).

38. Lischer, *The Preacher King,* 50-51.

39. Ibid.

40. Taylor, *How Shall They Preach,* 57.

41. Ibid., 63-64.

42. Ibid., 72.

43. Ibid., 81.

44. This is true as well of Taylor's suggestions for homiletical development in the *Proclamation* volume, of which he was coauthor. And it is true a fortiori of his actual sermons, including the four he uses to make his lectures a book-length volume as well as those in *Chariots Aflame.*

45. Taylor, *How Shall They Preach,* 13.

46. A good sample of this eloquence can be seen in ibid., 68-72, in the passage discussing the depression that has afflicted so many great preachers.

47. Kelly Miller Smith, *Social Crisis Preaching* (Macon, Ga.: Mercer University Press, 1984). An example of Smith's own preaching can be seen in *Outstanding Black Sermons,* vol. 2, ed. Walter B. Hoard (Valley Forge, Pa.: Judson, 1979), 107-13. Parenthetical references that follow in the text section are to page numbers in *Social Crisis Preaching.*

48. Smith provides a good list of the accomplishments of Dr. King in *Social Crisis Preaching,* 75-76.

49. For what is meant by inductive preaching, see the discussion of Fred Craddock below, pp. 800-6.

50. Sermon outline patterns were a favorite topic of mid-twentieth-century homiletics manuals; see, for example, Halford E. Luccock, *In the Minister's Workshop,* Notable Books on Preaching (Whitmore & Stone, 1944; reprint, Grand Rapids, Mich.: Baker, 1977), 134-47.

51. James Forbes, *The Holy Spirit in Preaching* (Nashville: Abingdon, 1989). Parenthetical references that follow in this text section are to page numbers from *The Holy Spirit in Preaching.*

52. In Forbes's lectures are a number of extended expositions of scripture that effectively turn them into sermons.

53. Samuel D. Proctor, *"How Shall They Hear?": Effective Preaching for Vital Christian Faith* (Valley Forge, Pa.: Judson, 1992).

54. Proctor has also written a "how-to" book on preaching, *The Certain Sound of the Trumpet: Crafting a Sermon of Authority* (Valley Forge, Pa.: Judson, 1994).

55. See Samuel Proctor's autobiography, *The Substance of Things Hoped For: A Memoir of African-American Faith* (New York: G. P. Putnam's Sons, 1996).

56. Proctor, *How Shall They Hear?,* 16-17.

57. Lischer calls Proctor "one of the most formidable black preachers of our century" and says that he may have been the only one tutored by Pius Barbour in Chester, Pennsylvania, who was more promising than King (Lischer, *The Preacher King,* 110, 70).

58. One of the three major historic African American churches in the Wesleyan tradition.

59. Hoyt's lectures have not yet been published in book form, although a cassette recording of them is available from Berkeley Divinity School at Yale, the Episcopal presence at Yale Divinity School. I am grateful to the former dean of Berkeley, Dr. William Franklin, for a set of these cassettes.

60. In contrast to the usual four.

61. A more nuanced view of Hoyt's hermeneutic than he was able to give in his lecture appears in "Interpreting Biblical Scholarship for the Black Church Tradition," the chapter he contributed to *Stony the Road We Trod: African American Biblical Interpretation,* ed. Cain Hope Felder (Minneapolis: Fortress, 1991), 17-39. This entire volume is useful for understanding contemporary African American preaching.

62. Even here there are differences in congregations. As Hoyt points out, some are largely composed of traditional folk hearers, others of bourgeois hearers (who expect a preacher with educational credentials whose sermons are rationally persuasive), and still others of a hybrid type that expects sermons to be both rationally persuasive and emotionally stirring.

63. This last element is especially characteristic of the folk-type church.

64. See above, pp. 716-19.

65. For example, his first work assignment was as director of the Freshman Experimental Program at Tuskegee Institute.

66. Peter Gomes, *The Good Book: Reading the Bible with Mind and Heart* (New York: William Morrow, 1996).

67. Unpublished in book format so far, they may be heard on cassettes recorded by Biomedical Communications, Audio Visual Services, Yale University School of Medicine and distributed through Yale's Student Book Supply under the title of *The Texture of Biblical Preaching: Songs, Letters, and Stories.*

68. Examples of Gomes's preaching can be seen in his *Sermons: Biblical Wisdom for Daily Living* (New York: William Morrow, 1998).

69. This could be misleading, since many African American congregations have a dual membership in the American Baptist Churches.

CHAPTER 29

MAINSTREAM PROPHECY

The civil rights movement did not affect preaching in African American churches alone. The mainstream denominations of the white majority in the United States were deeply challenged by the charges of complicity in the subjugation and exploitation that still victimized the descendants of slaves. Their guilt acknowledged and their consciences aroused, the white churches took up the cause of working with their black brothers and sisters to purge their institutions and the country as a whole of the racism that was as pervasive as it was contrary to the gospel.

One of the main agents employed in the purging was the prophetic voice of the pulpit. Yet churches had been so separated along racial lines that conventions of preaching in the white denominations were very different from those of the communions that had been mobilized into militant involvement by the sermons of Dr. King and his clerical comrades in the struggle. While white America was awestruck by the eloquence of the black pulpit, it would take more familiar rhetorical strategies to move its churches to accept the cause as their own. Thus there came to be developed a type of sermon on racial justice that fit into the homiletical tradition of white American churches that could still be called mainline at that time.

A CRISIS IN VALUES

The raising of this one major issue of social morality, however, was only the beginning. Soon it became apparent that there were many other injustices to be acknowledged and dealt with. The crisis in the social values of America was just beginning. The country was on the verge of another of what Mark Noll[1] has called its "turbulent decades."

The 1960s were so tumultuous that it is hard for even those who lived through them and participated in the events of the time to believe all that actually happened. When the decade began, Eisenhower was still president, and memories of McCarthyism were fresh. There was doubt whether a Roman Catholic like John F. Kennedy could be elected to the country's highest office. The Russians had already launched their first spaceship and would soon put the first human being into orbit around the earth. In addition to competition in space, the cold war produced the Cuban missile crisis and the Berlin Wall.

All that seems like a continuation of the 1950s, but change was in the air. Lunch-counter sit-ins had begun, and a voting rights bill had passed Congress. By 1961, African American and white Freedom Riders were challenging Jim Crow segregation of interstate travel facilities. The following year, the University of Mississippi admitted its first black student, James Meredith, even though three thousand federal troops were needed to quell riots. In some ways, the climax of the civil rights movement was the March on Washington of August 28, 1963, when Dr. King gave his "I Have a Dream" speech. The next summer saw campaigns to register African American voters in southern states—and the martyrdom of some of the workers in that effort. But it also saw the passage of the Civil Rights Act, which banned racial discrimination in voting, jobs, public accommodations, and federally funded programs.

That legislative accomplishment, however, did not mean racial problems were over for the country, as the riots that broke out in major cities during the rest of the decade demonstrated. The assassination of Dr. King on April 4, 1968, was tragic evidence of how far the struggle was from being over. Indeed, racism remains the most serious social problem in the United States at the time of this writing.

President Lyndon Johnson tried to involve the country in efforts to eliminate other social problems such as poverty, which, although one of the worst aspects of racism, was not confined to racial minorities. While he did get his War on Poverty Bill passed in the summer of 1964, he had already become embroiled in a cause that would put him at loggerheads with most of those who supported his efforts to create "the Great Society."

American cold war strategy had become captive to a metaphor. The manner in which one European country after another had become communist after World War II was compared to what happens to dominoes stood on end and in line with one another: If the first is tilted, they all will fall. When North Vietnam became Marxist after the expulsion of the French, this was understood not as a move for national self-determination, but as part of an international communist conspiracy that would initiate a domino effect throughout Southeast Asia.

As a result, a small cadre of American military advisers was sent to South Vietnam quite early on, and President Kennedy decided that they should protect themselves if fired upon. Johnson used an alleged attack on American naval vessels in the Gulf of Tonkin to obtain congressional approval for military action in Vietnam. As early as 1967, there were four hundred thousand American troops there, and a saturation bombing campaign was being carried out against the North.

By then the war had become increasingly unpopular at home, and a vast peace movement organized protests and demonstrations all over the country. After North Vietnam launched an all-out offensive in early 1968 and it became obvious how far the war was from being won, Johnson grew so discouraged that he stopped the bombing raids and decided not to run for another term as president. Six weeks later, peace talks began in Paris. After Richard Nixon took office and the peace negotiations dragged on, the protest movement increased in vehemence, culminating in a march of a quarter million people on Washington. The cease-fire and withdrawal of American troops did not occur until early 1973.

While the civil rights and the peace movements were the most obvious social actions in the sixties, other changes were occurring in society that would be just as far-reaching. The most obvious date assigned to the beginning of the sexual mores revolution that has changed so much in American social life is 1960, when approval was given for marketing the birth control "pill." The modern environmental movement may be said to have gotten its initial impulse from the publication of Rachel Carson's book *The Silent Spring* in late 1962. And the women's movement can be dated from the release of Betty Friedan's *The Feminine Mystique* a few months later. The growing ethnic and religious pluralism of the country was documented when the Supreme Court declared in 1963 that requiring prayers and Bible reading in public schools was unconstitutional. It was also seen in Cesar Chavez's organization of migrant farmworkers, not to mention the fact that somewhere along the way an interest in Eastern religions developed in the country.

The triumphal tour of the Beatles in 1964 demonstrated a basic shift in taste in popular music, a shift that had become complete by the summer of 1969 when a half million young people assembled for a music festival near Woodstock, New York. Woodstock also showed how far the sexual revolution had gone and how much drug use had become a part of youth culture. And, while Medicare for the nation's elderly was instituted in 1965, the decade belonged to the young. Thus a students' rights movement disrupted the nation's college campuses. Along with that occurred a free speech movement, which resulted in the entry into the public vocabulary of many words and expressions that had formerly been considered obscene or profane. Another cause supported in the sexual revolution was the gay rights movement, which began with the Stonewall Inn riot on June 27, 1969. A turbulent decade, indeed, and a decade during which more accepted values were in dispute than during any comparable period in American history.

A PRIVILEGED PROPHET

As in any dispute about values, clergy felt an obligation to speak out on the controversies of the sixties and early seventies, to try to cast some Christian light on the situation. While there was a great deal of advocacy for some of the changes being called for at the time, there was also a sense that others had to be resisted. And all clergy did not take the same side on a particular issue, nor did their parishioners always agree with them or favor their expressing opinions from the pulpit. While it was by no means a unanimous voice and may not even have been a majority voice, there did develop in the United States at the time a highly visible and even more audible strain of preaching. It intended to be prophetic, to rally Christians to work for social justice involving many conflicts of value and the confrontations of groups that disagreed vigorously and sometimes violently.

While in many ways this movement was the heir of the Social Gospel movement before World War I, it also differed from it markedly in a number of other ways. The earlier movement grew out of Romanticism and shared many of its liberal presuppositions. These included the understanding of the kingdom of God as the establishment of a perfect society on earth and the belief that, on the one hand, this society was to be the result of inevitable evolutionary progress in history, and that, on the other, it was to be brought in by the concerted efforts of Christians who could be exhorted by preaching to make the effort. Involved in this point of view is an optimistic understanding of human nature that considered people capable of such achievements if they would use their free will to accomplish them. Thus a distinction was made between evil institutions and essentially good human beings.

The prophetic preaching of the sixties, on the other hand, was influenced by the realism regarding human nature that came after two world wars and a depression in one generation, and by biblical scholarship that understood the kingdom of God in the teaching of Jesus as an eschatological and apocalyptic concept. Another difference between the social preaching in the two eras is that the first concentrated on labor questions, while the latter extended to all the questions of value raised in the 1960s. As a result, the main common factors between the two movements were a sense of Christian duty to improve society and an assumption that preaching could help effect such change.

As with many other movements in the history of preaching, this one can be studied mainly in the ministry of one cleric. It cannot be said that William Sloane Coffin Jr. (1924–) was the first to engage in such preaching or that he was typical of those who did, but he became by far the best-known exemplar of this homiletical trend. Not only that, he also did social protest preaching with a power and persuasiveness that few could achieve and with an integrity and wisdom that were hard to match.

It would be difficult to claim that Bill Coffin is typical of anything, since he came to his work with gifts and privileges few can equal. He was born into a position of affluence and social prominence. Much of the family wealth was lost in the Great Depression and more after his father died when Coffin was nine, but even in such relative financial straits, he was better off than most. He and his siblings were provided a secondary education in prep schools at home or abroad, and undergraduate and graduate schooling in the Ivy League.

Then, too, their social position remained secure. Very few clergy, for instance, have been lucky enough to have as an uncle someone like Henry Sloane Coffin, who had been, among other things, pastor of Madison Avenue Presbyterian Church in Manhattan, president of Union Theological Seminary, and moderator of the Presbyterian Church. But the family connections were not exclusively nor even mainly ecclesiastical.

Yet family and affluence are not the most extraordinary things about Coffin. His great talents in a number of areas are more impressive than anything else. He is so musically gifted, for instance, that when still high-school age, he was in Paris studying piano under Jacques Février and composition under the legendary Nadia Boulanger. The French virtuoso of the piano, Alfred Corot, told him that he had an enormous talent,[2] and, if World War II had not intervened, he probably would have achieved his ambition to become a conductor.

He also has a rare facility for languages. After living in Paris for a short while, he was able to pass himself off as French.[3] Later, as an army intelligence officer in the war, he learned enough Russian in three months to serve as a liaison officer between U.S. and Soviet military units stationed in Czechoslovakia.[4] Finally, he was a far better athlete than the majority of clergy. To cite but one instance: When he was in the sixth grade he was able to put up a respectable resistance to a muscular seventeen-year-old who was already boxing professionally.[5] In all of this Coffin finds "the source of the paradoxes and tensions" that complicated his later life: "I was an elitist who came to question such principles; a combative young squirt who espoused nonviolence; a boy with a gift for music and languages who became a preacher."[6]

When he returned home from World War II, Coffin went to Yale, where he received advanced placement for his various accomplishments. At the time he was anticipating a career in diplomacy and majored in political science, but already his interest was being captured by issues of good and evil as those were discussed by atheistic existentialists like Sartre and Camus and Christian theologians such as the Niebuhr brothers and Tillich.

After graduation he began to prepare for the ministry at Union Seminary, but the Korean War broke out in the summer after his first year, and his patriotism caused him to accept the CIA appointment he had considered before. He spent almost three years in Germany training anticommunist Russians for clandestine operations within the Soviet Union. Then he returned to his preparation for ordination—at Yale, however, rather than Union, so he could be near his aging mother in New Haven.

Coffin had originally hoped to serve in an inner-city slum parish, but his engagement to the daughter of the famous pianist Arthur Rubinstein led him to accept a call to be chaplain at Phillips Andover. After a year there and another at Williams College, he began the ministry through which he would become known to the Christian world: eighteen years as chaplain of his alma mater Yale. That attention came because of his public involvement in some of the most visible of the social protest movements. For the civil rights movement, that meant his participation in a "Freedom Ride" through Georgia and Alabama in the spring of 1961 to try to integrate travel facilities in accordance with the regulations of the Interstate Commerce Commission. He was also with Dr. King in Birmingham two years later.

His interest in the war in Vietnam was stimulated in the spring of 1964 by Paul Jordan, a graduate student in music. In the summer of 1965, he founded Americans for the Reappraisal of Far Eastern Policy, and the following winter he helped organize the National Emergency Committee of Clergy Concerned About Vietnam. He was convicted of conspiracy along with other prominent people like Dr. Benjamin Spock for counseling young men to turn in their draft cards. Nothing he did, however, shocked the country so much as his going with a delegation to Hanoi in 1972 to accept the release of three American prisoners of war. In a similar way, he went to Tehran during the Iran hostage crisis.

In 1977 he became senior minister of Manhattan's famous Riverside Church, which had been founded by another preacher against war, Harry Emerson Fosdick. Coffin held that position for ten years before he left to organize SANE/FREEZE, the country's largest peace and justice organization. As William J. Carl III has pointed out, each major phase of his ministry had its characteristic social issue:

> His practice has been to immerse himself in one major problem for a period of time. In the early sixties it was civil rights. In the late sixties to early seventies it was Vietnam. In the late seventies it was hunger and American intervention in places like El Salvador. In the eighties it has been the arms race.[7]

In retirement, he continues to witness for the justice demanded by the gospel.

Coffin's Homiletic

The difference between Coffin's social action preaching and any of his other sermons—or those of his contemporaries in the pulpit—was not so much in structure as in content. He usually preached from the lectionary, and he has said that his best sermons had an introduction, three points, and a conclusion.[8] Nor was his preaching exclusively about social issues. He said that he much preferred pastoral counseling to prophetic preaching,[9] and printed collections of his sermons include more dealing with pastoral than social issues—although the pastoral sermons are at least as aware of the social aspects of problems as they are of their personal dimensions.

Yet the issue here is how he preached social action sermons. The first point, then, is that he did so only occasionally. And the second is that he was well prepared when he did so. One of the most obvious features of his sermons is the large number of illustrations and quotations, drawn from a wide range of reading. He decries the fact that the average Christian cleric reads only a third as much as the average rabbi.[10] His own reading of the Bible, books, and magazines is voluminous, covering not only theology and ethics but also literature and technical studies of the topics with which he deals.[11] It is these latter that give authority to what he has to say on such subjects. To be taken seriously on social issues, clergy must make it obvious that they know whereof they speak. Not stated in so many words but clearly implied is the assumption that many clergy are not respected for what they say on controversial issues because they go off half-cocked without bothering to inform themselves on what they are talking about.

One of the reasons Coffin concentrated on one major problem at a time was so that his study of it could be cumulative and deep. "At Yale and at Riverside his practice has been to do his homework and make his statement clearly and early to the congregation only once, and not badger them with it week after week."[12]

Nor was his reading on just one side of the issue. He believes that one should be able to "state the opposition's position to the opposition's satisfaction."[13] It is easier for people to accept refutation of a position that they know has been understood and taken seriously. Of equal importance is the fact that fairness to the other side will show his hearers that they, too, are being taken seriously. Coffin thus often quoted with approval words spoken to him by a Yale freshman: "If it's both true and painful, say it softly."[14]

And on his own he said:

> Whenever possible, I believe we should challenge people kindly. Nothing, for example, prevents any of us, in the middle of a sermon, from saying, "What I now want to say is hard for me to say, so I can imagine how painful it's going to be for some of you to hear. But here we are in church, where unity is based not on agreement, but on mutual concern. So let me tell you what's on my mind and heart and, after the service, those of you who disagree can bring your coffee into the library and tell me where you think I went wrong."[15]

At the same time, however, he was insistent that the preacher's own need to be loved should not encourage soft-pedaling what ought to be proclaimed from the housetops.

In addition to being informed and pastoral, Coffin thought that social action preaching had also to be theological. It was only the theological dimension of the issue that made it an appropriate subject for preaching.

In this way he distinguished between what he himself did in press conferences and what he did from the pulpit. Yet "Coffin believes that we preachers should speak theologically about not only ecclesiastical but [*sic*] political matters. For this reason, he always speaks as a 'reverend,' whether he is in church or the local Rotary Club."[16]

He says that his own orthodoxy has increased over the years, but for theological rather than psychological reasons. He finds that the world is always bearing out the Bible, and the Bible is always illuminating the world.[17] He can, therefore, make it clear to people that his insistence on social justice derives from his concern for their souls.

A Case in Point

An example of the way Coffin practiced his own homiletical principles is a sermon on homosexuality. (For the text of this sermon, see **Vol. 2, pp. 580-85.**) It was published in *The Courage to Love*[18] in 1982 and had already appeared in the journal *Christianity and Crisis*[19] previously, so it must have been preached only about a decade after the Stonewall Inn riot, the beginning of the gay rights movement.[20] He introduces the question by asking his congregation if they know what a long list of famous and talented people of both sexes and many fields of endeavor have in common. By announcing that the common factor is homosexuality he has gained their attention and made them aware that the issue is serious.

He admits that the subject is the most divisive in the church since slavery, and, by identifying it with slavery, suggests on which side people should be. The previously unmentionable subject has become unavoidable because some Christian clergy are claiming that homosexuals are sinfully different from other people. "Gay men and women are being physically and psychologically abused; they are being excluded from their families, frozen out of churches, and discriminated against in a variety of painful legal ways" (40).

The basis for the claim of these clergy is their understanding of biblical teaching. To counter that, Coffin begins by interpreting his sermon's text, the story in Acts 10:1-20 of Peter's vision on a roof in Joppa in which he was commanded to eat nonkosher food. The revelation to Peter was that "God shows no partiality, but in every nation any one who fears him and does what is right is acceptable to him" (Acts 10:34 RSV). The passage seems likely to have been appointed in the lectionary, and, after studying it, the preacher must have asked what would be an apt application and extension of it in the present. He concludes that "in every sexual orientation any one who fears him and does what is right is acceptable to him" (41).

Coffin then quotes ethicist James B. Nelson to the effect that there are four primary theological stances toward homosexuality: the rejecting-punitive, the rejecting nonpunitive, the conditional acceptance, and the unconditional acceptance positions. These four attitudes become the four points discussed in the body of the sermon. Consideration of the rejecting-punitive stance involves a close look at what the Bible has to say on the subject of homosexuality. It is true that Leviticus calls a male homosexual act an abomination, but it uses the same Hebrew word *(toevah)* in reference to "eating pork, to misuse of incense, and to intercourse during menstruation" (41). Other passages are related to participating in pagan rites that included both male and female prostitutes, where the issue was idolatry. And others to anal rape as a way of humiliating captured enemy soldiers.

Further, the understanding of conception in that culture was that only the male seed carried life, "women providing only the incubating space." In a society in which it was desirable to have as many children as possible, any waste of sperm in homoerotic acts or masturbation was viewed as a form of abortion. As for Sodom and Gomorrah, their sin as viewed by Ezekiel, Isaiah, and Jesus seems to have been more a violation of hospitality than a sin against nature. In thus rejecting the interpretation of his opponents, Coffin shows that he takes the Bible more seriously than they do. He is not content with hurling proof texts; he exerts considerable effort to learn what the sacred writers meant.

In addressing the rejecting-nonpunitive position, Coffin responds to the charge that a homosexual orientation is a psychic disorder that needs to be cured. He points out that the psychotherapeutic community does not agree. Then he considers the conditional acceptance attitude, which would permit the ordination of homosexuals while not being able to "picture a gay spouse in the parsonage" (45). He sees an analogy between their position and that of those who think Jews should enjoy the same rights as Christians, but nevertheless consider Judaism inferior to Christianity. Recognizing the dilemma involved, he says, "The worst thing we can do with a dilemma is to resolve it prematurely because we lack the courage to live with uncertainty" (45).

Finally, with the unconditional acceptance stance that is his own, he points out analogies to "the black problem" and "the woman problem": "The 'homosexual problem' is really the homophobia of many heterosexuals" (45). While he was appalled at the promiscuity of some gays in those days before the AIDS epidemic, so were other gays, and it was no worse than straight promiscuity.

In his conclusion, Coffin returns to his text, saying that Peter widened his horizons and we should do the same, perceiving that God shows no partiality in regard to sexual orientation. And he ends by saying: "What St. Augustine called the duty of the preacher is the obligation of all: 'to teach what is right and to refute what is wrong, and in the performance of this task to conciliate the hostile [and] to rouse the careless'" (46). It would be hard to find a better statement of Coffin's homiletic or a better description of what he did than this sermon.

THE PERSPECTIVE OF THE UNDERPRIVILEGED

The prophetic preaching of mainstream clergy who spoke out on social issues was mostly delivered to middle-class whites by males of their own social group and reflected the group's attitudes toward its social role. This is not to question the sincerity of the clergy in call for change, but rather to say that they assumed that they and their audience, working with others like themselves, could effect the changes they called for. It is to say that they thought they could work within the social and economic system to improve it.

Another strain of social protest preaching that was never as large as the first in the United States was more in touch with the attitude of those oppressed by society and was more likely to assume that social and economic systems needed to be replaced rather than improved. This tradition was shaped by the liberation theology of Latin America and took as its model the preaching done in that area. (For an example of such preaching, see **Vol. 2, pp. 592-95.**) That point of view can be seen in a popular manual on preaching from a liberation perspective, *The Liberating Pulpit* by Justo L. González and Catherine G. González.[21] The five chapters of the book deal with the stance of liberation theology; impediments to understanding the Bible as the underprivileged do; resources for doing that; techniques to help in that endeavor; and the integration of biblical interpretation, preaching, and liturgy to communicate the insights gained.

The starting point of liberation theology is that traditional theology has carried an often unidentified agenda of oppression as the result of "an unconscious process through which the values, goals, and interests of those in power are read into scripture and expressed in supposedly universal theology" (16). That process began with the conversion of Constantine, although the greatest of the church fathers resisted this inclination. Centuries of such conditioning have led those speaking in the name of the church to offer theological justification for the continuation of oppressed people's suffering. Most of those who did this were not cruel so much as unaware of the way their theology had been shaped by the agenda of the powerful.

The corrective proposed by liberation theology is to notice that "the major portion of the Bible records the perspective of those who, in their own social situation, are the powerless and oppressed" (18). That being so, it becomes obvious that the Bible is best understood by those whose situation is most analogous to that of the people of God in Scripture. Often the only way the elite can hear what the Bible really says is to hear it from a powerless person. Such a hearing can be difficult to achieve because those who speak from this perspective are frequently regarded as communists and as advocates of violence and revolution. This reaction fails to note the violence by which subjugation has been maintained and the burning desire of those who have suffered from it to escape.

While liberation theology arises out of the concrete situation of oppressed people, it is not solely concerned with their own practical situation. Rather, their experience has given them important perspectives on every Christian doctrine. For them a basic insight is the recognition that the biblical principle of *Heilsgeschichte* ("redemption history") does not apply merely to Israel and the early church, but is relevant to all times and all places. Thus, "history is not simply the narration of past events. History is a project, both divine and human, for the redemption of God's creation" (24).

And part of this understanding of history as the arena of redemption is to notice that oppressive systems enslave not only the underprivileged but the elite as well, those for whom their comfort is the bribe for their compliance. That may be observed in our consumerist society, "where human beings are seen as either means of production or agents of consumption, and where the poor are valued according to how much they can produce, while the rich are valued according to how much they consume" (26).

Preaching that is shaped by a liberation perspective concentrates on interpreting the Bible from the point of view of the oppressed peoples about whom it was written rather than from the point of view of the powerful that has shaped post-Constantinian theology. So engrained is the elitist interpretation, however, that there are impediments to hearing the outlook of the original text. These impediments include the way that the Reformation principle of *sola scriptura* has led to the confusion of what the Bible actually says with the traditional elitist interpretation of its text. In fact, that traditional interpretation has been presupposed so reflexively that it has shaped translations of the Bible into other languages.

Furthermore, lectionaries, for all their merits, are drawn up by representatives of the mainline churches that use them and thus reflect their values; many texts that would raise issues of social justice are never read. Finally, biblical commentaries are often written from an Enlightenment perspective of rationality that assumes it knows what ancient documents originally meant and is unconcerned with what they might mean to people of faith today. For this reason, anyone who would expound the Bible from a liberation perspective has an uphill struggle to arrive at that interpretation.

The way to achieve the liberation interpretation always involves what Juan Luis Segundo has called "the hermeneutical circle."[22] This process begins when one brought up on the traditional interpretation becomes aware of oppression in the world and wants to do something about it as a Christian. At that point, representatives of the mainstream declare such an attitude unbiblical and unchristian. The circle is completed if, instead of giving in to the majority position, a person becomes suspicious of the methods of biblical interpretation that led to conclusions so apparently inconsistent with the attitude of Christ. The suspicion results in a new approach to the Bible, resulting in the discovery that it was written from the perspective of oppressed people and has to be interpreted in that light.

The rest of the book is concerned with exegesis in preparation for constructing a sermon and with the interrelation between biblical interpretation, the sermon, and the liturgy rather than with homiletics as such. Therefore, it need not be considered here.

More relevant to the actual history of preaching is the consideration of particular sermons constructed from the perspective of liberation theology. The most influential collection is from Latin America rather than the United States: *The Gospel in Solentiname,* edited by Ernesto Cardenal.[23]

Solentiname is an archipelago on Lake Nicaragua where Cardenal, a Roman Catholic priest, went with some companions to form a community or lay monastery.[24] The community worked with the local residents *(campesinos),* and a number of artistic and agricultural projects were begun, projects that attracted worldwide attention.[25] As a religious community, however, its activity was centered in Word and sacrament.

The sermons were not delivered by the priest alone, but were instead group reflections—or, as Cardenal calls them, dialogues—on the texts of the lectionary Gospels. At first Cardenal reconstructed these from memory, but then he began to record and transcribe them. Anyone reading through the collection will notice that most of the comments were made by a small group of regulars who become recognizable over time for their points of view.

> Marcelino is a mystic. Olivia is more theological. Rebeca, Marcelino's wife, always stresses love. Laureano refers everything to the Revolution. Elvis always thinks of the perfect society of the future. Felipe, another young man, is very conscious of the proletarian struggle. Old Tomás Peña, his father, doesn't know how to read, but he talks with great wisdom. Alejandro, Olivia's son, is a young leader, and his commentaries are usually directed toward everyone, and especially toward other young people. Pancho is a conservative. Julio Mairena is a great defender of equality. His brother Oscar always talks about unity. (Introduction, ix)

The discussion is led by the priest, and the two other founding adults of the community, the Colombian poet William Agudelo and his wife, Teresita, also make contributions.

The dialogues took place either at Mass or in a thatched hut afterward. Copies of the Gospel were distributed to those who could read and then read aloud for those who could not. The translation used was *Dios llega al hombre,* made by Protestants in the language of the campesinos. The passage was discussed verse by verse. The simplest way to convey the flavor of what took place is by quotation of randomly chosen facing pages. The text under consideration is the parable of the mustard seed from Matthew 13. (The full text of this sermon may be read in **Vol. 2, pp. 586-92.**) The pages begin with the conclusion of a remark by a visiting poet that started on the previous page. Then

> LAUREANO: "And the guerilla groups are small, insignificant, poor. And they're often wiped out. But they're going to change society. Can't we apply also to them the parable of the mustard seed?"
>
> MARCELINO, with his calm voice, said: "I don't know about the mustard seed, but I do know about the *guasima* seed, which is tiny. I'm looking at that *guasima* tree over there. It's very large, and the birds come to it too. I say to myself: that's what we are, this little community, a *guasima* seed. It doesn't seem there's any connection between a thing that's round and tiny, like a pebble, and that great big tree. It doesn't seem either that there's any connection between some poor *campesinos* and a just and well-developed society, where there is abundance and everything is shared. And we are the seed of that society. When the tree will develop we don't know. But we know that we are a seed and not a pebble."
>
> I [Cardenal] said: "The great tree with all its branches and its leaves is already present in the seed, even though in a hidden form. In the same way the kingdom of heaven, which is a cosmic kingdom, is already present in us, but in a hidden way. A tree is the product of the evolu-

> tion of a seed, and in nature everything is produced by a process of evolution. And it seems to me that with this parable of the seed Christ is also telling us here that the kingdom of heaven is the product of the same process of evolution that formed stars, plants, animals, people. And it grows in us impelled by the same forces of nature that impelled the evolution of the whole cosmos, which is to say that the kingdom of heaven is evolution itself."[26]
>
> ELVIS: "The birds that make their nests in the branches, it seems to me, are humanity now free: people who can go freely everywhere without borders of any kind and who will feel safe in the universe, without any of them ever being in need."
>
> TERESITA: "This parable also teaches us that we must be patient, because a tree isn't created in a single day, and all the processes of nature take their time."
>
> OLIVIA: "The kingdom of heaven or the kingdom of love begins with a tiny bit. When we work on it, that seed grows and grows."
>
> "I've seen that seed growing here, blessed be God," said DOÑA ADELITA in her faint voice.
>
> OLIVIA continued: "The kingdom of heaven is also taking shape in our homes with our growing children that we are shaping. They are growing up, and the kingdom of love is taking shape, which is the kingdom of heaven. It has to take shape in a child. And then it goes on developing, and if the children develop well they are going to extend that kingdom of love also. Yes, you can notice also how the kingdom of heaven is growing inside the child."[27]

In time a group of young people decided, precisely out of their Christian commitment, to participate in the Sandinista revolution against the Samoza dictatorship. In reprisal, Solentiname was devastated. The revolution succeeded, however, on July 19, 1979, and Ernesto Cardenal became the minister of culture for Nicaragua. The Sandinista government was voted out of office in 1990.

The preaching method devised by Cardenal for Solentiname has been taken up in other communities that see the cause of liberation to be related to the cause of the kingdom of God. It is used, for instance, in several ministries to homeless urban people. In commenting on the volumes collected by Cardenal, González and González say:

> There is . . . in the comments of many of these uneducated people an insight into the meaning of various texts, an ability to see what

> scholarly commentators hardly ever note, which seems to prove the contention that the poor and the oppressed have an edge when it comes to understanding the meaning of the Bible.[28]

That insight is ratified by those who have had the privilege of being present when this sermonic method was being used.[29]

Thus the practice of preaching for social justice that started in the black church spread quickly to others. Clergy in mainly white mainline churches began speaking out on all the social issues that came to be debated in the 1960s. No one exemplified the prophetic stance of such preaching better than William Sloane Coffin Jr. in his ministry as chaplain of Yale University and as senior pastor of Riverside Church in New York City. Coffin, a multitalented person who grew up in an atmosphere of privilege, offered a very responsible model of prophetic preaching by the way he informed himself thoroughly on any subject he discussed from the pulpit, alternated such preaching with a more pastoral kind, always showed fairness to those who disagreed, and had genuine concern for those to whom he preached.

There was always the danger in such mainline preaching, however, that it would be done from the perspective of the powerful rather than that of the oppressed. Those who really wanted to speak in the name of the least of Christ's brothers and sisters had to learn a new hermeneutic that recognized the Bible's "preferential option for the poor" and to preach from that perspective. The way to do that has been spelled out by Justo and Catherine González, and examples of it exist in abundance in the four volumes of *The Gospel in Solentiname.*

FOR FURTHER READING

Coffin, William Sloane, Jr. *Living the Truth in a World of Illusion.* San Francisco: Harper & Row, 1985.

———. *Once to Every Man: A Memoir.* New York: Athenaeum, 1977.

González, Justo L., and Catherine G. González. *The Liberating Pulpit.* Nashville: Abingdon, 1994.

The Gospel in Solentiname. Edited by Ernesto Cardenal. Translated by Donald D. Walsh. 4 vols. Maryknoll, N.Y.: Orbis Books, 1976–82.

Proclaiming the Acceptable Year: Sermons from a Perspective of Liberation. Edited by Justo González. Valley Forge, Pa.: Judson, 1982.

Notes

1. Mark Noll, *A History of Christianity in the United States and Canada* (Grand Rapids, Mich.: Eerdmans, 1992), 441-46.

2. William Sloane Coffin Jr., *Once to Every Man: A Memoir* (New York: Athenaeum, 1977), 20.

3. Ibid., 19.

4. Ibid., 52, 62. His ability to speak Russian was also an important factor in his being recruited by the CIA.

5. Ibid., 10-11.

6. Ibid., 14.

7. William J. Carl III, *Preaching Christian Doctrine* (Philadelphia: Fortress, 1984), 122.

8. Audiotape, "Discussion of Homiletics," at Union Theological Seminary, Richmond, Va., April 21, 1975, from the seminary's Reigner Recording Library. Other main sources for what Coffin says about preaching are his 1980 Beecher Lectures, "Preaching in the 80s," which were not published as such in book form, but are available in audiocassette from the Visual Educational Service of Yale Divinity School, and "Epilogue: A Word to the Preachers," in his *A Passion for the Possible: A Message to U.S. Churches* (Louisville: Westminster John Knox, 1993). The latter volume appears to be fragments of sermons and speeches integrated into a book. He describes his *The Courage to Love* as an edited form of sermons (San Francisco: Harper & Row, 1982), 8. The content of his *Living the Truth in a World of Illusion* (San Francisco: Harper & Row, 1985), however, is described simply as "sermons" (ix) and is probably closest to what was actually delivered from the pulpit. The first three of Coffin's four Beecher lectures were sermons, and they appear in edited form in *The Courage to Love.* (Indeed, like any preacher asked to speak often on the same subjects, Coffin reuses the language in which he phrases his thought as well as quotations and illustrations a number of times.) His fourth Beecher lecture, however, was addressed to clergy about the work he shares with them.

9. Coffin, *A Passion for the Possible,* 85. I can believe this from watching him conduct a workshop at the College of Preachers in 1994. He noted whenever a visitor appeared in the refectory for a meal and made a point of introducing himself and learning as much about that person as he could, without focusing any attention on himself as the celebrity that he was.

10. Ibid., 86. He also deals with this issue in the fourth Beecher lecture and in the "Discussion on Homiletics."

11. The indices and endnotes (if any) of his books show the range of his reading.

12. Carl, *Preaching Christian Doctrine,* 122.

13. Coffin, *A Passion for the Possible,* 86.

14. Ibid., 84.

15. Ibid., 85.

16. Carl, *Preaching Christian Doctrine,* 124. Carl identifies the position of Coffin with that of Reinhold Niebuhr: "They both reject political passivity and thoughtless activism and encourage a politically active posture informed by scripture, tradition,

and obedience to Christ" (120). He also sees similarities between Coffin's position and that of social-minded Evangelicals such as Richard Mouw and Richard Quebedeaux.

17. Coffin, "Discussion on Homiletics."

18. Coffin, *The Courage to Love,* 39-47. Hereafter, parenthetical references that follow in this text section are to page numbers in this work.

19. In the *Christianity and Crisis* issue for November 2, 1981, where it had a somewhat different form and appeared under the title "Homosexuality Revisited: Whose Problem?"

20. This means that it was preached before the AIDS epidemic had begun. The way that affected his thinking on the subject can be seen in the chapter called "Homophobia" in *A Passion for the Possible,* 62-68.

21. Justo L. González and Catherine G. González, *The Liberating Pulpit* (Nashville: Abingdon, 1994). This work is a thorough revision and expansion of their *Liberation Preaching: The Pulpit and the Oppressed* (Nashville: Abingdon, 1980). See also their article on "Liberation Preaching" in *Concise Encyclopedia of Preaching,* ed. William H. Willimon and Richard Lischer (Louisville: Westminster John Knox, 1995), 307-8. Hereafter, parenthetical references that follow in this text section are to page numbers in *The Liberating Pulpit.*

22. Juan Luis Segundo, *The Liberation of Theology* (Maryknoll, N.Y.: Orbis Books, 1976), 9; cited in González and González, *Liberation Preaching,* 32.

23. *The Gospel in Solentiname,* ed. Ernesto Cardenal, trans. Donald D. Walsh, 4 vols. (Maryknoll, N.Y.: Orbis Books, 1976–82). Justo González has also edited *Proclaiming the Acceptable Year: Sermons from a Perspective of Liberation* (Valley Forge, Pa.: Judson, 1982).

24. This information comes from an introduction that is the same in all four volumes and occupies pp. vii-x in each.

25. From the epilogue that also appears in each volume. Located at the end, its page numbers vary with the length of the individual volumes.

26. The evolutionary interpretation of Cardenal does not reflect older liberal Protestant theology, which interpreted parables as teaching progressive growth. More likely, it shows the influence of the thought of the French Jesuit Pierre Teilhard de Chardin, which was very popular in Roman Catholic circles at the time.

27. Ibid., 2:54-55.

28. González and González, *The Liberating Pulpit,* 59.

29. I have been very impressed by insights that emerged in such discussions at the Church of the Advocate, a church for the homeless formed in Asheville, North Carolina, by the Reverend Judith Whelchel and the Reverend William Jamieson.

CHAPTER 30

A GREAT COMPANY OF WOMEN[1]

Among the issues of social justice clamoring for attention in the 1960s was that of equal rights for women. At the same time as the feminist movement was getting started, an unprecedented number of women were entering the seminaries and ordained ministries of the mainline Christian churches in America. The exact correlation of the women's rights movement with the sudden increase in the number of ordained women is unclear.

On the one hand, most of the denominational decisions to permit such ordinations antedated the movement. Congregationalists and some Baptists were already ordaining women in the nineteenth century. The Methodists agreed to extend full ministerial privileges to women in 1956. Northern Presbyterians[2] decided that women could become teaching elders the same year, and their southern counterpart[3] followed suit eight years later. In 1970, the American Lutheran Church and the Lutheran Church in America both decided that women could become pastors.[4] And the General Convention of the Episcopal Church voted in 1976 to permit women to become priests. Since Sarah M. Evans calls the 1960s the "decade of discovery" for the feminist movement,[5] obviously it was possible for women to be ordained in some of the country's largest denominations before the movement really got under way.

Yet, on the other hand, the possibility that women could be ordained did not make it probable that many would be. Expectations of what women clergy might do were generally circumscribed until the influence of feminism was felt in the churches. There was, for instance, an article in *Monday Morning,* a Presbyterian weekly magazine for clergy, that welcomed the 1956 decision precisely because it saw the role of ordained women as subservient to that of male pastors:

> An ordained woman, among many other specializing tasks, can conduct junior congregations, relieve or supplement the pastor in calling, assist in the pulpit, take the sacraments to the sick and aged, perform certain types of personal work, counsel with young women on personal problems, even marry them, and lay away those of their sex.[6]

Small wonder there was not an immediate rush to the seminaries to prepare for such a challenging vocation.

When the influence of the women's rights movement came to be felt, however, and the possibility of full equality in ministry was opened, ministerial vocation came to be taken much more seriously by women in the churches in which they could be ordained. "In 1972 the Association of Theological Schools in the United States and Canada reported that barely 10 percent of the students in its member institutions were women, whereas by 1987 that figure had climbed to over 27 percent."[7] By 1998, the percentage had increased to 33.6, although only 29.9 percent were in the preordination degree program.[8] In the same year, women made up almost 10 percent of the total number of clergy in the country, an impressive number in view of the fact that three-quarters of American Christians belong to churches that do not ordain women.[9]

While the basic work of ministry in most of the churches that ordain women would appear very much the same to a casual observer, the relative timing of denominational decisions to ordain is related to the polity or form of governance in each body. The Congregationalists and Baptists needed only the agreement of the local congregation. For Methodists, the crucial issue was not so much the ministry of Word and sacrament as it was the full membership in an annual conference that entitled a cleric to a local church appointment. Presbyterians distinguished between ruling elders, who were the local governing board, and teaching elders, who preached and administered sacraments. Lutherans had only one order of ministry of Word and sacrament, that of pastors. Episcopalians claimed to have the threefold ministry of the early church and recognized as priests only those who were ordained by a bishop in apostolic succession.

As Barbara Brown Zikmund has pointed out, however, "in most mainstream denominations, no progress is made towards the recognition of women clergy until women gain significant power and influence as laity."[10] They have to be able to speak and vote in congregational meetings, serve on the local governing board, and be eligible for election as delegates to national bodies before service as ordained ministers becomes a likely possibility. Thus the issue is essentially one of power and the right of women to an equal share of it. Since that is the sort of issue feminists were calling attention to in all other structures of society, it is not surprising that it was raised in the churches.

Most of the women who had preached earlier had done so as evangelists, an activity that was not thought to require ordination. Even then they had functioned mainly in denominations that were in an early stage of transition from sect to church and at a time when there was a shortage of male clergy.[11] Therefore, the large numbers of women who began to be ordained in the 1970s represented a new stage in the histories of both the church and preaching, a stage in which a good deal of Christian preaching was to be done by women for the first time. What difference did that make in the way preaching was done?

PERCEIVED DIFFERENCES BETWEEN THE SPEAKING OF MEN AND WOMEN

An element of the ideology that previously had barred women from the pulpit was an assumption of differences in the psychological makeup of the two sexes. From classical antiquity at least, there had been an assumption that any public speaking done by women would be very different from that done by men:

> Because it was presumably driven by emotion, womanly speech was thought to be personal, excessive, disorganized, and unduly ornamental. Because it was presumably driven by reason, the manly style was thought to be factual, analytic, organized, and impersonal. Where womanly speech sowed disorder, manly speech planted order. Womanly speech corrupted an audience by inviting it to judge the case on spurious grounds; manly speech invited judicious judgment.[12]

Congregations in which some of the first ordained women served noted similar differences between the preaching of men and women. The

College of Preachers in Washington, D.C., held a conference on "Women and Preaching" in 1979 that was attended by about thirty female clergy from all over the country. Part of their preparation for the conference was to gather data from their congregations on the differences members perceived between the preaching of women and that of men. The approximately 150 responses revealed the pattern displayed in the table below.[13]

Perceived Gender Differences in Preaching

1980

Male		Female
	Content	
Intellectual		Down-to-earth
Theological		Emotional
Jargon		Personal
Hard questions		Experiential
Abstract		Life issues
Traditional and male illustrations		No point
		Too personal
	Delivery	
Confident		Solicitous
Controlled		Inviting
Voice-rich		Apologetic
Strong		Hesitant
Bigger		Animated
		Hard to hear
		Expressive
		Warm
	Style	
Formal		Informal
Forceful		Warm
Rational		Personal
Organized		Apologetic
Authoritarian		Ingratiating
Remote		

On the whole, men's preaching was considered more effective. Yet, when a similar poll was taken in 1994, the confidence that had come to women from experience and the greater exposure of congregations to women's preaching resulted in a much better scorecard for them.

> Women's preaching is described in more positive, receptive tones and words than in the earlier study. . . . Hearers appear to register a stronger feeling response to women preaching than to men.[14]

LEVELING THE PLAYING FIELD

One of the first efforts by a woman homiletician to delineate the strengths and weaknesses of preaching by members of her sex and to assist her sisters in building on the one and overcoming the other is **Carol Norén**'s book *The Woman in the Pulpit.*[15] The author, who moved from Duke into an endowed chair at North Park seminary in Chicago, begins by offering advice on overcoming hurdles in the process of becoming accepted as a candidate for ordination. Then she notes the lack of role models up until that time for women who would fill the pulpit. Next she says that women find it easier to claim authority in preaching and leading worship than in other parochial duties. This claim is made on the basis of polls taken among ordained women, and the author offers explanations of why both elements of the statement are true. She then goes on to suggest strategies for dealing with the imbalance.

Norén's fourth chapter is concerned with the way women preachers disclose themselves in the pulpit through their illustrations and autobiographical references and through their nonverbal communication. She says that when they preach from narrative texts in the Bible, they often identify with the character in the story who is weakest or who is "the object of the action rather than the initiator" (65). Sometimes, too, women preachers forget that personal illustrations are to be used when the speaker can be "the representative I" for all members of the congregation rather than for revealing their own need for intimacy. In these ways, the preachers are in danger of perpetuating stereotypes.

Noting that some authorities believe that 90 percent of a speaker's influence depends on nonverbal communication, Norén goes on to indicate the importance of pulpit attire that suggests professional competence. She points out that a woman who tilts or bobs her head while preaching, or breathes in a shallow way, crosses her legs like scissors, or has a rising inflection at the end of sentences is likely to suggest a daughterly diffidence to her congregation rather than spiritual leadership.

"More often," however, "the preacher's gestures and changes in posture communicate, 'Listen to your mother!'" (84).

In looking at ways in which the biblical interpretation of women preachers differs from that of men, Norén points out that "women's sermons regularly manifest several features in exegetical method that concur with liberation and/or feminist hermeneutics as set forth by Justo and Catherine González and Elisabeth Schüssler Fiorenza" (91). That often involves preaching from a familiar biblical text, but calling attention to aspects of it that had escaped notice or not been thought important before, especially the oppressiveness of patriarchy that can be discovered in many passages. Women also tend to show a more concrete relation than men do between the situation in the biblical text and the situation today. "Perhaps the strongest affinity between feminist/liberation hermeneutics and preaching by women in general is the way that both favor narrative/historical texts" (96). Another technique is to identify with the people addressed by a prophet rather than with the prophet, or otherwise "reassign the cast of characters." Finally, women's sermons assume implicitly that the congregation's task is to do everything possible to bring God's new social order to pass.

Female clergy have other characteristic ways of interpreting biblical texts that are not derived from a feminist hermeneutic. These include retelling the story of the text in an amplified way and then drawing an analogy to it in the present context. Often, too, the preachers studied by Norén identify with the least powerful character in the story and thus implicitly expect members of their congregation to do so. "A third characteristic of women's interpretive method is choosing to focus on the dynamics of relationship evidenced in the text, and preach a sermon that works for reconciliation in the divine-human and interpersonal relationships" (107). The last tendency shown by the preaching of the women studied was to interpret the text "from the perspective of the preacher's internal authority, based on her own experiences" (109).

Norén goes on to offer advice pertaining to the use of inclusive language about people and God and women's participation in liturgy, but these get away from characterizing the preaching of women as such. In summarizing what she has to say about the pulpit performance of ordained women, she does note some particular virtues, but on the whole directs her efforts toward helping her sisters avoid some of the practices that played into the hands of those who earlier had wished to denigrate their efforts.

Very different from Norén's book is one written a couple of years earlier, *Weaving the Sermon* by **Christine M. Smith.**[16] While Norén certainly does not want to make women preach like men, her primary goal is to help them avoid practices that could diminish the effectiveness of their proclamation. Smith, on the other hand, writes in a prescriptive way to encourage a new homiletical method that she thinks would result in a great improvement in preaching. That method is indicated in the book's subtitle, *Preaching in a Feminist Perspective.*[17]

The structure of Smith's book comes from the metaphor of weaving that appears in her title. This metaphor, she says, emerged in feminist writing "as an organizing image in women's lives" (7). Her entire project assumes that "there is some qualitative distinctiveness surrounding the preaching of feminist women" (9).[18] The metaphor of weaving points to that distinctiveness: "This image has at its heart the interlacing of conflict and struggle with vision and hope" (15). Or, again: "The essence of the craft [of weaving] is that it always involves the process of uniting and integrating separate strands into an interwoven whole" (21).

Each of Smith's chapters deals with an element of preaching to which an element of weaving is seen to be analogous. Inevitably, in the first the preacher is treated as the weaver. This is the only chapter in which Smith does not draw from feminists as such. Her sources here are women who have written on the psychology of their sex. It is necessary to point out that there is not one psychology for men and women; there are important differences between them:

> While men, particularly white men, appear to have autonomy, individuality, and detachment as integral focus points in their development and growth, women appear to have at the heart of their development qualities of affiliation and interconnectedness. (24)

The basic themes that recur in the psychological studies are of intimacy and relatedness. For the preaching task, this means "women preachers feel that the relationship established in the moment of preaching is as crucial to life and faith as the truths of the biblical witness" (40). It also means the experience of women will be a basic source and norm for that preaching. Anything untrue to that criterion has no place in feminist preaching.

The loom on which the feminist preacher weaves her sermons is her authority. It is, after all, a loom that holds the warp threads under tension and in order, so that the weft may be woven in to create a tapestry with its own pattern. But the authority of the feminist preacher is not "special rights, power, knowledge, and capacity to influence or transform" (46), which male preachers have traditionally claimed. Rather,

> many women would not speak of authority as that which gives them the "right" to speak. Authority has to do with a quality of content, a mode of communication, and an authenticity of message which makes the preaching craft and the moment of proclamation credible, honest, and life-transforming for speaker and listener alike. (47)

That quality, mode, and authenticity are the mutuality and solidarity that make up the loom of feminists' preaching: "The loom of our transforming, creative power, the loom of our life and faith weaving, is our woman's wisdom—a large source of our authority" (54).

The warp threads spread on the loom to undergird feminist preaching are a critique of traditional God language, Christology, and biblical hermeneutics. This is the prophetic dimension of such preaching. One approach to dealing with the traditional masculine and even macho language used about God has been to replace it with feminine images. Women need to hear such images, but that is not all that needs to be done:

> To incorporate the strands of our tradition that point to a prophetic God, a liberating sovereign, and a God who breaks through all idolatries is a much more radical stance in Christian preaching than to articulate equivalent female images in addition to male God images. (75)

Even more radical is the feminist critique of traditional Christology. It postulates that the male Jesus of Nazareth cannot be the normative model for all human beings. What is claimed instead is that "Jesus is not God, but Jesus' activity as justice bearer, healer of pain-filled humanity, and profound relational presence embodies and incarnates God in our world" (81). The most that can be said is that Jesus is a parable of God.[19] And, if feminist theology finds traditional God language and Christology wanting, how much more is it dissatisfied with biblical interpretation that ignores the way the Bible reflects the patriarchal societies in which it was written, and the consequent suppression in its text of women's lives, witness, and worth.[20]

The weft of feminist preaching is a vision for the transformation of the world. Such preaching could be called "weft-faced" because the threads that dominate it will not be those of tradition but those of transformation. This vision should come from feminist thought, music, art, and spirituality. It recognizes the interconnectedness of all forms of oppression; it is committed to peace, disarmament, and living in ecological and relational harmony with all creation; and draws on new feminist understandings of spirituality. While Smith lists as interconnected forms of oppression sexism, racism, classism, militarism, heterosexism, and lack of access, she highlights two: the oppression of the aged and the differently abled.[21] Then, referring to those who have suffered from the interconnected forms of oppressions, she says:

> Until all preachers are willing to open themselves to the voices in their communities and to be changed by those voices and insights, the preaching act will remain individualistic in nature, and the content of sermons will be less than inclusive, isolated from the needs and wisdom of the whole people of God. (123)

The commitment to peace and disarmament and to harmony with creation, the second weft thread of the transforming vision, is obvious enough. The third weft thread of feminist spirituality, however, needs to have its content specified in greater detail. Smith calls attention to three aspects of it: its recognition that spirituality that does not result in political action and social transformation is not worth the name; its affirmation and celebration of the human body; and an appreciation for a wide diversity of spiritual disciplines, perspectives, and practices. Preaching with these three weft threads will be prophetic preaching, shaped as it is by a vision for the transformation of society and individuals.

Design is the final element of weaving either fabrics or sermons. Noting the great freedom and creativity possible in sermon design, Smith quotes a weaving textbook: "One speaks of a design as being *effective* or *successful,* and any design is so when it satisfies the artist's aesthetic impulse and communicates with the audience."[22] The first element of design, proportion, is related to the phenomenon of beginning with women's lives, the process of naming. "One woman's weaving ought never to be more important in *proportion* to the whole, nor should one woman's weaving ever be less important in *proportion* to the whole" (144). The enterprise is collective!

Balance is the second element of design, and it is treated as the weft of transformation's relation to the warp of tradition. Even if the design is weft-faced, "to preach without a strong commitment to the tradition, even in the midst of transforming it, is to stand rootless as a preacher" (145). Emphasis is the element of design that catches and holds the viewer's attention. Two emphases noted in the preaching of women are their tendency to reveal themselves in their sermons and the greater imagination with which they preach. And on the rhythm of a feminist sermon Smith says: "At its very finest [it] should feel like an art piece and have the spirit of transformation" (150).

Preaching, then, that is woven by a woman on the loom of the authority given by mutuality and solidarity, in which the warp is Christian tradition that has undergone a feminist critique and the weft is the transforming vision of global feminism, that follows a design with the proportion of the one woman's voice to that of others, with a balance between tradition (as critiqued) and vision, the emphasis of self-revelation and imagination, and the balance of a work of art, will, in the opinion of Christine Smith, be transforming indeed.[23]

THE METAPHOR OF VOICE

Smith observed the importance of the weaving metaphor for feminist thought, but in more recent years another metaphor has occupied the attention of women homileticians, that of voice. For instance, **Lee McGee** of Yale Divinity School addressed that issue in *Wrestling with the Patriarchs*. Her title probably has a double reference. On the one hand, it refers to the difficulty many ordained women have experienced in preaching, a difficulty a seminarian described by saying:

> For me, the preaching experience is best conveyed in the image of God and Jacob wrestling. There is a combination of feelings, like a wound and a blessing. I'm never sure if I'm meeting an angel or a demon in the sermon preparation and delivery. (13, 29)

In this instance, the woman sees herself in analogy to the patriarch Jacob. On the other hand, a good bit of the struggle is caused by the way women have grown up in a patriarchal society in which their voices were not listened to or valued.

McGee was prompted to this study by her discovery of the way many women agonized over sermon preparation. This led her to research that Carol Gilligan and others engaged in as a collaborative endeavor of Harvard University and the Stone Center at Wellesley College.[24] Their work concerns the psychological development of girls and women. They have found that during adolescence, girls experience an increased desire for relationship, one result of which is their fear of saying anything that may alienate a male or female peer or adult.

A dramatic example of this desire's effect is revealed in the way girls at age fourteen say "I know" only a third as many times as they did at age twelve. Instead, they say "you know" to interviewers, teachers, or friends. This decline is referred to as "loss of voice." "[The girl] seems to be refusing to say what she knows, probably due to a loss of confidence about self, reality, and relationship security" (46).

The need to be true to God, her congregation, and herself while staying in relationship with her congregation is what McGee thinks is responsible for the anxiety women feel in preparing to preach. To help women deal with that anxiety, she developed a five-session workshop process, which she has used in her teaching and in conferences she has conducted. She gives the format for such a program in the last chapter of her book (97-113). In this process for "voice retrieval," women seminarians and clergy are invited to study the lives of great women in church history to see the barriers to being heard they faced and how they overcame them. Then they are exposed to the findings of the Harvard-Wellesley scholars on the psychological development of women and how that affects their willingness to speak.

Next they are taught an adaptation of a counseling method developed by Mary Ballou and Nancy Gabalac to help women overcome "harmful adaptation."[25] The method has five phases. The first is *separation*: "For the woman preacher this step involves separating herself from situations and persons who, either consciously or unconsciously, try to stifle, inhibit, or intimidate her voice" (74). The next step, *validation,* involves the preacher's stating her understanding of everything from personal relations to biblical interpretation to other women who reinforce those perceptions.

Then, by an *association* with other women during at least six sessions, she comes to see that her voice is valued because it is hers, rather than because everyone else shares or even welcomes her insight. After this association has gone on for a while, each member begins to feel an *authorization* of her voice by the group, because what she says is listened to with attention and respect for her situation. The final phase is one of *negotiation,* which involves testing the use of her voice and learning to weigh the relative costs and benefits of using it. "In this phase, women preachers attempt to make conscious decisions about and take risks with voice in preaching. Women preachers discuss how to alter sermon preparation so as to nurture voice" (80).

This, then, is the process McGee has developed to assist seminarians and ordained women to overcome the loss of voice they experienced in their adolescent development—the loss that made sermon preparation an agony for them—and to retrieve their voices so that they can freely and effectively share their insights with the church. Although they go over much the same ground, **Mary Donovan Turner** and **Mary Lin Hudson** have produced a very different book in their *Saved from Silence: Finding Women's Voices in Preaching.*[26] McGee has designed a process while Turner and Hudson have written an essay; their book is more discursive and analytical.

Turner and Hudson begin with a survey of feminist literature in which the metaphor of voice has been important. From that they abstract the following summary:

> "Voice" offers a new possibility for understanding the nature of self and world in relation to God and others. It is distinctive. It can call forth authentic selfhood. It is the self's authoritative expression. Sometimes it is resistant, but always it speaks of relationship. It opens the world to new perceptions, new action, and new ways of living. Voice subverts. Voice transforms. (17)

They go on to say that the metaphor also provides a new way of understanding "revelation, liberation, memory, longing, and justice" (17). They begin their justification for that claim with a two-chapter look at biblical revelation, with one chapter on the Old Testament and the other on the New. In the Bible, the God of Israel is one who speaks and one who listens. Persons and all things were brought into being when God spoke, and what God said came into being. And God is open to hearing the people God has made and responding to their distress; yet, the people of God are not always faithful and need to hear God's judgment spoken by the prophets. "God, through speech, discloses new meaning and becomes a living presence on our journey—even when we fail to be a hearing people" (33).

The authors limit their study of the New Testament to Luke–Acts, which carries forward the Israelite understanding of prophetic speech as an effect of the Holy Spirit:

> The Spirit breathes through Jesus in a limitless way, combining into one single voice the harmony of the voices of prophets throughout the ages. In turn, Jesus promises power to the disciples, and the Spirit sweeps through their silence and draws forth multiple voices alive with the presence of God. . . . They find that their voices offer a unique, unmistakable, essential tone to the sound of God's liberation of the world. (47)

Theological reflection on the biblical understanding of voice leads to the insight that "to be made in the image of God is to be made in the sound of God" (49). This is to say that after the death of Jesus, the prophetic authority of his voice was passed on to all his followers who seek God's realm. The authors say that this theology of voice challenges the traditional Protestant notion of an "unchanging and static Word that somehow comes to expression through women and men unaltered and unscathed" (54). Such a notion perpetuates the status quo and thus promotes disempowerment. On the other hand,

> a metaphor of "voice" suggests that the Holy Spirit still speaks, gives voice to ongoing revelation in the lives of many who have been silenced, often in the name of the very God who is thus represented. (55)

This means that the preacher must not only listen to the biblical text; she must also listen to her own experience in the world. In doing so, she would be trusting in the one who has called her all along and given her voice, rather than obeying the ecclesiastical authorities that have tried to stifle voices like hers through the centuries.

Like McGee, Turner and Hudson believe that women gain strength from the examples of women in church history who have resisted all efforts to silence them in order to use the voices God gave them. They cite New Testament examples and pay particular attention to Hildegard of Bingen among medieval models. They also look at Louisa Maria Layman Woolsey, ordained by the Cumberland Presbyterians in 1889. They look as well at Beverly Wildung Harrison, who rose to power in the United Presbyterian Church by conforming to masculine role models before she began to read feminists, who enabled her to accept herself as a woman and to begin to assist other women in holding on to their vocations.

The large numbers of women in seminaries today and in at least entry-level positions in ordained ministry could leave the impression that finding their voice is no longer a problem for women in the church. Turner and Hudson insist, however, that such is not the case. Referring to the research of Carol Gilligan and others that McGee also mentioned, and to numerous studies of adolescent girls in contemporary America, they show that outer and inner voices still conspire to silence women. Worse, they show that the church has colluded in this conspiracy to prevent women from speaking and to make them mistrust their own voices.

As a result, women are still hindered in their psychological, intellectual, and emotional development. And, since the descriptions of reality they hear come from those who oppress them, the descriptions often do not describe reality as they experience it. Thus there is a necessity for the woman in the church to begin a search, "looking for new theological language, new liturgical language to describe her experience of life, love, God, salvation, redemption, joy as true and good" (91). For a woman to be able to stand in the pulpit and speak that new theological language is a redemptive experience for her. It is also a prophetic act.

This means that for a woman, learning to preach is not just acquiring a set of skills to be added to others. It is the process by which she comes to value her own voice and to believe that she has something to say worth hearing. Key elements in reaching that assurance are imagination and listening: imaginative consideration of the possibilities that lead to a recognition that she has something valuable to say, and listening to voices from other silenced groups so that she will speak not just for herself but for all the oppressed.

Such imagining and listening will assist the preacher in "naming the old worlds out of which we would like to move" (111). Involved in this coming to voice through imagining, listening, and naming is the acquisition of new hermeneutical, exegetical, homiletic, narrative, and feminist and womanist theories. These theories "demand that the preacher bring forth the gospel in her own distinctive, authentic, authoritative, resistant, and relational voice, born of spirit and expressive of [her] own god-likeness" (99). When that happens, women in the church will have found their voice in preaching; they will have been saved from silence.[27]

PREACHING AS A MULTISTRANDED HELIX

While the metaphors of weaving and voice have been important to women homileticians, a different analogy has seemed more appropriate to an ethnographer who has made a specialty of studying women who preach. The work of Elaine J. Lawless, who teaches at the University of Missouri, was drawn on above in our study of women preachers in the Wesleyan/Holiness/ Pentecostal trajectory.[28] From there she has gone on to make the acquaintance of a sizable group of women clergy in mainline churches in the vicinity of Columbus, Missouri. In 1983, she began visiting their churches and recording their sermons. The first fruit of this work was a study of the women themselves, published as *Holy Women: Wholly Women: Sharing Ministries of Wholeness Through Life Stories and Reciprocal Ethnography.*[29] From there she went on, however, to make a study of the way they preach.[30] (**See Vol. 2, pp. 596-601,** for one of their sermons.)

Her method for doing this was to continue visiting the churches of the women and recording their sermons, but she added meeting with them in their groups. These included bimonthly luncheon meetings of as many as twenty-five women in ministry. More to the point was a smaller group that met weekly to study the readings from the Common Lectionary appointed for the following Sunday. She also met with a small number drawn from both groups who were interested in helping her with this book. In addition, there were some who met regularly as friends. In this way, she was in on the sermon preparation process and could also get reactions from the women to her efforts to interpret what they were doing; she calls her method "reciprocal ethnography" (4-6).

On the basis of this research, Lawless was able to find a list of qualities that characterize the preaching of her clergy friends. The qualities she found overlap with a number that have been mentioned above, but she finds all of these to be virtues, while some of the other analyses treat them as ambivalent.[31]

She found storytelling to be a key element in women's pulpit work: "I felt a concerted effort on their part to make the scriptures relevant to modern audiences, not in an ahistorical way, but by bringing the scriptures and people's lives into praxis through storytelling" (87).[32] "In their sermons, the speakers seem to be re-thinking the messages in biblical stories and in the process of preaching often disrupt the listeners' typical response to time-worn sermon analyses and expectations" (89). Thus "the sermons [are] unorthodox in the way they question things," and "some of them suggest that following the rules and regulations, the prescribed ways of doing things, is not necessarily the appropriate plan of action" (91).

The fact that the sermons are "about the outsider, the outcast, the marginal, the youngest, the meek, the quiet one, the unlikely one getting chosen by God" suggests to Lawless that the women are more concerned about "*Where* is God" than with "*Who* is God?" (91). And their sermons locate God in connection, relationship, the interconnectedness of all things, gratitude, the intuitive and the experienced (as opposed to the factual and the cerebral), dialogue, the fluid characteristics of an image, God's actions, their own stories, and being vulnerable (91-93).

Hence the sermons are rarely didactic (93). "Rhetorically, in these sermons, the women relate their beliefs 'about where God is' to their style of preaching by relinquishing typical pulpit hierarchical authority and claiming, instead, an authority based on equality and connection" (94). Appropriately, therefore, "the language used in these sermons is often poetic, powerful, sensuous, intimate, and evocative" (95).

Then, "above and beyond the significance of the characteristics outlined thus far in this chapter lies the power of personal experience stories used by women in their sermons to frame their messages" (95). Women do not use stories to illustrate sermons as men do, especially not canned material from encyclopedias of illustration. Lawless finds that amazing because the women were socialized to share with children the quality of being seen but not heard. "For the first time I am hearing women's stories and experiences from the pulpit. From whence comes the courage, the audacity, the willingness to take such a risk?... In these settings, women's stories become stories enhanced, sanctified, endorsed, validated, confirmed, experienced, enjoyed, shared, and celebrated" (96).

Through the stories, Lawless realized "just how much being female affected their sermons" (97). "Through their first-person stories, women's stories, the women were providing a new validation for the connection between women's lives and their personal, intimate relationship with the sacred. . . . The stories of the women authenticate the immediacy of an immanent God prepared and willing to enter into relationship with them and with all other humans, in mutual and collective connection in spite of differences" (97). "Their personal stories are poignant, deeply private, and sometimes angry" (98). But at any rate, they do not reflect a picture of God as "distant, judging, inaccessible, and 'watching'" (98) to catch them out.

Lawless says in summary, "Relationships, vulnerability, love, empathy, shared concerns, dialogue, and connection are the crucial themes that run throughout the sermons in every aspect—structure, language, storytelling, personal experience stories, and points of view" (99). On the basis of her study, Lawless concludes that there has been a paradigm shift in the church. She builds on Loren Mead's thesis that a shift from "the Christendom paradigm" to a "new paradigm," is occurring. She differs from Mead's belief that the shape of the new paradigm is not yet clear, insisting instead that it has emerged in the preaching of women (161).[33]

> Women's voices offer diverse approaches, reflective attitudes, different perspectives, and stimulating avenues for exploration. The women seem fearless to me, afraid of nothing. Speaking no longer only from the margins, they have broken through the fissures of the "old" Christendom paradigm and offer Christians new cooperative, reciprocal, and dialogic ways of being. (175)

Whether this is a new paradigm for Christianity remains to be seen, but it is clearly an improvement in the church.

BEECHER LECTURERS

In addition to these women who have written about the preaching of women, there have been others who delivered the prestigious Beecher Lectures on Preaching at Yale. Yet none of the four thus honored have chosen to focus on the preaching of women as such. The first, **Helen Kenyon,** was a member of a panel of laypersons[34] asked in 1950 to speak of the way preaching looked from the pew. At the time, Kenyon was moderator of the General Council of the Congregational Christian Churches, having served previously for six years as the chair of the Missions Council of the Congregationalists.

Her topic was "Walking Together."[35] She did not speak primarily as a woman, but rather as a nonprofessional layperson to the assembled clergy and future clergy. Speaking from the perspective of the old covenants between Puritan congregations and their pastors, she was concerned about how they should walk together into the presence of God. She addressed her audience as teachers, preachers, and pastors. She said laypeople need to be taught the Bible and to read good works of theology; they need to be taught to think—and to worship. She stated that preachers should train their congregations in worship, both private and corporate. And she called upon pastors to trust their people more, to allow a member of the congregation to preach occasionally, and to encourage lay evangelism.

Thirty-two years passed before another woman gave the lectures. By then the feminist movement was in full stride, and the distinguished scholar of the Hebrew Bible, **Phyllis Trible,** spoke on *Texts of Terror: Literary-Feminist Readings of Biblical Narratives.*[36] These lectures were written to be a companion volume to her earlier work, *God and the Rhetoric of Sexuality,*[37] although, as she says, the two books differ in emphasis and spirit: "The first is a time to laugh and dance; the second, a time to weep and mourn."[38] Neither book deals with preaching as such, but with the sort of exegetical work that should be done in preparation for preaching. In the first, Trible uses literary analysis to call attention to the way the power of women and life-giving images of their experience shine through essentially patriarchal texts in the stories in Genesis, Ruth, and the Song of Solomon. In her Beecher lectures, she shows how the brutalization, rape, and violation of women have been obscured in biblical accounts such as the stories of Hagar, Tamar, Jephthah's daughter, and the unnamed woman in Judges 19: Texts of Terror, indeed! Since, however, what Trible contributes is a resource for preaching rather than a consideration of the preaching of women as such, it cannot be considered at length here.

A similar verdict must be passed on the next Beecher lectures by a woman, those of **Peggy Brainard Way,** delivered in 1995.[39] Way has taught pastoral theology and directed field education at the University of Chicago Divinity School, the Urban Training Center, the Vanderbilt

Divinity School, and Eden Theological Seminary. She gave a marvelous series of lectures on the way that the voices of pastoral persons have been undervalued as resources for the privileged knowledge of the academic theological disciplines; they should be required listening for everyone involved in theological education or in church judicatories. Yet even though she is an ordained woman and a feminist, her lectures do not address the concerns of this chapter.

The only woman Beecher lecturer to speak about preaching as such is **Barbara Brown Taylor.** Her 1998 lectures were titled *Famine in the Land: Homiletical Restraint and the Silence of God,* but they were published as *When God Is Silent.*[40] An Episcopal priest, Taylor spent six years in administrative posts at the seminaries of Emory and Yale before she was ordained. For the next nine years she was on the staff of a large parish in Atlanta. Next she served as rector of the parish in Clarkesville, a small town in north Georgia.

Her preaching attracted attention from the beginning of her ordained life. She was, for example, asked to assist the legendary Fred Craddock in the instruction of preaching at Emory while she was in Atlanta. She won an award for the series of sermons she preached on *The Protestant Hour* in 1990, she was named by Baylor University as one of the twelve most effective preachers in the English-speaking world, and she has been widely invited to preach and to lecture on preaching. Now she holds an endowed chair at Piedmont College in Demorest, Georgia.[41]

Much of the literature about the preaching of women has dealt with difficulties they have experienced in that task. Therefore, it is helpful to be able to look at the work of Taylor, who has concentrated on preaching, to see how the Word's proclamation has been enriched by the ordination of women.[42] The qualities that make her such an effective preacher are also evident in her Beecher lectures.

The first of the lectures deals with a famine of the Word of God. Part of the problem, she recognizes, is with the way language has been abused. Some of that abuse has been by clergy: "most preachers wield words such as *God* or *faith* as if they were made of steel instead of air" (7). But our society is in crisis over a lack of trust in the power of words to convey meaning. Much of that is a result of consumerism, "which forces words to make promises they cannot keep" (9). Some of the fault also lies with journalism, which Taylor sees as a variety of consumerism. And more lies with the proliferation of words; their sheer quantity makes it hard for us to listen to any of them. She agrees with George Steiner that "we are living in the aftermath of the broken covenant between the word and the world."[43] As for preachers, "at best, we contribute more persuasive words to a world already glutted with them. At worst, we engage in more false advertising" (20). In the presence of so much sound, people are hungry for the Word of God. In all this noise, God seems silent.

In her second lecture, Taylor addresses the perceived silence of God. She says that of those who come to her for counseling,

> the large majority come because they cannot get God to say anything at all. They have asked as sincerely as they know how for answers, for guidance, for peace, but they are still missing those things. (51)

A search of the Scriptures, however, shows that this is not a new experience. "After the delivery of the commandments, God never spoke directly to the people again" (54). Only in Jesus did he speak again, but not all could recognize his voice there. Much of God's silence can be interpreted as for our protection. "Many people pray for an encounter with the living God. Those whose prayers are answered rarely ask for the same thing twice" (57). After hearing the voice of God directly at Sinai, the people of Israel decided they needed a mediator. After Mount Moriah, Abraham never again talked to God. And the resistance of the prophets to the word of God is "legendary."

How we have changed! "When we speak of God, we do not sound so much like people with fire shut up in our bones as we do like people who are blowing on gray coals" (65). We have turned away from God, but apparently God has also turned away from us. "This game of divine hide and seek is part of God's pedagogy in Isaiah, which makes silence a vital component of God's speech" (67). And silence is as much a characteristic of the Christian as of the Hebrew Scriptures. "Even when he spoke, Jesus created silence. Many of his sayings were so cryptic that no response was possible, while others were so offensive that replies were withheld" (75). Furthermore, Jesus himself experienced the silence of God when he prayed from the cross. And such things should surely produce silence in us.

> With the cross and the empty tomb, God has provided us with two events that defy all our efforts to domesticate them. Before them, and before the God who is present in them, our most eloquent words turn to dust. (80)

In her last lecture, Taylor talks about "how we may approach this God with all due respect, proclaiming the Word without violating the silence, by speaking with restraint" (80). Thus she disagrees with those who say that one should preach without restraint. "One big gulp of Gatorade is not the answer"[44] for people dying of thirst; what they need instead is a series of sips. Preaching exists in tension with the silence of God: "We must finally make peace with the incompleteness of our saying, which draws near to but cannot penetrate the silence of God's pure being" (90). Yet when we dare speak, what we say must give evidence of the time spent in waiting before the silence.

That, of course, raises the question: "How does one preach silence? More to the point, how does one preach without profaning God's silence?" (99). Taylor believes that three qualities are needed for such preaching: economy, courtesy, and reverence in the language we use. Preachers address both God and their people, acting as matchmakers between them. "Our job is to find the fewest, best words that will allow them to find one another and then to get out of the way" (101). The economy of preaching, then, will be expressed in short, well-crafted sermons. This means, among other things, that the words of the sermon will be the preacher's own, rather than those garnered from someone else; they must be the truest thing one can say about the subject. They must be like the food a hungry person finds crawling on her belly on the forest floor.

By courtesy in preaching, Taylor means the opposite of coercion. She means respecting the autonomy of those who hear. That involves "leaving partly described what can only be partly described" (111). The preaching of Jesus displayed this courtesy, this respect for the listener, with its stories and images that always have "great pockets of silence in them" (114). Too often preachers are made nervous by God's silence and compensate for it by talking more themselves. But,

> our job is not to pierce that mystery with our language, but to reverence it. Our understanding, such as it is, is never a result of trespassing the bounds of the holy but of knowing where they are, and of having the good sense not to say what cannot be said. (118-19)

This is true because "our duty in this time of famine is not to end the human hunger and thirst for God's word but to intensify it, until the whole world bangs its forks for God's food" (120).

Such a description of the preaching task is bound to raise the question of what sermons that meet these criteria would be like. One that comes very close is Taylor's Lenten sermon, "Life-Giving Fear."[45] For the text of this sermon, see **Vol. 2, pp. 601-4.**) She tells of making a hospital visit with the mother of a five-year-old girl who had a large tumor on her optic nerve. The mother was convinced that the child's illness was punishment for the mother's smoking. Taylor told her she did not believe in such a God, but saw that in doing so, what she said was more threatening than helpful. "If there was something wrong with her daughter, then there had to be a reason. She was even willing to be the reason. At least that way she could get a grip on the catastrophe" (70). In this the mother was much like the rest of us, who seek for a perspective that will give us some sense of control over the chaos of our lives.

Taylor is a lectionary preacher, and this sermon was for the Third Sunday in Lent, Year C. The Gospel is Luke 13:1-9, in which Jesus tells of the Galileans "whose blood Pilate mingled with their sacrifices." Jesus asks if those Galileans were worse sinners than all others. His answer to his own question seemed to give with one hand what was taken away with the other. "*No,* Jesus says, *there is no connection between the suffering and the sin.* Whew. *But unless you repent, you are going to lose some blood too.* Oh" (71).

Jesus responds to the panic the Galileans feel that the terrible things happening around them are the results of their failings. While he denies that to be the case, he recognizes the vulnerability the panic has caused, and urges them to take advantage of it and turn toward the light.

> That torn place your fear has opened up inside you is a holy place. Look around while you are there. Pay attention to what you feel. It may hurt you to stay there and it may hurt you to see, but it is not the kind of hurt that leads to death. It is the kind that leads to life. (72)

That sounds like preaching appropriate for a time when God is silent. It is also a good example of how Christian preaching has been enriched by the widespread ordination of women. It has most of the qualities that women homileticians have claimed are characteristic of the preaching of women. While Lawless may be premature in claiming that a shift of paradigms has occurred in church history, it is at least true that turning over the responsibility for a good bit of it to women has improved the quality of preaching.

FOR FURTHER READING

Lawless, Elaine J. *Women Preaching Revolution: Calling for Connection in a Disconnected Time.* Philadelphia: University of Pennsylvania Press, 1996.

McGee, Lee, with Thomas H. Troeger. *Wrestling with the Patriarchs: Retrieving Women's Voices in Preaching.* Nashville: Abingdon, 1996.

Norén, Carol. *The Woman in the Pulpit.* Nashville: Abingdon, 1991.

Smith, Christine M. *Weaving the Sermon.* Louisville: Westminster John Knox, 1989.

Taylor, Barbara Brown. *When God Is Silent.* Cambridge, Mass.: Cowley, 1998.

Turner, Mary Donovan, and Mary Lin Hudson. *Saved from Silence: Finding Women's Voices in Preaching.* St. Louis: Chalice, 1999.

Notes

1. "The Lord gave the word; great was the company of women who bore the tidings" (Ps. 68:11 BCP 1979 trans).

2. The Presbyterian Church in the USA.

3. The Presbyterian Church, U.S.

4. These were among the Lutheran bodies that merged in 1987 to become the Evangelical Lutheran Church in America.

5. Sarah M. Evans, *Born for Liberty: A History of Women in America* (New York: Free Press, 1989), 263-85.

6. Quoted by Barbara Brown Zikmund, "Winning Ordination for Women in Mainstream Protestant Churches," in Rosemary Radford Ruether and Rosemary Skinner Keller, *Women and Religion in America,* vol. 3 (San Francisco: Harper & Row, 1981), 367.

7. Mark A. Noll, *A History of Christianity in the United States and Canada* (Grand Rapids, Mich.: Eerdmans, 1992), 512. This figure is misleading in that it includes seminaries of denominations that do not yet ordain women, including the Roman Catholic Church and Southern Baptist Convention. There are, however, women students in some of these two churches' seminaries.

8. *Fact Book of Theological Education for the Academic Year 1998–99,* ed. Matthew Zyniewicz and Daniel Aleshire (Pittsburgh: ATS, 1999), 23.

9. *Employment and Earnings* 46 (1999): 214, gives the total number of clergy as 275,000, of whom 25,000 are women. The fraction of three-quarters is an estimate based on an awareness of the total number of Roman Catholics, Eastern Orthodox, Southern Baptists, and conservative evangelicals in the country.

10. Zikmund, "Winning Ordination for Women in Mainstream Protestant Churches," 339.

11. Catherine A. Brekus, *Strangers & Pilgrims: Female Preaching in America, 1740–1845: Gender and American Culture* (Chapel Hill: University of North Carolina Press, 1998).

12. Kathleen Hall Jamieson, *Eloquence in an Electronic Age: The Transformation of Political Speechmaking* (New York: Oxford University Press, 1988), 76. Some speeches delivered by men were considered feminine, but that was regarded as a disgraceful occurrence. Jamieson's thesis, however, is that television, with its scale of living room intimacy, has made what was previously regarded as feminine speech the currently most effective means of oral communication. "The intimate medium of tel-

evision requires that those who speak comfortably through it project a sense of private self, unself-consciously self-disclose, and engage the audience in completing messages that are mere dots and dashes on television's screen. The traditional male style is, in McLuhan's terms, too hot for the cool medium of television" (81). See my review article "Exempla 10," *ATR* 73 (1991): 188-93.

13. Lee McGee with Thomas H. Troeger, *Wrestling with the Patriarchs: Retrieving Women's Voices in Preaching* (Nashville: Abingdon, 1996), 26.

14. Ibid., 28.

15. Carol Norén, *The Woman in the Pulpit* (Nashville: Abingdon, 1991). Parenthetical references in the following text refer to page numbers in this book.

16. Christine M. Smith, *Weaving the Sermon: Preaching in a Feminist Perspective* (Louisville: Westminster John Knox, 1989). Parenthetical references in the following text refer to page numbers in this book.

17. Ibid. She considers what she says to be relevant to the preaching of men as well as that of women, as she frequently makes clear throughout the book.

18. She is aware that what she says applies most directly to the preaching of white Protestant women (ibid., 10), although she is very supportive of the "womanist" movement among African Americans, the "mujerista" movement among Hispanics, and movements in other ethnic groups.

19. Smith notes that African American womanists do not share this feminist critique of Christology (ibid., 89).

20. More will be said about feminist biblical interpretation below when the Beecher lectures of Phyllis Trible are discussed.

21. Smith discusses the need for preaching against most of these forms of oppression in *Preaching as Weeping, Confession, and Resistance: Radical Responses to Radical Evil* (Louisville: Westminster John Knox, 1992). A resource for those committed to doing such preaching is *Sermons Seldom Heard: Women Proclaim Their Lives,* ed. Annie Lally Milhaven, foreword Elisabeth Schüssler Fiorenza (New York: Crossroad, 1991). This collection includes sermons by women on all these topics and more, each followed by an autobiographical statement by the writer, and background information on the subject. A homiletics textbook not explicitly labeled as feminist but sharing much of Smith's perspective is the posthumously published work of Lucy Atkinson Rose, *Sharing the Word: Preaching in a Roundtable Church* (Louisville: Westminster John Knox, 1997).

22. Smith, *Weaving the Sermon,* 141. The quotation is from Shirley E. Held, *Weaving: A Handbook for Fiber Craftsmen* (New York: Holt, Rinehart & Winston, 1973), 310. This is but one of a number of books on weaving that are cited.

23. Similar, although much shorter, descriptions of feminine preaching occur in two introductions to collections of sermons by women, that by Edwina Hunter in the book she edited with David A. Farmer, *And Blessed Is She: Sermons by Women,* ed. David Albert Farmer and Edwina Hunter (San Francisco: Harper & Row, 1990), 91-97, and that by E. Lee Handcock in *The Book of Women's Sermons: Hearing God in Each Other's Voices* (New York: Riverhead, 1999), 1-11. An earlier anthology of sermons by women that has no introduction is *Spinning a Sacred Yarn: Women Speak from the Pulpit,* no editor named (New York: Pilgrim, 1982). Ella Pearson Mitchell has also edited two volumes of *Those Preaching Women: [More] Sermons by Black Women Preachers* (Valley Forge, Pa.: Judson, 1985–88).

24. The best-known publication of this group is *Making Connections: The*

Relational World of Adolescent Girls at Emma Willard School, eds. Carol Gilligan, Nona P. Lyons, and Trudy J. Hammer (Cambridge: Harvard University Press, 1988). Others are listed in McGee and Troeger, *Wrestling with the Patriarchs,* 125 (bibliography).

25. Mary Ballou and Nancy Gabalac, *A Feminist Position on Mental Health* (Springfield, Ill.: Thomas, 1985).

26. Mary Donovan Turner and Mary Lin Hudson, *Saved from Silence: Finding Women's Voices in Preaching* (St. Louis: Chalice, 1999). Turner teaches at Pacific School of Religion and Hudson at Memphis Theological Seminary.

27. The last chapter is followed by three sermons, one by each of the authors and one by Cheryl Cornish, with analyses that show how they exemplify the sort of preaching the book was written to encourage.

28. For Lawless's study of Pentecostal women preachers, see above, pp. 578-80.

29. Elaine J. Lawless, *Holy Women: Wholly Women: Sharing Ministries of Wholeness through Life Stories and Reciprocal Ethnography,* Publications of the American Folklore Society, n.s. (Philadelphia: University of Pennsylvania Press, 1993).

30. Elaine J. Lawless, *Women Preaching Revolution: Calling for Connection in a Disconnected Time* (Philadelphia: University of Pennsylvania Press, 1996). Just as in the former volume Lawless intercalated life stories of the women clergy with the chapters of her analysis, so in this one she interleaves sermons. Parenthetical references following in this section of text are to page numbers from this book.

31. Perhaps, as with other things, the shortcomings of an individual or group are the defects of their virtues.

32. Lawless used italics to set off her first mention of each quality from the discussion of it, but they have been omitted here since only these first mentions are quoted.

33. Her reference is to Loren B. Mead, *The Once and Future Church* (Washington, D.C.: Alban Institute, 1991).

34. The name of the series is "The Church and Its Ministry." The other members of the panel and their topics are, Henry M. Wriston, "The Preacher as Teacher"; Arthur S. Flemming, "The Objectives of the Local Church"; W. H. Auden, "The Witness of the Layman"; Edmund Sinnott, "The Church in an Age of Science"; and Charles P. Taft, "The Social and Economic Program of the Churches." The only one of these lectures that has been published is that of Sinnott, which was issued as a pamphlet by the Edward W. Hazen Foundation in 1950 as "Science and Religion—A Necessary Partnership."

35. Helen Kenyon, "Walking Together" (Cornwall, Conn.: privately printed at Hayloft Press, 1964). I am grateful to Martha Smalley of the Library of Yale Divinity School for providing me with a photocopy of this lecture.

36. Phyllis Trible, *Texts of Terror: Literary-Feminist Readings of Biblical Narratives,* OBT, no. 13 (Philadelphia: Fortress, 1984). The lectures were given two years earlier.

37. Phyllis Trible, *God and the Rhetoric of Sexuality* (Philadelphia: Fortress, 1978).

38. Ibid., xiii.

39. Peggy Brainard Way, *Pastoral Epistemology: Method, Metaphor, Metatheology* has not yet been published in print form. Cassette recordings of these lectures can be obtained from the Yale Divinity School bookstore.

40. Barbara Brown Taylor, *When God Is Silent* (Cambridge, Mass.: Cowley, 1998). Hereafter, parenthetical references that follow in this text section are to page numbers in this work.

41. There are autobiographical elements in the first five chapters of Taylor's *The Preaching Life* (1993); the second half of the book is sermons. Other volumes of her sermons are *Gospel Medicine* (1995), *Bread of Angels* (1997), and *Home by Another Way* (1999). All are published by Cowley Press of Cambridge, Massachusetts. I am grateful to Cynthia Shattuck, editor-in-chief at the time, for sending me copies of these volumes as they have appeared.

42. Although her writings make it obvious that Taylor has a strong social conscience in regard to women's issues as well as other problems, she does not often identify herself as a feminist or even as a woman.

43. Taylor, *Home by Another Way,* 71. Her reference is to George Steiner's *Language & Silence: Essays on Language, Literature, and the Inhuman* (New York: Atheneum, 1986).

44. Taylor quotes these words from the letter of an unnamed friend in ibid., 86.

45. Taylor, *Home by Another Way,* 69-72. This sermon was originally published in *Christian Century,* March 4, 1998.

CHAPTER 31

EVANGELISM IN AN ELECTRONIC AGE

Evangelistic preaching was the form of the earliest Christian proclamation, beginning with the apostles at Pentecost. Through the ages it has been a major activity of the church, especially as new populations have become open to the extension of the Christian community. There is a more restricted use of the term "evangelistic preaching," however, that applies particularly to a sort of preaching that began in the Scotch-Irish Presbyterian sacramental meetings in the seventeenth century. These, in turn, paved the way for the Evangelical Awakening in Britain and the Great Awakenings in America beginning in the eighteenth century. Since then, such evangelistic preaching has become almost indigenous to the United States, where charismatic leaders of revivals have been the instruments of periods of heightened spiritual interest and religious activity.[1]

Most of the chapters so far in this section have been concerned with the effects of social change of one sort or another on how preaching was done. This chapter explores the effects of technological change on the way evangelistic preaching occurs. While revivals have taken place all through the twentieth century and into the twenty-first,[2] technological change has critically influenced three forces in evangelistic preaching: the ministry of Billy Graham, televangelism, and megachurches.

THE CRUSADER FOR CHRIST[3]

Speaking of Billy Graham demands superlatives. In 1956, only seven years after Graham had become a national celebrity through his Los Angeles campaign, Stanley High, an editor of the *Reader's Digest,* said that "Billy Graham has probably preached to more people than any spokesman for the faith in all Christian history."[4] High reckoned the number then to have been twenty million, of whom one million were estimated to have made "decisions for Christ."[5] In the approximately fifty years that have passed since then, the yearly average has probably increased. Indeed, at his 1973 crusade in South Korea, crowds averaged around half a million, and attendance at the final service was more than one million. No other human being has ever had a larger live audience.

Technological change enabling Graham and his team to travel rapidly to all parts of the world made such numbers possible, but even these numbers are dwarfed by statistics for the audience reached by the extensions of his voice through advances in the technology of communication. As he has said, "It has literally become possible to proclaim the Gospel to the entire world."[6] That possibility can be documented by the fact that telecasts of his crusade in Hong Kong were translated into forty-eight languages and were heard by an estimated one hundred million viewers a night.[7] It is not improbable that more people have made decisions in response to his preaching than have even heard any other evangelist. His influence has been felt in yet further ways, such as his acquaintance with many world political leaders, especially his access to every American president since Truman.

Little wonder, then, that biographers have often asked of him the question the apostles asked of Jesus after he calmed the storm at sea: "What manner of man is this?"[8] The facts are fairly straightforward, however little they account for the phenomenon. He was born in Charlotte, North Carolina, on November 7, 1918, the son of a dairy farmer. He grew up in a devout Associate Reformed Presbyterian family, and was converted near his sixteenth birthday at a citywide revival conducted by Mordecai Ham. Although he was unaware of his vocation at a conscious level, he soon began doing things that were usual preparations for ministry. He enrolled at Bob Jones University but, finding it too strict, he transferred to Florida Bible Institute. After doing a good bit of preaching there, he acknowledged his vocation and was ordained as a Southern Baptist preacher.

With that vocational commitment, he felt the need for further education and went to Wheaton College in Illinois. Upon graduation he married classmate Ruth Bell, the daughter of a medical missionary to China and the one whom he identifies as his inspiration and closest adviser. He became pastor of Western Springs Baptist Church in a Chicago suburb and soon attracted enough attention to take over a weekly radio program with the help of singer George Beverly Shea, who has worked with him ever since. During the World War II years he considered the military chaplaincy, but gave that up to become the international organizer for Youth for Christ, a program being developed then to provide one-night rallies in cities that would be an alternative to nights on the town for service personnel on leave. It was through these rallies that he became an itinerant evangelist.

Even though he continued his work with Youth for Christ, Graham was persuaded in 1948 to become president of a Bible college in Minneapolis, Northwestern Schools, despite the facts that he was only thirty and had just a bachelor's degree. While the school grew under his leadership, his heart was truly in evangelism, and he had already begun holding citywide campaigns before he went to Northwestern.

He had previously led revivals in cities as large as Miami and Baltimore, but what he calls the watershed of his ministry was the 1949 campaign in Los Angeles. Held in a giant circus tent, the meeting was originally scheduled for three weeks; it lasted eight. The involvement of movie stars, a gangster, and other celebrities—and overall attendance in the hundreds of thousands and decisions in the thousands, brought media attention from all over the country. During the Los Angeles campaign, William Randolph Hearst instructed his chain of newspapers to "puff Graham." Since that time, few names have been so familiar or been able to open as many doors as that of Billy Graham.

Los Angeles was followed by other campaigns as spectacular, from New England to the South to the Northwest. He easily raised $25,000 in order to begin his weekly network radio program, and that was the occasion of the incorporation of the Billy Graham Evangelistic Association. By 1952, Graham had resigned his other jobs and was ready to devote himself full-time to evangelism.

Even before Los Angeles, however, he and the team he had formed had already drawn up the principles that would govern the conduct of all their campaigns and their strategy for waging them. First, to avoid the pitfalls into which other evangelists had stumbled, they would be strictly accountable for all funds while downplaying their efforts to raise them. They committed themselves to avoiding any situation that could possibly be thought conducive to sexual impropriety. They would cooperate fully with local churches instead of criticizing them. And they would never inflate reports of their results.[9] As a further hedge against any suggestion of avarice, they decided that team members would be compensated by salary alone, with Graham's salary to "compare favorably with that of a typical minister in any average large-city church."[10]

Their campaign strategy was always to have as broad-based an involvement of local churches as possible, to have widespread prayer in preparation for the meeting, and to have as much honest publicity in advance as they could arrange.[11] They also discovered the advantage of placing a member of their staff in the city to supervise preparation well in advance of the campaign. And they arranged for the recruitment and training of thousands of persons to serve as door-to-door callers, members of the choir, ushers, and counselors to those who made decisions. All the expenses for the campaign were to be raised and administered by the local committee and thoroughly audited.

By 1955, their crusades had extended to England and Scotland, with exploratory rallies on the Continent. The next year saw them in Asia, from India to Korea and Japan. It was not until the following year that they felt confident enough to carry their work into New York City. From May through August, the old Madison Square Garden was filled nightly, with even larger services in Yankee Stadium and Times Square. After that it was Australia, Africa, the Middle East, South and Central America, and eventually behind the Iron Curtain. In time, Graham was even allowed to preach in China and North Korea. And for fifty years the world over, the response was greater than anyone had anticipated. "He has preached in person to eighty million people in more than eighty countries and has seen more than two million respond to the invitation at the end of his sermons."[12]

Such statistics prompt the question of what sort of preaching could elicit such a response. The answer hardly seems adequate to the question, because everyone, including his team members and Graham himself, admits that homiletically they are not outstanding. To begin with, one has to note that he is an evangelist. His definition of that term is

> a person who has been called and especially equipped by God to declare the Good News to those who have not yet accepted it, with the goal of challenging them to turn to Christ in repentance and faith and to follow Him in obedience to His will.[13]

This means that the message of all his sermons is the same. God created human beings in his image, but we all have sinned. Yet God loves us still and wishes to forgive us so that we can live with him forever. To make that possible he sent his Son, Jesus Christ, to die on the cross for our salvation. In order to receive this salvation, we have to respond by confessing our sins and committing our lives to Christ as our Lord and Savior. Thus those in the congregation who have not already done so are invited to accept Jesus Christ. When they do that, they will be changed forever.[14]

This means, among other things, that his sermons are not expository.

> What he calls his "text" is actually an introductory Scripture to gain attention for John 3:16, which is invariably his real text. That is true whether he is dealing with "Teenage Vandalism," "Nonconformity to the World," or "The Ten Commandments." In each of these sermons he uses other "texts" to illustrate man's need, to describe a given human problem, to present an illustration of God's provision, or to state a condemnation of specific sins. In each case, however, he is presenting a lengthy introduction to his real business of inviting men to accept God's provision in Christ.[15]

While Graham has had essentially one message through his entire preaching career, his delivery has changed considerably over the years. In the beginning he had a frenetic style that Martin has called "assault."[16] He would move from one end of the platform to the other, with his arms in constant motion and his words coming in a constant flow, almost browbeating his congregation into submission. Through the years, however, he has evolved a calmer and quieter delivery. This moderation is not simply an effect of the aging process, but reflects as well a change of attitude. While earlier a great deal of anger was detected in his manner, he now realizes that the preacher's attitude toward rebellious sinners should be the compassion of the God who became incarnate in order to deliver them from sin. This is part and parcel of a mellowing process, an indication that he takes his own medicine and has continued to mature spiritually.

Attempts to explain the power of his attraction differ from writer to writer, depending on the disposition of each toward him. Some regard him as a special agent of the Holy Spirit sent to be a channel of redemption in a sinful age. Others would offer a demonic explanation if they believed in demons. Most, however, are convinced that besides being an extraordinarily charismatic person, he has a transparent conviction of his message's utter truth. His most persuasive argument is *ethos,* the trustworthiness of the speaker, rather than *logos,* reason, or *pathos,* the capacity to stir emotion.[17] To the extent that it can be accounted for, much of that impression seems to derive from his trust in the authority of the Bible.

His absolute conviction of that issue dates back to slightly before the Los Angeles campaign. His Youth for Christ colleague Chuck Templeton had intellectual doubts that activated Graham's own. On a moonlight stroll in the San Bernardino Mountains, he wrestled with his uncertainty until he was able to pray: "Father, I am going to accept this as thy Word—*by faith!* I'm going to allow faith to go beyond my intellectual questions and doubts, and I will believe this to be your inspired Word."[18] After that he never looked back. One of the traits of his preaching that has been noted most often is the absolute conviction with which he exclaims, "The Bible says . . . !"

Almost as remarkable as Graham's impact on those who have come into his presence, is the way he has taken advantage of technology to extend that impact. It goes back at least to his days as pastor of the Western Springs church when he took over a popular religious broadcast in the Chicago area. This was continued in 1950 when he began a weekly radio broadcast, *The Hour of Decision,* over ABC. That program grew until it was carried on a thousand stations and had an audience of more than twenty-five million. A few months after he began network broadcasting, he started writing a syndicated daily newspaper column, "My Answer," which soon had a daily circulation of twenty million.[19]

In 1951, the Billy Graham Evangelistic Association made the first of its many religious motion pictures. As early as his 1954 crusade in London, his sermons were relayed by telephone line to theaters and halls all over England so that four hundred thousand more people could hear his message. His use of television has already been mentioned. He was quick to see the advantage of satellites for extending the range of virtual presence at one of his meetings. Now BGEA is assessing the effectiveness of a Web site on the Internet, www.billygraham.org.

Along with the newspaper column, books he has written, and magazines he has founded, from *Christianity Today* to *Decision,* these uses of media technology have been extensions of his preaching as such.[20] They have multiplied his audiences beyond even the thousands and hundreds of thousands who could hear him preach in person, to millions at a time, a homiletical development of some significance.

All this is a demonstration of the tendency to fall into superlatives when discussing the ministry of Billy Graham. Yet he is not without fault, nor is he superior to others who proclaim God's Word, as he would be the first to say. Regret can be felt for what appears to be his tendency to dwell on the number of celebrities with whom he has come in contact—although it must be admitted that they seem just as eager to claim association with him. Those who have what they consider to be a more nuanced theological position may wish that his did not seem oversimplified to them, although, again, there has been development over the years, and he has suffered much from fellow evangelicals who think he has sold their faith down the river. These conservatives also deplore his willingness to work not only with liberal Protestants, but with Roman Catholics, Eastern Orthodox, and even Jews as well. Like him or not, one must admit that Christianity had no more visible advocate in the twentieth century.

TELEVANGELISTS

As effective at using television as Billy Graham has been, he has not attempted a weekly program—much less, a more frequent one—because of the high cost of doing so.[21] Where he has hesitated, however, others have not. Something about the very nature of Evangelicalism makes that inevitable. If the belief exists that anyone who has not been converted to Christ will spend eternity in hell, then there also exists the obligation to rescue as many as possible. And if conversion is understood as "the life-changing experience of turning one's life over to Jesus,"[22] then the obligation is to provide opportunities for that to occur.

Since evangelists concentrate on conversion rather than the pastoral care and spiritual development of parishioners with whom they are in a long-term relation, the impetus is to reach as many people as possible.[23] This motive is reinforced for many who are premillennialists[24] because of their interpretation of Matthew 24:14 (KJV): "And this gospel of the kingdom shall be preached in all the world for a witness unto all nations; and then shall the end come." Providing opportunity for everyone on earth to hear the gospel would hasten the second coming of Christ.[25]

Television's potential for reaching the widest possible audience is seen in the way that Billy Graham's 1990 Hong Kong telecasts were translated into forty-eight languages and heard nightly by one hundred million people. This technology magnifies enormously the number of people who can be reached by a given evangelist. Small wonder, then, that so many of this calling rushed to avail themselves of such an opportunity to maximize their efforts.

Of course, something of this potential for reaching larger audiences was already present in radio and many, including Graham, took advantage of it. The first radio station to broadcast on a regular basis was KDKA, Pittsburgh, which went on the air November 2, 1920. Two months later, it broadcast its first religious program by airing the evening service of Calvary Episcopal.[26] The promise of religious broadcasting was soon recognized, and many churches even experimented in owning radio stations. Stable patterns did not begin to appear, however, until the late 1920s, when networks of stations were first formed. The earliest of these, NBC, developed a policy toward the end of 1928 to protect itself from religious groups' requests for public service time. It decided that responsibility for Protestant airtime would be lodged with the Federal Council of Churches, while the National Council of Catholic Men and the Jewish Theological Seminary of America would administer the time allotted to their constituencies. At the same time, they said airtime would not be sold for religious broadcasts. CBS and ABC followed NBC's approach. Only Mutual dissented, deciding to make no free time available to religious groups, but to market it to those who were willing to pay.[27]

The effect of this was to virtually exclude from the airways representatives of the Evangelical and Pentecostal traditions. This arbitrary decision was not based on the percentage of the population represented by these different traditions. When the radio networks were being founded, conservative Christians were admittedly in decline as a result of the fundamentalist/modernist controversy, but their numbers were never small. The relevant distinction between them and the members of the Federal Council of Churches as far as this policy is concerned was social: they did not belong to the elite. There was a gulf of social class between the churches that were given public service time on radio and those that had to purchase their airtime. The Evangelicals and Pentecostals, who have since formed the National Association of Evangelicals, as well as those who agreed with them, were trying to convert a world in which they counted for little.

The first preacher to demonstrate television's potential for religious propagation was a Roman Catholic, Bishop Fulton J. Sheen, whose *Life Is Worth Living* series became a commercially sponsored part of ABC programming in 1952. He attracted an audience competitive with that for the entertainment provided by other channels for five years. When he stopped broadcasting, he did so because of ecclesiastical opposition rather than any decline in popularity.

By the 1950s, Billy Graham had begun televising his crusades, but he made no other use of the medium. Within a few years, Oral Roberts also began using TV to air his tent revival and healing services, but as his fame spread, he began to broadcast his program from a television studio instead. In the 1960s, Rex Humbard became the first evangelist to build a church especially for telecasting. In the early days of televangelism, the format of its programs came from evangelistic services in tents and stadia, but gradually some of the preachers began to develop approaches more compatible with the medium, as when Pat Robertson copied the structure of television talk shows for his *700 Club*. Robertson was also a pioneer in the next stage of religious telecasting, when he led the way in forming a network of stations and satellites to carry conservative Christian programs.

It is difficult to characterize the preaching of the televangelists because several have developed such individual styles. Perhaps the best that can be done is to follow the admittedly breezy taxonomy created by Jeffrey Hadden and Charles Swann to enumerate the main types of television preachers.[28] Their first category is "Supersavers," by which they mean the pioneers of religious telecasting. There are, however, distinctions to be made among them. Graham's sermons were simply those he preached at his crusades. Jerry Falwell's sermons on his *Old-Time Gospel Hour* are like Graham's in that they are what he prepared for a live audience. But they differ in that Falwell's were for the regular congregation of his seventeen-thousand-member Thomas Road Baptist Church in Lynchburg, Virginia, instead of for those attending an evangelistic meeting. When Oral Roberts moved to the studios of the university he founded in Tulsa, he set his sermons in the context of what was essentially a religious entertainment show, with music and guest stars. Rex Humbard was like Falwell in telecasting the services of his church (the Cathedral of Tomorrow in Akron, Ohio), but these had a format similar to Roberts's entertainment pattern.

The next category of Hadden and Swann, "Mainliner," has only one member, Robert Schuller, who is a minister of a nonfundamentalist denomination, the Reformed Church of America. His message, however, is not as typical of the mainline churches as it is of the "power of positive thinking" approach of his fellow RCA cleric, Norman Vincent Peale. The third category is "The Talkies," named for televangelists who use the format of a TV talk show, and includes Jim Bakker, Pat Robertson, and Paul Crouch. These shows do not have extended sermons as such, but fit short meditations into the flow of their magazine format.

"The Entertainers," which includes evangelists like Jimmy Swaggart, have essentially a musical show into which preaching is inserted. "The Teachers" includes evangelists with a more didactic style who conduct

Bible study from a set created to look like a living room. Richard De Haan, Paul Van Gorder, and Frank Pollard belong to this group. What "The Rising Stars"—James Robinson, Kenneth Copeland, and Jack Van Impe—have in common is not so much a style as a popularity that was increasing when *Prime Time Preachers* was published in 1981. The last category, "The Unconventional," is another that has only one member, Ernest Angley, who, the authors say, has been called "the lunatic fringe" of religious broadcasting because of his claim to have seen demons leaving those he healed, angels standing by his side, and even God.

Obviously, the medium of each of these televangelist groups colors the way they preach. Therefore, to find a common denominator for the preaching of the entire group, it is necessary to look at content rather than style. With the exception of Schuller, they share a theology and a worldview—though Pentecostals add an expectation of the gifts of the Holy Spirit to the evangelical creed. They all have a strong doctrine of biblical inspiration, and most are fundamentalists. They believe in a God who is intimately involved in the world and the lives of individuals and nations, so that nothing happens without divine causation or at least permission. And they tend to have great confidence in their ability to discern why God intervenes in a particular way.

God's overall purpose is the salvation of all, and the evangelists are God's agents in the conversion of souls. The Pentecostals also hope to be the media through whom people are baptized in the Holy Spirit and receive such charismata as the gift of tongues. Many of the televangelists also believe that God has given them the gift of healing the physical as well as spiritual ailments of those who hear them, and some also claim to be able to cast out demons.

All of them see the world as a battleground where the forces of God contend with those of Satan, and many of them think that the warfare is approaching a climax. They expect Jesus to return soon and begin his thousand-year reign, but before that happens they expect the "rapture," the instant and simultaneous taking-up into heaven of all saved souls. In the first seven years after the rapture, Jews will be converted to Christianity, and the antichrist will rise and contend against Israel. When the antichrist is defeated, Jesus will return.

What are regarded as biblical prophecies of these events are closely correlated with world events today in an effort to show that these are the last days. Even among those who put less emphasis on the approaching end, however, the United States is generally given a special role. Communism is often identified with the antichrist, and America has the vocation to oppose it. In order to do so, however, the nation will have to return to what are understood as the religious roots of the country. It will have to oppose evil in every form. Most of the evil tendencies in the culture are lumped together under the rubric of secular humanism, "man's attempt to solve his problems independently of God."[29] Crucial to this restoration of righteousness is the protection of the nuclear family from the threats of feminism, abortion, and homosexuality. The restoration of public prayer to the schools is also vital.[30]

Another item that has high priority on this agenda is the evangelists' ability to continue their ministries. First and foremost, that means they must continue to receive the donations necessary to purchase very expensive airtime, which has led to an emphasis on fund-raising that many have found distressing. While a few of the televangelists have been shown to have feathered their own nests by this means, such charlatanism does not seem to be the major dynamic in this emphasis on raising money. Most of the religious broadcasters seem to be sincere people who are caught up in the catch-22 of their situation. They feel the need to go on TV in order to save as many souls as possible. To do that, they have to meet an enormous regular budget. To meet this budget, they have to spend so much time encouraging donations that they have less time to preach the gospel. And some have been led by this necessity into a theology that promises material as well as spiritual benefits to those who both respond to God's grace and give financial support to the TV ministry.[31]

In the late 1980s, a series of scandals connected with television ministries left the impression with many people in the general culture that all such preachers' credibility had been so thoroughly damaged that they lost all influence and following. Jim Bakker was accused of adultery and later of wider sexual irregularity. It then transpired that he and his wife, Tammy Faye, had lived a life of luxury on the offerings to their ministry, and he consequently spent time in federal prison for a number of financial irregularities. Jimmy Swaggart was then discovered to have visited a prostitute, and Oral Roberts claimed that God would take his life unless he raised $8 million in a month.[32]

What has happened, however, is not that such broadcasting has disappeared or even lost its audience. Bobby C. Alexander said:

> By January 1989, almost two years after news of the Bakker scandal broke, television religion showed signs of recovering audiences and contributions. Many stations had returned controversial personalities to the air. The number of organizations producing religious television had increased. And contributions were holding steady.[33]

What really happened was that televangelism dropped from the consciousness of the mainstream of American culture. That, however, did little to diminish its audience, because that audience had always been composed largely of Evangelical and Pentecostal Christians who remained loyal to this expression of their faith.[34] In fact, these groups have become a progressively larger percentage of the American public without the rest of the country's having really noticed.[35] At the time of this writing, about half of the Christians in the United States are Roman Catholic. Approximately half of those remaining belong to liberal churches of the sort that make up the National Council of Churches, while the other half belong to conservative churches of the sort that belong to the National Association of Evangelicals.[36] Thus part of the significance of the public ado over televangelism in the 1970s and 1980s is that it brought a large segment of American Christianity into its overall consciousness.[37]

MEGACHURCHES

One of televangelism's curiosities is that while its audience is isolated individuals, it has the capacity to communicate to the viewer a sense of being part of a wider body, called the "virtual church." This phenomenon is to be accounted for in terms of the two main technologies these ministries use: television and the computer. It has been pointed out that the scale of television is living room intimacy. Listening to a person whose face seems almost life-sized in the comfort of home creates a sense of personally knowing the speaker.[38] Regulars on a program, especially the preacher, come to seem like old friends, far more familiar, for instance, than one's pastor. Then the capacity of the computer to personalize letters, to retrieve information about the addressee that can be fitted into the boilerplate of a solicitation, to take note of prayer requests, and to offer counseling increases further the sense of being a member of an intimate group. A person is known and valued as he or she knows and values the evangelist. Yet, obviously, this sense of intimacy is an illusion. A single listener among hundreds of thousands or millions can hardly rise to the consciousness of the broadcasters. The community is only virtual. Or, as a poster of the Episcopal Ad Project trenchantly expressed it: "You can't receive holy communion from a Sony!"

By contrast, the third phenomenon of late-twentieth-century evangelism to be considered, the megachurch, is far more ecclesial in its orientation than the evangelical community has traditionally been. As noted above, most of the effort in the past has gone to convert people, with the assumption that those who have been saved will somehow continue in the life of grace and become integrated into a local church. The megachurch movement, however, is congregationally based, uses its own worship to evangelize, and has as its goal the integration of converts into its life.

For instance, the vision of founder Bill Hybels for Willow Creek Community Church in the Chicago suburb of Barrington, the prototypical megachurch, is the second chapter of Acts as expounded by Trinity College professor Gilbert Bilezikian. As Hybels said:

> What motivated me twenty years ago, and what motivates me today, is the priceless goal of seeing redeemed people become the church. To one another. I am reenergized every time I see people who were formerly lost in darkness now giving and receiving love, walking through valleys with one another, rescuing each other, and helping each other with their physical and spiritual needs.[39]

The presentation of megachurches that follows is based primarily on Willow Creek.[40] Megachurches can be defined as "large churches with more than 2,000 persons in attendance at Sunday services."[41] A brief sketch of how this church, which averages sixteen thousand in weekend attendance, came into being provides a perspective from which megachurch preaching can be understood.

From a human point of view, it would seem that Willow Creek was begun almost by accident. Hybels did not start out to enter the ministry; in fact, to the best of my knowledge, he has never been ordained. While he was converted at summer camp when he was sixteen, and attended a "Christian" (i.e., evangelical) liberal arts college, he dropped out after two years to work in his father's successful wholesale produce business. There is an affluence and even a sophistication in his background that are rare in some evangelical circles. He learned to sail in his father's oceangoing yacht and fly in his plane, and was given a sporty car and a motorcycle of his own. He grew up in a Dutch evangelical culture that had begun in Michigan and spread through the Midwest, a culture that combined Calvinist orthodoxy with intense interest in education. While Evangelicalism makes up a larger proportion of the total population in the South than in other parts of the country,[42] there are European ethnic communities in the Midwest that have been an important part of the movement since at least the end of the nineteenth century.[43]

Even as Hybels threw himself into work in the family business, he began to have deeper vocational stirrings, wondering if God was calling him to some form of ministry. The following summer, that of 1972, he went, as had become his custom, to serve on the staff of the church camp where he had been converted. While there he was visited by Dave Holmbo, an old friend who had recently taken a job as assistant music director of a church in the Chicago suburb of Park Ridge. To provide the music at a contemporary service the church had recently begun offering, he had founded a Christian rock-and-roll group called Son City that was already giving concerts all around the area. By the end of the summer, Hybels had decided to move to Chicago and work for the association that sponsored his camp. Once he was there, Holmbo asked him to become one of the group's guitarists and to begin a Bible class for them on Wednesday evenings. Everything that happened later seems to have grown out of that.

The Bible study grew so rapidly that Hybels and Holmbo decided to organize a weekly outreach program to which the Christian young people could invite their unchurched friends. In planning for this, the Bible study class, most members of which attended a high school that placed great emphasis on the arts, insisted that the program be one that eliminated the "cringe factor" so frequently experienced by young evangelicals who invited their friends to church. Hybels, remembering this from his own efforts to evangelize as a teenager, said:

> The typical traditional church is no place for the unchurched. To anybody but the already convinced, the average church service seems grossly abnormal. It makes no sense to those who haven't grown up in it, to those who don't know the drill. The music we sing, the titles we choose, the way we dress, the language we use, the subjects we discuss, the poor quality of what we do—all of these lead the average unchurched person to say, "This is definitely not for me."[44]

The suggestions the young people made at that meeting were to determine the basic approach that Willow Creek Church would take when it was organized a couple of years later. They had to have a more attractive setting than the basement room in which they sat on carpet squares. The music had to be the sort of Christian rock and roll played by Son City. It would help to have a short dramatic presentation that raised the question dealt with by the sermon. A media presentation would add to the effect. And Hybels was not to do the sort of expository treatment of the next section of a biblical book that had characterized the Bible studies he had led. "Make a point that is biblical but relevant to the kids' lives, tell some good stories to illustrate it, and keep it down to about twenty-five minutes," he was told.[45] Within six months, the group had grown to three hundred. And, since the outreach program was designed for the unchurched, it was necessary to add a Sunday evening event in which the converted members could be fed spiritually. This was called Son Village, while the outreach program was designated by the band's name, Son City.

The high point of Son City was an evening in May 1974 when there was a major outreach program. Six hundred young people turned out and, when Hybels issued an altar call, half of the group made decisions for Christ. By that time, however, relations between the host church and Son City had become strained; the impact of so many excited teenagers on an ordinary congregation was too jarring, even though many approved of the good work.

At the same time, Hybels had been finishing his undergraduate degree at Trinity College in Deerfield, Illinois, where he was exposed to the vision of Dr. Bilezikian. In that context, Hybels began to wonder if this vision of Acts 2 could be applied to adults as well as high school students. By then Son City had an average attendance of twelve hundred young people, but Hybels resigned in May of 1975 to start a church, and Holmbo decided to help him. The core idea for the adult congregation was the sort of "seeker service," as they had come to call it, that they had used at Son City: "a regularly scheduled, high-quality, Spirit-empowered outreach service where irreligious people can come and discover that they matter to [God] and that Christ died for them."[46]

Many of the young people who had worked on the Son City team joined Hybels in founding Willow Creek. They decided that the nearby suburb of Palatine was the place to start, and they wanted to focus on the unchurched. To make sure they avoided the things that kept people away, they made a door-to-door survey, asking those who did not attend why they did not.[47] They were looking for things to avoid in their church, because it was not to be formed from Christians who transferred in from other congregations; it was to be recruited entirely from the unchurched. For a meeting place, they rented a local movie house for Sunday morning hours when it was unused, because it was easy to get to, had a large parking lot, and could seat nearly a thousand people. The theater was used for their evangelistic "seeker service," while, initially, the service for believers was held in a conference room they added on to a warehouse in which their equipment was stored. Placing the seeker event at the usual time for church services while asking church members to come on a weekday evening reversed what had been standard practice, but reflected the priority of putting evangelism first. And the seeker service followed the format of Son City's outreach programs, which was not dissimilar to that of televangelism's entertainment style.[48]

The opening service, which attracted 125 people, was held at Willow Creek Theater on October 12, 1975. The midweek New Community services for believers began the following January. Within two years, the Sunday service was filling the theater twice; within three, they had bought the ninety-acre property in South Barrington that has become their home, although they did not move into their own building until 1981. The story of how they came to their present system of four weekend services, almost filling their forty-five-hundred-seat auditorium for each, and two midweek New Community services is interesting. So is the way the team developed their program to meet needs and offer services.[49] Such information is not necessary, however, to understand the homiletical strategy of Willow Creek and other megachurches, both in their seeker and in their believer services.

People wishing to attend a weekend service at Willow Creek will turn from a major road onto a well-marked drive leading to an enormous parking lot, into which a corps of attendants welcomes and directs them. As seen from the road, the building could be any of a number of large corporate headquarters that dot the area. An elegant modern building sprawls above a pond on a spacious and well-landscaped tract. Entering the building through a vast open space with information booths and other services, the visitor is welcomed again and pointed toward the auditorium. It resembles an immense theater with unusually comfortable seats more than it does a church building as commonly conceived. There are several tiers of seating, and the area is wider than it is long. No traditional religious symbol is to be seen anywhere. The stage is wide, with a bandstand that accommodates a fifteen- to twenty-piece orchestra occupying the rear center. Up high on each side is an enormous television screen. The nearest thing to ordinary church furniture is a pulpit of sorts, but the resemblance is slight. It is made of Plexiglas and is hardly noticeable, even when it is being used. The center pedestal is narrow, but the ledge on which a manuscript, a Bible, and other things can be placed has room for all. There is an air of expectancy in the audience, and those who see friends visit with animation.

The service opens with an energetic prelude played by the orchestra. The TV screens magnify what is taking place on the stage as seen from a number of camera angles. A group of perhaps eight vocalists, male and female, clad in upscale, informal mod clothing, line up in front of the band with individual microphones and belt out the opening song. All the songs, like everything else in the service, are on the theme of the sermon that day—and could indeed be considered a part of it. There is no unscripted moment. For all that anyone unacquainted with the repertoire of Christian rock might know, the songs could have been written for the service, so well do they serve its theme.

The musicians then vacate the stage so that a short dramatic presentation can be given. On the last weekend in September 1999, this was a monologue by someone dressed as the Lone Ranger who talked about the way that American individualism and self-reliance often cut people off from the needed support of others. Next came a testimony to the difference that faith and a church family make. This September Sunday, it was given by a staff member who had experienced major illness in his family and had been given the support that made it endurable. After another song and announcements, an offering was taken, with the admonition that visitors were not expected to contribute. A seeker service ends with the "message" from Hybels or one of the other teachers. This particular Sunday, he began a series of sermons entitled "Nobody Stands Alone."[50] (For the sermon, see **Vol. 2, pp. 605-17.**)

He began by noting that persons who suddenly erupt into violence and kill a number of others are generally found to be loners. By the same token, the failure of a schoolchild to make friendships, or a potential mate's lack of relationships, is a serious warning sign. That is because friendships are so important in the scheme of things. There are few issues about which God is more concerned than friendships, especially the sort that move people from loneliness into rich, Christ-honoring community. The Bible is full of warnings about the danger of isolation. So the question is: How do we move from standing alone to standing together? And the answer grows out of the nature of true friendship. It is not about trying to get someone else to take care of you in one way or another, but about seeking that person's well-being.

Starting and building such friendships is a risky, inexact, lengthy, and frustrating challenge, but success is worth the effort. A tip to those accepting the challenge is to look for friends in an environment conducive to such mutual commitments. Willow Creek has been such an environment for many, since such relationships are one of the two main purposes for which the Christian church exists. Ways of going about trying to form these relationships include joining one of their many small groups,[51] volunteering for a ministry team at the church, or becoming a member of a sports or fitness group, but the person seeking such relationships has to take the initiative. The idea for Willow Creek originated because Hybels took the initiative in forming a friendship with Dr. Bilezikian.

When such preliminary initiative has been taken, ways to deepen the relationship involve asking questions that encourage confidences about what is going on in the life of the other. It is by forming such friendships that one discovers how much they are a part of what life is all about. Although there are thousands who attend Willow Creek who have never become more involved, Hybels's dream for the church is that no one will have to stand alone for the rest of their life. The closing prayer was for those who were still lonely and for the other members to reach out to them.

It is clear that this service as a whole followed Hybels's norms for a seeker service: it was "a regularly scheduled, high-quality, Spirit-empowered outreach service where irreligious people [could] come and discover that they matter to [God] and that Christ died for them." It is also obvious that this sermon met the criteria the teenagers had set for Hybels in the original Son City outreach program: "Make a point that is biblical but relevant to the kids' lives, tell some good stories to illustrate it, and keep it down to about twenty-five minutes."

This sermon was topical life-situation preaching, in which an alternative was offered to the meaninglessness of much of contemporary life. While intended to be entirely biblical, it did not depend on a single text, much less present an exposition of an extended passage. Instead, it sought to condense the meaning of the Bible as a whole, with a number of citations of particular verses (although these were often given a modern paraphrase) and general summaries of biblical teaching. The remedy for the diagnosed condition was not merely that the Willow Creek community was a good place to make friends, because there was always the implication that such relationships are a by-product of relationship with God through Christ. It was, as it was intended to be, an invitation to seekers to satisfy their longings in the Body of Christ.[52]

The other kind of services held at Willow Creek, the "New Community" midweek services for believers, begins with somewhere from one-half to three-quarters of an hour of praise to God in word and song. The Lord's Supper is celebrated once a month. And they "learn together, going through the Bible book by book and focusing on themes—such as 'downward mobility' from Philippians 2—that become rallying cries throughout the church."[53] So the preaching is the continuous exposition of a biblical book. Many evangelicals assume that such *lectio continuo* expository preaching is normative among the converted. Rick Warren shares that conviction:

> When preaching to believers I like to teach through books of the Bible, verse-by-verse. . . . Verse-by-verse, or book, exposition builds up the

> body of Christ. It works great when you're speaking to believers who accept the authority of God's Word and are motivated to learn the Scriptures.[54]

This acceptance of expository preaching as the norm for the faithful reflects the Reform tradition of Calvin and the Puritans, in which the public exegesis of Scripture is expected to convey grace *ex opere operato*. Not surprisingly, then, preaching is often spoken of as teaching, and Hybels designates those who deliver sermons as teachers more often than as preachers. He also does not refer to traditional orders of ministry, but instead has a charismatic understanding of office in the church, based on 1 Corinthians 12:28 and Galatians 5:22-23. He considers his own gifts to be leader,[55] evangelist, and teacher, in that order.[56]

His understanding of the relative relations of teaching and leadership is that both are vital to the church. "The church *needs* great teachers. Preaching is the core ministry of the church, and lives will not change without powerful and Spirit-inspired teaching from the Word of God." But,

> when teachers stand in front of people, their chief desire is to accurately and compellingly communicate biblical truth in the hopes of impacting lives. But when leaders have the microphone, there's another agenda. Usually they have a purpose, mission, or cause that they want to get people fired up about."[57]

Willow Creek is perhaps the only local church that has ever been studied by Harvard Business School to see how well it serves its constituents. In the discussion, a student was asked what she thought of the congregation's mission statement. Her reply was: "It sounds to me like they're . . . well . . . *they're trying to turn atheists into missionaries.* And frankly, I see that as one hell of a challenge!"[58] Hybels agrees. The church exists to transform the lives of all its members in the way lives were transformed in Acts 2, and the role of preaching in the transformation of lives is crucial.

> In a biblically functioning community, the leaders make sure the preaching is done only by those who have the appropriate spiritual gifts, who have yielded themselves to the spiritual disciplines, and who have been anointed by the Holy Spirit to teach. When that happens, life starts pulsating through a place.[59]

Megachurches that share the goal of Willow Creek do not see their purpose so much to be big as to be church.

The unifying theme of this chapter on late-twentieth-century evangelistic preaching has been the ways in which technology has been employed to make the preaching more effective. The uses of technology in megachurches have been implicit rather than explicit in the foregoing discussion, but it is easy enough to raise them to consciousness. The technologies have been mainly the television projection screens, which have made it possible for all the people in a large auditorium to have an intimate view of those leading in the worship; and the sound systems, which have enabled all to hear the music and the preaching without straining.[60] The combination has also made seekers feel at home in an environment as familiar as their TVs, computer screens, stereos, and the rock concerts they attend. This combination of the familiar and the ecstatic opens them to the proclaimed word of invitation. Therefore, the defining characteristic of evangelistic preaching in this era has been its use of technology.

FOR FURTHER READING

Alexander, Bobby C. *Televangelism Reconsidered: Ritual in the Search for Human Community.* American Academy of Religion Studies in Religion, no. 68. Atlanta: Scholars Press, 1994.

Graham, Billy. *Just As I Am: The Autobiography of Billy Graham.* San Francisco: HarperCollins, 1997.

________. *The Challenge: Sermons Delivered from Madison Square Garden.* New York: Doubleday, 1969.

Hadden, Jeffrey K., and Charles E. Swann. *Prime Time Preachers: The Rising Power of Televangelism.* Reading, Mass.: Addison-Wesley, 1981.

Hybels, Lynne and Bill. *Rediscovering Church: The Story and Vision of Willow Creek Community Church.* Grand Rapids, Mich.: Zondervan, 1995.

Warren, Rick. *The Purpose-Driven Church: Growth Without Compromising Your Message & Mission.* Grand Rapids, Mich.: Zondervan, 1995.

Notes

1. The process by which that was accomplished is the subject of chapters 18 and 19, in this book.

2. A sense of these can be gained from Richard M. Riss, *A Survey of 20th-Century Revival Movements in North America* (Peabody, Mass.: Hendrickson, 1988). Riss, however, is primarily interested in Pentecostal movements, and many important campaigns in other traditions are entered only by title.

3. This term was used by the *Boston Sunday Globe* in its January 1, 1950, report of the campaign begun in Boston the night before. Billy Graham, *Just As I Am: The Autobiography of Billy Graham* (San Francisco: HarperCollins, 1997), 160. Up until that time, Graham had referred to his meetings as "campaigns," but shortly after that he began to designate them as "crusades" on the advice of Willis Haymaker, who thought the term "campaign" had been tarnished by association with older and more sensational styles of evangelism (ibid., 163).

4. Stanley High, *Billy Graham: The Personal Story of the Man, His Message, and His Mission* (New York: McGraw-Hill, 1956), 3.

5. Graham's term for those who respond to the invitation for commitment he makes at the end of every sermon. These include converts to Christianity, lapsed Christians who renew their faith, and practicing Christians who rededicate their lives to God.

6. Graham, *Just As I Am,* 722.

7. Ibid., 638.

8. Mark 4:41 KJV.

9. Graham, *Just As I Am,* 128-29.

10. Ibid., 186.

11. Ibid., 125-26.

12. William Martin, "Graham, William Franklin ('Billy')," in *Concise Encyclopedia of Preaching,* ed. William H. Willimon and Richard Lischer (Louisville: Westminster John Knox, 1995), 167. Martin is author of the recent biography, *A Prophet With Honor: The Billy Graham Story* (New York: William Morrow, 1991). This recency is important not only for its view of Graham's entire career, but also for perspective. By contrast, Marshall Frady, who ended his biography with Watergate, ends up with an understanding of Graham as an innocent on the order of Melville's Billy Budd (*Billy Graham: A Parable of American Righteousness* [Boston: Little, Brown, 1979], 11, 437-39, 483-84).

13. Graham, *Just As I Am,* xv.

14. A summary of ibid., 727-29.

15. Clyde E. Fant Jr. and William M. Pinson Jr., eds., *20 Centuries of Great Preaching: An Encyclopedia of Preaching* (Waco, Tex.: Word, 1971), 12:295. The whole treatment of Graham's preaching, pp. 294-302, is very good. Oddly enough, there are in the literature few analyses of his preaching as such. Some of the best observations on it are in High, *Billy Graham,* 49-100.

16. Martin, "Graham, William Franklin ('Billy')," 168.

17. Martin gives an example of that *ethos* when he tells of Graham's appearance for an interview at the National Press Club, where those accustomed to facing most of the world's newsmakers "seemed to acknowledge the sheer physical presence radiated by the world's most famous preacher" (Martin, *A Prophet With Honor,* 23).

18. Graham, *Just As I Am,* 139.

19. He is as frank to acknowledge the help he receives in writing it as he is to acknowledge any other assistance he receives (Graham, *Just As I Am,* 283). He does the same for the autobiography itself (ibid., 731-35).

20. One of Graham's sermons is a regular feature of *Decision* magazine.

21. Graham, *Just As I Am,* 433.

22. Jeffrey K. Hadden and Charles E. Swann, *Prime Time Preachers: The Rising Power of Televangelism* (Reading, Mass.: Addison-Wesley, 1981), 91. Their chapter "The Sermon from the Satellite" (85-102) is a good summary of the theology motivating TV evangelism, although it is not theologically nuanced. Hadden is a sociologist, and Swann is a cleric with a doctorate in religious communications who managed a PBS station at the time of writing. As good a treatment of televangelists as this is, it is primarily concerned with the threat of political power falling into the hands of these preachers. This is even truer of a later book on which Hadden collaborated with another sociologist, Anson Shupe, *Televangelism: Power and Politics on God's Frontier* (New York: Henry Holt, 1988).

23. At the time of this writing, one evangelist, Morris Cerullo, felt called to see that everyone in the world would have had an opportunity to repent before the year 2000 was over. While he has been active in this project for a number of years, I heard him talk about it on the Inspiration network on March 2, 2000.

24. "The 'millennium' is a prophesied thousand-year period of events on the earth surrounding the second coming of Jesus. Premillennialists believe Jesus will return before the millennium, to reign for a thousand years, finally defeat all the forces of evil, and claim the world for God. Postmillennialists believe that Jesus will come to reign after the thousand-year period of seeing the gospel finally conquer the world. Most TV preachers are premillennialists" (Hadden and Swann, *Prime Time Preachers,* 95).

25. This motivation for evangelism has been effective at least since James Hudson Taylor began his China Inland Mission in 1865.

26. A church service had already been aired by the U.S. Army Signal Corps on August 24, 1919, but that was an experimental program rather than a regular broadcast. This was also an Episcopal service, one from Trinity Church in Washington.

27. The history of religious broadcasting is given in a number of places. Hadden and Swann, *Prime Time Preachers* (17-45, 69-83), gives a good orientation. A more concise presentation occurs in William F. Fore, *Television and Religion: The Shaping of Faith, Values, and Culture* (Minneapolis: Augsburg, 1987), 77-85. Fore was assistant general secretary for communications of the National Council of Churches. The perspective of the televangelists themselves may be seen in *The Electric Church* (Nashville: Thomas Nelson, 1979), by the executive director of their National Religious Broadcasters, Ben Armstrong.

28. Hadden and Swann, *Prime Time Preachers,* 20-45.

29. The definition comes from Tim LaHaye, a member of the board of the Moral Majority. It is quoted in ibid., 85. Most of this summary of the theology of televangelism is based on ibid., 85-102. For a more concise statement, see Fore, *Television and Religion,* 85-86. For an effort to show that the teachings of some televangelists are not orthodox according to evangelical teaching, see *The Agony of Deceit: What Some TV Preachers Are Really Teaching,* ed. Michael Horton (Chicago: Moody, 1990).

30. Quentin J. Schulze has perceptively claimed a particular compatibility of the message and method of the evangelists with the medium of television in his article "Television and Preaching," in Willimon and Lischer, *Concise Encyclopedia of Preaching,* 469-76. He has also written a book on the subject, *Television and*

American Culture: The Business of Popular Religion (Grand Rapids, Mich.: Baker, 1991), which I have not seen.

31. Hadden and Swann acutely observe that "the tube makes up less than half of the technology that supports the new social movement of evangelism. The other half comes in the form of the ubiquitous computer" that enables the evangelists to keep track of individual donors and to personalize their mailings (*Prime Time Preachers,* 104).

32. For details of these and other scandals, see Hadden and Shupe, *Televangelism,* 1-19 passim, and Steve Bruce, *Pray TV: Televangelism in America* (London: Routledge), 1990), 198-212.

33. Bobby C. Alexander, *Televangelism Reconsidered: Ritual in the Search for Human Community,* American Academy of Religion Studies in Religion, no. 68 (Atlanta: Scholars Press, 1994), 21.

34. Bruce, *Pray TV,* 234.

35. See, for instance, the table in Mark A. Noll, *A History of Christianity in the United States and Canada* (Grand Rapids, Mich.: Eerdmans, 1992), 465. Some effort, however, will be necessary to move from his groupings to an overall figure for conservative Christians.

36. The largest of such groups, however, the Southern Baptists, do not belong to the NEA, but they do share the theology of most of those who do.

37. Alexander's thesis in *Televangelism Reconsidered* is that this religious broadcasting is, among other things, a "battle waged by televangelism's followers against mainstream American society for greater inclusion" (2). He calls televangelism "redressive ritual" to accomplish that goal, and analyzes different religious broadcasts in terms of what they accomplish in this way for their constituents. Thus Jerry Falwell's program furnishes legitimation, while Pat Robertson's *700 Club* offers adaptation, and Jimmy Swaggart's program offers evangelicals an opportunity to take the offensive against a culture that has ignored them.

38. The literature on the way the medium affects the message in television is too vast for citation here, but a short introduction can be gained from Schulze, "Television and Preaching," pp. 471-75. See also what was said in chapter 29 concerning Kathleen Hall Jamieson, *Eloquence in an Electronic Age: The Transformation of Political Speechmaking* (New York: Oxford University Press, 1988).

39. Lynne and Bill Hybels, *Rediscovering Church: The Story and Vision of Willow Creek Community Church* (Grand Rapids, Mich.: Zondervan, 1995). On the cover and title page, the title is followed by what looks like a dictionary entry for the word *church:* "*n* 1. A building for public, esp. Christian worship. 2. People who demonstrate their love for God by loving and serving others."

40. It is based secondarily on Saddleback Community Church in Orange County, California, founded by Rick Warren, which has an average weekend attendance of ten thousand. See Warren's book *The Purpose-Driven Church: Growth Without Compromising Your Message & Mission* (Grand Rapids, Mich.: Zondervan, 1995).

41. Millard J. Erickson, "Evangelicalism: USA," *The Blackwell Encyclopedia of Modern Christian Thought,* ed. Alister E. McGrath (Oxford: Basil Blackwell, 1993), 191.

42. This can be seen, for example, in the percentages of audience for televangelists in different regions. Hadden and Swann, *Televangelism,* 60-61.

43. Indications of this may be seen in the way two of the most important publishers of evangelical books, Eerdmans and Zondervan, come from this tradition, and a number of televangelists have Dutch names.

44. Hybels and Hybels, *Rediscovering Church,* 32.

45. Ibid., 29-30.

46. Ibid., 40.

47. Ibid., 57-59. Warren also used such a survey in starting Saddleback Church. *The Purpose-Driven Church,* 39-40.

48. Schulze, "Television and Preaching," 470.

49. One of the most attractive features of the way the Hybelses tell the story in *Rediscovering Church* is the "warts and all" portrait they give that does not hesitate to mention mistaken judgments, crises that occurred, and the way personal failings of themselves and others threatened at times to shipwreck the entire operation.

50. There are four other "teachers" who share weekend and midweek preaching duties with Hybels, two of whom are women. Disagreeing with many evangelicals, Hybels believes that "when the Bible is interpreted correctly and in its entirety, it teaches the full equality of men and women in status, giftedness, and opportunities for ministry" (ibid., 211-12).

51. Small groups are a key element in the strategy of Willow Creek, Saddleback, and all megachurches for much the same reason as John Wesley insisted that his converts become members of classes (see above, 439-40).

52. Hybels's advice to preachers at seeker services is to watch out for going overboard with "felt-need" and "helpful" messages; overprotecting seekers and new believers; the shadow side of team teaching; the sizzle of programming talents; and the temptation to make everything produced and slick (ibid., 185). Rick Warren's formula for preaching at seeker services is to follow the example of Jesus in attracting crowds by meeting people's needs and teaching in a practical, interesting way (Warren, *The Purpose-Driven Church,* 219-34; for his more detailed suggestions for preaching at seeker services, see 293-306).

53. Hybels and Hybels, *Rediscovering Church,* 176.

54. Warren, *The Purpose-Driven Church,* 294.

55. First Corinthians 12:28 refers to the gift, *kubernēsis,* rather than the person who has it, *kubernēsis,* from which are derived the Latin *gubernator* and our "governor." The root concept is of steering a ship. Older translations called the gift "administration," but newer ones call it "leadership."

56. Hybels and Hybels, *Rediscovering Church,* 150.

57. Ibid., 149.

58. Ibid., 168.

59. Ibid., 158.

60. The effort to use technology to spread the faith continues at Willow Creek. An e-mail News Brief from Episcopal News Service of July 12, 2001, says they are planning to open up satellite churches, where gatherings will feature live music and piped-in sermons on huge video screens for the sake of people who live farther than thirty minutes from the main church.

CHAPTER 32

A CRISIS IN COMMUNICATION[1]

THE CHANGED SITUATION

The previous four chapters have dealt with changes in American society during the last four decades of the twentieth century. Movements for civil, women's, student, and gay rights, and for peace and the environment were developing simultaneously with the sexual revolution, experimentation with drugs, changes in standards of acceptable speech and taste in popular music, growing ethnic and religious pluralism, and a marked increase in the number of retired people in the country. During the same period the American people, like those of other nations, were having their consciousness shaped by the intimate medium of television. Computers became pervasive in every aspect of daily living.

Along with the other changes occurring during this period was the disappearance of many of the common assumptions that made American life a culture. Trust was eroded on every hand. The Vietnam War, Watergate, and other evidences that national leaders had feet of clay undermined public confidence in government. The resistance met by the various rights movements that prevented their living up to their promises encouraged cynicism among those who had tasted hope. Meanwhile, church membership and participation were plummeting. Deep suspicion of the threat to human life posed by thermonuclear weapons, combined with the damage done to the environment through technology, replaced the awe and optimism with which the scientific enterprise had previously been regarded. This dethroning of the idol of science was abetted by a change in the understanding of its goal: from discovering laws of the universe, to merely devising models or paradigms that would enable a more effective prediction of performance. There was even a loss of confidence in the ability of language to describe reality or to convey univocal meaning. Eternal verities were vanishing right and left.

A result of this erosion of trust in public institutions and loss of consensus in beliefs and values was a growing individualism and loss of commitment. Marriages were postponed or forsaken altogether, and those who married did not rush to have children. Many sought to find the meaning of their lives in their careers, only to come to doubt the worth of what they were doing and the integrity of the corporations they worked for. Consumption became the measure of success, and the hollowness of its victory was reflected in a bumper sticker that read: "The one who dies with the most toys wins." People seemed to live as isolated individuals, yearning for but achieving little sense of personal fulfillment.

DISCONTENT WITH THE PAST

Consciousness had changed so radically in the 1970s and 1980s as to leave little sense of continuity with what it had been like to be human just a few decades before. In the anxious uncertainty that characterized this period, there was also widespread dis-ease among clergy about the effectiveness of preaching. At first there was a despair of preaching's capacity to make any difference in people's lives. Then followed a series of efforts to discover new ways of going about the task of Christian proclamation, ways that would have integrity and might elicit a hearing in the new world in which clergy found themselves.

These proposals, which have been referred to generally as "the New Homiletic," are bound together more by diagnosis than prescription. In this changed environment, the style of preaching that had reigned at least since John A. Broadus had published *On the Preparation and Delivery of Sermons* in 1870 no longer seemed adequate. There was, however, much less agreement about what should be done instead.

A deep distrust of words and a preference for action over speech had been expressed in the 1960s, an attitude not restricted to preaching but extended to all speech. That pessimism was captured in the first and one of the most important books espousing a New Homiletic, Fred Craddock's *As One Without Authority*.[2] Craddock opens his book by saying, "We are all aware that in countless courts of opinion the verdict on preaching has been rendered and the sentence passed." Yet, "all this slim volume asks is a stay of execution until one other witness is heard." This questioning of the value of preaching he relates to a crisis in language, "a general experience of the loss of the power of words."[3]

He relates this loss of the power of words to six factors, the first of which is that people are bombarded by so many words. The second is contempt for religious language in a scientific age, a contempt that has been extended to language in general. The effect of television on the human sensorium, through which the aural has been replaced by the visual, is another. The crisis of confidence in the power of the pulpit by those who occupy it is a fourth. Closely related to that is the fifth: Christian belief, which had been a part of Western consciousness since before the Middle Ages, is no longer reinforced by the society at large. And, finally, talking to people about the most serious issues of life always has been difficult and remains so.

Craddock and the others who were to join him in proposing a New Homiletic were deeply aware of all the changes in consciousness that had transpired since the 1950s, but their concentration on preaching caused them to begin by focusing on the sort of preaching that had been done before and criticizing its adequacy. *This attack on the previous homiletic rather than proposals for what should be done instead is what unifies these writers.* All believe that the old way is bad, but they have different ideas about what should replace it.

The traditional sermon form has long been described as "three points and a poem," although some of the New Homileticians take this more as an adequate description than as a satirical reduction. Craddock is closer to the point when he calls the traditional form deductive. He says:

> There are basically two directions in which thought moves: deductive and inductive. Simply stated, deductive movement is from the general truth to the particular application or experience, while induction is the reverse. Homiletically, deduction means stating the thesis, breaking it down into points or sub-theses, explaining and illustrating these points, and applying them to the particular situations of the hearers.[4]

Craddock diagrams what he means by deductive development with a form of outline that looks like this:

I.
  A.
    1.
      a.
      b.
    2.
      a.
      b.

The terms "deductive" and "inductive" are used in a special way here.[5] Strictly speaking, to deduce is to reason syllogistically from major premise and minor premise to a conclusion, and induction is "logical reasoning that a general law exists because particular cases that seem to be examples of it exist."[6] Yet, since Craddock defined the sense in which he uses the terms and he uses them that way consistently, no confusion should exist.[7]

Craddock's objection to traditional preaching was that it was deductive. Other New Homileticians have seen it falling short in a number of other respects as well. Don M. Wardlaw has provided a rather comprehensive list of the contrasts made between the old and new ways of preaching.[8] He writes of a "flight" of *continua* between the poles of the old and the new that "show shifts in homiletical theory in a number of categories."

The first of these *continua* is between deductive and inductive, and by that he means what Craddock means. Next, he sees a movement from static to tensive, from an analytical development concerned with timeless truth to a development that has movement. The third continuum is from the denotative to the connotative, from the explicit to the suggestive.

His continuum from left brain to right brain reflects studies of the activity of the brain hemispheres that find the left side to be the center of analysis, while the right side functions in a less linear and more imaginative and intuitive way. The continuum from points to moves reflects the work of David Buttrick, which will be considered below. The next movement is from facticity to the evocative. Wardlaw also says that preaching has moved from being authoritarian to being relational. And, finally, he says that it has become more collaborative and is done in less isolation, calling attention to sermon preparation groups and other ways of involving congregation members in the pastor's sermon preparation.

Needless to say, all these changes in performance reflect changes in value and emerging convictions about what it takes for preaching to be effective in a culture that has undergone so much change.[9]

"A MORE EXCELLENT WAY"

While the New Homileticians were in agreement about the inadequacy of traditional preaching to meet the needs of men and women today, their ideas of what sort of preaching is needed instead are by no means so uniform. It is not so much that they make contradictory recommendations as that they come at the question from different angles and make proposals that have not been integrated into a comprehensive system. Thus to look at the program of the New Homiletic, one must look at several components, proposals made by a number of individuals that are not necessarily interlocking.

Fred Craddock's Inductive Method

A good bit has already been said about Craddock's pioneering role, but now his constructive suggestions need to be looked at in detail. A little about the man himself helps to understand his work. Born in Humboldt, Tennessee, in 1928, Fred B. Craddock is an ordained minister of the Disciples of Christ. Trained as a New Testament scholar, he began his teaching career in 1965 with a joint appointment in New Testament and preaching at one of his denomination's seminaries, the Graduate Seminary of Phillips University in Enid, Oklahoma. From there he went to Candler School of Theology at Emory University, where he occupied the Bandy chair in preaching and New Testament until his retirement in 1993. Influences in the development of his thought include the existentialism of Søren Kirkegaard and the "New Hermeneutic" of Gerhard Ebeling. He is also an advocate of John Dewey's educational theories.

All these influences are apparent in the inductive method of preaching that he advocates. Dewey's influence is seen in Craddock's insistence that the sermon begin with concrete experiences rather than with conclusions. "On the basis of these concrete thoughts and events, by analogy and by the listener's identification with what he[10] hears, conclusions are reached, new perspectives are gained, decisions made" (61-62). As a good Disciple who believes in the priesthood of all believers, he goes on to say that inductive preaching involves a "movement of material that respects the hearer as not only capable of but deserving the right to participate in that movement and arrive at a conclusion that is his own, not just the speaker's" (62). A corollary of this second point is a third, which says that the listeners should be allowed to complete the sermon. They can see the implications of what has been said and are perfectly capable of applying it to their own lives.

Craddock agrees with Martin Heidegger that "the primary function of language" is "letting be what is through evocative images rather than conceptual structures" (77), because images are more basic to thought, and it is by changing images that a mind is changed. His rules for the selection of images are that they be: drawn from their hearers' world of experience; specific and concrete;[11] economical in their use of words—especially modifiers; uninterrupted by self-conscious insertions such as "we find" or "we see"; and in the preacher's own language (92-97).

Effective sermons preached in the inductive mode are characterized by conceptual unity: good biblical preaching is based on a single pericope in which there is only one such idea. Thus the plotting of a sermon begins after the preacher is able to express its "central germinal idea in one simple affirmative sentence" (105). By the same token, the sermon based on that pericope should not be allowed to break apart with one section focused on the text and another on the congregation.

> If the text wrestles with serious questions and if the reader does also, then the reader's own questions are not extraneous intrusions on a "pure understanding" of the text. (114)

Bringing such questions from the contemporary church to the text is not, however, a shortcut that eliminates the need for study; it rather gives point to the study.

According to Craddock, part of the difficulty of deductive preaching, which begins with a general principle and moves on to apply it, is that in the presentation of a sermonic insight, the mental processes by which the preacher has arrived at that insight are reversed:

> If . . . the first stage (exegesis) is like ascending a hill . . . the second (sermonizing) is like the descent on the other side. . . . The shift consists of a transition from inductive to deductive movement of thought. (123-24)

He recommends that instead, the preacher take the congregation over the exploratory path in the sermon that she herself traversed in discovering the insight to be communicated, ending with the insight as a conclusion rather than beginning with it as an assumption. The sermon, therefore, is designed as a process that leads from the present experience of the congregation to the conclusion, and the design begins with the identification of the conclusion to which they are to be led.

That insight should not be into the "human situation" in general, but into "the issues facing the particular congregation participating in the sermon experience" (129). Therefore, the preacher's preparation is listening to the dialogue between the scriptural passage that is the text and the situation of the local congregation. And when the sermon is preached, the thought of the text is to be expressed in the language of the congregation. In the construction of such inductive sermons, "the sole purpose is to engage the hearer in the pursuit of an issue or an idea so that he will think his own thoughts and experience his own feelings in the presence of Christ and in the light of the gospel" (157).

An example of such inductive preaching is a sermon that Craddock preached in chapel while he was still teaching at Phillips. His congregation was made up of seminarians in Oklahoma at the height of the civil rights movement. Most of them were student pastors, and they were probably accustomed to delivering fiery "prophetic" sermons[12] to their small rural congregations. The title of Craddock's sermon is "Praying Through Clenched Teeth."[13] (For the text of this sermon, **see Vol. 2, pp. 618-23.**) The scripture read was Galatians 1:11-24, in which Paul speaks of his conversion from persecuting Christians.

Craddock begins by saying that he wants to say a word and have his hearers associate a face and a name with it. The word is *bitter,* and he quickly sketches in concrete images of bitter people, a series of vignettes: a dustbowl farmer, a forty-seven-year-old widow at the cemetery, a small grocer watching a large supermarket going in across the street, a pregnant young woman whose soldier husband is being shipped overseas. These images are drawn from the lives of the students, because any one of the people described could belong to the churches they serve. The last of the images is even closer to home, because it is of a young pastor being given a cast-off TV by a parishioner who expects deep gratitude for the pittance.

Then he gives the image of bitterness from his text, the Pharisee Saul of Tarsus, who is bitter that Christian preachers would make salvation available to Gentiles, whose ancestors had not suffered generations for their faith. It is like a seventeen-year-old child suddenly being told by his parents that they are adopting a brother for him, of the same age, who will be a full coheir to the family business. The seventeen-year-old would do everything in his power to stop it, as Saul would try to stop the

Christians. Of course, Paul knew that God loves all creation, but "it's one thing to know something; it's another thing to *know* it" (51).

Craddock then asks his hearers if they know anyone like that who is bitter, and, if so, how do they respond. He hopes they do not do so with bitterness themselves. "A few years ago, many of us found ourselves more prejudiced against prejudiced people than the prejudiced people were prejudiced" (51).

Then he tells the story of a family out for a Sunday drive in the country. Along the way they see a homeless kitten beside the road, and the children beg the father to stop for it. He is reluctantly persuaded by his wife to go back for the kitten and gets out to pick it up. He is rewarded for his pains by being scratched. A few weeks later, after the kitten has been fed into health and sports a sleek coat, the man feels the kitten rubbing up against his leg. Craddock asks if it is the same cat and answers: "No. It's not the same as that frightened, hurt, hissing kitten on the side of the road. Of course not. And you know as well as I what makes the difference" (52).

He then closes quickly by saying:

> Not too long ago God reached out his hand to bless me and my family. When he did, I looked at his hand; it was covered with scratches. Such is the hand of love, extended to those who are bitter.

He began with concrete images, showed respect for his listeners' ability to arrive at their own conclusions, and did not state any conclusion explicitly. He never mentioned "prophetic" preaching that "dumped" on people whose lives gave them grounds for bitterness. But it is hard to imagine that any of his hearers were unaware of the one point he was making, a point that was the result of the dialogue he had overheard between the situation in the text and the situation in the congregation.

A postscript to this consideration of inductive preaching is to note how much it was a response to the cultural climate at the time Craddock wrote *As One Without Authority,* a climate in which there was deep distrust of any form of public speech, especially preaching. His Beecher lectures were his next book, *Overhearing the Gospel,*[14] which was published seven years later. It deals with a different crisis in preaching—not that of a secular distrust of religion but that of a Christian audience that has heard the gospel so often as to be unable to pay attention to it. His text for that book is a quotation from Kirkegaard: "There is no lack of information in a Christian land; something else is lacking, and this is a something which the one man cannot directly communicate to the other."[15] He recommends an indirect method of preaching by which people who hear the gospel can overhear[16] it. And that method has much in common with inductive preaching.

By the time Craddock got around to publishing a general homiletics textbook in 1985, the climate had changed even more. Thus he can say in the introduction to *Preaching:*[17]

> After a generation of walking alone, the object of general ridicule and preoccupied in self-flagellation, preaching is again making new friends among other disciplines and renewing old acquaintances with biblical studies, literary criticism, and communication theory. (13)

He is no longer so critical of traditional homiletics (14), and even suggests that some of its sermon forms are able to be used with profit today (176-77). Much can be said also for deriving the form of the sermon from the form of the biblical text. But often it will be good for the preacher to create a form for the particular sermon that grows out of its own particular demands. And, although it is not labeled as such, that sermon form has much in common with inductive preaching:

> Beginning at that intersection of message and hearer, the sermon begins to unfold, moving from where they are, through the text, using analogies, examples, images, perhaps even pleasant interruptions in the form of asides or hints of roads not now to be taken, until preacher and congregation know the message has been said. (188)

The Phenomenological Approach of David Buttrick

A proposal for what should be done to overcome the shortcomings of traditional homiletics comparable to Craddock's in its significance and influence is that of David Buttrick, who recently retired as professor of homiletics and liturgics at the Divinity School of Vanderbilt University. A son of the distinguished preacher George Buttrick,[18] he was ordained as a Presbyterian minister and later went over to the United Church of Christ on a principle of conscience. He served as a parish minister and taught in several seminaries, including St. Meinrad's, a Roman Catholic Benedictine theologate, before going to Vanderbilt.

The quality that most distinguishes Buttrick from his colleagues in homiletics[19] is the wideness of his intellectual horizons. He has made an effort to understand the universe in which he lives as fully as possible, using especially the tools of the phenomenological school of philosophy, which goes back to the early-twentieth-century work of Edmund Husserl in German universities. Further developed by European thinkers such as Remey Kwant, Maurice Merleau-Ponty, Martin Heidegger, Michel Foucault, and Paul Ricoeur, this movement has had much influence on theology. One of the theologians to show that influence is Edward Farley, with whom Buttrick served on the faculty of Pittsburgh Theological Seminary near the beginning of his teaching career, and at Vanderbilt at the end of it. During all this time, he and Buttrick have been close friends and partners in theological conversation.

The significance of phenomenology's influence on Buttrick's homiletic is spelled out in a contribution to his Festschrift by his closest and most able disciple, David Greenhaw.[20] He points out that phenomenology is a philosophical approach to understanding reality that seeks to do greater justice to the complexity of that process than is done by common sense. Common sense assumes that things exist objectively in the world, and the mind perceives them as doing so. Phenomenology points out that while the things exist in the external world, what they are understood as being is at least as much a function of the perceiving mind as it is of the thing itself. Pieces of wood can be joined together in such a way that they have a shape we recognize as that of a table, but it is the mind's recognition that the assembly of wood is a flat surface at which one can sit to eat or write or that otherwise functions in a tabular way that constitutes the thing as a table. Or, more precisely, it is the perceiver's intention to use or regard it as a table that makes it a table rather than just a configuration of lumber.

The mind, furthermore, does not necessarily perceive things as wholes. A complex reality may be experienced from a number of different perspectives before it dawns that the awareness is of a single reality. An analogy to this can be seen in a series of photographs a person takes of a house she is contemplating buying: someone to whom she shows the photos may take a while to realize that they are not of different houses but of the same one seen from different angles. It then becomes the intention of the viewer to see the collection as different aspects of the same house, which permits him to go on and imagine the house as a whole. But again, the fullness of the reality will not be experienced until the viewer says: "Oh, this is where you are going to live!" It is this purposive act that makes what is viewed a house in the fullest sense.

This forming of a whole out of a combination of perspectival aspects is what Buttrick means by consciousness.

> It is not simply that we passively perceive objects in the world or even just aspects of objects. It is rather that through an intentional act, the

> perception is pulled together into a unitary experience, a lived experience, a formed consciousness.[21]

Therefore, "consciousness refers to lived experience, not simply an idea or a thought, but the formation of a world out of the various worlds that can be formed."[22] While the roof, walls, windows, and doors are all there, the house itself and as a whole is "there only *in lived experience,* not as a bundle of perceptions but *as a synthetic unity constituted by my purposive presence.*"[23] The point is that reality does not exist objectively in the world but is formed when perceptions of what exists come together with human intentionality in an act of consciousness.

It is this potentiality for the formation of a reality in consciousness that makes preaching so important in Buttrick's understanding. The sort of naming[24] that identified a series of photographs as a house could have had various other outcomes: the building could have been named prison, castle, ruin, or fortress. Everything can be named in a number of ways, or, more accurately, everything can be given a number of names. Things can be named mistakenly or accurately. And so Buttrick can say: "Evangelism rests on the open option that anything may be renamed gleefully into a consciousness of God."[25] "Preaching is to name God in consciousness, and by naming God, to construct the world of the church and the greater social order as a world in which we may live and love."[26]

The fundamental seriousness of the preaching enterprise should be recognized. What is at stake here is not just inspiration or even persuasion that such and such a view of an aspect of reality is the correct one. The formation of Christian consciousness in an individual or a congregation is essentially transformative.[27] Although Urban T. Holmes III was using the conceptual framework of Jungian psychology rather than that of phenomenology, his understanding of what preaching should accomplish is as radical as that of Buttrick. Saying that the object of preaching is "the inscape of existence, not the landscape," he insists that preaching is not teaching, but rather "an act of evangelizing the deep memory."[28] And he recognized that deep memory is a corporate as well as a personal possession.

While others of the New Homileticians are as committed as Buttrick to the view that the goal of preaching is transformation, his phenomenological approach may make his prescriptions for bringing that about through preaching a little more nuanced than some of the others'. Before looking at those prescriptions, however, it will be useful to notice what Buttrick finds wrong with traditional homiletics. He thinks that for two-thirds of the twentieth century American preaching was dominated by two models, that of the biblical theology movement and that of what Philip Rieff calls "the triumph of the therapeutic," reflected in preaching in the tradition of Harry Emerson Fosdick.[29] The former is dominated by a view of revelation that treats God as existing "out there" independently of human perception. That God exists independently of us is not the issue because we do not know God as God is in the Divine Self. God is known to us only as God is revealed to our perception; all we know about God is what we have perceived. The phenomenological perspective applies even to God.

As biblical theology posited an "out there" God, so the therapeutic tradition posited an "in here" me, a focus on existential self-awareness that isolates the self from its social milieu. Buttrick calls the two tendencies represented in traditional homiletics the "objective/subjective split," and he regards it as a trap. "The first isolates revelation from contact with human understanding, and the second reduces divine revelation to a region of the human psyche."[30]

The presentation of such a detailed theoretical basis has been necessary to communicate the depth of Buttrick's homiletical project. Otherwise, his prescriptions could appear as just another set of "how-to" tips. When it is seen, however, that what he is concerned with is how truth forms in consciousness, the seriousness of his recommendations becomes clear. He recognizes that what he is proposing is a new partnership of preaching with rhetoric. Aware of the bad press rhetoric has received and of the reductionism with which it is often dismissed as "mere rhetoric," he nevertheless devotes himself to an analysis of the conditions under which language can be transformative, which is what rhetoric is really all about.

Granting the validity of that approach, we should still note that in his prescriptions he makes a lot of what appear to be apodictic judgments regarding what will or will not form in consciousness, down to such details as the number of sentences an introduction can incorporate. His text is peppered with many remarks such as "research shows," remarks that appear to give an empirical basis to the limits set. The book is so long, however, that a decision was made to publish it without notes,[31] so the warrant for those claims is not available for the reader's inspection. The reader's only recourse, then, is to decide if the cogency of Buttrick's arguments in the text implies that he is also reliable at times when he simply must be taken at his word.

His book, *Homiletic,* is essentially a preaching rhetoric. It deals with two questions, the way individual building blocks of a sermon are to be constructed (moves) and their position relative to one another in the whole (structures). "Sermons," Buttrick says, "involve an ordered sequence—they are not glossolalia. Sermons are a movement of language from one idea to another, each idea being shaped in a bundle of words."[32] Such bundles, "formed modules of language," he calls "moves," rejecting the traditional term "points" because it implies a more exclusively rational, objective, and static character than many such modules possess. A move is a module of language that forms in consciousness to pattern an understanding. The sequence in which such modules appear is not governed by strict logic, but by the many forms of association by which one statement follows another in a conversation.

Attention span today allows only about four minutes per move, and yet it is hard for an idea to form in communal consciousness in any less time. Thus a twenty-minute sermon can consist of only five or, at most, six moves. Each move needs to begin with a statement of the idea it is to communicate and should end with a restatement of that idea. In between come "internal development systems" (moves within a move), which enable the hearers to acknowledge the truth of the idea when it is restated at the end of the move. These systems may be information about the subject, evidence or arguments to deal with anticipated congregational resistance to the idea (which Buttrick calls "contrapuntals"), "phenomenal lived experience" (most of what traditional homiletics has called "illustrations" or "support material"), or theological concerns. The type chosen will depend on what the preacher is trying to do in the move. In any case, each move must be unified—must point in only one direction—so that the idea will not fragment, but will form in consciousness. And it should achieve closure in the idea's restatement at the end of the move. Introductions and conclusions are special kinds of moves that have their own problems and, therefore, their special set of rules.

When he comes to the structures in which moves are joined, Buttrick rejects the numbered points with transitions between them favored by traditional homiletics. Rather, he says, the sermon should be regarded as a sequence of ideas with its own connective logic. Hence one of the most important steps in sermon preparation is to write out the sequence of ideas, listing the move statements in the order in which the moves occur. These statements are not topics but the theses of the moves stated in conversational language. When the five or six move statements for the sermon are thus set down, the connective logic[33] of the whole can be tested. Adjustments can then be made so that the flow of thought is justified and unimpeded.

Buttrick uses the term "modes" to refer to the patterns in which the sequence of ideas, or structure, in a sermon may fall, and he considers there to be three that are legitimate. These he calls the Immediate Mode, the Reflective Mode, and the Mode of Praxis. Those in the Immediate Mode are based on narrative passages of scripture, including parables; those in the Reflective Mode are based on expository (nonnarrative) passages of scripture; and those in the Mode of Praxis do not begin with a text but with an issue before the congregation, moving on to theological questions and relevant biblical passages.

Buttrick believes that sermons on narrative passages should preserve the story's suspense, and thus should not separate telling the story and applying it. Sermons in the Mode of Reflection intend to form in consciousness a contemporary theological understanding produced by the structure of the text combined with contemporary images drawn from lived experience. While sermons on narrative passages have to follow the story sequence, in sermons on expository passages the preacher can replot the movement of thought into a basic sermon structure.

By sermons in the Mode of Praxis, Buttrick means legitimate forms of what traditional homiletics calls topical sermons. In these the preacher has the role of the resident theologian in the parish and takes people through a consideration of a problem that faces them or the community or society, sets it in theological perspective, and then rereads the situation in the light of revelation, story, and symbol. The outcome should be a new understanding if the issue was one of being, or a new course of action if it was one of doing.

The foregoing summary of a long and closely argued book is dangerously curtailed, but it is what is possible in the space available. Perhaps, though, it has been possible to suggest Buttrick's understanding of how a new partnership of preaching with rhetoric can enable the formation of Christian consciousness in individuals and congregations.

Narrative Proposals

A number of New Homileticians' suggestions about what should be done instead of preaching in the traditional mode have centered on some concept of story or narrative. All of a sudden in 1980, at least three proposals of this sort were made, suggesting that the time had come for the homiletical community to reappraise the role of narrative in sermons. First, a distinguished retired professor at Union, **Edmund A. Steimle,** published *Preaching the Story*[34] with two of his former graduate students, **Morris J. Niedenthal** and **Charles L. Rice.**[35] Their volume was intended to be a preaching textbook for seminary classes, and chapters in it were written not only by the three themselves, but by others as well. The introduction deals with the concept of preaching as shared story, while the major divisions of the book consider that theme from the perspectives of the preacher, the listeners, the congregation, and the message. There is also a final chapter on learning to preach in a new context in which women as well as men occupy pulpits.

The significance of this seminal volume lies in the way that it named and thus raised an issue and set others clamoring to answer it. By saying "story," the authors seemed to say the magic word. How they understood the term can be learned from three sorts of evidence: the way the book itself was written (for its style and way of presenting its content seems to be the one recommended for sermons), the sermons printed at the end of each of the four major sections, and Steimle's discussion of the "fabric" of the sermon. Of the sermons included as examples, it can be said that none were extended narratives in the strict sense, thus indicating what they did not mean by "preaching the story."

The four qualities of a sermon that functions as story listed by Steimle are "its secularity, its dialogical character, its dramatic story-form in the indicative mood, and its lean and spare style."[36] By "dramatic story-form in the indicative mood," he seems to mean that the sermon will eschew the imperatives of exhortation and display what John McClure refers to as the "delay of the arrival of the preacher's meaning."[37] Or, as Steimle says, "The end . . . is still in doubt."[38] The example he gives of how such a sermon may be constructed (**see Vol. 2, pp. 623-27**) does not take the form of a story proper but rather that of an unfolding sequence of images, thus raising the question of how the authors use their key term of "story."

It turns out that what Eslinger says of Rice applies to all three authors: they use "metaphor," "image," and "story" interchangeably.[39] In that original publication,[40] then, they were not sufficiently clear about what they meant by "story" to make it easy for others to construct sermons according to their formula. That in a way, however, shows how attuned they were to the spirit of the times, because, as will be seen, others began to develop models for correcting traditional preaching using the narratives and images Steimle, Niedenthal, and Rice had elided into one.

Before moving on to consider the proposed remedies of image-based preaching, it will be appropriate to see what has been recommended in the way of narrative preaching. The discussion to follow will take account of only two of those forms of narrative preaching, that which gives a narrative shape to nonstory sermons and that in which sermons consist of one long story.[41]

Narrative form is given to nonstory sermons to maintain suspense by delaying the preacher's meaning until the end of the sermon—that is, giving the sermon a dramatic plot. The main advocate of this kind of preaching is **Eugene L. Lowry,** William K. McElvaney Professor of Preaching at St. Paul School of Theology in Kansas City, Missouri.

His distinction between the sort of preaching he advocates and traditional preaching begins with his understanding of what is to be ordered in a sermon: experience, not ideas. Thus the task of preparing a sermon is shaping rather than organizing. The form of the sermon is to be thought of as a process rather than a structure. The focus of the sermon is not so much theme as events. Its principle is the resolution of ambiguity rather than the presentation of substance. The product of the work of preparation will be, therefore, a plot instead of an outline. The means used to put the sermon across will be ambiguity and suspense rather than logic and clarity. And the goal the sermon is to achieve is a happening rather than an understanding.[42]

All of this is to say that he thinks the sermon's meaning should be withheld to the end in the way of a literary plot. By that he does not mean that sermons should be fictional stories, but that the "experiences" presented should have the sequence of a plot.

> The stages are: 1) upsetting the equilibrium, 2) analyzing the discrepancy, 3) disclosing the clue to the resolution, 4) experiencing the gospel, and 5) anticipating the consequences. [His] students have found it helpful to remember these steps with the following abbreviations: 1) Oops; 2) Ugh; 3) Aha; 4) Whee; and 5) Yeah.[43]

Lowry thereby suggests that we begin our sermons by pointing out the inconsistency between the way we think life ought to be and the way it actually is. Next, he suggests that we go on to analyze this discrepancy. For him, this analysis is the most important stage in the sermon. It seeks to move from behavior to the motivation behind the behavior, wherein lies the real trouble. It is, then, a diagnosis of sin, and must be done accurately so that it can be matched accurately with the remedy of grace that is proposed by the text.

Yet, at this stage of diagnosis, the problem is still stated in the language of ordinary human wisdom rather than in theological language. The reason for this is that the third stage, the disclosure of the clue to resolution, can come not only as a revelation, but also as something of a surprise. A reversal occurs so that the situation is no longer seen from the perspective of human wisdom, but from the perspective of the gospel. This brings us to the next stage, that of experiencing the gospel. It is in this section that the most substantial positive presentation is made. Finally, the last stage is to anticipate the consequences, to apply the insight to future living.[44]

One of the first to advocate preaching in which the entire sermon is a story was **Richard A. Jensen,** who did not suggest this as the only valid sermon form, but saw it instead as a way of giving variety to preaching. Jensen was trained in systematic theology rather than homiletics, but his duties as speaker for the national Lutheran Vespers radio broadcast made him a popular conductor of preaching workshops for clergy. He also taught in doctor of ministry programs. His 1980 book, *Telling the Story: Variety and Imagination in Preaching,*[45] gives almost equal treatment to three sermon forms. The first he calls "didactic," by which he means traditional sermons of the sort that the New Homiletics understands itself over against. Although 90 percent of the preaching he had heard and done was of that sort, and it still has some legitimate use, he does not consider it to be very effective anymore. He considers it to be more like a physician's explaining what is wrong with one's body than giving the medicine one needs to recover.

He calls the second sort of preaching he considers, his default style, "proclamatory" preaching. While it has much in common with the preaching of the biblical theology movement discussed in chapter 26, it has its theological basis not so much in the thought of Barth as in that of Bultmann and of his disciples who developed the "New Hermeneutic." This sort of preaching announces and offers the help that people need, God's grace for healing sinners.

However, it is the third type of preaching Jensen discusses, story preaching, that is relevant to the present discussion. He was motivated to consider such preaching by a number of currents in the theological air, ranging from Frederick Buechner's thoughts about "preaching as fairy tale" through the growing importance of story in theology, to research about the division of labor between the hemispheres of the brain. He also found persuasive Amos Wilder's suggestion that if the biblical text makes its point in story form, then preachers should consider doing the same.[46]

What he has in mind as story sermons are not those in which stories illustrate points, but those in which the story itself is the preaching. The aim of such sermons is for the listeners to participate and become involved in the gospel story. For that to happen, it helps if the stories are open-ended. The hearers need to recognize themselves in the story and experience the "good turn"[47] the story takes because of God's grace.

Jensen gives some helpful hints to preachers who are considering story preaching. They need to work on their narrative skills before they attempt such sermons in the pulpit. The stories should be based on a biblical text, but not a simple retelling of a Bible story. To be persuasive, they should have characters who are recognizable as real people. For particular occasions the story can be autobiographical.[48] The story should function more like a parable than an allegory. Sometimes a visual prop can elicit interest in what lies ahead. People are more open to the message at times when they overhear it as if it were spoken to someone else than when they hear it as directly addressed to them.[49]

A simple way of beginning to preach story sermons is to tell stories that parallel the story in that day's Gospel closely enough for listeners to make the connection. It sometimes helps to provide a period of silence in which people can identify themselves with the story. People can be led to meditate on a biblical story in the light of stories they know from literature, theater, cinema, TV, music, or human life when the juxtaposition of the two suggests insights. And the final bit of advice is that the preachers who read the book should try the method.

The examples of story sermons from Jensen's own preaching are, not surprisingly, congruent with his suggestions. The first, for instance, is a modern story that parallels the parable of the prodigal son in a way that makes the older story seem more real. Another, in effect, tells the story of the lost sheep from the perspective of a sheep, which, Jensen admits, seems to contradict his principle that the stories should be about real people. He also offers a sermon that combines elements of proclamatory and story preaching as an intermediate step in introducing a congregation to story preaching.

Since the purpose of the present chapter is to list proposals of alternatives to traditional preaching made by New Homileticians rather than to trace the development of each of the proposals after they are made, much literature on narrative preaching cannot be considered here. For present purposes, it is enough to say that such literature exists.[50]

Image and Imagination in Preaching

The alternatives to traditional preaching proposed under this rubric are the most difficult to summarize, because they are the most diffuse. They seem to range from the general assumption that preaching would be better if it were more imaginative, to something as specific as the recommendation that a single image be used to tie a sermon together. The most influential writer in this field is one who clearly practices what he preaches. **Thomas Troeger,** a Presbyterian minister who has also received

Episcopal ordination and who occupies an endowed chair in preaching at Iliff Theological Seminary in Denver, has published a volume of hymns and another of his poetry, and is an accomplished flautist as well. Colleagues will never forget the 1985 meeting of the Academy of Homiletics, at which there was a celebration of the three-hundredth anniversary of the birth of Johann Sebastian Bach. For that program, Troeger both played some of Bach's music and gave voice to a sermon in which he claimed that Bach was the preacher.[51] (A form of this sermon is found in **Vol. 2, pp. 634-37.**)

In the first of his two books on the use of imagination in preaching, *Creating Fresh Images for Preaching: New Rungs for Jacob's Ladder,*[52] Troeger models the sort of preaching he recommends in the way he writes the book. His thesis is that "there are more cures for incoherence [in a sermon] than logic."[53] Instead of depending on logical connection, "a preacher can glue a sermon together through the being of an image or story. A repeated phrase or vision can hold the preacher's words together."[54] There are many such phrases and visions that recur through the length of this book. One is indicated in the subtitle, "new rungs for Jacob's ladder." Noting that the angels descend to earth before they ascend to heaven, Troeger says, "Don't start in heaven. Don't start with the sweeping generality. . . . Start on earth. Start with the particular, with what we see and hear and touch."[55] Other visions include members of a congregation who heard a particular sermon and elders of a Presbyterian church with whom Troeger began a workshop by asking them to identify their dominant relationship with God. These and other such visions reappear briefly throughout the book.

The book is a joy to read. It moves from image to image rather than from point to point. One recognizes along the way that complete sermons of the author have been woven into the text as illustrations of what can be done by the imaginative preacher. Some are stories in the mode of Jensen, so that it is difficult to tell where image leaves off and story begins. Or a sermon may be a secular love story, a scripture reading, and a prayer that renders the theological meaning of the story. There are other sections that model the way a passage of scripture can be brought to light by visualizing its images rather than looking for its point. The whole is connected by the recurring images in the way a musical composition is tied together by the reprise of motifs and themes.

Interspersed along the way are bits of instruction about how the reader can accomplish similar results, but they are hard to isolate and systematize. For the most part, the preaching student is expected to learn by example.[56] Perhaps not enough did, because Troeger's second book,

Imagining a Sermon, seems to go over much the same territory in a more linear way—although it, too, has stunning products of the author's creativity introduced every so often, causing the reader to gasp for breath. This work operates on Ricoeur's principle that imagination is a rule-governed activity. "The imaginative process can be compared to the art of sailing a boat: We cannot make the wind blow, but we can trim the sails and tend the helm."[57] This understanding "disallows any purely Romantic understanding"[58] of the creative process.

Some of the rules for this rule-governed activity are the chapter titles of *Imagining a Sermon*. Each chapter thus furnishes instruction on how to obey the particular rule and examples of what it looks like in action. The rules are:

1. Alert the eye to keener sight.
2. Feel the bodily weight of truth.
3. Listen to the music of speech.
4. Draw parables from life.
5. Understand the church's resistance to imagination.
6. Dream of new worlds.
7. Return to the Source.[59]

This work also includes sample sermons constructed according to the principles taught in the chapter, and they show what variety of sermon forms can be encompassed in the term "imaginative." While all of them use imagery, at least one is a continuous story—showing how slippery the distinction between narrative and imaginative preaching is.

A work that concentrates on a method of using a single image to connect a sermon is *Imagery for Preaching* by **Patricia Wilson-Kastner.**[60] The author, who died prematurely, was a former Roman Catholic nun who became an Episcopal priest. She taught Historical and Constructive Theology at United Theological Seminary of the Twin Cities before becoming Trinity Church Professor of Preaching at the General Theological Seminary. After that she served several parishes out of a desire to put into practice her understanding of ministry, especially preaching. She begins her book with a discussion, similar to that in the other works surveyed, of changes in the way human access to truth has been understood in philosophy, depth psychology, anthropology, history of science, and theology—changes that call for a more imaginative and less linear approach to communicating the gospel.

As a case in point in the study of the way that all thinking begins with images, she looks at the use of imagery in the Bible. After listing some of the primary images of the Old Testament, she gives five questions to be posed in assessing the helpfulness of such images:

1. What is the root of this image in common human experience?
2. How does this image portray God?
3. What does this image imply about God's relationship to human beings?
4. What response to God does this image evoke in the hearer?
5. How is this image complemented by other images? (pp. 48-61)

In preparing to preach a sermon bound together by an image, the preacher needs to note the congruence between the image and the spiritual reality to which it is related, what that image has in common with our world, the multidimensional quality of all powerful images (and sermons should not be based on any other sort), the appealing quality of the image to the congregation, and the open-endedness of the image.

A notable quality of Wilson-Kastner's work is her insistence that since preaching is a part of the liturgy, it is a form of prayer and, therefore, it is only appropriate that one pray in preparation for doing it. She recommends a particular form of prayer as suitable for this task, the Ignatian meditation.[61] This method of prayer, which is fundamental to the formation of members of the Jesuit order, begins by reconstructing imaginatively the scene in the biblical passage being prayed. Then the one who meditates asks God to be allowed to pray in that place. "After this one enters into the event, applying one's memory, mind, and will" (67). The prayer ends with a resolve to put the insight gained through the meditation into practice in one's own life.

While the passage on which the preacher has meditated is often narrative, the suggested method for constructing the sermon is imagistic rather than narrative. An example of the way such a sermon works is preached by the author on the parable of Dives (the rich man) and Lazarus (Luke 16:19-31). (**See Vol. 2, pp. 638.**) Instead of retelling the story of the two, she sets up the contrast between these two vivid figures "who see but do not encounter one another" (87). She sees a modern parallel in the contrast between a luxury hotel in Dallas, where she attended a meeting of a scholarly society, and the run-down neighborhood where she grew up in the same city, which she visited after the meeting. She then asks why the contrast is allowed to continue. After accounting for it in terms of human sin, Wilson-Kastner calls the church to both judgment and hope. Thus the sermon is based on a static rather than a kinetic use of the figures, an image rather than a story.[62]

Fitting the Form of the Sermon to the Form of the Text

The last proposal for what should be done instead of traditional preaching is not so much a separate way of creating sermons as it is an element of all the other proposals made. That element was already in place when Fred Craddock wrote *As One Without Authority*. He said: "If the minister feels lost at first with a body of ideas without a skeleton, he may adopt the form in which the biblical text is presented."[63] While all the authors surveyed have enunciated this principle in one way or the other, it has also been the subject of entire books. Two examples illustrate the emphasis on this principle, one a collection of essays by various authors edited by **Don M. Wardlaw**[64] and the other written by Thomas G. Long alone.

Preaching Biblically,[65] the Wardlaw volume, grew out of the work of a panel assembled by the editor.[66] After listing the inadequacies of traditional homiletics, the editor says that the contributors suggest ways in which the shape of the sermon can be determined by that of the biblical passage on which it is based. The aspects of the text identified by the contributors as offering such direction include: its language, its context, its claim on the readers, its interplay with a metaphor, its structure, the interaction of its shape with the preacher's individuality, and its encounter with the preacher. Wardlaw sorts these into three groups: those that "accent particularly the shaping of the sermon from the preacher's personal experience of the text"; those that "concentrate on the experience of the faith community embedded in the text and see possibilities of structuring the shape of the human drama that gave rise to the text"; and those that "see significant sermon shapes arising from the language of the text itself." He goes on to say, "No contributor dwells exclusively in any of these three categories" (23). It can also be said that the suggestions of contributors to this volume whose proposals of what to do in place of traditional preaching have already been considered in this chapter are consistent with those proposals. (For Wardlaw's sermon from this book, see **Vol. 2, pp. 642-46.**)

Thomas Long, who taught for a number of years at Princeton Theological Seminary, now occupies Fred Craddock's old chair at the Candler School of Theology of Emory University and is the author of a number of books. His *Preaching and the Literary Forms of the Bible*[67] is based upon "the relatively simple idea that the literary form and dynamics of a biblical text can and should be important factors in the preacher's navigation of the distance between text and sermon."[68] To help the preacher complete that voyage, he offers five questions to ask of the biblical passage on which the sermon is planned:

1. What is the genre of the biblical text?
2. What is the rhetorical function of this genre?
3. What literary devices does this genre employ to achieve its rhetorical effect?
4. How in particular does the text under consideration, in its own literary setting, embody the characteristics and dynamics described in the previous questions?
5. How may the sermon, in a new setting, say and do what the text says and does in its setting?[69]

Then, to help the reader see how to pose those questions to particular texts, he models the interrogatory process in chapters on such literary forms as psalms, proverbs, narratives, the parables of Jesus, and epistles. And, finally, he lists four broad types of "text-to-sermon bonds," which have been illustrated in his consideration of the literary forms. These are:

1. Allow the movement of the sermon to follow the movement of the text.
2. Allow the opposing forces in the text to become the opposing forces in the sermon.
3. Allow the central insight of the text to be the central insight of the sermon.
4. Allow the mood of the text to set the mood of the sermon.[70]

While such a bare-bones outline can only suggest the strategies that Long counsels, a careful study of his book should equip readers with the tools to create sermons shaped by the text on which they are based, rather than according to a points and subpoints outline growing out of abstract principles extrapolated from the text.

CODA

This concludes the list of the major alternatives proposed by the New Homileticians to the traditional homiletics, which continued the Puritan preachers' practice of distilling from biblical texts a set of abstract theological propositions—"doctrines"—that were to be applied to their congregations as "uses." Their proposals have included inductive preaching, forming ideas in consciousness, preaching narratively, using imagination, and allowing the shape of a sermon's text to govern the shape of the sermon itself. These are not mutually exclusive alternatives, but neither do they comprise a single, coherent homiletic. They share a rejection of traditional preaching and offer a number of alternatives to it, none of which have succeeded in establishing themselves as the ruling paradigm.

Completing the list brings this history of Christian preaching to an end, because it concludes the homiletical activity that is now history. Not that thought about how to preach has ended! Far from it! But the New Homiletic is the last stage that has been completed. Its practitioners represent the phase of homiletical thought that Lucy Rose calls "Transformational."[71] Already she and others are offering strategies to supersede those of the group studied in this chapter. But these new strategies are only emerging; they are not yet history.

FOR FURTHER READING

Buttrick, David. *Homiletic: Moves and Structures*. Philadelphia: Fortress, 1987.

Chatfield, Don. *Dinner with Jesus and Other Left-handed Story-sermons: Meeting God Through the Imagination*. Ministry Resources Library. Grand Rapids, Mich.: Zondervan, 1988.

Craddock, Fred. *As One Without Authority*. 3rd edition. Nashville: Abingdon, 1978.

Greenhaw, David. "The Formation of Consciousness." In *Preaching as a Theological Task: World, Gospel, Scripture: In Honor of David Buttrick*. Edited by Thomas G. Long and Edward Farley, 1-16. Louisville: Westminster John Knox, 1996.

Long, Thomas. *Preaching and the Literary Forms of the Bible*. Philadelphia: Fortress, 1989.

Lowry, Eugene L. *The Homiletical Plot: The Sermon as Narrative Form*. Atlanta: John Knox, 1980.

Steimle, Edmund A., Morris J. Niedenthal, and Charles L. Rice. *Preaching the Story*. Philadelphia: Fortress, 1980.

Troeger, Thomas H. *Imagining a Sermon*. Abingdon Preacher's Library. Nashville: Abingdon, 1990.

Wilson-Kastner, Patricia. *Imagery for Preaching*. Fortress Resources for Preaching. Minneapolis: Fortress, 1989.

Notes

1. I am grateful to Professors Don Wardlaw and David Schlafer for suggestions for this chapter, but I take full responsibility for the way it is developed. The subject

matter is treated in Richard L. Eslinger, *A New Hearing: Living Options in Homiletic Method* (Nashville: Abingdon, 1987); Lucy Atkinson Rose, *Sharing the Word: Preaching in the Roundtable Church* (Louisville: Westminster John Knox, 1997), 59-85; and Don Wardlaw, "Postmodern Homiletics: Which Language for What Consciousness?," in *Papers for the 1994 Annual Meeting of the Academy of Homiletics* (privately published).

2. Fred Craddock, *As One Without Authority,* 3rd ed. Originally published by Phillips University Press, Enid, Oklahoma, in 1971. The edition consulted was the 3rd, published by Abingdon Press, Nashville, Tennessee, in 1978.

3. Ibid., 6.

4. Ibid., 54.

5. Charles L. Campbell, "Inductive Preaching," in *Concise Encyclopedia of Preaching,* ed. William H. Willimon and Richard Lischer (Louisville: Westminster John Knox, 1995), 270.

6. *Oxford American Dictionary,* 1st ed., def. 3. According to Aristotle, for such reasoning to be valid, one would have to list all the particulars. About two thousand years later, Francis Bacon proposed the inductive method, by which it could be inferred that what is true of a part is true of the whole to which it belongs.

7. Something more likely to be misleading, an error several of the New Homileticians fall into, however, is the identification of the pattern of reasoning Craddock calls deductive as something that originated with Aristotle (Craddock, *As One Without Authority,* 54). What is confusing about the statement is that it is consistent with neither what Aristotle said in his *Logic* nor with what he said in his *Rhetoric.* The *Logic* is concerned with the rules of valid reasoning rather than outlines. As for rhetoric, Aristotle did not consider rigorously deductive reasoning to be the means of persuasion appropriate to oral presentation. Instead, he favored the *enthymeme,* "a 'syllogism' in which the premises are only generally true"—that is to say, not rigorously logical (Richard A. Lanham, *A Handlist of Rhetorical Terms,* 2nd ed. [Berkeley and Los Angeles: University of California Press, 1991], 65).

Aristotle taught that in speeches there are three means of persuasion *(pisteis)* that can be used: reason, the trustworthiness of the speaker, and emotion. The two forms rational persuasion may take are the enthymeme and the example (the rhetorical version of inductive reasoning). But even when reason was the means of persuasion to be used, no ancient rhetoricians recommended the sort of outline described by Craddock. They usually presented the outline of a speech in court as the norm.

Nor did Greek outlines enter Christian preaching through Augustine or another of the Fathers. As we have often noted above, none of the standard rhetorical outlines were appropriate for Christian preaching, especially the sort of exegetical homily preached by the Fathers, because none provided for an explication of a text. In *De doctrina christiana,* Augustine assumed that preachers would have been trained in rhetoric since that was almost the only sort of education there was at the time, but he did not get his sermon form from rhetoric.

This excursus has been longer than desirable, but it seemed necessary to point out that whatever the faults of the outline form Craddock describes, they cannot be blamed on either Greek logic or rhetoric or on the Fathers of the early church. Truthfully, I do not know when such outlining began; my guess is that it was during the Enlightenment. It has parallels with the preaching of Calvin and the Puritans and with that of the latitudinarians.

8. In a letter to me dated April 26, 2000. As he says, it overlaps some with a list drawn up by Eugene L. Lowry, "The Revolution of Sermonic Shape," in *Listening to the Word: Studies in Honor of Fred Craddock,* ed. Gail R. O'Day and Thomas G. Long (Nashville: Abingdon, 1993), 93-112, but I find that of Wardlaw more satisfactory.

9. To list the shortcomings with which New Homileticians charge traditional sermons is not the same as saying the sermons had all those faults. A review of collections of traditional sermons such as *The Protestant Pulpit: An Anthology of Master Sermons from the Reformation to Our Own Day,* ed. Andrew W. Blackwood (New York and Nashville: Abingdon-Cokesbury, 1947), and *The Twentieth-Century Pulpit,* ed. James W. Cox, 2 vols. (Nashville: Abingdon, 1978, 1981), does not reveal the sermons to be consistently in the pattern they are portrayed as having. Rather, the traditional sermon of the New Homileticians is a construct that enables them to account for the inability of previous preaching to meet the needs of their greatly changed cultural situation.

10. In his preface to the third edition of *As One Without Authority,* Craddock admits the "highly male-oriented language" he used in 1971, but he did not change it because he recognized that the great expense in doing so would be passed on to his readers (viii). Hereafter, references to *As One Without Authority* are page numbers inserted into the text parenthetically.

11. "If the sermon revives the memory of the odor of burped milk on a blouse, it evokes more meaning than the most thorough analysis of 'motherhood'" (ibid., 93).

12. For Craddock's evaluation of such "prophetic" preaching, see ibid., 19.

13. It is published in James Cox, *The Twentieth-Century Pulpit* (Nashville: Abingdon, 1981), 2:47-52 and is reprinted, with permission, in volume 2 of this book.

14. Fred Craddock, *Overhearing the Gospel* (Nashville: Abingdon, 1978).

15. Quoted in ibid., 9.

16. Overhearing is a practice Craddock advocates for preachers in their approach to scripture in *As One Without Authority,* 137.

17. Fred Craddock, *Preaching* (Nashville: Abingdon, 1985). Hereafter, references to this work are page numbers inserted into the text parenthetically.

18. George Buttrick was born in England, the son of a Primitive Methodist minister. He, however, was ordained in the Congregational Church before migrating to America. In time he was called to Madison Avenue Presbyterian Church in New York City, where he served from 1927 to 1954, becoming one of the most influential preachers in America. From there he went to Harvard as both minister to the university and professor of homiletics. Before and after his Harvard stint, he taught at Union. He later taught at Garrett and Louisville seminaries. He wrote fifteen books, was general editor of *The Interpreter's Bible* (Nashville: Abingdon, 1951–57) and *The Interpreter's Dictionary of the Bible* (Nashville: Abingdon, 1962), and was twice a Beecher lecturer.

19. Among whom I include myself.

20. David Greenhaw, "The Formation of Consciousness," in *Preaching as a*

Theological Task: World, Gospel, Scripture: In Honor of David Buttrick, ed. Thomas G. Long and Edward Farley (Louisville: Westminster John Knox, 1996), 1-16. Greenhaw is now president and professor of homiletics at Eden Theological Seminary. Another major study of the contribution of Buttrick is that of Eslinger in *A New Hearing,* 133-69, which is the more remarkable in that it was published before the appearance of Buttrick's *Homiletic: Moves and Structures* (Philadelphia: Fortress, 1987).

21. Greenhaw, "The Formation of Consciousness," 5.

22. Ibid., 5-6.

23. The words in quotation marks were quoted by Greenhaw, ibid., from Erazim Kodak.

24. Note that the intentional act that forms reality in consciousness occurs in language.

25. Buttrick, *Homiletics,* 8; quoted in Greenhaw, "The Formation of Consciousness," 6.

26. Ibid., 7.

27. Lucy Rose has characterized most of the practitioners of the New Homiletic as transformational (*Sharing the Word,* 59-85). She has called attention to the way practitioners depend on the power of language to effect change: "Discussions of language under the transformational umbrella tend not to focus on the unchanging reality behind the words, as in traditional or kerygmatic theories. The focus instead is on the change in the human situation created by words" (ibid., 67). While she discusses the contribution of Buttrick very little, she does distinguish between him and other transformational theorists by recognizing that the others concentrate on change within individuals, while Buttrick sees that "the goal of preaching is transformation of congregational consciousness" (ibid., 142).

28. Urban T. Holmes III, *Turning to Christ: A Theology of Renewal and Evangelization* (New York: Seabury, 1981), 216. Conversion is the process by which Christ becomes the dominant metaphor of the deep memory (74).

29. Philip Rieff, *The Triumph of the Therapeutic: Uses of Faith after Freud* (New York: Harper & Row, 1966).

30. Greenhaw, "The Function of Consciousness," 8.

31. Buttrick, *Homiletic,* xi. The book runs to 512 pages. His original plan was to treat "Worship and Preaching" and "Preaching and the Social World" as well. With these sections and documentation, the work would have been enormous.

32. Ibid., 23. The summary of Buttrick's thought about moves and structures will be too compressed to permit extensive citation of the pages on which ideas are expressed. Tracking down a particular statement, however, should not be difficult for anyone with a copy of the book who follows its table of contents.

33. This connective logic is not deductive, but is rather the conversational association mentioned above.

34. Edmund A. Steimle, Morris J. Niedenthal, and Charles L. Rice, *Preaching the Story* (Philadelphia: Fortress, 1980).

35. Niedenthal taught at the Lutheran School of Theology at Chicago and Rice at the Theological School of Drew University.

36. Steimle, Niedenthal, and Rice, *Preaching the Story,* 174.

37. John McClure, "Narrative and Preaching: Sorting It All Out," in *Journal for Preachers* 15 (Advent 1991): 24-25, quoted by Lowry, "The Revolution of Sermonic Shape," 99.

38. Steimle, Niedenthal, and Rice, *Preaching the Story,* 171.

39. Eslinger, *A New Hearing,* 30.

40. Rice especially went on to develop what he meant. See the list of his articles in the footnotes to Eslinger's treatment of his work, in ibid., 38.

41. John McClure (in "Narrative and Preaching," 24-27) has pointed out that preaching has been characterized as narrative in four different respects:

1. When the literary form of its biblical text has an impact on the shape of a sermon (narrative hermeneutics),
2. When the shape of the sermon itself is narrative (narrative semantics),
3. When there is an exploration of the use of culture and human experience that links narrative elements such as metaphor and image with current interest in imagination (narrative enculturation), and
4. When a theological worldview or faith story is cultivated through preaching (narrative worldview).

Only two forms of his second category will be considered here.

42. Eugene L. Lowry, *Doing Time in the Pulpit: The Relationship between Narrative and Preaching* (Nashville: Abingdon, 1985), 11-28. He gives a longer list in "The Revolution of Sermonic Shape," 100-112.

43. Eugene L. Lowry, *The Homiletical Plot: The Sermon as Narrative Form* (Atlanta: John Knox, 1980), 25.

44. Since the publication of *The Homiletical Plot,* Lowry has gone on to publish a number of books that continue to explore the basic theme of this first work from a number of angles. For instance, in *Doing Time in the Pulpit,* he gives the justification for his theory from the perspective of literary criticism. In *How to Preach a Parable: Designs for Narrative Sermons,* Abingdon Preacher's Library (Nashville: Abingdon, 1989), he analyzes several sermons preached by himself and others from the perspective of the homiletical plot. *The Sermon: Dancing the Edge of Mystery* (Nashville: Abingdon, 1997) is his textbook for preaching classes that correlates various narrative forms of the New Homiletic from the perspective of his own theory into a presentation of the various tasks of sermon preparation and delivery.

45. Richard A. Jensen, *Telling the Story: Variety and Imagination in Preaching* (Minneapolis: Augsburg, 1980).

46. Ibid., 128. The Wilder work referred to is *Early Christian Rhetoric: The Language of the Gospel* (Cambridge: Harvard University Press, 1971), a work that has influenced many of the narrative homileticians. It is not surprising that Wilder should have had a great appreciation of narrative, since his brother was the novelist and playwright Thornton Wilder. Most of the New Homileticians agree that the form of the biblical text on which it is based should influence the shape of a sermon, as will be seen below.

47. The literary term is "eucatastrophe," which is used by J. R. R. Tolkien to describe how he wishes his stories to work.

48. A point with which many homileticians would take issue.

49. This point is derived from Fred Craddock's book *Overhearing the Gospel.*

50. For example, Don Chatfield has published a volume of sermons that never leave the narrative mode of stories in *Dinner with Jesus and Other Left-handed Story-sermons: Meeting God Through the Imagination,* Ministry Resources Library (Grand Rapids, Mich.: Zondervan, 1988). A sermon from this book appears in **Volume 2, pp. 627-34.** Many who have advocated story sermons have been influenced by the work of the Roman Catholic priest John Shea through such books as *Stories of God: An Unauthorized Biography* (Chicago: Thomas More, 1978). The work of Henry Mitchell, discussed above in chapter 28 on recent African American preaching, is recognized as an important contribution to the thought of the New Homiletics about narrative preaching. Narrative concerns have also influenced the homiletical thought of conservative evangelicals, as may be seen in Bruce C. Salmon, *Storytelling in Preaching: A Guide to the Theory and Practice* (Nashville: Broadman, 1988); and Calvin Miller, *Spirit, Word, and Story: A Philosophy of Preaching* (Dallas: Word, 1989).

51. A form of that sermon is the concluding chapter to Troeger's *Imagining a Sermon,* Abingdon Preacher's Library (Nashville: Abingdon, 1990), 135-40. Troeger edits the Abingdon Preacher's Library.

52. Thomas Troeger, *Creating Fresh Images for Preaching: New Rungs for Jacob's Ladder* (Valley Forge, Pa.: Judson, 1982).

53. Ibid., 19.

54. Ibid.

55. Ibid., 30.

56. At the opposite end of the spectrum is Paul Scott Wilson's *Imagination of the Heart: New Understandings in Preaching* (Nashville: Abingdon, 1988), which gives a completely analytical approach to preaching with imagination. Drawing on his University of London dissertation on the understandings of imagination displayed in the literary criticism of Samuel Coleridge, Leigh Hunt, William Hazlitt, and Charles Lamb, he defines imagination as "the bringing together of two ideas that might not otherwise be connected and developing the creative energy they generate" (32) in the way that wires connected to the positive and negative poles of a generator will spark if they are brought close together. Thus the sermon preparation process he recommends is a series of steps in bringing two sets of poles together: the biblical text and our situation, law and gospel/judgment and grace, story and doctrine, and pastor and prophet.

57. Troeger, *Imagining a Sermon,* 14.

58. Ibid.

59. Ibid., 29-30.

60. Patricia Wilson-Kastner, *Imagery for Preaching,* Fortress Resources for Preaching (Minneapolis: Fortress, 1989). Hereafter, references to this work are page numbers inserted into the text parenthetically.

61. Although she cites a much fuller bibliography on Ignatian meditation, Wilson-Kastner particulary acknowledges the importance for her of Elizabeth Canham, *Praying the Bible* (Cambridge, Mass.: Cowley, 1987).

62. An important study on both narrative and imagistic preaching is Richard L.

Eslinger, *Narrative & Imagination: Preaching the Worlds That Shape Us* (Minneapolis: Fortress, 1995), particularly in its theoretical first half. Eslinger has a deeper understanding and acquaintance with the philosophical and literary studies behind contemporary approaches to narrative and imagery than most homileticians, and thus is able to argue the implications of those theories more cogently than most. An example is his warning against the experiential-expressive model of storytelling preaching in which Christian references are used to illustrate principles of some other system of thought that is assumed to be primary. Such an approach undercuts all biblical authority (see p. 17). His discussion of imagination, while too detailed to be summarized here, would provide much theoretical insight to anyone wishing to know how to use it effectively in preaching.

63. Craddock, *As One Without Authority,* 153.

64. Before his retirement, Wardlaw taught homiletics and worship for many years at McCormick Theological Seminary.

65. *Preaching Biblically,* ed. Don M. Wardlaw (Philadelphia: Westminster, 1983). The other writers are Ronald J. Allen; Thomas G. Long; Charles Rice; William J. Carl III; Gardner Taylor; and Thomas H. Troeger.

66. Wardlaw edited another book, one produced by an Academy of Homiletics study group, a textbook on the instruction of preaching from the perspective of the New Homiletics titled *Learning Preaching: Understanding and Participating in the Process* (Lincoln, Ill.: Lincoln Christian College and Seminary Press for the Academy of Homiletics, 1989). The other members of the writing team were Fred Baumer; Donald F. Chatfield; Joan Delaplane; O. C. Edwards Jr.; James A. Forbes Jr.; Edwina Hunter; and Thomas H. Troeger. Wardlaw, like most of the other New Homileticians considered in this chapter, has served as president of the Academy of Homiletics.

67. Thomas Long, *Preaching and the Literary Forms of the Bible* (Philadelphia: Fortress, 1989).

68. Ibid., 11.

69. Ibid., 24-34.

70. Ibid., 24.

71. Rose, *Sharing the Word,* 59-85.

CONCLUSION[1]

At the end of this long survey, it is appropriate to ask what, if anything, has been learned about the nature of Christian preaching in this survey of its history. The answer begins with something that may be easily forgotten in preachers' daily preoccupation with their task: the importance of preaching. Most of the significant movements in the history of the church have involved preaching in their development and expansion.

That was true from the beginning, as may be seen in the way the gospel spread after Pentecost. In A.D. 49, just sixteen years after the classical date assigned to the crucifixion, the emperor Claudius ordered Jews out of Rome because of disturbances within their community resulting from the activity of Christian missionaries. In that short time, Christian preaching had moved from a backwater province of the empire to its very center, and was creating enough disturbance to come to the attention of the highest reaches of government. Fifteen years later, when the citizens of Rome believed the fire that had razed their city was set by the emperor Nero to inspire his poetic composition, he shifted the blame to the Christians, who in that short time had become the standard scapegoats on whom anything unpleasant could be blamed. Some very effective preaching must have been done to evangelize a Christian community in Rome large enough to have received so much public attention—even if it was largely negative.

It is certainly not coincidental that the period when Christianity finally displaced Greco-Roman religion as the official cult of the empire was a time when the church's greatest bishops and theologians had achieved success as sophists and teachers of rhetoric before ordination. Then, too, the church's response to the unchurched populations of the newly founded cities in the High Middle Ages was to create the mendicant orders of friars, itinerant preachers to be sent where the need was greatest. It belabors the obvious to mention the Reformation as a preaching movement.

These examples can be rounded off without being anywhere near exhausted by noting that the abolition movement in the nineteenth century and the civil rights movement in the twentieth century numbered preachers among their most effective leaders, and preaching was one of the major media through which they spread their message. Most of the great movements in church history have depended on preaching to accomplish their purposes.

This is not even to mention the importance of preaching in the ordinary life of the church. In a justly famous passage in *The Shape of the Liturgy,* Dom Gregory Dix listed the occasions on which the people of God have found making Eucharist to be their most appropriate activity.[2] A list of the times when preaching has seemed the natural thing to do would both overlap his to a considerable extent and, if anything, be even longer. And what Dix said about ordinary offerings of the Eucharist applies equally well to the preaching of sermons:

> Best of all, week by week and month by month, on a hundred thousand successive Sundays, faithfully, unfailingly, across all the parishes of Christendom, the pastors have done just this to *make* the *plebs sancta Dei*—the holy common people of God.[3]

That the same thing can be said of both the Eucharist and preaching should surprise no one because two of the main channels of grace in the church are Word and sacrament. Of the two, however, preaching has been the major means by which Christians have been converted and formed intellectually. As Paul said, "Faith comes from what is heard" (Rom. 10:17). Preaching thus gives specificity to the grace the Eucharist communicates sacramentally. Many historical examples could be given of the grace that has been communicated through preaching, but readers of this book probably do not need those because most can document that proposition from their own lives.

With such a reminder of the importance of preaching in the church's history, it is not surprising—though many would be surprised—that we have numerous examples of the sermons preached during most periods in church history. A case in point: For the years 1150 to 1350, a list of sermon manuscripts has been compiled that runs to nine volumes with a cumulative seventy-three hundred pages.[4] If the average number of sermons per page is consistent with a sample taken of forty-plus pages, more than eighty thousand sermons have been preserved in manuscript. Since this is one of the periods from which relatively few sermons could have been expected to survive, it can be taken as an indication of the number of sermons from the past that are still in existence.

It will amaze no one that most of the sermons that have come down from different periods of the Christian past are those of the homiletic equivalent of "the rich and famous," but we can assume that then as now ordinary preaching was very similar to that of the "tall steeple preachers" in form and content, since it would all reflect the consciousness of the church at the time. It cannot even be taken for granted that the sermons of the "giants of the pulpit" were necessarily more eloquent, profound, or filled with spiritual insight, because there have been too many excellent preachers whose reputation never reached beyond a small circle. By the same token, some proclaimers of the Word most esteemed in their own generation make a poor showing on the test of time.

Thus, while it can be said that ordinary preaching has been most important in the life of the church, it nevertheless remains true that for most Christian generations, we have to infer what that was like through sermons that have come down to us from the better-known preachers.

An example of what can be inferred about ordinary preachers from the ones whose sermons have not been lost is the qualities that have made all of them effective. A list of those qualities can begin with what F. Van der Meer said about his subject in *Augustine the Bishop:* "His real secret, which he shares with all orators who really succeed in fascinating us, is that he had such an enormous amount to say."[5] That recalls the old distinction between "sermons that have something to say and sermons that have to say something." There is no doubt about which sort is more memorable—or, perhaps more accurately, none about the sort from which one retains pleasant memories.

To break down the elements of having something to say, it can be noted that all truly effective preachers have at least three qualities in common. They all have a good mind, a rhetorical reflex, and personal holiness. Rhetorical reflex denotes a native sense of how to get one's point across when addressing a group; the meaning of the other two terms is obvious. It is likely that among the group of preachers respected in any given period there may be found all the possible ratios in which the relative strengths of these three elements may be combined. But preaching at its best requires each of these qualities in a high degree, because a lack of any one of the three will diminish the effect, and do so in a characteristic way.

In addition to the qualities of preachers, there must be considered as well the characteristics of the times in which they preached. There have been many different kinds of preaching in history, and they all were probably related to what was going on in the society in which they arose. More will be said of this later; the only point to be made right now is that these movements all draw on contemporary standards of what makes public speaking effective, and tastes in that have at times changed rapidly.

In most ages, a factor in the formation of taste in oratory has been Greco-Roman rhetoric. This is not surprising because that enterprise represents the best effort ever made to observe what does and does not work in public address, and to create a vocabulary with which to communicate that information.

Notice that the task of the discipline of rhetoric is value-free description. Rhetoric is often used in a pejorative sense in which it implies a lack of sincerity and a desire to manipulate an audience. It is to be understood instead as a body of observations that are value-neutral: These things seem to work and those do not. The choice to use what is more effective is up to the speaker, as are the speaker's motives in doing so. The issue has been stated by Augustine with utter clarity:

> Rhetoric, after all, being the art of persuading people to accept something, whether it is true or false, would anyone dare to maintain that truth should stand there without any weapons in the hands of its defenders against falsehood; that those speakers, that is to say, who are trying to convince their hearers of what is untrue, should know how to get them on their side, to gain their attention, and have them eating out their hands with their opening remarks, while those who are defending truth should not?[6]

Put that way, it becomes clear that rhetoric offers a speaker a set of tools, and all who have a message they want to get across, use the tools. Some do so by instinct and some because of training, but, as Cicero said, "when noble and elevated natural gifts are supplemented and shaped by the influence of theoretical knowledge, the result is then something truly remarkable and unique."[7] A case in point is Dr. Martin Luther King Jr., who developed his natural talent by analyzing the preaching of many clergy and by formally studying rhetoric.

In a pure form, however, the criteria of classical rhetoric have never served well as standards for Christian preaching. The reason is that none of the three classical *genera dicendi* (basic types of speech) provide for the explication of a text, and thus provide no place for the interpretation of passages from the Bible, which has been one of the most persistent elements in Christian preaching.

Incidentally, the method of choosing the text to be explicated has varied considerably over the centuries. Probably the use of a lectionary has been most common, but many preachers through the ages have seen virtue in preaching all the way through one biblical book before considering a passage from another *(lectio continua)*, even though this method is as fixed and artificial as following a lectionary. Other preachers have chosen the passage or verse that seemed to be the portion of the Bible most relevant to their congregation at the moment, the result being either expository or textual preaching, depending on the length of the passage chosen. And some have chosen a subject—a topic—to speak about, which they authorized scripturally by citations from various parts of the Bible.[8]

However the passage is chosen, it is nevertheless the case that the way text is explicated reflects the principles of biblical interpretation in vogue at the time. Or, more precisely, it reflects the hermeneutics of at least the community for which it was prepared, since at any given moment there is a variety of Christian communities, and each has its own characteristic method of discovering what a biblical passage means to and for them.

Within this overall variation, there nevertheless have been methods that have prevailed within large portions of the Christian community. Among these, the most dramatic shift has undoubtedly been from allegorical interpretation to use of the historical/critical method. Even that, however, has not made as much difference as one might think. While use of the two methods would produce very different understandings of the passage's original meaning, the way in which it is brought to bear on the life of the congregation would probably be very similar. The literal, grammatical, historical meaning of a biblical text is always the meaning it had for its first hearers or readers, and the relevance of the text to later congregations is necessarily always analogical.

That being so, it is disappointing that most Christians today can read few sermons of the past with much edification. (That probably is more a matter of different concerns preoccupying the churches than it is the result of changed methods of biblical interpretation.) In spite of this, it still can be seen that in every generation, the church has been able to turn to the Bible for necessary insight into its own situation. Somehow, through preaching, the Bible speaks to the condition of the local community of the people of God, whenever and wherever they are assembled. This capacity of the Scriptures to give needed insight into such an immense variety of situations is undoubtedly much of what is meant by calling them "inspired."

The rest of what is to be said about lessons to be learned from the history of preaching will be organized in terms of a speaker's five tasks, as recognized by Greco-Roman rhetoric: invention, disposition, elocution or style, memory, and delivery.

Invention consists of deciding what to say in a speech. Aristotle defined *rhetoric* as "an ability in each particular case to see the available means of persuasion."[9] Persuasion, as such, is not what we are trying to accomplish in all sermons, but preaching is motivated behavior—it is trying to accomplish something. A good list of the things we seek to do in preaching comes from Ronald E. Osborn:

> The skilful preacher attempts to catch the hearers' interest from the start and to sustain it throughout, engaging their problems and concerns, passing on the tradition, guiding understanding, correcting false impressions, answering objections, projecting a vision, undertaking to persuade, imparting grace.[10]

To have a chance of meeting these goals, preachers need to be strategic in their invention; they need to decide where they want their congregation to arrive, identify the obstacles that stand in the way of their getting there, and design a process to help them get by the roadblocks and arrive safely at their destination.

Part of all such processes is a demonstration that what is proposed is consistent with whatever is accepted as authoritative by members of the congregation. Most Christians have been willing to assume that the Bible is normative for their belief, but the way its authority has been brought to bear has varied enormously. Thus the preacher whose invention involves an appeal to the Bible has to make this appeal in accordance with the criteria acknowledged by those who will hear the sermon. While we all are probably familiar with some sort of proof-texting, that has by no means ever been the main way biblical warrant has been invoked for positions taken in sermons. Other appeals made in preaching have been to reason, emotion, and imagination.

The variety of possible combinations of these appeals can be seen in the sermons of five revivalists:

• **Jonathan Edwards** combined rigorous logic with acute psychological analysis to move people to love God's election of some to salvation and some to damnation.

• The published sermons of **John Wesley** seem to be instructions in Christian doctrine (modeled as they were on the Church of England's *Book of Homilies*), but in actual delivery, the calm voice of reason is not all that was heard. Horace Walpole, a litterateur and a pioneer in the Gothic Revival, has left an unsympathetic account of what it was like to hear Wesley preach: "He spoke his sermon, but so fast, and with so little accent, that I am sure he has often uttered it, for it was like a lesson; but towards the end he exalted his voice, and acted very ugly enthusiasm."[11]

• **George Whitefield,** on the other hand, preached in such a way that it was hard for people to remember afterward what he had said, but they did remember that it was enormously moving—as Benjamin Franklin testified in his autobiography. He went to hear Whitefield, intending to not give a penny to the orphanage in Georgia for which the preacher was trying to raise money, but he wound up emptying his pockets.

• **Charles Grandison Finney** had been trained in law rather than theology, and he argued to get a conviction, except that instead of trying to convince jurors that the defendant was guilty, he set out to make his hearers feel that they were.

• **Dwight L. Moody's** idea of a sermon, however, has been compared to the report of one businessman to another.

Since all these such different styles of preaching were for the single purpose of converting sinners to Christianity, we can see that sermon invention for all the many purposes of preaching must have varied enormously.

There has been equal variety in homiletical approaches to disposition. Greco-Roman rhetoric recognized three basic types of speech *(genera dicendi),* each with its characteristic outline. These were: (1) the forensic speech, the sort made in a law court, designed to persuade an audience about what happened in the past; (2) the deliberative, the type given in a legislative assembly to recommend what ought to be done in the future; and (3) the epideictic, made on public occasions to "point with pride" or to "view with alarm" some person or activity in the present life of the community—the sort of speech made on ceremonial occasions.

As noted earlier, sermons fit none of these three arrangements of a speech because none provide for the explication of a text. Nor was there one standard outline into which classical homilies fell.[12] A look through history reveals expository sermons with many different outlines:

- **Origen** would comment verse by verse as he went along, tossing out exegetical information and doing allegorical interpretation in which his application occurred, commenting on the biblical text the way a grammarian teaching in a secondary school at the time would comment on a classical text.
- Sometimes beginning with an introduction and sometimes not,[13] **Chrysostom** would do literal exegesis with no effort at application until he got to the last verse he had time to talk about. Even then, the moral lesson he found did not always come too obviously from the verse just exegeted.
- **Puritans** would go through three steps with each verse (or, sometimes, phrase): They would exegete it, state as a proposition the doctrine it taught (confirming that proposition from other passages in the Bible), and then find applications to the lives of the congregation or, as they called them, "uses."

Notice that this variety of disposition or outline occurs within a single basic type of sermon. How much greater the differences become when one considers the whole range of sermon forms can be imagined.

Incidentally, there seem to be more forms of preaching today than in all previous Christian centuries put together. That is probably because there are more Christians, more preachers, and consequently more sermons than ever before. This indicates how radically ad hoc all Christian preaching is. Just as at Pentecost all heard the good news in their own language, everyone always has to hear it not only in their own tongue, but in terms of the culture of which they are a part as well.

In classical rhetoric, the concept of *Elocutio* was not as inclusive as that of style today. It was generally limited to figures of sound and thought, that is, to figures of speech whose appeal lay in the way they struck the ear (such as alliteration or rhyme) and those that pleased the mind (metaphor, for example). It was recognized, however, that there were three levels of style, each with its characteristic use or abstention from figures: the plain style to teach, the middle to please, and the grand to move.

There has been a pendulum swing through the ages in the church's attitude toward the use of these figures. Some have thought that only plain style, which eschewed such ornamentation, was consistent with the gospel. Others have used great artistry to convey the Christian message. This alternation may be related to the dominance of the right brain or left brain in an individual or culture. It is certainly related to what Charles Williams has referred to as "the two chief approaches to God defined in Christian thought," the way of the rejection of images and that of the affirmation of them.[14]

It is a matter for reflection, for example, that Gregory the Great (ca. 540–604) was the first preacher in the history of the church to make much use of extended narratives to illustrate the points in his sermons, and his doing so was not widely imitated until the High Middle Ages when friars began using *exempla*.

I will combine memory and delivery in one of the few sweeping generalizations I can make about preaching through the ages, which is that, with rare exceptions, the most effective preachers have not preached from manuscripts. In not doing so they have to an extent honored the standard of the Greco-Roman rhetoricians, who either memorized their orations or spoke them extemporaneously.[15]

This generalization can be documented by noting that Augustine wanted never to impede his ability to gauge audience reactions to what he was saying. If he saw ready comprehension, he would move along, but if he saw uncertainty on his auditors' faces, he would go back over the point and offer analogies (*Doctr. chr.* 10.25). Bernard of Clairvaux did much the same. Indeed, the standard was so established that Archbishop William Laud apologized for using "papers" when he preached from the scaffold where he was beheaded. While Spurgeon would think all week about his sermon for the coming Sunday, he would wait until after Saturday afternoon tea to draw up the outline, which would be the only thing he took into the pulpit. Henry Ward Beecher would have several ideas for sermons going around in his mind at once and would decide on which to preach only Sunday morning after breakfast.

There are exceptions that prove this rule like any other, exceptions of the stature of Tillotson and Fosdick, but, nevertheless, the generalization that most of the greatest preachers spoke without a manuscript is the most sweeping I can make from the history of preaching.

With that, the only things left to be said are warnings voiced by far greater authorities than the present. Let us first hear from Dante:

> Christ did not say to his first company: "Go, and preach idle stories to the world," but he gave to them the true foundation; and that alone sounded in their mouths, so that to fight for kindling of the faith they made shield and lance of the Gospel. Now men go forth to preach with jests and with buffooneries, and so there be only a good laugh the cowl puffs up, and nothing more is asked.[16]

Or, to draw on an even more exalted authority, listen to the words of Paul:

> When I came to you, brothers and sisters, I did not come proclaiming the mystery of God to you in lofty words or wisdom. For I decided to know nothing among you except Jesus Christ, and him crucified. And I came to you in weakness and in fear and in much trembling. My speech and my proclamation were not with plausible words of wisdom, but with a demonstration of the Spirit and of power, so that your faith might rest not on human wisdom but on the power of God.
>
> Yet among the mature we do speak wisdom, though it is not a wisdom of this age or of the rulers of this age, who are doomed to perish. But we speak God's wisdom, secret and hidden, which God decreed before the ages for our glory. None of the rulers of this age understood this; for if they had, they would not have crucified the Lord of glory. But, as it is written,
>
> "What no eye has seen, nor ear heard,
> nor the human heart conceived,
> what God has prepared for those who love him"—
>
> these things God has revealed to us through the Spirit; for the Spirit searches everything, even the depths of God. For what human being knows what is truly human except the human spirit that is within? So also no one comprehends what is truly God's except the Spirit of God. Now we have received not the spirit of the world, but the Spirit that is from God, so that we may understand the gifts bestowed on us by God. And we speak of these things in words not taught by human wisdom but taught by the Spirit, interpreting spiritual things to those who are spiritual. (1 Cor. 2:1-13)

This is as far as the history that began with Melito of Sardis and the author of *Second Clement* can go—for the time being.

Earlier, it seemed appropriate to apply to preaching what Dom Gregory Dix said about the occasions on which it had seemed appropriate to offer the Holy Eucharist. In the same spirit, then, the sacristy prayer after St. Basil's liturgy of the altar can be applied at this point to this effort to write a history of the liturgy of the proclaimed Word:

> The mystery of thy dispensation, O Christ, our God,
> Hath been accomplished as far as in us lies.
> We have seen the memory of thy death;
> We have seen the type of thy Resurrection;
> We have been filled with thine endless life;
> We have enjoyed thy heavenly delights, of which

we pray thee make us more worthy hereafter;
Through the grace of God the Father, and of thy holy,
good, and life-giving Spirit, let us depart in peace.
Amen.[17]

Notes

1. An earlier form of this chapter was presented to the Consortium of Episcopal Homileticians, meeting at St. Paul's College, Washington, D.C., May 27-29, 1999.

2. Dom Gregory Dix, *The Shape of the Liturgy* (London: Dacre, 1945), 744.

3. Ibid.

4. J. B. Schneyer, *Reportium der lateinischen Sermones des Mittelalters für die Zeit von 1150–1350,* Beiträge zur Geschichte der Philosophie und Theolgie des Mittelalters, Band 43, Heften 1-9 (Münster: Aschendorffsche Verlagsbuchhandlung, 1969–80).

5. F. van der Meer, *Augustine the Bishop: The Life and Work of a Father of a Church,* trans. Brian Battershaw and G. R. Lamb (London and New York: Sheed & Ward, 1961), 432.

6. St. Augustine, "Teaching Christianity: *De Doctrina Christiana,*" intro., trans., and notes, Edmund Hill, ed. John E. Rotelle, *The Works of Saint Augustine: A Translation for the 21st Century* (Hyde Park, N.Y.: New City Press, 1996), 201.

7. "In Defence of the Poet Aulus Licinius Archias" 7.15, *Selected Political Speeches of Cicero,* trans. with intro. Michael Grant (Harmondsworth: Penguin, 1969), 156.

8. In practice, however, these methods of choosing the text to be explicated do not automatically produce sermons of clearly different forms. Preachers following a lectionary, for instance, can do either expository or textual or even topical preaching.

9. *Rhet.* 1.2. The translation given is that of *Aristotle* On Rhetoric, *A Theory of Civic Discourse Newly translated with Introduction, Notes, and Appendixes by George A. Kennedy* (New York: Oxford University Press, 1991), 36. The translation given in the Loeb Classics edition is: "the faculty of discovering the possible means of persuasion in reference to any subject whatever."

10. Ronald E. Osborn, *A History of Christian Preaching, Vol. 1, Folly of God: The Rise of Christian Preaching* (St. Louis: Chalice, 1999), xiii.

11. Letter to John Chute of October 10, 1766.

12. To the extent that "homily" has a technical meaning, it refers to sermons following the pattern of verse-by-verse interpretation of a biblical passage—what is referred to today as "expository preaching."

13. When one was used, however, it was not an introduction in our sense, that is, it did not necessarily "lead into" the topic that was to be discussed. Often it was a discussion of a moral issue that happened to be on his mind and did not have to be related to the passage being interpreted. Sometimes, however, it would relate that sermon to the one that had preceded it.

14. Charles Williams, *The Figure of Beatrice: A Study in Dante* (1943; reprint, Cambridge: D. S. Brewer, 1994), 8.

15. Both traditions were highly honored. On the one hand, rhetoricians devised

elaborate methods of memorization that are still called on by anyone offering to help people improve their memories. On the other, itinerant sophists made glamorous careers of raising to an art form the schoolboy exercise of giving impromptu orations on topics set by their audience, speeches that observed all the rules of rhetoric, including periodic sentences, the figures, and frequent quotations from classical literature.

16. *Par.* 29: 109-17, *The Divine Comedy of Dante Alighieri,* trans. Charles Eliot Norton (Boston: Houghton Mifflin, 1902).

17. *The Priest's Book of Private Devotion,* compiled and arranged by J. Oldknow and A. D. Crake, revised by J. F. Briscoe, new ed. (London: Mowbray, 1952), 486 (noted as "From the Liturgy of St. Basil").

APPENDIX ON PIETISM

Although the seventeenth-century British movements listed in chapter 17 had great importance for the Evangelical Awakenings in the United Kingdom and America, the story line will be clearer if the influence of continental Pietism is considered.

The Thirty Years' War, which ended with the Peace of Westphalia in 1648, had begun as a religious tug-of-war between the some three hundred Catholic and Protestant petty states of the Holy Roman Empire, most of which were German-speaking, and ended as a less disguised struggle for political power. The military conflict was prompted by theological polemics that were at least as fierce. Among Lutherans, the result of this dogmatic warfare was the hardening of their theological system into what is known as Lutheran Scholasticism. This theology was reflected in a formalization of church life in which all that was expected of the faithful was that they receive the sacraments, hear the faith proclaimed in sermons that were virtuoso exercises in the splitting of theological hairs, and apparently earn salvation by the intellectual good work of having a correct understanding of the Lutheran confessions and their teaching of justification by faith alone. So the caricature goes.

This was the atmosphere in which **Philipp Jakob Spener** (1635–1705), the "Father of Pietism," exercised his ministry and became one of the most influential pastors in the German-speaking world.[1] Many things about him upset the stereotypical expectations of what such a person must have been like. To begin with, he was not a rabble-rouser; rather, he was the son of an official in one of the small state courts, and much of his ministry was carried out in close association with members of the nobility and in influential pastorates that were court appointments. Nor was he an anti-intellectual; he earned a doctorate and took parishes, reluctantly at first because he hoped to have an academic career. Perhaps most surprisingly, he had not even had a dramatic conversion experience to which he could point, nor did he show any expectation that others would have one.

The orthodoxy of his own Lutheranism was a matter of great concern to him. The main difference between his theology and that of the Reformer was in the place where they felt the problem lay. For Luther, it had to do with the assurance that he had been justified. For Spener, living after a century and a half of Lutheranism, it had to do with the effect of justification on the lives of the elect. Should being truly reborn not have its repercussions in the nature of the internal disposition of faith and the outward expression of faith? Certainly one could not merit salvation by good works, but if one were truly justified, would they not be inevitable? Obviously, the move from self-love to love of God could not be made on self-initiative, but if God had effected that change, shouldn't the difference be felt?

Spener's appointments were some of the most distinguished in his age's Lutheranism, and his influence was so great in his lifetime and ever afterward that it is common to see him referred to by a title such as "the second Luther." Much of that influence was exercised through his preaching. Tastes have changed enough in the centuries since that it is hard for people today to read his sermons and sense the effects they had on their first audience.

Something of Spener's appeal must be seen as the result of what else was available at the time. The preaching of Lutheran Scholasticism was not only polemical in its theology but also rhetorically complex. In the words of Yngve Brilioth, "the preference for pomposity, and for the curving and swelling forms of baroque architecture and poetry, also left its imprint on preaching."[2] While there actually was not only some good preaching but even some good homiletical theory at the time, there were obvious abuses.

Unfortunately, some of the worst abuses were at the hands of J. B. Carpzov the younger, a professor at the University of Leipzig. The university was in the Electorate of Saxony, and Spener had just become preacher at the Elector's Court in Dresden. In his previous ministerial appointment in Frankfurt am Main, Spener's Pietism had met with opposition, and it seemed even less likely to be popular in Saxony. Carpzov at first welcomed Spener, but later turned against him when he felt that his homiletic had been attacked.[3]

The offending passage had appeared in Spener's *De impedimentis studii theologici,* in which he had complained of the results of homiletical teaching he had seen in examining ministerial candidates in Dresden. These caused him to oppose professors who stopped for a whole month to explain one chapter of the Bible. Carpzov took that as a reference to himself, since he had treated the first chapter of Isaiah in great detail.[4] Carpzov was even more notorious for his role in the concentration of scholastic homiletics on the *exordium* as the chief place to introduce variety into preaching on the same lectionary pericopes year after year, having provided a hundred different ways to introduce a sermon on Psalm 14:7.[5]

Spener himself had definite ideas about the way a sermon should be preached. He was convinced, first and foremost, that preaching was for the edification of the congregation, not for arguing fine points of theology. He proposed as the sixth point of his *Pia Desideria* that "sermons be so prepared by all that their purpose (faith and its fruits) may be achieved by the hearers in the greatest possible degree."[6]

Thus he thought that basing sermons on Luther's lectionary of Gospel pericopes every Sunday was not ideal. To begin with, that meant many excellent texts were never preached upon. Furthermore, since the Epistles spoke more directly to issues of personal faith than did the Gospels, they made more useful sermons texts.[7]

He also had objections to the rhetorical ostentation of scholastic preaching.

> Many preachers are more concerned to have the introduction shape up well and transitions be effective, to have an outline that is artful and yet sufficiently concealed, and to have all the parts handled precisely according to the rules of oratory and suitably embellished, than they are concerned that the materials be chosen and by God's grace be developed in such a way that the hearers may profit from the sermon in life and death.[8]

It must be remembered, however, that all of this emphasis on edification did not mean that his preaching exhibited the hypersubjectivity or the emphasis on conversion of later revivalism in America. As noted above, he made no claim to having had a conversion experience himself.[9] He did not even follow his hero Arndt in stressing the mystical union *(unio mystica)* between the soul and God, with the accompanying states of emotion. His interest was ever in practical piety.[10] Therefore, he did not confuse faith with feeling. "Persons can be reassured that they stand within the new birth when they have the desire and make the effort to live according to the divine will."[11]

In order to achieve the results he believed preaching should have in changed lives, Spener did not think that he had to change the sermon form. All of his preaching was expository rather than topical, with an almost word-for-word analysis of the text. His sermons began with an introduction of what the text was about and then moved into the body, which involved four steps: (1) explanation of the truth in the passage, (2) refutation of misunderstandings of it, (3) application that made suggestions for the improvement of one's life, and (4) a concluding word of comfort.

He was, however, exceptional in the length of his sermons: the average at the time was about half an hour, and he often preached for as long as two hours. While he did avoid the contemporary fault of lengthy quotations in Greek and Latin, he did not lighten his tone with illustrations. He read from his manuscript in an unemotional way, appealing to the reason of the congregation rather than stirring them up. No one was more aware than he of the faults of his preaching. This humility undoubtedly contributed to the real reason for his popularity: his presence in the pulpit as one who believed implicitly in what he said, his "whole face reflecting a serene tranquility with kindness."[12]

While in some ways Spener's closest disciple was **August Hermann Francke** (1663–1727), it is also true that the entire nature of Pietism was changed with Francke. To begin with, Francke was aggressive, while there was a certain passivity in the character of Spener. This can be seen in the number of institutions for good works that Francke started when he was at the University of Halle; a list made in 1698 totals twenty-three.[13] Further, the students of Halle carried Francke's ideal around the world, and the university became the hub from which this work was coordinated. Further, unlike Spener, Francke did undergo a conversion experience after a crisis precipitated by an invitation to preach, and that experience became normative for him in his expectations of others.[14] Both of these differences from Spener had a great deal to do with the way Francke preached.

Francke expressed his understanding of what makes good preaching in a letter he wrote to a friend.[15] The purpose of the letter was to tell

> how a faithful minister, who earnestly desires to save and to edify the souls of his hearers, to gain sinners unto Christ, and to inflame their

> hearts with a growing love to their Savior, may best adapt his preaching to these excellent purposes. (117)

He does this out of the conviction that "under-shepherds of the flock" (i.e., clergy, under the "great shepherd of the sheep") should "make it more designedly and zealously the purpose of their preaching to bring sinners" to Christ (122).

He begins by saying that the preacher should often list the differentia between the converted and unconverted so that members of the congregation will be able to recognize their own state. Later he says that preachers should often explain the renewing or change of mind involved in true religion. The distinction between mere morality and religion also needs to be made, and that between legal and evangelical religion is another such need. The necessity, nature, and progress of conversion should be delineated frequently.

The preacher needs to be filled with a zeal to win souls to Christ, and so the "excellency and glory of Christ's person" (123) ought to be a frequent topic, as should the love of Christ. The importance of prayer is to be stressed frequently. Indeed, "the whole faith and duty of a Christian" needs to be presented "in its most amiable and attractive light" (122). This includes calls to self-denial and warnings against worldliness. And parishioners should be encouraged both to read good evangelical books and to seek the counsel and prayers of more mature Christians.

Not much time in the sermon should be given to text explanation; only so much as is necessary to lead their hearers into "the true sense and meaning" (122). To preach in this way requires that the minister have a deep love for both Christ and the flock of Christ, a love that is expressed in deed as well as word. Thus the pastor needs to practice what is preached. The letter ends and is summarized in the prayer that

> none of (the clergy) vainly presume on their skill and ability to do any good by their preaching, and obtain any good success, but let them humbly wait upon you, and by fervent daily prayer let them seek for and obtain the aids of your grace, to enable them to dispense the word of life, and let your blessing render their preaching happily successful to the souls of those that hear them. (127)[16]

Pietistic preaching began to stress conversion and assumed a form that has characterized most evangelistic preaching since. But before Pietism was to exercise its influence on the Evangelical Awakening in the English-speaking world, it had to pass through another filter. That filter represents an alliance already noted between Pietism and the German nobility, but it also takes on its own unique hue. **Count Nikolaus Ludwig von Zinzendorf** (1700–1760), a godchild of Spener, began his higher education at Halle, but his family sent him to anti-Pietistic Wittenberg when they felt his "religious ideas" threatened the likelihood that he would perform the public and family duties his station required of him.

Zinzendorf dutifully served at the Saxon court until he felt free to devote himself to the Christian work to which he felt called. While that began in the characteristic institutional form of Halle, it soon took a turn when he became aware of the plight of the Bohemian[17] Brethren (the *Unitas Fratrum* or *Brüderunität*), a refugee remnant of the Hussite movement. He gave them a home on his estates, where they built their community, which they called *Herrnhut* ("the Lord's Watch").

In time, the count became more and more involved in the life of the community, eventually being ordained as a Lutheran pastor and then as a bishop by the Moravian Daniel Ernst Jablonski. The community experienced an awakening and began to send out missionaries to other parts of Europe and to the New World, especially Georgia and Pennsylvania. A particular sort of piety was cultivated at Herrnhut, one making much of bridal imagery and the blood of Christ, which has appeared sentimental and in bad taste to some other Christians. Nor did Zinzendorf place the emphasis on conversion that Francke did. Instead, he advocated a passive waiting upon the Lord, a "stillness" that had something in common with quietism.[18] His disciples, and later Zinzendorf himself, were to encounter a young Anglican missionary to Georgia and, through him, were to have great influence on the Awakenings in Britain and America.[19]

Notes

1. For this section on Pietism, I am grateful for the bibliographical suggestions of Prof. John Wyborg of North Park Theological Seminary.

2. Yngve Brilioth, *A Brief History of Preaching,* trans. Karl E. Mattson (Philadelphia: Fortress, 1965), 130.

3. Ibid., 133. "In Carpzov, technical homiletics not only reached its zenith but developed to the point of absurdity."

4. *De Impedimentis* appears in the volume of Spener's *Hauptschriften* edited by Paul Grünberg (Gotha, 1889), 184-231. Translations into English of Pietists' works are rare, but a selection from this treatise, which unfortunately does not include the passage under consideration, appears in *Pietists: Selected Writings,* ed. with intro. Peter C. Erb and pref. F. Ernest Stoeffler, Classics of Western Spirituality (New York: Paulist, 1983), 65-70. The only major biography of Spener in English is K. James Stein, *Philip Jakob Spener: Pietist Patriarch* (Chicago: Covenant, 1986). For the

Carpzov incident, see pp. 117-18. For more information on the incident, I am indebted to Professor Stein for his letter to me of June 2, 1992, and for his providing me with the relevant part of Hans Leube's article, "*Die Entscheidungsjahre der Reformbestrebungen Ph. J. Spener's,*" *Neue Kirchliche Zeitschrift,* 35:155-74.

5. Brilioth, *A Brief History of Preaching,* 131.

6. This short work, which Spener wrote as a preface to a new edition of the *Postil* of Johann Arndt, is translated in Erb, *Pietists,* 31-49. The passage quoted appears on p. 47.

7. Stein, *Philip Jakob Spener,* 78-79. When Spener moved from Frankfurt to Dresden, he began preaching on the Gospels again (p. 112), but in Berlin he interrupted preaching from the lectionary to do series of sermons on topics such as new birth and its results (p. 128).

8. *Pia Desideria* in Erb, *Pietists,* 47.

9. Stein, *Philip Jakob Spener,* 157.

10. Ibid., 169.

11. Quoted in ibid., 175.

12. The quoted words come from a description of Spener's preaching by his contemporary, Gottfried Olearius, quoted ibid., 268. This paragraph is based on pp. 267-69. For a sample of one of Spener's sermons (admittedly shortened drastically), see Erb, *Pietists,* 83-96.

13. This list may be seen in Erb, *Pietists,* 163-64.

14. The portion of his autobiography recounting this experience is translated in Erb, *Pietists,* 99-107.

15. "A Letter to a Friend Concerning the Most Useful Way of Preaching" appears in a modernization of a 1754 translation in Erb, *Pietists,* pp. 117-27. Hereafter, references to this work will be given parenthetically in the text by page number alone.

16. Several of Francke's sermons appear in Erb, *Pietists,* 128-62.

17. Also called Moravians.

18. For the identification of the views of the Moravians with those of Madame Guyon, see Wesley's *Journal* for June 5, 1742.

19. Biographical sketches of Zinzendorf can be found in, among others, Kurt Aland, *A History of Christianity,* trans. James L. Schaaf (Philadelphia: Fortress, 1986), 2:255-59, and Erb, *Pietists,* 19-24. A selection of his writings, including his "Litany of the Life, Suffering, and Death of Jesus Christ" appears in ibid., 289-330. Zinzendorf's encounter with John Wesley is treated and documented in Outler, *John Wesley,* pp. 353-76.

Scripture Index

SUBJECT INDEX

www.ingramcontent.com/pod-product-compliance
Lightning Source LLC
Chambersburg PA
CBHW060836100426
42814CB00013B/348
9781501833779